AutoCAD
and Its Applications
B A S I C S

2007

by

Terence M. Shumaker
Faculty Emeritus
Former Chairperson
Drafting Technology
Autodesk Premier Training Center
Clackamas Community College, Oregon City, Oregon

David A. Madsen
Faculty Emeritus, Former Department Chair Drafting Technology, Autodesk Premier
Training Center. Clackamas Community College, Oregon City, Oregon
Autodesk Developer Network Member
Director Emeritus, American Design Drafting Association

David P. Madsen
Instructor, Program Coordinator Drafting Technology
Northwest College, Powell, Wyoming
Autodesk Developer Network Member
SolidWorks Research Associate
American Design Drafting Association Member

Publisher
The Goodheart-Willcox Company, Inc.
Tinley Park, Illinois
www.g-w.com

Library of Congress Catalog Card Number 2006043555

International Standard Book Number-13: 987-1-59070-752-4
International Standard Book Number-10: 1-59070-752-4

1 2 3 4 5 6 7 8 9 – 07 – 10 09 08 07 06

The Goodheart-Willcox Company, Inc. Brand Disclaimer: Brand names, company names, and illustrations for products and services included in this text are provided for educational purposes only and do not represent or imply endorsement or recommendation by the author or the publisher.

The Goodheart-Willcox Company, Inc. Safety Notice: The reader is expressly advised to carefully read, understand, and apply all safety precautions and warnings described in this book or that might also be indicated in undertaking the activities and exercises described herein to minimize risk of personal injury or injury to others. Common sense and good judgment should also be exercised and applied to help avoid all potential hazards. The reader should always refer to the appropriate manufacturer's technical information, directions, and recommendations; then proceed with care to follow specific equipment operating instructions. The reader should understand these notices and cautions are not exhaustive.

The publisher makes no warranty or representation whatsoever, either expressed or implied, including but not limited to equipment, procedures, and applications described or referred to herein, their quality, performance, merchantability, or fitness for a particular purpose. The publisher assumes no responsibility for any changes, errors, or omissions in this book. The publisher specifically disclaims any liability whatsoever, including any direct, indirect, incidental, consequential, special, or exemplary damages resulting, in whole or in part, from the reader's use or reliance upon the information, instructions, procedures, warnings, cautions, applications, or other matter contained in this book. The publisher assumes no responsibility for the activities of the reader.

Library of Congress Cataloging-in-Publication Data
Shumaker, Terence M.
AutoCad and its applications basics 2007 / by Terence M. Shumaker, David A. Madsen, David P. Madsen.
  p. cm.
Includes index.
ISBN 1-59070-752-4
1. Computer graphics. 2. AutoCAD. I. Madsen, David A.
  II. Title.
T385.S46166 2006
620'.00420285536--dc22
                              2006043555

Introduction

AutoCAD and Its Applications—Basics is a text providing complete instruction in mastering fundamental AutoCAD® 2007 commands and drawing techniques. Typical applications of AutoCAD are presented with basic drafting and design concepts. The topics are covered in an easy-to-understand sequence and progress in a way that allows you to become comfortable with the commands as your knowledge builds from one chapter to the next. In addition, *AutoCAD and Its Applications—Basics* offers the following features:

- Step-by-step use of AutoCAD commands.
- In-depth explanations of how and why commands function as they do.
- Extensive use of font changes to specify certain meanings.
- Examples and discussions of industry practices and standards.
- Actual screen captures of AutoCAD and Windows features and functions.
- Professional tips explaining how to use AutoCAD effectively and efficiently.
- Over two hundred exercises to reinforce the chapter topics. These exercises also build on previously learned material.
- Chapter tests for review of commands and key AutoCAD concepts.
- A large selection of drafting problems supplementing each chapter. Problems are presented as 3D illustrations, industrial drawings, and engineering sketches.

With *AutoCAD and Its Applications—Basics*, you learn AutoCAD commands and become acquainted with information in other areas:

- Office practices for firms using AutoCAD systems.
- Preliminary planning and sketches.
- Linetypes and their uses.
- Drawing geometric shapes and constructions.
- Special editing operations that increase productivity.
- Making multiview drawings (orthographic projection).
- Dimensioning techniques and practices, based on accepted standards.
- Drawing section views and designing graphic patterns.
- Creating shapes and symbols for different uses.
- Creating and managing symbol libraries.
- Sketching with AutoCAD.
- Plotting and printing drawings.
- Using Windows Explorer for organizing and managing files and directories.

Features of the Textbook

Cautions alert you to potential problems.

Notes explain important aspects of a topic.

Learning Objectives identify the key items you will learn in the chapter.

Command Entry Graphics show command prompt, toolbar, and pull-down menu entry. Command options are also shown where applicable.

Prompt Sequences highlight procedures for entering commands and options.

Drawing Problems require application of chapter concepts and problem-solving techniques. Icons identify problems from various drafting disciplines.

Mechanical

Civil

Architectural

Graphic Design

Electronics

Piping

General

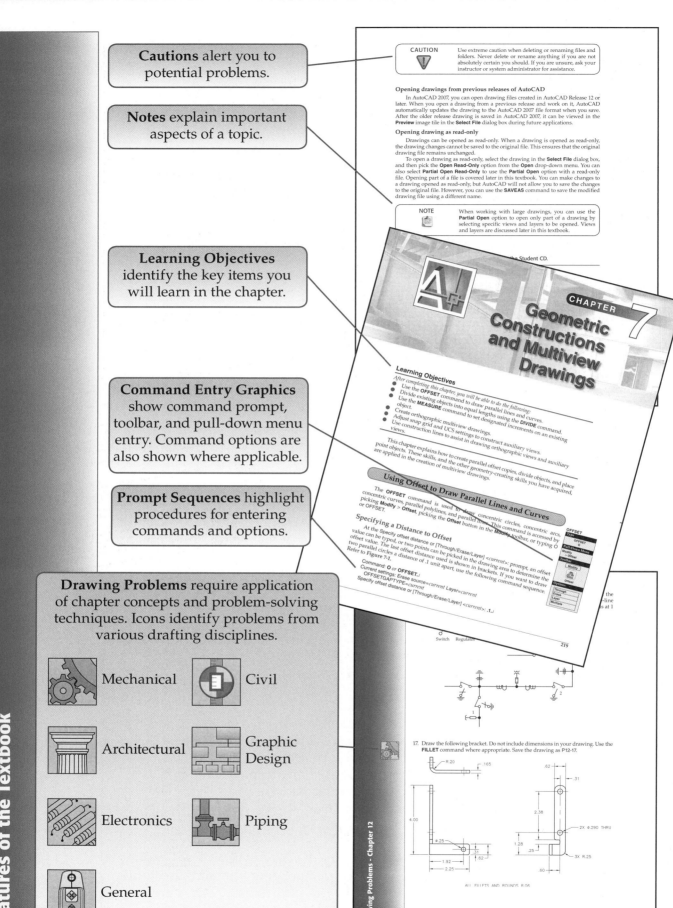

Illustrations, including AutoCAD "screen shots" and line art illustrations, make learning easy.

Professional Tips increase your productivity in using AutoCAD commands and techniques.

Exercise References identify when you should complete an Exercise from the Student CD.

Legacy Notes identify commands used more commonly in previous versions of AutoCAD.

Express Tool References identify when you should refer to Express Tool material from the Student CD.

Chapter Tests reinforce the knowledge gained while reading the chapter and completing the Exercises.

New Feature Graphics identify new and updated features for AutoCAD 2007.

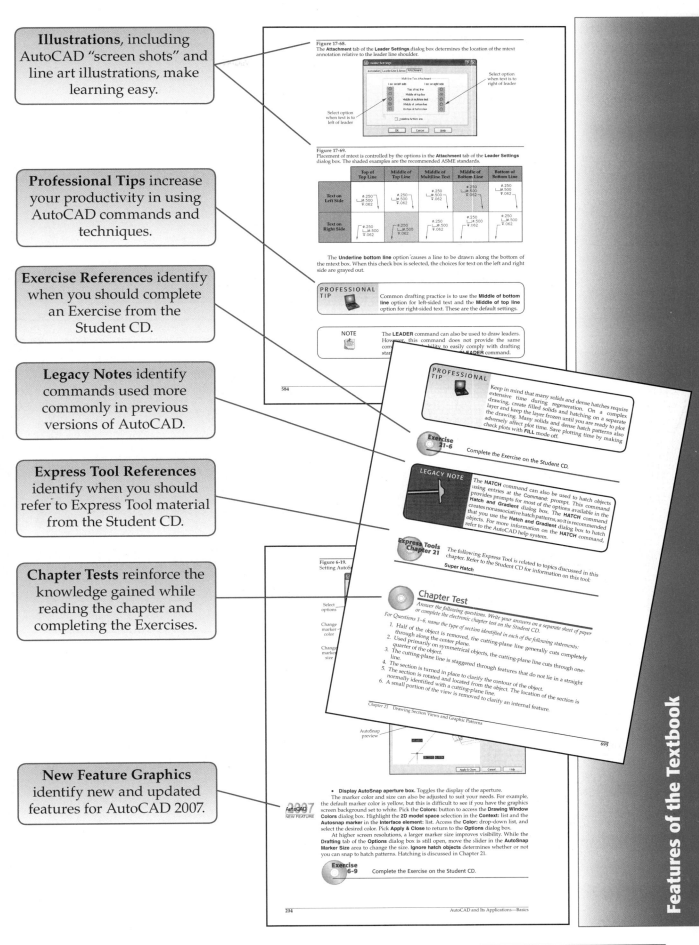

Features of the Textbook

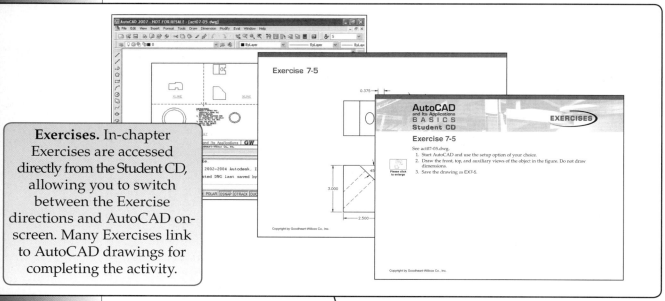

Exercises. In-chapter Exercises are accessed directly from the Student CD, allowing you to switch between the Exercise directions and AutoCAD on-screen. Many Exercises link to AutoCAD drawings for completing the activity.

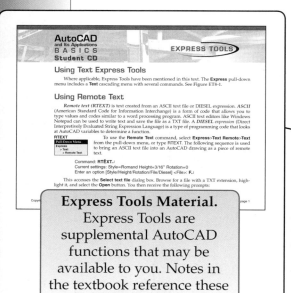

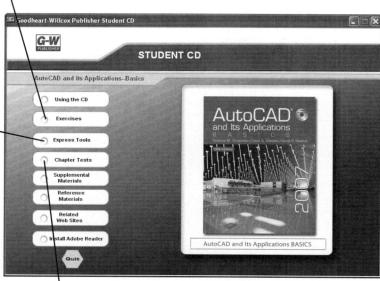

Express Tools Material. Express Tools are supplemental AutoCAD functions that may be available to you. Notes in the textbook reference these components.

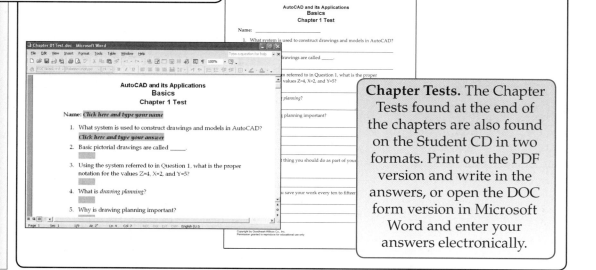

Chapter Tests. The Chapter Tests found at the end of the chapters are also found on the Student CD in two formats. Print out the PDF version and write in the answers, or open the DOC form version in Microsoft Word and enter your answers electronically.

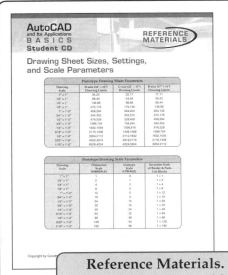

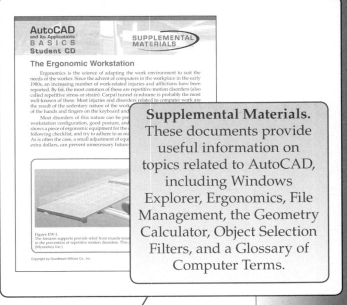

Supplemental Materials. These documents provide useful information on topics related to AutoCAD, including Windows Explorer, Ergonomics, File Management, the Geometry Calculator, Object Selection Filters, and a Glossary of Computer Terms.

Reference Materials. You will find these tables and charts useful both in the classroom and in the workplace. Access the material from your desktop, or print them and store in a binder.

Related Web Sites. Use this to access a wide variety of CAD/drafting Web sites.

Fonts Used in This Text

Different typefaces are used throughout this text to define terms and identify AutoCAD commands. The following typeface conventions are used in this textbook:

Text Element	Example
AutoCAD commands	**LINE** command
AutoCAD pulldown menu	**Draw > Arc> 3 Points**
AutoCAD system variables	**FILEDIA** system variable
AutoCAD toolbars and buttons	**Edit** toolbar, **Offset** button
AutoCAD dialog boxes	**Insert Table** dialog box
Keyboard entry (in text)	Type LINE
Keyboard keys	[Ctrl]+[1] key combination
File names, folders, and paths	C:\Program Files\AutoCAD 2007\my drawing.dwg
Microsoft Windows features	Start menu, Programs folder
Prompt sequence	Command:
Keyboard input at prompt sequence	Command: **L** *or* **LINE**↵
Comment at prompt sequence	Specify first point: *(pick a point or press* [Enter]*)*

Other Text References

For additional information, standards from organizations, such as ANSI (American National Standards Institute) and ASME (American Society of Mechanical Engineers) are referenced throughout the text. These standards are used to help you create drawings that follow industry, national, and international practices. The Student CD includes a list of many of these standards.

Also for your convenience, other Goodheart-Willcox textbooks are referenced. Referenced textbooks include *AutoCAD and Its Applications—Advanced*, *Geometric Dimensioning and Tolerancing*, and *Process Pipe Drafting*. All these textbooks can be ordered directly from Goodheart-Willcox.

AutoCAD and Its Applications—Basics covers basic AutoCAD applications. For a text covering the advanced AutoCAD applications, please refer to *AutoCAD and Its Applications—Advanced*.

Trademarks

Autodesk, the Autodesk logo, 3ds max, Autodesk VIZ, AutoCAD, DesignCenter, AutoCAD Learning Assistance, AutoSnap, and AutoTrack are either registered trademarks or trademarks of Autodesk, Inc. in the U.S.A. and/or other countries.

Microsoft, Windows, and Windows NT are registered trademarks of Microsoft Corporation in the United States and/or other countries.

Contents in Brief

About the Authors

Terence M. Shumaker is Faculty Emeritus, the former Chairperson of the Drafting Technology Department, and former Director of the Autodesk Premier Training Center at Clackamas Community College. Terence taught at the community college level for over 25 years. He has professional experience in surveying, civil drafting, industrial piping, and technical illustration. He is the author of Goodheart-Willcox's *Process Pipe Drafting* and coauthor of the *AutoCAD and Its Applications* series.

David A. Madsen is Faculty Emeritus, and former Chairperson of Drafting Technology at the Autodesk Premier Training Center at Clackamas Community College, in Oregon City, Oregon. David was awarded Director Emeritus of the American Design and Drafting Association. His education includes a Bachelor of Science degree in Technology Education, and a Master of Education in Vocational Administration. During his teaching career, David was an instructor and a department chair at Clackamas Community College for nearly thirty years. In addition to community college teaching experience, David was a Drafting Technology instructor at Centennial High School in Gresham, Oregon. David also has extensive experience in mechanical drafting, architectural design and drafting, and construction practices. He is the author of several Goodheart-Willcox drafting and design textbooks, including *Geometric Dimensioning and Tolerancing*, and coauthor of the *AutoCAD and Its Applications* series and *Architectural Drafting Using AutoCAD*.

David P. Madsen is the Instructor and Program Coordinator of Drafting Technology at Northwest College in Powell, Wyoming. Dave holds a Master of Science degree in Educational Policy, Foundations, and Administrative Studies with a specialization in Postsecondary, Adult, and Continuing Education; a Bachelor of Science degree in Technology Education; and an Associate of Science degree in General Studies and Drafting Technology. Dave has been involved in providing Drafting and Computer Aided Design and Drafting instruction to adult learners since 1999. Dave has extensive and varied experience in the drafting, design, and engineering fields. He has worked in the drafting industry for over ten years and has created everything from mechanical and electronic to architectural and civil drawings.

Acknowledgments

Special thanks from David Madsen to Ethan Collins, Eugene O'Day, and Ron Palma for their professional expertise in providing in-depth research and testing, technical assistance, reviews, and development of new materials for use throughout the text.

Special thanks from Terence Shumaker to Craig Black for his expert reviews, technical assistance, and contribution of new material for several chapters in this book. Craig is manager of the Autodesk Premier Training Center at Fox Valley Technical College in Appleton, Wisconsin.

Technical Assistance and Contribution of Materials

Margo Bilson of Willamette Industries, Inc.
Fitzgerald, Hagan, & Hackathorn
Bruce L. Wilcox, Johnson and Wales University School of Technology

Contribution of Photographs or Other Technical Information

Arthur Baker
Autodesk
CADalyst magazine
CADENCE magazine
Chris Lindner
EPCM Services, Ltd.
Harris Group, Inc.

International Source for Ergonomics
Jim Webster
Kunz Associates
Myonetics, Inc.
Norwest Engineering
Schuchart & Associates, Inc.
Willamette Industries, Inc.

Contents

CHAPTER 9

Working with Tables

CHAPTER 10

Drawing Display Options

CHAPTER 11

Layouts, Plotting, and Printing

Editing the Drawing

CHAPTER 12

Basic Editing Commands

CHAPTER 13

Automatic Editing

AutoCAD Applications

CHAPTER 14

Introduction to Polylines and Multilines

CHAPTER 15

Drawing and Editing Polylines and Splines

CHAPTER 16

Obtaining Information about the Drawing

Dimensioning and Tolerancing

CHAPTER 24

Assigning Attributes and Generating a Bill of Materials

CHAPTER 25

External Reference Drawings

CHAPTER 26

Sheet Sets

Advanced Applications

CHAPTER 27

Isometric Drawing

CHAPTER 28

Advanced Topics

Student CD Content

Using the Student CD

Textbook Exercises

Express Tools

Chapter Tests

Supplemental Materials
Working with AutoCAD Files
The Ergonomic Workstation
Managing the AutoCAD File System
Glossary of Computer Terms
Geometry Calculator
Object Selection Filters

Reference Materials
Drawing Sheet Sizes, Settings, and Scale Parameters
Command Aliases
AutoCAD Menu Tree
Drafting Standards and Related Documents
Drafting Symbols
Standard Tables
AutoCAD System Variables
AutoCAD Dimensioning Variables
Planning Sheet
AutoCAD Fonts
Shortcut Keys

Related Web Sites

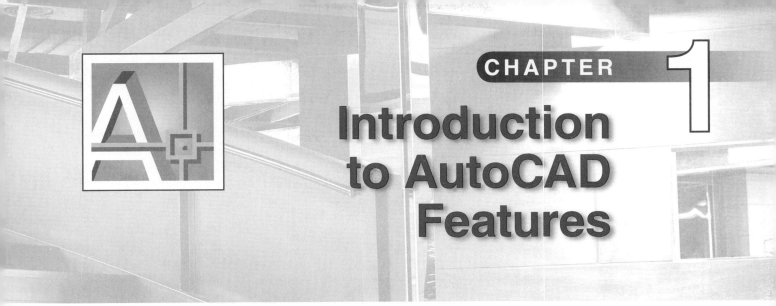

CHAPTER 1

Introduction to AutoCAD Features

Learning Objectives

After completing this chapter, you will be able to do the following:

- Describe the methods and procedures used in computer-aided drafting.
- Explain the value of planning your work and system management.
- Load AutoCAD from the Windows desktop.
- Describe the AutoCAD screen layout and user interface.
- Describe the function of dialog boxes.
- Identify the function of modeless dialog boxes.
- Use the features found in the **AutoCAD Help** window.
- Use function keys and control keys.

The Tools of CAD

The computer and software are the principal components of the present-day design and drafting workstation. These tools make up a system referred to as *CAD*—computer-aided design or computer-aided drafting. Drafters, designers, and engineers use CAD to develop designs and drawings and to plot them on paper or film. Additionally, drawings and designs can be displayed as three-dimensional (3D) models and animations or used in analysis and testing.

CAD has surpassed the use of manual drafting techniques because of the increase in speed, power, accuracy, and flexibility. However, designing with computers is not totally without its attendant problems and trade-offs. Although the uses of CAD designs are limited only by the imagination, it should be remembered that computer hardware is sensitive to the slightest electrical impulses and the human body is sensitive to the repetitive motions required when using this modern method.

The AutoCAD Toolbox

Drawings and models are constructed in AutoCAD using XYZ coordinates. The *Cartesian (rectangular) coordinate system* is used most often. Angular geometry is created by measuring angles in a counterclockwise direction. Drawings can be annotated with text and described with a variety of dimensioning techniques. In addition, objects can be given colors, patterns, and textures. AutoCAD also provides you with the tools to create basic pictorial drawings, called *isometrics*, and powerful 3D solid and surface models.

The Applications of AutoCAD

Using AutoCAD software and this text, you will learn how to construct, lay out, dimension, and annotate two-dimensional drawings. Should you wish to expand your study into the topics of 3D modeling, 3D rendering, and customization, *AutoCAD and Its Applications—Advanced* can provide you with detailed instruction. Your studies will enable you to create a wide variety of drawings, designs, and 3D models in any of the drafting, design, and engineering disciplines.

AutoCAD drawings can have hundreds of colors and *layers*, which contain different kinds of information. Objects can also be shown as 2D, 3D, or exploded assemblies. See **Figure 1-1.** In addition, objects in the drawing can be given "intelligence" in the form of *attributes*. These attributes are various kinds of data that turn a drawing into a graphical database. You can then ask questions of your drawing and receive a variety of information.

Using AutoCAD, you have the ability to construct 3D models that appear as wireframes or have surface colors and textures. The creation of solid models having physical properties, such as mass and density, that can be used for analysis is also possible with AutoCAD. The display in **Figure 1-2** is an example of a solid model created in AutoCAD. 3D drawings and models can be viewed in several ways. These models can also be colored and shaded, or *rendered*, to appear in a realistic format.

Figure 1-1.
A 3D model shown as an exploded assembly. (Thomas Short, Anthony Dudek)

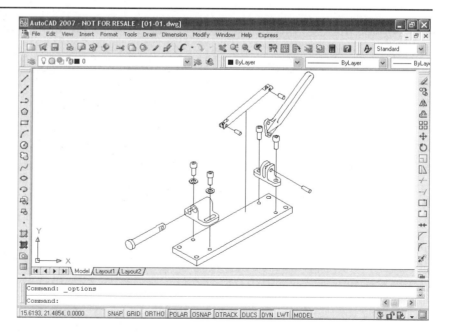

Figure 1-2.
A 3D model of a welding fixture illustrating the difference between a wireframe and a rendering. (Autodesk, Inc.)

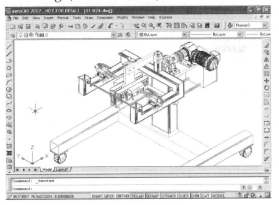

Wireframe

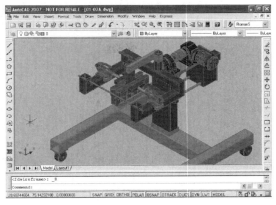

Rendering

A powerful application of CAD software and 3D models is animation. The simplest form of animation is to dynamically rotate the model in order to view it from any direction. See **Figure 1-3.** Drawings and models can also be animated so the model appears to move, rotate, and even explode into its individual components. An extremely useful form of animation is called a *walkthrough*. Using specialized software, you can plot a path through or around a model and replay it just like a movie. The logical next step in viewing the model is to actually be inside it and have the ability to manipulate and change the objects in it. This is called *virtual reality*, and it is achieved through the use of 3D models and highly specialized software and hardware.

Figure 1-3.
The welding fixture model can be rotated, zoomed in and out, and viewed from any location in 3D space. (Autodesk, Inc.)

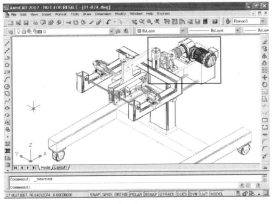

Initial Display

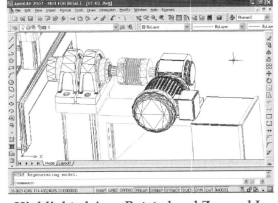

Highlighted Area Rotated and Zoomed In

Establishing an AutoCAD Drawing Method

All aspects of the project must be considered when developing a drawing plan. Careful use of the CAD system is required for the planning and drawing process. Therefore, it is important to be familiar with the AutoCAD tools and to know how they work and when they are best suited for a specific job. There is no substitute for knowing the tools, and the most basic of these is the Cartesian coordinate system.

Learning the XYZ Coordinate System

The XYZ coordinate system is the basic building block of any CAD drawing. The locations of points are described with XYZ coordinate values. These values are called *rectangular coordinates* and locate any point on a flat plane, such as a sheet of paper. The *origin* of the coordinate system is where the axes meet, usually the lower-left corner. See **Figure 1-4.** A distance measured horizontally from the origin is an X value. A distance measured vertically from the origin is a Y value.

Rectangular coordinates can also be measured in three-dimensional space. The third dimension rises up from the surface of the paper and is given a Z value. When describing coordinate locations, the X value is first, the Y value is second, and the Z value is third. Each value is separated by a comma. For example, the coordinate location of 3,1,6 represents three units from the origin in the X direction, one unit from the origin in the Y direction, and six units from the origin in the Z direction. A detailed explanation of rectangular coordinates is provided in Chapter 3.

Planning Your Drawing

Drawing planning involves looking at the entire process or project in which you are involved. A plan determines how a project is going to be approached. It includes the drawings to be created, the title and numbering conventions, the information to be presented, and the types of symbols needed to show the information.

More specifically, drawing planning applies to how you create and manage a drawing or set of drawings. This includes which view or feature you draw first and the coordinates and AutoCAD commands you use to draw it. Drafters who begin constructing a drawing from the seat of their pants—creating symbols and naming objects, shapes, and views as they go—do not possess a good drawing plan. Those who plan, use consistent techniques, and adhere to school or company standards are developing good drawing habits.

Throughout this text you will find aids to help you develop good drawing habits. One of the first steps in developing your skills is to learn how to plan your work. The importance of planning cannot be emphasized enough. There is no substitute.

Using Drafting Standards

Standards are guidelines for operating procedures, drawing techniques, and record keeping. Most schools and companies have established standards. It is important that standards exist and are used by all CAD personnel. Drawing standards may include the following items:
- Methods of file storage (location and name).
- File naming conventions.
- File backup methods and times.
- Drawing templates and title blocks.
- Drawing symbols.
- Dimensioning styles and techniques.

Figure 1-4.
The difference between the 2D and 3D rectangular coordinate systems is the Z axis.

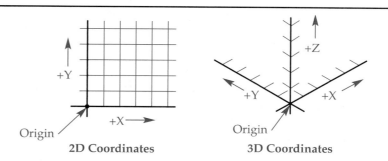

2D Coordinates   3D Coordinates

- Text styles.
- Table styles.
- Layer settings.
- Plot styles.

Your standards may vary in content, but the most important aspect of standards is that they are used. When standards are used, your drawings are consistent, you become more productive, and the classroom or office functions more efficiently.

Planning Your Work

As you begin your CAD training, plan your drawing sessions thoroughly to organize your thoughts. Sketch the problem or design, noting the sizes and locations of features. List the drawing commands needed in the order they are to be used. Schedule a regular time to use the computer and adhere to that time. Follow the standards your school or firm has set. These might include specific drawing names, project planning sheets, project logs, drawing layout procedures, special title blocks, and a location for drawing storage. Everyone using the computers in your school or company must follow the standards and procedures. Confusion may result if your drawings do not have the proper name, are stored in the wrong place, or have the wrong title block.

Develop the habit of saving your work regularly—at least every ten to fifteen minutes. The automatic save tool can be set to automatically save your drawings at predetermined intervals. Automatic save is covered in detail in Chapter 2. Drawings may be lost due to a software error, hardware malfunction, power failure, or your own mistakes. This is not common, but you should still be prepared for such an event.

You should develop methods of managing your work. This is critical to computer drafting and is discussed throughout the text. Keep the following points in mind as you begin your AutoCAD training:
- ✓ Plan your work and organize your thoughts.
- ✓ Learn and use your classroom or office standards.
- ✓ Save your work often.

If you remember to follow these three points, your grasp of the tools and methods of CAD will be easier. In addition, your experiences with the computer will be more enjoyable.

When you feel the need to dive blindly into a drawing or project, restrain yourself. Take the time needed for development of the project goals. Then proceed with the confidence of knowing where you are heading.

During your early stages of AutoCAD training, write down all the instructions needed to construct your drawing, especially for your first few assignments. This means documenting every command and every coordinate point (dimension) needed. Develop a planning sheet for your drawings. Following these suggestions will make your time with AutoCAD more productive and enjoyable.

Using Drawing Plan Sheets

A good work plan can save drawing time. Planning should include sketches. A rough preliminary sketch and a drawing plan can help by:
- Determining the drawing layout.
- Setting the overall size of the drawing by laying out the views and required free space.
- Confirming the drawing units, based on the dimensions provided.
- Predetermining the point entry system and locating the points.
- Establishing the grid and snap settings.
- Presetting some of the drawing variables, such as layers, linetypes, and line widths.
- Establishing how and when various activities are to be performed.

- Determining the best use of AutoCAD.
- Resulting in an even workload.
- Providing maximum use of equipment.

Planning Checklist

In the early stages of your AutoCAD training, it is best to plan your drawing projects carefully. There is a tendency to want things to happen immediately—for things to be "automatic"—but if you hurry and do little or no planning, you will become increasingly frustrated. Therefore, as you begin each new project, step through the following planning checklist so the execution of your project goes smoothly:

✓ Analyze the problem.
✓ Study all engineering sketches.
✓ Locate all available resources and list for future use.
✓ Determine the applicable standards for the project.
✓ Sketch the problem.
✓ Decide on the number and kinds of views required.
✓ Determine the final plotted scale of the drawing and of all views.
✓ Determine the drawing sequence, such as lines, features, dimensions, and notes.
✓ List the AutoCAD commands to be used.
✓ Follow the standards and refer to resources as you work.

PROFESSIONAL TIP

AutoCAD is designed so you can construct drawings and models using the actual dimensions of the object. *Always draw in full scale.* The proper text and dimension size is set using scale factors. This is covered in detail in later chapters. The final scale of the drawing should be planned early and displayed on the plot.

Working Procedures Checklist

As you begin learning AutoCAD, you will realize that several skills are required to become a proficient CAD user. The following checklist provides you with some hints to help you become comfortable with AutoCAD. These hints will also allow you to work quickly and efficiently. The following actions are discussed in detail in later chapters:

✓ Plan all work with pencil and paper before using the computer.
✓ Check the **Layers**, **Styles**, and **Properties** toolbars at the top of the display screen and the status bar at the bottom to see which object property settings and drawing aids are in effect.
✓ Read the prompts displayed by AutoCAD. Constantly check for the correct commands, instructions, or keyboard entry of data.
✓ Right-click to access shortcut menus; review available options.
✓ Think ahead. Know your next move.
✓ Learn new commands every day. Do not rely on just a few that seem to work. Find commands that can speed your work and do it more efficiently.
✓ Save your work every ten to fifteen minutes, in case a power failure or system crash deletes the drawing held in computer memory.
✓ If you are stumped, ask the computer for help. Become familiar with the AutoCAD help system so you will be comfortable using it.

Exercise 1-1

Complete the Exercise on the Student CD.

Starting AutoCAD

AutoCAD 2007 is designed to operate with Windows XP Professional, Windows XP Home, Windows XP Tablet PC, and Windows 2000 Professional. If you see illustrations in this text that appear slightly different than your screen, do not be concerned, as the AutoCAD feature is the same.

When AutoCAD is first installed, Windows creates a *program icon*, which is displayed on the desktop and in the list of programs available from the Start menu. An *icon* is a small picture representing an application, accessory, file, or command.

AutoCAD can be started using several different techniques. The quickest way to start AutoCAD is to double-click on the AutoCAD 2007 icon on the Windows desktop. See **Figure 1-5.**

A second method for starting AutoCAD is to pick the Start button at the lower-left corner of the Windows desktop. Move the pointer to Programs and either hold it there or pick. Pick Autodesk, AutoCAD 2007, and AutoCAD 2007 to start the program. See **Figure 1-6.**

Figure 1-5.
Double-click the AutoCAD 2007 icon on the Windows desktop to start AutoCAD.

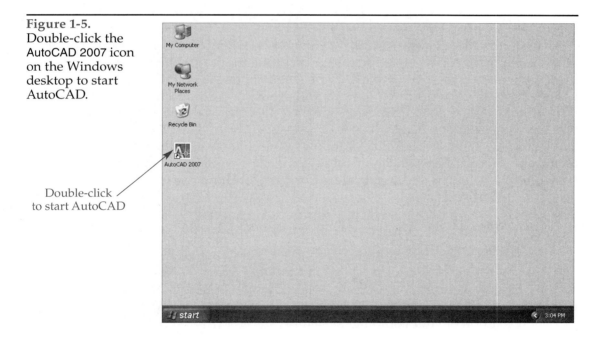

Double-click to start AutoCAD

Figure 1-6.
Pick AutoCAD 2007 in the AutoCAD 2007 menu to load the program.

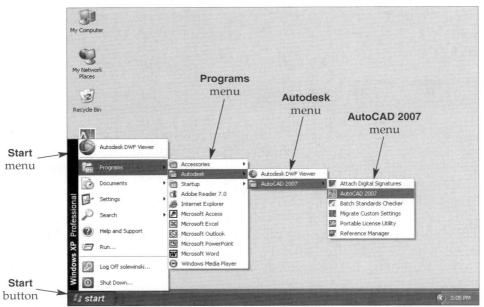

The AutoCAD Window

The AutoCAD window is similar to any other window within the Windows operating system. Minimizing, maximizing, and closing the program window or individual drawing windows is done by picking the small control icon in the upper-left corner, which displays a standard window control menu, or picking one of the appropriate icons in the upper-right corner. See **Figure 1-7.** Window sizing operations are done as with any other window.

AutoCAD uses the familiar Windows style interface with buttons, pull-down menus, and dialog boxes. Each of these items is discussed in detail in this chapter. Learning the layout, appearance, and proper use of these features will allow you to master AutoCAD quickly.

Standard Screen Layout

The standard screen layout provides a large drawing area. The drawing area is bordered by *toolbars* at the left, right, and top and by the *command window* at the bottom. Look at your screen now and study the illustration in **Figure 1-7.** Note that the proportional size of the AutoCAD window features may vary depending on the display resolution of your computer system.

Floating and docking

Some of the elements of the AutoCAD window are referred to as *floating*. This means the item can be freely resized or moved about the screen into new positions. Floating features are contained within a standard Windows border and display a title bar at the top. When you run AutoCAD for the first time, the AutoCAD window is displayed in a floating position on the desktop. A smaller window inside the AutoCAD window displays the drawing area for the currently open drawing file. Floating windows are moved and adjusted for size in the same manner as any other window, however, the drawing windows can only be adjusted and positioned within the AutoCAD window.

Figure 1-7.
The default standard AutoCAD window.

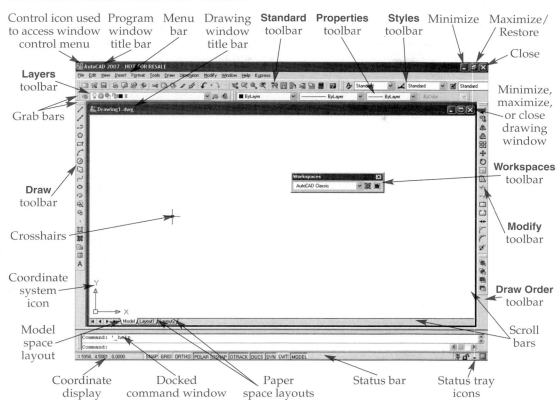

Docking a window or toolbar means the feature is moved to one of the edges of the AutoCAD window (top, bottom, left, or right) until it snaps into position. Once docked, the feature will lose its title bar and gain a grab bar. The term *grab bar* refers to the two thin bars at the top or left edge of a docked feature.

Locking toolbars and windows

The AutoCAD toolbars and open windows can be moved around to suit your working environment. To prevent them from being accidentally moved, each of the toolbars and windows can be locked in either a floating or docked state. To access the locking options, select **Lock Location** from the **Window** pull-down menu, pick the **Toolbar/Windows Positions** icon from the system tray area, or right-click over any toolbar and select **Lock Location** from the shortcut menu. The **Lock Location** menu options are displayed in **Figure 1-8.**

Select an option to lock the toolbars or windows that reside in that group as floating or docked. To unlock a group, select the option again. To quickly lock or unlock all of the toolbars and windows, select **Locked** or **Unlocked** from the **All** cascading menu. A locked toolbar or window can be moved without unlocking it by holding down the [Ctrl] key while moving the toolbar or window.

Areas of the AutoCAD window

Become familiar with the unique areas of the AutoCAD window and the information provided by each. The following list describes the function of each area. Each of these features will be discussed in detail later in this text:

Figure 1-8.
Toolbars and
windows can be
locked in position.

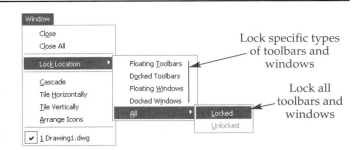

Lock specific types
of toolbars and
windows

Lock all
toolbars and
windows

- **Command window.** In its default position, the command window is docked at the bottom of the AutoCAD window. It displays the Command: prompt and reflects any command entries you make. It also displays prompts that supply information to you or request input. The command window is where your primary communications with AutoCAD are displayed, so watch for any information shown on this line.
- **Menu bar.** The menu bar appears just below the title bar and displays a number of menu names. As with standard Windows menus, use the cursor to point at a menu name and press the pick button. This displays a *pull-down menu*.
- **Scroll bars.** The scroll bars allow you to adjust your view of the drawing area by "sliding" the drawing from side to side or up and down.
- **Crosshairs.** This is your primary means of pointing to objects or locations within a drawing.
- **Coordinate system icon.** This indicates the current coordinate system and view orientation.
- **Toolbars.** Toolbars contain buttons that activate AutoCAD commands.
- **Standard toolbar.** In the default AutoCAD screen configuration, the **Standard** toolbar appears just above the **Layers** toolbar. When you move the cursor to the toolbar, the crosshairs change to the familiar Windows arrow pointer. The **Standard** toolbar contains a series of buttons that provide access to several of AutoCAD's drawing setup and control commands.
- **Styles toolbar.** In the default AutoCAD screen configuration, the **Styles** toolbar appears to the right of the **Standard** toolbar. This toolbar contains buttons and display fields relative to text, dimension, and table styles.
- **Layers and Properties toolbars.** In the default AutoCAD screen configuration, the **Layers** and **Properties** toolbars appear just above the drawing area, below the **Standard** and **Styles** toolbars. These toolbars contain buttons and display fields for setting and adjusting the properties of objects in a drawing.
- **Workspaces toolbar.** In the default AutoCAD screen configuration, the **Workspaces** toolbar appears to the left of the **Layers** toolbar. This toolbar is used to group and customize menus, toolbars, and windows. These workspaces allow you to display certain toolbars and AutoCAD windows based on your preferences. The menus, toolbars, and windows display only the options that are relative to the current workspace. For more information about these options and other customizing methods, refer to *AutoCAD and Its Applications—Advanced*.
- **Status bar.** This bar contains several buttons that display the current state of specific drawing control features and allow access for changing the settings of these features. To the right of the status bar is a tray with icons. These icons represent the presence of various drawing conditions. When a pull-down menu item is highlighted or you are pointing at a toolbar button, a brief explanation of the item is shown along the left side of the status bar.
- **Coordinate display.** This display field, found on the status bar, shows the XYZ crosshairs location, according to the current settings.

Buttons

Buttons are icons that are placed on a toolbar and, when picked, initiate a command. The image on the button indicates the command. As you move your cursor across a toolbar button, a 3D border is displayed around the previously flat button.

Holding the cursor motionless over a button for a moment displays a *tooltip*, which shows the name of the button in a small box at the cursor location. While the tooltip is visible, a brief explanation of what the button does is displayed along the status bar at the bottom-left edge of the window. *AutoCAD and Its Applications—Advanced* demonstrates how buttons can be created with custom images and commands.

Pull-Down Menus

The AutoCAD pull-down menus are located on the menu bar at the top of the screen. As with a toolbar, when you move the cursor to the menu bar, the crosshairs change to the arrow pointer. The default menu bar has eleven pull-down menu items: **File**, **Edit**, **View**, **Insert**, **Format**, **Tools**, **Draw**, **Dimension**, **Modify**, **Window**, and **Help**.

> NOTE
>
> During the AutoCAD installation process, an additional Express Tools menu is available. Installing this menu provides you with an **Express** pull-down menu, which includes additional tools for improved functionality and productivity during your drawing processes. Express Tools are discussed on the Student CD and referenced where appropriate throughout this textbook.

Menu items and commands are easily selected by picking a menu item with your mouse. Some commands in the pull-down menu may have a small arrow to the right. When one of these items is selected, a *cascading menu* appears that has additional options. Some of the menu selections are followed by an ellipsis (…). If you pick one of these items, a dialog box is displayed.

It is also possible to use the keyboard to access pull-down menu items by typing shortcuts. These shortcut keystrokes are called *menu accelerator keys.* The [Alt] key turns on the menu accelerator keys. To access any pull-down menu selection, use an [Alt]+[*key*] combination on the keyboard. For instance, the **View** pull-down menu can be accessed by first pressing the [Alt] key and then pressing the [V] key.

One character of each pull-down menu title or command is underlined. Once a pull-down menu is displayed, a menu item can be selected using that single character key. For example, to zoom in closer to your work, press [Alt]+[V] to access the **View** pull-down menu. Then, press [Z] to select the **Zoom** command, and [I] to select the **In** option.

Exercise 1-3   Complete the Exercise on the Student CD.

Toolbars

Toolbars are features containing various buttons that activate AutoCAD commands. Toolbars can be resized, modified, hidden, floating, and docked as needed. Some toolbar buttons show a small black triangle in the lower-right corner. These buttons are called *flyouts*. Press and hold the pick button while pointing at a flyout to display a set of related buttons.

Dialog Boxes

One of the most important aspects of AutoCAD is the graphical user interface (GUI) offered by the Microsoft Windows operating environment. A *graphical user interface* is how the software displays information, options, and choices for you. The most common component of the GUI is the dialog box. A *dialog box* is a box that may contain a variety of information. You can set variables and select items in a dialog box using your cursor. This eliminates typing, saving time and increasing productivity.

A pull-down selection followed by an ellipsis (…) displays a dialog box when picked. An example of a simple dialog box is shown in **Figure 1-9**. This dialog box is displayed when you pick **Insert** > **Block...** from the pull-down menu.

Buttons in a dialog box that are followed by an ellipsis (…) display another dialog box when they are picked. You must make a selection from the second dialog box before returning to the original dialog box. A button in a dialog box with an arrow symbol (<) requires you to make a selection in the drawing area.

There are standard parts to all dialog boxes. Knowing these parts will make it much easier to work with the dialog boxes. Detailed discussions are provided in later chapters.

- **Command buttons.** When you pick a command button, something happens immediately. The most common buttons are **OK**, **Cancel**, and **Help**. See **Figure 1-9**. If a button has a dark border, it is the default. Pressing the [Enter] key accepts the default. If a button is "grayed-out," it cannot be selected.
- **Text box.** You can type a name or single line of information using the text box. Refer to the text box in **Figure 1-9**.
- **Check box.** A check box, or toggle, displays a "✓" when it is on (active). If the box is empty, the option is off. See **Figure 1-10**.

Figure 1-9.
A dialog box is displayed when you pick an item that is followed by an ellipsis. The dialog box shown here appears after you select **Insert** > **Block...** from the pull-down menu. You can type a name, number, or single line of information in a text box.

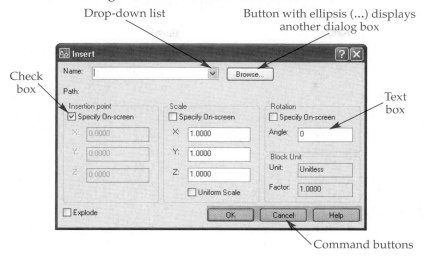

Drop-down list

Button with ellipsis (...) displays another dialog box

Check box

Text box

Command buttons

- **Radio buttons.** Only one item in a group of radio buttons can be highlighted or active at one time. See **Figure 1-10.**
- **Tab.** A dialog box tab is much like an index tab used to separate sections of a notebook or the label tab on the top of a manila file folder. Many dialog boxes in AutoCAD contain two or more "pages" or "panels," each with a tab at the top. See **Figure 1-10.**
- **List box.** A list box contains a list of items or options that you can scan through using the scroll bar (if present) or the keyboard arrow keys. Either highlight the desired item with the arrow keys and press [Enter] or simply select it with the mouse. See **Figure 1-11.**
- **Drop-down list box.** The drop-down list box is similar to the standard list box, except only one item is initially shown. The remaining items are hidden until you pick the drop-down arrow. When you pick the drop-down arrow, the drop-down list is displayed below the initial item. You can then pick from the expanded list or use the scroll bar to find the item you need. See **Figure 1-11.**

Figure 1-10.
Only one radio button in a group can be highlighted at a time. A "✓" in a check box indicates the item is active (on). Any number of check boxes can be active in a given group. A dialog box tab is much like an index tab used to separate sections of a notebook. Each tab displays a new set of related options.

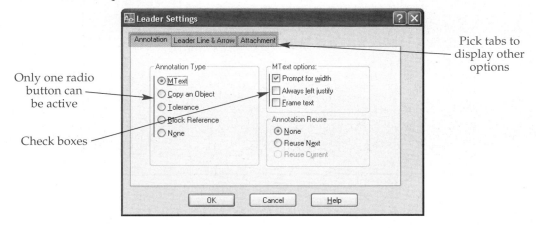

Pick tabs to display other options

Only one radio button can be active

Check boxes

Figure 1-11.
A list box contains a list of items related to the dialog box. A drop-down list is displayed when you pick the drop-down arrow.

List box

Drop-down list

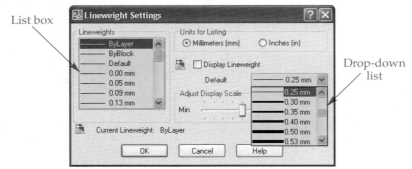

- **Preview box.** A preview box is an area of a dialog box that displays a "picture" of the item you select. See **Figure 1-12.**
- **Scroll bars and buttons.** Vertical scroll bars and buttons allow you to scroll up or down a list of items. Simply pick the up or down arrows. Horizontal scroll bars and buttons operate in the same manner. **Figure 1-13** shows the operation of a scroll bar.
- **Alerts.** Alerts may appear in the lower-left corner of the original dialog box, or as a separate alert dialog box. See **Figure 1-14.**
- **Help.** If you are unsure of any features of a dialog box, pick the question mark button in the upper-right corner of the dialog box. When the question mark appears next to your cursor, you can pick any feature in the dialog box to see a description of what that feature does. See **Figure 1-15.**
- **... (Ellipsis button).** Some dialog box features have an ellipsis button. The ellipsis button provides access to a related dialog box. See **Figure 1-15.**

Figure 1-12.
The file dialog box provides a simple means of locating files. An image tile displays the selected setting or file.

Current folder

Double-click on a name to open the drawing

Preview box showing the selected drawing

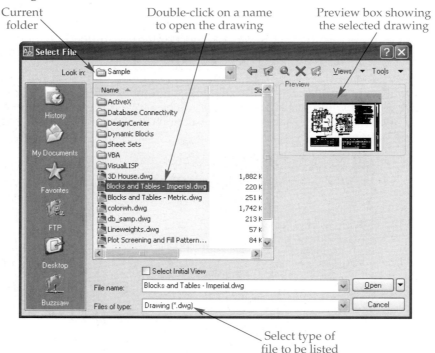

Select type of file to be listed

Figure 1-13.
Use scroll bars and buttons to scroll through a listing or to view sections of a drawing.

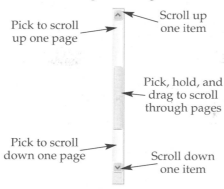

Scroll up one item

Pick to scroll up one page

Pick, hold, and drag to scroll through pages

Pick to scroll down one page

Scroll down one item

Figure 1-14.
An alert may appear as a separate dialog box.

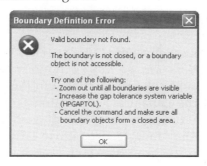

Figure 1-15.
The ... (ellipsis) button displays a dialog box providing additional options related to the dialog feature it is next to. The ellipsis button shown here is picked to display a dialog box for defining and modifying table styles.

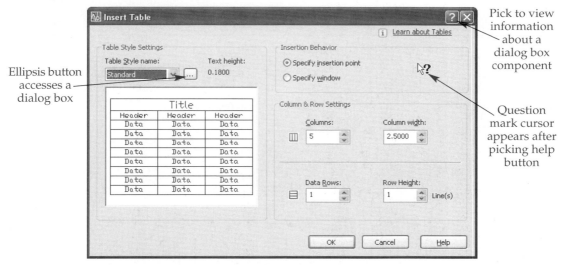

Ellipsis button accesses a dialog box

Pick to view information about a dialog box component

Question mark cursor appears after picking help button

Exercise 1-4

Complete the Exercise on the Student CD.

Shortcut Menus

AutoCAD makes extensive use of shortcut menus to simplify and accelerate command entries. Sometimes referred to as *cursor menus* because they are displayed at the cursor location, these context sensitive menus are accessed by right-clicking. Because they are context sensitive, the shortcut menu content varies based on the location of the pointer when you right-click and the current conditions, such as whether a command is active or whether an object is selected.

When you right-click in the drawing area with no command active, the first item displayed on the shortcut menu is typically an option to repeat the previously used command or operation. If you right-click while a command is active, the shortcut menu contains options specific to the command. See **Figure 1-16.**

Exercise 1-5

Complete the Exercise on the Student CD.

Modeless Dialog Boxes

Some AutoCAD features are presented in a special type of window that is sometimes referred to as a *modeless dialog box* or window. Features displayed in this manner include the **DesignCenter**, the **Properties** window, the **Sheet Set Manager**, the **Tool Palettes** window, and the **QuickCalc** calculator. Unlike standard dialog boxes, these windows can be docked or resized and do not need to be closed in order to type commands and work within the drawing. See **Figure 1-17.** If one of these windows has been docked, double-click on the grab bar to change it to the floating state. Double-click on the title bar to return to the docked position. When docked, the window's resizing bar allows you to adjust the size to suit your needs.

The **Auto-hide** button allows the window to minimize out of your way when the cursor is away from the window. Each modeless dialog box also contains a **Properties** button, which allows you to control how the window operates and displays within AutoCAD.

Figure 1-16.
Shortcut menus provide instant access to commands and options related to what you are doing at the time.

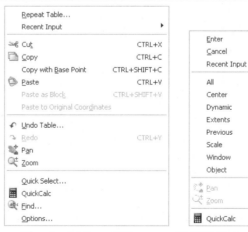

Shortcut Menu When No Active Command

ZOOM Command Shortcut Menu

Figure 1-17.
Modeless dialog boxes, such as the **QuickCalc** calculator, remain displayed on-screen as you work in the drawing area.

Title bar

Auto-hide button

Properties button

DesignCenter

DesignCenter is a powerful drawing information manager that provides a simple tool for effectively reusing and sharing drawing content. One of the primary productivity benefits of using CAD is that once something has been created, you can use it repeatedly in any number of drawings or drawing projects. Many types of drawing elements are similar or the same in numerous drawings, such as common drawing details, frequently used subassemblies or parts, and drawing layouts. **DesignCenter** lets you conveniently "drag and drop" drawing content to copy it from one drawing to another. When you first start **DesignCenter**, it is opened in the center of the AutoCAD window. The use of this powerful information management system is first discussed in Chapter 4 and additionally throughout the text where it applies.

Properties window

The **Properties** window lets you manage the properties of new and existing objects in a drawing. The actual use of the **Properties** window is explained where it applies throughout this text.

Sheet Set Manager

The **Sheet Set Manager** lets you create, organize, and manage sheets in a sheet set. A *sheet set* is a named collection of drawing sheets. The use of the **Sheet Set Manager** is explained in detail in Chapter 26.

Tool Palettes window

The **Tool Palettes** window provides access to frequently used commands, block symbols, and hatch fill patterns. These items can be organized into categories called palettes for easy management and use. **Figure 1-18** shows some sample tool palettes. The palettes can be customized with your own symbols, hatch patterns, or commands, and new palettes can also be created. This process is explained later in this text. The **Properties** button on this modeless dialog box includes a **Transparency...** option, which allows drawing geometry behind the palette to be viewed, as shown in **Figure 1-19**.

Figure 1-18.
Block symbols, hatch patterns, and commands can be organized into palettes. Mechanical fasteners and electrical symbols are available in these palettes.

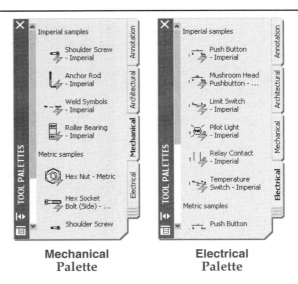

Mechanical Palette

Electrical Palette

Figure 1-19.
Tool palettes can be transparent by picking the **Properties** button in the title bar.

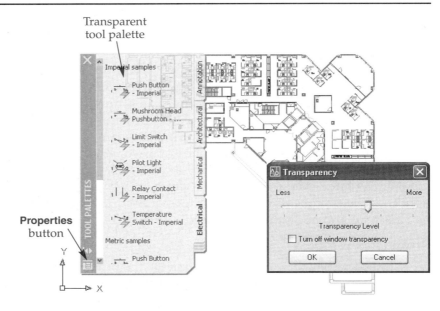

Transparent tool palette

Properties button

PROFESSIONAL TIP

You can move the modeless dialog boxes to the side of the AutoCAD window without docking them by holding the [Ctrl] key while positioning the windows.

QuickCalc calculator

The **QuickCalc** calculator allows you to perform mathematical, scientific, and trigonometric calculations. It also contains a units-of-measurement converter and allows variables to be created and saved for later use. The **QuickCalc** calculator is discussed in detail in Chapter 16.

Exercise 1-6   Complete the Exercise on the Student CD.

AutoCAD commands are selected using one of four primary ways:
- By picking a toolbar button.
- By selecting a pull-down menu item.
- By selecting a shortcut menu item.
- By typing at the keyboard.

The advantage of using toolbar buttons and shortcut menus is you do not need to remove your eyes from the screen. Typing commands may not require you to turn your eyes from the screen. You can also learn commands quickly by typing them.

Typing Commands at the Keyboard

Commands and options can be typed directly into AutoCAD by using Dynamic Input or the command line. When Dynamic Input is enabled, a temporary area for command input and command information is displayed at the crosshairs in the drawing area. When the command window is turned on, commands can be typed and command information can be read at the Command: prompts within the command window. Both of these features can be used at the same time or one of them can be disabled, depending on your working preference.

Using Dynamic Input

Dynamic Input allows you to keep your focus at the point where you are drawing. When a command is typed, it is displayed in the lower-right corner of the crosshairs. See **Figure 1-20.** To start a command, type the command name and press the [Enter] key. When a command is in process, the next action needed to proceed with the command is displayed along with additional command options, an input area, and additional information. Dynamic Input can be toggled on and off by either picking the **DYN** button on the status bar or by using the [F12] function key. If Dynamic Input is turned off, the command line is used for command input and information.

Figure 1-20.
Using Dynamic Input, commands can be typed in a temporary input area next to the crosshairs.

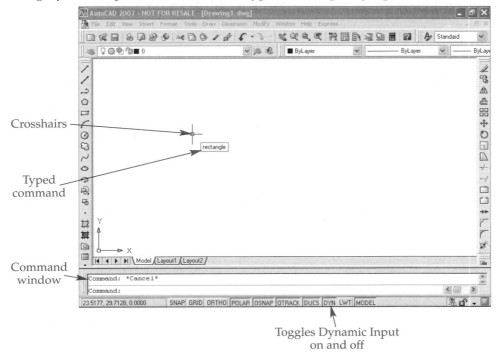

Crosshairs

Typed command

Command window

Toggles Dynamic Input on and off

Figure 1-21.
The Dynamic Input fields after the **RECTANGLE** command has been started.

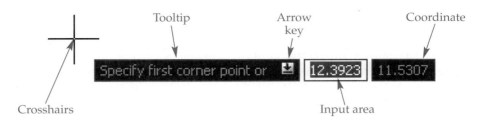

Depending on the command that is in process, different information and options are available in the Dynamic Input area. In **Figure 1-21**, the **RECTANGLE** command has been started and the available options are shown in the Dynamic Input area. The first part of the Dynamic Input area is the tooltip, which reads Specify first corner point or. In this case, you need to pick in the drawing area or type coordinates to specify the first corner of the rectangle, or use the arrow keys.

Pressing the down arrow key displays the available options associated with the current command. See **Figure 1-22**. Pressing the down arrow again cycles through the available options, which is indicated by a bullet next to the option. To select an option once it is bulleted, press [Enter]. The next available options and additional information are then displayed in the Dynamic Input area.

Once a command is started, the Dynamic Input area displays the appropriate tooltip, input field, and any other additional information for the current command. This information changes during the command depending on the action. In **Figure 1-23**, two different illustrations are shown during the process of using the **LINE** command. Additional options for Dynamic Input are discussed in Chapter 3.

Using the command window

AutoCAD commands can be typed only when the command window displays the Command: prompt. When a command is started, whether from a menu selection or by typing, AutoCAD either performs the specified operation or prompts you for any additional information. AutoCAD commands have a standard format, structured as follows:

Command: **COMMANDNAME**⏎
Current settings: Setting1 Setting2 Setting3
Instructional text [Option1/oPtion2/opTion3/...] <default option or value>:

Figure 1-22.
Using the down arrow key exposes additional options for the current command. The dot identifies the option to be selected. Use the up and down arrow keys to position the dot at the desired option and press the [Enter] key.

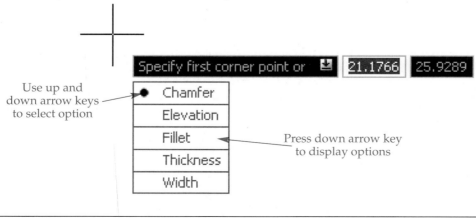

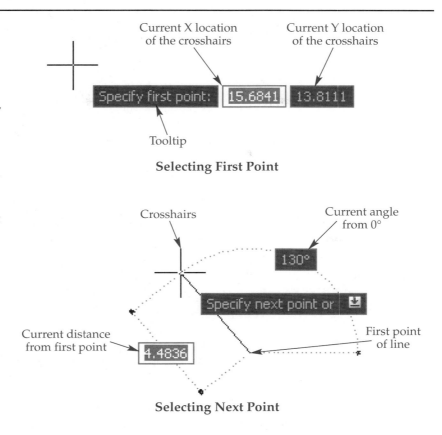

Figure 1-23.
The Dynamic Input fields change when using the **LINE** command. When picking the first endpoint of the line, the coordinates of the crosshairs are displayed. After the first endpoint is picked, the distance and angle of the crosshairs relative to the first endpoint are displayed.

Current X location of the crosshairs

Current Y location of the crosshairs

Tooltip

Selecting First Point

Crosshairs

Current angle from 0°

Current distance from first point

First point of line

Selecting Next Point

If the command has associated settings or options, these are displayed as shown. The instructional text indicates what you should do at this point, and all available options are shown within the square brackets. Each option has a unique combination of uppercase characters that can be entered at the prompt rather than typing the entire option name. If a default option is displayed in the angle brackets, you can press [Enter] to accept it rather than typing the value again.

The command window can be turned on and off by selecting **Tools** > **Command Line** or by using the [Ctrl]+[9] key combination. The command window can also be dragged into the drawing area and resized in the same manner as a toolbar.

Command entry shortcuts

AutoCAD provides you with the ability to select previously used commands by using the up and down arrow keys. When no command is active, press the up arrow key on the keyboard to display the previously used command. If you continue to press the up arrow key, AutoCAD continues to back track through the commands you have used. Then press [Enter] to activate a displayed command.

Right-clicking in the drawing area displays a shortcut menu with a cascading menu showing a list of commands you have used recently. See **Figure 1-24.** Pick a command name from the list to use that command again.

In addition, you can type the first letter (or several letters) of the command or system variable you wish to use, and then press the [Tab] key. This displays the first command or system variable beginning with the entered letter(s). Continue to press the [Tab] key to display all of the commands and system variables. When the desired command is displayed, press the [Enter] key.

Figure 1-24.
The shortcut menu displayed when you right-click in the drawing area offers a cascading menu listing commands you have used recently.

Repeat most recent commands

Cascading menu lists recent inputs

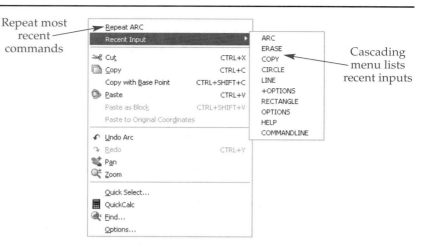

Exercise 1-7 Complete the Exercise on the Student CD.

Getting Help

If you need help with a specific command, option, or program feature, AutoCAD provides a powerful and convenient help system. There are several ways to access this feature. The fastest method is to press the [F1] function key. You can also pick the **?** button at the right end of the **Standard** toolbar, select **Help** > **Help** from the pull-down menu, or type **?** or **HELP**. Each of these methods displays the **AutoCAD Help** window.

NOTE

If you are unfamiliar with how to use a Windows help system, it is suggested you spend time now exploring all the topics under **AutoCAD Help** in the **Contents** tab of the **AutoCAD Help** window.

The **AutoCAD Help** window consists of two frames. See **Figure 1-25**. The left frame, which has three tabs, is used to locate help topics. The right frame displays the selected help topics. The tabs in the left frame are as follows:

- **Contents.** This tab displays a list of book icons and topic names. The book icons represent the organizational structure of books of topics within the AutoCAD documentation. Topics contain the actual help information; the icon used to represent a topic is a sheet of paper with a question mark. To open a book or a help topic, double-click on its name or icon. The **Contents** tab lists each of the help documents within the AutoCAD help system. The documents available

Figure 1-25.
The **AutoCAD Help** window.

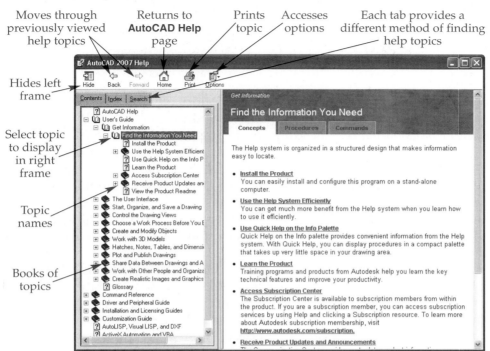

Moves through previously viewed help topics

Returns to **AutoCAD Help** page

Prints topic

Accesses options

Each tab provides a different method of finding help topics

Hides left frame

Select topic to display in right frame

Topic names

Books of topics

are **AutoCAD Help**; **User's Guide**; **Command Reference**; **Driver and Peripheral Guide**; **Installation and Licensing Guides**; **Customization Guide**; **AutoLISP, Visual LISP, and DXF**; and **ActiveX Automation and VBA**.

- **Index.** Although the **Contents** tab of the **AutoCAD Help** window is useful for displaying all the topics in an expanded table of contents manner, it is not very useful when searching for a specific item. In this case, most people refer to the index. This is the function of the **Index** tab.
- **Search.** This tab is used to search the help documents for specific words or phrases.

In addition to the two frames and four tabs, there are six buttons located at the top of the **AutoCAD Help** window. The **Hide/Show** button controls the visibility of the left frame. The **Back** button is used to view the previously displayed help topic. The **Forward** button is used to go forward to help pages you viewed before pressing the **Back** button. The **Home** button takes you to the AutoCAD Help page. The **Print** button is used to print a help topic. The **Options** button contains a cascading menu with a variety of items used to control other aspects of the **AutoCAD Help** window.

PROFESSIONAL TIP

AutoCAD's help function can also be used while you are in the process of using a command. For example, suppose you are using the **ARC** command and forget what type of information AutoCAD requires for the specific prompts on screen. Get help by pressing the [F1] function key, and the help information for the currently active command is displayed. This *context-oriented help* saves valuable time, since you do not need to scan through the help contents or perform any searches to find the information.

Exercise 1-8 Complete the Exercise on the Student CD.

The Info Palette

ASSIST

Type
ASSIST [Ctrl]+[5]
Pull-Down Menu
Help > Help

The **Info Palette** is a modeless dialog box that continually monitors your actions and displays help information for the active command or dialog box. With the **Info Palette**, you can display a list of procedures in a compact palette that takes up very little space in the drawing area. The **Info Palette** can also be docked on either side of the drawing area so you can work more efficiently. It can be accessed by selecting **Help > Info Palette**, by typing ASSIST, or by using the [Ctrl]+[5] key combination.

The **Info Palette** is shown in **Figure 1-26**. It remains active as you work in AutoCAD and updates the displayed help information as you start new commands. If you need to freeze the information displayed, you can lock the **Info Palette** by picking the **Lock to prevent content from changing** button.

To navigate through the **Quick Help** tab, print information, or lock the **Info Palette**, you can use the buttons across the top of the **Info Palette**. You can also right-click in the **Info Palette** to display the **Info Palette** shortcut menu.

The **Info Palette** has properties that can be changed when it is in the undocked state. To change these settings, click the **Properties** button at the lower end of the **Info Palette** title bar. The following options are available:

- **Move.** This option allows you to move the **Info Palette**.
- **Size.** This option allows you to change the size of the **Info Palette**.
- **Close.** This option closes the **Info Palette**.
- **Allow Docking.** This option controls whether or not the **Info Palette** docks when you drag it over a docking area at the side of the drawing area.
- **Anchor Left.** This option docks the **Info Palette** to the left of the drawing area.
- **Anchor Right.** This option docks the **Info Palette** to the right of the drawing area.

Figure 1-26.
The **Info Palette** provides help information for the current command.

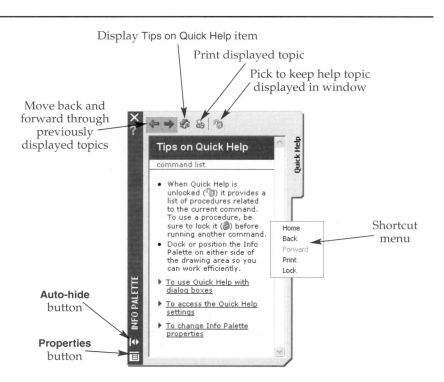

- **Auto-hide.** This option sets the **Info Palette** to display information only when the cursor is over the title bar. Make sure this option does not have a check mark if you want to display the **Info Palette** content at all times.
- **Transparency.** This option accesses the **Transparency** dialog box. This dialog box sets the display for the **Info Palette** to be opaque or transparent.

When you are finished using the **Info Palette**, you can click on the X to exit.

Using the Support Knowledge Base

AutoCAD's product support extends beyond the locally installed help system. There is additional support resources on the Autodesk Web site. To access this information, pick **Help > Additional Resources > Support Knowledge Base.** Your computer must have an Internet connection to access this information. Enter the topic in the text box to search the database.

Pull-Down Menu
Help
> Additional
Resources
> Support
Knowledge
Base

Exercise 1-9   Complete the Exercise on the Student CD.

Keyboard Keys

AutoCAD provides several ways of performing a given task. Many keys on the keyboard allow you to quickly perform many functions. Become familiar with the meaning of these keys to help improve your performance with AutoCAD.

The [Esc] Key

Any time it is necessary to cancel a command or dialog box, press the *escape key* [Esc] on your keyboard. This key is found on the upper-left corner of most keyboards and is typically labeled Esc. Some command sequences may require the [Esc] key to be pressed twice to completely cancel the operation.

Control Keys

Most computer programs use *control key* functions to perform common tasks. Control key functions are used by pressing and holding the [Ctrl] key while pressing a second key. These keys are also called *accelerator keys*. Print the list of control keys found on the Student CD. Keep the list close at hand and try the keys occasionally. If a command or key is noted as a "toggle," it is either on or off—nothing else.

Function Keys

Function keys provide instant access to commands. They can also be programmed to perform a series of commands. The function keys are located along the top of the keyboard and are numbered from [F1] to [F12]. The default commands for function keys are listed on the Student CD.

> **NOTE**
>
> The Reference Materials section of the Student CD includes lists of control key shortcuts and function key commands. Keep printouts of these reference sheets handy while you are learning AutoCAD.

Understanding Terminology

The following terms are used throughout the text and will help you select AutoCAD functions. You should become familiar with them.

- **Default.** A value maintained by the computer until you change it.
- **Pick or click.** Use the mouse to select an item on the screen.
- **Button.** One of the screen toolbar or mouse buttons.
- **Key.** A key on the keyboard.
- **Function key.** One of the keys labeled [F1]–[F12] along the top of the keyboard.
- **[Enter] (⏎).** The [Enter] key on the keyboard.
- **Command.** An instruction issued to the computer.
- **Option.** An aspect of a command that can be selected.

Exiting AutoCAD

EXIT

Type
EXIT
QUIT

Pull-Down Menu
File
> Exit

The **EXIT** command is the primary way to end an AutoCAD session. You can close the program by picking **File > Exit** or by typing EXIT or QUIT. If you attempt to exit before saving your work, AutoCAD gives you a chance to decide what you want to do with unsaved work.

Chapter Test

Answer the following questions. Write your answers on a separate sheet of paper or complete the electronic chapter test on the Student CD.

1. What system is used to construct drawings and models in AutoCAD?
2. Basic pictorial drawings are called _____.
3. Using the system referred to in Question 1, what is the proper notation for the values Z=4, X=2, and Y=5?
4. What is *drawing planning*?
5. Why is drawing planning important?
6. What is the first thing you should do as part of your planning checklist?
7. Why should you save your work every ten to fifteen minutes?
8. What are *standards*?
9. What scale should you use to draw in AutoCAD?
10. Name the two methods used to input data into AutoCAD.
11. Why should you read the prompts displayed in the dynamic input area and command window?
12. What is the quickest method for starting AutoCAD?
13. Which toolbars are displayed by default when AutoCAD is launched?
14. What is a *grab bar*?
15. What is the difference between a docked toolbar and a floating toolbar?
16. How do you select the locking options to lock the toolbars and windows in both their floating and docked states?
17. How do you move a toolbar or window that is locked, without unlocking it first?
18. What are *menu accelerator keys*? How are they used? Give an example.
19. What is an *option*?
20. What is a *flyout menu*?
21. What is the function of tabs in a dialog box?

22. What are the functions of the following control keys? (Refer to the *Shortcut Keys* document in the *Reference Materials* section of the Student CD.)
    A. [Ctrl]+[B]
    B. [Ctrl]+[C]
    C. [Ctrl]+[D]
    D. [Ctrl]+[G]
    E. [Ctrl]+[O]
    F. [Ctrl]+[S]
23. Name the function keys that execute the same tasks as the following control keys. (Refer to the *Shortcut Keys* document in the *Reference Materials* section of the Student CD.)
    A. [Ctrl]+[B]
    B. [Ctrl]+[D]
    C. [Ctrl]+[G]
    D. [Ctrl]+[L]
    E. [Ctrl]+[T]
24. What type of pull-down menu item has an arrow to the right?
25. What is *context oriented help,* and how is it accessed?
26. How do you open a folder in a file dialog box in order to see its contents?
27. What is the function of the ... (ellipsis) button?
28. How do you access a shortcut menu?
29. Why are shortcut menus considered context sensitive?
30. How do you access previously used commands?
31. Briefly explain the function of the [Esc] key.
32. Identify the quickest way to access the **AutoCAD Help** window.
33. What happens to the cursor when you pick the question mark in the upper-right corner of a dialog box? What is the purpose of the cursor?
34. Describe the purpose of the book icons in the **Contents** tab of the **AutoCAD Help** window.
35. Identify the tab in the **AutoCAD Help** window that allows you to do a detailed search based on one or more words.

Drawing Problems

1. Interview your drafting instructor or supervisor and try to determine what type of drawing standards exist at your school or company. Write them down and keep them with you as you learn AutoCAD. Make notes as you progress through this text on how you use these standards. Also note how the standards could be changed to better match the capabilities of AutoCAD.

2. Research your drafting department standards. If you do not have a copy of the standards, acquire one. If AutoCAD standards have been created, make notes as to how you can use these in your projects. If no standards exist in your department or company, make notes as to how you can help develop standards. Write a report on why your school or company should create CAD standards and how they would be used. Discuss who should be responsible for specific tasks. Recommend procedures, techniques, and forms, if necessary. Develop this report as you progress through your AutoCAD instruction and as you read through this book.

3. Develop a drawing planning sheet for use in your school or company. List items you think are important for planning a CAD drawing. Make changes to this sheet as you learn more about AutoCAD.

4. Launch AutoCAD and perform the following tasks:
   A. Open the **AutoCAD Help** window.
   B. In the **Contents** tab, expand the User's Guide category.
   C. In the right pane, pick the Get Information, Find the Information You Need, and Use the Help System Efficiently topics.
   D. If you have access to a printer, print the topic.
   E. Close the **AutoCAD Help** window, and then close AutoCAD.

5. Launch AutoCAD using the Start button on the Windows task bar.
   A. Move the pointer over the buttons in the **Standard** toolbar and read the notes on the status bar at the bottom of the screen.
   B. Slowly move the pointer over each of the buttons on the **Styles** and **Layers** toolbars and read the tooltips. Do the same on the **Draw** and **Modify** toolbars at the sides of the screen.
   C. Pick the **File** pull-down menu to display it. Using the right arrow key, move through all the pull-down menus. Use the left arrow key to return to the **Draw** pull-down menu. Use the down arrow key to move to the **Circle** command, then use the right arrow key to display the **Circle** options in the cascading menu.
   D. Press the [Esc] key to dismiss the menu.
   E. Close AutoCAD.

6. Draw a freehand sketch of the screen display. Label each of the screen areas. To the side of the sketch, write a short description of each screen area's function.

CHAPTER 2

Working with Drawings and Templates

Learning Objectives

After completing this chapter, you will be able to do the following:
- Start a new drawing.
- Save a drawing under a different name.
- Specify how often your work is automatically saved.
- Save AutoCAD drawings for older releases.
- Open a saved drawing.
- Search for AutoCAD files.
- Manage multiple drawings.
- Use the **CLOSE** and **EXIT** commands.
- Adjust grid and snap settings.
- Determine settings for linear and angular units and precision.
- Create a template drawing.

When using AutoCAD, you work with drawing files. In this chapter, you will learn how to create new drawing files, save drawing files, and open existing drawing files.

New drawings are typically created using templates. Templates allow you to start a new drawing with preset drawing aids and objects, such as borders or title blocks. Many templates are provided with AutoCAD, and you can also create custom templates.

Some of the basic drawing aids used in AutoCAD are discussed in this chapter. As you begin working with drawing files, you will find these and other types of settings a very useful starting point.

Starting a New Drawing

In AutoCAD, new drawings are typically started from templates. *Templates* store standard drawing settings and objects. All settings and contents of the template file are included in the new drawing.

Templates can be incredible productivity boosters. The provided template files may meet some personal needs, but creating new custom templates is where the greatest benefit is found. Custom templates allow you to use an existing drawing as a starting point for any new drawing. This option is extremely valuable for ensuring that everyone in a department, class, school, or company uses the same standards within their drawings.

When using a template, values defining the drawing settings are automatically set. Templates usually have the following values and drawing elements:

✓ Standard layouts with a border and title block.
✓ Grid and snap settings.
✓ Units and angle values.
✓ Text standards and general notes.
✓ Dimensioning styles.
✓ Layer definitions.
✓ Plot styles.

These items are discussed later in this textbook.

To start a drawing, select **File** > **New...**, type NEW, or use the [Ctrl]+[N] key combination. This displays the **Select template** dialog box, **Figure 2-1.**

The **Select template** dialog box lists the templates found in the default template folder. A variety of templates conforming to accepted industry standards are included with AutoCAD. You will notice all the files have a .dwt extension, which stands for *drawing template*. If you just want to open a blank file, use the acad.dwt template for English settings or the acadiso.dwt template for metric settings. To open a template file, double-click on the file or select the file and then pick the **Open** button.

Standard Templates

The template files provided with AutoCAD use a naming system indicating the drafting standard referenced, the size of the title block in the preset layout, and the plot style settings used. Plot styles are introduced in Chapter 11.

Drafters often think of the drawing size as sheet size. The *sheet size* is the size of the paper you will use to lay out and plot the final drawing. It takes into account the size of the drawing and additional space for dimensions, notes, and clear space between the drawing and border lines. The sheet size also includes room for the title block, the revision block, zoning, and an area for general notes. In AutoCAD, the sheet size is specified in the **Page Setup** dialog box when defining your drawing layout. The **Page Setup** dialog box is discussed in Chapter 11.

Figure 2-1.
The **Select template** dialog box allows you to begin a new drawing by selecting a template.

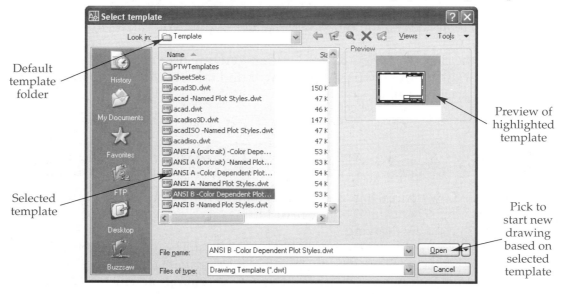

American Society of Mechanical Engineers (ASME) and American National Standards Institute (ANSI) standard sheet sizes and formats are specified in the documents ASME Y14.1, *Decimal Inch Drawing Sheet Size and Format,* and ASME Y14.1M, *Metric Drawing Sheet Size and Format.* ASME Y14.1 lists sheet size specifications in inches, as follows:

Size Designation	Size (in inches)
A	8 1/2 × 11 (horizontal format)
	11 × 8 1/2 (vertical format)
B	11 × 17
C	17 × 22
D	22 × 34
E	34 × 44
F	28 × 40
Sizes G, H, J, and K are roll sizes.	

ASME Y14.1M provides sheet size specifications in metric units. Standard metric drawing sheet sizes are designated as follows:

Size Designation	Size (in millimeters)
A0	841 × 1189
A1	594 × 841
A2	420 × 594
A3	297 × 420
A4	210 × 297

Longer lengths are referred to as elongated and extra-elongated drawing sizes. These are available in multiples of the short side of the sheet size. **Figure 2-2** shows standard ASME/ANSI sheet sizes.

All generic and ANSI templates provided with AutoCAD are based on decimal inches as the unit of measure. The architectural templates are set up for measurements in inches and feet, which is typical in architectural applications. DIN, Gb, ISO, and JIS template files are based on metric measurement settings.

NOTE   *DIN* refers to the German standard *Deutsches Institut Für Normung,* which was established by the German Institute for Standardization. *Gb* refers to Guo Biao (Chinese) standards, *ISO* is the International Organization for Standardization, and *JIS* is the Japanese Industry Standard.

The ANSI, DIN, Gb, ISO, and JIS templates provide layouts with the title block located in the lower-right corner. The architectural templates provide a title block on the right side of the sheet, which is common in the architectural industry. The Template folder also contains the acad.dwt template, for starting a drawing using feet and inches, and the acadiso.dwt template, for using metric units. These options do not have layouts or title blocks.

Figure 2-2.
A—Standard drawing sheet sizes (ASME Y14.1). B—Standard metric drawing sheet sizes (ASME Y14.1M).

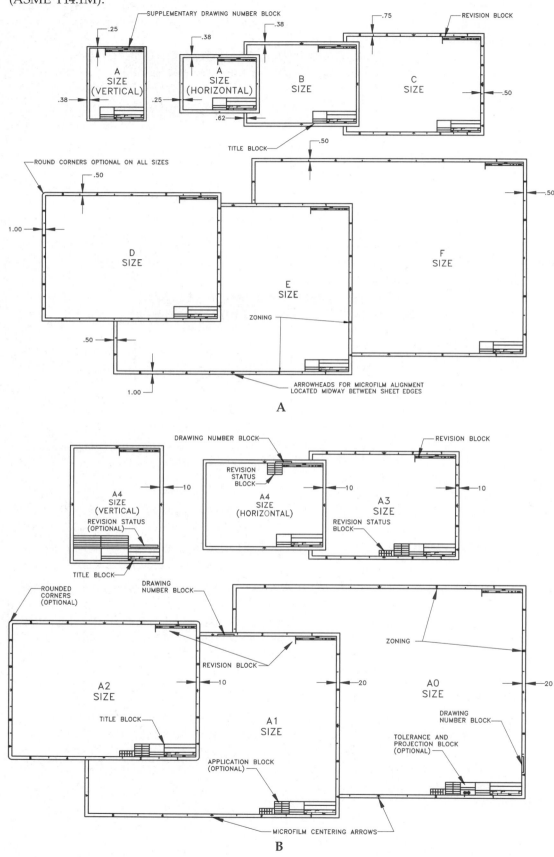

Exercise 2-1   Complete the Exercise on the Student CD.

Starting a Drawing Quickly

AutoCAD also provides methods of starting a new drawing from a preset template. This allows you to begin a drawing more quickly.

Before using the "quick start" feature, you must specify the template to be used for quick starts. This is done in the **Options** dialog box. To access the dialog box, pick **Tools** > **Options...**. In the **Files** tab, expand Template Settings, and then expand Default Template File Name for QNEW item. Either a template file name or None is displayed. See **Figure 2-3.** Pick the **Browse...** button to select a template.

To start a new drawing using this template, pick the **QNew** button from the **Standard** toolbar or type QNEW. A new drawing is started.

If the Default Template File Name for QNEW setting is None, typing the **QNEW** command or picking the **QNew** button opens the **Select template** dialog box.

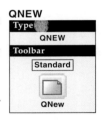

Figure 2-3.
Specifying a template file for the **QNEW** command.

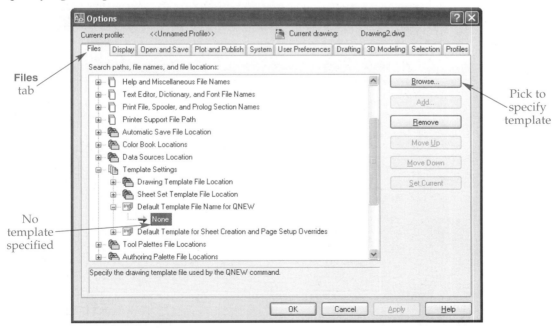

Other Options for Starting Drawings

You can also start a drawing without using a template. This is also called starting a drawing "from scratch." Doing so provides a "blank" drawing without a title block, layouts, or customized drawing settings. Use this option to "play it by ear" when just sketching or when the start or end of a drawing project is unknown.

To create a new drawing from scratch, pick the arrow next to the **Open** button in the **Select template** dialog box. See **Figure 2-4.** Select one of the **Open with no Template** options. Pick the option corresponding to the type of units to be used in the drawing.

LEGACY NOTE

AutoCAD provides an alternative method for drawing startup using a **Startup** dialog box. This method is inactive by default, but can be selected from the **System** tab of the **Options** dialog box. When this method is active, a **Startup** or **Create New Drawing** dialog box appears when AutoCAD is started and when the **NEW** command is issued. These dialog boxes allow you to select a template, start a drawing from scratch, or use a startup wizard to set drawing settings. It is recommended that you use the default settings instead of this alternative method.

Figure 2-4.
Starting a drawing without a template.

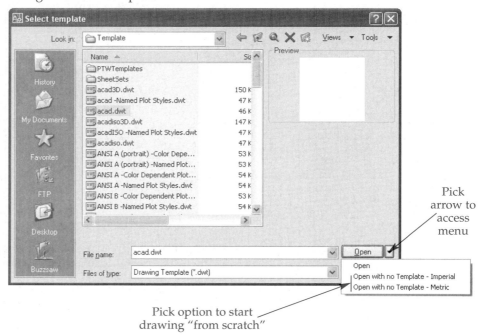

Pick arrow to access menu

Pick option to start drawing "from scratch"

Saving Drawings

After starting a drawing, you need to assign a name to the new drawing and save it. The following discussion provides you with detailed information about saving and quitting a drawing. When saving drawing files using either the **QSAVE** or **SAVEAS** command, you can use a dialog box or type everything at the Command: prompt.

PROFESSIONAL TIP

The appearance of dialog boxes is controlled by the **FILEDIA** system variable. A *system variable* is a setting that lets you change the way AutoCAD works. System variables are remembered by AutoCAD and remain in effect until you change them again. If the **FILEDIA** system variable is set to 1, the default, dialog boxes are displayed at the appropriate times. If **FILEDIA** is set to 0, dialog boxes do not appear. You must then type the desired information at the prompt line.

Naming Drawings

Drawing names may be chosen to identify a product by name and number—for example, VICE-101, FLOORPLAN, or 6DT1005. Your school or company probably has a drawing numbering system you can use. Drawing names should be recorded in a part numbering or drawing name log. Such a log serves as a valuable reference long after you forget what the drawings contain.

It is important to set up a system that allows you to determine the content of a drawing by the drawing name. Although it is possible to give a drawing file an extended name, such as Details for Top Half of Compressor Housing for ACME, Inc., Part Number 4011A, Revision Level C, this is normally not a practical way of sorting drawing information. Drawing titles should be standardized and may be most effective when making a clear and concise reference to the project, part number, process, sheet number, and revision level.

When a standardized naming system exists, a shorter name like ACME.4011A.C provides all the necessary information. If additional information is desirable for easier recognition, it can be added to the base name, for example: ACME 4011A.C Compressor Housing.Top.Casting Details. Always record drawing names and provide information related to the drawings. The following rules and restrictions apply to naming all files, including AutoCAD drawings:
- A maximum of 256 characters can be used.
- Alphabetical and numeric characters and spaces, along with most punctuation symbols, can be used.
- The following characters cannot be used: quotation mark ("), asterisk (*), question mark (?), forward slash (/), and backward slash (\).

Saving Your Work

You must save your drawing periodically to protect your work. While working in AutoCAD, you should save your drawing every 10 to 15 minutes. This is very important! If there is a power failure, a severe editing error, or another problem, all the work saved prior to the problem will be usable. If you save only once an hour, a power failure could result in an hour of lost work. Saving your drawing every 10 to 15 minutes results in less lost work if a problem occurs.

The **QSAVE**, **SAVEAS**, and **SAVE** commands allow you to save your work. Also, any command or option ending the AutoCAD session provides a warning asking if you want to save changes to the drawing. This gives you a final option to either save or not save changes to the drawing.

Using the Qsave Command

QSAVE

Type
QSAVE [Ctrl]+[S]
Pull-Down Menu
File > Save
Toolbar
Standard
Save

Of the three available saving commands, the most frequently used is the **QSAVE** command. **QSAVE** stands for *quick save*. The **QSAVE** command is accessed by picking the **Save** button from the **Standard** toolbar, picking **File** > **Save** from the pull-down menu, typing QSAVE, or pressing [Ctrl]+[S].

The **QSAVE** command response depends on whether or not the drawing already has a name. If the current drawing has a name, the **QSAVE** command updates the file based on the current state of the drawing. In this situation, **QSAVE** issues no prompts and displays no messages.

If the current drawing has not yet been named, the **QSAVE** command displays the **Save Drawing As** dialog box. See **Figure 2-5.** You must complete three steps in order to save your file:

1. Select the folder in which the file is to be saved.
2. Select the type of file to save, such as drawing (.dwg) or template (.dwt).
3. Type a name for the file.

When selecting the folder in which the file will be stored, first select the disk drive from the **Save in:** drop-down list. To move upward from the current folder, pick the **Up one level** button. To create a new folder in the current location, pick the **Create New Folder** button and type the name for the folder.

The **Files of type:** drop-down list offers options to save the drawing file in alternative formats. For most applications, this should be set to AutoCAD 2007 Drawing (*.dwg) when saving drawings. When saving a template file, this is set as AutoCAD Drawing Template (*.dwt).

Figure 2-5.
The **Save Drawing As** dialog box.

Select folder where drawing will be saved

Move up one level from current folder

Create a new folder

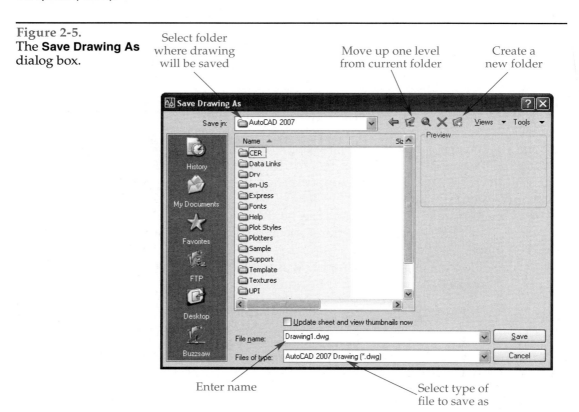

Enter name

Select type of file to save as

If the drawing has not yet been named, the name Drawing1 appears in the **File name:** text box. Change this to the desired drawing name. You do not need to include the .dwg extension.

Once you have specified the correct location and file name, pick the **Save** button to save the drawing file. Keep in mind that you can either pick the **Save** button or just press the [Enter] key to activate the **Save** button and save the drawing.

 NOTE The **Save Drawing As** dialog box is a standard file selection dialog box. The features of this dialog box are discussed more thoroughly later in this chapter.

Using the Saveas Command

The **SAVEAS** command is used in the following situations:
- When the current drawing already has a name and you need to save it under a different name.
- When you need to save the current drawing in an alternative format, such as a previous AutoCAD release format.
- When you open one of your drawing template files and create a drawing. This leaves the drawing template unchanged and ready to be used for other drawings.

The **SAVEAS** command is accessed by picking **File > Save As...** from the pull-down menu or by typing SAVEAS. This command always displays the **Save Drawing As** dialog box. If the current drawing has already been saved, the current name and location are displayed. Confirm that the **Save in:** drop-down list displays the current drive and directory folder you want and that the **Files of type:** drop-down list displays the desired file type. Type the new drawing name in the **File name:** text box and pick the **Save** button.

SAVEAS	
Type	SAVEAS
Pull-Down Menu	File > Save As...

 **LEGACY NOTE** The third command provided for saving a drawing is the **SAVE** command. The **SAVE** command is not commonly used and is only available by typing SAVE. The **SAVE** command displays the **Save Drawing As** dialog box, regardless of whether the drawing has been previously saved. Because of this, the **QSAVE** command is better for saving a drawing in progress, and the **SAVEAS** command is better for saving a drawing with a new name or location.

When saving a drawing to a different name, the **SAVE** command saves the drawing file with a different name, but leaves you in the current drawing. The **SAVEAS** command discards all changes to the original drawing file up to the last save.

Saving Your Work Automatically

AutoCAD can create an automatic backup copy of the active drawing. The backup file has a .bak extension and is created in the same folder where the drawing is located. When you save the drawing, the DWG file is updated, and the BAK file is overwritten by the old DWG file. Therefore, the backup file is always "one save behind" the drawing file.

Figure 2-6.
Use the **Open and Save** tab in the **Options** dialog box to save backup files and set the autosave feature.

Activates autosave

Autosave timer setting

Creates backup copies

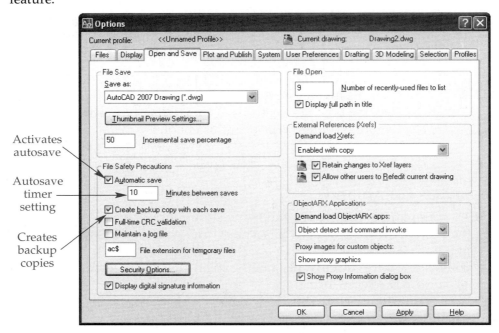

This feature can be activated using the **Create backup copy with each save** check box in the **Open and Save** tab of the **Options** dialog box. See **Figure 2-6**.

Before you can access a backup file, you must rename it. Use Windows Explorer to rename the file and change the file extension from .bak to .dwg. Once the file has been renamed, it can be opened in AutoCAD.

AutoCAD provides you with an automatic work-saving tool called *automatic save (autosave)*. Type the amount of time (in minutes) between saves in the **Open and Save** tab of the **Options** dialog box. The value is typed in the **Minutes between saves** text box in the **File Safety Precautions** area. See **Figure 2-6**, which shows a setting of 10 minutes.

The autosave timer starts as soon as a change is made to the drawing. The timer is reset when the drawing is saved. The drawing is automatically saved when the first command is given after the autosave timer has been reached. For example, if you set the timer to 10 minutes, work for 9 minutes, and then let the computer remain idle for 5 minutes, an automatic save is not executed until you return and execute a command. Therefore, be sure to manually save your drawing if you plan to be away from your computer for an extended period of time.

The autosave feature is intended to be used in case AutoCAD shuts down unexpectedly. Therefore, when you close a drawing file, the autosave file associated with that drawing is automatically deleted. If AutoCAD does shut down unexpectedly, the autosave file remains and can be used. The autosave drawing is always saved with the name of *DrawingName_n_n_nnnn*.sv$. If you need to use the autosave file, it must be renamed with a .dwg extension using Windows Explorer. Refer to the Student CD for more information on Windows Explorer.

> **NOTE**
>
> The **Automatic Save File Location** listing in the **Files** tab of the **Options** dialog box determines the folder where the autosave files are saved.

Saving AutoCAD Drawings to Older Release Formats

The drawing file type saved by AutoCAD 2007 is a different file format from the file types saved by previous releases of AutoCAD. AutoCAD 2007 drawings can be saved in a different file format, such as the AutoCAD 2004 format. This allows you to send AutoCAD 2007 drawings to businesses where older releases of AutoCAD are being used.

To save a drawing to an older release format, use the **SAVEAS** command. The **Save Drawing As** dialog box appears. Using the **Files of type:** drop-down list, select the AutoCAD 2004/LT2004 Drawing (*.dwg) option to save the drawing in the AutoCAD 2004 format. AutoCAD 2004, 2005, and 2006 all use AutoCAD 2004 format files.

When you save a version of a drawing in an earlier format, be sure to give it a different name from the AutoCAD 2007 version. This prevents you from accidentally overwriting your working drawing with the older format file.

NOTE Additional information on saving AutoCAD drawings in alternative formats can be found in the Windows Explorer material on the Student CD.

Opening Existing Drawings

An existing drawing is one that has been previously saved. There are various ways to open existing drawings. You can use the **OPEN** command, select from the **File** pull-down menu, or open a drawing from Windows Explorer. These methods are discussed in the following sections.

Using the Open Command

You can easily access any existing drawing with the **OPEN** command. To use the **OPEN** command, pick the **Open** button on the **Standard** toolbar, select **File** > **Open...** from the pull-down menu, press the [Ctrl]+[O] key combination, or type OPEN. The **Select File** dialog box appears. See **Figure 2-7.** This dialog box contains a list of folders and files. Double-click on a file folder to open it, and then double-click on the desired file to open it. In **Figure 2-7,** the AutoCAD 2007\Sample folder is shown open, with the sample drawings displayed.

When you select an existing drawing, a picture of the drawing is displayed in the **Preview** area. This provides an easy way for you to get a quick look at the drawing without loading it into AutoCAD. You can view each drawing until you find the one you want.

After picking a drawing file name to highlight it, you can quickly highlight another drawing in the list by using the keyboard arrow keys. Use the up and down arrow keys to move vertically between files and use the left and right arrow keys to move horizontally. This enables you to scan through the drawing previews very quickly.

OPEN

Type
OPEN
[Ctrl]+[O]

Pull-Down Menu
File
> Open...

Toolbar
Standard

Open

Exercise 2-2   Complete the Exercise on the Student CD.

Figure 2-7.
The **Select File** dialog box is used to select a drawing to open. Notice the db_samp drawing has been selected from the file list box and appears in the **File name:** text box.

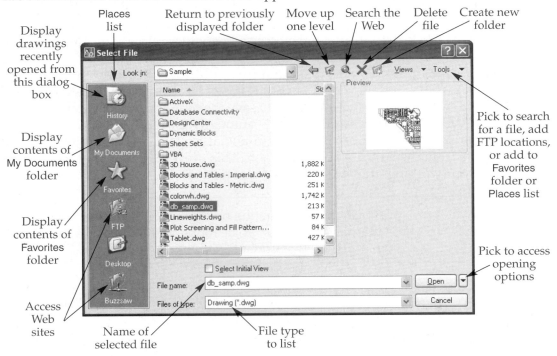

Display drawings recently opened from this dialog box

Places list

Return to previously displayed folder

Move up one level

Search the Web

Delete file

Create new folder

Display contents of My Documents folder

Display contents of Favorites folder

Access Web sites

Name of selected file

File type to list

Pick to search for a file, add FTP locations, or add to Favorites folder or Places list

Pick to access opening options

Opening Drawings from the File Pull-Down Menu List

By default, AutoCAD stores the names and locations of the last nine drawing files opened. These file names are listed at the bottom of the **File** pull-down menu, as shown in **Figure 2-8.** Any one of these files can be quickly opened by picking the file name.

If you try to open one of these drawing files after it has been deleted or moved to a different drive or directory, AutoCAD is unable to locate it. AutoCAD displays the message Cannot find the specified drawing file. Please verify that the file exists. AutoCAD then opens the **Select File** dialog box.

PROFESSIONAL TIP
You can specify the number of previous drawings displayed in the **File** pull-down menu by accessing the **Open and Save** tab of the **Options** dialog box. The setting that controls this function is the **Number of recently-used files to list** value in the **File Open** area.

Using Windows Explorer to Open Drawings

You can open drawing files through Windows Explorer. This can be done in two ways. You can double-click on the file, and it opens in AutoCAD. If AutoCAD is not already running, it starts and the file is opened. You can also drag-and-drop a file to the AutoCAD command line, and AutoCAD opens it. If AutoCAD is not running, you can drag-and-drop the file to the AutoCAD icon on your desktop. AutoCAD then starts and opens the drawing file. Refer to the Student CD for more information about Windows Explorer.

Figure 2-8.
The **File** pull-down
menu contains a
list of the last nine
edited drawings.

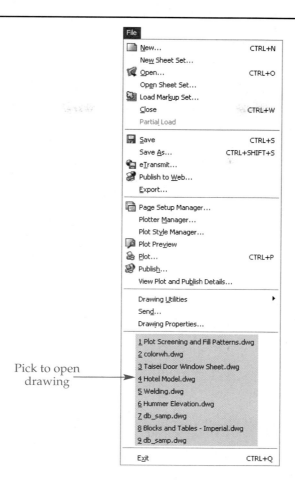

Pick to open
drawing

The Select File Dialog Box

The **Select File** dialog box includes the Places list along its left side. The Places list provides instant access to certain folders. The following buttons are available:

- **History.** Lists drawing files opened recently from the **Select File** dialog box.
- **My Documents.** Displays the files and folders contained in the My Documents folder for the current user.
- **Favorites.** Displays files and folders located in the Favorites folder on your hard drive.
- **FTP.** Displays available FTP (file transfer protocol) sites. To add or modify the listed FTP sites, select **Add/Modify FTP Locations** from the **Tools** menu in the **Select File** dialog box.
- **Desktop.** Lists the files, folders, and drives located on your desktop.
- **Buzzsaw.** Displays projects on the Buzzsaw Web site. Buzzsaw.com is designed for the building industry. After setting up a project hosting account, users can access drawings from a given construction project on the Web site. This allows the various companies involved in the project to have instant access to the drawing files.

The **Select File** dialog box includes other features for selecting folders and files:

- **Back button.** Shows the previously displayed folder contents.
- **Up one level button.** Displays the contents of the folder containing the currently displayed file or folder.
- **Search the Web button.** Accesses the **Browse the Web** dialog box, from which you can open files found on the Internet.
- **Delete button.** Deletes the selected file or folder.
- **Create New Folder button.** Creates a new folder within the folder being displayed.

- **Views menu.** Provides options for how file names are displayed in the **Select File** dialog box.

Finding files

You can search for files from the **Select File** dialog box by picking **Find...** in the **Tools** menu. This accesses the **Find** dialog box, **Figure 2-9.** If you know the file name for the drawing, type it in the **Named:** text box. If you do not know the name, you can use wildcard characters (such as *) to narrow the search.

Choose the type of file from the **Type:** drop-down list. You can search for DWG, DWS, DXF, or DWT files from the **Find** dialog box. If you are searching for another type of file, use the Windows Explorer search tool.

A search can be completed more quickly if you do not search the entire hard drive. If you know the folder in which the file is located, specify the folder in the **Look in:** text box. Pick the **Browse** button to select a folder from the **Browse for Folder** dialog box. Check the **Include subfolders** check box if you want the subfolders within the selected folder to be searched.

You can also search for files based on when they were last modified. The **Date Modified** tab provides options to search for files modified within a certain time period. This option is very useful if you wish to list all drawings modified within a specific week or month.

PROFESSIONAL TIP

While working in file dialog boxes, certain file management capabilities are available, similar to when you are using Windows Explorer. To rename an existing file or folder, pick it once and pause for a moment, then pick the name again. This places the name in a text box for editing. Type the new name and press [Enter].

For a full listing of all the available options, point to a desired file folder, and then right-click. This displays a shortcut menu of available options for working with the file folder. Use one of the options or pick somewhere off the menu to close it.

Figure 2-9.
The **Find** dialog box is used to locate drawing files.

Enter name of drawing or wildcards

Selected type of file to search for

Pick to search

Create new search

Selected folders to be searched

Found items listed here

Find:

Name & Location | Date Modified

Named:

Type: Drawing (*.dwg)

Look in: C:\Program Files\AutoCAD   Browse

☑ Include subfolders

Find Now

Stop

New Search

OK

Cancel

Help

Name | In Folder | Size | Type | Modified

AutoCAD and Its Applications—Basics

Opening drawings from previous releases of AutoCAD

In AutoCAD 2007, you can open drawing files created in AutoCAD Release 12 or later. When you open a drawing from a previous release and work on it, AutoCAD automatically updates the drawing to the AutoCAD 2007 file format when you save. After the older release drawing is saved in AutoCAD 2007, it can be viewed in the **Preview** image tile in the **Select File** dialog box during future applications.

Opening drawing as read-only

Drawings can be opened as read-only. When a drawing is opened as read-only, the drawing changes cannot be saved to the original file. This ensures that the original drawing file remains unchanged.

To open a drawing as read-only, select the drawing in the **Select File** dialog box, and then pick the **Open Read-Only** option from the **Open** drop-down menu. You can also select **Partial Open Read-Only** to use the **Partial Open** option with a read-only file. Opening part of a file is covered later in this textbook. You can make changes to a drawing opened as read-only, but AutoCAD will not allow you to save the changes to the original file. However, you can use the **SAVEAS** command to save the modified drawing file using a different name.

NOTE

When working with large drawings, you can use the **Partial Open** option to open only part of a drawing by selecting specific views and layers to be opened. Views and layers are discussed later in this textbook.

Exercise 2-3

Complete the Exercise on the Student CD.

Working with Multiple Drawings

AutoCAD allows you to have multiple drawings open at the same time. Most drafting projects are composed of a number of drawings, where each presents different aspects of a project. For example, in an architectural drafting project, required drawings might include a site plan, a floor plan, electrical and plumbing plans, and assorted detail drawings. Consider a mechanical assembly composed of several unique parts. The required drawings might include an overall assembly view, plus individual detail drawings of each component part. The drawings in such projects are closely related to one another. By opening two or more of these drawings at the same time, you can easily reference information contained in existing drawings while working in a new drawing. AutoCAD even allows you to directly copy all or part of the contents from one drawing directly into another, using a simple drag-and-drop operation.

When multiple drawings are open, there are several methods to control display. Controlling the arrangement of multiple drawing windows will help you avoid confusion.

Each drawing you open or start in AutoCAD is placed in its own drawing window. Based on AutoCAD's default behavior, drawing windows are displayed in a floating state. This means the drawing area is displayed within a smaller window inside the main AutoCAD window. When multiple drawings are open at the same time, they are placed in a cascading arrangement by default. The name of each drawing is displayed on the left side of its title bar.

AutoCAD's drawing windows have the same control options as program windows on your desktop. They can be resized, moved, minimized, maximized, restored, and closed, using the same methods used for program windows on your desktop. **Figure 2-10** shows a summary of the standard window control functions available for drawing windows.

The drawing windows and the AutoCAD window have the same relationship that program windows have with the Windows desktop. When a drawing window is maximized, it fills the available area in the AutoCAD window. Minimizing a drawing window displays it as a reduced size title bar along the bottom of AutoCAD's drawing area. Drawing windows cannot be moved outside the AutoCAD window. **Figure 2-11** illustrates drawing windows in a floating state and minimized.

Figure 2-10.
Drawing window control options.

Window Control Buttons		
Button	**Function**	**Description**
	Minimize	Displays window as a button along bottom of drawing window space in AutoCAD window.
	Restore	Returns window to floating state, at previous size and position, displays title bar.
	Maximize	Displays window at largest possible size, hides title bar.
	Close	Closes drawing, provides option to save drawing if any changes remain unsaved.
	Display window control menu	Displays pull-down menu with window control options.

Resizing Controls		
Cursor	**Function**	**Usage**
	Size window vertically	Press and hold pick button while pointing at top or bottom border of window, then move mouse.
	Size window horizontally	Press and hold pick button while pointing at left or right border of window, then move mouse.
	Size window diagonally	Press and hold pick button while pointing at any corner on border of window, then move mouse.
	Move window	Press and hold pick button while pointing at title bar of window, then move mouse.

Figure 2-11.
Drawing windows can be displayed in several ways. By default, drawings are displayed in floating windows. Minimized drawing windows are displayed as reduced size title bars. Pick the title bar drawing icon to display a window control menu.

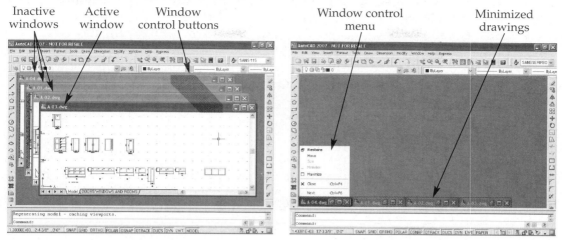

Floating Windows   Minimized Windows

To work on any currently open drawing, just pick its title bar if it is visible. Pressing the [Ctrl]+[F6] key combination allows you to cycle through all open drawings. To go directly to a specific drawing when the title bars are not visible, access the **Window** pull-down menu in AutoCAD. The name of each open drawing file is displayed, and the active drawing shows a check mark next to it. See **Figure 2-12A.** Pick the name of the desired drawing to make it current. Up to nine drawing names are displayed on this menu. If more than nine drawings are open, a **More Windows...** selection is displayed. Picking this displays the **Select Window** dialog box, **Figure 2-12B.**

The additional control options available in the **Window** pull-down menu include:
- **Close.** Closes the active drawing.
- **Close All.** Closes all open drawings.
- **Cascade.** Arranges the drawing windows that are not currently minimized in a cascade of floating windows, with the active drawing placed at the front.
- **Tile Horizontally.** Tiles the drawing windows that are not currently minimized in a horizontal arrangement, with the active drawing window placed in the top position.

Figure 2-12.
Selecting the active drawing window. A—Pick the name of a drawing displayed on the **Window** pull-down menu to make it current. This menu also offers additional drawing window control options. B—When more than nine drawings are open, pick **More Windows...** from the **Window** pull-down menu to display the **Select Window** dialog box.

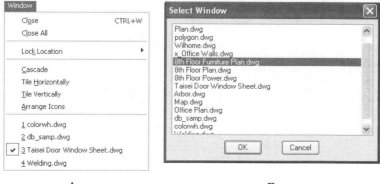

A   B

- **Tile Vertically.** Tiles the drawing windows that are not currently minimized in a vertical arrangement, with the active drawing window placed in the left position.
- **Arrange Icons.** Arranges minimized drawings neatly along the bottom of the AutoCAD drawing window area.
- **Lock Location.** Prevents toolbars and windows from being moved in the drawing area.

The effects of tiling the drawing windows vary, based on the number of windows being tiled and whether they are tiled horizontally or vertically. See **Figure 2-13.**

NOTE

Typically, you can change the active drawing as desired. There are some situations, however, when you cannot switch between drawings. For example, you cannot switch drawings while a dialog box is open. You must either complete or cancel the dialog box before switching is possible.

Exercise 2-4 Complete the Exercise on the Student CD.

Figure 2-13.
Tiled drawing windows.

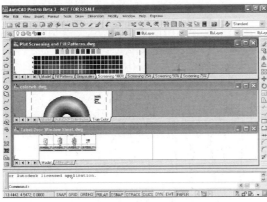

Horizontal Tiling

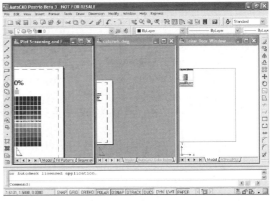

Vertical Tiling

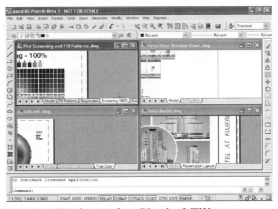

Horizontal or Vertical Tiling

Closing a Drawing

The **CLOSE** command is the primary way to exit out of a drawing file without ending the AutoCAD session. You can close the current drawing file by picking **File** > **Close** pull-down menu or by typing CLOSE. If you enter the **CLOSE** command before saving your work, AutoCAD gives you a chance to decide what you want to do with unsaved work. An AutoCAD alert box with the message Save Changes to *drawing*.dwg? appears. Pick the **Yes** button to save the drawing. You can also pick the **No** button if you plan to discard any changes made to the drawing since the previous save. Pick the **Cancel** button if you decide not to close the drawing and want to return to the drawing area.

Creating and Using Drawing Templates

Depending on the types of drawing projects with which you work, there may be many settings that are the same from one drawing to the next. These can include drawing aids, such as the use of snap and grid, and drawing settings, such as units. In most companies, standard borders and title blocks are used in all drawings. To save drawing setup time, templates are used.

When you use a template, all the settings saved in the template are applied to your new drawing. A template file can supply any settings and content normally saved in a drawing file. Many templates used by drafting companies are set up with standard borders and title blocks. When a new drawing is created from the template, these objects appear on screen. A template drawing also contains drawing setup options. As you continue through this text, you can add items to your templates, such as layer settings, company information, logos, text styles, plot styles, dimension styles, and table styles. All these settings can be designed to your company or school specifications and based on your drawing applications.

Creating Your Own Templates

If none of the predefined AutoCAD templates meet your needs, you can create and save your own custom templates. AutoCAD allows you to save *any* drawing as a template. A drawing template should be developed whenever several drawing applications require the same setup procedure. The template then allows the setup to be applied to any number of future drawings. Creating templates increases drafting productivity by decreasing setup requirements.

Some existing AutoCAD templates may be close to what you need and simply need fine-tuning. Some basic parameters that can be specified in a drawing template include settings for units, snap, and grid. These functions are discussed later in this chapter. You can also draw your own border and title block.

As you learn more about working with AutoCAD, you will find many other settings that can be included in your drawing templates. When you have everything needed in the template, the template is ready to save. Use the **SAVEAS** command to save a drawing template. This command displays the **Save Drawing As** dialog box. To specify that the drawing is to be saved as a drawing template, pick AutoCAD Drawing Template (*.dwt) from the **Files of type:** drop-down list. The file list window then shows all the drawing templates currently found in the Template folder. See **Figure 2-14**. You can store custom templates in another location, but it is recommended that they be stored in the Template folder. After specifying the name and location for the new template file, pick the **Save** button in the **Save Drawing As** dialog box. The **Template Description** dialog box is now displayed, **Figure 2-15**. Use the **Description** area to type

Figure 2-14.
Saving a template in the AutoCAD Template folder.

Folder where template is saved

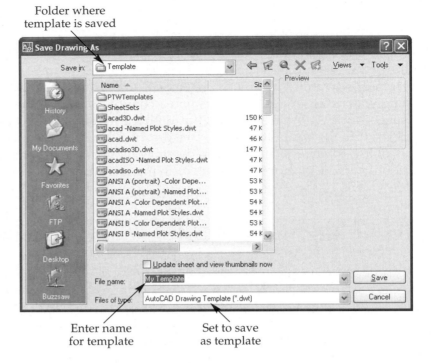

Enter name for template

Set to save as template

Figure 2-15.
Type a description of the new template in the **Template Description** dialog box.

Enter description for template

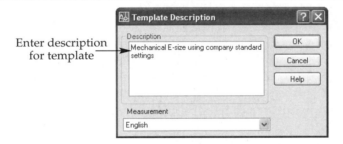

a description of the template file you are saving. A brief description usually works best. In the **Measurement** drop-down list, specify whether the units used in the template are English or Metric, and then pick the **OK** button.

The template name should relate to the template, such as Mechanical A size, for a mechanical drawing on an A-size sheet. The template might be named for the drawing application, such as Architectural floor plans. The template name might be as simple as Template 1. The name should be written in a reference manual, along with documentation about what is included in the template. This provides future reference for you and other users. The template drawing you create is saved for you to open and use whenever it is needed. Once you exit AutoCAD and start it up again, the template you created is ready for you to use for preparing a new drawing.

Planning Your AutoCAD Templates

Effective planning can greatly reduce the amount of time it takes to set up and complete a drawing. By creating a variety of templates with various setups, the basic drawing aids and drawing settings are already set when you begin the drawing.

The following sections discuss the most basic drawing aids for inclusion in your templates. These are Grid mode, Snap mode, and the basic units drawing settings. Additional items to be included in templates are discussed throughout this textbook.

Establishing a Grid on the Screen

AutoCAD provides a grid, or pattern of dots, on the screen to help you lay out a drawing. When the Grid mode is activated, this pattern of dots appears in the drawing area, as shown in **Figure 2-16.** The grid pattern may be set to show only within the drawing limits to help clearly define the working area. The spacing between dots can be adjusted.

Though there are many ways to control whether the grid is displayed on-screen, the most efficient way is to pick the **GRID** button on the status bar. Using this method means no typing is necessary because the grid can be toggled on or off with a mouse click.

Figure 2-17 shows the **Snap and Grid** tab of the **Drafting Settings** dialog box. This dialog box can be used to turn the grid on and off and to set the grid spacing and display. To access the **Drafting Settings** dialog box, right-click on the **GRID** or **SNAP** button in the status bar and select **Settings...** from the shortcut menu.

The grid spacing can be set in the **Grid spacing** area of the **Drafting Settings** dialog box. If the grid spacing you choose is too dense, AutoCAD adjusts the display automatically for the grid to be shown on-screen.

NOTE

You can access the **Drafting Settings** dialog box by selecting **Tools** > **Drafting Settings...** or by typing DSETTINGS, DS, or SE. The grid may be turned on or off by checking the **Grid On** checkbook inside the **Drafting Settings** dialog box. Other methods for turning the grid on and off include using the **ON** and **OFF** options of the **GRID** command, using the [Ctrl]+[G] key combination, pressing the [F7] function key, and using puck button 6.

Figure 2-16.
Dots represent the grid spacing when Grid mode is activated.

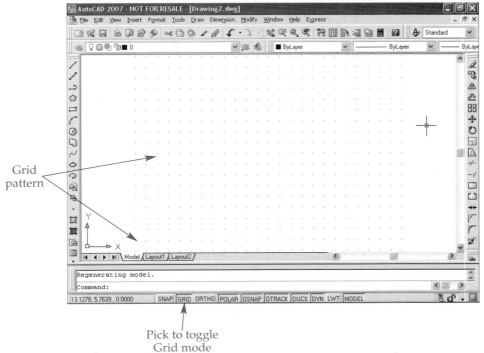

Grid pattern

Pick to toggle
Grid mode

Figure 2-17.
Grid settings can be made in the **Snap and Grid** tab of the **Drafting Settings** dialog box.

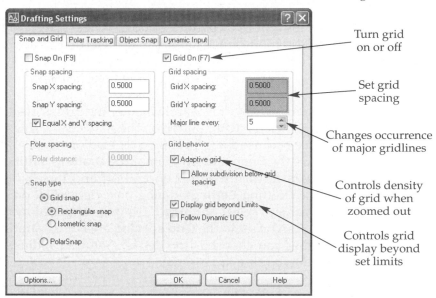

Turn grid on or off

Set grid spacing

Changes occurrence of major gridlines

Controls density of grid when zoomed out

Controls grid display beyond set limits

Setting Different Horizontal and Vertical Grid Units

When setting different values for horizontal and vertical grid spacing, first be sure the **Equal X and Y spacing** checkbox in the **Snap spacing** area of the **Drafting Settings** dialog box is turned off. Then, type the appropriate values in the **Grid X spacing:** and **Grid Y spacing:** text boxes. For example, **Figure 2-18** shows a horizontal spacing of 1 and a vertical spacing of .5.

Figure 2-18.
The X and Y grid spacing units can be set to different values. Notice that, here, the horizontal spacing is greater than the vertical spacing.

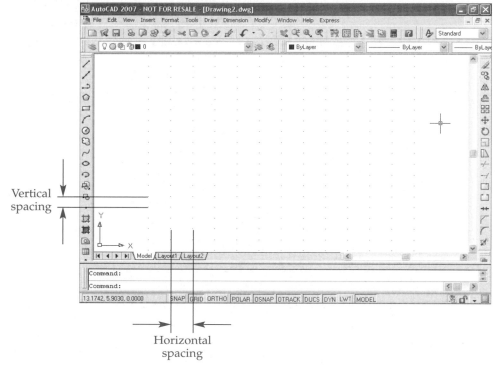

Vertical spacing

Horizontal spacing

Another option is to display major grid lines differently from minor grid lines. The **Major line every:** text box allows you to change the occurrence of major grid lines. This option is available for 3D applications.

Changing the Grid Display

The options in the **Grid behavior** area of the **Drafting Settings** dialog box allow you to set how the grid appears on the screen. When the **Adaptive Grid** check box is turned on, dense grids with small spacing values can be displayed when zoomed out. The **Display grid beyond Limits** option determines whether or not the grid shows only within the set drawing limits. The **Allow subdivision below grid spacing** and **Follow Dynamic UCS** options are used for 3D applications.

Setting Increments for Cursor Movement

When you move your pointing device, the crosshairs move freely on the screen. Sometimes it is hard to place a point accurately. You can set up an invisible grid that allows the cursor to move only in exact increments. This is called the *snap grid*, or *snap resolution*. Using the snap grid is different from using Grid mode. The snap grid controls the movement of the crosshairs, while Grid mode is only a visual guide. The grid and snap grid settings can, however, be used together. The AutoCAD defaults provide the same settings for both.

Picking the **SNAP** button on the status bar is an easy way to turn snap spacing on or off at any time. Properly setting the snap grid can greatly increase your drawing speed and accuracy. The snap grid spacing can be set in the **Snap and Grid** tab of the **Drafting Settings** dialog box. See **Figure 2-19.** Type the snap spacing values in the **Snap X spacing:** and **Snap Y spacing:** text boxes.

The value you set remains the same until changed. If you turn snap off, the same snap spacing is in effect when you turn snap on again.

Figure 2-19.
Snap grid settings can be made in the **Snap and Grid** tab of the **Drafting Settings** dialog box.

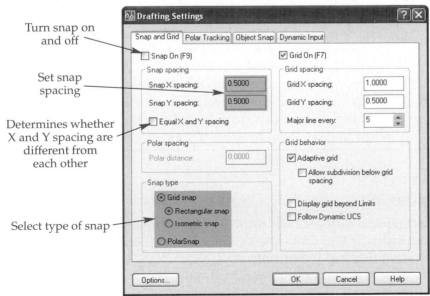

PROFESSIONAL TIP

The most effective use of the Snap mode quite often comes from setting an equal X and Y spacing to the lowest, or near lowest, increment of the majority of the feature dimensions. For example, this might be .0625 units in a mechanical drawing or 6″ in an architectural application. If many horizontal features conform to one increment and most vertical features correspond to another, then a snap grid can be set up using different X and Y values.

Setting the Snap Type and Style

The **Snap type** area of the **Drafting Settings** dialog box allows you to select one of two types of snap grids: **Grid snap** or **PolarSnap**. PolarSnap allows you to snap to precise distances along alignment paths when using polar tracking. Polar tracking is discussed in Chapter 6. **Grid snap** has two styles: **Rectangular snap** and **Isometric snap**. **Rectangular snap** is the standard style. **Isometric snap** is useful when creating isometric drawings (discussed in Chapter 27). Select the radio button(s) for the snap type and style you desire and pick the **OK** button. You can also use the **Type** and **Style** options of the **SNAP** command to change these settings. Use the **Type** option to select **Polar** or **Grid** and use the **Style** option to select **Standard** (rectangular) or **Isometric**.

PROFESSIONAL TIP

The Snap and Grid modes may be set at different values to complement each other. For example, the grid may be set at .5, and the snap may be set at .25. With this type of format, each mode plays a separate role in assisting drawing layout. This may also keep the grid from being too dense. You can quickly change these values at any time to have them best assist you.

Factors to Consider When Setting Drawing Aids

The following factors will influence the drawing aid settings you choose to use:
✓ **The drawing units.** If the units are decimal inches, set the grid and snap values to standard decimal increments, such as .0625, .125, .25, .5, and 1 or .05, .1, .2, .5, and 1. For architectural units, use standard increments, such as 1, 6, and 12 (for inches) or 1, 2, 4, 5, and 10 (for feet).
✓ **The drawing size.** A very large drawing might have a grid spacing of 1.00, while a small drawing may use a spacing of .5 or less.

✓ **The value of the smallest dimension.** If the smallest dimension is .125, then an appropriate snap value would be .125, with a grid spacing of .25.

✓ **The ability to change the settings.** You can change the snap and grid values at any time without changing the location of points or lines already drawn. This should be done when larger or smaller values would assist you with a certain part of the drawing. For example, suppose a few of the dimensions are in .0625 multiples, but the rest of the dimensions are .250 multiples. Change the snap spacing from .250 to .0625 when laying out the smaller dimensions.

✓ **Sketches prepared before starting the drawing.** Use the visible grid to help you place views and lay out the entire drawing.

✓ **Efficiency.** Use whatever method works best and quickest for you when setting or changing the drawing aids.

Exercise 2-5   Complete the Exercise on the Student CD.

Drawing Settings

Drawing settings determine the general characteristics of a drawing. These include the type of units used for linear and angular measurements, and the precision to which these measurements are displayed. The drawing units can be changed within a drawing, but it is best if the settings found in the template on which the drawing is based are not modified.

Drawing Units

Drawing units are set in the **Drawing Units** dialog box, **Figure 2-20.** To access this dialog box, pick **Format** > **Units...** or type UN or UNITS.

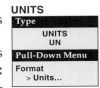

UNITS
| Type |
| UNITS |
| UN |
| **Pull-Down Menu** |
| Format |
| > Units... |

Both linear and angular units are set in the **Drawing Units** dialog box. Linear units are specified in the **Length** area. Select the desired linear units format from the **Type:** drop-down list and use the **Precision:** drop-down list to specify the linear unit's precision. The following options are illustrated in **Figure 2-21:**

- **Decimal.** Decimal units are used to create drawings in decimal inches or millimeters. Decimal units are normally used on mechanical drawings for manufacturing. This option conforms to the ASME Y14.5M dimensioning and tolerancing standard. The initial default precision is four decimal places.

Figure 2-20.
The **Drawing Units** dialog box.

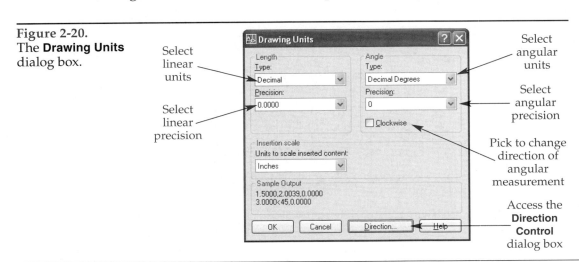

Select linear units

Select linear precision

Select angular units

Select angular precision

Pick to change direction of angular measurement

Access the **Direction Control** dialog box

Figure 2-21.
Linear unit formats available in the **Drawing Units** dialog box.

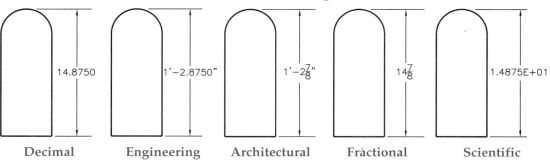

Decimal	Engineering	Architectural	Fractional	Scientific
14.8750	1'–2.8750"	1'–2⅞"	14⅞	1.4875E+01

- **Engineering.** Engineering units are often used in civil drafting projects, such as projects involving maps, plot plans, dam and bridge construction, and topography. The initial default precision is four decimal places.
- **Architectural.** Architectural, structural, and other drawings use architectural units when measurements are in feet, inches, and fractional inches. The initial default precision is 1/16".
- **Fractional.** This option is used for drawings having fractional parts of any common unit of measure. The initial default precision is 1/16.
- **Scientific.** Scientific units are used when very large or small values are applied to a drawing. These applications take place in industries such as chemical engineering and astronomy. The initial default precision is four decimal places. The unit precision E+01 means the base number is multiplied by 10 to the first power.

The angular unit format and precision is set in the **Type:** and **Precision:** drop-down lists in the **Angle** area of the **Drawing Units** dialog box. Selecting the **Clockwise** check box changes the direction for angular measurements to clockwise from the default setting of counterclockwise.

Pick the **Direction...** button to access the **Direction Control** dialog box. See **Figure 2-22.** The standard **East, North, West,** and **South** options are offered as radio buttons. Pick one of these buttons to set the compass orientation. The **Other** radio button activates the **Angle:** text box and the **Pick an angle** button. The **Angle:** text box allows an angle for zero direction to be typed. The **Pick an angle** button allows two points on the screen to be picked for establishing the angle zero direction.

The angular unit formats available are illustrated in **Figure 2-23** and described as follows:
- **Decimal Degrees.** This is the initial default setting. It is normally used in mechanical drafting, where degrees and decimal parts of a degree are commonly used.

Figure 2-22.
The **Direction Control** dialog box.

Set direction of 0°

Specify another angle

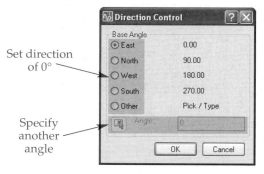

AutoCAD and Its Applications—Basics

Figure 2-23.
Angular unit formats available in the **Drawing Units** dialog box.

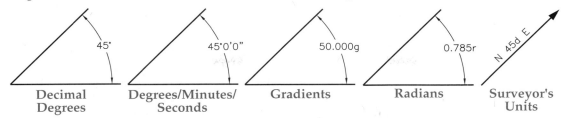

Decimal
Degrees

Degrees/Minutes/
Seconds

Gradients

Radians

Surveyor's
Units

- **Deg/Min/Sec.** This style is sometimes used in mechanical, architectural, structural, and civil drafting. There are 60 minutes in one degree and 60 seconds in one minute.
- **Grads.** *Grad* is the abbreviation for *gradient*. The angular value is followed by a g. Gradients are units of angular measurement based on one-quarter of a circle having 100 grads. A full circle has 400 grads.
- **Radians.** A *radian* is an angular unit of measurement in which 2π radians = $360°$ and π radians = $180°$. Pi (π) is approximately equal to 3.1416. For example, a $90°$ angle has $\pi/2$ radians and an arc length of $\pi/2$. Changing the precision displays the radian value rounded to the specified decimal place.
- **Surveyor.** Surveyor angles are measured using bearings. A *bearing* is the direction of a line with respect to one of the quadrants of a compass. Bearings are measured clockwise or counterclockwise (depending on the quadrant), beginning from either north or south. Bearings are measured in degrees, minutes, and seconds. An angle measuring 55°45′22″ from north toward west is expressed as N55°45′22″W. An angle measured 25°30′10″ from south toward east is expressed as S25°30′10″E. Use the **Precision:** drop-down list to set measurement to degrees, degrees/minutes, or degrees/minutes/seconds, or use it to set decimal display accuracy of the seconds part of the measurement.

After selecting the linear and angular units and precision, pick the **OK** button to exit the **Drawing Units** dialog box.

LEGACY NOTE

Every drawing has defined model space drawing limits. These limits are set using the **LIMITS** command. Model space drawing limits are intended to define the space in which all drawing objects are located. The drawing limits can be used to define an area to be plotted, to limit the area in which grid points are displayed, and to restrict the area in which objects can be located.

The **LIMITS** command asks you to specify the coordinates for the lower-left corner and the upper-right corner of the drawing area. The lower-left corner is usually 0,0, but you can specify a different value. The upper-right corner setting usually identifies the upper-right corner of the drawing area. The first value is the horizontal measurement, and the second value is the vertical measurement of the limits. A comma separates the values.

Exercise
2-6

Complete the Exercise on the Student CD.

PROFESSIONAL TIP

Generalized templates that set the units, snap settings, and grid settings to specifications are useful, but keep in mind you can create any number of drawing templates. Templates containing more detailed settings can dramatically increase drafting productivity. As you refine your setup procedure, you can revise the template files. When using the **SAVE** command, you can save a new template over an existing one. You can also use the **SAVEAS** command to save a new template from an existing one.

Chapter Test

Answer the following questions. Write your answers on a separate sheet of paper or complete the electronic chapter test on the Student CD.

1. By default, what is the name of the dialog box that opens when using the **NEW** command?
2. What is a drawing template?
3. What is *sheet size*?
4. What are the dimensions of an ASME/ANSI B-size sheet?
5. Is the size of an ASME/ANSI A2 sheet specified in inches or millimeters?
6. What does the .dwt file extension stand for?
7. How often should work be saved?
8. Name the command allowing you to quickly save your work without displaying a dialog box.
9. Name the system variable allowing you to control the dialog box display.
10. Name the pull-down menu where the **SAVE**, **SAVEAS**, and **OPEN** commands are located.
11. How do you set AutoCAD to automatically save your work at designated intervals?
12. If a drawing has been previously saved, what is the difference between using the **QSAVE** and **SAVE** commands?
13. How do you search for a drawing file from the **Select File** dialog box?
14. What is shown when you pick the **Favorites** button in the **Select File** dialog box?
15. From which pull-down menu can you select the name of a recently opened drawing file and open it?
16. How can you set the number of files listed in the pull-down menu described in Question 15?
17. How do you quickly cycle through all the currently open drawings in sequence?
18. Identify the command you would use if you wanted to exit a drawing file, but remain in the AutoCAD session.
19. What happens if you use the **CLOSE** command before saving your work?
20. How can you simultaneously close all open drawing windows?
21. How do you set grid spacing of .25?
22. How do you set snap spacing of .125?
23. Name the command used to place a pattern of dots on the screen.
24. How do you activate the Snap mode?
25. How do you set different horizontal and vertical snap units?
26. Name three ways to access the **Drafting Settings** dialog box.
27. How can you access the **Drawing Units** dialog box?
28. Name three settings that can be specified in the **Drawing Units** dialog box.
29. What does *read-only* mean?

Drawing Problems

1. Create a new drawing based on one of the templates supplied by AutoCAD. Save the new drawing as a file named P2-1.dwg.

The following problems can be done if the AutoCAD 2007\Sample file folder is loaded. All drawings listed are found in that folder.

2. Locate and preview or open the Lineweights drawing. Describe the drawing in your own words.

3. Locate and preview or open the TrueType drawing. Describe the drawing in your own words.

4. Locate and preview or open the Tablet drawing. Describe the drawing in your own words.

5. Locate and preview or open the 3D House drawing. Describe the drawing in your own words.

The following problems can be saved as templates for future use.

6. Create a template with decimal units with 0.0 precision, decimal degrees with 0.0 precision, default angle measure and orientation, a snap setting of .1 and a grid setting of .5. Save the template as P2-6.dwt. Enter an appropriate description for the template.

7. Create a template with architectural units with 0'-0" precision, decimal degrees with 0 precision, a snap setting of 1", and a grid setting of 6". Save the template as P2-7.dwt. Enter an appropriate description for the template.

AutoCAD includes many standard templates. These templates include settings and title blocks for many standard sheet sizes. Three such templates are shown here.

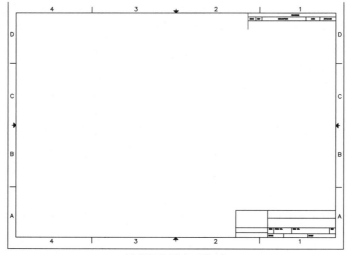

ANSI C Title Block

Architectural Title Block

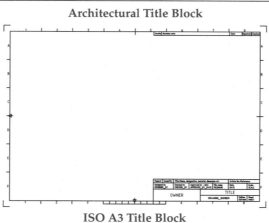

ISO A3 Title Block

Introduction to Drawing and Editing

Learning Objectives

After completing this chapter, you will be able to do the following:

- Use a variety of linetypes to construct an object.
- Select the **LINE** command to draw various objects.
- Use absolute, relative, and polar coordinate point entry systems.
- Use the screen cursor for point entry.
- Use Ortho mode and polar tracking.
- Use direct distance entry.
- Use Dynamic Input for efficient entry.
- Revise objects using the **ERASE** command and its options.
- Create selection sets using the **Window**, **Crossing**, **WPolygon**, **CPolygon**, and **Fence** options.
- Remove and add objects to a selection set.
- Clean up the screen with the **REDRAW** command.
- Use the **OOPS** command to bring back an erased object.
- Use the **U** command to undo a command.
- Select stacked objects.

This chapter introduces drawing and editing using the **LINE** and **ERASE** commands. There are many other drawing and editing commands discussed in later chapters of this textbook. All drawing commands require you to select points in the drawing area. AutoCAD provides many point entry methods, including coordinate entry, cursor selection, and direct distance entry. These point entry methods are discussed in this chapter. Similarly, nearly all editing commands require that you select one or more objects. There are many object selection methods. Several object selection methods are introduced in this chapter.

Line Conventions

Drafting is a graphic language using lines, symbols, and words to describe products to be manufactured. Line conventions are standards based on line thickness and type. These standards are designed to enhance the readability of drawings. This section introduces line standards.

The American National Standards Institute (ANSI) recommends two line widths to establish contrasting lines in a drawing. Lines are described as thick or thin. For manual drafting, thick lines are twice as thick as thin lines, with recommended widths of 0.6 mm and 0.3 mm, respectively. A single line width for all types of lines is acceptable, however, on drawings prepared with a CAD system. **Figure 3-1** shows recommended line width and type as defined in ASME Y14.2M, *Line Conventions and Lettering*.

Figure 3-1.
Line conventions. (Adapted from ASME Y14.2M)

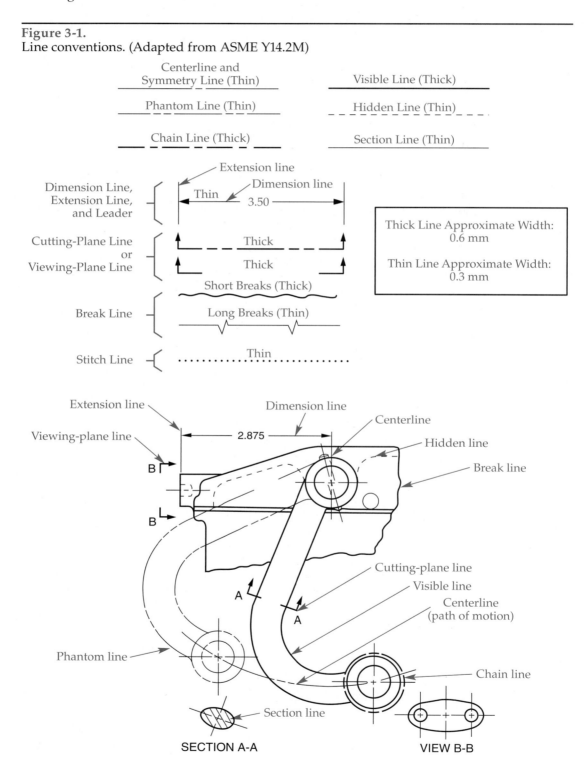

Figure 3-2.
This simple drawing
shows the different
line styles and line
thicknesses used in
drafting.

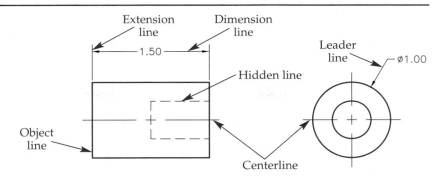

Object Lines

Object lines, also called *visible lines*, are thick lines used to show the outline or contour of an object. See **Figure 3-2.** Object lines are the most common type of lines used in drawings. These lines should be twice as thick as thin lines.

Hidden Lines

Hidden lines, often called *dashed lines*, are used to represent invisible features of an object, as shown in **Figure 3-2.** They are drawn thin so they clearly contrast with object lines. When properly drawn at full size, the dashes are .125" (3 mm) long and spaced .06" (1.5 mm) apart. Be aware that if the drawing is to be greatly reduced or scaled down during the plotting process, the dashes may appear too small.

Centerlines

Centerlines are thin lines consisting of alternating long and short dashes that locate the centers of circles and arcs and show the axis of a cylindrical or symmetrical shape. See **Figure 3-2.** The recommended dash lengths are .125" (3 mm) for the short dashes and .75" to 1.5" (19 mm to 38 mm) for the long dashes. These lengths can be altered, depending on the size of the drawing. Spaces approximately .06" (1.5 mm) long should separate the dashes. The small centerline dashes should cross only at the center of a circle.

Extension Lines

Extension lines are thin lines used to show the "extent" of a dimension, as shown in **Figure 3-2.** They begin a small distance from an object and extend .125" (3 mm) beyond the last dimension line. Extension lines may cross object lines, hidden lines, and centerlines, but they may not cross dimension lines. Centerlines become extension lines when they are used to show the extent of a dimension. When this is done, there is no space where the centerline joins the extension line.

Dimension Lines

Dimension lines are thin lines placed between extension lines to indicate a measurement. In mechanical drafting, the dimension line is normally broken near the center for placement of the dimension numeral, as shown in **Figure 3-2.** The dimension line normally remains unbroken in architectural and structural drawings. The dimension numeral is placed on top of an unbroken dimension line. Arrows terminate the ends of dimension lines, except in architectural drafting, where slashes or dots are often used.

Leader Lines

Leader lines are thin lines used to connect a specific note to a feature on a drawing. A leader line terminates with an arrowhead at the feature and has a small shoulder at the note. See **Figure 3-2.** Dimension and leader line usage is discussed in detail in Chapters 17 and 18.

Cutting-Plane and Viewing-Plane Lines

Cutting-plane lines are thick lines identifying the location of a section. *Viewing-plane lines* are drawn in the same style as cutting-plane lines, but identify the location of a view. Cutting-plane and viewing-plane lines can be drawn one of two ways, as shown in **Figure 3-1**. The uses of viewing-plane and cutting-plane lines are discussed in detail in Chapters 6 and 21.

Section Lines

Section lines are thin lines drawn in a section view to show where material has been cut away. See **Figure 3-3**. Types of section lines and applications are discussed in Chapter 21.

Break Lines

Break lines show where a portion of an object has been removed for clarity or convenience. For example, the center portion of a very long part can be broken out so the two ends can be moved closer together for a more convenient representation. There are several types of break lines shown in **Figure 3-4**.

Figure 3-3.
Section lines and cutting-plane lines.

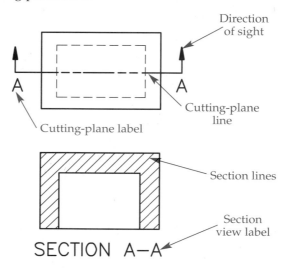

Figure 3-4.
Standard break lines.

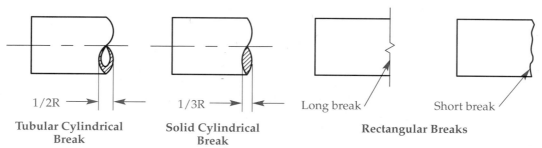

Phantom Lines

Phantom lines are thin lines with two short dashes alternating with long dashes. The short dashes are .125" (3 mm) long, and the long dashes range from .75" to 1.5" (19 mm to 38 mm) in length, depending on the size of the drawing. Spaces between dashes are .06" (1.5 mm). Phantom lines identify repetitive details, show alternate positions of moving parts, and locate adjacent positions of related parts. See **Figure 3-5**.

Chain Lines

Chain lines are thick lines of alternating long and short dashes. They show that the portion of the surface next to the chain line has special features or receives unique treatment. See **Figure 3-6**.

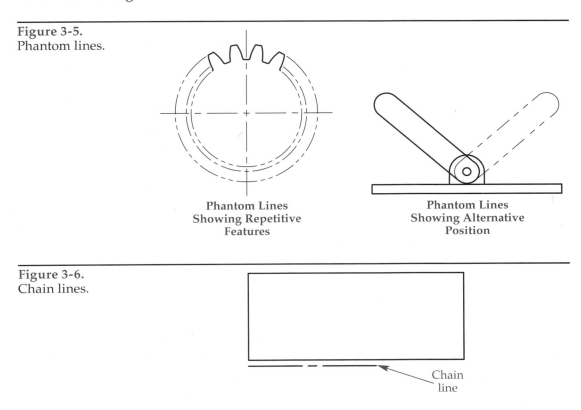

Figure 3-5.
Phantom lines.

Phantom Lines
Showing Repetitive
Features

Phantom Lines
Showing Alternative
Position

Figure 3-6.
Chain lines.

Chain
line

Drawing Lines with AutoCAD

Individual line segments are drawn between two points on the screen. This is referred to as *point entry*. Point entry is the simplest form of drafting. After selecting the **LINE** command, simply type the coordinates for each end of the line. Picking the **Line** button in the **Draw** toolbar, picking **Draw > Line**, or typing L or LINE or the pointer input field accesses the **LINE** command.

Using the Line Command and the Command Window

When using the **LINE** command, a prompt asks you to select a starting point (Specify first point:). When the first point is selected, you are asked for the second point (Specify next point or [Undo]:). When the next Specify next point or [Undo]: prompt is given, continue selecting additional points if you want to connect a series of lines. When you are finished, press the [Enter] key, the space bar, or right-click and select **Enter** to end the command.

AutoCAD provides a set of abbreviated commands called *command aliases*. Command aliases are also called *keyboard shortcuts* because they reduce the amount of typing needed when entering a command at the keyboard. Using command aliases allows you to enter commands more quickly. For example, instead of typing LINE, you can type L, which takes less time. Becoming familiar with the available command aliases can help you become more productive with AutoCAD.

Responding to AutoCAD Prompts with Numbers

Many of the AutoCAD commands require specific types of numeric data. Some of AutoCAD's prompts require you to enter a whole number. Other entries require whole numbers that may be positive or negative. A number is understood to be positive without placing the plus sign (+) before the number. The minus sign (–) must, however, precede a negative number.

Much of your data entry may not be whole numbers. In these cases, any real number can be used and expressed as a decimal, as a fraction, or in scientific notation. These numbers may be positive or negative. Here are some examples of acceptable real numbers:

    4.250
    -6.375
    1/2
    1-3/4
    2.5E+4 *(25,000)*
    2.5E-4 *(0.00025)*

When entering fractions, the numerator and denominator must be whole numbers greater than zero. For example, 1/2, 3/4, and 2/3 are all acceptable fraction entries. Fractional numbers greater than one must have a dash between the whole number and the fraction. For example, 2-3/4 is typed for two and three quarters. The dash (-) separator is needed because a space acts just like pressing [Enter] and automatically ends the input. The numerator may be larger than the denominator, as in 3/2, *only* if a whole number is not used with the fraction. For example, 1-3/2 is not a valid input for a fraction. When you enter coordinates or measurements, the values used depend on the units of measurement.

- Values on inch drawings are understood to be in inches without placing the inch marks (″) after the numeral. For example, 2.500 is automatically understood to be 2.500″.
- When your drawing is set up for metric values, any entry is automatically expressed as millimeters.
- If you are working in an engineering or architectural environment, any value greater than 1′ is expressed in inches, feet, or feet and inches. The values can be whole numbers, decimals, or fractions.
  - For measurements in feet, the foot symbol (′) must follow the number, as in 24′.
  - If the value is in feet and inches, there is no space between the feet and inch value. For example, 24′6 is the proper input for the value 24′-6″.
  - If the inch part of the value contains a fraction, the inch and fractional part of an inch are separated by a dash, such as 24′6-1/2.

Never mix feet with inch values greater than one foot. For example, 24′18″ is an invalid entry. In this case, you should type 25′6.

Placing the inch mark (″) after an inch value at the prompt line is acceptable, but not necessary. It takes more time and reduces productivity.

AutoCAD accepts the inch (″) and foot (′) symbols in the command line only when the drawing units are set to either **Architectural** or **Engineering**. If the drawing units are not set to one of these, a message on the command line will read Requires numeric distance or second point.

Point Entry Methods

There are several point entry techniques for drawing lines. Becoming skillful with these methods are very important. A combination of point entry techniques should be used to help reduce drawing time.

Each of the point entry methods uses the Cartesian, or rectangular, coordinate system. The *Cartesian coordinate system* is based on selecting distances from three intersecting axes. The point's distance from the intersection point, the *origin*, in respect to each of these axes defines a *location*. In standard two-dimensional (2D) drafting applications, objects are drawn in the XY plane, and the Z axis is not referenced. Using the Z axis is discussed in *AutoCAD and Its Applications—Advanced*.

In 2D drafting, the origin divides the coordinate system into four quadrants within the XY plane. Points are located in relation to the origin, or (0,0), where X = 0, and Y = 0. **Figure 3-7** shows the X,Y values of points located in the Cartesian coordinate system.

When using AutoCAD, the origin (0,0) is usually at the lower-left corner of the drawing. This setup places all points in the upper-right quadrant, where both X and Y coordinate values are positive. See **Figure 3-8.** Methods of establishing points in the Cartesian coordinate system include using absolute coordinates, relative coordinates, and polar coordinates.

Using absolute coordinates

Points located using the absolute coordinate system are measured from the origin (0,0). For example, when X = 4 and Y = 2 (4,2), a point is located four units horizontally and two units vertically from the origin, as shown in **Figure 3-9.** The coordinate display on the status bar registers the location of the selected point in XYZ coordinates.

Figure 3-7.
The Cartesian
coordinate system.

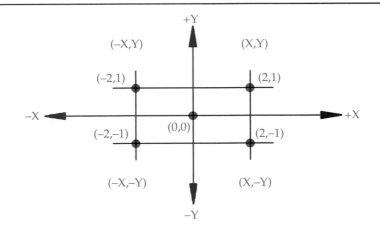

Figure 3-8.
The XY coordinate
axes on the screen.

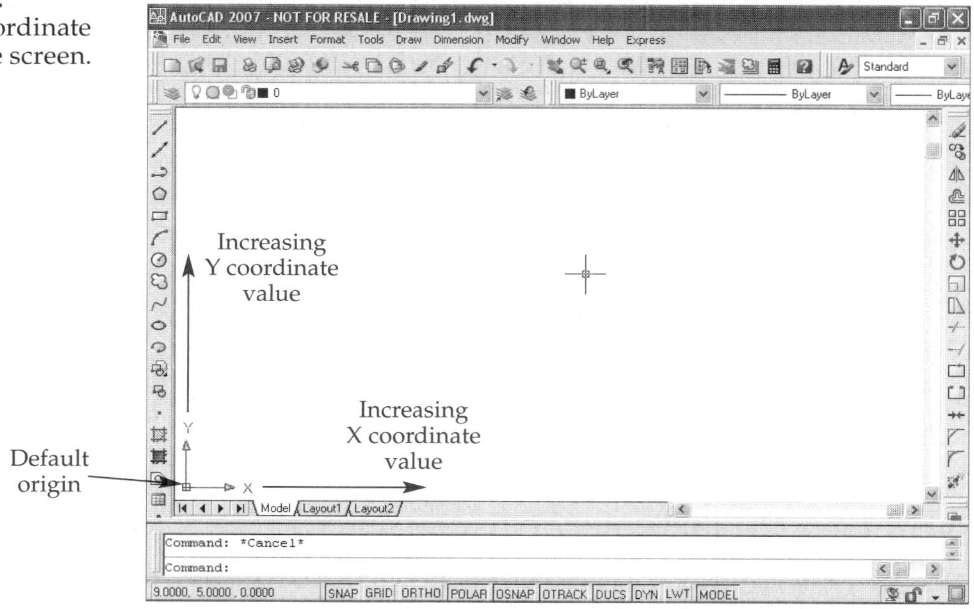

Increasing
Y coordinate
value

Increasing
X coordinate
value

Default
origin

Figure 3-9.
Locating points with
absolute coordinates.

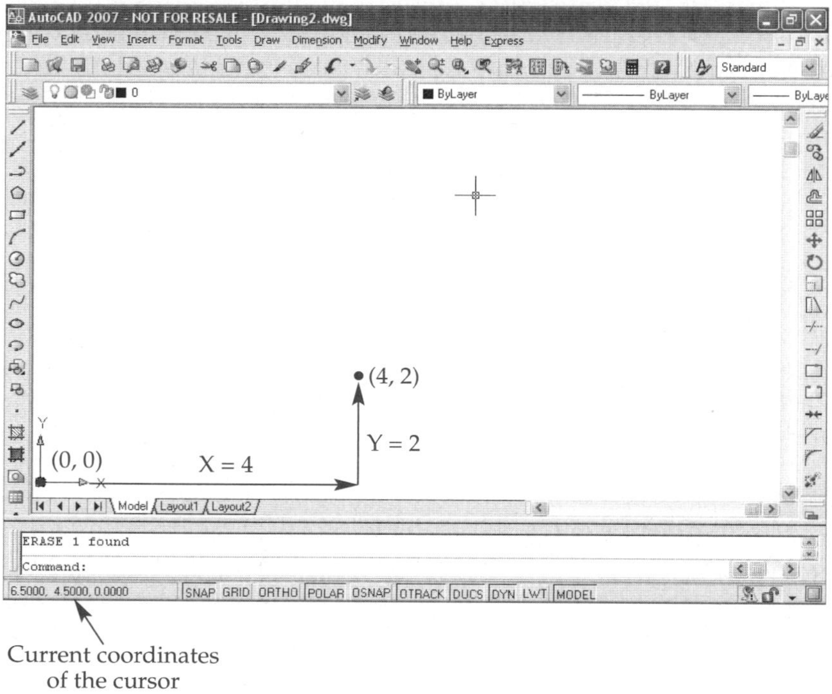

(4, 2)

Y = 2

(0, 0)   X = 4

Current coordinates
of the cursor

The discussion and examples in this chapter reference only the XY coordinates for 2D drafting. (The Z coordinate is used in 3D modeling.) Also note that the coordinate display reflects the current system of working units. Remember, when the absolute coordinate system is used, each point is located from 0,0. Follow these commands and point placements in the command window as you refer to **Figure 3-10:**

> Command: **L** *or* **LINE**↵
> Specify first point: **4,2**↵
> Specify next point or [Undo]: **7,2**↵
> Specify next point or [Undo]: **7,6**↵
> Specify next point or [Close/Undo]: **4,6**↵

Figure 3-10.
Drawing simple
shapes using the
LINE command and
absolute coordinates.

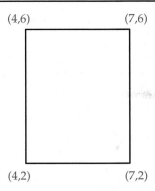

```
Specify next point or [Close/Undo]: 4,2↵
Specify next point or [Close/Undo]: ↵
Command:
```

When entering absolute coordinates using Dynamic Input with default settings, the pound sign (#) must be entered before the absolute coordinate value. Dynamic Input is discussed later in this chapter.

Exercise 3-1   Complete the Exercise on the Student CD.

Using relative coordinates

Relative coordinates are located from the previous position, rather than from the origin. The relationship of points in the Cartesian coordinate system, shown in **Figure 3-7**, must be clearly understood before using this method. When entering relative coordinates at the command window, the @ symbol must precede your entry. Holding the [Shift] key and pressing the [2] key at the top of the keyboard selects this symbol. Follow these commands and relative coordinate point placements, as you refer to **Figure 3-11:**

Figure 3-11.
Drawing a simple
shape using the
LINE command
and relative
coordinates. Notice
that the coordinates
are entered
counterclockwise
from the first point
(2,2). When typing
at the Command:
prompt, @ is
required for relative
polar coordinates.
When using
Dynamic Input, the
@ symbol may not
be needed.

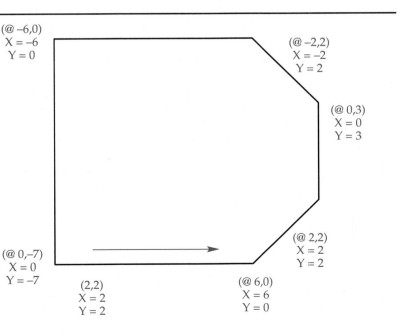

```
Command: L or LINE↵
Specify first point: 2,2↵
Specify next point or [Undo]: @6,0↵
Specify next point or [Undo]: @2,2↵
Specify next point or [Close/Undo]: @0,3↵
Specify next point or [Close/Undo]: @-2,2↵
Specify next point or [Close/Undo]: @-6,0↵
Specify next point or [Close/Undo]: @0,-7↵
Specify next point or [Close/Undo]: ↵
Command:
```

When using Dynamic Input with default settings, relative coordinate entry is assumed for "next point" selections. Dynamic Input is discussed later in this chapter.

Exercise 3-2   Complete the Exercise on the Student CD.

Using polar coordinates

A point located using **_polar coordinates_** is based on the distance from a fixed point at a given angle. The distance is entered, then the angle. A < symbol separates the two values.

The angular values used for the polar coordinate format are shown in **Figure 3-12**. Consistent with standard AutoCAD convention, 0° is to the right, or east. Angles are then measured counterclockwise.

When preceded by the @ symbol, a polar coordinate point is measured relative to the previous point. If the @ symbol is not included, the coordinate is located relative to the origin. If you want to draw a line four units long from point (1,1) at a 45° angle, the following information can be typed in the command window:

```
Command: L or LINE↵
Specify first point: 1,1↵
Specify next point or [Undo]: @4<45↵
Specify next point or [Undo]: ↵
Command:
```

Figure 3-13 shows the result of this command. The entry @4<45 means the following:
- **@.** Tells AutoCAD to measure from the previous point. This symbol must precede all relative coordinate inputs in the command window. When using Dynamic Input with default settings, this symbol does not need to be entered.
- **4.** Gives the distance, such as 4 units, from the previous point.

Figure 3-12.
Angles used in the polar coordinate system.

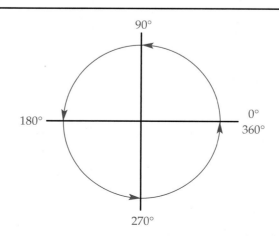

AutoCAD and Its Applications—Basics

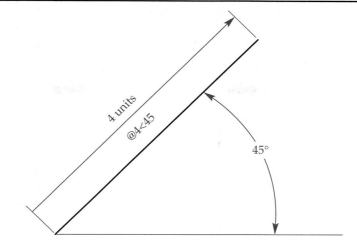

Figure 3-13.
Using polar
coordinates for the
LINE command.

4 units
@4<45
45°

- **<.** Establishes that a polar or angular increment is to follow.
- **45.** Specifies the angle, such as 45°, from 0°.

Now, follow these command window entries and polar coordinate points on your computer, as you refer to **Figure 3-14:**

```
Command: L or LINE↵
Specify first point: 2,6↵
Specify next point or [Undo]: @2.5<0↵
Specify next point or [Undo]: @3<135↵
Specify next point or [Close/Undo]: 2,6↵
Specify next point or [Close/Undo]: ↵
Command: ↵
LINE Specify first point: 6,6↵
Specify next point or [Undo]: @4<0↵
Specify next point or [Undo]: @2<90↵
Specify next point or [Close/Undo]: @4<180↵
Specify next point or [Close/Undo]: @2<270↵
Specify next point or [Close/Undo]: ↵
Command:
```

Exercise 3-3   Complete the Exercise on the Student CD.

Picking points using the crosshairs

Typically, object snap mode is used to select points using the crosshairs. This tool is discussed in Chapter 6. There are also some situations where Snap mode can be a useful aid in using the crosshairs for point entry. This assists in drafting presentation and maintains accuracy when using a mouse. With Snap mode on, the crosshairs move in designated increments without any guesswork.

Figure 3-14.
Using polar
coordinates to draw.

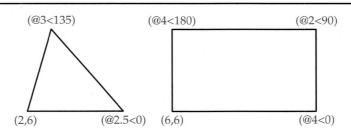

(@3<135)   (@4<180)   (@2<90)

(2,6)   (@2.5<0)   (6,6)   (@4<0)

When using a mouse, the command sequence is the same as when you are using coordinates. Points are picked when the crosshairs are at the desired location. After the first point is picked, the distance to the second point and the point's coordinates are displayed on the status line for reference. When picking points in this manner, there is a "rubberband" line connecting the first point and the crosshairs. The rubberband line moves as the crosshairs are moved, showing where the new line will be placed.

The Coordinate Display

The area to the left side of the status bar shows the coordinate display window. The drawing units setting determines the format and precision of the coordinate display. The coordinate display changes to represent the location of the cursor in relation to the origin. Each time a new point is picked or the cursor is moved, the coordinates are updated.

Picking the coordinate display in the status bar toggles the coordinate display on and off. With coordinates on, the coordinates constantly change as the crosshairs move. With coordinates off, the coordinate display is "grayed out," but still updates to display the coordinates of the last point selected.

There are two coordinate display modes: absolute and polar. Both display the current crosshairs location. When a command is active, the polar mode displays the crosshairs position as polar coordinate relative to the previously picked point.

Exercise 3-4　　Complete the Exercise on the Student CD.

Drawing in Ortho Mode

The term *ortho* comes from *orthogonal*, which means "at right angles." The Ortho mode constrains points selected while drawing and editing to be only horizontal or vertical. See Figure 3-15. To activate or deactivate Ortho mode, pick the **ORTHO** button on the status bar; use the [F8] function key or the [Ctrl]+[L] key combination; or type ORTHO. If Ortho mode is turned off, it can be temporarily turned on when drawing an object by holding down the [Shift] key.

Using Direct Distance Entry

Direct distance entry is a method of entering points by dragging the cursor to indicate direction and typing a number to specify distance. To draw a line using this point entry method, drag the cursor in any desired direction from the first point of the line. Type a numerical value indicating the distance from that point.

The direct distance entry method works best in combination with the Ortho mode or polar tracking. Figure 3-16 shows how to draw a rectangle using direct distance entry. Note that the Ortho mode is on for this example:

Figure 3-15.
Using Ortho mode. Angled lines cannot be drawn with a pointing device while Ortho mode is turned on. With Ortho mode turned off, angled lines can be drawn.

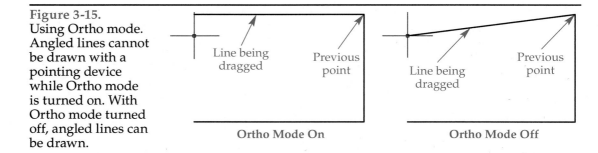

Ortho Mode On　　　　　　　　Ortho Mode Off

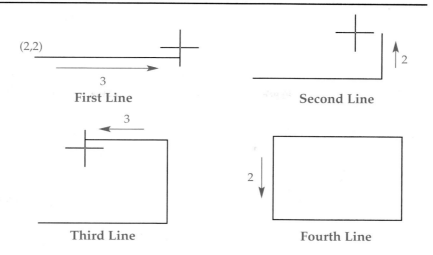

Figure 3-16.
Using direct distance entry to draw lines a designated distance from a current point. With Ortho mode on, move the cursor in the desired direction and type the distance.

(2,2)

First Line

3

Second Line

2

Third Line

3

Fourth Line

2

```
Command: L or LINE↵
Specify first point: 2,2↵
Specify next point or [Undo]: (drag the cursor to the right) 3↵
Specify next point or [Undo]: (drag the cursor up) 2↵
Specify next point or [Close/Undo]: (drag the cursor to the left) 3↵
Specify next point or [Close/Undo]: (drag the cursor down) 2↵
Specify next point or [Close/Undo]: ↵
Command:
```

PROFESSIONAL TIP

Direct distance entry is a convenient way to find points quickly and easily with a minimum amount of effort. Use direct distance entry with Ortho mode or polar tracking to draw objects with perpendicular lines. Direct distance entry can be used whenever AutoCAD expects a point coordinate value, including drawing and editing commands.

Using Polar Tracking

Polar tracking is similar to Ortho mode, except you are not limited to 90° angles. With polar tracking toggled on, you can cause the drawing crosshairs to "snap" to any predefined angle increment. To turn on polar tracking, pick the **POLAR** button on the status bar or use the [F10] function key. Polar tracking provides visual aids. As you move the cursor in the desired direction, AutoCAD displays an alignment path and tooltip when the cursor crosses the default polar angle increments of 0°, 90°, 180°, or 270°. Setting different polar alignment angles is explained in Chapter 6.

After you have specified a starting point in the **LINE** command and moved the cursor in alignment with a polar tracking angle, all you have to do is type the desired distance value and press [Enter] to have the line drawn. Polar tracking is used, as follows, to draw the lines shown in **Figure 3-17:**

```
Command: L or LINE↵
Specify first point: 2,2↵
Specify next point or [Undo]: 2 (drag the crosshairs while watching the tooltip; at 0°,
    press [Enter])
```

Figure 3-17.
Using polar tracking to draw lines at predefined angle increments.

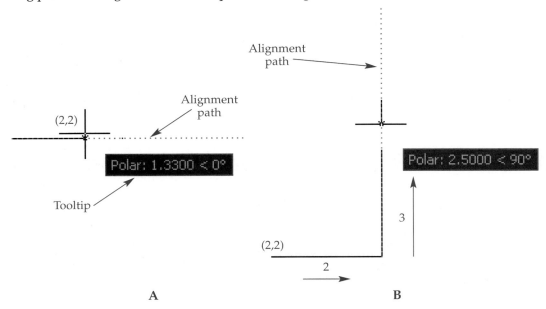

Specify next point or [Undo]: **3** *(drag the crosshairs while watching the tooltip; at 90°, press [Enter])*
Specify next point or [Close/Undo]: ⏎
Command:

Polar tracking is discussed in detail in Chapter 6.

Using Previously Picked Points

There are situations when you need to specify a point that has already been picked. AutoCAD provides several methods for picking previously selected points.

Typing @ and pressing [Enter] at a point selection prompt automatically picks the last point selected. In addition, you can access a list of recently picked points by right-clicking and picking the **Recent Input** cascading menu.

When using Dynamic Input, pressing the up arrow key at a point selection prompt displays the coordinates of the last picked point. You can continue to press the up arrow key to cycle through other previously picked points. As you scroll through the point coordinates in this way, a symbol appears on screen at the displayed point's location. This is a useful tool for reselecting points.

PROFESSIONAL TIP

Practice using the different point entry techniques and decide which method works best for certain situations. Keep in mind that you may mix methods to help enhance your drawing speed. For example, absolute coordinates may work best to locate an initial point or to draw a simple shape. These calculations are easy. Polar coordinates may work better to locate features in a circular pattern or at an angular relationship. Practice with Ortho mode, polar tracking, and direct distance entry to see the advantages and disadvantages of each.

Using the Close Line Option

A *polygon* is a closed plane figure with at least three sides. Triangles and rectangles are examples of polygons. Once you have drawn two or more line segments of a polygon, the endpoint of the last line segment can be connected automatically to the first line segment using the **Close** option. To use this option, type C or CLOSE. In Figure 3-18, the last line is drawn using the **Close** option, as follows:

```
Command: L or LINE↵
Specify first point: (pick Point 1)
Specify next point or [Undo]: (pick Point 2)
Specify next point or [Undo]: (pick Point 3)
Specify next point or [Close/Undo]: (pick Point 4)
Specify next point or [Close/Undo]: C↵
Command:
```

Using the Line Continue Option

Suppose you draw a line, then exit the **LINE** command, but decide to go back and connect a new line to the end of the previous one. Type L to begin the **LINE** command. At the Specify first point: prompt, simply press the [Enter] key, space bar, or right-click the mouse. This action automatically connects the first endpoint of the new line segment to the endpoint of the previous one. The **Continue** option can also be used for drawing arcs, as discussed in Chapter 5. The following command sequence is used for continuing a line:

```
Command: L or LINE↵
Specify first point: (press [Enter] or the space bar, and AutoCAD automatically picks
    the last endpoint of the previous line)
Specify next point or [Undo]: (pick the next point)
Specify next point or [Undo]: (press [Enter] to exit the command)
Command:
```

PROFESSIONAL TIP

Pressing the space bar or [Enter] repeats the previous command.

Figure 3-18.
Using the **Close** option to complete a box.

Undoing the Previously Drawn Line

When drawing a series of lines, you may find you made an error. To delete the mistake while still in the **LINE** command, type U at the Specify next point or [Undo]: prompt and press [Enter]. Doing this removes the previously drawn line and allows you to continue from the previous endpoint. You can use the **Undo** option repeatedly to continue deleting line segments until the entire line is gone. The results of the following prompt sequence are shown in **Figure 3-19:**

> Command: **L** or **LINE**⏎
> Specify first point: *(pick Point 1)*
> Specify next point or [Undo]: *(pick Point 2)*
> Specify next point or [Undo]: *(pick Point 3)*
> Specify next point or [Close/Undo]: *(pick Point 4)*
> Specify next point or [Close/Undo]: **U**⏎
> Specify next point or [Close/Undo]: **U**⏎
> Specify next point or [Undo]: *(pick Point 5)*
> Specify next point or [Close/Undo]: *(press* [Enter] *to exit the command)*
> Command:

Exercise 3-6   Complete the Exercise on the Student CD.

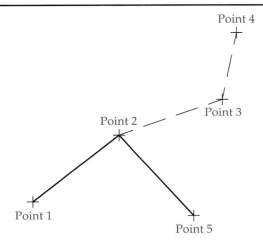

Figure 3-19.
Using the **Undo** option while in the **LINE** command.

Point 4

Point 2

Point 3

Point 1

Point 5

Dynamic Input

Earlier in this chapter, absolute, relative, and polar coordinates were discussed, and the command line method was used to demonstrate inputting values. Typing the same values when Dynamic Input is enabled produces the same results, but there are some additional techniques available when using Dynamic Input.

Dynamic Input and Coordinate Input

When the **LINE** command is started, the dynamic input tooltip reads Specify first point:, the X coordinate value is active, and the Y coordinate value is displayed. See **Figure 3-20.** At this point, the X and Y coordinates can be typed using the same method as with the command line. For example, typing 4,2 and pressing [Enter] starts the line 4 units on the X axis and 2 units on the Y axis. The 4 is typed into the X coordinate field,

Figure 3-20.
After starting the **LINE** command, Dynamic Input displays these items.

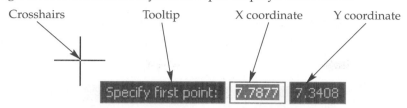

Crosshairs   Tooltip   X coordinate   Y coordinate

Specify first point: 7.7877 7.3408

and once the comma (,) is typed, the Y coordinate field becomes active. The 2 is then typed into the Y coordinate field. By typing the @ symbol before an entry to specify relative coordinates or typing the less than symbol (<) to specify polar coordinates, the dynamic input fields automatically change to anticipate the next entry, just as when a comma is entered. **Figure 3-21** shows the dynamic input fields when using relative and polar coordinates.

PROFESSIONAL TIP

The [Tab] key on the keyboard can be used to cycle through the dynamic input fields. You may find this more convenient than using characters such as the comma (,) and the less than symbol (<).

Dynamic Input Settings

Options for Dynamic Input can be found on the **Dynamic Input** tab of the **Drafting Settings** dialog box. To access this dialog box, right-click on the **DYN** button from the status bar, and then select **Settings**; pick **Tools > Drafting Settings...** from the pull-down menu; or type DSETTINGS or DS. **Figure 3-22** shows the **Dynamic Input** tab of the **Drafting Settings** dialog box.

When **Enable Pointer Input** is checked, commands are entered into the pointer input field next to the crosshairs. The X and Y coordinates are also displayed in the tooltip area, and values can be typed directly into these fields. When **Enable Pointer Input** is unchecked, typing occurs at the Command: prompt. Picking the **Settings...**

Figure 3-21.
A—After typing the @ symbol, it is displayed in the tooltip. B—When using the polar coordinates, the less-than symbol (<) is displayed in the tooltip just before the angle.

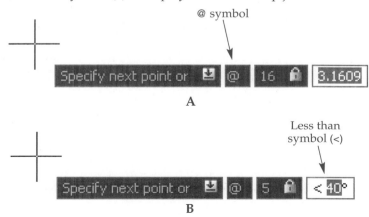

@ symbol

Specify next point or   @   16   3.1609

A

Less than symbol (<)

Specify next point or   @   5   < 40°

B

Figure 3-22.
Dynamic Input settings are found on the **Dynamic Input** tab of the **Drafting Settings** dialog box.

When this box is checked, commands are entered into the pointer input field

Diplays the **Pointer Input Settings** dialog box

Displays the **Tooltip Appearance** dialog box

When this box is checked, the dimension and angle values are displayed

Displays the **Dimension Input Settings** dialog box

Determines whether or not the command prompts and tooltips appear next to the crosshairs

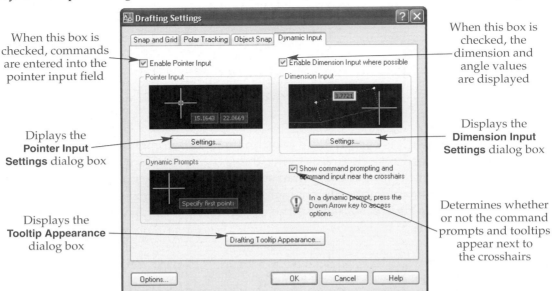

button in the **Pointer Input** area displays the **Pointer Input Settings** dialog box. See Figure 3-23. In the **Format** area, default options can be specified when selecting a second or next point. The following options are available:

- **Polar format.** The tooltip values are displayed in the polar format (distance and angle).
- **Cartesian format.** The tooltip values are displayed in the Cartesian format (X and Y values).
- **Relative coordinates.** The tooltip values are displayed relative to the last point picked.
- **Absolute coordinates.** The tooltip values are displayed in the absolute coordinate values.

Figure 3-23.
The **Pointer Input Settings** dialog box controls the format and visibility of the tooltip.

Tooltip values are displayed as a distance and an angle

Tooltip values are displayed as X and Y values

Tooltip values do not appear until a value is typed

X and Y coordinates are always displayed

Tooltip values are displayed relative to the last point picked

Tooltip values are displayed in the absolute coordinate values

Tooltip values appear when a command is in progress and prompts for a point to be selected

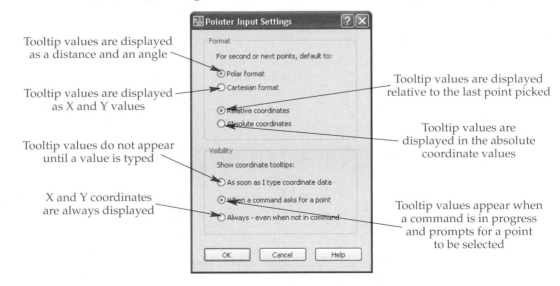

The **Visibility** area of the **Pointer Input Settings** dialog box controls when the tooltip values appear next to the crosshairs. When **As soon as I type coordinate data** is selected, the tooltip values do not appear until a value is typed. If **When a command asks for a point** is selected, the tooltip values appear when a command is in progress and the command is prompting for a point to be selected. To have the X and Y coordinates always displayed, select **Always - even when not in a command**.

When a second point or distance is requested, the dimension and angle values are displayed when **Enable Dimension Input where possible** is checked on the **Dynamic Input** tab. Values can be typed directly into these fields. As you move the crosshairs, the values dynamically update to reflect the current crosshair location relative to the last point picked. Pick the **Settings...** button in the **Dimension Input** area to open the **Dimension Input Settings** dialog box. This dialog box is shown in **Figure 3-24.** For the most part, these options apply to grip-editing, which is discussed in Chapter 13. The following options are available in the **Visibility** area:

- **Show only 1 dimension input field at a time.** Displays only the distance dimension value when creating and grip-editing objects.
- **Show 2 dimension input fields at a time.** Displays the distance and the angle value when creating and grip-editing objects.
- **Show the following dimension input fields simultaneously.** Lets you select any of the items to display when applicable for grip-editing objects.
  - **Resulting Dimension.** When grip-editing an object, the dynamic distance value is displayed while moving the crosshairs.
  - **Length Change.** Displays the change in length when grip-editing an object.
  - **Absolute Angle.** When grip-editing, the absolute angle is displayed.
  - **Angle Change.** When grip-editing, the change in angle is displayed.
  - **Arc Radius.** Displays the radius of an arc while it is being grip-edited.

In the **Dynamic Prompts** area of the **Dynamic Input** tab, the **Show command prompting and command input near the crosshairs** setting determines whether or not the command prompts and tooltips appear next to the crosshairs. If this option is turned off, the down arrow key on the keyboard can be pressed to show the command prompting and inputs. Picking the **Drafting Tooltip Appearance...** button at the bottom of the **Dynamic Input** tab displays the **Tooltip Appearance** dialog box. See **Figure 3-25.** In the **Color** area, the background color of the tooltip can be changed individually for model space and layout space. Pick the **Model Color** or **Layout color** button to change the color. In the **Size** area, a value can be typed, or the slider bar can be dragged to

Figure 3-24.
When grip-editing objects, different dimension values can be specified to display as tooltips from the **Dimension Input Settings** dialog box.

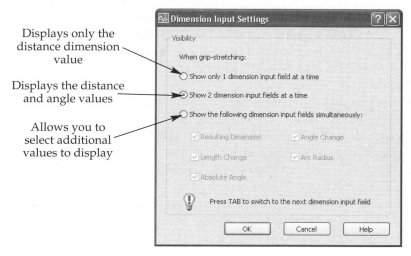

Displays only the distance dimension value

Displays the distance and angle values

Allows you to select additional values to display

Figure 3-25.
The tooltip color, size, and transparency settings can be specified in the **Tooltip Appearance** dialog box.

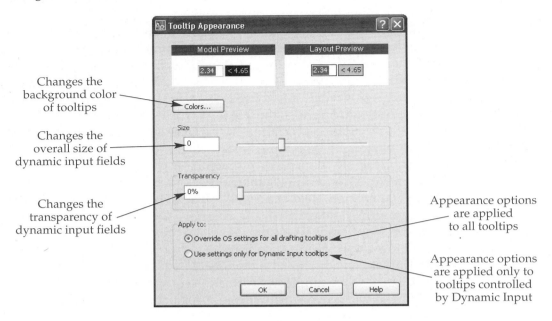

Changes the background color of tooltips

Changes the overall size of dynamic input fields

Changes the transparency of dynamic input fields

Appearance options are applied to all tooltips

Appearance options are applied only to tooltips controlled by Dynamic Input

change the overall size of the dynamic input fields. The **Transparency** setting can be changed so you can see through the dynamic input fields to the drawing area. Increasing the transparency value allows you to see through the dynamic input fields, but the fields are less visible. In the **Apply to:** area, there are two options that determine the tooltips where the settings are applied. If the first option, **Override OS settings for all drafting tooltips**, is selected, the appearance options are applied to all tooltips, overriding the operating system settings. When **Use settings only for Dynamic Input tooltips** is selected, the appearance options are applied only to tooltips controlled by Dynamic Input.

Canceling a Command

If you press the wrong key or misspell a word when typing a command or answering a prompt, use the [Backspace] key to correct the error. This works only if you notice your mistake *before* the [Enter] key is pressed. If you do enter an incorrect option or command, AutoCAD usually responds with an error message. You are then given another chance to enter the correct information or return to the Command: prompt. If you are not sure what has happened, reading the error message should tell you what you need to know.

Previous messages displayed in the command window may not be visible. Press the [F2] function key to display AutoCAD's text screen. This allows you to read the entire message. Also, you will be able to review the commands and options you entered. This may help you better understand what happened. You can press the [F2] key again to return to the graphics screen or use your cursor to pick any visible portion of the graphics screen to make it current again.

It is often necessary to stop the currently active command and return to AutoCAD's Command: prompt to either reenter a command or use another command. This can occur if an incorrect entry is made and you need to restart the command using the

AutoCAD and Its Applications—Basics

correct method or even if you simply decide to do something different. Pressing the [Enter] key or the space bar discontinues some commands, such as the **LINE** command. This exits the command and returns to the Command: prompt, where AutoCAD awaits a new command entry. There are many situations, however, in which this does not work.

You can cancel any active command or abort any data entry and return to the Command: prompt by pressing the [Esc] key. This key is usually located in the upper-left corner of your keyboard. It may be necessary to press the [Esc] key twice to completely cancel certain commands. Most of the toolbar buttons and pull-down menu options automatically cancel any currently active command before entering the new command. In a case in which you wish to abort the current command and start a new one, simply pick the appropriate pull-down menu option or toolbar button.

Introduction to Editing

Editing is the procedure used to correct mistakes or revise an existing drawing. There are many editing functions that help increase productivity. The basic editing operations **ERASE**, **OOPS**, and **U** are introduced in the next sections.

To edit a drawing, you must select items to modify. The Select objects: prompt appears whenever you need to select items in the command sequence. Whether you select only one object or hundreds of objects, a *selection set* is created. You can create a selection set using a variety of selection options, including the following:

- Window selection.
- Crossing selection.
- Window polygon selection.
- Crossing polygon selection.
- Selection fence.

When you become familiar with the selection set options, you will find that they increase your flexibility and productivity.

In the following discussion and examples, several of the selection set methods are introduced using the **ERASE** command. Keep in mind, however, that these techniques can be used with most of the editing commands in AutoCAD whenever the Select objects: prompt appears. Any of the selection set methods can be enabled from the prompt line.

Using the Erase Command

The **ERASE** command is similar to using an eraser in manual drafting to remove unwanted information. With the **ERASE** command, however, you have a second chance. If you erase the wrong item, it can be brought back with the **OOPS** or **UNDO** command. Picking **Modify > Erase**, picking the **Erase** button in the **Modify** toolbar, or typing E or ERASE accesses the **ERASE** command.

When you enter the **ERASE** command, you are prompted to select an object. When the Select objects: prompt appears, a small box replaces the screen crosshairs. This box is referred to as the *pick box*. Move the pick box over the item to be erased and pick that item. The object is highlighted, and the Select objects: prompt is redisplayed. You can then select another object to erase. If you are finished selecting objects, erase the selected objects by pressing the space bar, right-clicking and selecting **Enter** from the shortcut menu, or pressing [Enter]. See **Figure 3-26.**

Exercise 3-7   Complete the Exercise on the Student CD.

Figure 3-26.
Using the **ERASE** command to erase a single object.

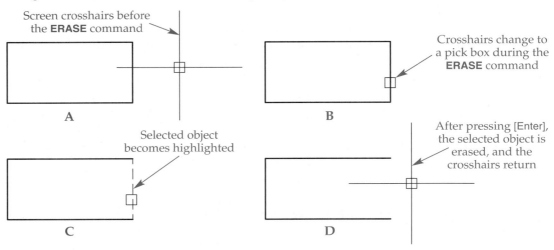

Screen crosshairs before the **ERASE** command

A

Crosshairs change to a pick box during the **ERASE** command

B

Selected object becomes highlighted

C

After pressing [Enter], the selected object is erased, and the crosshairs return

D

Using the Window selection option

The **W** or **Window** option can be used at any Select objects: prompt. This option allows you to draw a box, or "window," around an object or group of objects to select for editing. Everything entirely within the window can be selected at the same time. If portions of entities project outside the window, those entities are not selected.

When the Select objects: prompt is shown, the screen crosshairs change to a box-shaped cursor. Select a point clearly below and to the left of the object to be erased. The cursor is replaced by a selection box. This box grows as you move the corner to the right of the first point. The box is a solid line with a light blue background.

The Specify opposite corner: prompt is shown. Move the pointing device up and to the right so the box completely covers the object(s) to be erased. Pick to locate the second corner, as shown in **Figure 3-27**. All objects within the box become highlighted. When finished, press [Enter] or pick the right mouse button to complete the **ERASE** command.

You can also manually specify the **Window** selection option from the command line. You need to do this if the **PICKAUTO** variable (discussed later in this chapter) is set to 0. Type W at the Select objects: prompt to use the **Window** selection option. When you manually enter the **Window** option, you do not need to pick the first point to the left of the object(s) being erased. The box remains the **Window** box whether you move the cursor to the left or right.

Figure 3-27.
Using the **Window** selection option with the **ERASE** command.

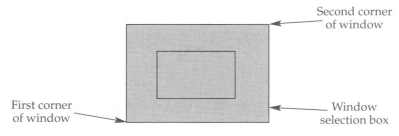

Second corner of window

First corner of window

Window selection box

Using the Crossing selection option

The **Crossing** selection option is similar to the **Window** option. With the **Window** option, objects contained within the box are selected. With the **Crossing** option, objects contained within the box *and object crossing the box* are selected. The **Crossing** box outline is dotted to distinguish it from the solid outline of the **Window** box.

To use the Crossing option, select a point to the right of the object to be erased when the Select objects: prompt is shown. After you select the first point, the cursor expands in size as you move the pointing device to the left.

Remember, the crossing box does not need to enclose the entire object to erase it, as the window box does. The crossing box needs only to cross part of the object. **Figure 3-28** shows how to erase three of the four lines of a rectangle using the **Crossing** option.

You can also manually specify the **Crossing** option by typing C at the Select objects: prompt. When you manually enter the **Crossing** option, you do not need to pick the first point to the right of the object(s) being erased. The box remains the **Crossing** box whether you move the cursor to the left or right.

Window and Crossing display options

By default, the **Window** selection window has a transparent blue background, and the **Crossing** selection window has a transparent green background. These colors and other selection window settings can be modified in the **Visual Effect Settings** dialog box. To access this dialog box, select **Tools** > **Options...** from the pull-down menu or type OP or OPTIONS. You can also right-click in the drawing area and select **Options...** from the shortcut menu. In the **Options** dialog box, pick the **Selection** tab. In the **Selection Preview** area, pick the **Visual Effect Settings...** button. The **Visual Effect Settings** dialog box is shown in **Figure 3-29**.

The **Indicate selection area** option determines if the selection window has a background color. If this option is checked, the window is filled with a background color. If it is unchecked, there is no background color, and only the solid and dashed border lines are displayed. The color of the window box background can be changed by selecting a different color from the **Window selection color:** drop-down list. The **Crossing selection color:** sets the background color when using a crossing box. The transparency of the background color can be set in the **Selection area opacity:** field. To make the background more opaque, type a larger value or move the slider bar to the right. To make it more transparent, type a smaller value or move the slider bar to the left.

Object selection preview

You may have noticed that when you move the crosshairs over an object and pause for a moment, the object changes to a thicker lineweight. When the crosshairs are moved off the object, its lineweight goes back to normal. This allows you to preview the object before you select it. When there are many objects in a small area, this feature helps you select the correct object the first time.

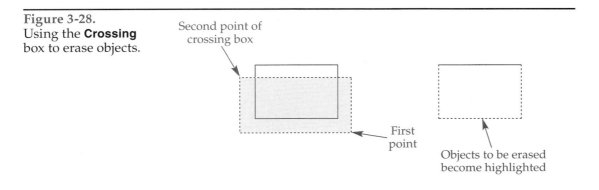

Figure 3-28.
Using the **Crossing** box to erase objects.

Second point of crossing box

First point

Objects to be erased become highlighted

Figure 3-29.
Display options for the selection windows can be set in the **Visual Effect Settings** dialog box.

Determines if the selection window has a background color

Changes the color of the window box background

Options for the selection preview border

Opens the **Advanced Preview Options** dialog box

Sets the transparency of the background color

Changes the color of the crossing box background

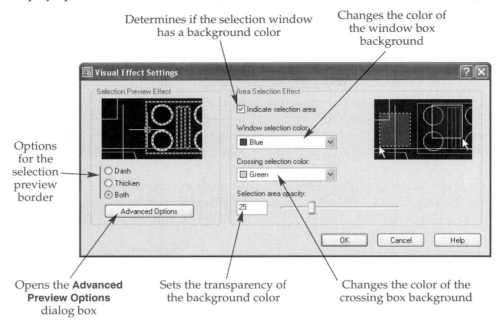

In the **Selection** tab of the **Options** dialog box, the **Selection Preview** area contains settings for this feature. If **When a command is active** is checked, the selection preview works in the middle of a command, and if **When no command is active** is checked, the preview works when the command line is at an empty prompt. If you find the selection preview distracting while you move the crosshairs around the drawing area, you can uncheck these boxes to turn the preview feature off.

The selection preview border can be set to **Dash**, **Thicken**, or **Both**. This setting can be accessed by picking the **Visual Effect Settings...** button in the **Selection Preview** area. Select one of the options in the **Selection Preview Effect** area. **Figure 3-30** illustrates the results of the three different options.

Picking the **Advanced Options** button opens the **Advanced Preview Options** dialog box. In this dialog box, certain types of objects can be excluded from using the selection preview settings.

Figure 3-30.
Before selecting an object, you can hover over it to have it display as dashed, thickened, or both.

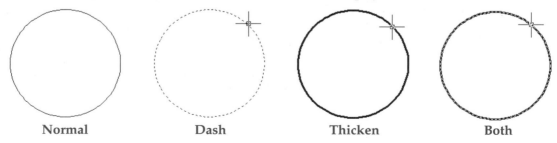

Normal   **Dash**   **Thicken**   **Both**

> **NOTE**
>
>
>
> The **PICKAUTO** system variable controls automatic windowing (also called *implied windowing*) when the Select objects: prompt appears. Change the **PICKAUTO** value by typing PICKAUTO and then entering 1 (on) or 0 (off). Automatic windowing is on by default. The type of selection box is determined by the direction you move the crosshairs to select the second point. When automatic windowing is deactivated, you can manually activate it by using the **Box** selection option.

Exercise 3-8   Complete the Exercise on the Student CD.

Using the WPolygon and CPolygon selection option

The **Window** selection option is a rectangle selection box, which may not allow you to select the items you need to erase. You can also draw a polygon as the selection set boundary by using the **WPolygon** selection option.

To use the **WPolygon** option, type WP at the Select objects: prompt. Draw a polygon enclosing the objects. As you pick corners, the polygon drags into place. The command sequence for erasing the five middle squares in **Figure 3-31** is as follows:

    Command: **E** *or* **ERASE**↵
    Select objects: **WP**↵
    First polygon point: *(pick Point 1)*
    Specify endpoint of line or [Undo]: *(pick Point 2)*
    Specify endpoint of line or [Undo]: *(pick Point 3)*
    Specify endpoint of line or [Undo]: *(pick Point 4)*
    Specify endpoint of line or [Undo]: ↵
    Select objects: ↵
    Command:

If you do not like the last polygon point you picked, use the **Undo** option by typing U at the Specify endpoint of line or [Undo]: prompt.

The **CPolygon** selection option is similar to the **WPolygon** selection option. With the **CPolygon** option, however, a crossing window is created. Type **CP** at the Select objects: prompt to access this selection option. **Figure 3-32** illustrates the **CPolygon** selection option.

Figure 3-31.
Using the **WPolygon** selection option to erase objects.

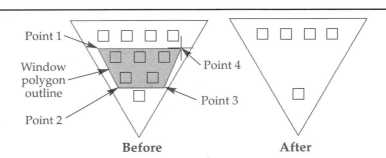

Figure 3-32.
Using the **CPolygon** selection option. Everything enclosed within and crossing the polygon is selected.

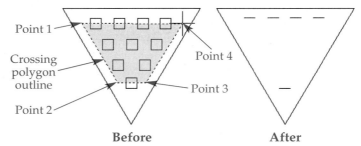

Before   After

PROFESSIONAL TIP

When using **WPolygon** or **CPolygon**, AutoCAD does not allow you to select a point that causes the lines of the selection polygon to intersect each other. Pick locations that do not result in an intersection. Use the **Undo** option if you need to go back and relocate a preceding pick point.

Using the Fence selection option

Fence is another selection option used to select several objects at the same time. When using the **Fence** option, you simply place a fence through the objects you want to select. Only the objects the fence passes through are included in the selection set. The fence can be straight or staggered, as shown in **Figure 3-33**. Type F at the Select objects: prompt to use the **Fence** option:

```
Command: E or ERASE↵
Select objects: F↵
Specify first fence point: (pick Point 1)
Specify next fence point or [Undo]: (pick Point 2)
Specify next fence point or [Undo]: (pick Point 3)
Specify next fence point or [Undo]: (pick Point 4)
Specify next fence point or [Undo]: (pick Point 5)
Specify next fence point or [Undo]: (pick Point 6)
Specify next fence point or [Undo]: ↵
Select objects: ↵
Command:
```

Figure 3-33.
Using the **Fence** selection option to erase objects. The fence can be either straight or staggered.

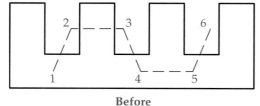

Before   After

Removing from and adding to the selection set

When editing a drawing, a common mistake is to accidentally select an object you do not want to select. The simplest way to remove one or more objects from the current selection set is by holding down the [Shift] key and reselecting the objects. This is possible only for individual picks and implied windows. For an implied window, the [Shift] key must be held down while picking the first corner and then can be released for picking the second corner. If you accidentally remove the wrong object from the selection set, release the [Shift] key and pick it again.

To use other methods for removing objects from a selection set or for specialized selection needs, you can switch to the **Remove** option by typing R at the Select objects: prompt. This changes the Select objects: prompt to Remove objects:. The command sequence is as follows:

> Command: **E** *or* **ERASE**↵
> Select objects: *(pick several objects, using any technique)*
> Select objects: **R**↵
> Remove objects: *(pick the objects you want removed from the selection set)*
> Remove objects: ↵
> Command:

Switch back to the selection mode by typing A (for add) at the Remove objects: prompt. This restores the Select objects: prompt and allows you to select additional objects.

Using the Oops Command

The **OOPS** command brings back the last object you erased. It is issued by typing OOPS. If you erased several objects in the same command sequence, all are brought back to the screen. Only the objects erased in the most recent erase procedure can be returned using **OOPS**.

Using the U Command

While the **OOPS** command brings back the last object you erased, the **U** command undoes the last command. The **U** command is issued by typing U or by using the [Ctrl]+[Z] key combination. **OOPS** can be used only one time in sequence, while **U** can be issued until every command used since the editing session began has been undone. Even **OOPS** can be undone with the **U** command.

Using the Last Selection

The **ERASE** command's **Last** option saves time if you need to erase the last entity drawn. For example, suppose you draw a line and then want to erase it. The **Last** option will automatically select the line. Typing L at the Select objects: prompt selects the **Last** option:

> Command: **E** *or* **ERASE**↵
> Select objects: **L**↵
> 1 found
> Select objects: ↵
> Command:

Keep in mind that using the **Last** option only highlights the last visible item drawn. You must press [Enter] for the object to be erased. If you need to erase more than just the last object, you can use the **ERASE** command and **Last** option repeatedly to erase items in reverse order. This is not as quick, however, as using the **ERASE** command and selecting the objects.

Using the Previous Selection

The object selection options given up to this point in the chapter have used the example of the **ERASE** command. These selection options are also used when moving objects, rotating objects, and performing other editing functions. These basic editing commands are explained in Chapter 12.

Often, more than one sequential editing operation needs to be carried out on a specific group of objects. In this case, the **Previous** selection option allows you to select the same object(s) you just edited. You can select the **Previous** selection set by typing P at the Select objects: prompt. In the following example, a group of objects is erased, and the **OOPS** command is used to recover them. The **ERASE** command is then issued again, this time using the **Previous** selection option to access the previously selected objects:

Command: **E** *or* **ERASE**↵
Select objects: *(pick several items, using any selection technique)*
Select objects: ↵
Command: **OOPS**↵
Command: **E** *or* **ERASE**↵
Select objects: **P**↵
Select objects: ↵
Command:

Selecting All Objects in a Drawing

Sometimes, you may want to select every object in the drawing. To do this, type ALL at the Select objects: prompt, as follows:

Command: **E** *or* **ERASE**↵
Select objects: **ALL**↵
Select objects: ↵
Command:

This procedure erases everything in the drawing. You can use the **Remove** option at the second Select objects: prompt to remove certain objects from the set. You can also type ALL after typing R to remove all objects from the set.

Exercise 3-10   Complete the Exercise on the Student CD.

Cycling through Stacked Objects

One way to deal with stacked objects is to let AutoCAD cycle through the overlapping objects. *Cycling* is repeatedly selecting one item from a series of stacked objects until the desired object is highlighted. This works best when several objects cross at the same place or are very close together. To begin cycling through objects, hold down the [Ctrl] key while you make your first pick.

Figure 3-34.
Cycling through a series of stacked circles until the desired object is highlighted.

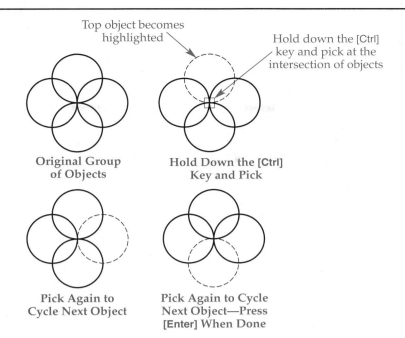

Top object becomes highlighted

Hold down the [Ctrl] key and pick at the intersection of objects

Original Group of Objects

Hold Down the [Ctrl] Key and Pick

Pick Again to Cycle Next Object

Pick Again to Cycle Next Object—Press [Enter] When Done

For the objects in **Figure 3-34**, pick the point where the four circles intersect. If there are two or more objects found crossing through the pick box area, the top object is highlighted. Now, you can release the [Ctrl] key. When you pick again, the top object returns, and the next one is highlighted. Every time you pick, another object becomes highlighted. In this way, you cycle through all the objects. When you have the desired object highlighted, press [Enter] to end the cycling process and return to the Select objects: prompt. The following command sequence is used to erase one of the circles in **Figure 3-34**, but you can use this for any editing function:

Command: **E** *or* **ERASE**↵
Select objects: *(hold down the* [Ctrl] *key and pick)* <Cycle on> *(pick until you high-light the desired object and press* [Enter]*)*
<Cycle off>1 found
Select objects: *(select additional objects or press* [Enter]*)*
Command:

LEGACY NOTE

The **MULTIPLE** command causes AutoCAD to continue to reissue a command until you press the [Esc] key. The **MULTIPLE** command is no longer practical, since you can repeat a command more easily by pressing the space bar or [Enter] key, or by right-clicking and picking **Repeat COMMAND** from the top of the shortcut menu.

LEGACY NOTE

Blips are used as visual aids when selecting points. The **BLIPMODE** system variable controls whether or not blips are used. Change the **BLIPMODE** value by typing BLIPMODE and then entering 1 (on) or 0 (off). You can remove blips by selecting **View > Redraw**.

Answer the following questions. Write your answers on a separate sheet of paper or complete the electronic chapter test on the Student CD.

1. Give the commands and entries to draw a line from Point A to Point B to Point C and back to Point A. Return to the Command: prompt:
   A. Command: _____
   B. Specify first point: _____
   C. Specify next point or [Undo]: _____
   D. Specify next point or [Undo]: _____
   E. Specify next point or [Close/Undo]: _____

2. Identify the following linetypes:

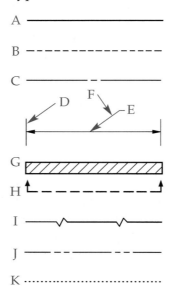

3. List two ways to discontinue drawing a line.
4. Name five point entry methods.
5. How can you turn on the coordinate display?
6. What does the polar coordinate display @2.750<90 mean?
7. What does the absolute coordinate display 5.250,7.875 mean?
8. How can you turn on the Ortho mode?
9. Identify how you can continue drawing another line segment from a previously drawn line.
10. Define *stacked objects*.
11. How do the appearances of a window and a crossing box differ?
12. Name the command used to bring back the last object(s) erased before issuing another command.
13. List five ways to select an object to erase.
14. Explain, in general terms, how direct distance entry works.
15. Where does the result of typing occur when Dynamic Input is turned on?

Drawing Problems

1. Open one of your templates from Chapter 2. Draw the specified objects as accurately as possible with grid and snap turned off. Use the **LINE** command and draw the following objects on only the left side of the screen:
   - Right triangle.
   - Isosceles triangle.
   - Rectangle.
   - Square.

   Save the drawing as P3-1.

2. Draw the same objects specified in Problem 1 on the right side of the screen. This time, make sure the snap grid is turned on. Observe the difference between having snap on for this problem and off for the previous problem. Save the drawing as P3-2.

3. Draw an object by connecting the following point coordinates. Save your drawing as P3-3. Make a print of your drawing if a printer is available.

Point	Coordinates	Point	Coordinates
1	2,2	8	@-1.5,0
2	@1.5,0	9	@0,1.25
3	@.75<90	10	@-1.25,1.25
4	@1.5<0	11	@2<180
5	@0,-.75	12	@-1.25,-1.25
6	@3,0	13	@2.25<270
7	@1<90		

4. With the absolute, relative, and polar coordinate entry methods, draw the following shapes. Set the limits to 0,0 and 22,17; units to decimal; grid spacing to .5; and snap spacing to .0625. Draw Object A three times, using a different point entry system each time. Draw Object B once, using at least two methods of coordinate entry. Do not draw dimensions. Save the drawing as P3-4. Make a print of your drawing if a printer is available.

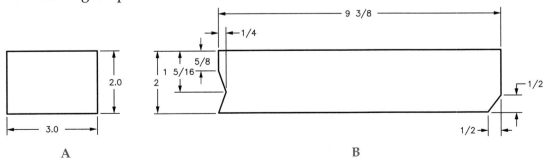

5. Draw the front elevation of this house. Create the features proportional to the given drawing. Save the drawing as P3-5.

6. Use Ortho mode and direct distance entry to draw the outline shown. Each grid square is one unit. Do not draw the grid lines. Save the drawing as P3-6.

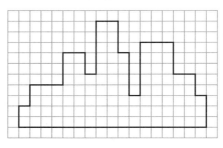

7. Use polar coordinate entry to draw the hexagon shown. Each side of the hexagon is 2 units. Begin at the start point, and draw the lines in the direction indicated by the arrows. Do not draw dimensions. Save the drawing as P3-7.

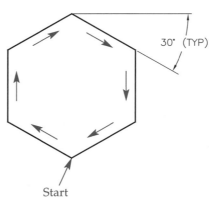

8. Draw the objects shown in A and B. Begin at the start point and then discontinue the **LINE** command at the point shown. Complete each object using the **Continue** option. Do not draw dimensions. Save the drawing as P3-8.

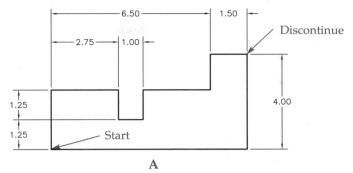

A

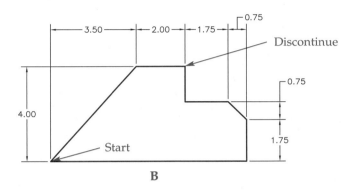

B

9. Draw the elevation of the desk shown. Do not draw dimensions. Save the drawing as P3-9.

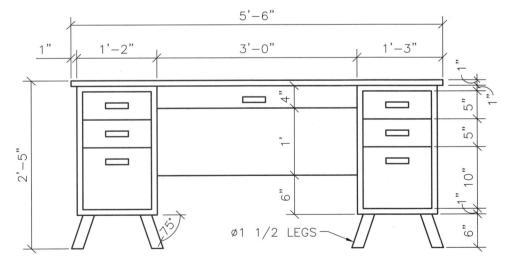

For Problems 10–14, draw the given part. Do not draw dimensions. Save the drawing as P3-10, P3-11, etc.

10.

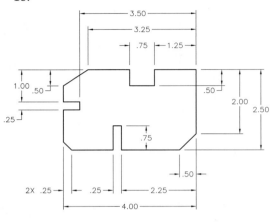

11.

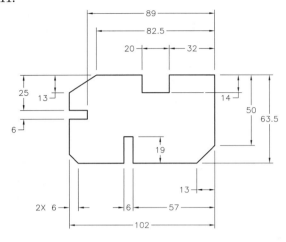

12.

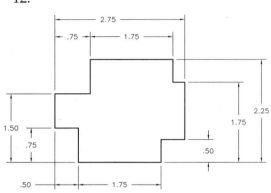

13.

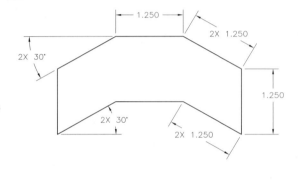

14.

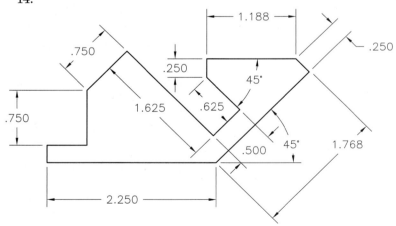

Using Layers, Modifying Object Properties, and Making Prints

Learning Objectives

After completing this chapter, you will be able to do the following:

- Draw objects on separate layers.
- Create and manage drawing layers.
- Draw objects with different colors, linetypes, and lineweights.
- Filter a list of layers.
- Use the **Properties** window to change layers, colors, linetypes, and lineweights.
- Use **DesignCenter** to copy layers and linetypes between drawings.
- Make prints of your drawings.

Chapter 3 introduced you to drawing and editing in AutoCAD. In addition to lines, many other types of objects are created in the course of producing most drawings. Many of these objects will be introduced in Chapter 5.

Regardless of the type of object drawn, all AutoCAD objects have properties. Some object properties, such as color and linetype, are common to many types of objects. Other properties, such as text height, are specific to a single object type. AutoCAD uses a layer system to simplify the process of assigning and modifying object properties. In addition, when using layer display options, you can create several different drawing sheets, views, and displays from a single drawing.

This chapter introduces the AutoCAD layer system and basic object properties. It also provides a brief introduction to printing and plotting. Printing and plotting will be covered in greater detail in Chapter 11.

Introduction to Layers

In drafting, different elements or components of drawings might be separated by placing them on different sheets. When each sheet is perfectly aligned with the others, you have what is called an *overlay system*. In AutoCAD, the components of this overlay system are referred to as *layers*. All the layers can be reproduced together to reflect the entire design drawing. Individual layers might also be reproduced to show specific details or components of the design. Using layers increases productivity in several ways:

- ✓ Specific information can be grouped on separate layers. For example, the floor plan can be drawn on one layer, the electrical plan on another, and the plumbing plan on a third.
- ✓ Several plot sheets can be referenced from the same drawing file by modifying layer visibility.
- ✓ Drawings can be reproduced in individual layers, or the layers can be combined in any desired format. For example, the floor plan and electrical plan can be reproduced together and sent to an electrical contractor for a bid. The floor plan and plumbing plan can be reproduced together and sent to a plumbing contractor.
- ✓ Each layer can be assigned a different color, linetype, and lineweight to help improve clarity.
- ✓ Each layer can be plotted in a different color or pen width, or it can be not plotted at all.
- ✓ Selected layers can be turned off or frozen to decrease the amount of information displayed on the screen or to speed screen regeneration.
- ✓ Changes can be made to a layer promptly, often while the client watches.

Layers Used in Different Drafting Fields

In mechanical drafting, views, hidden features, dimensions, sections, notes, and symbols might each be placed on separate layers. In architectural or civil drafting, there may be over one hundred layers. Layers can be created for floor plans, foundation plans, partition layouts, plumbing systems, electrical systems, structural systems, roof drainage systems, reflected ceiling systems, and HVAC systems. Interior designers may use floor plan, interior partition, and furniture layers. In electronics drafting, each level of a multilevel circuit board can be drawn on its own layer.

Current Layer

As you have worked through the exercises in this book, you may have noticed that "0" appears in the **Layer Control** drop-down list on the **Layers** toolbar. See **Figure 4-1**. Layer 0 is the AutoCAD default current layer. Until another layer is defined and set current, all objects drawn are placed on and belong to layer 0.

Figure 4-1.
0 appears in the **Layer Control** drop-down list on the **Layers** toolbar. Layer 0 is the AutoCAD default layer.

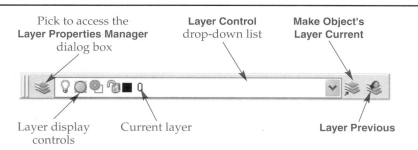

Pick to access the **Layer Properties Manager** dialog box

Layer Control drop-down list

Make Object's Layer Current

Layer display controls

Current layer

Layer Previous

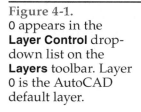

Naming Layers

Layers should be given names to reflect what is drawn on them. Layer names can have up to 255 characters and can include letters, numbers, and certain special characters, including spaces. Typical mechanical, architectural, and civil drafting layer names are as follows:

Mechanical	Architectural	Civil
Object	Walls	Property Line
Hidden	Windows	Structures
Center	Doors	Roads
Dimension	Electrical	Water
Construction	Plumbing	Contours
Hatch	Furniture	Gas
Border	Lighting	Elevations

For very simple drawings, layers can be named by linetype and color. For example, the layer name Continuous-White may have a continuous linetype drawn in white. The layer usage and color number, such as Object-7, can also be used to indicate an object line with color 7. Another option is to assign the linetype a numerical value. For example, object lines can be 1, hidden lines can be 2, and centerlines can be 3. If you use this method, keep a written record of your numbering system for reference.

Layers can also be given more complex names. The name might include the drawing number, color code, and layer content. The layer name Dwg100-2-Dimen, for example, could refer to drawing DWG100, color 2, and the fact that this layer is used for dimensions. The American Institute of Architects (AIA) has established a layer naming system for architectural and related drawings. This standard is found in the document *CAD Layer Guidelines*, published by AIA.

The Layer Properties Manager

The **LAYER** command opens the **Layer Properties Manager** dialog box. To display this dialog box, pick the **Layer Properties Manager** button from the **Layers** toolbar, select **Format** > **Layer...** from the pull-down menu, or type LA or LAYER. **Figure 4-2** shows the **Layer Properties Manager** dialog box. Only one layer is required in an AutoCAD drawing. This layer is named 0 and cannot be renamed or purged from the drawing. As discussed earlier, however, it is often useful to have more than one layer in a drawing. The most important layer is the *current* layer because whatever you draw is placed on this layer. It is useful to think of the current layer as the *top* layer.

LAYER

Type
LAYER
LA

Pull-Down Menu
Format
> Layer...

Toolbar
Layers

Layer Properties
Manager

Creating Layers

Layers should be added to a drawing to meet the needs of the current drawing project. To add a new layer, pick the **New Layer** button from the **Layer Properties Manager** dialog box. A new layer listing appears, using a default name of Layer1. See **Figure 4-3**. The layer name is highlighted when the listing appears, allowing you to type a new name.

You can also enter several new layer names at the same time. Typing a layer name and then pressing the comma key enters the first layer name and moves on to the next one. Entering several layer names in this manner saves time because it keeps you from having to pick the **New Layer** button each time. Pick the **OK** button when you are finished typing the new layer names. When you reopen the **Layer Properties Manager** dialog box, the new layer names are alphabetized, as shown in **Figure 4-4**.

Figure 4-2.
The **Layer Properties Manager** dialog box.

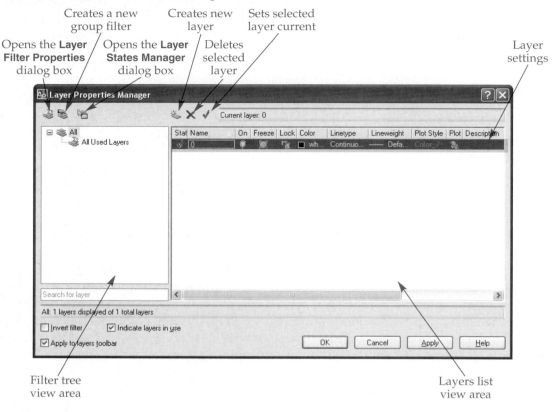

Creates a new group filter

Creates new layer

Sets selected layer current

Opens the **Layer Filter Properties** dialog box

Opens the **Layer States Manager** dialog box

Deletes selected layer

Layer settings

Filter tree view area

Layers list view area

Figure 4-3.
A new layer is named Layer1 by default.

Edit layer name

Figure 4-4.
Layer names are automatically placed in numerical and alphabetical order.

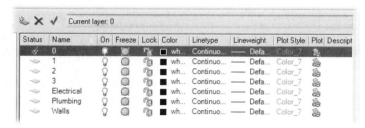

Deleting Layers

To delete a layer, select the layer and then pick the **Delete Layer** button. Pick the **Apply** button, and then the layer is erased from the list box. If the selected layer is not deleted, an object in the drawing has been drawn on this layer.

Setting the Current Layer

You can set a new current layer by double-clicking the layer name or highlighting the layer name in the layer list and then picking the **Set Current** button. To highlight the layer name, simply pick the name. The current layer is specified in the status line above the layer list in the **Layer Properties Manager** dialog box and in the **Layer Control** drop-down list in the **Layers** toolbar.

Exercise 4-1   Complete the Exercise on the Student CD.

Viewing the Status of Layers

The status of each layer is displayed in the **Layer Properties Manager** with icons to the right of the layer name. See **Figure 4-5**. If you position the pointer over an icon for a moment, a tooltip appears and tells what the icon refers to. Picking the icons changes layer settings.

- **Status.** The icon shown in this field indicates the status property of the layer. A green check mark indicates this is the current layer. If there are objects on the layer, the icon is a blue sheet of paper. A white sheet of paper indicates that there are no objects on the layer. If the filters are shown in the layer list, the same icons associated with the filters in the filter tree view list are used.
- **Changing the layer name.** The layer name list box contains all the layers in the drawing. To change an existing name, pick the name once to highlight it, pause for a moment, and then pick it again. When you pick the second time, the layer name is highlighted with a text box around it and a cursor for text entry, allowing you to type a new layer name. Layer 0 cannot be renamed.

Figure 4-5.
Layer settings can be changed by picking the icons in the **Layer Properties Manager** dialog box.

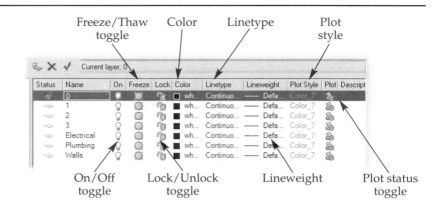

On   Off

Thawed Frozen

- **Turning layers on and off.** The lightbulb shows whether a layer is on or off. The yellow lightbulb means the layer is on; objects on that layer are displayed on-screen and can be plotted. If you pick on a yellow lightbulb, it turns gray, turning the layer off. If a layer is off, the objects on it are not displayed on-screen and are not plotted. Objects on a layer that has been turned off can still be edited when using advanced selection techniques and are regenerated when a drawing regeneration occurs.

- **Thawing and freezing layers.** Layers are further classified as thawed or frozen. Similar to turned off layers, frozen layers are not displayed and do not plot. Objects on a frozen layer, however, cannot be edited and are not regenerated when the drawing regenerates. Freezing layers containing objects that do not need to be referenced for current drawing tasks can greatly speed up your system performance. The snowflake icon is displayed when a layer is frozen. Layers are normally thawed, which means objects on the layer are displayed on-screen. The sun icon is displayed for thawed layers. Picking the sun/snowflake icon toggles it to the other icon.

NOTE

It is important to note that objects on frozen layers cannot be modified, but objects residing on turned off layers can be modified. For example, if you turn off half your layers and use the **All** selection option with the **ERASE** command, even the objects on the turned off layers will be erased! The **ERASE** command does not, however, affect frozen layers.

Locked Unlocked

- **Unlocked and locked layers.** The unlocked and locked padlock symbols are for locking and unlocking layers. Layers are unlocked by default, but you can pick on an unlocked padlock to lock it. A locked layer remains visible, but objects on it cannot be edited. New objects can be added to a locked layer.

- **Layer color.** The color swatch shows the current default color for objects created on each layer. When you need to change the color for an existing layer, pick the swatch to display the **Select Color** dialog box. Working with colors is discussed later in this chapter.

- **Layer linetype.** The current linetype setting for each layer is shown in the **Linetype** list. Picking the linetype name opens the **Select Linetype** dialog box, where you can specify a new linetype. Working with linetypes is discussed later in this chapter.

- **Layer lineweight.** The current lineweight setting for each layer is shown in the **Lineweight** list. Picking the lineweight name opens the **Lineweight** dialog box, where you can specify a new lineweight. Working with lineweights is discussed later in this chapter.
- **Layer plot styles.** This setting changes the plot style associated with the selected layers. The plot style setting is disabled when you are working with color-dependent plot styles (the **PSTYLEPOLICY** system variable is set to 1). Otherwise, picking the plot style displays the **Select Plot Style** dialog box. Plot styles are discussed in Chapter 11.
- **Layer plot/no plot.** Select this toggle to turn off plotting for a particular layer. The "no plot" symbol is displayed over the printer image when the layer is not available to be plotted. The layer is still displayed, but not plotted.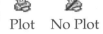
  Plot   No Plot
- **Description.** Provides an area to type a short description for the layer.

The following layer options appear only in paper space layout mode, which is discussed in Chapter 11:

- **Thawing and freezing layers in active and new viewports.** These settings, for floating model space views on layouts, are detailed later in this textbook. The options are visible only when a layout tab is active.

Exercise 4-2   Complete the Exercise on the Student CD.

Working with Layers

Any setting you change affects all currently selected layer names. Selecting layer names uses the same techniques used to select files. You can highlight a single name by picking it. Picking another name deselects the previous name and highlights the new selection. You can use the [Shift] key to select two layers and all layer names between them on the listing. Holding the [Ctrl] key while picking layer names highlights or deselects each selected name without affecting any other selections.

A shortcut menu is also available while your cursor is in the layer list area of the **Layer Properties Manager** dialog box. Press the right mouse button to display the shortcut menu shown in **Figure 4-6.** The options available on this menu are as follows:

- **Show Filter Tree.** Opens or closes the filter tree view area.
- **Show Filters in Layer List.** Displays all the layer filters, along with the layers, in the layer list area.
- **Set current.** Sets the selected layer current.
- **New Layer.** Creates a new layer.

Figure 4-6.
Right-clicking in the list box of the **Layer Properties Manager** dialog box produces this shortcut menu.

- **Delete Layer.** Sets the selected layer to be deleted.
- **Change Description.** Allows you to modify the description for the selected layer.
- **Remove From Group Filter.** This is only available if the selected layer is part of a group filter. When this option is available and chosen, the selected layer is removed from the group filter.
- **Select All.** Selects all layers.
- **Clear All.** Deselects all layers.
- **Select All but Current.** Selects all layers, except the current layer.
- **Invert Selection.** Deselects all selected layers and selects all deselected layers.
- **Invert Layer Filter.** Inverts the current filter setting. Filters are discussed later in this chapter.
- **Layer Filters.** Displays a submenu with predefined filters. The choices are **All** and **All Used Layers**.
- **Save Layer States.** Opens the **New Layer State to Save** dialog box, which is discussed later in this chapter.
- **Restore Layer State.** Opens the **Layer States Manager** dialog box, which allows you to restore a previously saved layer state.

Exercise 4-3   Complete the Exercise on the Student CD.

Setting the Layer Color

The number of layer colors available depends on your graphics card and monitor. Color systems usually support at least 256 colors, while many graphics cards support up to 16.7 million colors. Color settings can affect the appearance of plotted drawings. Lineweights can also be associated with drawing colors. This is discussed in Chapter 11. Colors should highlight the important features on the drawing and not cause eyestrain. AutoCAD allows you to assign colors to layers by selecting a color from the **Select Color** dialog box.

In order to assign a color to a layer, first highlight a layer name in the **Layer Properties Manager**, and then pick the color swatch associated with the layer name. AutoCAD displays the **Select Color** dialog box. See Figure 4-7. This dialog box includes three different color tabs from which a color can be selected for use in your highlighted layer. These tabs are the **Index Color** tab, the **True Color** tab, and the **Color Books** tab. Each of these tabs includes different methods of obtaining colors for assignment to a layer. The tabs are described in the following sections.

Index Color tab

This tab includes 255 color swatches from which you can choose a color. See Figure 4-8. This tab is commonly referred to as the AutoCAD Color Index (ACI), as layer colors are coded by name and number. The first seven colors in the ACI include both a numerical index number and a name:

Number	Color
1	red
2	yellow
3	green
4	cyan
5	blue
6	magenta
7	white

Figure 4-7.
The **Select Color** dialog box.

Index Color tab
255 colors

True Color tab
24 bit color

Color Books tab
Pantone colors

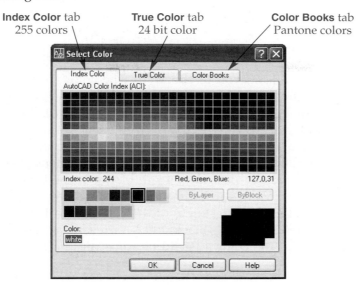

Figure 4-8.
The **Index Color** tab uses 255 indexed colors.

Selected color

Color index number

Standard colors #1–9

Selected color index number

Red, green, and blue colors mixed to make selected color

Previous selected color

New selected color

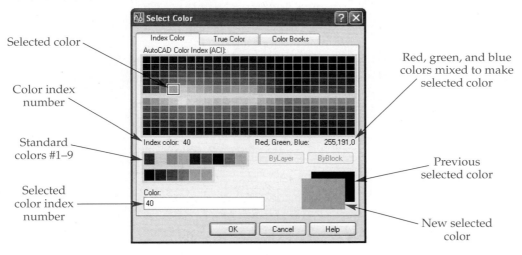

To select a color, you can either pick the color swatch displaying the desired color or type the color name or number in the **Color:** text box. The first seven basic colors are listed in the table on the previous page. The color white (number 7) refers to white if the graphics screen background is black, and it refers to black if the background is white. All other colors can be accessed by their ACI numbers.

As you move the cursor around the color swatches, the **Index color:** note updates to show you the number of the color over which the cursor is hovering. Beside the **Index color:** note is the **Red, Green, Blue:** (RGB) note. This indicates the RGB numbers used to mix the highlighted color. Once you pick a color, the **Index color:** note is entered into the **Color:** text box. On the lower right of the dialog box are a preview of the newly selected color and a sample of the previously assigned color. Two additional buttons are also included: **ByLayer** and **ByBlock**. These are special colors assigned to geometry in the drawing, but they cannot be assigned to a layer name. These are discussed later in this text.

An easy way to investigate the ACI numbering system is to pick a color swatch and see what number appears in the **Color:** text box. After selecting a color, pick the **OK** button when you are ready. The color you picked is now displayed as the color swatch for the highlighted layer name in the **Layer Properties Manager** dialog box.

True Color tab

The **True Color** tab allows you to specify a true color (24 bit color) using either Hue, Saturation, and Luminance (HSL) or Red, Green, and Blue (RGB) color models. **Figure 4-9A** shows the **True Color** tab with the **HSL** color model selected. The **True Color** tab is shown in **Figure 4-9B** with the **RGB** color model selected.

The **HSL** color model includes three text boxes allowing you to control the properties of the color. The **Hue:** value represents a specific wavelength of light within the visible spectrum. Valid hue values range from 0°–360°. The **Saturation:** value refers to the purity of the color. Valid saturation values range from 0%–100%. Finally, the **Luminance:** value specifies the brightness of the color. Valid luminance values range from 0%–100%, where 0% represents black, 100% represents white, and 50% represents the optimal brightness of the color. Instead of adjusting the HSL colors through the

Figure 4-9.
The **True Color** tab uses 24 bit color. A—HSL color model. B—RGB color model.

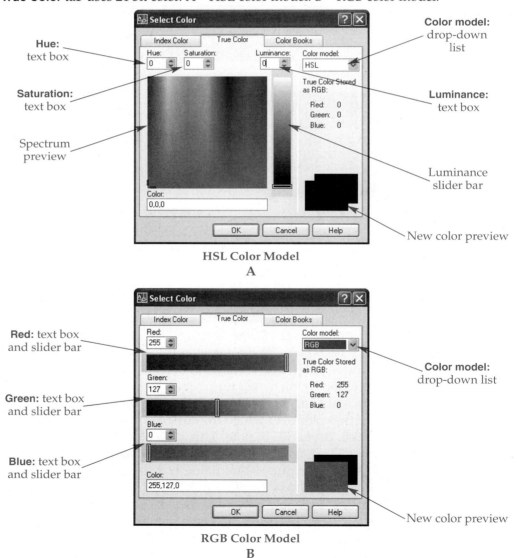

HSL Color Model
A

RGB Color Model
B

text boxes, you can move the cursors in the spectrum preview screen and luminance slider bar and pick the approximate color you want. The true color specified is then translated to RGB values, which are displayed in the **Color:** text box.

The **RGB** color model includes four text boxes and three slider bars. Adjusting the values in the **Red:**, **Green:**, and **Blue:** text boxes causes the slider bars to adjust, with the mixed color displayed in the new color preview. The cursors can also be used to slide the markers along each bar to mix the colors.

Color Books tab

The **Color Books** tab allows you to use third party color books, such as Pantone color books, to specify a color. See Figure 4-10. The **Color Book:** drop-down list includes several different color books, including several Pantone and RAL books. Once a book has been selected, the available colors within the book are displayed. (RAL colors, which were developed in Germany, are used internationally.) You can pick an area on the color slider or use the up and down keys to browse through the book. To select a color, use your pick button to pick on top of one of the color book swatches. As a color is selected, the equivalent RGB values are displayed on the right side of the dialog box, and the color is updated in the new color preview.

Exercise
4-4   Complete the Exercise on the Student CD.

Setting the Layer Linetype

You were introduced to line standards in Chapter 3. AutoCAD provides standard linetypes that can be used at any time to match the ASME standards or the standards for other drafting applications you are using. You can also create your own custom linetypes. In order to achieve different line widths, it is necessary to assign lineweights.

AutoCAD linetypes

AutoCAD maintains its standard linetypes in an external file named acad.lin. Before any of these linetypes can be used, they must be loaded, and then they must be set current or assigned to a layer. Three of AutoCAD's linetypes are required and cannot be deleted from the drawing. The Continuous linetype represents solid lines

Figure 4-10.
The **Color Books** tab uses Pantone and RAL colors.

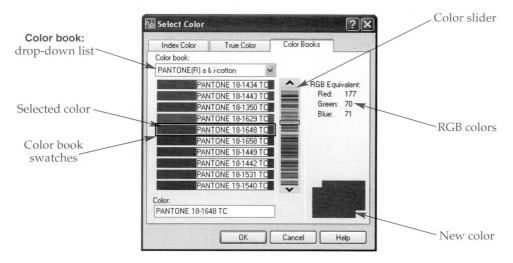

with no breaks. ByLayer and ByBlock are logical linetypes and represent the linetype assigned to an AutoCAD layer or block insertion. ByLayer and ByBlock are assigned to objects in the drawing and cannot be assigned to layers because they already represent the linetypes assigned to individual layers. ByLayer means "use the linetype, color, or lineweight of the object's layer." ByBlock means "use the linetype assigned to the block insertion." The AutoCAD linetypes are shown in **Figure 4-11.**

Figure 4-11.
The AutoCAD linetype library contains ACAD ISO, standard, and complex linetypes.

Continuous	————————	Acad_iso02w100	— — — — — —
Border	— — — — —	Acad_iso03w100	— — — —
Border2	– — – — – — –	Acad_iso04w100	— · — · — · —
Borderx2	—— —— ——	Acad_iso05w100	— ·· — ·· —
Center	—— – —— – ——	Acad_iso06w100	— ··· — ···
Center2	— · — · — · —	Acad_iso07w100	··················
Centerx2	—— — ——	Acad_iso08w100	—— – —— – ——
Dashdot	– · — · — · — · –	Acad_iso09w100	—— –– —— ––
Dashdot2	–·–·–·–·–·–·	Acad_iso10w100	— · — · — · —
Dashdotx2	—— · —— · ——	Acad_iso11w100	—— – —— – ——
Dashed	— — — — — —	Acad_iso12w100	— · · — · · —
Dashed2	– – – – – – – –	Acad_iso13w100	— ··· — ···
Dashedx2	—— —— ——	Acad_iso14w100	— · — · — · —
Divide	– · · — · · — · ·	Acad_iso15w100	— – ·· — – ··
Divide2	–··–··–··–··	Fenceline1	——o——o——o——
Dividex2	—— · · —— · ——	Fenceline2	——□——□——□——
Dot	· · · · · · · · · · ·	Gas_line	—— GAS —— GAS ——
Dot2	····················	Hot_water_supply	—— HW —— HW ——
Dotx2	· · · · · · · ·		
Hidden	– – – – – – – –	Tracks	+++++++++++++++
Hidden2	––––––––––––––		
Hiddenx2	— — — — — —	Zigzag	∧∧∧∧∧∧∧∧∧
Phantom	— – – —— – – ——		
Phantom2	–––·––––·––––	Batting	⌒MMMMMMMMMM⌒
Phantomx2	—— — — ——		

Figure 4-12.
The **Select Linetype**
dialog box.

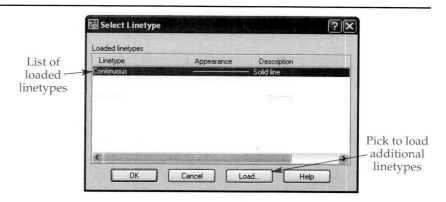

Changing linetype assignments

To change linetype assignments, select the layer name you want to change and pick its linetype name. This displays the **Select Linetype** dialog box, shown in Figure 4-12. The first time you use this dialog box, you may find only the Continuous linetype listed in the **Loaded linetypes** list box. You need to load any other linetypes to be used in the drawing.

If you need to add linetypes not included in the list, pick the **Load...** button to display the **Load or Reload Linetypes** dialog box, shown in Figure 4-13. The ACAD ISO, standard, and complex linetypes are named and displayed in the **Available Linetypes** list. Standard linetypes use only dashes, dots, and gaps. Complex linetypes can also contain special shapes and text.

Use the down arrow to look at all the linetypes. Select the linetypes you want to load. Use the [Shift] key and pick to select linetypes between your two picked linetypes. You can also use the [Ctrl] key and pick to select nonconsecutive linetypes. Pick the **OK** button to return to the **Select Linetype** dialog box, where the linetypes you selected are listed, as shown in Figure 4-14. In the **Select Linetype** dialog box, pick the desired linetype, and then pick **OK**. The HIDDEN linetype selected in Figure 4-14 is now the linetype assigned to Layer2, as shown in Figure 4-15.

NOTE

The acad.lin file is used by default. You can switch to the ISO library by picking the **File...** button in the **Load or Reload Linetypes** dialog box. This displays the **Select Linetype File** dialog box, where you can select the acadiso.lin file.

Figure 4-13.
The **Load or Reload Linetypes** dialog box.

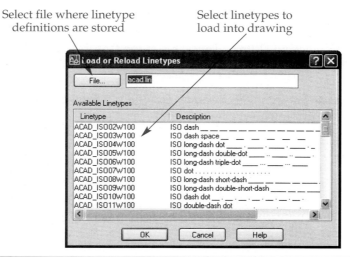

Figure 4-14.
Linetypes loaded from the **Load or Reload Linetypes** dialog box are added to the **Loaded linetypes** list box.

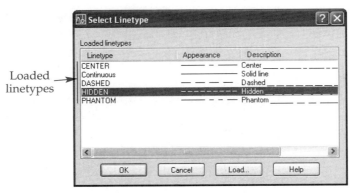

Loaded
linetypes

Figure 4-15.
Objects drawn on Layer 2 now have a HIDDEN linetype.

Linetype changed
to HIDDEN

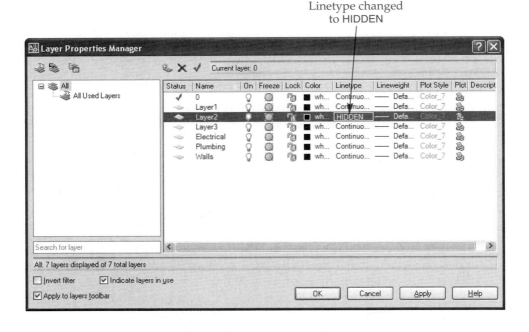

Managing linetypes

The **Linetype Manager** dialog box is a convenient place to load and access line-types. This dialog box can be accessed by selecting **Format** > **Linetype...** from the pull-down menu, selecting **Other...** in the **Linetype Control** drop-down list in the **Properties** toolbar, or typing LT or LINETYPE. See **Figure 4-16.**

This dialog box is similar to the **Layer Properties Manager** dialog box. Picking the **Load...** button opens the **Load or Reload Linetypes** dialog box. Picking the **Delete** button deletes any selected unused linetypes.

Changing lineweight assignments

Like linetypes, lineweights can also be assigned to objects. *Lineweight* adds width to objects for display and plotting. Lineweights can be set for objects or assigned to layers. Assigning lineweights to layers allows you to have the objects on specific layers set to their own lineweights. This allows you to control the display of line thickness to match ASME or other standards related to your drafting application.

Figure 4-16.
The **Linetype Manager** dialog box.

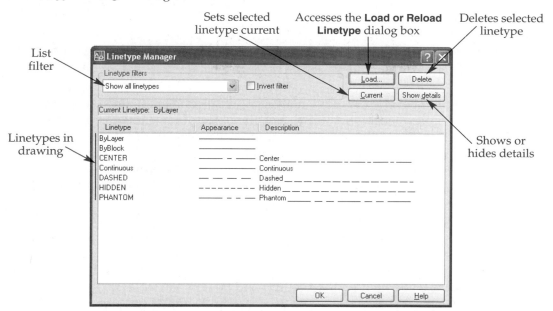

The layer lineweight settings are displayed on the screen when the lineweight is turned on. To toggle screen lineweights, pick the **LWT** button on the status bar.

To change lineweight assignments in the **Layer Properties Manager**, select the layer name you want to change and pick its lineweight setting. This displays the **Lineweight** dialog box, shown in **Figure 4-17.** Scroll through the **Lineweights:** list to select the desired lineweight. The **Lineweight** dialog box displays fixed lineweights available in AutoCAD for you to apply to the selected layer. The Default lineweight is the lineweight initially assigned to a layer when it is created.

The area near the bottom of the **Lineweight** dialog box lists the original lineweight (the lineweight previously assigned to the layer) and the new lineweight (the new lineweight assigned to the layer). In **Figure 4-17,** the **Original:** and **New:** specifications are the same, because the initial layer lineweight has not been changed from the default.

Figure 4-17.
The **Lineweight** dialog box.

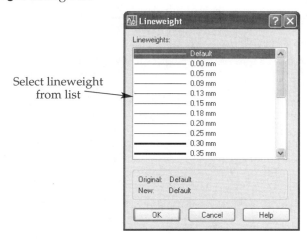

LINEWEIGHT
Type
LINEWEIGHT
LWEIGHT
LW
Pull-Down Menu
Format
> Lineweight...

Setting the current lineweight

Current lineweights are set in the **Lineweight Settings** dialog box, shown in **Figure 4-18.** The **Lineweight Settings** dialog box can be accessed by typing LW, LWEIGHT, or LINEWEIGHT; picking **Format** > **Lineweight...** from the pull-down menu; or right-clicking on the **LWT** button on the status bar and then selecting **Settings...** from the shortcut menu. The following describes the features of the **Lineweight Settings** dialog box:

- **Lineweights.** Set the current lineweight by selecting the desired setting from the list. If lineweight is set to ByLayer, the object lineweight corresponds to the lineweight of its layer. The Default option lineweight width is controlled by the Default list options. Settings other than ByLayer, ByBlock, or Default are used as overrides for lineweights of objects drawn with the selected option.
- **Units for Listing.** This area allows you to set the lineweight thickness to **Millimeters (mm)** or **Inches (in)**.
- **Display Lineweight.** This is another way to turn lineweight thickness on or off. Check this box to turn lineweight on.
- **Default.** Select a lineweight default value from the drop-down list. This becomes the default lineweight for layers. The initial default setting is 0.010" or 0.25 mm. This is also controlled by the **LWDEFAULT** system variable.
- **Adjust Display Scale.** This scale allows you to adjust the lineweight display scale to improve the appearance of different lineweight widths. Adjustment of the lineweight display scale toward the **Max** value can reduce AutoCAD performance. A setting near the middle of the scale or toward **Min** may be preferred.
- **Current Lineweight.** This indicates the current lineweight setting.

NOTE

An object's individual properties, such as color, linetype, and lineweight, can be assigned "by layer" or "by object." It is important to note that assigning properties "by object" overrides any assignments made "by layer." For example, if a line's color property is ByLayer, the line obtains its color from the color of the layer on which it is drawn. If that same line's color is changed "by object" to a green color, however, the line is green regardless of the layer color. This is also true for linetype and lineweight.

Figure 4-18.
The **Lineweight Settings** dialog box.

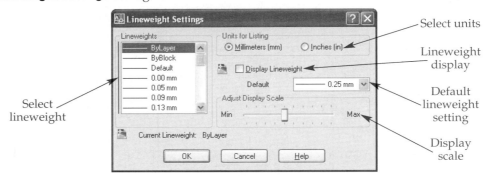

Layer States

Layer settings, such as on/off, frozen/thawed, plot/no plot, and locked/unlocked, determine whether or not a layer is displayed, plotted, and editable. The status of layer settings for all layers in the drawing can be saved as a named *layer state*. Once a layer state is saved, layer settings can be readjusted to meet your needs, giving you the ability to restore the previously saved layer state at any time.

For example, a basic architectural drawing uses the layers shown in **Figure 4-19**. From this drawing file, three different drawings are plotted: a floor plan, a plumbing plan, and an electrical plan. The following chart shows the layer settings for each of the three drawings:

	Floor Plan	Plumbing Plan	Electrical Plan
0	Off	Off	Off
Dimension-Electrical	Frozen	Frozen	On/Thawed
Dimension-Floor Plan	On/Thawed	Frozen	Frozen
Dimension-Plumbing	Frozen	On/Thawed	Frozen
Electrical	Frozen	Frozen	On/Thawed
Floor Plan Notes	On/Thawed	Frozen	Frozen
Plumbing	Frozen	On/Thawed	Frozen
Title Block	On/Thawed	Locked	Locked
Wall	On/Thawed	Locked	Locked
Windows and Doors	On/Thawed	Frozen	Frozen

Figure 4-19.
Layers for a basic architectural drawing.

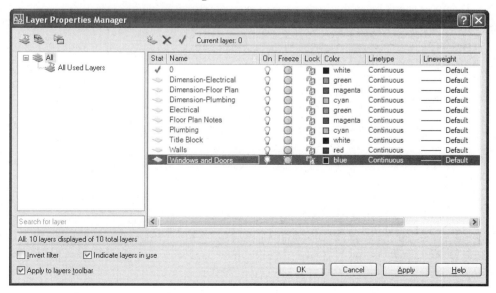

Each of the three groups of settings can be saved as an individual layer state. Once the layer state is created, the settings can be restored by simply restoring the layer state. This is easier than changing the settings for each layer individually.

To save a layer state, pick the **Layer States Manager** button from the **Layer Properties Manager** dialog box. The **Layer States Manager** dialog box appears as shown in **Figure 4-20**. In the **Layer settings to restore** area, place a check mark next to the layer properties you want to have saved with your layer state. To create a new layer state, pick the **New...** button. Type a name for the layer state in the **New layer state name:** field and enter a description (optional). Pick the **OK** button to save the new layer state. To restore a layer state, select the layer state in the **Layer States Manager** dialog box and pick the **Restore** button. The following buttons are available in the **Layer States Manager** dialog box:

- **New.** Opens the **New Layer State to Save** dialog box, in which a layer state can be saved.
- **Delete.** Deletes the selected layer state.
- **Import.** Accesses the **Import layer state** dialog box, where you can select an LAS file containing an existing layer state. Imported layer states are listed in the **Layer states** list in the **Layer State Manager**. Select the imported layer state and pick the **Restore** button to have the settings restored.
- **Export.** Saves the layer state as a LAS file and imports it into other drawings. This allows you to share layer states between drawings containing identical layers. Pick this button to access the **Export layer state** dialog box, where you can specify a name and location for the LAS file.
- **Restore.** Restores the layer settings saved in the selected layer state.

PROFESSIONAL TIP  If you have a drawing that does not contain layer names, importing a layer state file (.las) causes the layers from the layer state to be added to your drawing.

Figure 4-20.
The **Layer States Manager** allows you to save layer settings so they can be used later.

Select to create a new layer state

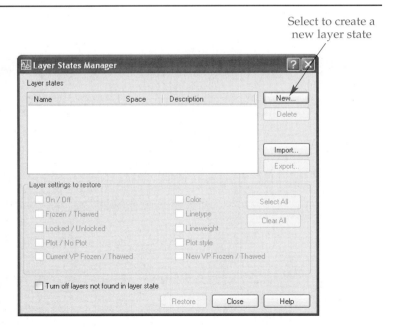

Layer Filters

In some applications, large numbers of layer names may be used to assist in drawing information management. Having all layer names showing at the same time in the layer list can make it more difficult to work with your drawing layers. *Layer filters* are used to screen, or filter, out any layers you do not want displayed in the **Layer Properties Manager** dialog box. The filter tree view area in the **Layer Properties Manager** dialog box was created to make working with filters easier. The options are explained below:

- **Invert filter.** You can invert, or reverse, the layer filter setting. For example, there is a choice to show all used layers, but what if you want to show all unused layers? In this case, you would check the **Invert filter** toggle to invert, or reverse, your choice.
- **Indicate layers in use.** When checked, a layer that has at least one object drawn on them will be indicated by a blue sheet of paper icon in the status column. A layer not being used is indicated by a white sheet of paper icon.
- **Apply to layers toolbar.** Check this toggle if you want only the layers matching the current filter displayed in the **Layers** toolbar. The **Layer Control** drop-down list tooltip shows when a filter is active.

The filter tree view area of the **Layer Properties Manager** dialog box is shown in Figure 4-21. The **All Used Layers** filter is a default filter created by AutoCAD. Selecting this filter hides all the layers that have no objects on them. To create a new filter, pick the **New Property Filter** button. This displays the **Layer Filter Properties** dialog box, Figure 4-22. Enter a name for the new filter in the **Filter name:** text box. The **Filter definition** area is where the parameters are defined to hide the unwanted layers from the **Layer Properties Manager** dialog box and the **Layer Control** drop-down list on the **Layers** toolbar. To create a definition, pick in any of the layer settings fields. Depending on the layer setting, the appropriate options become available. For most, there is a drop-down list from which to choose. Here are the filter definition options for each setting:

Figure 4-21.
Layer filters can be created and restored from the filter tree view area of the **Layer Properties Manager** dialog box.

Pick to create a new property filter   Pick to create a new group filter

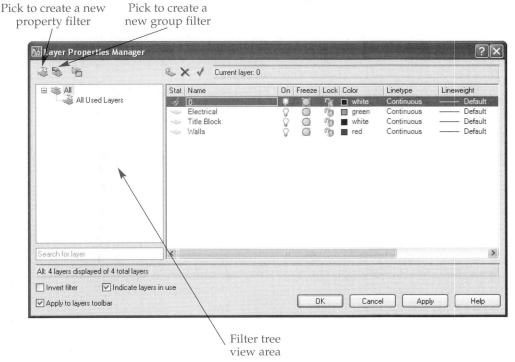

Filter tree view area

Figure 4-22.
New layer filters are created in the **Layer Filter Properties** dialog box.

Edit the layer properties to define the layer filter

Enter name for filter

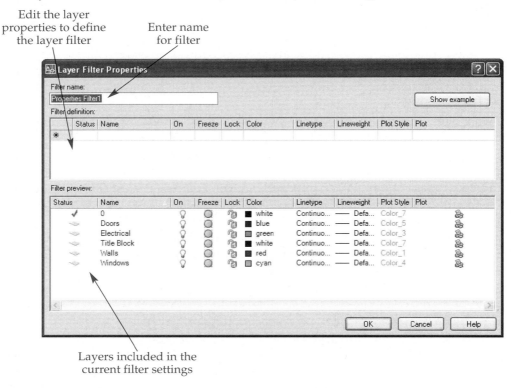

Layers included in the current filter settings

- **Status.** Use this filter to display the names of all layers, only used layers, or only unused layers.
- **Name.** This is a text field in which you can type a layer name or a partial layer name using the * wildcard character. If you want to see all the layers that start with an *A*, type **a***.
- **On.** Use this filter to display only the names of layers that are on or only those that are off.
- **Freeze.** Use this filter to display only frozen or only thawed layer names.
- **Lock.** Use this filter to display only locked or only unlocked layer names.
- **Color.** A color number or name can be typed, or the **...** button can be used to select a color from the **Select Color** dialog box.
- **Linetype.** A linetype name can be typed, or the **...** button can be used to select a linetype from the **Select Linetype** dialog box.
- **Lineweight.** A lineweight can be typed, or the **...** button can be used to select a lineweight from the **Lineweight** dialog box.
- **Plot Style.** Type a plot style name or select a plot style from the **Select Plot Style** dialog box by picking the **...** button. This option is only available if the current drawing is using named plot style tables.
- **Plot.** Use this filter to display the names of layers that plot or the names of layers that do not plot.
- **Current VP Freeze.** Use this filter to display only frozen or only thawed layer names. This option is only available in paper space.
- **New VP Freeze.** Use this filter to display only frozen or only thawed layer names. This option is only available in paper space.

Figure 4-23.
Multiple rows in the **Filter definition:** area can be used to create a filter.

Layer filter definitions   Filter name

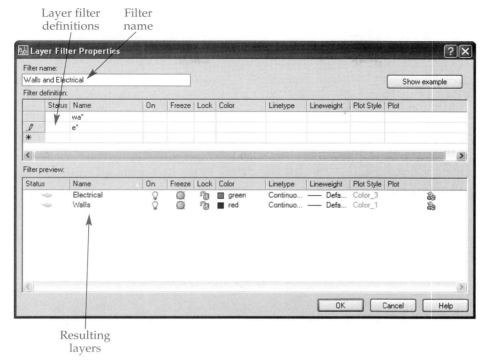

Resulting layers

Once a definition has been edited, another row is added to the **Filter definition:** area. This allows you to create simple to advanced filters. **Figure 4-23** shows a filter named Walls and Electrical, where two rows are used to filter out all the layers except Walls and Electrical. To save the filter, pick the **OK** button. The new filter now displays in the filter tree view area. To set it current, just select it once. The layers the filter defined are now displayed in the layer list area. To view all the layers again, pick the **All** filter at the top of the filter tree view area.

Another type of filter that can be created is a group filter. Layers can be added to a group filter, but the individual settings of the layers cannot be defined, as in a property filter. To add a group filter, select the **New Group Filter** button above the filter tree view area. A new group filter is created in the filter tree view area, and a name can be typed. To add a layer to a group filter, select a layer in the layer list, and then drag and drop it onto the group filter name. You can also add layers to a group filter by selecting the group filter and then right-clicking. From the shortcut menu, choose **Select Layers**. Select **Add** from the **Select Layers** cascading menu. The **Layer Properties Manager** temporarily hides, allowing you to select objects on the layers you wish to add to the group filter. After the objects are selected, right-click or press the [Enter] key to add the layers to the group filter.

Other options associated with filters are only accessible from the shortcut menu. To display the shortcut menu, right-click in the filter tree view area. The shortcut menu is displayed in **Figure 4-24.** Most of the options in the shortcut menu are the same for the filter types, but there are some options that are only available for a certain filter. Here is an explanation for the shortcut menu options:

- **Visibility.** Allows you to change the **On/Off** and **Thawed/Frozen** states of all the layers associated with the filter.
- **Lock.** Locks or unlocks all the layers.
- **Viewport.** Allows you to freeze or thaw all the layers in the current paper space viewport.

Figure 4-24.
The filter tree view shortcut menu displays options for the selected filter type.

- **Isolate Group.** Turns off all the layers in the drawing that are filtered out by the filter. It can be applied to all the viewports or just the current one.
- **New Properties Filter.** Opens the **Layer Filter Properties** dialog box so a new layer filter can be created.
- **New Group Filter.** Creates a new group filter.
- **Convert to Group Filter.** Converts a property filter to a group filter.
- **Rename.** Allows you to rename the selected filter.
- **Delete.** Deletes the selected filter.
- **Properties.** Allows you to edit a property filter.
- **Select Layers.** Gives the options to **Add** or **Replace** layers to an existing group filter.

Exercise 4-6   Complete the Exercise on the Student CD.

Quickly Setting a Layer Current

You can quickly make another layer current by using the **Layer Control** drop-down list located in the **Layers** toolbar. The name of the current layer is displayed in the box. Pick the drop-down arrow, and a layer list appears, as shown in **Figure 4-25.**

Pick a layer name from the list, and that layer is set current. When many layers are defined in the drawing, the vertical scroll bar can be used to move up and down through the list. Selecting a layer name to set as current automatically closes the list and returns you to the drawing editor. When a command is active, the drop-down button is grayed out, and the list is not available. The **Layer Control** drop-down list has the same status icons as the **Layer Properties Manager** dialog box. By picking an icon, you can change the state of the layer.

Figure 4-25.
The **Layer Control** drop-down list is located on the left side of the **Layers** toolbar. All layers are listed with icons representing their state and color. Pick on a layer name to make it current.

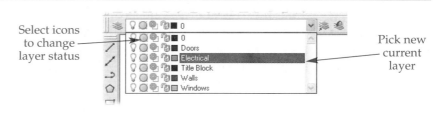

Layers are meant to simplify the drafting process. They separate different details of the drawing and can reduce the complexity of what is displayed. If you set color and linetype by layer, do not reset and mix object linetypes and color on the same layer. Doing so can mislead you and your colleagues when trying to find certain details. Always maintain accurate records of your template drawings.

Making the Layer of an Existing Object Current

Another quick way to set the current layer is to use the **Make Object's Layer Current** button in the **Layers** toolbar. When you pick this button, AutoCAD asks you to select an object on the layer you want to make current. Pick an object, and the object's layer is set as current. You can also select **Format** > **Layer tools** > **Make Object's Layer Current** to use this tool.

Pull-Down Menu

Format
  > Layer tools
    > Make Object's
      Layer Current

Toolbar
Standard
Make Object's Layer Current

Restoring the Previous Layer Settings

After changing layer properties, you can restore the previous layer settings by picking the **Layer Previous** button in the **Layers** toolbar, selecting the **Format** > **Layer tools** > **Layer Previous**, or typing LAYERP.

The **Layer Previous** command affects layer operations only. Therefore, after using commands to draw, modify, and zoom, you can use the **Layer Previous** command to restore the last layer state without affecting any other functions. The following layer properties are restored by the **Layer Previous** command:
- On/Off.
- Freeze/Thaw.
- Lock/Unlock.
- Color.
- Linetype.
- Lineweight.
- Plot style (if using named plot styles).
- Freeze/Thaw in current viewport.

The **Layer Previous** command does not affect layer name changes, recreate layers that have been purged, or delete layers that have been added.

LAYERP

Type
LAYERP
Pull-Down Menu

Format
  > Layer tools
    > Layer Previous

Toolbar
Layers
Layer Previous

Changing Object Properties

You should always draw objects on an appropriate layer, but layer settings are not permanent. You can change an object's layer if needed. You can also change other properties of the object, such as color and linetype. Using the **Properties** toolbar or the **Properties** window modifies these properties.

To modify properties using the **Properties** toolbar, select the object, and then use the drop-down lists in the appropriate control boxes to change the properties. After you have changed the properties, press [Esc] to deselect the object. To modify an object's properties using the **Properties** window, pick the **Properties** button in the **Standard** toolbar; select **Modify** > **Properties** from the pull-down menu; or type PROPS, CH, MO, or PROPERTIES. If an object has been selected, you can right-click on it and pick **Properties** from the shortcut menu. When you use one of these options, AutoCAD

PROPERTIES
Type
PROPERTIES PROPS CH MO
Pull-Down Menu
Modify   > Properties
Toolbar
Standard
Properties

Figure 4-26.
The **Properties**
window is used
to modify the
properties of the
selected object.

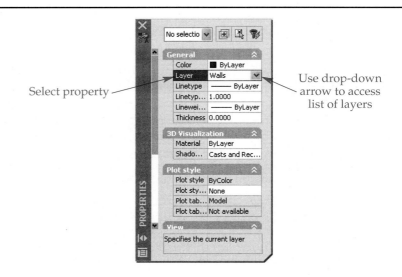

Select property

Use drop-down
arrow to access
list of layers

displays the **Properties** window, shown in Figure 4-26. You can also double-click on many objects to automatically select the object and open the **Properties** window.

The properties of the selected object are listed in the **Properties** window. The specific properties listed vary, depending on the type of object selected. Properties such as layer, linetype, and color are listed in the **General** category.

To modify a particular object property, first find the property in the **Properties** window, and then select its value. Depending on the type of value, a specific editing method is activated. Use this tool to change the value. For example, if you want to change an object's layer, pick **Layer** to highlight it, as in Figure 4-26. A drop-down arrow is displayed to the right of the layer name. Pick the arrow to access the **Layer** drop-down list. Pick the layer name you want to use for the selected object's layer. You can use this same process to change the color, linetype, or lineweight of a selected object.

You can work in AutoCAD with the **Properties** window open and available for use. By picking and holding on the title bar while you move the mouse, you can move the **Properties** window. If you want to close the **Properties** window, select the **X** in the upper-left corner.

NOTE

Modifying object properties using the **Properties** window is covered in greater depth in Chapter 13.

Exercise
4-7

Complete the Exercise on the Student CD.

Overriding Layer Settings

Color, linetype, and lineweight settings reference layer settings by default. This means when you create a layer, you also establish a color, linetype, and lineweight to go with the layer. This is what it means when the color, linetype, and lineweight are specified as ByLayer. This is the most common method for managing these settings. Sometimes, however, you may need objects to reference a specific layer, but have specific color, linetype, or lineweight properties different than the layer settings. In such a situation, the color, linetype, and lineweight can be set to an *absolute* value, and current layer settings are ignored. The term *absolute*, as used here and in future content, refers to an object being assigned specific properties that are not reliant on a layer or block for their definitions.

Exercise 4-8   Complete the Exercise on the Student CD.

Setting Color

The current object color can be easily set by selecting the **Color Control** drop-down list from the **Properties** toolbar. See **Figure 4-27**. The default setting is ByLayer. This is the recommended setting for most applications. To change this setting, pick another color from the list. If the color you want is not on the list, you can pick the item at the bottom of the list, labeled **Select Color**, to display the **Select Color** dialog box, or you can type COL or COLOR. Once an absolute color is specified, all new objects are drawn in the specified color, regardless of the current layer settings. Another way to set the current object color is by using the **CECOLOR** system variable.

Setting Lineweight

Similar to the current object color, you can set the current object lineweight to differ from the layer settings. To set the current object lineweight, pick the **Lineweight Control** drop-down list from the **Properties** toolbar and select the desired linetype. See **Figure 4-28.** You can also directly adjust the **CELWEIGHT** system variable, which controls the current object linetype.

Setting Linetype

Similar to the current object lineweight, you can set the current object linetype to be separate from any layer settings. To set the current object linetype, pick the **Linetype Control** drop-down list from the **Properties** toolbar and select the desired linetype. See **Figure 4-29.** If the linetype you want has not been loaded into the current drawing yet, it will not appear in the listing. You can select **Other...** from the list to load the **Linetype Manager** so new linetypes can be loaded. You can also directly adjust the **CELTYPE** system variable, which controls the current object linetype.

Figure 4-27.
The current object color is easily set by opening the **Color Control** drop-down list in the **Properties** toolbar. This control box is also used to change the color of selected objects.

Color Control
drop-down list

Figure 4-28.
The current object lineweight is easily set by opening the **Lineweight Control** drop-down list in the **Properties** toolbar.

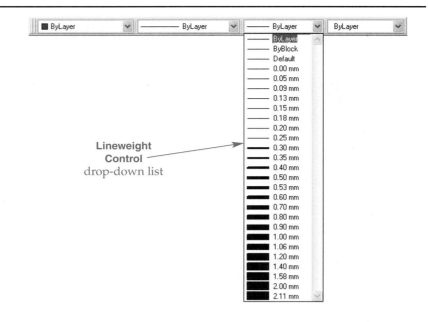

Lineweight
Control
drop-down list

Figure 4-29.
The current object linetype is easily set by opening the **Linetype Control** drop-down list in the **Properties** toolbar.

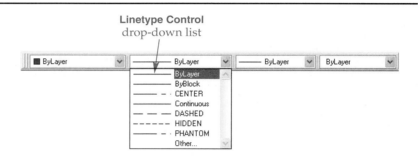

Linetype Control
drop-down list

NOTE

Colors, linetypes, and lineweights are often set as ByLayer. ByLayer is known as a logical color, while red, for instance, is known as an explicit color. If an object uses ByLayer as its color, its color is displayed as the color assigned to the layer on which the object resides. Explicit properties, however, override logical properties. Therefore, if an object's color is set explicitly to red, it will appear red regardless of the layer on which it resides. Change its color to ByLayer, and it will use the layer color. It is a common mistake for AutoCAD users to set object property override settings to some value other than ByLayer and then wonder why new objects do not use the color of the current layer!

Setting the linetype scale

The linetype scale sets the lengths of dashes and spaces in linetypes. When you start AutoCAD with a wizard or template, the global linetype scale is automatically set to match the units you select. The global linetype scale can, however, be overridden at the object level. A *global change* is a change affecting all linetypes in the current drawing.

The default object linetype scale factor is 1.0000. As with layers, the linetype scale can be changed at the object level. One reason for changing the default linetype scale is to make your drawing more closely match standard drafting practices.

Earlier, you were introduced to the **Properties** window. When a line object is selected to modify, a **Linetype scale** property is listed. You can change the linetype scale of the object by entering a new value in this field. A value less than 1.0 makes the dashes and spaces smaller than those in the global setting, while a value greater than 1.0 makes the dashes and spaces larger than those in the global setting. Using this information, you can experiment with different linetype scales until you achieve your desired results. Be careful when changing linetype scales to avoid making your drawing look odd, with a variety of line formats. **Figure 4-30** shows a diagram comparing different linetype scale factors.

Changing the global linetype scale

The **LTSCALE** variable can be used to make a global change to the linetype scale. The default global linetype scale factor is 1.0000. Any line with dashes initially assumes this factor.

To change the linetype scale for the entire drawing, type LTSCALE. The current value is listed. Enter the new value and press [Enter]. A Regenerating model message appears, as the global linetype scale is changed for all lines on the drawing.

Exercise 4-9   Complete the Exercise on the Student CD.

Figure 4-30.
Drawing the same linetype at different linetype scales.

Scale Factor	Line
0.5	— — — — — — — — — — — — — — — — — —
1.0	— — — — — — — — — — — —
1.5	— — — — — — — —

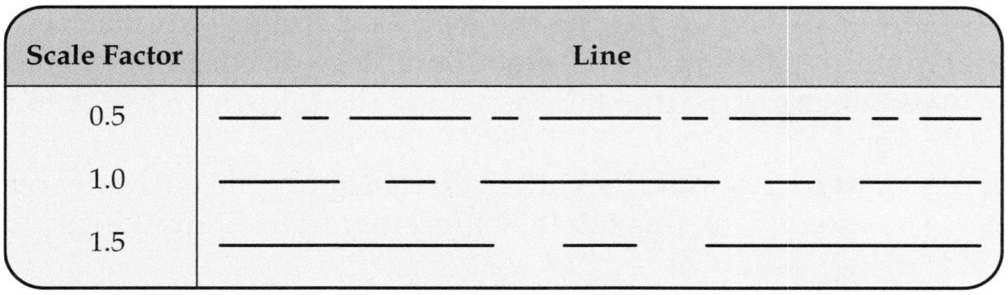

Reusing Drawing Content

In nearly every drafting discipline, individual drawings created as part of a given project are likely to share a number of common elements. All the drawings within a specific drafting project generally have the same set of standards. Drawing features, such as the text size and font used for annotation, standardized dimensioning methods and appearances, layer names and properties, drafting symbols, drawing layouts, and even typical drawing details, are often duplicated in many different drawings. These and other components of CAD drawings are referred to as *drawing content*. One of the most fundamental advantages of CAD systems is the ease with which content can be shared between drawings. Once a commonly used drawing feature has been defined, it can be used again as needed, in any number of drawing applications.

The creation and use of drawing template files was covered in Chapter 2. Drawing templates represents one way to reuse drawing content that has already been defined. Creating your own customized drawing template files provides an effective way to start each new drawing using standard settings.

Drawing templates, however, provide only a starting point. During the course of a drawing project, you may need to add content to the current drawing that has been defined previously in another drawing. Some drawing projects may require you to revise an existing drawing rather than start a completely new drawing. For other projects, you may need to duplicate the standards used in a drawing a client has supplied.

AutoCAD provides a powerful drawing content manager called **DesignCenter**. **DesignCenter** allows you to reuse drawing content that has already been defined in previous drawings by using a drag-and-drop operation. **DesignCenter** was introduced in Chapter 1.

DesignCenter is used to manage several categories of drawing content, including blocks, dimension styles, layers, layouts, linetypes, text styles, and externally referenced drawings. Layers and linetypes are discussed in this chapter, but the other content types are introduced in the chapters where they apply. The following discussion details the features of **DesignCenter** and shows how layer and linetype content found in existing drawings can be reused in other drawing projects.

Using DesignCenter to Copy Layers and Linetypes

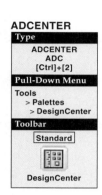

DesignCenter is activated by picking the **DesignCenter** button on the **Standard** toolbar, picking **Tools** > **Palettes** > **DesignCenter**, typing ADC or ADCENTER, or using the [Ctrl]+[2] key combination. This displays **DesignCenter**. See **Figure 4-31**.

It is not necessary to open a drawing in AutoCAD in order to view or access its content. **DesignCenter** allows you to directly load content from any accessible drawing. You can also use **DesignCenter** to browse through existing drawing files and view their contents, or you can use its advanced search tools to look for specific drawing content.

DesignCenter allows you to easily share content between drawings currently open in AutoCAD. To copy content, first select the drawing from which the content is to be copied. The drawing is selected from the tree view pane. If the tree view is not already visible, toggle it on by picking the **Tree View Toggle** button in the **DesignCenter** toolbar. The first three tabs on the **DesignCenter** toolbar control the tree view display:

- **Folders.** Pick this tab to display the folders and files found on the hard drive and network.
- **Open Drawings.** Pick this tab to list only the currently opened drawings.
- **History.** Pick this tab to list recently opened drawings.

Figure 4-31.
DesignCenter is used to copy content from one drawing to another.

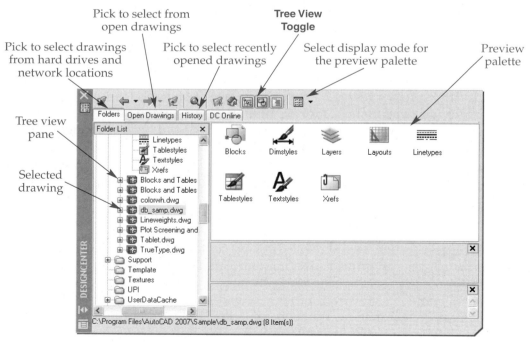

Figure 4-32.
Displaying the layers found in a drawing using **DesignCenter**.

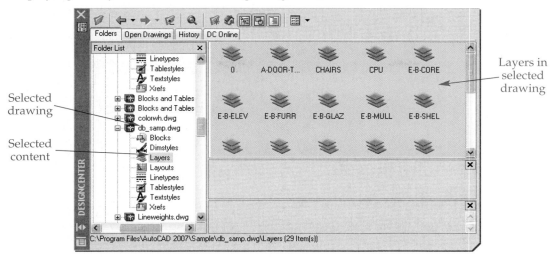

Selected drawing

Selected content

Layers in selected drawing

Pick the plus sign (+) next to a drawing icon to view the content categories for the drawing. Each category of drawing content is listed with a representative icon. Pick the Layers icon to load the palette with the layer content found in the selected drawing. The preview palette now displays all the available layer content. See **Figure 4-32**.

To select layers from the palette, use standard Windows selection methods. The [Shift] and [Ctrl] keys are used for selecting multiple items. In this example, the drawing is selected first, and the **Layers** content is picked. The preview palette displays the available content. Select the desired layers and use one of the following options to import them into the current drawing:

- **Drag and drop.** Move the cursor over the top of the desired icon in the preview palette. Press and hold down the pick button on your pointing device. Drag the cursor to the opened drawing. See **Figure 4-33**. Release the pick button, and the selected content is added to your current drawing file.
- **Add from shortcut menu.** Select the desired icon(s) in the preview palette and right-click to open the shortcut menu. Pick the **Add Layer(s)** option, and the selected content is added to your current drawing.
- **Copy from shortcut menu.** This option is identical to the **Add Layer(s)** option, except you select **Copy** from the shortcut menu instead of **Add Layer(s)**. Now, move the cursor to the drawing where you want the content added and right-click to open the shortcut menu. Select **Paste**, and the selected contents are added to the current drawing.

To select more than one icon at one time, hold down the [Shift] key and pick the first and last icons in a group. You can also hold down the [Ctrl] key to select multiple icons individually. The copied layers are now available in the active drawing. If the name of a layer being loaded already exists in the destination drawing, that layer name and its settings are ignored. The existing settings for the layer are preserved, and a message is displayed at the command line indicating the duplicate settings were ignored.

Linetypes can be copied using the same procedure. In the tree view, select the drawing containing the linetypes to be copied. Select **Linetypes** to display the linetypes in the preview palette. Select the linetypes to be copied, and then use drag and drop or the shortcut menu to add the linetypes to the current drawing.

NOTE

DesignCenter is a very powerful tool. Specific applications of **DesignCenter** are provided throughout this text.

Figure 4-33.
To copy layers shown in **DesignCenter** into the current drawing, first select the layers to be copied, and then drag and drop them into the drawing area of the current drawing.

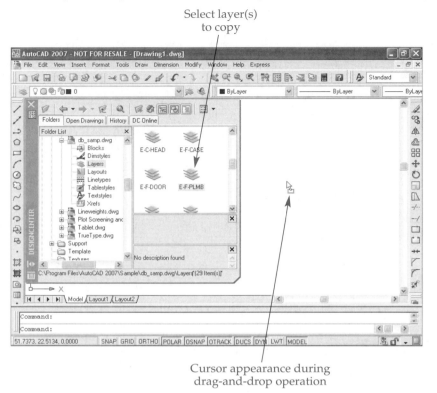

Select layer(s) to copy

Cursor appearance during drag-and-drop operation

Exercise 4-10

Complete the Exercise on the Student CD.

Additional Layer Tools

In addition to the standard layer tools discussed throughout this chapter, the **Format** pull-down menu includes a **Layer tools** cascading menu with several useful tools. A **Layers II** toolbar is also available by right-clicking in a docked toolbar area. Brief descriptions of the tools available are provided in the following list:

- **Layer Walk.** Selecting the **Layer Walk...** command opens the **LayerWalk - Layers:** *n* dialog box, shown in **Figure 4-34A.** This tool provides a list box with all the layers in the drawing. Selecting a layer name in the list causes all the layers in the drawing to be turned off, except for the selected layer. This provides a means for you to "walk" through a drawing full of layers to see which objects are drawn on which layers. You can select multiple layers to be displayed.

  You can also enter a character in the filter list to filter for layers with specific characters. Layers meeting your filter criteria are then displayed in the list box. See **Figure 4-34B.**

- **Layer Match.** Using this command allows you to select objects that need their layer to match another object's layer. First, select the objects whose layers will be changed, and then select an object whose layer will be matched.

AutoCAD and Its Applications—Basics

Figure 4-34.
The **LayerWalk - Layers:** *n* dialog box. A—Selected layers are displayed in the drawing area.
B—Entering a filter in the filter drop-down lists only layers matching the filter criteria.

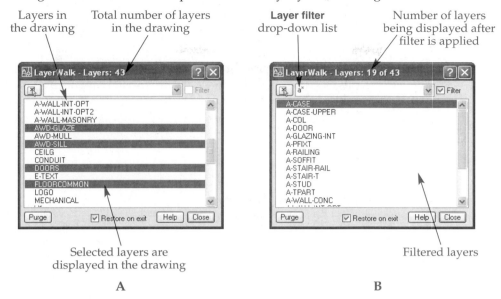

A

B

- **Change to Current Layer.** This command allows you to pick objects on a layer and have them moved to the current layer.
- **Copy Objects to New Layer.** Use this command to copy objects in the drawing to a new layer and move the copies to a new location. This command displays the **COPYTOLAYER** dialog box, where you can select the layer to which the objects will be moved. After selecting the layer, you have the option of choosing a base point from which to move the layers and a displacement point, or new location, for the copied objects.
- **Layer Isolate.** This command turns off all the layers in the drawing, except for the layer of an object you choose.
- **Isolate Layer to Current Viewport.** This command is similar to **Layer Isolate**, except it freezes the selected layer in all paper space viewports other than the current viewport. Layer control for paper space viewports is discussed later in this text.
- **Layer Unisolate.** This command restores layers to the state before a layer was isolated. Any changes made during **Layer Isolate** are kept after using this command.
- **Layer Off.** You can use this command when you desire to turn off a layer. Select an object whose layer you wish to turn off, and the layer is turned off.
- **Turn All Layers On.** This command turns on all layers that have been turned off.
- **Layer Freeze.** Similar to the **Layer Off** command, this command freezes the layer of an object you select.
- **Thaw All Layers.** This command thaws all frozen layers in the drawing.
- **Layer Lock.** Use this command to lock the layer of an object you select.
- **Layer Unlock.** Use this command to unlock any locked layers in the drawing.
- **Layer Merge.** This command causes you to merge objects on two layers to a single layer. First, select the objects that need to be moved to a different layer. Next, select an object on the layer where you want the first selected objects to be merged. Once you have done this, the layer of the first selected objects is deleted from the drawing.
- **Layer Delete.** This command deletes all objects on a layer you choose, and then it deletes the selected layer.

Introduction to Printing and Plotting

A drawing created with CAD can exist in two distinct forms: hard copy and soft copy. The term *hard copy* refers to a physical drawing a printer or plotter produces on paper. The term *soft copy* refers to the computer software version of the drawing, or the actual data file. The soft copy can only be displayed on the computer monitor, making it inconvenient to use for many manufacturing and construction purposes. If the power to the computer is turned off, the soft copy drawing is not available.

A hard copy drawing is extremely versatile. It can be rolled up or folded and taken down to the shop floor or out to a construction site. A hard copy drawing can be checked and redlined without a computer or CAD software. Although CAD is the standard throughout the world for generating drawings, the hard copy drawing is still a vital tool for communicating the design.

Hard copy drawings are created by printers or plotters. These terms can be used interchangeable, although *plotter* typically refers to a large-format printer. Printers take the soft copy images you draw in AutoCAD and transfer them onto paper.

There are two general classifications of printers: desktop printers and large-format printers. Desktop printers generally print 8 1/2″ × 11″ or possibly 11″ × 17″ drawings. These are the printers common to computer workstations. Desktop printers are used to print small drawings and to print reduced-size test prints. Large-format printers can print larger drawings, such as C-size and D-size. The most common types of both desktop and large-format printers are inkjet and laser printers. Pen plotters, which "draw" with actual ink pens, are still in use, but are not as common as they were in the past.

The information found in this chapter is provided to give you only the basics, so you can make your first plot. Chapter 11 explores the detailed aspects of printing and plotting. Prints and plots are made using the **Plot** dialog box. Access this dialog box by selecting **File > Plot...** from the pull-down menu, picking the **Plot** button in the **Standard** toolbar, pressing the [Ctrl]+[P] key combination, or typing PLOT. You can also right-click on a **Model** or layout tab and select **Plot...** from the shortcut menu.

The first step in making an AutoCAD drawing is to create a model. The *model* is composed of various objects, such as lines, circles, and text. The model is created by drawing in the **Model** tab at the bottom of the drawing area. See **Figure 4-35**. The model is created in an environment called *model space*.

Once the model is completed, a layout can be created. A *layout* can contain various views of the model, a title block, and other annotations. In addition, the layout includes page setup information (such as paper size and margins) and plotter configuration data (information related to the specific model of printer or plotter being used). Layouts are created using the layout tabs at the bottom of the drawing area. They are created in an environment called *paper space*. A single drawing can have multiple layouts.

PLOT

Type
PLOT [Ctrl]+[P]

Pull-Down Menu
File > Plot...

Toolbar
Standard

Plot

Figure 4-35.
The **Model** and **Layout** tabs at the bottom of the drawing area are used to access the model space and paper space environments.

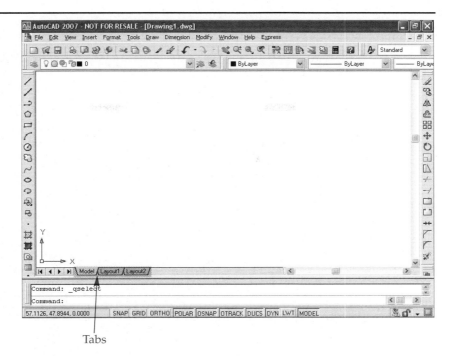

Tabs

Drawings can be plotted from the **Model** tab of the drawing area or from one of the layout tabs. The following discussion will address plotting from the **Model** tab only. Creating and plotting layouts is addressed in Chapter 11.

Making a Plot

There are many plotting options available. In this section, one method of creating a plot from the **Model** tab is discussed. Refer to **Figure 4-36** as you read through the following plotting procedure:

1. Access the **Plot** dialog box. If the column on the far right of the dialog box shown in **Figure 4-36** is not displayed, pick the **More Options** button (>) in the lower-right corner.
2. Check the plot device and paper size specifications in the **Printer/plotter** and **Paper size** areas.
3. Select what is to be plotted in the **Plot area** section. The following options are available:
   - **Display.** This option plots the current screen display.
   - **Extents.** This option plots only the area of the drawing where objects are drawn.
   - **Limits.** This option plots everything inside the defined drawing limits.
   - **Window.** Pick the **Window** option to manually select a rectangular area of the drawing to plot. When you pick the **Window** button, the drawing window returns, and you can select a window. After you select the second corner of the window, the **Plot** dialog box returns.
4. Select an option in the **Drawing orientation** area. Choose **Portrait** or **Landscape** to orient your drawing vertically (portrait) or horizontally (landscape). The **Plot upside-down** option rotates the paper 180°.
5. Set the scale in the **Plot scale** area. Because you draw full-scale in AutoCAD, you typically need to scale drawings either up or down to fit the paper. Scale is measured as a ratio of either inches or millimeters to drawing units. Select a predefined scale from the **Scale:** drop-down list or enter your own values into the custom fields. Choose the **Fit to paper** check box to let AutoCAD automatically shrink or stretch the plot area to fill the paper.

Figure 4-36.
The **Plot** dialog box.

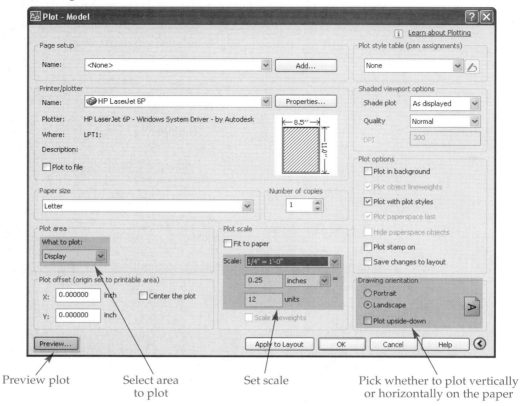

Preview plot   Select area   Set scale   Pick whether to plot vertically
to plot   or horizontally on the paper

6. If desired, use the **Plot offset (origin set to printable area)** area to set additional left and bottom margins around the plot or to center the plot.
7. Preview the plot. Pick the **Preview...** button to display the sheet as it will look when it is plotted. See **Figure 4-37.** The cursor appears as a magnifying glass with + and – symbols. The plot preview image zooms if you hold the left mouse button and move the cursor. Press [Esc] to exit the preview.
8. Pick the **OK** button in the **Plot** dialog box to send the data to the plotting device.

Before you pick the **OK** button to send your drawing to the plotter, there are several items you should check:
✓ The printer or plotter is plugged in.
✓ The cable from your computer to printer or plotter is secure.
✓ The printer has paper.
✓ Paper is properly loaded in the plotter, and grips or clamps are in place.
✓ The plotter area is clear for paper movement.

Exercise
4-11   Complete the Exercise on the Student CD.

Figure 4-37.
A preview of the plot shows exactly how the drawing will appear on the paper.

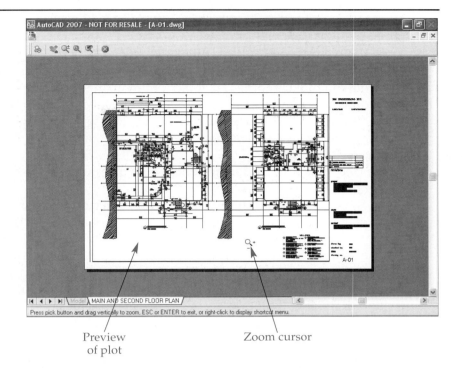

Preview
of plot

Zoom cursor

Chapter Test

Answer the following questions. Write your answers on a separate sheet of paper or complete the electronic chapter test on the Student CD.

1. Which pull-down menu contains the **Layer...** option?
2. Identify three ways to access the **Layer Properties Manager** dialog box.
3. How are new layer names entered when creating several layers at the same time without using the **New Layer** button in the **Layer Properties Manager** dialog box?
4. How do you make another layer current in the **Layer Properties Manager** dialog box?
5. How do you know if a layer is off, thawed, or unlocked in the **Layer Properties Manager** dialog box?
6. What is the state of a layer *not* displayed on the screen and *not* calculated by the computer when the drawing is regenerated?
7. Identify the following layer status icons:

   A.   D.

   B.   E.

   C.   F.

8. Are locked layers visible?
9. Describe the purpose of locking a layer.
10. How is the **Select Color** dialog box displayed from the **Layer Properties Manager** dialog box?
11. List the seven standard color names and numbers.
12. What is the default linetype in AutoCAD?
13. What condition must exist before a linetype can be used in a layer?
14. How do you load several linetypes at the same time from the **Load or Reload Linetypes** dialog box?
15. How do you change a layer's linetype in the **Layer Properties Manager** dialog box?
16. Why is ByLayer referred to as a logical color, linetype, and lineweight?

---

17. Which button in the **Layer Properties Manager** allows you to save layer settings so they can be restored at a later time?
18. Describe the purpose of layer filters.
19. Name the two types of filters.
20. How do you make another layer current by using the **Layers** toolbar?
21. How do you make the layer of an existing object current?
22. Identify two ways to directly access property options for changing the layer, linetype, or color of an existing object.
23. Define a *global change*.
24. In the tree view area of **DesignCenter**, how do you view the content categories of one of the listed open drawings?
25. How do you display all the available layers in a drawing using the **DesignCenter** preview palette?
26. Briefly explain how drag and drop works.
27. Define *hard copy* and *soft copy*.
28. Identify four ways to access the **Plot** dialog box.
29. Describe the difference between the **Display** and **Window** options in the **Plot area** section of the **Plot** dialog box.
30. What is a major advantage of doing a plot preview?

Drawing Problems

Before beginning these problems, set up template drawings with layer names, colors, linetypes, and lineweights for the type of drawing you are creating. Do not draw dimensions. Be sure to do preliminary planning for each drawing as discussed in this chapter.

1. Draw the plot plan shown below. Use the linetypes shown, which include Continuous, HIDDEN, PHANTOM, CENTER, FENCELINE2, and GAS_LINE. Make your drawing proportional to the example. Save the drawing as P4-1.

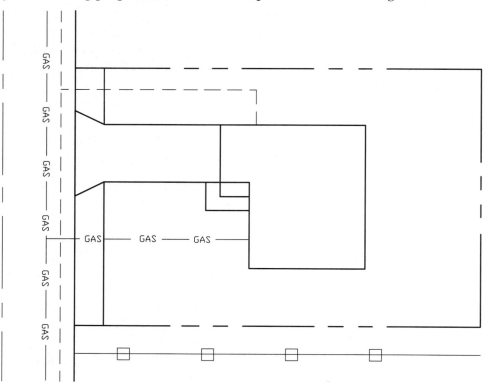

2. Draw the chart for the door schedule. Make the measurements for the rows and columns approximately the same as in the given problem. Do not draw the text. It will be added in Chapter 8. Save the drawing as P4-2.

DOOR SCHEDULE

SYM.	SIZE	TYPE	QTY.
①	36 x 80	S.C. R.P. METAL INSULATED	1
②	36 x 80	S.C. FLUSH METAL INSULATED	2
③	32 x 80	S.C. SELF CLOSING	2
④	32 x 80	HOLLOW CORE	5
⑤	30 x 80	HOLLOW CORE	5
⑥	30 x 80	POCKET SLDG.	2

3. Draw the line chart shown below. Use the linetypes shown, which include Continuous, HIDDEN, PHANTOM, CENTER, FENCELINE1, and FENCELINE2. Make your drawing proportional to the given example. Save the drawing as P4-3.

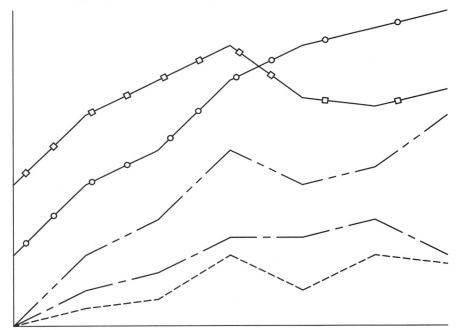

4. Draw the chart for the window schedule. Make the measurements for the rows and columns approximately the same as shown. Do not draw the hexagons or text. They will be added in Chapter 8. Save the drawing as P4-4.

	WINDOW SCHEDULE			
SYM.	SIZE	MODEL	ROUGH OPEN	QTY.
Ⓐ	12 x 60	JOB BUILT	VERIFY	2
Ⓑ	96 x 60	W4N5 CSM.	8'-0 3/4" x 5'-0 7/8"	1
Ⓒ	48 x 60	W2N5 CSM.	4'-0 3/4" x 5'-0 7/8"	2
Ⓓ	48 x 36	W2N3 CSM.	4'-0 3/4" x 3'-6 1/2"	2
Ⓔ	42 x 42	2N3 CSM.	3'- 6 1/2" x 3'-6 1/2"	2
Ⓕ	72 x 48	G64 SLDG.	6'-0 1/2" x 4'-0 1/2"	1
Ⓖ	60 x 42	G536 SLDG.	5'-0 1/2" x 3'-6 1/2"	4
Ⓗ	48 x 42	G436 SLDG.	4'-0 1/2" x 3'-6 1/2"	1
Ⓙ	48 x 24	A41 AWN.	4'-0 1/2" x 2'-0 7/8"	3

5. Draw the chart for the interior finish schedule. Make the measurements for the rows and columns approximately the same as in the given problem. Do not draw the solid circles or the text. They will be added in Chapters 5 and 8. Save the drawing as P4-5.

INTERIOR FINISH SCHEDULE											
ROOM	FLOOR					WALLS				CEILING	
	VINYL	CARPET	TILE	HARDWOOD	CONCRETE	PAINT	PAPER	TEXTURE	SPRAY	SMOOTH	BROCADE	PAINT
ENTRY					•							
FOYER			•			•			•			•
KITCHEN			•					•		•		•
DINING				•		•			•	•		•
FAMILY		•				•			•	•		•
LIVING		•				•		•		•		•
MSTR. BATH			•			•				•		•
BATH #2			•			•				•	•	
MSTR. BED		•				•		•		•		•
BED #2		•				•				•		•
BED #3		•				•				•		•
UTILITY	•					•				•	•	•

Drawing Problems - Chapter 4

6. Draw the integrated circuit block diagram. Make your drawing proportional to the given problem. Do not draw the circle, line connections, or text. Save the drawing as P4-6.

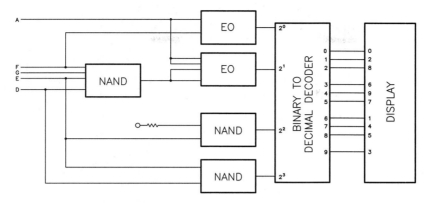

7. Draw the robotics system block diagram. Make your drawing proportional to the given problem. Do not draw the arrowheads or text. Save the drawing as P4-7.

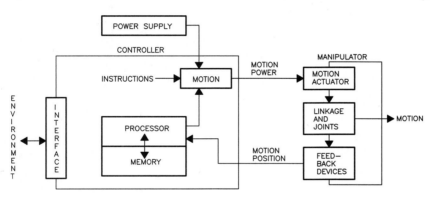

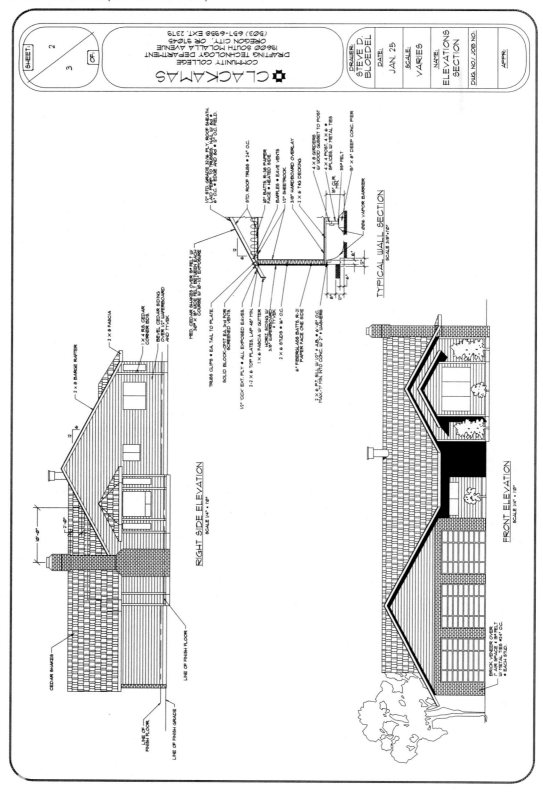

CHAPTER 5

Drawing Basic Shapes

Learning Objectives

After completing this chapter, you will be able to do the following:

● Use **DRAGMODE** to observe an object being dragged into place.
● Draw circles using the **CIRCLE** command options.
● Draw arcs using the **ARC** command options.
● Use the **ELLIPSE** command to draw ellipses and elliptical arcs.
● Draw polygons.
● Draw rectangles using the **RECTANG** command options.
● Draw donuts.
● Use the **Revision Cloud** tool to mark up drawings.

The decisions you make when drawing circles and arcs with AutoCAD are similar to those made when drawing the items manually. AutoCAD provides many ways to create circles and arcs using the **CIRCLE** and **ARC** commands. These methods require inputting the center location and radius or diameter or entering where the outline of the circle or arc should be located. AutoCAD also includes additional drawing tools, such as the **ELLIPSE**, **POLYGON**, **RECTANG**, and **DONUT** commands, to draw a wide variety of shapes. Other provided tools include the **Revision Cloud** tool, which is used to mark up drawings.

Watching Objects Drag into Place

Chapter 3 showed how the **LINE** command displays an image that is "dragged" across the screen before the second endpoint is picked. This image is called a *rubber band*. The **CIRCLE**, **ARC**, **ELLIPSE**, **POLYGON**, and **RECTANG** commands also display a rubberband image to help you decide where to place the object.

For example, when you draw a circle using the **Center, Radius** option, a circle image appears on the screen after you pick the center point. This image gets larger or smaller as you move the pointer. When the desired circle size is picked, a solid-line circle replaces the dragged image. See **Figure 5-1.**

Figure 5-1.
Dragging a circle to
its desired size.

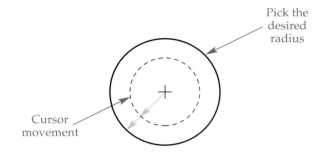

The **DRAGMODE** command affects the visibility of the rubberband. The options are **ON**, **OFF**, and **Auto**. To change the setting, type DRAGMODE:

Command: **DRAGMODE**↵
Enter new value [ON/OFF/Auto] <Auto>: *(type ON, OFF, or A, and press* [Enter]*)*

The current (default) mode is shown in brackets. The **Auto** option is set by default. Pressing the [Enter] key keeps the existing status. When the setting is **On**, you must enter DRAG during a command sequence to see the objects drag into place.

NOTE	This chapter covers the use of command line entry methods with drawing commands. When Dynamic Input is enabled, similar prompts and options are available.

CIRCLE

Type	
	CIRCLE
	C
Pull-Down Menu	
Draw	
> Circle	
Toolbar	
	Draw
	Circle
Options	
3P	
2P	
Ttr	

Drawing Circles

The **CIRCLE** command is activated by picking the **Circle** button in the **Draw** toolbar. You can also select **Draw > Circle** or type C or CIRCLE. The options available in the **Circle** cascading menu are shown in **Figure 5-2**.

Drawing a Circle by Radius

A circle can be drawn by specifying the center point and the radius. After accessing the **Center, Radius** option, you are asked to specify the center point, followed by the radius. You can enter the center point coordinates and a radius value by typing or by picking with the crosshairs. The following command sequence is used to draw the circle in **Figure 5-3**:

Pull-Down Menu	
Draw	
> Circle	
> Center,	
Radius	

Command: **C** *or* **CIRCLE**↵
Specify center point for circle or [3P/2P/Ttr (tan tan radius)]: *(select a center point)*
Specify radius of circle or [Diameter] <current>: *(drag the circle to the desired radius and pick, or type the radius size and press* [Enter]*)*

NOTE	The radius value you enter is stored as the **CIRCLERAD** system variable. This system variable is the default radius setting the next time you use the **CIRCLE** command. If **CIRCLERAD** is set to 0, no default radius is provided the next time you use the **CIRCLE** command.

Figure 5-2.
The **Circle** cascading menu in the **Draw** pull-down menu.

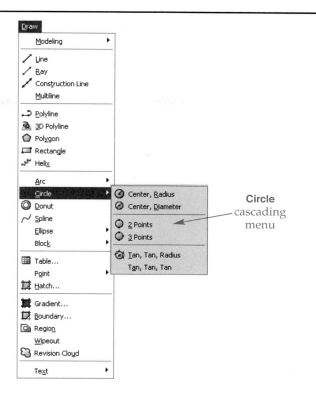

Figure 5-3.
Drawing a circle by specifying the center point and radius.

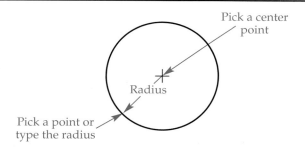

Pick a center point

Radius

Pick a point or type the radius

Drawing a Circle by Diameter

A circle can also be drawn by specifying the center point and the diameter. The command sequence for the **Center, Diameter** option is as follows:

Pull-Down Menu
Draw
> **Circle**
> **Center, Diameter**

Command: **C** *or* **CIRCLE**↵
Specify center point for circle or [3P/2P/Ttr (tan tan radius)]: *(select a center point)*
Specify radius of circle or [Diameter] *<current>*: **D**↵
Specify diameter of circle *<current>*: *(drag the circle to the desired diameter and pick, or type the diameter size and press* [Enter]*)*

Watch the screen carefully when using the **Center, Diameter** option. The pointer measures the diameter, but the circle passes midway between the center and the cursor. See **Figure 5-4.** The **Center, Diameter** option is convenient because most circular holes, shafts, and features are specified by the diameter.

After you draw a circle, its radius becomes the default for the next circle. If you use the **Diameter** option, the previous default setting is converted to a diameter. If you use the **Radius** option to draw a circle after using the **Diameter** option, AutoCAD changes the default to a radius measurement based on the previous diameter. If you set **CIRCLERAD** to a value such as .50, the default for a circle drawn with the **Diameter** option is automatically 1.00 (twice the default radius).

Figure 5-4.
Drawing a circle
using the **Center,
Diameter** option.
Notice that
AutoCAD calculates
the circle's position
as you move the
cursor.

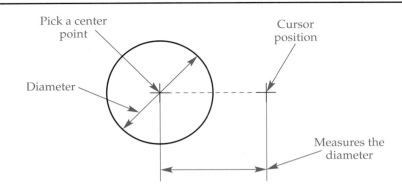

Drawing a Two-Point Circle

Pull-Down Menu

Draw
> Circle
 > 2 Points

A two-point circle is drawn by picking two points on opposite sides of the circle.
See **Figure 5-5**. The **2 Points** option is useful if the diameter of the circle is known, but
the center is difficult to find. One example of this is locating a circle between two lines.
The command sequence is as follows:

Command: **C** *or* **CIRCLE**↵
Specify center point for circle or [3P/2P/Ttr (tan tan radius)]: **2P**↵
Specify first end point of circle's diameter: *(select a point)*
Specify second end point of circle's diameter: *(select a point)*

AutoCAD automatically calculates the radius of the circle. This is the default radius
the next time the **CIRCLE** command is used.

Figure 5-5.
Drawing a circle by
selecting two points.

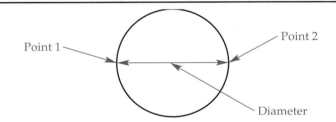

Drawing a Three-Point Circle

Pull-Down Menu

Draw
> Circle
 > 3 Points

If three points on the circumference of a circle are known, the **3 Points** option is
the best method to use. The three points can be selected in any order. See **Figure 5-6**.
The command sequence is as follows:

Command: **C** *or* **CIRCLE**↵
Specify center point for circle or [3P/2P/Ttr (tan tan radius)]: **3P**↵
Specify first point on circle: *(select a point)*
Specify second point on circle: *(select a point)*
Specify third point on circle: *(select a point)*
Command:

AutoCAD automatically calculates the radius of the circle. This becomes the default
radius the next time the **CIRCLE** command is used.

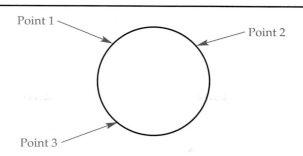

Figure 5-6.
Drawing a circle by picking three points on the circle.

Point 1

Point 2

Point 3

Drawing a Circle Tangent to Two Objects

The term *tangent* refers to a line, circle, or arc that comes into contact with an arc or circle at only one point. That point is called the *point of tangency*. A line drawn from the circle's center to the point of tangency is perpendicular to the tangent line. One drawn between the centers of two tangent circles passes through the point of tangency. You can draw a circle tangent to given lines, circles, or arcs.

Pull-Down Menu

Draw
> Circle
> Tan, Tan,
Radius

The **Tan, Tan, Radius** option creates a circle tangent to two objects. Once the **Tan, Tan, Radius** option is selected, select the lines, arcs, or circles to which the new circle will be tangent. The radius of the circle is also required. To assist you in picking the objects, AutoCAD uses the **Deferred Tangent** object snap by default. (Object snap modes are covered in Chapter 6.) The **Deferred Tangent** symbol is shown when you move the cursor to the objects you want to pick. The command sequence is as follows:

Command: **C** *or* **CIRCLE**↵
Specify center point for circle or [3P/2P/Ttr (tan tan radius)]: **T**↵
Specify point on object for first tangent of circle: *(pick the first line, circle, or arc)*
Specify point on object for second tangent of circle: *(pick the second line, circle, or arc)*
Specify radius of circle <current>: *(type a radius value and press [Enter])*

If the radius entered is too small, AutoCAD gives you the message Circle does not exist. AutoCAD automatically calculates the radius of the circle. This is the default radius the next time the **CIRCLE** command is used. Two examples of this option are shown in **Figure 5-7**.

Figure 5-7.
Two examples of drawing circles tangent to two given objects using the **Tan, Tan, Radius** option.

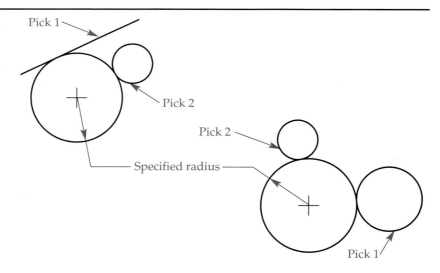

Pick 1

Pick 2

Specified radius

Pick 2

Pick 1

Drawing a Circle Tangent to Three Objects

Pull-Down Menu
Draw
> Circle
> Tan, Tan, Tan

The **Tan, Tan, Tan** option allows you to draw a circle tangent to three existing objects. This option creates a three-point circle using the three points of tangency. See **Figure 5-8.** Selecting the pull-down option is the same as using the **3 Points** option with the **Tangent** object snap:

Command: **C** *or* **CIRCLE**↵
Specify center point for circle or [3P/2P/Ttr (tan tan radius)]: **3P**↵
Specify first point on circle: **TAN**↵
to *(pick an object)*
Specify second point on circle: **TAN**↵
to *(pick an object)*
Specify third point on circle: **TAN**↵
to *(pick an object)*
Command:

Figure 5-8.
Two examples of drawing circles tangent to three given objects.

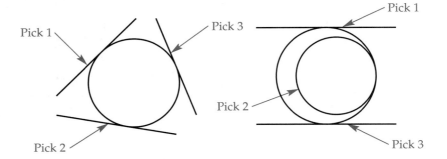

NOTE

Unlike the **Tan, Tan, Radius** option, the **Tan, Tan, Tan** option does not automatically recover when a point prompt is answered with a pick where no tangent exists. In such a case, the **Tangent** object snap must be manually reactivated for subsequent attempts to make that pick. The **Tangent** object snap is one of the object snaps discussed in Chapter 6 of this text. For now, if this happens, type TAN and press [Enter] at the point selection prompt. This returns the aperture box so you can pick again.

Exercise
5-1   Complete the Exercise on the Student CD.

Drawing Arcs

An *arc* is defined as any portion of a circle. Arcs are commonly dimensioned with a radius, but they can be drawn by a number of different methods. The **ARC** command can be accessed by selecting **Draw** > **Arc**. There are eleven arc construction options accessible in the **Arc** cascading menu. See **Figure 5-9.** This is the easiest way to access the **ARC** command and an arc option. The **ARC** command and its options, however, can also be accessed by picking the **Arc** button in the **Draw** toolbar or by typing A or ARC. The **3 Points** option is the default.

Drawing a Three-Point Arc

The **3 Points** option asks for the start point, the second point along the arc, and the endpoint. See **Figure 5-10.** The arc can be drawn clockwise or counterclockwise and is dragged into position as the endpoint is located. The command sequence is as follows:

Command: **A** *or* **ARC.**⏎
Specify start point of arc or [Center]: *(select the first point on the arc)*
Specify second point of arc or [Center/End]: *(select the second point on the arc)*
Specify end point of arc: *(select the arc's endpoint)*
Command:

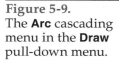

Figure 5-9.
The **Arc** cascading menu in the **Draw** pull-down menu.

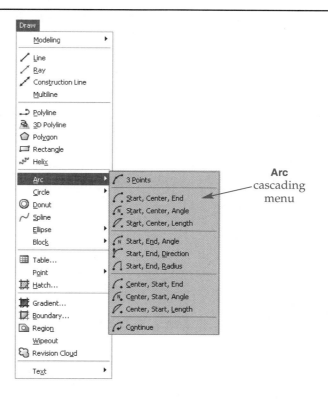

Figure 5-10.
Drawing an arc by picking three points.

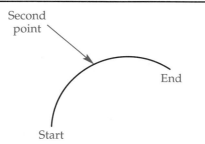

Drawing Arcs Using the Start, Center, End Option

Pull-Down Menu
Draw
> Arc
> Start, Center,
End

Use the **Start, Center, End** option when you know the start, center, and endpoint locations for the arc. With this method, arcs are drawn counterclockwise. Picking the start and center points establishes the arc's radius. The point selected for the endpoint determines the arc length. The selected endpoint does not have to be on the radius of the arc. See **Figure 5-11.** The command sequence is as follows:

Command: **A** *or* **ARC**↵
Specify start point of arc or [Center]: *(select the first point on the arc)*
Specify second point of arc or [Center/End]: **C**↵
Specify center point of arc: *(select the arc's center point)*
Specify end point of arc or [Angle/chord Length]: *(select the arc's endpoint)*
Command:

Drawing Arcs Using the Start, Center, Angle Option

Pull-Down Menu
Draw
> Arc
> Start, Center,
Angle

When the arc's included angle is known, the **Start, Center, Angle** option may be the best choice. The *included angle* is an angle formed between the center, start point, and endpoint of the arc. The arc is drawn counterclockwise, unless a negative angle is specified. See **Figure 5-12.** The following shows the command sequence with a 45° included angle:

Command: **A** *or* **ARC**↵
Specify start point of arc or [Center]: *(select the first point on the arc)*
Specify second point of arc or [Center/End]: **C**↵
Specify center point of arc: *(select the arc's center point)*
Specify end point of arc or [Angle/chord Length]: **A**↵
Specify included angle: **45**↵
Command:

Figure 5-11.
Using the **Start, Center, End** option. Notice the endpoint does not have to be on the arc.

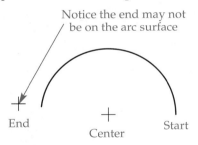

Figure 5-12.
How positive and negative angles work with the **Start, Center, Angle** option.

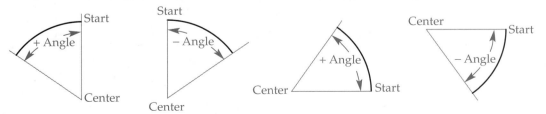

Drawing Arcs Using the Start, Center, Length Option

The chord length of an arc can be determined using a chord length table. (A chord length table is provided in the *Standard Tables* document in the *Reference Materials* section of the Student CD.) For example, a one-unit radius arc with an included angle of 45° has a chord length of .765 units. You can use the **Start, Center, Length** option to specify the chord length of an arc. With this method, arcs are drawn counterclockwise. A positive chord length gives the smallest possible arc with that length. A negative chord length results in the largest possible arc. See **Figure 5-13**. The following shows the command sequence with a chord length of .765:

Pull-Down Menu
Draw
> Arc
> Start, Center, Length

Command: **A** *or* **ARC↵**
Specify start point of arc or [Center]: *(select the first point on the arc)*
Specify second point of arc or [Center/End]: **C↵**
Specify center point of arc: *(select the arc's center point)*
Specify end point of arc or [Angle/chord Length]: **L↵**
Specify length of chord: *(type .765 for the smaller arc or −.765 for the larger arc, and press* [Enter]*)*
Command:

Exercise 5-2

Complete the Exercise on the Student CD.

Drawing Arcs Using the Start, End, Angle Option

An arc can also be drawn by picking the start point and endpoint and entering the included angle. A positive included angle draws the arc counterclockwise, while a negative angle produces a clockwise arc. See **Figure 5-14**. The command sequence is as follows:

Pull-Down Menu
Draw
> Arc
> Start, End, Angle

Command: **A** *or* **ARC↵**
Specify start point of arc or [Center]: *(select the first point on the arc)*
Specify second point of arc or [Center/End]: **E↵**
Specify end point of arc: *(select the arc's endpoint)*
Specify center point of arc or [Angle/Direction/Radius]: **A↵**
Specify included angle: *(type a positive or negative angle and press* [Enter]*)*
Command:

Figure 5-13.
How positive and negative chord lengths work with the **Start, Center, Length** option.

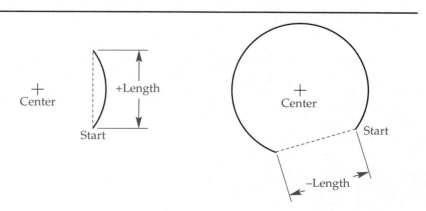

Figure 5-14.
How positive and
negative angles
work with the **Start,
End, Angle** option.

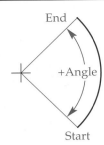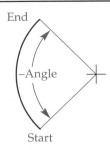

Drawing Arcs Using the Start, End, Direction Option

An arc can be drawn by picking the start point and endpoint and then using the mouse to specify the direction of rotation. The distance between the points and the direction the cursor is moved determine the arc's location and size. The arc is started tangent to the direction specified, as shown in **Figure 5-15.** The command sequence is as follows:

Command: **A** *or* **ARC**↵
Specify start point of arc or [Center]: *(select the first point on the arc)*
Specify second point of arc or [Center/End]: **E**↵
Specify end point of arc: *(select the arc's endpoint)*
Specify center point of arc or [Angle/Direction/Radius]: **D**↵
Specify tangent direction for the start point of arc: *(pick the direction from the start point, or type the direction in degrees and press* [Enter]*)*
Command:

Figure 5-15.
Using the **Start, End,
Direction** option.

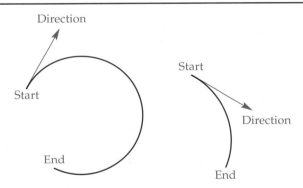

Drawing Arcs Using the Start, End, Radius Option

A positive radius value for the **Start, End, Radius** option results in the smallest possible arc between the start point and endpoint. A negative radius gives the largest arc possible. See **Figure 5-16.** Arcs can only be drawn counterclockwise with this option. The command sequence is as follows:

Command: **A** *or* **ARC**↵
Specify start point of arc or [Center]: *(select the first point on the arc)*
Specify second point of arc or [Center/End]: **E**↵
Specify end point of arc: *(select the arc's endpoint)*
Specify center point of arc or [Angle/Direction/Radius]: **R**↵
Specify radius of arc: *(pick or type a positive or negative radius and press* [Enter]*)*
Command:

Figure 5-16.
Using the **Start, End, Radius** option with a positive and negative radius.

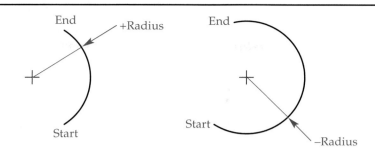

Exercise
5-3   Complete the Exercise on the Student CD.

Drawing Arcs Using the Center, Start, End Option

The **Center, Start, End** option is a variation of the **Start, Center, End** option. See Figure 5-17. Use the **Center, Start, End** option when it is easier to begin by locating the center. The command sequence is as follows:

Pull-Down Menu
Draw
> Arc
> Center, Start, End

Command: **A** *or* **ARC**↵
Specify start point of arc or [Center]: **C**↵
Specify center point of arc: *(pick the center point)*
Specify start point of arc: *(pick the start point)*
Specify end point of arc or [Angle/chord Length]: *(pick the arc's endpoint)*
Command:

Figure 5-17.
Using the **Center, Start, End** option. Note that the endpoint does not have to be on the arc.

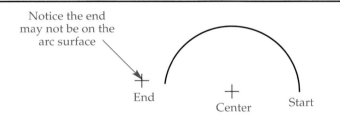

Drawing Arcs Using the Center, Start, Angle Option

The **Center, Start, Angle** option is a variation of the **Start, Center, Angle** option. Use the **Center, Start, Angle** option when it is easier to begin by locating the center. Figure 5-18 shows how positive and negative angles work with this option. The command sequence is as follows:

Pull-Down Menu
Draw
> Arc
> Center, Start, Angle

Command: **A** *or* **ARC**↵
Specify start point of arc or [Center]: **C**↵
Specify center point of arc: *(pick the center point)*
Specify start point of arc: *(pick the start point)*
Specify end point of arc or [Angle/chord Length]: **A**↵
Specify included angle: *(pick the included angle, or type a positive angle or negative angle and press [Enter])*
Command:

Figure 5-18.
How positive and negative angles work with the **Center, Start, Angle** option.

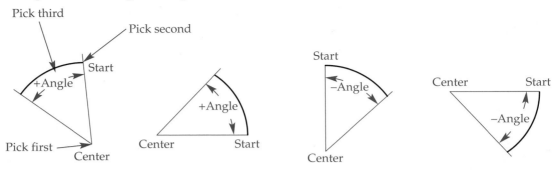

Drawing Arcs Using the Center, Start, Length Option

Pull-Down Menu

Draw
> Arc
> Center, Start,
Length

The **Center, Start, Length** option is a variation of the **Start, Center, Length** option. Use the **Center, Start, Length** option when it is easier to begin by locating the center. **Figure 5-19** shows how positive and negative chord lengths work with this option. The command sequence is as follows:

Command: **A** *or* **ARC**↵
Specify start point of arc or [Center]: **C**↵
Specify center point of arc: *(pick the center point)*
Specify start point of arc: *(pick the start point)*
Specify end point of arc or [Angle/chord Length]: **L**↵
Specify length of chord: *(pick or type the chord length, and press* [Enter]*)*
Command:

Figure 5-19.
How positive and negative chord lengths work with the **Center, Start, Length** option.

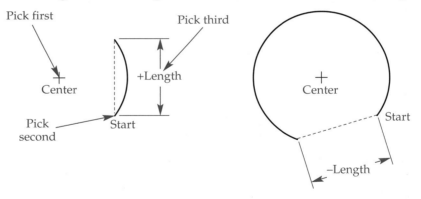

Continuing Arcs from a Previously Drawn Arc or Line

Pull-Down Menu

Draw
> Arc
> Continue

An arc can be continued from the previous arc or line. To do so, select **Draw** > **Arc** > **Continue**. The **Continue** option can also be accessed by beginning the **ARC** command and then pressing the [Enter] key, pressing the space bar, or selecting **Enter** from the shortcut menu when prompted to specify the start point of the arc:

Specify start point of arc or [Center]: *(press the space bar or* [Enter] *to place the start point of the arc at the end of the previous line or arc)*

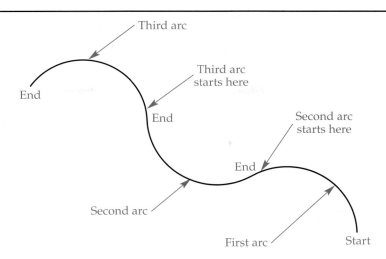

Figure 5-20.
Using the **Continue** option to draw three arcs.

Third arc

Third arc
starts here

End

Second arc
starts here

End

End

Second arc

First arc

Start

When a series of arcs are drawn in this manner, each consecutive arc is tangent to the object before it. The start point and direction are taken from the endpoint and direction of the previous arc. See **Figure 5-20.**

The **Continue** option can also be used to quickly draw an arc tangent to the endpoint of a previously drawn line. See **Figure 5-21.** The command sequence is as follows:

> Command: **L** *or* **LINE.**↵
> Specify first point: *(select a point)*
> Specify next point or [Undo]: *(select a second point)*
> Specify next point or [Undo]: ↵
> Command: **A** *or* **ARC.**↵
> Specify start point of arc or [Center]: *(press the space bar or* [Enter] *to place the start point of the arc at the end of the previous line)*
> Specify end point of arc: *(select the endpoint of the arc)*
> Command:

**Exercise
5-4**   Complete the Exercise on the Student CD.

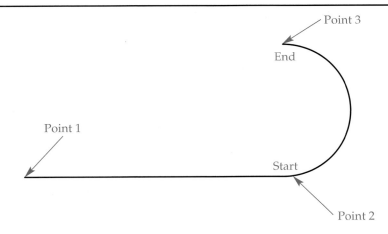

Figure 5-21.
An arc continuing from the previous line. Point 2 is the start of the arc, and Point 3 is the end of the arc.

Point 3

End

Point 1

Start

Point 2

ELLIPSE

Type
ELLIPSE
EL

Pull-Down Menu
Draw
> Ellipse

Toolbar
Draw

Ellipse

Options
Arc
Center
Rotation

Drawing Ellipses

When a circle is viewed at an angle, an elliptical shape is seen. For example, a 30° ellipse is created if a circle is rotated 30° from the line of sight. The parts of an ellipse are shown in **Figure 5-22**. The longer of the two axes is always the major axis. The **ELLIPSE** command can be accessed by selecting **Draw > Ellipse**, picking the **Ellipse** button in the **Draw** toolbar, or typing EL or ELLIPSE. An ellipse can be drawn using different options of the **ELLIPSE** command.

Figure 5-22.
The parts of an ellipse.

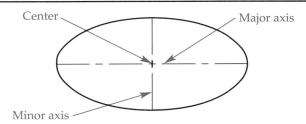

Drawing an Ellipse Using the Center Option

Pull-Down Menu
Draw
> Ellipse
> Center

An ellipse can be constructed by specifying the center point and one endpoint for each of the two axes. See **Figure 5-23**. The **Center** option in the **Ellipse** cascading menu of the **Draw** pull-down menu is used to draw an ellipse in this manner. The command sequence for this option is as follows:

Command: **EL** *or* **ELLIPSE**↵
Specify axis endpoint of ellipse or [Arc/Center]: **C**↵
Specify center of ellipse: *(select the ellipse's center point)*
Specify endpoint of axis: *(select the endpoint of one axis)*
Specify distance to other axis or [Rotation]: *(select the endpoint of the other axis)*

If you respond to the Specify distance to other axis or [Rotation]: prompt with R for **Rotation**, AutoCAD assumes you have selected the major axis with the first axis endpoint. The next prompt requests the angle at which the corresponding circle is rotated from the line of sight to produce the ellipse. The command sequence is as follows:

Specify distance to other axis or [Rotation]: **R**↵
Specify rotation around major axis: *(type a rotation angle, such as* 30, *and press* [Enter])
Command:

The 30 response draws an ellipse that is created when a circle is rotated 30° from the line of sight. A 0 response draws an ellipse with the minor axis equal to the major axis—that is, a circle. AutoCAD rejects any rotation angle between 89.99994° and 90.00006° or between 269.99994° and 270.00006°. **Figure 5-24** shows the relationship among several ellipses having the same major axis length, but different rotation angles.

Figure 5-23.
Drawing an ellipse by picking the center and endpoints of two axes.

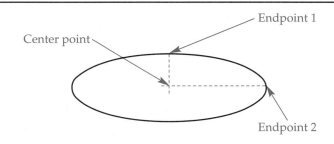

Figure 5-24.
Ellipse rotation angles.

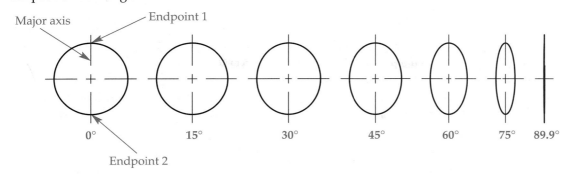

Drawing an Ellipse Using the Axis, End Option

Pull-Down Menu
Draw
> Ellipse
> Axis, End

The **Axis, End** option establishes the first axis and one endpoint of the second axis. The first axis may be either the major or minor axis, depending on what is entered for the second axis. After you pick the first axis, the ellipse is dragged by the cursor until the point is picked. The command sequence for the ellipses in **Figure 5-25** is as follows:

Command: **EL** *or* **ELLIPSE**↵
Specify axis endpoint of ellipse or [Arc/Center]: *(select an axis endpoint)*
Specify other endpoint of axis: *(select the other endpoint of the axis)*
Specify distance to other axis or [Rotation]: *(select a distance from the midpoint of the first axis to the end of the second axis and press [Enter])*
Command:

Exercise 5-5   Complete the Exercise on the Student CD.

Figure 5-25.
Constructing the same ellipse by choosing different axis endpoints.

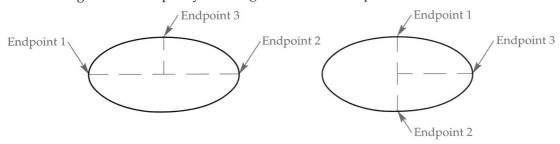

Drawing Elliptical Arcs

Pull-Down Menu
Draw
> Ellipse
> Arc

The **Arc** option of the **ELLIPSE** command is used to draw elliptical arcs. The command sequence for the **Arc** option is as follows:

Command: **EL** *or* **ELLIPSE**↵
Specify axis endpoint of ellipse or [Arc/Center]: **A**↵
Specify axis endpoint of elliptical arc or [Center]: *(pick the first axis endpoint)*
Specify other endpoint of axis: *(pick the second axis endpoint)*
Specify distance to other axis or [Rotation]: *(pick the distance for the second axis)*
Specify start angle or [Parameter]: **0**↵
Specify end angle or [Parameter/Included angle]: **90**↵
Command:

Once the second endpoint of the first axis is picked, you can drag the shape of a full ellipse. This can help you visualize the other axis. The distance for the second axis is from the ellipse's center to the point picked. Enter a start angle. The start and end angles are the angular relationships between the ellipse's center and the arc's endpoints. The angle of the elliptical arc is established from the angle of the first axis. A 0° start angle begins the arc at the first endpoint of the first axis. A 45° start angle begins the arc 45° counterclockwise from the first endpoint of the first axis. End angles are also established counterclockwise from the start point. Figure 5-26 shows the elliptical arc drawn with the previous command sequence and displays sample arcs with different start and end angles.

Using the Parameter option

The **Parameter** option requires the same input used for drawing other elliptical arcs, until the Specify start angle or [Parameter]: prompt. With the **Parameter** option, AutoCAD uses a different means of vector calculation to create the elliptical arc. The results are similar, but the command sequence is as follows:

> Specify start angle or [Parameter]: **P**↵
> Specify start parameter or [Angle]: *(pick the start point or enter a value)*
> Specify end parameter or [Angle/Included angle]: *(pick the endpoint or enter a value)*
> Command:

Using the Included angle option

The **Included angle** option establishes an included angle beginning at the start angle. An included angle is an angle that is formed by two sides, or in this case, the angle formed by the axis endpoints and center of the arc. This option requires the same input used for drawing other elliptical arcs until the Specify end angle or [Parameter/Included angle]: prompt. The command sequence is as follows:

> Specify end angle or [Parameter/Included angle]: **I**↵
> Specify included angle for arc <*current*>: *(enter the included angle)*
> Command:

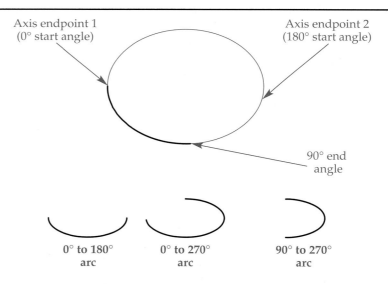

Figure 5-26.
Drawing elliptical arcs with the **Arc** option. Note the three examples at the bottom created by three different angle settings.

Rotating an elliptical arc around its axis

The **Rotation** option for drawing an elliptical arc is similar to the **Rotation** option used when drawing a full ellipse, which was discussed earlier. This option allows you to rotate the elliptical arc about the first axis by specifying a rotation angle. Refer to **Figure 5-24** for examples of various rotation angles. This option requires the same input used for drawing other elliptical arcs, until the Specify distance to other axis or [Rotation]: prompt. The command sequence is as follows:

Specify distance to other axis or [Rotation]: **R↵**
Specify rotation around major axis: *(enter rotation value)*
Specify start angle or [Parameter]: *(enter start angle)*
Specify end angle or [Parameter/Included angle]: *(enter end angle)*
Command:

Drawing an elliptical arc using the Center option

The **Center** option for drawing an elliptical arc lets you establish the center of the ellipse. See **Figure 5-27**. This option requires the same input used for drawing other elliptical arcs, until the Specify axis endpoint of elliptical arc or [Center]: prompt. The command sequence is as follows:

Specify axis endpoint of elliptical arc or [Center]: **C↵**
Specify center of elliptical arc: *(select the ellipse's center point)*
Specify endpoint of axis: *(select the endpoint of the axis)*
Specify distance to other axis or [Rotation]: *(select the endpoint of the other axis)*
Specify start angle or [Parameter]: *(enter start angle)*
Specify end angle or [Parameter/Included angle]: *(enter end angle)*
Command:

Figure 5-27.
Drawing elliptical arcs with the **Center** option.

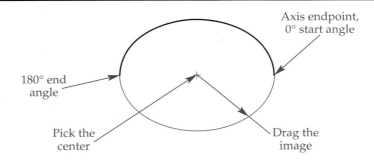

Axis endpoint, 0° start angle

180° end angle

Pick the center

Drag the image

NOTE

The setting of the **PELLIPSE** system variable affects the way an ellipse can be edited. An ellipse drawn when **PELLIPSE** is set at 0 is a true elliptical object, while an ellipse drawn when **PELLIPSE** is set at 1 is a polyline ellipse. A true elliptical object maintains its elliptical shape during grip editing. (Grip editing is discussed in Chapter 13 of this text.) The vertices of a polyline ellipse can be moved out of the elliptical shape. The **Arc** option of the **ELLIPSE** command is not available when **PELLIPSE** is set to 1.

Complete the Exercise on the Student CD.

Drawing Regular Polygons

A *regular polygon* is any closed-plane geometric figure with three or more equal sides and equal angles. For example, a hexagon is a six-sided regular polygon. The **POLYGON** command is used to draw any regular polygon with up to 1024 sides.

The **POLYGON** command can be accessed by selecting **Draw > Polygon**, picking the **Polygon** button in the **Draw** toolbar, or typing POL or POLYGON. Regardless of the method used to select the command, you are first prompted for the number of sides. If you want an octagon (a polygon with eight sides), enter 8 as follows:

Command: **POL** *or* **POLYGON**↵
Enter number of sides <*current*>: **8**↵
Specify center of polygon or [Edge]:

The number of sides you enter becomes the default for the next time you use the **POLYGON** command. (This value is saved as the **POLYSIDES** system variable.) Next, AutoCAD prompts for the center or edge of the polygon. If you reply by picking a point on the screen, this point becomes the center of the polygon. You are then asked if you want to have the polygon inscribed within or circumscribed outside of an imaginary circle. See **Figure 5-28.**

A polygon is *inscribed* when it is drawn inside a circle and its corners touch the circle. *Circumscribed* polygons are drawn outside of a circle, where the sides of the polygon are tangent to the circle. With either option, you must specify the radius of the circle. The command continues as follows:

Specify center of polygon or [Edge]: *(pick the center of the polygon)*
Enter an option [Inscribed in circle/Circumscribed about circle] <*current*>: *(respond with I or C, and press [Enter])*
Specify radius of circle: *(type the radius, such as 2, and press [Enter], or pick a point on the screen at the desired distance from the center)*
Command:

The **I** or **C** option you select becomes the default for the next polygon. The Specify center of polygon or [Edge]: prompt allows you to pick the center or specify the edge. Notice that picking the center is the default. If you want to draw the polygon by specifying the length of one of the edges, enter E for the **Edge** option and pick edge endpoints as follows:

Figure 5-28.
Drawing an inscribed and a circumscribed polygon.

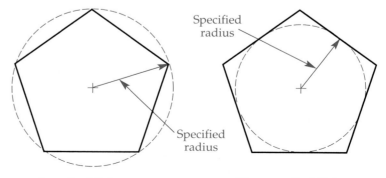

Inscribed Polygon   Circumscribed Polygon

Specify center of polygon or [Edge]: **E⏎**
Specify first endpoint of edge: *(pick a point)*
Specify second endpoint of edge: *(pick a second point)*
Command:

After you pick the endpoints of one side, the rest of the polygon sides are drawn counterclockwise, using the length specified by the two picked endpoints.

Polygons are polylines and can be easily edited using the **PEDIT** (polyline edit) command. The **PEDIT** command is discussed in Chapter 15 of this text.

Hexagons (six-sided polygons) are commonly drawn as bolt heads and nuts on mechanical drawings. Keep in mind that these features are normally dimensioned across the flats. To draw a polygon to be dimensioned across the flats, circumscribe it. The radius you enter is equal to one-half the distance across the flats. The distance across the corners is specified when the polygon must be confined within a circular area. In this case, use an inscribed polygon.

Exercise 5-7   Complete the Exercise on the Student CD.

Drawing Rectangles

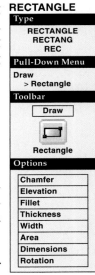

RECTANGLE

Type
RECTANGLE RECTANG REC
Pull-Down Menu
Draw > Rectangle
Toolbar
Draw
Rectangle
Options
Chamfer
Elevation
Fillet
Thickness
Width
Area
Dimensions
Rotation

The **RECTANG** command allows you to easily draw rectangles. When using this command, pick one corner and then the opposite diagonal corner to establish the rectangle. See **Figure 5-29**. The **RECTANG** command can be accessed by selecting **Draw > Rectangle**; by picking the **Rectangle** button in the **Draw** toolbar; or by typing REC, RECTANG, or RECTANGLE:

> Command: **REC, RECTANG,** *or* **RECTANGLE⏎**
> Specify first corner point or [Chamfer/Elevation/Fillet/Thickness/Width]: *(select the first corner of the rectangle)*
> Specify other corner point or [Area/Dimensions/Rotation]: *(select the second corner)*
> Command:

Rectangles are polylines and can be edited using the **PEDIT** command. Since a rectangle is a polyline, it is treated as one entity until it is exploded. After it is exploded, the individual sides can be edited separately. The **EXPLODE** command is discussed in Chapter 15 of this text.

Figure 5-29.
Using the **RECTANG** command. Simply pick opposite corners of the rectangle.

Other corner

First corner

Drawing Rectangles with Line Width

The **Width** option of the **RECTANG** command is used to adjust the width of the rectangle in the XY plane. Setting line width for rectangles is similar to setting width for polylines, which is discussed in Chapters 14 and 15.

The following sequence is used to create a rectangle with .03 wide lines:

Command: **REC**, **RECTANG**, *or* **RECTANGLE**↵
Specify first corner point or [Chamfer/Elevation/Fillet/Thickness/Width]: **W**↵
Specify line width for rectangles <*current*>: **.03**↵
Specify first corner point or [Chamfer/Elevation/Fillet/Thickness/Width]:

You can press [Enter] at the Specify line width for rectangles: prompt to have the rectangle polylines drawn with the default polyline width. If you enter a value at this prompt, the polylines are drawn using the specified width.

After setting the rectangle width, you can either select another option or draw the rectangle. Continue selecting options until you have set the characteristics correctly, and then draw the rectangle. If a width is set, any new rectangles drawn use the width you entered. To reset the width to the initial default, enter the **Width** option, and then specify a width of 0. Now, new rectangles are drawn using a standard "0 width" line.

Drawing Chamfered Rectangles

A *chamfer* is an angled corner on an object. Drawing chamfers is covered in detail in Chapter 12 of this text. This is a brief introduction to drawing chamfers on rectangles. To draw chamfers on rectangles, use the **Chamfer** option of the **RECTANG** command. The rectangle created will have chamfers drawn automatically.

After you select the **Chamfer** option, you must provide the chamfer distances. See **Figure 5-30.** The command sequence is as follows:

Command: **REC**, **RECTANG**, *or* **RECTANGLE**↵
Specify first corner point or [Chamfer/Elevation/Fillet/Thickness/Width]: **C**↵
Specify first chamfer distance for rectangles <*current*>: *(enter the first chamfer distance)*
Specify second chamfer distance for rectangles <*current*>: *(enter the second chamfer distance)*
Specify first corner point or [Chamfer/Elevation/Fillet/Thickness/Width]:

After setting the chamfer distances, you can either draw the rectangle or select another option. If you select the **Fillet** option, the chamfers will not be drawn.

Figure 5-30.
These drawings show rectangles with chamfers and fillets.

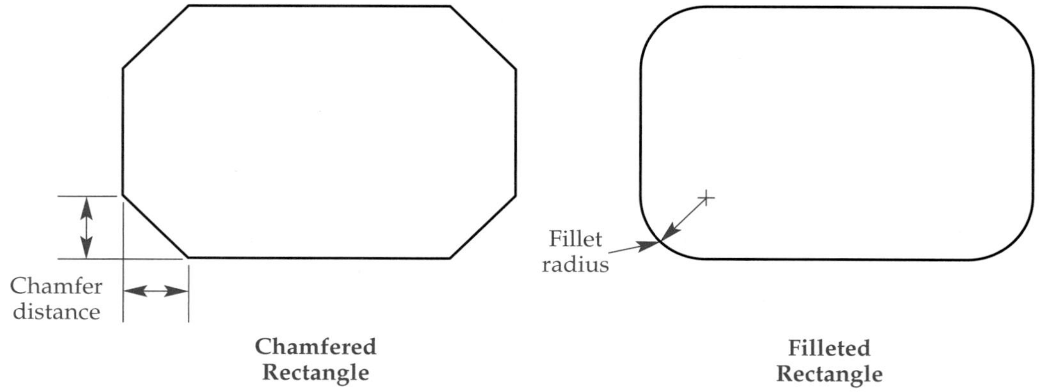

Chamfer distance

Chamfered
Rectangle

Fillet radius

Filleted
Rectangle

The default chamfer distances are the chamfer distances or fillet radius used to draw the previous rectangle. If the default for the first chamfer distance is zero, and you enter a different value, the new distance becomes the default for the second chamfer distance. If the default chamfer distances are nonzero values, however, a new value entered for the first distance does *not* become the default for the second distance. As with the **Width** option, if you set the **Chamfer** option's distances to a value greater than 0, any new rectangles created are automatically chamfered. New rectangles will continue to be created with chamfers until you reset the chamfer distances to 0 or use the **Fillet** option to create rounded corners.

Drawing Filleted Rectangles

A *fillet* is a rounded corner on an object. See Figure 5-30. Drawing fillets is covered in detail in Chapter 12 of this text. This is a brief introduction to drawing fillets on rectangles.

Fillets are automatically drawn on rectangles using the **Fillet** option of the **RECTANG** command. After selecting the option, you must enter the fillet radius:

> Command: **REC, RECTANG,** *or* **RECTANGLE.**↵
> Specify first corner point or [Chamfer/Elevation/Fillet/Thickness/Width]: **F**↵
> Specify fillet radius for rectangles <*current*>: *(enter a fillet radius or press* [Enter] *to accept the default)*
> Specify first corner point or [Chamfer/Elevation/Fillet/Thickness/Width]:

The default fillet radius is the radius of the previously drawn rectangle. Once a fillet radius is specified, the **RECTANG** command will automatically draw fillets on rectangles. In order to draw rectangles without fillets, the fillet radius must be set to 0.

Specifying Rectangle Areas

When you know the area of a rectangle and the length of one of its sides, the rectangle can be drawn using the **Area** option. This option is available after the first corner point of the rectangle is picked:

> Specify other corner point or [Area/Dimensions/Rotation]: **A**

You are then prompted to enter the total area for the rectangle. Enter a value that corresponds to the current units. The following sequence is used to draw a rectangle with an area of 45 in² when the length is known:

> Enter area of rectangle in current units <*current*>: **45**↵
> Calculate rectangle dimensions based on [Length/Width] <*current*>: **L**↵
> Enter rectangle length <*current*>: *(enter the length for the rectangle)*
> Command:

After entering the length, the width dimension is automatically calculated and the rectangle is drawn.

Specifying Rectangle Dimensions

AutoCAD provides a **Dimensions** option for the **RECTANG** command. The option is available after the first corner of the rectangle is picked.

Enter D to access the **Dimensions** option. You are then prompted to enter the length and width of the rectangle. In the following example, a 5 × 3 rectangle is specified:

> Specify other corner point or [Area/Dimensions/Rotation]: **D**↵
> Specify length for rectangles <*current*>: **5**↵
> Specify width for rectangles <*current*>: **3**↵
> Specify other corner point or [Area/Dimensions/Rotation]: *(move the crosshairs to the desired quadrant and pick a point)*
> Command:

Figure 5-31.
When using the **Dimensions** option of the **RECTANG** command, the orientation of the rectangle relative to the first corner point is determined by the second corner point.

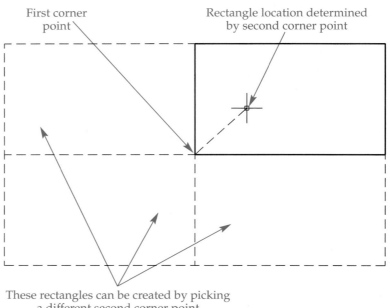

First corner point

Rectangle location determined by second corner point

These rectangles can be created by picking a different second corner point

After specifying the length and width, the Specify other corner point or [Area/Dimensions/Rotation]: prompt is displayed. If you wish to change the dimensions, select the **Dimensions** option again. If the dimensions are correct, you can specify the other corner point to complete the rectangle. When using the **Dimensions** option, the second corner point determines which of four possible rectangles is drawn. See **Figure 5-31.**

Drawing a Rotated Rectangle

A rectangle can be drawn at an angle by specifying a rotation angle after selecting the first point. To do so, use the **Rotation** option as follows:

Specify other corner point or [Area/Dimensions/Rotation]: **R↵**
Specify rotation angle or [Pick points] *<current>*: *(enter an angle, pick a point, or enter* P *to pick two reference points)*
Specify other corner point or [Area/Dimensions/Rotation]: *(pick the second point)*
Command:

When the **Pick points** option is used, you are prompted to select two points to define the angle. When a new value is specified with the **Rotation** option, it becomes the default angle.

Additional Rectangle Options

There are two other options available when using the **RECTANG** command. These options remain effective for multiple uses of the command:

- **Elevation.** This option sets the elevation of the rectangle along the Z axis. The default value is 0.
- **Thickness.** This option gives the rectangle depth along the Z axis. The default value is 0.

A combination of these options can be used to draw a single rectangle. For example, a rectangle can have fillets and a .03 line width.

Exercise 5-8   Complete the Exercise on the Student CD.

Drawing Donuts and Solid Circles

DONUT

Type
DONUT
DOUGHNUT
DO
Pull-Down Menu
Draw
> Donut

Donuts drawn in AutoCAD are actually polyline arcs with width. Drawing polylines is introduced in Chapter 14 and is covered in detail in Chapter 15. The **DONUT** command allows you to draw a thick circle. It can have any inside and outside diameters or be completely filled. See **Figure 5-32.**

The **DONUT** command can be accessed by selecting **Draw > Donut** or by typing DO, DONUT, or DOUGHNUT as follows:

Command: **DO**, **DONUT**, *or* **DOUGHNUT**⏎
Specify inside diameter of donut <*current*>: *(enter inside diameter)*
Specify outside diameter of donut <*current*>: *(enter outside diameter)*
Specify center of donut or <exit>: *(select the donut's center point)*
Specify center of donut or <exit>: *(select the center point for another donut, or press*
    [Enter] *to discontinue the command)*

The current diameter settings are shown in brackets. New diameters can be entered, or the current value can be accepted by pressing the [Enter] key. An inside diameter of 0 produces a solid circle.

After selecting the center point, the donut appears on the screen. You may pick another center point to draw the same size donut in a new location. The **DONUT** command remains active until you press [Enter] or cancel by pressing [Esc].

When the **FILL** mode is turned off, donuts appear as segmented circles or concentric circles. **FILL** can be used transparently by entering 'FILL while inside the **DONUT** command. Enter ON or OFF as needed. The fill display for previously drawn donuts is updated when the drawing is regenerated.

> **NOTE**
>
> The setting for the inside diameter of a donut is stored in the **DONUTID** system variable. The setting for the outside diameter is stored in the **DONUTOD** system variable. If the value of **DONUTID** is greater than the value of **DONUTOD**, the values are switched when the next donut is drawn.

Exercise 5-9   Complete the Exercise on the Student CD.

Figure 5-32.
Donuts can have outside diameters and can have inside diameters or be completely filled.

Fill On

Fill On
ID = 0

Fill Off

Fill Off
ID = 0

Figure 5-33.
A revision cloud can be used to identify areas of a drawing that have been modified.

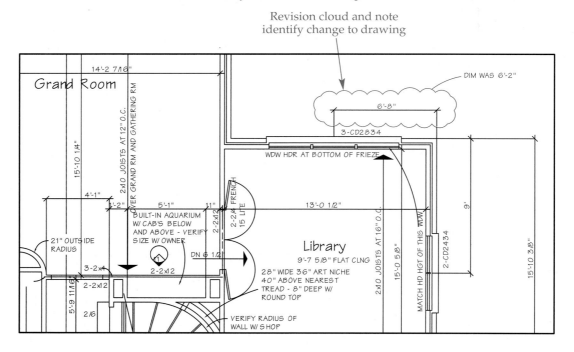

Revision cloud and note
identify change to drawing

Using the Revision Cloud

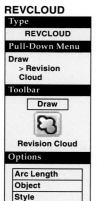

A *revision cloud* is a polyline of sequential arcs forming a cloud-shaped object. See **Figure 5-33.** This figure shows a note with a leader attached to the cloud. Revision clouds are typically used by people who review drawings and mark notes and changes. The revision cloud points the drafter to a specific portion of the drawing that may need to be edited.

To create a revision cloud, pick a starting location, move the cursor to shape the cloud, and then move the cursor toward the beginning of the cloud. AutoCAD automatically closes the cloud and ends the command. This command can be entered by selecting **Draw > Revision Cloud**, picking the **Revision Cloud** button from the **Draw** toolbar, or by typing REVCLOUD. The following prompt is displayed after entering this command:

Command: **REVCLOUD.↵**
Minimum arc length: *current*   Maximum arc length: *current*   Style: *current*
Specify start point or [Arc length/Object/Style] <*current option*>:

To begin drawing the revision cloud, pick a starting point in the drawing. After picking the starting point, the prompt tells you to Guide crosshairs along cloud path.... Move the cursor around the objects to be enclosed, until you come close to the starting point. AutoCAD then closes the cloud and prompts you with the message Revision cloud finished.

The size of the arcs can be set by entering the **Arc length** option. This value measures the length of an arc from its starting point to its ending point. You can change this value to any desired value. Upon entering the **Arc length** option, you are prompted for the following:

Specify start point or [Arc length/Object/Style] <*current option*>: **A**↵
Specify minimum length of arc <*current size*>: *(enter a minimum arc length)*
Specify maximum length of arc <*current size*>: *(enter a maximum arc length)*
Specify start point or [Arc length/Object/Style] <*current option*>: *(pick a starting point for the cloud)*

Varying the minimum and maximum values causes the revision cloud to have an uneven, hand-drawn look. The actual size of the arc is the length value multiplied by the dimension scale (**DIMSCALE** system variable), so revision clouds appear consistent in drawings with different scales.

Circles, closed polylines, ellipses, polygons, and rectangles can be converted to revision clouds by selecting the **Object** option. The command sequence follows:

Specify start point or [Arc length/Object/Style] <*current option*>: **O**↵
Select object: *(pick the object to convert to a revision cloud)*
Reverse direction [Yes/No] <*default*>: *(enter N, or enter Y to reverse the cloud arcs)*
Revision cloud finished.
Command:

The polyline and dimension scale topics related to this discussion are covered in detail later in this text.

The **Style** option of the **Revision Cloud** tool offers two different style choices: **Normal** and **Calligraphy.** The default style is **Normal**, in which the arcs are a consistent width. With the **Calligraphy** style, the individual arcs' start and end widths are different, creating a more stylish revision cloud. See **Figure 5-34.** To change the revision cloud style, the command sequence is as follows:

Specify start point or [Arc length/Object/Style] <*current option*>: **S**↵
Select arc style [Normal/Calligraphy] <*current*>: **C**↵
Arc style = Calligraphy
Specify start point or [Arc length/Object/Style] <*current option*>: *(pick a starting point for the cloud)*
Guide crosshairs along cloud path… *(move the cursor around the objects to be enclosed, until you come close to the starting point)*
Revision cloud finished.
Command:

Exercise 5-10   Complete the Exercise on the Student CD.

Figure 5-34.
Revision clouds can be created in two different styles, the **Normal** style and the **Calligraphy** style.

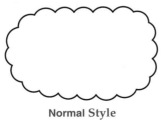

Normal Style

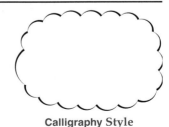

Calligraphy Style

Chapter Test

Answer the following questions. Write your answers on a separate sheet of paper or complete the electronic chapter test on the Student CD.

1. Give the command, entries, and actions required to draw a circle with a 2.5 unit diameter:
   A. Command: _____
   B. Specify center point for circle or [3P/2P/Ttr (tan tan radius)]: _____
   C. Specify radius of circle or [Diameter] *<current>*: _____
   D. Specify diameter of circle *<current>*: _____

2. Give the command, entries, and actions required to draw a circle that has a 1.75 unit radius and is tangent to an existing line and circle:
   A. Command: _____
   B. Specify center point for circle or [3P/2P/Ttr (tan tan radius)]: _____
   C. Specify point on object for first tangent of circle: _____
   D. Specify point on object for second tangent of circle: _____
   E. Specify radius of circle *<current>*: _____

3. Give the command, entries, and actions needed to draw a three-point arc:
   A. Command: _____
   B. Specify start point of arc or [Center]: _____
   C. Specify second point of arc or [Center/End]: _____
   D. Specify end point of arc: _____

4. Give the command, entries, and actions needed to draw an arc, beginning with the center point and having a 60° included angle:
   A. Command: _____
   B. Specify start point of arc or [Center]: _____
   C. Specify center point of arc: _____
   D. Specify start point of arc: _____
   E. Specify end point of arc or [Angle/chord Length]: _____
   F. Specify included angle: _____

5. Give the command, entries, and actions required to draw an arc tangent to the endpoint of a previously drawn line:
   A. Command: _____
   B. Specify start point of arc or [Center]: _____
   C. Specify end point of arc: _____

6. Give the command, entries, and actions needed to draw an ellipse with the **Axis, End** option:
   A. Command: _____
   B. Specify axis endpoint of ellipse or [Arc/Center]: _____
   C. Specify other endpoint of axis: _____
   D. Specify distance to other axis or [Rotation]: _____

7. Give the command, entries, and actions needed to draw a hexagon measuring 4" (102 mm) across the flats:
   A. Command: _____
   B. Enter number of sides *<current>*: _____
   C. Specify center of polygon or [Edge]: _____
   D. Enter an option [Inscribed in circle/Circumscribed about circle] *<current>*: _____
   E. Specify radius of circle: _____

8. Give the entries needed to draw two donuts with a .25 inside diameter and a .75 outside diameter:
   A. Command: _____
   B. Specify inside diameter of donut *<current>*: _____
   C. Specify outside diameter of donut *<current>*: _____

D. Specify center of donut or <exit>: _____
E. Specify center of donut or <exit>: _____
F. Specify center of donut or <exit>: _____

9. Define the term *included angle* as it applies to an arc.
10. List the three input options that can be used to draw an arc tangent to the endpoint of a previously drawn arc.
11. Given the distance across the flats of a hexagon, would you use the **Inscribed** or **Circumscribed** option to draw the hexagon?
12. Describe how a solid circle can be drawn.
13. Identify how to access the option that allows you to draw a circle tangent to three objects.
14. Identify two ways to access the **Arc** option for drawing elliptical arcs.
15. Name the AutoCAD system variable that lets you draw a true ellipse or a polyline ellipse with the **ELLIPSE** command.
16. Name the pull-down menu where the **RECTANG** command is found.
17. What is the default option if the **ARC** command is typed?
18. Give the easiest keyboard shortcut for the following commands:
    A. **CIRCLE**
    B. **ARC**
    C. **ELLIPSE**
    D. **POLYGON**
    E. **RECTANG**
    F. **DONUT**
19. Name the command option designed specifically for drawing rectangles with line width.
20. Name the command option used to draw rectangles with rounded corners.
21. Describe how you would draw a rectangle with different chamfer distances at each corner.
22. What is the **ELLIPSE** rotation angle that causes you to draw a circle?
23. Explain how to turn the **FILL** mode off while inside the **DONUT** command.
24. Name the system variable used to set the default radius when drawing circles.
25. How do you close a revision cloud?

Drawing Problems

Start AutoCAD and use a template or a setup option of your choice. Do not draw dimensions or text. Use your own judgment and approximate dimensions if needed.

1. You have just been given the sketch of a new sports car design (shown below). You are asked to create a drawing from the sketch. Use the **LINE** command and selected shape commands to draw the car. Do not be concerned with size and scale. Consider the commands and techniques used to draw the car, and try to minimize the number of entities. Save your drawing as P5-1.

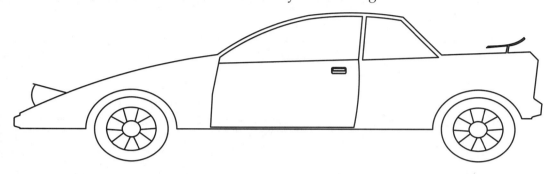

2. You have just been given the sketch of an innovative new truck design (shown below). You are asked to create a drawing from the sketch. Use the **LINE** command and selected shape commands to draw a truck resembling the sketch. Do not be concerned with size and scale. Save your drawing as P5-2.

3. Use the **LINE** and **CIRCLE** command options to draw the objects below. Do not include dimensions. Save the drawing as P5-3.

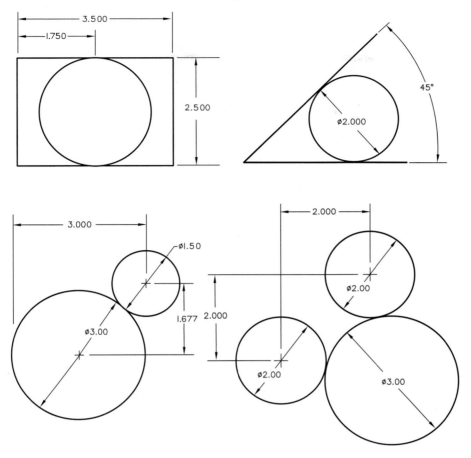

4. Use the **CIRCLE** and **ARC** command options to draw the object below. Do not include dimensions. Save the drawing as P5-4.

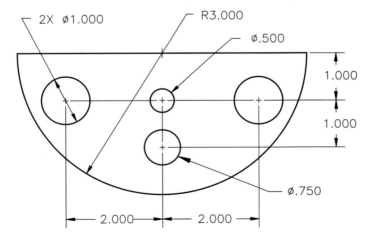

5. Draw the following object. Do not include dimensions.

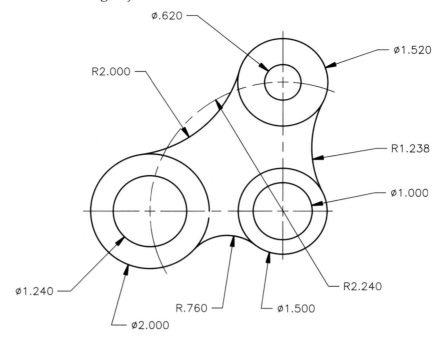

Ø.620
Ø1.520
R2.000
R1.238
Ø1.000
R2.240
Ø1.240
R.760
Ø1.500
Ø2.000

(Art courtesy of Bruce L. Wilcox)

6. Draw the pressure cylinder shown below. Use the **Arc** option of the **ELLIPSE** command to draw the cylinder ends. Do not draw the dimensions. Save the drawing as P5-6.

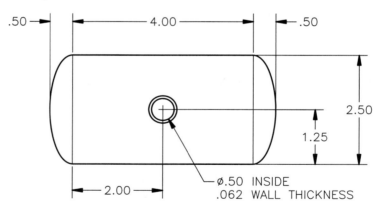

.50
4.00
.50
2.50
1.25
2.00
Ø.50 INSIDE
.062 WALL THICKNESS

7. Draw the hex head bolt pattern shown below. Do not draw dimensions. Save the drawing as P5-7.

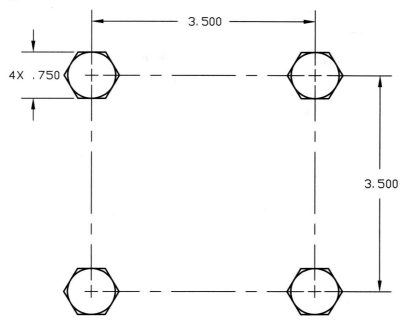

8. Draw the spacer below. Do not draw the dimensions. Save the drawing as P5-8.

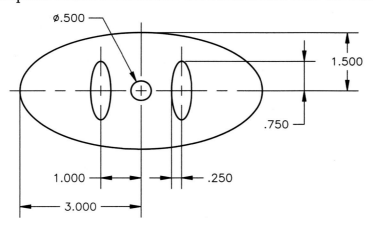

9. Draw the following object. Do not draw the dimensions. Save the drawing as P5-9.

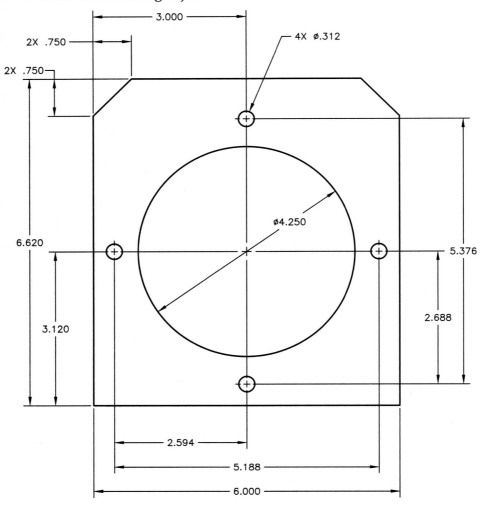

10. Draw the following object. Do not draw the dimensions. Save the drawing as P5-10.

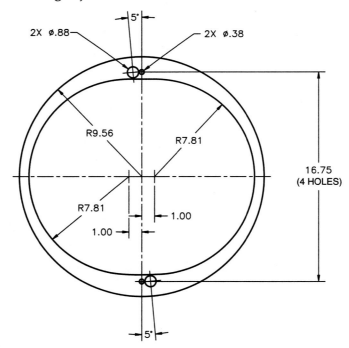

11. Create this controller integrated circuit diagram. Use a ruler or scale to keep the proportion as close as possible. Do not include the text. Save the drawing as **P5-11**.

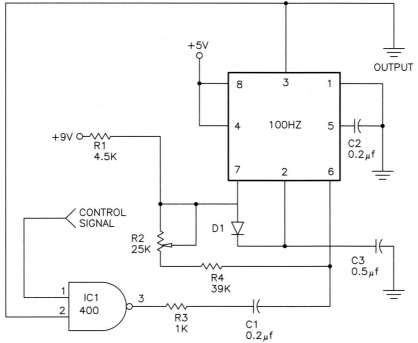

12. Draw this elevation using the **ARC**, **CIRCLE**, and **RECTANG** commands. Do not be concerned with size and scale. Save the drawing as **P5-12**.

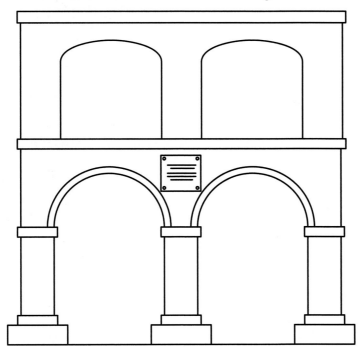

Drawing Problems - Chapter 5

13. Create a 1/2″ hex nut with 3/4″ across the flats and a .422″ root diameter as shown. Save the drawing as P5-13.

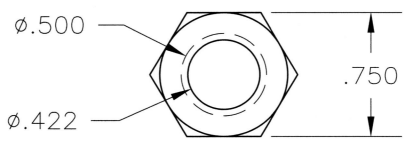

14. Open P4-5 and add the solid circles (donuts) to the cells in the schedule. Save the drawing as P5-14.

15. Draw the object shown below. Save the drawing as P5-15.

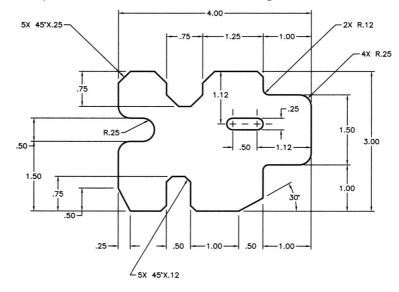

16. Draw the gasket shown below. Save the drawing as P5-16.

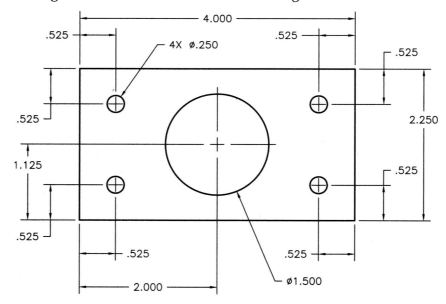

For Problems 17–22, draw the part shown. Save your drawing as **P15-***(problem number).*

17.

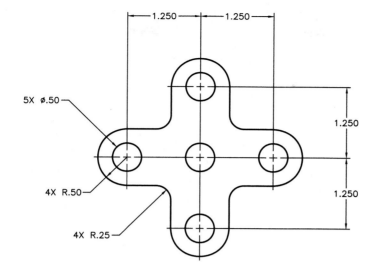

18.

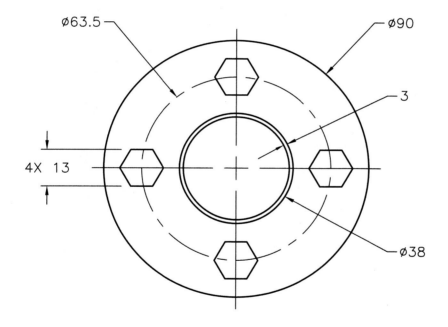

19.

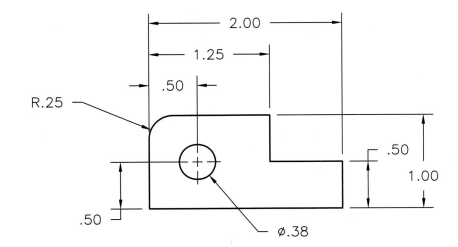

20.

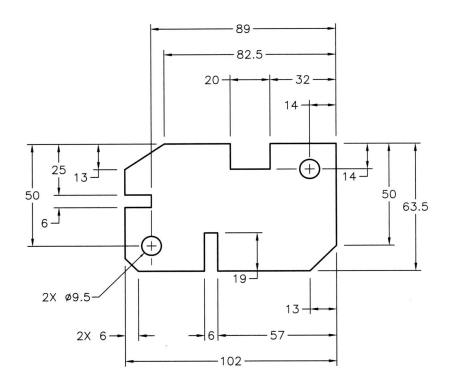

21.

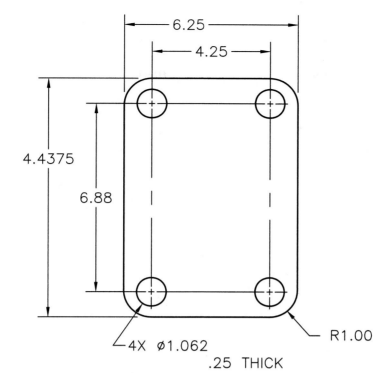

6.25

4.25

4.4375

6.88

4X ⌀1.062

.25 THICK

R1.00

22.

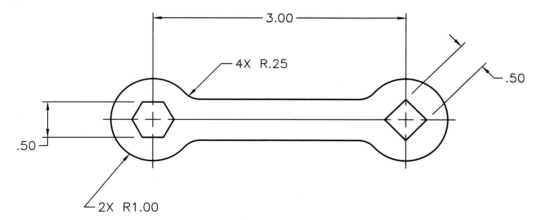

3.00

4X R.25

.50

.50

2X R1.00

23. Draw the pipe fitting shown. Save the drawing as P5-23.

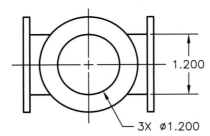

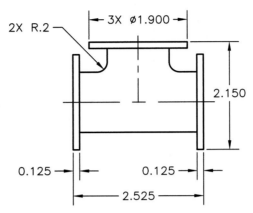

24. Draw the elbow shown. Save the drawing as P5-24.

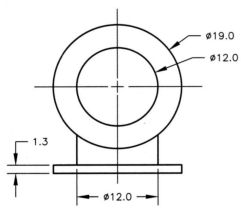

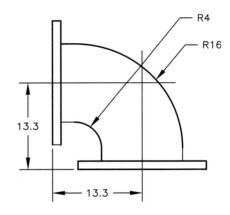

25. Draw the elbow shown. Save the drawing as P5-25.

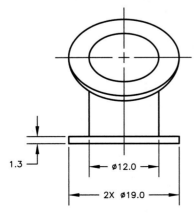

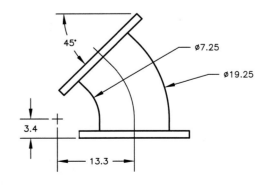

26. Draw a drift boat similar to the one shown below. Estimate dimensions. Save the drawing as P5-26.

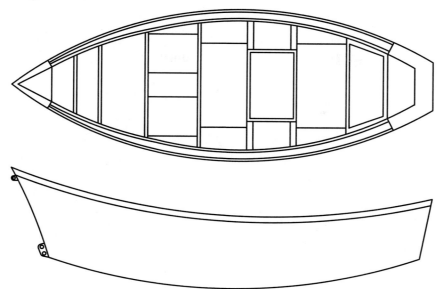

27. Draw the fishing boat shown. Save the drawing as P5-27.

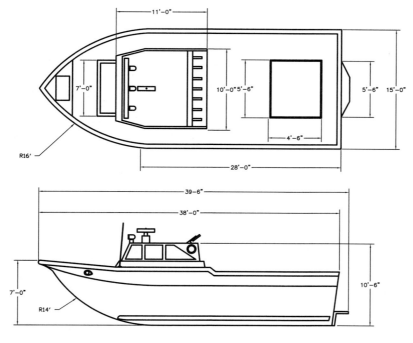

28. Draw the ellipse template shown. Save the drawing as P5-28.

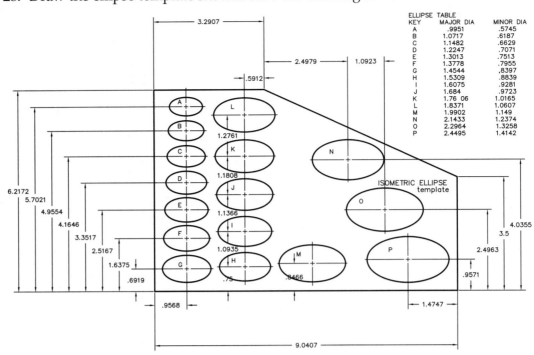

ELLIPSE TABLE

KEY	MAJOR DIA	MINOR DIA
A	.9951	.5745
B	1.0717	.6187
C	1.1482	.6629
D	1.2247	.7071
E	1.3013	.7513
F	1.3778	.7955
G	1.4544	.8397
H	1.5309	.8839
I	1.6075	.9281
J	1.684	.9723
K	1.76 06	1.0165
L	1.8371	1.0607
M	1.9902	1.149
N	2.1433	1.2374
O	2.2964	1.3258
P	2.4495	1.4142

ISOMETRIC ELLIPSE
template

CHAPTER 6

Object Snap and AutoTrack

Learning Objectives

After completing this chapter, you will be able to do the following:

- Use object snap modes to create precision drawings.
- Use object snap overrides for single point selections.
- Set running object snap modes for continuous use.
- Use the AutoSnap features to speed up point specifications.
- Adjust marker size based on point selection needs.
- Use temporary tracking and AutoTrack modes to locate points relative to other points in a drawing.
- Use polar tracking and polar snap.

This chapter explains how the powerful object snap and AutoTrack™ features are used when creating and editing your drawing. *Osnap* means *object snap*. Object snap can be used to visually preview and confirm point options prior to selection. AutoTrack creates and deletes construction lines automatically. After these features are detailed, you will learn how to take advantage of their strengths when creating geometry.

Object Snap

Object snap is one of the most useful tools found in AutoCAD. It increases your drafting performance and accuracy. *Snapping* is the process of picking a point near the intended position and having the cursor "snap" exactly to the specific point.

Object snap modes identify the object snap point. For instance, the **Endpoint** object snap mode automatically selects a line's endpoint, and the **Midpoint** object snap mode automatically selects a line's midpoint. The AutoSnap™ feature provides visual cues related to the active object snap modes. There are two methods of activating object snap modes: running object snaps and snap overrides. These topics are covered in more detail in the following sections.

The AutoSnap feature is enabled by default. With AutoSnap active, visual cues are displayed while snapping. This helps you in visualizing and confirming candidate points for object snap. These visual cues appear as *markers* displayed at the current selection point. **Figure 6-1** shows two examples of visual cues provided by AutoSnap.

Figure 6-1.
AutoSnap displays markers and related tooltips for object snap modes.

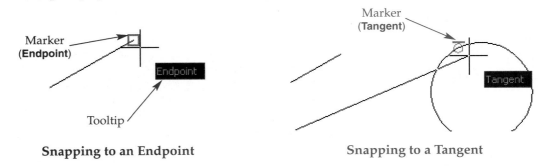

Snapping to an Endpoint   Snapping to a Tangent

The visual cue for an **Endpoint** object snap is shown as a square when the cursor is placed close to the line object. After a brief pause, a tooltip is displayed, indicating the object snap mode. The AutoSnap symbol for a tangency point is shown as a circle with a tangent horizontal line.

Object Snap Overrides

When you want to activate an object snap mode for a single point selection, use an *object snap override*. Activate the object snap override when you are prompted to select a point. This temporarily suspends any running object snap modes (which are defined later in this chapter). After you select the point, the running object snap modes are reactivated.

After entering a command, an object snap override can be activated in any of three ways:

- **Object Snap shortcut menu.** This shortcut menu lists the object snap modes. See **Figure 6-2.** To access the **Object Snap** shortcut menu when selecting a point, right-click and pick **Snap Overrides** or hold the [Shift] key and right-click.
- **Object Snap toolbar.** The **Object Snap** toolbar includes buttons for each object snap mode. See **Figure 6-3.** Pick the appropriate button to activate the snap override. To access this toolbar, right-click on any toolbar button and select **Object Snap** from the shortcut menu.

Figure 6-2.
The **Object Snap** shortcut menu provides quick access to object snap overrides.

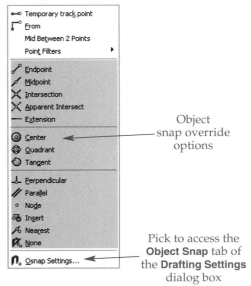

Object
snap override
options

Pick to access the
Object Snap tab of
the **Drafting Settings**
dialog box

Figure 6-3.
The **Object Snap** toolbar.

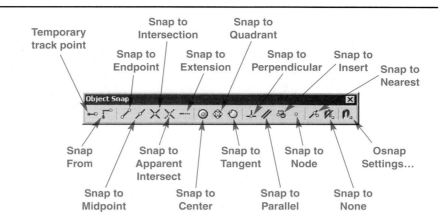

- **Keyboard entry.** Each object snap override can be activated by typing a three-letter abbreviation at a point selection prompt.

> **PROFESSIONAL TIP**
>
> Use the object snap modes not only when drawing, but also when editing. With practice, using object snaps becomes second nature, greatly increasing your productivity and accuracy.

Object Snap Modes

The table in **Figure 6-4** summarizes the object snap modes. Included with each mode is the marker that appears on-screen and its button from the **Object Snap** toolbar. Each object snap mode selects a different portion of an object.

> **PROFESSIONAL TIP**
>
> Remember that object snap overrides are not commands. They are, however, used in conjunction with commands. If you type MID when no command is active, for example, AutoCAD displays the following error message: Unknown command "MID". Press F1 for help.

Practice with the different object snap modes to find the ones that work best in various situations. Be sure to clear the previous object snap mode before activating the next one. Object snaps can be used during many commands, such as **LINE**, **CIRCLE**, **ARC**, **MOVE**, **COPY**, and **INSERT**. The most common uses for object snaps are discussed in the following sections.

Endpoint object snap

In many cases, you need to connect a line, an arc, or a center point of a circle to the endpoint of an existing line or arc. Select the **Endpoint** object snap mode and move the cursor past the midpoint of the line or arc, toward the end to be picked. A small square marks the endpoint that will be picked. Pick to begin drawing the new object. See **Figure 6-5.**

Figure 6-4.
The object snap modes.

Object Snap Modes			
Mode	**Marker**	**Button**	**Description**
Endpoint	□		Finds the nearest endpoint of a line, arc, polyline, elliptical arc, spline, ellipse, ray, solid, or multiline.
Midpoint	△		Finds the middle point of any object having two endpoints, such as a line, polyline, arc, elliptical arc, polyline arc, spline, ray, solid, xline, or multiline.
Center	○		Locates the center point of a radial object, including circles, arcs, ellipses, elliptical arcs, and radial solids.
Quadrant	◇		Picks the closest of the four quadrant points that can be found on circles, arcs, elliptical arcs, ellipses, and radial solids. (Not all of these objects may have all four quadrants.)
Intersection	×		Picks the closest intersection of two objects.
Apparent Intersection	⊠		Selects a visual intersection between two objects that appear to intersect on screen in the current view, but may not actually intersect each other in 3D space.
Extension	+		Finds a point along the imaginary extension of an existing line, polyline, arc, polyline arc, elliptical arc, spline, ray, xline, solid, or multiline.
Insertion	⬐		Finds the insertion point of text objects and blocks.
Perpendicular	⌐		Finds a point that is perpendicular to an object from the previously picked point.
Parallel	∥		Used to find any point along an imaginary line parallel to an existing line or polyline.
Tangent	ⵔ		Finds points of tangency between radial and linear objects.
Nearest	⊠		Locates the point on an object closest to the crosshairs.
Node	⊗		Picks a point object drawn with the **POINT**, **DIVIDE**, or **MEASURE** command.
None			Turns running object snap off.

Figure 6-5.
Using **Endpoint** object snap.

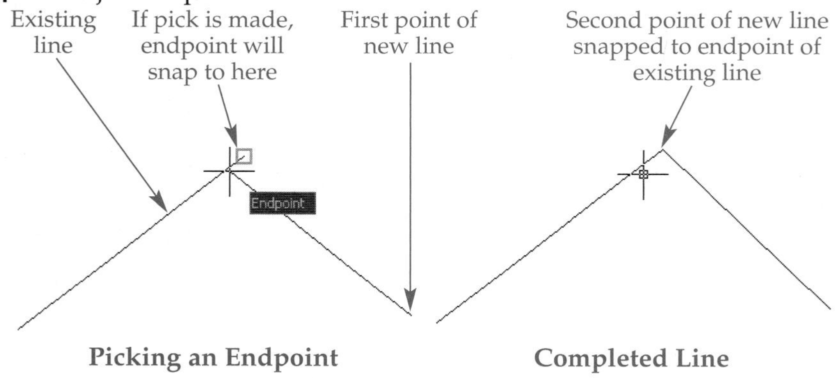

Existing line If pick is made, endpoint will snap to here First point of new line Second point of new line snapped to endpoint of existing line

Endpoint

Picking an Endpoint   Completed Line

The **Endpoint** object snap can be used to quickly select the endpoints of all types of lines and arcs. It is often selected as a running object snap.

Midpoint object snap

The **Midpoint** object snap mode finds and picks the midpoint of a line, a polyline, or an arc. During a command, type MID, pick the **Snap to Midpoint** button on the **Object Snap** toolbar, or select **Midpoint** from the **Object Snap** shortcut menu to activate this object snap mode. Position the cursor near the midpoint of the object. See **Figure 6-6**.

Exercise 6-1   Complete the Exercise on the Student CD.

Center object snap

The **Center** object snap mode allows you to snap to the center point of a circle, a donut, an ellipse, an elliptical arc, a polyline arc, or an arc. During a command, type CEN, pick the **Snap to Center** button on the **Object Snap** toolbar, or pick **Center** from the **Object Snap** shortcut menu.

Be sure to move the cursor near the perimeter, not the center point, of the object. For example, when locating the center of a large circle, the **Center** object snap mode will *not* locate the center if the cursor is not near the perimeter of the circle. See **Figure 6-7**.

Figure 6-6.
Using **Midpoint** object snap.

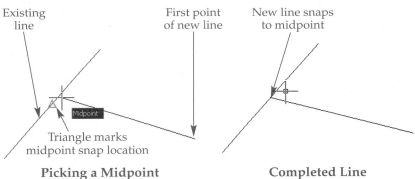

Picking a Midpoint   Completed Line

Figure 6-7.
Using **Center** object snap.

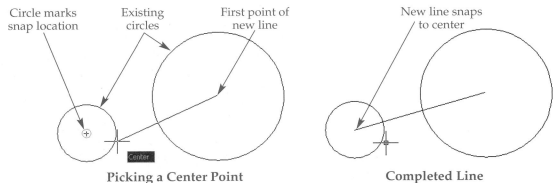

Picking a Center Point   Completed Line

Quadrant object snap

A *quadrant* is a quarter section of a circle, a donut, or an ellipse. The **Quadrant** object snap mode finds the 0°, 90°, 180°, and 270° positions on a circle, a donut, an ellipse, an elliptical arc, a polyline arc, or an arc. See **Figure 6-8.** When picking quadrants, locate the crosshairs near the intended quadrant on the circle, donut, ellipse, or arc.

NOTE	Quadrant positions are unaffected by the current angle zero direction, but they always coincide with the current world coordinate system (WCS). The WCS is discussed later in this chapter. The quadrant points of a circle, a donut, or an arc are at the top, bottom, left, and right, regardless of the rotation of the object. The quadrant points of ellipses and elliptical arcs, however, rotate with the objects.

Exercise 6-2 Complete the Exercise on the Student CD.

Intersection object snap

The **Intersection** object snap mode is used to snap to the intersection of two or more objects. This mode is activated by typing INT at the selection prompt, picking the **Snap to Intersection** button on the **Object Snap** toolbar, or picking **Intersection** from the **Object Snap** shortcut menu. Move the cursor near the intersection to cause a small "X" to appear at the intersection. See **Figure 6-9.**

Apparent Intersection object snap

The *apparent intersection* is the point where two objects created in 3D space appear to intersect based on the current view. Three-dimensional objects that are far apart may appear to intersect when viewed from certain angles. Whether they intersect or not, this option returns the coordinate point where the objects appear to intersect. This is a valuable option when working with 3D drawings. Creating and editing 3D objects is discussed in *AutoCAD and Its Applications—Advanced.*

Figure 6-8.
The four quadrant points of a circle can be selected with the **Quadrant** object snap.

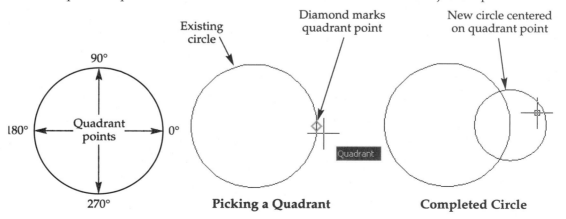

Figure 6-9.
Using **Intersection** object snap.

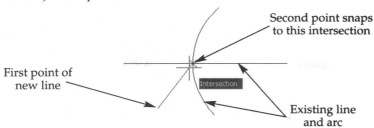

Second point snaps
to this intersection

First point of
new line

Intersection

Existing line
and arc

Extension object snap

The **Extension** object snap mode is used to find any point along the imaginary extension of an existing line, polyline, or polyline arc. This mode is activated by typing EXT at the selection prompt, picking the **Snap to Extension** button on the **Object Snap** toolbar, or picking **Extension** from the **Object Snap** shortcut menu. The **Extension** object snap differs from most other snaps because it requires more than one selection point. The initial point, called the *acquired point*, is not selected in the typical manner, but is found by simply moving the cursor over the line, polyline, or polyline arc from which the new object is to be extended. When the object is found, a (+) symbol marks the location. If the new object is to be created at the intersection of extensions from two objects, the cursor must be placed over the second object to locate its extension path. The last point, which is the actual snap point, can be placed anywhere along the extension path, including the intersection of two extension paths. The *extension path*, represented by a dashed line or arc, extends from the acquired point to the current location of the cursor.

Line A in **Figure 6-10** is an example of the way the **Extension** object snap can create a new line anywhere along the extension of an existing object. The first acquired point is found by moving the cursor directly over the upper-right corner of the rectangle. The tooltip for the extension is displayed, and the (+) marker becomes visible at the end of the line. While the dotted extension line is displayed, the first point can be

Figure 6-10.
The **Extension** object snap can be used to create a line from an extended intersection to an extended endpoint.

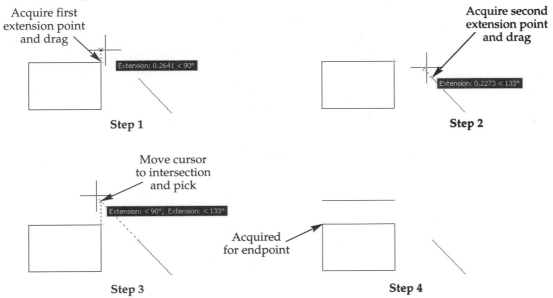

Acquire first
extension point
and drag

Extension: 0.2641 < 90°

Step 1

Acquire second
extension point
and drag

Extension: 0.2273 < 133°

Step 2

Move cursor
to intersection
and pick

Extension: < 90°, Extension: < 133°

Step 3

Acquired
for endpoint

Step 4

picked. The second acquired point is found in the same manner at the endpoint of the line on the right. Pick near the intersection of the extension lines to locate the starting point of the new line.

The **Extension** object snap can also be used to create the new line a specific distance away from the end of the old line. In **Figure 6-11**, the distance (0.8) is typed while the first extension is displayed.

Exercise 6-3   Complete the Exercise on the Student CD.

Extended Intersection object snap

There is one object snap that is available only as a snap override—*extended intersection*. When using **Extended Intersection**, you select the objects one at a time, and the intersection point is automatically located. This is especially useful when two objects do not actually intersect and you need to access the point where these objects would intersect if they were extended.

To activate **Extended Intersection**, select the **Intersection** object snap override and pick an object (rather than an intersection). If the cursor is near an object, but not close to an actual intersection, the tooltip reads Extended Intersection, and the AutoSnap marker is followed by an ellipsis (...). **Figure 6-12** shows the use of **Extended Intersection** to find an intersection point between a line and an arc.

If the intersection point is not in the currently visible screen area, the AutoSnap marker is not displayed when selecting the second object. You can still confirm the point, however, before picking. Keeping the cursor motionless over the second object will display the tooltip, which confirms the objects intersect somewhere beyond the currently visible area. When selecting two objects that could not intersect, no AutoSnap marker or tooltip is displayed, and no intersection point is found if the pick is made.

Exercise 6-4   Complete the Exercise on the Student CD.

Perpendicular object snap

In geometric construction, it is common to draw one object perpendicular to another. This is done using the **Perpendicular** object snap mode. To activate this mode, type PER at the selection prompt, pick the **Snap to Perpendicular** button in the **Object Snap** toolbar, or pick **Perpendicular** from the **Object Snap** shortcut menu. A small right-angle symbol appears at the snap point. This mode can be used with arcs, elliptical arcs, ellipses, splines, xlines, multilines, polylines, solids, traces, or circles.

Figure 6-11.
Using the **Extension** object snap to create a line 0.8 units away from a rectangle.

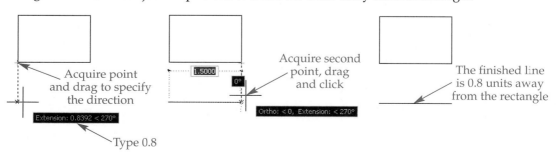

Figure 6-12.

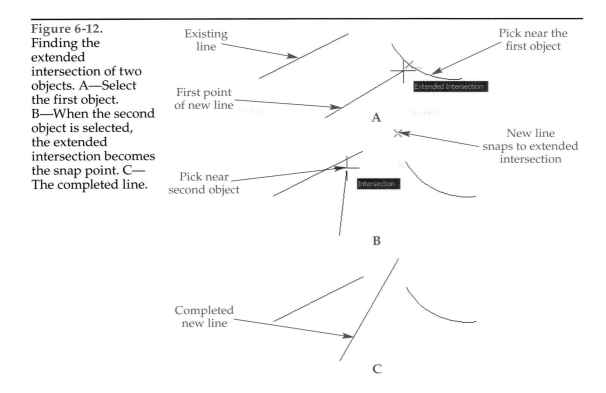

Figure 6-12.
Finding the
extended
intersection of two
objects. A—Select
the first object.
B—When the second
object is selected,
the extended
intersection becomes
the snap point. C—
The completed line.

Figure 6-13 shows the **Perpendicular** object snap being used to locate the second point of a line perpendicular to a vertical line, an angled line, and a circle. In **Figure 6-14**, the object snap is used to start the line perpendicular to each object. The tooltip reads Deferred Perpendicular, and the AutoSnap marker is followed by an ellipsis (...). The term *deferred perpendicular* means the calculation of the perpendicular point is delayed until another point is picked. The second endpoint determines the location of the entire line.

It is important to understand that perpendicularity is calculated from points picked and not as a relationship between objects. Also, perpendicularity is measured at the point of intersection. Therefore, it is possible to draw a line perpendicular to a circle or an arc.

Exercise 6-5   Complete the Exercise on the Student CD.

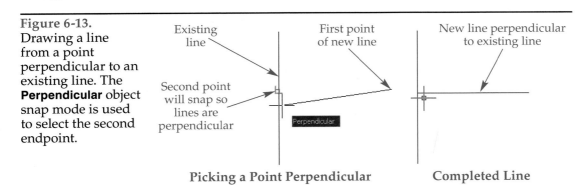

Figure 6-13.
Drawing a line
from a point
perpendicular to an
existing line. The
Perpendicular object
snap mode is used
to select the second
endpoint.

Figure 6-14.
Deferring the perpendicular location until the second point is selected. The **Perpendicular** object snap mode is used to select the first endpoint.

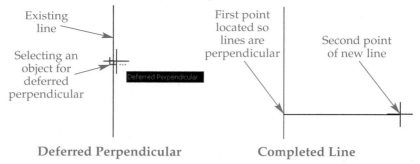

Deferred Perpendicular   Completed Line

Tangent object snap

The **Tangent** object snap is used to align objects tangentially to an arc, circle, ellipse, elliptical arc, and spline. To activate this mode, type TAN at the selection prompt, pick the **Snap to Tangent** button on the **Object Snap** toolbar, or pick **Tangent** from the **Object Snap** shortcut menu.

In Figure 6-15, the endpoint of a line is located using the **Tangent** object snap mode. The first point is selected normally. As the cursor is placed near the tangent point on the circle, AutoCAD determines the tangent point and places the snap point there.

When creating an object tangent to another object, multiple points may be needed to fix the tangency point. For example, the point where a line is tangent to a circle cannot be found without knowing the locations of both ends of the line. Until both points have been specified, the object snap specification is for *deferred tangency*. Once both endpoints are known, the tangency is calculated, and the object is drawn in the correct location. In Figure 6-16, a line is drawn tangent to two circles.

Exercise 6-6   Complete the Exercise on the Student CD.

Figure 6-15.
Using **Tangent** object snap.

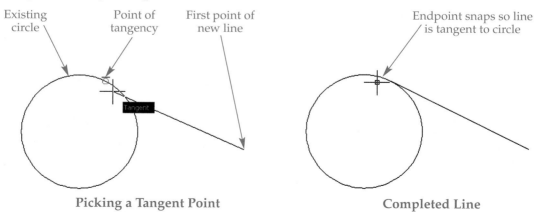

Picking a Tangent Point   Completed Line

Figure 6-16.
Drawing a line
tangent to two
circles.

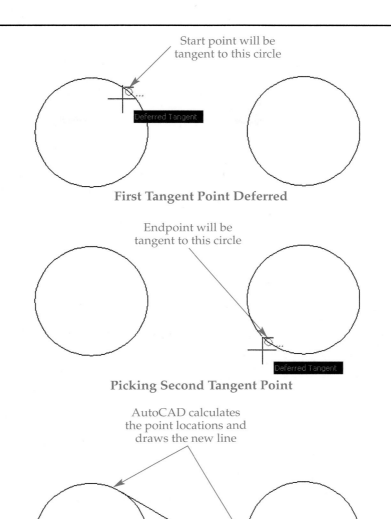

Start point will be
tangent to this circle

Deferred Tangent

First Tangent Point Deferred

Endpoint will be
tangent to this circle

Deferred Tangent

Picking Second Tangent Point

AutoCAD calculates
the point locations and
draws the new line

Completed Line

Parallel object snap

The process of drawing, moving, or copying objects that are not horizontal or vertical is improved with the **Parallel** object snap mode. This option is used to find any point along an imaginary line that is parallel to an existing line or polyline. Polylines are discussed in Chapter 14. To activate the **Parallel** object snap mode, type PAR at the selection prompt, pick the **Snap to Parallel** button on the **Object Snap** toolbar, or pick **Parallel** from the **Object Snap** shortcut menu.

The **Parallel** object snap is similar to the **Extension** object snap because it requires more than one selection point. The *acquired point* is found by pausing the cursor over any point on the line to which the new object is to be parallel. When the object is found and you move the cursor in a direction parallel to the existing line, a (//) symbol marks the existing line. A dashed line, parallel to the existing line, extends from the cursor's location. This line is known as the *parallel alignment path*. The last point, which is the actual snap point, can be placed anywhere along the parallel alignment path. When the alignment path is displayed, the **Parallel** snap marker appears on the line from which the parallel is used. Picking any location along the parallel alignment path creates the second point of the parallel line. Figure 6-17 shows an example of the **Parallel** object snap being used to draw a line parallel to an existing line.

Figure 6-17.
Using the **Parallel** object snap option to draw a line parallel to an existing line. A—Select the first endpoint for the new line, select the **Parallel** object snap, and then move the crosshairs near the existing line to acquire a point. B—After the parallel point is acquired, move the crosshairs near the location of the parallel line, and an extension path appears.

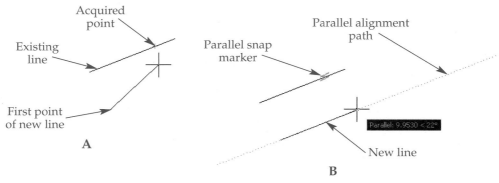

Exercise
6-7   Complete the Exercise on the Student CD.

Node object snap

Point objects can be snapped to using the **Node** object snap mode. In order for object snap to find the point object, the point must be in a visible display mode. Controlling the point display mode is covered later in this chapter.

Nearest object snap

When you need to specify a point that is on an object, but cannot be located with any of the other object snap modes, the **Nearest** mode can be used. This object snap locates the point on the object closest to the crosshair location. It should be used when you want an object to touch an existing object, but the location of the intersection is not critical.

Consider drawing a line object that is to end on another line. Trying to pick the point with the crosshairs is inaccurate because you are relying only on your screen and mouse resolution. The line you draw may fall short or extend past the line. Using **Nearest** ensures that the point is precisely on the object.

DDOSNAP

Type
DDOSNAP
OSNAP
OS
Pull-Down Menu
Tools
> Drafting
Settings...
Toolbar
Object Snap
Osnap Settings...

Running Object Snaps

You can set an object snap mode by using the **Object Snap** tab in the **Drafting Settings** dialog box. To access this dialog box, pick **Tools** > **Drafting Settings...** from the pull-down menu; pick the **Osnap Settings...** button from the **Object Snap** toolbar; right-click on the **OSNAP** or **OTRACK** button on the status bar and select **Settings...** from the shortcut menu; or type OS, OSNAP, or DDOSNAP. You can also type DSETTINGS to access the **Drafting Settings** dialog box.

The **Object Snap** tab of the **Drafting Settings** dialog box is shown in **Figure 6-18.** Notice that the **Endpoint**, **Intersection**, **Extension**, and **Parallel** modes are active. The object snaps that are selected in this dialog box are called *running object snaps*. You can use this dialog box at any time to discontinue a running object snap or to set additional modes.

When you need to make several point specifications without the aid of object snap, you can toggle running object snaps off by picking the **OSNAP** button on the status bar. The advantage of this method is that you can make several picks and then restore the same running object snap modes by picking the **OSNAP** button again. You

Figure 6-18.
Running object snap modes can be set in the **Drafting Settings** dialog box.

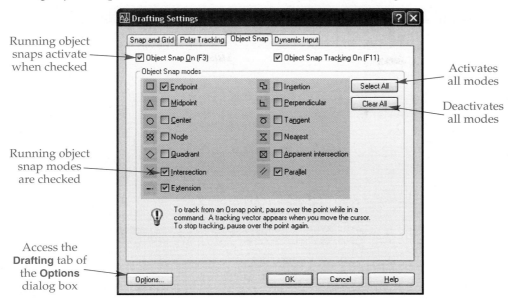

Running object snaps activate when checked

Running object snap modes are checked

Access the **Drafting** tab of the **Options** dialog box

Activates all modes

Deactivates all modes

can also right-click on the **OSNAP** button and pick **Off** from the shortcut menu (pick **On** to restore the running object snaps), pick the **Object Snap On (F3)** check box in the **Drafting Settings** dialog box, or press the [F3] key on your keyboard. Any of these options can be used to toggle running object snaps.

You can remove the active checks in the **Drafting Settings** dialog box as needed to disable running object snaps. You can also pick the **Clear All** button to disable all running modes. Select desired running object snaps by picking the associated boxes or pick the **Select All** button to activate all object snaps.

PROFESSIONAL TIP

By default, a keyboard entry overrides any currently running object snap modes. This behavior can be changed in the **Priority for Coordinate Data Entry** area in the **User Preferences** tab of the **Options** dialog box.

Exercise 6-8

Complete the Exercise on the Student CD.

AutoSnap Settings

To customize the appearance and functionality of the AutoSnap feature, access the **Object Snap** tab of the **Drafting Settings** dialog box and pick the **Options...** button in the lower-left corner. This opens the **Drafting** tab of the **Options** dialog box, shown in **Figure 6-19.** To activate an AutoSnap option, check the corresponding check box:

- **Marker.** Toggles the AutoSnap marker display.
- **Magnet.** Toggles the AutoSnap magnet. When active, the magnet snaps the cursor to the object snap point.
- **Display AutoSnap tooltip.** Toggles the tooltip display.

Figure 6-19.
Setting AutoSnap features.

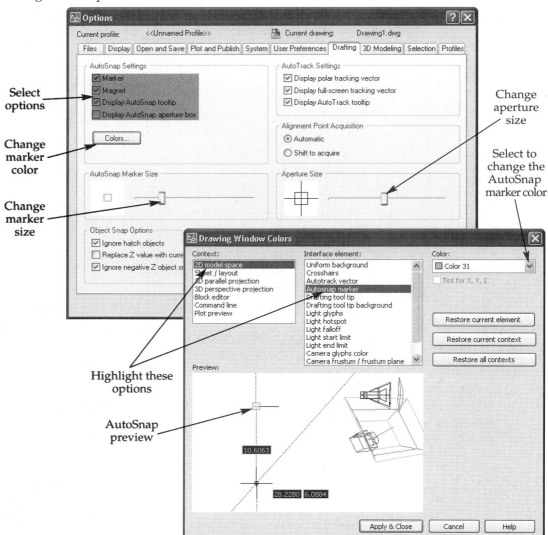

- **Display AutoSnap aperture box.** Toggles the display of the aperture.

The marker color and size can also be adjusted to suit your needs. For example, the default marker color is yellow, but this is difficult to see if you have the graphics screen background set to white. Pick the **Colors:** button to access the **Drawing Window Colors** dialog box. Highlight the **2D model space** selection in the **Context:** list and the **Autosnap marker** in the **Interface element:** list. Access the **Color:** drop-down list, and select the desired color. Pick **Apply & Close** to return to the **Options** dialog box.

At higher screen resolutions, a larger marker size improves visibility. While the **Drafting** tab of the **Options** dialog box is still open, move the slider in the **AutoSnap Marker Size** area to change the size. **Ignore hatch objects** determines whether or not you can snap to hatch patterns. Hatching is discussed in Chapter 21.

Exercise 6-9   Complete the Exercise on the Student CD.

Changing the aperture size

When selecting a point using object snaps, the cursor must be within a specific range of a candidate point before the point is located. The object snap detection system finds everything within a square area centered at the cursor location. This square area is called the *aperture* and is invisible by default.

To display the aperture, open the **Drafting Settings** dialog box and pick the **Options...** button from the **Object Snap** tab. The **Drafting** tab of the **Options** dialog box appears. Activate the **Display AutoSnap aperture box** check box. Having the aperture visible may be helpful when you are first learning to work with object snap.

To change the size of the aperture, move the slider in the **Aperture Size** area. Various aperture sizes are shown in **Figure 6-20.**

Keep in mind that the *aperture* and the *pick box* are different. The aperture is displayed on the screen when object snap modes are active. The pick box appears on the screen for any command that activates the Select objects: prompt.

Exercise 6-10   Complete the Exercise on the Student CD.

Figure 6-20. Aperture box size is measured in pixels. The three examples here are not shown in actual size, but they are provided to show the size relationships among different settings.

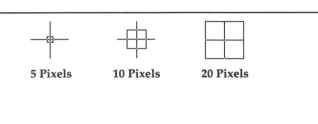

5 Pixels   10 Pixels   20 Pixels

AutoTrack

Creating geometry that lines up with existing geometry is very common in drafting and design. AutoTrack makes this procedure straightforward and accurate by creating alignment paths and tracking vectors when needed. *Alignment paths* are temporary lines and arcs that coincide with the position of existing objects. *Tracking vectors* are temporary lines that are displayed at specific angles, typically 0, 90, 180, and 270 degrees.

There are two AutoTrack modes: *object snap tracking* and *polar tracking*. Any commands requiring a point selection, such as the **COPY**, **MOVE**, and **LINE** commands, can make use of these modes.

Object Snap Tracking

Object snap tracking is always used in conjunction with object snaps. When this mode is active, placing the crosshairs near an AutoSnap marker will acquire the point. Once a point is acquired, horizontal and vertical alignment paths are available for locating points.

The [F11] function key and the **OTRACK** button on the status bar toggle object snap tracking on and off. This mode is only available for points selected by the currently active object snap modes. When running object snaps are active, all selected object

Figure 6-21.
Using object snap tracking to draw a line. A—The first endpoint is located at the midpoint of the existing line. The alignment path is displayed when the crosshairs are near. B—The completed line, with the second endpoint identified using direct distance entry along the alignment path.

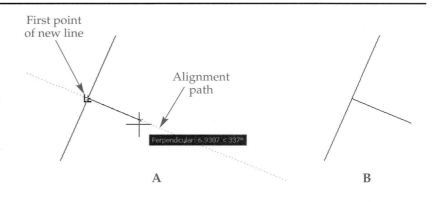

snap modes are available for object snap tracking. These modes are not available for object snap tracking, however, if running object snaps are deactivated.

In **Figure 6-21**, object snap tracking is used in conjunction with the **Perpendicular** and **Midpoint** running object snaps to draw a line that is 2 units long and perpendicular to the existing, slanted line. The running object snap modes are set before the following command sequence is initiated. The **OSNAP** and **OTRACK** buttons on the status bar are active.

> Command: **L** *or* **LINE**↵
> Specify first point: *(pick the midpoint of the existing line)*
> Specify next point or [Undo]: *(pause the crosshairs near the first point to acquire it, and then position the crosshairs as shown in Figure 6-21A to activate the perpendicular alignment path)* **2**↵
> Specify next point or [Undo]: ↵
> Command:

The previous example used object snap tracking to orient a new line based on an existing line. Object snap tracking can also be used to position new geometry based on the locations of existing geometry. In **Figure 6-22**, object snap tracking is used to position a circle directly above the midpoint of a horizontal line and to the right of the midpoint of an angled line, with only the **Midpoint** running object snap on. The **OSNAP** and **OTRACK** buttons on the status bar are active.

> Command: **C** *or* **CIRCLE**↵
> Specify center point for circle or [Undo]: *(pause the crosshairs near the midpoint of the horizontal line to acquire it, and then pause the crosshairs near the midpoint of the angled line to acquire it. Move the cursor to the position as shown in Figure 6-22B until two tracking vectors appear. Pick to locate the center of the circle.)*
> Specify radius of circle or [Undo]: *(drag the cursor to specify any radius and pick to complete the circle)*
> Command:

PROFESSIONAL TIP

AutoTracking is similar in performance to the **Extension** object snap. Experiment with a combination of just the **Endpoint** object snap mode and AutoTracking. Try a combination of **Endpoint** and **Extension** object snap modes without AutoTracking to see the difference. Notice that without object snap tracking, you cannot drag in a direction perpendicular to an endpoint.

Figure 6-22.
Object snap tracking is used to position this circle in line with the midpoints of each line.

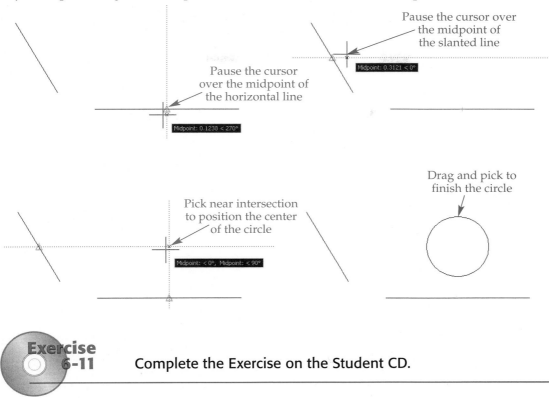

Pause the cursor over the midpoint of the slanted line

Pause the cursor over the midpoint of the horizontal line

Midpoint: 0.3121 < 0°

Midpoint: 0.1238 < 270°

Drag and pick to finish the circle

Pick near intersection to position the center of the circle

Midpoint: < 0°, Midpoint: < 90°

Exercise 6-11 Complete the Exercise on the Student CD.

Polar Tracking

Ortho mode, discussed in Chapter 3, forces the cursor movement to orthogonal (horizontal and vertical) orientations. When Ortho mode is turned on and the **LINE** command is in use, all new line segments are drawn at 0°, 90°, 180°, or 270°. Polar tracking works in much the same way, but it allows for a greater range of angles.

Selecting the **POLAR** button from the status bar or using the [F10] function key turns polar tracking on and off. AutoCAD automatically turns Ortho off when polar tracking is on, and it turns polar tracking off when Ortho is on. You cannot use polar tracking and Ortho at the same time.

When polar tracking mode is turned on, the cursor snaps to preset incremental angles if a point is being located relative to another point. For example, when using the **LINE** command, polar tracking is not active for the first endpoint selection, but it is available for the second and subsequent point selections. Polar tracking vectors are displayed as dashed lines whenever the cursor comes into alignment with any of these preset angles.

To set incremental angles, use the **Polar Tracking** tab in the **Drafting Settings** dialog box. To access this dialog box, right-click on the **POLAR** button from the status bar, and then select **Settings**; pick **Tools > Drafting Settings...** from the pull-down menu; or type DSETTINGS or DS. **Figure 6-23** shows the **Polar Tracking** tab of the **Drafting Settings** dialog box.

The following features are found in the **Polar Tracking** tab:
- **Polar Tracking On (F10).** Check this box, press the [F10] key, or pick the **POLAR** button on the status bar to turn polar tracking on.
- **Polar Angle Settings area.** This area of the dialog box allows you to set the desired polar angle increments. It contains the following items:

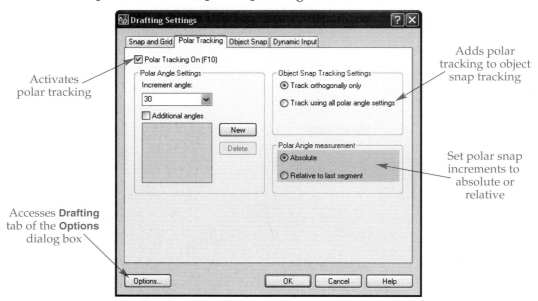

Activates polar tracking

Adds polar tracking to object snap tracking

Set polar snap increments to absolute or relative

Accesses **Drafting** tab of the **Options** dialog box

- **Increment angle.** This drop-down list is set at 90 by default. This setting provides angle increments every 90°. Open the drop-down list to select from a variety of preset angles. The setting in Figure 6-23 provides polar tracking in 30° increments. The increment angle can also be adjusted by changing the value of the **POLARANG** system variable.
- **Additional angles.** This check box activates your own angle increments. To do this, pick the **New** button to open a text box in the window. Type the desired angle. Pick the **New** button each time you want to add another angle. The additional angles are used together with the increment angle setting when you use polar tracking. Use the **Delete** button to remove angles from the list. You can make the additional angle(s) inactive by turning off the **Additional angles** check box. An additional angle can also be added or changed using the **POLARADDANG** system variable.
- **Object Snap Tracking Settings area.** This area is used to set the angles available with object snap tracking. If **Track orthogonally only** is selected, only horizontal and vertical alignment paths are active. If **Track using all polar angle settings** is selected, alignment paths for all polar snap angles are active.
- **Polar Angle measurement area.** This setting determines if the polar snap increments are constant or relative to the previous segment. If **Absolute** is selected, the polar snap angles are measured from the base angle of 0° set for the drawing. If **Relative to last segment** is selected, each increment angle is measured from a base angle established by the previously drawn segment.

Figure 6-24 shows a parallelogram being drawn with polar tracking active and set for 30° angle increments and absolute polar angle measurements. The following command sequence creates the parallelogram:

Command: **L** *or* **LINE**↵
Specify first point: *(select the first point)*
Specify next point or [Undo]: *(drag the cursor to the right while the polar alignment path indicates <0°)* **3**↵
Specify next point or [Undo]: *(drag the cursor to the 60° polar alignment path)* **1.5**↵
Specify next point or [Close/Undo]: *(drag the cursor to the 180° polar alignment path)* **3**↵
Specify next point or [Close/Undo]: **C**↵
Command:

Figure 6-24.
Using polar tracking with 30° angle increments to draw a parallelogram. A—After the first side is drawn, the alignment path and direct distance entry are used to create the second side. B—A horizontal alignment path is used for the third side. C—The parallelogram is completed with the **Close** option.

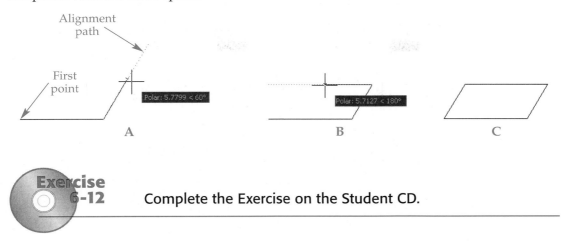

Exercise 6-12   Complete the Exercise on the Student CD.

Polar tracking with polar snaps

Polar tracking can also be used in conjunction with polar snaps. If polar snaps are used when drawing the parallelogram in Figure 6-24, there is no need to type the length of the line, because you set both the angle increment and a length increment. The desired angle and length increments are established in the **Snap and Grid** tab of the **Drafting Settings** dialog box. You can open this dialog box as previously described, or you can right-click on the status bar **SNAP** button and pick **Settings...** from the shortcut menu. This opens the **Drafting Settings** dialog box, as shown in Figure 6-25.

To activate polar snap, pick the **PolarSnap** button in the **Snap type & style** area of the dialog box. Picking this button activates the **Polar spacing** area and deactivates the **Snap** area. The length of the polar snap increment is set in the **Polar distance:** box. If the **Polar distance:** setting is 0, the polar snap distance will be the orthogonal snap distance. Figure 6-26 shows a parallelogram being drawn with 30° angle increments and length increments of .75. The lengths of the parallelogram sides are 1.5 and .75.

Using polar tracking overrides

It takes some time to set up the polar tracking and the polar snap options, but it is worth the effort if you have several objects to draw that can take advantage of this feature. If you want to perform polar tracking for only one point, you can use the polar tracking override to do this easily. This works for the specified angle if polar tracking is on or off. To activate a polar tracking override, type a left angle bracket (<) followed by the desired angle when AutoCAD asks you to specify a point. The following command sequence uses a 30° override to draw a line 1.5 units long:

> Command: **L** *or* **LINE**↵
> Specify first point: *(pick a start point for the line)*
> Specify next point or [Undo]: **<30**↵
> Angle Override: 30
> Specify next point or [Undo]: *(move the cursor in the desired 30° direction)* **1.5**↵
> Specify next point or [Undo]: ↵
> Command:

Exercise 6-13   Complete the Exercise on the Student CD.

Figure 6-25.
The **Snap and Grid** tab of the **Drafting Settings** dialog box is used to set the polar snap spacing.

Activates snap

Polar snap spacing

Select grid or polar snap

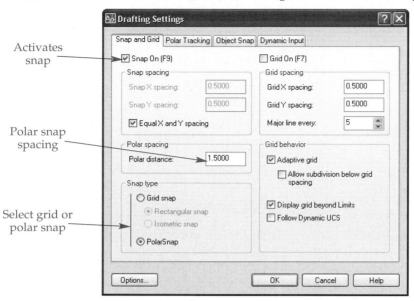

Figure 6-26.
Drawing a parallelogram with polar snap.

| A | B | C | D |

AutoTrack Settings

The settings that control the function of AutoTracking can be accessed through the **Options...** button on the **Drafting Settings** dialog box. This opens the **Options** dialog box to the **Drafting** tab. This tab was illustrated in **Figure 6-19.**

The following options are available in the **AutoTrack Settings** area:

- **Display polar tracking vector.** When this feature is selected, the alignment path is displayed. When this option is off, no polar tracking path is displayed.
- **Display full-screen tracking vector.** When this option is selected, the alignment path for object snap tracking extends across the length of the screen. If not checked, the alignment paths are shown only between the acquired point and the cursor location. Polar tracking vectors always extend from the original point to the extents of the screen.
- **Display AutoTrack tooltip.** When this box is checked, a temporary tooltip is displayed with the AutoTrack alignment paths.

The options in the **Alignment Point Acquisition** area determine how the object snap tracking alignment paths are selected:

- **Automatic.** When this option is selected, points are acquired whenever the cursor is paused over an object snap point.
- **Shift to acquire.** When this option is selected, the [Shift] key must be pressed to acquire an object snap point and use object snap tracking. AutoSnap markers are still displayed, and normal object snap can be used without pressing the [Shift] key. If many running object snaps are set, it may be useful to use this option to reduce the number of paths displayed across the screen.

The **TRACKPATH** system variable stores the alignment path display settings, and the **POLARMODE** system variable stores the alignment point acquisition method.

Temporary Tracking

There are additional tracking modes available that are not listed in the **Object Snap** tab of the **Drafting Settings** dialog box. These modes may be used whether object snap tracking is on or off. These modes are **Temporary track point**, **From**, and **Mid Between 2 Points**.

Temporary Track Point

Object snap tracking has two requirements: running object snap mode must be active and the cursor must pause over the selected point long enough to be acquired. Temporary track point can produce tracking vectors without either of these conditions.

To activate temporary tracking, pick the **Temporary track point** button from the **Object Snap** toolbar, type TT at the selection prompt, or pick **Temporary track point** from the **Object Snap** shortcut menu. For example, temporary tracking can be used to place a circle at the center of a rectangle. See **Figure 6-27**. The X coordinate of the rectangle's center corresponds to the midpoint of the horizontal lines. The Y coordinate of the rectangle's center corresponds to the midpoint of the vertical lines. Temporary tracking can be used to combine these two points to find the center of the rectangle using this sequence:

> Command: **C** *or* **CIRCLE**↵
> Specify center point for circle or [3P/2P/Ttr (tan tan radius)]: **TT**↵
> Specify temporary OTRACK point: **MID**↵
> of *(pick one of the vertical lines and move the cursor horizontally)*
> Specify center point for circle or [3P/2P/Ttr (tan tan radius)]: **TT**↵
> Specify temporary OTRACK point: **MID**↵
> of *(pick one of the horizontal lines and move the cursor vertically)*
> Specify center point for circle or [3P/2P/Ttr (tan tan radius)]: *(select the point where the two alignment paths intersect)*
> Specify radius of circle or [Diameter] <*current*>: ↵
> Command:

Figure 6-27.
Using temporary tracking to locate the center of a rectangle. A—The midpoint of the left line is acquired. B—The midpoint of the bottom line is acquired. C—The center point of the circle is located at the intersection of the alignment paths.

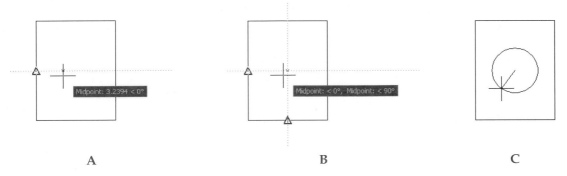

A   B   C

The direction of the orthogonal line determines whether the X or Y component is used. In the previous example, after picking the first tracking point, the cursor is moved horizontally. This means the Y axis value of the previous point is being used, and tracking is now ready for an X coordinate specification.

After moving the cursor horizontally, you may notice movement is locked in a horizontal mode. If you need to move the cursor vertically, move the cursor back to the previously picked point, and then drag vertically. Use this method anytime you need to switch between horizontal and vertical movements.

Using the From Point Selection Option

The **From** point selection mode is another tracking tool that can be used to locate points based on existing geometry. It allows you to establish a relative coordinate, polar coordinate, or direct distance entry from a specified reference base point. Access the **From** option by selecting the **Snap From** button in the **Object Snap** toolbar, selecting **From** in the **Object Snap** shortcut menu, or typing FRO at a point selection prompt. The example in **Figure 6-28** shows the center point for a circle being established as a polar distance from the midpoint of an existing line. The command sequence is shown here:

Command: **C** *or* **CIRCLE**⏎
Specify center point for circle or [3P/2P/Ttr (tan tan radius)]: **FRO**⏎
Base point: **MID**⏎
of *(pick line)*
<Offset>: **@2<45**⏎
Specify radius of circle or [Diameter] *<current>*: *(pick a radius)*
Command:

Using the Mid Between 2 Points Option

A point can be located at the midpoint of two picks by using the **Mid Between 2 Points** feature. This is different from the **Midpoint** object snap, which finds the midpoint of a selected object. **Mid Between 2 Points** picks the midpoint between any two points in the drawing area and can be used in conjunction with object snap modes.

Mid Between 2 Points can only be accessed from the **Object Snap** shortcut menu or by typing M2P at a point selection prompt. The following example (illustrated in **Figure 6-29**) locates the center of a circle between two line endpoints:

Command: **C** *or* **CIRCLE**⏎
Specify center point for circle or [3P/2P/Ttr (tan tan radius)]: **M2P**⏎
First point of mid: *(select first point)*
Second point of mid: *(select second point)*
Specify radius of circle or [Diameter] *<current>*: *(pick a radius)*
Command:

Figure 6-28.
Using the **From** point selection mode, following the command sequence given in the text.

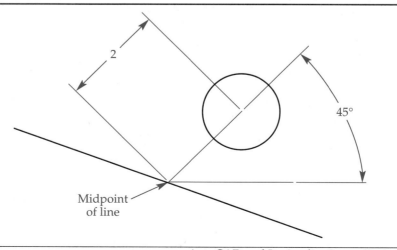

Midpoint
of line

Figure 6-29.
Creating a circle, in which the center is an exact equal distance between two points, using the **Mid Between 2 Points** option.

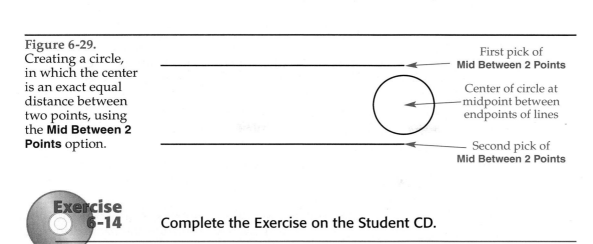

First pick of **Mid Between 2 Points**

Center of circle at midpoint between endpoints of lines

Second pick of **Mid Between 2 Points**

Exercise 6-14   Complete the Exercise on the Student CD.

Chapter Test

Answer the following questions. Write your answers on a separate sheet of paper or complete the electronic chapter test on the Student CD.

1. Give the command and entries needed to draw a line to the midpoint of an existing line:
   A. Command: _____
   B. Specify first point: _____
   C. Specify next point or [Undo]: _____
   D. of _____

2. Give the command and entries needed to draw a line tangent to an existing circle and perpendicular to an existing line:
   A. Command: _____
   B. Specify first point: _____
   C. to _____
   D. Specify next point or [Undo]: _____
   E. to _____

3. Define *AutoSnap*.
4. Define *object snap*.
5. What is an AutoSnap tooltip?
6. How do you activate the **Object Snap** shortcut menu?
7. Describe the object snap override.
8. Define *running object snap mode*.
9. Name the following AutoSnap markers:

A.   B.   C.

D.   E.   F.

G.   H.   I.

J.   K.   L.

10. Define *quadrant.*
11. What is the situation when the tooltip reads Extended Intersection?
12. What does it mean when the tooltip reads Deferred Perpendicular?
13. What is a deferred tangency?
14. What conditions must exist for the tooltip to read Tangent?
15. Which object snaps depend on "acquired points" to function?
16. How do you set running object snaps?
17. How do you access the **Drafting Settings** dialog box to change object snap settings?
18. If you are using running object snaps and you want to make a single point selection without the effects of the running object snaps, what do you do?
19. If you are using running object snaps and want to make several point specifications without the aid of object snap, but want to continue the same running object snaps after making the desired point selections, what is the easiest way to temporarily turn off the running object snaps?
20. How is the running object snap discontinued?
21. What do you do if there are multiple AutoSnap selection possibilities within range of the cursor and you want to select a specific one of the possibilities?
22. How do you turn off AutoSnap?
23. How do you change the color of the AutoSnap marker?
24. How do you change the aperture size?
25. What value would you specify to make the aperture half the default value?
26. Define *AutoTracking.*
27. Which feature should be used in conjunction with AutoTracking?

Drawing Problems

Load AutoCAD for each of the following problems, and use one of your templates or start a new drawing using your own variables.

1. Draw the object below using the object snap modes. Do not draw the dimensions. Save the drawing as P6-1.

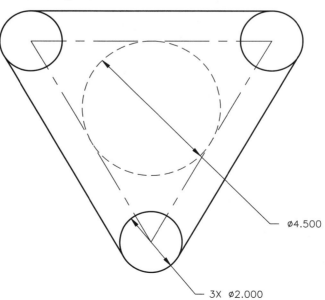

2. Draw the highlighted objects below, and then use the object snap modes indicated to draw the remaining objects. Save the drawing as P6-2.

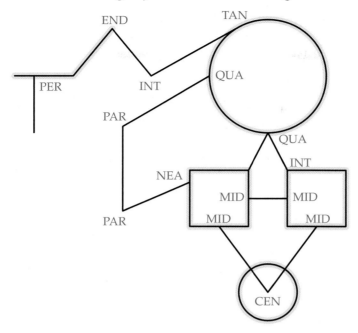

3. Draw the object below using the **Endpoint, Tangent, Perpendicular,** and **Quadrant** object snap modes. Save the drawing as P6-3.

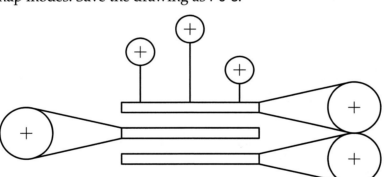

4. Use the **Midpoint, Endpoint, Tangent, Perpendicular,** and **Quadrant** object snap modes to draw these electrical switch schematics. Do not draw the text. Save the drawing as P6-4.

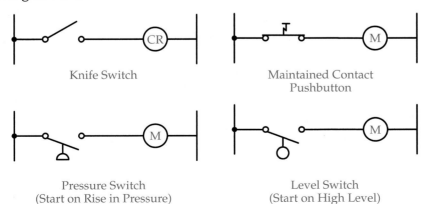

Knife Switch

Maintained Contact
Pushbutton

Pressure Switch
(Start on Rise in Pressure)

Level Switch
(Start on High Level)

Drawing Problems - Chapter 6

5. Use object snap modes to draw this elementary diagram. Do not draw the text. Save the drawing as P6-5.

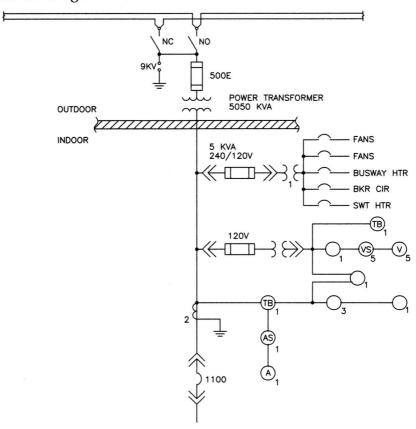

For Problems 6–11, use object snap modes and tracking to draw the objects shown. Do not draw dimensions. Save the drawing as P6-(problem number).

6.

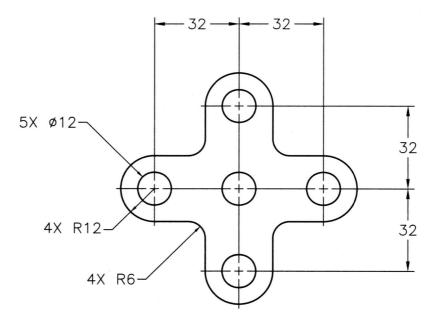

7.

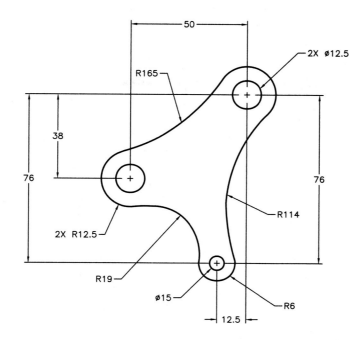

8.

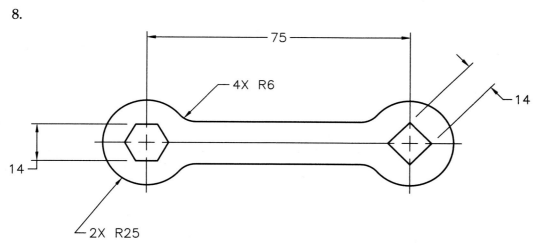

9.

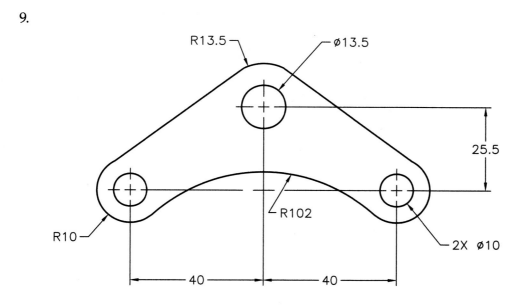

10.

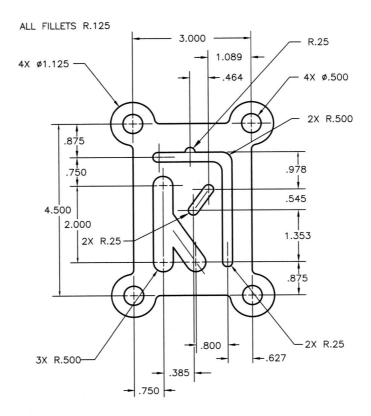

ALL FILLETS R.125

11.

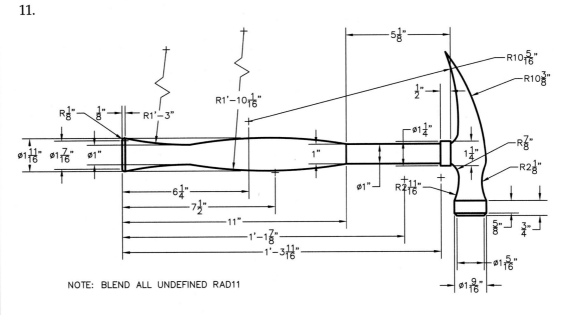

NOTE: BLEND ALL UNDEFINED RAD11

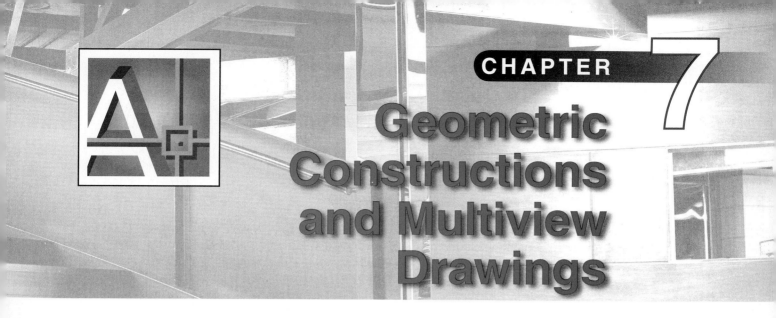

Learning Objectives

After completing this chapter, you will be able to do the following:
- Use the **OFFSET** command to draw parallel lines and curves.
- Divide existing objects into equal lengths using the **DIVIDE** command.
- Use the **MEASURE** command to set designated increments on an existing object.
- Create orthographic multiview drawings.
- Adjust snap grid and UCS settings to construct auxiliary views.
- Use construction lines to assist in drawing orthographic views and auxiliary views.

This chapter explains how to create parallel offset copies, divide objects, and place point objects. These skills, and the other geometry-creating skills you have acquired, are applied in the creation of multiview drawings.

Using Offset to Draw Parallel Lines and Curves

The **OFFSET** command is used to draw concentric circles, concentric arcs, concentric curves, parallel polylines, and parallel lines. This command is accessed by picking **Modify > Offset**, picking the **Offset** button in the **Modify** toolbar, or typing O or OFFSET.

Specifying a Distance to Offset

At the Specify offset distance or [Through/Erase/Layer] <*current*>: prompt, an offset value can be typed, or two points can be picked in the drawing area to determine the offset value. The last offset distance used is shown in brackets. If you want to draw two parallel circles a distance of .1 unit apart, use the following command sequence. Refer to **Figure 7-1**.

```
Command: O or OFFSET↵
Current settings: Erase source=current Layer=current
    OFFSETGAPTYPE=current
Specify offset distance or [Through/Erase/Layer] <current>: .1↵
```

Figure 7-1.
Drawing an offset
using a designated
distance.

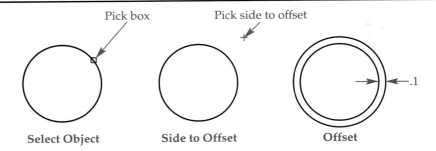

Pick box

Pick side to offset

.1

Select Object

Side to Offset

Offset

Select object to offset or [Exit/Undo] <*current*>: *(pick the object)*
Specify point on side to offset or [Exit/Multiple/Undo] <*current*>: *(pick the side of the object on which the offset will be drawn)*
Select object to offset or [Exit/Undo] <*current*>: *(select another object or press* [Enter]*)*
Command:

If the offset value is not known, but there are two reference points in the drawing area, instead of typing in an offset value, a first point can be picked, and then a second point. The distance between these two points is used as the offset value.

When the Select object to offset or [Exit/Undo] <*current*>: prompt first appears, the screen cursor turns into a pick box. After the object is picked, the screen cursor turns back into crosshairs. No other selection option (such as window or crossing) works with the **OFFSET** command. The other option is to pick a point through which the offset is drawn. Type T, as follows, to produce the results shown in **Figure 7-2**:

Command: **O** *or* **OFFSET**⏎
Current settings: Erase source=*current* Layer=*current* OFFSETGAPTYPE=*current*
Specify offset distance or [Through/Erase/Layer] <*current*>: **T**⏎
Select object to offset or [Exit/Undo] <*current*>: *(pick the object)*
Specify through point or [Exit/Multiple/Undo] <*current*>: *(pick the point through which the offset will be drawn)*
Select object to offset or [Exit/Undo] <*current*>: ⏎
Command:

Object snap modes can be used to assist in drawing an offset. For example, suppose you have a circle and a line and want to draw a concentric circle tangent to the line. Refer to **Figure 7-3** and the following command sequence:

Command: **O** *or* **OFFSET**⏎
Current settings: Erase source=*current* Layer=*current* OFFSETGAPTYPE=*current*
Specify offset distance or [Through/Erase/Layer] <*current*>: **QUA**⏎
of *(pick the existing circle)*
Specify second point: **PER**⏎
to *(pick the existing line)*
Select object to offset or [Exit/Undo] <*current*>: *(pick the existing circle)*
Specify point on side to offset or [Exit/Multiple/Undo] <*current*>: *(pick between the circle and line)*
Select object to offset or [Exit/Undo] <*current*>: ⏎
Command:

Figure 7-2.
Drawing an offset
through a given
point.

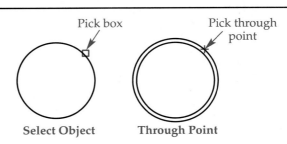

Pick box

Pick through point

Select Object

Through Point

AutoCAD and Its Applications—Basics

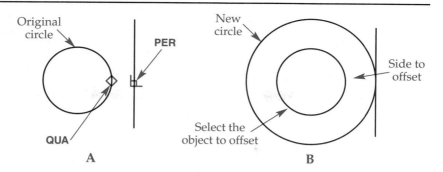

Figure 7-3.
Using **OFFSET** to draw a concentric circle tangent to a line.

Erasing the Original Object

When an object is being offset, you may want to remove the original object. Instead of offsetting the object and then erasing the source object, the source object can be erased when it is offset. After initiating the **OFFSET** command, select **Erase** and **Yes** from the shortcut menu to erase the source object. The **Yes** option remains as the default until it is changed to **No**. Be sure to change this option back to **No** if you do not want the source offset object to be erased the next time the **OFFSET** command is used.

Changing the Layer of the Offset Object

The **Layer** option allows you to have the offset object placed on the current layer. For example, if the offset source object resides on the Electrical layer and the offset object needs to be placed on the Lighting layer, this can be done during the command if Lighting is the current layer by following this command sequence:

Command: **O** *or* **OFFSET**↵
Current settings: Erase source=*current* Layer=*current* OFFSETGAPTYPE=*current*
Specify offset distance or [Through/Erase/Layer] <*current*>: **L**↵
Enter layer option for offset objects [Current/Source] <*current*>: **C**↵
Specify offset distance or [Through/Erase/Layer] <*current*>:

When **Current** is specified, the offset object is placed on the current layer. To have the offset object remain on the same layer as the offset source object, the **Source** option needs to be used.

Offsetting Multiple Times

Once the object to offset has been selected, the **Multiple** option can be used to offset an object more than once with the same distance between the objects. Initiate the **OFFSET** command, specify the offset distance, and pick the source object. You can then select **Multiple** and begin picking to specify the offset direction. See **Figure 7-4.** Whenever the **Undo** option is available, it can be used to undo the last offset without exiting the command. Using the **Exit** option by typing E or Exit, pressing [Enter], or right-clicking exits the **OFFSET** command.

Exercise 7-1   Complete the Exercise on the Student CD.

Figure 7-4.
The **Multiple** option can be use to create multiple offsets with the same distance, without having to start the command over again.

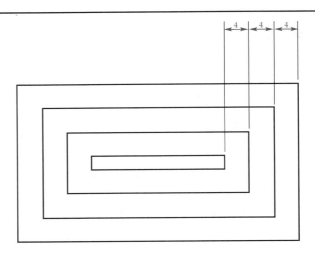

Drawing Points

POINT

Type
POINT
PO

Pull-Down Menu
Draw
> Point

Toolbar
Draw
▪
Point

Points are useful for identifying specific locations on a drawing and, as you will see in the next section, for marking positions on objects. You can draw points anywhere on the screen using the **POINT** command. To access this command, pick the **Point** button from the **Draw** toolbar, type PO or POINT, or select **Draw > Point** and one of the options. You can pick or type coordinates to place the points.

If you need to place only a single point object, use the keyboard command or select the **Single Point** option from the **Point** cascading menu. If you need to draw multiple points, use the **Point** button on the **Draw** toolbar or the **Multiple Point** option from the **Point** cascading menu. Press [Esc] to exit the command.

When the **POINT** command is used, the current point modes are listed at the command line. The **PDMODE** system variable specifies the type of point marker, and the **PDSIZE** system variable specifies the size of the point marker. The point style, which is set in the **Point Style** dialog box, controls the appearance of the point.

> **NOTE**
>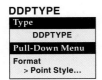
>
> If the point style is set as dots and blips are active, the blip covers the dot when the point is selected. Type REDRAW and press [Enter] to erase the blip.

DDPTYPE

Type
DDPTYPE

Pull-Down Menu
Format
> Point Style...

Setting Point Style

The style and size of points are set using the **Point Style** dialog box. See **Figure 7-5.** This dialog box is accessed by selecting **Format > Point Style...** or by typing DDPTYPE.

The **Point Style** dialog box contains twenty different point styles. The current point style is highlighted. To change the style, simply pick the graphic image of the desired style.

Figure 7-5.
The **Point Style** dialog box. This is a quick way to select the point style and change the point size.

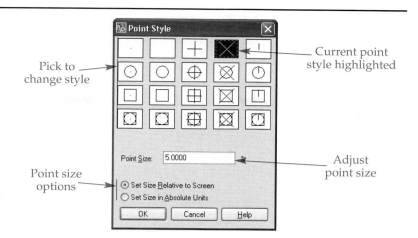

Pick to change style

Current point style highlighted

Point Size: 5.0000

Adjust point size

Point size options

Set Size Relative to Screen
Set Size in Absolute Units

OK   Cancel   Help

NOTE

The point style is stored in the **PDMODE** system variable. This variable can be changed at the Command: prompt. The **PDMODE** values of the point styles shown in the top row of the **Point Style** dialog box are 0 through 4, from left to right. These are the basic point styles. Add a circle (second row in dialog box) by adding 32 to the basic **PDMODE** value. Add 64 to draw a square (third row), and add 96 to draw a circle and square (bottom row). For example, a point display of an X inside a circle has a **PDMODE** value of 35. This is the sum of the X value of 3 and the circle value of 32.

Set the point size by entering a value in the **Point Size:** text box of the **Point Style** dialog box. Pick the **Set Size Relative to Screen** option button if you want the point size to change in relation to different display options. Picking the **Set Size in Absolute Units** option button makes the points appear the same size no matter what display option is used. The effects of these options are shown in **Figure 7-6.**

NOTE

The point size and relative/absolute settings can also be modified by changing the **PDSIZE** (point display size) system variable. Positive **PDSIZE** values change size in relation to different display options (relative to screen). Negative **PDSIZE** values make the points appear the same size no matter how much you zoom the drawing (absolute units).

Figure 7-6.
Points sized with the **Set Size Relative to Screen** setting change size as the drawing is zoomed. Points sized with the **Set Size in Absolute Units** setting remain a constant size.

Size Setting	Original Point Size	2X Zoom	0.5 Zoom
Relative to Screen	⊠	⊠	⊠
Absolute Units	⊠	⊠	⊠

Dividing an Object

A line, circle, arc, or polyline can be divided into an equal number of segments using the **DIVIDE** command. To start the **DIVIDE** command, select **Draw > Point > Divide** or type DIV or DIVIDE. The **DIVIDE** command does not break an object into multiple parts. It places point objects or blocks at the locations where the breaks would occur if the object were actually divided into multiple segments.

Suppose you have drawn a line and want to divide it into seven equal parts. Enter the **DIVIDE** command, select the object to divide, and then enter the number of segments. See Figure 7-7.

The **Block** option of the **DIVIDE** command allows you to place a block at each division point. To initiate the **Block** option, type B at the Enter the number of segments or [Block]: prompt. You are then asked if the block is to be aligned with the object. A *block* is a previously drawn symbol or shape. Blocks are discussed in detail in Chapter 22 of this text.

After the number of segments is given, the object is divided with points. By default, however, points are displayed as dots, which may not show very well. Change point style to make the points more visible.

Figure 7-7.
Using the **DIVIDE** command. Note that the default marks (points) have been changed to Xs.

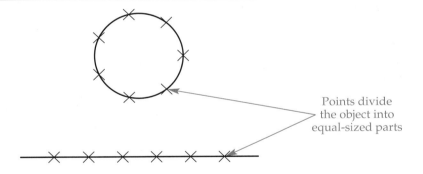

Points divide the object into equal-sized parts

Marking an Object at Specified Distances

Unlike the **DIVIDE** command, in which an object is divided into a specified number of parts, the **MEASURE** command places marks a specified distance apart. To activate the **MEASURE** command, pick **Draw > Point > Measure** from the pull-down menu or type ME or MEASURE. Pick the object and type in the distance. The line shown in Figure 7-8 is measured with .75 unit segments.

Measuring begins at the end closest to where the object is picked. All increments are equal to the entered segment length, except the last segment, which may be shorter. The point style determines the type of marks placed on the object, just as it does with the **DIVIDE** command. Blocks can be inserted at the given distances using the **Block** option of the **MEASURE** command.

Figure 7-8.
Using the **MEASURE** command. Notice that the last segment may be shorter than the others, depending on the total length of the object.

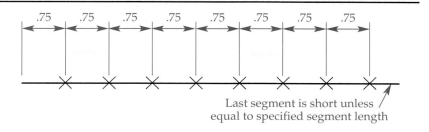

.75 .75 .75 .75 .75 .75 .75 .75

Last segment is short unless equal to specified segment length

Exercise 7-3   Complete the Exercise on the Student CD.

Orthographic Multiview Drawings

Each field of drafting has its own method to present views of a product. Architectural drafting uses plan views, exterior elevations, and sections. In electronics drafting, symbols are placed in a schematic diagram to show a circuit layout. In civil drafting, contour lines are used to show the topography of land. Mechanical drafting uses *multiview drawings*.

This section discusses multiview drawings. Multiview drawings are based on the standard ASME Y14.3M, *Multiview and Sectional View Drawings*. The views of a multiview drawing are created through orthographic projection. *Orthographic projection* involves projecting object features onto an imaginary plane. This imaginary plane is called a *projection plane*. The imaginary projection plane is placed parallel to the object. Thus, the line of sight is perpendicular to the object. This results in views that appear two-dimensional. See Figure 7-9.

Six two-dimensional views show all sides of an object. The six views are the front, right side, left side, top, bottom, and rear. The views are placed in a standard arrangement so others can read the drawing. The front view is the central, or most important, view. Other views are placed around the front view. See Figure 7-10. Notice in this figure that the horizontal and vertical edges illustrated in the front view are aligned with the corresponding edges in the other views. You will create the other views from the front view by using the object snapping and tracking features covered in Chapter 6.

There are very few products that require all six views. The number of views needed depends on the complexity of the object. Use only enough views to completely describe the object. Drawing too many views is time-consuming and can clutter the drawing. In some cases, a single view may be enough to describe the object. The object shown in Figure 7-11 needs only two views. These two views completely describe the width, height, depth, and features of the object.

Figure 7-9.
Obtaining a front view with orthographic projection.

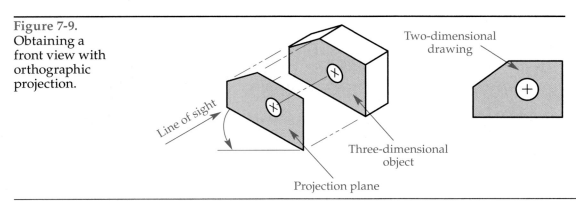

Two-dimensional drawing

Line of sight

Three-dimensional object

Projection plane

Figure 7-10.
Arrangement of the
six orthographic
views.

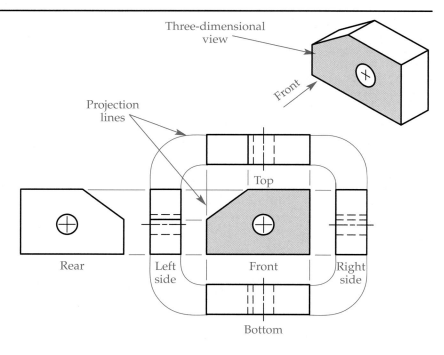

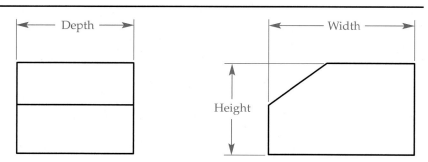

Figure 7-11.
The views you
choose to describe
the object should
show all height,
width, and depth
dimensions.

Selecting the Front View

The front view is usually the most descriptive view. The following attributes should be considered when selecting the front view:
- ✓ Most descriptive
- ✓ Most natural position
- ✓ Most stable position
- ✓ Provides the longest dimension
- ✓ Contains the least number of hidden features

Additional views are selected relative to the front view. Remember to choose only the number of views needed to completely describe the object's features.

Showing Hidden Features

Hidden features are parts of the object not visible in the view at which you are looking. A visible edge appears as a solid line. A hidden edge is shown with a hidden line. Hidden lines were discussed in Chapter 3. Notice in **Figure 7-12** how hidden features are shown as hidden lines. Hidden lines are thin to provide contrast to object lines.

Exercise 7-4   Complete the Exercise on the Student CD.

Figure 7-12.
Hidden features are shown with hidden lines.

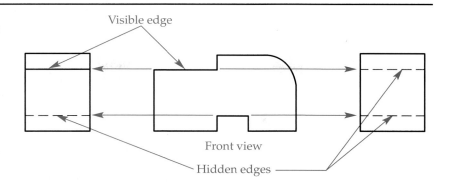

Visible edge

Front view

Hidden edges

One-View Drawings

In some instances, an object can be fully described using one view. A thin part, such as a gasket, can be drawn with one view. See **Figure 7-13**. The thickness is given as a note in the drawing or in the title block. A cylindrical object can also be drawn with one view. The diameter dimension is given to identify the object as cylindrical.

Showing Symmetry and Circle Centers

The centerlines of symmetrical objects and the centers of circles are shown with centerlines. For example, in one view of a cylinder, the axis is drawn as a centerline. In the other view, centerlines cross to show the center in the circular view. See **Figure 7-14**. The only place that the small centerline dashes should cross is at the center of a circle.

Figure 7-13.
A one-view drawing of a gasket. The thickness is given in a note.

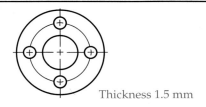

Thickness 1.5 mm

Figure 7-14.
Drawing centerlines.

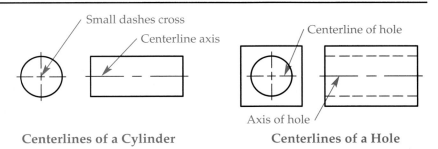

Small dashes cross

Centerline axis

Centerline of hole

Axis of hole

Centerlines of a Cylinder

Centerlines of a Hole

Drawing Auxiliary Views

In most cases, an object is completely described using a combination of one or more of the six standard views. Sometimes, however, the multiview layout is not enough to properly identify some object surfaces. It may then be necessary to draw an auxiliary view.

An *auxiliary view* is typically needed when a surface on the object is at an angle to the line of sight. This slanted surface is *foreshortened* in a standard view, meaning it is shorter than the true size and shape of the surface. To show this surface in true size, an auxiliary view is needed. Foreshortened dimensions are not recommended.

An auxiliary view is drawn by projecting lines perpendicular (90°) to a slanted surface. Usually, one projection line remains on the drawing. It connects the auxiliary view to the view where the slanted surface appears as a line. The resulting auxiliary view shows the surface in true size and shape. For most applications, the auxiliary view needs only to show the slanted surface, not the entire object. This is called a *partial auxiliary view* and is shown in **Figure 7-15**.

In many situations, there may not be enough room on the drawing to project directly from the slanted surface. The auxiliary view is then placed elsewhere. See **Figure 7-16**. A viewing-plane line is drawn next to the view where the slanted surface appears as a line. The *viewing-plane line* is drawn with a thick dashed or phantom line in accordance with ASME Y14.2M. It is terminated with bold arrowheads that point toward the slanted surface.

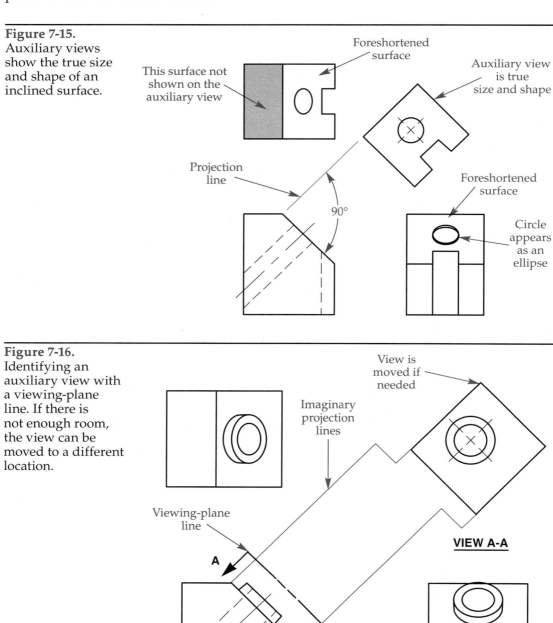

Figure 7-15.
Auxiliary views show the true size and shape of an inclined surface.

Figure 7-16.
Identifying an auxiliary view with a viewing-plane line. If there is not enough room, the view can be moved to a different location.

AutoCAD and Its Applications—Basics

Each end of the viewing-plane line is labeled with a letter. The letters relate the viewing-plane line with the proper auxiliary view. A title such as "VIEW A-A" is placed under the auxiliary view. When more than one auxiliary view is drawn, labels continue with B-B through Z-Z (if necessary). The letters *I*, *O*, and *Q* are not used because they may be confused with numbers. An auxiliary view drawn away from the standard view retains the same angle as if it is projected directly.

Using the User Coordinate System for Auxiliary Views

All the features on your drawing originate from the *world coordinate system (WCS)*. This system includes the X, Y, and Z coordinate values measured from the origin (0,0,0). The WCS is fixed. The *user coordinate system (UCS)*, on the other hand, can be moved to any orientation. The UCS is discussed in detail in ***AutoCAD and Its Applications—Advanced***.

In general, the UCS allows you to set your own coordinate origin. The UCS 0,0,0 origin has been in the lower-left corner of the screen for the drawings you have done so far. In many cases, this is fine, but when drawing an auxiliary view, it is best to have the measurements originate from a corner of the view. This, in turn, makes all auxiliary view features and the coordinate display true, as measured from the corner of the view. This method makes it easier to locate and later dimension the auxiliary view features.

Figure 7-17 shows an example of aligning the UCS to the auxiliary view. Draw the principal views, such as the front, top, and right side. Move the UCS origin to a location that coincides with a corner of the auxiliary view.

To move the UCS origin, type UCS, select the **3 Point** button on the **UCS** toolbar, or select **Tools > New UCS > 3 Point**. The command sequence is as follows:

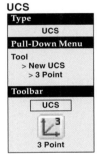

Command: **UCS**↵
Current ucs name: *current*
Enter an option [New/Move/orthoGraphic/Prev/Restore/Save/Del/Apply/?/World]
<World>: **N**↵
Specify origin of new UCS or [ZAxis/3point/OBject/Face/View/X/Y/Z] <0,0,0>: **3**↵
Specify new origin point <0,0,0>: *(select Point A, as shown in* ***Figure 7-17****)*
Specify point on positive portion of X-axis <*current*>: *(select Point B)*
Specify point on positive-Y portion of the UCS XY plane <*current*>: *(select Point C)*
Command:

Figure 7-17.
Relocating the origin and rotating the Z axis of the UCS system. A—Rotating the UCS to align with the auxiliary view angle. B—The UCS icon is displayed at the current UCS origin at the corner of the auxiliary view.

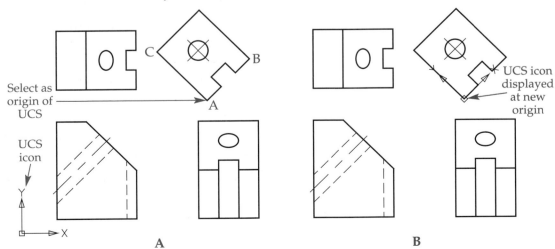

The icon is rotated and moved, as shown in **Figure 7-17B**. If you want the UCS displayed in the lower-left corner of the drawing area, select **Tools > Named UCS...** from the pull-down menu. This displays the **UCS** dialog box. In the **Settings** tab, uncheck the **Display at UCS origin point** check box.

Before you begin drawing the auxiliary view, use the **Save** option of the **UCS** command to name and save the new UCS:

Command: **UCS**↵
Current ucs name: *current*
Enter an option [New/Move/orthoGraphic/Prev/Restore/Save/Del/Apply/?/World]
    <World>: **S**↵
Enter name to save current UCS or [?]: **AUX**↵
Command:

Now, proceed by drawing the auxiliary view. When you have finished, select the **World UCS** button from the **UCS** toolbar or enter the **UCS** command and use the default **World** option to reset the UCS back to the WCS origin:

Command: **UCS**↵
Current ucs name: AUX
Enter an option [New/Move/orthoGraphic/Prev/Restore/Save/Del/Apply/?/World]
    <World>: ↵
Command:

PROFESSIONAL TIP   Polar tracking is another method that can be used to draw auxiliary views. It can be used in place of or in addition to the UCS method described in the previous section. Polar tracking was covered in Chapter 6.

Exercise 7-5   Complete the Exercise on the Student CD.

Construction Lines and Rays

The tracking vectors and alignment paths you used in the previous sections are efficient methods of creating geometry. This is because these types of lines appear only when they are needed. Sometimes, you may want the lines to stay visible while you continue to create the geometry. This is when you will want to use construction lines (**XLINE**) and rays (**RAY**). Both commands can be used for similar purposes, however, the **XLINE** command has more options and flexibility than the **RAY** command has.

Using the Xline Command

A construction line is an infinite length line used to help build accurate geometry. Although these lines are infinite, they do not change the drawing extents. This means they have no effect on zooming operations.

Construction lines can be modified by moving, copying, trimming, and other editing operations. Editing commands such as **TRIM** or **FILLET** change the object type. For example, if one end of a construction line is trimmed off, it becomes a ray. A *ray* is considered semi-infinite because it is infinite in one direction only. If the infinite end of a ray is trimmed off, it becomes a line object.

Construction lines and rays are drawn on the current layer and plot the same as other objects. This may cause conflict with the other lines on that layer. A good way to handle this problem is to set up a special layer just for construction lines.

The **XLINE** command can be accessed by picking the **Construction Line** button on the **Draw** toolbar, picking **Draw** > **Construction Line** in the pull-down menu, or typing XL or XLINE. You can specify two points through which the construction line passes. The first point of a construction line is called the *root point*. After you pick the first point, you can select as many points as you would like. Xlines are created between every point and the root point.

Figure 7-18 shows how construction lines can be used to help project features between views. Right-click the drawing area to see the following **XLINE** options in the shortcut menu:

- **Hor.** This option draws a horizontal construction line through a single specified point.
- **Ver.** This option draws a vertical construction line through a specified point.
- **Ang.** This option draws a construction line at a specified angle through a selected point. The default lets you specify an angle and then pick a point through which the construction line is to be drawn. This works well if you know the angle. You can also pick two points in the drawing to describe the angle. The **Reference** option allows you to use the angle of an existing line object as a reference angle for construction lines. This option is useful when you do not know the angle of the construction line, but you know the angle between an existing object and the construction line. **Figure 7-19** shows the **Ang** option used to draw construction lines establishing the location of an auxiliary view.

XLINE	
Type	
	XLINE
	XL
Pull-Down Menu	
Draw	
	> Construction
	Line
Toolbar	
	Draw
	Construction Line
Options	
	Hor
	Ver
	Ang
	Bisect
	Offset

Figure 7-18.
Creating horizontal construction lines using two points and the **Hor** option.

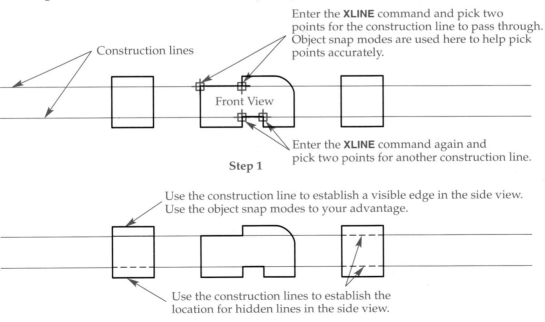

Enter the **XLINE** command and pick two points for the construction line to pass through. Object snap modes are used here to help pick points accurately.

Construction lines

Front View

Enter the **XLINE** command again and pick two points for another construction line.

Step 1

Use the construction line to establish a visible edge in the side view. Use the object snap modes to your advantage.

Use the construction lines to establish the location for hidden lines in the side view.

Step 2

Figure 7-19.
Using the **XLINE**
command **Ang**
option.

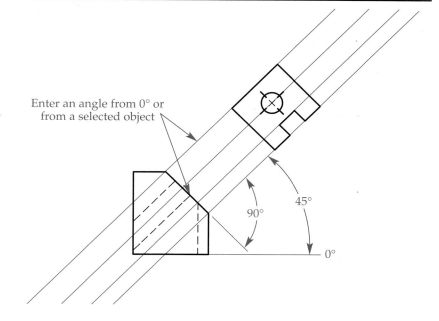

- **Bisect.** This option draws a construction line that bisects a specified angle. This is a convenient tool for use in some geometric constructions, as shown in Figure 7-20.
- **Offset.** This **XLINE** option draws a construction line a specified distance from a selected line object. You have the option of specifying an offset distance or using the **Through** option to pick a point through which to draw the construction line.

Exercise 7-6   Complete the Exercise on the Student CD.

Using the Ray Command

The **RAY** command is limited, compared to the **XLINE** command. The **RAY** command allows you to specify the point of origin and a point through which the ray passes. In this manner, the **RAY** command works much like the default option of the **XLINE** command. The ray, however, extends beyond only the second pick point. The **XLINE** command results in a construction line that extends both directions from the pick points.

Figure 7-20.
Using the **XLINE**
command **Bisect**
option.

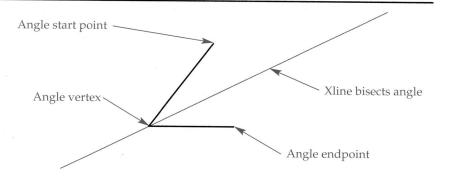

The **RAY** command can be accessed by picking **Draw** > **Ray** or by typing RAY. The RAY command sequence is as follows:

RAY
Type
RAY
Pull-Down Menu
Draw
> Ray

> Command: **RAY**↵
> Specify start point: *(pick a point)*
> Specify through point: *(pick a second point)*
> Specify through point: *(draw more construction lines or press* [Enter]*)*
> Command:

Both the **RAY** command and the **XLINE** command allow the creation of multiple objects. You must press [Enter] to end the command.

Editing Construction Lines and Rays

The construction lines you create using the **XLINE** and **RAY** commands can be edited and modified using standard editing commands. These commands are introduced in Chapter 12 and Chapter 13. The construction lines will change into a new object type when infinite ends are trimmed off. A trimmed xline becomes a ray. A ray that has its infinite end trimmed becomes a normal line object. Therefore, in many cases, your construction lines can be modified to become part of the actual drawing. This approach can save a significant amount of time in many drawings.

Chapter Test

Answer the following questions. Write your answers on a separate sheet of paper or complete the electronic chapter test on the Student CD.

1. Give the command and entries needed to divide a line into 24 equal parts:
   A. Command: _____
   B. Select object to divide: _____
   C. Enter the number of segments or [Block]: _____
2. List two ways to establish an offset distance using the **OFFSET** command.
3. What option of the **OFFSET** command is used to remove the source offset object?
4. If you use the **DIVIDE** command and nothing appears to happen, what should you do?
5. How do you access the **Point Style** dialog box?
6. What is the difference between the **DIVIDE** and **MEASURE** commands?
7. How do you draw a single point, and how do you draw multiple points?
8. How do you change the point size in the **Point Style** dialog box?
9. Provide at least four guidelines for selecting the front view of an orthographic multiview drawing.
10. When can a part be shown with only one view?
11. When is an auxiliary view needed, and what does an auxiliary view show?
12. What is the angle of projection from the slanted surface into the auxiliary view?
13. Name the AutoCAD command that allows you to draw construction lines.
14. Why is it a good idea to put construction lines on their own layer?
15. Name the option that can be used to bisect an angle with a construction line.
16. What is the difference between the construction lines drawn with the command identified in Question 13 and rays drawn with the **RAY** command?

Drawing Problems

Load AutoCAD for each of the following problems, and use one of your templates or start a new drawing using your own variables.

1. Draw the front and side views of this offset support. Use object snap modes and tracking. Do not draw the dimensions. Save your drawing as P7-1.

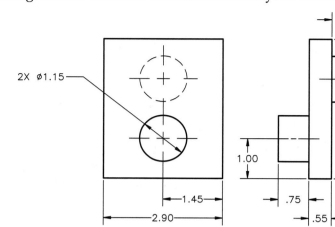

2. Draw the top and front views of this hitch bracket. Use object snap modes and tracking. Do not draw the dimensions. Save your drawing as P7-2.

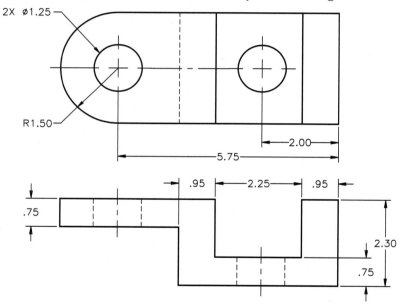

3. Draw this aluminum spacer. Use object snap modes and tracking. Do not draw the dimensions. Save the drawing as P7-3.

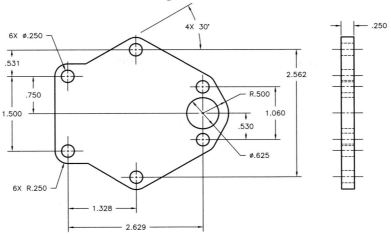

4. Draw this spring using the **OFFSET** command for material thickness. Do not draw the dimensions. Save the drawing as P7-4.

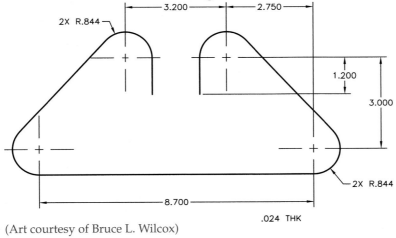

(Art courtesy of Bruce L. Wilcox)

5. Draw this gasket. Do not draw the dimensions. Save the drawing as P7-5.

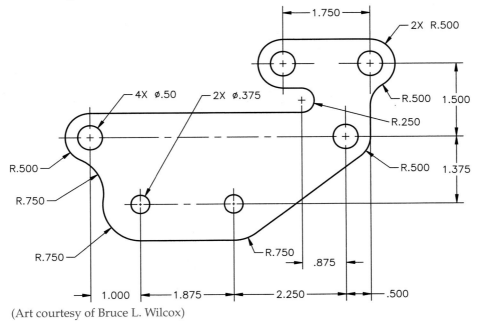

(Art courtesy of Bruce L. Wilcox)

6. Draw this sheet metal chassis. Do not draw the dimensions. Use object snap tracking and polar tracking to your advantage. Save the drawing as P7-6.

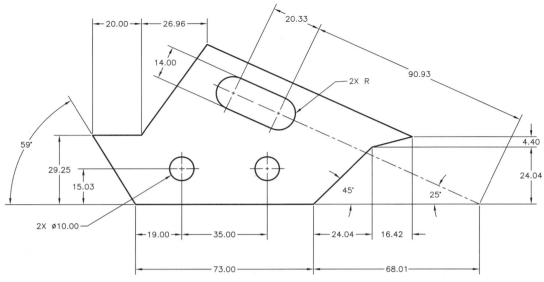

(Art courtesy of Bruce L. Wilcox)

7. Draw this cup. Do not draw the dimensions. Save the drawing as P7-7.

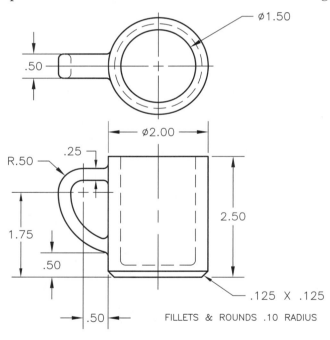

FILLETS & ROUNDS .10 RADIUS

8. Draw this bushing. Do not draw the dimensions. Save the drawing as P7-8.

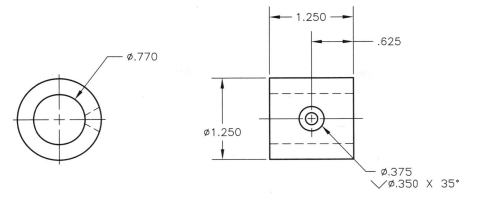

9. Draw this wrench. Do not draw the dimensions. Save the drawing as P7-9.

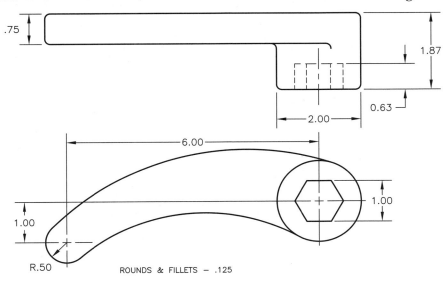

ROUNDS & FILLETS − .125

10. Draw this support. Do not draw the dimensions. Save the drawing as P7-10.

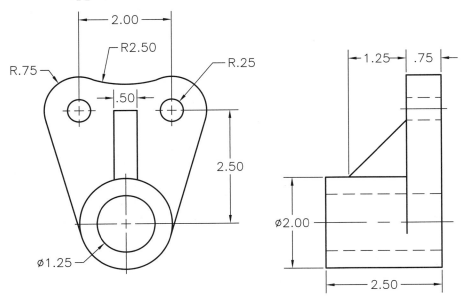

Drawing Problems - Chapter 7

In Problems 11 through 16, draw the views needed to completely describe the objects. Use object snap modes, AutoTrack modes, and offsets as needed. Do not dimension. Save the drawings as **P7-***(problem number).*

11.

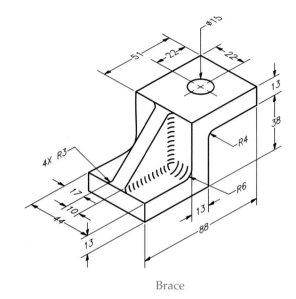

Brace

12.

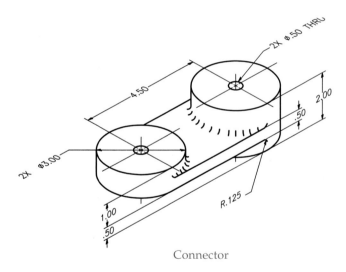

Connector

13.

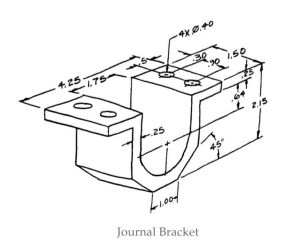

Journal Bracket

14.

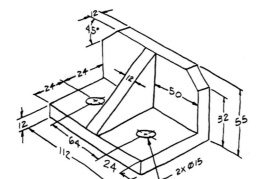

Angle Bracket
(Metric)

15.

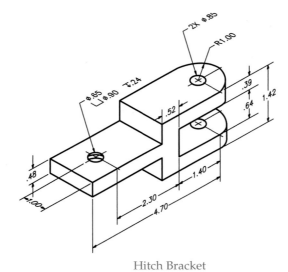

Hitch Bracket

16. Draw the views of this pillow block, including the auxiliary view. Do not draw the dimensions. Save your drawing as P7-16.

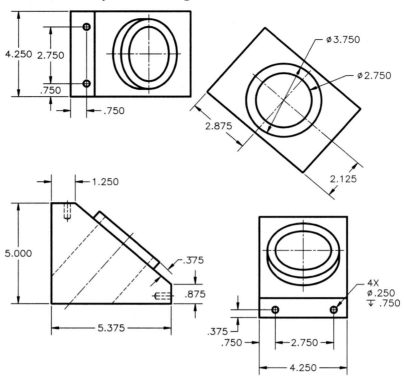

CHAPTER 8

Placing Text on Drawings

Learning Objectives

After completing this chapter, you will be able to do the following:

- Use and discuss proper text standards.
- Create text styles.
- Use **DesignCenter** to manage text styles.
- Make multiple lines of text with the **MTEXT** command.
- Insert drafting symbols into text.
- Use the **TEXT** command to create single-line text.
- Explain the purpose of the Quick Text mode and use the **QTEXT** command.
- Insert fields into text.
- Edit existing text.
- Check your spelling.
- Search for and replace material automatically.
- Design title blocks for your template drawings.

In manual drafting, words and notes on drawings have traditionally been added by hand lettering. This is a slow, time-consuming task. Computer-aided drafting programs have reduced the tedious nature of adding notes to a drawing. In computer-aided drafting, lettering is referred to as *text*.

There are advantages of computer-generated text over hand-lettering techniques. When performed by computer, lettering is fast, easier to read, and more consistent. This chapter shows how text can be added to drawings. Also explained are standards for proper text presentation based on ASME Y14.2M, *Line Conventions and Lettering*.

Text Standards

Company standards often dictate how text appears on a drawing. The minimum recommended text height on engineering drawings is .125" (3 mm). All dimension numbers, notes, and other text information should be the same height. Text for titles, subtitles, captions, revision information, and drawing numbers can be .188" to .25" (5 mm to 6.5 mm) high. Many companies specify a .188", or 5/32" (5 mm), lettering height for standard text. This text size is easy to read even after the drawing is reduced.

Figure 8-1.
Vertical and inclined text.

ABC.. abc.. 123..
ABC.. abc.. 123..

Vertical or inclined text may be used on a drawing, depending on company preference. See Figure 8-1. Do not use both text styles on the same drawing. The recommended slant for inclined text is 68° from horizontal. AutoCAD offers a variety of styles for specific purposes, such as titles or captions. Text on a drawing is normally uppercase, but lowercase letters are used in some instances.

Numbers in dimensions and notes are the same height as standard text. When fractions are used in dimensions, the fraction bar should be placed horizontally between the numerator and denominator using full-size numbers. Fractions can be stacked when using the **MTEXT** command. However, many notes placed on drawings have fractions displayed with a diagonal (/) fraction bar. A dash or space is usually placed between the whole number and the fraction. Examples of text for numbers and fractions in different unit formats are shown in Figure 8-2.

Figure 8-2.
Examples of text for different unit formats.

Decimal Inch	Fractional Inch			Millimeter		
2.750 .25	$2\frac{3}{4}$	2−3/4	2 3/4	2.5	3	0.7

Scale Factors for Text Height

Scale factors and text heights should be determined before beginning a drawing. They are best incorporated as settings within your template drawing files. The scale factor of a drawing is important because this value is used to make sure the text is plotted at the proper height. The scale factor is multiplied by the desired plotted text height to get the AutoCAD text height.

The scale factor is always a reciprocal of the drawing scale. For example, if you wish to plot a drawing at a scale of 1/2″ = 1″, calculate the scale factor as follows:

> 1/2″ = 1″
> .5″ = 1″
> 1/.5 = 2
> The scale factor is 2.

An architectural drawing that is to be plotted at a scale of 1/4″ = 1′-0″ has a scale factor calculated as follows:

> 1/4″ = 1′-0″
> .25″ = 12″
> 12/.25 = 48
> The scale factor is 48.

The scale factor of a civil engineering drawing that has a scale of 1″ = 60′ is calculated as follows:

1″ = 60′
1″ = (60 × 12)″
720/1 = 720
The scale factor is 720.

If your drawing is in millimeters with a scale of 1:1, the drawing can be converted to inches with the formula 1″ = 25.4 mm. Therefore, the scale factor is 25.4. When the metric drawing scale is 1:2, the scale factor for converting to inches is 1″ = 25.4 × 2, or 1″ = 50.8. The scale factor is 50.8.

After the scale factor has been determined, you should then calculate the height of the AutoCAD text. In a 1″ = 1″ scaled drawing, the scale factor equals 1. Therefore, the text height in the drawing will be 1/8″ high, because the text height multiplied by a scale factor of 1 equals 1/8″ high text. However, if you are working on a civil engineering drawing with a scale of 1″ = 60′, text drawn at 1/8″ high appears as a dot. Remember the drawing you are working on is 720 times larger than it is when plotted at the proper scale. Therefore, you must multiply the text height by the 720 scale factor to have text in correct proportion on the screen:

text height × scale factor = model space scaled text height
.125″ × 720 = 90″
The proper text height in model space is 90″.

An architectural drawing with a scale of 1/4″ = 1′-0″ has a scale factor of 48. Text that is to be 1/8″ high when printed should be drawn 6″ high (1/8″ × 48 = 6″).

Text Composition

Composition refers to the spacing, layout, and appearance of the text. With manual lettering, it is necessary to space letters freehand. Spacing is performed automatically with computer-generated text.

Notes should be placed horizontally on the drawing. AutoCAD automatically sets lines of text apart at an equal distance. This helps maintain the identity of individual notes.

The term *justify* means to align the text to fit a given location. For example, left-justified text is aligned along an imaginary left border. Most lines of text are left-justified.

AutoCAD Text Fonts

A *font* is a particular letter face design. Two of the standard AutoCAD text fonts are shown in **Figure 8-3**. The standard fonts have .shx file extensions.

The txt font is the AutoCAD default. The rough appearance of the txt font allows it to regenerate faster than other fonts. The Romans (roman simplex) font is smoother than txt. It closely duplicates the single-stroke lettering that has long been the standard for most drafting.

Several AutoCAD fonts provide special alphabets or symbols that are accessed from the **Character Map** dialog box, as shown in **Figure 8-4**.

TrueType fonts are scaleable and have an outline. *Scaleable* means the font can be displayed on the screen or printed at any size and still maintain proportional letter

Figure 8-3.
Standard AutoCAD fonts.

Fast Fonts

Txt   abcdABCD12345

Monotxt   abcdABCD12345

Simplex Fonts

Romans   abcdABCD12345

Italic   *abcdABCD12345*

Triplex Fonts

Romant   abcdABCD12345

Italict   *abcdABCD12345*

Complex Fonts

Romanc   abcdABCD12345

Italicc   *abcdABCD12345*

Figure 8-4.
The **Character Map** dialog box.

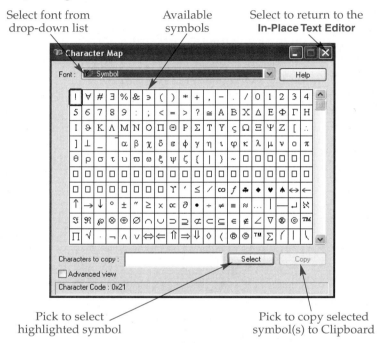

Select font from drop-down list

Available symbols

Select to return to the **In-Place Text Editor**

Pick to select highlighted symbol

Pick to copy selected symbol(s) to Clipboard

thickness. TrueType fonts appear filled in the AutoCAD window, but the **TEXTFILL** system variable controls whether the plotted fonts will be filled. The **TEXTFILL** default is **1**, which draws filled fonts. A setting of **0** draws the font outlines. A sample of a TrueType font, Stylus BT, is shown in **Figure 8-5.** This is an excellent choice for the artistic appearance desired on architectural drawings.

NOTE

Additional standard fonts, characters, and TrueType fonts can be seen by experimenting within AutoCAD or reviewing the *AutoCAD Fonts* document in the *Reference Material* section of the Student CD.

Figure 8-5.
A few of the many TrueType fonts available.

Swiss 721		Architect's Hand Lettered	
swiss (regular)	**abcdABCD12345**	stylus BT	abcdABCD I 2345
swissi (italic)	*abcdABCD12345*		
swissb (bold)	**abcdABCD1234**	**Vineta (shadow)**	
swissbi (bold italic)	***abcdABCD12345***	vinet (regular)	**abcdABCD12345**

PROFESSIONAL TIP

TrueType fonts and other complex text fonts can be taxing on system resources. They can slow down display changes and increase drawing regeneration time significantly. Use these fonts only when necessary. When you must use complex fonts, set your system variables to speed-optimized settings.

AutoCAD Text Styles

Text styles are variations of fonts. A *text style* gives height, width, obliquing angle (slant), and other characteristics to a text font. You may have several text styles that use the same font, but with different characteristics. By default, the Standard text style uses the txt font, a 0° rotation angle, a width of 1, and a 0° obliquing angle.

Text Style Settings

Text styles are created, modified, and deleted using the **Text Style** dialog box, shown in **Figure 8-6.** Access this dialog box by picking **Format** > **Text Style...** from the pull-down menu, selecting the **Text Style...** button in the **Styles** toolbar, or by typing ST or STYLE. The following describes the features found in this dialog box:

- **Style Name area.** Set a new current text style by making a selection from the drop-down list. Use the **New...** button to create a new text style and the **Rename...** button to rename a selected style. If you need to delete a style, use the **Delete** button.
- **Font area.** This area of the **Text Style** dialog box is where you select an available font, style of the selected font, and text height.
  - **Font Name.** This drop-down list is used to access the available fonts. The default font is txt.shx. All SHX fonts are identified with an AutoCAD compass symbol, while the TrueType fonts have the TrueType symbol.
  - **Font Style.** This drop-down list is inactive unless the selected font has options available, such as bold or italic. None of the SHX fonts have additional options, but some of the TrueType fonts may. For example, the SansSerif font has Regular, Bold, BoldOblique, and Oblique options. Each option provides the font with a different appearance.

Figure 8-6.
The **Text Style** dialog box is used to set the characteristics of a text style.

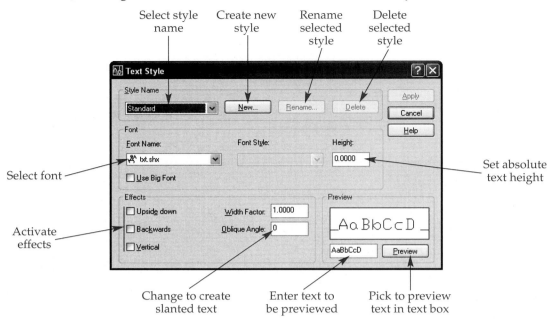

Select style name · Create new style · Rename selected style · Delete selected style

Select font

Set absolute text height

Activate effects

Change to create slanted text · Enter text to be previewed · Pick to preview text in text box

- **Height.** This text box is used to set the text height. The default is 0.0000. This allows you to set the text height with the **TEXT** command. If you set a value such as .125, the text height becomes fixed for this text style and you are not prompted for the text height. Setting a text height value other than zero saves time during the command process, but also eliminates your flexibility. ASME-recommended text heights were discussed earlier in this chapter.

NOTE

The default text height is stored in the **TEXTSIZE** system variable. When a text style has a height other than 0, the style height overrides any default value stored in this variable.

PROFESSIONAL TIP

It is recommended that a text height value of 0 be used for text styles used in dimensions. Dimension styles allow you to specify a text height value for the annotation text. By specifying a text height in the text style, the dimension text height is overridden. Dimension styles are discussed later in this text.

- **Use Big Font.** Asian and other large format fonts (called *Big Fonts*) are activated with this check box. The Big Font is used as a supplement to define many symbols not available in normal font files.
- **Effects area.** This area of the **Text Style** dialog box is used to set the text format. It contains the following options, which are shown in **Figure 8-7:**
  - **Upside down.** This check box is off by default. When it is checked, the text you draw is placed upside down.

Figure 8-7.
Special effects for
text styles can be set
in the **Effects** area of
the **Text Style** dialog
box.

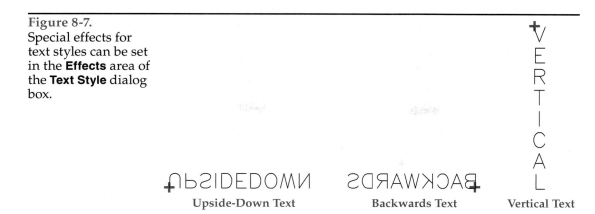

Upside-Down Text   Backwards Text   Vertical Text

- **Backwards.** When this check box is checked, text that you draw is placed backwards.
- **Vertical.** This check box is inactive for all TrueType fonts. A check in this box makes SHX font text vertical. Text on drawings is normally placed horizontally, but vertical text can be used for special effects and graphic designs. Vertical text works best when the rotation angle is 270°.

> **NOTE**
>
> The **In-Place Text Editor** displays the text horizontally, right-side up, and forward. Any special effects such as vertical, backwards, or upside down take effect when you pick **OK** to exit the editor.

- **Width Factor.** This text box provides a value that defines the text character width relative to the height. A width factor of 1 is the default. A width factor greater than 1 expands the characters, and a factor less than 1 compresses the characters. See **Figure 8-8.**
- **Oblique Angle.** This text box allows you to set an angle at which text is slanted. The zero default draws characters vertically. A value greater than 0 slants the characters to the right, while a negative value slants the characters to the left. See **Figure 8-9.** Some fonts, such as italic, are already slanted.

> **PROFESSIONAL TIP**
>
>
>
> Some drafting companies, especially those in structural drafting, like to slant text 15° to the right. Also, water features named on maps often use text that is slanted to the right.

Figure 8-8.
Width factor settings
for text.

Width Factor	Text
1	ABCDEFGHIJKLM
.5	ABCDEFGHIJKLMNOPQRSTUVWXY
1.5	ABCDEFGHI
2	ABCDEFG

Figure 8-9.
Oblique angle settings for text.

Obliquing Angle	Text
0	ABCDEFGHIJKLM
15	*ABCDEFGHIJKLM*
–15	ABCDEFGHIJKLM

- **Preview area.** The preview image allows you to see how the selected font or style will appear. This is a very convenient way to see what the font looks like before using it in a new style. **Figure 8-10** shows previews of various fonts. Specific characters can also be previewed. Simply type the characters in the text box and then pick the **Preview** button.

Exercise 8-1 Complete the Exercise on the Student CD.

Creating a New Text Style

If you start a new drawing with the AutoCAD default template, the only text style available is the Standard style. The Standard text style is based on the txt font.

What if you want to create a text style for mechanical drawings that uses the Romans font and characters .125″ high? You want to have this available as the most commonly used text on your drawings. Choose a style name that you can remember, such as ROMANS-125. It is also a good idea to record the names and details about the text styles you create and keep this information in a log for future reference.

Text style names can have up to 255 characters, including letters, numbers, dashes (–), underlines (_), and dollar signs ($). You can type uppercase or lowercase letters. The following explains the steps to use to create this text style:

1. Open the **Text Style** dialog box. Standard is the current style with txt.shx as the font, and a zero text height.
2. Pick the **New...** button. This opens the **New Text Style** dialog box, **Figure 8-11**. Notice style1 is in the **Style Name** text box. You can keep a text style name like style1 or style2, but this is not descriptive. Type ROMANS-125 in the box and then pick the **OK** button. See **Figure 8-11**. ROMANS-125 is now displayed in the **Style Name** text box of the **Text Style** dialog box.
3. Go to the **Font Name** drop-down list, find romans.shx, and pick it. The font is now romans.shx.
4. Change the value in the **Height** text box to .125. These settings are shown in **Figure 8-12**.
5. Pick the **Apply** button and then the **Close** button. The new ROMANS-125 text style is now part of your drawing.

Figure 8-10.
The **Preview** image shows a sample of the font. A—The Scripts font. B—The Gothice font. C—The Italic font.

A   B   C

Figure 8-11.
The **New Text Style** dialog box.

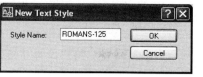

Default Style   New Style

Figure 8-12.
The **Text Style** dialog box showing the changes in the style, font, and height.

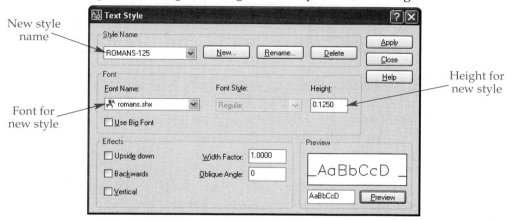

New style name → ... → Font for new style → ... → Height for new style

Now, ROMANS-125 is the default style when you use the **TEXT** or **MTEXT** command. If you want to create a similar text style for your architectural drawings, you might consider a style name called ARCHITECTURAL-125. For this style, set the font to Stylus BT and the height to .125.

PROFESSIONAL TIP

You can make the text style name the same as the font name if you wish. In some cases, this is a clear and concise way of naming the style.

Exercise 8-2

Complete the Exercise on the Student CD.

PROFESSIONAL TIP

To save valuable drafting time, add text styles to your template drawings. If only a single text height is needed in the template, set the text height for the style. Do not forget to consider the scale factor when typing the text height. Type the scaled text height for each style.

Changing, Renaming, and Deleting Text Styles

You can change the current text style without affecting existing text objects. The changes are applied only to text added using that style.

Existing text styles are easily renamed in the **Text Style** dialog box. Select the desired style name in the **Style Name** text box and pick the **Rename...** button. This opens the **Rename Text Style** dialog box, which is similar to the **New Text Style** dialog box. Change the text style name and pick the **OK** button.

> **NOTE**
> Styles can also be renamed using the **Rename** dialog box. You can access this dialog box by selecting **Format > Rename...** from the pull-down menu or by typing RENAME. Select **Text styles** in the **Named Objects** list to rename the style.

You can delete an existing text style in the **Text Style** dialog box by picking the desired style name in the **Style Name** drop-down list and then picking the **Delete** button. If you try to delete a text style that has been used to create text objects in the drawing, AutoCAD gives you the following message:

Style in use, can't be deleted.

This means that there are text objects in the drawing that reference this style. If you want to delete the style, change the text objects in the drawing to a different style. You cannot delete or rename the Standard style.

> **NOTE**
> If you change the font and orientation of an existing text style, all text items with that style are redrawn with the new values.

Importing Text Styles from Existing Drawings

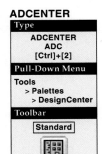

ADCENTER

Type
ADCENTER
ADC
[Ctrl]+[2]

Pull-Down Menu
Tools
> Palettes
> DesignCenter

Toolbar
Standard
DesignCenter

DesignCenter can be used to import text styles from existing drawing files. **DesignCenter** allows you to browse through drawing files to find desired text styles, and then add the needed style into your current drawing file.

DesignCenter can be accessed by picking the **DesignCenter** button on the **Standard** toolbar, selecting from the **Tools > Palettes > DesignCenter**, typing ADC or ADCENTER, or using the [Ctrl]+[2] key combination. See **Figure 8-13.**

The following procedure is used to import a text style into the current drawing:

1. In the tree view area, locate the existing drawing containing the text style to be copied.
2. Double-click on the file name or pick the plus (+) sign next to it to list the various types of content within the drawing.
3. Pick the Textstyles content listing in the tree view. This displays the text styles.
4. Select the text style or text styles to be copied into the drawing. You can then copy the text style in any of the following ways:
   - **Drag and drop.** Move the cursor over the top of the desired text style, press and hold the pick button on your pointing device, and drag the cursor to the drawing area of the opened drawing. Let go of the pick button and the text style is added to your current drawing file.

Figure 8-13.
DesignCenter allows you to copy a text style from an existing drawing into the current drawing.

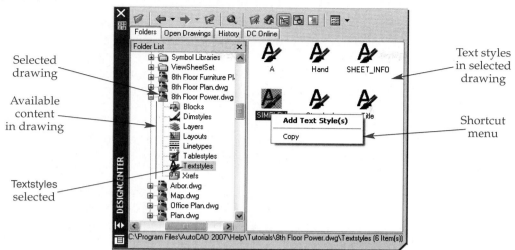

Selected drawing

Available content in drawing

Textstyles selected

Text styles in selected drawing

Shortcut menu

- **Shortcut menu.** Position the cursor over the desired text style and right-click to open the shortcut menu. Refer to **Figure 8-13.** Pick the **Add Text Style(s)** option, and the text style is added to your current drawing.
- **Copy and paste.** Use the shortcut menu as described in the previous method, but select the **Copy** option. Move the cursor to the drawing where you want the text style added, then right-click your mouse button and select the **Paste** option from the shortcut menu. The copied text style is added to the current drawing.

PROFESSIONAL TIP

To select more than one text style at one time to import into your current drawing file, hold down the [Shift] key and pick the first and last text styles in a group of text styles, or hold down the [Ctrl] key to select multiple text styles individually.

Exercise 8-3

Complete the Exercise on the Student CD.

LEGACY NOTE

New text styles can be created with the **-STYLE** command. After typing the command, you are prompted to type the new style name and properties (such as font, height, and obliquing angle). It is typically more efficient to use the **Text Style** dialog box to create text styles.

Using AutoCAD to Draw Text

AutoCAD provides two basic systems for creating text. There is line text for creating single-line text objects, and multiline text for preparing paragraphs of text. The **MTEXT** command is used to create paragraph text. This text is typed in the **In-Place Text Editor**. The **TEXT** command is used to create single-line text. This text is typed at the command line. Each command is used differently, but the options are similar.

Multiline Text

The **MTEXT** command is used to create multiline text objects. All the lines are part of the same object. The **MTEXT** command is accessed by picking the **Multiline Text** button in the **Draw** or **Text** toolbar, picking **Draw > Text > Multiline Text...** in the pull-down, or typing T, MT, or MTEXT.

After typing the **MTEXT** command, AutoCAD asks you to specify the first and opposite corners of the text boundary. The *text boundary* is a box within which your text will be placed. When you pick the first corner of the text boundary, the cursor changes to a box with grayed-out letters that represent the current text height. Move the box until you have the desired size for your paragraph and pick the opposite corner. See **Figure 8-14.**

When drawing the text boundary, an arrow in the boundary shows the direction of text flow. While the width of the boundary provides a limit to the width of the text paragraphs, it does not affect the possible height. The boundary height is automatically resized to fit the actual text typed. The direction of the flow indicates where the boundary is expanded, if necessary.

After picking the text boundary, the **In-Place Text Editor** appears. See **Figure 8-15.** The **In-Place Text Editor** is divided into the **Text Formatting** toolbar and the *text editor.* The **Text Formatting** toolbar controls the properties of text typed into the text editor. The text editor includes a paragraph ruler where indent stops and an indent marker are located. A cursor is located within the text editor. This cursor is the height set in the **Text Formatting** toolbar. This is where text is typed to create a paragraph. The text editor is transparent so that you can see how the text you type will appear on-screen in relation to other objects.

As mentioned earlier, notes in drawings are often presented using uppercase text. Picking the **Options** button in the **Text Formatting** toolbar displays the **Options** menu. The **AutoCAPS** option is found in this menu. Selecting this option turns on the caps lock

Figure 8-14.
The text boundary is a box within which your text will be placed. The arrow indicates the direction of text flow.

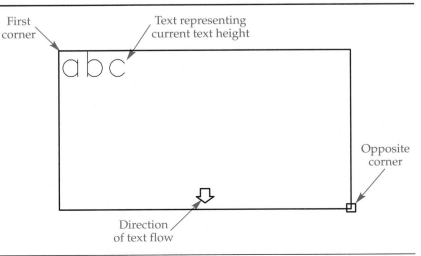

Figure 8-15.
The **In-Place Text Editor** is used to create multiline text.

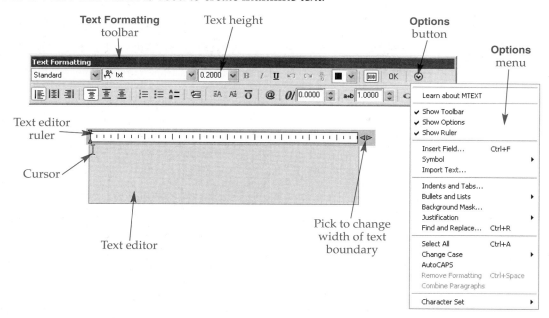

on the keyboard each time the **In-Place Text Editor** is accessed. The caps lock is turned off when you exit the text editor so text in other programs is not all uppercase.

When the text editor is filled with text and a new line is added, previous lines begin to be hidden and a scroll bar is displayed at the right. Use the scroll bar to move up and down to access lines in the text editor. Pressing the [Enter] key causes a new line to be entered. Pressing [Enter] twice creates a blank line between lines of text. Tabs can also be used to line up columns of text. If you need to change the width of the text editor, pick and drag one of the arrows at the end of the paragraph ruler. When finished typing text in the editor, pick the **OK** button in the **Text Formatting** toolbar to exit the text editor.

> **NOTE**
>
>
>
> You can also change the width of a paragraph of multiline text by right-clicking on the text editor ruler and selecting **Set Mtext Width...** from the shortcut menu. This displays the **Set Mtext Width** dialog box, where a new width for the paragraph can be specified.

Exercise 8-4   Complete the Exercise on the Student CD.

Using the In-Place Text Editor

The **In-Place Text Editor** is displayed after you define the text boundary. The **Text Formatting** toolbar controls the properties of the text typed in the text editor. Additional text controls can be accessed by picking the **Options** button to display the **Options** menu. You can also right-click within the text editor to display the text editor shortcut menu. This section describes the features within the toolbar, text editor, **Options** menu, and text editor shortcut menu.

While typing text in the **In-Place Text Editor**, there are a number of keystroke combinations that are available. These combinations are as follows:

Keystroke	Function
[↑] [←] [↓] [→]	The arrow keys move the cursor through the text one position in the direction indicated by the arrow.
[Ctrl]+[→] [Ctrl]+[←]	These key combinations move the cursor one word in the direction indicated.
[Home]	Moves the cursor to the start of the current line.
[End]	Moves the cursor to the end of the current line.
[Delete]	Deletes the character immediately to the right of the cursor.
[Backspace]	Deletes the character immediately to the left of the cursor.
[Ctrl]+[Backspace]	Deletes the word immediately to the left of the cursor.
[Ctrl]+[C]	Copies selection to the Clipboard. The Clipboard is an internal storage area that temporarily stores information that you copy or cut from a document.
[Ctrl]+[V]	Pastes Clipboard contents to the selection or current cursor location.
[Ctrl]+[X]	Cuts selection to Clipboard.
[Ctrl]+[Z]	Performs an undo.
[Enter]	Ends the current paragraph, starting a new one on the next line.
[Page Up] [Page Down]	These keys move the cursor position up to 28 rows in the indicated direction.
[Ctrl]+[Page Up] [Ctrl]+[Page Down]	These keys move the cursor to the top or bottom of the currently visible page of text.
[Ctrl]+[Home]	Moves the cursor to Line 1, Column 1.
[Ctrl]+[End]	Moves the cursor to the last character position.
[Ctrl]+[A]	Selects all text in the current multiline text object.
[Shift]+[→] [Shift]+[←]	Selects or deselects text. Increases or decreases the selection by one character at a time, depending on the direction indicated.
[Shift]+[↑] [Shift]+[↓]	Selects or deselects text. Increases or decreases the selection by one line at a time, depending on the direction indicated.
[Ctrl]+[Shift]+[→] [Ctrl]+[Shift]+[←]	Selects or deselects text. Increases or decreases the selection by one word at a time, depending on the direction indicated.
[Esc]	Closes the **In-Place Text Editor** and loses any changes made.

Text can be pasted from any text-based application into the **In-Place Text Editor**. For example, you can copy text from an application such as Microsoft® Word, and then paste it into the **In-Place Text Editor**. The pasted text retains its properties. Likewise, text copied or cut from the **In-Place Text Editor** can be pasted into another text-based application.

As you move the cursor into the editing window, it changes shape. If you have used other Windows text editors, this is a familiar text cursor shape. Pointing to a character position within the text and pressing the pick button causes the cursor to be placed at the selected location. You can then begin typing or editing as needed. If you begin typing where the text cursor is initially placed, your text begins in the upper-left corner of the text boundary.

Text is selected as it is with most standard Windows text editors. Place the cursor at one end of the desired selection, then press and hold the pick button. Drag the cursor until the desired text is highlighted, then release the pick button. Now, any editing operations you perform affect the highlighted text. For example, a copy or cut operation places the highlighted text on the Clipboard. One other way to highlight text is to move your mouse to the word you would like to highlight and double-click it with the pick button. To entirely replace the highlighted text with new text, either paste the new text from the Clipboard or begin typing. The selection is erased and the new text appears in its place.

Using the Text Formatting toolbar

The features in the **Text Formatting** toolbar are shown in **Figure 8-16**. The following list describes the features in the top row of the toolbar. Keep in mind as you review these features that *selected text* refers to text that you have highlighted in the text editor:

- **Style.** This drop-down list includes a list of the different text styles available. A text style sets the font, size, obliquing angle, orientation, and other text characteristics. Creating text styles is covered in detail later in this chapter.
- **Font.** Pick the down arrow to open the drop-down list of available text fonts. Picking one of the options allows the selected text to have its font changed or newly typed text to use this font type. This overrides the font used in the current style. Txt is the default text font.

Figure 8-16.
The **Text Formatting** toolbar.

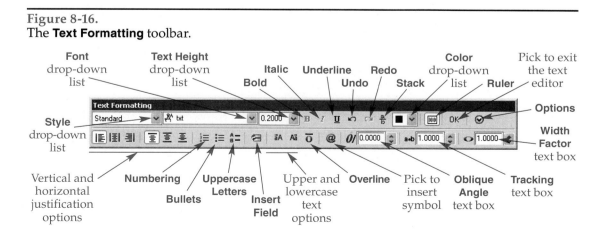

- **Text Height.** This option allows selected text or new text to have its height changed. This overrides the current setting of the **TEXTSIZE** system variable and the text height set within the text style.
- **Bold.** Pick this button to have the selected text become bold. This only works with some TrueType fonts. The SHX fonts do not have this capability.
- **Italic.** Pick this button to have the selected text become italic. This only works with some TrueType fonts. The SHX style fonts do not have this capability.
- **Underline.** Picking this button underlines selected text.

NOTE If you select text that is already bold, picking the **Bold** button returns the text to its normal appearance. This is also true for the **Italic** and **Underline** functions.

- **Undo.** Pick this button to undo the previous activity.
- **Redo.** Pick this button to redo undone operations.
- **Stack.** Picking this button stacks selected text vertically or diagonally. To use this feature for drawing a vertically stacked fraction, place a forward slash between the top and bottom items. Then select the text with your pointing device and pick the button. This button is also used for unstacking text that has been previously stacked. You can also use the caret (^) character between text if you want to stack the items without a fraction bar. This is called a *tolerance stack.* Typing a number sign (#) between selected numbers results in a diagonal fraction bar. See **Figure 8-17.**
- **Color.** The color is set to ByLayer by default, but you can change the text color by picking one of the colors in the **Color** drop-down list.
- **Ruler.** Picking this button turns the display of the paragraph ruler on or off.

Picking the **OK** button closes the **In-Place Text Editor** and displays the text typed on-screen. As previously discussed, picking the **Options** button displays the **Options** menu with additional options for multiline text.

NOTE The formatting of text within the **In-Place Text Editor** may not always appear exactly as it does in the drawing. This is most commonly true when a substitute font is used for display in the editor. A substitute font may be wider or narrower than the font used in the drawing. AutoCAD automatically reformats the text to fit within the boundary defined in the drawing.

Figure 8-17.
Different types of stack characters.

	Selected Text	Stacked Text
Vertical Fraction	1/2	$\frac{1}{2}$
Tolerance Stack	1^2	$\frac{1}{2}$
Diagonal Fraction	1#2	½

The features in the bottom row of the **Text Formatting** toolbar contain options for justifying text, creating lists, and other functions. Refer to **Figure 8-16**. The first series of buttons determines the vertical and horizontal justification of the text paragraph. The **Left, Center,** and **Right** buttons determine how the text is aligned vertically, and the **Top, Middle,** and **Bottom** buttons control the alignment of the text horizontally. **Figure 8-18** displays the different options for vertical and horizontal justification and how they relate to multiline text.

The **Numbering, Bullets,** and **Uppercase Letters** options allow you to create numbered, bulleted, or lettered lists for the text you type. These features are discussed in detail in the *Creating Lists* section of this chapter.

Picking the **Insert Field** button opens the **Field** dialog box, which allows you to insert text that can be updated. There are many different preset fields, including formatting options. For example, you could insert the **Date** field into a title block. The field is then updated automatically with the current date throughout the life of the drawing file. When a field is inserted into the **In-Place Text Editor,** it is highlighted in gray to indicate the text is a field. Fields are discussed later in this chapter.

Picking the **UPPERCASE** button changes all of the selected text to uppercase formatting. When no text is selected, this button is grayed out. Picking the **lowercase** button changes all of the selected text to lowercase formatting. This button is also grayed out if no text is selected.

The **Overline** option is used to place a line over selected text. If no text is selected and this button is picked, it turns on overline formatting. When text is typed, it is automatically created with the overline. To turn this feature off, pick the button again.

Picking the **Symbol** button displays a list of special symbols that can be inserted into the text editor. These symbols are not found on a typical keyboard. Included are a number of drafting symbols and other characters. Unique symbols can also be inserted using the **Character Map** dialog box. This is explained later in this chapter.

Figure 8-18.
The justification options for multiline text.

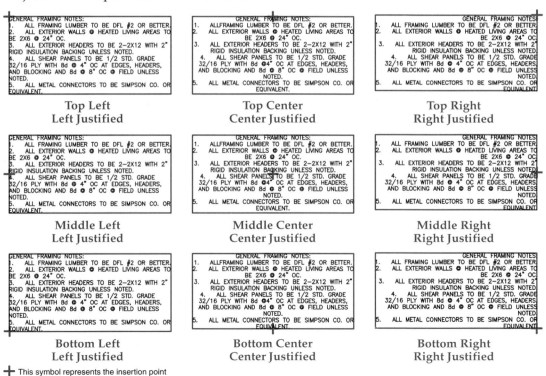

This symbol represents the insertion point

The **Oblique Angle**, **Tracking**, and **Width Factor** options are used to modify the slant angle, spacing, and width of the text characters. The **Oblique Angle** text box setting determines whether text characters are slanted to the left or right with an obliquing angle. The **Width Factor** text box setting is used to change the text character width. The **Oblique Angle** and **Width Factor** settings can be assigned to text styles. These options are discussed in greater detail later in this chapter. The **Tracking** text box setting determines the amount of space between text characters. The default value is 1, which results in normal spacing. The higher the value, the more space added between characters. The lower the value, the tighter the spacing between characters. You can enter a value between 0.75 and 4.0. See **Figure 8-19**. To change the **Oblique Angle**, **Tracking**, or **Width Factor** settings for multiline text, first select the text in the text editor. Then select the value in the text box and type a new value or use the arrow buttons.

Exercise 8-5   Complete the Exercise on the Student CD.

Using the text editor shortcut menu

The text editor shortcut menu was briefly introduced earlier in this chapter. This shortcut menu is accessed by right-clicking while the cursor is in the text editor. The menu and its options are displayed and explained in **Figure 8-20**. Most of the same options can be accessed by picking the **Options** button from the **Text Formatting** toolbar. All of the options listed in the **Options** menu are available in the text editor shortcut menu. Refer to **Figure 8-15**.

Some of the options in the text editor shortcut menu have already been discussed. The options that have not been discussed are covered in this section and the sections that follow.

At the top of the text editor shortcut menu are the **Undo** and **Redo** options and the Windows Clipboard functions. The Clipboard functions allow you to cut, copy, or paste text to or from the text editor. Selecting the **Learn about MTEXT** option provides access to help-related information about multiline text.

The fourth section of the text editor shortcut menu contains options that control the display of items. These options are described as follows:
- **Show Toolbar.** This option determines whether the **Text Formatting** toolbar is displayed. Unchecking this option hides the toolbar.
- **Show Options.** This option, when checked, displays the second row of buttons on the **Text Formatting** toolbar. The row can be hidden by unchecking this option.
- **Show Ruler.** This option controls the display of the ruler at the top of the text editor window. The ruler is hidden when the option is unchecked.

Figure 8-19.
The **Tracking** option for multiline text determines the spacing between characters.

AutoCAD tracking
Normal Spacing

AutoCAD tracking
Tracking = 0.75

A u t o C A D   t r a c k i n g
Tracking = 2.0

Figure 8-20.
The text editor shortcut menu is accessed by right-clicking while the cursor is in the text editor.

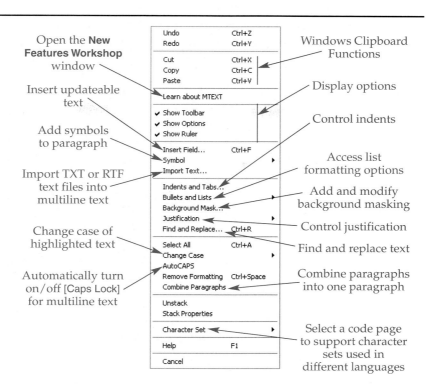

Open the **New Features Workshop** window

Insert updateable text

Add symbols to paragraph

Import TXT or RTF text files into multiline text

Change case of highlighted text

Automatically turn on/off [Caps Lock] for multiline text

Windows Clipboard Functions

Display options

Control indents

Access list formatting options

Add and modify background masking

Control justification

Find and replace text

Combine paragraphs into one paragraph

Select a code page to support character sets used in different languages

The fifth section of the text editor shortcut menu includes options for inserting fields, symbols, and text files into multiline text. Picking **Insert Field...** allows you to insert a field in text. Creating fields is discussed later in this chapter. The next section discusses the use of symbols and imported text.

Importing text and symbols

Symbol characters can be inserted into the text editor by selecting the **Symbol** option in the text editor shortcut menu. This displays the cascading menu, **Figure 8-21.** This option allows the insertion of symbols at the text cursor location. The first two sections in the **Symbol** menu contain commonly used symbols. The third section contains the **Non-breaking Space** option, which keeps two separate words together. The **Other...** option opens the **Character Map** dialog box, shown in **Figure 8-4.** To use this dialog box, pick the desired symbols from the **Font:** drop-down list. The following are the steps for using a symbol or symbols:

Figure 8-21.
The **Symbol** menu options.

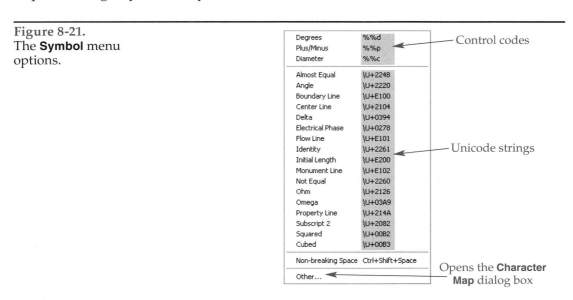

Control codes

Unicode strings

Opens the **Character Map** dialog box

1. Pick the desired symbol and then pick the **Select** button. The selected symbol is displayed in the **Characters to copy:** box.
2. Pick the **Copy** button to have the selected symbol or symbols copied to the Clipboard.
3. Pick the **Close** button to close the dialog box.
4. In the **In-Place Text Editor**, place the text cursor where you want the symbols displayed.
5. Move the screen cursor to anywhere inside the text editor and right-click to display the text editor shortcut menu. Pick the **Paste** option to paste the symbol at the cursor location.

The **Import Text** option allows you to import text from an existing text file directly into the **In-Place Text Editor**. The text file can be either a standard ASCII text file (TXT) or an RTF (rich text format) file. The imported text becomes a part of the current multi-line text object.

When this option is selected, the **Select File** dialog box is displayed. Select the text file to be imported and pick the **Open** button. The text is then inserted at the current cursor location.

Exercise 8-6 Complete the Exercise on the Student CD.

Setting indents and tabs

Indents and tabs are used to offset the starting points of lines of text. Indents are typically used when paragraphs are started, and tabs are used to line up rows of text. Selecting the **Indents and Tabs...** option in the text editor shortcut menu opens the **Indents and Tabs** dialog box, **Figure 8-22.** This dialog box allows you to set up the indentation for the first line of a paragraph of text as well as the remaining portion of a paragraph. Each time a new paragraph is started, the **First line** indent is used. As text is typed in the editor and wrapped to the next line, the **Paragraph** indent is used. The **Tab stop position** text box allows you to set up a cursor stop position when the [Tab] key is pressed. Typing a new value and picking the **Set** button allows you to set up several additional tab locations in the paragraph. Picking the **Clear** button removes the highlighted tab location.

Creating lists

Lists are commonly used to organize information. They provide a way to arrange related items in a logical order. They also help make lines of text more readable. There are examples of bulleted and numbered lists throughout this text. List formatting can be applied to multiline text using the **Bullets and Lists** option in the text editor shortcut menu. You can also use the **Numbering**, **Bullets**, and **Uppercase Letters** buttons in the **Text Formatting** toolbar. These tools are used to create numbered, bulleted, and alphabetical lists.

Figure 8-22.
The **Indents and Tabs** dialog box is used to set up indentations within a multiline text object.

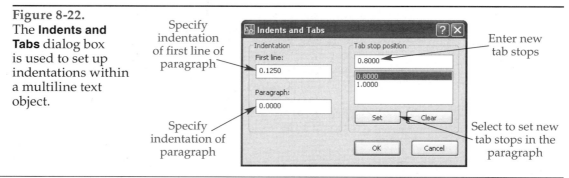

AutoCAD and Its Applications—Basics

AutoCAD allows you to apply list formatting to existing text or create lists as you enter text. The numbering or lettering adjusts automatically if items are added to a list or removed. Lists can be set up to contain sublevel items. Sublevel items are designated with double numbers, letters, or bullets. Default tab settings are used in lists by AutoCAD unless you make settings in the **Indents and Tabs** dialog box.

Picking the **Bullets and Lists** option in the text editor shortcut menu displays the cascading menu shown in **Figure 8-23.** To start a list, select **Lettered, Numbered,** or **Bulleted.** By default, the **Allow Auto-list** option is active. When this option is turned on, a list can be created by starting a line of text with a symbol, one or more numbers, or one or more letters. If you are creating a numbered or lettered list, the number or letter you enter must be followed by punctuation (such as a period, parenthesis, or colon) and a tab. After the line of text is typed and the [Enter] key is used to start a new line, the next line uses the same formatting and the next consecutive number or letter. To end the list, press [Enter] twice. A numbered list is shown in **Figure 8-24.**

When creating a bulleted list, selecting the **Bulleted** option places a solid circle at the beginning of the line of text. The solid circle is used as the default bullet symbol by AutoCAD. When a new line of text is started, the next line is also bulleted.

Other symbols can be used as bullet characters when formatting a list. You can use a typical keyboard character (such as a hyphen) by typing the character at the beginning of a line, entering a tab, and then typing the line of text. When the [Enter] key is pressed, the line is formatted as a bulleted item and the next line uses the same bullet symbol and formatting. See **Figure 8-25.** Examples of bullet characters include the following:

Hyphen   –
Tilde   ~
Asterisk   *
Angle bracket   <
Open parenthesis   (
Open bracket   [

Figure 8-23.
Options for creating lists. This menu is accessed by selecting **Bullets and Lists** in the text editor shortcut menu.

Figure 8-24.
Framing notes arranged in a numbered list.

FRAMING NOTES:
1. ALL FRAMING NOTES TO DFL #2 OR BETTER.
2. ALL HEATED WALLS @ HEATED LIVING AREA TO BE 2 X 6 @16" OC. FRAME ALL EXTERIOR NON-BEARING WALLS W/2 X 6 STUDS @ 24"OC.
3. USE 2 X 6 NAILER AT THE BOTTOM OF ALL 2-2 X 12 OR 4 X HEADERS @ EXTERIOR WALLS, BACK HEADER W/2" RIGID INSULATION.
4. BLOCK ALL WALLS OVER 10"-0' HIGH AT MID HEIGHT.

Figure 8-25.
In addition to the regular bullet symbol, other keyboard characters can be used for items in bulleted lists.

- An elevation of the beam with end views or sections
- Complete locational dimensions for holes, plates, and angles
- Length dimensions

Bulleted List with Bullet Symbols

~Connection specifications
~Cutouts
~Miscellaneous notes for the fabricator

Bulleted List with Tilde Characters

Multiple lines of text can be converted to a list by selecting all of the lines of text and then picking a list formatting option. AutoCAD detects where the [Enter] key was used to start a new line of text and lists the lines in sequence. When creating a list in this manner, space is automatically placed after the number, letter, or symbol preceding the text. The size of the space can be adjusted by setting tabs and indents.

Other options for creating lists are available in the **Bullets and Lists** cascading menu. These options are described as follows:

- **Off.** Selecting this option removes any list characters or bulleting from selected text.
- **Lettered.** Selecting this option creates an alphabetical list. There are two options available after selecting this option. Select the **Uppercase** option to use uppercase lettering or the **Lowercase** option to use lowercase lettering. The **Uppercase** option is set by default.
- **Numbered.** Selecting this option creates a numbered list.
- **Bulleted.** Selecting this option creates a bulleted list.
- **Restart.** This option is used to renumber or reletter selected items in a new sequence. The numbering or lettering starts from the beginning (using 1 or A). For example, if an item in a numbered list is selected and the current number is 12, selecting the **Restart** option renumbers the item as 1. Items below the selected item are renumbered using the new sequence.
- **Continue.** This option is used to add selected items to a list that exists above the currently selected item. The selected item is renumbered so that it continues the previous list. Items below the selected item are also renumbered.
- **Allow Auto-list.** This option enables AutoCAD to detect characters that are used to start a list and automatically assign the first list item. For example, if a line of text begins with a numeral or letter and a period, AutoCAD assumes that you are starting a list and any additional lines of text are formatted to continue the list.
- **Use Tab Delimiter Only.** This option determines how AutoCAD applies list formatting when text is typed. By default, automatic list formatting is only applied when a tab follows the initial number, letter, or bullet character. If the option is unchecked, list formatting is applied when a space or tab follows the initial list item character. This option limits unwanted list formatting by instructing AutoCAD to only recognize tabs when starting a list.
- **Allow Bullets and Lists.** This option enables the creation of lists by AutoCAD and is active by default. Unchecking this option converts any list items in the text object to plain text characters and disables the other options in the menu.

Exercise 8-7   Complete the Exercise on the Student CD.

Using a background mask

Sometimes text has to be placed over existing objects in a drawing, such as cross-hatch patterns, making the text hard to read. A *background mask* can be used to hide any portion of the objects behind and around the text, so that no objects obstruct the text. To mask objects behind text, select **Background Mask...** from the text editor shortcut menu. This displays the **Background Mask** dialog box, Figure 8-26.

To apply the mask settings to the current multiline text object, check the **Use background mask** check box. The **Border offset factor:** text box is where you set how much of the underlying objects are masked out. This value, from 1 to 5, works with the text height value. If the border offset factor is set to 1, then the mask occurs directly within the boundary of the text. To offset the mask beyond the text boundary, use a value greater than 1. If the text height is 1/8″ and the border offset factor is set to 2, the text is masked along with the area exceeding 1/8th of an inch from the text boundary. The calculation is border offset factor × text height = total masking distance from the bottom of the text. See Figure 8-27. The **Fill Color** area of the **Background Mask** dialog box allows you to apply color to the mask using the background color or a different color.

Searching for text

AutoCAD allows you to search for text in a paragraph and replace it with a different piece of text. When the **Find and Replace...** option is picked from the text editor shortcut menu, the **Find and Replace** dialog box is displayed. See Figure 8-28. Enter the text you are searching for in the **Find what:** text box. Then pick the **Find**

Figure 8-26.
The **Background Mask** dialog box is used to specify settings for a text mask.

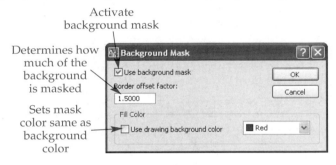

Figure 8-27.
The border offset factor determines the size of the background mask. The text in the figure is 1/8″ with different border offset factor values.

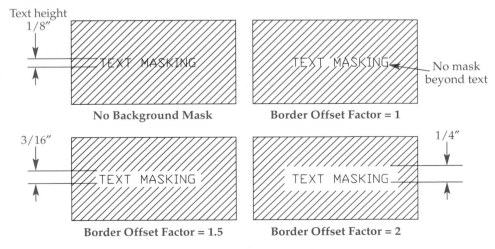

Figure 8-28.
Using the **Find and Replace** option.

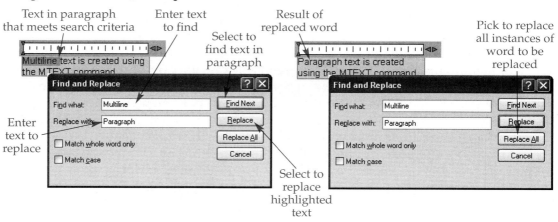

Searching for Text   Replacing Text

Next button to highlight it. Next, enter the text that will be substituted in the **Replace with:** text box. You can then pick the **Replace** or the **Replace All** button to replace the highlighted text or all words that match your search criteria.

The **Match whole word only** check box is used to specify a search for a whole word, and not part of another word. For example, if **Match whole word only** is not checked, a search for the word *the* would find those letters wherever they occur—including as part of other words, such as o**the**r or wea**the**r. You can also select the **Match case** check box if you are searching for words that are case specific.

Other text editing and formatting options

The remaining options in the text editor shortcut menu control how text is created, formatted, and selected. The following options are available:

- **Select All.** This option selects all lines of text within the multiline text object being created or modified.
- **Change Case.** Selecting this option displays a cascading menu with **UPPERCASE** and **lowercase** options. These options are the same as those found in the **Text Formatting** toolbar.
- **AutoCAPS.** This option was described earlier in this chapter. When selected, this option causes the [Caps Lock] button on the keyboard to be turned on so text will be typed in uppercase.
- **Remove Formatting.** Selecting this option removes formatting such as bold, italic, or underline from any highlighted text in the text editor.
- **Combine Paragraphs.** Selecting this option causes any lines of highlighted text that form multiple paragraphs to be combined into a single paragraph.
- **Character Set.** Selecting this option displays a menu of code pages. A code page provides support for character sets used in different languages. Select a code page to apply it to the selected text.

Stacking Text

Earlier in this chapter, the **Stack** button on the **Text Formatting** toolbar was discussed. When you enter a fraction in the **In-Place Text Editor** for the first time, the **AutoStack Properties** dialog box is displayed. See **Figure 8-29.** This dialog box allows you to enable AutoStacking, which causes the entered fraction to stack with a horizontal or diagonal fraction bar. You can also choose to remove the leading space between a whole number and the fraction. This dialog box is displayed each time a fraction is entered. If you decide that you do not want this dialog box to pop up each

Figure 8-29.
The **AutoStack Properties** dialog box.

Check to activate AutoStacking

Select style for fraction

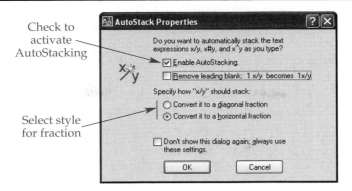

time you create a fraction, you can pick the **Don't show this dialog again; always use these settings** check box. Selecting this option causes new fractions to be created with the last settings you specified.

If you highlight a fraction and right-click, the text editor shortcut menu appears with two additional options. The first option is **Unstack**, which causes the fraction to unstack. The upper and lower values are placed on a single line with the appropriate character (^, #, or /) displayed between the numbers. The second option is **Stack Properties**, which displays the **Stack Properties** dialog box. The features of this dialog box are described in **Figure 8-30**.

Setting Line Spacing and Rotating Text

Most of the options for creating and formatting multiline text are found in the **In-Place Text Editor**. However, there are additional options that are not available in the text editor. These options are for line spacing and text rotation. They can be accessed in the **Properties** window after selecting a multiline text object. You can open this window by selecting the text object, right-clicking, and selecting **Properties** from the shortcut menu. Using this window to edit text is discussed in detail later in this chapter.

There are three line spacing options for multiline text in the **Properties** window. *Line spacing* is the vertical distance from the bottom of one line of multiline text to the bottom of the next line. AutoCAD line spacing for single lines of text is equal to 1.66 times the text height. The **Line space factor** setting is used to specify a multiple of single-line spacing. For example, single-spaced lines have a value of 1, and double-spaced lines have a value of 2. The default value is 1. The **Line space distance** setting sets an absolute value for the line spacing. The default value is 0.3333. Changing either the **Line space factor** setting or the **Line space distance** setting updates the other setting.

Figure 8-30.
The **Stack Properties** dialog box.

Top and bottom numbers in stack

Set horizontal, diagonal, or tolerance style

Select bottom, center, or top alignment

Stacked character size as percentage of normal text size

Save settings or return to default settings

Access the **AutoStack Properties** dialog box

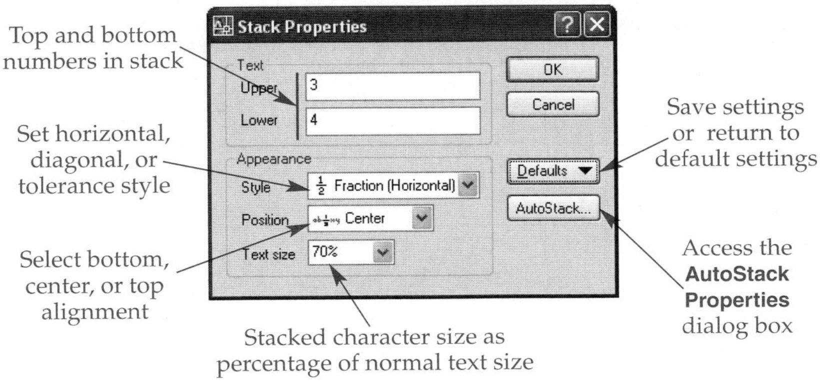

The **Line space style** setting has two options. The **At least** option automatically adds spaces between lines based on the height of the character in the line. The **Exactly** option forces the line spacing to be the same for all lines of the multiline text object.

You can specify a rotation angle for multiline text by using the **Rotation** option in the **Properties** window. With the text object selected, type a rotation value in degrees. After the value is typed, the multiline text object is rotated at the desired angle.

NOTE

The **-MTEXT** command can be used to enter a multiline text object without using the **In-Place Text Editor**. The options at the Command: prompt are identical to the options for the **MTEXT** command. Lines of text are typed at the MText: prompt, or in the drawing area if Dynamic Input is enabled.

Single-Line Text

TEXT

Type
TEXT

Pull-Down Menu
Draw
> Text
> Single Line Text

Toolbar
Text
Single Line Text

The **TEXT** command allows you to create single-line text. This means that each line of text is a single text object. The **TEXT** command is most useful for text items that require only one line of text. Whenever the text has more than one line or requires mixed fonts, sizes, or colors, multiline text should be used.

The **TEXT** command can be issued by picking **Draw > Text > Single Line Text**, picking the **Single Line Text** button in the **Text** toolbar, or typing TEXT.

After specifying the height and rotation angle, a text cursor box equal in size to the text height appears on the screen at the text start point. As text is typed, the text cursor box increases in size to display the characters. See **Figure 8-31.** You can enter multiple lines of text simply by pressing [Enter] at the end of each line. The text cursor automatically moves to the start point one line below the preceding line. Press [Enter] twice to exit the command and keep what you have typed. You can cancel the command at any time by pressing the [Esc] key. This action erases any incomplete lines of text.

When typing text on-screen with the **TEXT** command, a number of options are available by right-clicking to display a shortcut menu. There are options for using Windows Clipboard functions, inserting fields, and changing text to uppercase or lowercase. The key functions to reposition the cursor and edit entered material are the same as used when in the **MTEXT** command.

LEGACY NOTE

In previous releases of AutoCAD, the **DTEXT** command was used to create single-line text. This command has been replaced by the **TEXT** command. If you type DTEXT or its alias, DT, the **TEXT** command is activated.

Figure 8-31.
Text is entered in a text cursor box with the **TEXT** command.

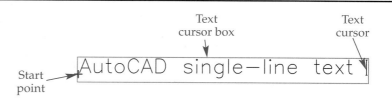

The Start Point Option

After entering the **TEXT** command, you are given the Specify start point of text or [Justify/Style]: prompt. The default option allows you to select a point on the screen where you want the text to begin. This point becomes the lower-left corner of the text. After you pick the start point, you are asked to enter the text height. The default value is 0.2000. This is where the scaled text height needs to be entered. For example, if you want letters that are .5 units high, then enter .5.

The next prompt asks for the text's rotation angle. The default value is 0, which places the text horizontally. The values rotate text in a counterclockwise direction. The text pivots about the starting point as shown in **Figure 8-32**.

After entering a value for the rotation angle, the text cursor box appears on-screen. Type the desired text and press [Enter]. If no other justification is selected, the text is left-justified, as shown in **Figure 8-33**.

NOTE If the default angle orientation or direction (**ANGBASE** or **ANGDIR** system variable) is changed, the text rotation is affected.

The Justify Option

The **TEXT** command offers a variety of justification options. Left justification is the default. If you want another option, type J at the Specify start point of text [Justify/Style]: prompt. When you select the **Justify** option, you can use one of several text alignment options.

When the **Align** option is selected, AutoCAD automatically adjusts the text height to fit between the start point and endpoint. The height varies according to the distance between the points and the number of characters. The **Fit** option is similar to the **Align** option, except you can select the text height. AutoCAD adjusts the letter width to fit between the two given points, while keeping text height constant. See **Figure 8-34** to see the effects of the **Align** and **Fit** options.

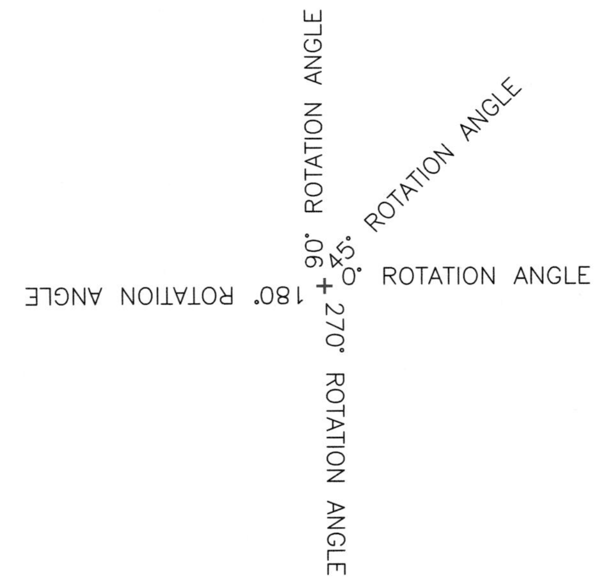

Figure 8-32.
Different rotation angles for text. The starting point is indicated here with a plus sign.

ROTATION ANGLE

Figure 8-33.
Left-justified text with the start point shown.

AUTOCAD LEFT–JUSTIFIED TEXT

Figure 8-34.
Examples of aligned and fit text. With aligned text, the text height is adjusted. With fit text, the text width is adjusted.

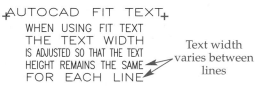

Text height varies between lines

Text width varies between lines

Align Option

Fit Option

PROFESSIONAL TIP

The **TEXT** command is not recommended for aligned text because the text height for each line is adjusted according to the width. One line may run into another.

The **Center** option allows you to select the center point for the baseline of the text. The **Middle** option allows you to center text both horizontally and vertically at a given point. The **Right** option justifies text at the lower-right corner. The letter height and rotation can also be changed when using these options. **Figure 8-35** compares the **Center**, **Middle**, and **Right** options.

There are a number of text alignment options that allow you to place text on a drawing in relation to the top, bottom, middle, left side, or right side of the text. These alignment options are shown in **Figure 8-36**. These options are shown as abbreviations that correlate to the **TEXT** prompt line. To use one of these options, type the two letters for the desired option and press [Enter].

Figure 8-35.
Three text justification options with start point shown.

AUTOCAD CENTERED TEXT

Center Option

AUTOCAD MIDDLE TEXT

Middle Option

AUTOCAD RIGHT—JUSTIFIED TEXT

Right Option

Figure 8-36.
Using the **TL**, **TC**, **TR**, **ML**, **MC**, **MR**, **BL**, **BC**, and **BR** text alignment options. Notice what the abbreviations stand for.

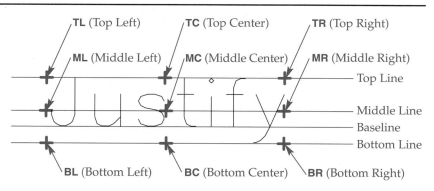

If you already know which text alignment option you want to use in your drawing, you can type it at the Specify start point of text or [Justify/Style]: prompt without typing J. Just type the letter or letters of the desired option and press [Enter].

Exercise 8-8   Complete the Exercise on the Student CD.

Inserting Symbols

Many drafting applications require special symbols for text and dimensions. In order to insert a symbol with the **TEXT** command, AutoCAD requires a control code. The *control code sequence* for a symbol begins with two percent signs (%%). The next character you enter represents the symbol. Control code sequences are used for single-line text objects that are generated with the **TEXT** command. The common control code sequences available with the **TEXT** command are shown in **Figure 8-21**.

For example, in order to add the note ⌀2.75, the control code sequence %%C2.75 is entered in the text cursor box. See **Figure 8-37A**.

A single percent sign can be added normally. However, when a percent sign must precede another control code sequence, %%% can be used to force a single percent sign. For example, suppose you want to type the note 25%±2%. You must enter 25%%%%%P2%.

Drawing Underscored or Overscored Text

Text can be underscored (underlined) or overscored with the **TEXT** command by typing a control code sequence in front of the line of text. The control code sequences are:

%%O = overscore
%%U = underscore

For example, the note <u>UNDERSCORING TEXT</u> must be entered as %%UUNDERSCORING TEXT. The resulting text is shown in **Figure 8-37B**. A line of text may require both underscoring and overscoring. For example, the control code sequence %%O%%ULINE OF TEXT produces the note with both underscore and overscore.

The %%O and %%U control codes are toggles that turn overscoring and underscoring on and off. Type %%U preceding a word or phrase to turn underscoring on. Type %%U after the desired word or phrase to turn underscoring off. Any text following the second %%U then appears without underscoring. For example, <u>DETAIL A</u> HUB ASSEMBLY would be entered as %%UDETAIL A%%U HUB ASSEMBLY.

Figure 8-37.
A—The control code sequence %%C creates the ⌀ (diameter) symbol.
B—The control code sequence %%U underscores text.

⌀2.75

A

<u>UNDERSCORING TEXT</u>

B

Many drafters prefer to underline labels such as <u>SECTION A-A</u> or <u>DETAIL B</u>. Rather than draw line or polyline objects under the text, use **Middle** or **Center** justification modes and underscoring. The view labels are automatically underlined and centered under the views or details they identify.

Exercise 8-9   Complete the Exercise on the Student CD.

Using Quick Text Mode

Text often requires a great deal of time to regenerate, redraw, and plot because each character is drawn with many individual vectors (line segments). To speed regeneration and plotting time, Quick Text mode can be used. This mode makes text appear as rectangles equal to the height and length of each text string. Quick Text mode is turned on and off with the **QTEXT** (quick text) command. **Figure 8-38** shows a comparison between displays when Quick Text mode is on and off.

The **QTEXT** command must be typed. If the last setting was off, the command line appears as follows:

Command: **QTEXT**↵
Enter mode [ON/OFF] <Off>:

Type **ON** to activate Quick Text mode and quicken the regeneration time. New text that you create is displayed in this mode. If you have existing text on-screen, it will not be displayed in Quick Text mode until the next time the drawing is regenerated. You can regenerate the drawing with the **REGEN** command. This command is discussed in Chapter 9.

Quick Text mode can also be activated by selecting the **Show text boundary frame only** option in the **Display performance** area of the **Display** tab in the **Options** dialog box. This dialog box can be accessed by selecting **Tools** > **Options...** from the pull-down menu.

NOTE

If you print with Quick Text mode on, the text prints as box outlines, not as actual text. If you want the actual text to print, turn Quick Text mode off before printing.

Figure 8-38.
Quick Text mode causes text to be displayed as rectangular boundaries.

Quick Text Mode On

THE QUICK TEXT MODE IS USED TO
SPEED REGENERATION TIME IN
COMPLEX DRAWINGS.

Quick Text Mode Off

Revising Text with Ddedit

Text editing is accomplished using the **DDEDIT** command. This command is accessed by picking **Modify > Object > Text > Edit...** from the pull-down menu, typing ED or DDEDIT, or selecting the **Edit...** button on the **Text** toolbar. The **DDEDIT** command can also be accessed by selecting the text object, right-clicking, and selecting **Mtext Edit...** or **Edit...** from the shortcut menu.

If you pick single-line text, you can edit it in-place in a text cursor box. Type the new text string or modify a piece of the text. Then pick outside of the text cursor box and press the [Enter] key to apply the changes. If you pick text that was drawn with the **MTEXT** command, you get the **In-Place Text Editor**.

DDEDIT

Type

DDEDIT
ED

Pull-Down Menu

Modify
> Object
> Text
> Edit...

Toolbar

Text

Edit

PROFESSIONAL TIP

You can double-click on a text object to edit it. Double-clicking on a single-line text object allows you to edit the text in-place. Double-clicking on a multiline text object opens the **In-Place Text Editor**.

NOTE

Multiline text is also drawn with the **QLEADER** command, which is used to create annotation leaders. This type of text is also editable with the **DDEDIT** command. The **QLEADER** command is discussed in Chapter 17.

Exercise 8-10

Complete the Exercise on the Student CD.

Changing Text with the Properties Window

The **Properties** window can be used to change text. The **Properties** window can be opened by picking the **Properties** button on the **Standard** toolbar, selecting **Modify > Properties**, or typing CH, MO, PROPS, or PROPERTIES. You can also open the **Properties** window by selecting the desired text and then right-clicking and selecting **Properties** from the shortcut menu.

You have two options for selecting text to change. You can select the desired text and then display the **Properties** window, or you can display the **Properties** window and then select the desired text. If you display the **Properties** window first, you may need to move the window before you can select the text (if the window covers the text you want to pick). Either way, the **Properties** window is opened, as shown in **Figure 8-39**.

Notice the top of the window displays Text in the box. This informs you that a single-line text object has been selected. If multiple objects are selected, the drop-down list is used to select which object has its properties displayed.

The properties of the text object are displayed in different categories within the window. Picking on top of a property allows you to modify its value. The text properties are divided into the following categories:

PROPERTIES

Type

PROPERTIES
PROPS
CH
MO

Pull-Down Menu

Modify
> Properties

Toolbar

Standard

Properties

Figure 8-39.
The **Properties** window shows the properties of the selected text. The properties of text created with the **TEXT** command are slightly different from the properties of text created with the **MTEXT** command.

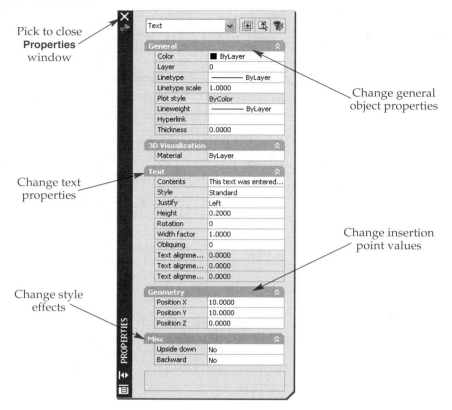

Pick to close **Properties** window

Change general object properties

Change text properties

Change insertion point values

Change style effects

- **General.** These general properties are found in nearly all AutoCAD object types. The general properties include color, layer, linetype, linetype scale, plot style, lineweight, hyperlink, and thickness.
- **3D Visualization.** Contains the properties for an object's material. This feature is used in 3D applications.
- **Text.** Most text properties are common to text and multiline text objects. These properties were explained earlier in this chapter and include items such as style and justification. The different text category settings available for single-line text and multiline text are identified later in this section.
- **Geometry.** The geometry properties are the X, Y, and Z coordinate locations of the text insertion point.
- **Misc.** The miscellaneous settings are the Upside down and Backward properties. These properties are not listed for multiline text objects.

To change a property, pick the property or property setting with the cursor. The property setting can then be edited. For some properties, a drop-down list can be used to select other settings. See **Figure 8-40.**

After you make the desired changes to your text, press [Enter] to apply the changes or pick the "X" in the **Properties** window title bar to close the **Properties** window. Then press the [Esc] key to deselect the text.

When the **Properties** window is opened with single-line text selected, some of the text category properties listed are different from those listed with multiline text. The **Width factor** property sets the text character width. The **Obliquing** property sets the slant angle for the text characters. These properties are editable for multiline text in the **In-Place Text Editor.** The **Text alignment X**, **Text alignment Y**, and **Text alignment Z** properties are unique to single-line text. These properties set the location of the alignment point for the text based on the justification setting.

Figure 8-40.
Modifying a property using the **Properties** window. When the **Justify** property is picked, the drop-down arrow appears next to the Left setting. Picking the arrow displays the drop-down list shown.

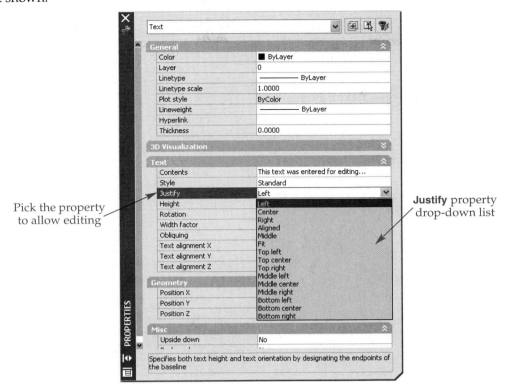

Pick the property to allow editing

Justify property drop-down list

When the **Properties** window is opened with multiline text selected, MText is identified as the selected object. See **Figure 8-41.** The properties listed are similar to those listed for a single-line text object. The properties that differ are described below:

- **Contents.** Picking the button at the right opens the **In-Place Text Editor**.
- **Direction.** The horizontal or vertical direction of the multiline text object is specified with this property.
- **Width.** This property allows you to specify the paragraph width of the multiline text object.
- **Background mask.** This property is used to set a background for the text.

The **Line space factor**, **Line space distance**, and **Line space style** settings are used for line spacing for multiline text. These options were discussed earlier in this chapter.

Exercise 8-11   Complete the Exercise on the Student CD.

 NOTE   The **CHANGE** command can also be used to modify single-line text objects. This command is accessed by typing -CH or CHANGE. After selecting the text, you can change the text style, height, rotation angle, insertion point, object properties, and other settings on the command line.

Figure 8-41.
The **Properties** window with a multiline text object selected. Note the list of text properties is slightly different from the list for a single-line text object.

Selected object type

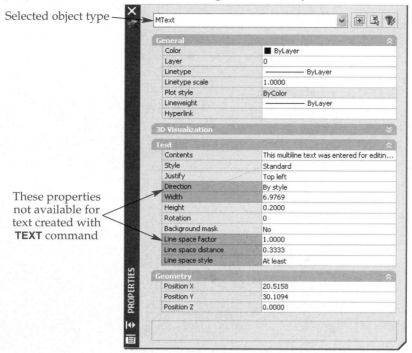

These properties not available for text created with **TEXT** command

Scaling Text

Changing the height of text objects can be accomplished using the **SCALETEXT** command. The **SCALETEXT** command allows you to scale text objects in relation to their individual insertion points or in relation to a single base point. **SCALETEXT** is accessed by picking **Modify** > **Object** > **Text** > **Scale**, typing SCALETEXT, or selecting the **Scale** button on the **Text** toolbar.

The **SCALETEXT** command works with single-line and multiline text objects. You can select both types of text objects simultaneously when using the **SCALETEXT** command. The prompts for the **SCALETEXT** command are as follows:

Command: **SCALETEXT**⏎
Select objects: *(select the text object(s) to be scaled)*
Enter a base point option for scaling [Existing/Left/Center/Middle/Right/TL/TC/TR/
    ML/MC/MR/BL/BC/BR] <Existing>: *(specify justification for base point)*
Specify new height or [Match object/Scale factor] <default>: *(specify scaling option)*
Command:

All the justification options except **Existing** and **Left** are shown in **Figure 8-35** and **Figure 8-36**. Using the **Existing** option scales the text objects using their existing justification setting as the base point. Using the **Left** option scales the text objects using their lower-left point as the base point. **Figure 8-42** shows text with different justification points being scaled using the **Existing** option. Notice how the text is scaled in relation to its own justification setting.

After specifying the justification to be used as the base point, AutoCAD prompts for the scaling type. The **Specify new height** option (default) is used to type a new value for the text height. All the selected text objects change to the new text height. The **Match object** option allows you to pick an existing text object. The selected text object's

Figure 8-42. Using the **Existing** option of the **SCALETEXT** command, text objects are scaled using their individual justification settings.

BL Justification
MC Justification
TR Justification

Original Text

BL Justification
MC Justification
TR Justification

Text Scaled Using
Existing Base Point Option

height adopts the text height from the picked text object. Use the **Scale factor** option to scale text objects that have different heights in relation to their current heights. Using a scale factor of 2 scales all the selected text objects to twice their current size.

Changing Text Justification

If you use the **Properties** window to change the justification setting of a text object, the text object(s) move to adjust to the new justification point. The justification point does not move. To change the justification point without moving the text, use the **JUSTIFYTEXT** command. This command is accessed by picking **Modify** > **Object** > **Text** > **Justify**, typing JUSTIFYTEXT, or by selecting the **Justify** button on the **Text** toolbar.

Exercise 8-12   Complete the Exercise on the Student CD.

Working with Fields

A *field* is a special type of text object. A field displays a specific property value, setting, or characteristic. Fields can display information related to a specific object, general drawing properties, or information related to the current user or computer system.

The text displayed in the field can change if the value being displayed changes. AutoCAD can update the field information automatically. This makes fields useful tools for displaying information that may change throughout the course of a project.

Inserting Fields

Fields can be inserted in both multiline and single-line text. To insert a field in multiline text, pick the **Insert Field** button from the **Text Formatting** toolbar or right-click in the text editor to display the text editor shortcut menu and pick **Insert Field...** to display the **Field** dialog box. You can also use the [Ctrl]+[F] key combination to access this dialog box from the **In-Place Text Editor**. To insert a field in single-line text, right-click and select **Insert Field...** from the shortcut menu while entering text on-screen. You can also insert a field without first accessing the **MTEXT** or **TEXT** commands by picking **Insert** > **Field...** from the pull-down menu.

Regardless of the method used, the **Field** dialog box is displayed when you select to insert a field. See **Figure 8-43**. Many preset fields can be selected from the **Field** dialog box. To make it easier to locate a specific field, they are separated into categories, **Figure 8-44**. When you select a category from the **Field category** drop-down list, only the fields within the category are displayed in the **Field names** list box. This makes it much easier to locate a desired field.

Figure 8-43.
Select fields using the **Field** dialog box.

Selected field

Current value for field

Select category to limit field list

All available fields listed

Select text format for field

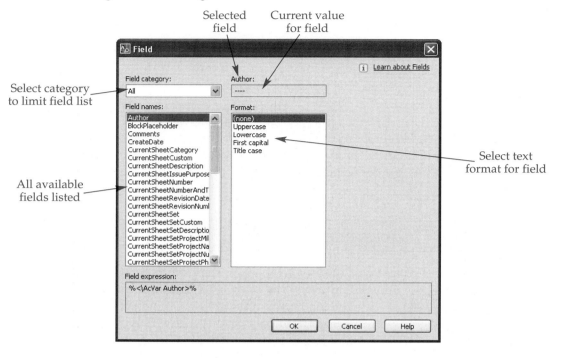

Figure 8-44.
Fields are separated into categories.

Categories

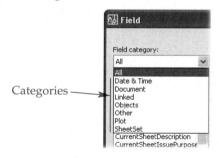

Pick the field category, and then pick the field to be inserted from the **Field name** list box. The selected field and its current value are displayed in the center of the **Field** dialog box. You can also select from a list of formats to determine the display of the field. The **Format** list varies, depending on the selected field.

Once you have selected the field and format, pick the **OK** button to insert the field. The field assumes the current text style properties, such as font type and size. By default, the field text has a gray background. See **Figure 8-45.** This keeps you aware that the text is actually a field, so the value displayed may change. You can deactivate the background in the **Fields** area of the **User Preferences** tab of the **Options** dialog box, **Figure 8-46.** If you inserted the field from the **Insert** pull-down menu, the field is inserted as a multiline text object.

Updating Fields

Once a field is inserted into a drawing, the value being displayed may change. For example, a field displaying the current date changes value every date. A field displaying the file name will change if the file name changes. A field displaying the value of an object property will change if the object is modified and the property is

Figure 8-45.
A date and time field inserted into multiline text. The gray background identifies the text as a field.

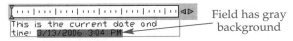

Field has gray background

Figure 8-46.
The **Fields** area of the **User Preferences** tab in the **Options** dialog box contains field settings.

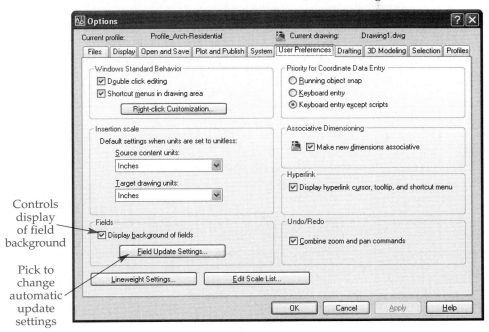

Controls display of field background

Pick to change automatic update settings

changed. *Updating* is the process of AutoCAD checking the value of the field and changing the display if needed.

Updating can be completed automatically or manually. Automatic updating is set using the **Field Update Settings** dialog box, **Figure 8-47.** To access this dialog box, pick the **Field Update Settings...** button in the **Fields** area of the **User Preferences** tab of the **Options** dialog box. Whenever a selected event (such as saving or regenerating) occurs, all fields are automatically updated.

You can also update fields manually by selecting **Update Fields** from the **Tools** pull-down menu (**UPDATEFIELD** command). After picking the command, select the fields to be updated. You can use the **All** selection option to quickly update all fields.

Editing Fields

There may be instances in which you wish to edit a field. Typically, you would do so to select a different display format.

To edit a field, you must first select the text object containing the field for editing. Then, double-click on the field to display the **Field** dialog box. You can also right-click on the field and pick **Edit Field...** from the shortcut menu. Use the **Field** dialog box to modify the field settings and pick **OK** to have the changes applied.

You can also convert a field to standard text. When you convert a field, the current value displayed becomes text, the association to the field is lost, and the value will no longer update. To convert a field to text, select the text for editing, right-click on the field, and pick the **Convert Field To Text** option.

Figure 8-47.
The **Field Update Settings** dialog box.

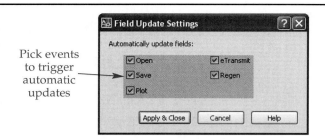

Pick events to trigger automatic updates

NOTE

Fields can be used in conjunction with many AutoCAD tools, including inquiry commands, drawing properties, attributes, and sheet sets. Specific field applications are discussed where appropriate throughout this textbook.

Exercise 8-13

Complete the Exercise on the Student CD.

Checking Your Spelling

You have been introduced to editing text on the drawing using the **DDEDIT** command and the **Properties** window. You can use these methods to change lines of text and even correct spelling errors. However, AutoCAD has a powerful and convenient tool for checking the spelling on your drawing.

To check spelling, type SP or SPELL or pick **Tools > Spelling**. After entering the command, you are asked to select the text to be checked. You need to pick each line of single-line text or make one pick on multiline text to select the entire paragraph. You can enter the **All** selection method to select all text in the drawing.

The **Check Spelling** dialog box is displayed. See **Figure 8-48**. The following describes the features found in the **Check Spelling** dialog box:

- **Current dictionary: American English.** The dictionary being used is identified at the top of the dialog box. You can change to a different dictionary by picking the **Change Dictionaries...** button.

SPELL

Type
SPELL
SP
Pull-Down Menu
Tools
> Spelling

Figure 8-48.
The **Check Spelling** dialog box.

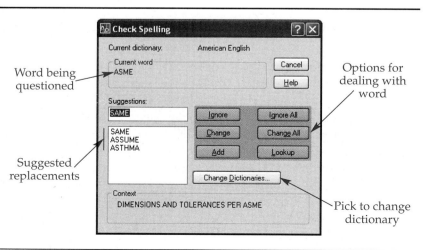

Word being questioned

Suggested replacements

Options for dealing with word

Pick to change dictionary

- **Current word.** Displayed is a word that may be spelled incorrectly.
- **Suggestions.** This area gives you a list of possible correct spellings for the current word. The highlighted word in the first box is AutoCAD's best guess. Following the highlighted word is a list of other choices. If there are many choices, a scroll bar is available for you to use. If you do not like the word that AutoCAD has highlighted, move the cursor to another word and pick it. The word you pick then becomes highlighted in the list and is shown in the **Suggestions** text box. If none of the words in the **Suggestions** text box or list are correct and the current word is not correct either, you can enter the correct word in the text box.
- **Ignore.** Pick this button to skip the current word. In Figure 8-48, ASME is not a misspelled word, it just is not recognized by the dictionary. Select the **Ignore** button and the spell check goes on to the next word.
- **Ignore All.** Pick this button if you want AutoCAD to ignore all words that match the currently found misspelled word.
- **Change.** Pick this button to replace the current word with the word in the **Suggestions** text box.
- **Change All.** Pick this button if you want to replace the current word with the word in the **Suggestions** text box throughout the entire selection set.
- **Add.** Pick this button to add the current word to the custom dictionary. You can add words with up to 63 characters.
- **Lookup.** This button asks AutoCAD to check the spelling of the word you enter in the **Suggestions** text box.
- **Context.** At the bottom of the dialog box, AutoCAD displays the line of text where the current word was found.

Changing Dictionaries

AutoCAD provides you with several dictionaries for spelling: one American English, two British English, and two French. There are also dictionaries available for 24 different languages. Pick the **Change Dictionaries...** button to access the **Change Dictionaries** dialog box. See Figure 8-49.

The features of the **Change Dictionaries** dialog box include the following:
- **Main dictionary area.** This is where you can select one of the many language dictionaries to use as the current dictionary. To change the main dictionary, pick the down arrow to access the drop-down list. Next, pick the desired language dictionary from the list. The main dictionary is protected and cannot be added to.
- **Custom dictionary area.** This area displays the name of the current custom dictionary, sample.cus by default. You can create your own custom dictionary by entering a new file name with a .cus extension. Words can be added or deleted and dictionaries can be combined using any standard text editor. If you use a word processor such as Microsoft Word, be sure to save the file as *text only*, with no special text formatting or printer codes.

PROFESSIONAL TIP You can create custom dictionaries for various disciplines. For example, when in a mechanical drawing, common abbreviations and brand names might be added to a mech.cus file. A separate file named arch.cus might contain common architectural abbreviations and frequently used brand names.

Figure 8-49.
The **Change Dictionaries** dialog box.

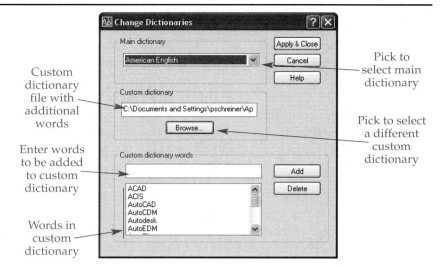

Custom dictionary file with additional words

Enter words to be added to custom dictionary

Words in custom dictionary

Pick to select main dictionary

Pick to select a different custom dictionary

- **Browse....** Pick this button to access the **Select Custom Dictionary** dialog box.
- **Custom dictionary words area.** Type a word in the text box that you either want to add or delete from the custom dictionary. For example, ASME Y14.5M is custom text used in engineering drafting. Pick the **Add** button to accept the custom word in the text box, or pick the **Delete** button to remove the word from the custom dictionary. Custom dictionary entries may be up to 63 characters in length.

NOTE

The current main and custom dictionaries are stored in the **DCTMAIN** and **DCTCUST** system variables, respectively.

Exercise 8-14

Complete the Exercise on the Student CD.

Finding and Replacing Text

FIND

Type
FIND

Pull-Down Menu
Edit
> Find...

Toolbar
Text

Find

You can use the **SPELL** command to check and correct the spelling of text in a drawing. If you want to find a piece of text in your drawing and replace it with an alternative piece of text in a single instance or throughout your drawing, you should use the **FIND** command.

To find a string of text in the drawing, type FIND, pick **Edit > Find...** from the pull-down menu, or pick the **Find...** button on the **Text** toolbar. After you type the command, AutoCAD displays the **Find and Replace** dialog box. See **Figure 8-50.**

The **Find and Replace** dialog box contains the following elements:
- **Find text string.** Specify the text string that you want to find in this text box. Type a string, or choose one of the six most recently used strings from the drop-down list.
- **Replace with.** Specify the text string you want to replace with in this text box. Enter a string, or choose one of the most recently used strings from the drop-down list.

Figure 8-50.
The **Find and Replace** dialog box.

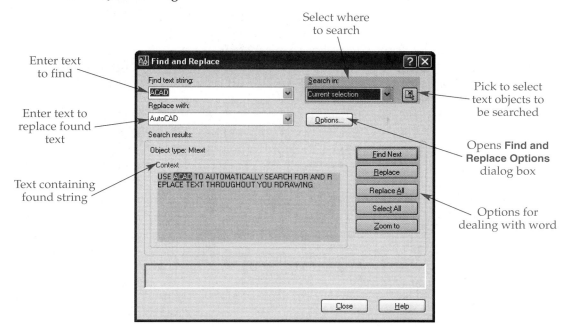

Select where
to search

Enter text
to find

Enter text to
replace found
text

Text containing
found string

Pick to select
text objects to
be searched

Opens **Find and
Replace Options**
dialog box

Options for
dealing with word

- **Search in.** Specify whether to search the entire drawing or only the current selection. If there is a current selection set, **Current selection** is the default value. If there is no current selection set, **Entire drawing** is the default value. Picking the **Select Objects** button closes the dialog box temporarily, allowing you to select objects in your drawing. Press [Enter] to return to the dialog box.
- **Options....** Picking this button displays the **Find and Replace Options** dialog box, in which you can define the search criteria for the text you want to find. See **Figure 8-51.** The following options are available:
    - **Include area.** This area contains the types of objects you want to include in the search. By default, all options are selected.
    - **Match case.** This check box allows you to include the case of the text in the **Find text string** text box as part of the search criteria.
    - **Find whole words only.** This check box allows you to find only whole words that match the text in the **Find text string** text box.
- **Context.** This area displays and highlights the currently found text string in its surrounding context. If you choose **Find Next**, AutoCAD refreshes the **Context** area and displays the next found text string in its surrounding context.

Figure 8-51.
The **Find and Replace Options** dialog box.

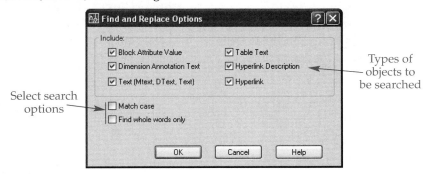

Select search
options

Types of
objects to
be searched

- **Find/Find Next.** This button allows you to find the text in the **Find text string** text box. Once you find the first instance of the text, the **Find** button becomes the **Find Next** button, which you can use to find the next instance.
- **Replace.** Use this button to replace found text with the text entered in the **Replace with** text box.
- **Replace All.** This button allows you to find all instances of the text entered in the **Find text string** text box and replace all occurrences with the text in the **Replace with** text box.
- **Select All.** This button is used to find and select all loaded objects containing instances of the text in the **Find text string** text box. This option is available only when searching the **Current selection**. When you pick this button, the dialog box closes and AutoCAD displays a message indicating the number of objects found and selected.
- **Zoom to.** Picking this button displays the area in the drawing that contains the found text.

 NOTE The find and replace strings are saved with the drawing file and may be reused.

Additional Text Tips

Text presentation is important on any drawing. It is a good idea to plan your drawing using rough sketches to allow room for text and notes. Some things to consider when designing the drawing layout include:

- ✓ Arrange text to avoid crowding.
- ✓ Place related notes in groups to make the drawing easy to read.
- ✓ Place all general notes in a common location. Locate notes in the lower-left corner or above the title block when using ASME standards. Place notes in the upper-left corner when using military standards.
- ✓ Always use the spell checker.

 **Express Tools Chapter 8** The following Express Tools are related to topics discussed in this chapter. Refer to the Student CD for information on these tools:

Remote Text	**Text Fit**
Text Mask	**Unmask Text**
Explode Text	**Convert Text to MTEXT**
Arc-Aligned Text	**Rotate Text**
Enclose Text with Object	**Automatic Text Numbering**
Change Text Case	**Justify Text**

Chapter Test

Answer the following questions. Write your answers on a separate sheet of paper or complete the electronic chapter test on the Student CD.

1. List three ways to access the **TEXT** command.
2. Give the control code sequence required to draw the following symbols when using the **TEXT** command:
   A. 30°
   B. 1.375 ± .005
   C. ⌀24
   D. <u>NOT FOR CONSTRUCTION</u>
3. When typing text in the **In-Place Editor**, how do you remove the character located in front of the text cursor?
4. When typing text, how do you move the text cursor to the left without removing text characters?
5. When typing text, how do you remove all of the text to the right of the text cursor?
6. Name the command that lets you create multiline text objects.
7. How does the width of the multiline text boundary affect what you type?
8. What happens if the multiline text that you are entering exceeds or is not as long as the boundary length that you initially establish?
9. How do you move the text cursor down one line at a time in the **In-Place Text Editor**?
10. When you are in the **In-Place Text Editor**, how do you open the text editor short-cut menu?
11. What happens when you pick the **Other...** option in the **Symbol** cascading menu of the text editor shortcut menu?
12. Name the internal storage area that temporarily stores information you copy or cut from a document.
13. What is the purpose of *tracking*?
14. Explain the function of the **Allow Auto-list** option.
15. Explain how to convert multiple lines of text into a numbered list using the text editor shortcut menu.
16. What text feature allows you to hide parts of objects behind and around text?
17. How do you draw stacked fractions when using the **MTEXT** command?
18. Define *line spacing*.
19. Outline at least five steps that are used to create a new text style with the **Text Style** dialog box.
20. Describe how to create a text style that has the name ROMANS-125_15, uses the romans.shx font, has a fixed height of .125, a text width of 1.25, and an obliquing angle of 15.
21. How would you specify vertical text?
22. What does a width factor of .5 do to text when compared to the default width factor of 1?
23. When setting text height in the **Text Style** dialog box, what value do you enter so text height can be altered each time the **TEXT** command is used?
24. Determine the AutoCAD text height for text to be plotted .188″ high using a half (1″ = 2″) scale. (Show your calculations.)
25. Determine the AutoCAD text height for text to be plotted .188″ high using a scale of 1/4″ = 1′-0″. (Show your calculations.)
26. Identify and briefly describe two methods that can be used to import an existing text style from **DesignCenter** to another drawing when you right-click over the desired text style.
27. How do you turn on Quick Text mode if it is currently off using the Command: prompt?
28. Why use Quick Text mode rather than have the actual text displayed on the screen?

29. Identify the command used to revise existing single-line text on the drawing by editing the text in-place.
30. Name two commands that allow you to edit multiline text.
31. What appears if you double-click on multiline text?
32. Describe two ways to select text objects to change when using the **Properties** window.
33. Explain how to edit text in the **Properties** window.
34. When using the **SCALETEXT** command, which base point option would you select to keep the text object's current justification point?
35. What is the difference between using the **JUSTIFYTEXT** command and using the **Properties** window to change the justification point of a text object?
36. What is a *field*?
37. What is different about the on-screen display of fields compared to that of text?
38. How can you access the **Field Update Settings** dialog box?
39. Identify three ways to access the AutoCAD spell checker.
40. What is the purpose of the word found in the **Current word** box of the **Check Spelling** dialog box?
41. How do you change the **Current word** if you do not think the word that is displayed in the **Suggestions:** text box of the **Check Spelling** dialog box is the correct word, but one of the words in the list of suggestions is the correct word?
42. What is the purpose of the **Add** button in the **Check Spelling** dialog box?
43. How do you change the main dictionary for use in the **Check Spelling** dialog box?
44. Name the command that allows you to find a piece of text and replace it with an alternative piece of text in a single instance or for every instance in your drawing.

Drawing Problems

1. Start AutoCAD, use the setup option of your choice, and create text styles as needed. Use the **TEXT** command to type the following information. Change the text style to represent each of the four fonts named. Use a .25 unit text height and 0° rotation angle. Save the drawing as P8-1.

   TXT–AUTOCAD'S DEFAULT TEXT FONT WHICH IS AVAILABLE FOR USE WHEN YOU BEGIN A DRAWING.
   ROMANS–SMOOTHER THAN TXT FONT AND CLOSELY DUPLICATES THE SINGLE-STROKE LETTERING THAT HAS BEEN THE STANDARD FOR DRAFTING.
   ROMANC–A MULTISTROKE DECORATIVE FONT THAT IS GOOD FOR USE IN DRAWING TITLES
   ITALICC–AN ORNAMENTAL FONT SLANTED TO THE RIGHT AND HAVING THE SAME LETTER DESIGN AS THE COMPLEX FONT.

2. Start AutoCAD, use the setup option of your choice, and create text styles as needed. Change the options as noted in each line of text. Then use the **TEXT** command to type the text, changing the text style to represent each of the fonts named. Use a .25 unit text height. Save the drawing as P8-2.

   TXT–EXPAND THE WIDTH BY THREE.
   MONOTXT–SLANT TO THE LEFT –30°.
   ROMANS–SLANT TO THE RIGHT 30°.
   ROMAND–BACKWARDS.
   ROMANC–VERTICAL.
   ITALICC–UNDERSCORED AND OVERSCORED.
   ROMANS–USE 16d NAILS @ 10″ OC.
   ROMANT–∅32 (812.8).

3. Start AutoCAD and use the setup option of your choice. Create text styles with a .375 height with the following fonts: Arial, BankGothic Lt BT, CityBlueprint, Stylus BT, Swis721 BdOul BT, Vineta BT, and Wingdings. Use the **TEXT** command to type the complete alphabet and numbers 1–10 for the text styles. Also, type all symbols available on the keyboard and the diameter, degree, and plus/minus symbols. Save the drawing as P8-3.

4. Use the **MTEXT** command to type the following text using a text style with the Romans font and a .125 text height. The heading text height is .25. Check your spelling. Save the drawing as P8-4.

NOTES:
1.   INTERPRET DIMENSIONS AND TOLERANCES PER ASME Y14.5M−1994.
2.   REMOVE ALL BURRS AND SHARP EDGES.

CASTING NOTES UNLESS OTHERWISE SPECIFIED:
1.   .31 WALL THICKNESS.
2.   R.12 FILLETS.
3.   R.06 ROUNDS.
4.   1.5°−3.0° DRAFT.
5.   TOLERANCES:
   ± 1° ANGULAR
   ±.03 TWO PLACE DIMENSIONS.
6.   PROVIDE .12 THK MACHINING STOCK ON ALL MACHINE SURFACES.

5. Use the **MTEXT** command to type the following text using a text style with the Stylus BT font and a .125 text height. The heading text height is .188. After typing the text exactly as shown, edit the text with the following changes:
A. Change the \ in item 7 to 1/2.
B. Change the [in item 8 to 1.
C. Change the 1/2 in item 8 to 3/4.
D. Change the ^ in item 10 to a degree symbol.
E. Check your spelling after making the changes.
F. Save as drawing P8-5.

COMMON FRAMING NOTES:

1.   ALL FRAMING LUMBER TO BE DFL #2 OR BETTER.
2.   ALL HEATED WALLS @ HEATED LIVING AREAS TO BE 2 X 6 @ 24" OC.
3.   ALL EXTERIOR HEADERS TO BE 2-2 X 12 UNLESS NOTED, W/ 2" RIGID INSULATION BACKING UNLESS NOTED.
4.   ALL SHEAR PANELS TO BE 1/2" CDX PLY W/8d @ 4" OC @ EDGE, HDRS, & BLOCKING AND 8d @ 8" OC @ FIELD UNLESS NOTED.
5.   ALL METAL CONNECTORS TO BE SIMPSON CO. OR EQUAL.
6.   ALL TRUSSES TO BE 24" OC. SUBMIT TRUSS CALCS TO BUILDING DEPT. PRIOR TO ERECTION.
7.   PLYWOOD ROOF SHEATHING TO BE \ STD GRADE 32/16 PLY LAID PERP TO RAFTERS. NAIL W/8d @ 6" OC @ EDGES AND 12" OC @ FIELD.
8.   PROVIDE [1/2" STD GRADE T&G PLY FLOOR SHEATHING LAID PERP TO FLOOR JOISTS. NAIL W/10d @ 6" OC @ EDGES AND BLOCKING AND 12" OC @ FIELD.
9.   BLOCK ALL WALLS OVER 10'-0" HIGH AT MID.
10. LET-IN BRACES TO BE 1 X 4 DIAG BRACES @ 45^ FOR ALL INTERIOR LOAD BEARING WALLS.

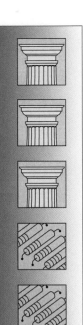
6. Open P4-4 and complete the window schedule by creating text using a text style with the Stylus BT font. Create a layer for the text. Draw the hexagonal symbols in the SYM column. Save the drawing as P8-6.

7. Open P4-2 and complete the door schedule by creating text using a text style with the Stylus BT font. Create a layer for the text. Draw the circle symbols in the SYM column. Save the drawing as P8-7.

8. Open P5-14 and complete the finish schedule by creating text using a text style with the Stylus BT font. Save the drawing as P8-8.

9. Open P4-6 and complete the block diagram by creating text using a text style with the Romans font. Create a layer for the text. Save the drawing as P8-9.

10. Open P4-7 and complete the block diagram by creating text using a text style with the Romans font. Create a layer for the text. Save the drawing as P8-10.

11. Open P5-11 and add text to the circuit diagram. Use a text style with the Romans font. Create a layer for the text. Save the drawing as P8-11.

12. Add title blocks, borders, and text styles to the template drawings you created in earlier chapters. Create a Border layer for the border lines and thick title block lines. Create a Title block layer for thin title block lines and text. Make three template drawings with borders and title blocks for your future drawings. Use the following guidelines:
    A. Template 1 used for A-size, 8 1/2 × 11 drawings, named TITLEA–MECH.
    B. Template 2 used for B-size, 11 × 17 drawings, named TITLEB–MECH.
    C. Template 3 used for C-size, 17 × 22 drawings, named TITLEC–MECH.
    D. Set the following values for the drawing aids:
       Units = three-place decimal
       Grid = .500
       Snap = .250
    E. Draw a border 1/2″ from the drawing limits.
    F. Design a title block using created text styles. Place it in the lower-right corner of each drawing. The title block should contain the following information: Company or school name, address, date (field), drawn by, approved by, scale, title, drawing number, material, revision number. See the example below.
    G. Record the information about each template in a log.

SPECIFICATIONS			R -	CHANGE		DATE	ECN
			HYSTER COMPANY				
			THIS PRINT CONTAINS CONFIDENTIAL INFORMATION WHICH IS THE PROPERTY OF HYSTER COMPANY. BY ACCEPTING THIS INFORMATION THE BORROWER AGREES THAT IT WILL NOT BE USED FOR ANY PURPOSE OTHER THAN THAT FOR WHICH IT IS LOANED.				
UNLESS OTHERWISE SPECIFIED DIMENSIONS ARE IN INCHES MILLIMETERS AND TOLERANCES FOR: ____ PLACE DIMS± _____ : _____ PLACE DIMS± _____ ANGLES ± _____ : WHOLE DIMS± _____			DR.		SCALE		DATE
			CK. MAT'L.		CK. DESIGN		REL. ON ECN
			NAME				
MODEL	DWG. FIRST USED	SIMILAR TO					
DEPT.	PROJECT	LIST DIVISION	H	PART NO.			R

13. Start a new drawing using your C-size template drawing. Draw a small parts list connected to the title block, similar to the one shown below.
    A. Enter PARTS LIST with a style containing a complex font.
    B. Enter the other information using text and the **TEXT** command.
    C. Save the drawing as TITLEC-PARTS.
    D. Record the information about the template in a log.

3	HOLDING PINS	12
2	SIDE COVERS	3
1	MAIN HOUSING	1
KEY	DESCRIPTION	QTY

PARTS LIST

UNLESS OTHERWISE SPECIFIED ALL DIMENSIONS IN		
INCHES		
AND TOLERANCES FOR:		
1 PLACE DIMS: ±.1		
2 PLACE DIMS: ±.01		
3 PLACE DIMS: ±.005		
ANGULAR: ±30'		
FRACTIONAL: ±.1/32		
FINISH: 125? in.		

JANE'S DESIGN

DR: JANE	SCALE: FULL	DATE: XX–XX–XX	APPD:
MATERIAL: MILD STEEL			
NAME: XXX–XXXX			

FIRST USED ON:	SIMILAR TO:

B

PART NO: 123–321	REV: 0

14. Create an architectural template for a 17″ × 22″ or 22″ × 34″ sheet size with a title block along the right side similar to the one shown below. Use the same guidelines given for Problem 12. Save the drawing as ARCH. Record the information about the template in a log.

15. Draw title blocks with borders for your electrical, piping, and general drawings. Use the same guidelines provided in Problem 12. The title block can be similar to the one displayed with Problem 12, but the area for mechanical drafting tolerances is not required. Research sample title blocks to come up with your design. Save the drawings as templates named ELEC A, ELEC B, PIPE A, PIPE B, or use names related to the drawing type and sheet size.

16. Draw the AND/OR schematic shown below. Save your drawing as P8-16.

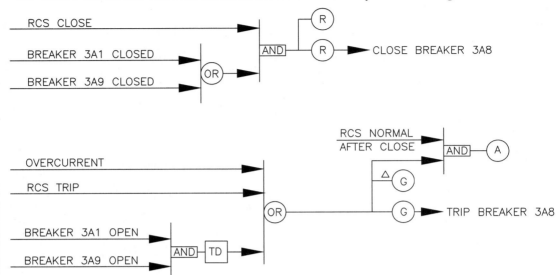

17. Draw the controller schematic shown below. Save your drawing as P8-17.

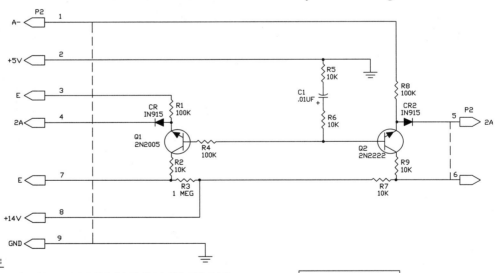

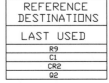

18. Draw the general caulking notes shown below. Save your drawing as **P8-18**.

CAULKING NOTES:

CAULKING REQUIREMENTS BASED ON 1992
OREGON RESIDENTIAL ENERGY CODE

1. SEAL THE EXTERIOR SHEATHING AT CORNERS, JOINTS, DOORS, WINDOWS, AND FOUNDATION SILL WITH SILICONE CAULK.
2. CAULK THE FOLLOWING OPENINGS W/ EXPANDED FOAM, BACKER RODS, OR SIMILAR:
   - ANY SPACE BETWEEN WINDOW AND DOOR FRAMES
   - BETWEEN ALL EXTERIOR WALL SOLE PLATES AND PLY SHEATHING
   - ON TOP OF RIM JOIST PRIOR TO PLYWOOD FLOOR APPLICATION
   - WALL SHEATHING TO TOP PLATE
   - JOINTS BETWEEN WALL AND FOUNDATION
   - JOINTS BETWEEN WALL AND ROOF
   - JOINTS BETWEEN WALL PANELS
   - AROUND OPENINGS

19. Draw the basic organizational chart shown below. Save your drawing as **P8-19**.

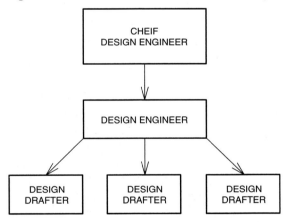

20. Draw the finish schedule shown below. Save your drawing as **P8-20**.

ROOM	FLOOR				WALLS					CEIL	
	CARPET	VINYL	TILE	HARDWOOD	PAINT	PAPER	TEXTURE	SPRAY	SMOOTH	BROCADE	PAINT
FOYER			•		•		•			•	•
KITCHEN			•			•		•	•		•
DINING				•	•		•			•	•
FAMILY	•				•		•			•	•
LIVING	•				•		•			•	•
MAST BED	•				•		•			•	•
MAST BATH		•				•		•	•		•
BATH 2		•				•		•	•		•
BED 2	•				•		•			•	•
BED 3	•				•		•			•	•
UTILITY		•				•		•	•		•

INTERIOR FINISH SCHEDULE

21. Draw the flow chart shown below. Save your drawing as P8-21.

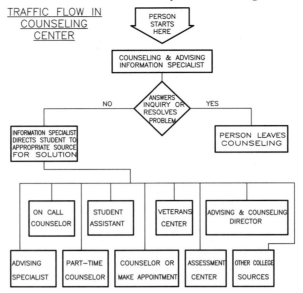

22. Draw the engineering change notice form shown below. Save your drawing as P8-22.

Engineering Change Notice

ECN NO.

Disposion of production stock:
A =Alter or rework U=Use in production
T=Transfer to service stock   S=Scrap

Qty.	Drawing Size Part No.	R/N	Description	Change	Other Usage in Production	D/S
01						
02						
03						
04						
05						
06						
07						
08						
09						
10						
11						
12						
13						
14						
15						
16						
17						
18						

Reason:

Castings & forgings affected? ☐ Yes ☐ No	Design engineer:	Supervisor approval:	Release date:	Page

CHAPTER 9

Working with Tables

Learning Objectives

After completing this chapter, you will be able to do the following:

- Create a table for use in a specific drafting discipline.
- Enter text into a table.
- Edit a table.
- Insert formulas into table cells to perform calculations on numeric data.
- Create table styles.

A *table* consists of rows and columns that organize data to make it easier to read. Tables are commonly used in drafting to show information such as bills of materials, door and window schedules, legends, and title block information.

Inserting Tables

The **TABLE** command allows you to insert a table by specifying the number of rows and columns. Once the table is inserted, text can be typed into the table cells. You can also insert blocks and fields into table cells. Tables can contain specific format settings defined in styles. The style settings can be used in the same drawing or even other drawing files. This saves valuable drafting time and ensures that school or company standards are followed.

To insert a table, pick **Draw > Table…**, pick the **Table** button in the **Draw** toolbar, or type TB or TABLE. This opens the **Insert Table** dialog box, **Figure 9-1.** In the **Table Style Settings** area, a table style can be selected from the **Table Style name** drop-down list, or the ellipsis (**…**) button can be selected to create or modify a style. The **Text height** setting indicates the current text height for the table style and the preview area shows a preview of a table with the current table style settings. The preview area does not adjust to the column and row settings, but shows table style properties such as text font, text color, and background color.

A table can be inserted by picking an insertion point or by windowing an area. This option is set in the **Insertion Behavior** area. If **Specify insertion point** is selected, picking the **OK** button prompts for an insertion point. When this option is used, the table is created by using the values in the **Column & Row Settings** area. A table created with three columns and five data rows using the **Insertion point** option is shown in **Figure 9-2A.**

TABLE

Type	
TABLE	
TB	
Pull-Down Menu	
Draw	
> Table…	
Toolbar	
Draw	
Table	

Figure 9-1.
The **Insert Table** dialog box.

Create a new style or modify an existing one

Determines the insertion mode

Current table style

Preview area

Specify the column settings

Specify the row settings

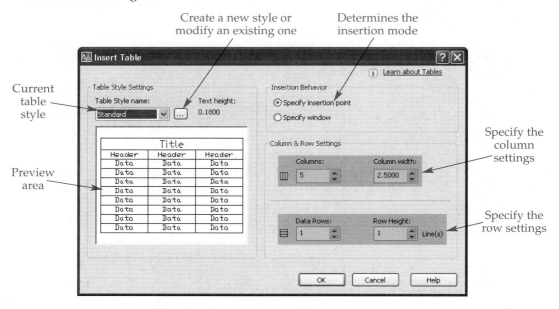

Figure 9-2.
There are two ways to insert a table. A—Specifying a single insertion point. B—Windowing an area with two pick points.

Column width and number of rows determined by size of window

Insertion point

First point of window

Second point of window

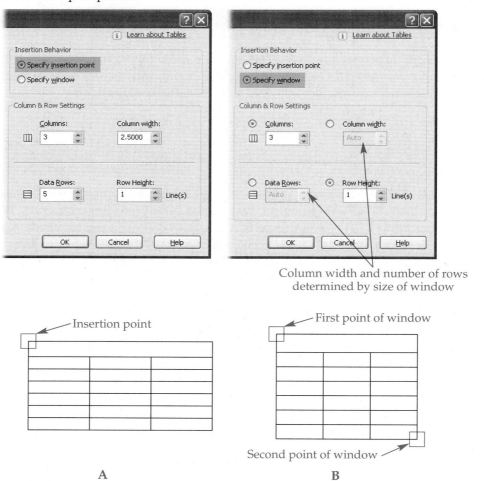

A

B

If you need to create a table to fit into a designated area, the **Specify window** option can be used. When this option is selected, only one column setting and one row setting are available. The option buttons control which settings are active. If you want to set a fixed number of columns, for example, activate the **Columns** option button. The **Column width** setting becomes unavailable and the table width you pick determines the column width. If you want to set a fixed number of rows, activate the **Data Rows** option button. The row height is determined by the height of the table picked. After you make these settings and pick the **OK** button, you are prompted to select the upper-left and lower-right corners for the table. The fixed **Column & Row Settings** values are used and the other settings are adjusted to fit the window. A table created with three columns and five data rows using the **Specify window** option is shown in **Figure 9-2B**. After a table is inserted, the values in the **Column & Row Settings** area can be adjusted, so it is not critical that the exact numbers of columns and rows are entered before the table is created.

The number of data rows you set in the **Insert Table** dialog box does not include the title and header rows. If you set the **Data Rows** setting to 1, for example, the table will have three rows because the top two rows are used for the table title and content headers. Refer to **Figure 9-1**. The default value for the row height is based on the text height and cell margin settings in the current table style.

Exercise 9-1   Complete the Exercise on the Student CD.

Entering Text into a Table

Once a table is inserted, the **Text Formatting** toolbar appears above the table and the text cursor is placed in the top cell ready for typing. See **Figure 9-3**. The active cell is indicated by a dashed line around its border and a light gray background. The columns and rows making up the table have identifying letters and numbers. These appear in a grid along the outer border. This grid is called the *table indicator*. It is used to identify individual cells in the table. This identification system is used to assign formulas to table cells for calculation purposes. This is discussed later in this chapter.

Figure 9-3.
The **Text Formatting** toolbar is used to modify the appearance of the table's components. The active cell is indicated by a blinking cursor, a dashed border, and a light gray background.

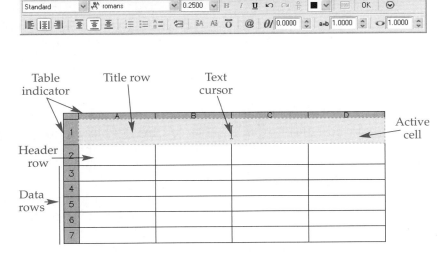

Before typing text in a cell, adjust the text settings in the **Text Formatting** toolbar, if needed. Holding the [Alt] key and pressing [Enter] inserts a return within the cell. When you are done entering the text in the active cell, press the [Tab] key to move to the next cell. Holding the [Shift] key and pressing the [Tab] key moves the cursor backward (to the left or up) and makes the previous cell active. Pressing the [Enter] key makes the cell directly below the current one active. The arrow keys on the keyboard can also be used to navigate through the cells in a table. When you are done entering text in the table, pick the **OK** button on the **Text Formatting** toolbar or pick anywhere in the drawing area to exit the **TABLE** command. **Figure 9-4** shows a completed table.

| NOTE | Text heights and other display options for the text letters and numbers in the table indicator are determined by the text heights and display settings in the current table style. Creating table styles is discussed later in this chapter. |

Exercise 9-2   Complete the Exercise on the Student CD.

Figure 9-4.
A completed parts list table.

Parts List		
Part Number	Part Type	Qty
100−SCR−45	Screw	18
202−BLT−32	Bolt	18
340−WSHR−06	Washer	18

Editing Tables

There are two levels of table editing. You can edit individual table cells or the entire table layout. For example, you may need to modify the text contents within a cell or change the text formatting (such as the font type or text height). Changes can also be made to the table layout. These types of changes include adding and resizing cells. These topics are discussed in the following sections.

Editing Table Cells

You can edit the text in a table cell by double-clicking inside the cell, typing TABLEDIT and then selecting the cell, or by picking inside the cell, right-clicking, and selecting **Edit Cell Text** from the table cell shortcut menu. This makes the selected cell active and displays the **Text Formatting** toolbar.

Right-clicking in an active cell displays the shortcut menu shown in **Figure 9-5**. This shortcut menu includes the Windows Clipboard functions. There are options for inserting fields, symbols, and imported text. There are also options for text justification and uppercase and lowercase formatting. These options are also used with multiline text. Refer to Chapter 8 for a full discussion of these options and multiline text.

Figure 9-5.
This shortcut menu is displayed after right-clicking in the active table cell.

Undo	Ctrl+Z
Redo	Ctrl+Y
Cut	Ctrl+X
Copy	Ctrl+C
Paste	Ctrl+V
Learn about MTEXT	
✔ Show Toolbar	
✔ Show Options	
Insert Field...	Ctrl+F
Symbol	▶
Import Text...	
Justification	▶
Find and Replace...	Ctrl+R
Select All	Ctrl+A
Change Case	▶
AutoCAPS	
Remove Formatting	Ctrl+Space
Combine Paragraphs	
Character Set	▶
Help	F1
Cancel	

Exercise 9-3   Complete the Exercise on the Student CD.

Editing the Table Layout

In many cases, you will find it necessary to add new columns or rows to a table in order to insert more data. The size of the table may also need to be adjusted so all of the content fits into a certain area. These changes and others can be made after a table has been created. To access the table layout options, pick inside a cell to activate its grips, and then right-click. This displays the table cell shortcut menu. This menu is different from the shortcut menu that appears when you right-click after double-clicking inside of a cell to make it active. Make sure you pick completely inside of the cell with the screen cursor. If one of the cell borders is selected, then the entire table becomes the selected object. The table cell shortcut menu is shown in **Figure 9-6.**

The first section of the shortcut menu contains the Windows Clipboard functions. When one of these options is selected, it affects the entire contents of the cell. Selecting **Recent Input** displays a list of previously entered commands. The rest of the options in the shortcut menu are discussed in the following sections.

Editing cell properties

The **Cell Alignment**, **Cell Borders...**, and **Match Cell** options allow you to set the cell justification, change the cell border properties, and match the cell properties to another cell. Selecting the **Cell Alignment** option displays a cascading menu of alignment options for text. These options set the text justification within the cell. The text is located in relation to the cell borders. Selecting the **Cell Borders...** option opens the **Cell Border Properties** dialog box. See **Figure 9-7**. In the **Border Properties** area, the lineweight and color of the cell grid can be set. The **Apply to** area allows you to apply the properties to all borders, outside borders, inside borders, or no borders.

The data formatting controls can be accessed in the **Table Cell Format** dialog box, which is found by selecting the **Format...** option in the shortcut menu. The **Data Type** area lists, in alphabetical order, options for formatting the selected table cell: **Angle**, **Date**, **Decimal Number**, **General**, **Point**, **Text**, and **Whole Number**. Selecting each of these options presents different formats in the **Format:** area. See **Figure 9-8.** You may be able to preview or see an example of the format, after a specific format is selected.

AutoCAD 2007
NEW FEATURE

Figure 9-6.
The table cell shortcut menu contains options for editing cell properties, cell content, column settings, and row settings.

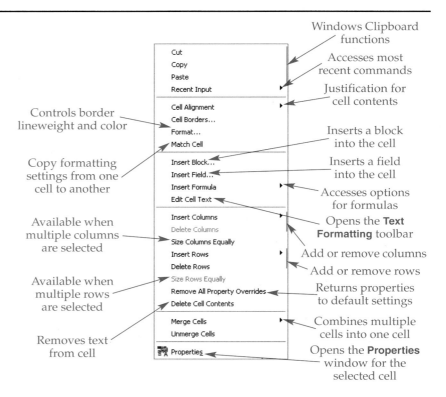

Windows Clipboard functions

Accesses most recent commands

Justification for cell contents

Controls border lineweight and color

Copy formatting settings from one cell to another

Inserts a block into the cell

Inserts a field into the cell

Accesses options for formulas

Opens the **Text Formatting** toolbar

Available when multiple columns are selected

Add or remove columns

Add or remove rows

Available when multiple rows are selected

Returns properties to default settings

Removes text from cell

Combines multiple cells into one cell

Opens the **Properties** window for the selected cell

Figure 9-7.
The **Cell Border Properties** dialog box allows you to apply lineweight and color settings to the borders of individual table cells.

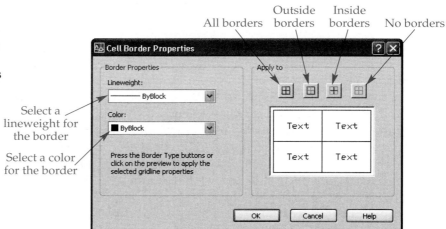

All borders   Outside borders   Inside borders   No borders

Select a lineweight for the border

Select a color for the border

The **Match Cell** option allows you to copy formatting settings from one cell to another. First, select the cell that has the settings you wish to copy. Right-click and select **Match Cell** from the shortcut menu. You are then prompted to select a destination cell. Pick the cell to which you want to copy the settings. Select another cell or right-click to exit.

If you are changing cell alignment or cell border properties, the changes can be applied to multiple cells at once. This can be done by first selecting multiple cells in the table. Changes to the layout are applied to each cell selected. For example, you can select multiple cells by picking in a cell and dragging the window over the other cells. When the pick button is released, all of the cells touching the window become selected. An example of this is shown in **Figure 9-9A.** Multiple cells can also be selected by picking a cell, holding down the [Shift] key, and then picking another cell. The picked cells and the cells in between the picked cells are then selected. See **Figure 9-9B.**

Figure 9-8.
There are many
different data types
available when
formatting a table
cell.

Table Cell Data Format Option

Data Type	Formats
Angle	Current units Decimal degrees Deg/min/seconds Grads Radians Surveyor's units
Date	*26 options for displaying the following items:* Day of the week Month and date Year Time
Decimal number	Current units Decimal Architectural Engineering Fractional Scientific
General	*No additional options*
Point	Current units Decimal Architectural Engineering Fractional Scientific
Text	Uppercase Lowercase First capital Title case
Whole number	*No additional options*

NOTE

The default cell alignment and cell border properties are defined in the current table style. If you are making significant changes to cell properties, it is better to modify the table style or create a new style. Working with table styles is discussed later in this chapter.

Inserting and editing content

In addition to text, table cells can contain AutoCAD blocks, fields, and formulas. Blocks are useful when creating a legend, or when you want to display images of parts in a parts list table. Blocks are discussed in detail in Chapter 22 of this text. The options for inserting a block in a table are briefly discussed here.

Figure 9-9.
Selecting multiple cells in a table for editing. A—Using the pick and drag method.
B—Picking a range of cells using the [Shift] key.

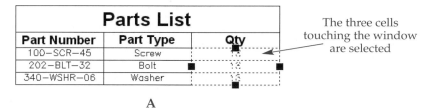

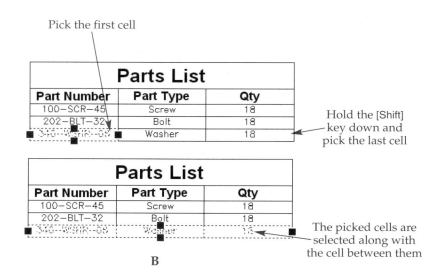

To insert a block into a table cell, select the **Insert Block...** option from the table cell shortcut menu. This opens the **Insert a Block in a Table Cell** dialog box, **Figure 9-10.** The following options are available:

- **Name.** A block that is stored in the current drawing can be selected from the drop-down list.
- **Browse.** Picking this button displays the **Select Drawing File** dialog box, where a drawing file can be selected and inserted into the table cell as a block.
- **Cell alignment.** This option determines the justification of the block in the cell. The setting overrides the current cell alignment setting.
- **Scale.** Enter a block insertion scale in this text box. A value of 2 inserts the block at twice its original size. A value of 0.5 inserts the block at half its created size. If the **AutoFit** check box is checked, the **Scale** option is not available.
- **AutoFit.** Checking the check box scales the block automatically to fit inside the cell.
- **Rotation angle.** Entering a value rotates the block to the specified angle.

> **NOTE**
>
>
>
> A text object and a block cannot reside in the same table cell. If a block is inserted into a cell that contains text, the text is erased and the block is inserted. Double-clicking in a cell that contains a block opens the **Insert a Block in a Table Cell** dialog box.

Figure 9-10.
The **Insert a Block in a Table Cell** dialog box.

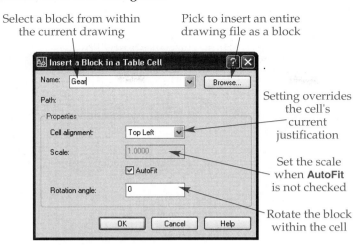

Select a block from within the current drawing

Pick to insert an entire drawing file as a block

Setting overrides the cell's current justification

Set the scale when **AutoFit** is not checked

Rotate the block within the cell

You can insert a field into a table cell by selecting the **Insert Field...** option from the table cell shortcut menu. This opens the **Field** dialog box. There are many uses for fields in text. For example, you can insert a field for a hyperlink, the current date, or the drawing file name. When creating a sheet list table for a sheet set, sheet numbers and names can be inserted into table cells as fields. Sheet sets are discussed in Chapter 26 of this text.

Formulas used in table cells are inserted as fields. Selecting **Insert Formula** from the table cell shortcut menu displays a cascading menu with formula options. Formulas are discussed later in this chapter.

Selecting **Edit Cell Text** from the table cell shortcut menu opens the **Text Formatting** toolbar and makes the current cell active. This is the same as double-clicking in a cell, as discussed earlier in this chapter.

Adding and resizing columns and rows

Columns and rows can be added, deleted, and resized after a table is created. Selecting **Insert Columns** from the table cell shortcut menu places a new column to the right or left of the selected cell. Selecting **Delete Columns** deletes the entire column (or set of columns) containing the selected cell(s). Selecting **Size Columns Equally** automatically sizes the selected columns to the same width. This option is only available when cells belonging to multiple columns are selected. The **Insert Rows** option is used to place a new row in the table above or below the selected cell. The **Delete Rows** option is used to delete the row (or set of rows) containing the selected cell(s). Selecting **Size Rows Equally** automatically sizes the selected rows to the same height. This option is only available when cells belonging to multiple rows are selected.

Editing and merging cells

There are additional options for editing the contents and properties of cells in the table cell shortcut menu. You can restore default settings, delete the cell contents, and access the **Properties** window. You can also combine adjacent cells by merging the cells.

Selecting **Remove All Property Overrides** from the table cell shortcut menu returns all property settings of the selected cell to the default settings. Selecting **Delete Cell Contents** deletes the contents in the selected cell. This is the same as selecting a cell and pressing the [Delete] key. The **Merge Cells** option allows you to merge multiple cells. To use this option, multiple cells need to be selected first. Select the cells, then pick **Merge Cells** to merge the cells together. Selecting **All** from the cascading menu merges all cells into one space. The **By Row** and **By Column** options allow you to merge cells in multiple rows or columns without removing the horizontal or vertical borders. The **Unmerge Cells** option is used to separate merged cells back into individual cells.

Selecting the **Properties** option from the table cell shortcut menu opens the **Properties** window, displaying the settings of the selected cell. The options that are not available in the table cell shortcut menu or the **Text Formatting** toolbar are shown in **Figure 9-11** and are explained as follows:

- **Cell width.** Enter a value to adjust the cell width. This also affects the other cells in the column.
- **Cell height.** Enter a value to adjust the cell height. This also affects the other cells in the row.
- **Background fill.** Select a color from the drop-down list to change the cell background color.
- **Text rotation.** Enter a value to rotate the text in the current cell.

Exercise 9-4   Complete the Exercise on the Student CD.

PROFESSIONAL TIP

The size of the columns and rows in a table can also be adjusted using grips. Selecting any of the cell borders activates the grips. To resize a column or row, select a grip and then move the mouse and pick. Grips are discussed in detail in Chapter 13.

Figure 9-11.
The **Properties** window displayed while a table cell is selected. Some of the cell settings can only be modified in the **Properties** window.

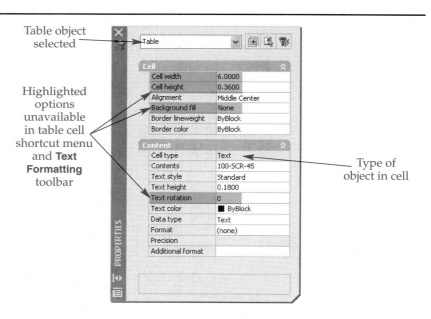

Calculating Values in Tables

It is frequently necessary to perform calculations on data in tables. For example, in a parts list, it is common to add the number of parts and show the total. In a door or window schedule, a total count of the doors or windows is commonly calculated. In a room schedule, square footage is often calculated and listed for various areas. Mathematical expressions called *formulas* can be created in tables to automatically calculate sums and other computations. Formulas are used to calculate operations based on numeric data in table cells. AutoCAD allows you to write formulas for sums, averages, counts, and other basic mathematical functions.

Table cells are identified in formulas with their column letter and row number. As discussed earlier in this chapter, the table indicator grid appears when a table cell is being edited. This grid provides a numbering system for the cells. Columns are identified with letters, and rows are identified with numbers. For example, the cell located in Column A and Row 3 is identified as A3. This system of cell identification is illustrated in **Figure 9-12.** In the table shown, the cell identified as C6 is highlighted.

Creating Formulas

Formulas are mathematical expressions used to make calculations of table data. When inserted into a cell, a formula evaluates values from other cells and displays the resulting value. Formulas are field objects. As with other types of fields, both the expression and value are displayed with a gray background. The value can change if values in the corresponding expression change. This enables you to automatically update data in a table cell when updating the data in other cells.

Table cells with existing numeric values are used for writing formulas. For example, you may want to add all of the values in a single column and display the total at the bottom of the column. You can define a formula that evaluates a range of continuous cells or cells that do not share a common border.

When writing a formula, the common symbols used for mathematical functions are entered as operators in the expression. These basic symbols are shown below:

Symbol	Function
+	Addition
–	Subtraction
*	Multiplication
/	Division
^	Exponentiation

Figure 9-12.
Table cells are identified by column letter and row number. The table indicator grid provides a reference for identifying each cell.

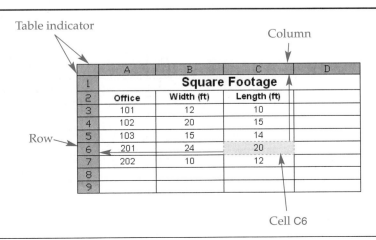

Parentheses are used to enclose expressions for table cell formulas. To perform an operation correctly, the proper syntax must be entered in the table cell. The syntax uses the following conventions:

Entry	Description
=	The equal sign is used to begin an expression. This tells AutoCAD that you want to perform a calculation.
(	An open parenthesis is used to start the expression.
)	A closing parenthesis is used to close the expression.
(*expression*)	Write the expression by typing the cells to be evaluated and the desired operator symbol(s).

A complete expression is shown below. This expression tells AutoCAD to add the value of C3 and the value of D4 together and display the sum in the current cell:

=(C3+D4)

Note that when identifying a cell in an expression, the letter must come before the number. For example, you cannot enter 3C to designate the cell identified as C3. If you enter an incorrect expression or an expression evaluating cells without numeric data, AutoCAD displays the pound sign character (#) to indicate the error.

NOTE

Parentheses are not needed in all expressions, but some expressions will not be calculated without them. It is good practice to use parentheses in all expressions.

After entering an expression, press [Enter], pick outside the table, or pick **OK** on the **Table Formatting** toolbar to close the toolbar and save the changes. An example of a multiplication formula is shown in **Figure 9-13**. The expression =(B3*C3) is entered in cell D3. The result is shown in the cell after pressing [Enter].

Figure 9-13. Entering a multiplication formula. A—The expression is typed in the table cell with the correct syntax. B—The resulting value is displayed after the expression is calculated.

	A	B	C	D
1	Square Footage			
2	Office	Width (ft)	Length (ft)	Sq Ft
3	101	12	10	=(B3*C3) ← Expression
4	102	20	15	
5	103	15	14	
6	201	24	20	
7	202	10	12	
8				
9				

A

Square Footage			
Office	Width (ft)	Length (ft)	Sq Ft
101	12	10	120 ← Result
102	20	15	
103	15	14	
201	24	20	
202	10	12	

B

Grouped expressions can also be used in writing formulas. The expression sets are enclosed in parentheses. Two examples are shown below. The first operation multiplies the sum of E1 and F1 by E2. The second operation multiplies the sum of E1 and F1 by the sum of E2 and F2 and divides the product by G6:

=(E1+F1)*E2
=(E1+F1)*(E2+F2)/G6

Creating sum, average, and count formulas

In addition to entering basic mathematical formulas in table cells manually, you can select from one of AutoCAD's formula types. The options for these formulas are in the table cell shortcut menu. These allow you to create formulas to calculate the sum, average, or count of a range of cells. The formula options can be accessed by selecting a cell, right-clicking, and then picking **Insert Formula** from the table cell shortcut menu. The **Insert Formula** cascading menu is displayed. See **Figure 9-14.**

The **Sum** option allows you to add the values of a range of cells by specifying a selection window on screen. After selecting this option, AutoCAD prompts you to pick the first corner of a window defining the cell range. The range you specify can include cells from several columns and rows. Pick inside the top or bottom cell that you wish to include in the calculation. Then, move the cursor and pick inside the lowest or highest cell, making sure that all of the cells to be included in the formula are included in the window selection. See **Figure 9-15.** When the second point is selected, the expression is automatically entered into the cell. In the example shown, the square footage for each office is first calculated in the Sq Ft column on the right in **Figure 9-15A.** The values are then selected for a sum formula that calculates the total square footage of all of the offices. Refer to **Figure 9-15B.**

Notice in **Figure 9-15B** that the resulting expression is =Sum(D3:D7). This formula specifies that the selected cell is equal to the sum of cells D3 through D7. The colon symbol (:) is used to indicate the range of cells for the calculation.

The **Average** and **Count** options are similar to the **Sum** option. The **Average** option creates a formula that gives the average value of the cells you select. The average is the sum of the selected cells divided by the number of cells selected. The **Count** option creates a formula that counts the number of selected cells. Only cells that contain a value are included in the count.

Figure 9-14.
The **Insert Formula**
cascading menu.

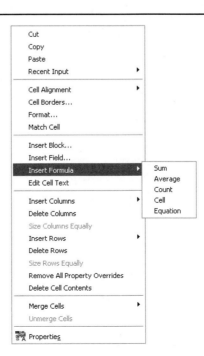

Figure 9-15.
Creating a sum
formula in a table
cell. A—A range
of cells is selected
for the formula by
windowing around
the cells. B—After
the second point
of the window is
picked, the formula
displays in the cell.

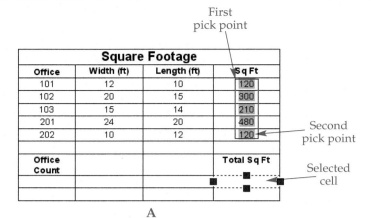

First pick point

Square Footage			
Office	Width (ft)	Length (ft)	Sq Ft
101	12	10	120
102	20	15	300
103	15	14	210
201	24	20	480
202	10	12	120
Office Count			Total Sq Ft

Second pick point

Selected cell

A

	A	B	C	D
1	Square Footage			
2	Office	Width (ft)	Length (ft)	Sq Ft
3	101	12	10	120
4	102	20	15	300
5	103	15	14	210
6	201	24	20	480
7	202	10	12	120
8				
9	Office Count			Total Sq Ft
10				=Sum(D3:D7)
11				

Sum formula

B

Sum, average, and count formulas can be typed directly into a cell without using the **Insert Formula** cascading menu. If you are calculating a value over a range of cells, use the colon symbol to designate the range. You can also write an expression that evaluates individual cells instead of a range. The cells do not have to share a common border. To write an expression in this manner, the comma (,) is used. For example, if cells D1, D3, and D6 need to be averaged, type the following expression:

=Average(D1,D3,D6)

This formula calculates the average of the cell values for cells D1, D3, and D6.

A range of cells and individual cells can be included in the same expression. For example, if cells A1 through B10 need to be counted in addition to cells C4 and C6, enter the following expression:

=Count(A1:B10,C4,C6)

Examples of sum, average, and count formulas are shown in Figure 9-16.

> **NOTE**
>
>
>
> When using architectural units in a drawing, the foot (') and inch (") symbols can be typed in table cells for use in values and formulas. When the foot symbol is used for a cell value, a formula in another cell automatically converts the resulting value to inches and feet.

Figure 9-16.
Sum, average, and count formulas and their resulting values.

	A	B	C	D
1	Square Footage			
2	Office	Width (ft)	Length (ft)	Sq Ft
3	101	12	10	120
4	102	20	15	300
5	103	15	14	210
6	201	24	20	480
7	202	10	12	120
8				
9	Office Count	Average Sq Ft Per Room		Total Sq Ft
10	5	246		1230

=Count(A3:A7) =Average(D3:D7) =Sum(D3:D7)

Other formula options

The **Insert Formula** cascading menu contains additional options for writing table formulas. The **Cell** option allows you to select a table cell from a different table and insert its contents in the current cell. The cell value can then be used in a new formula. After selecting the **Cell** option, AutoCAD prompts you to select the cell. The value of the selected cell is then displayed in the current cell.

The **Equation** option in the **Insert Formula** cascading menu is used to enter an expression manually. Selecting this option places an equal sign (=) in the current cell. You can then type the expression.

NOTE

You can use the **FIELD** command to insert and edit table cell formulas. Selecting **Formula** from the **Field names** list in the **Field** dialog box displays option buttons for creating sum, average, and count formulas. You can also select a cell value from a different table as a starting point. Table cells are selected on screen to define the formula. The **Formula** text box in the **Field** dialog box can be used for adding to or editing the formula. Unit format options are also available.

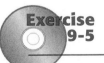

Exercise 9-5

Complete the Exercise on the Student CD.

Table Styles

TABLESTYLE
Type
TABLESTYLE
TS
Pull-Down Menu
Format
> Table Style...
Toolbar
Styles
Table Style...

In many drafting companies, standards are developed for items such as text and dimensions to create a consistent appearance of the drawings. Other types of standards are commonly used on projects for special purposes. Formatting standards are also used in tables. They can include settings such as the text height, text font, spacing, and alignment. These settings and others can be preset in tables by creating table styles.

Figure 9-17.
The **Table Style** dialog box.

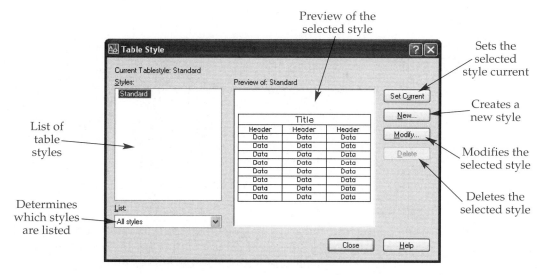

Preview of the
selected style

Sets the
selected
style current

Creates a
new style

Modifies the
selected style

List of
table
styles

Determines
which styles
are listed

Deletes the
selected style

Working with Table Styles

The **Table Style** dialog box allows you to create and modify table styles. To open the **Table Style** dialog box, select **Format > Table Style...**, pick the **Table Style...** button in the **Styles** toolbar, or type TS or TABLESTYLE. The **Table Style** dialog box can also be opened from the **Insert Table** dialog box by picking the ellipsis (...) button (shown in **Figure 9-1**). The **Table Style** dialog box is shown in **Figure 9-17**.

The **Styles** list box displays all of the table styles available in the current drawing when the **List** drop-down list is set to All styles. When the **List** drop-down list is set to Styles in use, only the table styles used in the drawing appear in the list box. The **Preview of** area shows a preview of the currently selected style. To select a style, pick it once in the **Styles** list box. Picking the **Set Current** button sets the selected style current. When a table is inserted into the drawing, it uses the formatting settings from the current table style. Use the **New** button to create a new table style. To modify a style, select the style in the **Styles** list box and pick the **Modify** button. Picking the **Delete** button deletes the selected style. You cannot delete the current style or a style that is being used in the drawing.

Creating and Formatting a Table Style

To create a new table style, pick the **New...** button in the **Table Style** dialog box. The **Create New Table Style** dialog box is displayed. See **Figure 9-18**. In the **New Style Name** text box, type a name for the new table style. The new table can be based on the

Figure 9-18.
In the **Create New Table Style** dialog box, specify the new table style's name and the existing style that will be copied.

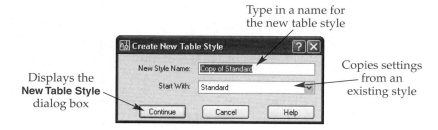

Type in a name for
the new table style

Displays the
New Table Style
dialog box

Copies settings
from an
existing style

Figure 9-19.
When creating a new table style, the formatting properties are specified in the **New Table Style** dialog box.

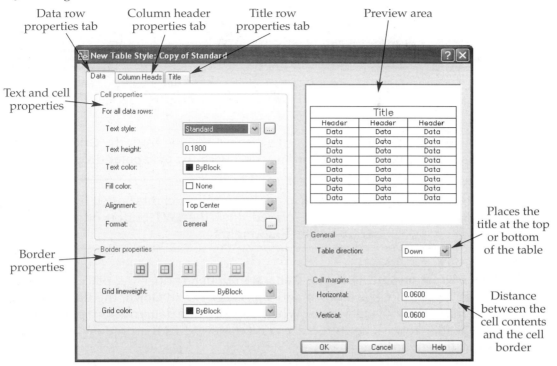

Data row properties tab

Column header properties tab

Title row properties tab

Preview area

Text and cell properties

Border properties

Places the title at the top or bottom of the table

Distance between the cell contents and the cell border

formatting settings from an existing table by selecting the name of the table style from the **Start With** drop-down list. After these settings are specified, pick the **Continue** button to open the **New Table Style** dialog box. See **Figure 9-19.**

The tabs at the top left of the **New Table Style** dialog box allow for the data rows, column header rows, and the title row to have their own formatting properties. Picking a tab displays the properties for the corresponding element. In **Figure 9-19**, the **Data** tab is selected.

The text and cell formatting properties are set in the **Cell properties** area. The following options are available:

- **Text style.** This drop-down list displays all of the text styles that are in the current drawing. If you want a cell to use text settings such as bold or italicized, these can be preset in a text style. If a new text style needs to be created or an existing one needs to be modified, picking the ellipsis (**...**) button to the right of the drop-down list opens the **Text Style** dialog box. Text styles were discussed in Chapter 8.

- **Text height.** This text box is used to specify the height of the text. The default setting for data row and column header cells is 0.1800. If a text height other than 0 has been set in the text style, this setting is grayed out.

- **Text color.** This drop-down list is used to set the color of the text.

- **Fill color.** This setting is the background color of the cells. The default setting is None. This forces the cells to use the background color of the current drawing. If you want the cell background color to be different from the drawing background, select the color from the drop-down list.

- **Alignment.** This drop-down list contains the different cell justification options.

Cell borders can be set to different lineweights and colors. There are options for different border styles in the **Border properties** area of the current tab. The five buttons at the top of this area show the different border styles that are available. An example of each border style is shown in **Figure 9-20.** The options are **All Borders**, **Outside Borders**, **Inside Borders**, **No Borders**, and **Bottom Border**.

Figure 9-20.
There are five border options for table cells. The settings shown are for data rows only.

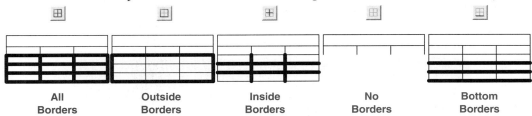

| All Borders | Outside Borders | Inside Borders | No Borders | Bottom Borders |

To assign a lineweight to the cell borders, select a value from the **Grid lineweight** drop-down list. The color of the cell borders is set with the **Grid color** drop-down list.

> **NOTE**
>
> AutoCAD displays border lineweights only if lineweights are being displayed. Pick the **LWT** button on the status bar to display lineweights.

The **Table direction** setting in the **General** area determines the placement of the data rows. The two options are **Down** and **Up**. When set to **Down**, the data rows are placed below the title and header rows. When set to **Up**, the data rows are placed above the title and header rows. The difference can be viewed in the preview window by selecting the different options.

The spacing between the cell content and the borders is set in the **Cell margins** area. This spacing applies to both text and blocks. The values in the **Horizontal** and **Vertical** text boxes determine the spacing between the content and the cell border. The default setting is 0.06.

The **Column Heads** and **Title** tabs have the same format settings that are found in the **Data** tab. The **Column Heads** and **Title** tabs have additional settings that allow you to turn off the column header and title rows if they are not needed. If the **Include Header row** check box in the **Column Heads** tab is checked, the header row is used. If unchecked, the header row is hidden. See **Figure 9-21.** The **Title** tab has a similar option called **Include Title row.**

When you are done making settings for the table style, pick **OK** to return to the **Table Style** dialog box. Then, pick the **Set Current** button to set the style current.

> **NOTE**
> If a cell's formatting properties have been specified in the **Text Formatting** toolbar, the table cell shortcut menu, or the **Properties** window, these settings override the table style settings.

> **PROFESSIONAL TIP**
>
> If table data has already been created in Microsoft® Excel, the table can be inserted into AutoCAD. This process is discussed in Chapter 28.

Exercise 9-6
Complete the Exercise on the Student CD.

Figure 9-21.
The **Include Header row** option is found in the **Column Heads** tab. The **Include Title row** option is located in the **Title** tab.

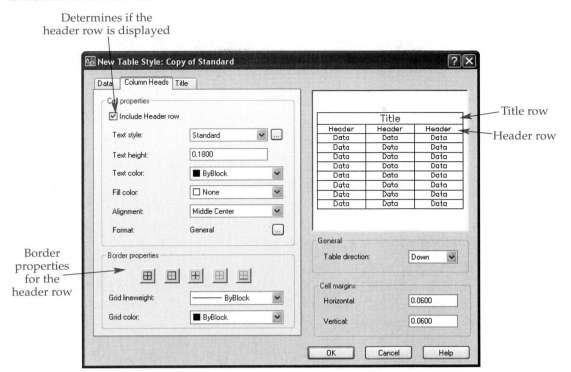

Determines if the header row is displayed

Title row

Header row

Border properties for the header row

Chapter Test

Answer the following questions. Write your answers on a separate sheet of paper or complete the electronic chapter test on the Student CD.

1. List three ways to open the **Insert Table** dialog box.
2. Describe the two ways to insert a table and explain how the methods differ.
3. By default, what toolbar opens after a table has been inserted?
4. If you are done typing in one cell and want to move to the next cell in the same row, what two keyboard keys can be used?
5. List two ways to make a cell active for editing.
6. By default, what two types of rows are at the top of a table when it is inserted?
7. Explain how to insert a block into a table cell.
8. How do you insert a new row at the bottom of a table?
9. What is the purpose of creating a table style?
10. What does the **Alignment** setting in the **New Table Style** dialog box do?
11. Which setting would you adjust in the **New Table Style** dialog box to increase the spacing between the text and the top of the cell?
12. How can you hide the title row in a table?
13. How are table cells identified?
14. Give the table cell formula that adds the value of C3 plus the value of D4.
15. What is the difference between a sum formula and a count formula?
16. What is the function of the colon symbol (:) in the formula =Sum(D3:D7)?
17. Explain how to write a formula that calculates a function for cells that do not share common borders.
18. Give the table cell formula that averages the values of cells D1, D3, and D6.

Drawing Problems

For each of the following problems, use one of your templates or start a new drawing using your own setup option.

1. Create a bill of materials for a mechanical drawing with the content of your choice, or locate a drawing with a bill of materials and make a similar drawing.

2. Create a door and window schedule for an architectural drawing with the content of your choice, or locate a drawing with a door and window schedule and make a similar drawing.

3. Create a legend for a civil drawing with the content of your choice, or locate a drawing with a legend and make a similar drawing.

4. Create a parts list for a mechanical drawing with the content of your choice, or locate a drawing with a parts list and make a similar drawing.

5. Create the door schedule shown below. Make the measurements for the rows and columns approximately the same as in the given table. Save the drawing as P9-5.

DOOR SCHEDULE

SYM.	SIZE	TYPE	QTY.
①	36x80	S.C. RP. METAL INSULATED	1
②	36x80	S.C. FLUSH METAL INSULATED	2
③	32x80	S.C. SELF CLOSING	2
④	32x80	HOLLOW CORE	5
⑤	30x80	HOLLOW CORE	5
⑥	30x80	POCKET SLDG.	2

6. Create the window schedule shown below. Make the measurements for the rows and columns approximately the same as in the given table. Save the drawing as P9-6.

WINDOW SCHEDULE

SYM.	SIZE	MODEL	ROUGH OPEN	QTY.
Ⓐ	12x60	JOB BUILT	VERIFY	2
Ⓑ	96x60	W4N5 CSM.	8'–0 3/4" x 5'–0 7/8"	1
Ⓒ	48x60	W2N5 CSM.	4'–0 3/4" x 5'–0 7/8"	2
Ⓓ	48x36	W2N3 CSM.	4'–0 3/4" x 3'–6 1/2"	2
Ⓔ	42x42	2N3 CSM.	3'–6 1/2" x 3'–6 1/2"	2
Ⓕ	72x48	G64 SLDG.	6'–0 1/2" x 4'–0 1/2"	1
Ⓖ	60x42	G536 SLDG.	5'–0 1/2" x 3'–6 1/2"	4
Ⓗ	48x42	G436 SLDG.	4'–0 1/2" x 3'–6 1/2"	1
Ⓙ	48x24	A41 AWN.	4'–0 1/2" x 2'–0 7/8"	3

7. Create the interior finish schedule shown below. Make the measurements for the rows and columns approximately the same as in the given table. Save the drawing as P9-7.

INTERIOR FINISH SCHEDULE

ROOM	FLOOR					WALLS				CEILING		
	VINYL	CARPET	TILE	HARDWOOD	CONCRETE	PAINT	PAPER	TEXTURE	SPRAY	SMOOTH	BROCADE	PAINT
ENTRY					•							
FOYER			•			•			•			•
KITCHEN			•				•			•		•
DINING				•		•			•		•	•
FAMILY		•				•			•		•	•
LIVING		•				•		•			•	•
MSTR. BATH			•			•				•		•
BATH #2			•			•			•	•		•
MSTR. BED		•				•		•			•	•
BED #2		•				•			•		•	•
BED #3		•				•			•		•	•
UTILITY	•					•			•	•		•

8. Create the parts list shown below. Make the measurements for the rows and columns approximately the same as in the given table. Save the drawing as **P9-8**.

KEY	QTY	NAME	DESCRIPTION	PART NO.
	1	CAPS	1/2−12 UNC HEX NUT	210014−29
	1	CAPS	1/2 FLAT WASHER	320014−33
	2	CAPS	7/16 EXTERNAL SNAP RING	632043−43
	2	CAPS	1/4−20 UNC WING NUT	255010−41
	2	CAPS	3/4X1/4−20 UNC BOLT	803010−11
KEY	QTY	NAME	DESCRIPTION	PART NO.
PARTS LIST				

CHAPTER 10

Drawing Display Options

Learning Objectives

After completing this chapter, you will be able to do the following:
● Explain the differences between the **REDRAW** command and the **REGEN** command.
● Magnify a small part of the drawing to work on details.
● Move the display window to reveal portions of the drawing outside the boundaries of the monitor.
● Create named views that can be recalled instantly.
● Define the terms *model space* and *paper space*.
● Create multiple viewports in the graphics window.
● Control display order.

You can view a specific portion of a drawing using the AutoCAD display commands. The **ZOOM** command is used to enlarge or reduce the amount of the drawing displayed. The portion displayed can also be moved using the **PAN** command. *Panning* is similar to looking through a camera and moving the camera across the drawing. A mouse with a scroll wheel allows you to zoom out to show the entire drawing, move a specific area to the center of the screen, and zoom in to see the details of that area without having to type any commands. Use the **View Manager** to create and name specific views of the drawing. When further drawing or editing operations are required, the view can be quickly and easily recalled.

Display functions allow you to work in model space or paper space. *Model space* is used for drawing and designing, while *paper space* is used for plotting. Detailed information on the use of model space and paper space to prepare multiview drawings is provided in Chapter 11.

This chapter also discusses the differences between the **REDRAW** and **REGEN** commands. Additionally, using the **REGENAUTO** and **VIEWRES** commands to achieve optimum display speeds and quality is covered.

Redrawing and Regenerating the Screen

REDRAW

Type
REDRAW
R

Pull-Down Menu
View
> Redraw

The **REDRAW** command is used to refresh the display of objects. To redraw the screen, select **View** > **Redraw** or type R or REDRAW.

The **REDRAW** command simply refreshes the current screen. To recalculate all drawing object coordinates and regenerate the display based on the current zoom magnification, regenerate the screen with the **REGEN** command. For example, if you have zoomed in and curved objects appear as straight segments, use **REGEN** to smooth the curves.

REGEN

Type
REGEN
RE

Pull-Down Menu
View
> Regen

To access the **REGEN** command, pick **View** > **Regen** or type RE or REGEN. The screen is immediately regenerated.

LEGACY NOTE A *blip* is a small cross that is displayed when a point is picked on the screen. These blips are not part of your drawing; they are visual indicators of pick positions that stay on the screen until it is redrawn. Blips are off by default, which eliminates the need for redraws. Blips can be turned on or off by typing **BLIPMODE** and then entering either ON or OFF as desired. Turning **BLIPMODE** on affects the current drawing only. If you want blips to be on in new drawings, turn **BLIPMODE** on in the template drawing.

Getting Close to Your Work

Zooming in (magnifying) gives designers the ability to create extremely small items, such as the electronic circuits found in a computer. The **ZOOM** command is a helpful tool that you will use often. The different options of the **ZOOM** command are discussed in the next sections.

The Zoom Options

Each of the **ZOOM** options can be accessed by its corresponding button in the **Standard** toolbar, or by selecting the option in the **Zoom** cascading menu from the **View** pull-down menu. All the buttons in the **Zoom** flyout are also found in the **Zoom** toolbar. See **Figure 10-1.** All **ZOOM** options except **In** and **Out** are available when Z or ZOOM is typed:

ZOOM

Type
ZOOM
Z

Pull-Down Menu
View
> Zoom

Options
real time
All
Center
Dynamic
Extents
Previous
Scale
Window
Object

Command: **Z** *or* **ZOOM**↵
Specify corner of window, enter a scale factor (nX or nXP), or
[All/Center/Dynamic/Extents/Previous/Scale/Window/Object] <real time>:

The **ZOOM** options are as follows:
- **real time.** This interactive zooming is the default option. Zooming is done by holding the left mouse button while moving the cursor up or down.
- **All.** Zooms to the edge of the drawing limits. If objects are drawn beyond the limits, the **All** option zooms to the edges of your geometry. Always use this option after you change the drawing limits.

Figure 10-1.
ZOOM command options. A—The **Zoom** flyout button on the **Standard** toolbar. B—The **Zoom** cascading menu. C—The **Zoom** toolbar contains the same buttons as the **Zoom** flyout.

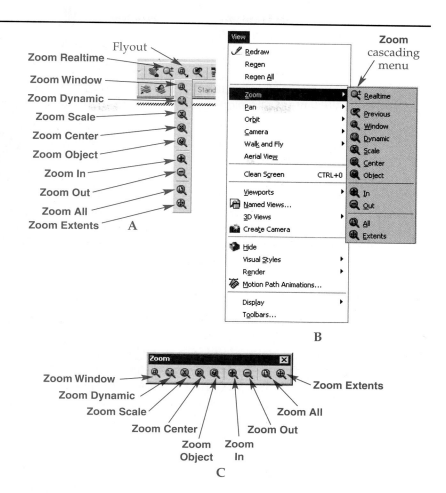

- **Center.** Zoom the center of the display screen to a picked point. If you want to zoom to the center of an area of the drawing and want to magnify the view as well, then pick the center and height of the area in the drawing. Rather than a height, a magnification factor can be entered by typing a number followed by an X, such as 4X. The current value represents the height of the screen in drawing units. Entering a smaller number enlarges the image size, while a larger number reduces it.
- **Dynamic.** Allows for a graphic pan and zoom with the use of a view box that represents the screen. This option is discussed in detail later in the chapter.
- **Extents.** Zooms to the extents (or edges) of the geometry in a drawing. This is the portion of the drawing area that contains drawing objects.
- **Window.** Pick opposite corners of a box. Objects in the box enlarge to fill the display. The **Window** option is the default if you pick a point on the screen upon entering the **ZOOM** command.
- **Scale.** The following prompt appears when you select the **Scale** option:

    Enter a scale factor (nX or nXP):

    There are two options, **nX** or **nXP**. The **nX** option scales the display relative to the current display. To use this option, type a positive number, then X, and then press [Enter]. For example, enter 2X to magnify the current display "two times." To reduce the display, enter a number less than 1. For example, if you enter .5X, objects appear half as large as they did in the previous display.

    The **nXP** option is used in conjunction with model space and paper space. It scales a drawing in model space relative to paper space and is used primarily in the layout of scaled multiview drawings.

Both of the **Scale** options can be entered at the initial **ZOOM** command prompt. For example, enter the following to enlarge the current display by a factor of three:

Command: **Z** *or* **ZOOM**↵
[All/Center/Dynamic/Extents/Previous/Scale/Window/Object] <real time>: **3X**↵
Command:

- **Previous.** Returns to the previous display. You can go back ten displays, one at a time.
- **Object.** After the command is executed, select an object or set of objects. The selection is zoomed in on and centered to fill the display area.
- **In.** This option is available only on the toolbar and the pull-down menu. It automatically executes a 2X zoom scale factor.
- **Out.** This option is available only on the toolbar and the pull-down menu. It automatically executes a .5X zoom scale factor.

The Vtenable System Variable

When using the **ZOOM** command and any of its associated options, the zoom operation is performed in a smooth transition from the current display to the new display. This feature is controlled by the **VTENABLE** system variable. To turn off zoom smooth transitions, type VTENABLE and enter a value of 0. To turn on zoom smooth transitions, type VTENABLE and enter a value of 3, which is the default setting.

The **VTENABLE** system variable also is used to change the smooth transitions for changes of view angle and for scripts. This variable also can be changed in the **View Transitions** dialog box, which is accessed by typing VTOPTIONS. See **Figure 10-2**.

Performing Realtime Zoom

When using the command line, the default option of the **ZOOM** command is **real time**. A *realtime* zoom can be viewed as it is performed. It is activated by pressing [Enter] at the **ZOOM** command prompt, by picking the **Zoom Realtime** button in the **Standard** toolbar, by picking **View > Zoom > Realtime**, or by right-clicking in the drawing area and selecting **Zoom** in the shortcut menu.

Realtime zooming allows you to see the model move on the screen as you zoom. The Zoom cursor (a magnifying glass icon with a plus and minus) is displayed when realtime zoom is executed. Press and hold the left mouse button (pick button) and move the pointer up to zoom in (enlarge) and down to zoom out (reduce). When you

Figure 10-2.
The **View Transitions** dialog box is used to change the smooth transitions for zooming and panning operations, changes of view angle, and scripts.

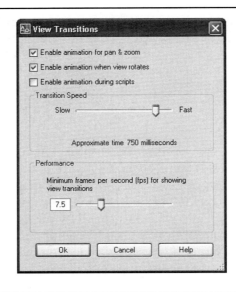

have achieved the display you want, release the button. If the display needs further adjustment after the initial zoom, press and hold the left mouse button again and move the pointer to get the desired display. To exit once you are done, press the [Esc] key, the [Enter] key, or right-click to get the shortcut menu and pick **Exit**.

If you right-click while the Zoom cursor is active, a shortcut menu is displayed. See **Figure 10-3**. This menu appears at the Zoom cursor location and contains six viewing options.

- **Pan.** Activates the **PAN Realtime** option. This allows you to adjust the placement of the drawing on the screen. If additional zooming is required, right-click again to display the shortcut menu and pick **Zoom**. In this manner you can toggle back and forth between **PAN** and **ZOOM Realtime** to accurately adjust the view. A detailed explanation of the **PAN** command is given later in the chapter.
- **Zoom.** Activates the **ZOOM Realtime** option. A check appears to the left of this option if it is active.
- **3D Orbit.** When this is selected, your point of view around your drawing can change. Similar to **ZOOM**, this option is used to move around a 3D object. A detailed explanation of **3D Orbit** is provided later in this chapter.
- **Zoom Window.** Activates the **ZOOM Window** option and changes the cursor display. See **Figure 10-4**. You can pick opposite corners of a window but, unlike the typical zoom window, you must press and hold the pick button while dragging the window box to the opposite corner, then release the pick button.
- **Zoom Original.** Restores the previous display before any realtime zooming or panning had occurred. This is a handy function if the current display is not to your liking, and it would be easier to start over rather than to make further adjustments.
- **Zoom Extents.** Zooms to the extents of the drawing geometry. This can also be accomplished by double-clicking a wheel mouse.

Figure 10-3.
This shortcut menu appears at the Zoom cursor location and contains six viewing options.

Exit
Pan
✔ Zoom
3D Orbit
Zoom Window
Zoom Original
Zoom Extents

PROFESSIONAL TIP

AutoCAD supports most mice that have a scroll wheel. This is a wheel between the two mouse buttons that usually scrolls the display up or down. Within AutoCAD, the scroll wheel has these basic functions:

- Roll the wheel forward (away from you) to zoom in.
- Roll the wheel backward (toward you) to zoom out.
- Press and hold the wheel button and move the mouse to pan.
- Double-click the wheel to zoom to the drawing extents.

The **ZOOMFACTOR** system variable controls the incremental movement of the wheel. By default, the zoom factor is set to 60 percent. Thus, each increment in the wheel rotation changes the zoom level by 60 percent.

Figure 10-4.
The cursor changes when **Zoom Window** is selected from the shortcut menu.

Accurate Displays with a Dynamic Zoom

The **ZOOM Dynamic** option allows you to accurately specify the portion of the drawing you want displayed. This is done by constructing a *view box*. This view box is proportional to the size of the display area of your screen. If you are looking at a zoomed-in view when **ZOOM Dynamic** is selected, the entire drawing is displayed on the screen. To practice using this command, load any drawing into AutoCAD. Then, select the **ZOOM Dynamic** option.

The screen is now occupied by three boxes. See **Figure 10-5.** The third box (panning view box) changes to a zooming view box during the process. Each box has a specific function:

- **Drawing extents.** (blue dotted line) This box shows the area of the drawing that is occupied by drawing objects. It is the same area that is displayed with **ZOOM Extents.**
- **Current view.** (green dotted line) This is the view that was displayed before you selected **ZOOM Dynamic.**
- **Panning view box.** (X in the center) Move the pointing device to find the center point of the desired zoomed display. When you press the pick button, the zooming view box appears.
- **Zooming view box.** (arrow on right side) This box allows you to decrease or increase the area you wish to zoom. Move the pointer to the right and the box increases in size. Move the pointer to the left and the box shrinks. You can also pan up or down with the zooming view box. The only restriction is that you cannot move the box to the left.

Figure 10-5.
Features of the **ZOOM Dynamic** option.

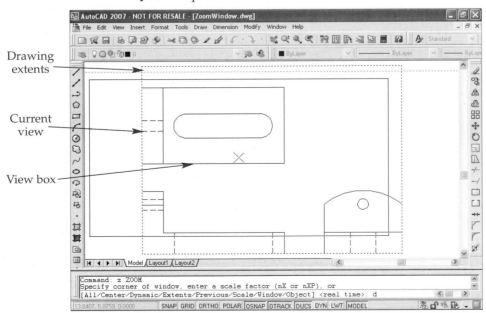

AutoCAD and Its Applications—Basics

The **ZOOM Dynamic** command is not complete until you press [Enter]. If you press the pick button to select the zooming view box, you can resize the viewing area. Press the pick button again and the panning view box reappears. The panning view box can then be repositioned over the area desired. In this manner, you can fine-tune the exact display needed. This is also helpful in defining permanent views, which is discussed later in this chapter.

Exercise
10-1   Complete the Exercise on the Student CD.

Moving Around the Display Screen

The **PAN** command is used to move your viewpoint around the drawing without changing the magnification factor. It is typically used in conjunction with the **ZOOM** command to change the display.

PAN
| Type |
| PAN |
| P |
| Pull-Down Menu |
| View |
| > Pan |
| > Realtime |
| Toolbar |
| Standard |
| Pan Realtime |

Performing Realtime Pan

A *realtime pan* allows you to see the drawing move on the screen as you pan. It is the quickest and easiest method for adjusting the view around the drawings on the screen. To activate realtime panning, pick **View > Pan > Realtime**, pick the **Pan Realtime** button on the **Standard** toolbar, or type P or PAN.

After starting the command, press and hold the pick button and move the pointing device in the direction you wish to pan. The pan icon of the hand is displayed when a realtime pan is used. A right-click displays the shortcut menu shown in **Figure 10-3**.

If you pan to the edge of your drawing, a bar is displayed on one side of the hand cursor. The bar correlates to the side of the drawing. For example, if you reach the left side of the drawing, a bar and arrow appear on the left side of the hand. These icons are shown in **Figure 10-6**.

Using Scroll Bars to Pan

The scroll bars found at the bottom and to the right of the drawing area can also be used to pan the display. See **Figure 10-7**. Pick the arrows at the end of the scroll bar to pan in small increments. Select the scroll bar itself to pan in larger increments. Position the cursor over the box in the scroll bar, pick and hold the left mouse button, and then move the mouse to see realtime panning in the horizontal or vertical direction.

Figure 10-6.
A bar and arrow appear by the hand cursor when you pan to the edge of the drawing.

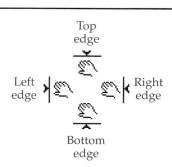

Top edge

Left edge   Right edge

Bottom edge

Figure 10-7.
The drawing area
scroll bars can be
used for panning
operations.

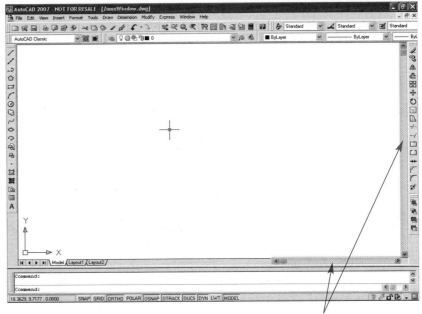

Use vertical and horizontal
scroll bars to pan drawing

NOTE

The drawing area scroll bars can be activated and deactivated by selecting the **Display scroll bars in drawing window** option in the **Window Elements** area of the **Display** tab of the **Options** dialog box. To access this dialog box, select **Tools > Options...** from the pull-down menu or right-click in the drawing area and select **Options...** from the shortcut menu.

Undoing Pan and Zoom Operations

There are times when you are working in one area of a drawing and you need to reference another area for some information. It may take a few zoom and pan operations to get to the other area. By using the **UNDO** command, you can get back to the working area of the drawing in just one undo. This is because AutoCAD groups together pan and zoom commands that are operating at the same time. This allows you to pan and zoom around the drawing and then get back to the original view quickly. To use this feature, select **Edit > Undo**, pick the **Undo** button from the **Standard** toolbar, type UNDO, or right-click and select **Undo** from the shortcut menu. This feature is controlled by the **Combine zoom and pan commands** option in the **Undo/Redo** area of the **User Preferences** tab of the **Options** dialog box. Deactivating this option makes each pan and zoom operation count as an individual undo even if they are performed at the same time. The **UNDO** command is discussed in more detail in Chapter 14.

AutoCAD provides two additional panning tools: pan displacement and pan presets. These options are available in the **View > Pan** cascading menu. Pick the **Point** option to specify a pan displacement. You specify the pan displacement by picking two points, with the drawing panning so that the first point is relocated to the second point. The pan presets options—**Left, Right, Up**, and **Down**—pan the drawing in the selected direction by a set increment. Using realtime panning is more effective than pan displacement and pan presets.

Setting View Resolution for Quick Displays

AutoCAD can save you time on zooming and panning at the expense of display accuracy. AutoCAD can also provide a highly accurate display at the expense of zoom and pan speed. The main factor is the view resolution.

The *view resolution* refers to the number of lines used to draw circles and arcs. High resolution values display smooth circles and arcs. Low resolution values display segmented circles and arcs. The view resolution can be set in the **Options** dialog box. To access this dialog box, pick **Tools > Options...** from the pull-down menu, and then pick the **Display** tab. In the **Display resolution** area in the upper-right corner of the dialog box is the **Arc and circle smoothness** text box. This contains the current **VIEWRES** setting. See **Figure 10-8**.

Figure 10-8.
The view resolution (**VIEWRES**) variable can be set in the **Options** dialog box.

Change number to change the view revolution (**VIEWRES**)

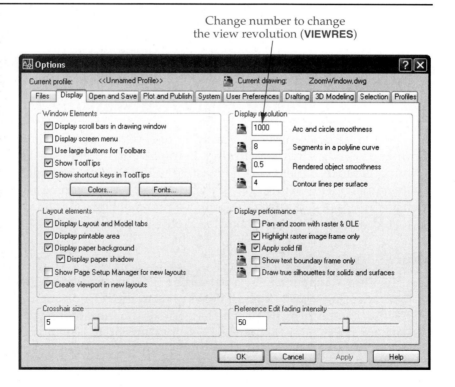

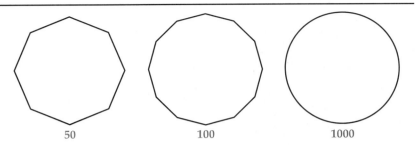

Figure 10-9.
The higher the
VIEWRES value, the
smoother a circle
will appear.

The display smoothness of circles and arcs is controlled by the **VIEWRES** setting. It can vary between 1 and 20000. The default setting is 1000, which produces a relatively smooth circle. A number smaller than 1000 causes circles and arcs to be drawn with fewer vectors (straight lines). See **Figure 10-9**. A number larger than 1000 causes more vectors to be included in the circles.

It is important to remember that the **VIEWRES** setting is a display function only and has no effect on the plotted drawing. A drawing is plotted using an optimum number of vectors for the size of circles and arcs. In other words, even if a circle you draw looks like a polygon in the drawing area before **REGEN** is used, it will still look like a circle when the drawing is plotted.

NOTE	You can change the **VIEWRES** setting by typing VIEWRES. A Do you want fast zooms? prompt appears. This prompt is no longer useful, but remains in AutoCAD so programs written for earlier versions will still function properly.

Exercise
10-2   Complete the Exercise on the Student CD.

NEW FEATURE

Creating Your Own Working Views

On a large drawing with a number of separate details, using the **ZOOM** and **PAN** commands can be time-consuming. Being able to quickly specify a certain part of the drawing is much easier. This is possible with the **View Manager**, which allows you to create named views of any area of the drawing. A view can be a portion of the drawing, such as the upper-left quadrant, or it can represent an enlarged portion. After the view is created, you can instruct AutoCAD to display it at any time.

View Manager

The **View Manager** can be accessed by picking the **Named Views** button in the **View** toolbar, selecting **View** > **Named Views...** from the pull-down menu, or typing V, VIEW, or DDVIEW. See **Figure 10-10**. The left side of the **View Manager** contains a list of view types. Each node can be expanded, except **Current**, to reveal any saved views:
- **Current.** Select this to display the properties of the current view.
- **Model Views.** This node contains a list of saved views.
- **Layout Views.** This node contains a list of viewports.
- **Preset Views.** All orthogonal and isometric views are listed in this node.

Figure 10-10.
Select a different view in the **Views** area of the **View Manager** dialog box. Create a new view by selecting the **New...** button.

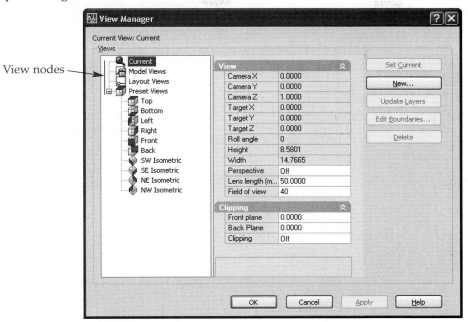

Picking one of the view types will cause the middle section of the **View Manager** to display information about the view type. See **Figure 10-11.** The right side of the **View Manager** contains buttons to control or modify the selected view or view type. These actions are also available in a shortcut menu when you right-click on the view or view type. When a view type is selected, the only button and shortcut selection available is the **New...** option. Select this to open the **New View** dialog box.

Figure 10-11.
Select each view type and read its description. The shortcut menu is the same as the buttons on the right of the **View Manager**.

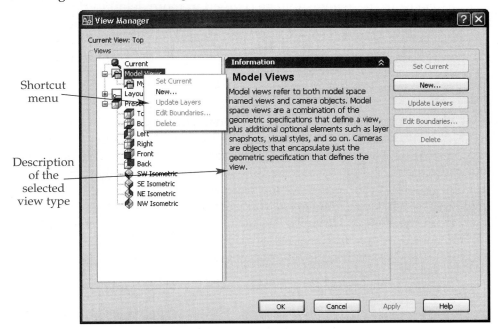

Figure 10-12.
Select a named view to see its properties and a preview image.

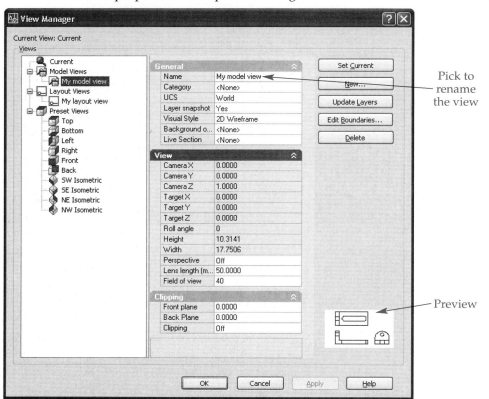

Picking one of the view names causes the middle area of the dialog box to display information related to the current view. See **Figure 10-12.** The first section, **General**, contains details such as the name of the view, layer settings saved with the view, and other settings pertinent to the type of view. This section is not visible while the **Current** node is selected. The settings in the **View** section include camera position, target position, and perspective status. The **Clipping** section controls front plane and back plane location and the clipping status. Some of these items will be covered in more detail in this chapter; others are reserved for later chapters, where the information is more relevant.

The lower-right corner of the **View Manager** shows a preview image of the selected view. This image is only visible when one of the named model or layout views is selected.

Preset views

The **Preset Views** node is used to quickly choose one of the ten preset views. See **Figure 10-13.** Notice that the icons highlight the side of the drawing that will be viewed. There are orthogonal views such as Top, Bottom, Front, Back, Left, and Right. Picking any of these icons, then pressing the **Set Current** button changes the view in AutoCAD so you are looking at your drawing from the selected direction. There are isometric views such as Southwest, Southeast, Northeast, and Northwest. These views can also be selected from the **View** > **3D Views** cascading menu or from the **View** toolbar. See **Figure 10-14.** Selecting any of these icons displays a 3D (isometric) view of the drawing. Orthogonal and isometric views are covered in greater depth in *AutoCAD and Its Applications—Advanced*.

Figure 10-13.
The preset views are available in the **Views** section of the **View Manager**.

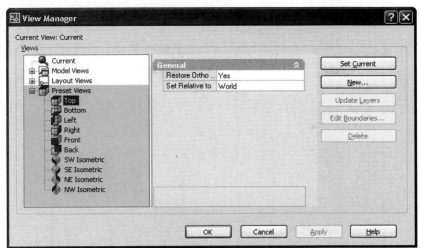

Figure 10-14.
Preset orthographic and isometric views can also be selected in the **3D Views** cascading menu in the **View** pull-down menu or from the **View** toolbar.

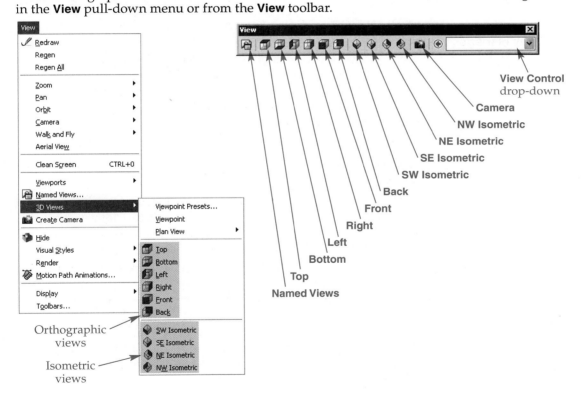

New view

If you want to save the current display as a view, pick the **New...** button to access the **New View** dialog box, **Figure 10-15.** Type the desired view name in the **View name:** edit box. The **Current display** radio button is the default. Click **OK** and the view name is added to the list. AutoCAD creates a view from what is currently being displayed in the graphics window.

If you want to use a window to define the view, pick the **Define window** radio button in the **New View** dialog box and then pick the **Define view window** button. You are prompted to Specify first corner. Pick two points to define a window. After the

Figure 10-15.
In the **New View** dialog box, you can save the current display or define a window.

Defines new view as current display

Check to save the current layer settings with the view

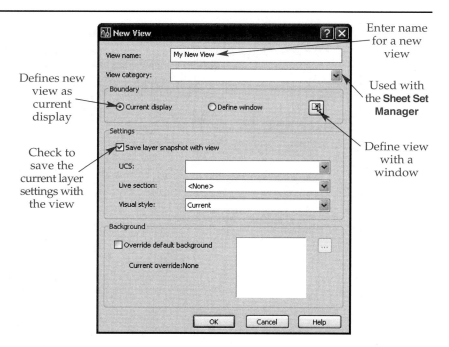

Enter name for a new view

Used with the **Sheet Set Manager**

Define view with a window

second corner is selected, the **New View** dialog box reappears. Pick the **OK** button and the **View Manager** is updated to reflect the new view.

If the named view is associated with a category in the **Sheet Set Manager**, the category can be selected from the **View category** drop-down list. The **Sheet Set Manager** is discussed in Chapter 26.

When a view is saved, the current layer settings can also be saved with the view. These layer settings are recalled each time the view is set current. To do this, check the **Save layer snapshot with view** check box.

NOTE

When creating a view, it is possible to save a named UCS (user coordinate system) to the particular view being created. The world coordinate system is the default system in AutoCAD. It determines where the 0,0,0 point is for the X, Y, and Z axes. The **UCS** command is introduced in Chapter 6 of this text and covered in depth in *AutoCAD and Its Applications—Advanced*.

To display one of the listed views, pick its name from the list in the **Views** area of the **View Manager** and pick the **Set Current** button. The name of the current view appears in the **Current View:** label above the **Views** area. Now, pick the **OK** button and the screen displays the selected view.

PROFESSIONAL TIP

Part of your project planning should include view names. A consistent naming system guarantees that all users know the view names without having to list them. The views can be set as part of the template drawings.

Using Transparent Display Commands

To begin a new command, you usually need to complete or cancel the current command. Most menu picks automatically cancel the command in progress before initiating the new one. However, some commands function without canceling an active command.

A *transparent command* temporarily interrupts the active command. After the transparent command is completed, the command that was interrupted is resumed. Therefore, it is not necessary to cancel the initial command. Many display commands can be used transparently, including **REDRAW**, **PAN**, and **ZOOM**.

Suppose that while drawing a line, you need to place one end somewhere off the screen. One option is to cancel the **LINE** command, zoom out to see more of the drawing, and select **LINE** again. A more efficient method is to use **PAN** or **ZOOM** while still in the **LINE** command. To do so, begin the **LINE** command and pick the first point. At the Specify next point: prompt, pick the **Pan** or **Zoom** button or use the wheel mouse to pan and zoom. When the drawing is displayed correctly, pick the second point of the line.

PROFESSIONAL TIP

The **Pan**, **Zoom**, and **View** buttons and pull-down menu selections activate commands transparently. The wheel mouse also works transparently.

You can also activate commands transparently by typing. To do so, type an apostrophe (') before the command name. For example, to enter the transparent **ZOOM** command, type 'Z or 'ZOOM.

PROFESSIONAL TIP

A transparent redraw is executed when **Redraw** is picked from the **View** pull-down menu. Commands such as **GRID**, **SNAP**, and **ORTHO** can be used transparently, but it is quicker to activate these modes with the appropriate function keys or from the status bar.

Exercise 10-3   Complete the Exercise on the Student CD.

Model Space and Paper Space

Model space can be thought of as the space where you draw and design in AutoCAD. The term *model* has more meaning when working in 3D, but you can consider any drawing or design as a model, even if it is two-dimensional. An introduction of user coordinate systems and the UCS icon is given in Chapter 6 of this text, and a detailed discussion is in *AutoCAD and Its Applications—Advanced.*

Paper space is a *space* you use to lay out a drawing or model to be plotted. Basically, it is as if you place a sheet of paper on the screen, then insert, or *reference*, one or more drawings to the paper. In order to enter paper space, you can pick one of the layout tabs at the bottom of the screen. See **Figure 10-16.** You can also use the **MODEL** or **PAPER** button on the status bar to switch between model space and paper space. The button displays the current environment, and picking it switches to the other environment.

Remember that you should create all your drawings and designs in the **Model** tab, not in a layout tab. Only paper layouts for plotting purposes should be created in a layout tab. To return to model space, pick the **Model** tab.

Do not be confused by model space and paper space. The discussion in Chapter 11 provides you with additional understanding. Right now, think of these terms in the following manner:

View Type	Environment	Status Bar Button	Activity
Model	Model space	**MODEL**	Drawing and design
Layout	Paper space	**PAPER**	Plotting and printing

Figure 10-16.
The layout tabs are located at the bottom of the drawing area window. The **PAPER** button indicates the paper space environment is active. The button reads **MODEL** when you are working in model space.

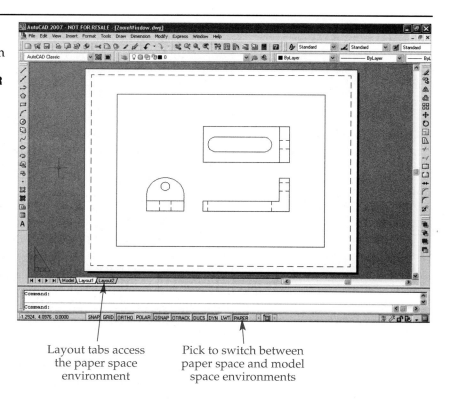

Layout tabs access the paper space environment

Pick to switch between paper space and model space environments

Tiled Viewports

The **Model** tab drawing area can be divided into various viewports. These viewports are called *tiled viewports*. Another type of viewport, *floating viewport*, can be created in a layout tab. Tiled viewports are created in model space; floating viewports are created in paper space.

By default, there is only one viewport in the drawing area. Additional viewports can be added. The edges of tiled viewports butt against one another like floor tile. The tiled viewports cannot overlap.

Figure 10-17.
An example of three tiled viewports in model space. All viewports contain the same objects, but the display in each viewport can be unique.

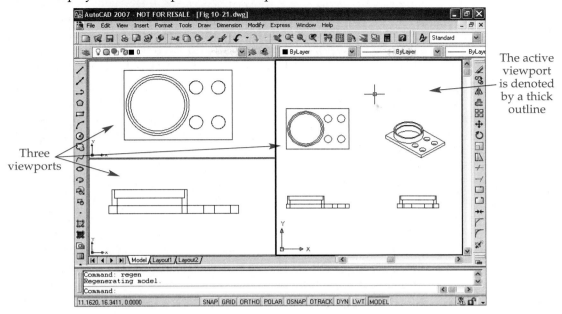

Three viewports

The active viewport is denoted by a thick outline

Viewports are different views in the same drawing. Only one viewport can be active at any given time. The active viewport has a bold outline around its edges. See **Figure 10-17.**

Creating Tiled Viewports

Viewports can be created using the **Viewports** dialog box, **Figure 10-18.** Picking the **Display Viewports Dialog** button from either the **Layouts** or **Viewports** toolbar can access this dialog box. You can also type VPORTS, or select **View > New Viewports > Viewports...** from the pull-down menu.

VPORTS

Type
VPORTS

Pull-Down Menu

View
> Viewports
> New
Viewports...

Toolbar

Layouts
Viewports

Display Viewports
Dialog

Figure 10-18.
Specify the number and arrangement of tiled viewports in the **New Viewports** tab of the **Viewports** dialog box.

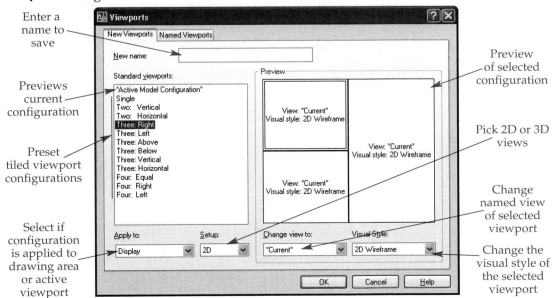

Enter a name to save

Previews current configuration

Preset tiled viewport configurations

Select if configuration is applied to drawing area or active viewport

Preview of selected configuration

Pick 2D or 3D views

Change named view of selected viewport

Change the visual style of the selected viewport

The **New Viewports** tab is shown in Figure 10-18. The **Standard viewports:** list contains many preset viewport configurations. The configuration name identifies the number of viewports and the arrangement or location of the largest viewport. These configurations are shown in Figure 10-19. Select one, and a preview appears in the **Preview** area. Select *Active Model Configuration* to preview the current configuration.

You can create a unique viewport configuration and save it. Enter a name in the **New name:** text box. When you pick the **OK** button, the new named viewport configuration is recorded in the **Named Viewports** tab. Use a descriptive name. For example, if you are going to configure four viewports, you might name this as Four Viewports.

The **Apply to:** drop-down list allows you to specify if the viewport configuration is applied to the graphics window or to the active viewport. Select **Display** to have the configuration applied to the entire drawing area. Select **Current Viewport** to have the new configuration in the active viewport only. See Figure 10-20.

The default setting in the **Setup:** drop-down list is **2D**. When this is selected, all viewports show the top view of the drawing. If the **3D** option is selected, the different viewports display various 3D views of the drawing. At least one viewport is set up with an isometric view. The other viewports have different views, such as a top view or side view. The viewpoint is displayed within the viewport in the **Preview** image. To change a view in a viewport, pick the viewport in the **Preview** image and then select the new viewpoint from the **Change view to:** drop-down list.

Figure 10-19.
Preset tiled viewport configurations are available in the **New Viewports** tab of the **Viewports** dialog box.

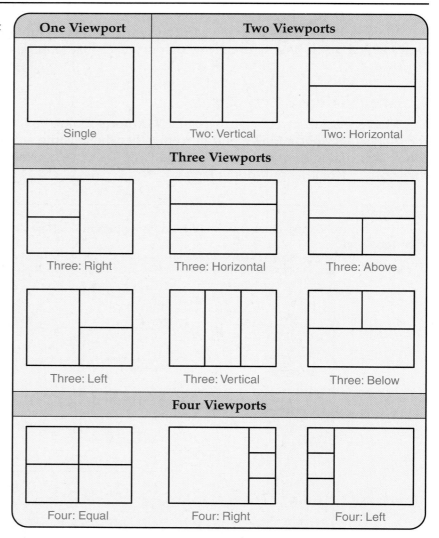

Figure 10-20.
Viewport configurations can be applied to the drawing area or the active viewport. A—Original configuration (Three: Right). B—Use the **Current Viewport** option to create additional viewports within the active viewport. Here, the Two: Vertical configuration is specified for the active viewport.

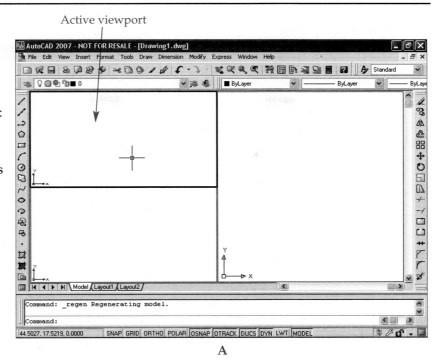

Active viewport

A

New configuration applied to active viewport

B

The **Named Viewports** tab displays the names of saved viewport configurations and gives you a preview of each. See **Figure 10-21**. Select the named viewport configuration and pick **OK** to apply it to the drawing area. Named viewport configurations cannot be applied to the active viewport.

You can also select a viewport configuration from the **View** > **Viewports** cascading menu, shown in **Figure 10-22**. The following configuration options are available:

- **1 Viewport.** This option replaces the current viewport configuration with a single viewport.

Figure 10-21.
The **Named Viewports** tab.

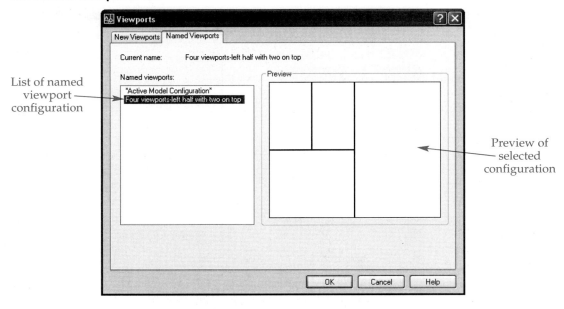

List of named viewport configuration

Preview of selected configuration

Figure 10-22.
The **Viewports** cascading menu in the **View** pull-down menu.

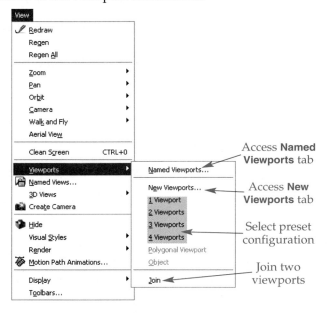

Access **Named Viewports** tab

Access **New Viewports** tab

Select preset configuration

Join two viewports

- **2 Viewports.** When you select this option, you are prompted to select a vertical or horizontal arrangement. The arrangement you choose is then applied to the active viewport. This configuration does not replace the current viewport configuration.
- **3 Viewports.** The following options are available: **Horizontal, Vertical, Above, Below, Left**, and **Right**. The arrangement you choose is then applied to the active viewport. This configuration does not replace the current viewport configuration.
- **4 Viewports.** This option creates four equal viewports within the active viewport.

Once you have selected the viewport configuration and returned to the drawing area, move the pointing device around and notice that only the active viewport contains crosshairs. The pointer is represented by an arrow in the other viewports. To make a different viewport active, move the pointer into it and pick.

As you draw in one viewport, the image is displayed in all viewports. Try drawing lines and other shapes and notice how the viewports are affected. Use a display command, such as **ZOOM**, in the active viewport and notice the results. Only the active viewport reflects the use of the **ZOOM** command.

If you want to join two viewports together, you can do so by picking **View** > **Viewports** > **Join**. Once **Join** is selected, you are prompted to Select dominant viewport. Select the viewport that has the view you want to keep in the joined viewport.

Once the dominant viewport is selected, you are prompted to Select viewport to join. Select the viewport that you want to join with the active viewport. Once you select a viewport to join, AutoCAD "glues" the two viewports together and retains the dominant view. The two viewports you are joining cannot create an L-shape viewport. In other words, the two edges of the viewports must be the same size in order to join them.

Uses of Tiled Viewports

Viewports in model space can be used for both 2D and 3D drawings. They are limited only by your imagination and need. See *AutoCAD and Its Applications—Advanced* for examples of the tiled viewports in 3D. The nature of 2D drawings, whether mechanical multiview, architectural construction details, or unscaled schematic drawings, lend themselves well to viewports.

Exercise 10-4   Complete the Exercise on the Student CD.

Floating Viewports

The layout tabs are used to set up a page to be printed or plotted. The paper space environment is activated when you switch from the **Model** tab to a layout tab. Viewports created in paper space are called floating viewports. These *floating viewports* are actually holes cut into the paper in the layout tab so that the model space drawing can be seen. These viewports are separate objects and can be moved around and even overlap, thus the term *floating viewports*.

After floating viewports are created, display commands are used to modify the model space "showing through" the viewport. Editing commands such as **MOVE**, **ERASE**, and **COPY** can be used in paper space to modify the viewports.

As you work through the following sections describing floating viewports, be sure a layout tab is selected on your AutoCAD screen.

Creating Floating Viewports

The process of creating floating viewports in paper space is nearly identical to the process of creating tiled viewports in model space. A viewport configuration can be selected from the **Viewports** dialog box, which was discussed earlier in this chapter. Also, the **MVIEW** command options can be used to create single or multiple viewports.

As discussed earlier, when model space is active, the **Viewports** dialog box creates tiled viewports. When paper space is active, it creates floating viewports. This dialog box differs slightly depending on the current environment—model space or paper space. The **Apply to:** drop-down list found in model space becomes the **Viewport spacing:** text box in paper space. Use this setting to specify the space around the edges of the floating viewports. See **Figure 10-23.**

Floating viewports can also be created using the **MVIEW** command.

Command: **MV** *or* **MVIEW.**↵
Specify corner of viewport or [ON/OFF/Fit/Shadeplot/Lock/Object/Polygonal/
    Restore/2/3/4] <Fit>:

The default option is to define a rectangular floating viewport by selecting opposite corners. See **Figure 10-24.**

The **2**, **3**, and **4** options provide preset viewport configurations similar to the **Viewports** dialog box. These options can also be selected from the **View** > **Viewports** cascading menu, as was discussed for tiled viewports.

The remaining options are described as follows:

- **ON and OFF.** These options activate and deactivate the model space display within a viewport. When you enter the **OFF** option, you are prompted to select the viewports to be affected. Use the **ON** option to reactivate the viewport.
- **Fit.** This default option creates a single rectangular floating viewport that fills the entire printable area on the sheet.
- **Shadeplot.** Specifies how viewports in layouts appear when plotted. This option is covered in greater detail in *AutoCAD and Its Applications—Advanced.*
- **Lock.** This option allows you to lock the view in one or more viewports. When a viewport is locked, objects within the viewport can still be edited and new objects can be added, but you are unable to use display commands such as **ZOOM** and **PAN.** This option is also used to unlock a locked viewport.

Figure 10-23.
When paper space is active, the **New Viewports** tab in the **Viewports** dialog box contains the **Viewport Spacing:** setting.

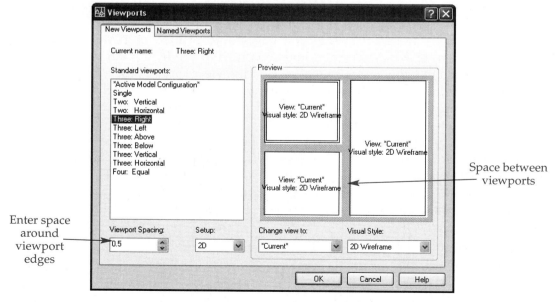

Enter space around viewport edges

Space between viewports

Figure 10-24.
Creating a rectangular floating viewport using the **MVIEW** command.

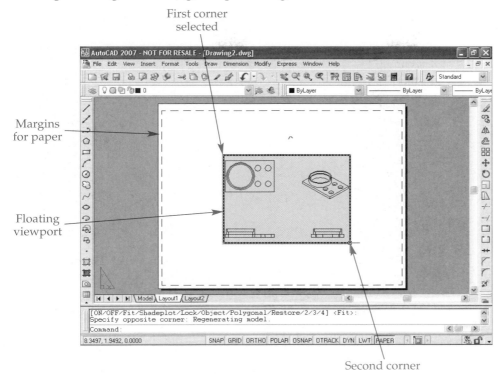

First corner selected

Margins for paper

Floating viewport

Second corner

- **Object.** Use this option to change a closed object drawn in paper space into a floating viewport. Circles, ellipses, polygons, and other closed shapes can be used as floating viewport outlines. See **Figure 10-25.** This option can also be accessed by picking the **Convert Object to Viewport** button in the **Viewports** toolbar or by selecting **View > Viewports > Object**.

- **Polygonal.** Use this option to draw a floating viewport outline using a polyline. Polylines are discussed in Chapter 14. The viewport shape can be any closed shape composed of lines and arcs. This option can also be accessed by picking the **Polygonal Viewport** button in the **Viewports** toolbar or by selecting **View>Viewports>Polygonal Viewport**.

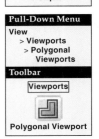

- **Restore.** Converts saved viewport configurations into individual floating viewports.

Redrawing and Regenerating Viewports

Since each viewport is a separate screen, you can redraw or regenerate a single viewport at a time without affecting the others. The **REGEN** (regenerate) command instructs AutoCAD to recalculate all objects in the drawing. This takes considerably longer than a **REDRAW,** especially if the drawing is large. However, **REGEN** can clarify a drawing by smoothing out circles, arcs, ellipses, and splines.

To redraw all viewports, use the **REDRAWALL** command or pick **View > Redraw**. If you need to regenerate all viewports, use the **REGENALL** command or pick **View > Regen All**.

Figure 10-25.
Viewports can be
created from closed
objects. A—Draw
the objects in paper
space. B—Objects
converted to
viewports.

Objects drawn in
layout space

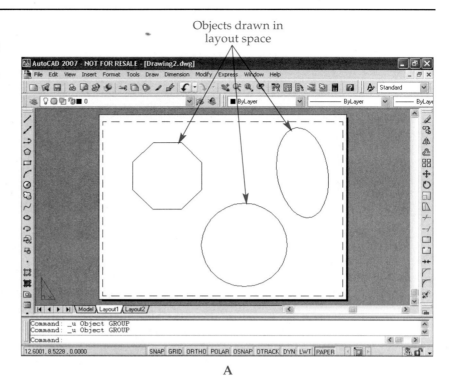

A

Objects converted to
floating viewports

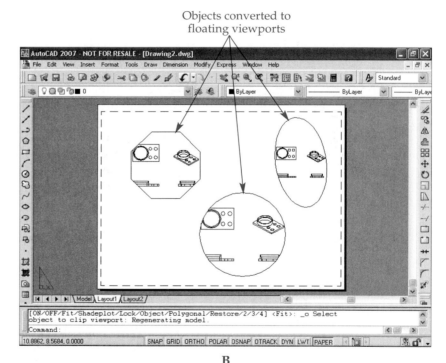

B

Controlling Automatic Regeneration

When developing a drawing, you may use a command that changes certain aspects
of the entities. When this occurs, AutoCAD does an automatic regeneration to update
the objects. This may not be of concern to you when working on small drawings, but
this regeneration may take considerable time on large and complex drawings. In addition, it may not be necessary to have a regeneration of the drawing at all times. If this
is the case, set the **REGENAUTO** command to off.

Command: **REGENAUTO**↲
Enter mode [ON/OFF] <*current*>: **OFF**↲
Command:

Some of the commands that may automatically cause a regeneration are **PLAN**, **HIDE**, and **VIEW Restore**.

Controlling the Order of Display

Drawings can have objects that overlap each other, but since most objects are made of thin lines, the overlap is unseen. Controlling the order of display is better illustrated with an object that has some width, such as a donut. See **Figure 10-26**. The bracket was drawn before the donuts, with inner diameters of 0.0, were added. The donuts, and all other objects, can be moved above or below selected objects and to the front or back of all objects.

DRAWORDER
Type
DRAWORDER
DR
Pull-Down Menu
Tools
> Draw Order

To change the order of an object, use the **DRAWORDER** command, pick **Tools > Draw Order** from the pull-down menu, pick a button in the **Draw Order** toolbar, or type DR or DRAWORDER. The order and arrangement functions are handled by the following **DRAWORDER** options:

- **Above objects.** The selected object is moved above the reference object.
- **Under objects.** The selected object is moved below the reference object.
- **Front.** The selected object is placed to the front of the drawing.
- **Back.** The selected object is placed to the back of the drawing.

These options can also be accessed from the selected object shortcut menu.

Figure 10-26.
The order of objects can be changed to put them in under or above the other objects.

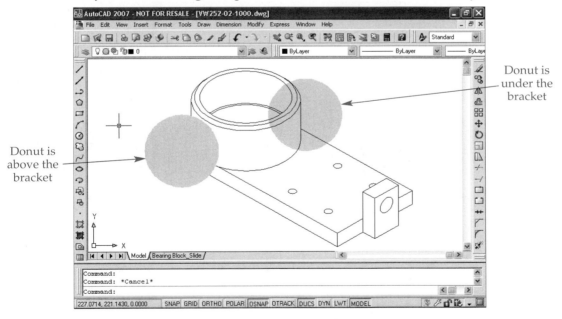

Donut is under the bracket

Donut is above the bracket

Clearing the Screen

The AutoCAD window can become crowded in the course of a drawing session. Each toolbar and modeless dialog box displayed reduces the size of the drawing area. As the drawing area gets smaller, less of the drawing is visible. This can make drafting difficult. You can quickly maximize the size of the drawing area using the **Clean Screen** tool.

This tool clears the AutoCAD window of all toolbars, modeless dialog boxes, and title bars. See **Figure 10-27**. The **Clean Screen** tool is accessed by picking **View** > **Clean Screen** or using the [Ctrl]+[0] (zero) key combination. To return to the normal display, use the [Ctrl]+[0] (zero) key combination.

Type
[Ctrl]+[O]
Pull-Down Menu
View
> Clean Screen

Figure 10-27.
Using the **Clean Screen** tool. A—
Initial display with default toolbars displayed. B—
Display after using the **Clean Screen** tool.

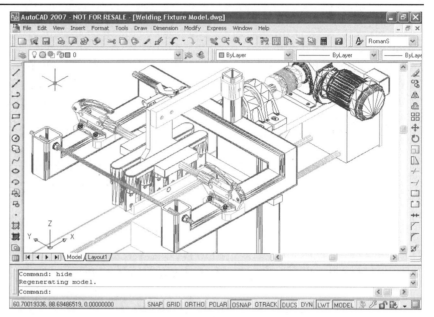

A

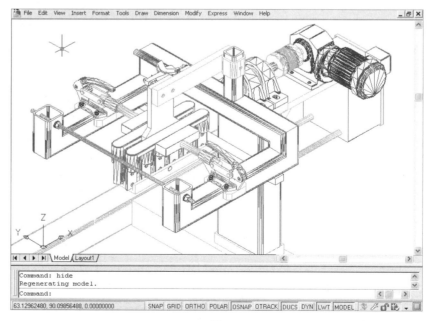

B

Chapter Test

Answer the following questions. Write your answers on a separate sheet of paper or complete the electronic chapter test on the Student CD.

1. What is the difference between the **REDRAW** and **REGEN** commands?
2. Give the proper command option and value to automatically zoom to a 2X scale factor.
3. What is the difference between **ZOOM Extents** and **ZOOM All**?
4. During the drawing process, when should you use **ZOOM**?
5. How many different boxes are displayed during the **ZOOM Dynamic** command?
6. When using the **ZOOM Dynamic** option, what represents the current view?
7. What is the purpose of the **PAN** command?
8. Explain how scroll bars can be used to pan the drawing display.
9. What is *view resolution*?
10. In which dialog box is *circle and arc smoothness* set?
11. How do you create a named view of the current screen display?
12. How do you display an existing view?
13. How would you obtain a listing of existing views?
14. How is a transparent display command entered at the keyboard?
15. Explain the difference between model space and paper space.
16. What type of viewport is created in model space?
17. What type of viewport is created in paper space?
18. What is the purpose of the **Preview** area of the **Viewports** dialog box?
19. Explain the procedures and conditions that need to exist when joining viewports.
20. Which command regenerates all of the viewports?

Drawing Problems

1. Open the drawing named 3D House.dwg found in the AutoCAD 2007\Sample folder.
   Perform the following display functions on the drawing:
   A. **ZOOM Extents**.
   B. Create a view named Rendering.
   C. Replace the view with the Top view.
   D. Create a view named Plan using **Define Window** in the **New View** dialog box.
   E. Use realtime pan and realtime zoom to create a display of the dining room in the top-right area of the Plan view.
   F. Create a view of this display named Dining Room.
   G. Display the view named Rendering.
   H. Save the drawing as P10-1.

2. Load one of your own mechanical template drawings that contains a border and title block. Do the following:
   A. Zoom into the title block area. Create and save a view named Title.
   B. Zoom to the extents of the drawing and create and save a view named All.
   C. Determine the area of the drawing that will contain notes, parts list, or revisions. Zoom into these areas and create views with appropriate names such as Notes, Partlist, and Revisions.
   D. Divide the drawing area into commonly used multiview sections. Save the views with descriptive names such as Top, Front, Rightside, and Leftside.
   E. Restore the view named All.
   F. Save the drawing as P10-2, or as a template.

3. Load one of your own template drawings used for architectural layout that contains a border and title block. Do the following:
   A. Zoom into the title block area. Create and save a view named Title.
   B. Zoom to the extents of the drawing and create and save a view named All.
   C. Determine the area of the drawing that will contain notes, schedules, or revisions. Zoom into these areas and create views with appropriate names such as Notes, Schedules, and Revisions.
   D. Restore the view named All.
   E. Save the drawing as P10-3, or as a template.

CHAPTER 11

Layouts, Plotting, and Printing

Learning Objectives

After completing this chapter, you will be able to do the following:

- Print and plot a drawing.
- Set up layouts using title blocks and viewports.
- Create new layouts.
- Manage layouts.
- Select a plotting device and modify a plotting device configuration.
- Explain plot styles, plot style tables, and plot style modes.
- Create and modify plot styles and plot style tables.
- Attach plot style tables to drawings and layouts.
- Assign plot styles to drawings, layers, and objects.
- Select plot settings.
- Calculate scale factors based on drawing scale.
- Create a plot file.
- Plot a group of drawings using the Batch Plot utility.
- Explain keys to efficient plotting.

Often, the end result of your AutoCAD work will be a printed or plotted drawing. It is easier for a construction crew in the field to use a printed copy of the drawing rather than use a computer to view the DWG file. Therefore, it is important for you to understand the various plotting options available in AutoCAD.

Paper space, model space, the **Model** tab, and layout tabs were discussed in Chapter 10. Each layout tab can be set to plot different views of the objects using different plotting settings. This allows you to create several different plots using a single drawing.

Plotting Procedure

You can create plots from the **Model** tab (model space) and from the layout tabs (paper space). The general procedures for both cases are similar. The following steps are explained later in this chapter:

1. Create the drawing objects in the **Model** tab (model space). If you are creating a layout, create the floating viewports, title block, and other desired items in a layout tab (paper space).

2. Configure the plotting device if it is not already configured.
3. Access the **Page Setup Manager** or **Plot** dialog box and specify values for the plotting settings. Each tab (**Model** and layout) can have its own settings, so each layout can produce a different plot.
4. Plot the drawing.

Layout and Plotting Terms

It is important to understand the terminology used when discussing model space, paper space, layouts, and plotting. Therefore, this section provides you with a quick overview of the commands and functions that enable you to lay out and plot a drawing. These terms are described in greater detail later in this chapter.

- **Model space.** This is the drawing environment in which the drawing objects are constructed. Model space is active when the **Model** tab is selected. Model space is also activated when you double-click inside a floating viewport in a layout tab.
- **Paper space.** This is the drawing environment used to create plotting layouts, which are arrangements of various objects (such as floating viewports, title blocks, and annotations) on the page to be plotted. Paper space is active by default when a layout tab is selected. If you double-click inside a floating viewport in a layout tab, the viewport becomes active and model space is entered. To switch back to paper space, double-click in an area outside the floating viewport.
- **Layouts.** A layout is the manner in which a drawing is arranged in paper space. A layout may contain a title block, one or more viewports, and annotations. Each drawing can have multiple layouts, and each layout is shown as a tab along the bottom of the drawing area. Each layout can have different page setups and plotting settings.
- **Page setups.** A page setup is the manner in which the drawing is displayed on a sheet of paper in order to create a layout. Most of the aspects of how the drawing is plotted can be established in a page setup, from the plot device to pen settings to scales. Other included settings are paper size and drawing units, paper orientation, plot area, plot scale, plot offset, and plot options. These settings can even be saved in the drawing file as a named page setup, which can be recalled each time the drawing is plotted.
- **Plotters window.** The **Plotters** window allows you to add, delete, configure, and reconfigure plotters. It can be accessed by selecting **File** > **Plotter Manager...** from the pull-down menu. When a device is configured, the settings are saved in a PC3 file.
- **Plot styles.** Plot styles contain settings that are applied to objects when they are plotted. A *color-dependent plot style* is applied to all objects with a specific color. A *named plot style* can be assigned to an object or layer.
- **Plot style tables.** A plot style table is a collection of plot styles. There are two types of plot style tables: color-dependent and named. A plot style table can only contain plot styles of a single *plot style mode* (either color-dependent or named). The **Model** tab and each layout tab can have a unique plot style table attached. Only plot styles in the attached plot style table can be used within a tab.
- **Plot Styles window.** The **Plot Styles** window allows you to manage all your plot style table files. From here you can open and edit the plot styles within a plot style table. You can also create new plot style tables.

- **Plot settings.** These settings are created in the **Plot** dialog box and include many of the same items found in the **Page Setup** dialog box. They control how the drawing is printed on paper. Although this may seem like the last step in the process, plot settings can be created at the beginning of a project and then saved for use later.

Layout Settings

A *layout* shows the arrangement of objects on a sheet of paper for plotting purposes. A layout may include a title block, floating viewports showing your model space drawing, and annotation.

A single drawing can have multiple layouts. Named layouts are displayed as tabs along the bottom of the drawing area. Each layout tab represents a different paper space configuration.

When you start AutoCAD, a new drawing is started automatically. This drawing is based on a template file containing default settings and has two layouts by default. These layouts are identified by the **Layout1** and **Layout2** tabs below the drawing area. When you pick a layout tab for the first time, the layout will be displayed using default settings primarily based on an 8.5″ × 11″ sheet of paper in a landscape orientation.

When a layout tab is selected, an image showing a preview of the final printed drawing is shown. See Figure 11-1. The dashed line around the edge of the paper represents the page margins. The solid lines show the outline of a floating viewport. By default, a single viewport is created.

Figure 11-1.
A layout is displayed when a layout tab is selected. The layout provides a preview of how the plotted drawing will appear.

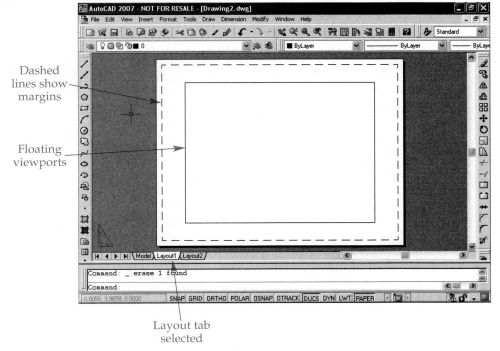

Dashed lines show margins

Floating viewports

Layout tab selected

Working in Layout Tabs

A layout can contain many types of objects, including floating viewports, a title block, and various types of annotation, such as general notes, revision levels and descriptions, and a bill of material. Assembling these items in a layout allows you to see exactly what the final plot will look like.

Several settings that affect the display of layouts are contained in the **Layout elements** area of the **Display** tab in the **Options** dialog box. See **Figure 11-2**. Access this dialog box by selecting **Tools > Options...** from the pull-down menu. Use the default settings until you are comfortable working with layouts.

Inserting a title block

Most layouts contain a title block. Title blocks are generally saved in a template file and then inserted as a block when needed. A block is a single object comprising multiple individual objects. See Chapter 22 for a complete discussion on blocks.

It is best to insert a title block into the layout and then save it as a template file. You can then start a new drawing based on the template, and the layout with the title block will already be created.

To insert a title block, select **Insert > Block...** from the pull-down menu to access the **Insert** dialog box. Pick the **Browse...** button and select the title block drawing to be inserted. **Figure 11-3** shows the ANSI A title block inserted into a layout.

NOTE

You can also copy a layout containing the title block from an existing drawing using **DesignCenter**. This is discussed later in this chapter.

Working with floating viewports

Chapter 10 explained how to create floating viewports in a layout. Once the viewports are created, the display within the viewport must be set to show the correct part of the model space drawing.

Figure 11-2.
Layout display options are found in the **Options** dialog box.

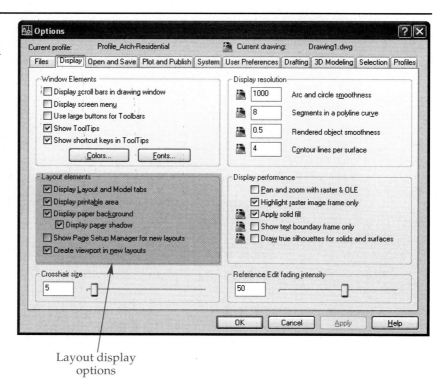

Layout display options

Figure 11-3.
The ANSI A title block inserted into the layout. Note the viewport created by default has been deleted.

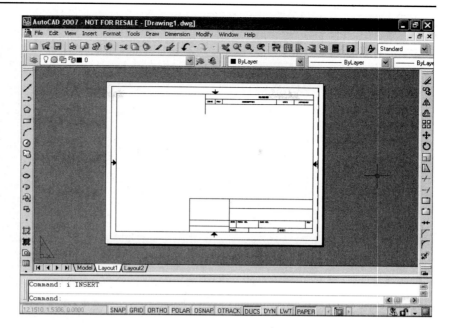

Create the floating viewports after the title block has been inserted. This will allow you to position the viewports so they do not interfere with the title block. Floating viewports are created using the **Viewports** dialog box or the **MVIEW** command.

Figure 11-4 illustrates the following procedure for establishing the display in two floating viewports:

1. Create the first viewport using the **Viewports** dialog box. The model space drawing is visible in the viewport.
2. Create a second viewport.
3. Double-click in the new viewport to enter model space.
4. Use the **XP** option of the **ZOOM** command or the scale drop-down list on the **Viewports** toolbar to scale the drawing. Use realtime panning to display the part of interest in the drawing.
5. Double-click outside of the viewports to activate paper space. Use grips or the **STRETCH** command to resize the viewport.

Using multiple viewports in a layout allows you to illustrate different aspects of the drawing. Using multiple layouts, various types of drawings can be created from a single drawing model. This is a very simple example of the use of floating viewports within a layout. Figure 11-5 shows the viewports created by the **Std. 3D Engineering Views** option available in the **Create Layout** wizard. The viewports show the three primary orthographic views and an isometric view. The **Create Layout** wizard is discussed later in this chapter.

> **CAUTION**
>
>
>
> If you use zoom to adjust the drawing inside the viewport, the drawing may no longer be to scale. Always use the **ZOOM XP** option or the scale drop-down list on the **Viewports** toolbar as the final step prior to plotting to be certain the drawing is scaled inside the viewport.

Exercise 11-1   Complete the Exercise on the Student CD.

Figure 11-4.
These steps illustrate the procedure for adding viewports to a simple layout outlined in the text.

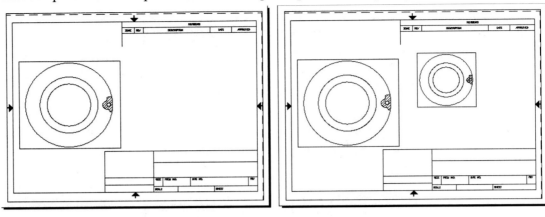

Step 1—Create viewport.   Step 2—Create second viewport.

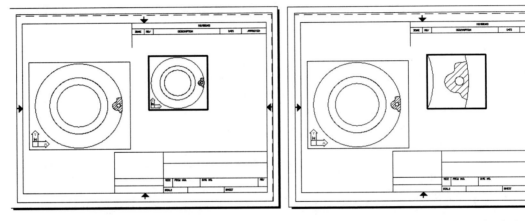

Step 3—Make second viewport active.   Step 4—Zoom and pan display in second viewport.

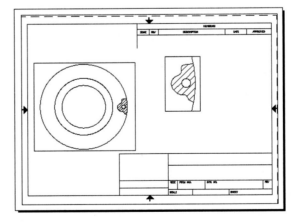

Step 5—Resize viewport.

Managing Layouts

The **LAYOUT** command allows you to manage layouts. To access this command, enter LO or LAYOUT. You are prompted to select a **LAYOUT** command option. Some of these options are also available in the **Layouts** toolbars or the **Insert** > **Layout** cascading menu. You can also position the cursor over a layout tab and right-click to display the layout shortcut menu, Figure 11-6. This shortcut menu also contains many **LAYOUT** command options.

Figure 11-5.
This example shows the ANSI D title block and the **Std. 3D Engineering Views** viewport configuration. This configuration is available in the **Create Layout** wizard.

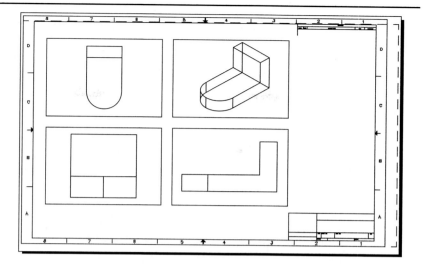

Figure 11-6.
Right-click on a layout tab to display the layout shortcut menu. Many options for managing layouts are available.

New layout
From template...
Delete
Rename
Move or Copy...
Select All Layouts

Activate Previous Layout
Activate Model Tab

Page Setup Manager...
Plot...

Hide Layout and Model tabs

Setting the current layout

The current layout is identified by the highlighted tab at the bottom of the drawing area. To set the current layout, pick the layout tab using the cursor. You can also use the **Set** option of the **LAYOUT** command to specify the current layout.

PROFESSIONAL TIP

If you are selecting options from the layout shortcut menu, you must have the appropriate layout set as current before selecting the command. For example, if you select **Delete** from the layout shortcut menu, the current layout is deleted. If you type the **LAYOUT** command, the current layout is the default but you can specify a different layout.

Listing layouts

If a drawing has several layouts or layouts with fairly long names, all layout tabs may not be visible. When this is the case, you can use the four buttons to the left of the tab list to view the tabs. See **Figure 11-7**. The two outer arrows display the left and right ends of the tab list. The inner arrows move the list one tab in the indicated direction. Changing the display of the tab list does not affect the current tab. You must still pick a tab to set it as current.

The **?** option of the **LAYOUT** command can be used to list all layouts within the drawing. After selecting this option, you must switch to the **AutoCAD Text Window** to view the list. To do this, select **View** > **Display** > **Text Window** or use the [F2] function key.

Figure 11-7.
Use the arrows to select which layout tabs are displayed.

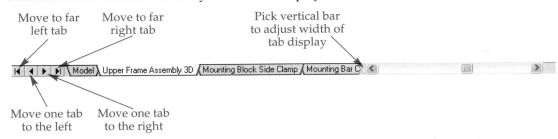

Creating a new layout

There are several methods of creating new layouts. A new layout can be created from scratch or it can be copied from an existing drawing or template file. Finally, a layout within the drawing can be copied to create a new layout. These methods are described as follows:

- **New layout from scratch.** Use the **New** option of the **LAYOUT** command to create a new layout. You can also create a new layout by selecting **Insert** > **Layout** > **New Layout**, picking the **New Layout** button in the **Layouts** toolbar, or by right-clicking on a layout tab and selecting **New layout** from the layout shortcut menu. If you select the option from the command line, toolbar, or pull-down menu, you are prompted to enter the layout name. If you use the **New layout** option in the layout shortcut menu, the new layout is created with the default name. You can then use the **Rename** option to change the name.

- **New layout from template.** This option creates a new layout based on a layout stored in an existing drawing or template file. Select this option by using the **Template** option of the **LAYOUT** command, selecting **Insert** > **Layout** > **Layout from Template...** from the pull-down menu, or picking the **Layout from Template** button in the **Layouts** toolbar. You can also right-click on a layout tab and select **From template...** in the layout shortcut menu.

  When you select this option, the **Select Template From File** dialog box is displayed, **Figure 11-8A.** The Template folder in the path set by the AutoCAD Drawing Template File Location is selected by default.

  Select the drawing file or template file containing the layout to be copied and pick the **Open** button. The **Insert Layout(s)** dialog box appears, see **Figure 11-8B.** This dialog box lists all layouts in the selected file. Highlight the layout(s) you want to copy and pick the **OK** button.

- **Copy layout in drawing.** You can create a new layout by copying an existing layout. If you use the **Copy** option of the **LAYOUT** command, enter the name of the layout to copy, and then enter the name for the new copy. The current layout is the default layout to copy. If a name for the copy is not entered, AutoCAD uses the current layout name plus a number in parentheses.

  You can also copy an existing layout by selecting **Move or Copy...** from the layout shortcut menu. This option provides no opportunity to change the layout to be copied; the current layout tab is copied. When you select this option, the **Move or Copy** dialog box appears, **Figure 11-9.** Activate the **Create a copy** check box, and then select which layout the new layout tab should be to the left of. The default name is automatically assigned to the new layout. Use the **Rename** option to change it.

- **Using the Create Layout wizard.** You can create a new layout using the **Create Layout** wizard. To access this wizard, select **Insert** > **Layout** > **Layout Wizard** or select **Tools** > **Wizards** > **Create Layout...** from the pull-down menu. The pages of the wizard allow you to specify a title block, viewports, and many page setup values. These page setup values are discussed later in this chapter.

Figure 11-8.
Creating a new layout from another drawing or template. A—Select the drawing or template containing the layout. B—Highlight the layout(s) to be added to the current drawing.

Template folder
opened by default

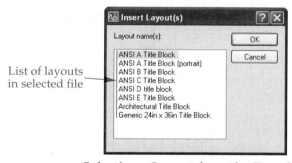

Step 1—Selecting a Template

List of layouts
in selected file

Selecting a Layout from the Template

Figure 11-9.
The **Move or Copy** dialog box is used to reorganize the layout tabs and to copy layout tabs within a drawing. It is accessed through the layout shortcut menu.

Select location
of new
layout tab

Check to create
a copy of the
current layout

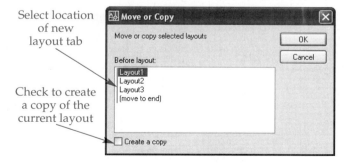

ADCENTER

Type
ADCENTER
ADC
[Ctrl]+[2]

Pull-Down Menu
Tools
> Palettes
> DesignCenter

Toolbar
Standard

DesignCenter

Copying layouts with DesignCenter

Layouts are included as a type of content that can be viewed using **DesignCenter**. To access **DesignCenter,** select **Tools** > **Palettes** > **DesignCenter** from the pull-down menu, pick the **DesignCenter** button in the **Standard** toolbar, enter ADC or ADCENTER, or use the [Ctrl]+[2] key combination.

To copy a layout from an existing drawing or template, first locate the drawing in the **DesignCenter** tree view. Then select Layouts to display the layouts within the drawing. See **Figure 11-10.** Select the layout(s) to be copied and then use the **Add Layout(s)** or **Copy** and **Paste** options from shortcut menus or drag-and-drop to insert the layouts in the current drawing.

Renaming a layout

The name of the layout appears on its tab. Layouts created by default are named **Layout***n*, where *n* is a number. A layout created by copying another layout has the same name as the initial layout, followed by a number in parentheses. For example, the first copy of **Layout2** is named **Layout2 (2)**.

Layouts are easier to work with when they have a descriptive name. Layouts can be renamed using the **Rename** option of the **LAYOUT** command. When you select the **Rename** option of the **LAYOUT** command, you are prompted to enter the name of the layout to be renamed. The current layout is provided as a default. Once you have entered the layout to be renamed, you are prompted to enter the new layout name.

You can also rename a layout by right-clicking on the layout tab and selecting **Rename** from the layout shortcut menu. This accesses the **Rename Layout** dialog box. If you select this option, you can rename only the current layout. Enter the new name in the text box and pick the **OK** button. After the layout has been renamed, the new name is displayed on the tab.

Deleting a layout

When a layout is no longer useful, it can be deleted. You can delete a layout using the **Delete** option of the **LAYOUT** command. You can also delete the active layout by right-clicking on the layout tab and selecting **Delete** from the layout shortcut menu.

When you use the **Delete** option of the **LAYOUT** command, you are prompted to enter the name of the layout to be deleted. The current layout is provided as the default.

If you select **Delete** from the layout shortcut menu, an alert box warns you that the layout will be permanently deleted. Pick the **OK** button to delete the layout.

Figure 11-10.
Layouts can be shared between drawings using **DesignCenter**.

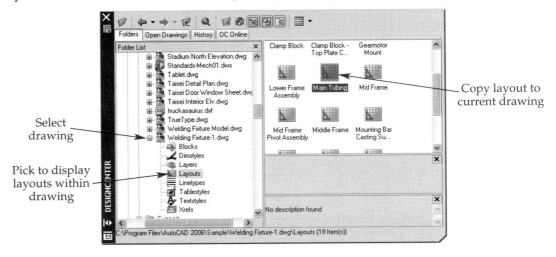

Select drawing

Pick to display layouts within drawing

Copy layout to current drawing

Saving a layout

The **Saveas** option of the **LAYOUT** command is used to save a single layout as a drawing template or drawing file. The following is the command sequence:

Command: **LO** *or* **LAYOUT**↵
Enter layout option [Copy/Delete/New/Template/Rename/SAveas/Set/?] <set>: **SA**↵
Enter layout to save to template <*current layout*>: (*enter name of layout or accept default*)

After you specify the layout to save, the **Create Drawing File** dialog box appears. You can save the layout in a DWT, DWG, or DXF file. Enter the file name and pick the **SAVE** button. The layout is now saved in the new file.

Exercise 11-2   Complete the Exercise on the Student CD.

Page Setups for Plotting

A *page setup* contains the settings required to create a finished plot of the drawing. Most aspects of how the drawing is plotted can be established in a page setup, from the plot device to pen settings to scales. In fact, the only difference between the **Page Setup** and **Plot** dialog boxes is that the **Page Setup** dialog box does not provide a plot preview button.

Each layout can have a unique page setup. Therefore, the **Page Setup Manager** dialog box is always tied to the active **Model** tab or layout tab. These settings can even be saved in the drawing file as a named page setup, which can be recalled each time the drawing is plotted. Therefore, the setup becomes a productivity tool since it decreases the amount of time required to prepare a drawing for plotting.

PAGESETUP

| Type |
| PAGESETUP |
| **Pull-Down Menu** |
| File |
| > Page Setup |
| Manager... |
| **Toolbar** |
| Layouts |
| Page Setup Manager |

The settings that compose the page setup are set in the **Page Setup** dialog box. This dialog box is accessed by selecting **File > Page Setup Manager...** from the pull-down menu, picking the **Page Setup Manager** button in the **Layouts** toolbar, entering PAGESETUP, or right-clicking on a layout tab and selecting **Page Setup Manager...** from the layout shortcut menu. The **Page Setup Manager** dialog box is shown in **Figure 11-11A**.

The initial dialog box of **Page Setup Manager** is divided into two areas: **Page setups** in the upper area and **Selected page setup details** below. The **Page setups** area shows a list of the available page setups on the left. On the right are buttons labeled **Set Current**, **New**, **Modify**, and **Import**.

The **Set Current** button attaches the highlighted page setup from the list of available page setups to the current layout. The **New...** button allows you to create a new page setup. The **New Page Setup** dialog box will be displayed as shown in **Figure 11-11B**. The **Modify...** button allows you to change the settings of an existing page setup. The **Page Setup** dialog box will be displayed after picking the **Modify...** button and after picking **OK** from the **New Page Setup** dialog box. See **Figure 11-11C**. The **Import...** button allows you to bring in previously created page setups from an existing drawing.

The page setup consists of many settings including printer selection, plot style (pen settings) choices, paper size and orientation, scale, and other settings that define how the model is going to appear on the final plotted output. All of these settings will be discussed later in this chapter.

> **PROFESSIONAL TIP**
>
> In the planning stages of your work, create one or more page setups for the drawing and save them in a template drawing.

Figure 11-11.
Creating a new page setup in the **Page Setup** dialog box.

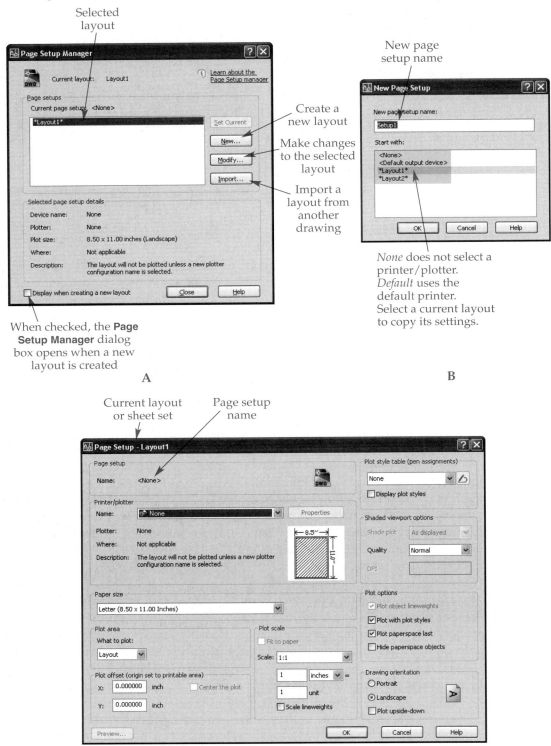

Selected layout

New page setup name

Create a new layout

Make changes to the selected layout

Import a layout from another drawing

None does not select a printer/plotter. *Default* uses the default printer. Select a current layout to copy its settings.

When checked, the **Page Setup Manager** dialog box opens when a new layout is created

A

B

Current layout or sheet set

Page setup name

C

Plot Device Selection and Management

Before printing or plotting, make sure that your output device is configured properly. AutoCAD displays information about the currently configured printer or plotter in the **Printer/plotter** area of the **Page Setup** dialog box that appears when you press either the **New...** button or the **Modify...** button on the **Page Setup Manager** dialog box. See **Figure 11-12**.

You can use this tab to change many of the printer or plotter specifications. The current device is displayed in the **Printer/plotter** area of the **Page Setup** dialog box. When additional devices are configured, you can make a different one current by picking it from the **Name:** drop-down list.

> **NOTE**
>
>
> You can add printers and plotters to the list by selecting **File > Plotter Manager...** from the pull-down menu. This executes the **PLOTTERMANAGER** command and displays the **Plotters** window. Select the Add-A-Plotter Wizard icon to add, modify, and remove printing and plotting devices. When a plotter or printer is installed using the **Add Plotter** wizard, a PC3 (plot configuration) file is created. This file contains all the settings required for the plotter to function.

Figure 11-12.
The **Printer/Plotter** area of the **Page Setup** dialog box.

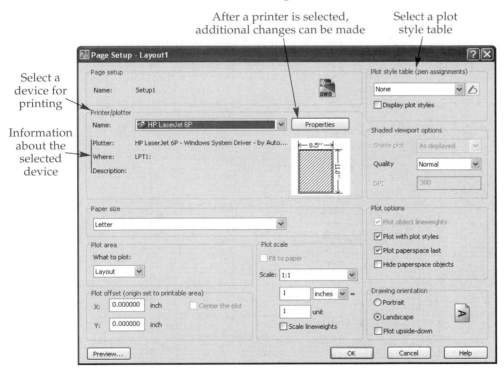

Modifying the Plotter Configuration

To change the properties of the current plot device, pick the **Properties...** button in the **Printer/plotter** area. This opens the **Plotter Configuration Editor** dialog box. See Figure 11-13. Three tabs provide access to the plotting device property settings:

- **General tab.** General information about the current plotter is displayed in this tab. The only item you can change is the description.
- **Ports tab.** Use this tab to pick a port to send the plot to, plot to a file, or select **AutoSpool**. Using **AutoSpool**, plot files can be sent to a *plot spooler* file, which automatically plots the drawing in the background while you continue to work.
- **Device and Document Settings tab.** This tab displays a tree list of all the settings applicable to the current plotting device. Clicking on the desired icon enables you to modify specific settings. Items in this list that are displayed in brackets (< >) can be changed. The **Custom Properties** item is highlighted by default because it contains the properties most often changed. Pick the **Custom Properties...** button to display the properties dialog box specific to your plotter. Pick the **Save As...** button to save your changes to a PC3 file.

CAUTION

Avoid editing and saving modified PC3 files unless you have been instructed to do so. These files are critical to the proper functioning of your plotter.

Specifying a Plot Style Table

The **Plot style table** area is located in the upper right of the **Page Setup** dialog box. This area allows you to list and select customized pen assignment files for specialized plotting purposes. Use the default of **None** until you possess a good understanding of plot style tables. Plot style tables are discussed in the following section.

Figure 11-13.
The **Plotter Configuration Editor** dialog box. The **Device and Document Settings** tab is shown here.

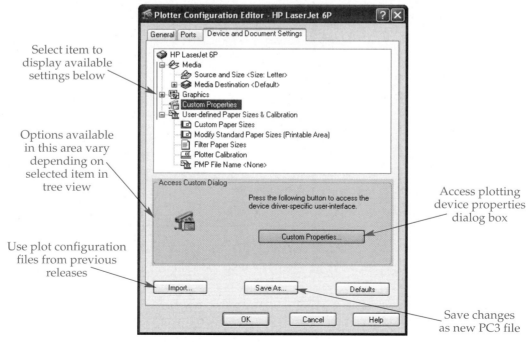

Exercise 11-3

Complete the Exercise on the Student CD.

Plot Styles

The properties of objects in an AutoCAD drawing, such as color, layer, linetype, and lineweight, are used as defaults for plotting. This means that all colors, linetypes, and lineweights will be plotted exactly as they appear in the drawing. You also have the ability to create multiple plots of the same drawing using different plot style tables. A *plot style table* is a named file that provides complete control over pen settings for plotted drawings.

Plot styles are basically a variety of pen settings that control, among other things, the color, thickness, linetype, line end treatment, and fill style of drawing objects. Plot styles can be assigned to any object or layer.

Plot Style Attributes

By default, objects are drawn without a plot style. When no plot style is applied, objects are plotted according to their assigned properties, such as color, linetype, and lineweight. The finished plot appears identical to the on-screen display.

A plot style is a collection of several properties. When a plot style is assigned to an object, the plot style properties replace the object's properties *for plotting purposes only*. For example, assume a drawing has a layer named Blue, which has blue selected as its color. A line drawn on this layer appears blue on screen. If no plot style is assigned to the line, it will plot as blue also. Now assume a plot style is created with the color red set as one of its properties. This plot style is assigned to the line. The line will now be plotted as red. However, the line still appears blue on screen, because the plot style only takes effect when the object is plotted.

The following properties can be set in a plot style:

- **Color.** A color specified in a plot style will override the object color in the drawing. Use object color is the default setting. This setting plots the object with the same color shown on screen. The following options related to color could also be specified:
  - **Dithering.** *Dithering* is the intermingling of dots of various colors to produce what appears to be a new color. Dithering is either enabled or disabled. It is ignored if the plotter does not support it. Dithering may create incorrect linetypes when plotting pale colors or thin lines. It is best to test dithering to see if it produces the expected results. Dithering can be used regardless of the object color selected.
  - **Convert to Grayscale.** If this option is selected, the object's colors are converted to grayscale if the plotter supports it. If this is not selected, the object colors are used. This option is illustrated in **Figure 11-14.**

Figure 11-14.
The effects of the Convert to grayscale plot style setting.

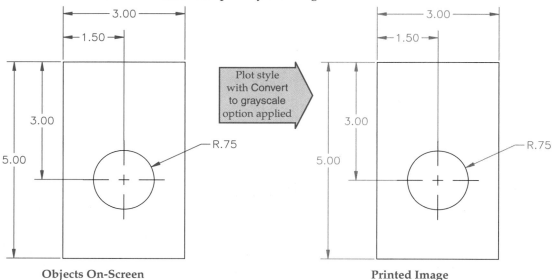

Objects On-Screen   Printed Image

- **Use Assigned Pen Number.** This setting only applies to pen plotters. Available pens range from 1 to 32. The assigned pen number cannot be changed if the plot style color is set to Use object color, or if you are editing a plot style in a color-dependent plot style table. In this case, the value is set to Automatic. If you enter 0 for pen number, the field reads Automatic. AutoCAD selects a pen based on the plotter configuration.
- **Virtual Pen Number.** Pen numbers between 1 and 255 allow non-pen plotters to simulate pen plotters using virtual pens. A 0 or Automatic setting instructs AutoCAD to assign a virtual pen from the AutoCAD Color Index (ACI).
- **Screening.** This affects the amount of ink placed on the paper while plotting. A value of 0 produces the color white, and 100 plots the color's full intensity. The effects of screening are shown in **Figure 11-15.**
- **Linetype.** If you select a plot style linetype, it overrides the object's linetype when plotted. The default value (Use object linetype) plots the object using the linetype displayed on-screen. An adaptive adjustment setting adjusts the linetype scale to keep the linetype pattern complete. This is activated by default.
- **Lineweight.** Select a lineweight from this list if you want the plotted lineweight to override the object property in the AutoCAD drawing. The default value is Use object lineweight.
- **Line End Style.** If you select a line end style from this list, the line end style is added to the endpoints when plotted. **Figure 11-16** illustrates the end style options. Note that the lines must be relatively thick for the end styles to be noticeable. The default setting is Use object end style.
- **Line Join Style.** If you select a line join style from this list, it overrides the object's line join style when the drawing is plotted. The default setting is Use object join style, but you can select one of the following line end styles: Miter, Bevel, Round, and Diamond.
- **Fill Style.** If you select a fill style from this list, it overrides the object's fill style when the drawing is plotted. The default setting is Use object fill style, but you can select one of the fill styles shown in **Figure 11-17.**

Figure 11-15.
Using the screening plot style settings.

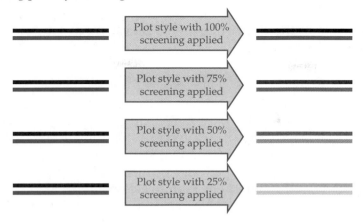

Figure 11-16.
End line style options can be specified within a plot style.

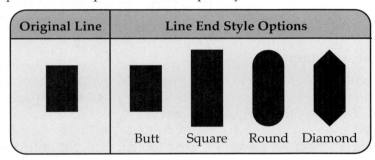

Figure 11-17.
These fill styles can be set for a plot style.

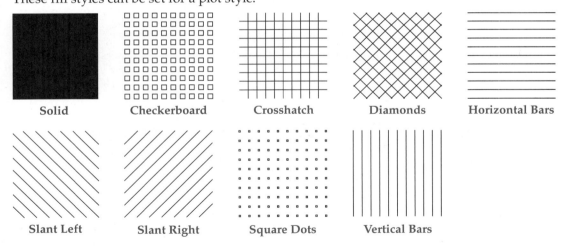

Plot Style Modes

There are two plot style modes: color-dependent and named. You can create a *color-dependent plot style* in which each color can be assigned values for the various plotting properties. These settings are saved in a *color-dependent plot style table* file with a .ctb extension.

A *named plot style* is assigned to objects. The settings in the named plot style override the object properties when the object is plotted. *Named plot style tables* are saved in a file with an .stb extension. These tables allow you to use color properties in the drawing without having the object's color tied to its plotting characteristics. These tables are useful if, for example, you are working on a multiphase project in which different components of the drawing must be highlighted, subdued, or plotted in a specific lineweight or linetype.

Plot Style Tables

AutoCAD is supplied with several plot style tables. You can also create and save your own customized tables. Plot style tables are given file names with .ctb or .stb extensions. These files are saved in the path set by the AutoCAD Plot Style Table Search Path. To verify the location of AutoCAD plot style table, access the **Files** tab in the **Options** dialog box and check the path listed under the Plot Style Table Search Path, after expanding the **Printer Support File Path** selection.

To view the available plot style tables, select **File** > **Plot Style Manager...** from the pull-down menu or type STYLESMANAGER. The **Plot Styles** window is displayed. See **Figure 11-18.**

The **Plot Styles** window displays icons for each of the saved plot style tables. There is also an icon to access the **Add Plot Style Table** wizard. You can double-click on an icon to access the **Plot Style Table Editor** dialog box. This dialog box, which is discussed later in the chapter, is used to edit the plot style table.

Creating a plot style table

Create a named plot style table if you know that components of the drawing or project, such as layouts, layers, and objects, will be plotted at different times using different colors, linetypes, lineweights, or area fills.

Plot style tables are created using the **Add Plot Style Table** wizard. To access this wizard, select **Tools** > **Wizards** > **Add Plot Style Table...** from the pull-down menu. You can also select the Add-A-Plot Style Table Wizard icon in the **Plot Styles** window, which is discussed later in the chapter. The **Add Plot Style Table** wizard is displayed. Read the introductory page and pick **Next** to access the **Begin** page. See **Figure 11-19.** Four options are available:

Figure 11-18.
Double-click on an icon to edit the plot style table. Select the Add-A-Plot Style Table Wizard icon to create a new table.

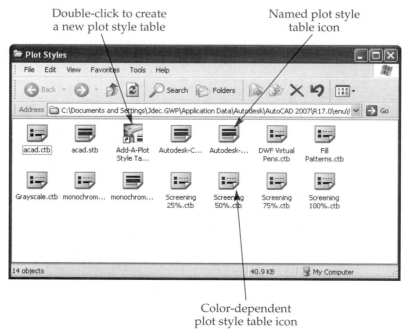

Double-click to create
a new plot style table

Named plot style
table icon

Color-dependent
plot style table icon

AutoCAD and Its Applications—Basics

Figure 11-19.
Select the basis for the plot style table in the **Begin** page of the **Add Plot Style Table** wizard.

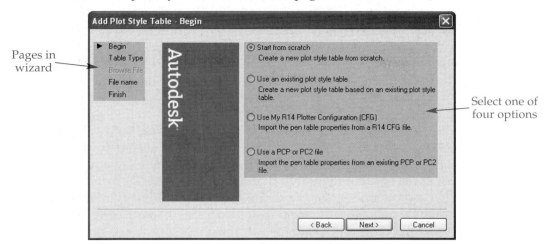

Pages in wizard

Select one of four options

- **Start from scratch.** Constructs a new plot style table. The **Browse File** page is skipped with this option because the new plot style table is not based on any existing settings.
- **Use an existing plot style table.** Copies an existing plot style table to be used as a template for a new one. The **Table Type** page is skipped when this option is selected because the plot style mode is determined by the file selected as the template.
- **Use My R14 Plotter Configuration (CFG).** Copies the pen assignments from the acad14.cfg file to be used as a template for a new one. This option should be used if you did not save either a PCP or PC2 file in Release 14.
- **Use a PCP or PC2 file.** Pen assignments saved previously in a Release 14 PCP or PC2 file are used to make a new plot style table.

After you have selected the beginning plot style table option, pick **Next** to go to the **Table Type** page. See **Figure 11-20.** This page is not displayed if the **Use an existing plot style table** option was selected. Select the **Named Plot Style Table** option to use the named plot style mode, and then pick **Next**.

Figure 11-20.
Select the plot style mode in the **Table Type** page. This page does not appear if the new table is based on an existing plot style table.

Select plot style mode

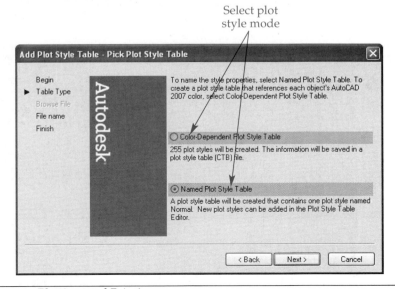

Select the file on which the plot style table is to be based in the **Browse File** page. This page is not displayed if the **Start from scratch** option was selected. Enter the file name in the text box or pick the **Browse...** button to display a **Select File** dialog box. The type of file you select depends on the selected beginning plot style table option. If you are using a CFG file, you must also select the plotter or printer to use.

After selecting the appropriate file, pick the **Next** button to access the **File name** page. See **Figure 11-21.** Enter a name for the new plot style table. A .ctb extension is added to color-dependent plot style tables, and an .stb extension is added to named plot style tables.

Once you have entered the plot style table name, pick **Next** to display the **Finish** page. See **Figure 11-22.** Pick the check box at the bottom of the page to attach this plot style table to all new drawings by default. That is, the plot style table will be listed in the **Plot style table area** of the **Page Setup** dialog box. This check box is only available if you are creating a plot style using the mode (color-dependent or named) specified in the **Default plot style behavior for new drawings** area of the **Plot Style Table Settings** dialog box. This dialog box is discussed later in the chapter.

Figure 11-21.
Enter the name for the plot style table in the **File name** page.

Enter name for plot style table

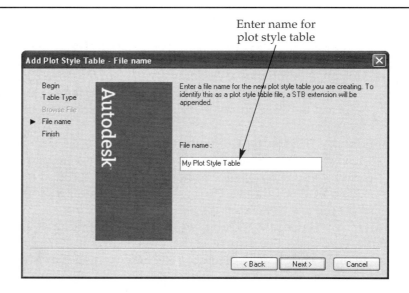

Figure 11-22.
The **Finish** page allows you to edit the new plot style table immediately and to attach the new table to all new drawings (if the plot style mode matches the setting in the **Options** dialog box).

Pick to edit plot style table

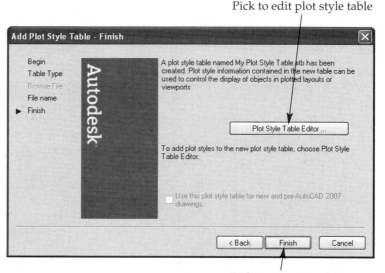

Pick to exit wizard

You can edit the new plot style table by selecting the **Plot Style Table Editor...** button, which accesses the **Plot Style Table Editor** dialog box. This is discussed later in the chapter.

Pick **Finish** and the new plot style table is created. The new file is saved in the folder path set by the Plot Style Table Search Path. To verify the location of this file, access the **Files** tab in the **Options** dialog box and check the path listed under the Plot Style Table Search Path after expanding the **Printer Support File Path** selection. A corresponding icon is added to the **Plot Styles** window.

NOTE The **Wizards** cascading menu also contains an **Add Plot Style Table...** or **Add Color-Dependent Plot Style Table...** option. The plot style mode set for the drawing determines which option is available. The pages in these wizards are identical to the **Add Plot Style Table** wizard with the following exceptions:

- On the **Begin** page, the **Use an existing plot style table** option is not available.
- There is no **Table Type** page.
- The **Finish** page includes an option to attach the new plot style table to the current drawing.

Exercise 11-4   Complete the Exercise on the Student CD.

Editing a plot style table

Plot style properties are set in the **Plot Style Table Editor** dialog box. To access this dialog box, double-click on the icon for the desired plot style table in the **Plot Styles** window. You can also select the button next to the drop-down list in the **Plot style table** area in the **Page Setup** dialog box.

The **Plot Style Table Editor** dialog box is used to edit both color-dependent and named plot style tables. Color-dependent plot style tables contain 255 preset plot styles—one for each ACI color. A new named plot style table contains one preset plot style, Normal.

The **Plot Style Table Editor** contains three tabs. The **General** tab contains information about the plot style table. See **Figure 11-23**. Enter a description in the text box. The **Apply global scale factor to non-ISO linetypes and fill patterns** option scales all non-ISO linetypes and fill patterns by the value entered in the **Scale factor** text box.

The **Table View** and **Form View** tabs are used to set the plot style attributes and, for named plot style tables, to create and delete plot styles. These tabs are shown in **Figure 11-24**.

When editing a named plot style table, the Normal plot style is created automatically. This plot style cannot be modified, and is assigned to all layers by default. To create a new plot style, pick the **Add Style** button. In the **Table View** tab, this inserts a new table with the name Style *n* highlighted at the top. Enter a new name. In the **Form View** tab, the **Add Plot Style** dialog box appears. Enter a new name and pick the **OK** button.

If you wish to delete a named plot style, pick the **Delete Style** button in either tab. If the **Form View** tab is displayed, the current style is deleted. If the **Table View** tab is displayed, first pick in the gray bar above the name of the plot style to be deleted, then pick the **Delete Style** button.

Figure 11-23.
Information about
a plot style table is
contained in the
General tab of the
**Plot Style Table
Editor** dialog box.

Plot style table
being edited

Enter a description
for the plot style table

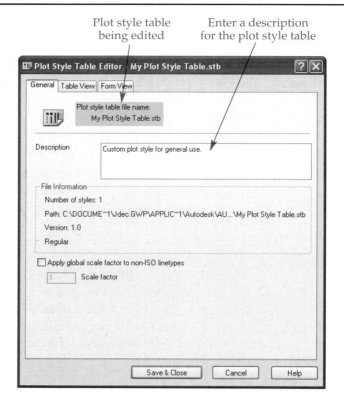

To modify plot style attributes in the **Table View** tab, first use the scroll bar to display the plot style to be edited. Pick the value to be changed and you can modify it with a text box or drop-down list. This editing procedure is similar to changing object properties in the **Properties** window.

The **Form View** tab lists all the attributes in a different format. To view all of the settings for a specific plot style, simply pick the plot style in the **Plot styles:** list box. The properties of the selected plot style are listed in the **Properties** area. Modify the properties using the drop-down lists provided.

Pick the **Save As...** button to change the table name, or pick the **Save & Close** button to save the current file and exit.

NOTE Once a plot style table is created, it can be used on new drawings and drawings created in previous releases of AutoCAD.

Exercise
11-5   Complete the Exercise on the Student CD.

Applying Plot Styles

In order to assign plot styles, plot style tables must be specified in the drawing. The **Model** tab and each individual layout tab can be assigned one plot style table each. Only the styles within the attached plot style table can be applied within the layout.

The plot style mode (color-dependent or named) for a drawing is determined when the drawing is first created. The setting is found in the **Plot and Publish** tab of the **Options** dialog box. To access the **Options** dialog box, select **Tools** > **Options...** from

Figure 11-24.
Plot style table settings are modified in the **Plot Style Table Editor** dialog box.

Plot style
attribute

Create new
named plot
style

Delete named
plot style

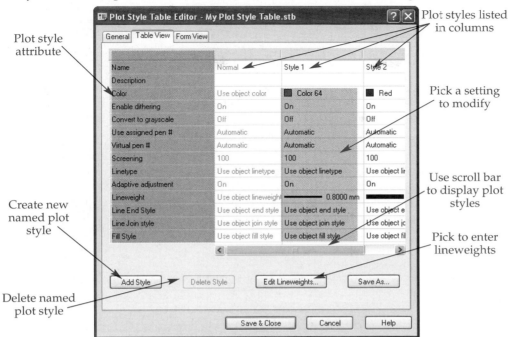

Plot styles listed
in columns

Pick a setting
to modify

Use scroll bar
to display plot
styles

Pick to enter
lineweights

Table View Tab for Named Plot Style Table

Select plot
style

List of plot
styles in table

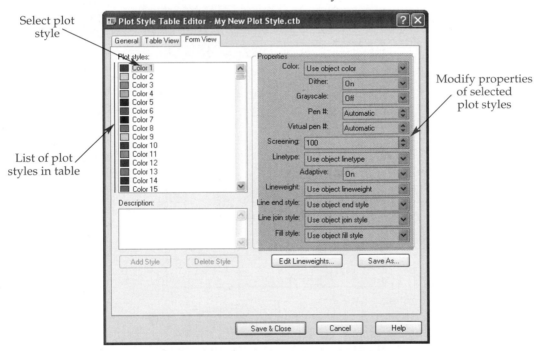

Modify properties
of selected
plot styles

Form View Tab for Color-Dependent Plot Style Table

the pull-down menu or enter OP or OPTIONS. You can also right-click in the drawing area and select **Options...** from the shortcut menu.

The **Plot and Publish** tab of the **Options** dialog box is shown in **Figure 11-25A.** Options having to do with plot styles are accessed by picking the **Plot Style Table Settings...** button at the lower-right corner of the **Plot and Publish** tab. The **Plot Style Table Settings** dialog box is displayed in **Figure 11-25B.** The plot style mode for new drawings is determined by the setting in the **Default plot style behavior for new**

Figure 11-25.
Use the **Plot and Publish** tab of the **Options** dialog box to set default plot style modes and tables for new drawings.

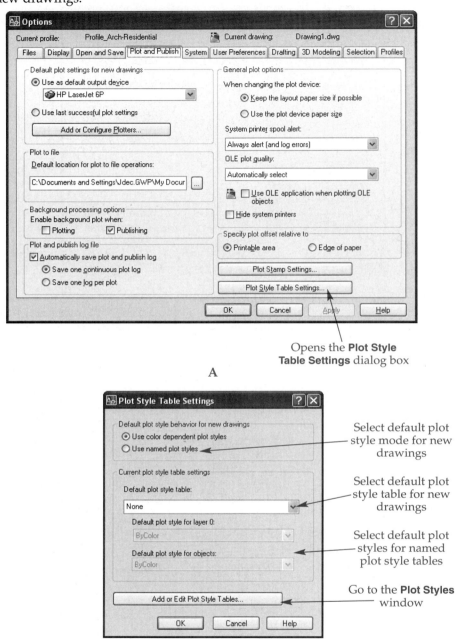

Opens the **Plot Style Table Settings** dialog box

A

Select default plot style mode for new drawings

Select default plot style table for new drawings

Select default plot styles for named plot style tables

Go to the **Plot Styles** window

B

drawings area. By default, the **Use color dependent plot styles** option is selected. When this option is selected, new drawings are set to use only color-dependent plot styles. The default plot style behavior setting can also be set using the **PSTYLEPOLICY** system variable (0 for named plot style mode and 1 for color-dependent mode).

The **Default plot style table** drop-down list can be used to set a default plot style table. When None is selected, objects in the new drawing are plotted based on their on-screen properties. The default plot style table is applied to the **Model** tab and layout tabs in new drawings. However, the plot style table can be changed at any time in the **Page Setup** dialog box.

If you select the **Use named plot styles** option, the drop-down lists below the default plot style table are activated. You can select the default plot styles for layer 0 and for objects. You can select any plot styles from the default plot style table.

The **Add or Edit Plot Style Tables...** button accesses the **Plot Styles** window. This window is where you edit existing plot style tables and create new plot style tables.

Applying color-dependent plot styles

Color-dependent plot style tables contain 255 plot styles—one for each color available for display in AutoCAD. You cannot add or delete plot styles in a color-dependent table. When you assign a color-dependent plot style table to a layout, the property values set for the plot styles override the on-screen display values during plotting.

Color-dependent plot styles can only be applied to drawings created while the **Use color dependent plot styles** option was selected as the default plot style behavior in the **Options** dialog box. Each of the **Model** and layout tabs can have a different plot style table assigned.

To assign a color-dependent plot style table, access the **Page Setup Manager**, then select the **Modify...** button, and then pick the plot style table from the **Plot style table** drop-down list of the **Page Setup** dialog box. See Figure 11-26. The selected plot style table is applied to the active **Model** or layout tab.

NOTE

A color-dependent plot style table cannot be attached to layers or objects because they may be composed of a variety of colors. Remember that a color-dependent plot style table should be used only when you want to show all lines of a single color plotted exactly the same.

Exercise 11-6   Complete the Exercise on the Student CD.

Applying named plot styles

In order for named plot styles to be used in a drawing, the drawing must have been created with the **Use named plot styles** option selected as the default plot style behavior in the **Options** dialog box. The drawing could also be based on a template with named plot styles.

Figure 11-26.
Selecting a plot style table for a page setup.

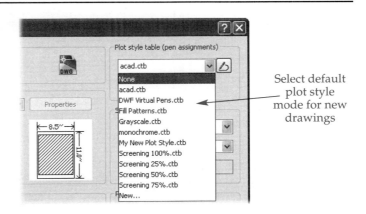

Select default plot style mode for new drawings

The **Model** tab and each layout tab can have a named plot style table attached. When you select a plot style table for the **Model** tab, you are also presented the option of selecting the plot style table for all layout tabs. However, each layout tab can have a different plot style table.

Once the named plot style tables have been assigned to the **Model** tab and layout tabs, plot styles can be assigned to objects and layers. A plot style assigned to an object overrides a plot style assigned to a layer, just as a color or linetype assigned to an object overrides the layer setting.

Plot styles can be assigned to layers in the **Layer Properties Manager** dialog box only when the drawing was created with a named plot style. See **Figure 11-27**. To access this dialog box, pick the **Layer Properties Manager** button from the **Layers** toolbar, select **Format > Layer...** from the pull-down menu, or enter LA or LAYER.

To modify the plot style, pick the current plot style listed for the layer. The **Select Plot Style** dialog box is displayed, **Figure 11-28**. This dialog box lists the plot styles available in the plot style table attached to the current tab. You can select a different plot style table from the **Active plot style table:** drop-down list. If you cannot select another plot style, the drawing was created with a color-dependent plot style. If you select another plot style table, the change is reflected in the **Plot style table** area of the **Page Setup** dialog box. Pick the **Editor...** button to access the **Plot Style Table Editor** dialog box.

Named plot styles can also be applied to objects. When a plot style is applied to an object, the plot style remains attached to the object in all layout tabs. If the plot style attached to the object is contained in the plot style table attached to the layout tab, the object will be plotted with the plot style settings. However, if the plot style assigned to the object is not found within the plot style table attached to the layout tab, the object is plotted according to its on-screen display settings.

Modifying an object's plot style is similar to modifying an object's layer, color, or linetype. You can select the new plot style from the **Plot Style Control** drop-down list in the **Properties** toolbar, **Figure 11-29A**, or you can use the **Properties** window to change the plot style, **Figure 11-29B**. Selecting the **Other...** option accesses the **Select Plot Style** dialog box.

LAYER

Type
LAYER
LA

Pull-Down Menu
Format
> Layer...

Toolbar
Layers

Layer Properties
Manager

Figure 11-27.
Named plot styles can be assigned to layers using the **Layer Properties Manager** dialog box.

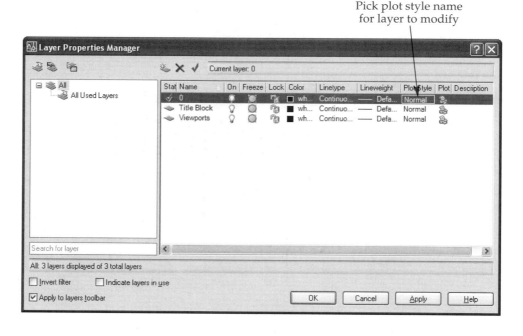

Pick plot style name
for layer to modify

AutoCAD and Its Applications—Basics

Figure 11-28.
Use the **Select Plot Style** dialog box to select a plot style for a layer.

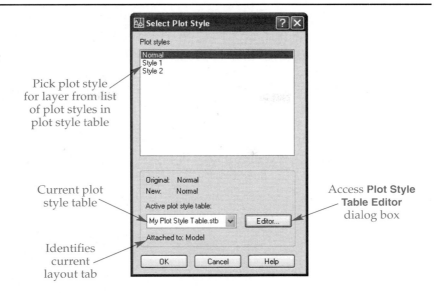

Pick plot style for layer from list of plot styles in plot style table

Current plot style table

Identifies current layout tab

Access **Plot Style Table Editor** dialog box

Figure 11-29.
Assigning a new plot style to an object. A—Using the **Plot Style Control** drop-down list in the **Properties** toolbar. B—Using the **Properties** window.

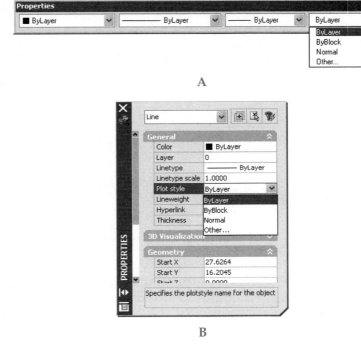

A

B

NOTE

Every AutoCAD object and layer is automatically assigned a plot style. If the current drawing is set to use a named plot style table, the default plot style for objects in the drawing is ByLayer. This means that objects retain the properties of their layers. The default plot style for a layer is Normal. Objects plotted with these settings keep their original properties.

Exercise 11-7   Complete the Exercise on the Student CD.

Viewing Plot Style Effects before You Plot

The display of lineweights in an AutoCAD drawing is controlled by the **LWDISPLAY** system variable. If **LWDISPLAY** is on, lineweights are displayed on-screen. Similarly, it is possible to display plot style effects on-screen to see how they will appear. To do so, pick the **Display plot styles** check box in the **Plot style table** area in the **Page Setup** dialog box. Keep in mind that these two display features can increase the time required to regenerate drawings and may decrease the performance of AutoCAD.

A quicker method is to use the print preview option, which is discussed later in the text. This displays all lineweights and plot styles exactly as they will appear on the plotted drawing.

Plot Settings

A majority of the settings that must be considered prior to plotting can be established and saved in layouts, viewports, layers, plot style tables, and template drawings. If you plan your work well, there should be very few settings, if any, you will have to adjust prior to plotting. Take a look at some of the items required for plotting, and where they can be saved.

Item	Location
Border and title block	Layout
View scales	Viewport (**Zoom XP**)
Text height	Drawing
Object color, lineweight, and end style	Layers and plot style tables
Plot device	Page setup
Plot style table	Page setup
Paper size and drawing orientation	Page setup
Plot scale, area, offset, and options	Page setup

If you prepare for plotting as soon as you begin a new drawing, the act of plotting may mean just a few clicks of your pointing device.

Selecting the desired output device and plot style table was discussed earlier in this chapter. Once these settings are complete, you can elaborate on the plot settings in the **Plot** dialog box or in the **Page Setup** dialog box of the **Page Setup Manager**. See **Figure 11-30**.

Paper Size, Units, and Drawing Orientation

The **Paper size** area of the **Plot** dialog box controls the paper size. Select the appropriate paper size from the drop-down list. Paper sizes are listed in inches or millimeters.

The **Drawing orientation** area of the **Plot** dialog box controls the plot rotation. You may need to select the ">" (more options) button in the lower right of the **Plot** dialog box to see this area. *Portrait* orients the long side of the paper vertically, and is the standard orientation for most written documents printed on 8.5 × 11 paper. *Landscape* orients the long side of the paper horizontally, and is the default for AutoCAD drawings. If you consider landscape format to be a rotation angle of 0°, the following table should help you determine how to use the **Plot upside-down button** option to achieve several rotation angles.

Figure 11-30.
A—The **Plot** dialog box. B—The **Page Setup** dialog box of the **Page Setup Manager**.

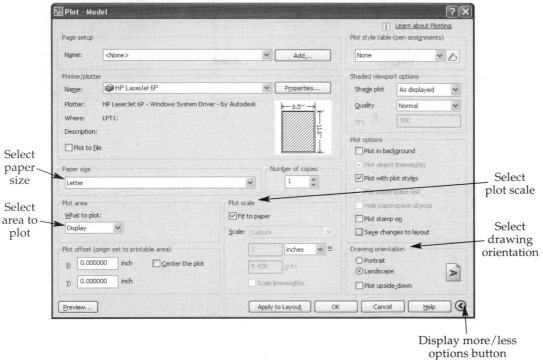

Select paper size

Select area to plot

Select plot scale

Select drawing orientation

Display more/less options button

A

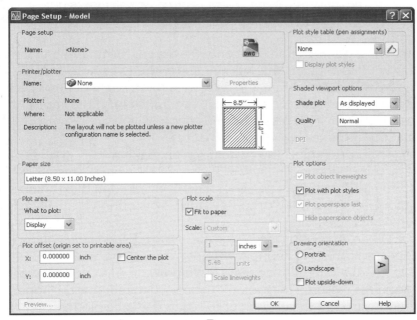

B

Orientation Buttons	Rotation Angle
Landscape	0°
Portrait	90°
Upside-down landscape	180°
Upside-down portrait	270°

Figure 11-31.
The long side of
the plot is oriented
vertically in a 90°
portrait rotation.

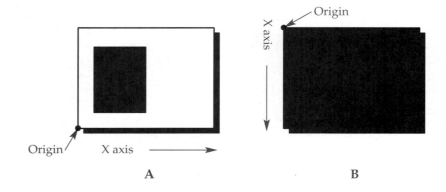

Origin / X axis ⟶

A

B

In AutoCAD, the horizontal screen measurement relates to the long side of the paper (landscape format). However, you might create a drawing, form, or chart in portrait format. This format orients the long side of the plot vertically. AutoCAD rotates plots in 90° increments, as shown in the previous table. **Figure 11-31** illustrates the result of a 90° portrait rotation.

Plotting Area

The **Plot area** region of the **Plot** dialog box allows you to choose the portion of the drawing to be plotted, and how it is to be plotted. The options contained in the drop-down list are described as follows:

- **Layout/Limits.** The **Layout** option is displayed when plotting a layout. Everything inside the margins of the layout is plotted. The **Limits** option is displayed when plotting from the **Model** tab. This option plots everything inside the defined drawing limits.

- **Extents.** The **Extents** option plots only the area of the drawing in which objects are drawn. Before using this option, zoom the extents to include all drawn objects to verify exactly what will be plotted. Be aware that border lines around your drawing (like the title block) may be clipped off if they are at the extreme edge of the screen. This often happens because you are requesting the plotter to plot at the extreme edge of its active area.

- **Display.** This option plots the current screen display.

- **View.** Use this option to plot named views, which were discussed in Chapter 10. This option is not shown if no views have been saved in the drawing. Select the name of the view from the drop-down list. This option is available only when the **Model** tab is current.

- **Window.** When this option is selected, the dialog disappears so that you can pick two opposite corners to define a window around the area to be plotted. After doing so, the dialog will reappear. A **Window...** button will now be displayed in the **Plot area** region. This button can be used to redefine the opposite corners of a window around the portion of the drawing to be plotted.

NOTE

If the window you define is too close to an object, some portion of that object may be clipped off in your plot. If this happens, simply adjust the window size the next time you plot. You can prevent these errors by using the plot preview option to see what exactly will be plotted.

Shaded Viewport Options

AutoCAD allows viewports to be plotted in shaded modes. You may need to select the ">" button in the lower right of the **Plot** dialog box to see this area. If a viewport has been designated to be plotted in **Wireframe** or **Hidden** mode, no options from this area of the **Plot** dialog box are editable. If a viewport is designated to be plotted in **As Displayed** or **Rendered** mode, you have the option of setting the quality of the shading for the viewports. Each predefined quality setting has a certain dots-per-inch (dpi) setting associated with it. If you choose **Custom** in the **Quality:** drop-down list, enter a value in the **DPI:** text box.

Plot Offset

The **Plot offset** area controls how far the drawing is offset from either the lower-left corner of the paper or the lower-left corner of the printable area. See **Figure 11-32.** This depends on how the **Specify plot offset relative to** area has been set in the **Publish and Plot** tab of the **Options** dialog box.

To begin plotting a drawing at the origin (either the lower-left corner of the plot media or the lower-left corner of the printable area, as described in the previous paragraph), leave the values shown in the **X:** and **Y:** text boxes at 0.00. If you want to move the drawing away from the default origin, change the required values in the text boxes. For example, to move the drawing four units to the right and three units above the plotter origin, enter 4 in the **X:** text box, and 3 in the **Y:** text box.

Other Plotting Options

The **Plot options** area of the **Plot** dialog box contains a list of items that can affect how, and if, objects appear on your plots, especially relating to paper space and model space objects. You may need to select the ">" button in the lower right of the **Plot** dialog box to see this area. Apply these options only when required for the plot by picking the appropriate check box. The following options are available:

- **Plot in background.** This option allows you to continue working in AutoCAD while your computer processes the plot.
- **Plot object lineweights.** Lines having a lineweight other than 0 are plotted using the appropriate thickness. This box is checked by default.
- **Plot with plot styles.** All plot styles attached to the drawing and its components are plotted.
- **Plot paperspace last.** Paper space objects are plotted first by default. If this box is checked, paper space objects are plotted last. Since there are no paper space objects present in the **Model** tab, this option is available only when plotting from a layout tab.

Figure 11-32.
The **Plot offset** area controls how far the drawing is offset from the lower-left corner of the paper.

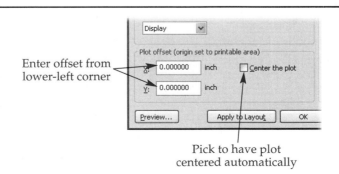

Enter offset from lower-left corner

Pick to have plot centered automatically

- **Hide paperspace objects.** This option removes hidden lines from 3D objects that have been created in paper space. This option is only available when you are plotting from a layout tab. This option affects only objects drawn in paper space. It does not affect any 3D objects within a viewport. To plot objects within viewports with hidden lines removed, you must change the Shade plot property of the viewport. To do this, select the layout tab, pick the viewport, and open the **Properties** window. Pick the Shade plot property and change the setting to Hidden. See **Figure 11-33.**
- **Plot stamp on.** Checking this option will attach a plot stamp along the edge of the plot. See the "Adding a Plot Stamp" section later in this chapter.
- **Save changes to layout.** This option allows any changes that are made to the settings in the **Plot** dialog box to be saved to the layout as the default page setup for the layout.

Determining Drawing Scale Factors

The proper scale factor is vitally important because it ensures that text, dimension values, and dimensioning entities (such as arrowheads and tick marks) are plotted at the proper size. The scale factor of the drawing should already be established by the time you are ready to plot. The scale factor should be an integral part of your template drawings. To obtain the correct text height, the desired plotted text height is multiplied by the scale factor. The scale factor is also used in scaling dimensions.

 NOTE Determine the plot scale and scale factor when you begin the drawing. If you find the drawing scale factor does not correspond to the plotting scale, you will need to update dimensions and text.

The scale factor is always the reciprocal of the drawing scale. For example, if you wish to plot a mechanical drawing at a scale of 1/2″ = 1″, calculate the scale factor as follows:

$1/2″ = 1″$
$.5″ = 1″$
$1 \div .5 = 2$ *(The scale factor is 2)*

An architectural drawing to be plotted at a scale of 1/4″ = 1′-0″ has a scale factor calculated as follows:

$1/4″ = 1′-0″$
$.25″ = 12″$
$12 \div .25 = 48$ *(The scale factor is 48)*

The scale factor of a civil engineering drawing that has a scale of 1″ = 60′ is calculated as follows:

$1″ = 60′$
$1″ = 60 \times 12 = 720″$ *(The scale factor is 720)*

Once the scale factor of the drawing has been determined, calculate the height of the text in AutoCAD. If text height is to be plotted at 1/8″, it should not be drawn at that height unless the drawing will be plotted at full scale. Remember, all geometry created in AutoCAD should be drawn at full scale.

For example, if you are working on a civil engineering drawing with a scale of 1″ = 60′, the scale factor equals 720. Text drawn 1/8″ high appears as a dot. The full-size civil engineering drawing in AutoCAD is 720 times larger than it will be when plotted at the proper scale. Therefore, you must multiply the text height by 720 in order to get text that appears in correct proportion on the screen. For 1/8″ high text to appear correctly on-screen, calculate the AutoCAD text height as follows:

$1/8″ \times 720$
$.125 \times 720 = 90$ *(The proper height of the text is 90)*

Figure 11-33.
In order to plot objects in a floating viewport with hidden lines removed, the Shade plot setting for the viewport must be Hidden.

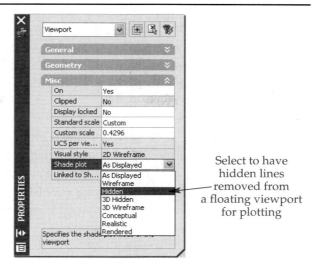

Select to have hidden lines removed from a floating viewport for plotting

Remember, scale factors and text heights should be determined before beginning a drawing. The best method is to incorporate these as values within your template drawing files.

Scaling the plot

AutoCAD drawing geometry is created at full scale, and the drawing is scaled at the plotter to fit on the sheet size. The **Plot scale** area of the **Plot** dialog box is used to specify the plot scale. The **Scale:** drop-down list contains a selection of 33 different decimal and architectural scales, including Custom. See **Figure 11-34.** The text boxes below the predefined scales drop-down list allow you to specify the plot scale as a ratio of plotted units to drawing units. An architectural drawing to be plotted at 1/4″ = 1′-0″ can be entered in the text boxes as:

$$1/4″ = 1′ \text{ or } .25 = 12 \text{ or } 1 = 48$$

A mechanical drawing to be plotted at a scale of 1/2″ = 1″ can be entered in the text boxes as:

$$1/2″ = 1″ \text{ or } .5 = 1 \text{ or } 1 = 2$$

Figure 11-34.
The **Scale:** drop-down list contains a selection of 33 different decimal and architectural scales, including Custom.

Select **Fit to paper** if scale is not a concern

Enter values here for a custom plot scale

Adjust lineweights as the plot scale changes

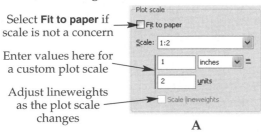

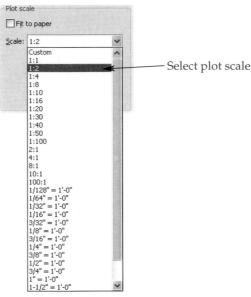

Select plot scale

Pick the **Fit to paper** check box above the predefined scales drop-down list if you want AutoCAD to automatically adjust your drawing to fit on the paper. This is useful if you have a C-size pen plotter but need to plot a D-size or E-size drawing. However, keep in mind that you may have considerable blank space left on the paper, depending on the size and proportions of your drawing.

The **Fit to paper** option is also useful if you are printing a large drawing on a printer that can only use A-size sheets. The drawing is automatically scaled down to fit the size of the printer paper.

Calculating the drawing area and limits

To calculate the available area on a sheet of paper at a specific scale, use this formula:

Scale factor × Media size = Limits

For example, the limits of a B-size (17″ × 11″) sheet of paper at 1/2″ = 1″ scale (scale factor = 2) can be calculated as follows:

2 × 17 = 34 (X distance)
2 × 11 = 22 (Y distance)

Thus, the limits of a B-size sheet at the scale of 1/2″ = 1″ are 34,22. The same formula applies to architectural scales. The limits of a C-size architectural sheet (24″ × 18″) at a scale of 1/4″ = 1′-0″ (scale factor = 48) can be determined as follows:

48 × 24 = 1152″ = 96′ (X distance)

Use the same formula to calculate the Y distance for the 18″ side of the paper. Refer to the *Drafting Sheet Sizes* chart in the *Reference Material* section of the Student CD to find the limits for common scales on various paper sizes for each drafting field.

CAUTION

Before you plot a drawing, always check the **LTSCALE** and **PSLTSCALE** system variables. These variables control model space and paper space linetype scaling. The **LTSCALE** variable is set to a value representing the scale factor to be applied to linetypes that contain dashes and spaces. The **PSLTSCALE** variable is a toggle that can be set to either 1 or 0, "on" or "off" respectively.

When working in the **Model** tab, **LTSCALE** should be set to the inverse of the plotting scale. For example, if the plotting scale is to be 1/48 (1/4″ = 1′-0″), **LTSCALE** should be set to 48. This way, unless you are zoomed in extremely close, the linetypes will be readily apparent. If the drawing is to be plotted from the **Model** tab, **LTSCALE** should remain set to this value. The **PSLTSCALE** variable setting has no effect when working and plotting from the model tab.

When plotting from a layout tab, especially with viewports of two or more differing scales, the **LTSCALE** should be set to 1, and **PSLTSCALE** should be set to 1 ("on"). Setting **PSLTSCALE** to 1 allows the zoom scale factor of the viewport to control the scale factor of the linetypes. In this case, the linetypes will be displayed through the viewports at a scale factor based on the product of the viewport zoom scale factor multiplied by the **LTSCALE** setting (which should be 1). Differently scaled viewports will display and plot linetypes at the same size, relative to paper space.

When plotting from a layout tab with a single viewport, or multiple viewports zoomed to the same scale, the **LTSCALE** can be set to the inverse of the zoom scale factor of the viewport(s) and the **PSLTSCALE** variable can be set to 0 ("off"). For the sake of consistency, if your school or company is using layouts, it might be a good idea to standardize on the linetype scaling method outlined in the previous paragraph.

AutoCAD and Its Applications—Basics

Previewing the Plot

Depending on their size and complexity, drawings can require long plotting times. By previewing a plot before it is sent to the output device, you can catch errors, saving material and valuable plot time. This feature is controlled by the **Preview...** button at the lower-left corner of the **Plot** dialog box.

Pick the **Preview...** button to display the drawing as it will actually appear on the plotted hard copy. The display reflects any plot style tables that have been attached to the drawing if the **Plot with plot styles** button is checked in the **Plot options** area. Displaying the preview takes the same amount of time as a drawing regeneration. Therefore, the drawing size determines how quickly the image is produced.

The drawing is displayed inside a paper outline. The Zoom cursor appears. Press and hold the pick button as you move the cursor up to enlarge and down to reduce. Right-click to display the shortcut menu shown in **Figure 11-35.** It provides several display options, a **Plot** option, and an **Exit** option. The shortcut menu is handy because it allows you to closely examine the drawing before you commit to plotting. When you are finished previewing, press [Esc] or [Enter] to return to the **Plot** dialog box.

A preview is also displayed by picking **File** > **Plot Preview**. This selection bypasses the **Plot** dialog box.

Before you pick **OK** in the **Plot** dialog box, there are several items you should check:

✓ The printer or plotter is plugged in and turned on.
✓ The printer's data cable is secure.
✓ The paper and ink/toner are loaded correctly.
✓ The printer or plotter area is clear for unblocked paper movement.

Once you are satisfied with all plotter parameters and are ready to plot, pick the **OK** button to exit the **Plot** dialog box. Depending on the type of plotter or printer you are using, one or more dialog boxes may be displayed, showing the drawing name and a meter showing the percentage of the file that has been regenerated and sent to the printer.

Adding a Plot Stamp

A plot stamp is specific text information included on a printed or plotted drawing. A plot stamp may include information such as the drawing name or the date and time the drawing was printed.

In the **Plot** dialog box, the **Plot stamp on** area in the **Plot options** area allows you to activate and modify the plot stamp. See **Figure 11-36.** If the **On** check box is activated, a **Plot Stamp Settings...** button appears next to the check box and a plot stamp will be printed on the drawing. You can also specify the items to be included in the plot stamp by picking the **Plot Stamp Settings...** button. This accesses the **Plot Stamp** dialog box, which is shown in **Figure 11-37.**

Specify the information to be included in the plot stamp in the **Plot stamp fields** area of the **Plot Stamp** dialog box. The following items can be included:

- Drawing name.
- Layout name.
- Date and time.
- Login name.
- Device name.
- Paper size.
- Plot scale.

Figure 11-35.
Right-click to display the shortcut menu when a plot preview is displayed.

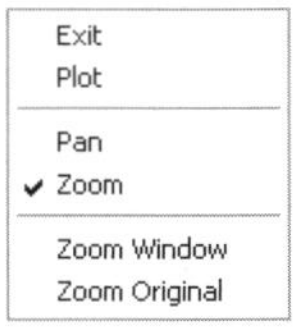

| Exit |
| Plot |
| Pan |
| ✓ Zoom |
| Zoom Window |
| Zoom Original |

Figure 11-36.
Activate the plot stamp in the **Plot options** area of the **Plot** dialog box. Pick the **Plot Stamp Settings...** button to access the **Plot Stamp** dialog box.

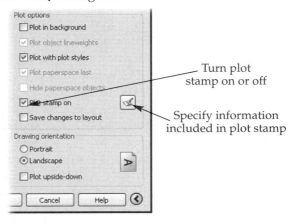

Turn plot stamp on or off

Specify information included in plot stamp

Figure 11-37.
Use the **Plot Stamp** dialog box to specify the information included in the plot stamp. You can save plot stamp settings as PSS files.

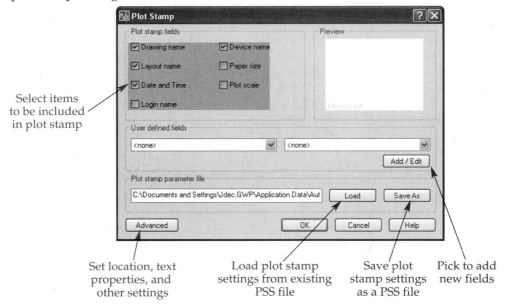

Select items to be included in plot stamp

Set location, text properties, and other settings

Load plot stamp settings from existing PSS file

Save plot stamp settings as a PSS file

Pick to add new fields

You can create additional plot stamp items in the **User defined fields** area. For example, you could add a field for the client name, the project name, or the contractor who will be using the drawing.

The **Preview** area provides a preview of the location and orientation of the plot stamp. The preview does not show the actual plot stamp text.

Plot stamp settings can be saved in a PSS (plot stamp parameter) file. If you load an existing PSS file, the settings saved in the file are automatically set in the **Plot Stamp** dialog box.

Additional plot stamp options are set in the **Advanced Options** dialog box. To access this dialog box, pick the **Advanced...** button in the **Plot Stamp** dialog box. The **Advanced Options** dialog box is shown in **Figure 11-38.** The following options are available:

Figure 11-38.
Specify the plot stamp location, orientation, text font and size, and units in the **Advanced Options** dialog box.

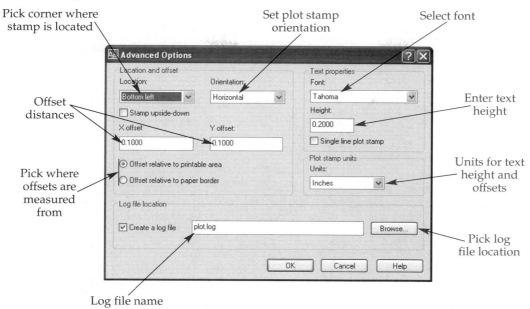

Pick corner where stamp is located

Set plot stamp orientation

Select font

Offset distances

Enter text height

Pick where offsets are measured from

Units for text height and offsets

Pick log file location

Log file name

- **Location and offset.** Pick the corner where the plot stamp begins from the drop-down list. If you want the plot stamp to print upside-down, pick the **Stamp upside-down** check box. The orientation is set by picking Horizontal or Vertical from the **Orientation** drop-down list. The X offset and Y offset distance is entered in the text boxes. The offset distances are measured relative to the printable area or paper border.
- **Text properties.** Specify the text font and height. Pick the **Single line plot stamp** check box if you want the plot stamp constrained to a single line. If this check box is not checked, the plot stamp will be printed in two lines.
- **Plot stamp units.** Select the plot stamp units. The plot stamp units can be different from the drawing units.
- **Log file location.** Pick the **Create a log file** check box to create a log file of plotted items. Specify the name of the log file in the text box. Pick **Browse...** to specify the location of the log file.

NOTE

The log file settings are independent of the plot stamp settings. Thus, you can produce a log file without creating a plot stamp or have a plot stamp without producing a log file.

Additional Plotting Options

The **Plot and Publish** tab of the **Options** dialog box contains general plotting settings, some of which will seldom have to be changed. See **Figure 11-39.** To access this dialog box, select **Tools** > **Options...** from the pull-down menu. The **Plot and Publish** tab provides several general plotting options. The areas are discussed briefly here.

- **Default plot settings for new drawings.** The default setting is **Use as default output device**. The device can be selected from the drop-down list. The **Use last successful plot settings** option retains the previous plot settings. Picking the **Add or Configure Plotters** button displays the **Plotters** window.

Figure 11-39.
General plotting settings are found in the **Plot and Publish** tab of the **Options** dialog box.

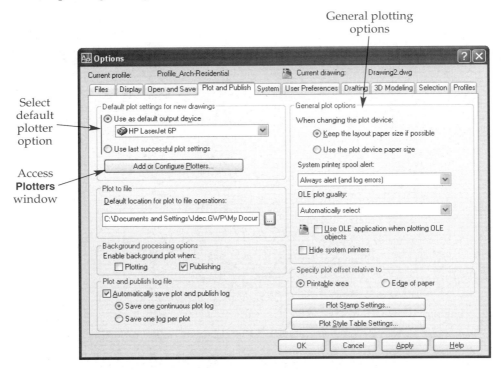

- **General plot options.** This area allows you to use either the **Keep the layout paper size if possible** option, regardless of the plotter selected, or the **Use the plot device paper size** option. If you choose to keep the layout size, AutoCAD will use the paper size specified in the **Page Setup** dialog box. If this size cannot be plotted, AutoCAD defaults to the size listed in the plotter's PC3 file.
  - **System printer spool alert.** If a port conflict occurs during plotting and a drawing is spooled to a system printer, AutoCAD can display an alert and log the error. This drop-down list gives four options for alerting and logging errors.
  - **OLE plot quality.** *OLE* is an acronym for *object linking and embedding* and refers to any text or graphic object that is imported from another software application. This drop-down list allows you to select the type of OLE objects that will be plotted.
  - **Use OLE application when plotting OLE objects.** If this check box is activated, applications used to create OLE objects are launched. This may be desirable if you wish to use the OLE software to adjust the quality of the object.

Alternative Plotting

Typically, the end result of executing the plotting procedures is a paper drawing, also known as a hardcopy. Largely because of the growth of the Internet, many drawings are being exchanged as electronic files instead of paper drawings. AutoCAD can generate two types of electronic files: design web format (DWF) and plot (PLT). The DWF file may be e-mailed, uploaded to the Internet, or posted on a company's internal Web site. The file is viewed using Autodesk's free application, *DWF Viewer®*. The other electronic file, PLT, is eventually sent to a printer or plotter. The reason for creating this file instead of plotting directly to paper is to save time. PLT files can be created during the workday and sent to the plotter at night, when the plotter is not busy. Sometimes the PLT files are sent to a plot spooler so your computer is not waiting for the plotter to finish.

Using Publish to Create a DWF File

A DWF file is created from the **Publish** dialog box. You can also send the drawings to a plotter from the **Publish** dialog box. This technique will be presented along with the DWF procedure. You can access this dialog box by picking the **Publish** button on the **Standard** toolbar, picking **File > Publish**, or typing PUBLISH. The listing of sheets to publish will be empty unless the **Model** or layout tabs have been initialized. If open, close the **Publish** dialog box and create some geometry and text in the **Model** view. Pick each layout tab to initialize them. Open the **Publish** dialog box again and notice the three sheets listed in the **Sheets to publish** area. It should say No errors under the status title for each sheet. See **Figure 11-40.**

The eight buttons below the **Sheets to publish** area are:
- **Preview.** Same as **Plot Preview.**
- **Add Sheets.** Add a sheet from another drawing.
- **Remove Sheets.** Remove the selected sheet from the list.
- **Move Sheet Up.** The published sheets are viewed or plotted in the order shown in the list.
- **Move Sheet Down.** Used with the button above to reorder the sheets.
- **Load Sheet List.** Loads a previously saved list of sheets to publish.
- **Save Sheet List.** This button is available after the current drawing is saved.
- **Plot Stamp Settings.** Same as the **Plot Stamp Settings** in the **Plot** dialog box.

Below these buttons is the **Publish to** area containing two destinations. The first, **Plotter named in page setup**, sends each sheet directly to the plotter designated in its page setup. Each sheet plots using the page setup named in the **Sheets to Publish** area. The second, **DWF File**, creates a design web format file that can be used as described in the first paragraph of this chapter. The location of this file, along with other options, can be found by picking the **Publish Options** button.

Other features to note are the **Number of copies** text box and the **Include when adding sheets** area. The number of copies only applies when the destination is a plotter and the page setup is not plotting to a file. The type of sheets, model or layout, to include when publishing is controlled in the second area mentioned. After configuring the necessary options, pick **Publish** to create the DWF file or send the sheets to a plotter.

Figure 11-40.
DWF files and paper copies can be created from the **Publish** dialog box.

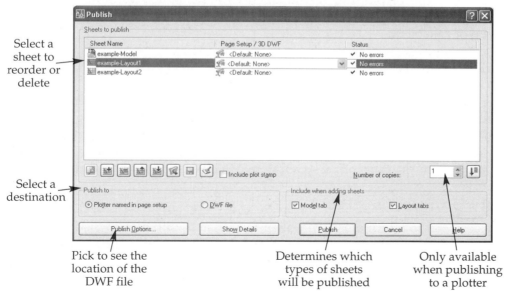

Select a sheet to reorder or delete

Select a destination

Pick to see the location of the DWF file

Determines which types of sheets will be published

Only available when publishing to a plotter

Creating a PLT File

The PLT file is generated within the **Plot** dialog box. All of the options that you would configure for a paper plot have to be considered when creating the PLT file. Even the plotter has to be selected for a file to be created. Open the **Plot** dialog box, as described in the previous sections, and prepare all of the options as you would when making a hardcopy. Make sure that you have chosen a plotter. Now, put a check in the **Plot to file** check box located in the **Printer/plotter** area. See **Figure 11-41**. Pick the **OK** button and the **Browse for Plot File** dialog box will pop up. If necessary, you can change the file name and location before saving the file.

Figure 11-41.
PLT files are created from the **Plot** dialog box.

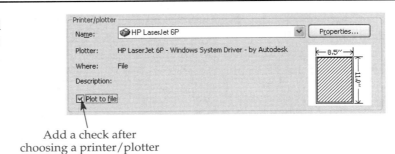

Add a check after
choosing a printer/plotter

Plotting Hints

Plotting can slow down productivity in an office or a classroom if not done efficiently. Establish and follow a procedure for using the plotter, and instruct all drafters, engineers, and other plotter users of the proper operating procedures. Post these in strategic locations.

Planning Your Plots

Planning is again the key word when dealing with plots. In the same way you planned the drawing, you must plan the plot. The following items need to be considered when planning:

- ✓ Size and type of plotting media, such as bond paper, vellum, or polyester film.
- ✓ Type of title block.
- ✓ Location and scale of multiple views.
- ✓ Origin location and scale of the drawing.
- ✓ Orientation of 3D views.
- ✓ Portion to be plotted: layout, view, window, display, limits, or extents.

This is only a sample of decisions that should be made before you begin plotting. Usually, the plotter is the funnel that all drawings must go through before they are evaluated, approved, and sent to production or the client. When a bottleneck develops at the plotter, the time savings of a CAD system can be drastically reduced.

Eliminate Unnecessary Plots

The easiest way to eliminate the problems associated with plotting is to eliminate plotting. Make plots *only* when absolutely necessary. This results in time and money savings. A few additional suggestions include the following:

- ✓ Obtain approvals of designs while the drawings are on-screen.
- ✓ Transfer files for the checker's comments.

✓ Create a special layer with a unique color for markups. Freeze or erase this layer when finally making a plot.

✓ Use a "redlining" software package that enables the checker to review the drawing and apply markups to it without using AutoCAD.

✓ Check drawings on disk. Use a special layer for comments.

✓ Use a printer when check prints are sufficient.

✓ Avoid making plots for backups. Rather, establish a reliable backup procedure. This may be accomplished using tape cartridges, optical disks, or other external storage devices.

If You Must Plot...

Industry still exists on a paper-based system. Therefore, it is important that plotters are used efficiently. This means using the plotter only for what is required. Here are a few hints for doing just that.

✓ Ask yourself, "Do I *really* need a plot?" If the answer is an unqualified *yes*, then proceed.

✓ Plan your plot!

✓ Pick the least busy time to make the plot.

✓ Select the smallest piece of paper possible.

✓ Use the lowest quality paper possible.

✓ Create batch plot files and use batch plotting at times when plotter and printer use is light.

Producing Quality Plots

When you must plot the highest quality drawing for reproduction, evaluation, or presentation, use your plotter in a manner that does the job right the first time. Keep in mind these points before making that final plot.

✓ Choose the device that will produce the quality of print needed. Select the right tool for the job.

✓ Choose the paper type and size appropriate for the project.

✓ If using wet ink pens, select the proper ink for your climate.

✓ Apply the appropriate plot style table for color plotting.

Chapter Test

Answer the following questions. Write your answers on a separate sheet of paper or complete the electronic chapter test on the Student CD.

1. What is paper space?
2. Which drawing environment (space) is active when the **Model** tab is selected?
3. What is a layout?
4. How do you create floating viewports in a layout?
5. When working in a layout tab, how do you activate a viewport in order to zoom or pan the viewport display?
6. List three methods used to create a new layout tab.
7. When creating a new layout by copying an existing layout, why is it better to select the command option from the shortcut menu rather than using the toolbar button?
8. How can you rename a layout?
9. If all layout tabs are not visible on screen, how do you select a tab that is not currently visible?
10. List the types of files a layout can be saved as.

11. How do you access the **Plotter Configuration Editor** from the **Page Setup** dialog box?
12. List five properties that can be set within a plot style.
13. Name the two plot style modes and the file extensions for their plot style tables.
14. What is a plot style table?
15. How do you access the **Plot Styles** window?
16. How do you create a new plot style table?
17. When you create a new color-dependent plot style table, how many plot styles does it contain?
18. When you create a new named plot style table, how many plot styles does it contain?
19. List two ways to access the **Plot Style Table Editor.**
20. What determines the plot style mode for a drawing?
21. Explain how you can specify a plot style table to be attached to all new drawings by default.
22. How does a color-dependent plot style table attached to a layout affect the plotting of the layout?
23. Plot styles of which plot style mode can be attached to layers and objects?
24. Explain how to assign a plot style to a layer.
25. Name two methods of assigning a plot style to an object.
26. What setting is used to have the effect of plot styles displayed in a layout?
27. Calculate the scale factors for drawings with the following scales:
    A. 1/4″ = 1″
    B. 1/8″ = 1′-0″
    C. 1″ = 30′
28. Calculate the drawing limits for the following scales and sheet sizes:
    A. 2″ = 1″ scale, 17 × 11 sheet size
    B. 1/2″ = 1′-0″ scale, 48 × 36 sheet size
    C. 1″= 10′ scale, 36 × 24 sheet size
29. Define *plot file* and explain how it is used.
30. What do you enter in the **Plot** dialog box to make the plotted drawing twice the size of the soft copy drawing?
31. What do you enter to specify a plot scale of 1/4″ = 1′-0″?
32. What system variable controls paper space linetype scaling?
33. Name the pull-down menu where the **Plot...** command is found.
34. How do you add a printer or plotter to the **Printer/plotter** area of the **Plot** dialog box?
35. What is the difference between a PC2 file and a PC3 file?
36. How do you save a plot file named PLOT1 to a specific folder?
37. Identify the two types of paper orientation.
38. Cite two advantages of the preview format.
39. Can you zoom while viewing a preview?
40. Explain why you should plan your plots.

For Questions 41–45, specify if the statement is true or false.

41. Plot styles can be added to and deleted from color-dependent plot style tables.
42. Plot styles can be added to and deleted from named plot style tables.
43. The plot style mode of a drawing cannot be changed.
44. A plot style assigned to a layer will override a plot style assigned to an object on the layer when the drawing is plotted.
45. If a drawing has multiple layouts, all layouts must use the same plot style table.

Drawing Problems

1. Create a new B-size decimal template drawing for use with mechanical (machine) parts. Use the following guidelines:
   A. Create a layout with the border and title block.
   B. Establish the appropriate settings to make this a half-scale (1″ = 2″) drawing.
   C. Create three different text styles: one to plot at 1/8″ high, another at 3/16″ high, and a third at 1/4″ high. Set the text heights and linetype scale according to the values given in the chart on the Student CD.
   D. Save the drawing template as MECH-B-HALF.DWT.

2. Create a new C-size architectural template drawing. Use the following guidelines:
   A. Create a layout with the border and title block. Set units to architectural and set the area to 160′ × 120′. Select to work on the drawing without the layout visible.
   B. Establish the appropriate settings to make this a 1/8″ = 1′-0″ scale drawing.
   C. Create three different text styles: one to plot at 1/8″ high, another at 3/16″ high, and a third at 1/4″ high. Set the text heights and linetype scale according to the values given in the chart on the Student CD.
   D. Save the drawing as ARCH-C-EIGHTH.DWT.

3. Create a new C-size civil engineering template drawing. Use the following guidelines:
   A. Create a layout with the border and title block. Set units to engineering, angle to surveyor, angle measure to east, angle direction to counterclockwise, and set the area to 1000′ × 750′. Select to work on the drawing while viewing the layout.
   B. Establish the appropriate settings to make this a 1″ = 50′ scale drawing.
   C. Create three different text styles: one to plot at 1/8″ high, another at 3/16″ high, and a third at 1/4″ high. Set the text heights and linetype scale according to the values given in the chart on the Student CD.
   D. Save the drawing as CIVIL-C-1=50.DWT.

4. Open one of your drawings from Chapter 8. Plot the drawing on B-size paper using the **Limits** option. Use different color pens for each color in the drawing.

5. Zoom in on a portion of the drawing used for Problem 4 and select the **Display** plotting option. Rotate the plot 90° and fit it on the paper.

6. Using the same drawing used in Problem 4, use the **Window** option. Window a detailed area of the drawing. Plot the drawing to fit the paper size chosen.

Drawing Problems – Chapter 11

7. Draw the views needed to describe the object completely. Set up appropriate layers, colors, and linetypes. Do not dimension the drawing. Plot from a layout tab using a scale of 1:1. Save the problem as P11-7.

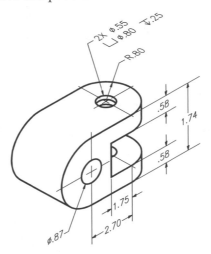

8. Draw the shown stainless steel stud on a B-size sheet at a scale of 2:1 (2 times actual size). Use a template drawing with a single floating model space viewport. Do not dimension the drawing. Be sure that paper space is active before using the **PLOT** command. Set the plot scale at 1:1. Save the drawing as P11-8.

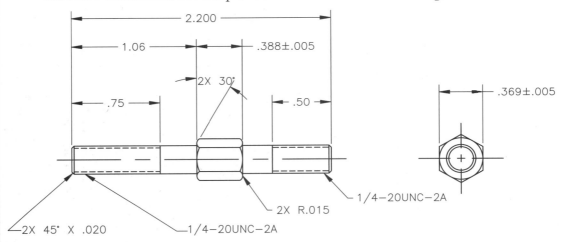

9. On an A-size sheet draw, at full scale, the schematic shown. Keep the proportions of each component and the entire drawing as shown. Using color-dependent plot styles, have the equipment (shown in color in the diagram) plot with a lineweight of 0.8 mm and 80% screening. Plotted text height should be 1/8". Plot in paper space at 1:1. Save the drawing as P11-9.

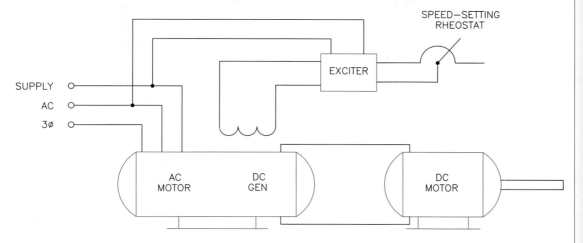

10. On a B-size sheet draw, at full scale, the schematic shown. Keep the proportions of each component and the entire drawing as shown. Plotted text height should be 1/8". Create four layouts with the names and displays as follows:
   A. The **Entire Schematic** layout plots the entire schematic.
   B. The **3 Wire Control** layout plots only the 3 Wire Control diagram.
   C. The **Motor** layout plots the motor symbol and connections in the lower-center of the schematic.
   D. The **Schematic** layout plots schematic without the 3 Wire Control and motor components.
   Plot in paper space at 1:1. Save the drawing as P11-10.

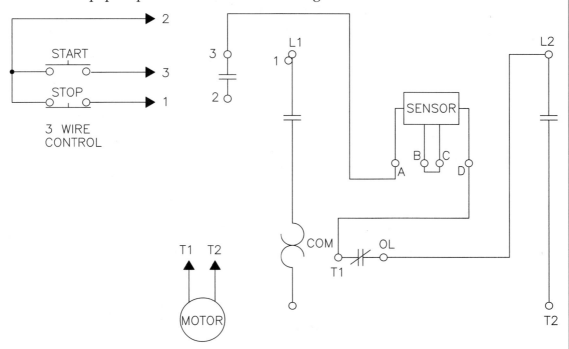

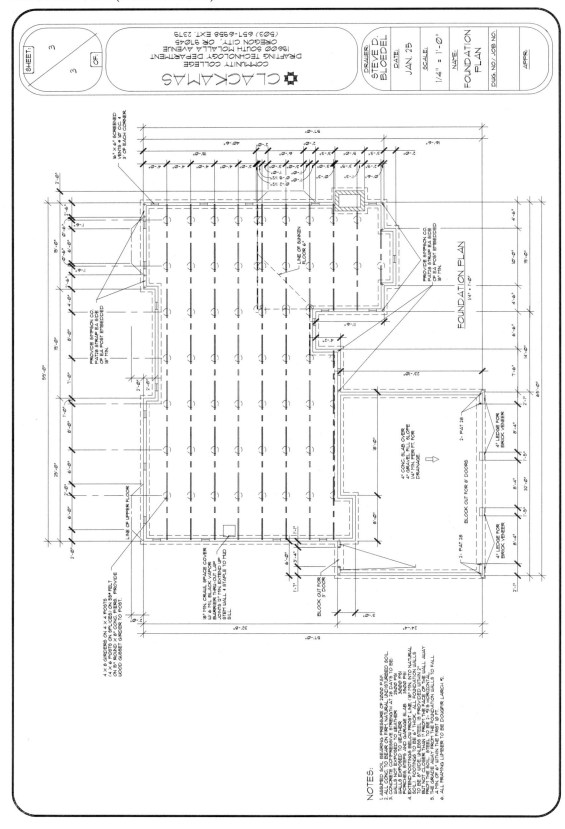

FOUNDATION PLAN
1/4" = 1'-0"

CHAPTER 12

Basic Editing Commands

Learning Objectives

After completing this chapter, you will be able to do the following:

- Draw chamfers and angled corners with the **CHAMFER** command.
- Use the **FILLET** command to draw fillets, rounds, and other rounded corners.
- Remove portions of lines, circles, and arcs using the **BREAK** command.
- Use the **TRIM** and **EXTEND** commands to edit the length of objects.
- Relocate objects using the **MOVE** command.
- Make single and multiple copies of existing objects using the **COPY** command.
- Draw mirror images of objects using the **MIRROR** command.
- Change the angular positions of objects using the **ROTATE** command.
- Create arrangements of objects using the **ARRAY** command.
- Use the **ALIGN** command to simultaneously move and rotate objects.
- Change the size of objects using the **SCALE** command.
- Modify the lengths and heights of objects using the **STRETCH** and **LENGTHEN** commands.
- Combine objects using the **JOIN** command.
- Use selection set filters using the **Quick Select** dialog box.
- Create object groups using the **GROUP** command.

This chapter explains commands and methods for changing a drawing. With manual drafting techniques, editing and modifying a drawing can take hours or even days. AutoCAD, however, makes the same editing tasks simpler and quicker. In Chapter 3, you learned how to draw and erase lines. The **ERASE** command is one of the most commonly used editing commands. You also learned how to select objects by picking with the cursor or using a window box, crossing box, window polygon, crossing polygon, or fence. The items selected are referred to as a *selection set*. You will learn various commands that increase the efficiency of creating selection sets.

Many of the same selection methods and techniques can be used for the editing commands discussed in this chapter. You will learn how to draw angled and rounded corners and how to move, copy, rotate, scale, and create mirror images of existing objects. These features are found in the **Modify** toolbar and the **Modify** pull-down menu. The editing commands discussed in this chapter are basically divided into two general groups: editing individual features of a drawing and editing major portions of a drawing. Commands typically used to edit individual features of a drawing include the following:

- **CHAMFER**
- **FILLET**
- **BREAK**
- **TRIM**
- **EXTEND**
- **LENGTHEN**

The following commands are used to edit entire drawings or major portions of a drawing, though they can also be used to edit individual features:

- **MOVE**
- **COPY**
- **ROTATE**
- **ARRAY**
- **MIRROR**
- **SCALE**
- **STRETCH**
- **GROUP**

> **NOTE**
>
>
>
> The editing commands discussed in this chapter include many options. When you access a command, its options can be accessed by right-clicking and selecting the option from the shortcut menu, by pressing the down arrow key with Dynamic Input and picking the option, or by typing the first letter of the option (typically) and pressing [Enter]. As you work through this chapter, experiment with each type of option selection method to see which is the most effective in different situations.

Drawing Chamfers

CHAMFER

Type
CHAMFER CHA
Pull-Down Menu
Modify > Chamfer
Toolbar
Modify
Chamfer
Options
Undo
Polyline
Distance
Angle
Trim
Method
Multiple

A *chamfer* in mechanical drafting is a small angled surface used to relieve a sharp corner. AutoCAD defines a *chamfer* as "any angled corner on the drawing." A chamfer's distance from the corner determines the chamfer's size. A 45° chamfer is the same distance from the corner in each direction. See **Figure 12-1**. Chamfers were introduced in Chapter 5.

These corners are drawn between two lines that may or may not intersect. They can also connect polylines, xlines, and rays. Selecting the **Chamfer** button in the **Modify** toolbar, picking **Modify > Chamfer**, or typing CHA or CHAMFER accesses the **CHAMFER** command.

The current settings are displayed for your reference. Chamfers are defined by two distances or one distance and an angle. The defaults are zero units for the lengths and the angle. A value of 0.5 for both distances produces a 45° × 0.5 chamfered corner. The following is a brief description of each **CHAMFER** option:

- **Undo.** Discards the previous chamfer when using **Multiple** mode.
- **Polyline.** Use this option if you want to chamfer all the eligible corners on a polyline. The term *eligible* means the chamfer distance is small enough to work on the corner.
- **Distance.** This option lets you set the chamfer distance for each line from the corner.
- **Angle.** This option uses a chamfer distance on the first selected line and applies a chamfer angle to determine the second line chamfer.

Figure 12-1.
Examples of different chamfers.

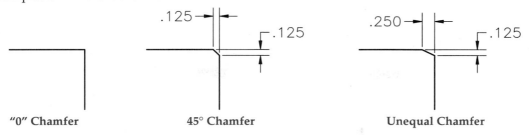

"0" Chamfer   45° Chamfer   Unequal Chamfer

- **Trim.** Enter this to set the Trim mode. If **Trim** is on, the selected lines are trimmed or extended as required from the corner, before the chamfer line is created. If **No trim** is active, the Trim mode is off. In this case, the selected lines are not trimmed or extended, and only the chamfer line is added.
- **mEthod.** This is a toggle that sets the chamfer method to either **Distance** or **Angle**. **Distance** and **Angle** values can be set without affecting each other.
- **Multiple.** Using this option repeats the chamfer command until you press the [Enter] or [Esc] key. This option is useful when you have several corners to chamfer.

Setting the Chamfer Distance

The chamfer distances must be set before you can draw a chamfer. The distances you set remain in effect until changed. The chamfer distances are usually exact values, but you can pick two points to set each distance. To set the chamfer distance, initiate the **CHAMFER** command, type D, and press [Enter]. After entering each distance, select each of the two lines that will be chamfered. After the lines are picked, AutoCAD automatically chamfers the corner.

Objects can be chamfered even when the corners do not meet. AutoCAD extends the lines as required to generate the specified chamfer and complete the corner if Trim mode is on. If Trim mode is off, AutoCAD does not extend the lines to complete the corner. This is discussed later.

If the specified chamfer distance is so large that the chamfered objects disappear, AutoCAD does not perform the chamfer. Instead, a message, such as Distance is too large *Invalid*, is given. If you want to chamfer additional corners, press [Enter] to repeat the **CHAMFER** command. The results of several chamfering operations are shown in **Figure 12-2.**

> **NOTE**
>
>
>
> For the distance method, the first and second chamfer distance values are stored in system variables. The first distance is stored in the **CHAMFERA** system variable. The second distance is stored in the **CHAMFERB** system variable.

Chamfering Square Corners

When the chamfer distances are set to zero, you can use the **CHAMFER** command to join two lines. You can also create a "zero distance" chamfer without setting the distance to zero by holding the [Shift] key when you pick the second line. This is a convenient way to join objects at a corner.

Figure 12-2.
Using the **CHAMFER**
command.

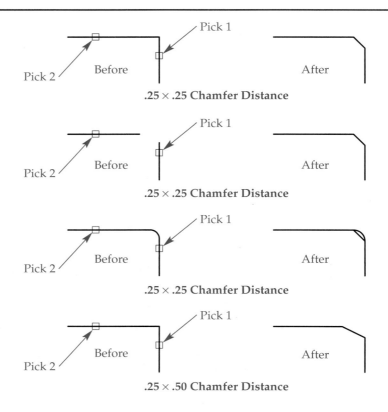

Pick 1

Pick 2

Before

After

.25 × .25 Chamfer Distance

Pick 1

Pick 2

Before

After

.25 × .25 Chamfer Distance

Pick 1

Pick 2

Before

After

.25 × .25 Chamfer Distance

Pick 1

Pick 2

Before

After

.25 × .50 Chamfer Distance

Chamfering the Corners of a Polyline

Polylines are objects that can be made up of many different widths and shapes. Drawing and editing polylines are discussed further in Chapter 14 and Chapter 15. All corners of a closed polyline can be chamfered at one time. Enter the **CHAMFER** command, select the **Polyline** option, and then select the polyline. The corners of the polyline are chamfered to the distance values set. If the polyline was drawn without using the **Close** option, the beginning corner is not chamfered, as shown in **Figure 12-3**.

Setting the Chamfer Angle

Instead of setting two chamfer distances, you can set the chamfer distance for one line and set an angle to determine the chamfer to the second line. See **Figure 12-4**. To do this, start the **CHAMFER** command and use the **Angle** option. After entering the distance and angle, select each of the two lines that will be chamfered. After the lines are picked, AutoCAD automatically chamfers the corner.

Figure 12-3.
Using the
Polyline option
of the **CHAMFER**
command.

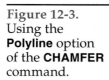
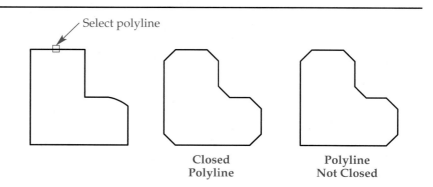

Select polyline

Closed
Polyline

Polyline
Not Closed

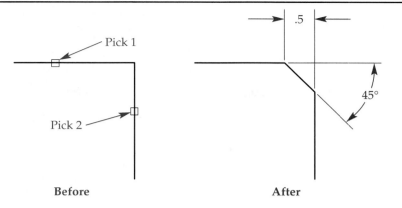

Figure 12-4.
Using the **Angle** option of the **CHAMFER** command with the chamfer length set at .5 and the angle set at 45°.

Before   After

NOTE

For the angle method, the chamfer distance and angle values are stored in system variables. The chamfer distance is stored in the **CHAMFERC** system variable. The chamfer angle is stored in the **CHAMFERD** system variable.

Exercise 12-1   Complete the Exercise on the Student CD.

Setting the Chamfer Method

When you set chamfer distances or a distance and an angle, AutoCAD maintains the setting until you change it. You can set the values for each method without affecting the other. Use the **Method** option if you want to toggle between drawing chamfers by **Distance** and **Angle**.

Setting the Chamfer Trim Mode

You can have the selected lines automatically trimmed with the chamfer, or you can have the selected lines remain in the drawing after the chamfer, as shown in **Figure 12-5**. To set this, enter the **Trim** option, and then select either T for **Trim** or N for **No trim**.

You can also use the **TRIMMODE** system variable to set **Trim** or **No trim** by typing TRIMMODE. A setting of 1 trims the lines before chamfering, while 0 does not trim the lines.

Making Multiple Chamfers

To make several chamfers on the same object, select the **Multiple** option of the **CHAMFER** command. The prompt for a first line repeats. When you have made all the chamfers needed, press [Enter] or [Esc]. When using the **Multiple** option, the previous chamfer can be undone by typing U for **Undo**.

NOTE

The **TRIMMODE** system variable affects both the **FILLET** and **CHAMFER** commands. If the **Polyline** option is used with the **No trim** option active, any chamfer lines created are not part of the polyline.

Figure 12-5.
Comparison of the **Trim** and **No trim** options with the **CHAMFER** command.

Before Chamfer	Chamfer with Trim	Chamfer with No Trim

PROFESSIONAL
TIP

When the **CHAMFER** or **FILLET** command is set to **Trim**, lines not connecting at a corner are automatically extended, and the chamfer or fillet is applied. These lines are not extended, however, when the **No trim** option is used, but the chamfer or fillet is drawn anyway. If you have lines drawn short of a corner and you want them to connect to the chamfer or fillet, you need to extend the lines when you draw with the **No trim** option active.

Exercise 12-2   Complete the Exercise on the Student CD.

Drawing Rounded Corners

FILLET

Type	
FILLET	
F	

Pull-Down Menu
Modify
 > Fillet

Toolbar
Modify

Fillet

Options
Undo
Polyline
Radius
Trim
Multiple

In mechanical drafting, an inside rounded corner is called a *fillet*. An outside rounded corner is called a *round*. AutoCAD refers to all rounded corners as *fillets*.

Fillets were introduced in Chapter 5 as a corner option on rectangles created with the **RECTANG** command. The **FILLET** command draws a rounded corner between intersecting and nonintersecting lines, circles, and arcs. To access the **FILLET** command, pick the **Fillet** button on the **Modify** toolbar, select **Modify > Fillet**, or type F or FILLET. See Figure 12-6.

The size of a fillet is determined by the fillet radius. You must set this value before selecting the corner to be filleted. After initiating the **FILLET** command, type R to access the **Radius** option, and enter the fillet radius dimension. You can then select the objects to be filleted.

Figure 12-6.
Using the **FILLET** command.

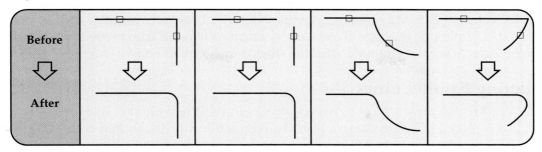

Exercise 12-3   Complete the Exercise on the Student CD.

Filleting Square Corners

When the fillet radius is set to zero, you can use the **FILLET** command to join two lines. You can also create a "zero radius" fillet without setting the radius to zero by holding the [Shift] key when you pick the second line. This is a convenient way to join objects at a corner.

Rounding the Corners of a Polyline

Fillets can be drawn at all corners of a closed polyline by selecting the **Polyline** option. The current fillet radius is used with this option. Polylines are fully explained in Chapter 14 and Chapter 15. See **Figure 12-7**.

AutoCAD tells you how many lines were filleted. If the polyline was drawn without using the **Close** option, the beginning corner is not filleted.

Figure 12-7.
Using the **Polyline** option of the **FILLET** command.

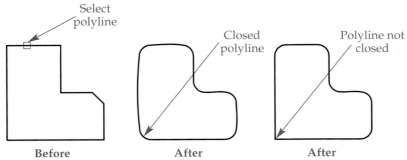

Setting the Fillet Trim Mode

The **TRIMMODE** system variable and the **Trim** option control whether or not the **FILLET** command trims object segments extending beyond the fillet radius point. When the Trim mode is active, objects are trimmed. When the Trim mode is inactive, the filleted objects are not changed after the fillet is inserted, as shown in **Figure 12-8**.

Filleting Parallel Lines

You can also draw a fillet between parallel lines. When parallel lines are selected, a radius is placed between the two lines. In Trim mode, the line picked second is either extended or trimmed to match the length of the line picked first. When Trim mode is off, the original lines are unaltered. In both cases, the fillet is placed at the end of the first line picked. The radius of a fillet between parallel lines is always half the distance between the two lines, regardless of the radius setting for the **FILLET** command.

Making Multiple Fillets

To make several fillets on the same object, select the **Multiple** option of the **FILLET** command. The prompt for a first object repeats. When you have made all the fillets needed, press [Enter] or [Esc]. When in **Multiple** mode, use the **Undo** option to discard the previous fillet.

Exercise 12-4   Complete the Exercise on the Student CD.

Figure 12-8. Comparison of the **Trim** and **No trim** options with the **FILLET** command.

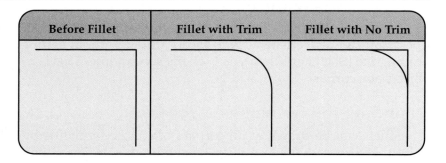

Before Fillet	Fillet with Trim	Fillet with No Trim

BREAK

Type
BREAK BR

Pull-Down Menu
Modify > Break

Toolbar
Modify
Break

Removing a Section from an Object

The **BREAK** command is used to remove a portion of a line, a circle, an arc, a trace, or a polyline. This command can also be used to divide a single object into two objects. Picking the **Break** button in the **Modify** toolbar, picking **Modify** > **Break**, or typing BR or BREAK accesses the **BREAK** command.

The **BREAK** command requires you to select the object to be broken, the first break point, and the second break point. When you select the object, the point you pick is also used as the first break point by default. If you wish to select a different first break point, type F at the Specify second break point or [First point]: prompt to select the **First point** option. After both break points are specified, the part of the object between the two points is deleted. See **Figure 12-9**.

The **BREAK** command can also be used to split an object in two without removing a portion. Selecting the same point for both the first and second break points does this. This can be accomplished by entering @ at the Specify second break point or [First point]: prompt. The @ symbol repeats the coordinates of the previously selected point.

AutoCAD and Its Applications—Basics

Figure 12-9.
Using the **BREAK** command to break an object. The first pick can be used to select both the object and the first break point.

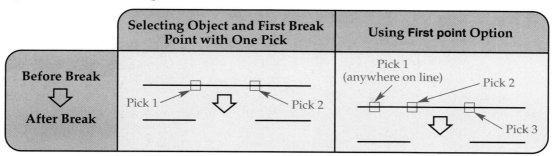

	Selecting Object and First Break Point with One Pick	Using First point Option
Before Break ⇩ **After Break**	Pick 1 → ⇩ ← Pick 2	Pick 1 (anywhere on line) → Pick 2 → ⇩ → Pick 3

You can also pick the **Break at Point** button in the **Modify** toolbar to break an object at a single point with a single pick. Using the **BREAK** command without removing a portion of the object is shown in **Figure 12-10**.

Toolbar
Modify
Break at Point

When breaking arcs or circles, always work in a counterclockwise direction. Otherwise, you may break the portion of the arc or circle you want to keep. If you want to break off the end of a line or an arc, pick the first point on the object. Pick the second point slightly beyond the end to be cut off. See **Figure 12-11**. When you pick a second point not on the object, AutoCAD selects the point on the object nearest the point you picked.

PROFESSIONAL TIP

You may want to turn running object snaps off if they conflict with the points you are trying to pick when using the **BREAK** command. Picking the **OSNAP** button on the status bar is an easy way to temporarily deactivate the running object snaps.

Exercise 12-5   Complete the Exercise on the Student CD.

Figure 12-10.
Using the **BREAK** command to break an object at a single point without removing any of the object. Select the same point as the first and second break points, or use the **Break at Point** button.

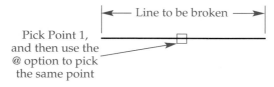

Line to be broken

Pick Point 1, and then use the @ option to pick the same point

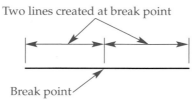

Two lines created at break point

Break point

Figure 12-11.
Using the **BREAK** command on circles and arcs.

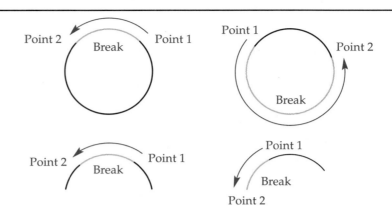

Trimming Sections of Lines, Circles, and Arcs

The **TRIM** command cuts lines, polylines, circles, arcs, ellipses, splines, xlines, and rays extending beyond a desired point of intersection. To access the **TRIM** command, pick the **Trim** button in the **Modify** toolbar, pick **Modify > Trim**, or type TR or TRIM.

The **TRIM** command requires you to pick a "cutting edge" and the object(s) to trim. The *cutting edge* can be an object such as a line, an arc, or text defining the point where the object you are trimming will be cut. If two corners of an object overrun, select two cutting edges and two objects. Refer to **Figure 12-12** as you go through the following sequence:

Command: **TR** *or* **TRIM**↵
Current settings: Projection=UCS, Edge=*current*
Select cutting edges …
Select objects or <select all>: *(pick the first cutting edge)*
1 found
Select objects: *(pick second cutting edge)*
1 found, 2 total
Select objects: ↵
Select object to trim or shift-select to extend or [Fence/Crossing/Project/Edge/
    eRase/Undo]: *(pick the first object to trim)*
Select object to trim or shift-select to extend or [Fence/Crossing/Project/Edge/
    eRase/Undo]: *(pick the second object to trim)*
Select object to trim or shift-select to extend or [Fence/Crossing/Project/Edge/
    eRase/Undo]: ↵
Command:

Figure 12-12.
Using the **TRIM** command. Note the cutting edges.

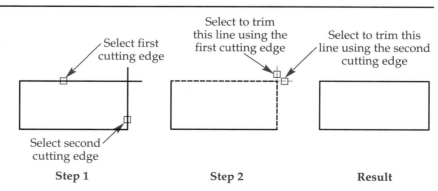

NOTE

You can access the **EXTEND** command while using the **TRIM** command. After selecting the cutting edge, hold the [Shift] key while selecting an object to extend the object to the cutting edge. The **EXTEND** command is discussed later in this chapter.

Trimming without Selecting a Cutting Edge

You can quickly trim objects back to the nearest intersection by hitting the [Enter] key at the first Select objects or <select all>: prompt, instead of picking a cutting edge. Picking an object that intersects with another object trims the selected object to the first object. If there are multiple objects intersecting the object to be trimmed, it is trimmed back to the first intersection. After trimming an object, you can select other objects to be trimmed without having to restart the command. When you are done trimming, press the [Enter] key to exit the command.

Trim Selection Options

When multiple lines need to be trimmed, the **Fence** option can be used to draw a temporary cutting line. Using this option is just like drawing a line. Any objects the fence line crosses are trimmed back to the cutting edge. See **Figure 12-13**.

The **Crossing** option allows you to select objects to be trimmed using a crossing box. This works similarly to the **Fence** option. After the objects have been selected as the cutting edges, you are prompted to specify a first corner and a second corner. Any lines crossing any of the four lines that make up the crossing window are trimmed back to the cutting edge. See **Figure 12-14**.

PROFESSIONAL
TIP

You do not need to use the **Crossing** option to select objects using a crossing box. If you pick a point in the drawing area when selecting objects to trim, the point becomes the first corner of a crossing box. You can then select the second corner.

Figure 12-13.
The **Fence** option can be used to make selections around objects.

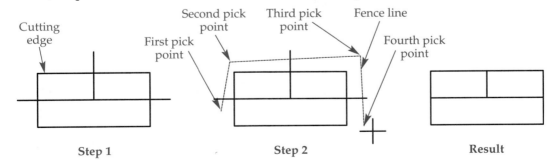

Figure 12-14.
The only objects trimmed with the **Crossing** option are those that cross the edges of the selection window.

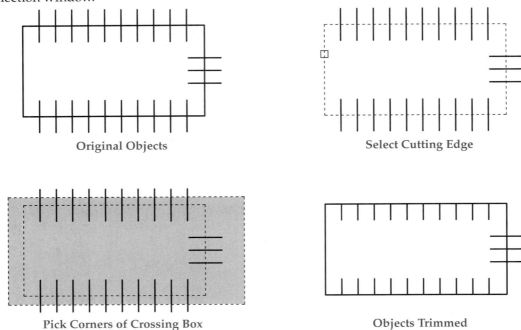

Original Objects

Select Cutting Edge

Pick Corners of Crossing Box

Objects Trimmed

Trimming to an Implied Intersection

An *implied intersection* is the point where two or more objects would meet if they were extended. Trimming to an implied intersection is possible using the **Edge** option of the **TRIM** command. When you enter the **Edge** option, the choices are **Extend** and **No extend**. When **Extend** is active, AutoCAD checks to see if the cutting edge object will extend to intersect the object to be trimmed. If so, the implied intersection point can be used to trim the object. This does not change the cutting edge object at all. The command sequence for setting **Extend** mode and performing the **TRIM** operation shown in **Figure 12-15** is as follows:

Command: **TR** *or* **TRIM**↵
Current settings: Projection=UCS, Edge=*current*
Select cutting edges …
Select objects or <select all>: *(pick the cutting edge)*
1 found
Select objects: ↵
Select object to trim or shift-select to extend or [Fence/Crossing/Project/Edge/
    eRase/Undo]: **E**↵
Enter an implied edge extension mode [Extend/No extend] <*current*>: **E**↵

Figure 12-15.
Trimming to an implied intersection is possible when **Extend** mode is active.

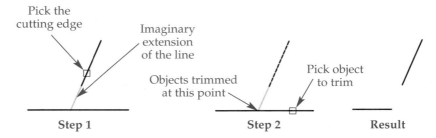

Pick the cutting edge

Imaginary extension of the line

Objects trimmed at this point

Pick object to trim

Step 1

Step 2

Result

Select object to trim or shift-select to extend or [Fence/Crossing/Project/Edge/
    eRase/Undo]: *(pick the object to trim)*
Select object to trim or shift-select to extend or [Fence/Crossing/Project/Edge/
    eRase/Undo]: ↵
Command:

The **Edge** option can also be set using the **EDGEMODE** system variable. The **EDGEMODE** settings are 1 (**Extend** mode) and 0 (**No extend** mode). This setting affects both the **TRIM** and **EXTEND** commands.

Using the Erase Option

While trimming objects, there may be some unneeded objects left over. Sometimes construction lines are used as trimming edges or boundaries and need to be erased after the trimming operation. While in the **TRIM** command, the **eRase** option can be used to delete objects. Once the objects are deleted, the **TRIM** command resumes. After the objects have been selected, they are highlighted. Pressing [Enter] deletes the objects.

Using the Undo Option

The **TRIM** command has an **Undo** option that allows you to cancel the previous trimming without leaving the command. This is useful when the result of a trim is not what you expected. To undo the previous trim, simply type U immediately after performing an unwanted trim. The trimmed portion returns, and you can continue trimming other objects.

Introduction to the Project Mode

In a 3D drawing environment, some lines may appear to intersect, but not actually touch. In such a case, using the **Project** option of the **TRIM** command can allow trimming operations. Using AutoCAD for 3D drawing is explained in *AutoCAD and Its Applications—Advanced.*

Extending Lines

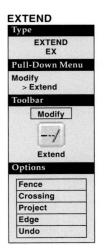

The **EXTEND** command is used to lengthen lines, elliptical arcs, rays, open polylines, and arcs to meet other objects. **EXTEND** does not work on closed polylines because an unconnected endpoint does not exist.

To use the **EXTEND** command, pick the **Extend** button in the **Modify** toolbar, select **Modify > Extend**, or type EX or EXTEND. The command format is similar to **TRIM**. You are asked to select boundary edges, as opposed to cutting edges. *Boundary edges* are objects, such as lines, arcs, or text, to which the selected objects are extended. The command sequence is shown below and illustrated in **Figure 12-16:**

Command: **EX** *or* **EXTEND**↵
Current settings: Projection=UCS, Edge=*current*
Select boundary edges ...
Select objects or <select all>: *(pick the boundary edge)*
1 found
Select objects: ↵
Select object to extend or shift-select to trim or [Fence/Crossing/Project/Edge/
    Undo]: *(pick the object to extend)*
Select object to extend or shift-select to trim or [Fence/Crossing/Project/Edge/Undo]: ↵
Command:

Figure 12-16.
Using the **EXTEND** command. Note the boundary edges.

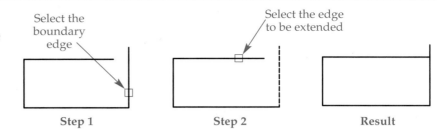

Select the boundary edge

Select the edge to be extended

Step 1   Step 2   Result

If there is nothing for the selected line to meet, AutoCAD gives the message Object does not intersect an edge.

NOTE

You can access the **TRIM** command while using the **EXTEND** command. After selecting the boundary edge, hold the [Shift] key while selecting an object to trim the object at the boundary edge.

Extending without Selecting a Boundary Edge

You can quickly extend objects to the nearest object by hitting the [Enter] key at the first Select objects or <select all>: prompt, instead of picking a boundary edge. Using this method, the selected object automatically extends it to the nearest object in its path. If there is no object to which to extend it, a message on the command line reads Object does not intersect an edge. After extending an object, you can select other objects to be extended or press the [Enter] or [Esc] key to exit the command. **Figure 12-17** illustrates how to combine extend and trim, without a boundary edge, to insert a wall in a drawing.

Extend Selection Options

Multiple lines can be extended to boundary edges at the same time by using the **Fence** option of the **EXTEND** command. After selecting F for **Fence**, you are prompted to draw a fence line. The fence line can have multiple segments. Any lines crossing the fence line are extended to the nearest boundary edge. See **Figure 12-18.**

Similar to the **Fence** option, the **Crossing** option can be used to select objects to be extended using a crossing box. After the objects have been selected as the boundary edges, you are prompted to specify a first corner and an opposite corner. This creates the crossing window. Any lines that cross the window lines are extended to the boundary edge. See **Figure 12-19.**

Figure 12-17.
To extend objects to the nearest object, press [Enter] instead of picking a boundary edge.

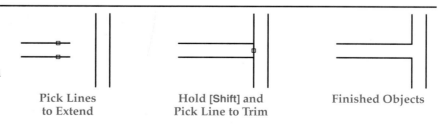

Pick Lines to Extend

Hold [Shift] and Pick Line to Trim

Finished Objects

Figure 12-18.
Multiple lines can be extended to a boundary edge by using the **Fence** option.

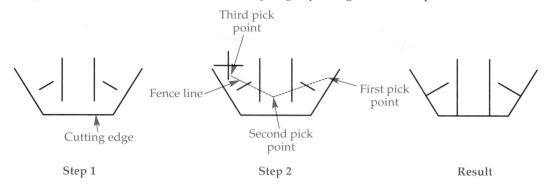

Figure 12-19.
The only objects extended with the **Crossing** option are those that cross the edges of the selection window.

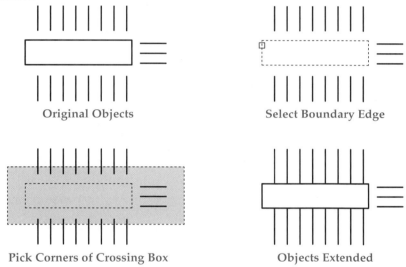

PROFESSIONAL TIP

As with the **TRIM** command, you do not need to use the **Crossing** option to select objects using a crossing box. If you pick a point in the drawing area when selecting objects to trim, the point becomes the first corner of a crossing box. You can then select the second corner.

Extending to an Implied Intersection

You can extend an object to an implied intersection when **Extend** mode is active. **Extend** mode is set using the **Edge** option. The **Edge** option setting affects both **TRIM** and **EXTEND** commands. When **Extend** mode is active, the boundary edge object is checked to see if it intersects an object when it is extended. If so, the implied intersection point can be used as the boundary for the object to be extended, as shown in **Figure 12-20.** This does not change the boundary edge object at all. The **Edge** option can also be set using the **EDGEMODE** system variable, as previously discussed with the **TRIM** command.

Figure 12-20.
Extending to an implied intersection with **Extend** mode.

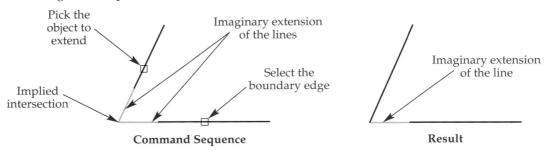

Pick the
object to
extend

Imaginary extension
of the lines

Select the
boundary edge

Imaginary extension
of the line

Implied
intersection

Command Sequence

Result

Using the Undo Option

The **Undo** option in the **EXTEND** command can be used to reverse the previous operation without leaving the **EXTEND** command. The command sequence is the same as discussed for the **TRIM** command.

The Project Mode of the Extend Command

In a 3D drawing, some lines may appear to intersect in a given view, but not actually intersect. In such a case, you can use the **Project** option, as explained for the **TRIM** command.

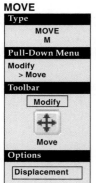

Exercise 12-6   Complete the Exercise on the Student CD.

Moving an Object

In many situations, you may find that the location of a view or feature is not where you want it. This problem is easy to fix using the **MOVE** command. Picking the **Move** button in the **Modify** toolbar, picking **Modify > Move**, or typing M or MOVE accesses the **MOVE** command.

After the **MOVE** command is accessed, AutoCAD asks you to select the objects to be moved. Use any of the selection set options to select the objects. Once the items are selected, the next prompt requests the base point or displacement. The *base point* provides a reference point. Most drafters select a point on an object, the corner of a view, or the center of a circle. The next prompt asks for the second point. This is the new position. All selected entities are moved the distance from the base point to the displacement point. See **Figure 12-21.**

Using the First Point As Displacement

In the previous **MOVE** command, you selected a base point and then selected a second point. The object moved the distance and direction you specified. You can also move the object relative to the first point. This means the coordinates you use to select the base point are automatically used as the coordinates for the direction and distance for moving the object. Follow this command sequence to do this:

    Command: **M** *or* **MOVE**↵
    Select objects: *(select the objects to move)*
    n found

Figure 12-21.
Using the **MOVE** command. When you select the object to be moved, it becomes highlighted.

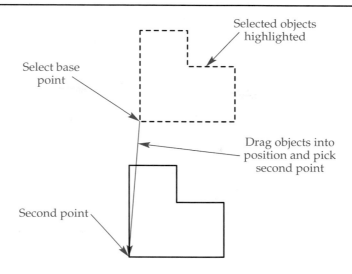

Select base point

Selected objects highlighted

Drag objects into position and pick second point

Second point

Select objects: ↵
Specify base point or [Displacement] <Displacement>: **2,4**↵
Specify second point or <use first point as displacement>: ↵ *(the object moves a distance and direction equal to the coordinates specified for the base point, which is 2 units in the X direction and 4 units in the Y direction, for this example)*
Command:

PROFESSIONAL TIP

Always use object snap modes to your best advantage with editing commands. For example, suppose you want to move an object to the center point of a circle. Use the **Center** object snap mode to select the center of the circle.

Copying Objects

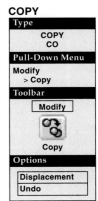

COPY
Type
COPY
CO
Pull-Down Menu
Modify
> Copy
Toolbar
Modify
Copy
Options
Displacement
Undo

The **COPY** command is used to make a copy of an existing object or objects. To access the **COPY** command, pick the **Copy** button in the **Modify** toolbar, select **Modify > Copy**, or type CO or COPY. The command prompts are the same as the **MOVE** command. When a second point is picked, however, the original object remains, and a copy is drawn. See **Figure 12-22**.

The **COPY** command is similar to the **MOVE** command. You can either specify a base point and a second point or simply specify a displacement. If you specify a displacement, a copy of the object is made at the specified location.

Making Multiple Copies

To make several copies of the same object, specify a point of displacement at the Specify second point of <use first point as displacement>: prompt. The prompt for a second point repeats until you end the command. When you have made all the copies needed, press [Enter] or [Esc]. The results are shown in **Figure 12-23**. To undo the previous copy, use the **Undo** option.

Figure 12-22.
Using the **COPY**
command.

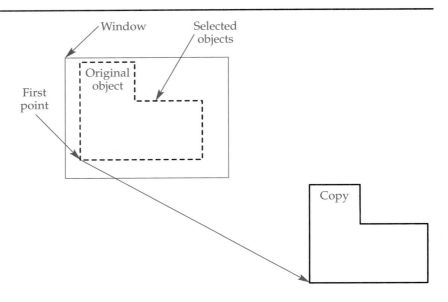

Figure 12-23.
Using the **COPY**
command to make
multiple copies.

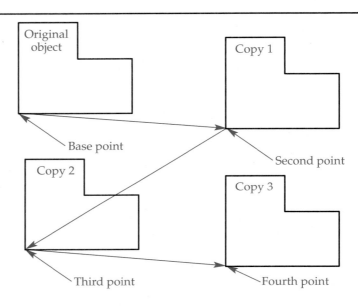

Exercise 12-7

Complete the Exercise on the Student CD.

MIRROR

Type
MIRROR MI

Pull-Down Menu
Modify > Mirror

Toolbar
Modify
Mirror

Drawing a Mirror Image of an Object

It is often necessary to draw an object in a reflected, or mirrored, position. The **MIRROR** command performs this task. Mirroring an entire drawing is common in architectural drafting, when a client wants a plan drawn in reverse. Picking the **Mirror** button in the **Modify** toolbar, selecting **Modify > Mirror**, or typing MI or MIRROR accesses the **MIRROR** command.

Figure 12-24.
When an object is reflected about a mirror line, the space between the object and the mirror line is also mirrored.

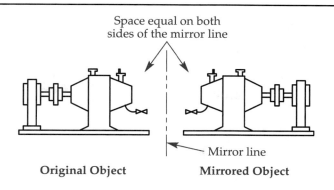

Space equal on both sides of the mirror line

Mirror line

Original Object   Mirrored Object

Selecting the Mirror Line

When you enter the **MIRROR** command, you select the objects to mirror and then select a mirror line. The *mirror line* is the hinge about which objects are reflected. The objects and any space between the objects and the mirror line are reflected. See **Figure 12-24.**

The mirror line can be placed at any angle. Once you pick the first endpoint, a mirrored image appears and moves with the cursor. Once you select the second mirror line endpoint, you have the option to delete the original objects. See **Figure 12-25.**

Exercise 12-8   Complete the Exercise on the Student CD.

Mirroring Text

The **MIRROR** command can reverse any text associated with the selected object. Backward text is generally not acceptable, although it is used for reverse imaging. To keep the text readable, the **MIRRTEXT** system variable must be 0. This is the default value. There are two values for **MIRRTEXT**, as shown in **Figure 12-26:**

- **1.** Text is mirrored in relation to the original object.
- **0.** Prevents text from being reversed. This is the default value.

To draw a mirror image of an existing object and reverse the text, set the **MIRRTEXT** variable to 1 by typing MIRRTEXT and entering 1. Proceed to the **MIRROR** command.

Exercise 12-9   Complete the Exercise on the Student CD.

Figure 12-25.
Using the **MIRROR** command. You have the option to delete the old objects.

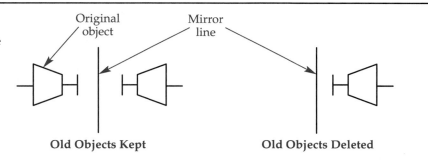

Original object

Mirror line

Old Objects Kept   Old Objects Deleted

Figure 12-26.
The **MIRRTEXT** system variable options.

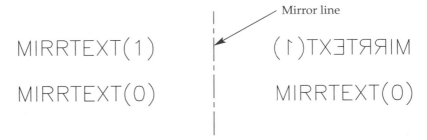

Rotating Existing Objects

Design changes often require an object, a feature, or a view to be rotated. For example, an office furniture layout may have to be moved, copied, or rotated for an interior design. AutoCAD allows you to easily revise the layout to obtain the final design.

To rotate selected objects, pick **Modify** > **Rotate** from the pull-down menu, pick the **Rotate** button on the **Modify** toolbar, or type RO or ROTATE. Objects can be selected using any of the selection set options. Once the objects are selected, pick a base point and enter a rotation angle. A negative rotation angle revolves the object clockwise. A positive rotation angle revolves the object counterclockwise. See **Figure 12-27.**

If an object is already rotated and you want a different angle, you can change the angle in two ways. Both ways involve using the **Reference** option after selecting the object for rotation. The first way is to specify the existing angle and then the new angle. See **Figure 12-28A:**

Specify rotation angle or [Copy/Reference] <current>: **R↵**
Specify the reference angle <current>: (specify a reference angle, such as 135, and press [Enter])
Specify the new angle or [Points] <current>: (specify a new angle, such as 180, and press [Enter])
Command:

The other method is to pick a reference line on the object and rotate the object in relationship to the reference line. See **Figure 12-28B:**

Specify rotation angle or [Copy/Reference] <current>: **R↵**
Specify the reference angle <current>: (pick an endpoint of a reference line that forms the existing angle)

Figure 12-27.
Rotation angles.

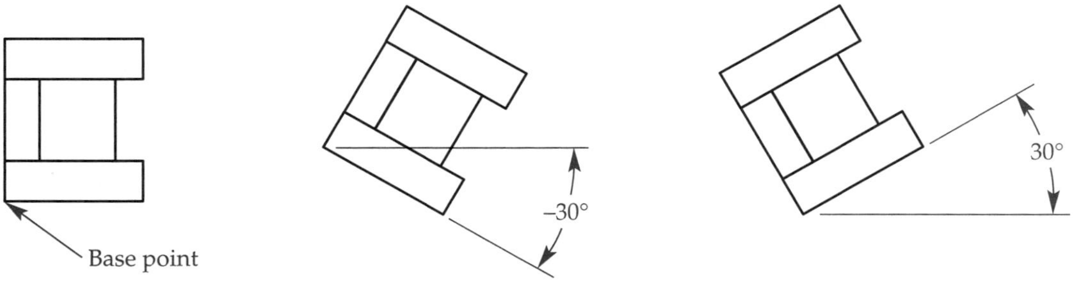

Base point

−30° Rotation

30° Rotation

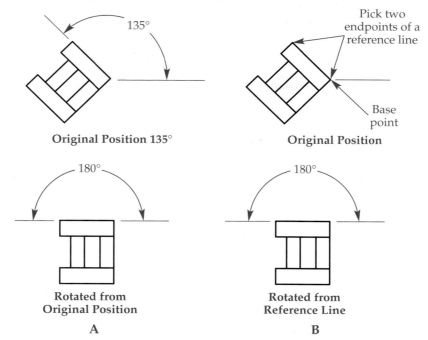

Figure 12-28.
Using the **Reference** option of the **ROTATE** command.
A—Entering reference angles.
B—Selecting points on a reference line.

135°

Original Position 135°

Pick two endpoints of a reference line

Base point

Original Position

180°

Rotated from Original Position

A

180°

Rotated from Reference Line

B

Specify second point: *(pick the other point of the reference line that forms the existing angle)*
Specify the new angle or [Points] *<current>*: *(specify a new angle, such as* **180**, *and press* [Enter])
Command:

An object can be copied and rotated at the same time, leaving the original object in place. This can be done by using the **Copy** option when prompted to Specify rotation angle or [Copy/Reference] *<current>*. After specifying the rotation angle, a new object is created and rotated, and the source object is left unchanged.

PROFESSIONAL TIP

Always use the object snap mode to your best advantage when editing. For example, suppose you want to rotate an object. It may be difficult to find an exact corner without using object snap mode. To select the base point, use the **Endpoint** or **Intersection** object snap mode.

Exercise 12-10   Complete the Exercise on the Student CD.

Moving and Rotating an Object at the Same Time

The **ALIGN** command is used when you want to move and rotate an object. The command sequence for 3D applications requires you to select objects and specify three source points and three destination points. For 2D applications, you only need two source points and two destination points. Press [Enter] when the prompt requests the third source and destination points. The *source points* define a line related to the object's original position. The *destination points* define the location of this line relative to the object's new location. See **Figure 12-29.** To access the **ALIGN** command, pick **Modify > 3D Operation > Align**, or type AL or ALIGN. The command sequence is as follows:

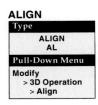

ALIGN

Type
> ALIGN
> AL

Pull-Down Menu

Modify
> 3D Operation
> Align

Command: **AL** *or* **ALIGN**⏎
Select objects: *(select the objects)*
n found
Select objects: ⏎
Specify first source point: *(pick the first source point)*
Specify first destination point: *(pick the first destination point)*
Specify second source point: *(pick the second source point)*
Specify second destination point: *(pick the second destination point)*
Specify third source point or <continue>: ⏎
Scale objects based on alignment points? [Yes/No] <N>: *(enter Y to scale the object if the distance between the source points is different than the distance between the destination points, and press* [Enter]*)*
Command:

The last prompt, Scale objects based on alignment points? [Yes/No] <N>:, allows you to change the size of the object that is being moved. **Figure 12-30** illustrates this process by moving, rotating, and scaling a rectangle to match a side of a hexagon.

Exercise 12-11   Complete the Exercise on the Student CD.

Figure 12-29.
Using the **ALIGN** command to move and rotate a kitchen cabinet layout against a wall.

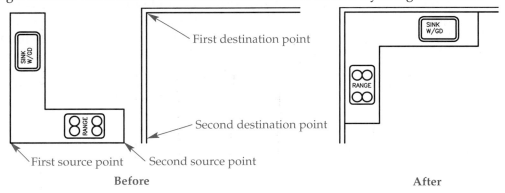

Before   After

Figure 12-30.
The **Scale** option of the **ALIGN** command is used to change the size of an object while it is moved and rotated.

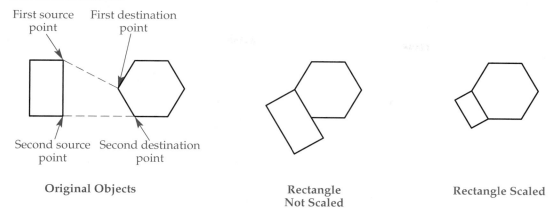

First source point First destination point

Second source point Second destination point

Original Objects

Rectangle Not Scaled

Rectangle Scaled

Creating Multiple Objects with Array

Some designs require a rectangular or circular pattern of the same object. For example, office desks are often arranged in rows. Suppose your design calls for five rows, each having four desks. You can create this design by drawing one desk and copying it nineteen times. This operation, however, is time-consuming. A quicker method is to create an array.

There are two types of arrays: rectangular and polar. A *rectangular array* creates rows and columns of the selected items, and you must provide the spacing. A *polar array* constructs a circular arrangement. For a circular array, you must specify the number of items to array, the angle between items, and the center point of the array. Some examples are shown in **Figure 12-31**.

ARRAY

Type
ARRAY
AR

Pull-Down Menu
Modify
> Array...

Toolbar
Modify

Array

Arrays are specified using the **Array** dialog box. To access this dialog box, pick the **Array** button in the **Modify** toolbar, select **Modify > Array...** from the pull-down menu, or type AR or ARRAY. All input needed to create the array is specified in the **Array** dialog box. See **Figure 12-32**. Use the **Rectangular Array** and **Polar Array** radio buttons to specify the type of array. Pick the **Select objects** button to return to the AutoCAD window and pick the objects to be included in the array.

Arranging Objects in a Rectangular Pattern

A rectangular array places objects in line along the X and Y axes. You can specify a single row, a single column, or multiple rows and columns. *Rows* are horizontal, and *columns* are vertical.

To create a rectangular pattern for a 0.5 unit square having three rows, three columns, and a 0.5 spacing between objects, enter 3 in the **Rows:** and **Columns:** text boxes and 1.0000 in the **Row offset:** and **Column offset:** text boxes. This is shown in **Figure 12-33**. Notice that the distances do not refer to the space between the objects, but the distances between the same points on the objects.

The distances can also be entered by picking points—there are two methods available. You can also use the **Pick Row Offset** and **Pick Column Offset** buttons in the **Array** dialog box to specify each distance separately. The second method uses the **Pick Both Offsets** button to specify both distances in one pick. **Figure 12-34** illustrates the second **Pick Both Offsets** method. You can use any point selection method—such as object snap modes, relative coordinates, and polar coordinates—to pick the second point.

Figure 12-31.
Examples of arrays.

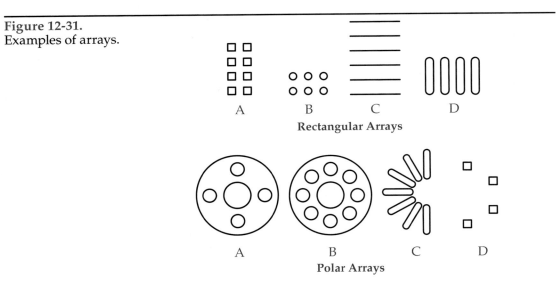

Rectangular Arrays

Polar Arrays

Figure 12-32.
The **Array** dialog box options for a rectangular array.

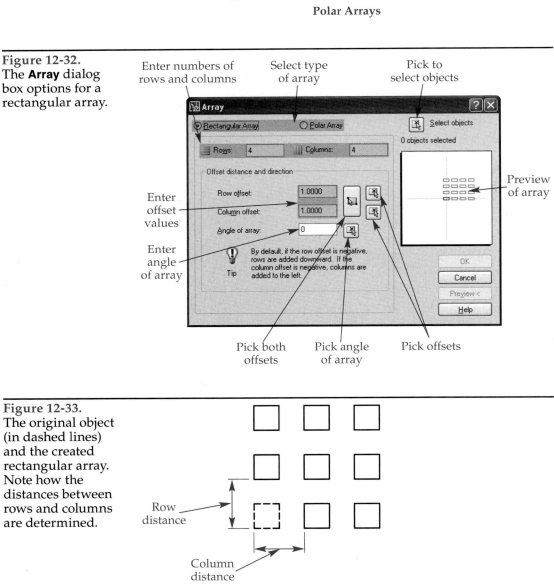

Enter numbers of rows and columns

Select type of array

Pick to select objects

Enter offset values

Enter angle of array

Pick both offsets

Pick angle of array

Pick offsets

Preview of array

Figure 12-33.
The original object (in dashed lines) and the created rectangular array. Note how the distances between rows and columns are determined.

Row distance

Column distance

Figure 12-34.
The spacing of rows and columns in an array can be specified with a single point.

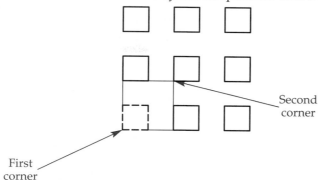

Second corner

First corner

Using the preview area of the **Array** dialog box, **Figure 12-35** shows the four directions an array can grow. The direction is based on the use of positive and negative distance values for row and column offsets.

You can also create an angled rectangular array. Enter the angle in the **Angle of array:** text box or pick the **Pick Angle of Array** button to specify the angle with the crosshairs. The column and row alignments are rotated, not the objects. See **Figure 12-36.**

Arranging Objects around a Center Point

A polar array creates a circular pattern with the selected object. To create a polar array, pick the **Polar Array** radio button in the **Array** dialog box. See **Figure 12-37.** Pick the **Select objects** button to return to the drawing area and select the object to be arrayed. Once you have selected the object, the **Array** dialog box returns.

The next step in creating a polar array is to specify the center point. This is the point about which the objects in the array will be rotated. Enter the coordinates for the center point in the **X:** and **Y:** text boxes or pick the **Pick Center Point** button to select the center point in the drawing area.

Figure 12-35.
The use of positive and negative offset distances determines the direction an array will grow.

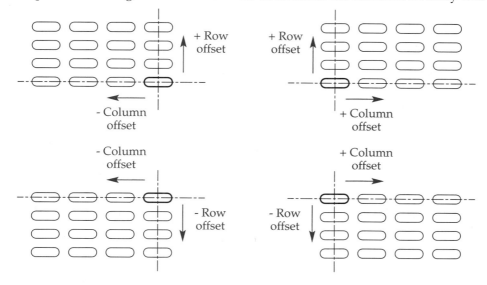

Figure 12-36.
Rectangular arrays can be arranged using the **Angle of array:** setting.

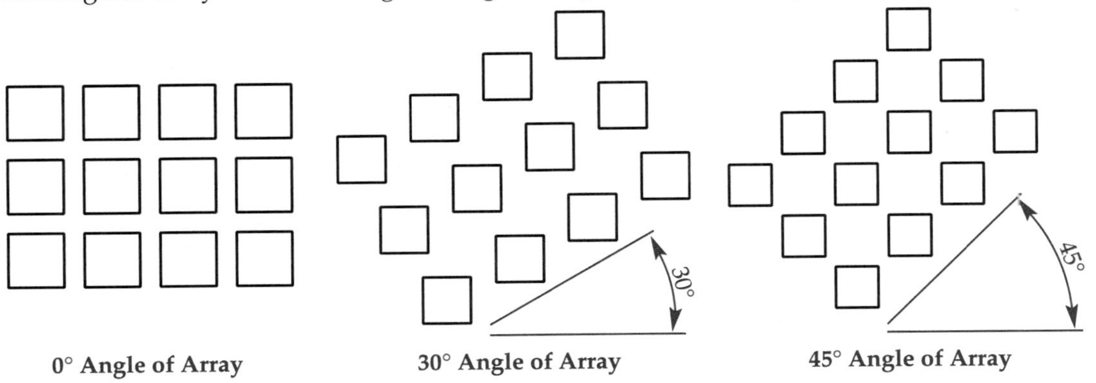

0° Angle of Array   30° Angle of Array   45° Angle of Array

Figure 12-37.
The **Array** dialog box options for a polar array.

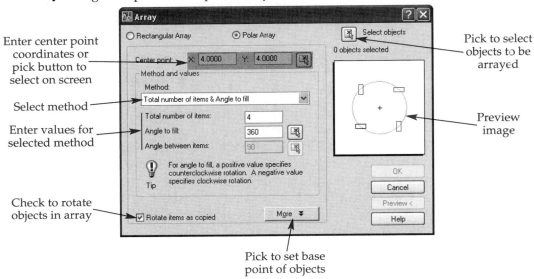

Enter center point coordinates or pick button to select on screen

Select method

Enter values for selected method

Check to rotate objects in array

Pick to select objects to be arrayed

Preview image

Pick to set base point of objects

After selecting the center point, you must specify the type of polar array to be created using the **Method:** drop-down list. The selected method determines which settings in the dialog box are available. Three methods are available:

- Total number of items & Angle to fill.
- Total number of items & Angle between items.
- Angle to fill & Angle between items.

The **Total number of items:** setting is the total number of objects to be in the array, including the originally selected object. If you do not know how many items will be in the array, use the Angle to fill & Angle between items method. The **Angle to fill:** setting can be positive or negative. To array the object in a counterclockwise direction, enter a positive angle. To array the object in a clockwise direction, enter a negative angle. Enter 360 to create a complete circular array. The **Angle between items:** setting specifies the angular distance between adjacent objects in the array. For example, if you are creating a circular pattern of five items spaced 18° apart, enter 5 in the **Total number of items:** text box and 18 in the **Angle between items:** text box.

You can have the objects rotated as they are copied around the center point by checking the **Rotate items as copied** check box. This keeps the same face of the object always pointing toward the center point. If objects are not rotated as they are copied, they remain in the same orientation as the original object. See **Figure 12-38.**

Figure 12-38.
Rotating objects in a polar array. A—The square is rotated as it is arrayed. B—The square is not rotated as it is arrayed.

A

B

When AutoCAD creates a polar array, the base point of the object is rotated and remains at a constant distance from the center point. The default base point varies for different types of objects, as shown in the following table:

Object Type	Default Base Point
Arc, circle, ellipse	Center
Rectangle, polygon	First corner
Line, polyline, donut	Starting point
Block, text	Insertion point

If the default base point does not produce the desired array, you can select a different base point for the selected object. Pick the **More** button in the **Array** dialog box to display the **Object base point** area. Deactivate the **Set to object's default** check box. Enter a new base point in the text boxes or pick the button to select a base point on screen.

Exercise 12-12   Complete the Exercise on the Student CD.

Changing the Size of an Object

A convenient editing command that saves hours of drafting time is the **SCALE** command. This command lets you change the size of a single object or an entire drawing. The **SCALE** command enlarges or reduces the entire object proportionately. If associative dimensioning is used, the dimensions also change to reflect the new size. This is discussed in Chapter 18.

To scale objects, pick the **Scale** button in the **Modify** toolbar, pick **Modify > Scale**, or type SC or SCALE. Pick a *base point*, the point where the selected objects move away from or toward. The next step is to specify the scale factor. Enter a number to indicate the amount of enlargement or reduction. For example, if you want to double the scale, type 2 at the Specify scale factor or [Copy/Reference] <current>: prompt, as shown in **Figure 12-39**. The chart in **Figure 12-40** shows sample scale factors.

Creating a Copy while Scaling

If an object needs to be copied and then scaled, these changes can be made at the same time in the **SCALE** command. The **Copy** option of the **SCALE** command copies the selected object and scales it, leaving the original object unchanged.

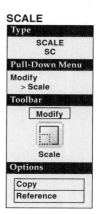

SCALE

Type
SCALE
SC

Pull-Down Menu
Modify
> Scale

Toolbar
Modify
Scale

Options
Copy
Reference

Figure 12-39.
Using the **SCALE** command. The base point does not move, but every other point in the object does.

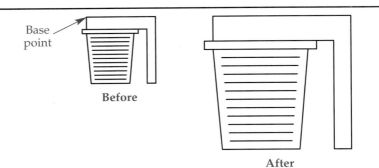

Figure 12-40.
Different scale factors and the resulting sizes.

Scale Factor	Resulting Size
10	10 × bigger
5	5 × bigger
2	2 × bigger
1	Equal to existing size
.75	3/4 of original size
.50	1/2 of original size
.25	1/4 of original size

Using the Reference Option

An object can also be scaled by specifying a new size in relation to an existing dimension. For example, suppose you have a shaft that is 2.50″ long, and you want to make it 3.00″ long. To do so, use the **Reference** option as follows, as shown in **Figure 12-41:**

Specify scale factor or [Copy/Reference] <*current*>: **R**↵
Specify reference length <*current*>: **2.5**↵
Specify new length or [Points] <*current*>: **3**↵
Command:

NOTE

The **SCALE** command changes all dimensions of an object proportionately. If you want to change only the width or length of an object, use the **STRETCH** or **LENGTHEN** command.

Exercise 12-13 Complete the Exercise on the Student CD.

Figure 12-41.
Using the **Reference** option of the **SCALE** command.

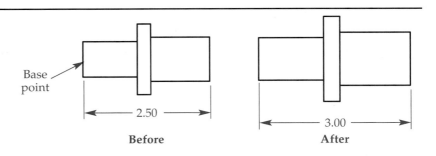

Stretching an Object

The **SCALE** command changes the length and width of an object proportionately. The **STRETCH** command changes only one dimension of an object. It is common to increase the length of a part, while leaving the diameter or width the same. In architectural design, room sizes may be stretched to increase the square footage.

When using the **STRETCH** command, you can select objects with a crossing window or crossing polygon. To use a crossing window, pick the right corner of the box first and then the left corner. To access the **STRETCH** command, pick the **Stretch** button in the **Modify** toolbar, pick **Modify** > **Stretch**, or type S or STRETCH. Use a crossing window or a crossing polygon to select only the objects that will be stretched, as shown in **Figure 12-42.** If you select the entire object, the **STRETCH** command works like the **MOVE** command.

After selecting the object(s) to be stretched, you are asked to pick the base point. This is the point from which the object will be stretched. Pick a new position for the base point. As you move the screen cursor, the object is stretched or compressed. When the displayed object is stretched to the desired position, pick the new point.

STRETCH

Type
STRETCH
S

Pull-Down Menu
Modify
> Stretch

Toolbar
Modify
Stretch

Using the Displacement Option

The **Displacement** option works the same with the **STRETCH** command as with the **MOVE** and **COPY** commands. After selecting the objects to be stretched, enter a displacement, as shown in the following:

> Specify base point or [Displacement] <Displacement>: *(enter an X and Y displacement, such as 2,3)*↵
> Specify second point or <use first point as displacement>: ↵
> Command:

When you press [Enter] at the Specify second point or <use first point as displacement>: prompt, the object is automatically stretched as you specified with the X and Y coordinates. In this case, the object is stretched 2 units in the X direction and 3 units in the Y direction.

Figure 12-42.
Using the **STRETCH** command.

Select objects using crossing window or polygon

Option 1, 25 Gallon Tank

Stretching

Option 2, 50 Gallon Tank

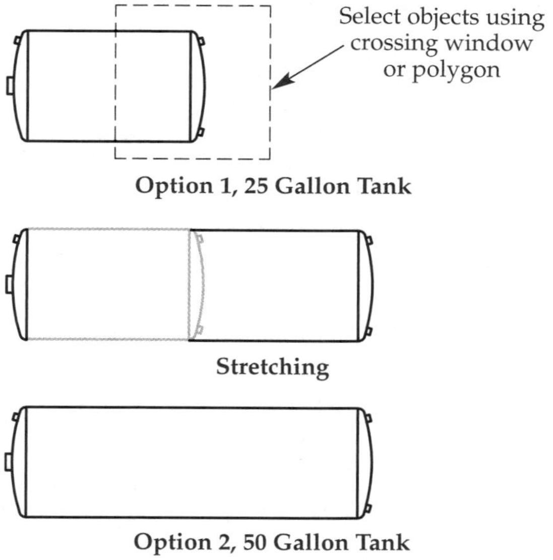

It may not be common to have objects lined up in a convenient manner for using the crossing box selection method with the **STRETCH** command. You should consider using the crossing polygon selection method to make selecting the objects easier. If the stretched object is not what you expected, cancel the command with the [Esc] key. The **STRETCH** command and other editing commands discussed in this chapter work well with Ortho mode or polar tracking activated.

Exercise 12-14   Complete the Exercise on the Student CD.

Changing the Length of an Object

The **LENGTHEN** command can be used to change the length of objects and the included angle of an arc. Only one object can be lengthened at a time. The **LENGTHEN** command does not affect closed objects. For example, you can lengthen a line, a polyline, an arc, an elliptical arc, or a spline, but you cannot lengthen a closed polygon or circle.

To access the **LENGTHEN** command, pick **Modify** > **Lengthen** or type LEN or LENGTHEN. When you select an object, AutoCAD gives you the current length if the object is linear, or the included angle if the object is an arc. There are four **LENGTHEN** command options available:

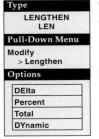

LENGTHEN
Type
LENGTHEN
LEN
Pull-Down Menu
Modify
> Lengthen
Options
DElta
Percent
Total
DYnamic

- **DElta.** The **DElta** option allows you to specify a positive or negative change in length, measured from the endpoint of the selected object. The lengthening or shortening happens closest to the selection point and changes the length by the amount entered. See **Figure 12-43.** The **DElta** option has an **Angle** suboption that lets you change the included angle of an arc by a specified angle. See **Figure 12-44.**
- **Percent.** The **Percent** option allows you to change the length of an object or the angle of an arc by a specified percentage. If you consider the original length to be 100 percent, you can make the object shorter by specifying less than 100 percent or longer by specifying more than 100 percent. See **Figure 12-45.**

Figure 12-43.
Using the **DElta** option of the **LENGTHEN** command with values of .75 and –.75.

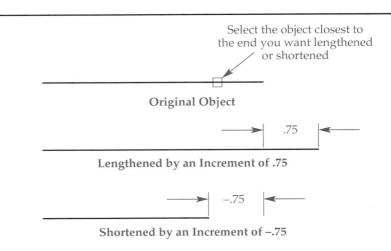

Select the object closest to the end you want lengthened or shortened

Original Object

Lengthened by an Increment of .75

Shortened by an Increment of –.75

Figure 12-44.
Using the **Angle**
suboption of
the **LENGTHEN**
command's **DElta**
option.

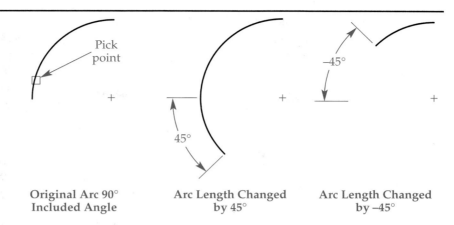

Original Arc 90°   Arc Length Changed   Arc Length Changed
Included Angle   by 45°   by –45°

Figure 12-45.
Using the **Percent**
option of the
LENGTHEN
command.

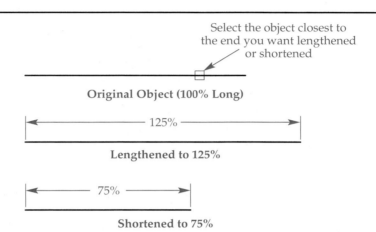

Select the object closest to
the end you want lengthened
or shortened

Original Object (100% Long)

125%

Lengthened to 125%

75%

Shortened to 75%

- **Total.** The **Total** option allows you to set the total length or angle to the value you specify. You do not have to select the object before entering one of the options, but doing so lets you know the current length and, if it is an arc, the angle of the object. See **Figure 12-46.**
- **DYnamic.** This option lets you drag the endpoint of the object to the desired length or angle with the screen cursor. See **Figure 12-47.** It is helpful to have the grid and snap set to usable increments when using this option.

Figure 12-46.
Using the **Total**
option of the
LENGTHEN
command.

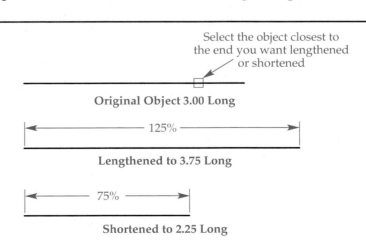

Select the object closest to
the end you want lengthened
or shortened

Original Object 3.00 Long

125%

Lengthened to 3.75 Long

75%

Shortened to 2.25 Long

Figure 12-47.
Using the
DYnamic option
of the **LENGTHEN**
command.

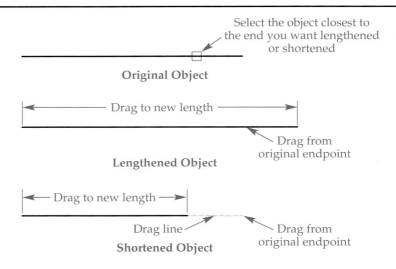

Select the object closest to
the end you want lengthened
or shortened

Original Object

Drag to new length

Lengthened Object

Drag from
original endpoint

Drag to new length

Drag line

Drag from
original endpoint

Shortened Object

NOTE

Only lines and arcs can be lengthened dynamically. A spline's length can only be decreased. Splines are discussed in Chapter 15.

Exercise
12-15

Complete the Exercise on the Student CD.

Joining Objects Together

It is common to have unneeded objects in a drawing after working on the drawing for a while. After using some commands that edit objects, the result often is multiple objects that should be one object. These multiple objects make the drawing file size larger and the drawing more cumbersome.

Certain objects can be joined together to make one object by using the **JOIN** command. To access this command, pick the **Join** button in the **Modify** toolbar, select **Modify > Join**, or type J or JOIN. This command can be used on lines, polylines, splines, arcs, and elliptical arcs. Only objects of the same type can be joined together. For example, a line can be joined to another line, but a line cannot be joined to a polyline. Also, joined objects must be in the same plane.

JOIN
Type
JOIN
J
Pull-Down Menu
Modify
> Join
Toolbar
Modify
Join

Joining Lines

For each type of object, there are different rules for joining. To join lines, the lines must be collinear. The lines can be touching, have gaps between them, or be overlapping. See Figure 12-48.

Joining Polylines and Splines

To join polylines together, the polylines must have a common endpoint. There cannot be gaps between the segments, and they cannot be overlapping. See Figure 12-49. The rules for joining splines together are the same as for polylines. The spline objects must share a common endpoint.

Figure 12-48.
Lines must be collinear to be joined, but there can be gaps and overlaps between the lines.

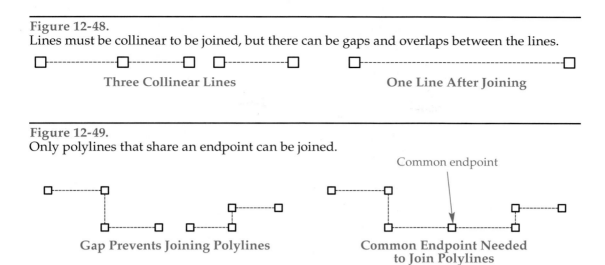

Three Collinear Lines   One Line After Joining

Figure 12-49.
Only polylines that share an endpoint can be joined.

Common endpoint

Gap Prevents Joining Polylines   Common Endpoint Needed
                                         to Join Polylines

Joining Arcs and Elliptical Arcs

Arcs that share the same center point and reside on the same circular path can be joined together. The arcs can be overlapping or have a gap between them. In Figure 12-50, two arcs with a gap have been joined together. When there is more than one gap between two arcs to be joined, using the **JOIN** command may close a gap other than the one you desired. When closing gaps in arcs, make sure to pick the arcs in a counterclockwise direction.

Elliptical arcs can be joined together using the same rules as the arc. The elliptical arcs must reside on the same elliptical path. They can, however, overlap or have gaps between them.

Both arcs and elliptical arcs can be closed by using the **JOIN** command. When using the **cLose** option on an arc, it becomes a circle. Using this option on an elliptical arc creates an ellipse.

Creating Selection Sets

When creating complex drawings, you often need to perform the same editing operation to many objects. For example, assume you have designed a complex metal part with over 40 holes for 1/8" bolts. A design change occurs, and you are notified that 3/16" bolts will be used instead of 1/8" bolts. Therefore, the hole size will also change. You could select and modify each circle individually, but it would be more efficient to create a selection set of all the circles and then modify them simultaneously.

Figure 12-50.
A—Arcs can have a gap or be overlapping, but they must share the same circular path.
B—The two arcs after being joined together.

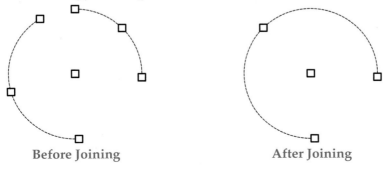

Before Joining   After Joining

AutoCAD provides two methods of creating selection sets: the **Quick Select** dialog box and the **Object Selection Filter** dialog box. The **Quick Select** dialog box is used to create simple selection sets by specifying object types and property values for selection. The **Object Selection Filter** dialog box provides additional selection criteria and allows you to save selection sets.

NOTE

The following section describes the **Quick Select** dialog box. This is the more common tool of the two for creating selection sets, since it is easier to access and use. The **Object Selection Filter** dialog box does provide some additional options, including the capability of saving selection set filters. Refer to the *Object Selection Filter* document in the *Supplemental Material* section of the Student CD for more information on this advanced tool.

Using Quick Select to Create Selection Sets

QSELECT
Type
   QSELECT
Pull-Down Menu
Tools
   > Quick Select...

With the **Quick Select** dialog box, you can quickly create a selection set based on the filtering criteria you specify. To access this dialog box, pick **Tools > Quick Select...** from the pull-down menu, type QSELECT, or right-click in the drawing area and choose **Quick Select...** from the shortcut menu. See **Figure 12-51.** You can also open the **Quick Select** dialog box by picking the **Quick Select** button if the **Properties** window is open.

A selection set can be defined in several ways using the **Quick Select** dialog box:

- Pick the **Select objects** button and select the objects on screen.
- Specify an object type (such as text, line, or circle) to be selected throughout the drawing.
- Specify a property (such as a color or layer) that objects must possess in order to be selected.

Figure 12-51.
Selection sets can be defined in the **Quick Select** dialog box.

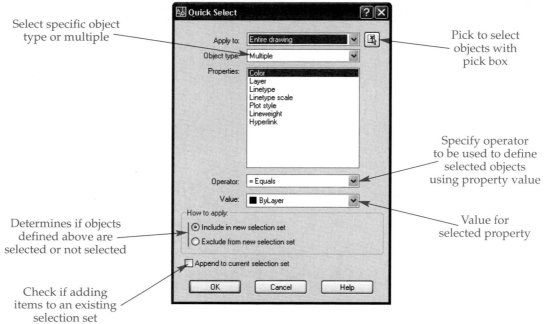

Figure 12-52.
Creating selection sets with the **Quick Select** dialog box. A—Objects in drawing. B—Selection set containing objects with the display color specified. C—Circle object added to initial selection set.

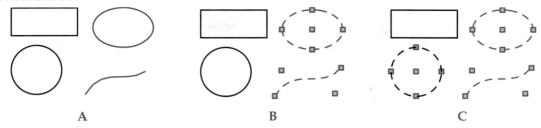

A   B   C

Once the selection criteria are defined, you can use the radio buttons in the **How to apply:** area to include or exclude the defined objects.

Look at **Figure 12-52** as you follow this example that uses the **Quick Select** command:

1. Select **Tools** > **Quick Select...** to open the **Quick Select** dialog box.
2. In the **Apply to:** drop-down list, select **Entire drawing**. If you access the **Quick Select** dialog box after a selection set is defined, there is also a **Current selection** option that allows you to create a subset of the existing set.
3. In the **Object type:** drop-down list, select **Multiple**. This will allow you to select any object type. The drop-down list contains all the object types in the drawing.
4. In the **Properties:** list, select **Color**. The items in the **Properties:** list vary depending on what is specified in the **Object type:** drop-down list.
5. In the **Operator:** drop-down list, select **= Equals**.
6. The **Value:** drop-down list contains values corresponding to the entry in the **Properties:** drop-down list. In this case, color values are listed. Select the color of the right-hand objects in **Figure 12-52A**.
7. Under the **How to apply:** area, pick the **Include in new selection set** radio button.
8. Pick the **OK** button.

AutoCAD selects all objects with the color specified in the **Value:** drop-down list, as shown in **Figure 12-52B**.

Once a set of objects has been selected, the **Quick Select** dialog box can be used to refine the selection set. Use the **Exclude from new selection set** option to exclude objects or use the **Append to current selection set** option to add objects. The following procedure refines the selection set created above to include any circles in the drawing that have a black color.

1. While the initial set of objects is selected, right-click in the drawing area and select **Quick Select...** from the shortcut menu to open the **Quick Select** dialog box.
2. Check the **Append to current selection set** check box at the bottom of the dialog box. AutoCAD automatically selects the **Entire drawing** option in the **Apply to:** drop-down list.
3. Select **Circle** in the **Object type:** drop-down list, **Color** in the **Properties:** drop-down list, **= Equals** in the **Operator:** drop-down list, and **Black** (or **ByLayer**, as appropriate) in the **Value:** drop-down list.
4. In the **How to apply:** area, pick the **Include in new selection set** radio button.
5. Pick the **OK** button. The selection now appears as shown in **Figure 12-52C**.

A *group* is a named selection set. These selection sets are saved with the drawing and, therefore, exist between multiple drawing sessions. Objects can be members of more than one group, and groups can be nested. *Nesting* means placing one group inside another group. By default, selecting one object within a group causes the entire group to be selected.

An object existing in multiple groups creates an interesting situation. For example, if a line and an arc are grouped, and the arc is then grouped with a circle, moving the first group moves the line and arc, and moving the second group moves the arc and circle. Nesting can be used to place smaller groups into larger groups for easier editing. Groups can be deactivated in the **Selection** tab of the **Options** dialog box, with the **Object grouping** check box in the **Selection Modes** area.

GROUP

Type
GROUP
G

Typing G or GROUP accesses the **Object Grouping** dialog box, in which groups can be defined and modified. See **Figure 12-53**. There are many elements found in the **Object Grouping** dialog box. The text box displays the **Group Name** and lists whether or not the group is selectable. If a group is selectable, picking any object in it selects the entire group. Making a group nonselectable allows individual objects within the group to be edited.

The **Group Identification** area has several components:
- **Find Name.** This button displays a dialog list of all groups with which an object is associated. When you pick this button, a Pick a member of a group prompt appears. Once you pick an object, the **Group Member List** dialog box lists any groups with which the object is associated.
- **Highlight.** This button allows a group name to be specified and then highlights all its members in the drawing editor. This allows you to see the parts of the drawing identified as members of that group. Pick the **Continue** button or press [Enter] to return to the **Object Grouping** dialog box.
- **Include Unnamed.** This check box causes unnamed groups to be listed with named groups. Unnamed groups are given a default name by AutoCAD in the format of *Ax, where x is an integer value that increases with each new group, such as *A6. Unnamed groups can be named later using the **Rename** option.

The **Create Group** area contains the options for creating a new group:
- **New.** This button creates a new group from the selected objects using the name entered in the **Group Name:** text box. AutoCAD issues a Select objects for grouping: Select objects: prompt after you enter a new name in the **Group Name:** text box.

Figure 12-53.
The various elements of the **Object Grouping** dialog box.

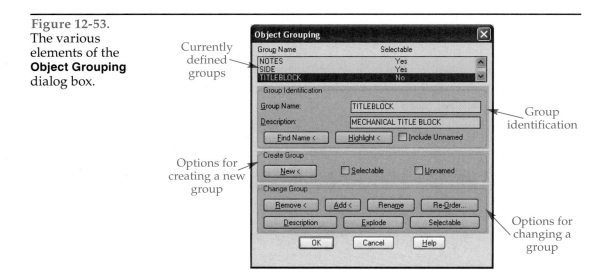

- **Selectable.** A check in this box sets the initial status of the **Selectable** value as Yes for the new group. This is indicated in the **Selectable** list described earlier. No check here specifies No in the **Selectable** list. This can be changed later.
- **Unnamed.** This indicates whether or not the new group will be named. If this box is checked, AutoCAD assigns its own default name as detailed previously.

The **Change Group** area of the **Object Grouping** dialog box shows the options for changing a group:
- **Remove.** Pick this button to remove objects from a group definition.
- **Add.** This button allows objects to be added to a group definition.
- **Rename.** Pick this button to change the name of an existing group. Unnamed groups can be renamed.
- **Re-Order.** Objects are numbered in the order they are selected when defining the group. The first object is numbered 0, not 1. This button allows objects to be reordered within the group. For example, if a group contains a set of instructions, you can reorder the instructions to create tool paths. The **Order Group** dialog box is displayed when you pick this button. The elements of this dialog box are briefly described as follows:
  - **Group Name.** Displays the name of the selected group.
  - **Description.** Displays the description for the selected group.
  - **Remove from position (0-*n*).** Position number of the object to reorder, where *n* is one less than the total number of objects found in the group. You place the desired order in the text boxes to the right of this feature and the next two features.
  - **Enter new position number for the object (0-*n*).** Position to which the object is being moved, where *n* is one less than the total number of objects found in the group.
  - **Number of objects (1-*n*).** Displays the number of objects or the range to reorder, where *n* is the total number of objects found in the group.
  - **Reverse Order.** Pick this button to have the order of all members in the group reversed.
- **Description.** Updates the group with the new description entered in the **Description:** text box.
- **Explode.** Pick this button to delete the selected group definition, but not the group's objects. The group name is removed, and the original group is exploded. Copies of the group become unnamed groups. By selecting the **Include Unnamed** check box, these unnamed groups are displayed and can then be exploded, if needed.
- **Selectable.** Toggles the selectable value of a group. This is where you can change the value in the **Selectable** list.

Exercise 12-16   Complete the Exercise on the Student CD.

LEGACY NOTE   The **SELECT** command can be used to define a selection set. After defining the selection set with this command, select the set by using the **Previous** section option at a Select objects: prompt. It is typically more effective to simply define the selection set within the initial editing command or to simply highlight the objects to be modified.

 The following Express Tool is related to topics discussed in this chapter. Refer to the Student CD for information on this tool:

Get Selection Set
Fast Select

Chapter Test

Answer the following questions. Write your answers on a separate sheet of paper or complete the electronic chapter test on the Student CD.

1. Give the command and entries used to draw a .125 × .125 chamfer:
   A. Command: _____
   B. (TRIM mode) Current chamfer *current*
      Select first line or [Undo/Polyline/Distance/Angle/Trim/mEthod/Multiple]: _____
   C. Specify first chamfer distance <*current*>: _____
   D. Specify second chamfer distance <*current*>: _____
   E. Select first line or [Undo/Polyline/Distance/Angle/Trim/mEthod/Multiple]: _____
   F. Select second line or shift-select to apply corner: _____

2. Give the command and entries required to produce .50-unit radius fillets on all corners of a closed polyline:
   A. Command: _____
   B. Current settings: Mode = *current*, Radius = *current*
      Select first object or [Undo/Polyline/Radius/Trim/Multiple]: _____
   C. Specify fillet radius <*current*>: _____
   D. Select first object or [Undo/Polyline/Radius/Trim/Multiple]: _____
   E. Select 2D polyline: _____

3. Give the command, entries, and actions required to move an object from Position A to Position B:
   A. Command: _____
   B. Select objects: _____
   C. 1 found
      Select objects: _____
   D. Specify base point or [Displacement] <Displacement>: _____
   E. Specify second point or <use first point as displacement>: _____

4. Give the command and entries needed to make two copies of the same object:
   A. Command: _____
   B. Select objects: _____
   C. 1 found
      Select objects: _____
   D. Specify base point or [Displacement] <Displacement>: _____
   E. Specify second point or <use first point as displacement>: _____
   F. Specify second point or [Exit/Undo] <Exit>: _____

5. Give the command and entries necessary to draw a reverse image of an existing object and remove the existing object:
   A. Command: _____
   B. Select objects: _____
   C. 1 found
      Select objects: _____
   D. Specify first point of mirror line: _____
   E. Specify second point of mirror line: _____
   F. Erase source objects? [Yes/No] <N>: _____

6. Give the command and entries needed to rotate an object 45° clockwise:
   A. Command: _____
   B. Current positive angle in UCS: ANGDIR=counterclockwise
      ANGBASE=0
      Select objects: _____
   C. 1 found
      Select objects: _____
   D. Specify base point: _____
   E. Specify rotation angle or [Copy/Reference] <*current*>: _____
7. Give the command and entries required to reduce the size of an entire drawing by one-half:
   A. Command: _____
   B. Select objects: _____
   C. *n* found
      Select objects: _____
   D. Specify base point: _____
   E. Specify scale factor or [Copy/Reference] <*current*>: _____
8. What is the purpose of the **mEthod** option in the **CHAMFER** command?
9. How is the size of a fillet specified?
10. Name the system variable used to preset the fillet radius.
11. Describe the difference between the **Trim** and **No trim** options when using the **CHAMFER** and **FILLET** commands.
12. How can you split an object in two without removing a portion?
13. In what direction should you pick points to break a portion out of a circle or an arc?
14. Name the command that trims an object to a cutting edge.
15. The **EXTEND** command is the opposite of the _____ command.
16. Name the command associated with boundary edges.
17. Name the option in the **TRIM** and **EXTEND** commands allowing you to trim or extend to an implied intersection.
18. List two locations drafters normally choose as the base point when using the **MOVE** or **COPY** commands.
19. Define the term *displacement,* as it relates to the **MOVE** and **COPY** commands.
20. Explain the difference between the **MOVE** and **COPY** commands.
21. Name the command that can be used to move and rotate an object simultaneously.
22. What is the difference between polar and rectangular arrays?
23. What four values should you know before you create a rectangular array?
24. Suppose an object is 1.5″ (38 mm) wide and you want to create a rectangular array with .75″ (19 mm) spacing between objects. What should you specify for the distance between columns?
25. How do you specify a clockwise polar array rotation?
26. What values should you know before you create a polar array?
27. The **MOVE, COPY, TRIM, EXTEND,** and **STRETCH** commands are located in the _____ pull-down menu.
28. How do you cancel the **STRETCH** command?
29. Give the keyboard shortcuts for the following commands:
   A. **CHAMFER**
   B. **FILLET**   H. **MIRROR**
   C. **BREAK**   I. **ROTATE**
   D. **TRIM**   J. **ALIGN**
   E. **EXTEND**   K. **ARRAY**
   F. **MOVE**   L. **SCALE**
   G. **COPY**   M. **LENGTHEN**

30. Identify the **LENGTHEN** command option corresponding to each of the following descriptions:
    A. Allows a positive or negative change in length from the endpoint.
    B. Changes a length or an arc angle by a percentage of the total.
    C. Sets the total length or angle to the value specified.
    D. Drags the endpoint of the object to the desired length or angle.
31. What is a *selection set*?
32. Define a *group*.
33. How do you access the **Object Grouping** dialog box?
34. Describe how you create a new group.
35. Identify four ways to open the **Quick Select** dialog box.

Drawing Problems

Use your templates as appropriate for each of the following problems. Start a new drawing for each problem, unless indicated otherwise.

1. Draw Object A using the **LINE** and **ARC** commands. Make sure the corners overrun and the arc is centered, but does not touch the lines. Use the **TRIM**, **EXTEND**, and **MOVE** commands to make Object B. Save the drawing as **P12-1**.

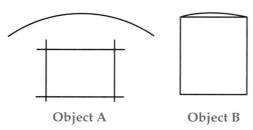

Object A   Object B

2. Open drawing P12-1 for further editing (Object A). Using the **STRETCH** command, change the shape to Object B. Make a copy of the new revision. Change the copy to represent Object C. Save the drawing as **P12-2**.

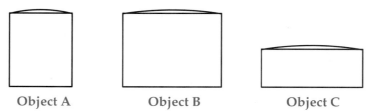

Object A   Object B   Object C

3. Refer to **Figure 12-42** in this chapter. Draw and make three copies of the object shown in Option 1. Stretch the first copy to twice its length, as shown in Option 2. Stretch the second copy to twice its height. Double the size of the third copy using the **SCALE** command. Save the drawing as **P12-3**.

4. Draw Objects A, B, and C, shown below, without dimensions. Move Objects A, B, and C to new positions. Select a corner of Object A and the centers of Objects B and C as the base points. Save the drawing as P12-4.

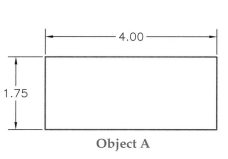

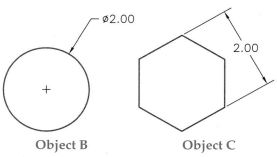

Object A   Object B   Object C

5. Draw Objects A, B, and C, shown in Problem 12-4, on the left side of the screen. Make a copy of Object A two units to the right. Make four copies of Object B three units, center to center, to the right, using the **Multiple** option. Make three copies of Object C three units, center to center, to the right. Save the drawing as P12-5.

6. Draw the object shown using the **ELLIPSE**, **COPY**, and **LINE** commands. The rotation angle of the ellipse is 60°. Use the **BREAK** or **TRIM** command when drawing and editing the lower ellipse. Save the drawing as P12-6.

7. Open drawing P12-6 for further editing. Shorten the height of the object using the **STRETCH** command, as shown below. Next, add to the object as indicated. Save the drawing as P12-7.

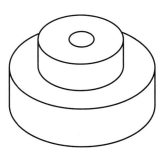

8. You have been given an engineer's sketches and notes to construct a drawing of a sprocket. Create a front and side view of the sprocket using the **ARRAY** command. Place the drawing on one of your templates. Do not add dimensions. Save the drawing as P12-8.

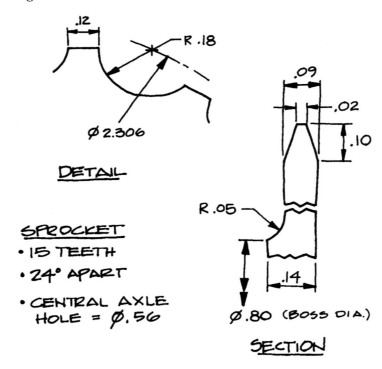

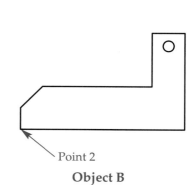

9. Draw Object A without dimensions. Use the **CHAMFER** and **FILLET** commands to your best advantage. Draw a mirror image as Object B. Now, remove the original view and move the new view so Point 2 is at the original Point 1 location. Save the drawing as P12-9.

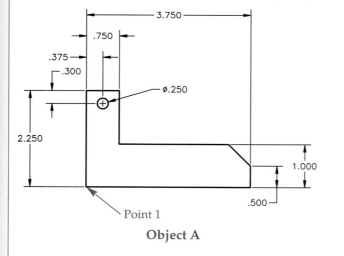

10. Draw the object shown below without dimensions. The object is symmetrical; therefore, draw only one half. Mirror the other half into place. Use the **CHAMFER** and **FILLET** commands to your best advantage. All fillets and rounds are 0.125. There are two places to use the **JOIN** command. Save the drawing as P12-10.

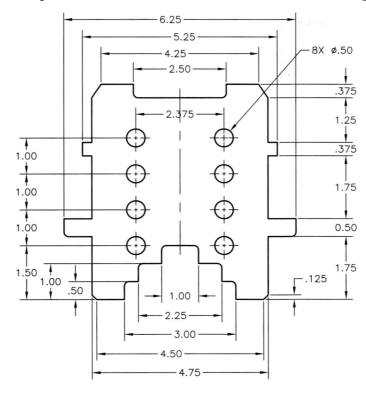

11. Use the **TRIM** and **OFFSET** commands to assist you in drawing this object. Do not draw centerlines or dimensions. Save the completed drawing as P12-11.

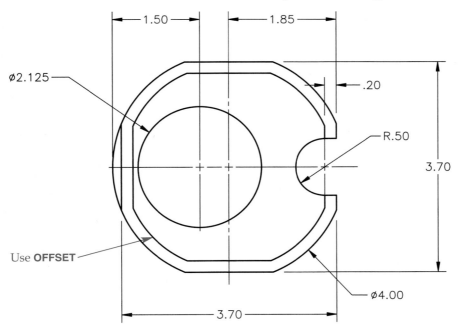

12. Draw the object shown below without dimensions. Mirror the right half into place. Use the **CHAMFER** and **FILLET** commands to your best advantage. Save the drawing as P12-12.

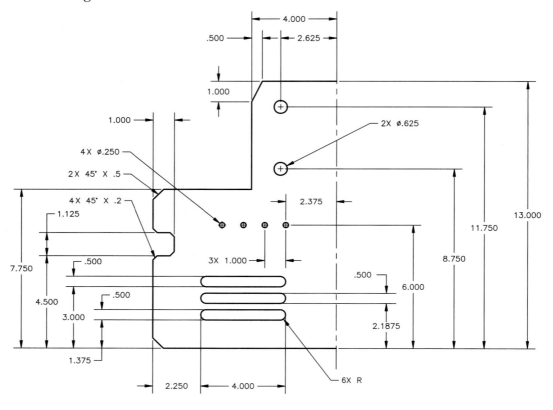

13. Redraw the objects shown below. Mirror the drawing, but have the text remain readable. Delete the original image during the mirroring process. Save the drawing as P12-13.

2b1

TRANSFER

5a2 4a1 8a1

LTS. HTRS. FANS

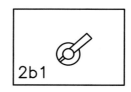

2b1

1b1

RESET

11b1

BYPASS

14. Draw the following object views using the dimensions given. Use **ARRAY** to construct the hole and tooth arrangements. Use one of your templates for the drawing. Do not add dimensions. Save the drawing as P12-14.

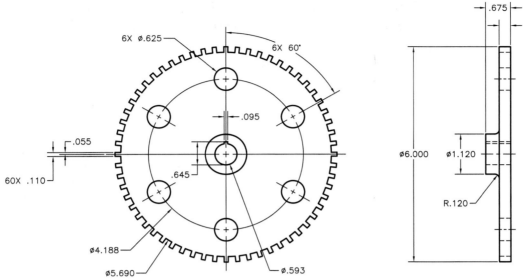

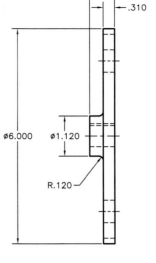

15. Draw the following object without dimensions. Use the **TRIMMODE** setting to your advantage. Save the drawing as P12-15.

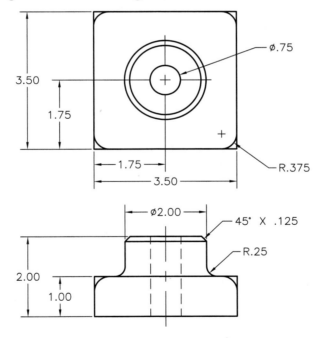

16. Draw the objects shown below. Use the **GROUP** command to name each of the objects with the names below them. Use the object groups to draw the one-line electrical diagram shown below. Use the **Explode** option to edit the symbols at 1 and 2 in the diagram, as shown. Save the drawing as P12-16.

Switch   Regulator   Ground-switch   Ground-overcurrent   Fuse

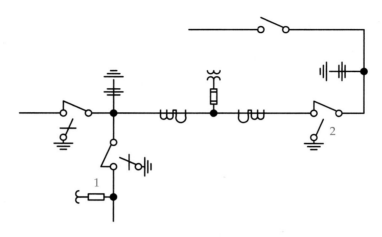

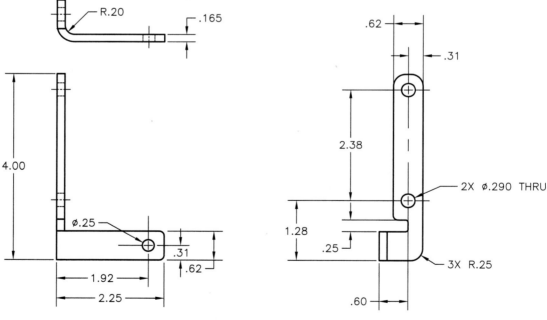

17. Draw the following bracket. Do not include dimensions in your drawing. Use the **FILLET** command where appropriate. Save the drawing as P12-17.

ALL FILLETS AND ROUNDS R.06

18. Draw this refrigeration system schematic. Save the drawing as P12-18.

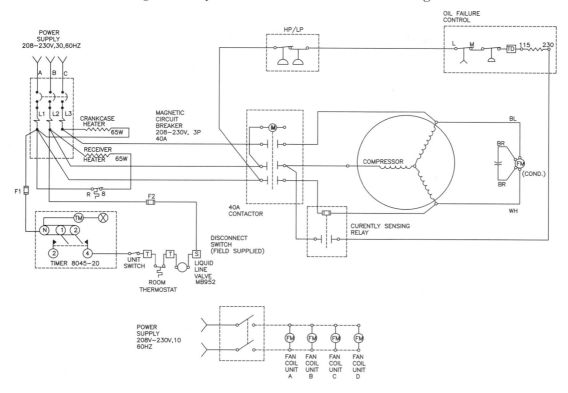

19. Draw this timer schematic. Save the drawing as P12-19.

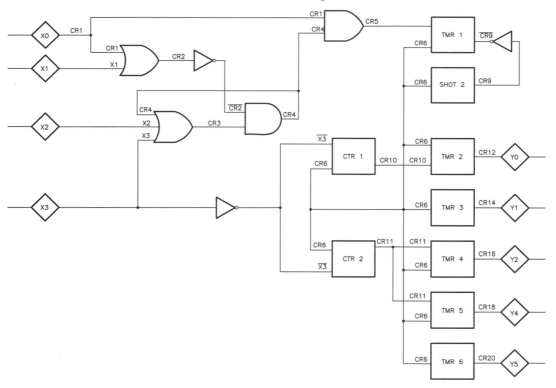

Drawing Problems - Chapter 12

20. The following engineering sketch shows a steel column arrangement on a concrete floor slab for a new building. The *I*-shaped symbols represent the steel columns. The columns are arranged in "bay lines" and "column lines." The column lines are numbered *1*, *2*, and *3*. The bay lines are labeled *A* through *G*. The width of a bay is 24'-0". Line balloons, or tags, identify the bay and column lines. Draw the arrangement, using **ARRAY** for the steel column symbols and the tags. Do not dimension the drawing. The following guidelines will help you:

A. Begin a new drawing, named P12-20, or use an architectural template.

B. Select architectural units and specify a 36 × 24 sheet size. Determine the scale required for the floor plan to fit on this sheet size and specify your limits accordingly.

C. Draw the steel column symbol to the dimensions given.

D. Set the grid spacing at 2'-0" (24").

E. Set the snap spacing at 12".

F. Draw all other objects.

G. Place text inside the balloon tags. Set the running object snap mode to **Center** and justify the text to **Middle**. Make the text height 6".

H. Place a title block on the drawing.

I. Save the drawing as P12-20.

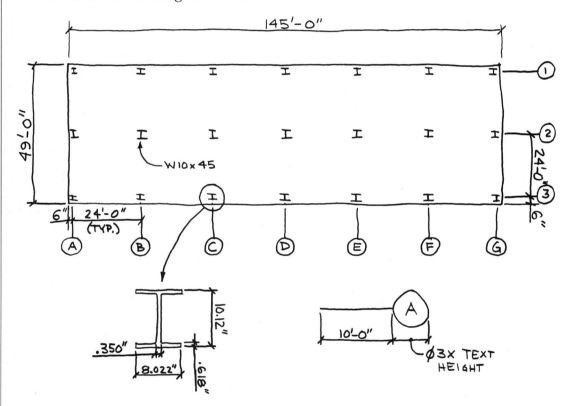

21. The engineering sketch given is a proposed office layout of desks and chairs. One desk is shown with the layout of a chair, keyboard, monitor, and tower-mounted computer (drawn with dotted lines). All the desk workstations should have the same configuration. The exact sizes and locations of the doors and windows are not important for this problem. Use the following guidelines to complete this problem:

A. Begin a new drawing, called P12-21.

B. Choose architectural units.

C. Select a C-size template drawing and be sure to create the drawing in model space. Use the **ZOOM nXP** option to display the drawing at a scale fitting the C-size layout.

D. Use the appropriate drawing and editing commands to complete this problem quickly and efficiently.

E. Draw the desk and computer hardware to the dimensions given.

F. Do not dimension the drawing. Plot a paper space layout tab at a one-to-one scale.

G. Save the drawing as P12-21.

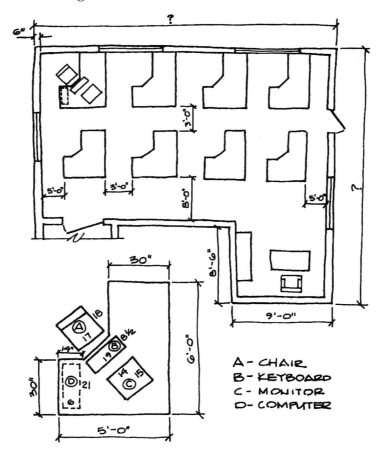

A - CHAIR
B - KEYBOARD
C - MONITOR
D - COMPUTER

22. Use tracking and object snaps to draw the object shown below based on these instructions:
    A. Draw the outline of the object first, followed by the ten (10) Ø.500 holes (A).
    B. The holes labeled B are located vertically halfway between the centers of the holes labeled A. They have a diameter one-quarter the size of the holes labeled A.
    C. The holes labeled C are located vertically halfway between the holes labeled A and B. Their diameter is three-quarters of the diameter of the holes labeled B.
    D. The holes labeled D are located horizontally halfway between the centers of the holes labeled A. These holes have the same diameter as the holes labeled B.
    E. Draw the rectangles around the circles as shown.
    F. Do not draw dimensions, notes, or labels.
    G. Use the **Quick Select** dialog box to erase all circles less than Ø.500.
    H. Save the drawing as P12-22.

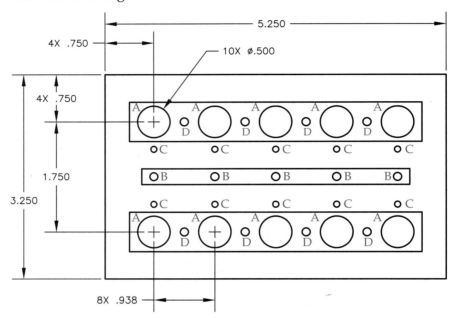

23. Draw the following roof plan. Do not dimension. Then, use the **Quick Select** dialog box to change the color of the roof and the linetype to CENTER. Finally, use the **Quick Select** dialog box to change the building outline to a continuous linetype. Save the drawing as P12-23.

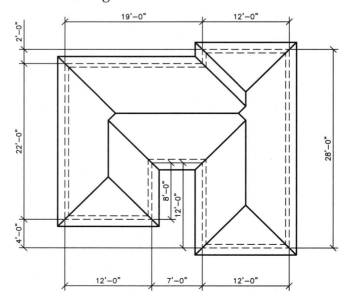

24. Draw the portion of the gasket shown on the left. Do not include dimensions. Use the **MIRROR** command to complete the gasket as shown on the right. Save the drawing as P12-24.

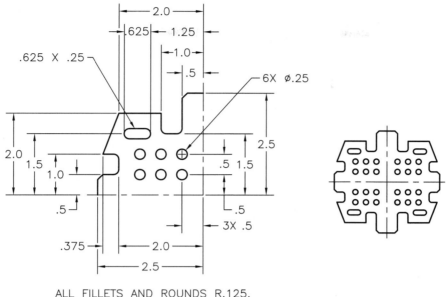

ALL FILLETS AND ROUNDS R.125.
CHAMFERS 45° X .125

25. Draw the padded bench. Do not include dimensions. Use the **COPY** and **ARRAY** commands as needed. Save the drawing as P12-25.

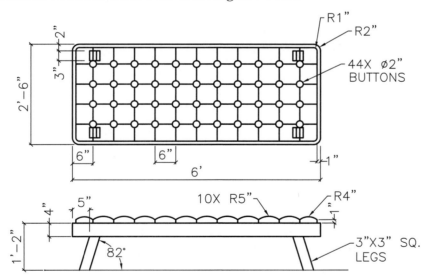

26. Draw the hand wheel shown below. Do not draw dimensions. Use the **ARRAY** command to draw the spokes. Save the drawing as P12-26.

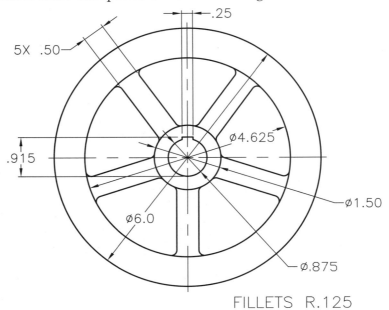

FILLETS R.125

27. Draw the control diagram. Draw one branch (including text) and use the copy command to your advantage. Use text editing commands as needed. Save the drawing as P12-27. (Design and drawing by EC Company, Portland, Oregon)

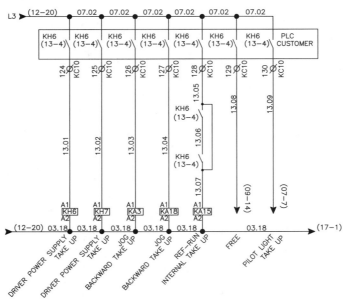

CHAPTER 13

Automatic Editing

Learning Objectives

After completing this chapter, you will be able to do the following:

● Use grips to do automatic editing with the **STRETCH**, **COPY**, **MOVE**, **ROTATE**, **SCALE**, and **MIRROR** commands.
● Identify the system variables used for automatic editing.
● Perform automatic editing with the **Properties** window.
● Use the **MATCHPROP** command to match object properties.

In Chapter 12, you learned how to use commands that let you do a variety of drawing and editing activities with AutoCAD. These editing commands give you maximum flexibility and increase productivity. This chapter takes editing a step further, however, by allowing you to first select an object and then automatically perform editing operations.

Automatic Editing with Grips

Hold, *grab*, and *grasp* are all words synonymous with *grip*. In AutoCAD, grips are features on an object that are highlighted with small boxes. For example, the grips on a straight line are the endpoints and midpoint. When grips are used for editing, you can select an object to automatically activate the grips. Pick any of the small boxes to perform **STRETCH**, **COPY**, **MOVE**, **ROTATE**, **SCALE**, or **MIRROR** operations.

When grips are enabled and there is no command active, a pick box is located at the intersection of the screen crosshairs. You can pick any object to activate the grips. **Figure 13-1** shows what grips look like on several different objects. For text, the grip box is located at the insertion point.

DDGRIPS

Type
DDGRIPS
GR

Pull-Down Menu
Tools
> Options...

You can control grip settings in the **Selection** tab of the **Options** dialog box. The **Options** dialog box is opened by picking **Tools** > **Options...** from the pull-down menu or by right-clicking in the drawing area and selecting **Options...** from the shortcut menu. You can access the **Selection** tab of the **Options** dialog box directly by typing GR or DDGRIPS. The **Selection** tab in the **Options** dialog box is shown in **Figure 13-2**.

The **Pickbox Size** scroll bar lets you adjust the size of the pick box. The sample in the image tile gets smaller or larger as you move the scroll bar. Stop when you have the desired size. The pick box size is also controlled by the **PICKBOX** system variable, in which the desired size is set in pixels.

Figure 13-1.
Grips are placed at strategic locations on objects.

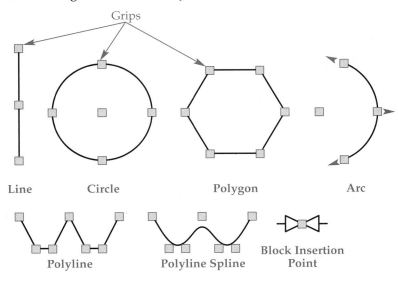

Line	Circle	Polygon	Arc

Polyline	Polyline Spline	Block Insertion Point

Figure 13-2.
The **Selection** tab of the **Options** dialog box contains grip control settings.

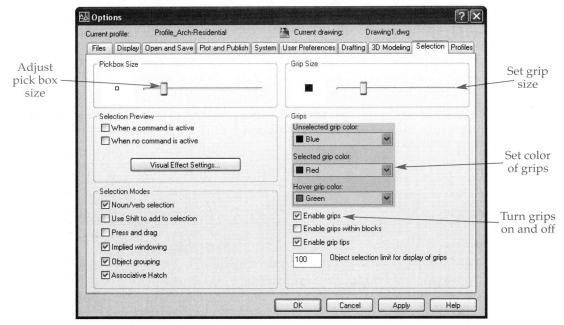

The **Grip Size** scroll bar in the **Selection** tab of the **Options** dialog box lets you graphically change the size of the grip box. The sample in the image tile gets smaller or larger as you move the scroll bar. Change the grip size to whatever works best for your drawing. Very small grip boxes may be difficult to pick. The grips may overlap, however, if they are too large. The grip size can be given a numerical value using the **GRIPSIZE** system variable. To change the default setting of 5, enter GRIPSIZE, and then type a desired size in pixels.

The three color drop-down lists allow you to change the color of grips. The grips displayed when you first pick an object are referred to as *unselected grips* because you have not yet picked them to perform an operation. An unselected grip is a filled-in square the color of the **Unselected grip color:** setting. Unselected grips are Blue by default and are called *warm*.

After you pick a grip, it is called a *selected grip*. A selected grip appears as a filled-in square that is the color specified by the **Selected grip color:** setting. Selected grips are Red by default and are called *hot*. If more than one object is selected (has warm grips), what you do with the hot grips affects all the selected objects. Objects having warm and hot grips are highlighted and are part of the selection set.

You can remove highlighted objects from a selection set by holding down the [Shift] key and picking the objects to be removed. The [Shift] key can also be used to add or remove hot grips. If you want to make more than one grip hot, hold the [Shift] key down, and then select the grip. To add more grips to the hot grip selection set, continue to hold the [Shift] key down and select the other grips. With the [Shift] key held down, selecting a hot (red) grip returns it to the warm (blue) stage. Figure 13-3 shows two different circles being modified by using hot grips. Moving the crosshairs over a warm grip and pausing changes the color of the grip to the **Hover grip color:** setting found in the **Selection** tab of the **Options** dialog box. By default, this color is set to Green. This is useful when multiple grips are close together. Pausing over the warm grip and letting it change color ensures that you select the correct grip.

You can also control grip color with the **GRIPCOLOR**, **GRIPHOT**, and **GRIPHOVER** system variables. **GRIPCOLOR** controls the color of warm grips, and **GRIPHOT** regulates the color of hot grips. The hover grip color can be changed by using the **GRIPHOVER** system variable. When you enter one of these variables, simply set the color number as desired.

Notice the three check boxes in the **Grips** area. Pick the **Enable grips** check box to turn grips on or off. This setting can also be set using the **GRIPS** system variable.

Pick the **Enable grips within blocks** check box to have grips displayed on every subobject of a block. A *block* is a special symbol designed for multiple uses. Blocks are discussed in detail in Chapter 22. When this check box is off, the grip location for a block is at the insertion point, as shown in Figure 13-1. Grips in blocks can also be controlled with the **GRIPBLOCK** system variable.

When the **Enable grip tips** box is checked, a tip displays relating to the selected object. This option only works on custom objects supporting grip tips. Standard AutoCAD objects do not have grip tips. The **GRIPTIPS** system variable also controls this option.

Figure 13-3.
You can modify multiple objects by using the [Shift] key to select grips to make them hot.

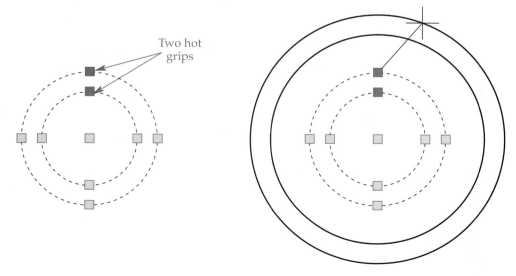

Using Grips

To activate grips, move the pick box to the desired object and pick. The object is highlighted, and the warm grips are displayed. To select a grip, move the pick box to the desired grip and pick it. Notice the crosshairs snap to a grip. When you pick a grip, the command line shows the following prompt:

```
** STRETCH **
Specify stretch point or [Base point/Copy/Undo/eXit]:
```

This activates the **STRETCH** command. All you have to do is move the cursor to make the selected object stretch, as shown in **Figure 13-4**. If you pick the middle grip of a line or an arc or the center grip of a circle, the object moves. These are the other options:

- **Base point.** Type B and press [Enter] to select a base point other than the hot grip.
- **Copy.** Type C and press [Enter] if you want to make one or more copies of the selected object.
- **Undo.** Type U and press [Enter] to undo the previous operation.
- **eXit.** Type X and press [Enter] to exit the command. The hot grip is gone, but the warm grips remain. You can also use the [Esc] key to cancel the command. Canceling twice removes the selected and unselected grips.

You can pick objects individually or use a window or crossing box. **Figure 13-5** shows how you can stretch features of an object after selecting all the objects. Step 1 in **Figure 13-5A** stretches the first corner, and Step 2 stretches the second corner. You can also make more than one grip hot at the same time by holding down the [Shift] key as you pick the grips, as shown in **Figure 13-5B**. Here are some general rules and guidelines that can help make grips work for you:

- ✓ Be sure grips are enabled.
- ✓ Pick an object or group of objects to activate grips. Objects in the selection set are highlighted.
- ✓ Pick a warm grip to make it hot.
- ✓ Make multiple grips hot by holding the [Shift] key while picking warm grips.
- ✓ If more than one object has hot grips, they are all affected by the editing commands.
- ✓ Remove objects from the selection set by holding down the [Shift] key and picking them, thus making the grips warm.
- ✓ Return objects to the selection set by picking them again.
- ✓ Remove hot grips from the selection set by pressing the [Esc] key to cancel. Cancel again to remove all grips from the selection set. You can also right-click and select **Deselect All** from the shortcut menu to remove all grips.

Figure 13-4.
Using the automatic **STRETCH** command. Note the selected grip.

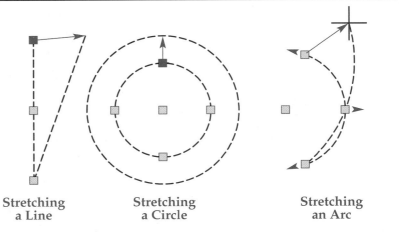

Stretching
a Line

Stretching
a Circle

Stretching
an Arc

Figure 13-5.
Stretching an object. A—Select corners to stretch individually. B—Select several hot grips by holding down the [Shift] key.

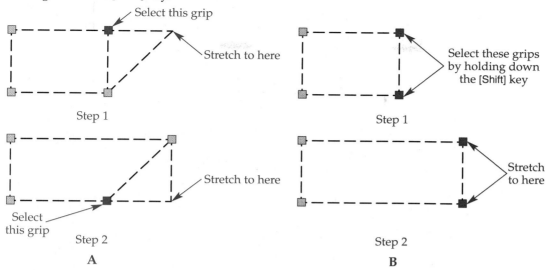

PROFESSIONAL TIP

When editing with grips, you can enter coordinates to help improve your accuracy. Remember that any of the coordinate entry methods work.

Exercise 13-1   Complete the Exercise on the Student CD.

You can also use the **MOVE, ROTATE, SCALE,** and **MIRROR** commands to automatically edit objects. All you have to do is pick the object, and then select one of the grips. When you see the ** STRETCH ** Specify stretch point or [Base point/Copy/Undo/eXit]: prompt, press [Enter] to cycle through the command options:

```
** STRETCH **
Specify stretch point or [Base point/Copy/Undo/eXit]: ↵
** MOVE **
Specify move point or [Base point/Copy/Undo/eXit]: ↵
** ROTATE **
Specify rotation angle or [Base point/Copy/Undo/Reference/eXit]: ↵
** SCALE **
Specify scale factor or [Base point/Copy/Undo/Reference/eXit]: ↵
** MIRROR **
Specify second point or [Base point/Copy/Undo/eXit]: ↵
** STRETCH **
Specify stretch point or [Base point/Copy/Undo/eXit]:
```

As an alternative to cycling through the command options, you can enter the first two characters of the desired command from the keyboard. Type MO for **MOVE,** MI for **MIRROR,** RO for **ROTATE,** SC for **SCALE,** and ST for **STRETCH.**

AutoCAD also allows you to right-click and access a grips shortcut menu, as shown in **Figure 13-6.** This menu is only available after a hot grip has been activated. The shortcut menu allows you to access the five grip editing options without using the keyboard.

Figure 13-6.
The grips shortcut menu appears when a grip is selected and you right-click.

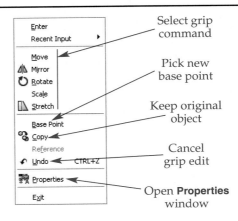

Select grip command

Pick new base point

Keep original object

Cancel grip edit

Open **Properties** window

PROFESSIONAL TIP

Many of the conventional AutoCAD editing operations can be performed when warm grips are displayed on screen. For example, the **ERASE** command can be used to clear the screen of all objects displayed with warm grips by first picking the objects and then selecting the **ERASE** command. This technique is available if **Noun/verb selection** is enabled (**Selection Modes** are of the **Selection** tab in the **Options** dialog box.)

Moving an Object Automatically

If you want to move an object with grips, select the object, pick a grip to use as the base point, and then press [Enter] to cycle through the commands until you get to this prompt:

```
** MOVE **
Specify move point or [Base point/Copy/Undo/eXit]:
```

The selected grip becomes the base point. Move the object to a new point by picking the new location. You may want to use object snap mode or coordinates to place it in a new location. The **MOVE** operation is complete, as shown in **Figure 13-7.** If you accidentally pick the wrong grip or want to have a base point other than the selected grip, type B and press [Enter] for the **Base point** option. Pick a new base point.

Exercise 13-2   Complete the Exercise on the Student CD.

Copying an Object Automatically

The **Copy** option is found in each of the editing commands. When using the **STRETCH** command, the **Copy** option allows you to make multiple copies of the object you are stretching. The **Copy** option in the **MOVE** command is the true form of the **COPY** command.

The **Copy** option works similarly in each of the editing commands. Try it with each to see what happens. You can also access the **Copy** option directly by picking the right mouse button to open the grips shortcut menu.

Figure 13-7.
The automatic
MOVE command.
The selected grip
becomes the base
point for the move.

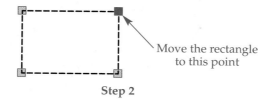

Pick a grip to be
a base point

Step 1

Move the rectangle
to this point

Step 2

Exercise 13-3   Complete the Exercise on the Student CD.

Rotating an Object Automatically

To automatically rotate an object, select the object, pick a grip to use as the base point, and press [Enter] until you see this prompt:

```
** ROTATE **
Specify rotation angle or [Base point/Copy/Undo/Reference/eXit]:
```

Now, move your pointing device to rotate the object. Pick the desired rotation point or enter a rotation angle at the prompt.

Type R and press [Enter] if you want to use the **Reference** option. The **Reference** option may be used when the object is already rotated at a known angle and you want to rotate it to a new angle. The reference angle is the current angle, and the new angle is the desired angle. **Figure 13-8** shows the **ROTATE** options.

Exercise 13-4   Complete the Exercise on the Student CD.

Figure 13-8.
The rotation angle
and **Reference**
option of the
ROTATE command.

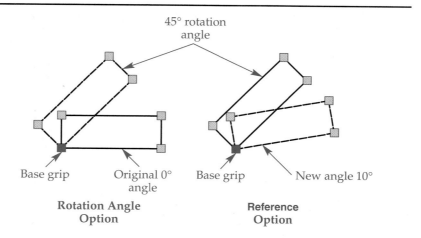

45° rotation
angle

Base grip   Original 0°   Base grip   New angle 10°
                 angle

Rotation Angle   Reference
Option   Option

Scaling an Object Automatically

If you want to scale an object with grips, cycle through the editing options until you get this prompt:

```
** SCALE **
Specify scale factor or [Base point/Copy/Undo/Reference/eXit]:
```

Move the screen cursor and pick when the object is dragged to the desired size. You can also enter a scale factor to automatically increase or decrease the scale of the original object. If you know a current length and a desired length, you can use the **Reference** option. The selected base point remains in the same place when the object is scaled. **Figure 13-9** shows the two **SCALE** options.

 **Exercise 13-5**   Complete the Exercise on the Student CD.

Mirroring an Object Automatically

If you want to mirror an object using grips, the selected grip becomes the first point of the mirror line. Press [Enter] to cycle through the editing commands until you get this prompt:

```
** MIRROR **
Specify second point or [Base point/Copy/Undo/eXit]:
```

Use the **Base point** option to reselect the first point of the mirror line. Pick another grip or any point on the screen as the second point of the mirror line. See **Figure 13-10**. Unlike the standard **MIRROR** command, the automatic **MIRROR** command does not give you the option to delete the old objects. The old objects are deleted automatically. If you want to keep the original object while mirroring, use the **Copy** option in the **MIRROR** command.

 **Exercise 13-6**   Complete the Exercise on the Student CD.

Figure 13-9.
When using the automatic **SCALE** command, you can enter a scale factor or use the **Reference** option.

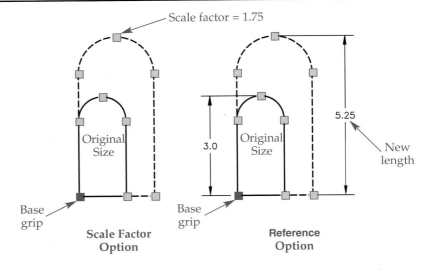

Figure 13-10.
When using the automatic **MIRROR** command, the selected grip becomes the first point of the mirror line, and the original object is automatically deleted.

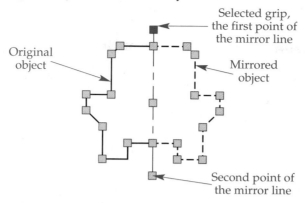

Selected grip, the first point of the mirror line

Original object

Mirrored object

Second point of the mirror line

Selection Options for Editing

In Chapter 12, you were introduced to basic editing. Basic editing allows you to first enter a command and then select the desired object to be edited. You can also enable settings so you first select the desired objects and then enter the desired command. The automatic editing features discussed in this chapter use grips and related editing commands to edit an object automatically, after first selecting the object.

The **Selection Modes** area of the **Selection** tab in the **Options** dialog box allows you to control the way you use editing commands. See **Figure 13-11.** Select or deselect the following options, based on your own preferences:

Figure 13-11.
The **Selection Modes** area of the **Selection** tab in the **Options** dialog box.

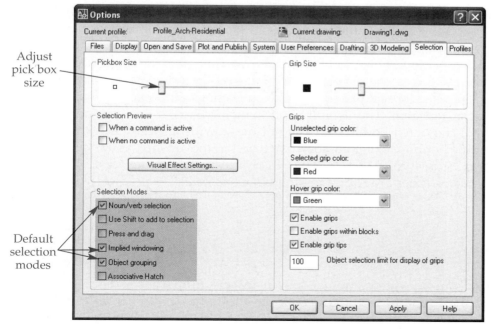

Adjust pick box size

Default selection modes

- **Noun/verb selection.** When you first select objects and then enter a command, it is referred to as the *noun/verb* format. The pick box is displayed at the screen crosshairs. A "✓" in this check box means the noun/verb method is active. The **PICKFIRST** system variable can also be used to set the **Noun/verb selection**. When using the *verb/noun* format, you enter the command before selecting the object. Remove the "✓" from the **Noun/verb selection** check box to enter the command before making a selection.

NOTE Some editing commands, such as **FILLET**, **CHAMFER**, **DIVIDE**, **MEASURE**, **OFFSET**, **EXTEND**, **TRIM**, and **BREAK**, require you to enter the command before you select the object.

- **Use Shift to add to selection.** When this check box is off, every object or group of objects you select is highlighted and added to the selection set. If you pick this check box, it changes the way AutoCAD accepts objects you pick. For example, if you pick an object, it is highlighted and added to the selection set. If you pick another object, however, it is highlighted, and the first one is removed from the selection set. This means you can only select one object by picking or one group of objects with a selection window. If you want to add more items to the selection set, you must hold down the [Shift] key as you pick them. Turning off the **PICKADD** system variable does the same thing as turning on this feature.
- **Press and drag.** This is the same as turning on the **PICKDRAG** system variable. With **Press and drag** on, you create a selection window by picking the first corner and moving the cursor while holding down the pick button. Release the pick button when you have the desired selection window. By default, this option is off. This means you need to pick both the first and second corners of the desired selection window.
- **Implied windowing.** By default, this option is on. This means you can automatically create a window box by picking the first point and moving the cursor to the right to pick the second point, or you can make a crossing box by picking the first point and moving the cursor to the left to pick the second point. This is the same as turning on the **PICKAUTO** system variable.
- **Object grouping.** This option controls whether or not AutoCAD recognizes grouped objects as singular objects. When it is off, the individual elements of a group can be selected for separate editing without having to first explode the group.
- **Associative Hatch.** The default is off, which means, if an associative hatch is moved, the hatch boundary does not move with it. Select this toggle if you want the boundary of an associative hatch to move when you move the hatch pattern. It is a good idea to have this on for most applications. Hatches and hatch boundaries are fully explained in Chapter 21.

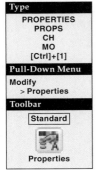

PROPERTIES
Type
PROPERTIES
PROPS
CH
MO
[Ctrl]+[1]
Pull-Down Menu
Modify
> Properties
Toolbar
Standard
Properties

Using the Properties Window

An object can be edited automatically using the **Properties** window. To edit an object using the **Properties** window, pick the **Properties** button from the **Standard** toolbar; pick **Modify > Properties**; or type MO, CH, PROPS, or PROPERTIES. You can also toggle the **Properties** window on and off using the [Ctrl]+[1] key combination. If an object has already been selected, you can access the **Properties** window by right-clicking and selecting **Properties** from the shortcut menu.

Figure 13-12.
The **Properties** window can be used to modify different properties of an object.

Type of object selected

Category

Properties within category (pick to modify)

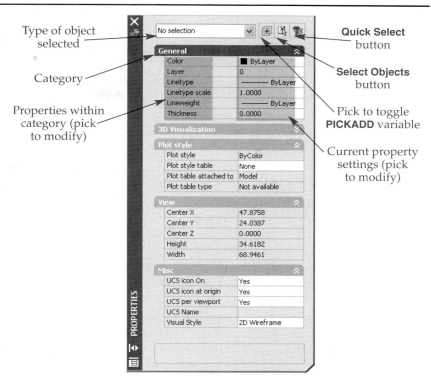

Quick Select button

Select Objects button

Pick to toggle **PICKADD** variable

Current property settings (pick to modify)

PROPERTIES	No selection		
General			
	Color	■ ByLayer	
	Layer	0	
	Linetype	——— ByLayer	
	Linetype scale	1.0000	
	Lineweight	——— ByLayer	
	Thickness	0.0000	
3D Visualization			
Plot style			
	Plot style	ByColor	
	Plot style table	None	
	Plot table attached to	Model	
	Plot table type	Not available	
View			
	Center X	47.8758	
	Center Y	24.0387	
	Center Z	0.0000	
	Height	34.6182	
	Width	68.9461	
Misc			
	UCS icon On	Yes	
	UCS icon at origin	Yes	
	UCS per viewport	Yes	
	UCS Name		
	Visual Style	2D Wireframe	

The **Properties** window is shown in **Figure 13-12.** The **Properties** window can be docked in the drawing area, similarly to the way a toolbar can be docked. This was discussed in Chapter 1. While the **Properties** window is displayed, you can enter commands and continue to work in AutoCAD. You can close the box by picking the **X** in the top left corner, picking the **Properties** button on the **Modify** toolbar, or using the [Ctrl]+[1] key combination.

When you access the **Properties** window without first selecting an object, No selection can be seen in the top drop-down list. This means AutoCAD does not have any objects selected to modify. The four categories—**General**, **Plot style**, **View**, and **Misc**—list the current settings for the drawing.

Underneath each category is a list of object properties. For example, in **Figure 13-12,** the current color is ByLayer. To change a property, pick the property or its current value. Once the property is highlighted, one of the following methods is used to set the new value:

• A drop-down arrow with a list of values.
• A pick point button, which allows you to pick a new coordinate location.
• A text box, which is opened when you select certain properties, such as the radius of an arc. Entering a new value in this box allows you to change the radius.

Once a property to be modified has been selected, a description of what that property does is shown at the bottom of the dialog box.

In the upper-right portion of the **Properties** window are three buttons. Pick the **Quick Select** button to access the **Quick Select** dialog box, where you can create object selection sets. This dialog box is discussed in Chapter 12. Picking the **Select Objects** button deselects the currently selected objects and changes the crosshairs to a pick box. The third button toggles the value of the **PICKADD** system variable, which determines whether or not you need to hold the [Shift] key when adding objects to a selection set.

In order to modify an object, the **Properties** window must be open, and an object must be selected. For example, if a circle and a line are drawn and you need to modify the circle, first pick on the circle to make the grips appear, and then use one of the methods to open the **Properties** window. The **Properties** window displays the categories that can be modified for the circle. All objects have a **General** category. The **General** category allows you to modify properties such as **Color**, **Layer**, **Linetype**, **Linetype scale**, **Plot style**, **Lineweight**, **Hyperlink**, and **Thickness**. For example, do the following to change the color of the circle:

1. Select the **Color** property in the window by picking on the word **Color**. A drop-down arrow appears to the right of the current color.
2. Select the drop-down arrow, and a list of available colors appears.
3. Select the new color. If the desired color is not on the list, choose **Select Color…** from the bottom of the list. This displays the **Select Color** dialog box, from which a color can be selected.

Once a color has been selected, the **Properties** window displays the current color for the circle.

A description of each of the properties in the **General** category follows:

- **Color.** Pick this property to display a drop-down list from which a color can be selected. At the bottom of the drop-down list is the **Select Color…** option, which displays the **Select Color** dialog box showing all the colors available.
- **Layer.** Select the desired layer for the object here. Layers are discussed in Chapter 4.
- **Linetype.** Select the desired linetype for the object.
- **Linetype scale.** To change the individual object's linetype, highlight the value and type a new scale value. The linetype scale for an individual object is a multiplier of the **LTSCALE** system variable. This was discussed in Chapter 4.
- **Plot style.** Picking on this property displays a drop-down list with various plot styles. Initially, only one style is available: ByColor. In order to create a list of plot styles, you must create a plot style table. Plotting and plot styles are discussed in Chapter 11.
- **Lineweight.** Select the desired lineweight for the object. Lineweights are discussed in Chapter 4.
- **Hyperlink.** Picking on this property displays an **…** (ellipsis) button. By selecting this button, you can access the **Insert Hyperlink** dialog box. Use this dialog box to add a hyperlink to a graphical object or a description or URL address to an object.
- **Thickness.** This property allows you to change the thickness of a 3D object in a text box.

Exercise 13-7   Complete the Exercise on the Student CD.

As stated earlier, all objects have a **General** category. Depending on the type of object that has been selected for modification, other categories are also displayed. See **Figure 13-13.** One of the most common categories is **Geometry**. Although most objects have a **Geometry** category, the properties within the categories vary, depending on the type of object. Typically, there are three properties that allow you to change the absolute coordinates for the object by specifying the X, Y, and Z coordinates. Pick one of these properties, and a pick button is displayed. The button allows you to pick a point in your drawing for the new location. In addition to the option of choosing a point with the pick button, the value for the coordinate can also be changed in a text box.

When multiple objects are selected, you can use the **Properties** window to modify all the objects, or you can pick only one of the selected objects to be modified. The drop-down list displays the types of objects selected. See **Figure 13-14.** Select All (*n*) to change the properties of all selected objects. Only properties shared by all selected objects are displayed when All (*n*) is selected. To modify only one object, select the appropriate object type.

Figure 13-13.
The **Properties** window with a Line object selected. Notice there are only three categories that can be modified for the line object.

Type of object selected

General properties

These values cannot be directly modified, but change if endpoints are modified

Start point and endpoint coordinates

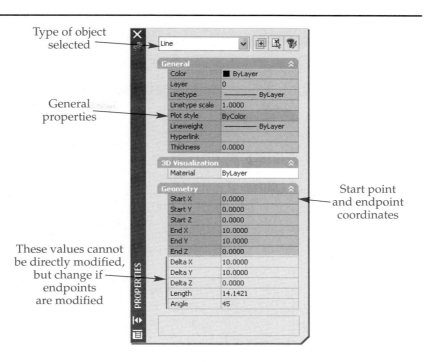

Figure 13-14.
The **Properties** window with three objects selected. You can edit the objects individually or all together by selecting All (3).

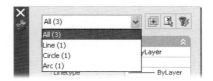

When all the changes to the object have been made, press the [Esc] button on the keyboard to clear the grips and remove the object from the **Properties** window. The object is now displayed in the drawing window with the desired changes. For example, if you select a circle, three categories appear in the **Properties** window—**General, 3D Visualization**, and **Geometry**. See **Figure 13-15**. The **Geometry** category displays the current location of the center of the circle by showing three properties: **Center X, Center Y**, and **Center Z**. To choose a new center location for the circle, select the appropriate property. Pick a new point or type the coordinate values. There are also other properties that can be modified for the circle, such as the **Radius, Diameter, Circumference**, and **Area**. By changing any of these values, you are modifying the size of the circle.

NOTE

The **Properties** window is discussed where appropriate throughout this text.

Exercise 13-8

Complete the Exercise on the Student CD.

Figure 13-15.
The **Properties** window with a Circle object selected for editing.

Type of
object selected

Pick to modify
location

Pick button

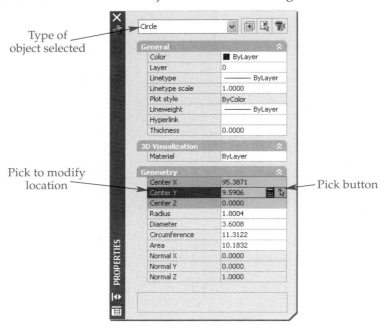

Editing between Drawings

One of the advantages of AutoCAD is the capability of editing in more than one drawing at a time. This allows you to copy objects from one drawing to another drawing. You can also refer to another drawing to obtain information (such as a distance) while working in a different drawing.

To take a look at how this works, open drawing EX13-8, and then open drawing EX13-7. Two drawings have now been opened in AutoCAD. Pick **Window > Tile Horizontally**. This "tiles" the two open drawings. See **Figure 13-16**.

Figure 13-16.
Multiple drawings can be tiled to make editing easier.

Docked
Properties
window

EX 13-8

EX 13-7

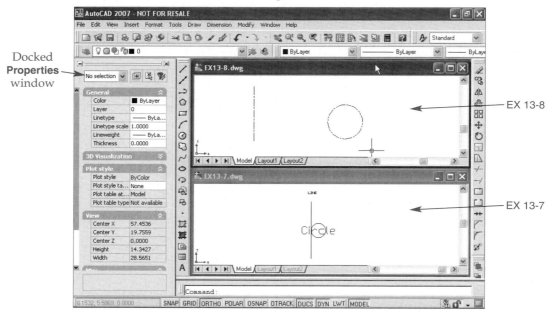

The Windows function *copy and paste* is used to copy an object from one drawing to another. To use this feature in AutoCAD, the object you intend to copy must be selected with grips. For example, if you want to copy the circle from drawing EX13-8 to drawing EX13-7, you would first select the circle. Once the circle is selected, right-click to get the shortcut menu shown in **Figure 13-17.** The shortcut menu has two options allowing you to copy to the Windows Clipboard:

- **Copy.** This option takes selected objects from AutoCAD and places them on the Windows Clipboard to be used in another application or AutoCAD drawing.
- **Copy with Base Point.** This option also copies the selected objects to the Clipboard, but it allows you to specify a base point to position the copied object when it is pasted. When using this option, AutoCAD prompts you to select a base point. Select a logical base point, such as a corner or center point of the object.

Once you have selected one of the two copy options, make the second drawing active by picking inside of it. Right-click, and a shortcut menu is displayed, as shown in **Figure 13-18.** Notice the copy options remain available, but three paste options are now available below the copy options. The paste options are only available if there is something on the Clipboard. The three options are described below:

- **Paste.** This option pastes any information from the Clipboard into the current drawing. If the **Copy with Base Point** option was used to place objects in the Clipboard, the objects being pasted are attached to the crosshairs at the specified base point.

Figure 13-17.
Right-click to access this shortcut menu to select one of the copy options.

Copy options

Figure 13-18.
Right-click to access this shortcut menu and select one of the paste options to paste an object from the Clipboard to a drawing.

Paste options

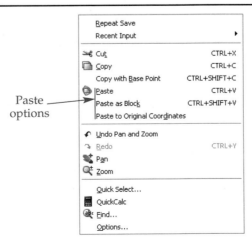

- **Paste as Block.** This option "joins" all objects in the Clipboard when they are pasted into the drawing. The pasted objects act like a block in that they are single objects joined together to form one object. Blocks are covered in Chapter 22. Use the **EXPLODE** command to get the objects to act individually again.
- **Paste to Original Coordinates.** This option pastes the objects from the Clipboard to the same coordinates at which they were located in the original drawing.

Exercise 13-9   Complete the Exercise on the Student CD.

MATCHPROP
Type
MATCHPROP
MA
PAINTER
Pull-Down Menu
Modify
  > Match Properties
Toolbar
Standard

Match Properties

Matching Properties

The **MATCHPROP** command allows you to copy properties from one object to one or more objects. This can be done in the same drawing or between drawings. To access the **MATCHPROP** command, select the **Match Properties** button from the **Standard** toolbar; select **Modify > Match Properties**; or enter MA, MATCHPROP, or PAINTER.

When you first access the **MATCHPROP** command, AutoCAD prompts you for the source object. The source object is the object with all the properties you would like to copy to another object or series of objects. Once the source object has been selected, AutoCAD displays the properties it will paint to the destination object. The next prompt allows you to pick the objects you want to receive the properties of the source object. If you want the properties painted to all objects in the drawing, type ALL at this prompt.

To change the properties to be painted, access the **Settings** option by typing S and pressing [Enter]. The **Property Settings** dialog box now appears, showing the types of properties that can be painted. See **Figure 13-19.** The following describes the major areas of the **Property Settings** dialog box:

- **Basic Properties.** This area lists the general properties of the selected object. If you do not want a specific property to be copied, deselect the appropriate check box. All active properties will be transferred to the destination objects.
- **Special Properties.** In addition to general properties, you can also paint over dimension styles, text styles, and hatch patterns. These properties are replaced in the destination object if these check boxes are active.

Figure 13-19.
The **Property Settings** dialog box for the **MATCHPROP** command. Select the properties to paint onto a new object.

Properties to be painted to other objects

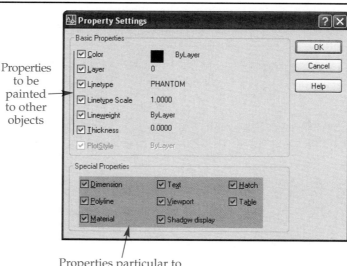

Properties particular to specific objects

For example, if you want to paint only the color property and text style of one text object to another text object, uncheck all boxes except the **Color** and **Text** property check boxes.

NOTE

To use the **MATCHPROP** command between drawings, select the source object from one drawing and the destination object from another.

PROFESSIONAL TIP

Use the **Partial Open** option in the **OPEN** command to partially open existing drawings to be used as source objects for copying or property matching. **Partial Open** is discussed in Chapter 2.

Exercise 13-10   Complete the Exercise on the Student CD.

LEGACY NOTE

The **CHANGE** and **CHPROP** commands can also be used to modify some object properties. The **CHANGE** command also provides a stretch option. Using **CHANGE** and **CHPROP** is typically less efficient than using the **Properties** window, **Properties** toolbar, and grip editing.

Chapter Test

Answer the following questions. Write your answers on a separate sheet of paper or complete the electronic chapter test on the Student CD.

1. Name the editing commands that can be accessed automatically using grips.
2. Identify two ways to access the **Options** dialog box.
3. Explain two ways to change the pick box size.
4. What is the purpose of the **Selection** tab found in the **Options** dialog box?
5. Name the three system variables controlling the color of grips.
6. How do you turn grips on and off?
7. When grips are active, how do you cycle through the available automatic commands?
8. How do you access the grips shortcut menu?
9. What is the purpose of the **Base Point** option in the grips shortcut menu?
10. Explain the function of the **Undo** option in the grips shortcut menu.
11. Describe the purpose of the **Properties** option in the grips shortcut menu.
12. What happens when you choose the **Exit** option from the grips shortcut menu?
13. Which option of the automatic **ROTATE** command would you use to rotate an object from an existing 60° angle to a new 25° angle?
14. What scale factor is used to scale an object to become three-quarters of its original size?

15. Name the system variable allowing you to set the "noun/verb" selection.
16. Explain the difference between "noun/verb" selection and "verb/noun" selection.
17. What does **Use Shift to add to selection** mean?
18. Describe how the **Press and drag** option works.
19. Name the system variable used to turn on the **Press and drag** option.
20. Name the system variable that turns on the **Implied windowing** option.
21. Identify the pull-down menu and the item you pick from this menu to access the **Properties** window.
22. How do you change the color of an object using the **Properties** window?
23. How would you change the linetype of an object using the **Properties** window?
24. How do you change existing text reading AutoCAD to read AutoCAD 2007 by using the **Properties** window?
25. Explain how you would change the radius of a circle from 1.375 to 1.875 using the **Properties** window.
26. Name the option used to have a group of objects joined as a block when they are pasted.
27. When you use the option described in Question 26, how do you separate the objects back into individual objects?
28. What command is used to quickly change the properties of objects to match the properties of a different object?

Drawing Problems

Use templates as appropriate for each of the following problems. Use grips and the associated editing commands or other editing techniques discussed in this chapter.

1. Draw the objects labeled A, below, and then use the **STRETCH** command to make them look like the objects labeled B. Do not include dimensions. Save the drawing as P13-1.

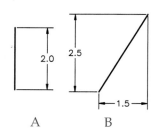
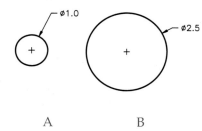
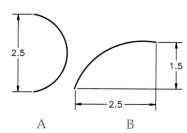

2. Draw the object labeled A, below. Using the **Copy** option of the **MOVE** command, copy the object to the position labeled B. Edit Object A so it resembles Object C. Edit Object B so it looks like Object D. Do not include dimensions. Save the drawing as P13-2.

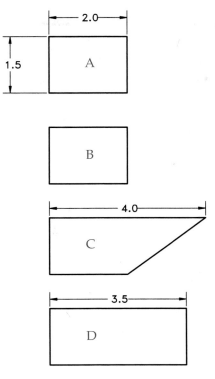

3. Draw the object labeled A, below. Copy the object, without rotating it, to a position below, as indicated by the dashed lines. Rotate the object 45°. Copy the rotated object labeled B to a position below, as indicated by the dashed lines. Use the **Reference** option to rotate the object labeled C to 25°, as shown. Do not include dimensions. Save the drawing as P13-3.

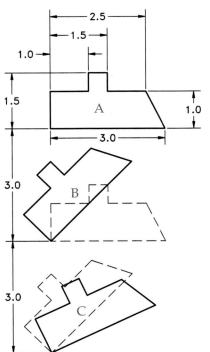

4. Draw the individual objects (vertical line, horizontal line, circle, arc, and *C* shape) in A, below, using the dimensions given. Use grips and the editing commands to create the object shown in B. Do not include dimensions. Save the drawing as P13-4.

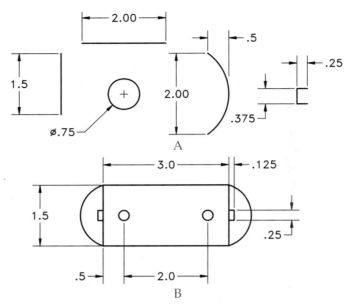

5. Use the completed drawing from Problem 13-4. Erase everything except the completed object and move it to a position similar to A, below. Copy the object two times to positions B and C. Use the automatic **SCALE** command to scale the object in position B to 50 percent of its original size. Use the **Reference** option of the **SCALE** command to enlarge the object in position C from the existing 3.0 length to a 4.5 length, as shown in C. Do not include dimensions. Save as P13-5.

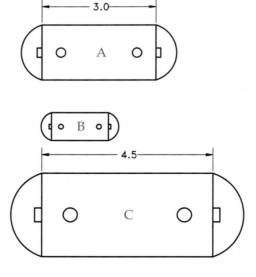

6. Draw the dimensioned partial object shown in A. Do not include dimensions. Mirror the drawing to complete the four quadrants, as shown in B. Change the color of the horizontal and vertical parting lines to Red and the linetype to CENTER. Save the drawing as P13-6.

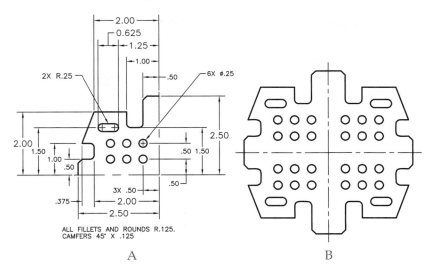

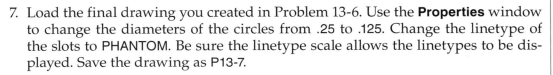

A   B

7. Load the final drawing you created in Problem 13-6. Use the **Properties** window to change the diameters of the circles from .25 to .125. Change the linetype of the slots to PHANTOM. Be sure the linetype scale allows the linetypes to be displayed. Save the drawing as P13-7.

8. Use the editing commands discussed in this chapter to assist you in drawing the following object. Draw the object within the boundaries of the given dimensions. All other dimensions are flexible. Do not include dimensions in the drawing. Save the drawing as P13-8.

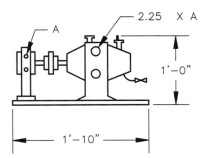

9. Draw the following object within the boundaries of the given dimensions. All other dimensions are flexible. Do not include dimensions. After drawing the object, create a page for a vendor catalog, as follows:
   - All labels should be ROMAND text, centered directly below the view. Use a text height of .125".
   - Label the drawing ONE-GALLON TANK WITH HORIZONTAL VALVE.
   - Keep the valve the same scale as the original drawing in each copy.
   - Copy the original tank to a new location and scale it so it is 2 times its original size. Rotate the valve 45°. Label this tank TWO-GALLON TANK WITH 45° VALVE.
   - Copy the original tank to another location and scale it so it is 2.5 times the size of the original. Rotate the valve 90°. Label this tank TWO- AND ONE-HALF GALLON TANK WITH 90° VALVE.
   - Copy the two-gallon tank to a new position and scale it so it is 2 times this size. Rotate the valve to 22°30'. Label this tank FOUR-GALLON TANK WITH 22°30' VALVE.
   - Left-justify this note at the bottom of the page: Combinations of tank size and valve orientation are available upon request.
   - Use the **Properties** window to change all tank labels to ROMANC, .25" high.
   - Change the note at the bottom of the sheet to ROMANS, centered on the sheet, using uppercase letters.
   - Save the drawing as P13-9.

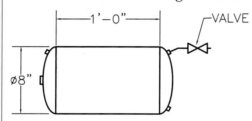

10. Draw the half of the gasket shown below. Do not include dimensions. Mirror the drawing to complete the bottom half. Save the drawing as P13-10.

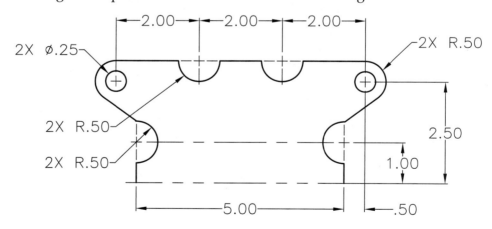

Drawing Problems - Chapter 13

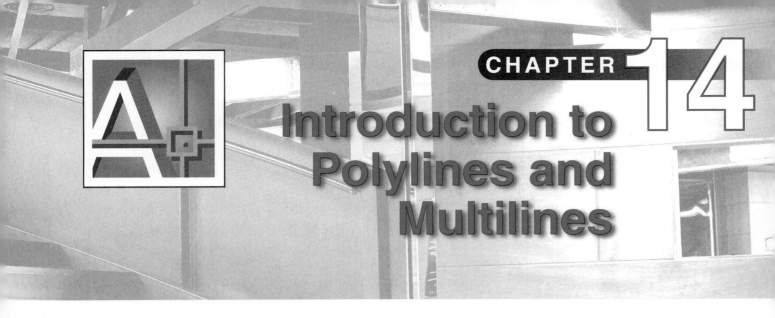

CHAPTER 14

Introduction to Polylines and Multilines

Learning Objectives

After completing this chapter, you will be able to do the following:

- Use the **PLINE** command to draw polyline objects.
- Explain the functions of the **UNDO** and **REDO** commands.
- Compare the results of turning the **FILL** mode on and off.
- Use the **MLINE** command to draw multilines.
- Create your own multiline styles with the **MLSTYLE** command.
- Edit multiline intersections, corners, and vertices.

Polylines and multilines are two AutoCAD features that provide you with special line creation abilities. This chapter introduces you to the use of polylines and fully explains how to create drawing features with multilines. A complete discussion of drawing polyline arcs and editing polylines is provided in Chapter 15.

The term *polyline* is composed of *poly-* and *line*. *Poly-* means "many." A *polyline* is a single object made up of one or more line segments. Each line segment can vary in width. Polylines are drawn with the **PLINE** command and its various options.

Multilines are combinations of parallel lines consisting of individual lines called *elements*. They can have up to 16 individual line elements. You can offset the elements as needed to create a desired pattern for any field of drafting (for example, architectural, schematic, or mechanical drafting). Multilines are drawn using the **MLINE** command and its options.

Introduction to Drawing Polylines

The **PLINE** command is used to draw polylines and any related objects made up of line segments. Polylines have advantages over normal lines because of the following:

- They can be drawn as thick or tapered lines.
- Polylines have much more flexibility than lines drawn with the **TRACE** command.
- They can be used with any linetype.
- Polylines can be edited using advanced editing features.
- They can be drawn as closed polygons.
- Polylines have areas and perimeters that can be determined easily.

- They can be used to draw a single object comprised of arcs and straight lines of varying thicknesses.

The function of the **PLINE** command is similar to the function of the **LINE** command. There are, however, additional command options. Also, all segments of a polyline are treated as a single object. To draw a polyline, you can pick the **Polyline** button on the **Draw** toolbar, pick **Draw > Polyline**, or type PL or PLINE.

A line width of 0.0000 produces a line of minimum width. If this is acceptable, select the endpoint of the line segment. If additional line segments are drawn, the endpoint of the first line segment automatically becomes the starting point of the next line segment. When you are done drawing line segments, press [Enter] or [Esc] to end the **PLINE** command.

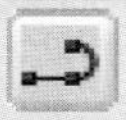

Setting the Polyline Width

If it is necessary to change the width of a line segment, enter the **PLINE** command, select the first point, and use the **Width** option. When the **Width** option is selected, you are asked to specify the starting and ending widths of the line. The starting width value becomes the default setting for the ending width. Therefore, to draw a line segment with one width, press [Enter] at the second prompt. If a tapered line segment is desired, enter different values for the starting and ending widths. After the widths are specified, the rubberband line from the first point reflects the width settings. **Figure 14-1** shows a 4″ long polyline with starting and ending widths of .25″. Notice that the starting and ending points of the line are located at the center of the line segment's width.

Drawing a Tapered Polyline

By entering different starting and ending width values, a tapered polyline is drawn. In the example shown in **Figure 14-2**, the starting width is .25 units, and the ending width is .5 units.

The **Width** option of the **PLINE** command can be used to draw an arrowhead. To do so, specify 0 as the starting width, and then use any desired ending width.

Using the Halfwidth Option

The **Halfwidth** option of the **PLINE** command allows you to specify the width of the polyline from the center to one side. After picking the first point of the polyline, enter the **Halfwidth** option. Specify starting and ending values. Notice that the polyline in **Figure 14-3** is twice as wide as the polyline in **Figure 14-2**, even though the same values are entered.

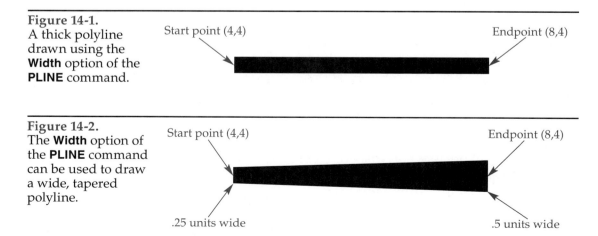

Figure 14-1.
A thick polyline drawn using the **Width** option of the **PLINE** command.

Start point (4,4)   Endpoint (8,4)

Figure 14-2.
The **Width** option of the **PLINE** command can be used to draw a wide, tapered polyline.

Start point (4,4)   Endpoint (8,4)

.25 units wide   .5 units wide

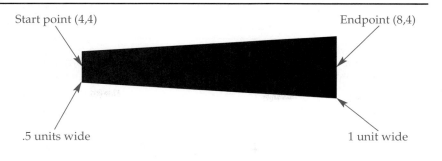

Figure 14-3.
Specifying the width of a polyline with the **Halfwidth** option of the **PLINE** command. Notice that a starting value of .25 produces a polyline width of .5 units and an ending value of .5 produces a polyline width of 1 unit.

Start point (4,4)   Endpoint (8,4)

.5 units wide   1 unit wide

Using the Length Option

The **Length** option of the **PLINE** command allows you to draw a polyline parallel to the previous polyline or line. After drawing a polyline, reissue the **PLINE** command and pick a starting point. Enter the **Length** option and give the desired length. The second polyline is drawn parallel to the previous polyline with the length you specified.

Undoing Previously Drawn Polylines

While inside the **PLINE** command, you can use the **Undo** option of the command to erase the last line segment. To do so, type U press [Enter]. Each time you use the **Undo** option, another line segment is erased. The segments are removed in reverse order (from the order in which they were drawn). This is a quick way to go back and correct the polyline while remaining in the **PLINE** command.

After you press [Enter], the last polyline segment drawn is automatically removed. The rubberband is attached to the end of the line segment that was drawn before the undone segment. You can now continue to draw additional line segments or undo another segment. You can use the **Undo** option to remove all the polyline segments up to the first point of the polyline. You cannot, however, specify a new first point for the polyline.

The **U** command (*not* the **Undo** option of the **PLINE** command) is also used to undo actions. It is, however, used to undo the actions of the previous command. After a command has been completed, pick the **Undo** button on the **Standard** toolbar, pick **Edit** > **Undo** *current*, press the [Ctrl]+[Z] key combination, or type U. The **U** command can also be activated by right-clicking in the drawing area and selecting **Undo** *current* from the shortcut menu. AutoCAD indicates which command was undone on the prompt line:

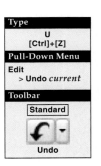

Type
U
[Ctrl]+[Z]

Pull-Down Menu
Edit
> Undo *current*

Toolbar
Standard

Undo

> Command: **U**↲
> PLINE
> Command:

In this example, the **PLINE** command was the last command. Therefore, it was the command whose actions were undone. You can reissue the **U** command to continue undoing commands, but you can only undo one command at a time. The commands must be undone in the order in which they were used. The **UNDO** command has a number of options not available with the **U** command, including the ability to undo more than one command. It is discussed later in this chapter.

Exercise 14-1   Complete the Exercise on the Student CD.

UNDO

Type
UNDO

Options
1
Auto
Control
BEgin
End
Mark
Back

As mentioned earlier in this chapter, the **UNDO** command is different from the **U** command. The **UNDO** command offers several options that allow you to undo a single command or a number of commands at once. After entering the command, the prompt reads Enter the number of operations to undo or [Auto/Control/BEgin/End/Mark/Back] <1>:. The default option allows you to designate the number of previous command sequences you wish to remove. For example, if you enter 1, the previous command sequence is undone. If you enter 2, the previous two command sequences are undone. AutoCAD tells you which commands were undone with a message on the prompt line.

Undo Options

There are several other options for the **UNDO** command. When the **Auto** option is on, any commands that are part of a group and used to perform a single operation are removed together. For example, when a command contains other commands, all the commands in that group are removed as one single command. The **Auto** option is active by default. If it is turned off, each command in a group of commands is treated individually.

The **Control** option allows you to specify how many of the **UNDO** command options you want active. You can even disable the **UNDO** command altogether. To use the **Control** option, type C after issuing the **UNDO** command. Selecting the **All** suboption keeps the full range of **UNDO** command options active. This is the default setting. The **None** suboption disables the **U** and **UNDO** commands. When the **U** command is entered, the prompt indicates the command is disabled. It then tells you to reactivate the **U** and **UNDO** commands by entering the **All** suboption of the **UNDO** command.

The **One** suboption limits **UNDO** to one operation only. If you attempt to enter a number higher than one when this suboption is active, you get an error message. You can type C at the Enter an option [Control] <1>: prompt to display the **Control** suboptions.

The **Combine** option determines whether or not **PAN** and **ZOOM** operations are combined together.

PROFESSIONAL TIP

When you use the **UNDO** command, AutoCAD maintains an "undo" file. This file saves previously used **UNDO** commands. All **UNDO** entries saved before disabling **UNDO** with the **None** suboption of the **Control** option are discarded. This frees up some disk space and may be valuable information for you to keep in mind if you ever get close to having a full disk. Using the **One** suboption of the **UNDO** command's **Control** option allows you to keep using the **U** and **UNDO** commands to a limited extent, while freeing up disk space holding current information about **UNDO**.

The **BEgin** and **End** options of the **UNDO** command are used together to perform several undo operations at once. They allow you to group a series of commands and treat them as a single command. Once the group is defined, the **U** command is then used to remove the commands that follow the **BEgin** option, but precede the **End** option. These options are useful if you can anticipate the possible removal of several commands entered consecutively. For example, if you think you may want to undo the next three commands altogether, start by entering the **BEgin** option of the **UNDO** command. Execute the three drawing commands. Then, enter the **End** option of the **UNDO** command. Since the three commands were executed between the **BEgin** and **End** options, the **U** command treats them as one command and undoes all three. The **BEgin** option must precede the command sequence and the **End** option must immediately follow the last command in the group to be undone.

The **Mark** option of the **UNDO** command allows you to insert a marker in the undo file. The **Back** option of the **UNDO** command undoes all commands issued after the marker was inserted. For example, if you do not want certain work to be undone by the **Back** option, enter the **Mark** option after completing the work. Then, continue working. To undo all work since the marker was inserted, reissue the **UNDO** command and enter the **Back** option. If no marker has been inserted, everything in the entire drawing is undone. AutoCAD issues the prompt This will undo everything. OK? <Y>. If you want everything you have drawn and edited to be undone, press [Enter]. If not, type N or NO and press [Enter], or press the [Esc] key.

PROFESSIONAL TIP

The **Mark** option of the **UNDO** command can be used to assist in the design process. For example, if you are working on a project and have completed a portion of the design, you can mark the spot with the **Mark** option and then begin work on the next design phase. If anything goes wrong with this part of the design, you can simply use the **Back** option of the **UNDO** command to remove everything back to the mark.

CAUTION

Be very careful when using the **Back** option of the **UNDO** command. Entering this option can undo everything in the entire drawing. You can bring back what you have undone if you use the **REDO** command immediately after using the **Back** option of the **UNDO** command. If you use any other command, even **REDRAW**, after using **UNDO Back**, the drawing is lost forever. The **REDO** command is explained later in this chapter.

Using the Undo List

The **Undo** list allows you to graphically select a number of commands to undo. Using this feature performs the same function as using the **UNDO** command and entering a number. Access the **Undo** list by picking the down arrow to the right of the **Undo** button on the **Standard** toolbar. A small window containing a sequential list of commands is displayed below the button. See **Figure 14-4**. The first (top) command in the list is the most recent command. Commands must be undone in reverse order. To select a number of commands, move the cursor down. The commands that will be undone are highlighted. To execute the undo operation, pick the last command to undo. All commands executed after the one selected will be undone, along with the selected command. Using this list is an easy way to undo back to an exact command without having to figure out how many commands have been issued since.

Figure 14-4.
The **Undo** list accessed from the **Standard** toolbar.

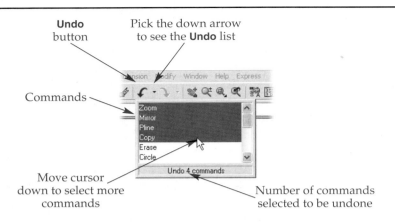

Undo button

Pick the down arrow to see the **Undo** list

Commands

Move cursor down to select more commands

Number of commands selected to be undone

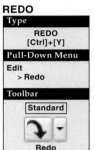

REDO

Type
REDO
[Ctrl]+[Y]

Pull-Down Menu
Edit
> Redo

Toolbar
Standard
Redo

Redoing the Undone

The **REDO** command is used to reverse the action of the **UNDO** and **U** commands. Type REDO, pick **Edit** > **Redo**, press the [Ctrl]+[Y] key combination, or pick the **Redo** button from the **Standard** toolbar to activate the command. The **REDO** command works only *immediately* after undoing something. The **REDO** command does *not* bring back polyline segments that were removed using the **Undo** option of the **PLINE** command.

If multiple undos are performed, any or all of the commands that were undone can be redone using the **REDO** list. Pick the down arrow next to the **Redo** button on the **Standard** toolbar. The list window is displayed, which shows the commands that were undone and can be redone. This list functions in the same way as the **UNDO** list discussed earlier.

Exercise 14-2 Complete the Exercise on the Student CD.

Filling Polylines and Traces

In the discussion of the **PLINE** command earlier in this chapter, the results were shown as if the objects were solid, or filled in. You can have polylines filled in, or you can show them as an outline. See **Figure 14-5**. These functions are controlled by the **Apply solid fill** setting in the **Display performance** area of the **Display** tab in the **Options** dialog box. This setting can also be changed by typing FILL or FILLMODE.

> **PROFESSIONAL TIP**
>
> When there are many wide polylines in a drawing, it is best to have solid fills turned off. This saves time when redrawing, regenerating, or plotting a check copy of the drawing. Activate solid fills for the final plotting.

Exercise 14-3 Complete the Exercise on the Student CD.

Figure 14-5.
Examples of the **FILL**
mode on and off.

FILL Mode On

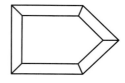

FILL Mode Off

Drawing Multilines

Multilines are objects that can consist of up to 16 parallel lines. The lines in a multiline are called *elements*. The **MLINE** command is used to draw multilines. A multiline configuration, or style, can be set using the **MLSTYLE** command. The default AutoCAD multiline style has two elements and is called STANDARD.

The **MLINE** command is accessed by picking **Draw > Multiline** or typing ML or MLINE. The prompts and options for the **MLINE** command are similar to those for the **LINE** command. You can use the **Close** option at the last prompt to close a polygon. Enter U during the command sequence to undo the previously drawn multiline segment. AutoCAD's STANDARD multiline style consists of two parallel lines. If you pick on one line to display grips, you can see that the entered coordinates correspond to both lines.

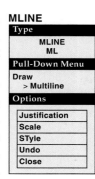

Multiline Justification

Multiline justification determines how the resulting lines are offset from the definition points provided. *Definition points* are the points you pick or coordinates you enter when drawing multilines. The justification is based on counterclockwise movement and can be specified only once during a single **MLINE** command sequence. The **Justification** options are **Top** (default), **Zero**, and **Bottom**.

To change the justification, type J at the first prompt displayed after entering the **MLINE** command. Enter the first letter of the desired justification format (T, Z, or B). The results of the three different **Justification** options using identical point entries are shown in **Figure 14-6**. Observe each orientation as you go through the following command sequence:

```
Command: ML or MLINE↵
Current settings: Justification = current, Scale = current, Style = current
Specify start point or [Justification/Scale/STyle]: J↵
Enter justification type [Top/Zero/Bottom] <current>: (type T, Z, or B, and press
    [Enter])
Current settings: Justification = specified value, Scale = current, Style = current
Specify start point or [Justification/Scale/STyle]: 2,2↵
Specify next point: 6,2↵
Specify next point or [Undo]: 6,6↵
Specify next point or [Close/Undo]: 2,6↵
Specify next point or [Close/Undo]: C↵
Command:
```

The current multiline justification setting is stored in the **CMLJUST** system variable. You can change the setting by entering 0 for the **Top** option, 1 for the **Zero** option, or 2 for the **Bottom** option.

Figure 14-6.
Multilines drawn using each of the three justification options. The definition points (represented by plus symbols) are picked in a counterclockwise rotation.

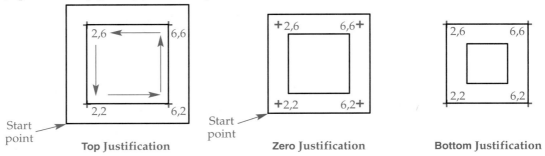

Top Justification   Zero Justification   Bottom Justification

PROFESSIONAL TIP

As shown in **Figure 14-6**, the multiline **Justification** options control the direction of the offsets for elements of the current style. The multiline segments in these examples are drawn in a counterclockwise direction. Unexpected results can sometimes occur when using the **MLINE** command, depending on the justification and drawing direction.

Exercise 14-4   Complete the Exercise on the Student CD.

Adjusting the Multiline Scale

The **Scale** option of the **MLINE** command is a multiplier applied to the offset distance specified in the multiline style. The multiline style is defined with the **MLSTYLE** command. The multiplier is stored in the **CMLSCALE** system variable. The example in the previous section used a scale setting of 1 (default). With this setting, the distance between multiline elements is equal to 1 times the offset distance. For example, if the offset distance is 0.5, the distance between multiline elements is 0.5 when the multiline scale is 1. If the multiline scale is specified as 2, however, the distance between multiline elements is 1 (0.5 × 2). Multilines drawn with different scale settings are shown in Figure 14-7.

Exercise 14-5   Complete the Exercise on the Student CD.

Changing the Multiline Style

You can specify the current multiline style by using the **STyle** option of the **MLINE** command. Before a new multiline style can be accessed, however, it must be created and saved using the **Multiline Style** dialog box. To use a saved multiline style, enter ST to access the **STyle** option, and then enter the style name.

Figure 14-7.
Multiline scale
settings.

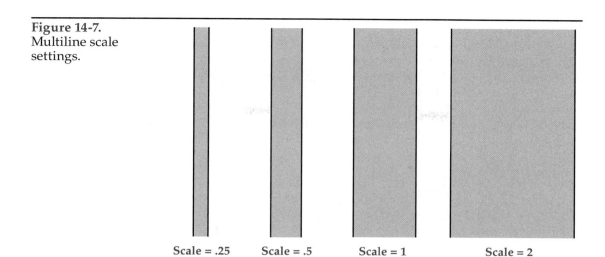

Scale = .25   Scale = .5   Scale = 1   Scale = 2

If you forget the name of the desired multiline style, you can enter ? at the Enter
mline style name or [?]: prompt. The text window is opened, and the currently loaded
multiline styles are listed. See **Figure 14-8.** Type the name of the style you want to use.

If you try to specify a multiline style that is not loaded, the **Load multiline style
from file** dialog box is displayed. You can look for the desired multiline style in the
acad.mln file library, or you can pick the **Tools** button and then **Find...** to open the **Find:**
dialog box.

Creating Multiline Styles

Multiline styles are defined using the **Multiline Style** dialog box. The current style
is stored in the **CMLSTYLE** system variable. The **Multiline Style** dialog box can be
accessed by picking **Format** > **Multiline Style...** from the pull-down menu or by typing
MLSTYLE.

MLSTYLE

Type	
	MLSTYLE
Pull-Down Menu	
Format	
	> Multiline Style...

The **Multiline Style** dialog box is shown in **Figure 14-9.** This is where multiline
styles can be defined, edited, and saved. Styles can be saved to an external file so they
can be used in other drawings. The image tile in the lower area of the **Multiline Style**
dialog box displays a representation of the selected multiline style.

Picking the **New...** button in the **Multiline Style** dialog box displays the **Create New
Multiline Style** dialog box shown in **Figure 14-10.** In the **New Style Name:** text box,
enter a name for the new multiline style. The properties from an existing style can be
used for the new style by selecting it from the **Start With:** drop-down list.

Once a name has been entered, the **Continue** button is active. Picking this button
opens the **New Multiline Style** dialog box. The options in this dialog box define the
appearance of the multiline. See **Figure 14-11.** The **Description:** field is optional, but it
can be used to enter a brief description of the multiline style.

Figure 14-8.
A list of loaded
multiline styles can
be displayed in the
text window.

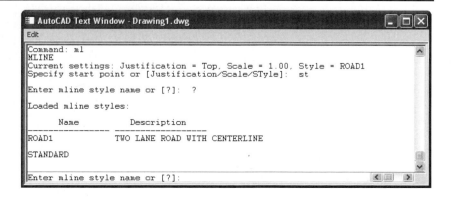

Figure 14-9.
The **Multiline Style** dialog box is used to define, edit, and save multiline styles.

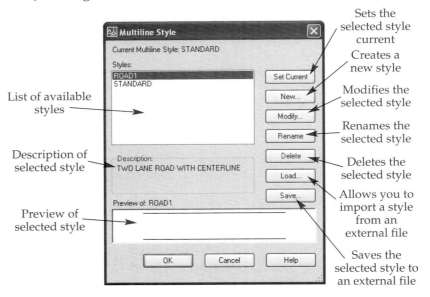

List of available styles

Description of selected style

Preview of selected style

Sets the selected style current

Creates a new style

Modifies the selected style

Renames the selected style

Deletes the selected style

Allows you to import a style from an external file

Saves the selected style to an external file

Figure 14-10.
To create a new multiline style, a name and existing multiline style settings are specified in the **Create New Multiline Style** dialog box.

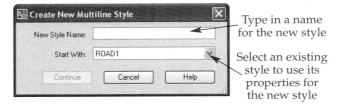

Type in a name for the new style

Select an existing style to use its properties for the new style

Figure 14-11.
The options in the **New Multiline Style** dialog box control all the settings for a multiline.

Description of the style

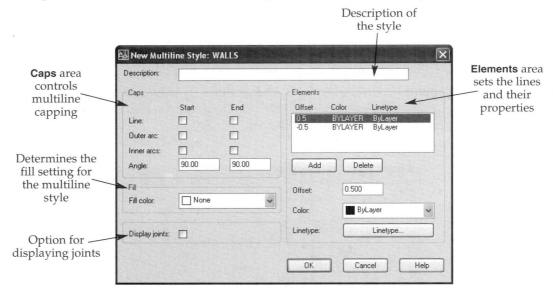

Caps area controls multiline capping

Determines the fill setting for the multiline style

Option for displaying joints

Elements area sets the lines and their properties

Using the caps, fill, and joints settings

The settings in the **Caps** area control the placement of caps on multilines. *Caps* are lines connecting the corresponding vertices of the beginning or ending points of the multiline elements. Using the check boxes, caps can be set at the start points, endpoints, or both. Several examples of different cap options are shown in **Figure 14-12**. The caps can be drawn as arcs. Arcs can be set to connect the ends of the outermost elements only, pairs of inner elements, or both the outer and inner elements. There must be at least two multiline elements for outer arcs to be drawn. Arcs are drawn tangent to the elements they connect. You can change the angle of the caps relative to the direction of the multiline elements. To do this, enter values in the **Angle:** text boxes. There is a text box for the start points, and there is another one for the endpoints.

The **Fill color:** setting in the **Fill** area allows a solid multiline to be created. When the **Fill color:** setting is set to **None**, there is no fill. A fill can be specified by selecting a color from the **Fill color:** drop-down list. Multilines drawn with and without fills are shown in **Figure 14-13**.

When **Display joints:** is checked, joints are displayed on the multiline. *Joints* are lines connecting the vertices of adjacent multiline elements. They are also referred to as *miters*. Multilines drawn with and without joints are shown in **Figure 14-14**.

Setting the element properties

The **Elements** area is where more elements (lines) can be added or deleted from the multiline style and the properties of each element are specified. The options in this area allow you to change properties including linetype, color, and offset. Once the properties have been set, pick **OK** to apply the properties to the new multiline style. The new style is then added to the **Multiline Style** dialog box.

Exercise 14-6   Complete the Exercise on the Student CD.

Figure 14-12.
Various cap options used with multilines.

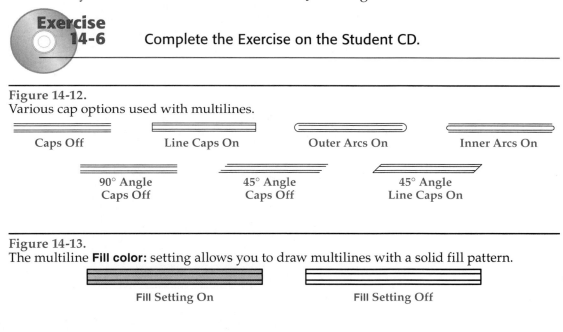

Caps Off   Line Caps On   Outer Arcs On   Inner Arcs On

90° Angle   45° Angle   45° Angle
Caps Off   Caps Off   Line Caps On

Figure 14-13.
The multiline **Fill color:** setting allows you to draw multilines with a solid fill pattern.

Fill Setting On   Fill Setting Off

Figure 14-14.
Multilines can be drawn with or without displayed joints.

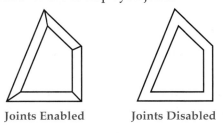

Joints Enabled   Joints Disabled

Editing Multilines

MLEDIT

Type
MLEDIT

Pull-Down Menu
Modify
> Object
> Multiline...

The **MLEDIT** command permits limited editing operations for multiline objects. To display the **Multilines Edit Tools** dialog box, pick **Modify** > **Object** > **Multiline...** from the pull-down menu or type MLEDIT. See **Figure 14-15**. This dialog box contains four columns of image buttons. Each column contains three image buttons of related command options. The image on each button gives you an example of what to expect when using the editing option.

Once you pick an image button, the dialog box is closed. You are prompted to continue with the command. The command options are described in the following sections.

Editing Intersections

The first (left) column in the **Multilines Edit Tools** dialog box displays three different types of multiline intersections. Picking a button allows you to create the type of intersection shown. The effects of the buttons in the first column are shown in **Figure 14-16** and described below.

- **Closed Cross.** When using this option, the first multiline selected is called the background, and the second multiline is called the foreground. A *closed cross* is created by trimming the background, while the foreground remains unchanged. The trimming is apparent, not actual. This means the line visibility of the background multiline is changed, but it is still a single multiline.

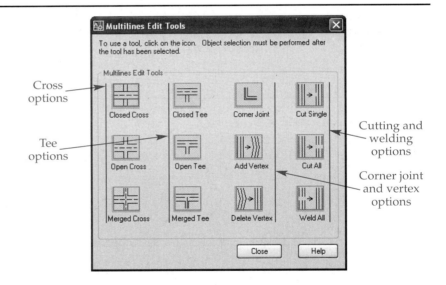

Figure 14-15.
The **Multilines Edit Tools** dialog box has twelve different options. Refer to the text for an explanation of each option.

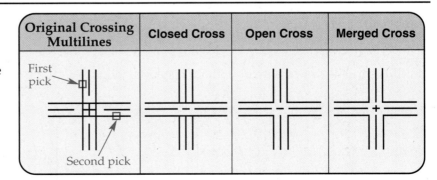

Figure 14-16.
Creating a **Closed Cross**, **Open Cross**, and **Merged Cross** intersection with the **MLEDIT** command.

- **Open Cross.** Select the **Open Cross** image button to trim all the elements of the first multiline and only the outer elements of the second multiline, as shown in **Figure 14-16.** The command sequence is the same as that used for the **Closed Cross** option.
- **Merged Cross.** The **Merged Cross** image button allows you to trim the outer elements of both multilines. The inner elements are not changed. See **Figure 14-16.**

Exercise 14-7   Complete the Exercise on the Student CD.

Editing Tees

The image buttons in the second column of the **Multilines Edit Tools** dialog box are used for editing multiline tees. The results of using the tee options are illustrated in **Figure 14-17.** The three options are the following:

- **Closed Tee.** Pick the **Closed Tee** option to have AutoCAD trim or extend the first selected multiline to its intersection with the second multiline.
- **Open Tee.** The **Open Tee** option is similar to the **Closed Tee** option. It allows you to trim the elements where a trimmed or extended multiline intersects with another multiline. The first pick specifies the multiline to trim or extend, and the second pick specifies the intersecting multiline. The intersecting multiline is trimmed and left open where the two multilines join.
- **Merged Tee.** The **Merged Tee** option is similar to the **Open Tee** option. It trims the intersecting multiline after the first multiline is trimmed or extended. The inner elements, however, are joined. This creates an open appearance with the outer elements, while merging the inner elements.

Exercise 14-8   Complete the Exercise on the Student CD.

Editing Corner Joints and Multiline Vertices

The image buttons in the third column of the **Multilines Edit Tools** dialog box provide options for creating corner joints and editing multiline vertices. The three options are the following:

- **Corner Joint.** This option allows you to create a corner joint between two multilines. The first multiline is trimmed or extended to its intersection with the second multiline, as shown in **Figure 14-18.**

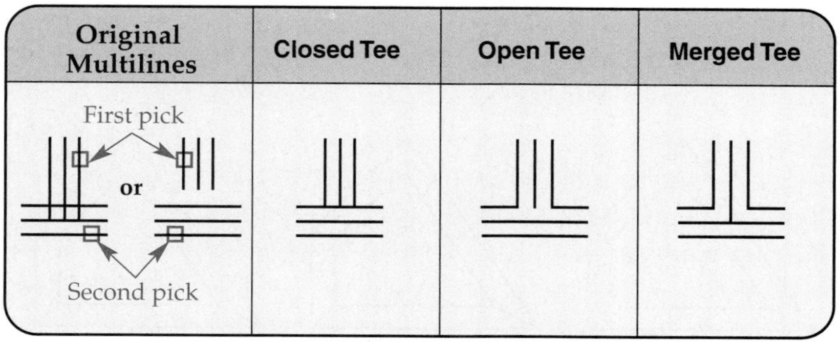

Figure 14-17.
Using the tee options of the **MLEDIT** command to edit multiline tees.

Original Multilines	Closed Tee	Open Tee	Merged Tee
First pick or Second pick			

Figure 14-18.
A corner joint can be created between two multilines using the **Corner Joint** option of the **MLEDIT** command.

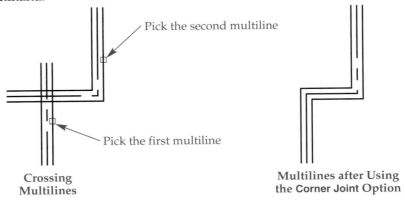

Pick the second multiline

Pick the first multiline

Crossing
Multilines

Multilines after Using
the **Corner Joint** Option

- **Add Vertex.** This option adds a vertex to an existing multiline at the location you pick. See **Figure 14-19.** The command sequence differs slightly from the sequences used with the other **MLEDIT** options. After you select the **Add Vertex** option, you are prompted to pick a location for the vertex.
- **Delete Vertex.** This option allows you to remove a vertex from an existing multiline. The vertex closest to the location you pick is deleted. See **Figure 14-19.** The command sequence is the same as for the **Add Vertex** option.

Exercise 14-9 Complete the Exercise on the Student CD.

Cutting and Welding Multilines

The fourth column of image buttons in the **Multilines Edit Tools** dialog box is used for *cutting* a portion out of a single multiline element or the entire multiline. The spaces between multiline elements can also be connected. AutoCAD refers to the connecting operation as *welding.* The **MLEDIT** cutting and welding options are the following:

- **Cut Single.** This option allows you to cut a single multiline element between two specified points, as shown in **Figure 14-20.** Cutting only affects the visibility of elements and does not separate a multiline object. The multiline is still a single object. After selecting the **Cut Single** option, you are prompted to pick the cutting points.

Figure 14-19.
The **Add Vertex** and **Delete Vertex** options of the **MLEDIT** command are used to edit multiline vertices.

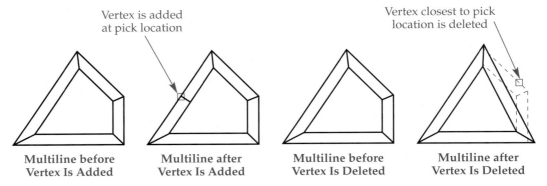

Vertex is added
at pick location

Vertex closest to pick
location is deleted

Multiline before
Vertex Is Added

Multiline after
Vertex Is Added

Multiline before
Vertex Is Deleted

Multiline after
Vertex Is Deleted

Figure 14-20.
The **MLEDIT** cutting
options allow you to
cut single multiline
elements or entire
multilines between
two specified points.

Original Multiline	Cut Single	Cut All
	Pick points	

- **Cut All.** This option cuts all elements of a multiline between specified points.
  See **Figure 14-20**. The multiline is still a single object, even though it appears to
  be separated.
- **Weld All.** This option allows you to repair all cuts in a multiline. Select the **Weld
  All** button, and select a point on each side of the cut multiline. The multiline is
  restored to its precut condition.

PROFESSIONAL TIP

Multiline objects can be converted to individual line
segments with the **EXPLODE** command. This command is
explained in Chapter 22.

Exercise
14-10   Complete the Exercise on the Student CD.

LEGACY NOTE

The **TRACE** command creates objects similar to polylines.
However, the **TRACE** command is difficult to access and
the trace objects are difficult to edit. In nearly all situations,
it is better to use polylines in your drawings.

The **SKETCH** command provides an alternative method of
drawing objects with multiple segments. This command
has some unique options and methods. In most situations,
using lines, polylines, and splines in the drawing is more
effective than using the **SKETCH** command.

Chapter Test

Answer the following questions. Write your answers on a separate sheet of paper or complete the electronic chapter test on the Student CD.

1. Give the command and entries needed to draw a multiline with zero justification and the saved style ROAD1.
   A. Command: _____
   B. Current settings: Justification = *current*, Scale = *current*, Style = *current*
      Specify start point or [Justification/Scale/STyle]: _____
   C. Enter mline style name or [?]: _____
   D. Current settings: Justification = *current*, Scale = *current*, Style = ROAD1
      Specify start point or [Justification/Scale/STyle]: _____
   E. Enter justification type [Top/Zero/Bottom] <*current*>: _____
   F. Current settings: Justification = Zero, Scale = *current*, Style = ROAD1
      Specify start point or [Justification/Scale/STyle]: _____
   G. Specify next point: _____
   H. Specify next point or [Undo]: _____
2. How do you draw a filled arrow using the **PLINE** command?
3. Name two commands that can be used to draw wide lines.
4. Which **PLINE** command option allows you to specify the width from the center to one side?
5. What is an advantage of leaving solid fills turned off?
6. What is the difference between picking **Edit** > **Undo** and entering the **UNDO** command?
7. Name the command used to bring back an object that was previously removed using **UNDO**.
8. Name the **MLINE** command option that establishes how the resulting lines are offset based on the definition points provided.
9. Name the option that controls the multiplier value for the offset distances specified with the **MLINE** command.
10. How do you access the **Multiline Style** dialog box?
11. Define *caps*.
12. Define *joints*.
13. What is displayed when you enter the **MLEDIT** command?
14. How do you access one of the **MLEDIT** options?
15. List the three options used for editing multiline intersections with the **MLEDIT** command.
16. Name the **MLEDIT** option in which the intersecting multiline is trimmed and left open after the first multiline is trimmed or extended to its intersection with the intersecting multiline.
17. Name the **MLEDIT** option that allows you to remove a vertex from an existing multiline.
18. Name the **MLEDIT** option that lets you remove a portion from an individual multiline element.
19. Name the **MLEDIT** option that removes all the elements of a multiline between two specified points.
20. Name the **MLEDIT** option that repairs all cuts in a multiline between two selected points.

Drawing Problems

1. Use the **PLINE** command to draw the following object with a .032 line width. Do not draw dimensions. Save the drawing as P14-1.

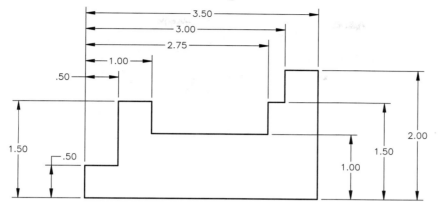

2. Use the **PLINE** command to draw the following object with a .032 line width. Do not draw dimensions. Save the drawing as P14-2.

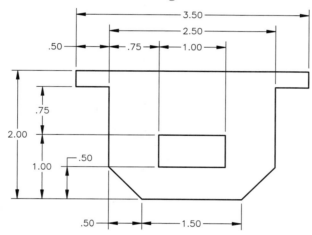

3. Use the **PLINE** command to draw the following object with a .032 line width. Do not draw dimensions.
   A. Deactivate solid fills and use the **REGEN** command, and reactivate solid fills and reissue the **REGEN** command.
   B. Observe the difference with solid fills enabled.
   C. Save the drawing as P14-3.

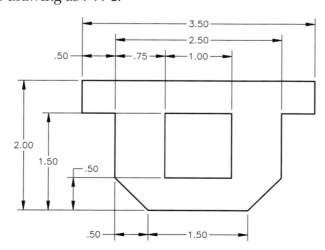

4. Use the **PLINE** command to draw the filled rectangle shown below. Do not draw dimensions. Save the drawing as P14-4.

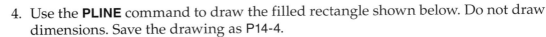

5. Draw the objects shown below. Do not draw dimensions. Use the **UNDO** command to remove Object B. To bring Object B back, use the **REDO** command. Save the drawing as P14-5.

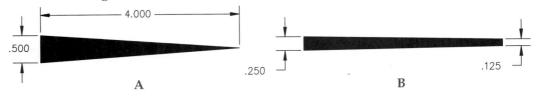

6. Draw the object shown below. Do not draw dimensions. Set decimal units; .25 grid spacing; .0625 snap spacing; and limits of 11,8.5. Save the drawing as P14-6.

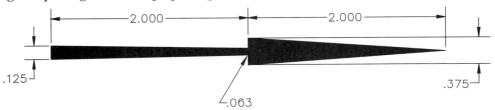

7. Open P4-7 and add the arrowheads. Draw one arrowhead using the **PLINE** command, and then use the necessary editing commands to place the rest. Refer to the original problem. Save the drawing as P14-7.

8. Draw the objects shown using the **MLINE** command. Use the justification options indicated with each illustration. Set the limits to 11,8.5; grid spacing to .50; snap spacing to .25; and the offset for the multiline elements to .125. Do not add text or dimensions. Save the drawing as P14-8.

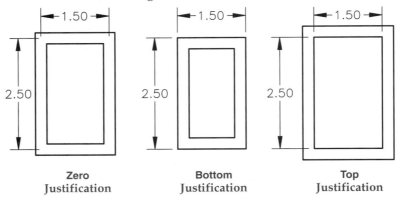

9. Draw the partial floor plan shown using the multiline commands. Carefully observe how the dimensions correlate with the multiline elements to determine your justification settings. Also, use the appropriate cap and multiline editing options. Use architectural units. Set the limits to 88",68"; grid spacing to 24"; and snap spacing to 12". Make all walls 6" thick. Do not add text or dimensions. Save the drawing as P14-9.

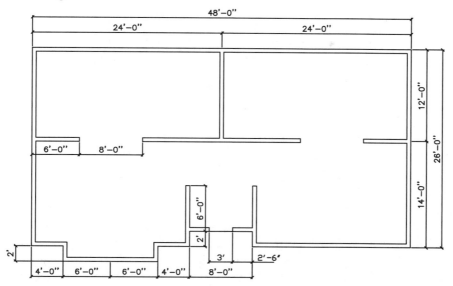

10. Draw the proposed subdivision map using the multiline commands. The roads are 30' wide. Use a centerline linetype for the center of each road. Adjust the linetype scale as needed. Do not include dimensions. Save the drawing as P14-10.

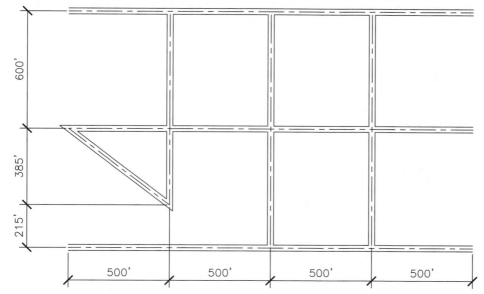

11. Draw the partial floor plan shown below using multilines for the walls. Do not dimension the floor plan. Save the drawing as P14-11.

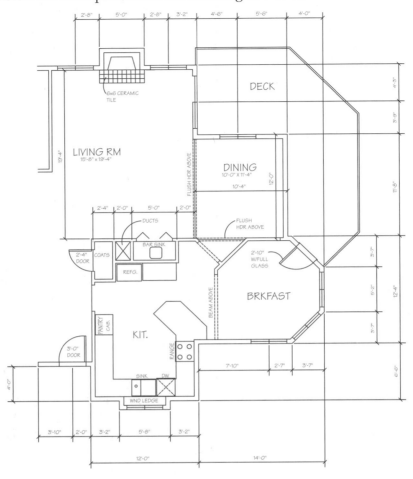

12. Draw the proposed electrical circuit using the multiline commands. Establish a line offset proportional to the given layout. Use a phantom linetype for the center of each run. Do not draw the grid, which is provided as a drawing aid. Save the drawing as P14-12.

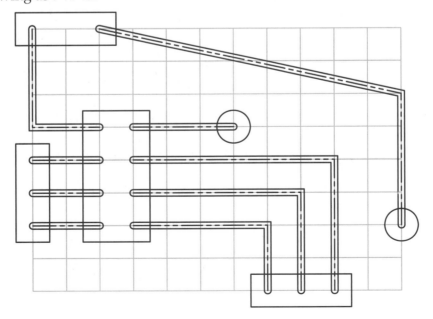

13. Draw the flow chart shown below. Use polylines to draw the connecting lines, arrows, and diamonds. Use Grid mode to locate points. Save the drawing as P14-13.

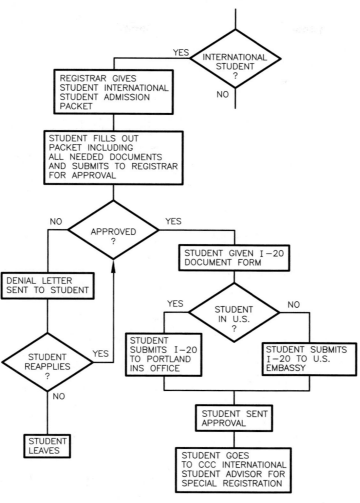

14. Draw the flow chart shown below. Use polylines to draw the connecting lines, arrows, and diamonds. Use Grid mode to locate points. Save the drawing as P14-14.

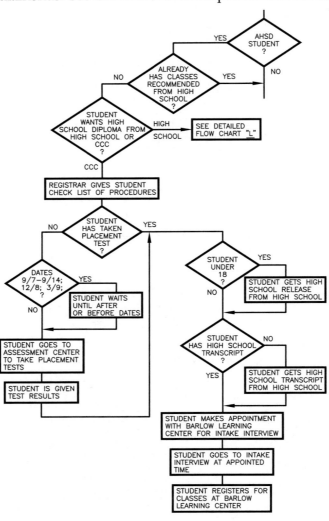

Drawing and Editing Polylines and Splines

Learning Objectives

After completing this chapter, you will be able to do the following:

- Use the **PLINE** command to draw straight and curved polylines.
- Edit existing polylines with the **PEDIT** command.
- Describe the function of each **PEDIT** command option.
- Use the **EXPLODE** command to change polylines into individual line and arc segments.
- Draw and edit spline curves.
- Create a polyline boundary.

PLINE	
Type	
	PLINE
	PL
Pull-Down Menu	
Draw	
	> Polyline
Toolbar	
	Draw
	Polyline
Options	
Arc	
Halfwidth	
Length	
Undo	
Width	

The **PLINE** command was introduced in Chapter 14 as a way to draw thick and tapered lines. The discussion focused on line-related options, such as **Width**, **Halfwidth**, and **Length**. The editing functions were limited to the **ERASE** and **UNDO** commands. As you will find in this chapter, the **PLINE** command can also be used to draw a variety of special shapes, limited only by your imagination. This chapter explains how to use the **PLINE** command to create polyline arcs and introduces advanced editing commands for polylines. It also discusses how to convert polylines into smooth curves and how to create and edit true spline curves. The **PLINE** command can be accessed by picking the **Polyline** button in the **Draw** toolbar, selecting **Draw > Polyline**, or typing PL or PLINE.

Drawing Polyline Arcs

The **Arc** option of the **PLINE** command is similar to the **ARC** command, except that the **Width** and **Halfwidth** options of the **PLINE** command can be used to set an arc width. The arc width can range from 0 to the radius of the arc. A polyline arc can also be drawn with different starting and ending widths, using the **Width** option, **Figure 15-1**. The **Width** and **Arc** options can be entered in either order.

A polyline arc continued from a previous line or polyline is tangent to the last object drawn by default. The arc's center is determined automatically, but you can pick a new center. You can also specify settings with one of the **Arc** suboptions of the **PLINE** command. These suboptions are **Angle**, **CEnter**, **Direction**, **Radius**, **Second pt** (second point), and **CLose**. The options are very similar to the **ARC** command options and are explained in the following sections.

Figure 15-1.
A polyline arc with
different starting
and ending widths.

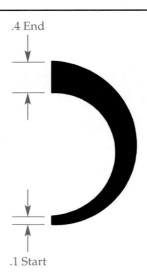

.4 End

.1 Start

Specifying the Included Angle

The **Angle** suboption inside the **Arc** option of the **PLINE** command sequence specifies an included angle for a polyline arc. The angle value is based on the number of degrees in a circle. Therefore, a value of 180 draws a half circle, 270 draws 3/4 of a circle, and so on. The values 0 and 360 cannot be entered. A negative value draws the arc in a clockwise direction. **Figure 15-2** shows a polyline arc with an included angle of 60°.

Using the Center Suboption

When a polyline arc is drawn as a continuation of a polyline segment, the center point of the arc is automatically calculated. You may want to pick a new center point if the polyline arc does not continue from another object or if the center point calculated is not suitable. The **CEnter** suboption allows you to specify a new center point for the arc. When you pick the center point for the polyline arc, the arc's radius is set as the distance from the center point to the starting point. You then have three methods to complete the polyline arc:

- Pick the endpoint of the arc.
- Use the **Angle** option to specify the included angle.
- Use the **Length** option to specify the chord length of the arc.

Figure 15-2.
Drawing a polyline
arc with a 60°
included angle
specified with **Angle**
suboption.

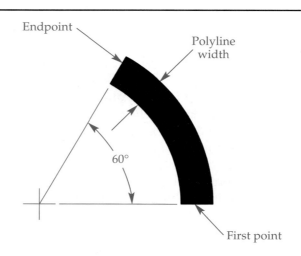

Endpoint

Polyline
width

60°

First point

Using the Direction Suboption

The **Direction** suboption alters the bearing of the arc. By default, a polyline arc is created tangent to the last polyline, arc, or line drawn. The **Direction** suboption is used to change this and can also be entered when you are drawing an unconnected polyline arc. It functions much like the **Direction** option of the **ARC** command.

After selecting the **Direction** suboption inside the **Arc** option of the **PLINE** command, you specify the tangent direction for the start point of the arc. You can enter a numeric angle value, or you can pick a point to define the angle (relative to the start point).

Drawing a Polyline Arc by Radius

Polyline arcs can be drawn by giving the arc's radius. Enter the **Radius** suboption inside the **Arc** option of the **PLINE** command sequence.

Specifying a Three-Point Polyline Arc

A three-point polyline arc can be drawn using the **Second pt** suboption. After entering the **Second pt** suboption, you are prompted to pick the second point and endpoint of the arc.

Using the Close Suboption

The **CLose** suboption saves drafting time by automatically adding the last segment to close a polygonal shape. Using this suboption inside the **Arc** option of the **PLINE** command sequence closes the shape with a polyline arc segment, rather than a straight polyline. See **Figure 15-3**. CL is entered at the prompt line to distinguish this option from the **CEnter** suboption.

Exercise 15-1   Complete the Exercise on the Student CD.

Figure 15-3.
Using the **CLose** suboption inside the **Arc** option of the **PLINE** command sequence to close a polygonal shape.

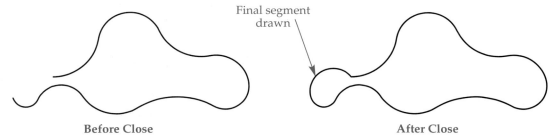

Final segment drawn

Before Close

After Close

Revising Polylines Using the Pedit Command

Polylines are drawn as multiple segments. A single polyline may be drawn as a straight segment joined to an arc segment and completed with another straight segment. Even though you have drawn separate segments, AutoCAD puts them all together. The result is one polyline treated as a single object. When editing a polyline, you must edit it as one object or divide it into its individual segments. These changes are made with the **PEDIT** and **EXPLODE** commands. The **EXPLODE** command is discussed later in this chapter.

PEDIT

Type
PEDIT
PE

Pull-Down Menu
Modify
> Object
> Polyline

Toolbar
Modify II
Edit Polyline

Options
Close/Open
Join
Width
Edit vertex
Fit
Spline
Decurve
Ltype gen
Undo

The **PEDIT** command is accessed by picking the **Edit Polyline** button on the **Modify II** toolbar, typing PE or PEDIT, or selecting **Modify > Object > Polyline**. You can also select a polyline, right-click in the drawing area, and choose **Polyline Edit** from the shortcut menu.

When selecting a wide polyline, you must pick on the edge of a polyline segment rather than in the center. If you want to edit more than one polyline, type M before selecting to access the **Multiple** option. If the object you select is a line or an arc object, AutoCAD issues a prompt that gives you the option to turn it into a polyline. The command then continues. Its options are explained later in this chapter.

You can have AutoCAD automatically turn lines and arcs into polylines without displaying the prompt. The value of the **PEDITACCEPT** system variable controls this feature. When it is set to 0, you are prompted when a line or an arc is selected. AutoCAD automatically turns selected lines and arcs into polylines when the system variable is set to 1. The command then continues normally.

Circles drawn with the **CIRCLE** command cannot be changed to polylines for editing purposes. Polyline circles can be created by using the **Arc** option of the **PLINE** command and drawing two 180° arcs or by using the **DONUT** command.

PROFESSIONAL TIP  A group of connected lines and arcs can be turned into a continuous polyline by using the **Join** option of the **PEDIT** command. This option is discussed later in this chapter.

Revising a Polyline as One Unit

A polyline can be edited as a single object, or it can be divided into individual segments. The segments can then be revised individually. This section discusses the options for changing the entire polyline. There is no default option for the **PEDIT** command; you must select one of the options.

Opening and Closing a Polyline

You may decide you need to close an open polyline or open a closed polyline. These functions are performed with the **Open** and **Close** options of the **PEDIT** command. Open and closed polylines are shown in **Figure 15-4**.

The **Open** option is only available if the polyline was closed using the **Close** option of the **PLINE** command. It is not displayed if the polyline was closed by manually drawing the final segment. Instead, the **Close** option is displayed. If you select an open polyline, the **Close** option is displayed instead of the **Open** option. Enter this option to close the polyline.

Joining Polylines to Other Polylines, Lines, and Arcs

Connected polylines, lines, and arcs can be joined to create a single polyline. This is done with the **Join** option of the **PEDIT** command. The **Join** option works only if the polyline and other existing objects meet *exactly*. They cannot cross, nor can there be any spaces or breaks between the objects. See **Figure 15-5**.

Select each object to be joined or group the objects with one of the selection set options. The original polyline can be included in the selection set, but it does not need to be. See **Figure 15-6**. If you select lines and arcs to join, AutoCAD automatically converts these objects to polylines, regardless of the **PEDITACCEPT** setting.

Figure 15-4.
Open and closed polylines.

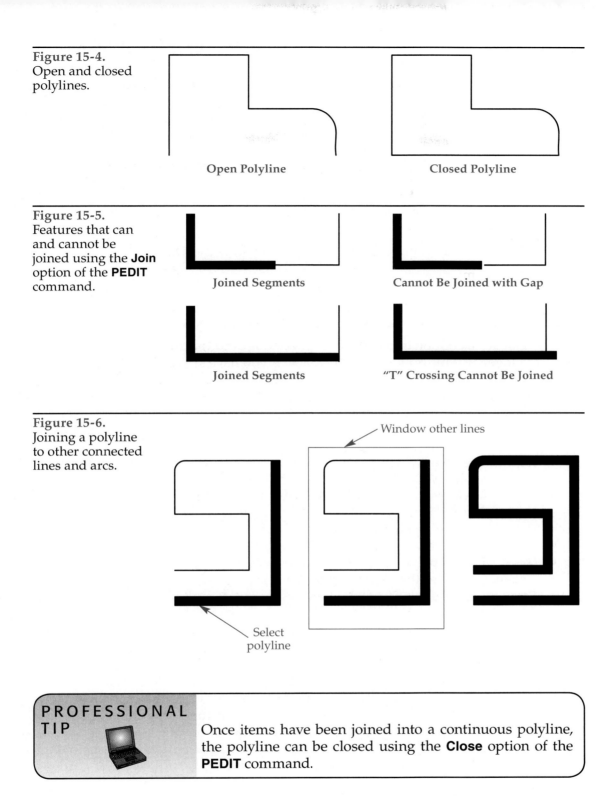

Open Polyline   Closed Polyline

Figure 15-5.
Features that can and cannot be joined using the **Join** option of the **PEDIT** command.

Joined Segments   Cannot Be Joined with Gap

Joined Segments   "T" Crossing Cannot Be Joined

Figure 15-6.
Joining a polyline to other connected lines and arcs.

Window other lines

Select polyline

PROFESSIONAL TIP

Once items have been joined into a continuous polyline, the polyline can be closed using the **Close** option of the **PEDIT** command.

Changing the Width of a Polyline

The **Width** option of the **PEDIT** command allows you to change a polyline width to a new width. The width of the original polyline can be constant, or it can vary. *All* segments will be changed, however, to the constant width you specify. An unedited polyline and a new polyline after using the **Width** option of the **PEDIT** command are shown in **Figure 15-7.** The width of donuts can be changed using this procedure as well.

Figure 15-7.
Changing the width
of a polyline.

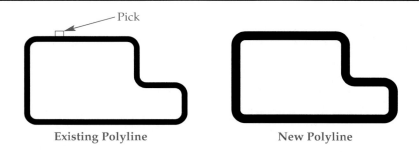

Pick

Existing Polyline

New Polyline

Exercise
15-2

Complete the Exercise on the Student CD.

Editing a Polyline Vertex or Point of Tangency

The **Edit vertex** option of the **PEDIT** command is used to edit polyline vertices and points of tangency. This option is not available if you have selected multiple polylines for editing. A polyline *vertex* is where straight polyline segments meet, and a *point of tangency* is where straight polyline segments or polyline arcs join other polyline arcs. When you enter the **Edit vertex** option, an "X" marker appears on the screen at the first polyline vertex or point of tangency. The **Edit vertex** option has 10 suboptions, as explained in the following:

- **Next.** Moves the "X" marker on screen to the next vertex or point of tangency on the polyline.
- **Previous.** Moves the "X" marker to the previous vertex or point of tangency on the polyline.
- **Break.** Breaks the polyline between two vertices or points of tangency.
- **Insert.** Adds a new polyline vertex at a selected point.
- **Move.** Moves a polyline vertex to a new location.
- **Regen.** Generates the revised version of the polyline.
- **Straighten.** Straightens polyline arc segments or multiple segments between two points.
- **Tangent.** Specifies a tangent direction for curve fitting when using the **Fit** option of the **PEDIT** command.
- **Width.** Changes the width of a polyline segment.
- **eXit.** Returns to the **PEDIT** command prompt.

Only the current point identified by the "X" marker is affected by editing functions. In **Figure 15-8**, the marker is moved clockwise through the points using the **Next** option and counterclockwise using the **Previous** option. If you edit the vertices of a polyline and nothing appears to happen, use the **Regen** option to regenerate the polyline.

Making breaks in a polyline

You can break a polyline into two separate polylines with the **Break** option of the **Edit vertex** option of the **PEDIT** command. Once the **Edit vertex** option is entered, use the **Next** or **Previous** option to move the "X" marker to the first vertex where the polyline is to be broken. Enter the **Break** option. A marker is placed at the first break point. After moving to the second vertex of the break, enter the **Go** option.

The **Go** option instructs AutoCAD to remove the portion of the polyline between the two points. You can also break the polyline without removing a segment by specifying **Go** without moving to a second vertex. The results of the following command sequence are illustrated in **Figure 15-9**. The polyline was drawn clockwise.

AutoCAD and Its Applications—Basics

Figure 15-8.
Using the **Next** and **Previous** vertex editing options to specify polyline vertices. Note the different positions of the "X" marker.

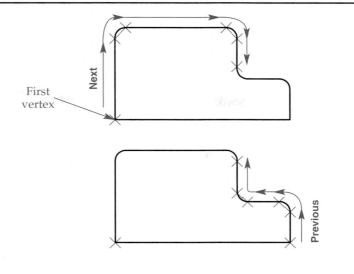

Figure 15-9.
Using the **Break** vertex editing option to break a polyline and remove a portion.

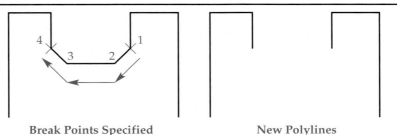

Break Points Specified   New Polylines

Enter a vertex editing option
[Next/Previous/Break/Insert/Move/Regen/Straighten/Tangent/Width/eXit] <N>: *(use* **Next** *to move to Point 1)*
Enter a vertex editing option
[Next/Previous/Break/Insert/Move/Regen/Straighten/Tangent/Width/eXit] <N>: **B**↵ *(specifies Point 1)*
Enter an option [Next/Previous/Go/eXit] <N>: **P**↵ *(specifies Point 2)*
Enter an option [Next/Previous/Go/eXit] <P>: ↵ *(specifies Point 3)*
Enter an option [Next/Previous/Go/eXit] <P>: ↵ *(specifies Point 4)*
Enter an option [Next/Previous/Go/eXit] <P>: **G**↵ *(breaks the polyline between Points 1 and 4)*
Enter a vertex editing option
[Next/Previous/Break/Insert/Move/Regen/Straighten/Tangent/Width/eXit] <P>:

Inserting a new vertex in a polyline

A new vertex can be added to a polyline using the **Insert** vertex editing option. The new vertex can be inserted on an existing polyline segment, but does not need to be. First, use the **Next** or **Previous** option to locate the vertex next to where you want the new vertex. After using the **Insert** option, pick the new vertex location. See **Figure 15-10.**

Moving a polyline vertex

The **Move** vertex editing option enables you to move a polyline vertex to a new location. The "X" marker must first be placed on the vertex you want to move. Enter the **Move** option and specify the new vertex location. See **Figure 15-11.**

Figure 15-10.
Using the **Insert** vertex editing option to add a new vertex to a polyline.

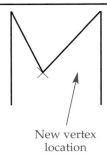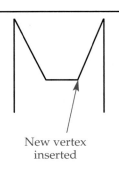

New vertex
location

New vertex
inserted

Figure 15-11.
Using the **Move** vertex editing option to place a polyline vertex at a new location.

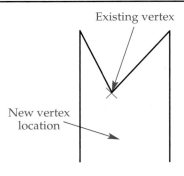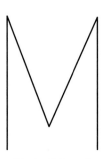

Existing vertex

New vertex
location

Vertex Moved

Straightening polyline segments or arcs

The **Straighten** vertex editing option allows you to straighten polyline segments or arcs between two points. Position the "X" marker at one end of the polyline segment to be straightened. Enter the **Straighten** option. The **Straighten** option has four suboptions: **Next**, **Previous**, **Go**, and **Exit**. Use the **Next** and **Previous** options to position the "X" mark at the end of the segment to be straightened. Then enter the **Go** option to straighten the polyline segment. If the "X" marker is not moved before G is entered, AutoCAD straightens the segment from the marked point to the next vertex. This provides a quick way to straighten an arc. See **Figure 15-12.**

Changing polyline segment widths

The **Width** vertex editing option is used to change the starting and ending widths of an individual polyline segment. To change a segment width, move the "X" marker to the beginning vertex of the segment to be altered. Enter the **Width** option and specify the new width.

Figure 15-12.
The **Straighten** vertex editing option is used to straighten polyline segments.

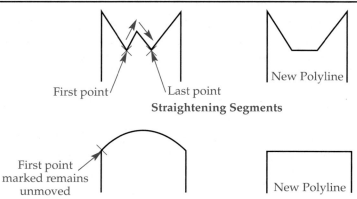

First point

Last point

New Polyline

Straightening Segments

First point
marked remains
unmoved

New Polyline

Straightening an Arc

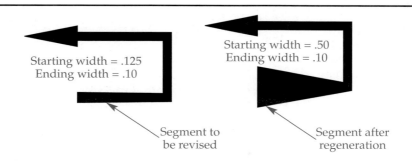

Figure 15-13.
Changing the width of a polyline segment with the **Width** vertex editing option. Use the **Regen** option to display the change.

Starting width = .125
Ending width = .10

Starting width = .50
Ending width = .10

Segment to be revised

Segment after regeneration

The default starting width value is the current width of the segment to be changed. The default ending width value is the same as the revised starting width. If nothing appears to happen to the segment when you specify the ending width and press [Enter], enter the **Regen** option to have AutoCAD draw the revised polyline. See Figure 15-13.

Exercise 15-3   Complete the Exercise on the Student CD.

Making Smooth Curves out of Polylines

In some situations, you may need to convert a polyline into a series of smooth curves. One example of this is a graph. A graph may show a series of plotted points as a smooth curve rather than straight segments. This process is called *curve fitting* and is accomplished using the **Fit** option and the **Tangent** vertex editing option of the **PEDIT** command.

The **Fit** option allows you to construct pairs of arcs passing through control points. You can specify the control points, or you can simply use the vertices of the polyline. The more closely spaced the control points are, the smoother the curve will be.

Prior to curve fitting, each vertex can be given a tangent direction. AutoCAD then fits the curve based on the tangent directions you set. You do not, however, need to enter tangent directions. Specifying tangent directions is a way to edit vertices when the **Fit** option of the **PEDIT** command does not produce the best results.

The **Tangent** vertex editing option is used to edit tangent directions. After entering the **PEDIT** command and the **Edit vertex** option, move the "X" marker to each vertex to be changed. Enter the **Tangent** option for each specified vertex, and enter a tangent direction in degrees or pick a point in the expected direction. An arrow placed at the vertex then indicates the direction you chose.

Continue by moving the marker to each vertex you want to change, entering the **Tangent** option for each vertex, and selecting a tangent direction. Once the tangent directions are given for all vertices to be changed, enter the **Fit** option of the **PEDIT** command.

You can also enter the **PEDIT** command, select a polyline, and then enter the **Fit** option without adjusting tangencies, if desired. The polyline shown in Figure 15-14 was made into a smooth curve using the **Fit** option. If the resulting curve does not look like what you had anticipated, enter the **Edit vertex** option. Make changes using the various vertex editing options, as necessary.

Using the Spline Option

When a polyline is edited with the **Fit** option of the **PEDIT** command, the resulting curve passes through each of the polyline's vertices. The **Spline** option of the **PEDIT** command also smoothes the corners of a straight-segment polyline. This option,

Figure 15-14.
Using the **Fit**
option of the **PEDIT**
command to turn
a polyline into a
smooth curve.

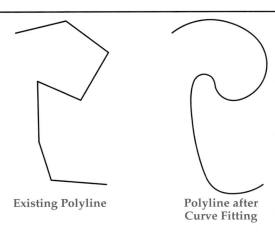

Existing Polyline   Polyline after
                           Curve Fitting

however, produces different results. The resulting curve passes through the first and last control points or vertices only. The curve *pulls* toward the other vertices, but does not pass through them.

The results of using the **Fit** and **Spline** options on a polyline are illustrated in **Figure 15-15**.

Straightening All Segments of a Polyline

The **Decurve** option of the **PEDIT** command returns a polyline edited with the **Fit** or **Spline** options to its original form. The information entered for tangent directions is kept, however, for future reference. You can also use the **Decurve** option to straighten the curved segments of a polyline. See **Figure 15-16**.

PROFESSIONAL TIP

If you make a mistake while editing a polyline, remember that the **Undo** option is available inside the **PEDIT** command. Using the **Undo** option more than once allows you to step backward through each operation.

Exercise
15-4   Complete the Exercise on the Student CD.

Figure 15-15.
A comparison of
polylines edited
with the **Fit** and
Spline options of the
PEDIT command.

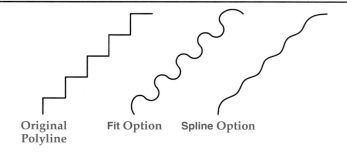

Original   Fit Option   Spline Option
Polyline

Figure 15-16.
The **Decurve** option of the **PEDIT** command is used to straighten the curved segments of a polyline.

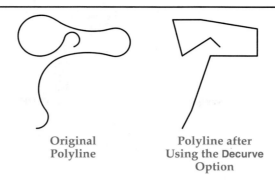

Original
Polyline

Polyline after
Using the **Decurve**
Option

Changing the Appearance of Polyline Linetypes

The **Ltype gen** (linetype generation) option of the **PEDIT** command determines how linetypes other than Continuous appear in relation to the vertices of a polyline. For example, when a Center linetype is used and the **Ltype gen** option is disabled, the polyline has a long dash at each vertex. When the **Ltype gen** option is activated, the polyline is generated with a constant pattern in relation to the polyline as a whole. The difference between having the **Ltype gen** option off and on is illustrated in Figure 15-17. Also shown are the effects these settings have on splined polylines.

You can also change the **Ltype gen** option setting for new polylines with the **PLINEGEN** system variable. This variable must be set before the polyline is drawn. Changing the setting does not affect existing polylines. The settings for the **PLINEGEN** system variable are 0 (off) and 1 (on).

Figure 15-17.
A comparison of polylines with the **Ltype gen** option of the **PEDIT** command on and off.

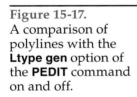
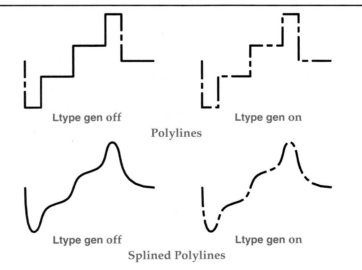

Ltype gen off

Ltype gen on

Polylines

Ltype gen off

Ltype gen on

Splined Polylines

Converting a Polyline into Individual Line and Arc Segments

A polyline is a single object composed of line and arc segments. The **EXPLODE** command allows you to change a polyline into a series of individual lines and arcs. You can then edit each segment individually. The resulting segments are not, however, polylines. When a wide polyline is exploded, the resulting line or arc is redrawn along the centerline of the original polyline. See **Figure 15-18.**

Figure 15-18.
Exploding a wide
polyline.

Original Polyline   Exploded Polyline

EXPLODE

Type
EXPLODE
X
Pull-Down Menu
Modify
> Explode
Toolbar
Modify

Explode

To explode an object, select **Modify** > **Explode**, pick the **Explode** button on the **Modify** toolbar, or type X or EXPLODE. You are then asked to select the objects to be exploded.

The **EXPLODE** command removes all width characteristics and tangency information. If you explode a wide polyline, AutoCAD reminds you of this fact. Using the **UNDO** command will bring back the polyline as it was.

Exercise 15-5 Complete the Exercise on the Student CD.

Additional Methods for Smoothing Polylines

The methods for smoothing polylines introduced earlier in this chapter focused on using the **Fit** and **Spline** options of the **PEDIT** command. With the **Fit** option, the resulting *fit curve* passes through the polyline vertices. The **Spline** option creates a *spline curve* that passes through the first and last control points or vertices. The resulting curve *pulls* toward the other vertices, but does not pass through them.

The **Spline** option creates a curve that approximates a true B-spline. AutoCAD's **SPLINE** command creates a true B-spline curve. You can choose between two types of calculations used by the **Spline** option to create the curve—cubic and quadratic. A *cubic curve* is extremely smooth. A *quadratic curve* is not as smooth as a cubic curve, but it is smoother than a curve produced with the **Fit** option. Like a cubic curve, a quadratic curve passes through the first and last control points. The remainder of the curve is tangent to the polyline segments between the intermediate control points, as shown in **Figure 15-19**.

The **SPLINETYPE** system variable determines whether AutoCAD draws cubic or quadratic curves. The default setting is 6. At this setting, a cubic curve is drawn when using the **Spline** option of the **PEDIT** command. If the **SPLINETYPE** system variable is set to 5, a quadratic curve is generated. The only valid values for **SPLINETYPE** are 5 and 6.

Exercise 15-6 Complete the Exercise on the Student CD.

The **SPLINESEGS** system variable controls the number of line segments used to construct spline curves. It can be set by typing SPLINESEGS or by entering a value in the **Segments in a polyline curve** text box in the **Display resolution** area of the **Display** tab of the **Options** dialog box. The **SPLINESEGS** default value is 8, which creates a fairly smooth spline curve with moderate regeneration time. If you decrease the value,

Figure 15-19.
A comparison of curves drawn with the **Fit** and **Spline** options of the **PEDIT** command. The **SPLINETYPE** system variable controls whether a quadratic or cubic curve is drawn with the **Spline** option.

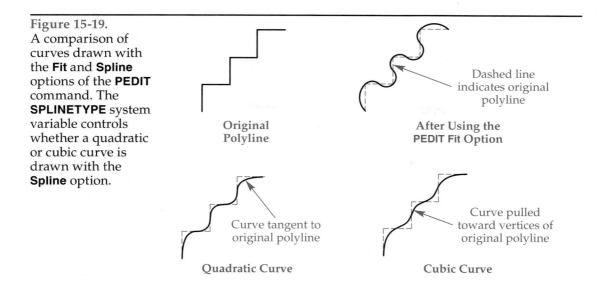

Original
Polyline

After Using the
PEDIT Fit Option

Dashed line
indicates original
polyline

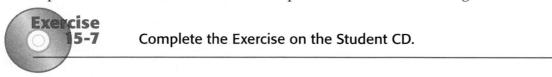

Curve tangent to
original polyline

Quadratic Curve

Curve pulled
toward vertices of
original polyline

Cubic Curve

the resulting spline curve is less smooth. The resulting spline curve is smoother if you increase the value, but the regeneration time and drawing file size are increased. The relationship between **SPLINESEGS** values and spline curves is shown in Figure 15-20.

Exercise 15-7   Complete the Exercise on the Student CD.

Figure 15-20.
A comparison of curves drawn with different settings for the **SPLINESEGS** system variable.

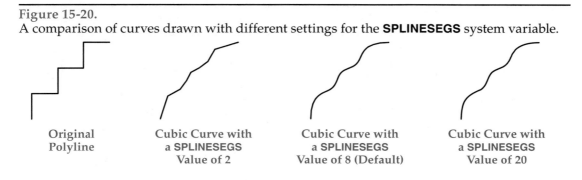

Original
Polyline

Cubic Curve with
a SPLINESEGS
Value of 2

Cubic Curve with
a SPLINESEGS
Value of 8 (Default)

Cubic Curve with
a SPLINESEGS
Value of 20

Drawing Curves Using the Spline Command

The **SPLINE** command is used to create a special type of curve called a nonuniform rational B-spline (NURBS). A *NURBS* curve is considered to be a true spline. A spline created by fitting a spline curve to a polyline is merely a linear approximation of a true spline and is not as accurate. An additional advantage of spline objects over smoothed polylines is that splines use less disk space. To access the **SPLINE** command, pick the **Spline** button on the **Draw** toolbar, pick **Draw > Spline**, or type SPL or SPLINE. A spline is created by specifying the control points using any standard coordinate entry method.

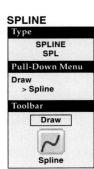

SPLINE

Type
   SPLINE
   SPL
Pull-Down Menu
Draw
   > Spline
Toolbar
   Draw

   Spline

```
Command: SPL or SPLINE↵
Specify first point or [Object]: 2,2↵
Specify next point: 4,4↵
Specify next point or [Close/Fit tolerance] <start tangent>: 6,2↵
Specify next point or [Close/Fit tolerance] <start tangent>: ↵
Specify start tangent: ↵
Specify end tangent: ↵
Command:
```

After you have given all the necessary points along the spline, pressing [Enter] ends the point specification process and allows the start tangency and end tangency to be entered. Specifying the tangents changes the direction in which the spline curve begins and ends. Pressing [Enter] at these prompts accepts the default direction, as calculated by AutoCAD, for the specified curve. The results of the previous command sequence are shown in Figure 15-21.

NOTE
If only two points are specified along the spline curve, an object that looks like a line is created, but the object is a spline.

Drawing Closed Splines

The **Close** option of the **SPLINE** command enables you to draw closed splines. See Figure 15-22. After closing a spline, you are prompted to specify a tangent direction for the start point or endpoint of the spline. Pressing [Enter] accepts the default calculated by AutoCAD.

Figure 15-21.
A spline drawn with the **SPLINE** command using the AutoCAD defaults for the start and end tangents.

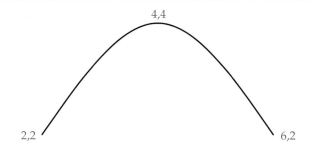

Figure 15-22.
Using the **Close** option of the **SPLINE** command with AutoCAD default tangents to draw a closed spline. Compare this spline to the object shown in Figure 15-21.

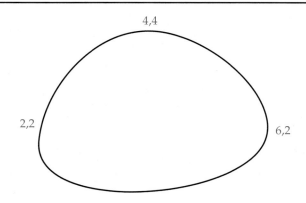

Altering the Fit Tolerance Specifications

When drawing splines, different results can be achieved by altering the specifications used with the **Fit tolerance** option. The outcomes of different settings vary, depending on the configuration of the individual spline object. The setting specifies a tolerance within which the spline curve falls as it passes through the control points.

Specifying the Start and End Tangents

The previous **SPLINE** command examples used AutoCAD's default start and end tangents. You can set start and end tangent directions by entering values at the prompts that appear after you pick the points of the spline. The tangency is based on the tangent direction of the selected point. The results of using the horizontal and vertical tangent directions using Ortho mode are shown in Figure 15-23.

Converting a Spline-Fitted Polyline to a Spline

A spline-fitted polyline object can be converted to a spline object using the **Object** option of the **SPLINE** command. This option works for either 2D or 3D objects.

Exercise 15-8. Complete the Exercise on the Student CD.

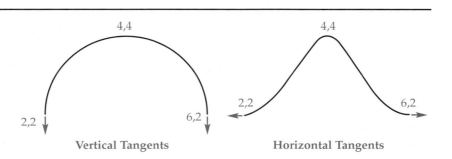
Figure 15-23. These splines were drawn through the same points, but they have different start and end tangent directions. The arrows indicate the tangent directions.

Vertical Tangents   Horizontal Tangents

Editing Splines

SPE

Type
SPE
SPLINEDIT

Pull-Down Menu
Modify
> Object
> Spline

Toolbar
Modify II
Edit Spline

Options
Fit data
Open
Move vertex
Refine
rEverse
Undo

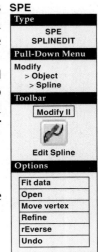

The **SPLINEDIT** command allows you to edit spline objects. Several editing options are available. Control points can be added, moved, or deleted to alter the shape of an existing curve. A spline can also be opened or closed. In addition, you can change the start and end tangents.

To access the **SPLINEDIT** command, pick the **Edit Spline** button on the **Modify II** toolbar, pick **Modify > Object > Spline**, or type SPE or SPLINEDIT. You are prompted to select the spline to be edited. When you pick a spline, the control points are identified by grips, as shown in Figure 15-24. You must then select one of the six **SPLINEDIT** options. These are described in the following sections.

Editing Fit Data

The **Fit data** option of the **SPLINEDIT** command allows spline control points to be edited. Spline control points are called *fit points*. The **Fit data** option has several suboptions:

```
Command: SPE or SPLINEDIT↵
Select spline: (pick a spline)
Enter an option [Fit data/Close/Move vertex/Refine/rEverse/Undo]: F↵
Enter a fit data option
[Add/Close/Delete/Move/Purge/Tangents/toLerance/eXit] <eXit>:
```

Chapter 15   Drawing and Editing Polylines and Splines

Figure 15-24.
The control points on a spline are displayed as grips when using the **SPLINEDIT** command.

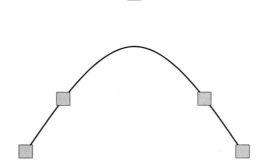

Each of the **Fit data** suboptions is explained next. See **Figure 15-25** for examples of using these options.

- **Add.** This suboption allows you to add new fit points to a spline definition. When adding, a fit point can be located by picking a point or entering coordinates. Fit points appear as unselected grips. When one is selected, it becomes highlighted along with the next fit point on the spline. You can then add a fit point between the two highlighted points. If the endpoint of the spline is selected, only the endpoint becomes highlighted. If the start point of the spline is selected, you are asked whether you want the new fit point inserted before or after the existing one. Respond by entering A or B accordingly. When a fit point is added, the spline curve is refit through the added point. See **Figure 15-25.**

Figure 15-25.
Examples of using the **Fit data** options of the **SPLINEDIT** command to edit a spline. Compare the original spline to each of the edited objects.

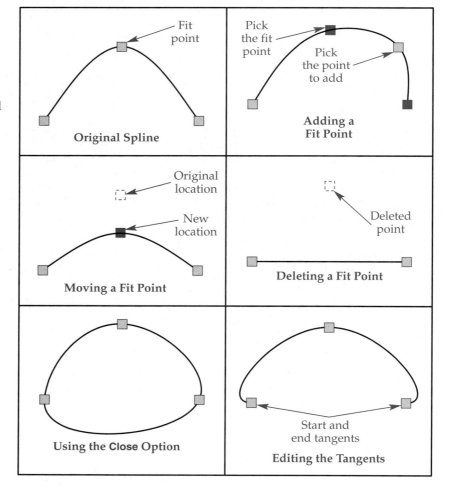

The **Add** suboption functions in a running mode. This means you can continue to add points as needed. By pressing [Enter] at a Specify new point <exit>: prompt, you can select other existing fit points. Therefore, points can be added anywhere on the spline.

- **Close/Open.** If the selected spline is open, the **Close** suboption is displayed. If the spline is closed, the **Open** suboption is displayed. These options allow you to open a closed spline or close an open spline.
- **Delete.** The **Delete** suboption allows you to delete fit points as needed. At least two fit points, however, must remain. Even when only two points remain, the object is still defined as a spline, although it looks like a line. Like the **Add** suboption, the **Delete** suboption operates in a running mode, allowing as many deletions as needed. The spline is recurved through the remaining fit points.
- **Move.** This suboption allows fit points to be moved as necessary. When the **Move** option is entered, the start point of the spline is highlighted. You can specify a different location simply by picking a new point with your left mouse button. You can also specify other fit points to move. The options are explained as follows:
  - **Specify new location.** This suboption allows you to move the currently highlighted point to a specified location.
  - **Next.** This suboption highlights the next fit point. It is activated by pressing [Enter].
  - **Previous.** Entering this suboption highlights the previous fit point.
  - **Select point.** This suboption allows you to pick a different fit point to move, rather than using the **Next** or **Previous** options.
  - **eXit.** This suboption returns you to the **Fit data** option prompt.
- **Purge.** This suboption lets you remove fit point data from a spline. After using this option, the resulting spline is not as easy to edit. In very large drawings where many complex splines are created, such as Geographical Information Systems (GIS) drawings, purging fit point data reduces the file size by simplifying the definition. Once a spline is purged, the **Fit data** option is no longer displayed by the **SPLINEDIT** command for the purged spline.
- **Tangents.** This suboption allows editing of the start and end tangents for an open spline and editing of the start tangent for a closed spline. The tangency is based on the direction of the selected point. You can also use the **System default** option to set the tangency values to the AutoCAD defaults.
- **toLerance.** Fit tolerance values can be adjusted using this suboption. The results are immediate, so the fit tolerance can be adjusted as necessary to produce different results.
- **eXit.** Entering this suboption returns you to the **SPLINEDIT** command option prompt.

Opening or Closing a Spline

The **Open** and **Close** options of the **SPLINEDIT** command are alternately displayed, depending on the current status of the spline object being edited. If the spline is open, the **Close** option is displayed. The **Open** option is displayed if the spline is closed.

Moving a Vertex

The **Move vertex** option of the **SPLINEDIT** command allows you to move the fit points of a spline. When you access this option, you can specify a new location for a selected fit point. The options displayed are identical to those used with the **Move** suboption inside the **Fit data** option of the **SPLINEDIT** command sequence.

```
Command: SPE or SPLINEDIT↵
Select spline: (pick a spline)
Enter an option [Fit data/Close/Move vertex/Refine/rEverse/Undo]: M↵
Specify new location or [Next/Previous/Select point/eXit] <N>:
```

You can pick a new location for the highlighted fit point using your left mouse button, or you can enter a suboption. The **Move vertex** suboptions are explained below:

- **Specify new location.** Move the currently highlighted point to a specified location.
- **Next.** Highlight the next fit point.
- **Previous.** Highlight the previous fit point.
- **Select point.** Pick a different fit point to move, rather than cycling through points with the **Next** or **Previous** suboptions.
- **eXit.** Return to the **SPLINEDIT** command prompt.

Exercise
15-9   Complete the Exercise on the Student CD.

Smoothing or Reshaping a Section of the Spline

The **Refine** option of the **SPLINEDIT** command allows fine-tuning of the spline curve. Fit points can be added to help smooth or reshape a section of the spline. When you use this option, the fit point data is removed from the spline. The command sequence is as follows:

Command: **SPE** *or* **SPLINEDIT**↵
Select spline: *(pick a spline)*
Enter an option [Fit data/Close/Move vertex/Refine/rEverse/Undo]: **R**↵
Enter a refine option [Add control point/Elevate order/Weight/eXit] <eXit>:

The following refining options are available:
- **Add control point.** Specify new fit points on a spline as needed.
- **Elevate order.** The *order* of a spline is the degree of the spline polynomial + 1. In simple terms, it is the degree of refinement of the spline. For example, a cubic spline has an order of 4. Elevating the order of a spline causes more control points to appear on the curve for greater control. In **Figure 15-26,** the order of the spline is elevated from 4 to 6. The order setting can be from 4 to 26, but it cannot be adjusted downward. For example, if the order is set to 24, the only remaining settings are 25 and 26.

Figure 15-26. The effects of elevating the order of a spline and increasing the weight of an individual control point.

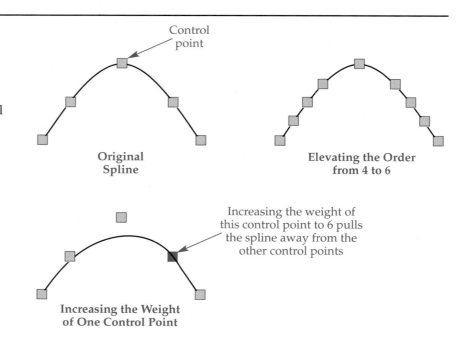

- **Weight.** When all control points have the same weight, they exert the same amount of pull on the spline. When a weight value is lessened for a control point, the spline is not pulled as close to the point as before. Likewise, when a weight value is increased, the control point exerts more pull on the spline. See **Figure 15-26.** The default setting of 1.0000 can be adjusted to a higher or lower value. The weight setting must be positive. The control point selection suboptions of the **Weight** option are the same as those used with the **Move vertex** option of the **SPLINEDIT** command. You can specify a new weight for the highlighted control point by using the **Enter new weight** option.

Reversing the Order of Spline Control Points

The **rEverse** option of the **SPLINEDIT** command allows you to reverse the listed order of the spline control points. This makes the previous start point the new endpoint and the previous endpoint the new start point. Using this option affects the various control point selection options as a result.

Undoing Splinedit Changes

The **Undo** option of the **SPLINEDIT** command undoes the previous change made to the spline. You can also use this option to undo changes back to the beginning of the current **SPLINEDIT** command sequence.

Exercise 15-10   Complete the Exercise on the Student CD.

Creating a Polyline Boundary

When you draw an object with the **LINE** command, each line segment is a single object. You can create a polyline boundary of an area made up of closed line segments using the **BOUNDARY** command. To do so, pick **Draw > Boundary...** from the pull-down menu or type BO or BOUNDARY. This displays the **Boundary Creation** dialog box. See **Figure 15-27.**

The **Object type:** drop-down list contains two options—**Polyline** and **Region**. The **Polyline** option is the default. If set to **Polyline**, AutoCAD creates a polyline around the area. If set to **Region**, AutoCAD creates a closed 2D area. A region may be used for area calculations, shading, extruding a solid model, or other purposes.

BOUNDARY

Type	
	BOUNDARY
	BO
Pull-Down Menu	
Draw	
	> Boundary...

Figure 15-27.
The **Boundary Creation** dialog box.

Pick to create a polyline or region boundary

Check to do automatic island detection

Select the boundary set

Select the type of boundary object

Pick to define a new boundary set

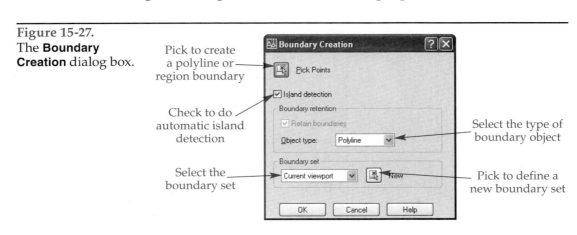

Chapter 15   Drawing and Editing Polylines and Splines

The **Boundary set** drop-down list has the **Current viewport** setting active. A *boundary set* is the portion or area of the drawing that AutoCAD evaluates when defining a boundary. The **Current viewport** option defines the boundary set from everything visible in the current viewport, even if it is not in the current display. The **New** button, located to the right of the drop-down list, allows you to define a boundary set. When you pick this button, the **Boundary Creation** dialog box closes, and the Select objects: prompt appears. You can then select the objects you want to use to create a boundary set. After you are done, press [Enter]. The **Boundary Creation** dialog box returns with **Existing set** active in the **Boundary set** drop-down list. This means the boundary set is defined from the objects you selected.

The **Island detection** setting is used to specify whether or not objects within the boundary are used as boundary objects. Objects inside a boundary are called *islands*. See **Figure 15-28**. When **Island detection** is checked, islands within a boundary will be detected and turned into their own boundaries.

The only other active feature in the **Boundary Creation** dialog box is the **Pick Points** button, which is located in the upper-left corner. When you pick this button, the **Boundary Creation** dialog box closes, and the Pick internal point: prompt appears. If the point you pick is inside a closed polygon, the boundary is highlighted, as shown in **Figure 15-29**. The **Boundary Definition Error** alert box appears if the point you pick is not within a closed polygon. Pick **OK**, and try again.

Figure 15-28.
Objects within a boundary, called islands, can be included or excluded when defining a boundary set.

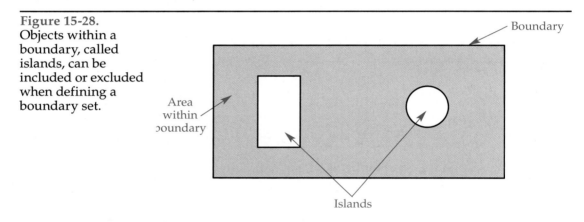

Figure 15-29.
When you select a point inside a closed polygon, the boundary is highlighted. Boundaries must be defined by closed objects.

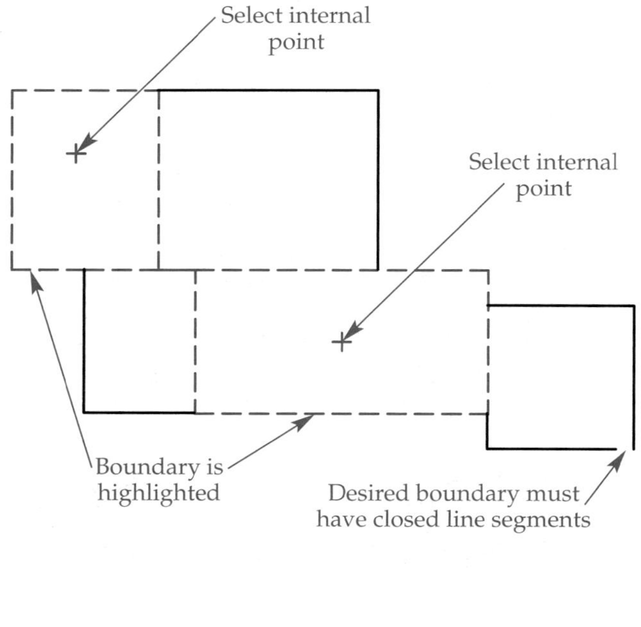

Unlike an object created with the **Join** option of the **PEDIT** command, a polyline boundary created with the **BOUNDARY** command does not replace the original objects from which it was created. The polyline simply traces over the defining objects with a polyline. Thus, the separate objects still exist and are underneath the newly created boundary. To avoid duplicate geometry, move the boundary to another location on screen, erase the original defining objects, and then move the boundary back to its original position.

PROFESSIONAL TIP

Area calculations can be simplified by first using the **BOUNDARY** command or joining objects with the **Join** option of the **PEDIT** command, before issuing the **AREA** command. Use the **Object** option of the **AREA** command to perform the area calculation. The **AREA** command is covered in Chapter 16. If you want to retain the original separate objects and the **Join** option of the **PEDIT** command was used, explode the joined polyline after the area calculation. Simply erase the polyline boundary after the calculation, if the **BOUNDARY** command was used.

Chapter Test

Answer the following questions. Write your answers on a separate sheet of paper or complete the electronic chapter test on the Student CD.

1. Give the command required to turn three connected lines into a single polyline.
2. Which system variable controls the automatic conversion of lines and arcs to polylines when they are selected within the **PEDIT** command?

*For Questions 3 through 9, give the **Edit vertex** option of the **PEDIT** command that relates to the definition given.*

3. Moves the "X" marker to the next position.
4. Moves a polyline vertex to a new location.
5. Breaks a polyline at a point or between two points.
6. Generates the revised version of a polyline.
7. Specifies a tangent direction.
8. Adds a new polyline vertex.
9. Returns you to the **PEDIT** command prompt.

10. Which **PEDIT** command option and suboption allow you to change the starting and ending widths of a polyline?
11. Why might it appear that nothing happens, after you change the starting and ending widths of a polyline?
12. Name the **PEDIT** command option and the **Edit vertex** suboption used for curve fitting.
13. Which command will remove all width characteristics and tangency information from a polyline?
14. Which two **PEDIT** command options allow you to open a closed polyline and close an open polyline?
15. When you enter the **Edit vertex** option of the **PEDIT** command, where is the "X" marker placed by AutoCAD?

16. How do you move the "X" marker to edit a different polyline vertex?
17. Can you use the **Fit** option of the **PEDIT** command without using the **Tangent** vertex editing suboption first?
18. Explain the difference between a fit curve and a spline curve.
19. Compare a quadratic curve, cubic curve, and fit curve.
20. Discuss the appearance of a quadratic curve.
21. Which **SPLINETYPE** system variable setting allows you to draw a quadratic curve?
22. Which **SPLINETYPE** setting allows you to draw a cubic curve?
23. Name the system variable that can be set to adjust the smoothness of a spline curve.
24. Name the pull-down menu selections used to access the polyline editing options.
25. Explain how you can adjust the way polyline linetypes are generated using the **PEDIT** command.
26. Name the system variable that allows you to alter the way polyline linetypes are generated.
27. Name the command used to create a polyline boundary.
28. Name the command that can be used to create a true spline.
29. How do you accept the AutoCAD defaults for the start and end tangents of a spline?
30. Name the **SPLINE** command option that allows you to turn a spline-fitted polyline into a true spline.
31. Name the command that allows you to edit splines.
32. What is the purpose of the **Add** suboption of the **Fit data** option of the **SPLINEDIT** command?
33. What is the minimum number of fit points for a spline?
34. Name the **SPLINEDIT** option that allows you to move the fit points in a spline.
35. What is the purpose of the **Refine** option of the **SPLINEDIT** command?
36. Identify the **Refine** suboption of the **SPLINEDIT** command that lets you increase, but not decrease, the number of control points appearing on a spline curve.
37. Name the **Refine** option of the **SPLINEDIT** command that controls the pull exerted by a control point on a spline.
38. How many operations can you undo inside the **SPLINEDIT** command with the **Undo** option?

Drawing Problems

Start a new drawing for each of the following problems. Specify your own units, limits, and other settings to suit each problem.

1. Draw the single polyline shown below. Use the **Arc**, **Width**, and **Close** options of the **PLINE** command to complete the shape. Set the polyline width to 0, except at the points indicated. Save the drawing as P15-1.

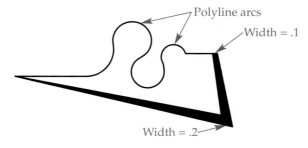

2. Draw the two curved arrows shown below using the **Arc** and **Width** options of the **PLINE** command. The arrowheads should have a starting width of 1.4 and an ending width of 0. The body of each arrow should have a beginning width of .8 and an ending width of .4. Save the drawing as P15-2.

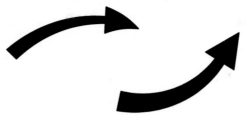

3. Open drawing P15-1 and make a copy of the original object to edit. Use the **PEDIT** command to change the object drawn into a rectangle. Use the **Decurve** and **Width** options and the **Straighten, Insert**, and **Move** vertex editing options of the **PEDIT** command. Save the completed drawing as P15-3.

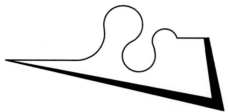

4. Open drawing P15-2 and make the following changes. Save the drawing as P15-4.
   A. Combine the two polylines using the **Join** option of the **PEDIT** command.
   B. Change the beginning width of the left arrow to 1.0 and the ending width to .2.
   C. Draw a polyline .062 wide, similar to Line A, as shown.

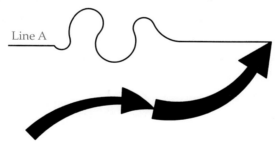

Line A

5. Draw a polyline .032 wide, using the following absolute coordinates.

Point	Coordinates	Point	Coordinates	Point	Coordinates
1	1,1	5	3,3	9	5,5
2	2,1	6	4,3	10	6,5
3	2,2	7	4,4	11	6,6
4	3,2	8	5,4	12	7,6

Copy the polyline three times so there are four polylines. Use the **Fit** option of the **PEDIT** command to smooth the first copy. Use the **Spline** option of the **PEDIT** command to turn the second copy into a quadratic curve. Make the third copy into a cubic curve. Use the **Decurve** option of the **PEDIT** command to return one of the three copies to its original form. Save the drawing as P15-5.

Drawing Problems – Chapter 15

6. Use the **PLINE** command to draw a patio plan similar to the one shown in Example A below. Draw the house walls 6″ wide. Copy the drawing three times and use the **PEDIT** command to create the remaining designs shown. Use the **Fit** option for Example B, a quadratic spline for Example C, and a cubic spline for Example D. Change the **SPLINETYPE** system variable as required. Save the drawing as P15-6.

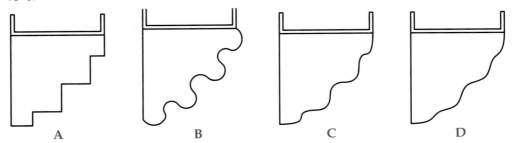

A   B   C   D

7. Open drawing P15-6 and create four new patio designs. This time, use grips to edit the polylines and create designs similar to Examples A, B, C, and D below. Save the drawing as P15-7.

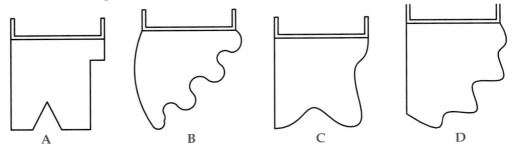

A   B   C   D

8. Use **SPLINE** and other commands, such as **ELLIPSE**, **MIRROR**, **OFFSET**, and **PLINE**, to design an architectural door knocker similar to the one shown. Use an appropriate text command and font to place your initials in the center. Save the drawing as P15-8.

9. Use the **SPLINE** command to draw the curve for the cam displacement diagram below. Use the following guidelines and the given drawing to complete this problem:
   A. The total rise equals 2.000.
   B. The total displacement can be any length.
   C. Divide the total displacement into 30° increments.
   D. Draw a half circle divided into 6 equal parts on one end.
   E. Draw a horizontal line from each division of the half circle to the other end of the diagram.
   F. Draw the displacement curve with the **SPLINE** command by picking points where the horizontal and vertical lines cross.
   G. Label the displacement increments along the horizontal scale as shown. Save the drawing as P15-9.

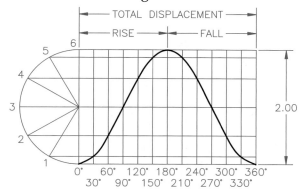

10. Draw a spline similar to the original spline shown below. Copy the spline seven times to create a layout similar to the one given. Perform the **SPLINEDIT** operations identified under each of the seven copies. Save the drawing as P15-10.

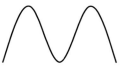
Original Spline

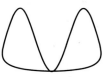
Close

Move a Control Point

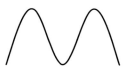
Elevate the Order to 10

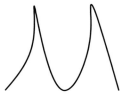
Add Two Control Points

Delete a Control Point

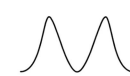
Edit the Tangents

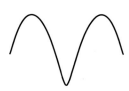
Increase the Weight of a Control Point to 4

Chapter 15 Drawing and Editing Polylines and Splines

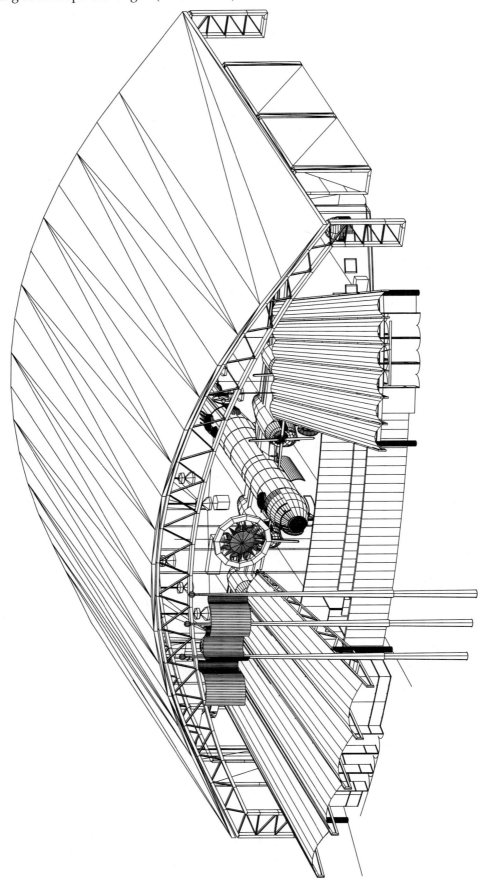

CHAPTER 16

Obtaining Information about the Drawing

Learning Objectives

After completing this chapter, you will be able to do the following:

- Use the **AREA** command to calculate the area of an object by adding and subtracting objects.
- Display object properties in a drawing using fields.
- List data related to a single point, an object, a group of objects, or an entire drawing.
- Find the distance between two points.
- Identify a point location.
- Determine the amount of time spent in a drawing session.
- Determine the status of drawing parameters.
- Perform basic and advanced mathematical calculations using the **QuickCalc** calculator.
- Convert units using the **QuickCalc** calculator.

When working on a drawing, you may need to ask AutoCAD for information about the drawing, such as object distances and areas. You can also ask AutoCAD to tell you how much time you have spent on a drawing. The commands to do this include **AREA**, **DBLIST** (database list), **DIST** (distance), **ID** (identification), **LIST**, **STATUS**, and **TIME**.

These commands are accessed from the **Tools > Inquiry** cascading menu. You can also access these commands from the **Inquiry** toolbar. See **Figure 16-1**. To display this toolbar, right-click on any visible toolbar and select **Inquiry** from the shortcut menu.

> **NOTE**
>
> The **Region/Mass Properties** button and pull-down menu entry provide data related to the properties of a 2D region or 3D solid. This topic is discussed in *AutoCAD and Its Applications—Advanced*.

Figure 16-1.
The inquiry commands are grouped on the **Inquiry** toolbar and in the **Inquiry** cascading menu in the **Tools** pull-down menu.

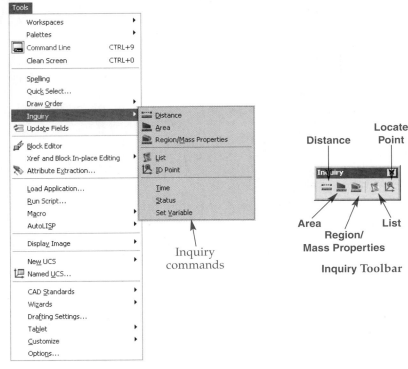

Inquiry Cascading Menu

Inquiry Toolbar

Finding the Area of Shapes and Objects

AREA

Type	
AREA	
AA	

Pull-Down Menu

Tools
> **Inquiry**
> **Area**

Toolbar

Inquiry

Area

Options

Object
Add
Subtract

The most basic function of the **AREA** command is to find the area of any object, circle, polygon, polyline, or spline. The command sequence to find the area of a circle is as follows:

Command: **AA** *or* **AREA**↵
Specify first corner point or [Object/Add/Subtract]: **O**↵
Select objects: (*pick the circle*)
Area = *n.nnnn*, Circumference = *n.nnnn*
Command:

The two numeric values represented by *n.nnnn* indicate the area and circumference of the circle. The second value returned by the **AREA** command varies, depending on the type of object selected, as shown in the following table:

Object	Value returned
Line	Selected value does not have an area (no value given)
Polyline	Length or Perimeter
Circle	Circumference
Spline	Length or Perimeter
Rectangle	Perimeter

Shapes drawn with polylines do not need to be closed for AutoCAD to calculate their areas. AutoCAD calculates the area as if a line segment connects the first and last points. To find the area of a shape created with the **LINE** command, pick all the vertices of that shape. This is the default mode of the **AREA** command. Setting a running object snap mode, such as **Endpoint** or **Intersection**, helps you pick the vertices. See **Figure 16-2.**

Command: **AREA**↵
Specify first corner point or [Object/Add/Subtract]: *(pick point 1)*
Specify next corner point or press ENTER for total: *(pick point 2)*
Specify next corner point or press ENTER for total: *(continue picking points until all corners of the object have been selected, and then press [Enter])*
Area = *n.nnnn*, Perimeter = *n.nnnn*
Command:

If you use the **Add** option of the **AREA** command, you can pick multiple objects or areas. As you add objects or areas, a running total of the area is automatically calculated. The **Subtract** option allows you to remove objects or areas from the selection set. Once either of these options is entered, the **AREA** command remains in effect until canceled.

The next example shows how to use these two options in the same operation. Refer to **Figure 16-3** as you go through the following command sequence:

Command: **AREA**↵
Specify first corner point or [Object/Add/Subtract]: **A**↵
Specify first corner point or [Object/Subtract]: **O**↵
(ADD mode) Select objects: *(pick the polyline)*
Area = 13.7854, Perimeter = 20.1416
Total area = 13.7854
(ADD mode) Select objects: ↵
Specify first corner point or [Object/Subtract]: **S**↵
Specify first corner point or [Object/Add]: **O**↵
(SUBTRACT mode) Select objects: *(pick the first circle)*
Area = 0.7854, Circumference = 3.1416
Total area = 13.0000
(SUBTRACT mode) Select objects: *(pick the second circle)*
Area = 0.7854, Circumference = 3.1416
Total area = 12.2146
(SUBTRACT mode) Select objects: ↵
Specify first corner point or [Object/Add]: ↵
Command:

Figure 16-2.
Pick all vertices to find the area of an object drawn with the **LINE** command.

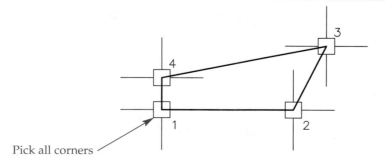

Pick all corners

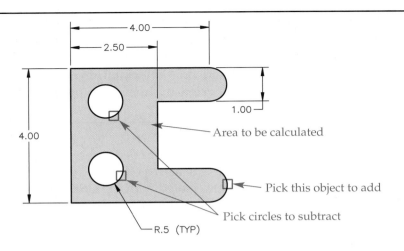

Figure 16-3.
To calculate the area of an object drawn with the **PLINE** command, first select the outer boundary of the object using the **Add** option of the **AREA** command. Select the inner boundaries (the circles) using the **Subtract** option of the **AREA** command. This will calculate the area of the object.

The total area of the object in **Figure 16-3** after subtracting the areas of the two holes is 12.2146. An area value and a perimeter or circumference value are given for each object as it is selected. These values are not affected by the adding or subtracting functions.

Notice in the previous command sequence that, when you are finished adding objects and wish to subtract, you must press [Enter] at the (ADD mode) Select objects: prompt. You can also right-click the mouse and then enter S to enter Subtract mode. If you have completed subtracting and wish to add, you must press [Enter] at the (SUBTRACT mode) Select objects: prompt or right-click the mouse and then enter A to enter Add mode.

PROFESSIONAL TIP
Calculating area, circumference, and perimeter values of shapes drawn with the **LINE** command can be time-consuming. You must pick each vertex on the object. If you need to calculate areas, it is best to create lines and arcs with the **PLINE** or **SPLINE** command. Use the **Object** option of the **AREA** command when adding or subtracting objects.

Exercise 16-1   Complete the Exercise on the Student CD.

Displaying Information with Fields

You can list some object properties and drawing information using fields. A *field* is a text object that displays a set property, setting, or value for an object, a drawing, or a computer system. If the value of the field setting changes, the text is updated automatically to reflect the change. Fields were introduced in Chapter 8. Each object type, such as a line, circle, or polyline, has different properties that can be displayed in a field. For example, using fields, you can place text next to a circle listing the circle's area and circumference.

To display an object property value using a field, access the **Field** dialog box by selecting **Insert > Field...** from the pull-down menu. In the **Field** dialog box, pick Objects from the **Field category:** drop-down list, and then pick Object in the **Field names:** list box. See **Figure 16-4**. Pick the **Select object** button to return to the drawing window and pick the object.

When you select the object, the **Field** dialog box reappears with the available properties listed. See **Figure 16-5**. Pick the property, select the format, and pick **OK** to have the field inserted in the text object. Once the field is created, whenever the object is modified, the value displayed in the field automatically updates. In addition to the object property settings, such as layer, linetype, lineweight, and plot style, many inquiry properties can be included in a field. The table in **Figure 16-6** lists some of the inquiry data that can be displayed in fields for various object types.

Exercise 16-2   Complete the Exercise on the Student CD.

Figure 16-4.
Pick the Object field to add a property for a specific object to a field. Pick the **Select object** button to select the object.

Listing Drawing Data

The **LIST** command enables you to display data about any AutoCAD object. Line lengths, circle and arc locations and radii, polyline widths, and object layers are just a few of the items you can identify with the **LIST** command. You can select several objects to list. The command sequence is as follows:

> Command: **LI**, **LS**, *or* **LIST**↵
> Select objects: *(pick one or more objects using any selection method)*
> *n* found
> Select objects:

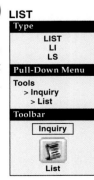

LIST
Type
LIST
LI
LS

Pull-Down Menu
Tools
> Inquiry
> List

Toolbar
Inquiry

List

Figure 16-5.
After picking the object, properties specific to the object type are listed. Pick the property and format for the field.

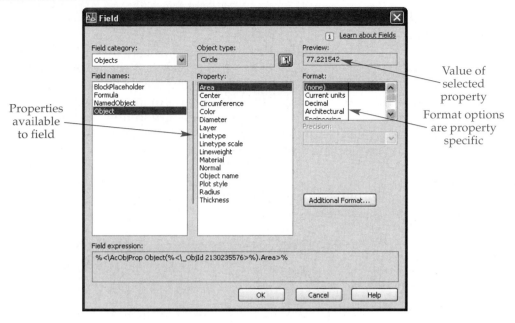

Properties available to field

Value of selected property

Format options are property specific

Figure 16-6.
This table is a partial listing of inquiry properties available for various object types.

Object Properties Available for Display in Fields			
Line Object	**Circle Object**	**Polyline Object**	**Rectangle Object**
Length	Area	Area	Area
Angle	Circumference	Length	Length
Delta	Diameter		
Start	Radius		
End	Center		
Arc Object	**Ellipse Object**	**Spline Object**	**Region Object**
Area	Area	Area	Area
Arc length	Center	Degree	Perimeter
Radius	Major axis	Start tangent	
Center	Minor axis	End tangent	
Total angle	Major radius		
Start	Minor radius		
End	Radius ratio		
Start angle	Start		
End angle	End		
	Start angle		
	End angle		

When you press [Enter], the data for each of the objects picked are displayed in the text window. The following data are given for a line:

```
LINE Layer:      "layer name"
           Space: Model or Paper space
       Handle = nn
from point,    X= nn.nnnn     Y= nn.nnnn     Z=  0.0000
to point,      X= nn.nnnn     Y= nn.nnnn     Z= 0.0000
Length = nn.nnnn,    Angle in XY Plane = nnn
Delta X = nn.nnnn,    Delta Y = nn.nnnn, Delta Z = 0.0000
```

The Delta X and Delta Y values indicate the horizontal and vertical distances between the *from point* and *to point* of the line. These two values, along with the length and angle, provide you with four measurements for a single line. An example of the data and measurements provided for two-dimensional lines is shown in **Figure 16-7**. If a line is three-dimensional, the **LIST** command displays an additional line of information:

```
3D Length = nn.nnnn,  Angle from XY Plane = nnn
```

The **LIST** command can also be used to determine information about text and multiline text. The data given for text, multiline text, circles, and splines are the following:

```
TEXT          Layer: "layer name"
          Space: Model or Paper space
          Layout: Only in Paper space
     Handle = nn
     Style = "name"
     Font file = name
     start point,    X= n.nnnn       Y= n.nnnn       Z= 0.0000
     height          n.nnnn
     text    text contents
     rotation        angle    n
     width scale factor       n.nnnn
     obliquing       angle    n
     generation      normal
     MTEXT          Layer: "layer name"
          Space: Model or Paper space
     Handle = nn
Location:       X= n.nnnn       Y= n.nnnn       Z= 0.0000
Width:  n.nnnn
Normal:X= n.nnnn       Y= n.nnnn       Z= 0.0000
Rotation:       n
Text style:     "style name"
Text height:    n.nnnn
Line spacing:   Multiple (n.nnnnnnx    =       n.nnnn)
```

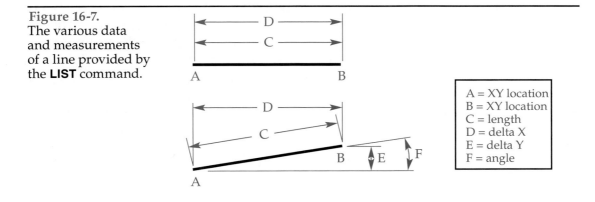

Figure 16-7.
The various data and measurements of a line provided by the **LIST** command.

A = XY location
B = XY location
C = length
D = delta X
E = delta Y
F = angle

Attachment:	*corner of multiline text insertion point*	
Flow direction:	*direction text is read based on language*	
Contents:	*multiline text contents*	
CIRCLE	Layer:	*"layer name"*
Space:	*Model or Paper* space	
Handle = *nn*		

center point, X= *n.nnnn* Y= *n.nnnn*   Z= 0.0000

radius *n.nnnn*

circumference   *n.nnnn*

area *n.nnnn*

SPLINE	Layer:	*"layer name"*
Space:	*Model or Paper* space	
Handle = *nn*		
Length:	*n.nnnn*	
Order:	*n*	
Properties:	Planar, Non-Rational, Non-Periodic	
Parametric Range:	Start *n.nnnn*	
	End *n.nnnn*	

Number of control points: *n*

Control Points: X = *n.nnnn*   , Y= *n.nnnn*   , Z = 0.0000
       (the XYZ of all control points are listed)

Number of fit points: *n*

User Data: Fit Points
      X = *n.nnnn*   , Y = *n.nnnn*   , Z = 0.0000
      (the XYZ of all fit points are listed)

Fit point tolerance: *n.nnnn*

PROFESSIONAL TIP

The **LIST** command is the most powerful inquiry command in AutoCAD. It provides all the information you need to know about an object. Also, when selecting an object from the polyline family, the **LIST** command reports the area and perimeter of the object so you do not need to use the **AREA** command. The **LIST** command also reports an object's color and linetype, unless both are BYLAYER.

Listing Drawing Data for All Objects

The **DBLIST** (database list) command lists all data for every object in the current drawing. This command is initiated by typing DBLIST. The information is provided in the same format used by the **LIST** command. As soon as you enter the **DBLIST** command, the information begins to quickly scroll up the screen in the text window. The scrolling stops when a complete page (or screen) is filled with database information. Press [Enter] to scroll to the end of the next page. Use the scroll buttons to move forward and backward through the listing. If you find the data you need, press the [Esc] key to exit the **DBLIST** command. You can exit the text window by pressing the [F2] function key.

Finding the Distance between Two Points

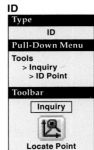

DIST

Type

DIST
DI

Pull-Down Menu

Tools
> Inquiry
> Distance

Toolbar

Inquiry

Distance

The **DIST** (distance) command is used to find the distance between two points. As with the **AREA** command, use object snap modes to accurately pick locations. The **DIST** command provides the distance between the points and the angle of the line from the positive X axis. It also gives delta X, Y, and Z dimensions. To access the **DIST** command, pick the **Distance** button in the **Inquiry** toolbar, select **Tools > Inquiry > Distance**, or type DI or DIST. The button and pull-down selections issue the command transparently and can be used within other commands.

> Command: **DI** or **DIST**↵
> Specify first point: *(select point)*
> Specify second point: *(select point)*
> Distance = *n.nnnn*,   Angle in XY Plane = *n*, Angle from XY Plane = *n*
> Delta X = *n.nnnn*,   Delta Y = *n.nnnn*,   Delta Z = 0.0000
> Command:

Identifying Point Locations

ID

Type

ID

Pull-Down Menu

Tools
> Inquiry
> ID Point

Toolbar

Inquiry

Locate Point

The **ID** command gives the coordinate location of a single point on screen. This command can be used to find the coordinates of a line endpoint or the center of a circle. Simply pick the point to be identified when the Specify point: prompt appears. Use the object snap modes for accuracy.

> Command: **ID**↵
> Specify point: *(select the point)*
> X = *n.nnnn*   Y = *n.nnnn*   Z = 0.0000
> Command:

In conjunction with "blip" mode, the **ID** command can help you identify where a coordinate is on the screen. Suppose you want to see where the point X=8.75, Y=6.44 is located. Enter these numbers at the Specify point: prompt. AutoCAD responds by placing a blip at that exact location. In order to use this feature, the **BLIPMODE** system variable must be on.

> Command: **BLIPMODE**↵
> Enter mode [ON/OFF] *<current>*: **ON**↵
> Command: **ID**↵
> Specify point: **8.75,6.44**↵
>   X = 8.7500   Y = 6.4400   Z = 0.0000
> Command:

Exercise 16-3   Complete the Exercise on the Student CD.

Checking the Time

TIME

Type

TIME

Pull-Down Menu

Tools
> Inquiry
> Time

The **TIME** command allows you to display the current time, time related to your drawing, and time related to the current drawing session. The following is an example of the information displayed in the text window when the **TIME** command is entered:

```
Command: TIME↵
Current time:     Monday, February 13, 2006       13:39:22:210 PM
Times for this drawing:
  Created:        Saturday, February 11, 2006      10:24:48:130 AM
  Last updated: Saturday, February 11, 2006      14:36:23:460 PM
  Total editing time:        0 days 01:23:57:930
  Elapsed timer (on):     0 days 00:35:28:650
  Next automatic save in:           0 days 01:35:26:680
Enter option [Display/ON/OFF/Reset]:
```

There are a few things to keep in mind when checking the text window display after issuing the **TIME** command. First, the drawing creation time starts when you begin a new drawing, not when a new drawing is first saved. Second, the **SAVE** command affects the Last updated: time. If you exit AutoCAD and do not save the drawing, however, all time in that session is discarded. Finally, you can time a specific drawing task by using the **Reset** option of the **TIME** command to reset the elapsed timer.

When the **TIME** command is issued, the times shown in the text window are static. This means that none of the times are being updated. You can request an update by using the **Display** option at the following prompt:

Enter option [Display/ON/OFF/Reset]:

When you enter the drawing area, the timer is on by default. If you want to stop the timer, simply enter OFF at the Enter option [Display/ON/OFF/Reset]: prompt. If the timer is off, enter ON to start it again.

NOTE

The Windows operating system maintains the date and time settings for the computer. You can change these settings in the Windows Control Panel. To access the Control Panel, pick Settings and then Control Panel from the start menu.

Exercise
16-4

Complete the Exercise on the Student CD.

Determining the Drawing Status

STATUS

Type

STATUS

Pull-Down Menu

Tools
> Inquiry
> Status

While working on a drawing, you may forget some of the drawing parameters, such as the limits, grid spacing, or snap values. All the information about a drawing can be displayed using the **STATUS** command. Access this command by typing STATUS or selecting **Tools** > **Inquiry** > **Status**. The drawing information is displayed in the text window. See **Figure 16-8**.

The number of objects in a drawing refers to the total number of objects—both erased and existing. Free dwg disk (C:) space: represents the space left on the drive

Figure 16-8.
The drawing information listed by the **STATUS** command is shown in the text window.

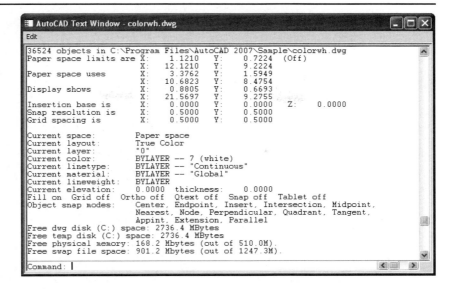

```
AutoCAD Text Window - colorwh.dwg
Edit

36524 objects in C:\Program Files\AutoCAD 2007\Sample\colorwh.dwg
Paper space limits are X:     1.1210    Y:      0.7224   (Off)
                       X:    12.1210    Y:      9.2224
Paper space uses       X:     3.3762    Y:      1.5949
                       X:    10.6823    Y:      8.4754
Display shows          X:     0.8805    Y:      0.6693
                       X:    21.5697    Y:      9.2755
Insertion base is      X:     0.0000    Y:      0.0000    Z:      0.0000
Snap resolution is     X:     0.5000    Y:      0.5000
Grid spacing is        X:     0.5000    Y:      0.5000

Current space:         Paper space
Current layout:        True Color
Current layer:         "0"
Current color:         BYLAYER -- 7 (white)
Current linetype:      BYLAYER -- "Continuous"
Current material:      BYLAYER -- "Global"
Current lineweight:    BYLAYER
Current elevation:     0.0000   thickness:      0.0000
Fill on  Grid off  Ortho off  Qtext off  Snap off  Tablet off
Object snap modes:     Center, Endpoint, Insert, Intersection, Midpoint,
                       Nearest, Node, Perpendicular, Quadrant, Tangent,
                       Appint, Extension, Parallel
Free dwg disk (C:) space: 2736.4 MBytes
Free temp disk (C:) space: 2736.4 MBytes
Free physical memory: 168.2 Mbytes (out of 510.0M).
Free swap file space: 901.2 Mbytes (out of 1247.3M).

Command: |
```

containing your drawing file. Drawing aid settings are shown along with the current settings for layer, linetype, and color. These topics are discussed in later chapters of this text. When you have completed reviewing the information, press [F2] to close the text window. You can also switch to the graphics window without closing the text window by picking anywhere inside the graphics window or using the Windows [Alt]+[Tab] feature.

> **NOTE**
>
> Another way to move between the graphics window and the text window is provided with the AutoCAD commands **GRAPHSCR** and **TEXTSCR**. Typing TEXTSCR displays the text window. Typing GRAPHSCR closes the text window. You can also open the text window by selecting **View** > **Display** > **Text Window**.

Using QuickCalc

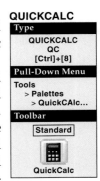

QUICKCALC

Type
QUICKCALC
QC
[Ctrl]+[8]

Pull-Down Menu
Tools
> Palettes
> QuickCAlc...

Toolbar
Standard

QuickCalc

AutoCAD commands require precise input. Often, the input is variable and based on objects or locations within a drawing. **QuickCalc** is a window that contains a basic calculator, a scientific calculator, a units converter, and a variables feature.

When professionally drafting, most days will find you grabbing for your handheld calculator. You may be working from a sketch with missing dimensions, you may need to calculate a distance or an angle, or some dimensions may need to be double-checked. **QuickCalc** can be used to do these things and much more. **QuickCalc** can be used like a basic calculator or it can be used while drafting, by passing values to the command line while in the middle of a command. **QuickCalc** is a window that can be opened by picking the **QuickCalc** button in the **Standard** toolbar, picking **Tools** > **Palettes** > **QuickCalc**, typing QC or QUICKCALC, or using the [Ctrl]+[8] key combination.

The QuickCalc Window

The **QuickCalc** window consists of a built-in toolbar, calculation and history areas, and calculation tools. See **Figure 16-9**. The different areas are briefly explained in the following list and discussed in depth throughout this section.

Figure 16-9.
All the different
areas of the
QuickCalc window
can be used to do
calculations.

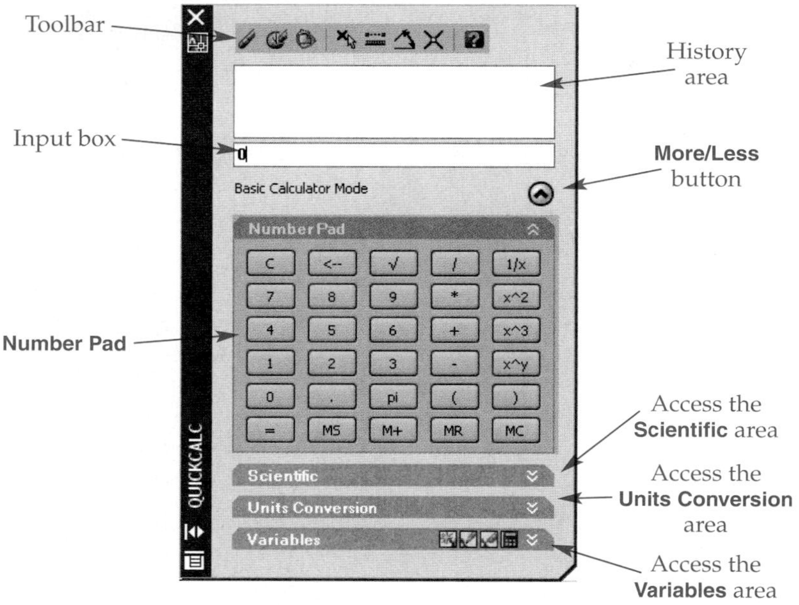

- **Toolbar.** Contains commands for clearing the calculator, passing values to the Command: prompt, and getting values from the drawing.
- **History area.** Stores a history of the previously used expressions.
- **Input box.** This is where expressions are typed or passed from the other tools.
- **Number Pad.** Serves as a basic calculator where numbers and symbols are used to calculate arithmetic expressions.
- **Scientific area.** Allows for performing more advanced calculations, such as trigonometry and geometry.
- **Units Conversion area.** Converts length, area, volume, and angular units from one unit type to another.
- **Variables area.** Contains predefined constants and functions variables, and allows you to create and store new ones.

Typing in Expressions

The basic mathematical functions used in numeric expressions include addition, subtraction, multiplication, division, and exponential notation. Parentheses are used to group symbols and values into sets. The symbols used for the basic mathematical operators are shown in the following table:

Symbol	Function	Example
+	Addition	3+26
−	Subtraction	270–15.3
*	Multiplication	4*156
/	Division	256/16
^	Exponent	22.6^3
( )	Grouped expressions	2*(16+2^3)

Expressions can be typed directly into the input box by using the number pad and symbols on the keyboard. Once the expression is typed, press [Enter] to have the expression evaluated. The result displays in the input box and the expression is moved to the history area. **Figure 16-10** displays the **QuickCalc** window after calculating 96.27 + 23.58. The following are examples of different expressions that can be entered in the input box:

Figure 16-10.
A—Type expressions
into the input box.
B—After typing the
expression, press
the [Enter] key to
have the expression
evaluated. The
expression and
result get stored in
the history area.

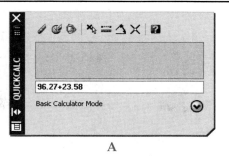

A

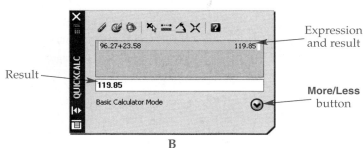

Result

Expression
and result

More/Less
button

B

```
268+182↵
450

49.2-19.8↵
29.4

49*12↵
588

15/4.5↵
3.333

6^4↵
1296
```

NOTE

If you move the pointer outside of the **QuickCalc** window,
the drawing area automatically becomes active. To make
QuickCalc active, pick anywhere inside of the **QuickCalc**
window.

Grouped expressions can be entered by using parentheses to break up the expressions that need to be calculated separately. For example, to calculate the result of 6 + 2 and then to multiply the result by 4, enter (6+2)*4. If the parentheses are not added, the result will be wrong.

When a mistake is made in the input box, you do not need to clear the input box and start over again. The left and right arrow keyboard keys can be used to move through the field. Right-clicking in the input box displays the shortcut options for copying and pasting text.

When using only the input box of **QuickCalc**, the additional sections can be hidden to save valuable drawing space. To do this pick the **More/Less** button below the input box. See Figure 16-10. When the **QuickCalc** window displays all of the areas, the button is an up arrow and its tooltip reads **Less**. To display the areas after they have been hidden, pick the button again.

Clearing the Input and History areas

After pressing the [Enter] key to evaluate an expression, a new expression can be typed without having to clear the last result. AutoCAD automatically starts a new expression. The input box can be cleared manually when needed by either placing the cursor in the input box and using the [Backspace] or [Delete] key from the keyboard, or by picking the **Clear** button from the **QuickCalc** toolbar. The history area can also be cleared by picking the **Clear History** button. See **Figure 16-11**.

CAUTION

If an expression is entered that cannot be evaluated, AutoCAD displays an **Error in Expression** dialog box. Pick the **OK** button, correct the error, and try it again.

Using the Number Pad

Expressions can also be entered by picking the numbers and symbols with the pointing device in the **Number Pad**. Picking a number or symbol places that item into the input box. The **Number Pad** offers some options that are not available from the keyboard. These options are displayed in **Figure 16-12**.

Figure 16-11.
The input box and history areas can be cleared by using the buttons on the **QuickCalc** toolbar.

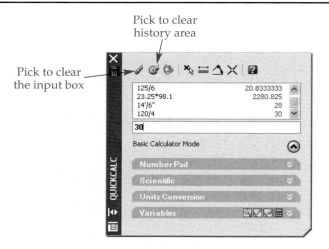

Figure 16-12.
The basic **Number Pad** area contains additional options that cannot be accessed using the keyboard.

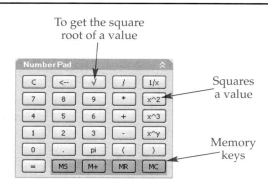

Figure 16-13.
The **Scientific** expressions available in **QuickCalc**.

	1	2	3	4	5
A	Sine	Cosine	Tangent	Base–10 Log	Base–10 Exponent
B	Arcsine	Arccosine	Arctangent	Natural Log	Natural Exponent
C	Convert Radians to Degrees	Convert Degrees to Radians	Absolute Value	Round	Truncate

Advanced Calculations

Trigonometry functions, some geometry functions, and exponential functions can be found in the **Scientific** area of **QuickCalc**. See **Figure 16-13**. To use one of the expressions, type a value in the input box, pick the appropriate expression button, and then press [Enter]. When the expression button is picked, the input box value is put into parentheses after the expression. For example, to get the *sine* of 14, clear the input box, type 14 in the input box, and pick the **sin** button. The input box now reads sin(14). Press the [Enter] key to get the result. Trigonometry functions are covered in more detail later in this supplement.

> **NOTE**
>
>
>
> The expression button can be picked first, but it puts a default value of 0 in parentheses. The cursor can then be placed in the input box to type a different number in the parentheses if needed.

Converting Units

The **Units Conversion** area allows you to convert one unit type to another. The unit types available are **Length, Area, Volume**, and **Angular**. To use the unit converter to convert 23 centimeters to inches, pick in the **Units type** field to display the drop-down list. See **Figure 16-14.** Pick the drop-down list button to display the different unit types and select Length. Activate the **Convert from** field and select Centimeters from the drop-down list. Activate the **Convert to** field and select Inches from the drop-down list. Type 23 in the **Value to convert** field and press the [Enter] key. The **Converted value** field now displays the converted units.

The converted value can be passed to the input box to use in an expression by picking the **Return Conversion to Calculator Input Area** button. See **Figure 16-15.** If the button is not visible, pick once on the converted units in the **Converted value** field.

Using Variables

If you use an expression or value frequently, it can be saved as a variable so you do not have to type it every time. This can be done in the **Variables** area of **QuickCalc**. The **Variables** area includes two types of predefined variables: **Constants** and **Functions**. A *constant* is an expression or value that stays the same—remains constant. A *function* is an expression that asks for user input to get values that can be passed to the expression.

Figure 16-14.
Picking on the current unit type activates the field and displays the drop-down list button.

Drop-down list button

Figure 16-15.
Once a value has been converted it can be passed to the input box.

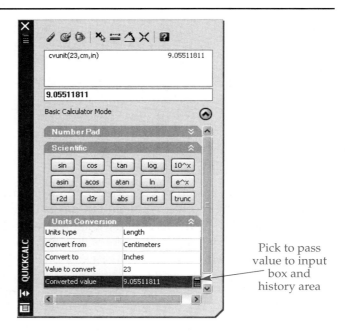

Pick to pass value to input box and history area

In the **Variables** area, variables can be created, edited, deleted, and passed to the input box. See **Figure 16-16.** The tool buttons contain the following functions:

- **New Variable.** Opens the **Variable Definition** dialog box where a new variable can be created.
- **Edit Variable.** Opens the **Variable Definition** dialog box with the information for the selected variable. If no variable is selected, this button is grayed out.
- **Delete.** Deletes the selected variable.
- **Return Variable to Input Area.** Passes the selected variable to the input box. The variable can also be passed to the input box by double-clicking on the variable name.

Figure 16-16.
The **Variables** area of **QuickCalc** allows you to store values and expressions for later use.

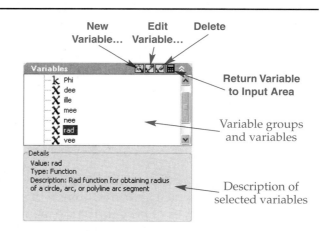

New Variable...

Edit Variable...

Delete

Return Variable to Input Area

Variable groups and variables

Description of selected variables

These commands can also be accessed by right-clicking in the **Variable** area to display the shortcut menu. The following two additional options are available:

- **New Category.** Creates a new category for saving variables.
- **Rename.** Allows you to rename the selected variable. This also can be accessed by selecting the variable, pausing, and then selecting it again.

Creating a new variable

To create a new variable, select the **New Variable...** button or right-click and select **New Variable...** from the shortcut menu. This opens the **Variable Definition** dialog box shown in **Figure 16-17.** Type a name for the variable in the **Name:** field. Select a group for the variable to reside in the **Group with:** field. In the **Value or expression:** field, type the value or the expression for the variable. Give a description for the variable in the **Description** field. Pick the **OK** button to save the variable and have it display in the **Variables** section.

PROFESSIONAL TIP

The predefined variables and their functions are explained in the AutoCAD help file. To view these, select **Help** > **Help** to open the **AutoCAD Help** window. Pick the **Search** tab, type QUICKCALC, and then pick the **Ask** button. In the results, pick on **QuickCalc** calculator to view the page. On the **Commands** tab of the page, pick the **Variables Area** link and then scroll down to the bottom of the page.

Getting and passing values from the AutoCAD window

Values can be passed from the input box to be used with commands, and values can be obtained from the AutoCAD drawing and passed to the input box. These commands are accessed from the **QuickCalc** toolbar. See **Figure 16-18.** The following commands are available:

- **Paste value to command line.** Picking this button places the current input box value on the Command: prompt. This button is typically used while in the middle of a command.

Figure 16-17.
A new variable is defined in the **Variable Definition** dialog box.

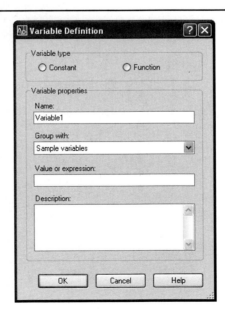

Figure 16-18.
Values can be passed from **QuickCalc** to AutoCAD, and they can be retrieved from AutoCAD and passed to **QuickCalc**.

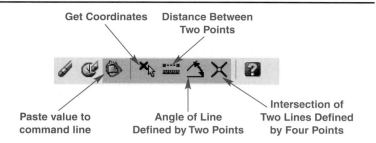

Get Coordinates   Distance Between Two Points

Paste value to command line

Angle of Line Defined by Two Points

Intersection of Two Lines Defined by Four Points

- **Get Coordinates.** Temporarily hides the **QuickCalc** window so a point can be selected from the drawing area. The X,Y,Z coordinates of the selected point are placed in the input box.
- **Distance Between Two Points.** Temporarily hides the **QuickCalc** window so two points can be selected from the drawing area. The distance between the two selected points is placed in the input box.
- **Angle of Line Defined by Two Points.** Allows you to select two points on a line and then the angle of the line is calculated and placed in the input box.
- **Intersection of Two Lines Defined by Four Points.** Allows you to find the intersection of two lines by picking points on the two lines. The X,Y,Z coordinates of the intersection is placed in the input box.

Using QuickCalc with commands

While drafting, there may be an unknown distance or angle that needs to be calculated before an object can be drawn. During a command, **QuickCalc** can be used to help with these calculations. To use **QuickCalc** during a command, start the command and then when prompted for the value that needs to be calculated, pick the **QuickCalc** button from the **Standard** toolbar or enter 'QC or 'QUICKCALC. The **QuickCalc** window opens in command mode. See **Figure 16-19.** Use the necessary tools of **QuickCalc** to evaluate an expression and then press the **Apply** button to pass the value back to the command. **QuickCalc** can also be in the middle of a command to do calculations without passing the result back to the command. To not have the result passed back to the command, pick the **Close** button. The following procedure draws a line a distance of 14'8" + 26'3" horizontally from the selected point:

Figure 16-19.
When **QuickCalc** is opened during a command, the active command is displayed and the **Apply** and **Close** buttons are available at the bottom of the window.

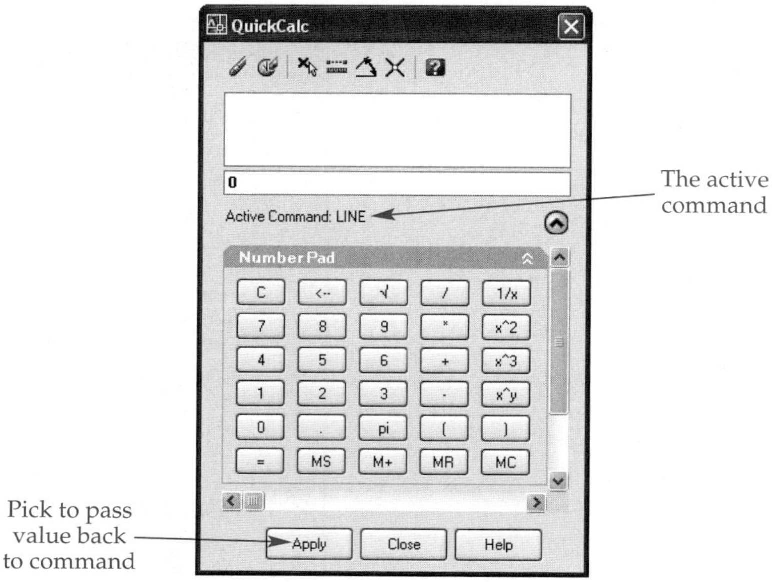

The active command

Active Command: LINE

Pick to pass value back to command

Apply   Close   Help

Command: **LINE**↵
Specify first point: *(pick a point)*
Specify next point or [Undo]: *(with polar tracking on, drag the mouse to the right of the first selected point so the line is at 0°)* '**QC**↵

In the input box of the **QuickCalc** window enter 14'8" + 26'3" and press [Enter]. The result is 40'11". Pick the **Apply** button and this value is passed as the distance for the Y coordinate. Press [Enter] and the line is drawn.

PROFESSIONAL TIP

When using **QuickCalc**, the unit used must match the drawing units. With the following example, architectural units are used. The drawing units must be set to architectural. If needed, use the **Drawing Units** dialog box to change the drawing units to Architectural.

Using QuickCalc with object properties

QuickCalc can also be used to calculate expressions for an object in the **Properties** window. When the **Properties** window is open, picking a field that contains a numeric value displays the calculator icon. In **Figure 16-20**, a circle is selected, and the **Radius** field in the **Properties** window is active. Picking the calculator icon opens the **QuickCalc** window in property calculation mode. Expressions and values can be used in the same manner as when using **QuickCalc** in the middle of a command. When the expression has been evaluated in the input box, pick the **Apply** button to pass the value to the property field in the **Properties** window. The object automatically updates based on the new value.

Additional QuickCalc Options

The history area contains some settings and features that can only be accessed from the right-click shortcut menu. This menu is displayed when right-clicking anywhere in the history area. See **Figure 16-21**. The following options are available:

- **Expression Font Color.** Allows you to change the color of the expression font.
- **Value Font Color.** Allows you to change the color of the value font.
- **Copy.** Copies the expression and value to the Windows clipboard.
- **Append Expression to Input Area.** Passes the expression to the input box.

Figure 16-20.
The calculator icon is displayed after selecting a numeric field in the **Properties** window.

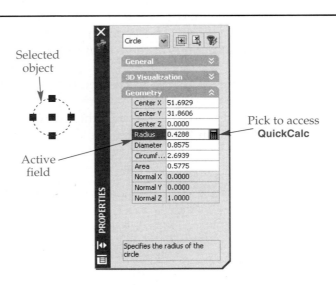

Selected object

Active field

Pick to access **QuickCalc**

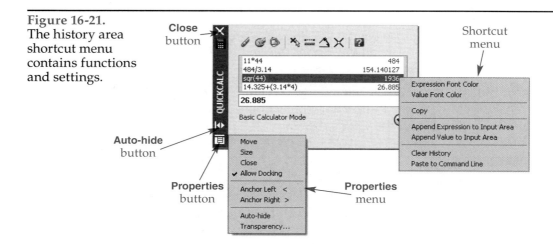

Figure 16-21.
The history area shortcut menu contains functions and settings.

- **Append Value to Input Area.** Passes the value to the input box.
- **Clear History.** Clears the history area.
- **Paste to Command Line.** Passes the value to the Command: prompt.

Picking the **Properties** button displays the **Properties** menu. Some of these options control the appearance of the **QuickCalc** window. The **Allow Docking** settings determine if the window can be docked on the side of the AutoCAD screen. If this is unchecked, the **QuickCalc** window does not try to dock automatically when it is moved near the edge of the AutoCAD screen. When **Auto-hide** is on, the main area of **QuickCalc** is hidden when the pointer is moved into the drawing area—only the title bar remains. Moving the pointer over the title bar expands the **QuickCalc** window to its full state. The feature can also be turned on and off by picking the **Auto-hide** button on the title bar. Picking **Transparency...** opens the **Transparency** dialog box and allows you to set a transparency level for the **QuickCalc** window. Entering in a higher value makes the window more transparent, allowing you to see through the window into the drawing area.

The Geometry Calculator

The *geometry calculator* is used by entering expressions at the Command: prompt. Fundamental math calculations and drafting applications are presented using the geometry calculator. Complex mathematical calculations are also possible.

AutoCAD's geometry calculator allows you to extract and use existing information in your drawing. The geometry calculator also allows you to perform basic mathematical calculations at the command line or supply an expression as input to a prompt.

The geometry calculator is accessed by typing **CAL**. You are then prompted for an expression. After you type the mathematical expression and press [Enter], AutoCAD automatically simplifies, or "solves," the expression and returns the result. For additional information on the geometry calculator, refer to the *Geometry Calculator* document in the *Supplemental Material* section of the Student CD.

Chapter Test

Answer the following questions. Write your answers on a separate sheet of paper or complete the electronic chapter test on the Student CD.

1. To add the areas of several objects when using the **AREA** command, when do you select the Add option?
2. Explain how picking a polyline when using the **AREA** command is different from picking an object drawn with the **LINE** command.
3. What information is provided by the **AREA** command?
4. For what is the **LIST** command used?
5. Describe the meanings of delta X and delta Y.
6. What is the function of the **DBLIST** command?
7. How do you cancel the **DBLIST** command?
8. What are the two purposes of the **ID** command?
9. What information is provided by the **TIME** command?
10. When does the drawing creation time start?
11. List at least three ways to open the **QuickCalc** window.
12. Name the four sections of the **QuickCalc** window.
13. Give the proper symbol to use for the following math functions:
    A. Addition.
    B. Subtraction.
    C. Multiplication.
    D. Division.
    E. Exponent.
    F. Grouped expressions.
14. Under which section of the **QuickCalc** window can the square root function be found?
15. Under which section of the **QuickCalc** window can the arccosine function be found?
16. When using one of the scientific functions, which should you do first: pick the scientific function button or type in the value to be used in the input box?
17. Name the three types of units that can be converted using **QuickCalc**.
18. A(n) _____ is a text item that represents another value that can be accessed later as needed.
19. Which tool button is used to pass the value in the input box to the command line?
20. Name the three ways to start **QuickCalc** while in the middle of a command.
21. When using **QuickCalc** in the middle of a command, how do you pass the value to the command line?
22. When the **Properties** window is open, what do you need to do first to see the calculator icon, so **QuickCalc** can be used?

Drawing Problems

*Use **QuickCalc** to calculate the result of the following equations.*

1. 27.375 + 15.875
2. 16.0625 – 7.1250
3. 5 × 17'-8"
4. 48'-0" ÷ 16
5. (12.625 + 3.063) + (18.250 – 4.375) – (2.625 – 1.188)
6. 7.25^2
7. Show the calculation and answer that would be used with the **LINE** command to make an 8" line 1.006 in./in. longer in a pattern to allow for shrinkage in the final casting. Show only the expression and answer.
8. Solve for the deflection of a structural member. The formula is written as $PL^3/48EI$, where P = pounds of force, L = length of beam, E = Modulus of Elasticity, and I = moment of inertia. The values to be used are P = 4000 lbs, L = 240", and E = 1,000,000 lbs/in². The value for I is the result of the beam (Width × Height³)/12, where Width = 6.75" and Height = 13.5".
9. Convert 4.625" to millimeters.
10. Convert 26 mm to inches.
11. Convert 65 miles to kilometers.
12. Convert 5 gallons to liters.
13. Calculate the coordinate located at 4,4,0 + 3<30.
14. Calculate the coordinate located at (3 + 5,1 + 1.25,0) + (2.375,1.625,0).
15. Find the square root of 360.
16. Calculate 3.25 squared.

Given the following right triangle, make the required trigonometry calculations.

17. Length of side c (hypotenuse).
18. Sine of angle *A*.
19. Sine of angle *B*.
20. Cosine of angle *A*.
21. Tangent of angle *A*.
22. Tangent of angle *B*.

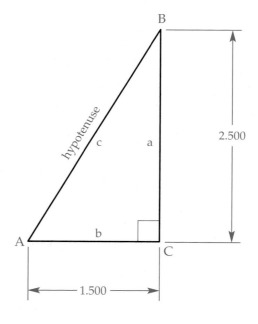

23. Draw the object shown below using the dimensions given. Check the time when you start the drawing. Draw all the features using the **PLINE** and **CIRCLE** commands. Use the **Object, Add,** and **Subtract** options of the **AREA** command to calculate the following measurements:
   A. The area and perimeter of Object A.
   B. The area and perimeter of Object B.
   C. The area and circumference of one of the circles.
   D. The area of Object A, minus the area of Object B.
   E. The area of Object A, minus the areas of the other three features.

   Enter the **TIME** command and note the editing time spent on your drawing. Save the drawing as P16-23.

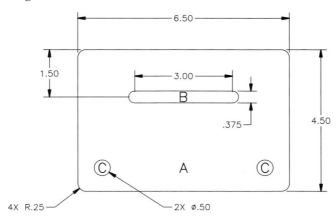

24. Draw the deck shown below using the **PLINE** command. Using the **POLYGON** command, draw the hexagon. Use the following guidelines to complete this problem:
   A. Specify architectural units for your drawing. Use 1/2″ fractions and decimal degrees. Leave the remaining settings for the drawing units at the default values.
   B. Set the limits to 100′,80′ and use the **All** option of the **ZOOM** command.
   C. Set the grid spacing to 2′ and the snap spacing to 1′.
   D. Calculate the measurements listed below.
      a. The area and perimeter of Object A.
      b. The area and perimeter of Object B.
      c. The area of Object A, minus the area of Object B.
      d. The distance between Point C and Point D.
      e. The distance between Point E and Point C.
      f. The coordinates of Points C, D, and F.
   E. Enter the **DBLIST** command and check the information listed for your drawing.
   F. Enter the **TIME** command and note the total editing time spent on your drawing.
   G. Save the drawing as P16-24.

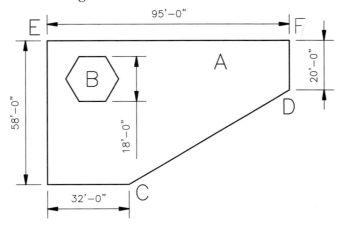

25. The drawing below is a view of the gable end of a house. Draw the house using the dimensions given, and draw the windows as single lines only (the location of the windows is not important). The spacing between each of the second-floor windows is 3″. The width of this end of the house is 16′-6″. The length of the roof is 40′. You may want to use the **PLINE** command to assist in creating specific shapes in this drawing, except as noted above. Save the drawing as P16-25. Calculate the following:

A. The total area of the roof.

B. The diagonal distance from one corner of the roof to the other.

C. The area of the first-floor window.

D. The total area of all second-floor windows, including the 3″ spaces between each of them.

E. Siding will cover the house. What is the total area of siding for this end?

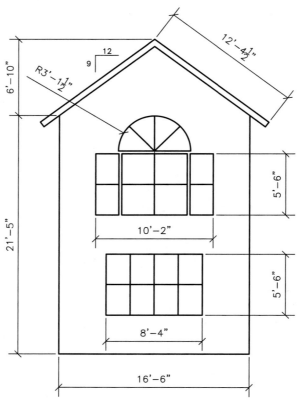

26. The drawing shown below is a side view of a pyramid. The pyramid has four sides. Create an auxiliary view showing the true size of a pyramid face. Save the drawing as **P16-26**. Using inquiry techniques, calculate the following:
    A. The area of one side.
    B. The perimeter of one side.
    C. The area of all four sides.
    D. The area of the base.
    E. The true length (distance) from the midpoint of the base on one side to the apex.

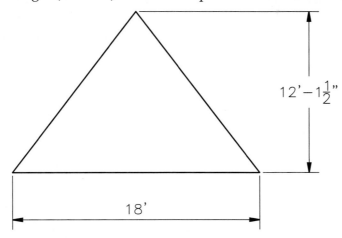

27. Draw the property plat shown below. Label property line bearings and distances only if required by your instructor. Calculate the area of the property plat in square feet and convert to acres. Save the drawing as **P16-27**.

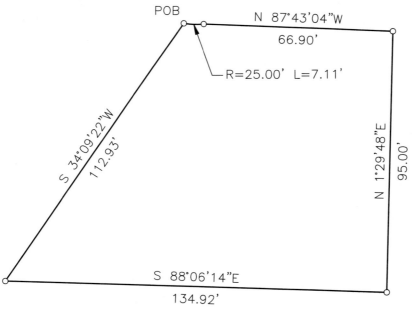

Drawing Problems – Chapter 16

28. Draw the subdivision plat shown below. Label the drawing as shown. Calculate the acreage of each lot and record each value as a label inside the corresponding lot (for example, .249 AC). Save the drawing as P16-28.

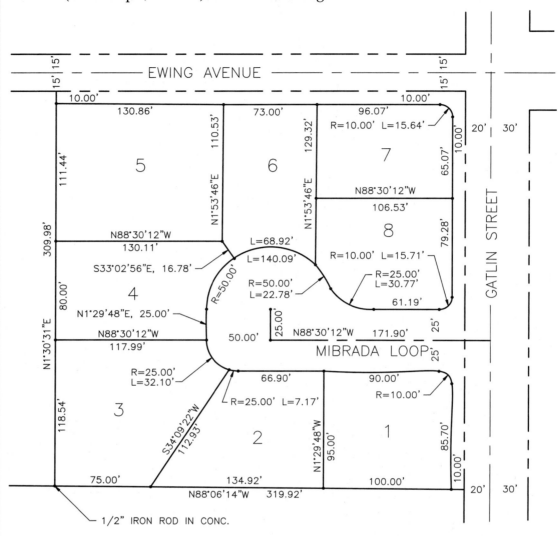

CHAPTER 17

Basic Dimensioning Practices

Learning Objectives

After completing this chapter, you will be able to do the following:

- Use AutoCAD dimensioning commands to dimension objects to ASME and other drafting standards.
- Create and use dimension styles.
- Create dimension style overrides.
- Control the appearance of dimensions.
- Add linear, angular, diameter, and radius dimensions to a drawing.
- Set the appropriate units and decimal precision for dimension text.
- Use text size and style standards consistent with ASME and other professional standards.
- Insert common drafting symbols within dimension text.
- Place general notes on drawings.
- Draw datum and chain dimensions.
- Add dimensions for multiple items using the **QDIM** command.
- Dimension curves.
- Draw oblique dimensions.
- Use the **QLEADER** command to draw specific notes with linked leader lines.
- Dimension objects with arrowless tabular dimensions.
- Prepare thread symbols and notes.

Dimensions are given to describe the size, shape, and location of features on an object or structure. The dimension may consist of numerical values, lines, symbols, and notes. Typical AutoCAD dimensioning features and applications are shown in Figure 17-1.

Each drafting field (such as mechanical, architectural, civil, and electronics drafting) uses a different type of dimensioning technique. It is important for a drafter to place dimensions in accordance with company and industry standards. The standard emphasized in this text is ASME Y14.5M-1994, *Dimensioning and Tolerancing*. The *M* in Y14.5M means the standard is written with metric numeric values for dimensions. ASME Y14.5M-1994 is published by the American Society of Mechanical Engineers (ASME). This text discusses the correct application of both inch and metric dimensioning.

Figure 17-1.
Dimensions describe size and location. Follow accepted conventions when dimensioning.

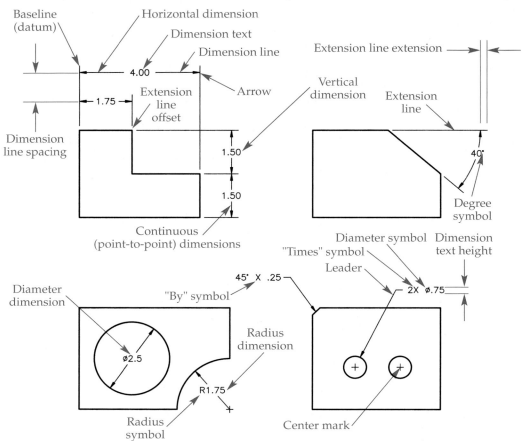

AutoCAD's dimensioning functions provide you with unlimited flexibility. Commands allow you to dimension linear distances, circles, and arcs. You can also place a note with an arrow and leader line pointing to the feature. In addition to these commands, dimension styles allow you to control the height, width, style, and spacing of the individual components of a dimension.

This text covers the comprehensive elements of AutoCAD dimensioning in four chapters. This chapter covers fundamental standards and practices for dimensioning. Chapter 18 covers editing procedures for dimensions. Chapter 19 covers dimensioning applications with tolerances. Chapter 20 covers geometric dimensioning and tolerancing practices. If you use AutoCAD for mechanical drafting in the manufacturing industry, you may want to study all four dimensioning chapters. If you are involved in another field, such as architectural design, you may want to learn the basics covered in Chapters 17 and 18 and skip Chapters 19 and 20.

This chapter will get you started dimensioning immediately with AutoCAD. As you progress, you will learn about dimension settings that can be used to control the way dimensions are presented. You can control conventions such as the space between dimension lines; arrowhead size and type; and text style, height, and position. You will also learn how to create dimension styles that have settings appropriate for the types of drawings done at your company or school.

When you dimension objects with AutoCAD, the objects are automatically measured exactly as you have them drawn. This makes it important for you to draw accurate original objects and features. Use object snap modes to your best advantage when dimensioning.

Dimension Arrangement

Dimensions communicate information about the drawing. Different industries and companies apply similar techniques for presenting dimensions. The two most accepted arrangements of text are unidirectional and aligned.

Unidirectional Dimensioning

Unidirectional dimensioning is typically used in the mechanical drafting field. The term **unidirectional** means *one direction*. This system has all dimension numbers and notes placed horizontally on the drawing. The dimensions are read from the bottom of the sheet.

Unidirectional dimensions normally have arrowheads on the ends of dimension lines. The dimension number is usually centered in a break near the center of the dimension line. See **Figure 17-2**.

Aligned Dimensioning

Aligned dimensions are typically placed on architectural or structural drawings. The term **aligned** means the dimension numbers are lined up with the dimension lines. The dimension numbers for horizontal dimensions read horizontally. Dimension numbers for vertical dimensions are placed so they are read from the right side of the sheet. See **Figure 17-3**. Numbers for dimensions placed at an angle read at the same angle as the dimension line. Notes are usually placed so they read horizontally.

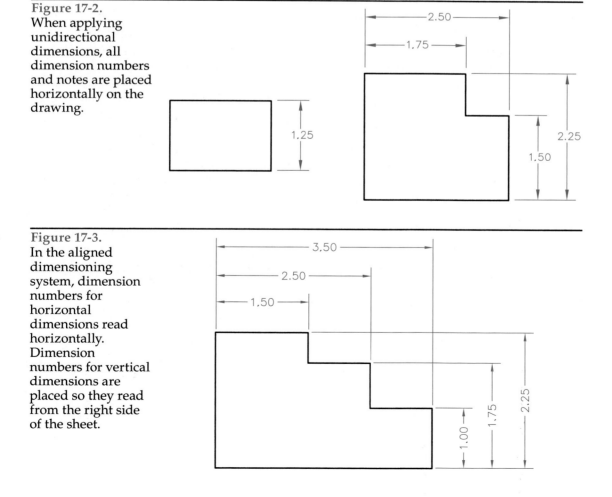

Figure 17-2.
When applying unidirectional dimensions, all dimension numbers and notes are placed horizontally on the drawing.

Figure 17-3.
In the aligned dimensioning system, dimension numbers for horizontal dimensions read horizontally. Dimension numbers for vertical dimensions are placed so they read from the right side of the sheet.

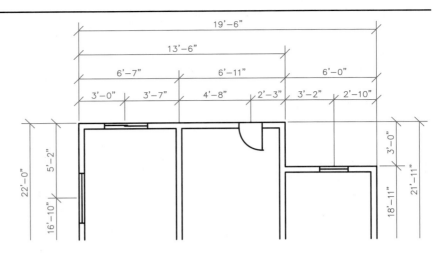

Figure 17-4.
An example of aligned dimensioning in architectural drafting. Notice the tick marks used in place of the arrowheads and the placement of the dimensions above the dimension line.

When using the aligned system, terminate dimension lines with tick marks, dots, or arrowheads. In architectural drafting, the dimension number is generally placed above the dimension line and tick marks are used as terminators. See **Figure 17-4**.

Dimension Styles

The appearance of dimensions, from the size and the style of the text to the color of the dimension line, is controlled by over 70 different settings. *Dimension styles* are saved configurations of these settings.

A dimension style is created by changing the dimension settings as needed to achieve the desired appearance for your drafting application. For example, the dimension style for mechanical drafting probably has the Romans text font placed in a break in the dimension line and the dimension lines are terminated with arrowheads. Refer to **Figure 17-3**. The dimension style for architectural drafting may use the CityBlueprint or Stylus BT text font placed above the dimension line and dimension lines are terminated with slashes. Refer to **Figure 17-4**.

The dimension style can have dimensions based on national or international standards, or it may be set up to match company or school applications and standards. The default dimension style is the Standard dimension style. This dimension style uses the AutoCAD default settings.

Creating Dimension Styles

You might think of dimension styles as the dimensioning standards you use. Dimension styles are usually established for a specific type of drafting field or application. You can customize dimension styles to correspond to drafting standards such as ASME/ANSI, International Organization for Standardization (ISO), military (MIL), architectural, structural, or civil standards, or your own school or company standards.

Dimension styles are created using the **Dimension Style Manager** dialog box. See **Figure 17-5.** This dialog box is accessed by picking the **Dimension Style...** button on the **Dimension** toolbar, selecting **Format > Dimension Style...** in the pull-down menu, or selecting **Dimension > Dimension Style...** in the pull-down menu. You can also type D, DST, DDIM, DIMSTY, or DIMSTYLE.

The current dimension style, which is initially Standard, is noted at the top of the **Dimension Style Manager** dialog box. The **Styles:** box displays the dimension styles found within the current drawing. The selection in the **List:** drop-down list controls whether all styles or only the styles in use are displayed in the **Styles:** box.

If there are external reference drawings (xrefs) within the current drawing, the **Don't list styles in Xrefs** box can be checked to eliminate xref-dependent dimension styles from the **Styles:** box. This is often valuable because xref dimension styles cannot be used to create new dimensions. External references are discussed in Chapter 25.

The **Description** area and **Preview of:** image provide information about the selected dimension style. The Standard dimension style is the AutoCAD default. If you change any of the AutoCAD default dimension settings without first creating a new dimension style, the changes are automatically stored in a dimension style override.

There are additional options found in the **Dimension Style Manager** dialog box. These include:

- **Set Current.** This button makes the dimension style selected in the **Styles:** box current. When a dimension style is current, all new dimensions are created in that style. Existing dimensions are not affected by a change to the current style. Xref-dependent dimension styles cannot be set current.
- **New.** Use this button to create a new dimension style. When you pick this button, the **Create New Dimension Style** dialog box is displayed. See **Figure 17-6.** The following options are available in this dialog box:
  - **New Style Name.** Give your new dimension style a descriptive name, such as Architectural or Mechanical.
  - **Start With.** This option helps you save time by basing the settings for a new style on an existing dimension style. Xref dimension styles can be selected from this dialog box only if they were displayed in the **Dimension Style Manager** dialog box.

DIMSTYLE

Type
DIMSTYLE
D
DST
DDIM
DIMSTY

Pull-Down Menu
Dimension > **Dimension Style...**
Format > **Dimension Style...**

Toolbar
Dimension

Dimension Style...

Figure 17-5.
The **Dimension Style Manager** dialog box. The Standard dimension style is the AutoCAD default.

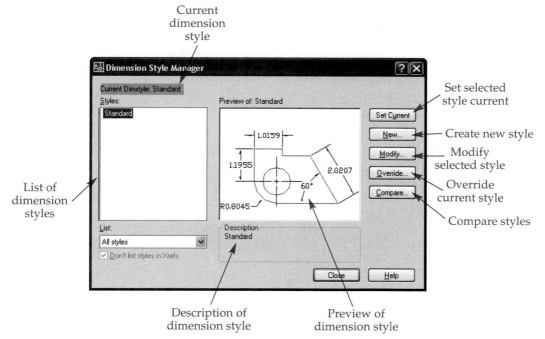

Current dimension style

List of dimension styles

Set selected style current

Create new style

Modify selected style

Override current style

Compare styles

Description of dimension style

Preview of dimension style

Figure 17-6.
The **Create New Dimension Style** dialog box.

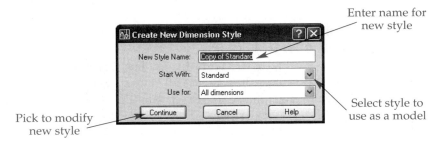

Enter name for new style

Pick to modify new style

Select style to use as a model

- **Use for.** The choices in this drop-down list are **All dimensions, Linear dimensions, Angular dimensions, Radius dimensions, Diameter dimensions, Ordinate dimensions,** and **Leaders and Tolerances.** Use the **All dimensions** option to create a new dimension style. If you select one of the other options, you create a "substyle" of the dimension style specified in the **Start With:** text box. The settings in the new style are applied to the dimension type selected in this drop-down list.
- **Continue.** Pick this button to access the **New Dimension Style** dialog box.
- **Modify.** Selecting this button opens the **Modify Dimension Style** dialog box, which allows you to make changes to the style highlighted in the **Styles** list. Xref styles cannot be modified.
- **Override.** An *override* is a temporary change to the current style settings. Including a text prefix for just a few of the dimensions on a drawing is an example of an override. Picking this button opens the **Override Current Style** dialog box. This button is only available for the current style. Once an override is created, it is made current and is displayed as a branch, called the *child*, of the style from which it is created. The dimension style from which the child is created is called the *parent*. The override settings are lost when any other style, including the parent, is set current.
- **Compare.** Sometimes it is useful to view the details of two styles to determine the differences. When the **Compare...** button is selected, the **Compare Dimension Styles** dialog box is opened. You can compare two styles by entering the name of one style in the **Compare:** drop-down list and the name of the other in the **With:** drop-down list. The differences between the selected styles are displayed in the dialog box.

The **New Dimension Style, Modify Dimension Style,** and **Override Current Style** dialog boxes have the same tabs. The **Lines** tab is shown in **Figure 17-7.** The **Lines, Symbols and Arrows, Text, Fit, Primary Units, Alternate Units,** and **Tolerances** tabs access the settings used for changing the way dimensions are displayed. These tabs are discussed in the next sections.

After completing the information on all tabs, pick the **OK** button to return to the **Dimension Style Manager** dialog box. Select **Set Current** to have all new dimensions take on the qualities of your newly created or modified style.

Figure 17-7.
The **Lines** tab of the **Modify Dimension Style** dialog box.

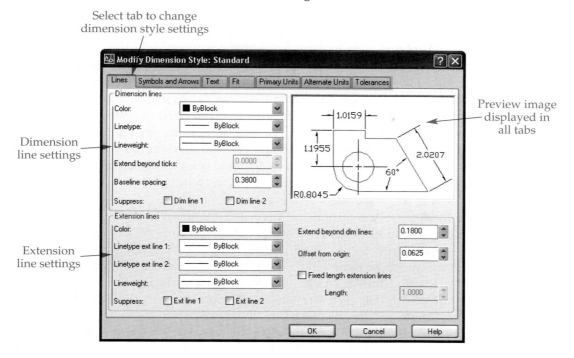

Select tab to change
dimension style settings

Preview image
displayed in
all tabs

Dimension
line settings

Extension
line settings

 NOTE   The values of dimension style settings are stored in
AutoCAD system variables called *dimension variables.*
For example, the center mark type setting in the **Center
marks** area of the **Symbols and Arrows** tab is stored in the
DIMCEN dimension variable. A change to a dimension style
setting changes the current value of the corresponding
dimension variable.

Changing the values of dimension variables by entering the
variable name on the command line is not a recommended
method for setting or changing dimension style settings.
Changes made in this manner can introduce inconsis-
tencies with other dimensions. Changes to dimensions
are best made by redefining styles or performing style
overrides. These methods are discussed later in this
chapter. Dimension variables have limited practical uses,
and are more likely to be used in advanced applications
such as scripting and customizing. For a listing of the
dimension variables in AutoCAD, see the *Reference
Materials* section on the Student CD.

Using the Lines Tab

When the **New** (or **Modify**) button is selected from the **Dimension Style Manager**
dialog box, the **New** (or **Modify**) **Dimension Style** dialog box is displayed with six tabs:
Lines, Symbols and Arrows, Text, Fit, Primary Units, Alternate Units, and **Tolerances**. As
adjustments are made to the current dimension style, an image on each tab updates to
graphically reflect those changes. The **Lines** tab controls all settings for the display of
the dimension and extension lines. Refer to **Figure 17-7**.

The **Dimension lines** area is used to change the format of the dimension line with the following settings:

- **Color.** By default, the dimension line color is set to ByBlock, which indicates that the line assumes the currently active color setting of all elements within the dimension object. The ByBlock color setting means that the color assigned to the created block is used for the component objects of the block. All associative dimensions are created as block objects. Blocks are symbols designed for multiple use and are explained in Chapter 22. Associative dimensions are discussed in this chapter and in Chapter 18. If the current entity color is set to ByLayer when the dimension block is created, then it comes in with a ByLayer setting. The component objects of the block then take on the color of the layer where the dimensions are created. If the current object color is an absolute color, then the component objects of the block take on that specific color regardless of the layer where the dimension was created.

- **Linetype.** By default, the dimension line linetype is set to ByBlock, which indicates that the line assumes the currently active linetype of all elements within the dimension object. To change the dimension style to use something other than ByBlock, select the drop-down list button. The currently loaded linetypes are available from the list. To use one of these, select it from the list. To use a linetype not in the list, pick the **Other...** option to open the **Select Linetype** dialog box. Linetypes are discussed in Chapter 4.

- **Lineweight.** By default, the dimension line lineweight is set to ByBlock, which indicates that the line assumes the currently active lineweight setting of all elements within the dimension object. The ByBlock lineweight setting means that the lineweight assigned to the created block is used for the component objects of the block. If the current object lineweight is set to ByLayer when the dimension block is created, then it comes in with a ByLayer setting. The component objects of the block then take on the lineweight of the layer where the dimensions are created. If the current object lineweight is an absolute lineweight, the component objects of the block take on that specific lineweight regardless of the layer where the dimension was created.

- **Extend beyond ticks.** This text box is inactive unless you are using tick marks instead of arrowheads. Architectural tick marks or oblique arrowheads are often used when dimensioning architectural drawings. The different settings for arrowhead styles are explained later in this chapter. In this style of dimensioning, the dimension lines often cross extension lines. The extension represents how far the dimension line extends beyond the extension line. See **Figure 17-8**. The 0.00 default is used to draw dimensions that are not extended past the extension lines.

- **Baseline spacing.** This text box allows you to change the spacing between the dimension lines of baseline dimensions created with the **DIMBASELINE** command. The default spacing is 0.38 units, which is generally too close for most drawings. Try other values to help make the drawing easy to read. **Figure 17-9** shows the dimension line spacing.

Figure 17-8.
Using the **Extend beyond ticks** setting to allow the dimension line to extend past the extension line. With the default value of 0, the dimension line does not extend.

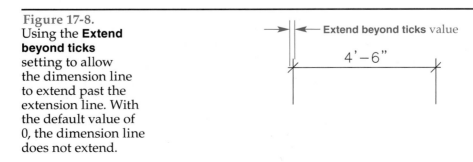

Figure 17-9.
The **Baseline spacing** setting controls the spacing between dimension lines.

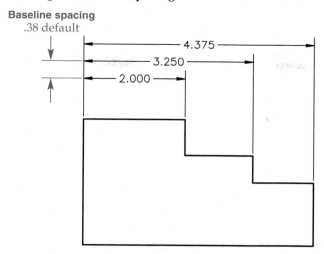

Figure 17-10.
Using the **Dim line 1** and **Dim line 2** dimensioning settings. "Off" is equivalent to an unchecked **Suppress** check box in the **Lines** tab.

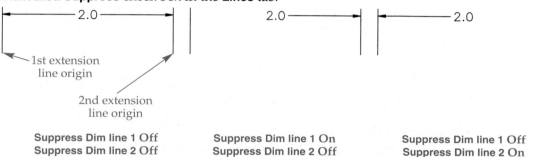

- **Suppress.** This option has two toggles that prevent the display of the first, second, or both dimension lines and their arrowheads. The **Dim line 1** and **Dim line 2** check boxes refer to the first and second points picked when the dimension is created. Both dimension lines are displayed by default. The results of using these options are shown in **Figure 17-10**.

The **Extension lines** area of the **Lines** tab is used to change the format of the extension lines with the following dimension settings:

- **Color.** The color choice made here controls the extension line color. The default value is ByBlock.
- **Linetype ext line 1.** This setting specifies the linetype to be used for the first extension line. The first extension line is determined by the first point picked when creating the dimension.
- **Linetype ext line 2.** The linetype of the second extension line is determined by this setting.
- **Lineweight.** The lineweight setting controls the lineweight of the extension lines.
- **Extend beyond dim lines.** This text box is used to set the extension line extension, which is the distance the extension line runs past the last dimension line. See **Figure 17-11**. The default value is 0.18; an extension line extension of 0.125 is common on most drawings.

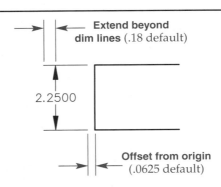

Figure 17-11.
The extension line extension and the extension line offset settings.

- **Offset from origin.** This text box is used to change the distance between the object and the beginning of the extension line. See **Figure 17-11.** Most applications require this small offset. The default is 0.0625. When an extension line meets a centerline, use a setting of 0.0 to prevent a gap.
- **Fixed length extension lines.** This setting allows you to set a given length for extension lines. When this option is checked, the **Length** text box becomes active. The value in this text box is then used to set a restricted length for the extension lines. The length is measured from the dimension line toward the extension line origin.
- **Length.** This option is activated when the **Fixed length extension lines** option is turned on, and sets the length of the extension lines.
- **Suppress.** This option is used to suppress the first, second, or both extension lines using the **Ext line 1** and **Ext line 2** check boxes. Extension lines are displayed by default. An extension line might be suppressed, for example, if it coincides with an object line. See **Figure 17-12.**

Using the Symbols and Arrows Tab

The settings in the **Symbols and Arrows** tab are used to control the appearance of arrowheads, center marks, and other symbol components of dimensions. See **Figure 17-13.** The **Arrowheads** area provides several different arrowhead options and controls the arrowhead size. Use the appropriate drop-down list to select the arrowhead used for the **First** arrowhead, **Second** arrowhead, and **Leader** arrowhead. The default arrowhead is closed filled; other options are shown in **Figure 17-14.** If you pick a new arrowhead in the **First:** drop-down list, AutoCAD automatically makes the same selection for the **Second:** drop-down list. Check your drafting standards and then select the appropriate arrowhead.

Notice in **Figure 17-14** there is no example of a user arrow. This option is used to access an arrowhead of your own design. For this to work, you must first design an arrowhead and save it as a block. Blocks are discussed in Chapter 22 of this text. When you pick **User Arrow...** in an **Arrowheads** drop-down list, the **Select Custom Arrow Block** dialog box is displayed. Type the name of your custom arrow block in the **Select from Drawing Blocks:** text box and then pick **OK** to have the arrow used for the style. The name of the block is then displayed in the **Arrowheads** drop-down list.

Figure 17-12.
Suppressing extension lines.

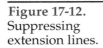

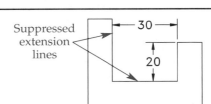

Figure 17-13.
The **Symbols and Arrows** tab of the **Modify Dimension Style** dialog box.

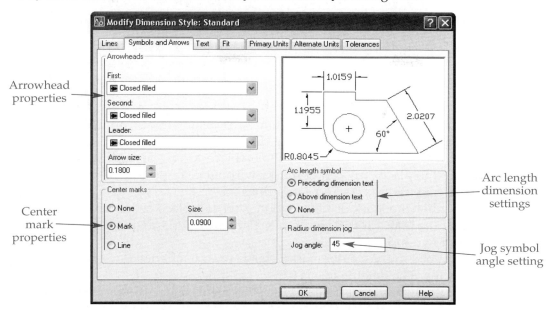

Figure 17-14.
Examples of dimensions drawn using the options found in the **Arrowheads** drop-down lists.

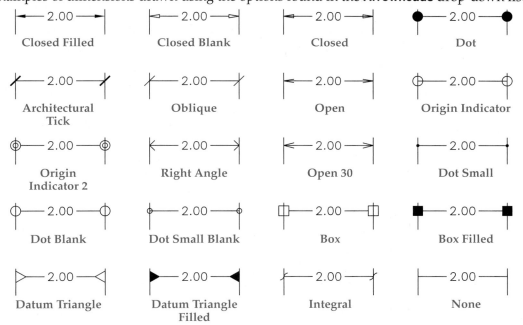

When you select the oblique or architectural tick arrowhead, the **Extend beyond ticks:** text box in the **Lines** tab is activated. This allows you to enter a value for a dimension line projection beyond the extension line. The default value is zero, but some architectural companies like to project the dimension line past the extension line. Refer to **Figure 17-8**.

The **Arrow size:** text box allows you to change the size of arrowheads. The default value is 0.18. An arrowhead size of 0.125″ is common on mechanical drawings. **Figure 17-15** shows the arrowhead size value.

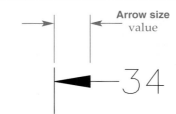

Figure 17-15.
The default arrow
size is 0.18.

The **Center marks** area of the **Symbols and Arrows** tab allows you to select the way center marks are placed in circles and arcs. The options are:

- **None.** Provides for no center marks to be placed in circles and arcs.
- **Mark.** Used to place only center marks without centerlines.
- **Line.** Places center marks and centerlines.

After selecting either the **Mark** or **Line** option, you can place center marks on circles and arcs by using the **DIMCENTER** command. The results of drawing center marks and centerlines are shown in **Figure 17-16.**

The **Size:** text box in the **Center marks** area is used to change the size of the center mark and centerline. The default size is 0.09.

The **Arc Length Symbol** area controls the placement of the arc length symbol when using the **DIMARC** command. The **Preceding dimension text** option is the default. This places the symbol in front of the dimension value. If **Above dimension text** is selected, the arc length symbol is placed over the length value. See **Figure 17-17.** To have the symbol not show, use the **None** option.

The **Jog angle** setting in the **Radius dimension jog** area controls the appearance of the break line used for the jog symbol when using the **DIMJOGGED** command. This value sets the incline formed by the line connecting the extension line and dimension line. The default angle is 45°.

Figure 17-16.
Arcs and circles
displayed with
center marks and
centerlines.

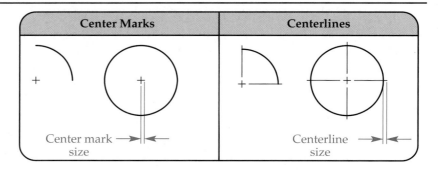

Figure 17-17.
The arc length
symbol can be
placed in front of or
above the dimension
text when using the
DIMARC command.

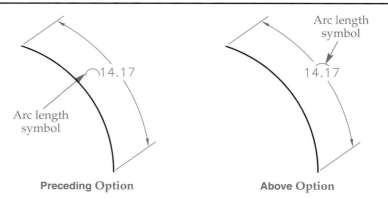

Exercise 17-1   Complete the Exercise on the Student CD.

Using the Text Tab

Changes can be made to dimension text by picking the **Text** tab in the **New** (or **Modify**) **Dimension Style** dialog box. See **Figure 17-18**.

The **Text appearance** area is used to set the dimension text style, color, height, and frame. The options in this area are:

- **Text style.** The dimension text style uses the Standard text style by default. Text styles must be loaded in the current drawing before they are available for use in dimension text. Pick the desired text style from the drop-down list.
- **Text color.** The dimension color default is ByBlock. Use the drop-down list to select a color for the text. If the color is not in the drop-down list, pick **Select Color...** to select a color from the **Select Color** dialog box.
- **Text height.** The dimension text height is set by entering the desired value in this text box. Dimension text height is commonly the same as the text height for items found on the rest of the drawing except for titles, which are larger. The default dimension text height is 0.18, which is an acceptable standard. Many companies use a text height of 0.125. The ASME standard recommends text height between 0.125 and 0.188. The text height for titles and labels is usually between 0.18 and 0.25.
- **Fraction height scale.** This setting controls the height of fractions for architectural or fractional unit dimensions. The value in this box is multiplied by the text height value to determine the height of the fraction. A value of 1.0 creates fractions that are the same text height as regular (nonfractional) text, which is the normally accepted standard. A value less than 1.0 makes the fraction smaller than the regular text height.
- **Draw frame around text.** If checked, AutoCAD draws a rectangle around the text. The distance between the text and the frame is determined by the setting for the **Offset from dim line** value, which is explained later in this section.

Figure 17-18.
The **Text** tab of the **Modify Dimension Style** dialog box.

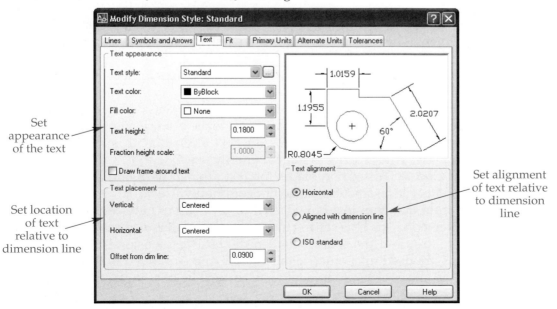

Figure 17-19.
Dimension text justification options. A—Vertical justification options, with the horizontal Centered justification. B—Horizontal justification options, with the vertical Centered justification.

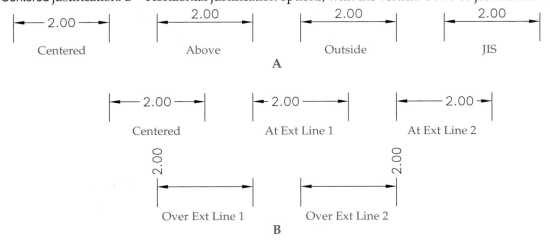

The **Text placement** area of the **Text** tab is used to place the text relative to the dimension line. See **Figure 17-19.** The preview image changes to represent the selections you make. The **Vertical:** drop-down list has the following options for the vertical justification:

- **Centered.** This option is the default. It places dimension text centered in a gap provided in the dimension line. This is the dimensioning practice commonly used in mechanical drafting and many other fields.
- **Above.** This option is generally used for architectural drafting and building construction. The dimension text is placed horizontally and above horizontal dimension lines. For vertical and angled dimension lines, the text is placed in a gap provided in the dimension line. Architectural drafting commonly uses aligned dimensioning, where the dimension text is aligned with the dimension lines and all text reads from either the bottom or right side of the sheet. An additional setting to provide this type of dimensioning is discussed later.
- **Outside.** This option places the dimension text outside the dimension line and either above or below a horizontal dimension line or to the right or left of a vertical dimension line. The direction you move the cursor determines the above/below and left/right placement.
- **JIS.** This is the option to use when dimensioning for Japanese Industrial Standards.

In addition to the vertical placement of the dimension text, you can control the horizontal placement. The **Horizontal:** drop-down list has the following options for the horizontal justification:

- **Centered.** This option is the AutoCAD default. It places dimension text centered between the extension lines.
- **At Ext Line 1.** This option locates the text next to the extension line placed first.
- **At Ext Line 2.** This option locates the text next to the extension line placed second.
- **Over Ext Line 1.** This option places the text aligned with and over the first extension line. This practice is not commonly used.
- **Over Ext Line 2.** This option places the text aligned with and over the second extension line. This practice is also not commonly used.

The **Offset from dim line:** text box is used to set the gap between the dimension line and the dimension text. This setting also controls the distance between the leader shoulder and the text, and the space between the basic dimension box and the text. Basic dimensions are used in geometric tolerancing and explained in Chapter 20. The default gap is 0.09. The gap should be set to half the text height. **Figure 17-20** shows the gap in linear and leader dimensions.

Figure 17-20.
The gap (offset) for text used in a linear dimension and a leader dimension.

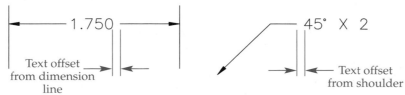

Text offset from dimension line

Text offset from shoulder

The **Text alignment** area of the **Text** tab allows you to control the alignment of dimension text. This area is used when you want to draw unidirectional dimensions or aligned dimensions, which were discussed earlier in this chapter. The **Horizontal** option draws unidirectional dimensions commonly used for mechanical manufacturing drafting applications. The **Aligned with dimension line** option creates aligned dimensions, which are typically used for architectural dimensioning. The **ISO Standard** option creates aligned dimensions when the text falls between the extension lines and horizontal dimensions when the text falls outside the extension lines.

Using the Fit Tab

The **Fit** tab in the **New** (or **Modify**) **Dimension Style** dialog box is used to establish the way in which dimension text and arrowheads are placed on the drawing. The **Fit** tab is shown in **Figure 17-21** with default settings.

The **Fit options** area of the **Fit** tab controls how text and arrows should behave if they do not fit within the given area between two extension lines. These effects are most obvious on dimensions where space is limited. Watch the preview image change as you try each of the following options. This should help you understand how each option acts. Notice that these options are radio buttons, which means only one option can be active at any given time:

- **Either text or arrows (best fit).** This is the default setting and allows AutoCAD to place text and dimension lines with arrowheads inside extension lines if space is available. Dimension lines with arrowheads are placed outside of extension lines if space is limited. Everything is placed outside of extension lines if there is not enough space between extension lines.

Figure 17-21.
The **Fit** tab of the **Modify Dimension Style** dialog box.

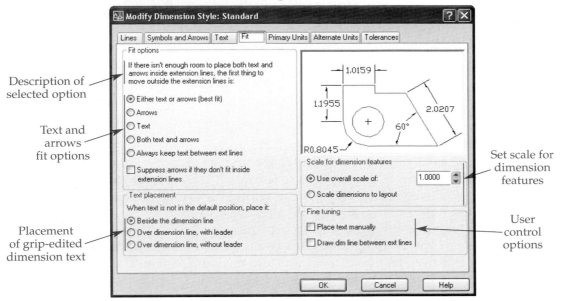

Description of selected option

Text and arrows fit options

Placement of grip-edited dimension text

Set scale for dimension features

User control options

- **Arrows.** The text, dimension line, and arrowheads are placed inside the extension lines if there is enough space. The text is placed outside if there is enough space for only the arrowheads and dimension line inside the extension lines. Everything is placed outside if there is not enough room for anything inside.
- **Text.** The text, dimension line, and arrowheads are placed inside the extension lines if there is enough space for everything. If there is enough space for only the text inside the extension lines, then the dimension lines and arrowheads are placed outside. Everything is outside if there is not enough room for the text inside.
- **Both text and arrows.** When this option is used, AutoCAD places the text, dimension line, and arrowheads inside the extension lines if there is enough space, or everything is placed outside the extension lines if there is not enough space.
- **Always keep text between ext lines.** This option always places the dimension text between the extension lines. This may cause problems when there is limited space between extension lines.
- **Suppress arrows if they don't fit inside extension lines.** This option removes the arrowheads if they do not fit inside the extension lines. Use this option with caution because it can create dimensions that violate standards.

Sometimes it becomes necessary to move the dimension text from its default position. The text can be moved by grip editing the text portion of the dimension. The options in the **Text placement** area of the **Fit** tab instruct AutoCAD how to handle these grip-editing situations. The following options are available:

- **Beside the dimension line.** When the dimension text is grip edited and moved, the text is constrained to move with the dimension line and can only be placed within the same plane as the dimension line.
- **Over dimension line, with leader.** When the dimension text is grip edited and moved, the text can be moved in any direction away from the dimension line. A leader line is created that connects the text to the dimension line.
- **Over dimension line, without leader.** When the dimension text is grip edited and moved, the text can be moved in any direction away from the dimension line without a connecting leader.

PROFESSIONAL TIP

To return the dimension text to its default position, select the dimension, right-click to display the shortcut menu, and select **Home text** from the **Dim Text position** cascading menu.

The **Scale for dimension features** area of the **Fit** tab is used to set the scale factor for all dimension features in the drawing. The **Use overall scale of:** value sets a multiplier for dimension settings, such as text height and the offset from origin. For example, if the height of the dimensioning text is set to 0.125 and the value for the overall scale is set to 100, then the dimension text can be measured within the drawing to be 12.5 units (100 × 0.125). If the drawing is plotted with a plot scale of 1 = 100, the size of the dimension text on the paper measures 0.125 units.

Select the **Scale dimensions to layout (paperspace)** option if you are dimensioning in a floating viewport in a layout (paper space) tab. It allows the overall scale to adjust according to the active floating viewport by setting the overall scale equal to the viewport scale factor.

The **Fine tuning** area of the **Fit** tab provides you with maximum flexibility in controlling where you want to place dimension text. The **Place text manually** option gives you control over text placement and dimension line length outside extension lines. The text can be placed where you want it, such as to the side within the extension lines, or outside of the extension lines.

The **Draw dim line between ext lines** option forces AutoCAD to place the dimension line inside the extension lines, even when the text and arrowheads are outside. The default application is with the dimension line and arrowheads outside the extension lines. See **Figure 17-22.** Forcing the dimension line inside the extension lines is not an ASME standard, but it may be preferred by some companies.

PROFESSIONAL TIP

When dimensioning mechanical drawings, it is common to have **Place text manually** on, centered horizontal and vertical justification, and horizontal text alignment.

For architectural drafting, it is typical to have **Place text manually** on, **Draw dim line between ext lines** on, centered horizontal justification, above vertical justification, and text aligned with dimension lines.

Exercise 17-2   Complete the Exercise on the Student CD.

Using the Primary Units Tab

The **Primary Units** tab of the **New** (or **Modify**) **Dimension Style** dialog box is used to set units for linear and angular dimensions. The **Linear dimensions** area is used to make settings for linear dimensions. See **Figure 17-23.** This area has the following options:

- **Unit format.** Select the type of units for dimension text from this drop-down list. The default selection is **Decimal** units. Definitions and examples of the different types of units are provided in Chapter 2 of this text.
- **Precision.** This drop-down list allows you to decide how many zeros follow the decimal place when decimal-related units are selected. The default is 0.0000; the 0.00 and 0.000 settings are also common in mechanical drafting. When fractional units are selected, the precision values are related to the smallest desired fractional denominator. The default is 1/16″ but you can choose other options ranging from 1/256″ to 1/2″; 0″ displays no fractional values. A variety of dimension precision may be found on the same drawing.
- **Fraction format.** The options for controlling the display of fractions are **Diagonal**, **Horizontal**, and **Not Stacked**. The **Fraction format** option is only available if the **Architectural** or **Fractional** style is selected for the unit format.
- **Decimal separator.** Decimal numbers may use commas, periods, or spaces as separators. The **'.' (Period)** option is the default. The **Decimal separator** option is not available if the **Architectural** or **Fractional** style is selected for the unit format.

Figure 17-22.
The effects of the **Draw dim line between ext lines** option of the **Fine tuning** area of the **Fit** tab.

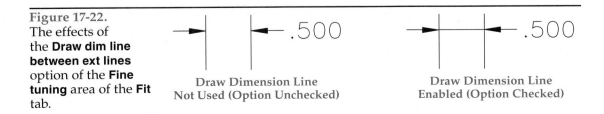

Draw Dimension Line
Not Used (Option Unchecked)

Draw Dimension Line
Enabled (Option Checked)

Figure 17-23.
The **Primary Units** tab of the **Modify Dimension Style** dialog box.

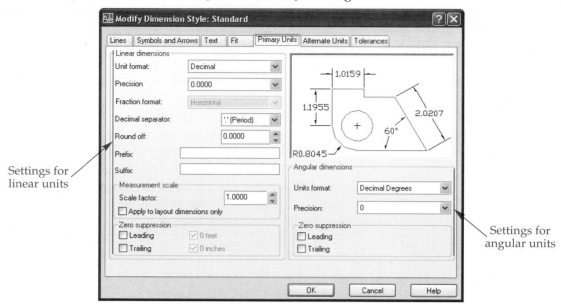

Settings for
linear units

Settings for
angular units

- **Round off.** This text box specifies the accuracy of rounding for dimension numbers. The default is zero, which means that no rounding takes place and all dimensions are placed exactly as measured. If you enter a value of 0.1, all dimensions are rounded to the closest 0.1 unit. For example, an actual measurement of 1.188 is rounded to 1.2.
- **Prefix.** *Prefixes* are special notes or applications placed in front of the dimension text. A typical prefix might be SR3.5 where SR means spherical radius. When a prefix is used on a diameter or radius dimension, the prefix replaces the ⌀ or R symbol.
- **Suffix.** *Suffixes* are special notes or applications placed after the dimension text. A typical suffix might be 3.5 MAX, where MAX is the abbreviation for maximum. The abbreviation IN can also be used when one or more inch dimensions are placed on a metric dimensioned drawing. Another example is using a suffix of MM on one or more millimeter dimensions placed on an inch drawing.

PROFESSIONAL TIP

Usually, a prefix or suffix is not used on every dimension in the drawing. A prefix or suffix is normally a special specification and might be used in only a few cases. Because of this, you might set up a special dimension style for these applications or enter them when needed by using the **MText** or **Text** option of the related dimensioning command.

The **Measurement scale** area in the **Linear dimensions** area of the **Primary Units** tab is used to set the scale factor of linear dimensions. Set the value in the **Scale factor:** text box. If a value of 1 is set, dimension values are displayed the same as they are measured. If the setting is 2, dimension values are twice as much as the measured amount. For example, an actual measurement of 2 inches is displayed as 2 with a scale factor of 1, but the same measurement is displayed as 4 when the scale factor is 2. Placing a check in the **Apply to layout dimensions only** check box makes the linear scale factor active only when dimensioning in a layout tab.

The **Zero suppression** area provides four check boxes. The following options are used to suppress leading and trailing zeros in the primary units:

- **Leading.** This option is unchecked by default, which leaves a zero on decimal units less than 1, such as 0.5. This option is used when placing metric dimensions as recommended by the ASME standard. Check this box to remove the 0 on decimal units less than 1, as recommended by the ASME standard for inch dimensioning. The result is a decimal dimension such as .5. This option is not available for architectural units.
- **Trailing.** This option is unchecked by default, which leaves zeros after the decimal point based on the precision setting. This is usually off for inch dimensioning because the trailing zeros often control tolerances for manufacturing processes. Check this box for metric dimensions to conform to the ASME standard. This option is not available for architectural units.
- **0 feet.** This option is checked by default. It removes the zero in feet and inch dimensions when there are zero feet. For example, when unchecked, a dimension may read 0'-11". When checked, however, the dimension reads 11". This option is only available for architectural or engineering units.
- **0 inches.** This option is checked by default. It removes the zero when the inch part of feet and inch dimensions is less than one inch, such as 12'-7/8". If checked, the same dimension reads 12'-0 7/8". Also, this option removes the zero from a dimension with no inch value; for example, 12' is used rather than 12'-0". This option is only available for architectural or engineering units.

The **Angular dimensions** area of the **Primary Units** tab is used to set the desired type of angular units for dimensioning. Angular units are discussed in the section in Chapter 2 on the **Drawing Units** dialog box. (The **Drawing Units** dialog box does not control the type of units used for dimensioning.) The following settings are found in the **Angular dimensions** area:

- **Units format.** The default setting is **Decimal Degrees**. The other options are **Degrees Minutes Seconds**, **Gradians**, and **Radians**. Select the desired option from the drop-down list.
- **Precision.** This value sets the desired precision of the angular dimension value. Select an option from the drop-down list.

The **Zero suppression** area has check boxes for the **Leading** and **Trailing** suppression options. These options are used to keep or remove leading or trailing zeros on the angular dimension.

Using the Alternate Units Tab

The **Alternate Units** tab of the **New** (or **Modify**) **Dimension Style** dialog box is used to set alternate units. See **Figure 17-24**. *Alternate units*, or *dual dimensioning* units, have inch measurements followed by millimeters in brackets, or millimeters followed by inches in brackets. Dual dimensioning practices are no longer a recommended ASME standard. ASME recommends that drawings be dimensioned using inch or metric units only. However, alternate units can be used in many other applications.

The **Display alternate units** check box must be checked in order to activate the settings. The tab has many of the same settings found in the **Primary Units** tab. The **Multiplier for alt units** setting is multiplied by the primary unit to establish the value for the alternate unit. The default is 25.4 because an inch value is multiplied by 25.4 to convert it to millimeters. The **Placement** area controls the location of the alternate-unit dimension. The two options are **After primary value** and **Below primary value**.

NOTE The final tab in the **Modify Dimension Style** dialog box, **Tolerances**, is discussed in Chapter 19.

Figure 17-24.
The **Alternate Units** tab of the **Modify Dimension Style** dialog box.

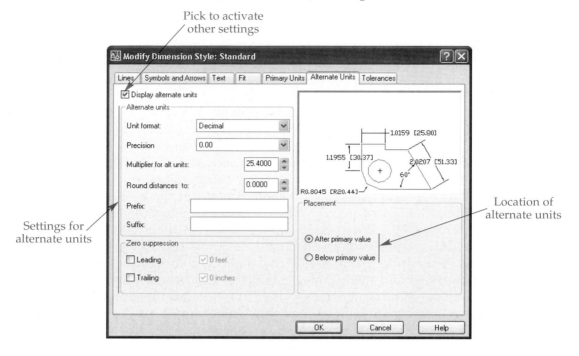

Pick to activate other settings

Settings for alternate units

Location of alternate units

Exercise 17-3   Complete the Exercise on the Student CD.

Making Your Own Dimension Styles

Creating and recording dimension styles is part of your AutoCAD management responsibility. You should carefully evaluate the items contained in the dimensions for the type of drawings you do. During this process, be sure to carefully check school, company, or national standards to verify the accuracy of your plan. Then, make a list of features and values for the dimensioning settings you use based on what you have learned in this chapter. When you are ready, use the **Dimension Style Manager** dialog box options to establish dimension styles named to suit your drafting practices.

The chart in **Figure 17-25** provides possible settings for two dimension styles. One list is for mechanical manufacturing and the other is for architectural drafting applications. For settings not listed here, use the AutoCAD defaults.

Exercise 17-4   Complete the Exercise on the Student CD.

Figure 17-25.
This chart shows dimension settings for typical mechanical and architectural drawings.

Setting	Mechanical (Inch)	Architectural
Dimension line spacing	.50	1/2″
Extension line extension	.125	1/8″
Extension line offset	.0625	3/32″
Arrowhead options	Closed filled, closed, or open	Architectural tick, dot, closed filled, oblique, or right angle
Arrowhead size	.125	1/8″
Center	Line	Mark
Center size	.25	1/4″
Text placement	Manually	Manually
Vertical justification	Centered	Above
Text alignment	Horizontal	Aligned with dimension line
Primary units	Decimal (default)	Architectural
Dimension precision	0.000	1/16″
Zero suppression (metric)	Leading off	Leading off
	Trailing on	Trailing on
Zero suppression (inch)	Leading on	Leading on
	Trailing off	Trailing off
Angles	Decimal degrees (default)	Decimal degrees
Tolerances	By application	None
Text style	gdt	Stylus BT
Text height	.125	1/8″
Text gap	.05	1/16″

Overriding Existing Dimension Style Settings

Generally, it is appropriate to have one or more dimension styles set to perform specific tasks that relate to your dimensioning practices. However, there are situations where a few dimensions require settings that are not covered by your basic styles. These situations may be too few and far between to warrant creating a new style. For example, assume you have the value for **Offset from origin** set at 0.0625, which conforms to ASME standards. However, in your final drawing there are three dimensions that require a 0 **Offset from origin** setting. For these dimensions, you can perform a *dimension style override* and temporarily alter the settings for the dimension style without actually modifying the style.

Dimension Style Overrides for Existing Dimensions

PROPERTIES

Type

PROPERTIES
PROPS
CH
MO
[Ctrl]+[1]

Pull-Down Menu

Modify
> Properties

Toolbar

Standard

Properties

To override the dimension style of an existing dimension, first select the dimension. Then, open the **Properties** window by picking the **Properties** button on the **Standard** toolbar, selecting **Modify** > **Properties** from the pull-down menu, or typing PROPERTIES. You can also right-click in the viewport and select **Properties** from the shortcut menu or double-click on the selected dimension.

The dimension properties listed in the **Properties** window are broken down into eight categories. See **Figure 17-26**. To change an existing property or value, access the proper category and pick the property to highlight it. You can then change the corresponding value. Refer to Chapter 13 for a discussion on how to make changes in the **Properties** window.

The changes made in the **Properties** window are overrides to the dimension style for the selected dimension. The changes do not alter the original dimension style. Also, the changes are not applied to new dimensions.

Figure 17-26.
The **Properties** window can be used to edit dimension properties and create a dimension style override.

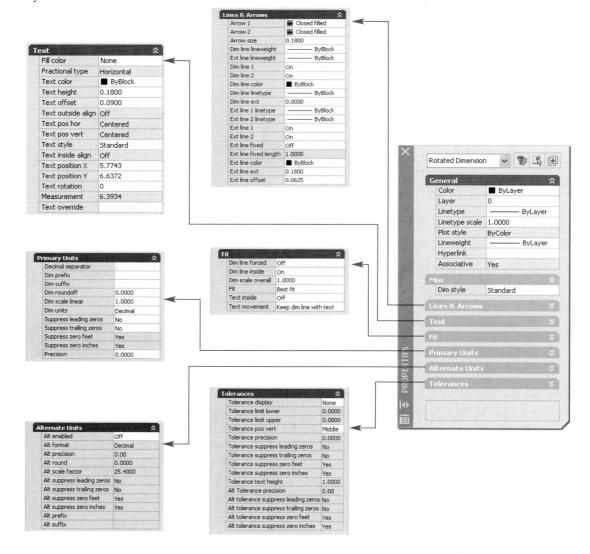

Dimension Style Overrides for New Dimensions

To override the dimension style for dimensions you are about to draw, open the **Dimension Style Manager**. Then, select the dimension style that you are going to override from the **Styles** list. Finally, pick the **Override...** button to display the **Override Current Style** dialog box. This dialog box has the same features as the **New** (or **Modify**) **Dimension Style** dialog box. Make any changes to the style and pick the **OK** button. The style you overrode now has a branch under it labeled **<style overrides>**, which is set as the current style. Close the **Dimension Style Manager** and draw the needed dimensions.

To clear the overrides, return to the **Dimension Style Manager** and set any other style current. However, this will discard the overrides. If you want to incorporate the overrides into the style that was overridden, right-click on the **<style overrides>** name and select **Save to current style** from the shortcut menu. To save the changes to a new style, pick the **New...** button. Then, select **<style overrides>** in the **Start With** drop-down list in the **Create New Dimension Style** dialog box. Finally, in the **New Dimension Style** dialog box, simply pick **OK** to save the overrides as a new style.

PROFESSIONAL TIP

Carefully evaluate the dimensioning requirements in a drawing before performing a style override. It may, in fact, be better to create a new style. For example, if a number of the dimensions in the current drawing require the same overrides, generating a new dimension style is a good idea. If only one or two dimensions need the same overrides, performing an override may be more productive.

Drawing Dimensions with AutoCAD

AutoCAD has a variety of dimensioning applications that fall into five fundamental categories: linear, angular, diameter, radius, and ordinate. These applications allow you to perform nearly every type of dimensioning practice needed for your discipline.

Drawing Linear Dimensions

Linear means straight. In most cases, dimensions measure straight distances, such as horizontal, vertical, or slanted surfaces. The **DIMLINEAR** command allows you to measure the length of an object and place the dimension line, extension lines, dimension text, and arrowheads automatically. To do this, pick the **Linear** button in the **Dimension** toolbar, select **Dimension > Linear** from the pull-down menu, or type DLI or DIMLINEAR.

Once the command is initiated, you are asked to pick the origin of the first extension line. Then you are asked for the origin of the second extension line. The points you pick are the extension line origins. See **Figure 17-27**. Place the crosshairs directly on the corners of the object where the extension lines begin. Use object snap modes for accuracy.

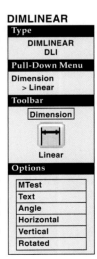

DIMLINEAR

Type
DIMLINEAR DLI

Pull-Down Menu
Dimension > Linear

Toolbar
Dimension
Linear

Options
MTest
Text
Angle
Horizontal
Vertical
Rotated

Figure 17-27.
Establishing
extension line
origins. The
Endpoint and
Intersection object
snap modes are
useful in accurately
locating the origins.

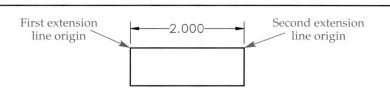

The **DIMLINEAR** command allows you to generate horizontal, vertical, or rotated dimensions. After selecting the object or points of origin for dimensioning, you are given the Specify dimension line location or [Mtext/Text/Angle/Horizontal/Vertical/Rotated] prompt. The options are as follows:

- **Specify dimension line location.** This is the default. Simply drag the dimension line to a desired location and pick. See **Figure 17-28.** This is where preliminary plan sheets and sketches help you determine proper distances to avoid crowding. The extension lines, dimension line, dimension text, and arrowheads are automatically drawn after the location is picked.

- **Mtext.** This option accesses the **In-Place Text Editor** and the **Text Formatting** toolbar, **Figure 17-29.** Here you can provide a specific measurement or text format for the dimension. See Chapter 8 for a complete description of the **In-Place Text Editor** and the **Text Formatting** toolbar. The highlighted value represents the current dimension value. Edit the dimension text and pick **OK.** For example, the ASME standard recommends that a reference dimension be displayed enclosed in parentheses. Type an open and closed parenthesis around the value to create a reference dimension. If you want the current dimension value changed, pick on the value and type the new value.

- **Text.** This option allows you to use the command line to change dimension text. This is convenient if you prefer to type the desired text rather than use the **In-Place Text Editor.** The **Text** and **Mtext** options both create multiline text objects. The **Text** option displays the current dimension value in brackets. Pressing [Enter] accepts the current value. If you need to modify the text, type the new text. For example, you can type parentheses around the value to create a reference dimension.

- **Angle.** This option allows you to change the dimension text angle. This option can be used when creating rotated dimensions or for adjusting the dimension text to a desired angle. The desired angle is entered at the Specify angle of dimension text: prompt.

- **Horizontal.** This option sets the dimension being created to a horizontal distance only. This may be helpful when dimensioning the horizontal distance of a slanted surface. The **Mtext, Text,** and **Angle** options are available again in case you want to change the dimension text value or angle.

Figure 17-28.
Establishing the
dimension line's
location.

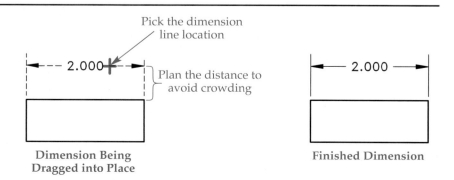

Figure 17-29.
When you use the **Mtext** option, the **In-Place Text Editor** and **Text Formatting** toolbar appear. The highlighted value represents the dimension value AutoCAD has calculated.

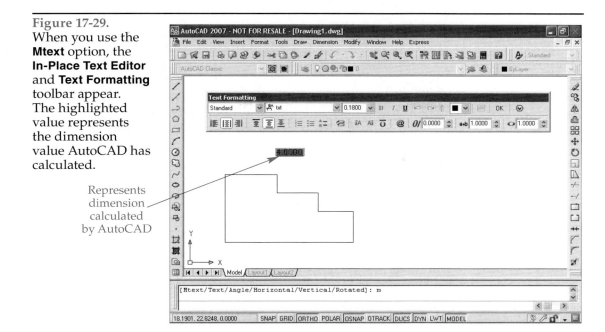

Represents dimension calculated by AutoCAD

- **Vertical.** This option sets the dimension being created to a vertical distance only. This may be helpful when dimensioning the vertical distance of a slanted surface. As with the **Horizontal** option, the **Mtext**, **Text**, and **Angle** options are available.
- **Rotated.** This option allows an angle to be specified for the dimension line. A practical application is dimensioning to angled surfaces and auxiliary views. This technique is different from other dimensioning commands because you are asked to provide a dimension line angle. See **Figure 17-30.** At the Specify angle of dimension line <0>: prompt, enter a value, such as 45, or pick two points on the line to be dimensioned.

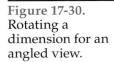

Exercise 17-5   Complete the Exercise on the Student CD.

Figure 17-30.
Rotating a dimension for an angled view.

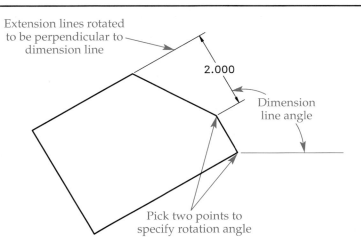

Extension lines rotated to be perpendicular to dimension line

2.000

Dimension line angle

Pick two points to specify rotation angle

Selecting an Object to Dimension

In the previous discussion, the extension line origins were picked in order to establish the extents of the dimension. Another powerful AutoCAD dimensioning option allows you to pick a single line, circle, or arc to dimension. This works when you are using the **DIMLINEAR**, **DIMALIGNED**, and **QDIM** commands; the latter two are discussed later. You can use this option any time you see the Specify first extension line origin or <select object>: prompt. Press [Enter] and then pick the object being dimensioned. When you select a line or arc, AutoCAD automatically begins the extension lines from the endpoints. If you pick a circle, the extension lines are drawn from the closest quadrant and its opposite quadrant. See **Figure 17-31**.

PROFESSIONAL TIP

Dimensioning in AutoCAD should be performed as accurately and neatly as possible. You can achieve consistently professional results by using the following guidelines:

- Always construct drawing geometry accurately. Never truncate, or round off, decimal values when entering locations, distances, or angles. For example, enter .4375 for 7/16 rather than .44.
- Set the desired precision level before beginning your dimensioning. Most drawings have varying levels of precision for specific drawing features, so select the most common precision level to start with and adjust the precision as needed for each dimension. Setting the dimension precision is explained later in this chapter.
- Always use the precision drawing aids to ensure the accuracy of dimensions. If the point being dimensioned does not coincide with a snap point or a known coordinate, use an appropriate object snap override.
- *Never* type a different dimension value than what appears in the brackets. If a dimension needs to change, revise the drawing or dimensioning settings accordingly. The ability to change the dimension in the brackets is provided by AutoCAD so that a different text format can be specified for the dimension. Prefixes and suffixes can also be added to the dimension in the brackets. A typical example of a prefix might be to specify the number of times a dimension occurs, such as 4X 1.750. Other examples of this capability appear later in this chapter.

Figure 17-31.
AutoCAD can automatically determine the extension line origins if you select a line, arc, or circle.

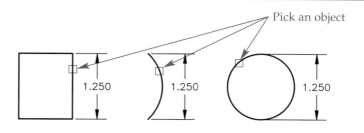

Exercise
17-6

Complete the Exercise on the Student CD.

Dimensioning Angled Surfaces and Auxiliary Views

When dimensioning a surface drawn at an angle, it may be necessary to align the dimension line with the surface. For example, auxiliary views are normally placed at an angle. In order to properly dimension these features, the **DIMALIGNED** command or the **Rotated** option of the **DIMLINEAR** command can be used.

Using the Dimaligned Command

The **DIMALIGNED** command can be accessed by picking the **Aligned** button in the **Dimension** toolbar, picking **Dimension > Aligned** in the pull-down menu, or typing DAL or DIMALIGNED. The results of the **DIMALIGNED** command are shown in **Figure 17-32.** Notice the difference between the aligned dimension in this figure and the rotated dimension in **Figure 17-30.**

Exercise
17-7

Complete the Exercise on the Student CD.

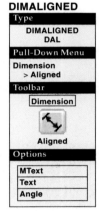

DIMALIGNED

Type
DIMALIGNED DAL

Pull-Down Menu
Dimension > Aligned

Toolbar
Dimension

Aligned

Options
MText
Text
Angle

Figure 17-32.
The **DIMALIGNED** dimensioning command allows you to place dimension lines parallel to angled features.

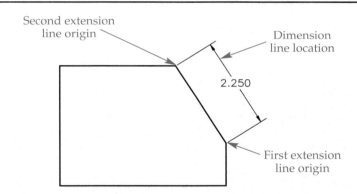

Second extension line origin

Dimension line location

2.250

First extension line origin

Dimensioning Angles

Coordinate and angular dimensioning are both accepted for dimensioning angles. In *coordinate dimensioning* of angles, dimensions locate the corner of the angle, as shown in **Figure 17-33.** This can be accomplished with the **DIMLINEAR** command.

Angular dimensioning locates one corner with a dimension and provides the value of the angle in degrees. See **Figure 17-34.** You can dimension the angle between any two nonparallel lines. The intersection of the lines is the angle's vertex. AutoCAD automatically draws extension lines if they are needed. The angular unit of measure is set in the dimension style, which is discussed later in this chapter.

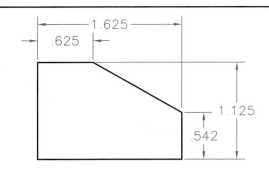

Figure 17-33.
Coordinate dimensioning of angles.

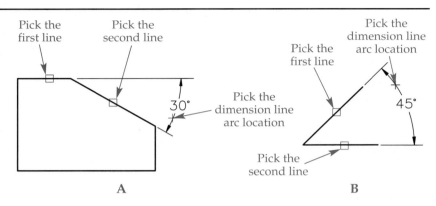

Figure 17-34.
Two examples of drawing angular dimensions.

Pick the first line   Pick the second line

Pick the dimension line arc location

Pick the first line

Pick the dimension line arc location

30°

Pick the dimension line arc location

45°

Pick the second line

A   B

DIMANGULAR

Type
DIMANGULAR DAN
Pull-Down Menu
Dimension > Angular
Toolbar
Dimension
Angular

The **DIMANGULAR** command is used for the angular method. It is accessed by picking the **Angular** button in the **Dimension** toolbar, picking **Dimension > Angular** in the pull-down menu, or by typing DAN or DIMANGULAR. The dimension in **Figure 17-34A** was drawn with the following sequence:

Command: **DAN** *or* **DIMANGULAR**↵
Select arc, circle, line, or <specify vertex>: *(pick the first leg of the angle to be dimensioned)*
Select second line: *(pick the second leg of the angle to be dimensioned)*
Specify dimension arc line location or [Mtext/Text/Angle]: *(pick the desired location of the dimension line arc)*
Dimension text = 30
Command:

The last prompt asks you to pick the dimension line arc location. If there is enough space, AutoCAD places the dimension text, dimension line arc, and arrowheads inside the extension lines. If there is not enough room between extension lines for the arrowheads and text, AutoCAD automatically places the arrowheads outside and the text inside the extension lines. If space is very tight, AutoCAD may place the dimension line arc and arrowheads inside and the text outside, or place everything outside of the extension lines. See **Figure 17-35.**

Placing Angular Dimensions on Arcs

The **DIMANGULAR** command can be used to dimension the included angle of an arc. The arc's center point becomes the angle vertex and the two arc endpoints are the origin points for the extension lines. See **Figure 17-36.**

Placing Angular Dimensions on Circles

The **DIMANGULAR** command can also be used to dimension a portion of a circle. The circle's center point becomes the angle vertex and two picked points are the origin points for the extension lines. See **Figure 17-37.** The point you pick on the circle is the endpoint of the first extension line. You are then asked for the second angle endpoint, which is the endpoint of the second extension line.

Figure 17-35.
The dimension line arc location determines where the dimension line arc, text, and arrows are displayed.

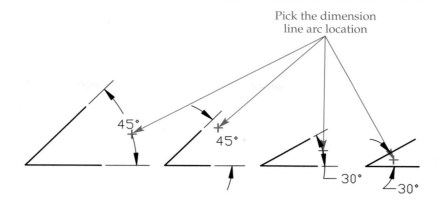

Figure 17-36.
Placing angular dimensions on arcs.

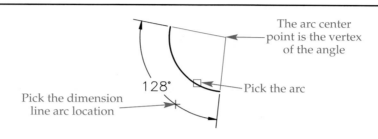

Figure 17-37.
Placing angular dimensions on circles.

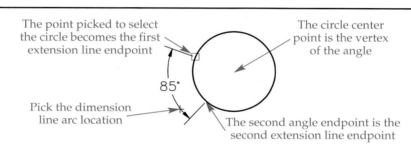

PROFESSIONAL TIP

Using angular dimensioning for circles increases the number of possible solutions for a given dimensioning requirement, but the actual uses are limited. One professional application is dimensioning an angle from a quadrant point to a particular feature without having to first draw a line to dimension. Another benefit of this option is the ability to specify angles that exceed 180°.

Angular Dimensioning through Three Points

You can also establish an angular dimension through three points. The points are the angle vertex and two angle line endpoints. See **Figure 17-38.** To do this, press [Enter] after the first prompt, pick the vertex, and then pick the two endpoints. This method also dimensions angles over 180°.

Exercise 17-8   Complete the Exercise on the Student CD.

Figure 17-38.
Placing angular
dimensions using
three points.

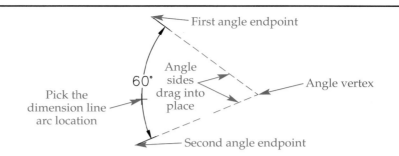

First angle endpoint

Angle
sides
drag into
place

60°

Angle vertex

Pick the
dimension line
arc location

Second angle endpoint

Dimensioning Practices

Dimensioning practices often depend on product requirements, manufacturing accuracy, standards, and tradition. Dimensional information includes size dimensions, location dimensions, and notes. Two methods that identify size and location are chain and datum dimensioning. The method used depends on the accuracy of the product and the drafting field. Both methods are covered later in this chapter.

Size Dimensions and Notes

Size dimensions provide the size of physical features. They include lines, notes, or dimension lines and numbers. Size dimensioning practices depend on the methods used to dimension different geometric features. See **Figure 17-39.** A *feature* is considered to be any physical portion of a part or object, such as a surface, hole, window, or door. Dimensioning standards are used so an object designed in one place can be manufactured or built somewhere else.

Specific notes and general notes are the two types of notes on a drawing. *Specific notes* relate to individual or specific features on the drawing. They are attached to the feature being dimensioned using a leader line. *General notes* apply to the entire drawing and are placed in the lower-left corner, upper-left corner, or above or next to the title block. Where they are placed depends on company or school practice.

Figure 17-39.
Size dimensions and
specific notes.

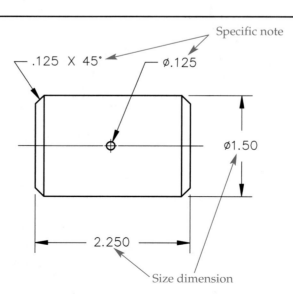

Specific note

.125 X 45°

Ø.125

Ø1.50

2.250

Size dimension

Dimensioning Flat Surfaces and Architectural Features

In mechanical drafting, flat surfaces are dimensioned by giving measurements for each feature. If there is an overall dimension provided, you can omit one of the dimensions. The overall dimension controls the omitted dimension. In architectural drafting, it is common to place all dimensions without omitting any of them. The idea is that all dimensions should be shown to help make construction easier. See **Figure 17-40.**

Dimensioning Cylindrical Shapes

Both the diameter and length of a cylindrical shape can be dimensioned in the view in which the cylinder appears rectangular. See **Figure 17-41.** The diameter symbol next to the dimension indicates that the part is a cylinder. This allows the view in which the cylinder appears as a circle to be omitted.

Dimensioning Square and Rectangular Features

Square and rectangular features are usually dimensioned in the views in which the length and height are shown. The square symbol can be used preceding the dimension for the square feature. See **Figure 17-42.** The square symbol must be created as a block and inserted. Blocks are discussed in Chapter 22 of this text.

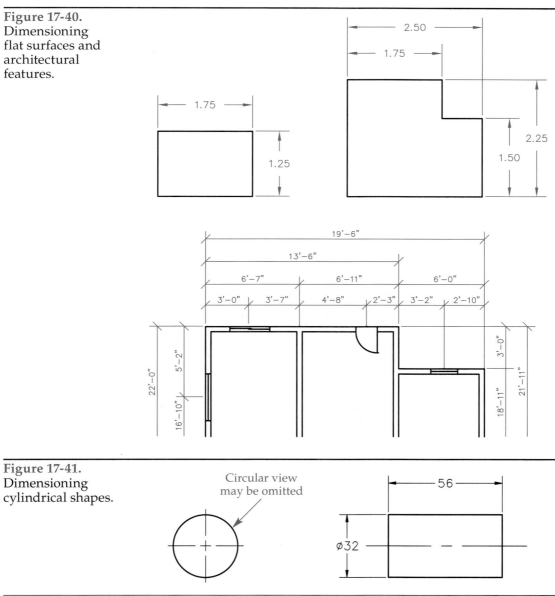

Figure 17-40. Dimensioning flat surfaces and architectural features.

Figure 17-41. Dimensioning cylindrical shapes.

Figure 17-42.
Dimensioning square and rectangular features.

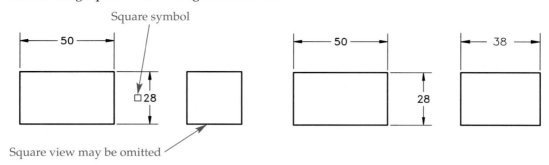

Dimensioning Cones and Hexagonal Shapes

There are two ways to dimension a conical shape. One method is to dimension the diameters at both ends and the length. See **Figure 17-43**. Another method is to dimension the taper angle and the length. Hexagonal shapes are dimensioned by giving the distance across the flats and the length.

Exercise 17-9   Complete the Exercise on the Student CD.

Figure 17-43.
Dimensioning cones and hexagonal cylinders.

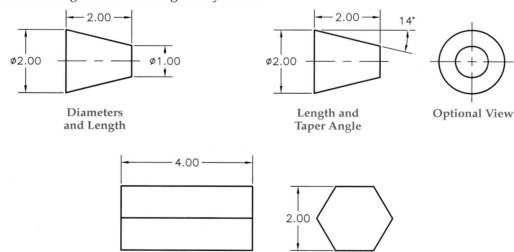

Location Dimensions

Location dimensions are used to locate features on an object. These dimensions do not specify the size of the feature. Holes and arcs are dimensioned to their centers in the view in which they appear circular. Rectangular features are dimensioned to their edges. See **Figure 17-44**. In architectural drafting, windows and doors are dimensioned to their centers on the floor plan.

The rectangular coordinate system and the polar coordinate system are the two basic systems used for creating location dimensions. See **Figure 17-45**. The *rectangular* *coordinate system* uses linear dimensions to locate features from surfaces, centerlines, or center planes. AutoCAD performs this type of dimensioning using a variety of dimensioning commands. The most frequently used linear dimensioning command is the **DIMLINEAR** command. The *polar coordinate system* uses angular dimensions to locate features from surfaces, centerlines, or center planes. Angular dimensions in the polar coordinate system are drawn using AutoCAD's **DIMANGULAR** command.

Figure 17-44.
Location dimensions are used to locate circular and rectangular features.

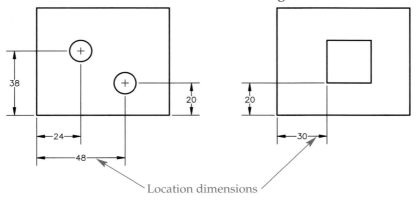

Figure 17-45.
A—Rectangular coordinate location dimensions. B—Polar coordinate location dimensions.

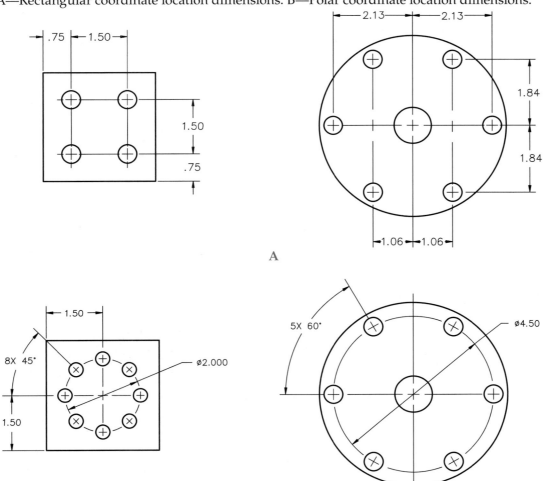

A

B

Datum and Chain Dimensioning

With *datum dimensioning*, or *baseline dimensioning*, dimensions on an object originate from common surfaces, centerlines, or center planes. Datum dimensioning is commonly used in mechanical drafting because each dimension is independent of the others. This achieves more accuracy in manufacturing. **Figure 17-46** shows an object dimensioned with surface datums.

Chain dimensioning, also called *point-to-point dimensioning*, places dimensions in a line from one feature to the next. Chain dimensioning is sometimes used in mechanical drafting. However, there is less accuracy than with datum dimensioning since each dimension is dependent on other dimensions in the chain. Architectural drafting uses chain dimensioning in most applications. **Figure 17-47** shows two examples of chain dimensioning. In mechanical drafting, it is common to leave one dimension blank and provide an overall dimension. Architectural drafting practices usually show dimensions all the way across features plus an overall dimension.

Figure 17-46.
Datum dimensioning.

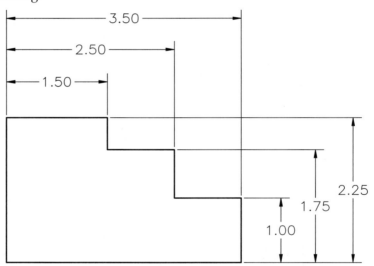

Figure 17-47.
Chain dimensioning.

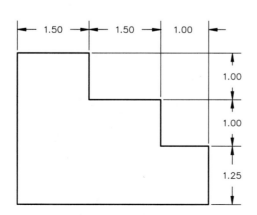
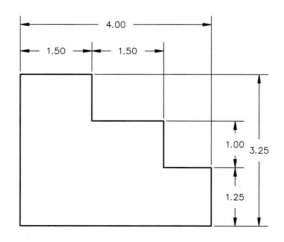

Making Datum and Chain Dimensioning Easy

AutoCAD refers to datum dimensioning as *baseline* dimensioning and chain dimensioning as *continued* dimensioning. Datum dimensioning is controlled by the **DIMBASELINE** command. Chain dimensioning is controlled by the **DIMCONTINUE** command. The **DIMBASELINE** and **DIMCONTINUE** commands are used in the same manner. The prompts and options are the same. Use the **Undo** option in the **DIMBASELINE** or **DIMCONTINUE** command to undo previously drawn dimensions.

Datum Dimensions

Datum dimensions are created by picking the **Baseline** button in the **Dimension** toolbar, picking **Dimension > Baseline** in the pull-down menu, or by typing either DBA or DIMBASELINE. Baseline dimensions can be created with linear, ordinate, and angular dimensions. Ordinate dimensions are discussed later in this chapter.

When you enter the **DIMBASELINE** command, AutoCAD asks you to Specify a second extension line origin. This is because a baseline dimension is a continuation of an existing dimension. Therefore, a dimension must exist before using the command. AutoCAD automatically selects the most recently drawn dimension as the base dimension unless you specify a different one. As you add datum dimensions, AutoCAD automatically places the extension lines, dimension lines, arrowheads, and text. For example, use the following procedure to dimension the series of horizontal baseline dimensions shown in **Figure 17-48**:

```
Command: DLI or DIMLINEAR↵
Specify first extension line origin or <select object>: (pick the first extension line origin)
Specify second extension line origin: (pick the second extension line origin)
Specify dimension line location or
[Mtext/Text/Angle/Horizontal/Vertical/Rotated]: (pick the dimension line location)
Dimension text = 2.000
Command: DBA or DIMBASELINE↵
Specify a second extension line origin or [Undo/Select] <Select>: (pick the next second extension line origin)
Dimension text = 3.250
Specify a second extension line origin or [Undo/Select] <Select>: (pick the next second extension line origin)
Dimension text = 4.375
Specify a second extension line origin or [Undo/Select] <Select>: ↵
Select base dimension: ↵
Command:
```

Figure 17-48.
Using the **DIMBASELINE** command. AutoCAD automatically places the extension lines, dimension lines, arrowheads, and text.

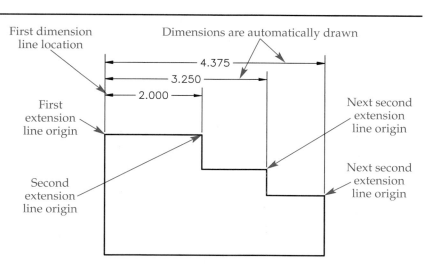

You can continue to add baseline dimensions until you press [Enter] twice to return to the Command: prompt. Notice as additional extension line origins are picked, AutoCAD automatically places the dimension text; you do not specify a location.

If you want to add datum dimensions to an existing dimension other than the most recently drawn one, use the **Select** option by pressing [Enter] at the first prompt. At the Select base dimension: prompt, pick the dimension to serve as the base. When picking a dimension to use as the baseline, the extension line nearest the point where you select the dimension is used as the baseline point. Then, select the new second extension line origins as described earlier.

You can also draw baseline dimensions to angular features. First, draw an angular dimension. Then, enter the **DIMBASELINE** command. You can also pick an existing angular dimension other than the one most recently drawn. **Figure 17-49** shows angular baseline dimensions.

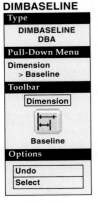

DIMBASELINE

Type
DIMBASELINE
DBA

Pull-Down Menu
Dimension
> Baseline

Toolbar
Dimension
Baseline

Options
Undo
Select

Chain Dimensions

As previously mentioned, when creating chain dimensions, you will receive the same prompts and options received while creating datum dimensions. Chain dimensioning is shown in **Figure 17-50**. Chain dimensions (continued dimensions) are created by picking **Dimension > Continue** in the pull-down menu, picking the **Continue** button in the **Dimension** toolbar, or by typing DCO or DIMCONTINUE. Continued dimensions can be created with linear, ordinate, and angular dimensions. Ordinate dimensions are discussed later in this chapter.

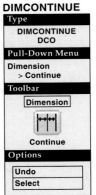

DIMCONTINUE

Type
DIMCONTINUE
DCO

Pull-Down Menu
Dimension
> Continue

Toolbar
Dimension
Continue

Options
Undo
Select

PROFESSIONAL TIP

You do not have to use **DIMBASELINE** or **DIMCONTINUE** immediately after a dimension that is to be used as a base or chain. You can come back later and use the **Select** option as previously discussed. Then, select the dimension you want to use and draw the datum or chain dimensions that you need.

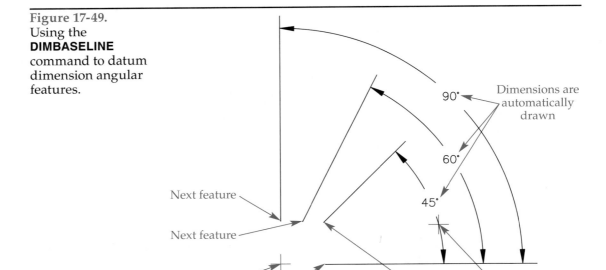

Figure 17-49.
Using the **DIMBASELINE** command to datum dimension angular features.

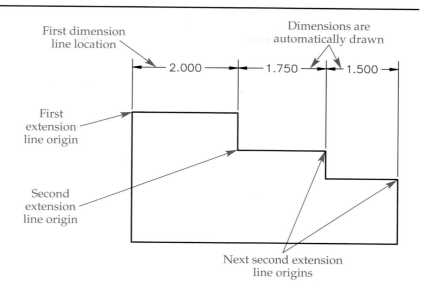

Figure 17-50.
Using the
DIMCONTINUE
command to create
chain dimensions.

First dimension
line location

Dimensions are
automatically drawn

2.000 — 1.750 — 1.500

First
extension
line origin

Second
extension
line origin

Next second extension
line origins

**Exercise
17-10**

Complete the Exercise on the Student CD.

Using Qdim to Dimension

The **QDIM**, or quick dimension, command makes chain and datum dimensioning easy by eliminating the need to define the exact points being dimensioned. Often, the points that need to be selected for dimensioning are the endpoints of lines or the center points of arcs. AutoCAD automates the process of point selection in the **QDIM** command by finding those points for you. The **QDIM** command can be accessed by selecting **Dimension > Quick Dimension** from the pull-down menu, picking the **Quick Dimension** button in the **Dimension** toolbar, or typing QDIM.

The type of geometry selected affects the **QDIM** output. If a single polyline is selected, **QDIM** attempts to draw linear dimensions to every vertex of the polyline. If a single arc or circle is selected, then **QDIM** draws a radius or diameter dimension. If multiple objects are selected, linear dimensions are drawn to the vertex of every line or polyline and to the center of every arc or circle. In each case, AutoCAD finds the points automatically. The command sequence is:

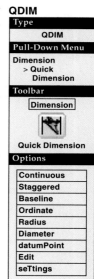

Command: **QDIM**↵
Associative dimension priority = Endpoint
Select geometry to dimension: (*pick several lines, polylines, arcs, and/or circles*)
Select geometry to dimension: ↵
Specify dimension line position, or
[Continuous/Staggered/Baseline/Ordinate/Radius/Diameter/datumPoint/Edit/
    seTtings] <*current*>: (*pick a position for the dimension lines*)
Command:

Figure 17-51 shows examples of different types of objects being dimensioned with the **QDIM** command. The upper dimensions are created by selecting each object separately. The lower dimensions are created by selecting all objects at once.

The **Continuous** option creates chain dimensions. The **Baseline** option creates datum dimensions. The **Staggered** option creates staggered (noncontinuous) dimensions. The **Ordinate, Radius**, and **Diameter** options are discussed later in this chapter. In **Figure 17-51**, the polyline labeled as Object A was dimensioned with the **Baseline** option of the **QDIM** command. The command sequence is:

Figure 17-51.
The **QDIM** command can dimension multiple features or objects at the same time.

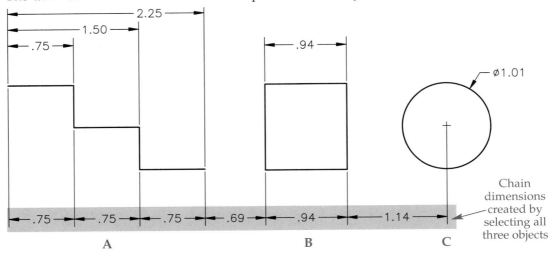

Command: **QDIM.⏎**
Select geometry to dimension: *(pick the polyline shown in Figure 17-51A)*
Specify dimension line position, or
[Continuous/Staggered/Baseline/Ordinate/Radius/Diameter/datumPoint/Edit/seTtings]
<Continuous>: **B⏎**
Specify dimension line position, or
[Continuous/Staggered/Baseline/Ordinate/Radius/Diameter/datumPoint/Edit/seTtings]
<Baseline>: *(pick a position for the dimension line)*
Command:

The dimensions at the bottom of **Figure 17-51** were created by using the **Continuous** option of the **QDIM** command and selecting all three objects.

The **datumPoint** option can be used to change the datum point for datum or chain dimensions. The **Settings** option allows you to set the object snap mode for establishing the extension line origins to **Endpoint** or **Intersection**.

The **QDIM** command can also be used as a way to edit any existing associative dimension. Editing dimensions and a description of the **Edit** option of the **QDIM** command are discussed in Chapter 18.

Including Symbols with Dimension Text

After you select a feature to dimension, AutoCAD responds with the measurement (dimension text). In some cases, such as when you are dimensioning radii and diameters, AutoCAD automatically places the radius (R) or diameter (∅) symbol before the dimension number. However, in other cases, this is not automatic. The recommended ASME standard for a diameter dimension is to place the diameter symbol (∅) before the number. This can be done using the **Mtext** option of the dimensioning commands. When the **In-Place Text Editor** appears, place the cursor in the location where you want the symbol, such as in front of the text. Then, pick **Symbol** from the **Text Formatting** toolbar or right-click to display the shortcut menu and select **Diameter** from the **Symbol** cascading menu. After you pick **OK** in the text editor, the command continues and you are asked to pick the dimension line location.

Other symbols are also available from the **Symbol** cascading menu. You can also use the control codes to place symbols. The **In-Place Text Editor** and drawing special symbols are covered in Chapter 8 of this text.

AutoCAD and Its Applications—Basics

Another way to place symbols with your dimension text is to create a dimension style that has a text style using the gdt.shx font. Establishing a dimension style with a desired text style is explained later in this chapter. A text style with the gdt.shx font allows you to place commonly used dimension symbols with the lowercase letter keys. This font is used for placing geometric dimensioning and tolerancing (GD&T) symbols. Often-used ASME symbols are shown in **Figure 17-52**. The letter in parentheses is the lowercase letter that you press at the keyboard to make the symbol. Additional GD&T symbols are available by pressing other keyboard keys. GD&T is covered in Chapter 20.

Figure 17-52.
Common dimensioning symbols and how to draw them. The lowercase letter displayed in parentheses with some symbol names is the keystroke for placing the symbol with the gdt.shx font.

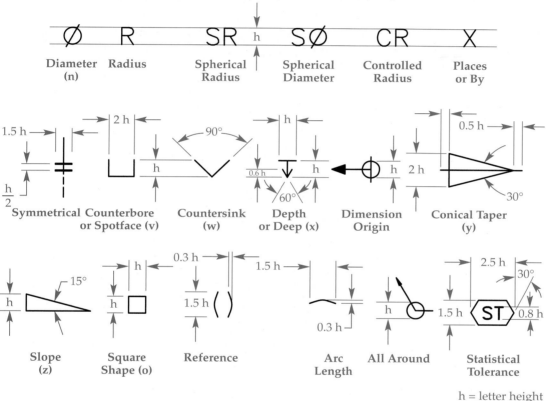

h = letter height

Drawing Center Dashes or Centerlines in a Circle or Arc

When small circles or arcs are dimensioned, the **DIMDIAMETER** and **DIMRADIUS** commands leave center dashes. If the dimension of a large circle crosses through the center, the dashes are left out. However, you can manually add center dashes and centerlines with the **DIMCENTER** command. This command is accessed by picking the **Center Mark** button in the **Dimension** toolbar, picking **Dimension > Center Mark** in the pull-down menu, or typing DCE or DIMCENTER. Once the command is entered, you are prompted to pick an arc or circle.

When the circle or arc is picked, center marks are automatically drawn. The size of the center marks or the amount that the centerlines extend outside the circle or arc is controlled by the **Center marks** area in the **Symbols and Arrows** tab of the **Modify Dimension Style** dialog box.

Dimensioning Circles

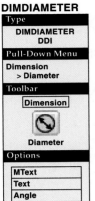

DIMDIAMETER

Type
DIMDIAMETER DDI

Pull-Down Menu
Dimension > Diameter

Toolbar
Dimension
Diameter

Options
MText
Text
Angle

Circles are normally dimensioned by giving the diameter. The ASME standard for dimensioning arcs is to give the radius. However, AutoCAD allows you to dimension either a circle or an arc with a diameter dimension. Diameter dimensions are produced by picking the **Diameter** button in the **Dimension** toolbar, picking **Dimension > Diameter** in the pull-down menu, or typing DDI or DIMDIAMETER. You are then prompted to select the arc or circle.

When using the **DIMDIAMETER** command, a leader line and diameter dimension value are attached to the cursor when you pick the desired circle or arc. You can drag the leader to any desired location and length. Pick the location and length and the dimension is placed. The resulting leader points to the center of the circle or arc just as recommended by the ASME standard. See Figure 17-53.

You also have the **Mtext**, **Text**, and **Angle** options that were introduced earlier. Use the **Mtext** or **Text** option if you want to change the text value or the **Angle** option if you want to change the angle of the text.

Exercise 17-11   Complete the Exercise on the Student CD.

Dimensioning Holes

Holes are dimensioned in the view in which they appear as circles. Give location dimensions to the center and a leader showing the diameter. Leader lines can be drawn using the **DIMDIAMETER** command, as previously discussed. The center mark type and size are controlled in the dimension style, which is discussed later in this chapter. Multiple holes of the same size can be noted with one hole dimension, such as 2X ∅.50. See Figure 17-54. Use the **Mtext** or **Text** option to create this dimension. The **Angle** option can be used to change the angle of the text numbers, but this is not commonly done.

Figure 17-53.
Using the **DIMDIAMETER** command with AutoCAD dimensioning defaults.

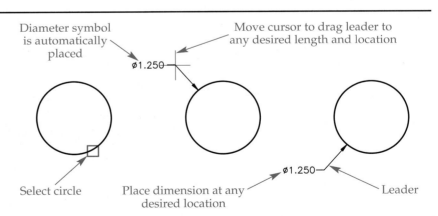

Diameter symbol is automatically placed

Move cursor to drag leader to any desired length and location

∅1.250

Select circle

Place dimension at any desired location

∅1.250

Leader

Figure 17-54.
Dimensioning holes.

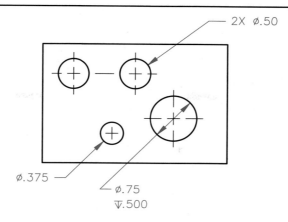

PROFESSIONAL TIP

The ASME standard recommends a small space between the object and the extension line. This happens when the **Offset from origin** setting within the dimension style is set to its default or some other desired positive value. This is very useful *except* when providing dimensions to centerlines for the location of holes. When the endpoint of the centerline is picked, a positive value leaves a space between the centerline and the beginning of the extension line. This is not a preferred practice. Change the **Offset from origin** setting to 0 to remove the gap. Be sure to change back to the positive setting when dimensioning other objects.

Use of the **Dimension Style Manager** dialog box to set this and other dimensioning settings is fully explained later in this chapter.

Dimensioning for Manufacturing Processes

A *counterbore* is a larger-diameter hole machined at one end of a smaller hole. It provides a place for the head of a bolt. A *spotface* is similar to a counterbore except that it is not as deep. The spotface provides a smooth, recessed surface for a washer. A *countersink* is a cone-shaped recess at one end of a hole. It provides a mating surface for a screw head of the same shape. Notes for these features are provided in drawings using symbols. First, locate the centers in the circular view. Then, place a leader providing machining information in a note. See **Figure 17-55**.

Symbols for these types of applications can be customized as blocks, as discussed in Chapter 22. These symbols can also be drawn by creating a dimension style with a text style using the gdt.shx font, as explained earlier in this chapter. The symbols and related gdt.shx keyboard characters used to make the symbols are shown in **Figure 17-52**.

The **DIMDIAMETER** command gives you multiline text to use during the creation of the dimension. Additional text can be added by editing the dimension text, since it is actually an mtext object.

Figure 17-55.
Dimension notes for machining processes. The symbols can be inserted as blocks or with lowercase letters when the gdt.shx font is used.

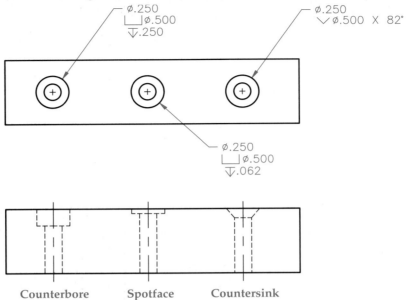

Counterbore   Spotface   Countersink

PROFESSIONAL TIP

After creating any dimension, the dimension text can be directly edited using the **Properties** window. Editing dimensions is covered in Chapter 18 of this text.

Dimensioning Repetitive Features

Repetitive features refer to many features having the same shape and size. When this occurs, the number of repetitions is followed by an X, a space, and the size dimension. The dimension is then connected to the feature with a leader. See Figure 17-56.

Exercise 17-12   Complete the Exercise on the Student CD.

Figure 17-56.
Dimensioning repetitive features (shown in color).

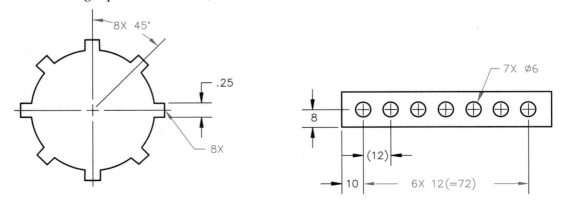

Dimensioning Arcs

The standard for dimensioning arcs is a radius dimension. A radius dimension is placed with the **DIMRADIUS** command. Access this command by picking the **Radius** button on the **Dimension** toolbar, picking **Dimension > Radius** in the pull-down menu, or typing either DRA or DIMRADIUS.

When you pick the desired arc or circle to dimension, a leader line and radius dimension value are attached to the cursor. You can drag the leader to any desired location and length. Pick the location and length and the dimension is placed. The resulting leader points to the center of the arc or circle as recommended by the ASME standard. See **Figure 17-57**.

As with the previously discussed dimensioning commands, you can use the **Mtext** or **Text** option to change the dimension text. You can also use the **Angle** option to change the angle of the text value.

Dimensioning Arc Length

The length of an arc can be dimensioned using the **DIMARC** command. The length measures the distance along the arc segment. To access the **DIMARC** command, pick the **Arc Length** button on the **Dimension** toolbar, pick **Dimension > Arc Length** from the pull-down menu, or type DAR or DIMARC.

After selecting the arc to be dimensioned, the arc length symbol and dimension value are attached to the cursor. By default, the symbol is placed before the text. To place the dimension, move the text to the desired location and pick once. An arc dimensioned with the **DIMARC** command is shown in **Figure 17-58**.

Before placing the dimension, you can change the dimension text with the **Mtext** or **Text** option. The **Angle** option can be used to change the angle of the text. Use the **Partial** option if you do not want to dimension the length of the entire arc. Entering this option prompts you to select a first point on the arc and a second point. The length between these two points is dimensioned. The **Leader** option allows you to add a leader pointing to the arc being dimensioned.

Dimensioning Large Circles and Arcs

When a circle or arc is so large that its center point is not displayed on the layout, the **DIMJOGGED** command can be used. This command allows you to draw a radius dimension by selecting a center point origin and placing a jog symbol with the dimension line. A *jog symbol* is a long break line symbol. To access the **DIMJOGGED** command, pick the **Jogged** button in the **Dimension** toolbar, pick **Dimension > Jogged** from the pull-down menu, or type JOG or DIMJOGGED. Refer to **Figure 17-59** as you go through the following command sequence:

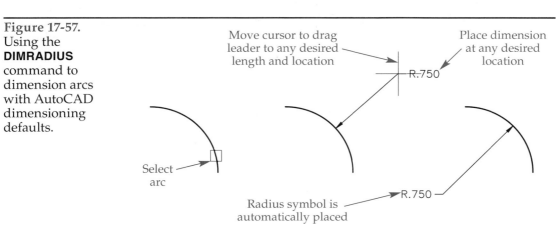

Figure 17-57.
Using the **DIMRADIUS** command to dimension arcs with AutoCAD dimensioning defaults.

Move cursor to drag leader to any desired length and location

Place dimension at any desired location

R.750

Select arc

R.750

Radius symbol is automatically placed

Figure 17-58.
Using the **DIMARC** command to dimension the length of an arc.

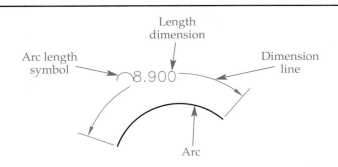

Figure 17-59.
Using the **DIMJOGGED** command to place a radius dimension for an arc.

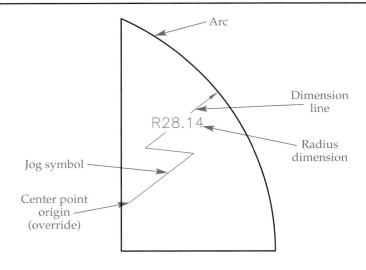

```
Command: JOG or DIMJOGGED↵
Select arc or circle: (pick the arc or circle)
Specify center location override: (pick a point for the origin of the center location)
Specify dimension line location or [Mtext/Text/Angle]: (pick to place the dimension line)
Specify jog location: (pick a point to place the jog symbol)
Command:
```

After the dimension line location is specified, pick a point to locate the center of the jog symbol. The different components of the dimension can be moved by using grip editing after the dimension is placed.

Dimensioning Fillets and Rounds

Small inside arcs are called *fillets*. Small arcs on outside corners are called *rounds*. Fillets are designed to strengthen inside corners. Rounds are used to relieve sharp corners. Fillets and rounds can be dimensioned individually as arcs or in a general note. See Figure 17-60. On mechanical drawings, it is common to place a general note such as ALL FILLETS AND ROUNDS R.125 UNLESS OTHERWISE SPECIFIED near the title block.

Exercise 17-13

Complete the Exercise on the Student CD.

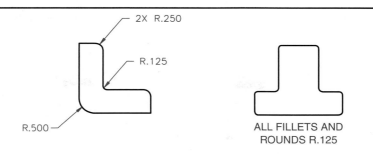

Figure 17-60.
Dimensioning fillets
and rounds.

ALL FILLETS AND
ROUNDS R.125

Dimensioning Curves

When possible, curves are dimensioned as arcs. When they are not in the shape of a constant-radius arc, they should be dimensioned to points along the curve using the **DIMLINEAR** command. See **Figure 17-61**.

Dimensioning Curves with Oblique Extension Lines

The curve shown in **Figure 17-61** is dimensioned using the normal practice, but, in some cases, spaces may be limited and oblique extension lines are used. First, dimension the object using the **DIMLINEAR** command as appropriate, even if dimensions are crowded or overlap. See **Figure 17-62A**.

DIMEDIT
Type
DIMEDIT
Pull-Down Menu
Dimension
> Oblique

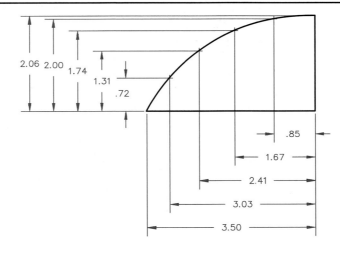

Figure 17-61.
Dimensioning
curves that do not
have a constant
radius.

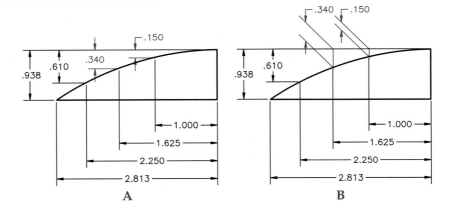

Figure 17-62.
Drawing
dimensions with
oblique extension
lines.

The .150 and .340 dimensions are to be placed at an oblique angle above the view. The **Oblique** option of the **DIMEDIT** command is used to draw oblique dimensions. The **DIMEDIT** command and other dimension editing commands are discussed in Chapter 18. The command option is accessed by picking **Dimension** > **Oblique** in the pull-down menu. First, you are asked to select the objects. Pick the dimensions to be redrawn at an oblique angle. In this case, the .150 and .340 dimensions are selected.

Next, you are asked for the obliquing angle. Careful planning is needed to make sure the correct obliquing angle is entered. Obliquing angles originate from 0° East and revolve counterclockwise. In the example shown in **Figure 17-62B,** the obliquing angle for the extension lines is 135°.

Drawing Leader Lines

The **DIMDIAMETER** and **DIMRADIUS** commands automatically place leaders on the drawing. The **QLEADER** command allows you to begin and end a leader line where you desire. You can also place single or multiple lines of text with the leader. This command is ideal for:

- Adding specific notes to a drawing.
- Staggering a leader line to go around other drawing features. Keep in mind that staggering leader lines is not a recommended ASME standard.
- Drawing a double leader. Drawing two leaders from one note is not a recommended ASME standard.
- Making custom leader lines.
- Drawing curved leaders for architectural applications.

The **QLEADER** command creates leader lines and related notes. This command provides you with the flexibility to place tolerances and multiple lines of text with the leader. Multiple-segment leaders can also be created. Some of the leader line characteristics, such as the arrowhead size, are controlled by the dimension style settings. Other features, such as the leader format and annotation style, are controlled by the **Settings** option within the **QLEADER** command. An *annotation* is text on a drawing (such as a note or dimension).

The **QLEADER** command is accessed by picking the **Quick Leader** button in the **Dimension** toolbar, selecting **Dimension** > **Leader** in the pull-down menu, or typing LE or QLEADER. The first two prompts look like those used with the **LINE** command, with the Specify from point: and Specify to point: prompts. This allows you to pick where the leader begins and ends.

In mechanical drafting, properly drawn leaders have one straight segment extending from the feature to a horizontal shoulder that is 1/4″ (6 mm) long. While most other fields also use straight leaders, AutoCAD provides the option of drawing curved leaders, which are commonly used in architectural drafting. This is done with the **Settings** option of the command.

Qleader Settings

The **Settings** option available at the beginning of the **QLEADER** command can be used to give you greater control over the leader and its associated text. For example, the leader can be set to have the first segment always drawn at a 45° angle and the second segment (or shoulder) always horizontal.

When you enter the **Settings** option of the **QLEADER** command, the **Leader Settings** dialog box is displayed. This dialog box has three tabs: **Annotation, Leader Line & Arrow,** and **Attachment.** The appearance of the arrow and leader line is determined by the settings in the **Leader Line & Arrow** tab. The settings found in the **Annotation** and **Attachment** tabs determine the appearance of the text portion of the leader.

QLEADER

Type
QLEADER
LE

Pull-Down Menu
Dimension > Leader

Toolbar
Dimension
Quick Leader

Options
Settings

Figure 17-63.
The **Leader Line & Arrow** tab of the **Leader Settings** dialog box.

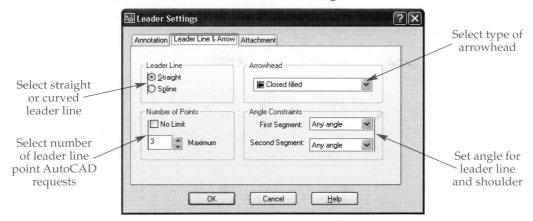

Select type of arrowhead

Select straight or curved leader line

Select number of leader line point AutoCAD requests

Set angle for leader line and shoulder

Leader line and arrow settings

The **Leader Line & Arrow** tab of the **Leader Settings** dialog box is shown in **Figure 17-63.** The settings in this tab determine the type of arrowhead, the type of leader line, the angles for the leader line and shoulder, and the number of requested points.

The **Leader Line** area is used to specify the shape of the leader line. A leader with straight-line segments is drawn by picking the **Straight** radio button. A curved leader is drawn by picking the **Spline** radio button. The spline leader is commonly used in architectural drafting. **Figure 17-64** shows examples of the spline and straight leader lines.

You can also set the maximum number of vertices on the leader line. This value is set in the **Number of Points** area. Set a maximum number of vertices in the **Maximum** text box or select the **No Limit** check box to have an unlimited number. After the maximum number is reached, the **QLEADER** command automatically stops drawing the leader and asks for text information. To use less than the maximum number of points, press the [Enter] key at the Specify next point prompt. If the leader is a line object, a value of three for the maximum number of points defines a maximum total of two line segments.

The **Arrowhead** area uses the default value assigned to leaders within the current dimension style. To change the appearance of the arrowhead, pick the drop-down list and select a terminator from the full range of choices. Changing the **Arrowhead** setting creates a dimension style override, which is discussed later in this chapter.

Figure 17-64.
The type of leader line (straight or spline) is set in the **Leader Line & Arrow** tab of the **Leader Settings** dialog box.

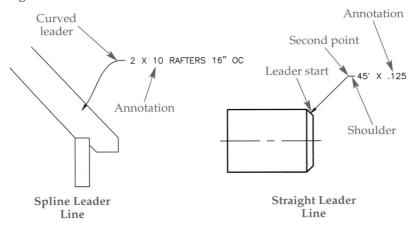

Curved leader

2 X 10 RAFTERS 16" OC

Annotation

Spline Leader Line

Annotation

Second point

Leader start

45° X .125

Shoulder

Straight Leader Line

The first two segments of the leader line can be restricted to certain angles. These angles are set in the **Angle Constraints** area. The options for each segment are **Any angle**, **Horizontal**, **90°**, **45°**, **30°**, and **15°**. The Ortho mode setting overrides the angle constraints so it is advisable to turn Ortho mode off while using this command.

PROFESSIONAL TIP

The ASME standard for leaders does not recommend a leader line that is less than 15° or greater than 75° from horizontal. Use the **Angle Constraints** settings in the **Leader Settings** dialog box to help maintain these standards.

Leader text settings

The **Annotation** and **Attachment** tabs of the **Leader Settings** dialog box control the way text is used with the leader line. The **Annotation tab** contains settings that specify the type of object used for annotation, additional options for mtext objects, and tools that automatically repeat annotations. The **Attachment** tab has options for specifying the point where the leader line shoulder meets an mtext annotation object.

The **Annotation** tab is shown in **Figure 17-65**. The **Annotation Type** area determines which type of object is inserted and attached to the end of the leader line. The following options are available:

- **MText.** This is the default setting, causing a multiline text object to be inserted after the leader lines are drawn. See **Figure 17-66A**.

Figure 17-65.
The **Annotation** tab of the **Leader Settings** dialog box.

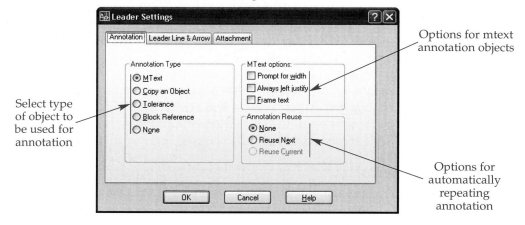

Figure 17-66.
The annotation type is selected in the **Annotation** tab of the **Leader Settings** dialog box.

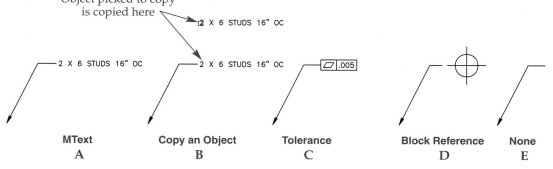

MText	Copy an Object	Tolerance	Block Reference	None
A	B	C	D	E

- **Copy an Object.** This option allows an mtext, text, block, or tolerance object to be copied from the current drawing and inserted at the end of the current leader line. This is useful when the same note or symbol is required in many places throughout a drawing. After drawing the leader line, the Select an object to copy: prompt appears. The selected object is placed at the end of the shoulder. See **Figure 17-66B**.
- **Tolerance.** This option displays the **Geometric Tolerance** dialog box for creation of a feature control frame after the leader line is drawn. See **Figure 17-66C**. Geometric tolerancing is explained in detail in Chapter 20 of this text.
- **Block Reference.** This option inserts a specified block at the end of the leader. A *block* is a symbol that was previously created and saved. Multiple-use symbols are explained in detail in Chapter 22 of this text. Blocks can be scaled during the insertion process. A special symbol block named Target is inserted in **Figure 17-66D**.
- **None.** This option ends the leader with no annotation of any kind. See **Figure 17-66E**. The **None** option can be used as a way to create multiple leaders for a single leader annotation, as shown in **Figure 17-67**. Multiple leaders are not a recommended ASME standard, but they are used for some applications, such as welding symbols. The welding symbol shown in **Figure 17-67B** was created as a block and then inserted using the **Block Reference** annotation option.

You can automatically repeat the previous leader annotation using the options in the **Annotation Reuse** area. The default option is **None**. This allows you to specify the annotation when creating a leader. If you wish to use an annotation repeatedly, select the **Reuse Next** option and then create the first leader and annotation. When you create another leader, the setting automatically changes to **Reuse Current** and the annotation is inserted. The annotation is repeated for all new leaders until the **Annotation Reuse** setting is changed back to **None**.

The **MText options** area of the **Annotation** tab is only available if **MText** is selected as the annotation type. These settings can be overridden by selecting the **MText** option during the **QLEADER** command. The following options are available:
- **Prompt for width.** If checked, you are prompted to define the size of the mtext box. If this option is not checked, a value of 0 (no text wrapping) is assigned to the mtext box.
- **Always left justify.** This option forces the mtext to be left justified, regardless of the direction of the leader line.
- **Frame text.** This option creates a box around the mtext text box. The default properties of the frame are controlled by the settings of the current dimension style.

The **Attachment** tab is only available when the **MText** option is selected in the **Annotation Type** area of the **Annotation** tab. This tab contains options that determine how the mtext object is positioned relative to the endpoint of the leader line shoulder. See **Figure 17-68**. Different options can be specified for mtext to the right of the leader line and mtext to the left of the leader line. These options are shown in **Figure 17-69**.

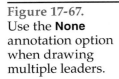

Figure 17-67.
Use the **None** annotation option when drawing multiple leaders.

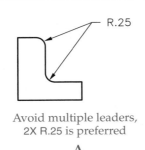

R.25

Avoid multiple leaders,
2X R.25 is preferred

A

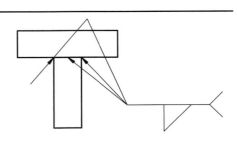

B

Figure 17-68.
The **Attachment** tab of the **Leader Settings** dialog box determines the location of the mtext annotation relative to the leader line shoulder.

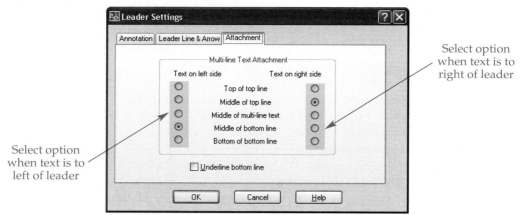

Select option when text is to right of leader

Select option when text is to left of leader

Figure 17-69.
Placement of mtext is controlled by the options in the **Attachment** tab of the **Leader Settings** dialog box. The shaded examples are the recommended ASME standards.

	Top of Top Line	Middle of Top Line	Middle of Multiline Text	Middle of Bottom Line	Bottom of Bottom Line
Text on Left Side	⌀.250 ⌐⌐ø.500 ⊽.062	⌀.250 ⌐⌐ø.500 ⊽.062	⌀.250 ⌐ø.500 ⊽.062	⌀.250 ⌐ø.500 ⊽.062	⌀.250 ⌐ø.500 ⊽.062
Text on Right Side	⌀.250 ⌐ø.500 ⊽.062	⌀.250 ⌐ø.500 ⊽.062	⌀.250 ⌐ø.500 ⊽.062	⌀.250 ⌐ø.500 ⊽.062	⌀.250 ⌐ø.500 ⊽.062

The **Underline bottom line** option causes a line to be drawn along the bottom of the mtext box. When this check box is selected, the choices for text on the left and right side are grayed out.

PROFESSIONAL TIP

Common drafting practice is to use the **Middle of bottom line** option for left-sided text and the **Middle of top line** option for right-sided text. These are the default settings.

NOTE

The **LEADER** command can also be used to draw leaders. However, this command does not provide the same convenience and ability to easily comply with drafting standards in comparison to the **QLEADER** command.

Exercise 17-14   Complete the Exercise on the Student CD.

Dimensioning Chamfers

A *chamfer* is an angled surface used to relieve sharp corners. The ends of bolts are commonly chamfered to allow them to engage the threaded hole better. Chamfers of 45° are dimensioned with a leader giving the angle and linear dimension, or with two linear dimensions. This can be accomplished using the **QLEADER** command. See Figure 17-70.

Chamfers other than 45° must have either the angle and a linear dimension or two linear dimensions placed on the view. See Figure 17-71. The **DIMLINEAR** and **DIMANGULAR** commands are used for this purpose.

Exercise 17-15   Complete the Exercise on the Student CD.

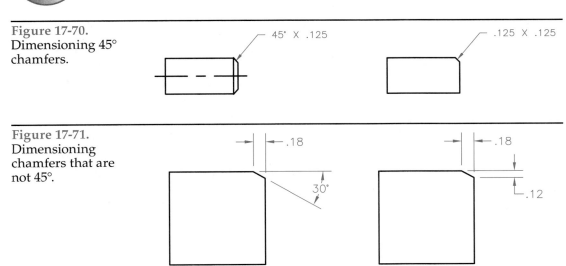

Figure 17-70.
Dimensioning 45°
chamfers.

Figure 17-71.
Dimensioning
chamfers that are
not 45°.

Alternate Dimensioning Practices

It is becoming common to omit dimension lines in industries where computer-controlled machining processes are used. Arrowless, tabular, and chart dimensioning are three types of dimensioning that omit dimension lines.

Arrowless Dimensioning

Arrowless dimensioning is becoming popular in mechanical drafting. It is also used in electronics drafting, especially for chassis layout. This type of dimensioning has only extension lines and text. Dimension lines and arrowheads are omitted. The dimension text is aligned with the extension lines. Each dimension represents a measurement originating from a common point. This starting, or 0, dimension is typically known as a *datum*, or *baseline*. Holes or other features are labeled with identification letters. Sizes for these features are given in a table placed on the drawing. See Figure 17-72.

Figure 17-72.
Arrowless dimensioning.

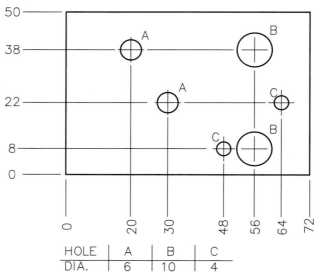

HOLE	A	B	C
DIA.	6	10	4

Tabular Dimensioning

Tabular dimensioning is a form of arrowless dimensioning where dimensions to features are shown in a table. Each feature is labeled with a letter or number that correlates to the table. The table gives the location of features from the X and Y axes. It also provides the depth of features from a Z axis, when appropriate. See **Figure 17-73.**

Chart Dimensioning

Chart dimensioning may take the form of unidirectional, aligned, arrowless, or tabular dimensioning. It provides flexibility in situations where dimensions change as

Figure 17-73.
Tabular dimensioning. (Doug Major)

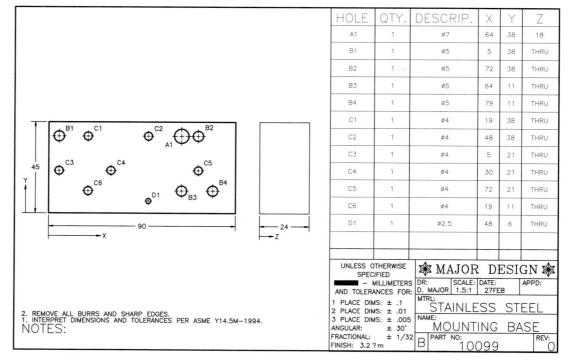

HOLE	QTY.	DESCRIP.	X	Y	Z
A1	1	⌀7	64	38	18
B1	1	⌀5	5	38	THRU
B2	1	⌀5	72	38	THRU
B3	1	⌀5	64	11	THRU
B4	1	⌀5	79	11	THRU
C1	1	⌀4	19	38	THRU
C2	1	⌀4	48	38	THRU
C3	1	⌀4	5	21	THRU
C4	1	⌀4	30	21	THRU
C5	1	⌀4	72	21	THRU
C6	1	⌀4	19	11	THRU
D1	1	⌀2.5	48	6	THRU

NOTES:
1. INTERPRET DIMENSIONS AND TOLERANCES PER ASME Y14.5M—1994.
2. REMOVE ALL BURRS AND SHARP EDGES.

UNLESS OTHERWISE SPECIFIED
█ – MILLIMETERS AND TOLERANCES FOR:
1 PLACE DIMS: ± .1
2 PLACE DIMS: ± .01
3 PLACE DIMS: ± .005
ANGULAR: ± 30'
FRACTIONAL: ± 1/32
FINISH: 3.2 ?m

❋ MAJOR DESIGN ❋
DR: D. MAJOR | SCALE: 1.5:1 | DATE: 27FEB | APPD:
MTRL: STAINLESS STEEL
NAME: MOUNTING BASE
B | PART NO: 10099 | REV: 0

Figure 17-74.
Chart dimensioning.

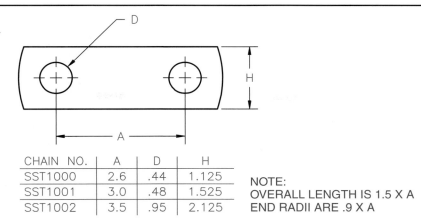

CHAIN NO.	A	D	H
SST1000	2.6	.44	1.125
SST1001	3.0	.48	1.525
SST1002	3.5	.95	2.125

NOTE:
OVERALL LENGTH IS 1.5 X A
END RADII ARE .9 X A

requirements of the product change. The views of the product are drawn and variable dimensions are shown with letters. The letters correlate to a chart where the different options (possible dimensions) are given. See **Figure 17-74.**

WCS and UCS

The world coordinate system (WCS) origin, the 0,0,0 coordinate, has been in the lower-left corner of the screen for the drawings you have already completed. In most cases, this is fine. However, when using arrowless dimensioning on a drawing, it is best to have the dimensions originate from a primary datum, which is often a corner of the object. Depending on how the object is drawn, this point may or may not align with the WCS origin.

The WCS is fixed; the user coordinate system (UCS), on the other hand, can be moved to any orientation desired. The UCS is discussed in detail in *AutoCAD and Its Applications—Advanced.* As a general practice, the UCS allows you to set your own coordinate system.

Arrowless dimensions are drawn in AutoCAD with the **DIMORDINATE** command, which is discussed in the next section. Measurements made with this command originate from the current UCS origin. By default, this is the 0,0 origin. You can move the UCS origin to the corner of an object or an appropriate datum feature by selecting **Tools > Move UCS.** You are then prompted to specify a new origin point. Use an object snap mode to select the corner of the object or the appropriate datum feature. In **Figure 17-75A,** the UCS is moved to an appropriate location.

When done drawing arrowless dimensions from a datum, you can leave the UCS origin at the datum or move it back to the WCS origin. To return to the WCS, select **Tools > New UCS > World.**

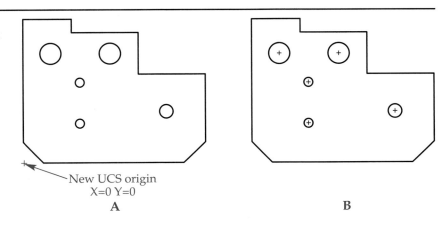

Figure 17-75.
A—Draw the object and move the UCS origin to the appropriate datum location. B—Add the center marks to the circular features using the **DIMCENTER** command.

New UCS origin
X=0 Y=0

A

B

Drawing Arrowless Dimensions

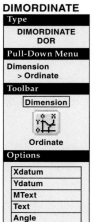
AutoCAD refers to arrowless dimensioning as *ordinate dimensioning*. Ordinate dimensions are drawn using the **DIMORDINATE** command, which is accessed by picking the **Ordinate** button on the **Dimension** toolbar, picking **Dimension** > **Ordinate** in the **Dimension** pull-down menu, or typing DOR or DIMORDINATE. When using this command, AutoCAD automatically places an extension line and a dimension at the location you pick. The dimension is measured as an X or Y coordinate distance.

Since you are working in the XY plane, it is often best to have Ortho mode on. Also, if there are circles on your drawing, use the **DIMCENTER** command to place center marks in the circles, as shown in **Figure 17-75B**. This makes your drawing conform to ASME standards and provides something to pick when dimensioning the circle locations.

Now, you are ready to start placing the ordinate dimensions. Enter the **DIMORDINATE** command. When the Specify feature location: prompt appears, move the screen cursor to the point or feature to be dimensioned. If the feature is the corner of the object, pick the corner. If the feature is a circle, pick the end of the center mark. This leaves the required space between the center mark and the extension line. Zoom in if needed and use the object snap modes. The next prompt asks for the leader endpoint. This actually refers to the extension line endpoint, so pick the endpoint of the extension line.

If the X axis or Y axis distance between the feature and the extension line endpoint is large, the default axis used for the dimension by AutoCAD may not be the desired axis. When this happens, use the **Xdatum** or **Ydatum** option to tell AutoCAD the axis from which the dimension originates. The **Mtext**, **Text**, and **Angle** options are identical to the options available with other dimensioning commands. Pick the leader endpoint to complete the command.

Figure 17-76A shows the ordinate dimensions placed on the object. Notice the dimension text is aligned with the extension lines. Aligned dimensioning is standard with ordinate dimensioning. Finally, complete the drawing by adding any missing lines, such as centerlines or fold lines. Identify the holes with letters and correlate a dimensioning table. See **Figure 17-76B**.

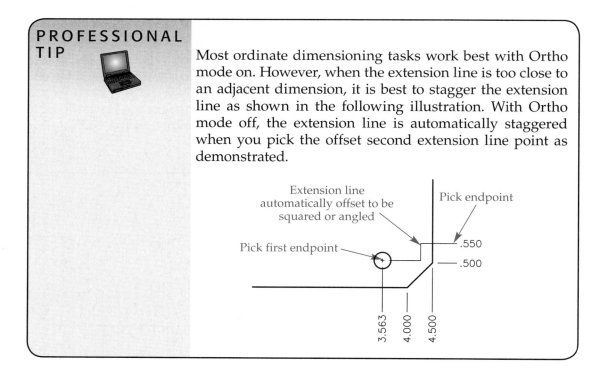

PROFESSIONAL TIP

Most ordinate dimensioning tasks work best with Ortho mode on. However, when the extension line is too close to an adjacent dimension, it is best to stagger the extension line as shown in the following illustration. With Ortho mode off, the extension line is automatically staggered when you pick the offset second extension line point as demonstrated.

Figure 17-76.
A—Placing ordinate
dimensions.
B—Completing the
drawing.

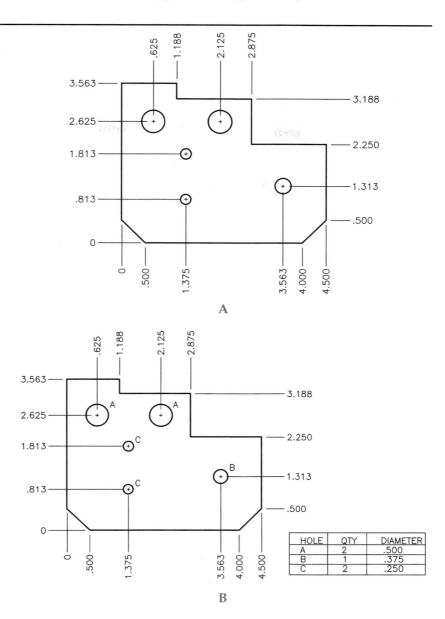

A

B

HOLE	QTY	DIAMETER
A	2	.500
B	1	.375
C	2	.250

**Exercise
17-16**   Complete the Exercise on the Student CD.

Thread Drawings and Notes

There are many different thread forms. The most common forms are the Unified and metric screw threads. The parts of a screw thread are shown in **Figure 17-77.**

Threads are commonly shown on a drawing with a *simplified* representation. Thread depth is shown with a hidden line. This method is used for both external and internal threads. See **Figure 17-78.** A chamfer is often placed on the external thread. This makes it easier to engage the mating thread.

Figure 17-77.
Parts of a screw
thread.

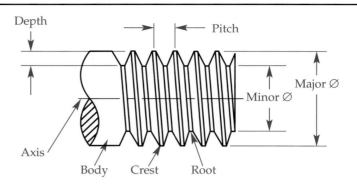

Figure 17-78.
Simplified thread
representations.

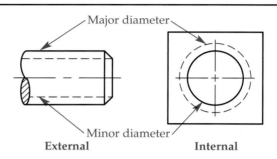

Showing the Thread Note

The objects show the reader that a thread exists, but the thread note gives exact specifications. The thread note is typically connected to the thread with a leader. See **Figure 17-79.** The thread note for Unified screw threads must be specified in the following format:

3/4 -   10UNC -   2A
(1)   (2) (3)   (4) (5)

(1) Major diameter of thread. Given as a fraction or number.
(2) Number of threads per inch.
(3) Thread series. UNC = Unified National Coarse. UNF = Unified National Fine.
(4) Class of fit. 1 = large tolerance. 2 = general purpose tolerance. 3 = tight tolerance.
(5) Thread type. A = external thread. B = internal thread.

The thread note for metric threads is specified in the following format:

M 14 X 2
(1) (2) (3)

(1) M = metric thread.
(2) Major diameter in millimeters.
(3) Pitch in millimeters.

There are too many Unified and metric screw threads to discuss here. Refer to the *Machinery's Handbook,* available from Goodheart-Willcox Publisher, or a comprehensive drafting text for more information.

Figure 17-79.
Displaying the
thread note with a
leader.

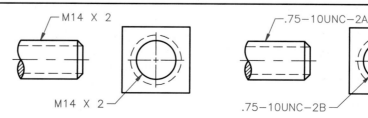

Dimensions can be drawn in either model space or layout (paper) space. Model space and layout space are discussed in Chapters 10 and 11. Model space dimensions must be scaled by the drawing scale factor to achieve the correct feature sizes, such as text height and arrow size. Associative paper space dimensions automatically adjust to model modifications and do not need to be scaled. Also, if you dimension in paper space, you can dimension the model differently in two viewports. However, paper space dimensions are not visible when working in the **Model** tab, so you must be careful not to move a model space object into a paper space dimension. Avoid using nonassociative paper space dimensions.

Exercise 17-17   Complete the Exercise on the Student CD.

LEGACY NOTE   Dimensions can also be created in dimensioning mode. To access dimensioning mode, type DIM. The Command: prompt becomes the Dim: prompt and you can enter dimensioning commands. To exit dimensioning mode, press the [Esc] key and the Command: prompt is displayed.

This method was common in earlier releases of AutoCAD, but has become a relatively inefficient method of command entry. Newer dimensioning commands, such as **QLEADER** and **QDIM**, cannot be accessed from the Dim: prompt.

Chapter Test

Answer the following questions. Write your answers on a separate sheet of paper or complete the electronic chapter test on the Student CD.

1. Name the dialog box that is used to create dimension styles.
2. Identify at least three ways to access the dialog box identified in Question 31.
3. Define an AutoCAD *dimension style.*
4. Name the dialog box tab used to control the appearance of dimension lines and extension lines.
5. Name the dialog box tab used to control dimensioning settings that adjust the location of dimension lines, dimension text, arrowheads, and leader lines.
6. Name the dialog box tab used to control the dimensioning settings that display the dimension text.
7. Name at least four arrowhead types that are available in the **Symbols and Arrows** tab for common use on architectural drawings.
8. Name the area in the **Modify Dimension Style** dialog box in which vertical justification of text can be set.
9. Which option for the vertical justification mentioned in Question 38 is commonly used in mechanical drafting?
10. Define *primary units.*

11. Given the following dimension text examples, identify if the application is for inch decimal drawings, metric decimal drawings, or architectural drawings.
    A. 12'-6"
    B. 0.5
    C. .500
12. What are the recommended standard units of measure for mechanical drawings?
13. Name the units of measure commonly used in architectural drafting. Show an example.
14. What is the recommended height for dimension numbers and notes on drawings?
15. Name the pull-down menu where the **Linear**, **Aligned**, and **Radius** dimensioning commands are found.
16. Name the two dimensioning commands that provide linear dimensions for angled surfaces.
17. Name the **DIMLINEAR** option that opens the **In-Place Text Editor** for changing the dimension text.
18. What is the keyboard shortcut (command alias) for the **DIMBASELINE** command?
19. Which command other than **DIMBASELINE** can be used to create baseline dimensions?
20. Name at least three modes of dimensioning available through the **QDIM** command.
21. Name the command used to dimension angles in degrees.
22. AutoCAD refers to chain dimensioning as _____ dimensioning.
23. AutoCAD refers to datum dimensioning as _____ dimensioning.
24. The command used to provide diameter dimensions for circles is _____.
25. The command used to provide radius dimensions for arcs is _____.
26. What does the *M* mean in the title of the standard ASME Y14.5M-1994?
27. Does a text style have to be loaded before it can be accessed for use in dimension text?
28. How do you place a datum dimension from the origin of the previously drawn dimension?
29. How do you place a datum dimension from the origin of a dimension that was drawn during a previous drawing session?
30. Which type of dimensions are created when you select multiple objects in the **QDIM** command?
31. Oblique extension lines are drawn using the _____ command and by accessing the _____ option.
32. Define *annotation*.
33. Identify how to access the **QLEADER** command using:
    A. Toolbar.
    B. Pull-down menu.
    C. Command: prompt.
34. Text placed using the **QLEADER** command is a _____ text object.
35. Describe the purpose of the **Copy an Object** option in the **Leader Settings** dialog box.
36. Define *arrowless dimensioning*.
37. AutoCAD refers to arrowless dimensioning as _____ dimensioning.
38. What is the importance of the user coordinate system (UCS) when drawing arrowless dimensions?
39. Identify the elements of this Unified screw thread note: 1/2-13UNC-2B.
    A. 1/2
    B. 13
    C. UNC
    D. 2
    E. B
40. Identify the elements of this metric screw thread note: M 14 X 2.
    A. M
    B. 14
    C. 2
41. How does the arrowhead specified for the dimension style affect the arrowhead used with the **QLEADER** command?

Drawing Problems

Use the startup option of your choice or use one of your templates. Set limits, units, dimension styles, and other parameters as needed. Use the following general guidelines.

A. Use dimension styles and text fonts that match the type of drawing as discussed in this chapter.
B. Use object snap modes to your best advantage.
C. Apply dimensions accurately using ASME or other related industry/architectural standards. Dimensions are in inches, or feet and inches, unless otherwise specified.
D. Set separate layers for dimensions and other features.
E. Plot drawings with proper lineweights.
F. For mechanical drawings, place the following general notes 1/2" from the lower-left corner:

> 3. UNLESS OTHERWISE SPECIFIED, ALL DIMENSIONS ARE IN INCHES (or MILLIMETERS as applicable).
> 2. REMOVE ALL BURRS AND SHARP EDGES.
> 1. INTERPRET DIMENSIONS AND TOLERANCES PER ASME Y14.5M-1994.
> NOTES:

G. Save each drawing as P17-*(problem number)*.

1.

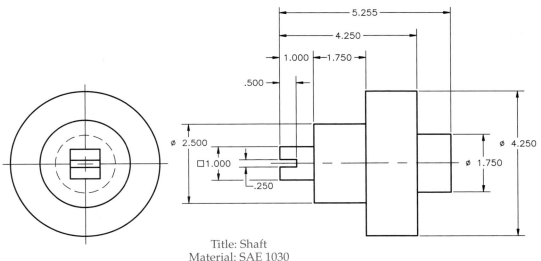

Title: Shaft
Material: SAE 1030

2.

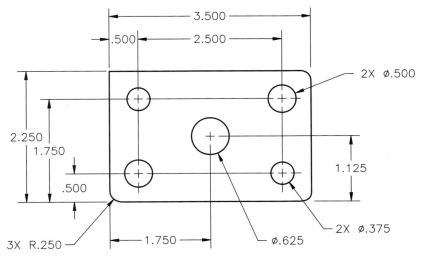

Title: Gasket

3.

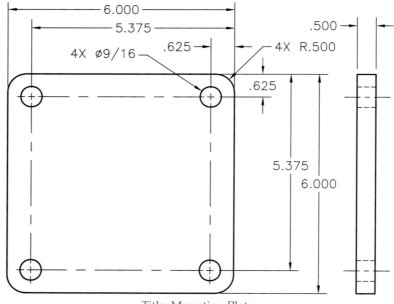

Title: Mounting Plate
Material: Mild Steel

4.

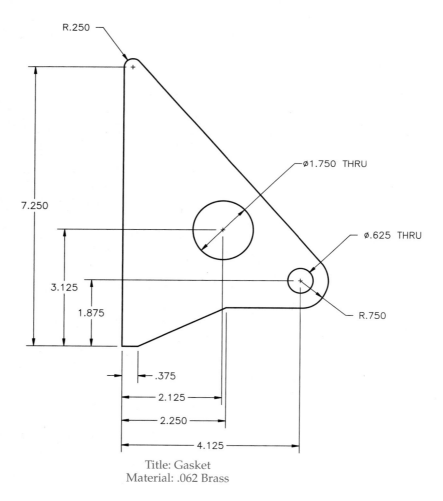

Title: Gasket
Material: .062 Brass

5.

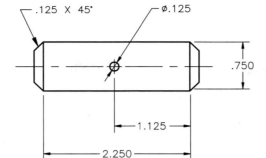

.125 X 45°
Ø.125
.750
1.125
2.250

Title: Pin
Material: SAE 4320

6.

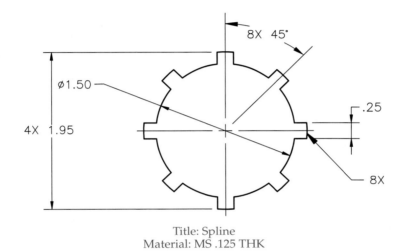

8X 45°
Ø1.50
4X 1.95
.25
8X

Title: Spline
Material: MS .125 THK

7.

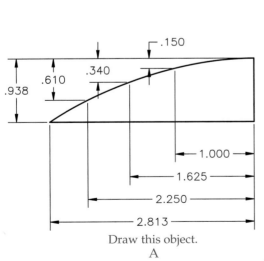

.150
.340
.610
.938
1.000
1.625
2.250
2.813

Draw this object.
A

.340 .150
.610
.938
1.000
1.625
2.250
2.813

Modify the dimensions as shown here.
B

Title: Shim

8.

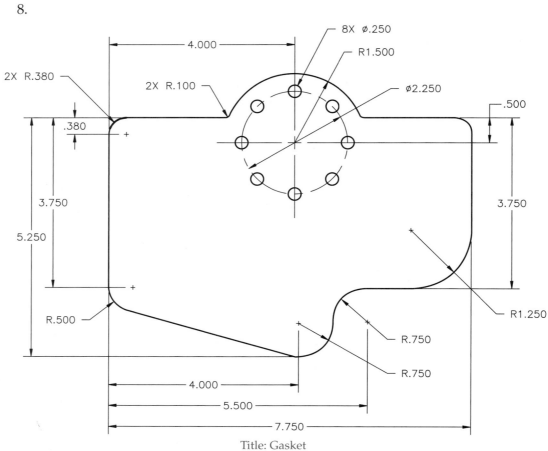

Title: Gasket
Material: 00 Phosphor Bronze

9.

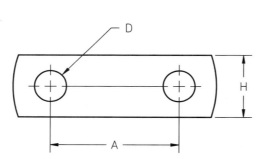

CHAIN NO.	A	D	H
SST1000	2.6	.44	1.125
SST1001	3.0	.48	1.525
SST1002	3.5	.95	2.125

Note:
Overall Length is 1.5XA
end radii are .9XA

Title: Chain Link
Material: Steel

10. Convert the given drawing to a drawing with the holes located using arrow-less dimensioning based on the X and Y coordinates given in the table. Place a table above your title block with Hole (identification), Quantity, Description, and Depth (Z axis).

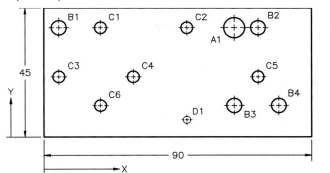

HOLE	QTY	DESC	X	Y	Z
A1	1	⌀7	64	38	18
B1	1	⌀5	5	38	THRU
B2	1	⌀5	72	38	THRU
B3	1	⌀5	64	11	THRU
B4	1	⌀5	79	11	THRU
C1	1	⌀4	19	38	THRU
C2	1	⌀4	48	38	THRU
C3	1	⌀4	5	21	THRU
C4	1	⌀4	30	21	THRU
C5	1	⌀4	72	21	THRU
C6	1	⌀4	19	11	THRU
D1	1	⌀2.5	48	6	THRU

Title: Base
Material: Bronze

11.

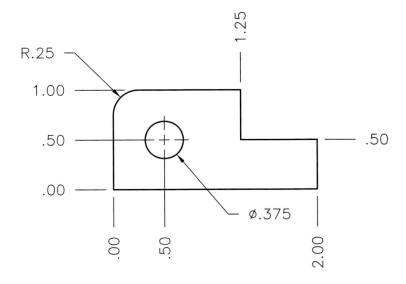

12.

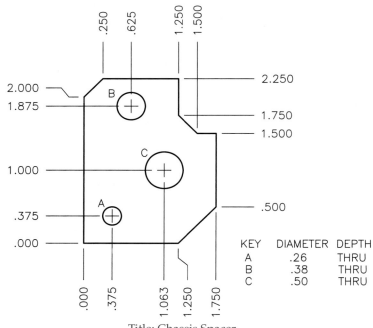

KEY	DIAMETER	DEPTH
A	.26	THRU
B	.38	THRU
C	.50	THRU

Title: Chassis Spacer
Material: .008 Aluminum

13.

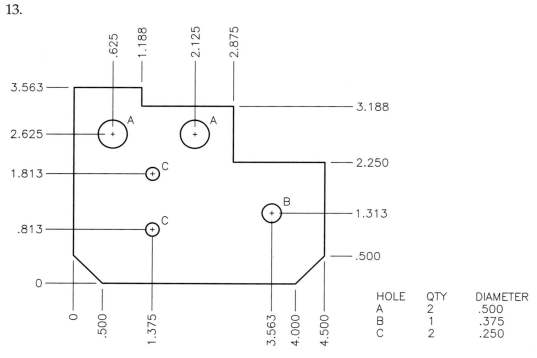

HOLE	QTY	DIAMETER
A	2	.500
B	1	.375
C	2	.250

Title: Chassis
Material: Aluminum .100 THK

14.

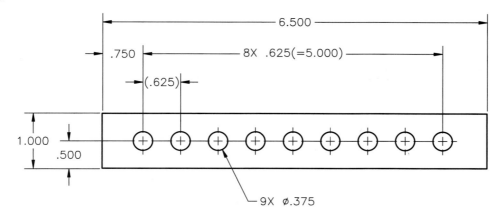

9X ⌀.375

15.

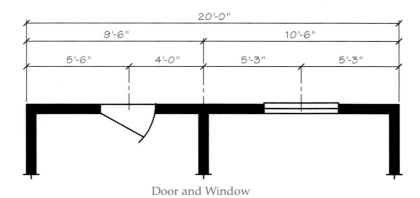

Door and Window

16.

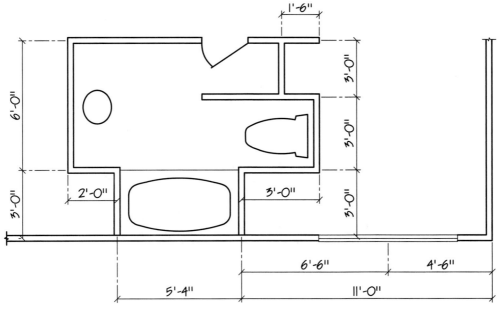

Title: Bathroom Area

Drawing Problems - Chapter 17

For Problems 17–22, use the isometric drawing provided to create a multiview orthographic drawing for the part. Include only the views necessary to fully describe the object. Dimension according to the ASME standards discussed in this chapter using a dimension style appropriate for mechanical drafting.

17.

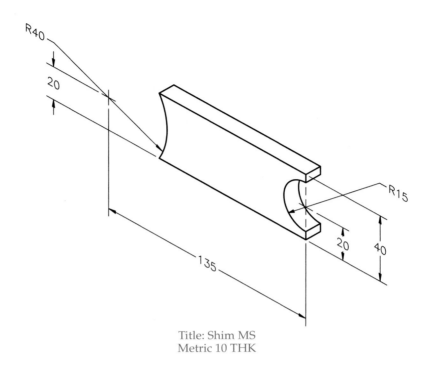

Title: Shim MS
Metric 10 THK

18. Half of the object is removed for clarity. The entire object should be drawn.

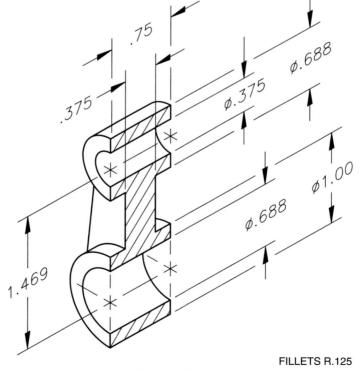

FILLETS R.125

Title: Shaft Support
Material: Cast Iron (CI)

19. Half of the object is removed for clarity. The entire object should be drawn.

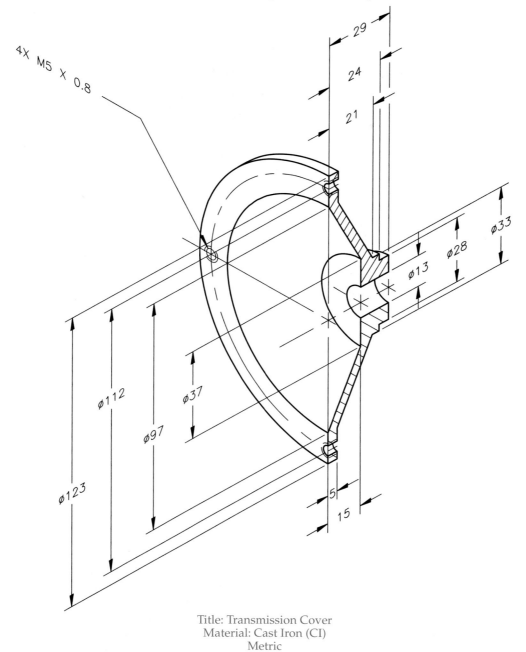

Title: Transmission Cover
Material: Cast Iron (CI)
Metric

20.

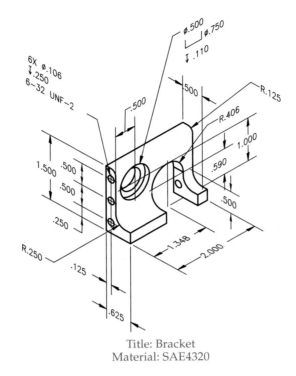

Title: Bracket
Material: SAE4320

21.

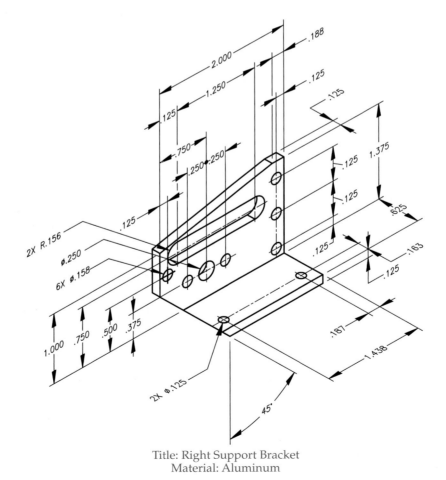

Title: Right Support Bracket
Material: Aluminum

22.

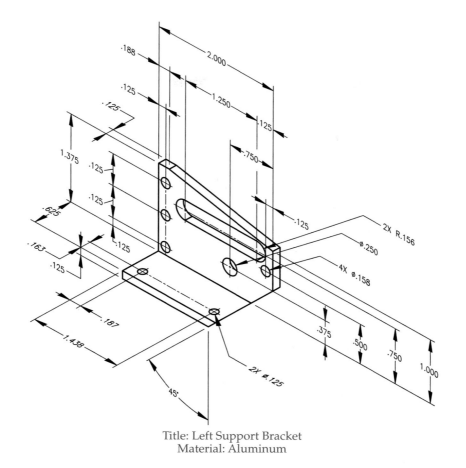

Title: Left Support Bracket
Material: Aluminum

23.

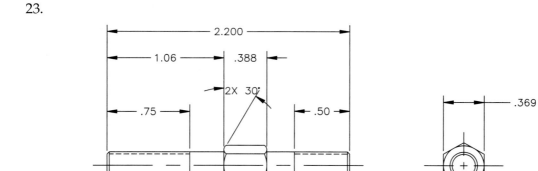

Title: Stud
Material: Stainless Steel

24. Draw this floor plan. Size the windows and the doors to your own specifications.

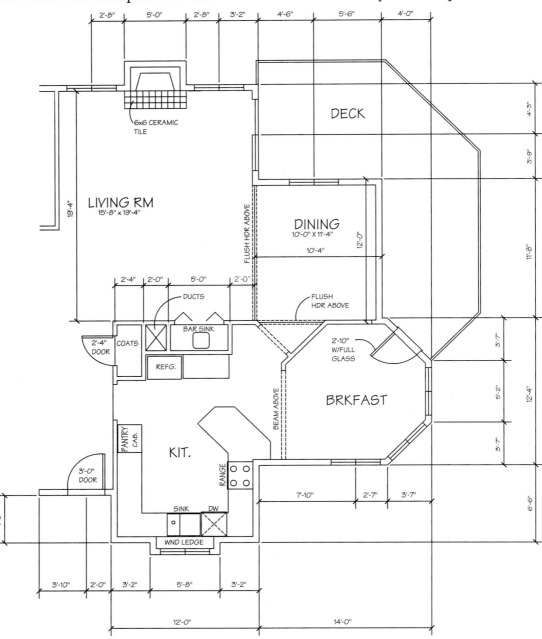

25.

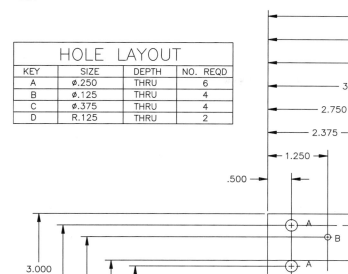

HOLE LAYOUT			
KEY	SIZE	DEPTH	NO. REQD
A	⌀.250	THRU	6
B	⌀.125	THRU	4
C	⌀.375	THRU	4
D	R.125	THRU	2

Title: Chassis Base (datum dimensioning)
Material: 12 gage Aluminum

26.

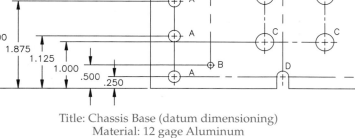

HOLE LAYOUT			
KEY	SIZE	DEPTH	NO. REQD
A	⌀.250	THRU	6
B	⌀.125	THRU	4
C	⌀.375	THRU	4
D	R.125	THRU	2

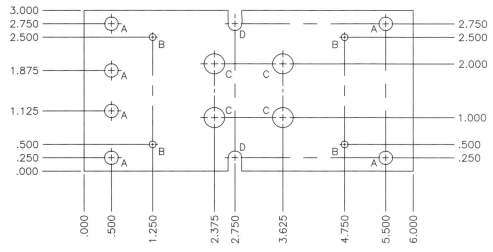

Title: Chassis Base (arrowless dimensioning)
Material: 12 gage Aluminum

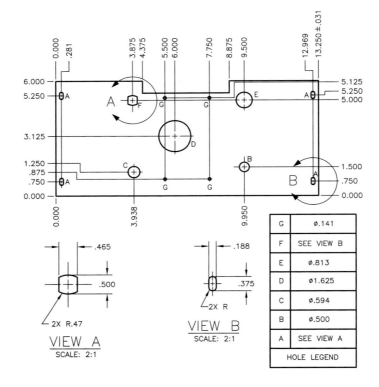

	HOLE LEGEND	
G	⌀.141	
F	SEE VIEW B	
E	⌀.813	
D	⌀1.625	
C	⌀.594	
B	⌀.500	
A	SEE VIEW A	

VIEW A
SCALE: 2:1

VIEW B
SCALE: 2:1

28.

HOLE LAYOUT				
KEY	X	Y	SIZE	TOL
A1	.500	2.750	⌀.250	±.002
A2	.500	1.875	⌀.250	±.002
A3	.500	1.125	⌀.250	±.002
A4	.500	.250	⌀.250	±.002
A5	5.500	2.750	⌀.250	±.002
A6	5.500	.250	⌀.250	±.002
B1	1.250	2.500	⌀.125	±.001
B2	1.250	.500	⌀.125	±.001
B3	4.750	2.500	⌀.125	±.001
B4	4.750	.500	⌀.125	±.001
C1	2.375	2.000	⌀.375	±.005
C2	2.375	1.000	⌀.375	±.005
C3	3.625	2.000	⌀.375	±.005
C4	3.625	1.000	⌀.375	±.005
D1	2.750	2.750	R.125	±.002
D2	2.750	.250	R.125	±.002

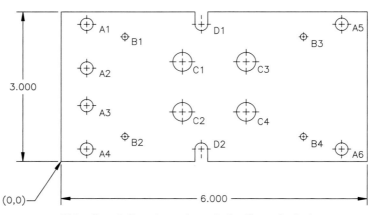

Title: Chassis Base (arrowless tabular dimensioning)
Material: 12 gage Aluminum

29.

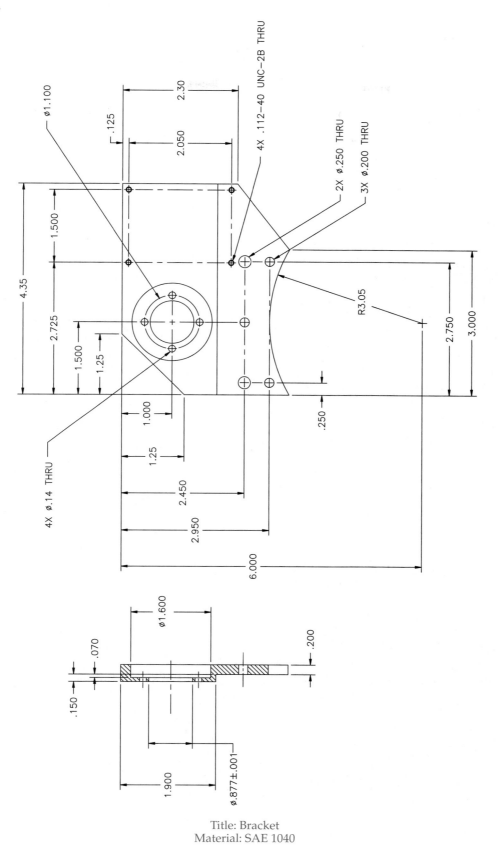

Title: Bracket
Material: SAE 1040

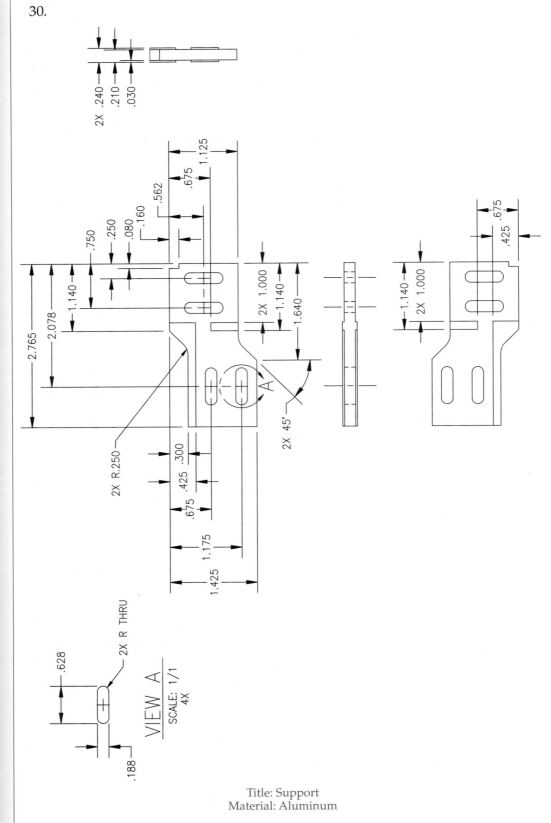

VIEW A
SCALE: 1/1
4X

Title: Support
Material: Aluminum

CHAPTER 18

Editing Dimensions

Learning Objectives

After completing this chapter, you will be able to do the following:

- Make changes to existing dimensions.
- Update a dimension to reflect the current dimension style.
- Import dimension styles from another drawing.
- Use the **Properties** window to edit individual dimension properties.
- Edit individual elements of associative dimensions.

The tools used to edit dimensions vary from simple erasing techniques to object editing commands. You may find it necessary to edit the placement of dimension text, a text value, or the settings in a dimension style. When an object with associative dimensions is edited, the dimensions are automatically updated to reflect the changes. This chapter provides you with a variety of useful techniques for editing dimensions.

Erasing Dimensions

Earlier in this text, you were introduced to the **ERASE** command. Among the many selection options used with this command are **Last**, **Previous**, **Window**, **Crossing**, **WPolygon**, **CPolygon**, and **Fence**.

Erasing existing features such as large groups of dimensions often becomes difficult. For example, the objects may be very close to other parts of the drawing. When there are many objects, it is usually time-consuming to erase each one individually. When this situation occurs, the **Crossing**, **CPolygon**, and **Fence** selection options of the **ERASE** command are useful. A comparison of using the **Window** and **Crossing** selection options with the **ERASE** command on a group of dimensions is shown in **Figure 18-1**. For a review of these techniques, refer to Chapter 3.

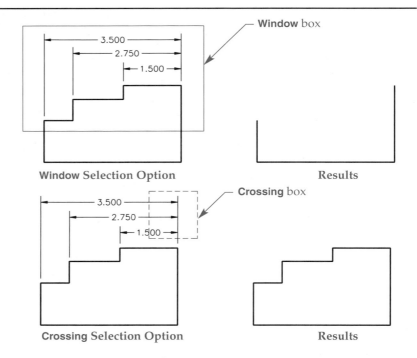

Figure 18-1.
Using the **Window** and **Crossing** selection options of the **ERASE** command to erase dimensions.

Window box

3.500
2.750
1.500

Window Selection Option

Results

Crossing box

3.500
2.750
1.500

Crossing Selection Option

Results

PROFESSIONAL TIP

Dimensions are treated as block objects within AutoCAD. After erasing dimensions, use the **PURGE** command to purge the erased dimension blocks. The **PURGE** command is discussed in Chapter 22.

Editing Dimension Text Values

The **DDEDIT** command can be used to edit existing dimension text. You can add a prefix or suffix to the text, or edit the dimension text format. This is useful when you wish to alter dimension text without creating a new dimension. For example, a linear dimension does not automatically place a diameter symbol with the text value. Using the **DDEDIT** command is one way to place this symbol on the dimension once it has already been placed in the drawing.

You can access the **DDEDIT** command by picking **Modify > Object > Text > Edit...** or typing ED or DDEDIT. When this command is issued, the Select an annotation object or [Undo]: prompt is displayed.

After you select a dimension to edit, the dimension value is highlighted and the **Text Formatting** toolbar is displayed. See **Figure 18-2.** The dimension value is highlighted in blue in a text window. In this selection mode, the cursor is placed at the beginning of the text string. You can then add a symbol in front of the value. You can move to the end of the value by pressing the right arrow key on the keyboard. Picking once on the dimension value highlights the value in the text window. This selection mode indicates that the entire dimension value is selected and typing new text replaces the existing text. To add a diameter symbol to the text, place the cursor at the position where you want to add the symbol and then select the **Symbol** button from the **Text Formatting** toolbar. Then, select **Diameter** from the **Symbol** menu. You can also right-click and select **Diameter** from the **Symbol** cascading menu. This adds the diameter

DDEDIT

Type
DDEDIT
ED

Pull-Down Menu
Modify
> Object
> Text
> Edit...

Toolbar
Text
Edit...

AutoCAD and Its Applications—Basics

Figure 18-2.
The **DDEDIT** command allows you to edit dimension text using a text window and the **Text Formatting** toolbar.

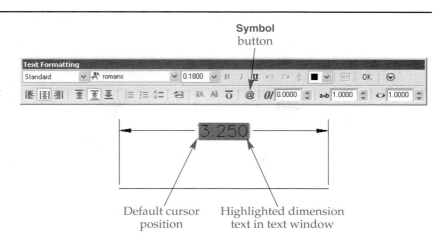

Symbol button

Default cursor position

Highlighted dimension text in text window

symbol to the text object. Pick the **OK** button on the **Text Formatting** toolbar to close the text window and exit the command. The result of changing an existing dimension in this manner is shown in **Figure 18-3.**

When using the **DDEDIT** command to edit dimension text, remember that the value is initially highlighted in blue. Any text that you type is added to the existing text. If you pick on the text, the entire text string is selected and the highlight color changes. Any text that you type replaces the entire string. You can change back to the initial selection mode by picking to the left of the text value or pressing the left arrow key on the keyboard. You can also pick to the right of the text value or press the right arrow key on the keyboard. The highlight color turns back to blue, indicating the dimension value is not discarded, but that the new text or symbol is added to it.

PROFESSIONAL TIP    You can replace the highlighted text representing the dimension value with numeric values. However, if the dimension is subsequently stretched, trimmed, or extended, the dimension text value will not change. Therefore, try to leave the default value.

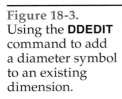 **Exercise 18-1**   Complete the Exercise on the Student CD.

Figure 18-3.
Using the **DDEDIT** command to add a diameter symbol to an existing dimension.

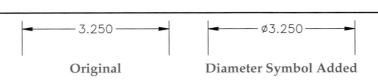

3.250

Original

Ø3.250

Diameter Symbol Added

Editing Dimensions with the Qdim Command

QDIM

Type

QDIM

Pull-Down Menu

Dimension
> Quick
Dimension

Toolbar

Dimension

Quick Dimension

Options

Continuous

Staggered

Baseline

Ordinate

Radius

Diameter

datumPoint

Edit

seTtings

The **QDIM** command can be used to place a new dimension in a drawing. This was discussed in Chapter 17. The **QDIM** command can also be used to perform several dimension editing operations. You can change the arrangement of existing dimensions, add an additional dimension, or remove an existing dimension. The **QDIM** command can be accessed by picking the **Quick Dimension** button on the **Dimension** toolbar, picking **Dimension** > **Quick Dimension**, or typing QDIM.

The **Continuous** option allows you to change the arrangement of a selected group of dimensions to chain dimensions. In chain, or continuous, dimensioning the dimensions are placed next to each other in a line, or end to end. This is discussed in Chapter 17. An example of continuous dimensioning is shown in **Figure 18-4**.

The **Baseline** option allows you to create a series of baseline dimensions from an existing dimension arrangement. In baseline dimensioning, all dimensions originate from common features. Baseline dimensions are drawn in **Figure 18-4**. In this example, the **Baseline** option has been used to change the dimensioning arrangement from continuous to baseline.

The **Edit** option allows you to add dimensions to, or remove dimensions from, a selected group and then automatically reorder the group. You can use the **Add** suboption of the **Edit** option to add a dimension. The **Remove** option is used to remove a dimension. The command sequence to add the dimension shown in **Figure 18-4** to the baseline dimensions is:

Command: **QDIM**↵
Associative dimensions priority = Endpoint
Select geometry to dimension: *(select all dimensions in the group to change)*
Select geometry to dimension: ↵
Specify dimension line position, or
[Continuous/Staggered/Baseline/Ordinate/Radius/Diameter/datumPoint/Edit/
   seTtings] <Baseline>: **E**↵
Indicate dimension point to remove, or [Add/eXit] <eXit>: **A**↵
Indicate dimension point to add, or [Remove/eXit] <eXit>: *(pick the location or feature for which the dimension is to be added)*
One dimension point added.
Indicate dimension point to add, or [Remove/eXit] <eXit>: ↵
Specify dimension line position, or
[Continuous/Staggered/Baseline/Ordinate/Radius/Diameter/datumPoint/Edit/
   seTtings] <Baseline>: *(pick a location for the baseline dimension arrangement)*

Figure 18-4.
The **QDIM** command can be used to change existing dimension arrangements and add or remove dimensions.

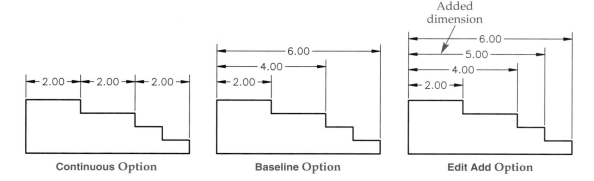

Continuous Option   Baseline Option   Edit Add Option

The dimensions are then automatically realigned after you pick a location for the arrangement. You do not have to pick all of the dimensions in the group. However, if you do not pick the entire group, you must select the location carefully. The spacing for the edited dimension and the dimensions in the group that were not selected may not be consistent.

 **Exercise 18-2** Complete the Exercise on the Student CD.

Editing Dimension Text Placement

Good dimensioning practice requires dimensions that are clear and easy to read. This may involve moving the text of adjacent dimensions. As an example, in **Figure 18-5**, one of the dimensions has been moved to a new location to separate the text elements. The **DIMTEDIT** command allows you to change the placement and orientation of an existing associative dimension text value. An *associative dimension* is one in which all elements of the dimension (including the dimension line, extension lines, arrowheads, and text) are connected to the object being dimensioned. Thus, if the object is modified, the dimension updates automatically. Associative dimensioning is controlled by the **DIMASSOC** system variable and is active by default.

To access the **DIMTEDIT** command, pick the **Dimension Text Edit** button on the **Dimension** toolbar, pick **Dimension > Align Text** and one of the options from the pull-down menu, or type DIMTEDIT. After entering the command, select the dimension to be altered.

If the dimension is associative, the text of the selected dimension automatically drags with the screen cursor. This allows you to relocate the text with your pointing device. If you pick a point, AutoCAD automatically moves the text and reestablishes the break in the dimension line. You can also select from the options offered at the Specify new location for dimension text or [Left/Right/Center/Home/Angle]: prompt.

- **Left.** Moves horizontal text to the left and vertical text down.
- **Right.** Moves horizontal text to the right and vertical text up.
- **Center.** Centers the dimension text on the dimension line.
- **Home.** Moves relocated text back to its original position.
- **Angle.** Allows you to place dimension text at an angle. When the **Angle** option is entered, you are asked to specify a rotation angle. The text is then rotated about its middle point.

The result after using each of the **DIMTEDIT** command options is shown in **Figure 18-6**.

Figure 18-5.
Using the **DIMTEDIT** command to stagger dimension text.

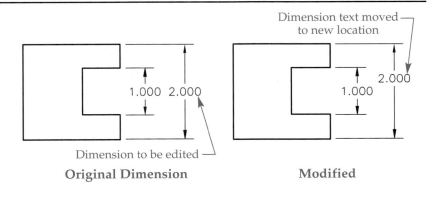

Original Dimension   Modified

Figure 18-6.
A comparison of
the options used
with the **DIMTEDIT**
command.

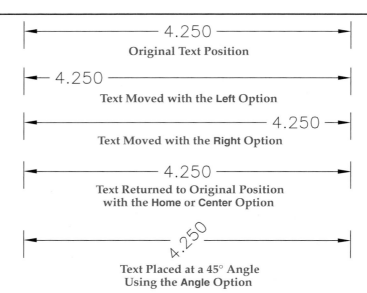

Original Text Position

Text Moved with the **Left** Option

Text Moved with the **Right** Option

Text Returned to Original Position
with the **Home** or **Center** Option

Text Placed at a 45° Angle
Using the **Angle** Option

PROFESSIONAL TIP

If you wish to relocate existing dimension text, using grips is the quickest way to adjust the text position. This method requires only picks and no command entry. Pick the dimension, pick the dimension text grip, and drag the text to the new location.

NOTE

When creating new dimensions, dimension text can be placed more easily by activating the **Place text manually** check box in the **Fit** tab of the **New** (or **Modify**) **Dimension Style** dialog box. This option allows you to locate the text as desired without using automatic horizontal justification.

Using Shortcut Menu Options

If you select a dimension and right-click, a shortcut menu is displayed. See **Figure 18-7.** The shortcut menu contains the following dimension-specific options:

- **Dim Text position.** The options in this cascading menu automatically move the dimension text.
- **Precision.** The options in this cascading menu allow you to easily adjust the number of decimal places displayed in a dimension text value.
- **Dim Style.** This cascading menu allows you to create a new dimension style based on the properties of the selected dimension. You can also change the dimension style of the dimension. In addition to the **Dim Style** option in the shortcut menu, there are other methods of changing the dimension style of an existing dimension. These are discussed in the next section, *Changing the Dimension Style.*

Figure 18-7.
Select a dimension and then right-click to access this shortcut menu.

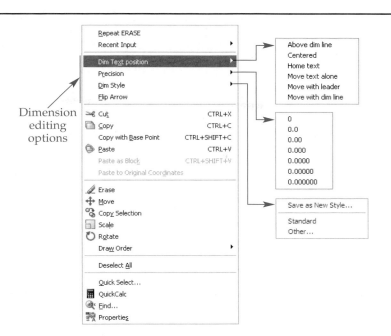

Dimension editing options

Menu items:
- Repeat ERASE
- Recent Input ▶
- **Dim Text position** ▶
  - Above dim line
  - Centered
  - Home text
  - Move text alone
  - Move with leader
  - Move with dim line
- Precision ▶
  - 0
  - 0.0
  - 0.00
  - 0.000
  - 0.0000
  - 0.00000
  - 0.000000
- Dim Style ▶
  - Save as New Style...
  - Standard
  - Other...
- Flip Arrow
- Cut   CTRL+X
- Copy   CTRL+C
- Copy with Base Point   CTRL+SHIFT+C
- Paste   CTRL+V
- Paste as Block   CTRL+SHIFT+V
- Paste to Original Coordinates
- Erase
- Move
- Copy Selection
- Scale
- Rotate
- Draw Order ▶
- Deselect All
- Quick Select...
- QuickCalc
- Find...
- Properties

- **Flip Arrow.** This option allows you to flip the direction of a dimension arrow-head to the opposite side of the extension line or object that it is touching. For example, if the arrowheads and the dimension value are crowded inside the extension lines, the arrowheads can quickly be flipped to the outside of the extension lines to make the dimension easier to read. When this option is used with a dimension that has a first and second arrowhead, only one of the arrowheads is flipped at a time. This allows you to control the arrowheads independently. The arrowhead that is flipped is determined by which arrowhead is closer to the point picked when selecting the dimension (not the right-click point).

> **NOTE**
>
>
>
> The **DIMEDIT** command can also be used to edit dimensions. The command options are similar to those available with other commands previously discussed. The **New** option allows you to edit the dimension text value. The **Home** and **Rotate** options are similar to the **Home** and **Angle** options used with the **DIMTEDIT** command. The **Oblique** option is not available with other commands. It allows you to change the angle of the extension lines of an existing dimension. This method is useful for overlapping or crowded dimensions and is discussed in Chapter 17.

Exercise 18-3   Complete the Exercise on the Student CD.

Changing the Dimension Style

So far you have learned how to edit dimension text, text placement, dimension group arrangements, and other elements of existing dimensions. In addition to these operations, you will often find it necessary to change the dimension style of a dimension. You can also import dimension styles from a separate drawing for use in the current drawing. These methods are discussed in the following sections.

As discussed in Chapter 17, you can create dimension styles by specifying settings for text styles, positioning elements, and other properties in the **Dimension Style Manager** dialog box. When there are a number of dimension styles used in your drawing, you may need to change the style of an existing dimension to a different style. A dimension's style can be changed using any of the following methods:

- **Dim Style cascading menu in the shortcut menu.** Select the dimension and right-click to display the shortcut menu. Select a new dimension style from the cascading menu.
- **Dim Style Control drop-down list in the Dimension toolbar.** Select the dimension and then select the new dimension style from this drop-down list. See **Figure 18-8.**
- **Dim Style Control drop-down list in the Styles toolbar.** Select the dimension and then select the new dimension style from this drop-down list.
- **Properties window.** Select a new dimension style in the **Misc** category. Refer to Chapter 13 for a discussion on how to change settings in the **Properties** window.
- **Update option.** The **Update** dimension command changes the style of the selected dimension to the current dimension style. This command can be accessed by picking the **Dimension Update** button on the **Dimension** toolbar or by selecting **Dimension** > **Update**.

Pull-Down Menu
Dimension
> Update
Toolbar
Dimension
Dimension Update

Figure 18-8.
The **Dim Style Control** drop-down list on the **Dimension** toolbar can be used to change the style of an existing dimension.

Pick to access the
Dim Style Control
drop-down list

Copying Dimension Styles between Drawings

ADCENTER
Type
ADCENTER
ADC
[Ctrl]+[2]
Pull-Down Menu
Tools
> Palettes
> DesignCenter
Toolbar
Standard
DesignCenter

DesignCenter can be used to import existing dimension styles from other drawing files. **DesignCenter** is opened by picking the **DesignCenter** button on the **Standard** toolbar, picking **Tools** > **Palettes** > **DesignCenter**, typing ADC or ADCENTER, or using the [Ctrl]+[2] key combination. Once **DesignCenter** is open, use the following procedure to copy dimension styles from an existing drawing into the current drawing.

1. In the tree view of **DesignCenter**, locate the drawing from which the dimension styles are to be copied.
2. Expand the drawing tree and highlight Dimstyles.
3. The dimension styles in the drawing are shown in the preview palette. See **Figure 18-9.**

Figure 18-9.
Copying dimension
styles using
DesignCenter.

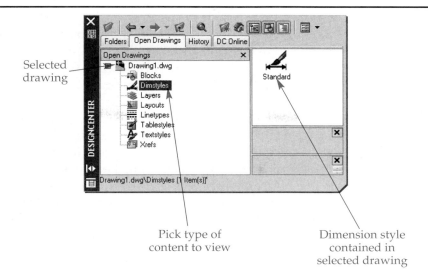

Selected
drawing

Pick type of
content to view

Dimension style
contained in
selected drawing

4. Select the dimension style(s) to be copied. Use the [Ctrl] and [Shift] keys to
    select multiple items. Then, right-click and select **Add Dimstyle(s)** from the
    shortcut menu to copy the styles to the current drawing. You can also use the
    Cut and **Paste** options from the shortcut menus or simply drag the dimension
    style icon and drop it into the drawing area.

Exercise
18-4   Complete the Exercise on the Student CD.

Using the Properties Window to Edit Dimensions

The **Properties** window can be used to change the various text, justification, and
formatting properties of selected dimensions. However, as discussed in Chapter 17,
doing so creates a dimension style override for the edited dimensions. Also, as discussed
earlier in this chapter, you can assign a different style to the selected dimension(s)
using the **Properties** window.

Exercise
18-5   Complete the Exercise on the Student CD.

Using the Matchprop Command

The dimension editing methods presented in this chapter have focused on updating
individual dimension properties and changing dimensions to a different dimension
style. You can also edit dimensions by matching the properties of one dimension to
another. The **MATCHPROP** command allows you to select the properties of one dimension and apply those properties to one or more existing dimensions.

MATCHPROP
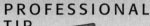
Type

MATCHPROP
MA

Pull-Down Menu

Modify
> Match Properties

Toolbar

Standard

Match Properties

The **MATCHPROP** command can be accessed by picking the **Match Properties** button on the **Standard** toolbar, selecting **Modify > Match Properties**, or typing MA or MATCHPROP. Pick the source dimension that has the desired properties and then pick the dimensions that will change. Press [Enter] and all of the destination dimensions are updated to reflect the properties of the source dimension. This command is covered more completely in Chapter 13.

For the **MATCHPROP** command to work with dimensions, the **Dimension** setting must be active. You can check this after you have selected the source object. When the Current active settings: prompt line appears, Dim should appear with the other settings. (Notice that the **Dimension** setting is active in the previous command sequence.) If this setting does not appear when you are prompted to select a destination object, type S for the **Settings** option. This displays the **Property Settings** dialog box. Activate the **Dimension** check box in the **Special Properties** area and pick **OK**. Then, select the destination dimensions.

PROFESSIONAL TIP

The style of the source dimension is applied to the destination dimensions. If the dimension style of the source dimension has been overridden, the "base" style is applied along with the dimension style override. Reapplying the "base" style will remove the overrides.

Exercise 18-6   Complete the Exercise on the Student CD.

Editing Associative Dimensions

As discussed earlier in this chapter, an associative dimension is made up of a group of individual elements and treated as a single object. When an associative dimension is selected for editing, the entire group of elements is highlighted. If you use the **ERASE** command, for example, you can pick the dimension as a single object and erase all elements at once.

One benefit of associative dimensioning is that it permits existing dimensions to be updated as an object is edited. This means that when a dimensioned object is edited, the dimension value automatically changes to match the edit. The automatic update is only applied if you accepted the default text value during the original dimension placement. This provides you with an important advantage when editing an associative-dimensioned drawing. Any changes to objects are automatically transferred to the dimensions.

NOTE

You can determine whether a dimension is associative by selecting the dimension, displaying the **Properties** window, and verifying the **Associative** property value in the **General** area.

Associative dimensioning is controlled by the **DIMASSOC** dimension variable. **DIMASSOC** is set by typing DIMASSOC. You can also open the **Options** dialog box and select the **User Preferences** tab. Then, check or uncheck the **Make new dimensions associative** option in the **Associative Dimensioning** area.

There are three settings for the **DIMASSOC** dimension variable: 0, 1, and 2. A setting of 0 turns off associative dimensioning. In this case, elements of the dimension are created separately, as if the dimension is exploded. The dimension is not updated when the object is edited. With a setting of 1, the components that make up a dimension are grouped together, but the dimension is not associated with an object. If you edit the object, you also have to edit the dimension.

If **DIMASSOC** is set to 2, the components that make up a dimension are grouped and the dimension is associated with the object. If the object is stretched, trimmed, or extended, the dimension updates automatically. See **Figure 18-10**. An associative dimension also updates when using grips or the **MOVE, MIRROR, ROTATE,** or **SCALE** commands.

In the **Options** dialog box, checking the **Make new dimensions associative** check box sets **DIMASSOC** to 2. If you uncheck the check box, the **DIMASSOC** value is changed to a previous value other than 2 (either 1 or 0).

NOTE   Associative dimensions in paper space attached to model space objects also automatically update when the object is edited.

Nonassociative dimensions can be converted to associative dimensions using the **DIMREASSOCIATE** command. To access this command, select **Dimension > Reassociate Dimensions** or type DRE or DIMREASSOCIATE. You are prompted to select the dimensions to be associated. After selecting the dimensions, an X marker appears at the first extension line endpoint. Select the point on an object with which to associate this extension line. Then, select the associated point for the second extension line.

Use the **Next** option to advance to the next definition point. You can also use the **Select object** option to select an object with which to associate the dimension. The extension line endpoints are then automatically associated with the object endpoints.

To disassociate a dimension from an object, type DDA or DISASSOCIATE and then select the dimension. The dimension objects are still grouped together, but the dimension will not be associated with an object.

DIMREASSOCIATE
Type
DIMREASSOCIATE
DRE
Pull-Down Menu
Dimensions
> Reassociate
Dimensions

DISASSOCIATE
Type
DISASSOCIATE
DDA

Figure 18-10.
The original drawing was created with associative dimensions. The drawing was revised using grips to change the rectangle dimensions and the **Properties** window to modify the circle diameter. The dimensions automatically updated to the new object geometry.

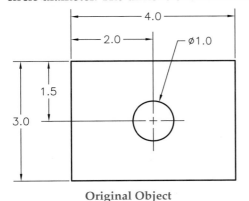

Original Object

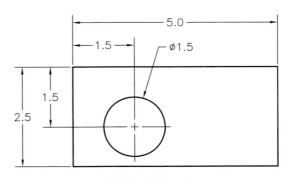

Revised Drawing

Exercise
18-7

Complete the Exercise on the Student CD.

EXPLODE

Type
EXPLODE
X

Pull-Down Menu
Modify
> Explode

Toolbar
Modify

Explode

Exploding an Associative Dimension

As previously discussed, the component parts of an associative dimension cannot be edited separately. An associative dimension is treated as one object even though it consists of extension lines, a dimension line, arrowheads, and text. At times, you may find it necessary to edit the individual parts. For example, you may want to erase the text without erasing the dimension line, arrowheads, or extension lines. To do this, you must first explode the dimension using the **EXPLODE** command.

Always be careful when exploding dimensions because they can lose their layer assignment. Also, an exploded dimension loses its association with the related feature.

PROFESSIONAL TIP   One way to edit individual dimension properties without removing the associative dimensioning feature is to use the **Properties** window to create a dimension style override.

Dimension Definition Points

When you draw an associative dimension, the points used to specify the dimension location and the center point of the dimension text are called the *definition points*, or *defpoints*. When a dimension location is redefined, the revised position is based on the definition points. The definition points are located on the Defpoints layer. This layer is automatically created by AutoCAD. The definition points are displayed with the dimension.

Normally, the Defpoints layer does not plot. The definition points are plotted only if the Defpoints layer is renamed and the layer is set to plot. The definition points are displayed when the dimensioning layer is on, even if the Defpoints layer is turned off.

If you select an object for editing and wish to include the dimensions in the edit, then you must include the definition points of the dimension in the selection set. If you need to snap to a definition point only, use the **Node** object snap.

Chapter Test

Answer the following questions. Write your answers on a separate sheet of paper or complete the electronic chapter test on the Student CD.

1. Name three selection options that can be used to easily erase a group of dimensions surrounding an object without erasing any part of the object.
2. Explain how to add a diameter symbol to a dimension text value using the **DDEDIT** command.
3. Which command and option can you use to add a new baseline dimension to an existing set of baseline dimensions?
4. Define *associative dimension*.
5. Name the command that allows you to control the placement and orientation of an existing associative dimension text value.
6. Which four command options related to dimension editing are available in the shortcut menu accessed when a dimension is selected?
7. Name three methods of changing the dimension style of a dimension.
8. How does the **Dimension Update** command affect selected dimensions?
9. Name three methods of copying dimension styles from the preview palette of **DesignCenter** into the current drawing.
10. When using the **Properties** window to edit a dimension, what is the effect on the dimension style?
11. How do you access the **Property Settings** dialog box?
12. Why is it important to have associative dimensions for editing objects?
13. Describe the differences between the dimensions created using the three **DIMASSOC** settings.
14. Which **Options** dialog box setting controls associative dimensioning?
15. Which command is used to convert nonassociative dimensions to associative dimensions?
16. Which command is used to convert associative dimensions to nonassociative dimensions?
17. What are definition points?
18. The definition points are automatically located on which layer?

1. Open P17-1 and edit as follows.
   A. Erase the left side view.
   B. Stretch the vertical dimensions to provide more space between dimension lines. Be sure the space you create is the same between all vertical dimensions.
   C. Stagger the existing vertical dimension text numbers if they are not staggered as shown in the original problem.
   D. Erase the 1.750 horizontal dimension and then stretch the 5.255 and 4.250 dimensions to make room for a new datum dimension from the baseline to where the 1.750 dimension was located. This should result in a new baseline dimension that equals 2.750. Be sure all horizontal dimension lines are equally spaced.
   E. Save the drawing as P18-1.

2. Open P17-2 and edit as follows.
   A. Stretch the total length from 3.500 to 4.000, leaving the holes the same distance from the edges.
   B. Fillet the upper-left corner. Modify the 3X R.250 dimension accordingly.
   C. Save the drawing as P18-2.

3. Open P17-5 and edit as follows.
   A. Use the existing drawing as the model and make four copies.
   B. Leave the original drawing as it is and edit the other four pins in the following manner, keeping the ∅.125 hole exactly in the center of each pin.
   C. Make one pin have a total length of 1.500.
   D. Create the next pin with a total length of 2.000.
   E. Edit the third pin to a length of 2.500.
   F. Change the last pin to a length of 3.000.
   G. Organize the pins on your drawing in a vertical row ranging in length from the smallest to the largest. You may need to change the drawing limits.
   H. Save the drawing as P18-3.

4. Open P17-6 and edit as follows.
   A. Modify the spline to have twelve projections, rather than eight.
   B. Change the angular dimension, linear dimension, and 8X dimension to reflect the modification.
   C. Save the drawing as P18-4.

5. Open P17-14 and edit as follows.
   A. Stretch the total length from 6.500 to 7.750.
   B. Add two more holes that continue the equally spaced pattern of 0.625 apart.
   C. Change the 8X .625(=5.00) dimension to read 10X .625(=6.250).
   D. Save the drawing as P18-5.

6. Open P17-16 and edit as follows.
   A. Make the bathroom 8'-0" wide by stretching the walls and vanity that are currently 6'-0" wide to 8'-0". Do this without increasing the size of the water closet compartment. Provide two equally spaced oval sinks where there is currently one.
   B. Save the drawing as P18-6.

7. Open P17-26 and edit as follows.
   A. Lengthen the part 0.250 on each side for a new overall dimension of 6.500.
   B. Change the width of the part from 3.000 to 3.500 by widening an equal amount on each side.
   C. Save the drawing as P18-7.

8. Open P17-23 and edit as follows.
   A. Shorten the 0.75 thread on the left side to 0.50.
   B. Shorten the 0.388 hexagon length to 0.300.
   C. Save the drawing as P18-8.

CHAPTER 19

Dimensioning with Tolerances

Learning Objectives

After completing this chapter, you will be able to do the following:
- Define and use dimensioning and tolerancing terminology.
- Identify different types of tolerance dimensions.
- Create dimension styles with specified tolerance settings.
- Prepare drawings with dimensions and tolerances from engineering designs, sketches, and layouts.

This chapter discusses the basics of tolerancing and explains how to prepare dimensions with tolerances for mechanical manufacturing drawings. Chapter 17 introduced you to the creation of dimension styles and explained how to set the specifications for dimension geometry, fit format, primary units, alternate units, and text. Dimensioning for mechanical drafting usually uses the following AutoCAD settings, depending on company practices.

Lines and Arrows

- The dimension line spacing for baseline dimensioning is usually more than the .38 default.
- The extension line extension is .125, and the extension line offset is .0625.
- Arrowheads are closed filled, closed blank, closed, or open.
- A small dot is used on a leader pointing to a surface.
- The centerline option is used for center marks for circles and located arcs. Fillets and rounds generally have no center marks.

Fit Format

- The manually defined format is convenient for flexible text placement.
- The best-fit option for text and arrows is common, but other format options work better for some applications.
- Horizontal and vertical justifications are usually in centered format.
- Text placement is normally inside and outside horizontal for unidirectional dimensioning.

Primary Units, Text, and Tolerances

- Objects are dimensioned in inches or millimeters.
- The primary units are typically decimal, with the number of decimal places controlled by the feature tolerance.
- Using alternate units for dual dimensioning is not a recommended ASME practice.
- The text is usually placed using the Romans font, a height of .125, and a gap of .0625.
- The tolerance method depends on the application.

Tolerancing Fundamentals

A *tolerance* is the total amount a specific dimension is permitted to vary. Tolerances are not given to values identified as reference, maximum, minimum, or stock sizes. A tolerance may be applied directly to the dimension, indicated by a general note, or identified in the drawing title block. See **Figure 19-1**.

The *limits* of a dimension are the largest and smallest numerical values the feature can be. In **Figure 19-2**, the dimension stated as 12.50±0.25 is referred to as *plus-minus dimensioning*. The tolerance of this dimension is the difference between the maximum and minimum limits. The upper limit is 12.75 (12.50 + 0.25), and the lower limit is 12.25 (12.50 – 0.25). If you take the upper limit and subtract the lower limit, the tolerance is .50.

The specified dimension is the part of the dimension from where the limits are calculated. In **Figure 19-2**, the specified dimension of the feature shown is 12.50. A tolerance on a drawing may be calculated and shown as *limits dimensioning*. Many schools and companies prefer this method because the limits are given and calculations are not required.

Figure 19-1.
Tolerances can be specified on the dimension, in a general note, or in the drawing title block.

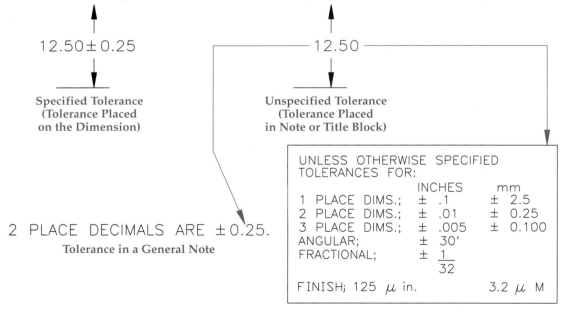

Figure 19-2.
Examples of plus-minus dimensioning and limits dimensioning.

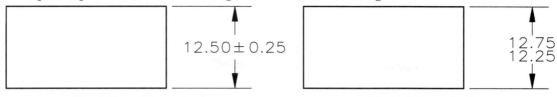

Plus-Minus Dimensioning   Limits Dimensioning

A *bilateral tolerance* permits variance in both the positive and negative directions from the specified dimension. An *equal bilateral tolerance* has the same variance in both directions. In an *unequal bilateral tolerance,* the variance from the specified dimension is not the same in both directions. See **Figure 19-3.** A *unilateral tolerance* permits an increase or a decrease in only one direction from the specified dimension. See **Figure 19-4.**

Figure 19-3.
Examples of bilateral tolerances.

$$24^{+0.08}_{-0.20} \qquad .750^{+.002}_{-.003}$$

Metric   Inch

Unequal Bilateral Tolerance

$$24\pm0.1 \qquad .750\pm.005$$

Metric   Inch

Equal Bilateral Tolerance

Figure 19-4.
The variance of a unilateral tolerance is in only one direction from the specified dimension.

$$24^{\;\;0}_{-0.2} \qquad .625^{+.000}_{-.004}$$

$$24^{+0.2}_{\;\;0} \qquad .625^{+.004}_{-.000}$$

Metric   Inch

Assigning Decimal Places to Dimensions and Tolerances

The ASME Y14.5M—*Dimensioning and Tolerancing* standard has separate recommendations for the way the number of decimal places is displayed in inch and metric dimensions. Examples of decimal dimension values in inches and metric units are shown in **Figure 19-3** and **Figure 19-4.** The following are some general rules.

Inch Dimensioning

- A specified inch dimension is expressed to the same number of decimal places as its tolerance. Zeros are added to the right of the decimal point if needed. For example, the inch dimension .250±.005 has an additional zero added to the .25 to match the three-decimal tolerance. Similarly, the dimensions 2.000±.005 and 2.500±.005 both have zeros added to match the tolerance.

- Both values in a plus and minus tolerance for an inch dimension have the same number of decimal places. Zeros are added to fill in where needed. The following is an example:

+.005   *not*   +.005
−.010   −.01

Metric Dimensioning

- The decimal point and zeros are omitted from the dimension when the metric dimension is a whole number. For example, the metric dimension 12 has no decimal point followed by a zero. This rule is true unless tolerance values are displayed.
- When a metric dimension includes a decimal portion, the last digit to the right of the decimal point is not followed by a zero. For example, the metric dimension 12.5 has no zero to the right of the 5. This rule is true unless tolerance values are displayed.
- Both values in a plus and minus tolerance for a metric dimension have the same number of decimal places. Zeros are added to fill in where needed.
- Zeros are not added after the specified dimension to match the tolerance. For example, both 24±0.25 and 24.5±0.25 are correct. Some companies prefer to add zeros after the specified dimension to match the tolerance, however, in which case 24.00±0.25 and 24.50±0.25 are both correct.

Setting Primary Units

DDIM

Type	
	DDIM
	D
Pull-Down Menu	
Format	
> Dimension	
Style...	
Toolbar	
Dimension	
Dimension Style...	

As discussed in Chapter 17, a dimension style can be created with specific formatting, justification, and text settings. The **Dimension Style Manager** dialog box is used to create dimension styles. See **Figure 19-5**. This dialog box is accessed by picking the **Dimension Style...** button on the **Dimension** toolbar, picking **Format > Dimension Style...** from the pull-down menu, or typing D or DDIM.

In the **Dimension Style Manager** dialog box, highlight the style you want to modify and pick the **Modify...** button to access the **Modify Dimension Style** dialog box. The **Primary Units** tab is used to set the type of units and precision of the dimension. The **Tolerances** tab allows you to set the tolerance format values. See **Figure 19-6**.

Figure 19-5.
The **Dimension Style Manager** dialog box.

Pick to access
the **Modify Dimension Style**
dialog box

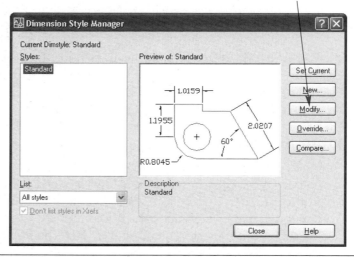

Figure 19-6.
Settings for the unit format and precision of linear dimensions are located in the **Primary Units** tab. The **Tolerances** tab contains formatting settings for tolerance dimensions.

Set the precision for specified dimensions

Settings should match the **Zero suppression** tolerance format settings in the **Tolerances** tab

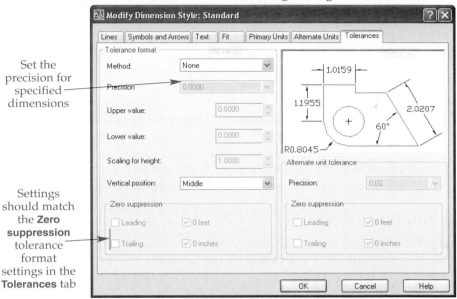

Primary Units Tab

Select a tolerance method

Set the precision for tolerance dimensions

Settings should match the **Zero suppression** linear dimension settings in the **Primary Units** tab

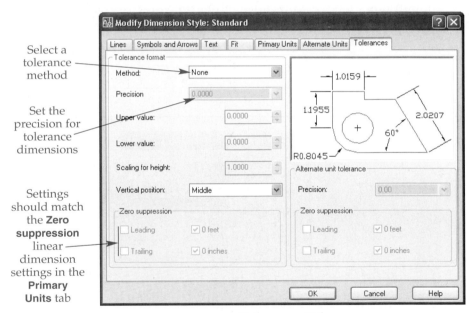

Tolerances Tab

In the **Linear dimensions** area of the **Primary Units** tab, the **Precision** drop-down list allows you to specify the number of zeros displayed after the decimal point of the specified dimension. The ASME standard recommends that the precision for the dimension and the tolerance be the same for inch dimensions, but it may be different for metric values, as previously discussed. After setting the primary unit precision, AutoCAD will automatically make the default for the tolerance precision in the **Tolerances** tab the same unit precision.

The **Zero suppression** settings were explained in Chapter 17. The suppression settings for linear dimensions in the **Primary Units** tab should be the same as the **Zero suppression** tolerance format settings in the **Tolerances** tab. The **Leading** options should be off, and the **Trailing** options should be on, for metric dimensions. For inch dimensions, the **Leading** options should be on, and the **Trailing** options should be off. AutoCAD does not automatically match the tolerance setting to the primary units setting. Changing the tolerance zero suppression is discussed later in this chapter.

Setting Tolerance Methods

The **Tolerances** tab is used to apply a tolerance method to your drawing. Refer to **Figure 19-6.** The default option in the **Method:** drop-down list is None. This means no tolerance method is used with your dimensions. As a result, most of the options in this area are disabled. If you pick a tolerance method from the drop-down list, the resulting image in the tab reflects the method selected. The drop-down list options are shown in **Figure 19-7.** These options are discussed in the following sections.

Symmetrical Tolerance Method

The symmetrical tolerance dimensioning option is used to draw dimension text that displays an equal bilateral tolerance in the plus-minus format. When the Symmetrical option is selected, the **Upper value:** text box, **Scaling for height:** text box, and **Vertical position:** drop-down list are activated. The preview image displays an equal bilateral tolerance. See **Figure 19-8.** You can enter a tolerance value in the **Upper value:** text box. Although it is inactive, you can see that the value in the **Lower value:** text box matches the value in the **Upper value:** text box.

Exercise 19-1   Complete the Exercise on the Student CD.

Figure 19-7.
A tolerance dimensioning method can be selected from the options in the **Method:** drop-down list, located in the **Tolerance format** area of the **Tolerances** tab.

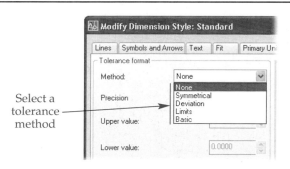

Select a tolerance method

Figure 19-8.
Setting the Symmetrical tolerance method option current, with an equal bilateral tolerance value of 0.005.

Specified tolerance method

Equal bilateral tolerance value

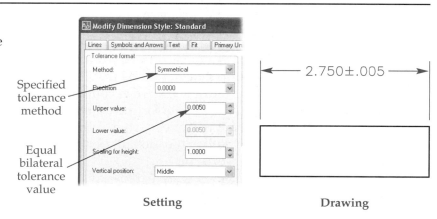

Setting   Drawing

Deviation Tolerance Method

AutoCAD refers to an unequal bilateral tolerance as a *deviation*. This means the tolerance deviates (departs) from the specified dimension within two different values. The deviation tolerance method can be set by selecting **Deviation** in the **Method:** drop-down list of the **Tolerances** tab. After selecting this option, the **Upper value:** and **Lower value:** text boxes are activated so you can enter the desired upper and lower tolerance values. See **Figure 19-9.** The preview image in the tab changes to match a representation of an unequal bilateral tolerance.

The deviation option can also be used to draw a unilateral tolerance by entering 0 for either the **Upper value:** or **Lower value:** setting. If you are using inch units, AutoCAD includes the plus or minus sign before the zero tolerance. When metric units are used, the sign is omitted for the zero tolerance. See **Figure 19-10.**

Exercise 19-2   Complete the Exercise on the Student CD.

Limits Tolerance Method

In limits dimensioning, the tolerance limits are given, and no calculations from the specified dimension are required (unlike plus-minus dimensioning). The limits tolerance method can be set by picking Limits in the **Method:** drop-down list in the **Tolerances** tab. When this option is set, the **Upper value:** and **Lower value:** text boxes are activated. You can then enter the desired upper and lower tolerance values that are added and subtracted from the specified dimension. The values you enter can be the same or different. See **Figure 19-11.**

Figure 19-9.
Setting the Deviation tolerance method option current, with unequal bilateral tolerance values.

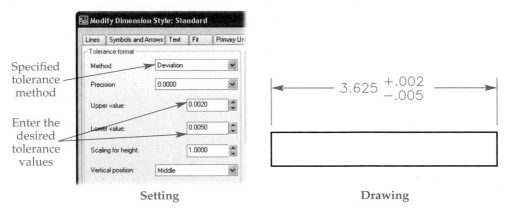

Specified tolerance method

Enter the desired tolerance values

Setting   Drawing

Figure 19-10.
When a unilateral tolerance is specified, AutoCAD automatically places the plus or minus symbol in front of the zero tolerance, if English units are used. The symbol is omitted with metric units.

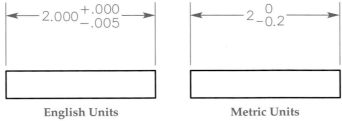

English Units   Metric Units

Figure 19-11.
Selecting the Limits tolerance method and setting limit values.

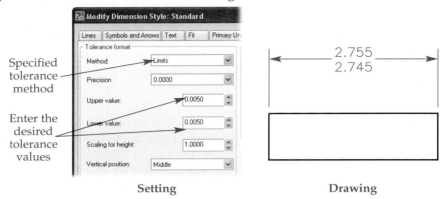

Setting   Drawing

Exercise
19-3   Complete the Exercise on the Student CD.

Basic Tolerance Method

The basic tolerance method is used to draw basic dimensions. A *basic dimension* is considered to be a theoretically perfect dimension and is used in geometric dimensioning and tolerancing, which is covered in Chapter 20. The basic tolerance method can be set by picking Basic in the **Method:** drop-down list in the **Tolerances** tab. With this setting, the **Upper value:** and **Lower value:** options in the **Tolerance format** area are disabled because a basic dimension has no tolerance. A basic dimension is distinguished from other dimensions by a rectangle placed around the dimension number, as shown in **Figure 19-12.**

Tolerance Precision and Zero Suppression

After a tolerance method is specified in the **Method:** drop-down list of the **Tolerances** tab, you can set the precision of the tolerance. By default, this setting matches the precision in the **Primary Units** tab. If the setting does not reflect the level of precision you want, change it using the **Precision** drop-down list in the **Tolerance format** area.

Figure 19-12.
The basic tolerance method is used for basic dimensioning. The dimension text for a basic dimension is placed inside a rectangle.

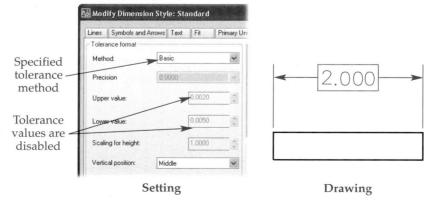

Setting   Drawing

As is the case with the precision settings, a tolerance method must be selected before the **Zero suppression** tolerance format options can be specified. AutoCAD does not automatically match the tolerance setting to the primary units setting.

Tolerance Method Review

✓ Each tolerance method option you pick is represented by an image preview in the **Modify Dimension Style** dialog box.

✓ When drawing inch tolerance dimensions, you should activate the **Leading** check box in the **Zero suppression** area of the **Tolerances** tab. The same option should be activated for linear dimensions in the **Primary Units** tab. You can then properly draw inch tolerance dimensions without placing the zero before the decimal point, as recommended by ASME standards. These settings allow you to draw a tolerance dimension such as .625±.005.

✓ When drawing metric tolerance dimensions, deactivate the **Leading** check box in the **Zero suppression** area of the **Tolerances** tab. Deactivate the same option for linear dimensions in the **Primary Units** tab. This allows you to place a metric tolerance dimension with the zero before the decimal point, as recommended by ASME standards (for example, a dimension such as 12±0.2).

Tolerance Justification

Using the options in the **Vertical position:** drop-down list in the **Tolerance format** area of the **Tolerances** tab, you can control the alignment, or justification, of deviation tolerance dimensions. The **Middle** option centers the tolerance with the specified dimension and is the default. This is also the recommended ASME practice. The other justification options are **Top** and **Bottom**. Deviation tolerance dimensions displaying each of the justification options are shown in **Figure 19-13.**

Tolerance Height

You can set the text height of the tolerance dimension in relation to the text height of the specified dimension. This is done using the **Scaling for height:** text box in the **Tolerance format** area of the **Tolerances** tab. The default of 1.0000 makes the tolerance dimension text the same height as the specified dimension text. This is the recommended ASME standard. If you want the tolerance dimension height to be three-quarters as high as the specified dimension height, type .75 in the **Scaling for height:** text box. Some companies prefer this practice to keep the tolerance part of the dimension from taking up additional space. Examples of tolerance dimensions with different text heights are shown in **Figure 19-14.**

Exercise 19-4   Complete the Exercise on the Student CD.

Figure 19-13.
Examples of the tolerance justification options for deviation tolerance dimensions.

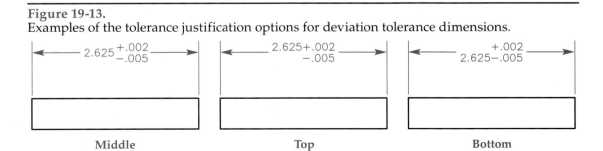

Middle   Top   Bottom

Figure 19-14.
Using different scale settings for the text height of tolerance dimensions.

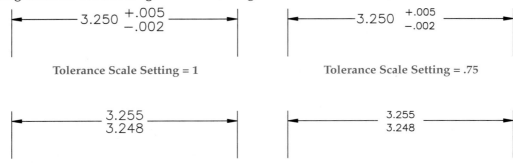

Tolerance Scale Setting = 1   Tolerance Scale Setting = .75

Tolerance Scale Setting = 1   Tolerance Scale Setting = .75

Chapter Test

Answer the following questions. Write your answers on a separate sheet of paper or complete the electronic chapter test on the Student CD.

1. Define the term *tolerance*.
2. Give an example of an equal bilateral tolerance in inches and in metric units.
3. Give an example of an unequal bilateral tolerance in inches and in metric units.
4. What are the limits of the tolerance dimension 3.625±.005?
5. Give an example of a unilateral tolerance in inches and in metric units.
6. Which dialog box is used to create dimension styles? How is it accessed?
7. How do you open the **Tolerances** tab?
8. How do you set the number of zeros displayed after the decimal point for a tolerance dimension?
9. Which **Zero suppression** settings should be specified for linear and tolerance dimensions when using metric units?
10. Which **Zero suppression** settings should be specified for linear and tolerance dimensions when using inch units?
11. What is the purpose of the symmetrical tolerance method option?
12. What is the purpose of the deviation tolerance method option?
13. What is the purpose of the limits tolerance method option?
14. What happens to the preview image in the **Tolerances** tab when a tolerance method option is picked from the **Method:** drop-down list?
15. Name the tolerance dimension justification option recommended by the ASME standards.
16. Explain the results of setting the **Scaling for height:** option to 1 in the **Tolerances** tab.
17. What setting would you use for the **Scaling for height:** option if you wanted the tolerance dimension height to be three-quarters of the specified dimension height?

Drawing Problems

Set the limits, units, dimension style options, and other parameters as needed for the following problems. Use the guidelines given below.

A. Draw and dimension the necessary views for the following drawings to exact size. These problems are presented in 3D. Draw the proper 2D views for each.

B. Apply dimensions accurately using ASME standards. Create dimension styles that suit the specific needs of each drawing. For example, save different dimension styles for metric and inch dimensions.

C. Create separate layers for the views and dimensions.

D. Plot the drawings with 0.6 mm object lines and 0.3 mm thin lines.

E. Place the following general notes in the lower-left corner of each drawing.
3. UNLESS OTHERWISE SPECIFIED, ALL DIMENSIONS ARE IN MILLIMETERS. (*or* INCHES, *as applicable*)
2. REMOVE ALL BURRS AND SHARP EDGES.
1. INTERPRET PER ASME Y14.5M-1994.
NOTES:

F. Save the drawings as P19-1 through P19-7.

1.

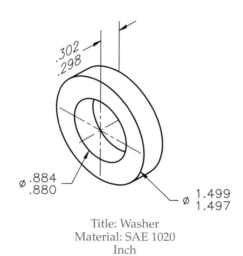

Title: Washer
Material: SAE 1020
Inch

2.

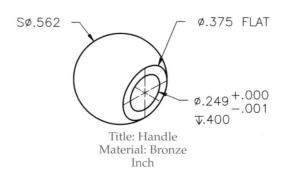

Title: Handle
Material: Bronze
Inch

3.

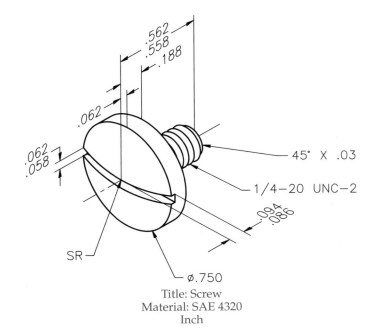

.562
.558
.188
.062
.062
.058
45° X .03
1/4—20 UNC—2
.094
.086
SR
⌀.750

Title: Screw
Material: SAE 4320
Inch

4.

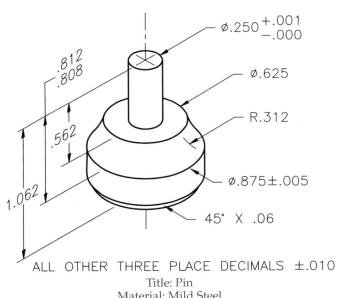

⌀.250 +.001 −.000
.812
.808
⌀.625
R.312
.562
⌀.875±.005
1.062
45° X .06

ALL OTHER THREE PLACE DECIMALS ±.010

Title: Pin
Material: Mild Steel
Inch

5. This object is shown as a section for clarity. Do not draw a section.

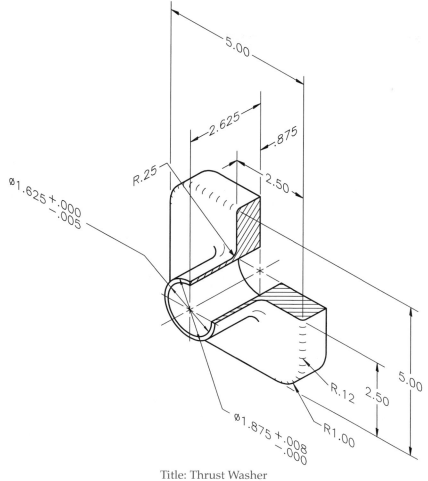

Title: Thrust Washer
Material: SAE 5150
Inch

6.

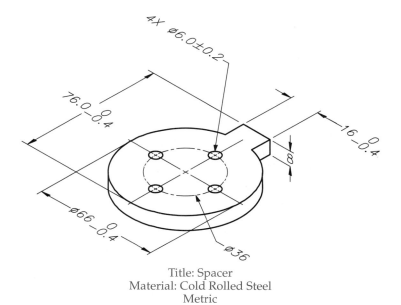

Title: Spacer
Material: Cold Rolled Steel
Metric

7.

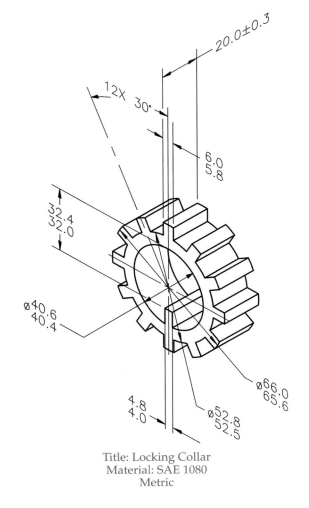

Title: Locking Collar
Material: SAE 1080
Metric

8. Draw the vise clamp shown below. Save the drawing as P19-8.

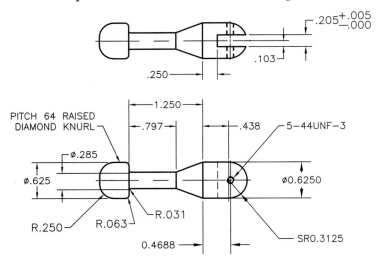

AutoCAD and Its Applications—Basics

CHAPTER 20

Geometric Dimensioning and Tolerancing

Learning Objectives

After completing this chapter, you will be able to do the following:

● Identify symbols used in geometric dimensioning and tolerancing (GD&T).
● Use the **TOLERANCE**, **QLEADER**, and **LEADER** commands to create geometric tolerancing symbols.
● Draw and edit feature control frames.
● Draw datum feature symbols.
● Place basic dimensions on a drawing.

This chapter is an introduction to geometric dimensioning and tolerancing (GD&T) principles, as adopted by the American National Standards Institute (ANSI) and published by the American Society of Mechanical Engineers (ASME) for engineering and related document practices. The standard is ASME Y14.5M-1994, *Dimensioning and Tolerancing*. **Geometric tolerancing** is a general term that refers to tolerances used to control the form, profile, orientation, runout, and location of features on an object.

The drafting applications covered in this chapter use the AutoCAD geometric tolerancing capabilities and additional recommendations to comply with the ASME Y14.5M-1994 standard. This chapter is only an introduction to GD&T. For complete coverage of GD&T, refer to *Geometric Dimensioning and Tolerancing*, published by Goodheart-Willcox Publisher. Before beginning this chapter, it is recommended that you have a solid understanding of dimensioning and tolerancing standards and AutoCAD applications. This introductory material is presented in Chapters 17, 18, and 19 of this text. The discussion in this chapter divides the dimensioning and geometric tolerancing symbols into five basic types:

- Dimensioning symbols.
- Geometric characteristic symbols.
- Material condition symbols.
- Feature control frames.
- Datum feature symbols.

When you draw GD&T symbols, it is recommended that you place them on a dimensioning layer, so the symbols and text can be plotted as lines that have the same thickness as extension and dimension lines (0.01″ or 0.3 mm). The suggested text font is Romans. These practices correspond with the standard ASME Y14.2M-1992, *Line Conventions and Lettering*.

Dimensioning Symbols

Symbols represent specific information that would be difficult and time-consuming to duplicate in note form. They must be clearly drawn to the required size and shape so they communicate the desired information uniformly. ASME Y14.5M recommends symbols because the language of symbols is international; they are read the same way in any country. In an international economy, it is important to have effective communication on engineering drawings. Symbols make this communication process uniform. ASME Y14.5M also states that the adoption of dimensioning symbols does not prevent the use of equivalent terms or abbreviations in situations where symbols are considered inappropriate.

Symbols aid in clarity, the presentation of the drawing, and a reduction of drawing time. Creating and using AutoCAD symbols is covered later in this chapter and in Chapter 22. A sample group of recommended dimensioning symbols is shown in **Figure 20-1.**

Geometric Characteristic Symbols

In GD&T, symbols are used to provide specific controls related to the form of an object, orientation of features, outlines of features, relationship of features to an axis, or location of features. These symbols are known as *geometric characteristic* symbols. Geometric characteristic symbols are separated into five types: form, profile, location, orientation, and runout. See **Figure 20-2.**

Figure 20-1.
Dimensioning symbols recommended by ASME Y14.5M-1994.

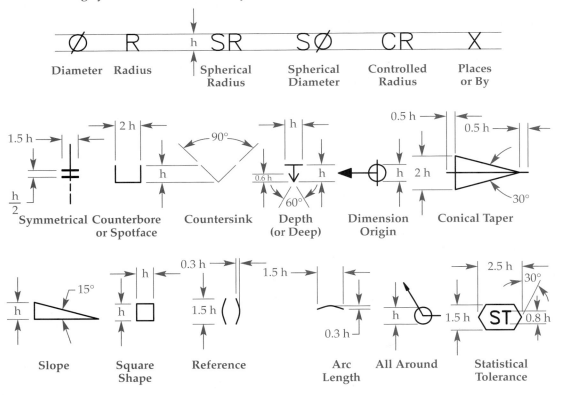

h = Letter height

Figure 20-2.
Geometric
characteristic
symbols
recommended by
ASME Y14.5M-1994.

	—	Straightness
Form	⬭	Flatness
	○	Circularity
	⌓	Cylindricity
Profile	⌒	Profile of a line
	⌓	Profile of a surface
	⊕	Position
Location	◎	Concentricity
	≡	Symmetry
	//	Parallelism
Orientation	⊥	Perpendicularity
	∠	Angularity
Runout	↗ or ↗	Circular runout
	↗↗ or ↗↗	Total runout

Material Condition Symbols

Material condition symbols are often referred to as *modifying symbols* because they modify the geometric tolerance, in relation to the produced size or location of the feature. These symbols are only used in geometric dimensioning applications. The symbols used in a feature control frame to indicate maximum material condition (MMC) or least material condition (LMC) are shown in **Figure 20-3.**

Surface control, regardless of feature size (RFS)

When there is no material condition symbol following the geometric tolerance in a feature control frame, regardless of feature size (RFS) is assumed as the material condition. *Regardless of feature size (RFS)* means the geometric tolerances remain the same, regardless of the actual produced size. The term *produced size*, when used here, means the actual size of the feature, when measured after manufacture.

When a feature control frame is connected to a feature surface with a leader or an extension line, it is referred to as *surface control*. See **Figure 20-4.** The geometric characteristic symbol shown is straightness, but the format is the same for any characteristic.

Look at the chart in **Figure 20-4** and notice how the possible sizes range from 6.20 (MMC) to 5.80 (LMC). With surface control, perfect form is required at MMC. *Perfect form* means the object cannot exceed a true geometric form boundary established at MMC. The geometric tolerance at MMC is zero, as shown in the chart. As the produced size varies from MMC in the chart, the geometric tolerance increases, until it equals the amount specified in the feature control frame.

Figure 20-3.
Material condition
symbols. In ASME
Y14.5M-1994, there
is no symbol for
regardless of feature
size (RFS), since RFS
is assumed unless
otherwise specified.

Ⓜ MMC, maximum
material condition

RFS, regardless of
feature size.
No symbol; RFS is
assumed unless
otherwise specified.

Ⓛ LMC, least material
condition

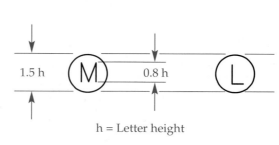

1.5 h   Ⓜ   0.8 h   Ⓛ

h = Letter height

Figure 20-4.
The drawing on the left specifies surface control, regardless of feature size (RFS). The actual meaning of the geometric tolerance is shown on the right.

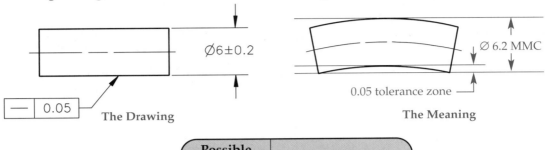

The Drawing

The Meaning

	Possible produced sizes	Maximum out-of-straightness
MMC	6.20	* 0
	6.10	0.05
	6.00	0.05
	5.90	0.05
LMC	5.80	0.05

* Perfect form required

Axis control, regardless of feature size (RFS)

Axis control is indicated when the feature control frame is shown with a diameter dimension. See **Figure 20-5.** Regardless of feature size (RFS) is assumed. With axis control, perfect form is not required at MMC. Therefore, the specified geometric tolerance stays the same at every produced size. See the chart in **Figure 20-5.**

Maximum material condition (MMC) control

If the material condition control is *maximum material condition (MMC)*, the symbol for MMC must be placed in the feature control frame. See **Figure 20-6.** When this application is used, the specified geometric tolerance is held at the MMC produced

Figure 20-5.
The drawing on the left specifies axis control, regardless of feature size (RFS). The actual meaning of the geometric tolerance is shown on the right.

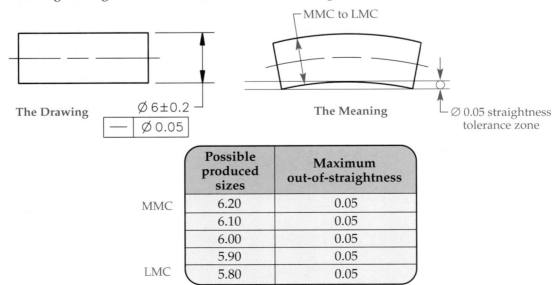

	Possible produced sizes	Maximum out-of-straightness
MMC	6.20	0.05
	6.10	0.05
	6.00	0.05
	5.90	0.05
LMC	5.80	0.05

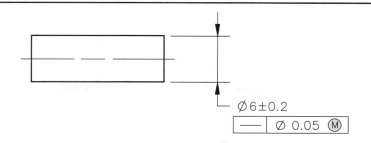

Figure 20-6.
The drawing specifies maximum material condition (MMC) applied to a feature. The symbol for MMC is shown highlighted.

Ø6±0.2

	Possible produced sizes	Maximum out-of-straightness
MMC	6.20	0.05
	6.10	0.15
	6.00	0.25
	5.90	0.35
LMC	5.80	0.45

size. See the chart in **Figure 20-6.** As the produced size varies from MMC, the geometric tolerance increases, equal to the change. The maximum geometric tolerance is at the LMC produced size.

Least material condition (LMC) control

If the material condition control is *least material condition (LMC)*, the symbol for LMC must be placed in the feature control frame. When this application is used, the specified geometric tolerance is held at the LMC produced size. As the produced size varies from LMC, the geometric tolerance increases, equal to the change. The maximum geometric tolerance is at the MMC produced size.

Feature Control Frame

The geometric characteristic, geometric tolerance, material condition, and datum reference (if any) for an individual feature are specified by means of a feature control frame. The *feature control frame* is divided into compartments containing the geometric characteristic symbol in the first compartment, followed by the geometric tolerance. Where applicable, the geometric tolerance is preceded by the diameter symbol, which describes the shape of the tolerance zone, and is followed by a material condition symbol (if other than RFS). See **Figure 20-7.**

When a geometric tolerance is related to one or more datums, the datum reference letters are placed in compartments following the geometric tolerance. *Datums* are considered theoretically perfect surfaces, planes, points, or axes. When there is a reference to multiple datums, both datum reference letters are separated by a dash and placed in a single compartment after the geometric tolerance. A *multiple datum reference* is established by two datum features, such as an axis established by two datum diameters. Several feature control frames with datum references are shown in **Figure 20-8.**

There is a specific order used to display elements in a feature control frame. See **Figure 20-9.** Notice the datum reference letters can be followed by a material condition symbol where applicable.

Figure 20-7.
Feature control frames containing the geometric characteristic symbol, geometric tolerance, and diameter symbol (as applicable). There is no material condition symbol for regardless of feature size (RFS), since RFS is assumed. Note that the geometric tolerance is expressed as a total, not a plus-minus value.

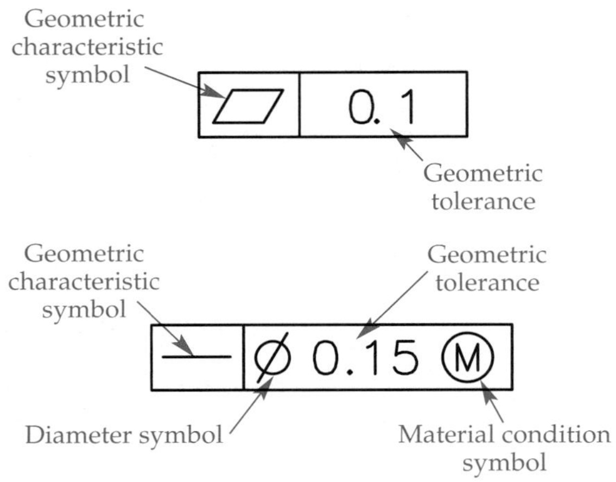

Geometric characteristic symbol

Geometric tolerance

Geometric characteristic symbol

Geometric tolerance

Diameter symbol

Material condition symbol

Figure 20-8.
Examples of datum references indicated in feature control frames.

Datum reference letter

Material condition symbol (when used)

Primary datum reference

Secondary datum reference

Primary datum reference

Tertiary datum reference

Secondary datum reference

Primary multiple datum reference

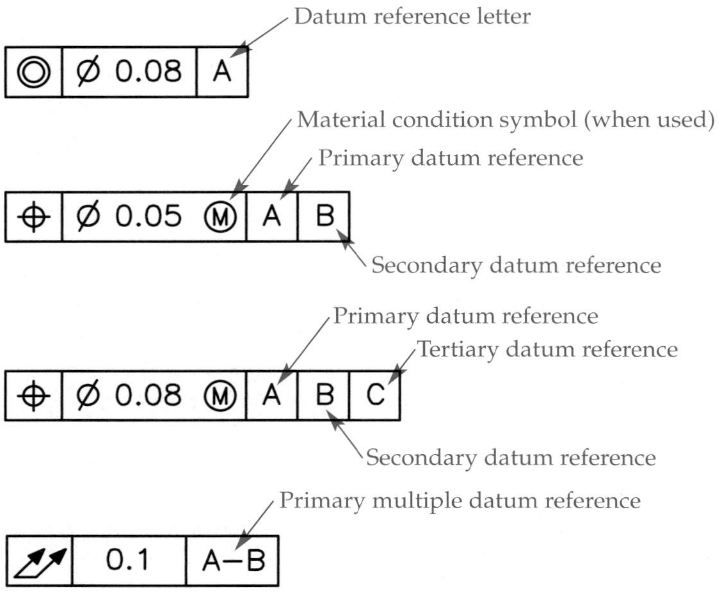

Figure 20-9.
The order of elements in a feature control frame.

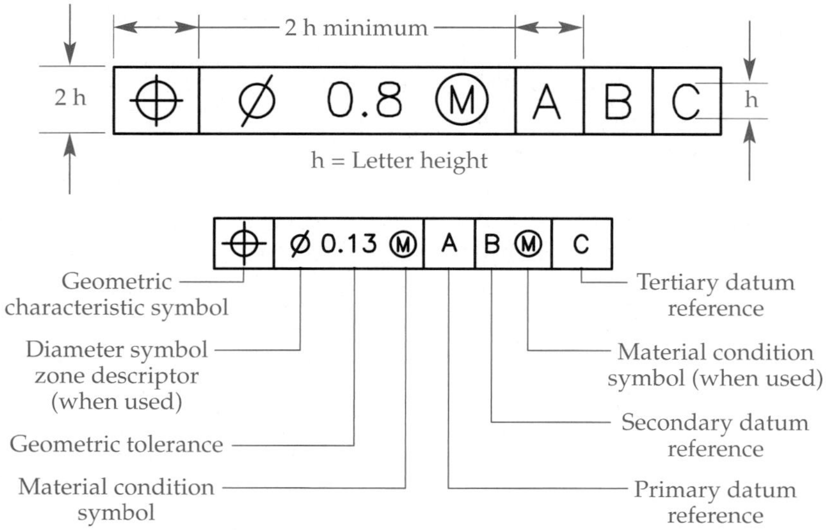

2 h minimum

2 h

h

h = Letter height

Geometric characteristic symbol

Diameter symbol zone descriptor (when used)

Geometric tolerance

Material condition symbol

Tertiary datum reference

Material condition symbol (when used)

Secondary datum reference

Primary datum reference

Basic Dimensions

A *basic dimension* is considered a theoretically perfect dimension. Basic dimensions are used to describe the theoretically exact size, profile, orientation, and location of a feature. These dimensions provide the basis from which permissible variations are established by tolerances on other dimensions, in notes, or in feature control frames. In simple terms, a basic dimension tells you where the geometric tolerance zone or datum target is located.

Basic dimensions are shown on a drawing with a rectangle placed around the dimension text, as shown in Figure 20-10. A general note can also be used to identify basic dimensions in some applications. For example, the note UNTOLERANCED DIMENSIONS LOCATING TRUE POSITION ARE BASIC indicates the basic dimensions. The basic dimension rectangle is a signal to the reader to look for a geometric tolerance in a feature control frame related to the features being dimensioned.

Figure 20-10.
Basic dimensions are identified with a rectangle drawn around the text.

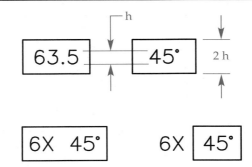

The number of times or places may be applied to a basic dimension by placement inside or outside of the basic dimension symbol.

h = Letter height

Additional Symbols

Other symbols commonly used in GD&T are shown in Figure 20-11. These symbols are used for specific applications and are identified as follows:

- **Free state.** Free state describes distortion of a part after the removal of forces applied during manufacture. The free state symbol is placed in the feature control frame after the geometric tolerance and the material condition (if any), if the feature must meet the tolerance specified while in free state.
- **Tangent plane.** A tangent plane symbol is placed after the geometric tolerance in the feature control frame when it is necessary to control a feature surface by contacting points of tangency.
- **Projected tolerance zone.** A projected tolerance zone symbol is placed in the feature control frame to inform the reader that the geometric tolerance zone is projected away from the primary datum.
- **Between.** The between symbol is used with profile geometric tolerances to identify where the profile tolerance is applied.

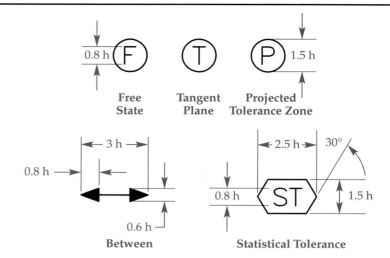

Figure 20-11.
Additional
recommended
dimensioning
symbols.

0.8 h — Free State

Tangent Plane

Projected Tolerance Zone 1.5 h

3 h

0.8 h

0.6 h

Between

2.5 h   30°

0.8 h   1.5 h

Statistical Tolerance

- **Statistical tolerance.** The statistical tolerance symbol is used to indicate that a tolerance is based on statistical tolerancing. *Statistical tolerancing* is the assigning of tolerances to related dimensions, based on the requirements of statistical process control (SPC). *Statistical process control (SPC)* is a method of monitoring and adjusting a manufacturing process based on statistical signals. The statistical tolerancing symbol is placed after the dimension or geometric tolerance that requires SPC. See **Figure 20-12.** When the feature can be manufactured by either SPC or conventional means, both the statistical tolerance with the statistical tolerance symbol and the conventional tolerance must be shown. An appropriate general note should accompany the drawing. Either of the two following notes is acceptable:
  - FEATURES IDENTIFIED AS STATISTICAL TOLERANCED SHALL BE PRODUCED WITH STATISTICAL PROCESS CONTROL.
  - FEATURES IDENTIFIED AS STATISTICAL TOLERANCED SHALL BE PRODUCED WITH STATISTICAL PROCESS CONTROL, OR THE MORE RESTRICTIVE ARITHMETIC LIMITS.

Figure 20-12.
Different ways to
apply a statistical
tolerance. The
statistical tolerance
symbol is shown
here highlighted.

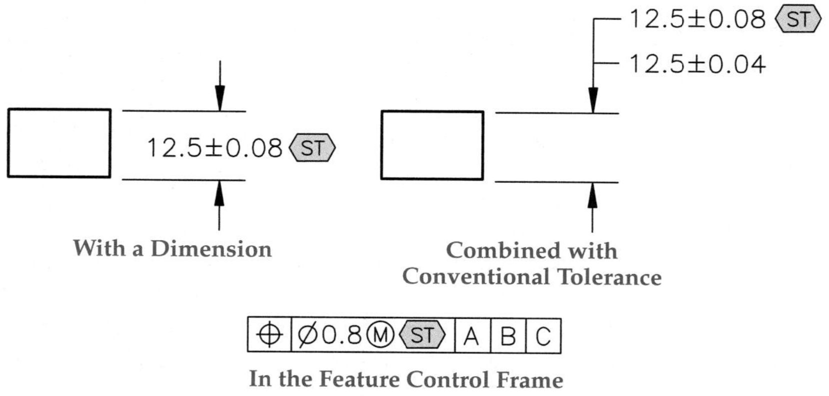

12.5±0.08 ⟨ST⟩

12.5±0.04

12.5±0.08 ⟨ST⟩

With a Dimension

Combined with Conventional Tolerance

⊕ | Ø0.8Ⓜ⟨ST⟩ | A | B | C

In the Feature Control Frame

Datum Feature Symbols

As discussed previously, datums refer to theoretically perfect surfaces, planes, points, or axes. In this introduction to datum-related symbols, the datum is assumed. In GD&T, the datums are identified with a *datum feature symbol*.

Each datum feature requiring identification must have its own identification letter. Any letter of the alphabet can be used to identify a datum, except *I, O,* or *Q.* These letters can be confused with the numbers *1* or *0.* On drawings where the number of datums exceeds 23, double letters are used, starting with *AA* through *AZ* and then continuing with *BA* through *BZ.* Datum feature symbols can be repeated only as necessary for clarity.

In **Figure 20-13**, the datum feature symbol recommended by ASME Y14.5M-1994 is shown. The datum feature symbol used in drawings prior to the release of ASME Y14.5M-1994 is distinctively different. The previously used datum feature symbol is shown in **Figure 20-14**.

When a surface is used to establish a datum plane on a part, the datum feature symbol is placed on the edge view of the surface or on an extension line in the view where the surface appears as a line. See **Figure 20-15**. A leader line can also be used to connect the datum feature symbol to the view.

When the datum is an axis, the datum feature symbol can be placed on the drawing using one of the following methods. See **Figure 20-16**.

Figure 20-13.
The datum feature symbol, based on ASME Y14.5M-1994.

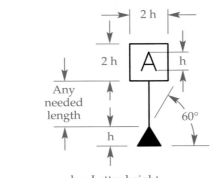

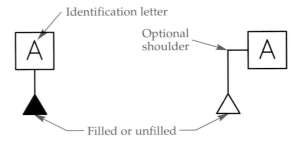

Figure 20-14.
The datum feature symbol, based on ANSI Y14.5M-1982. The standard was revised to ASME Y14.5M-1994.

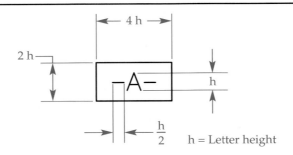

Figure 20-15.
Datum feature symbols used to identify datum planes.

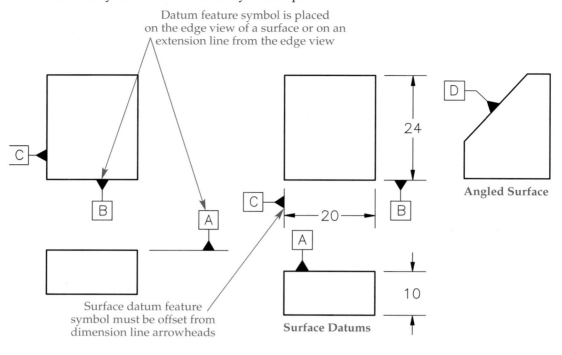

Datum feature symbol is placed on the edge view of a surface or on an extension line from the edge view

Surface datum feature symbol must be offset from dimension line arrowheads

Surface Datums

Angled Surface

Figure 20-16.
Different methods of using the datum feature symbol to represent a datum axis.

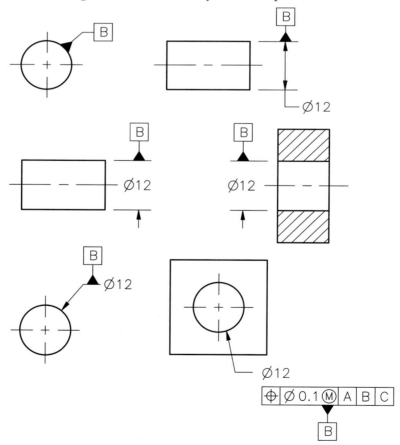

- The symbol can be placed on the outside surface of a cylindrical feature.
- The symbol can be centered on the opposite side of the dimension line arrowhead.
- The symbol can replace the dimension line and arrowhead when the dimension line is placed outside the extension lines.
- The symbol can be placed on a leader line shoulder.
- The symbol can be placed below, and attached to, the center of a feature control frame.

Elements on a rectangular symmetrical part or feature can be located and dimensioned in relationship to a datum center plane. Datum center plane symbols are shown in **Figure 20-17.**

Figure 20-17.
Placing datum center plane symbols. Axis and center plane datum feature symbols must align with, or replace, the dimension line arrowhead, or the datum feature symbol must be placed on the feature, leader shoulder, or feature control frame.

Geometric Dimensioning and Tolerancing (GD&T) with AutoCAD

This chapter has given you an introduction to the appearance and use of geometric dimensioning and tolerancing (GD&T) symbols. AutoCAD provides you with the ability to add GD&T symbols to your drawings. The feature control frame and related GD&T symbols can be created using the TOLERANCE, QLEADER, and LEADER commands. These commands are discussed in the following sections.

Using the Tolerance Command

The **TOLERANCE** command provides tools for creating GD&T symbols and feature control frames. To access this command, pick the **Tolerance...** button on the **Dimension** toolbar, pick **Dimension > Tolerance...** from the pull-down menu, or type TOL or TOLERANCE. This displays the **Geometric Tolerance** dialog box. See **Figure 20-18.**

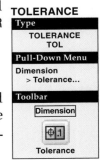

TOLERANCE
Type
TOLERANCE
TOL
Pull-Down Menu
Dimension
> Tolerance...
Toolbar
Dimension

Tolerance

Figure 20-18.
The **Geometric Tolerance** dialog box is used to draw geometric dimensioning and tolerancing (GD&T) symbols and feature control frames to desired specifications.

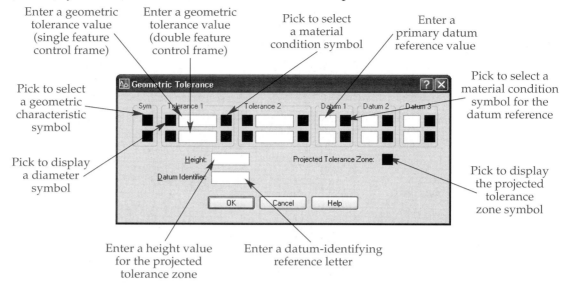

Enter a geometric tolerance value (single feature control frame)

Enter a geometric tolerance value (double feature control frame)

Pick to select a material condition symbol

Enter a primary datum reference value

Pick to select a material condition symbol for the datum reference

Pick to select a geometric characteristic symbol

Pick to display a diameter symbol

Enter a height value for the projected tolerance zone

Enter a datum-identifying reference letter

Pick to display the projected tolerance zone symbol

The **Geometric Tolerance** dialog box is divided into areas containing compartments that relate to the components found in a feature control frame. The compartments in the two **Tolerance** and three **Datum** areas allow you to specify geometric tolerance and datum reference values. There are two levels in each area that can be used to create a feature control frame. The first, or upper, level is used to make a single feature control frame. The lower level is used to create a double feature control frame. There are also options for displaying a diameter symbol and a modifying symbol. In addition, the **Geometric Tolerance** dialog box allows you to display a projected tolerance zone symbol and value and part of the datum feature symbol. The options and features in the **Geometric Tolerance** dialog box are explained in the following sections.

Selecting a geometric characteristic symbol

Geometric characteristic symbols can be accessed in the **Sym** area located at the far left of the **Geometric Tolerance** dialog box. This area has two image tile buttons that can be used to display one or two geometric characteristic symbols. Keep in mind that the corresponding text boxes along the upper row in each area are used for a single feature control frame. The text boxes in the lower row are used to create a double feature control frame.

Picking one of the image tile buttons in the **Sym** area opens the **Symbol** dialog box. See **Figure 20-19.** Pick a symbol to have it displayed in the **Sym** image tile you selected. After making a selection, the **Geometric Tolerance** dialog box returns. You can pick the same image tile again to select a different symbol, if you wish. To remove a previously selected symbol, pick the blank image tile in the lower-right corner of the **Symbol** dialog box.

Tolerance 1 area

The **Tolerance 1** area of the **Geometric Tolerance** dialog box allows you to enter the first geometric tolerance value used in the feature control frame. If you are drawing a single feature control frame, enter the desired value in the upper text box. Also enter a value in the lower text box, if you are drawing a double feature control frame. Double feature control frames, discussed later in this chapter, are used for applications such as unit straightness, unit flatness, composite profile tolerance, composite positional tolerance, and coaxial positional tolerance. You can add a diameter symbol by picking the image tile to the left of the text box. Pick the diameter image tile again to remove the diameter symbol.

Figure 20-19.
The **Symbol** dialog box is used to select a geometric characteristic symbol for use in a feature control frame.

Figure 20-19.
The **Symbol** dialog box is used to select a geometric characteristic symbol for use in a feature control frame.

Pick the desired symbol

Pick to remove a symbol from the **Sym** area

The image tile to the right of the text box is used to place a material condition symbol. When you pick this image tile, the **Material Condition** dialog box appears. See **Figure 20-20.** Pick the desired symbol to have it displayed in the image tile you selected. In the example given, an MMC symbol is selected. To remove a material condition symbol, pick the blank tile in the **Material Condition** image tile menu. The RFS symbol in **Figure 20-20** was used in ANSI Y14.5M-1982. The symbol is not used in ASME Y14.5M-1994 because RFS is assumed unless otherwise specified.

In **Figure 20-21**, a position symbol is shown in the **Sym** image tile, and 0.5 is entered as the tolerance value in the upper text box in the **Tolerance 1** area. The tolerance value is preceded by a diameter symbol and followed by an MMC symbol. Remember that a zero precedes metric decimals, but not inch decimals.

Tolerance 2 area

The **Tolerance 2** area of the **Geometric Tolerance** dialog box is used for the addition of a second geometric tolerance to the feature control frame. This is not a common application, but it may be used in some cases where there are restrictions placed on the geometric tolerance specified in the first compartment. For example, a second geometric tolerance value of 0.8 MAX means that the specification given in the first compartment is maintained, but it cannot exceed 0.8.

Figure 20-20.
The **Material Condition** dialog box. Pick the desired material condition symbol for the geometric tolerance and datum reference, as needed. Notice the symbol for regardless of feature size (RFS) is available. This symbol is not used in ASME Y14.5M-1994, but it may be needed when editing older drawings.

Old RFS symbol

Pick the desired symbol

Pick to remove a selected symbol

Figure 20-21.
The **Geometric Tolerance** dialog box with a diameter symbol, geometric tolerance value, and maximum material condition (MMC) symbol added to the **Tolerance 1** area.

The tolerance value, diameter symbol, and material condition symbol are entered

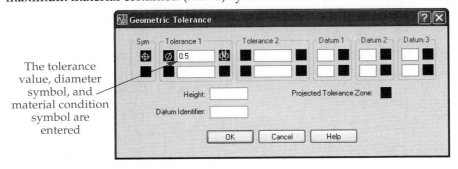

Datum areas

The **Datum 1** area of the **Geometric Tolerance** dialog box is used to establish the information needed for the primary datum reference compartment. Like the **Tolerance** areas, this area offers two levels of text boxes to create single or double feature control frames. You can also specify a material condition symbol for the datum reference by picking the image tile next to the corresponding text box to open the **Material Condition** dialog box. The **Datum 2** and **Datum 3** areas are used to specify the secondary and tertiary datum reference information. Refer to **Figure 20-9** to see how the datum reference and related material condition symbols are placed in the feature control frame.

Projected Tolerance Zone image tile and Height text box

The **Projected Tolerance Zone:** image tile can be picked to display a projected tolerance zone symbol in the feature control frame. The **Height:** text box is used to specify the height of a projected tolerance zone. The projected tolerance zone symbol and the height value are used together when a projected tolerance zone is applied to the drawing. The use of a projected tolerance zone in a drawing is discussed later in this chapter.

Datum Identifier text box

The **Datum Identifier:** text box is used to enter a datum-identifying reference letter to be used as part of the datum feature symbol. An uppercase letter should be entered. If you want to comply with ASME Y14.5M-1994, however, you need to design a datum feature symbol and save it as a block. Creating your own dimensioning symbols is discussed later in this chapter, and blocks are discussed in Chapter 22.

Completing the command

After you have entered all the desired information in the **Geometric Tolerance** dialog box, pick **OK**. The following prompt is then displayed on the command line:

> Enter tolerance location: *(pick the location for the feature control frame to be drawn)*
> Command:

The feature control frame for the given example is shown in **Figure 20-22**.

Figure 20-22.
When the desired values have been specified in the **Geometric Tolerance** dialog box, pick **OK**. In this example, primary, secondary, and tertiary datum reference values have been added and are shown highlighted, along with the geometric tolerance value. The feature control frame created by the values specified in the dialog box is shown.

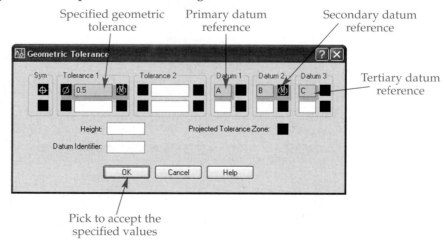

Feature Control Frame

![Exercise 20-1 CD icon] **Exercise 20-1** Complete the Exercise on the Student CD.

Using the Qleader and Leader Commands to Place GD&T Symbols

In many cases, leader lines are connected to feature control frames or other GD&T symbols in order to identify toleranced features. The **QLEADER** and **LEADER** commands enable you to draw leader lines and access the dialog boxes used to create feature control frames in one operation. Refer to Chapter 17 for a complete discussion of the **QLEADER** command.

The **QLEADER** command can be accessed by picking the **Quick Leader** button on the **Dimension** toolbar, picking **Dimension > Leader**, or by typing LE or QLEADER. When you enter this command, use the **Settings** option to open the **Leader Settings** dialog box. See **Figure 20-23**. Pick the **Tolerance** radio button in the **Annotation** tab to connect a feature control frame or datum feature symbol to a leader line. When asked to specify the first leader point, pick the leader start point. Now, pick the next leader point. Press [Enter] to end the leader line. After pressing [Enter], the **Geometric Tolerance** dialog box is displayed. Specify the desired settings and values for the feature control frame. Pick the **OK** button. The feature control frame is connected to the leader line in your drawing, as shown in **Figure 20-24**.

The **LEADER** command can also be used to connect a feature control frame to a leader line. After picking a start point and a second leader point, enter the **Annotation** option. The command sequence is as follows:

QLEADER	
Type	
	QLEADER
	LE
Pull-Down Menu	
	Dimension
	> Leader
Toolbar	
	Dimension
	[icon]
	Quick Leader

LEADER	
Type	
	LEADER
	LEAD

```
Command: LEAD or LEADER
Specify leader start point: (pick the leader start point)
Specify next point: (pick the next point of the leader)
Specify next point or [Annotation/Format/Undo] <Annotation>: ↵
Enter first line of annotation text or <options>: ↵
Enter an annotation option [Tolerance/Copy/Block/None/Mtext] <Mtext>: T
Enter an annotation option [Tolerance/Copy/Block/None/Mtext] <Mtext>:
```

Figure 20-23.
The **Leader Settings** dialog box. Activate the **Tolerance** radio button when placing a feature control frame with the **QLEADER** command.

Figure 20-24.
After completing the **QLEADER** command, the feature control frame is connected to the leader line.

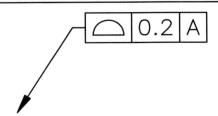

Entering the **Tolerance** suboption of the **Annotation** option displays the **Geometric Tolerance** dialog box. You can then establish the feature control frame information. When you pick **OK**, the feature control frame is connected to the leader shoulder.

Exercise 20-2   Complete the Exercise on the Student CD.

Introduction to Projected Tolerance Zones

In some situations where positional tolerance is used entirely in out-of-squareness, it may be necessary to control perpendicularity and position next to the part. The use of a *projected tolerance zone* is recommended when variations in perpendicularity of threaded or press-fit holes may cause the fastener to interfere with the mating part. A projected tolerance zone is usually specified for a fixed fastener, such as the threaded hole for a bolt or the press-fit hole for a pin. The length of a projected tolerance zone can be specified as the distance the fastener extends into the mating part, the thickness of the part, or the height of a press-fit stud. The normal positional tolerance extends through the thickness of the part.

This application, however, can cause an interference between the location of a thread or press-fit object and its mating part. This is because the actual angle of a threaded hole controls the attitude of the fixed fastener. There is no clearance available to provide flexibility. For this reason, the projected tolerance zone is established at true position and extends away from the primary datum at the threaded feature. The projected tolerance zone provides a larger tolerance because it is projected away from the primary datum, rather than within the thread. A projected tolerance is also easier to inspect than the tolerance applied to the pitch diameter of the thread. This is because a thread gauge with a post projecting above the threaded hole can be used to easily verify the projected tolerance zone with a coordinate measuring machine (CMM).

Representing a Projected Tolerance Zone

One method for displaying the projected tolerance zone is to place the projected tolerance zone symbol and height in the feature control frame after the geometric tolerance and related material condition symbol. The related thread specification is then connected to the section view of the thread symbol. With this method, the projected tolerance zone is assumed to extend away from the threaded hole at the primary datum. See **Figure 20-25**.

To provide additional clarification, the projected tolerance zone can be shown using a chain line in the view where the related datum appears as an edge and the minimum height of the projection is dimensioned. See **Figure 20-26**. The projected tolerance zone symbol is shown alone in the feature control frame after the geometric tolerance and material condition symbol (if any). The meaning is the same as previously discussed.

Drawing the Projected Tolerance Zone

AutoCAD specifies projected tolerance zones according to the 1982 standard. When following this standard, enter the desired geometric tolerance, diameter symbol, material condition symbol, and datum reference, as previously discussed. Pick the **Projected Tolerance Zone:** image tile and enter the height in the **Height:** text box. See **Figure 20-27**. Now, place the feature control frame in the desired location in the drawing. Notice that AutoCAD displays the projected tolerance zone height in a separate compartment below the feature control frame, in accordance with ANSI Y14.5M-1982.

Figure 20-25.
A projected tolerance zone representation with the length of the projected tolerance zone given in the feature control frame. The projected tolerance zone symbol is shown highlighted.

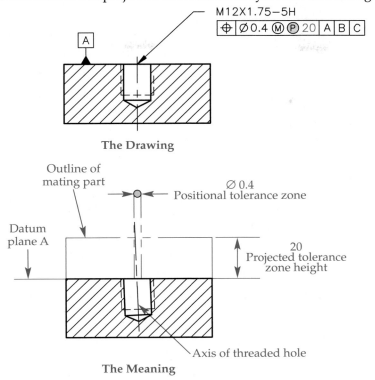

Figure 20-26.
A projected tolerance zone representation with the length of the projected tolerance zone shown with a chain line and a minimum dimension in the adjacent view.

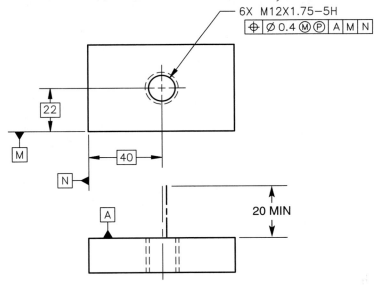

To specify a projected tolerance zone according to the 1994 standard, create a feature control frame with any modifier letters and the letter P after the tolerance value. The height of the projected tolerance zone is typed after the P. Leave one space between each letter and the height value. See **Figure 20-28.** When completed, use the **CIRCLE** command to draw a circle around the modifier and the letter P. You can group the feature control frame and circle so they can be selected as a single object.

Figure 20-27.
To add projected tolerance zone specifications to the feature control frame, enter the projected tolerance zone height and symbol in the **Geometric Tolerance** dialog box.

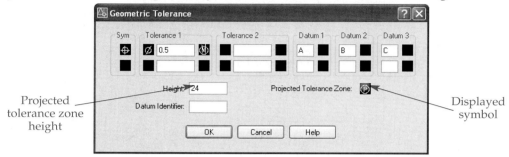

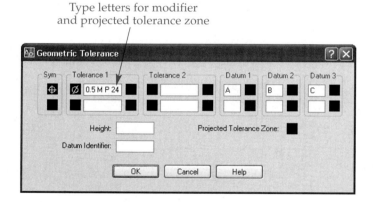

Feature Control Frame

Figure 20-28.
Specifying a projected tolerance zone in accordance with ASME Y14.5M-1994.

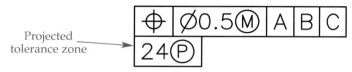

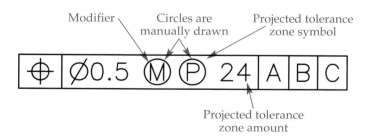

Feature Control Frame

Exercise 20-3

Complete the Exercise on the Student CD.

Drawing a Double Feature Control Frame

Several GD&T applications require that the feature control frame be doubled in height, with two sets of geometric tolerancing values provided. These applications include unit straightness and flatness, composite positional tolerance, and coaxial positional tolerance. To draw a double feature control frame, first use the **TOLERANCE** command and create the desired first level of the feature control frame in the **Geometric Tolerance** dialog box, as previously discussed. You can also use the **QLEADER** or **LEADER** command, if you are connecting the feature control frame to a leader line. Next, pick the lower image tile in the **Sym** area. When the **Symbol** dialog box is displayed again, pick another geometric characteristic symbol. This results in two symbols displayed in the **Sym** area. Continue specifying the needed information in the lower-level **Tolerance** and **Datum** compartments. Sample entries for a double feature control frame are shown in **Figure 20-29**.

If the two symbols in the **Sym** image tiles are the same, the double feature control frame is drawn with one geometric characteristic symbol displayed in a single compartment. This is called a *composite frame*. Some situations require the same geometric characteristic symbol twice, one in the upper frame and another in the lower frame. These are two single-segment feature control frames. To create this type, draw two separate feature control frames and group them. If you are drawing a double feature control frame with different geometric characteristic symbols for a combination control, the feature control frame must have two separate compartments. See **Figure 20-30**.

Exercise 20-4 Complete the Exercise on the Student CD.

Figure 20-29.
Specifying information for a double feature control frame in the **Geometric Tolerance** dialog box.

Pick to select a second geometric characteristic symbol

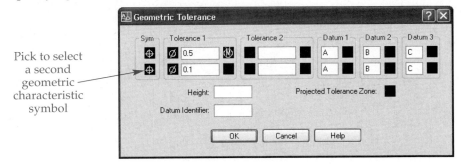

Figure 20-30.
If the same geometric characteristic symbol is entered in both **Symbol** boxes of the **Geometric Tolerance** dialog box, only one symbol is shown in the first compartment of the double feature control frame. Create two separate feature control frames to display the same symbol in both frames. If two different symbols are used, they are displayed in separate compartments.

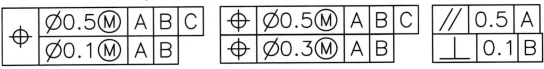

Same Symbol for Both Control Frames — **Create Separate Single Control Frames to Repeat Symbol** — **Double Feature Control Frame with Different Symbols**

Drawing Datum Feature Symbols

As discussed earlier in this chapter, datums in a drawing are identified by datum feature symbols. You can draw datum feature symbols using the **TOLERANCE**, **QLEADER**, or **LEADER** command. When you access the **Geometric Tolerance** dialog box, enter the desired datum reference letter in the **Datum Identifier:** text box. See **Figure 20-31.**

After picking **OK**, place the datum feature symbol at the desired location in your drawing. You can also draw a datum feature symbol connected to a feature control frame by selecting the desired geometric characteristic symbol and entering the necessary information in the **Geometric Tolerance** dialog box. In **Figure 20-32,** datum feature symbols are shown with and without a feature control frame. Notice the symbols are placed inside squares. This complies with the ANSI Y14.5M-1982 standard, rather than ASME Y14.5M-1994. In order to match the ASME Y14.5M-1994 standard, the symbols need to be drawn as shown previously in **Figure 20-13.** One way to do this is to create your own symbols, which you can insert as needed. Creating and saving your own symbols are discussed in Chapter 22.

Before you learn how to create your own symbols, you can modify the symbols shown in **Figure 20-32** by establishing a dimension style with leader line terminators set to **Datum triangle** or **Datum triangle filled**. These leader options are available in the **Symbols and Arrows** tab of the **Modify Dimension Style** dialog box. Creating dimension styles with the **Dimension Style Manager** and the **Modify Dimension Style** dialog boxes is discussed in Chapter 17.

After creating a dimension style that uses datum triangles for leader arrowheads, enter the **QLEADER** or **LEADER** command to draw a leader segment that connects to the datum feature symbol, as shown in **Figure 20-33A.** This modifies the symbol in

---

Figure 20-31.
Using the **Geometric Tolerance** dialog box to enter a datum-identifying reference letter. This letter is used to create the datum feature symbol.

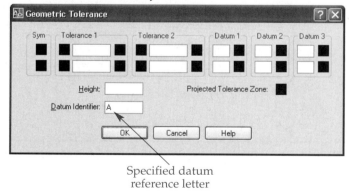

Specified datum
reference letter

Figure 20-32.
A—A datum feature symbol drawn without a feature control frame. B—A datum feature symbol drawn with a feature control frame. Note the symbols in A and B do not comply with the ASME Y14.5M-1994 standard.

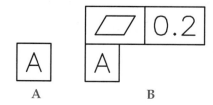

A   B

Figure 20-32A. Use the object snap modes to help you properly position the leader with the symbol. If you use the **QLEADER** command, make sure the **Annotation Type** setting is set to **MText**. Pick the leader start point and endpoint, and then press [Enter]. When prompted for the text width, press the [Esc] key. If you use the **LEADER** command, pick the leader line points, and then use the **None** suboption of the **Annotation** option to specify no annotation text.

To modify the datum feature symbol shown in **Figure 20-32B**, you must draw the datum feature symbol, the feature control frame, and the leader line separately. First, draw the datum feature symbol as previously discussed. Use the **QLEADER** or **LEADER** command to draw a connecting leader segment, as shown in **Figure 20-33B**. Finally, draw the feature control frame and connect it to the datum triangle as shown. The datum feature symbol and the feature control frame can be moved as needed to allow for proper positioning.

PROFESSIONAL TIP

Chapter 22 of this text provides a detailed discussion on how to create your own symbol libraries. A *symbol library* is a related group of symbols. It is recommended that you design dimensioning symbols that are not available in AutoCAD, such as the datum feature symbol recognized by ASME Y14.5M-1994. This symbol is shown in **Figure 20-13**.

Your symbol library might include the counterbore, countersink, depth, and other dimensioning symbols illustrated in **Figure 20-1**. These symbols are easily drawn if you establish a dimension style that uses the gdt.shx font. Chapter 17 explains how to create such a dimension style to help you draw these symbols when needed.

Exercise 20-5   Complete the Exercise on the Student CD.

Figure 20-33.
A—To draw a datum feature symbol in accordance with ASME Y14.5M-1994, create a dimension style using the **Datum triangle** or **Datum triangle filled** leader arrowhead option. Use the **QLEADER** or **LEADER** command to connect a leader arrow to the existing symbol. B—If a feature control frame is to be used, the datum feature symbol, leader line, and feature control frame must be drawn separately.

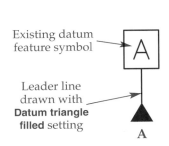
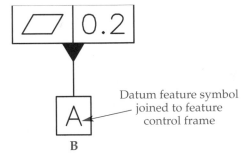

Existing datum feature symbol

Leader line drawn with **Datum triangle filled** setting

A

Datum feature symbol joined to feature control frame

B

Controlling the Height of the Feature Control Frame

Referring to **Figure 20-9**, the height of the feature control frame is twice the height of the text. Text on engineering drawings is generally drawn at a height of 0.125" (3 mm), which makes the feature control frame height 0.25" (6 mm). As a result, the distance from the text to the feature control frame should be equal to half the text height. For example, if the height of the drawing text is 0.125", the space between the text and the feature control frame should be 0.0625" to result in a 0.25" high frame.

The distance from the text to the feature control frame is controlled by the **Offset from dim line:** text box in the **Text placement** area of the **Text** tab in the **Modify Dimension Style** dialog box. See **Figure 20-34**. The default value is 0.0900. The setting also controls the gap between the dimension line and the dimension text for linear dimensions and the space between the dimension text and the rectangle for basic dimensions. Basic dimensions are discussed in the next section.

Figure 20-34.
The **DIMGAP** dimension variable setting controls the distance from the text to the feature control frame.

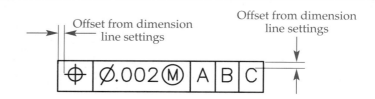

Drawing Basic Dimensions

A basic dimension is shown in **Figure 20-35**. Basic dimensions can be automatically drawn by setting a **Basic** tolerance in the **Tolerances** tab of the **Modify Dimension Style** dialog box, as discussed in Chapter 19. It is recommended that you establish a separate dimension style for basic dimensions because not all of your dimensions on a drawing will be basic. The **Offset from dim line:** setting in the **Text** tab of the **Modify Dimension Style** dialog box controls the space between the basic dimension text and the rectangle around the dimension.

Figure 20-35.
An AutoCAD basic dimension.

Exercise
20-6   Complete the Exercise on the Student CD.

Editing Feature Control Frames

A feature control frame acts as one object. When you pick any location on the frame, the entire object is selected. You can edit feature control frames using AutoCAD editing commands such as **ERASE**, **COPY**, **MOVE**, **ROTATE**, and **SCALE**. The **STRETCH** command only allows you to move a feature control frame. This effect is similar to the results of using the **STRETCH** command with text objects.

You can edit the values inside a feature control frame by using the **DDEDIT** command. To access the command, double-click on the feature control frame you wish to edit, select **Modify > Object > Text > Edit...** from the pull-down menu, or type ED or DDEDIT. When you enter this command and select the desired frame, the **Geometric Tolerance** dialog box is displayed with all the current values listed. After you make the desired changes, pick **OK** to update the feature control frame.

You can also use the **DDEDIT** command to edit basic dimensions. When you select a basic dimension for editing, the **In-Place Text Editor** is displayed. You can then edit the basic dimension as you would any other dimension.

DDEDIT

Type
DDEDIT
ED

Pull-Down Menu
Modify
> **Object**
> **Text**
> **Edit...**

> **NOTE**
>
> If you double-click on a dimension, AutoCAD opens the **Properties** window instead of the **In-Place Text Editor**.

Sample GD&T Applications

This chapter is intended to give you a general overview of GD&T applications and basic instructions on how to draw GD&T symbols using AutoCAD. If you are in the manufacturing industry, you may have considerable use for GD&T. The support information presented in this chapter may be a review, or it may inspire you to learn more about this topic. The drawings in **Figure 20-36** are intended to show you some common GD&T applications using the available dimensioning and geometric characteristic symbols.

Figure 20-36.
Examples of typical geometric dimensioning and tolerancing (GD&T) applications using various dimensioning and geometric characteristic symbols.

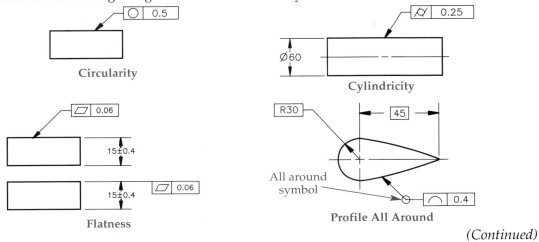

(Continued)

Figure 20-36 *(Continued)*

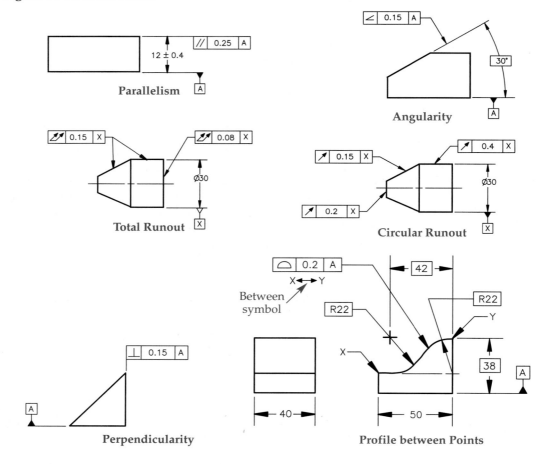

Parallelism

Angularity

Total Runout

Circular Runout

Perpendicularity

Profile between Points

Chapter Test

Answer the following questions. Write your answers on a separate sheet of paper or complete the electronic chapter test on the Student CD.

1. Identify each of the following geometric characteristic symbols:

A. ——   H. ◎

B. ⟋⟋   I. ≡

C. ○   J. //

D. ⌀   K. ⊥

E. ⌒   L. ∠

F. ◠   M. ↗

G. ⊕   N. ⤢

2. Identify the parts of the feature control frame shown below.

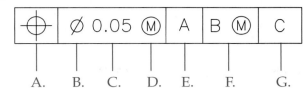

    A.   B.   C.   D.   E.   F.   G.

3. Name the current standard for dimensioning and tolerancing adopted by the American National Standards Institute (ANSI) and published by the American Society of Mechanical Engineers (ASME).
4. Name three commands that can be used to draw a feature control frame.
5. Identify the dialog box containing settings used to create a feature control frame.
6. How do you access the **Symbol** dialog box, in which a geometric characteristic symbol can be selected?
7. How do you remove a geometric characteristic symbol from one of the image tiles in the **Sym** area of the **Geometric Tolerance** dialog box?
8. Describe the procedure used to draw a feature control frame connected to a leader line.
9. Describe how to place a projected tolerance zone symbol and height value with the feature control frame, based on ANSI Y14.5M-1982.
10. Explain how to create a double feature control frame.
11. Which AutoCAD setting allows you to draw basic dimensions? How is it accessed?
12. Identify the AutoCAD setting controlling the space between the text in a feature control frame and the surrounding frame.
13. Describe how to draw a datum feature symbol without an attached feature control frame. How do you add a leader line with a filled datum triangle to the symbol?
14. Name the command that can be used to edit the existing values in a feature control frame.

Drawing Problems

Create dimension styles that will assist you with the following problems. Draw fully dimensioned multiview drawings. The required number of views depends on the problem and is to be determined by you. Apply geometric tolerancing as discussed in this chapter. Modify the available AutoCAD drawing applications to comply with ASME Y14.5M-1994 standards. The problems are presented in accordance with ASME Y14.5M-1994.

1. Open drawing P19-5. Edit the drawing by adding the geometric tolerancing applications shown below. Untoleranced dimensions are ±.02 for two-place decimal precision and ±.005 for three-place decimal precision. If you did not draw P19-5, start a new drawing and draw the problem now. The problem is shown as a cutaway for clarity. You do not need to draw a section. Save the drawing as P20-1.

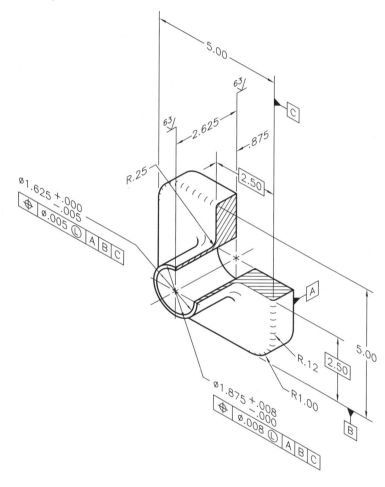

2. Open drawing P19-6. Edit the drawing by adding the geometric tolerancing applications shown below. Untoleranced dimensions are ±0.5. If you did not draw P19-6, start a new drawing and draw the problem now. Save the drawing as P20-2.

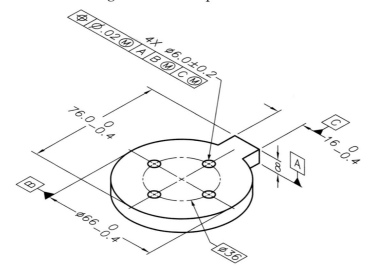

3. Open drawing P19-7. Edit the drawing by adding the geometric tolerancing applications shown below. If you did not draw P19-7, start a new drawing and draw the problem now. Save the drawing as P20-3.

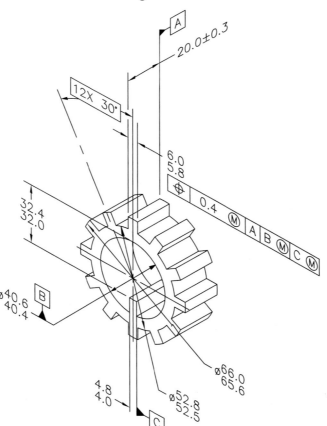

Chapter 20   Geometric Dimensioning and Tolerancing

Drawing Problems - Chapter 20

663

4. Draw the following object as previously instructed. Untoleranced dimensions are ±0.3. Save the drawing as P20-4.

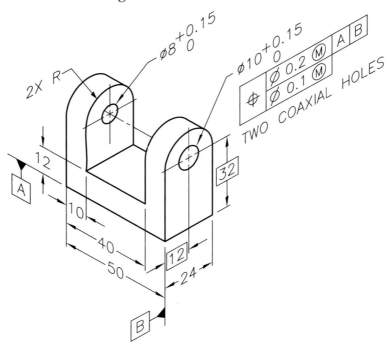

5. Draw the following object as previously instructed. The problem is shown with a full section for clarity. You do not need to draw a section. Untoleranced dimensions are ±.010. Save the drawing as P20-5.

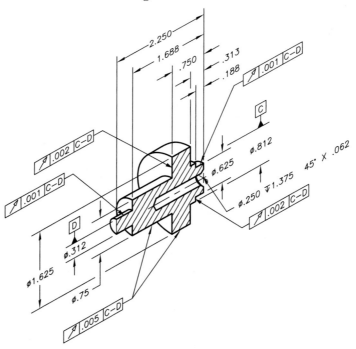

6. Open drawing P17-29. Edit the drawing by adding the geometric tolerancing applications shown below. If you did not draw P17-29, start a new drawing and draw the problem now. Save the drawing as P20-6.

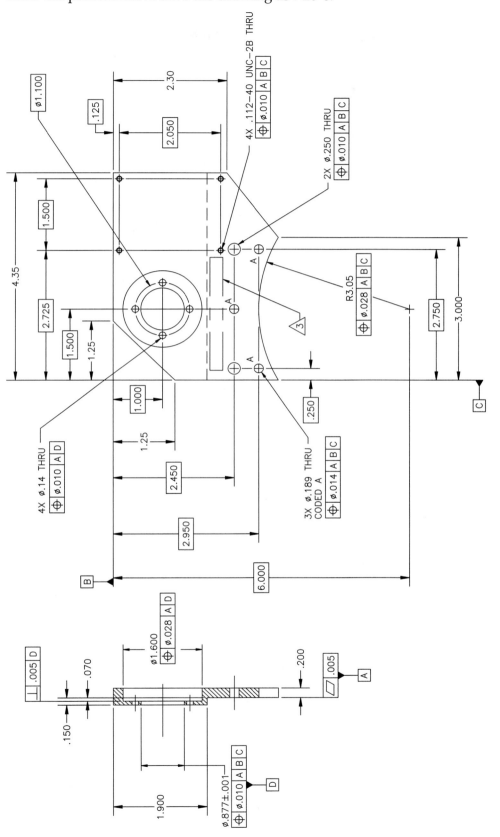

7. Draw the following object as previously instructed. The problem is shown with a half section for clarity. You do not need to draw a section. Untoleranced dimensions are ±.010. Save the drawing as P20-7.

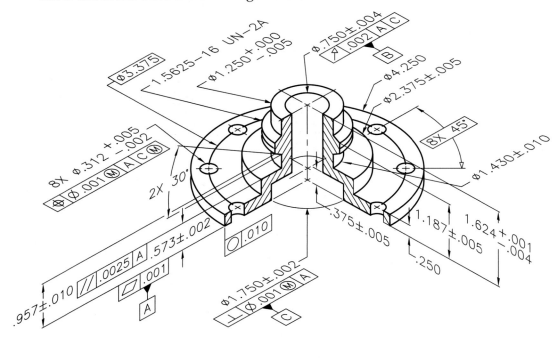

Drawing Section Views and Graphic Patterns

Learning Objectives

After completing this chapter, you will be able to do the following:

- Identify sectioning techniques.
- Use sections and dimensioning practices to draw objects given in engineering sketches.
- Draw section material using the **BHATCH** and **SOLID** commands.
- Insert hatch patterns into drawings using **DesignCenter** and tool palettes.
- Edit existing hatch patterns with the **HATCHEDIT** command.

In mechanical drafting, internal features in drawings appear as hidden lines. It is poor practice to dimension to hidden lines, but these features must be dimensioned. Therefore, section views are used to clarify the hidden features.

Section views show internal features as if a portion of the object is cut away. They are used in conjunction with multiview drawings to completely describe the exterior and interior features of an object.

When sections are drawn, a ***cutting-plane line*** is placed in one of the views to show where the cut was made. The cutting-plane is the *saw* that cuts through the object to expose internal features. The cutting-plane line is drawn with a thick dashed or phantom line in accordance with ASME Y14.2M, *Line Conventions and Lettering*. The arrows on the cutting-plane line indicate the line of sight when looking at the section view.

The cutting-plane lines are often labeled with letters that relate to the proper section view. A title, such as SECTION A-A, is placed under the view. When more than one section view is drawn, labels continue with B-B through Z-Z. The letters *I*, *O*, and *Q* are not used because they may be confused with numbers.

Labeling section views is necessary for drawings with multiple sections. When only one section view is present and its location is obvious, a label is not needed. Section lines are used in the section view to show where the material has been cut away. See **Figure 21-1**.

Sectioning is also used in other drafting fields, such as architectural and structural drafting. Cross sections through buildings show the construction methods and materials. See **Figure 21-2**. The cutting-plane lines used in these fields are often composed of letter and number symbols. This helps coordinate the large number of sections found in a set of architectural drawings.

Figure 21-1.
A three-view
multiview drawing
with a full section
view.

Direction
of sight

Cutting-plane label

Cutting-
plane line

A   A

Regular
Multiviews

Section
lines

SECTION A—A

Section-view label

Section View

Figure 21-2.
An architectural
section view. (Alan
Mascord Design
Associates)

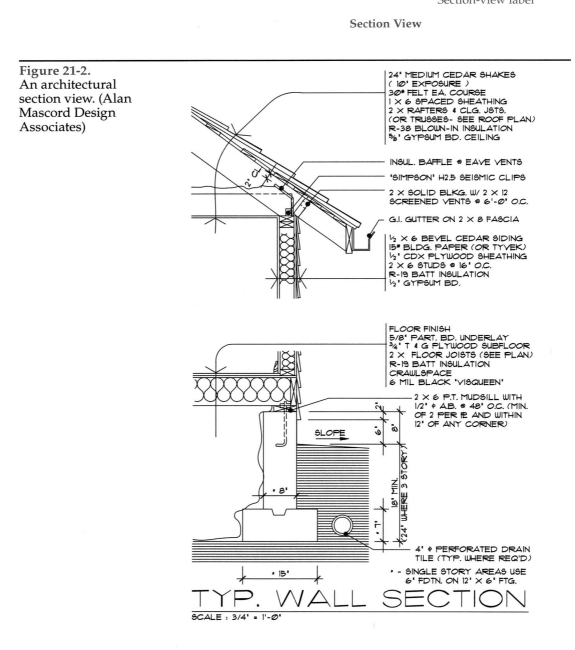

24" MEDIUM CEDAR SHAKES
(10" EXPOSURE)
30# FELT EA. COURSE
1 X 6 SPACED SHEATHING
2 X RAFTERS & CLG. JSTS.
(OR TRUSSES- SEE ROOF PLAN)
R-38 BLOWN-IN INSULATION
5/8" GYPSUM BD. CEILING

INSUL. BAFFLE @ EAVE VENTS

'SIMPSON' H2.5 SEISMIC CLIPS

2 X SOLID BLKG. W/ 2 X 12
SCREENED VENTS @ 6'-0" O.C.

G.I. GUTTER ON 2 X 8 FASCIA

1/2 X 6 BEVEL CEDAR SIDING
15# BLDG. PAPER (OR TYVEK)
1/2" CDX PLYWOOD SHEATHING
2 X 6 STUDS @ 16" O.C.
R-19 BATT INSULATION
1/2" GYPSUM BD.

FLOOR FINISH
5/8" PART. BD. UNDERLAY
3/4" T & G PLYWOOD SUBFLOOR
2 X FLOOR JOISTS (SEE PLAN)
R-19 BATT INSULATION
CRAWLSPACE
6 MIL BLACK 'VISQUEEN'

2 X 6 P.T. MUDSILL WITH
1/2" ø A.B. @ 48" O.C. (MIN.
OF 2 PER ℗ AND WITHIN
12" OF ANY CORNER)

SLOPE

18" MIN.
(24" WHERE 3 STORY)

4' ø PERFORATED DRAIN
TILE (TYP. WHERE REQ'D)

* - SINGLE STORY AREAS USE
6' FDTN. ON 12' X 6' FTG.

TYP. WALL SECTION
SCALE : 3/4' = 1'-0'

There are many types of sections available for the drafter to use. The section used depends on the detail to be sectioned. For example, one object may require the section be taken completely through the object. Another may only need to remove a small portion to expose the interior features.

Full sections remove half the object. Refer to **Figure 21-1**. In this type of section, the cutting-plane passes completely through the object along a center plane.

Offset sections are the same as full sections, except the cutting-plane is staggered. This allows you to cut through features that are not in a straight line. See **Figure 21-3**.

Half sections show one-quarter of the object removed. The term *half* is used because half of the view appears in section and the other half is shown as an exterior view. Half sections are commonly used on symmetrical objects. A centerline is used to separate the sectioned part of the view from the unsectioned portion. Hidden lines are normally omitted from the unsectioned side. See **Figure 21-4**.

Aligned sections are used when a feature is out of alignment with the center plane. In this case, an offset section will distort the image. The cutting-plane cuts through the feature to be sectioned. It is then rotated to align with the center plane before projecting into the section view. See **Figure 21-5**.

Revolved sections clarify the contour of objects that have the same shape throughout their length. The section is revolved in place within the object, or part of the view may be broken away. See **Figure 21-6**. This type of section makes dimensioning easier.

Removed sections serve much the same function as revolved sections. The section view is removed from the regular view. A cutting-plane line shows where the section has been taken. When multiple removed sections are taken, the cutting planes lines and related views are labeled. Drawing only the ends of the cutting-plane lines simplifies the views. See **Figure 21-7**.

Broken-out sections show only a small portion of the object removed. This type of section is used to clarify a hidden feature. See **Figure 21-8**.

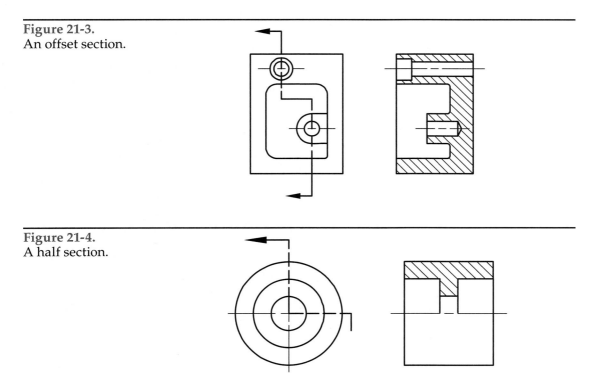

Figure 21-3.
An offset section.

Figure 21-4.
A half section.

Figure 21-5.
An aligned section.

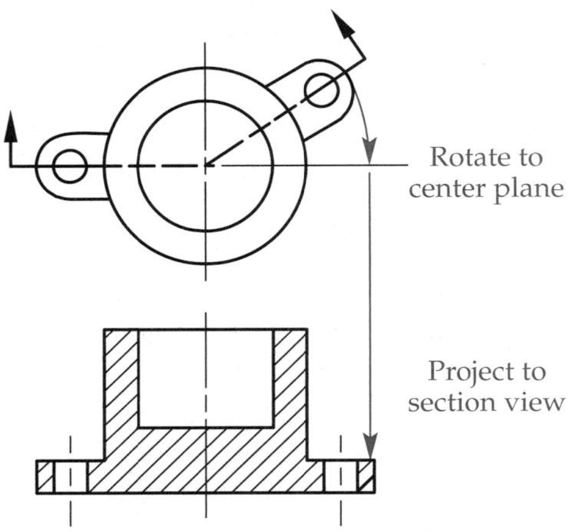

Rotate to
center plane

Project to
section view

Figure 21-6.
A revolved section.

Figure 21-7.
Removed sections.

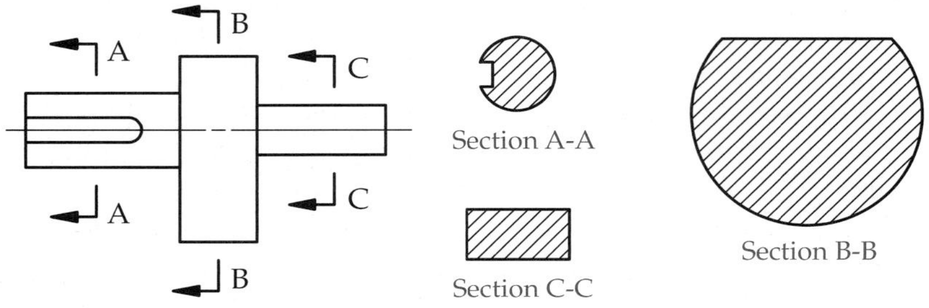

Section A-A

Section C-C

Section B-B

Figure 21-8.
A broken-out
section.

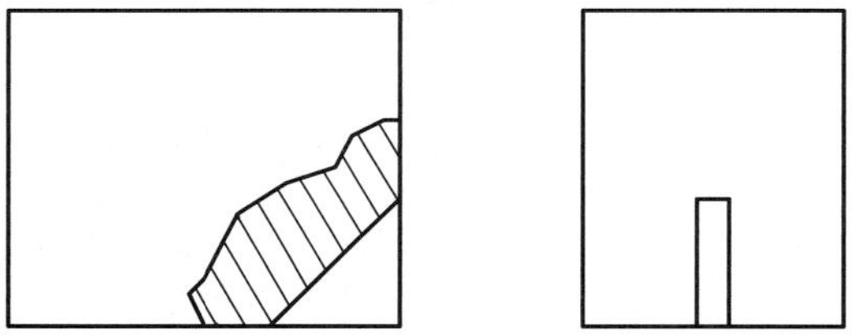

Section Line Symbols

Section line symbols are placed in the section view to show where material has been cut away. The ANSI32 symbol is used for sectioning steel. A sampling of other standard AutoCAD hatch patterns is shown in **Figure 21-9.** The following rules govern section line symbol usage:

- Section lines are placed at 45° unless another angle is required to satisfy the next two rules.
- Section lines should not be drawn parallel or perpendicular to any other adjacent lines on the drawing.
- Section lines should not cross object lines.
- Avoid section lines placed at angles greater than 75° or less than 15° from horizontal.

AutoCAD and Its Applications—Basics

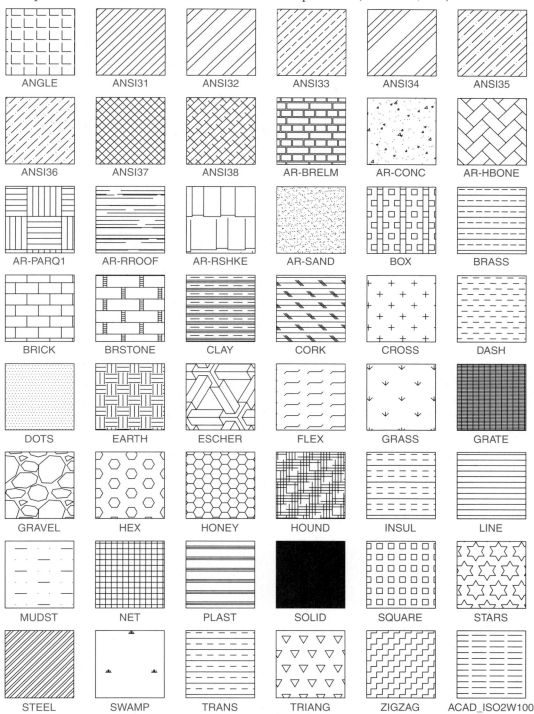

Section lines may be drawn using different patterns to represent the specific type of material. Equally spaced section lines represent a general application. This is adequate in most situations. Additional patterns are not necessary if the type of material is clearly indicated in the title block. Different section line material symbols are needed when connected parts of different materials are sectioned.

AutoCAD has standard section line symbols available. These are referred to as *hatch patterns*. These symbols are defined in the acad.pat file. The AutoCAD pattern labeled ANSI31 is the general section line symbol and is the default pattern in a new drawing. It is also used when representing cast iron in a section. When you change to a different hatch pattern, the new pattern becomes the default in the current drawing until it is changed.

When very thin objects are sectioned, the material may be completely blackened or filled in to clarify features. AutoCAD refers to this as *solid*. The ASME Y14.2M standard recommends that very thin sections be drawn without section lines or solid fill.

Drawing Section Lines and Hatch Patterns

BHATCH

Type	
BHATCH	
H	
Pull-Down Menu	
Draw	
> Hatch...	
Toolbar	
Draw	
Hatch	

AutoCAD hatch patterns are not limited to sectioning. They can be used as artistic patterns in a graphic layout for an advertisement or promotion. They might also be added as shading on an architectural elevation or technical illustration.

The **BHATCH** command simplifies the hatching process by automatically hatching any enclosed area. Hatch patterns are selected and applied using the **Hatch and Gradient** dialog box. Access this dialog box with the **BHATCH** command by picking the **Hatch** button on the **Draw** toolbar, by picking **Draw > Hatch...** in the pull-down menu, or by typing H or BHATCH.

The **Hatch and Gradient** dialog box is divided into the **Hatch** and **Gradient** tabs. See **Figure 21-10**. The **Hatch** tab is separated into different areas that control the hatch settings.

Figure 21-10.
The **Hatch** tab of the **Hatch and Gradient** dialog box.

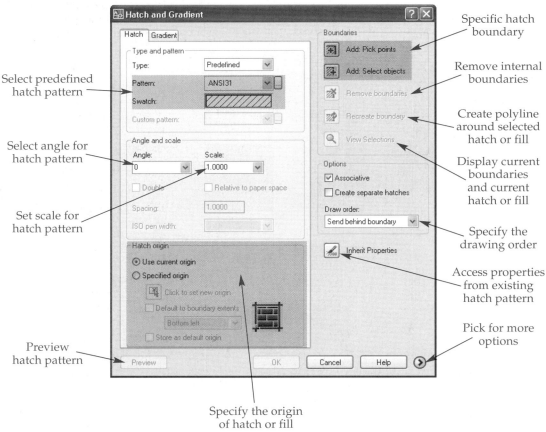

Selecting a Hatch Pattern

The hatch pattern is selected in the **Type and pattern** area under the **Hatch** tab of the **Hatch and Gradient** dialog box. The following three categories of hatch patterns are available in the **Type:** drop-down list:

- **Predefined.** These predefined AutoCAD patterns are stored in the acad.pat and acadiso.pat files.
- **User defined.** Selecting this option creates a pattern of lines based on the current linetype in your drawing. You can control the angle and spacing of the lines.
- **Custom.** Selecting this option allows you to specify a pattern defined in any custom PAT file that you have added to the AutoCAD search path. (To use the patterns in the supplied acad.pat and acadiso.pat files, choose Predefined.)

Predefined hatch patterns

AutoCAD has many predefined hatch patterns. These patterns are contained in the acad.pat and acadiso.pat files. To select a predefined hatch pattern, select **Predefined** in the **Type:** drop-down list and then select the predefined pattern. You can select the pattern from the **Pattern:** drop-down list, or you can pick the ellipsis (...) button next to the **Pattern:** drop-down arrow to display the **Hatch Pattern Palette** dialog box. See **Figure 21-11.**

The **Hatch Pattern Palette** dialog box provides sample images of the predefined hatch patterns. The hatch patterns are divided among the four tabs: **ANSI, ISO, Other Predefined,** and **Custom.** Select the desired pattern from the appropriate tab, and pick the **OK** button to return to the **Hatch and Gradient** dialog box. The selected pattern is displayed in the **Swatch:** tile and listed in the **Pattern:** text box. You can also access the **Hatch Pattern Palette** dialog box by picking the image displayed in the **Swatch:** tile.

You can control the angle and scale of any predefined pattern using the **Angle:** and **Scale:** drop-down lists located in the **Angle and scale** area. For predefined ISO patterns, you can also control the ISO pen width using the **ISO pen width:** drop-down list.

An object can be hatched solid by selecting the Solid predefined pattern or selecting an option from the **Gradient** tab. This is discussed later in this chapter.

Figure 21-11.
The **Hatch Pattern Palette** dialog box can be used to select a predefined or custom hatch pattern.

Select a tab to see other patterns

Select icon for desired hatch pattern

Pick to return to **Hatch and Gradient** dialog box

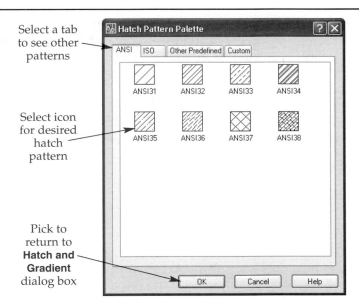

User defined hatch patterns

A user defined hatch pattern is a pattern of lines drawn using the current line-type. The angle for the pattern relative to the X axis is set in the **Angle:** text box, and the spacing between the lines is set in the **Spacing:** text box. Both of these options are located in the **Angle and scale** area of the **Hatch and Gradient** dialog box.

You can also specify double hatch lines by selecting the **Double** check box. This check box is only available when User defined is selected in the **Type:** drop-down list. **Figure 21-12** shows examples of user defined hatch patterns.

Custom hatch patterns

You can create custom hatch patterns and save them in PAT files. When you select Custom in the **Type:** drop-down list, the **Custom pattern:** drop-down list is enabled. You can select a custom pattern from this drop-down list, or pick the ellipsis (…) button to select the pattern from the **Custom** tab of the **Hatch Pattern Palette** dialog box. You can set the angle and scale of custom hatch patterns, just as you can with predefined hatch patterns.

Setting the Hatch Pattern Scale

Predefined and custom hatch patterns can be scaled by entering a value in the **Scale:** text box. The drop-down list contains common scales broken down in 0.25 increments. The scales in this list start with 0.25 and progress to a scale of 2, although you can type any scale in the text box.

The pattern scale default is 1 (full scale). If the drawn pattern is too tight or too wide, enter a new scale. **Figure 21-13** shows examples of different scales.

The **Relative to paper space** check box in the **Angle and scale** area is used to scale the hatch pattern relative to paper space units. Use this option to easily display hatch patterns at a scale appropriate for your layout.

PROFESSIONAL TIP

When hatching large areas, enter a larger scale factor. This makes your section lines look neater and saves regeneration and plot time. For metric drawings, set the hatch scale to 25.4, because 1″ = 25.4 mm.

Figure 21-12.
Examples of user defined hatch patterns with different hatch angles and spacing.

Angle	0°	45°	0°	45°
Spacing	.125	.125	.250	.250
Single Hatch				
Double Hatch				

Figure 21-13.
Hatch pattern scale factors.

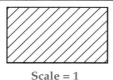
Scale = 1

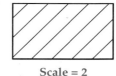
Scale = 2

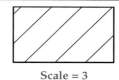
Scale = 3

Setting the Hatch Origin Point

When creating hatch patterns, there are times when you want lines on the hatch pattern to line up with an exiting object. This could be the case when using one of the brick hatch patterns, for example. By default, the current UCS origin point is used as the defining point for how the hatch pattern is created and how it repeats itself. The pattern of a hatch can be started in a different location by specifying a custom origin point.

In the **Hatch origin** area of the **Hatch and Gradient** dialog box, the default setting is **Use current origin**. This refers to using the current UCS origin. To specify a different origin point, select **Specified origin**. See **Figure 21-14.** When this option is selected, the other settings become available. Picking the **Click to set new origin** button temporarily hides the **Hatch and Gradient** dialog box so a different origin can be selected in the drawing area. For example, if you want a hatch pattern to start in the lower-left corner of a rectangle, use the **Endpoint** object snap to select the corner of the rectangle. In **Figure 21-15A**, the **Use current origin** setting is used. In **Figure 21-15B**, notice how it seems that the hatch pattern starts perfectly from the lower-left corner of the rectangle. This is because this corner was picked to be the origin point. After a point is selected, the **Hatch and Gradient** dialog box is displayed again.

The hatch origin point can be aligned with specific points on the hatch boundary. To use this setting, check the **Default to boundary extents** box. When this is checked, the drop-down list below it becomes available. The options in the drop-down list are **Bottom left, Bottom right, Top right, Top left,** and **Center.** The hatch origin is defined at the selected point on the boundary.

Figure 21-14.
The **Specified origin** setting in the **Hatch origin** area of the **Hatch** tab activates the other hatch origin settings.

Pick to specify a different origin point

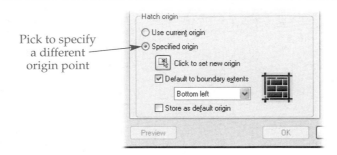

Figure 21-15.
A—The **Use current origin** setting is used. B—The **Specified origin** option is selected and the **Click to set new origin** button is used to select the lower-left corner of the rectangle.

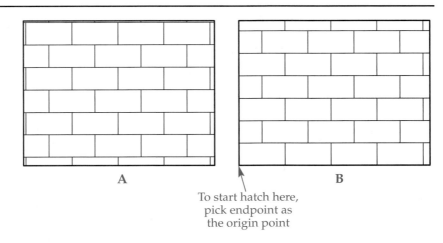

A

B

To start hatch here, pick endpoint as the origin point

The custom origin point can be saved by checking **Store as default origin**. The X and Y coordinates are then saved to the **HPORIGIN** variable. This new coordinate is then used as the default for new hatch patterns.

Selecting Areas to Be Hatched

Areas to be hatched can be selected by one of two methods: picking points or selecting objects. Both of these selection methods are accessed by picking a button in the **Boundaries** area of the **Hatch and Gradient** dialog box.

Using the **Add: Pick points** button is the easiest method of defining an area to be hatched. When you pick the button, the drawing returns. Pick a point within the region to be hatched, and AutoCAD automatically defines the boundary around the selected point.

More than one internal point can be selected. When you are finished selecting points, press [Enter] and the **Hatch and Gradient** dialog box returns. Then pick the **OK** button, and the feature is automatically hatched. See **Figure 21-16**.

<table>
<tr><td>NOTE
</td><td>When you are at the Select internal point: prompt, you can enter U or UNDO to undo the last selection, in case you picked the wrong area. You can also undo the hatch pattern by typing U after the pattern is drawn. However, you can preview the hatch before applying it to save time.</td></tr>
</table>

The **Add: Select objects** button is used to define the hatch boundary if you have items that you want to hatch by picking the object, rather than picking inside the object. See **Figure 21-17**. These items can be circles, polygons, or closed polylines. This method works especially well if the object to be hatched is crossed by other objects, such as the

Figure 21-16.
Defining the hatch boundary by picking a point.

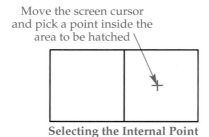

Figure 21-17.
Selecting objects to be hatched.

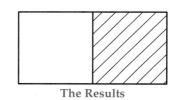

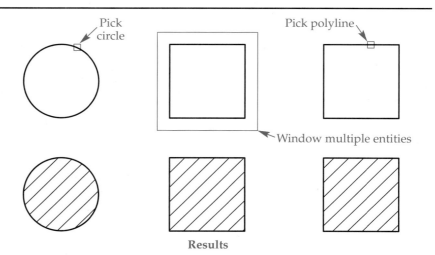

Figure 21-18.
A—Applying a hatch pattern to objects that cross each other using the **Add: Pick points** button. B—Applying a hatch pattern to a closed polygon using the **Add: Select objects** button.

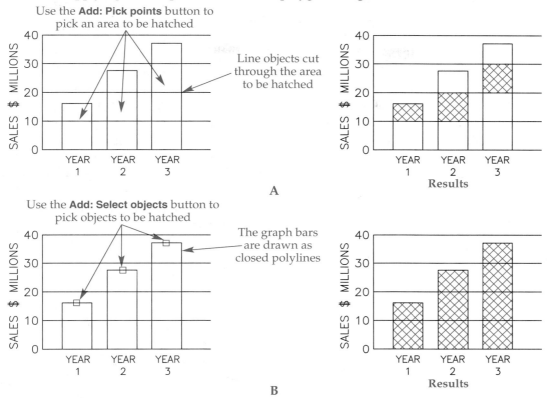

graph lines that cross the bars in **Figure 21-18.** Picking a point inside the bar results in the hatch displayed in **Figure 21-18A.** You can pick inside each individual area of each bar, but this can be time-consuming. If the bars were drawn using a closed polyline, all you have to do is use the **Add: Select objects** button to pick each bar. See **Figure 21-18B.**

The **Add: Select objects** button can also be used to pick an object inside an area to be hatched to exclude it from the hatch pattern. An example of this is the text shown inside the hatch area of **Figure 21-19.**

The **Remove boundaries** button is active after either points or objects have been selected. Picking this button returns you to the drawing screen and allows you to select objects for removal of their boundaries from the hatch area. Once the objects have been selected, press [Enter] to display the **Hatch and Gradients** dialog box. Boundaries can also be removed by using the **remove Boundaries** option at the Command: prompt while using the **Add: Pick points** button or the **Add: Select objects** button.

Specifying the Hatch Pattern Composition

The **BHATCH** command creates associative hatch patterns by default, but can be set to create nonassociative patterns. *Associative hatch patterns* update automatically when the boundary is edited. If the boundary is stretched, scaled, or otherwise edited, the hatch pattern automatically fills the new area with the original hatch pattern. Associative hatch patterns can be edited using the **HATCHEDIT** command, which is discussed later in this chapter.

The **Options** area of the **Hatch and Gradient** dialog box has the **Associative** option. This option is on by default. When unchecked, a nonassociative hatch, which is independent of its boundaries, is created. This means that if you pick only the hatch boundary to edit, the hatch pattern does not change with it. For example, if you pick

Figure 21-19.
Using the **Add: Select objects** button to exclude an object from the hatch pattern.

1. Select the object to be hatched inside

2. Pick the object to be removed from the hatch pattern

Results

a hatch boundary to scale, only the boundary is scaled while the pattern remains the same. You need to select both the boundary and the pattern before editing if you want to modify both.

To create multiple hatch patterns, multiple areas and objects can be selected during a single procedure. By default, these hatch patterns are the same object. This means that if you select one, they are all selected. Editing the properties of one of the hatch patterns edits all of them. This may not always be the result that you want. Checking the **Create separate hatches** check box in the **Options** area before applying the hatch patterns creates individual hatch patterns for each boundary.

Exercise 21-1   Complete the Exercise on the Student CD.

Defining the Drawing Order

A hatch pattern can be displayed in front of or behind other objects when it is placed in the drawing. The **Draw order** options in the **Options** area of the **Hatch and Gradient** dialog box control the order of display when the hatch pattern overlaps another object. The following options are available in the **Draw order** drop-down list:

- **Send behind boundary.** This is the default option. The hatch pattern appears behind the boundary that defines the hatch pattern area.
- **Bring in front of boundary.** The hatch pattern appears on top of the boundary that defines the hatch pattern area.
- **Do not assign.** No drawing order setting is assigned to the hatch pattern.
- **Send to back.** The hatch pattern is sent behind all other objects in the drawing. Any objects that are in the hatching area appear as if they are on top of the hatch pattern.
- **Bring to front.** The hatch pattern is in front, or on top of, all other objects in the drawing. Any objects that are in the hatching area appear as if they are behind the hatch pattern.

If the draw order setting needs to be changed after the hatch pattern is created, use the **DRAWORDER** command. You can also select the hatch pattern, right-click, and then select the appropriate shortcut menu option from the **Draw Order** cascading menu.

Selecting an Existing Pattern

You can specify the hatch pattern by selecting an identical hatch pattern from the drawing. Picking the **Inherit Properties** button allows you to select a previously drawn hatch pattern and use it for the current hatch pattern settings. The prompts look like this:

Select associative hatch object: (*pick the desired hatch pattern*)
Inherited Properties: Name <*hatch name*>, Scale <*hatch scale*>, Angle <*hatch angle*>
Select internal point: (*pick a point inside the new area to be hatched*)

After picking the internal point desired, press [Enter] to return to the **Hatch and Gradient** dialog box. The dialog box is displayed with the settings of the selected pattern. At the Select internal points or [Select objects/remove Boundaries]: prompt, typing S for **Select objects** allows you to select additional objects for the hatch pattern. Type B for **remove Boundaries** to remove objects from the current selection set being hatched.

Previewing the Hatch

Before applying a hatch pattern to the selected area, you can use preview tools to be sure the hatch pattern and hatch boundary settings are correct. The following buttons, which are found in the **Hatch and Gradient** dialog box, can be used to preview the boundary and hatch pattern:

- **View Selections button (Boundaries area).** You can instruct AutoCAD to let you see the boundaries of selected objects. The **View Selections** button is available after picking objects to be hatched. Pick this button and the drawing is displayed with the hatch boundaries highlighted. When you are finished, press [Enter] or right-click to return to the **Hatch and Gradient** dialog box.
- **Preview button.** Pick the **Preview** button if you want to look at the hatch pattern before you apply it to the drawing. This allows you to see if any changes need to be made before the hatch is drawn. When using this option, AutoCAD temporarily places the hatch pattern on your drawing. You can press [Enter] or right-click to accept the results. If you want to make changes after previewing the hatch, press [Esc] to return to the **Hatch and Gradient** dialog box. Change the hatch pattern, scale, or rotation angle as needed and preview the hatch again. When you are satisfied with the preview of the hatch, pick the **OK** button in the **Hatch and Gradient** dialog box to have it applied to the drawing.

Hatching Objects with Islands

Boundaries inside another boundary are known as *islands*. AutoCAD can either ignore these internal boundary objects and hatch through them or consider them as islands and hatch around them. See **Figure 21-20.**

When you use the **Add: Pick points** button to hatch an internal area, islands are left unhatched by default, as shown in **Figure 21-20B**. However, if you want islands to be hatched, use the **remove Boundaries** option or pick the **Remove boundaries** button in the **Hatch and Gradient** dialog box after selecting the internal point. The drawing window returns with the following prompts:

Select objects or [Add boundaries]: *(pick the islands to remove)*
Select objects or [Add boundaries//Undo]: ↵

Select the islands to remove and press [Enter] to return to the dialog box. The island objects are now hatched. See **Figure 21-20C.**

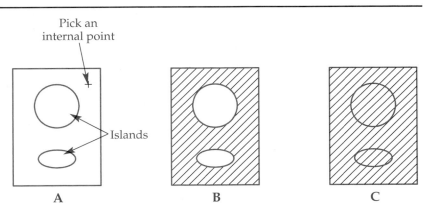

Figure 21-20.
A—Original objects.
B—Using the **Add: Pick points** button to hatch an internal area leaves islands unhatched. C—After picking an internal point, use the **Remove boundaries** button and pick the islands. This allows the islands to be hatched.

Pick an internal point

Islands

A   B   C

The island detection style and method is set in the **Islands** area of the **Hatch and Gradient** dialog box. By default, this area is hidden. Expand the dialog to show this area by picking the **More Options** button in the lower-right corner of the dialog box. See **Figure 21-10**. This area of the **Hatch and Gradient** dialog box can be hidden again by picking the **Less Options** button in the lower-right corner. The **Islands** area is shown in **Figure 21-21**.

If no islands exist, specifying an island detection style has no effect. There are three options that allow you to choose the features to be hatched. These options are illustrated by the image tiles in the dialog box. The three style options are:

- **Normal.** This option hatches inward from the outer boundary. If AutoCAD encounters an island, it turns off hatching until it encounters another island. Then the hatching is reactivated. Every other closed boundary is hatched with this option.
- **Outer.** This option hatches inward from the outer boundary. AutoCAD turns hatching off when it encounters an island and does not turn it back on. AutoCAD hatches only the outermost level of the structure and leaves the internal structure blank.
- **Ignore.** This option ignores all islands and hatches everything within the selected boundary.

Figure 21-21.
The **Islands** area of the **Hatch and Gradient** dialog box is displayed by picking the **More Options** button.

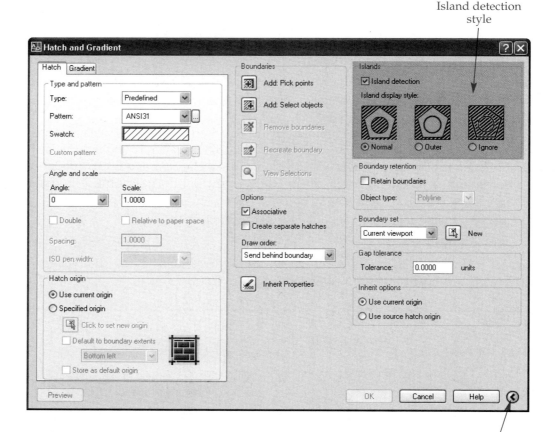

Island detection style

Pick to hide right column of dialog box

Improving Boundary Hatching Speed

In most situations, boundary hatching works with satisfactory speed. Normally, AutoCAD evaluates the entire drawing visible on screen to establish the boundary. This process can take some time on a large drawing.

You can improve the hatching speed and resolve other problems using options in the expanded **Hatch and Gradient** dialog box. See **Figure 21-22**. The drop-down list in the **Boundary set** area specifies what is evaluated when hatching. The default setting is Current viewport. If you want to limit what AutoCAD evaluates when hatching, you can define the boundary area so the **BHATCH** command only considers a specified portion of the drawing. To do this, pick the **New** button. Then at the Select objects: prompt, use a window to select the features of the object to be hatched. This is demonstrated in **Figure 21-23**.

Figure 21-22.
The **Boundary retention** and **Boundary set** areas of the **Hatch and Gradient** dialog box provides options to improve hatching efficiency.

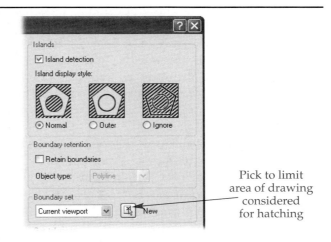

Pick to limit area of drawing considered for hatching

Figure 21-23.
The boundary set limits the area that AutoCAD evaluates during a boundary hatching operation.

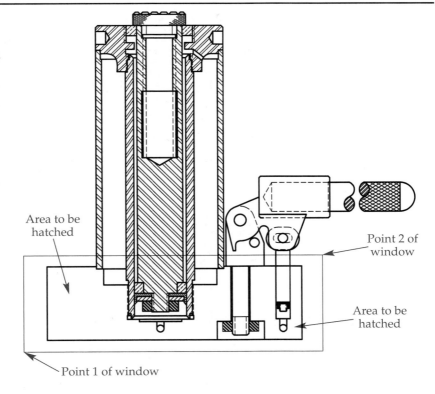

After selecting the object(s), the **Hatch and Gradient** dialog box returns. Notice in the **Boundary set** area that the drop-down list now displays Existing set as shown in **Figure 21-24.** The drawing with hatch patterns applied is shown in **Figure 21-25.**

You can make as many boundary sets as you wish. However, the last one made remains current until another is created. The **Retain boundaries** check box in the **Boundary retention** area can be selected as soon as a boundary set is made. Checking this box allows you to keep the boundary of a hatched area as a polyline, and new boundaries will continue to be saved as polylines whenever you create a boundary area. The default is no check in this box, so the hatched boundaries are not saved as polylines.

When you pick an internal area to be hatched, AutoCAD automatically creates a temporary boundary around the area. If the **Retain boundaries** check box is unchecked, the temporary boundaries are automatically removed when the hatch is complete. However, if you check the **Retain boundaries** check box, the hatch boundaries are kept when the hatch is completed.

When the **Retain boundaries** check box is checked, the **Object type:** drop-down list is activated. See **Figure 21-26.** Notice that the drop-down list has two options: Polyline (the default) and Region. If Polyline is selected, the boundary is a polyline object around the hatch area. If Region is selected, the hatch boundary is the hatched region. A *region* is a closed two-dimensional area.

Figure 21-25.
Results of hatching the drawing in **Figure 21-23** after selecting a boundary set.

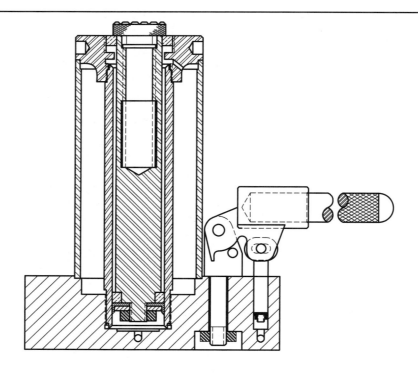

Figure 21-26.
There are two object type options for saving a boundary. These options are only available if the **Retain boundaries** option is checked.

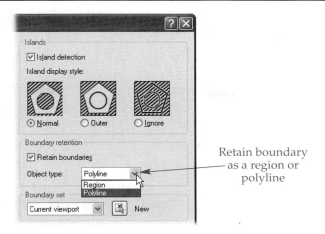

Retain boundary as a region or polyline

There are a number of techniques that can help you save time when hatching, especially with large and complex drawings. These include the following:

- Zoom in on the area to be hatched to make it easier for you to define the boundary. When you zoom into an area to be hatched, the hatch process is much faster because AutoCAD does not have to search the entire drawing to find the hatch boundaries.
- Preview the hatch before you apply it. This allows you to easily make last-minute adjustments.
- Turn off layers where there are lines or text that might interfere with your ability to accurately define hatch boundaries.
- Create boundary sets of small areas within a complex drawing to help save time.

Hatching Unenclosed Areas and Correcting Boundary Errors

The **BHATCH** command works well unless you have an error in the hatch boundary or pick a point outside a boundary area to be hatched. The most common error is a gap in the boundary. This can be very small and difficult to detect, and happens when you do not close the geometry. However, AutoCAD is quick to let you know by displaying the **Boundary Definition Error** alert box. See **Figure 21-27**. This alert notifies you that the area cannot be hatched unless you close the boundary or specify a gap tolerance value. The *gap tolerance* controls the amount of gap allowed for the opening in the boundary when hatching. The gap tolerance can be set in the **Gap Tolerance** area of the **Hatch and Gradient** dialog box. See **Figure 21-28**. The value in the **Tolerance:** text box is set to 0 by default. Setting a different value allows you to hatch an unenclosed boundary. Any gaps in the boundary equal to or smaller than the gap tolerance are ignored when applying the hatch. Before the hatch is generated, AutoCAD issues a warning to remind you that the boundary is not closed.

If you encounter the **Boundary Definition Error** alert box and decide you want to find and correct the problem, pick **OK** and return to the drawing. **Figure 21-29** shows an object where the corner does not close. The error is too small to see on the screen, but using the **ZOOM** command reveals the problem. Fix the error and use the **BHATCH** command again.

Figure 21-27.
The **Boundary Definition Error** alert box is displayed if problems occur in your hatching operation.

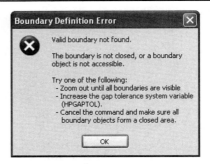

Figure 21-28.
The **Tolerance** setting controls whether hatching can be applied to open boundaries.

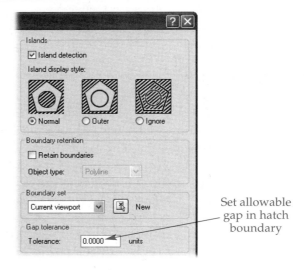

Set allowable gap in hatch boundary

Figure 21-29.
Using the **ZOOM** command to find the source of the hatching error.

Zoom view of error

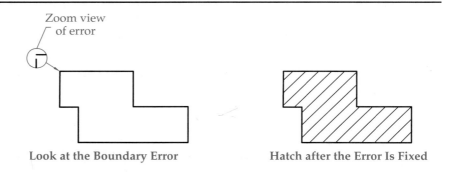

Look at the Boundary Error

Hatch after the Error Is Fixed

PROFESSIONAL TIP

When creating an associative hatch, it is best to specify only one internal point per hatch block placement. If you specify more than one internal point in the same operation, AutoCAD creates one hatch object from all points picked. This can cause unexpected results when trying to edit what appears to be a separate hatch object.

AutoCAD and Its Applications—Basics

Defining Inherit Options

The **Inherit Properties** button allows you to use the settings from an existing hatch pattern in the drawing by selecting it. This button was discussed earlier in this chapter. When this button is used, the **Inherit options** area in the **Hatch and Gradient** dialog box controls the hatch origin. See **Figure 21-30.**

The default option is **Use current origin**. When this option is selected, the hatch being created uses the origin point setting specified in the **Hatch origin** area on the **Hatch** tab in the **Hatch and Gradient** dialog box. Selecting the **Use source hatch origin** option causes the hatch being created to use the origin point of the hatch that was selected with the **Inherit Properties** button.

Creating Solid Hatch Patterns

As discussed earlier in this chapter, solid hatches can be created with the Solid predefined hatch pattern. See **Figure 21-31.** This pattern can be accessed from the **Pattern:** drop-down list in the **Hatch and Gradient** dialog box or the **Other Predefined** tab in the **Hatch Pattern Palette** dialog box. The pattern can be assigned a color. However, the hatching options used with other predefined hatches are not available. This is a quick way to fill a closed object solid. Filled objects can also be created with the **SOLID** command. This command is discussed later in this chapter.

More advanced types of fills can be applied to closed objects by using the gradient fill hatching options available with the **BHATCH** command. A *gradient fill* is a shading transition between the tones of one color or two separate colors. Gradient fills can be used to simulate color-shaded objects. There are nine different gradient fill patterns available. They are accessed in the **Gradient** tab of the **Hatch and Gradient** dialog box. See **Figure 21-32.**

The fills are based on linear sweep, spherical, radial, and curved shading. They create the appearance of a lit surface with a gradual transition from an area of highlight to a filled area. When two colors are used, a transition from light to dark between the colors is simulated.

As with other types of hatch patterns, gradient fills are associative when applied by default. They can also be edited in the same way as other hatch patterns with the **HATCHEDIT** command.

Figure 21-30.
The **Inherit options** area of the **Hatch and Gradient** dialog box is displayed by picking the **More Options** button.

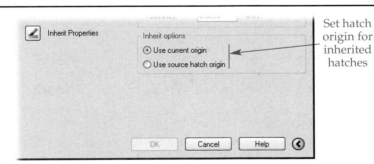

Set hatch origin for inherited hatches

Figure 21-31.
Using the Solid hatch pattern to make a basic solid hatch object.

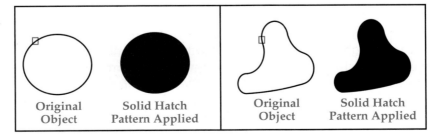

Original Object   Solid Hatch Pattern Applied   Original Object   Solid Hatch Pattern Applied

---

Figure 21-32.
The **Gradient** tab of the **Hatch and Gradient** dialog box contains options for creating gradient fill hatch patterns. There are nine types of gradient patterns available.

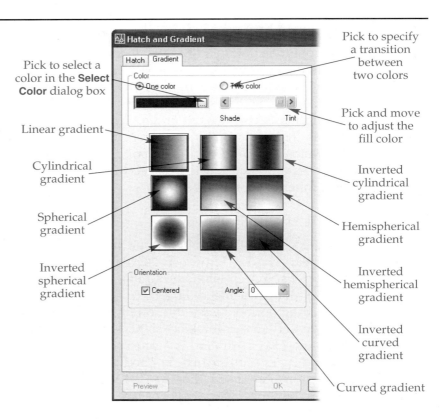

Pick to select a color in the **Select Color** dialog box

Linear gradient

Cylindrical gradient

Spherical gradient

Inverted spherical gradient

Pick to specify a transition between two colors

Pick and move to adjust the fill color

Inverted cylindrical gradient

Hemispherical gradient

Inverted hemispherical gradient

Inverted curved gradient

Curved gradient

The options in the **Gradient** tab of the **Hatch and Gradient** dialog box include settings for one or two fill colors, gradient configuration, and fill angle. The options are as follows:

- **One color.** This is the default option. It specifies a fill that has a smooth transition between the darker shades and lighter tints of one color. To select a color, pick the ellipsis (...) button next to the color swatch to access the **Select Color** dialog box. When the **One color** option is active, the **Shade** and **Tint** slider bar appears.
- **Two color.** This option allows you to specify a fill using a smooth transition between two colors. A color swatch with an ellipsis (...) button is displayed for each color.
- **Shade and Tint.** This slider bar allows you to specify the tint or shade of a color used for a one-color gradient fill. A *shade* is a specific color mixed with gray or black. A *tint* is a specific color mixed with white.
- **Centered.** This option is used to specify the gradient configuration. Picking the check box applies a symmetrical configuration. If this option is not selected, the gradient fill is shifted to simulate the projection of a light source from the left of the object.
- **Angle.** This option is used to specify the angle of the gradient fill. The default angle is 0°. The fill can be rotated by selecting a different angle from the drop-down list. The specified angle is relative to the current UCS and is independent of the angle setting for hatch patterns.

Using DesignCenter to Insert Hatch Patterns

Hatch patterns can be readily located and previewed before they are inserted using **DesignCenter**. To insert a hatch pattern into the current drawing, you can use a drag-and-drop operation. To access **DesignCenter**, pick the **DesignCenter** button on the **Standard** toolbar, select **Tools** > **DesignCenter**, type ADC or ADCENTER, or use the [Ctrl]+[2] key combination. To drag and drop a hatch pattern from **DesignCenter**, you need to select a PAT file. Once the PAT file is selected, the hatch patterns it contains are displayed in the preview palette. See **Figure 21-33.**

Figure 21-33.
Pick a PAT file in
DesignCenter to
display the available
hatch patterns in the
preview palette.

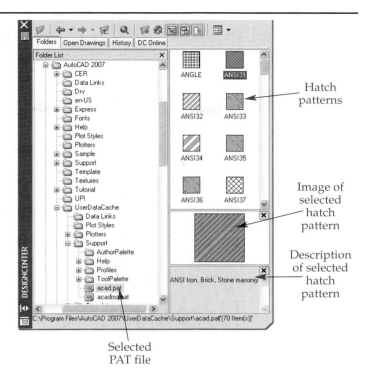

Hatch
patterns

Image of
selected
hatch
pattern

Description
of selected
hatch
pattern

Selected
PAT file

NOTE

AutoCAD includes two PAT files: acad.pat and acadiso.pat. Both are AutoCAD support files located in the Documents and Settings folder path set by the AutoCAD Support File Search Path. To verify the location of AutoCAD support files, access the **Files** tab in the **Options** dialog box and check the path listed under the Support File Search Path.

Pick a hatch pattern in the preview palette to display a preview of the pattern. Use one of the following three methods to transfer a hatch pattern from **DesignCenter** into the active drawing:

- **Drag and drop.** Pick the hatch pattern from **DesignCenter** and hold the mouse button. Move the cursor into the active drawing, and a hatch pattern symbol is displayed under the cursor, **Figure 21-34A.** Place the cursor within the area to be hatched, and release the pick button. The hatch is applied automatically. See **Figure 21-34B.**
- **Hatch and Gradient dialog box.** Right-click on a hatch pattern in **DesignCenter** and select **BHATCH...** from the shortcut menu to access the **Hatch and Gradient** dialog box. The selected hatch pattern is displayed automatically.
- **Copy and paste.** Hatch patterns can also be inserted using a copy and paste operation. Right-click on the hatch pattern in **DesignCenter** and pick **Copy** from the shortcut menu. Move the cursor into the active drawing, right-click, and select **Paste** from the shortcut menu. The hatch pattern symbol is displayed beneath the cursor. Pick within the area to be hatched, and the hatch pattern is automatically applied.

When hatch patterns are inserted from **DesignCenter**, the angle, scale, and island detection settings match the settings of the previous hatch pattern. If you wish to change these settings after inserting the hatch pattern, use the **HATCHEDIT** command.

Figure 21-34.
When a hatch pattern is selected in the preview palette, a preview image appears. A—The hatch pattern symbol appears under the cursor during the drag-and-drop and paste operations. B—The hatch pattern added to the drawing.

Selected hatch pattern

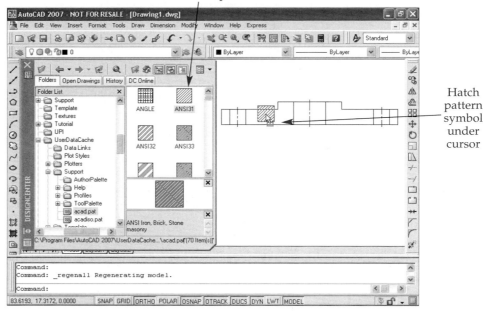

Hatch pattern symbol under cursor

A

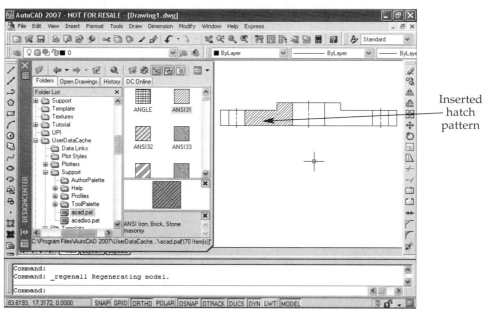

Inserted hatch pattern

B

NOTE

If you drag and drop or paste a hatch pattern into an area that is not a closed boundary, AutoCAD displays the Valid hatch boundary not found message at the Command: prompt.

Exercise 21-2

Complete the Exercise on the Student CD.

Using Tool Palettes

The **Tool Palettes** window provides a number of ways to manage frequently used blocks, hatch patterns, and other types of objects, such as gradients, images, tables, and external reference files. This section discusses the various features in the **Tool Palettes** window.

To open the **Tool Palettes** window, pick the **Tool Palettes** button on the **Standard** toolbar, select **Tools > Tool Palettes Window**, type TP or TOOLPALETTES, or use the [Ctrl]+[3] key combination. The **Tool Palettes** window is shown in **Figure 21-35**.

TOOLPALETTES
Type
TOOLPALETTES TP [Ctrl]+[3]
Pull-Down Menu
Tools > Tool Palettes Window
Toolbar
Standard
Tool Palettes

> **NOTE**
>
>
>
> Tool palettes can be used to store many different types of drawing content and tools, such as AutoCAD drawing and editing commands, customized commands, user-defined macros, script files, and AutoLISP routines. Examples of custom tools are provided in the **Command Tools** tool palette. For more discussion on AutoCAD customization, refer to *AutoCAD and Its Applications—Advanced*.

Locating and Viewing Content

Each tool palette in the **Tool Palettes** window has its own tab. There are a number of ways to navigate through the tools, or content, in each palette. In addition, viewing options are available to display the content in different ways.

To view the content in a tool palette, pick on the related tab to open it. If the **Tool Palettes** window contains more palettes than what is displayed on screen, pick on the edge of the lowest tab to display a selection menu listing the palette tabs. Locate the name of the tab to access the related tool palette.

Figure 21-35.
The **Tool Palettes** window can be used to access and insert hatch patterns.

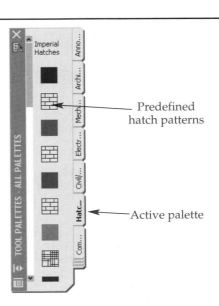

Predefined hatch patterns

Active palette

Chapter 21 Drawing Section Views and Graphic Patterns

The tool palette can be navigated by using one of two scroll methods. If all of the content of a selected tool palette does not fit in the window, the remainder can be viewed by using the scroll bar or the scroll hand. The scroll hand appears when the cursor is placed in an empty area in the tool palette. Picking and dragging scrolls the tool palette up and down.

By default, the tools in each palette are represented by icons. The appearance of the tools can be adjusted to suit user preference. To access the viewing options in a tool palette, right-click in the tool area to display the shortcut menu. See **Figure 21-36**. The **View Options...** listing is used to set viewing options. The options in the lower areas of the menu are used to create, delete, rename, and rearrange tool palettes. These options and the **Paste** option are discussed in the sections that follow.

Picking **View Options...** displays the **View Options** dialog box, **Figure 21-37**. The size of the preview image for a tool can be adjusted by moving the **Image size:** slider. The **View style:** radio button options control how the content is displayed. The three options are described as follows:

- **Icon only.** This setting displays just the icon (a preview image).
- **Icon with text.** This setting displays the icon and the name of the tool.
- **List view.** This setting displays the icon and the name of each tool in the palette in a single-column format.

In the **Apply to:** drop-down list, you can specify how the view settings are assigned. The settings can be applied to the current palette only or to all palettes.

Insert Hatch Patterns Using Tool Palettes

Inserting hatch patterns with the **Tool Palettes** window is similar to inserting them with **DesignCenter**. As with **DesignCenter**, a pattern can be previewed in a window before it is applied.

Figure 21-36.
Viewing options for each tool palette can be accessed by right-clicking in the tool palette to display the shortcut menu.

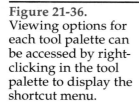

Figure 21-37.
Settings in the **View Options** dialog box control how the content is displayed in each tool palette.

Set size of tools on tool palette

Select tool display style

Apply settings to current tool palette or all tool palettes

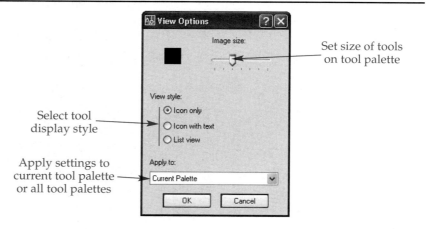

To drag and drop a hatch pattern from the **Tool Palettes** window, access the tool palette in which the pattern resides. There are two ways to drag the pattern for insertion into the drawing. You can pick the pattern and drag the image into the drawing while holding down the mouse button, or you can place the cursor over the hatch pattern image and pick once. When you then move the cursor into the drawing area, the hatch pattern is attached to the crosshairs automatically. The location where the crosshairs and the hatch pattern are connected is defined by the insertion point of the hatch pattern. Drag the pattern image to the desired boundary area and pick.

Once the hatch pattern is inserted, you can make modifications with the **HATCHEDIT** command. Hatch editing is discussed later in this chapter.

Adding Hatch Patterns to a Tool Palette

Hatch patterns and gradient fills can be added to tool palettes using a drag-and-drop procedure. The pattern must be in the current drawing or defined in an AutoCAD hatch pattern file. If you are adding a hatch pattern or gradient fill to a tool palette from the current drawing, first open the desired palette in the **Tool Palettes** window. Select the hatch pattern or gradient object in the drawing to highlight it. Then pick anywhere over the hatch pattern or gradient (do not select the grip) and drag it onto the tool palette.

As previously mentioned, the predefined hatch patterns provided with AutoCAD are stored in the acad.pat and acadiso.pat files. If you want to add a predefined pattern to a tool palette, one of the files must be located in **DesignCenter**. By default, these files are AutoCAD support files stored in the Support File Search Path folder. This path location can be determined by accessing the **Files** tab in the **Options** dialog box and identifying the path listed under Support File Search Path.

Once a hatch pattern file is located, its contents can be displayed in the **Content** area of **DesignCenter**. You can then add one or more hatch patterns to a tool palette.

To create a palette that contains all of the hatch patterns in a single PAT file, right-click on the hatch pattern file in the **Tree View** area and select **Create Tool Palette of Hatch Patterns** from the shortcut menu. To add an individual hatch pattern to a palette, drag-and-drop the pattern from the **Content** area into the desired palette.

Exercise 21-3   Complete the Exercise on the Student CD.

Editing Hatch Patterns

You can edit hatch boundaries and hatch patterns with grips and editing commands such as **ERASE, COPY, MOVE, ROTATE, SCALE,** and **TRIM.** If a hatch pattern is associative, whatever you do to the hatch boundary is automatically done to the associated hatch pattern. As explained earlier, a hatch pattern is associative if the **Associative** option in the **Options** area of the **Hatch and Gradient** dialog box is active.

A convenient way to edit a hatch pattern is by using the **HATCHEDIT** command. You can access this command by picking **Modify > Object > Hatch...** from the pull-down menu, picking the **Edit Hatch** button on the **Modify II** toolbar, or typing HE or HATCHEDIT. You can also double-click on the hatch pattern you wish to edit.

When you select a hatch pattern or patterns to edit, the **Hatch Edit** dialog box is displayed. See **Figure 21-38.** The **Hatch Edit** dialog box has the same features as the **Hatch and Gradient** dialog box, except that the **Recreate Boundary** button in the **Boundaries** area is available.

HATCHEDIT

Type

HATCHEDIT
HE

Pull-Down Menu

Modify
> Object
> Hatch...

Toolbar

Modify II

Edit Hatch

Figure 21-38.
The **Hatch Edit** dialog box is used to edit hatch patterns. Notice that only the options related to hatch characteristics are available.

Pick to recreate boundary

The **Recreate boundary** button can be used to create a new boundary for the hatch pattern. It basically redraws a new boundary on top of the existing boundary. If the current boundary is made up of several different lines, this command can be used to draw the boundary very quickly in one object. When the **Recreate boundary** button is picked, the **Hatch Edit** dialog box is temporarily hidden. You then decide if the boundary type will be a region or a polyline. The next query asks if you want the hatch pattern to be associated with the new boundary.

The **Hatch Edit** dialog box then displays again. The other features work just like they do in the **Hatch and Gradient** dialog box. You can change the pattern type, scale, or angle; remove the associative qualities; or set the inherit properties of an existing hatch pattern. You can also preview the edited hatch before applying it to your drawing.

PROFESSIONAL TIP
The **MATCHPROP** command can also be used to inherit the properties of an existing hatch pattern and apply it to the hatch pattern you wish to edit. This command can be used to apply existing hatch patterns to objects in the current drawing file or to objects in other drawing files that are open in AutoCAD.

Exercise 21-4   Complete the Exercise on the Student CD.

Figure 21-39.
Editing objects with associative hatch patterns. The hatch pattern changes to match the edit.

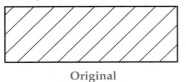

Original

Object Stretched

A

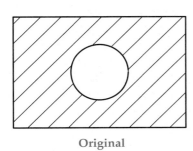

Original

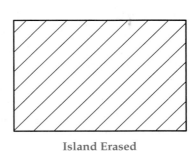

Island Erased

B

Editing Associative Hatch Patterns

When you edit an object with an associative hatch pattern, the hatch pattern changes to match the edit. For example, the object in **Figure 21-39A** is stretched and the hatch pattern matches the new object. When the island in **Figure 21-39B** is erased, the hatch pattern is automatically revised to fill the area where the island was located. As long as the original boundary is being edited, the associative hatch will update.

Drawing a new object and associating it with an existing hatch pattern will create a new island. See **Figure 21-40**. After a rectangle is drawn, double-click on the hatch pattern to open the **Hatch Edit** dialog box. Picking the **Add: Select objects** button hides the dialog box and allows you to pick the rectangle. Press [Enter] and the **OK** button to finish. The rectangle is now an associated island.

Exercise 21-5   Complete the Exercise on the Student CD.

Figure 21-40.
Objects can be added to a hatch pattern boundary after the pattern is created.

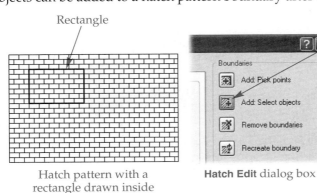

Drawing Objects with Solid Fills

In previous chapters, you learned that polylines, polyarcs, trace segments, and donuts may be filled in solid when **FILL** mode is on. When **FILL** mode is off, these objects are drawn as outlines only. The **SOLID** command works in much the same manner except that it fills objects or shapes that are already drawn and fills areas that are simply defined by picking points.

The **SOLID** command is accessed by picking **Draw** > **Modeling** > **Meshes** > **2D Solid** or typing SO or SOLID. You are then prompted to select points. If the object to fill solid is rectangular, pick the corners in the numbered sequence shown in **Figure 21-41**.

Notice that AutoCAD prompts you for another third point after the first four. This prompt allows you to fill in additional parts of the same object, if needed. AutoCAD assumes that the third and fourth points of the previous solid are now points one and two for the next solid. The subsequent points you select fill in the object in a triangular fashion. Continue picking points, or press [Enter] to stop. See **Figure 21-42**.

Different types of solid arrangements can be drawn by altering the numbering sequence. See **Figure 21-43**. Also, the **SOLID** command can be used to draw filled shapes without prior use of the **LINE**, **PLINE**, or **RECTANG** commands; simply pick the points. Consider using various object snap modes when picking the points of existing geometry.

SOLID

Type
SOLID
SO

Pull-Down Menu
Draw
> Modeling
> Meshes
> 2D Solid

Figure 21-41.
Using the **SOLID** command. Select the points in the order shown.

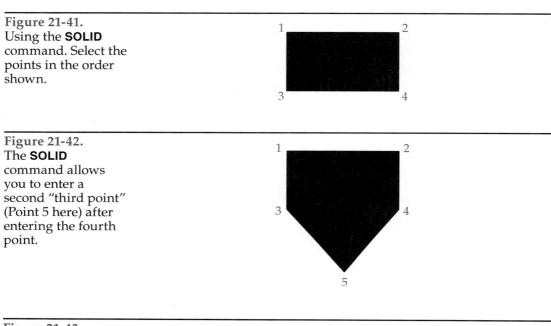

Figure 21-42.
The **SOLID** command allows you to enter a second "third point" (Point 5 here) after entering the fourth point.

Figure 21-43.
Using a different numbering sequence for the **SOLID** command will give you different results.

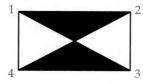

PROFESSIONAL TIP

Keep in mind that many solids and dense hatches require extensive time during regeneration. On a complex drawing, create filled solids and hatching on a separate layer and keep the layer frozen until you are ready to plot the drawing. Many solids and dense hatch patterns also adversely affect plot time. Save plotting time by making check plots with **FILL** mode off.

Exercise 21-6   Complete the Exercise on the Student CD.

LEGACY NOTE

The **HATCH** command can also be used to hatch objects using entries at the Command: prompt. This command provides prompts for most of the options available in the **Hatch and Gradient** dialog box. The **HATCH** command creates nonassociative hatch patterns, so it is recommended that you use the **Hatch and Gradient** dialog box to hatch objects. For more information on the **HATCH** command, refer to the AutoCAD help system.

Express Tools Chapter 21   The following Express Tool is related to topics discussed in this chapter. Refer to the Student CD for information on this tool:

Super Hatch

Chapter Test

Answer the following questions. Write your answers on a separate sheet of paper or complete the electronic chapter test on the Student CD.

For Questions 1–6, name the type of section identified in each of the following statements:

1. Half of the object is removed, the cutting-plane line generally cuts completely through along the center plane.
2. Used primarily on symmetrical objects, the cutting-plane line cuts through one-quarter of the object.
3. The cutting-plane line is staggered through features that do not lie in a straight line.
4. The section is turned in place to clarify the contour of the object.
5. The section is rotated and located from the object. The location of the section is normally identified with a cutting-plane line.
6. A small portion of the view is removed to clarify an internal feature.

7. AutoCAD's standard section line symbols are called _____.
8. In which pull-down menu can you select **Hatch...** to display the **Hatch and Gradient** dialog box?
9. Name the two files that contain hatch patterns that can be copied from **DesignCenter**.
10. Explain the purpose and function of the ellipsis (...) buttons in the **Hatch and Gradient** dialog box.
11. Identify two ways to select a predefined hatch pattern in the **Hatch and Gradient** dialog box.
12. Explain how you set a hatch scale in the **Hatch and Gradient** dialog box.
13. Explain how to use an existing hatch pattern on a drawing as the current pattern for your next hatch.
14. Describe the purpose of the **Preview** button found in the **Hatch and Gradient** dialog box.
15. What is the purpose of the **Gap tolerance** setting in the **Hatch and Gradient** dialog box?
16. How do you limit AutoCAD hatch evaluation to a specific area of the drawing?
17. Define *associative hatch pattern*.
18. How do you change the hatch angle in the **Hatch and Gradient** dialog box?
19. Describe the fundamental difference between using the **Add: Pick points** and the **Add: Select objects** buttons in the **Hatch and Gradient** dialog box.
20. If you use the **Add: Pick points** button inside the **Hatch and Gradient** dialog box to hatch an area, how do you hatch around an island inside the area to be hatched?
21. How do you hatch an object with text inside without hatching the text?
22. Name the command that may be used to edit existing associative hatch patterns.
23. How does the **Hatch Edit** dialog box compare to the **Hatch and Gradient** dialog box?
24. Explain the three island detection style options.
25. What happens if you erase an island inside an associative hatch pattern?
26. What is the result of stretching an object that is hatched with an associative hatch pattern?
27. In addition to the **BHATCH** command, what command can be used to fill an object solid?
28. What are gradient fill hatch patterns? How are they created with the **BHATCH** command?
29. Explain how to use drag and drop to insert a hatch pattern from **DesignCenter** into an active drawing.
30. Explain two ways to use drag and drop for inserting a hatch pattern from a tool palette into the drawing.

Drawing Problems

For Problems 1–4, use the following guidelines:

A. Use an appropriate template with a mechanical drawing title block.
B. Create separate layers for views, dimensions, and section lines.
C. Place the following general notes 1/2" from the lower-left corner.
   2. REMOVE ALL BURRS AND SHARP EDGES
   1. INTERPRET DIMENSIONS AND TOLERANCES PER ASME Y14.5M-1994
   NOTES:

1. Draw the full section shown on the right. Save the drawing as P21-1.

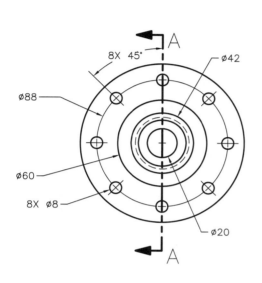

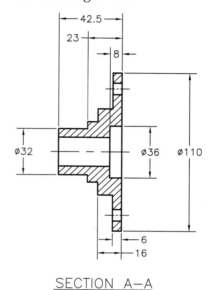

SECTION A—A

Name: Hub
Material: Cast Iron

2. Draw the half section shown in the center. Add the following notes: OIL QUENCH 40-45C, CASE HARDEN .020 DEEP, and 59-60 ROCKWELL C SCALE. Save the drawing as P21-2.

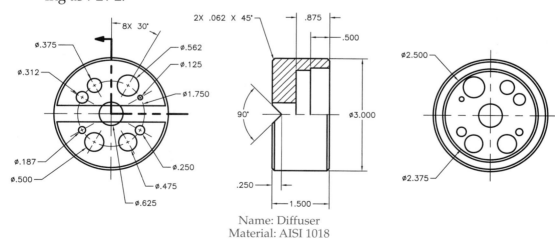

Name: Diffuser
Material: AISI 1018

3. Draw the given views, including aligned section shown on the right. Add the following notes: FINISH ALL OVER 1.63 mm UNLESS OTHERWISE SPECIFIED and ALL DIMENSIONS ARE IN MILLIMETERS. Save the drawing as P21-3.

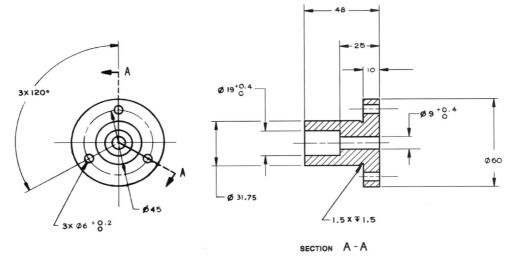

SECTION A-A

Name: Bushing
Material: SAE 1030

4. Draw these views, which include aligned and broken-out sections. Add the following notes: FINISH ALL OVER 1.63 mm UNLESS OTHERWISE SPECIFIED and ALL DIMENSIONS ARE IN MILLIMETERS. Save the drawing as P21-4.

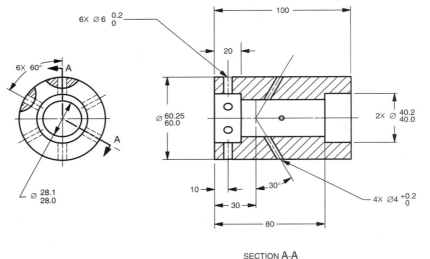

SECTION A-A

Name: Nozzle
Material: Phosphor Bronze

5. Draw the views of the chain guide as shown. Save the drawing as **P21-5**.

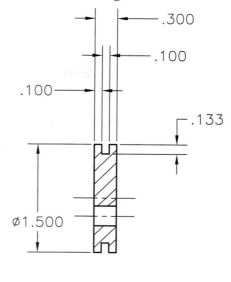

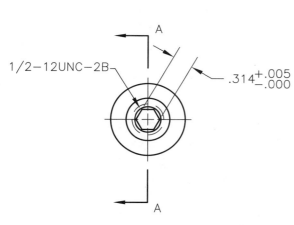

6. Draw the views of the sleeve and notes as shown. Save the drawing as **P21-6**.

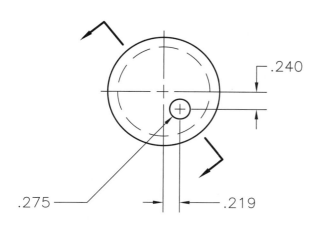

1/2−12UNC−2B

$.314^{+.005}_{-.000}$

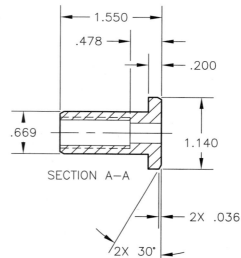

1.550

.478

.200

.669

1.140

SECTION A−A

2X .036

2X 30°

4. PAINT ACE GLOSS BLACK ALL OVER.
3. CASE HARDEN 45−50 ROCKWELL
2. REMOVE ALL BURRS AND SHARP
   EDGES.
1. INTERPRET ALL DIMENSIONS AND
   TOLERANCES PER ASME
   Y14.5M−1994.

7. Draw the views of the toe hook as shown. Save the drawing as P21-7.

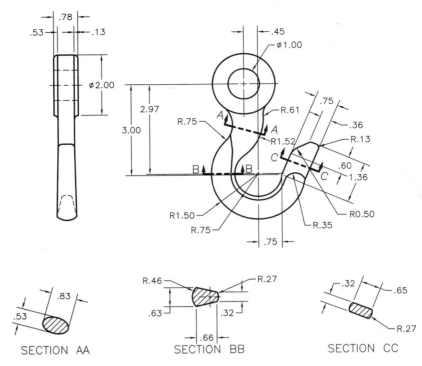

Draw the following problems using commands discussed in this chapter and in previous chapters. Use an appropriate template for each problem. Use text styles that correlate with the problem content. Place dimensions and notes when needed. Make your drawings proportional to the given problems when dimensions are not given. Save each of the drawings as P21-(problem number).

8.

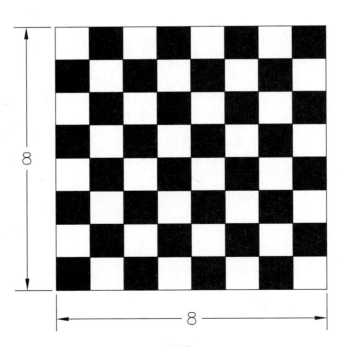

9.

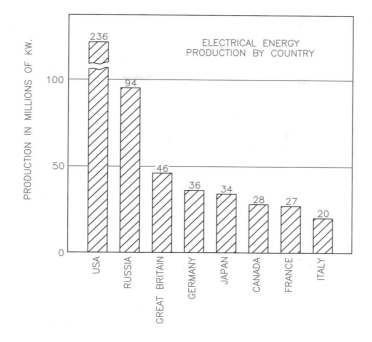

10.

COMPONENT LAYOUT

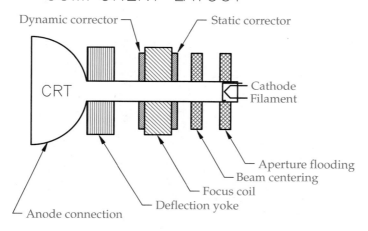

11.

SOLOMAN SHOE COMPANY

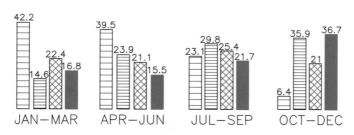

12.

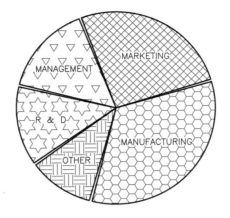

DIAL TECHNOLOGIES
EXPENSE BUDGET
FISCAL YEAR

13.

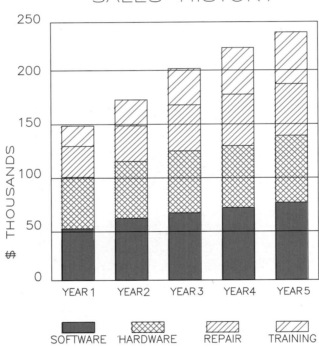

SALES HISTORY

14.

1" R-5 FOAM
SHEATHING

WALL AT GARAGE

SLOPE GRADE AWAY FROM
FOUNDATION @ 5" IN
FIRST 10'-10" (TYP)

8" MIN.

DEPTH AS REQD BY
CODE OR LOCAL FROST
LINE 2' MINIMUM

#5 DOWELS
@ 4'-0" O.C.

16" x 8" FTG.
W/ (2)#5 CONT.

FILL TOP 2 COURSES
W/ GROUT AT BOLTS

1/2" EXPANSION JOINT

4" CONC. SLAB W/
6X6 10/10 WWM

W/ 1/2" DIA. ANCHOR BOLTS
AT 4' O.C.
EMBEDDED PER LOCAL CODE

6 MIL VAPOR BARRIER

4" SAND CUSHION
OR CRUSHED STONE

#5 AT 4' O.C.
FILL BLKS SOLID W/
CONC. AT VERT. #5

8" C-90 CONC. BLK. (# OF
COURSES DETERMINED BY
FROST LINE)

15.

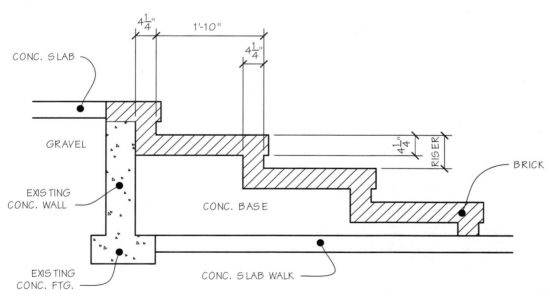

CONC. SLAB

GRAVEL

EXISTING
CONC. WALL

EXISTING
CONC. FTG.

CONC. SLAB WALK

CONC. BASE

$4\frac{1}{4}$"

1'-10"

$4\frac{1}{4}$"

$4\frac{1}{4}$"

RISER

BRICK

16.

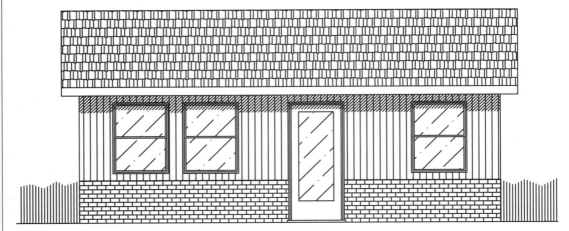

17.

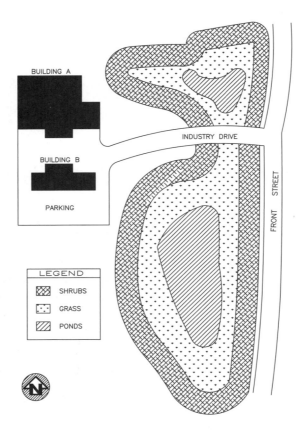

18.

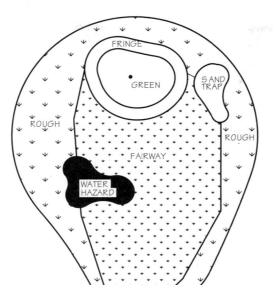

19.

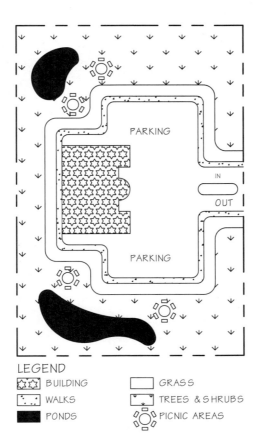

LEGEND

BUILDING		GRASS	
WALKS		TREES & SHRUBS	
PONDS		PICNIC AREAS	

Drawing Problems – Chapter 21

20.

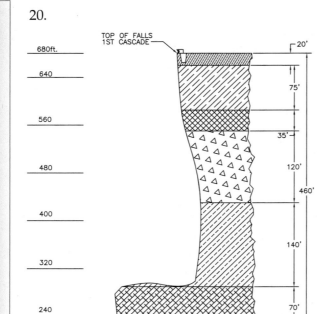

TOP OF FALLS
1ST CASCADE

680ft.

640

560

480

400

320

240

20'

75'

35'

120'

140'

70'

460'

SCALE 1:480

40' 30' 10' 40' 120'
40' 20' 0' 80'

PROFILE OF MULTNOMAH FALLS
&
GEOLOGIC INFORMATION

20' COLLONADE OF AN 80-FOOT THICK FLOW, NOTCHED BY MULTNOMAH CREEK.

75' PILLOW LAVA

35' A GLASSY FLOW, WITH WELL-FORMED ENTABLATURE AND COLLONADE.

120' CONSISTING OF TWO TIERS OF HACKLY-JOINTED BASALT, WITH NO COLLONADE.

140' ENTABLATURE WITH THIN COLUMNS, TOPPED BY A VESICULAR ZONE.

70' OF ENTABLATURE BENEATH THE LOWER FALLS.

BRIEF DESCRIPTION OF TERMS.
COLONNADE: THE LOWER PORTION OF A LAVA FLOW OF COLUMNAR-JOINTED BASALT.
ENTABLATURE: THE UPPER MASSIVE OF A LAVA FLOW OF HACKLY-JOINTED BASALT.

* INFORMATION TAKEN FROM:
"THE MAGNIFCENT GATEWAY"
AUTHOR: JOHN ELIOT ALLEN
PAGES: 89-91

Creating Symbols for Multiple Use

Learning Objectives

After completing this chapter, you will be able to do the following:

- Create and save blocks.
- Insert blocks into a drawing.
- Edit a block and update it in a drawing.
- Insert blocks and other objects into drawings using tool palettes.
- Create blocks that are saved independent of the drawing.
- Construct and use a symbol library of blocks.
- Add block insertion tools to tool palettes.

One of the greatest benefits of AutoCAD is its ability to store symbols for future use. These symbols, or *blocks*, can be inserted into a drawing, scaled, and rotated in one operation. If a block is edited, drawings containing the block can be updated to include the new version.

There are two types of blocks used in AutoCAD. A *block* created with the **BLOCK** command is stored within a drawing. A *wblock* created with the **WBLOCK** command is saved as a separate drawing file. Both types of blocks can be shared between drawings. Blocks can be copied between drawings using **DesignCenter** or the **Tool Palettes** window, and wblocks can be inserted into drawings using **DesignCenter**, the **Tool Palettes** window, and the **INSERT** command. Both types of blocks can be used to create a *symbol library*, which is a related group of symbols.

When a drawing is inserted or referenced, it becomes part of the drawing on screen, but its content is not added to the current drawing file. Any named objects, such as blocks and layers, are referred to as *dependent symbols*. Dependent symbols contained within a drawing are automatically updated by AutoCAD the next time the drawing is opened.

The ability to draw and store symbols is one of the greatest time-saving features of AutoCAD. The **BLOCK** command is used to create a symbol within a specific drawing file. The **INSERT** command can then be used to insert the block as many times as needed into the drawing in which it was defined. The block can also be copied into other drawings using **DesignCenter** or tool palettes. A block created with the **WBLOCK** command can be inserted as many times as needed into *any* drawing. When inserted, both types of blocks can be scaled and rotated to meet the drawing requirements.

There are advantages to creating and storing symbols as blocks rather than as individual drawing files. However, the best method for block usage depends on the needs of the user and the project. This chapter discusses the construction and management of blocks, wblocks, and symbol libraries. Blocks are discussed in the following sections.

Constructing Blocks

A block can be any shape, symbol, view, or drawing. Before constructing a block, review the drawing you are working on. This is where a sketch of your drawing can be useful. Look for any shapes, components, notes, and assemblies that are used more than once. These features can be drawn once and then saved as blocks for multiple use.

PROFESSIONAL TIP

Multiple features that are identical except for scale can be created from a single block. In these cases, the base block should be drawn to fit inside a one-unit square. It does not matter if the object is measured in feet, inches, or millimeters. This makes it easy to scale the symbol later when you insert it into a drawing.

Drawing the Block Components

Draw a block as you would any other drawing geometry. When you finish drawing the object, determine the best location on the symbol to use as an insertion point. When you insert the block into a drawing, the symbol is placed with its insertion point on the screen cursor. Several examples of commonly used blocks are shown in **Figure 22-1** with their insertion points highlighted.

In order for the block to assume the color and linetype of the layer on which it will be inserted, the objects forming the block must be drawn on layer 0. If the objects are drawn on a different layer, use the **Properties** window or **Properties** toolbar to place all the objects on layer 0 before using the **BLOCK** command. To have the block maintain a specific color and linetype regardless of the layer it is to be used on, set the color and linetype before drawing the objects. If the block should assume the current color and linetype when the block is inserted into a drawing, set the current object color and linetype to ByBlock.

To set the color to ByBlock, pick **ByBlock** in the **Color Control** drop-down list of the **Properties** toolbar, or pick the **ByBlock** button in the **Select Color** dialog box. See **Figure 22-2**.

To set the linetype to ByBlock, pick **ByBlock** in the **Linetype Control** drop-down list of the **Properties** toolbar, or set ByBlock current using the **Linetype Manager** dialog box. See **Figure 22-3**.

Figure 22-1.
Common drafting symbols and their insertion points for placement on drawings. The insertion points are shown as colored dots.

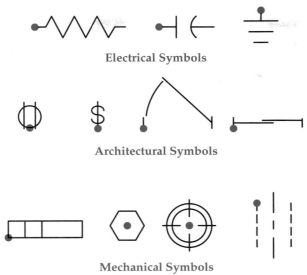

Electrical Symbols

Architectural Symbols

Mechanical Symbols

Figure 22-2.
After picking **Format** > **Color...** from the pull-down menu to display the **Select Color** dialog box, pick the **ByBlock** button to have the block assume the current color when it is inserted into a drawing.

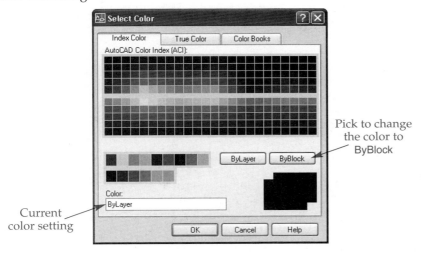

Pick to change the color to ByBlock

Current color setting

Once the current color and linetype are both set to ByBlock, you can create blocks. A block created with these settings assumes the current color and linetype when it is inserted into a drawing, regardless of the current layer setting.

Creating Blocks

When you draw a shape or symbol, you have not yet created a block. To save your object as a block, pick the **Make Block** button on the **Draw** toolbar, pick **Draw** > **Block** > **Make...** from the pull-down menu, or type B, BLOCK, or BMAKE. Any one of these methods displays the **Block Definition** dialog box, **Figure 22-4**. The process for creating a block is:

1. In the **Name:** text box, enter a name for the block, such as PUMP. The name cannot exceed 255 characters. It can include numbers, letters, and spaces, as well as the dollar sign ($), hyphen (-), and underscore (_).

BLOCK

Type
BLOCK
B
BMAKE

Pull-Down Menu
Draw
> Block
> Make...

Toolbar
Draw

Make Block

Figure 22-3.
To set the ByBlock linetype current, pick ByBlock in the **Linetype** list of the **Linetype Manager** dialog box and then pick the **Current** button.

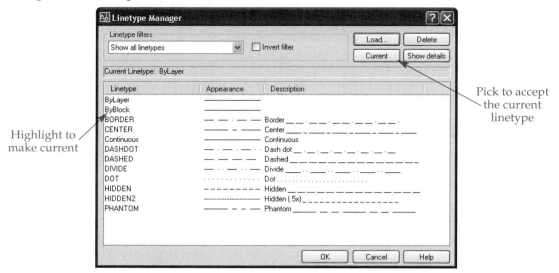

Highlight to make current

Pick to accept the current linetype

Figure 22-4.
Blocks are created using the **Block Definition** dialog box.

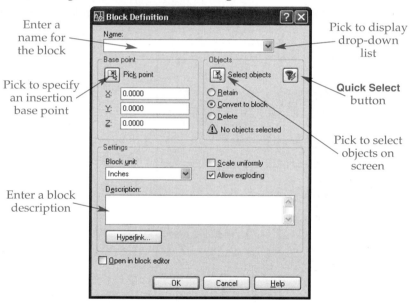

Enter a name for the block

Pick to specify an insertion base point

Enter a block description

Pick to display drop-down list

Quick Select button

Pick to select objects on screen

2. In the **Objects** area, pick the **Select objects** button to use your pointing device to select objects for the block definition. The drawing area returns and you are prompted to select objects. Select all the objects that will make up the block. Press [Enter] when you are done. The **Block Definition** dialog box is redisplayed and the number of selected objects is shown in the **Objects** area. If you want to create a selection set, use the **Quick Select** button to define a filter for your selection set.

3. In the **Objects** area, specify whether to retain, convert, or delete the selected objects. If you want to keep the selected objects in the current drawing (in their original state), pick the **Retain** radio button. If you want to replace the selected objects with one of the blocks you are creating, pick the **Convert to block** radio button. If you want to remove the selected objects after the block is defined, pick the **Delete** radio button.

4. In the **Base point** area, enter the coordinates for the insertion base point or pick the **Pick point** button to use your pointing device to select an insertion point.

5. In the **Settings** area, specify the insertion units of the block by selecting a unit type from the **Block unit** drop-down list.

6. If **Scale uniformly** is checked, you do not have the option of specifying different X and Y scale factors when the block is inserted into a drawing.

7. The **Allow exploding** setting determines if the block can be exploded. If this check box is unchecked, the block cannot be exploded either when it is inserted or after it is on the drawing.

8. If the **Open in block editor** check box is checked, the new block is immediately opened in the **Block Definition Editor** after the block is created. The **Block Definition Editor** is discussed later in this chapter.

9. In the **Description:** text box, enter a textual description to help identify the block for easy reference, such as This is a vacuum pump symbol.

10. After you have finished defining the block, pick **OK**.

If you select the **Delete** option and then decide that you want to keep the original geometry in the drawing after you have defined the block, you can enter the **OOPS** command. This returns the original objects to the screen, whereas typing U or picking the **Undo** button from the **Standard** toolbar removes the block from the drawing.

NOTE   The **Block Definition** dialog box contains a **Hyperlink...** button. Pick this button to access the **Insert Hyperlink** dialog box to insert a hyperlink in the block.

To verify that the block was saved properly, open the **Block Definition** dialog box. Then, pick the **Name:** drop-down list button to display a list of all blocks in the current drawing. The block names are organized in numerical and alphabetical order.

The **-BLOCK** command can also be used to create new blocks and list existing blocks. Access this command by typing -B or -BLOCK. When the **-BLOCK** command is entered, the options in the **Block Definition** dialog box are presented as prompts on the command line. To display a list of all block names, type ?, press [Enter], and press [Enter] again. The following information is then displayed in the **AutoCAD Text Window**:

-BLOCK

Type
-BLOCK
-B

```
Defined blocks.
  "PUMP"
User   External      Dependent   Unnamed
Blocks References    Blocks      Blocks
  1      0             0           0
```

This listing reports each block name, as well as the different types of blocks and the number of each type in the drawing. When you create a block, you have actually created a *block definition*. Therefore, the first entry in the block listing is that of *defined* blocks. *User blocks* are those created by you. *External references* are drawings referenced with the **XREF** command. (External references are discussed in Chapter 25.) Blocks that reside in a referenced drawing are called *dependent blocks*. *Unnamed blocks* are objects such as associative and nonassociative dimensions.

Step through the process of creating a block again. Draw a one-unit square and name it PLATE. See **Figure 22-5**. After creating the block, be sure to confirm that the PLATE block was saved by using the **-BLOCK** command.

Figure 22-5.
The procedure for
drawing a one-
unit square and
defining it as a
block. A—Draw the
block. B—Pick the
insertion base point.
C—Select the square
using the **Window**
selection option or
any other suitable
option.

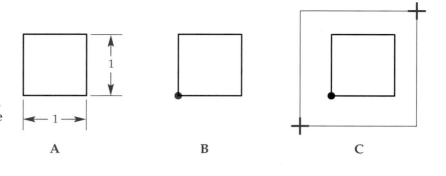

A   B   C

PROFESSIONAL TIP

Blocks can be used when creating other blocks. Suppose you design a complex part or view that will be used repeatedly. You can insert existing blocks into the view and then save the entire object as a block. This is called *nesting*, where blocks contain other blocks. The "top-level" block must be given a name that is different from any nested block. Proper planning and knowledge of all existing blocks can speed up the drawing process and the creation of complex parts.

Exercise 22-1   Complete the Exercise on the Student CD.

Using Blocks in a Drawing

Once a block has been created, it is easy to insert it into a drawing. First, determine the proper size and rotation angle for the block. Blocks are normally inserted on specific layers, so set the proper layer *before* inserting the block. Once a block has been inserted into a drawing, it is referred to as a *block reference*.

Inserting Blocks

INSERT

Type
INSERT
I
DDINSERT

Pull-Down Menu
Insert
> Block...

Toolbar
Insert

Insert Block

Blocks and wblocks are placed in a drawing with the **INSERT** command. Type I, INSERT, or DDINSERT, pick the **Insert Block** button on the **Draw** or **Insert** toolbar, or pick **Insert > Block...** from the pull-down menu. This opens the **Insert** dialog box, **Figure 22-6.**

Pick the **Name:** drop-down list button to show the blocks defined in the current drawing. Then, select the name of the block you wish to insert. You can also type the name of the block in the **Name:** text box. Once the desired block has been specified, you must specify the insertion location, scale, and rotation angle. You can also specify whether to explode the block while inserting it. The features in the **Insert** dialog box are:

- **Browse... button.** Pick this button to display the **Select Drawing File** dialog box in which you can select a drawing file (wblock) for insertion into the current drawing.

Figure 22-6.
The **Insert** dialog box allows you to select and prepare a block for insertion. Select the block you wish to insert from the drop-down list or enter the block name in the **Name:** text box.

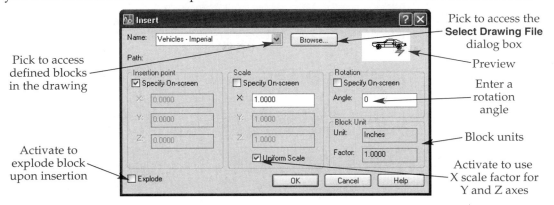

- **Insertion point area.** If the **Specify On-screen** check box is activated, the block is inserted dynamically when you pick **OK** and you must pick an insertion point on screen. If you wish to insert the block using absolute coordinates, disable the check box and enter the coordinates in the **X:**, **Y:**, and **Z:** text boxes.
- **Scale area.** The **Scale** area allows you to specify scale values for the block in relation to the X, Y, and Z axes. By default, the **Specify On-screen** check box is inactive. If the check box is inactive, you can enter scale values in the **X:**, **Y:**, and **Z:** text boxes. If you want to be prompted for the scale at the command line when inserting the block, activate the **Specify On-screen** check box.

  If you activate the **Uniform Scale** check box, you can simply specify a scale value for the X axis. The same value is then used for the Y and Z axes when the block is inserted. If the block was created with the **Scale uniformly** check box checked in the **Block Definition** dialog box, only the **X** value is active. The Y and Z coordinates also use this value so the block stays uniform.
- **Rotation area.** The **Rotation** area allows you to insert the block at a specified angle. By default, the **Specify On-screen** check box is inactive and the block is inserted at an angle of zero. If you want to use a different angle, enter a value in the **Angle:** text box. If you want to be prompted for the rotation angle at the command line when inserting the block, check the **Specify On-screen** check box.
- **Explode check box.** When a block is created, it is saved as a single object. Therefore, it is defined as a single object when inserted in the drawing, no matter how many objects were used to create the block. Activate the **Explode** check box if you wish to explode the block into its original objects for editing purposes. If you explode the block on insertion, it assumes its original properties, such as its original layer, color, and linetype. If **Allow exploding** was unchecked when the block was created, the **Explode** check box in the **Insert** dialog box is inactive.
- **Block Unit area.** This area displays information about the selected block. The **Unit:** text box indicates the units for the block. This is the value of the **INSUNIT** system variable. The **Factor:** text box indicates the scale factor based on the **INSUNIT** system variable. These text boxes are read-only.

When you pick the **OK** button, prompts appear for any values defined as **Specify On-screen** in the **Insert** dialog box. If you are specifying the insertion point on screen, the following prompt appears:

Specify insertion point or [Basepoint/Scale/X/Y/Z/Rotate/PScale/PX/PY/PZ/
    PRotate]: *(pick the point to insert the block)*

If you select one of the options, the new value overrides any setting in the **Insert** dialog box. The options allow you to specify a different base point, enter a value for the overall scale, enter independent scale factors for the X, Y, and Z axes, enter a rotation angle, and preview the scale of the X, Y, and Z axes or the rotation angle before entering actual values. The following prompt appears if you are specifying the X scale factor on screen:

Enter X scale factor, specify opposite corner, or [Corner/XYZ] <1>: *(pick a point or enter a value for the scale)*

Moving the cursor dynamically scales the block as it is dragged. If you want to scale the block visually, pick a point when the object appears correct. You can also use the **Corner** option to dynamically scale the block.

If you enter an X scale factor or press [Enter] to accept the default scale value, you are then prompted with the following:

Enter Y scale factor <use X scale factor>: *(enter a value or press [Enter] to accept the same scale specified for the X axis)*

The X and Y scale factors allow you to stretch or compress the block to suit your needs, **Figure 22-7.** This is why it is a good idea to draw blocks to fit inside a one-unit square. It makes the block easy to scale because you can enter the exact number of units for the X and Y dimensions. If you want the block to be three units long and two units high, respond with the following:

Enter X scale factor, specify opposite corner, or [Corner/XYZ] <1>: **3**↲
Enter Y scale factor <use X scale factor>: **2**↲

The base point that was specified to create the block may not always be the best point when inserting the block. Instead of inserting the block and then moving it, the **Basepoint** option can be used to specify a different base point before inserting the block. To use this option type B for **Basepoint** when prompted to specify the insertion point. The block is then temporarily placed on the screen. Pick the new desired base point for the block and then the block is reattached to the crosshairs at that point. A message appears on the command line indicating that the command is resuming and you are prompted to specify the insertion point.

PROFESSIONAL TIP

A block's rotation angle can be based on the current UCS. If you want to insert a block at a specific angle based on the current UCS or an existing UCS, be sure the proper UCS is active. Then insert the block and use a rotation angle of zero. If you decide to change the UCS later, any inserted blocks retain their original angle.

Figure 22-7.
A comparison of different X and Y scale factors used for inserting the PLATE block.

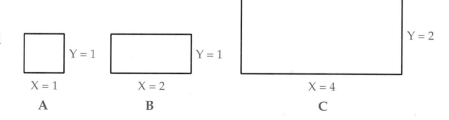

Block Scaling Options

It is possible to create a mirror image of a block by simply entering a negative value for the scale factor. For example, entering –1 for both the X scale factor and the Y scale factor mirrors the block to the opposite quadrant of the original orientation specified and retains the original size. Different mirroring techniques are shown in **Figure 22-8.** The insertion point is indicated by a dot.

In addition to the scaling options previously discussed, a block that is scaled during insertion can be classified as a *real block,* a *schematic block,* or a *unit block.* A **real block** is one that is drawn at a one-to-one scale. It is then inserted into the drawing using 1 for both the X and Y scale factors. Examples of real blocks could include a car design, a bolt, or a pipe fitting. See **Figure 22-9A.**

A **schematic block** is a block that is originally drawn at a one-to-one scale. It is then inserted into the drawing using the scale factor of the drawing for both the X and Y scale values. Examples of schematic blocks could include notes, detail bubbles, or section symbols. See **Figure 22-9B.**

A **unit block** is also originally drawn at a one-to-one scale. There are three different types of unit blocks. One example of a **1D unit block** is a 1″ line object that is turned into a block. A **2D unit block** is any object that can fit inside a 1″ × 1″ square. A **3D unit block** is any object that can fit inside a 1″ cube. To use a unit block, insert the block and determine the individual scale factors for each axis. For example, a 1D unit block could be inserted at a scale of 4, which would turn the line into a 4″ line. A 2D unit block could be assigned different scale factors for the X and Y axes, such as 48 for the X axis and 72 for the Y axis. See **Figure 22-9C.** A 3D unit block could be inserted at different scales for the X, Y, and Z axes.

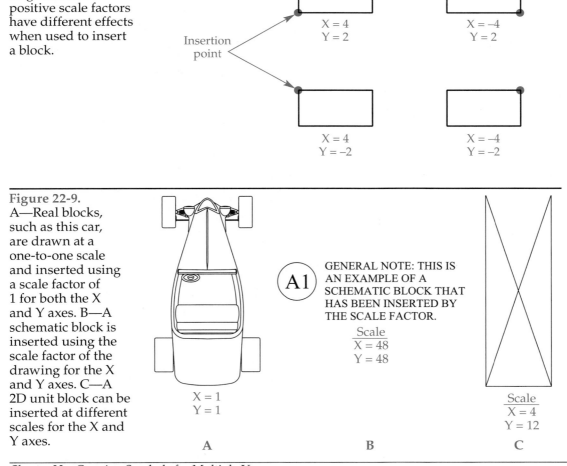

Figure 22-8.
Negative and positive scale factors have different effects when used to insert a block.

Insertion point

X = 4
Y = 2

X = –4
Y = 2

X = 4
Y = –2

X = –4
Y = –2

Figure 22-9.
A—Real blocks, such as this car, are drawn at a one-to-one scale and inserted using a scale factor of 1 for both the X and Y axes. B—A schematic block is inserted using the scale factor of the drawing for the X and Y axes. C—A 2D unit block can be inserted at different scales for the X and Y axes.

X = 1
Y = 1

A

A1 GENERAL NOTE: THIS IS AN EXAMPLE OF A SCHEMATIC BLOCK THAT HAS BEEN INSERTED BY THE SCALE FACTOR.

Scale
X = 48
Y = 48

B

Scale
X = 4
Y = 12

C

Changing the Layer, Color, and Linetype of a Block

If you insert a block on the wrong layer or if you wish to change the color or line-type properties of the block, you can use the **Properties** window to modify it. Select the block to modify and its properties are listed. See **Figure 22-10**. Notice that Block Reference is specified in the drop-down list. You can now modify the selected block.

To modify the layer of the selected block, pick **Layer** in the **General** category of the **Properties** window. A drop-down arrow appears allowing you to access the layer you want to use for the block. Once the new layer has been selected, pick the close button (**X**) at the upper-right corner of the **Properties** window to close the window. The block is now changed to the proper layer.

You may also want to change the color or linetype of a block. This can be done if the block was originally created on layer 0 and the color/linetype properties were set up as ByLayer. If the block was originally created on layer 0, it will assume the color and linetype of the current layer when it is inserted. If it was created on another layer, it will retain its original color and linetype.

If you wish to change the color or linetype of an inserted block, you can access the **Properties** window and select the corresponding property in the **General** section after selecting the block. Select the desired color or linetype from the corresponding drop-down list.

PROFESSIONAL TIP

If you want to change the properties of several blocks, you can use the **Quick Select** dialog box to create a selection set of block reference objects. Once the blocks are selected, change the properties using the **Properties** window or **Object Properties** toolbar. The **Quick Select** dialog box is discussed in Chapter 12.

Figure 22-10.
The **Properties** window allows you to change the layer, color, linetype, and other properties of a block.

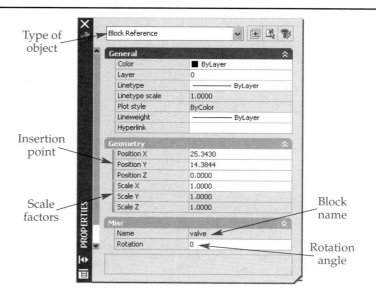

Type of object

Insertion point

Scale factors

Block name

Rotation angle

Inserting Multiple Copies of a Block

The features of the **INSERT** and **ARRAY** commands are combined using the **MINSERT** (multiple insert) command. This method of inserting and arraying blocks saves time and disk space. Type MINSERT to access the **MINSERT** command.

An example of an application using the **MINSERT** command is the arrangement of desks on a drawing. Suppose you want to draw the layout shown in **Figure 22-11**. First, specify architectural units and set the limits to 30′,22′. Draw a 4′ × 3′ rectangle and save it as a block named DESK. The arrangement is to be three rows and four columns. Make the horizontal spacing between desks 2′, and the vertical spacing 4′. Use the following command sequence:

> Command: **MINSERT**↵
> Enter block name or [?]: <*current*>: **DESK**↵
> Units: Inches   Conversion: 0′-1″
> Specify insertion point or [Basepoint/Scale/X/Y/Z/Rotate/PScale/PX/PY/PZ/
>   PRotate]: (*pick a point*)
> Enter X scale factor, specify opposite corner, or [Corner/XYZ] <1>: ↵
> Enter Y scale factor <use X scale factor>: ↵
> Specify rotation angle <0>: ↵
> Enter number of rows (- - -) <1>: **3**↵
> Enter number of columns (|||) <1>: **4**↵
> Enter distance between rows or specify unit cell (- - -): **7′**↵
> Specify distance between columns (|||): **6′**↵

The resulting arrangement is shown in **Figure 22-11**. The complete pattern takes on the characteristics of a block, except that an array created with the **MINSERT** command cannot be exploded. Since the array cannot be exploded, you must use the **Properties** window to modify the number of rows and columns, change the spacing between objects, or change the layer, color, or linetype properties. If the initial block is rotated, all arrayed objects are also rotated about their insertion points. If the arrayed objects are rotated about the insertion point while using the **MINSERT** command, all objects are aligned on that point.

Figure 22-11.
Creating an arrangement of desks using the **MINSERT** command.

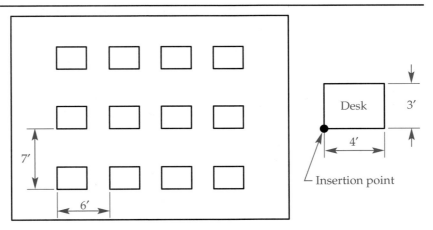

Exercise 22-3   Complete the Exercise on the Student CD.

Inserting Entire Drawings

In addition to blocks and wblocks, the **INSERT** command can be used to insert an entire drawing file into the current drawing. To do so, type INSERT and pick the **Browse…** button in the **Insert** dialog box to access the **Select Drawing File** dialog box. You can then select a drawing file to insert, as discussed earlier in this chapter.

When one drawing is inserted into another, the inserted drawing becomes a block reference. As a block, it may be moved to a new location with a single pick. The drawing is inserted on the current layer, but it does not inherit the color, linetype, or thickness properties of that layer. You can explode the inserted drawing back to its original objects if desired. Once exploded, the drawing objects revert to their original layers. A drawing that is inserted brings any existing block definitions, layers, linetypes, text styles, and dimension styles into the current drawing.

By default, every drawing has an insertion point of 0,0,0. This is the insertion point used for a drawing file when you insert it into the current drawing. If you want to change the insertion point of the drawing, use the **BASE** command. Pick **Draw > Block > Base** or type BASE, and select a new insertion point. The new base point now becomes the insertion point for the drawing. Save the drawing before inserting it into another drawing.

BASE

Type
BASE

Pull-Down Menu

Draw
  > Block
    > Base

Exercise 22-4

Complete the Exercise on the Student CD.

Using DesignCenter to Insert Blocks

DesignCenter is a dockable window that allows you to readily locate and preview blocks or drawing files before they are inserted into a drawing. You can insert blocks or entire drawings into your current drawing using the drag-and-drop capability of **DesignCenter**. You can also browse through existing drawings for blocks, show images of blocks and drawings, and display other information about saved blocks or files.

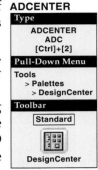

To access **DesignCenter**, pick the **DesignCenter** button on the **Standard** toolbar, pick **Tools** > **Palettes** > **DesignCenter**, type ADC or ADCENTER, or use the [Ctrl]+[2] key combination. When **DesignCenter** opens, it displays the content that was last selected in it.

The **Folders** tab shows the hierarchy of files and folders on your computer, including network drives. Navigating in the tree view is similar to using Windows Explorer. The **Open Drawings** tab displays all of the drawing files open in the current AutoCAD session. The **History** tab displays the most recently accessed files in **DesignCenter**. The **DC Online** tab gives you access to drawing content that can be downloaded from the Internet. See **Figure 22-12**.

To view the blocks contained within a drawing, select the **Blocks** branch in the tree view or double-click on the **Blocks** icon in the content area. Once the desired block has been found, you can use a drag-and-drop operation or the **Insert** dialog box to insert it into the current drawing.

To use the drag-and-drop method, move the cursor over the top of the block in the content area, press and hold down the pick button and drag the cursor to the drawing editor. Release the pick button and the block is inserted into the drawing where the cursor is located. The block is inserted based on the type of block units specified when the block was created. For example, if the original block was a 1 × 1 square and the block units were specified as feet when the block was created, then the block will be a 12″ × 12″ square when it is inserted from **DesignCenter**.

Figure 22-12.
DesignCenter Online provides many sources for blocks and other drawing content.

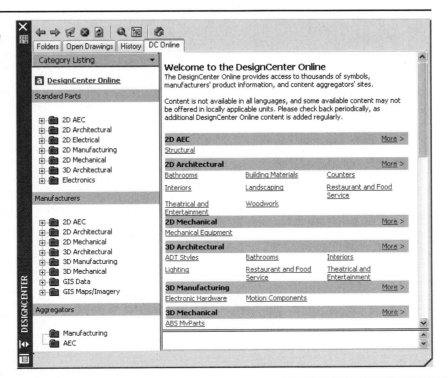

To use the **Insert** dialog box while inserting a block from **DesignCenter**, right-click on the block icon in the content area to display the shortcut menu. Then, select **Insert Block...** from the shortcut menu to activate the **INSERT** command. This allows you to scale, rotate, or explode the block during insertion.

To insert an entire drawing using **DesignCenter**, select the folder in the tree view that contains the drawing. Any drawings in the selected folder appear in the content area. Drag-and-drop the desired drawing into the current drawing. You can also right-click on a drawing icon in the content area and select **Insert as Block...** from the shortcut menu.

PROFESSIONAL TIP In addition to blocks and drawings, **DesignCenter** can be used to insert dimension styles, layers, layouts, linetypes, table styles, text styles, and external references.

Using the Tool Palettes Window to Insert Blocks

TOOLPALETTES

Type
TOOLPALETTES TP [Ctrl]+[3]
Pull-Down Menu
Tools > Palettes > Tool Palettes Window
Toolbar
Standard
Tool Palettes Window

The **Tool Palettes** window is a dockable window that provides another quick way to access blocks for insertion into a drawing. This feature is similar to **DesignCenter** in the way that blocks can be previewed before inserting them. To open the **Tool Palettes** window, pick the **Tool Palettes Window** button on the **Standard** toolbar, pick **Tools** > **Palettes** > **Tool Palettes**, type TP or TOOLPALETTES, or use the [Ctrl]+[3] key combination. The **Tool Palettes** window is shown in **Figure 22-13.** The window is divided into tool palettes, each indicated by a tab along the side of the window. The tool palettes are used to store blocks, hatch patterns, and commands.

To insert a block from the **Tool Palettes** window, select the tool palette tab in which the block resides and locate the block. Use the scroll bar on the side of the window to move up or down in the tool palette, if needed. When the block is located, place the cursor over the block icon. Help text appears next to the cursor describing the block, if the block contains a description. You can use the drag-and-drop method to insert the block, or you can pick once on the block icon. Then, move the cursor into the drawing area and pick again to place the block. With either method, the block is attached to

Figure 22-13.
The **Tool Palettes** window. Blocks may be inserted into the current drawing from a selected tab.

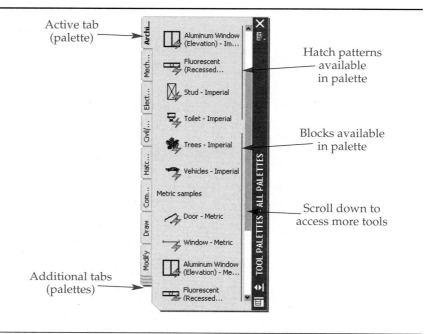

the crosshairs once the cursor is moved into the drawing area. The location where the crosshairs and the block are connected is defined by the insertion point of the block.

When inserting a block with the "pick-pick" method, you can access scaling and rotation options for the block on the command line before picking an insertion point. Enter **S** to scale the block along the XYZ axes or **R** to specify a rotation angle for the block. Blocks inserted from tool palettes are automatically scaled based on a ratio of the current drawing scale to the scale used in the original block definition.

Exercise 22-5   Complete the Exercise on the Student CD.

Editing Blocks

A block inserting in a drawing is edited as if it were a single object. That is, an inserted block be moved, rotated, copied, and mirrored. However, the separate objects within the block cannot be modified directly. In order to modify the block, you must use the **Block Editor**, or you must explode the block. These methods are discussed in the following sections.

Using the Block Editor

You can edit a block in-place by using the **BEDIT** command. This command is accessed by typing BEDIT, picking the **Block Editor** button on the **Standard** toolbar, or by picking **Tools > Block Editor** from the pull-down menu. Once you activate the **BEDIT** command, the **Edit Block Definition** dialog box appears. See **Figure 22-14**.

To edit an existing block, select the name of the block from the list of blocks. A preview and the description of the selected block are shown. A new block can be created by typing a name for the new block in the **Block to create or edit** field. Then, pick the **OK** button to open the selected block (or new block) in the **Block Editor**. See **Figure 22-15**.

The **Block Editor** consists of the **Block Editor** toolbar, the **Block Authoring Palettes** window, and the drawing area in block edit mode (indicated by a different background color). If a block was selected for editing, it is displayed in the drawing area. If a new block name was entered, the drawing area is empty so the new block can be created. All other objects in the drawing are hidden.

BEDIT
Type
  BEDIT
Pull-Down Menu
Tools
  > Block Editor
Toolbar
  Standard
  Block Editor

Figure 22-14.
The **Edit Block Definition** dialog box.

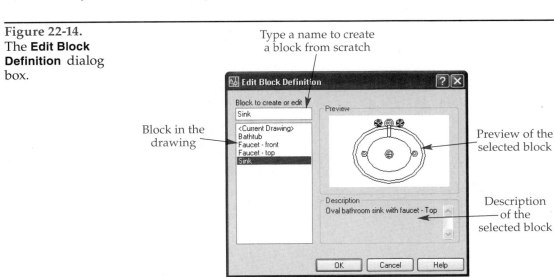

Type a name to create a block from scratch

Block in the drawing

Preview of the selected block

Description of the selected block

Figure 22-15.
When in block editing mode, the **Block Editor** toolbar and the **Block Authoring Palettes** window are available. The background of the drawing area in the **Block Editor** is, by default, tan.

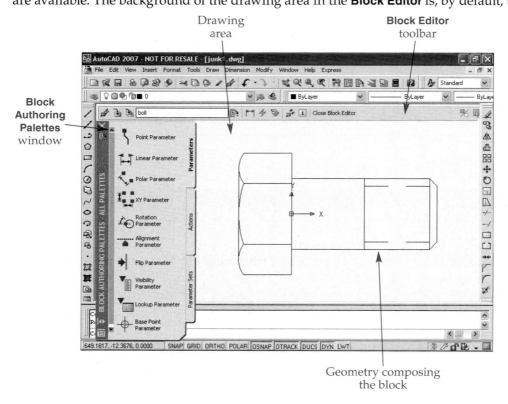

Use drawing and editing commands to create or modify the block. Some commands are not available in the **Block Editor**. When you have finished editing, close the **Block Editor**.

To exit block editing mode and return to the drawing, pick the **Close Block Editor** button on the **Block Editor** toolbar or type BCLOSE. If changes have not been saved, a dialog box appears asking if you wish to save the changes. Pick **Yes** to save the changes, **No** to discard the changes, or **Cancel** to return to block editing mode.

The commands in the **Block Editor** toolbar are used to create blocks and block geometry. Refer to **Figure 22-16.** The following describes the buttons at the left side of the toolbar:

- **Edit or Create Block Definition.** Opens the **Edit Block Definition** dialog box, which is the same dialog box displayed when entering block editing mode. You can select a different block to edit or specify the name of a new one to create from scratch.
- **Save Block Definition.** Saves the changes and updates the block.
- **Save Block As.** Opens the **Save Block As** dialog box. This dialog box allows you to save a copy of the current block under a different name.
- **Block definition name.** This label displays the name of the current block being edited.
- **Authoring Palettes.** Toggles the **Block Authoring Palettes** window off and on.

The remaining buttons in the **Block Editor** toolbar are discussed in Chapters 23 and 24.

Figure 22-16.
The **Block Editor** toolbar is displayed in the **Block Editor**.

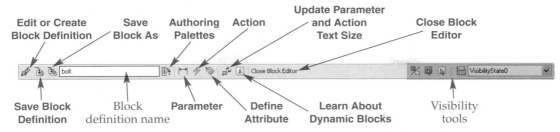

PROFESSIONAL
TIP

A block can be opened directly in the **Block Editor** by right-clicking on the block in the drawing and selecting **Block Editor** from the shortcut menu. A block can also be opened directly in the **Block Editor** when it is created by checking the **Open in block editor** check box in the **Block Definition** dialog box.

Adding a Block Description within Block Editor

You are able to add a description to a block in the **Block Definition** dialog box when the block is created. This description can be changed in the **Block Editor**. To modify a description, open the **Block Editor** and open the **Properties** window with no objects selected. In the **Properties** window, scroll down to the **Block** category and find the **Description** property. Make any changes to the description here. Pick the **Save Block Definition** button and the **Close Block Editor** button to return to the drawing.

Exercise 22-6   Complete the Exercise on the Student CD.

Exploding a Block

As previously discussed, you can explode a block as it is inserted using the **Insert** dialog box. This is useful when you want to edit the individual objects of the block. You can also use the **EXPLODE** command after the block is inserted to break it apart into its individual objects.

The **EXPLODE** command is used to break apart any existing block, polyline, or dimension. To access this command, pick the **Explode** button on the **Modify** toolbar, pick **Modify > Explode**, or type X or EXPLODE. Once the command is activated, you are prompted to select objects. When done selecting objects, press [Enter] to explode them.

When a block is exploded, its component objects are quickly redrawn. The individual objects can then be edited individually. To see if the **EXPLODE** command worked properly, select any object that was formerly part of the block. Only that object should be highlighted. If so, the block was exploded properly.

EXPLODE

Type
EXPLODE
X

Pull-Down Menu
Modify
> Explode

Toolbar
Modify
Explode

Redefining Existing Blocks

As you have seen, one way to edit a block is to use the **BEDIT** command. Once the block is modified and the changes saved, all instances of that block in the drawing are also updated. This can also be accomplished by what is referred to as *redefining a block* by using the **EXPLODE** and **BLOCK** commands together. To redefine an existing block, follow this procedure:

1. Insert the block to be redefined anywhere in your drawing.
2. Make sure you know where the insertion point of the block is located.
3. Explode the inserted block using the **EXPLODE** command.
4. Edit the components of the block as needed.
5. Recreate the block definition using the **BLOCK** command.
6. Give the block the same name and insertion point as it originally had.
7. Select the objects to be included in the block.
8. Pick **OK** in the **Block Definition** dialog box to save the block. When a message from AutoCAD appears and asks if you want to redefine the block, pick **Yes**.
9. When the **BLOCK** command is complete, all insertions of the block are updated.

A common mistake is to forget to use the **EXPLODE** command before redefining the block. When you try to create the block again with the same name, an alert box indicating the block references itself is displayed. This means you are trying to create a block that already exists. Once you press the **OK** button, the alert box disappears and the **Block Definition** dialog box is redisplayed. Press the **Cancel** button, explode the block to be redefined, and try again.

Understanding the Circular Reference Error

As described in the previous example, when you try to redefine a block that already exists using the same name, AutoCAD informs you that the block references itself or that it has not been modified. The concept of a block *referencing itself* may be a little difficult to grasp at first without fully understanding how AutoCAD works with blocks. A block can be composed of any objects, including other blocks. When using the **BLOCK** command to incorporate an existing block into a new block, AutoCAD must make a list of all the objects that compose the new block. This means AutoCAD must refer to any existing block definitions that are selected to be part of the new block. If you select an instance, or reference, of the block being redefined as a component object for the new definition, a problem occurs. You are trying to redefine a block name using a previous version of the block with the same name. In other words, the new block refers to a block of the same name, or *references itself*.

For example, assume you create a block named BOX that is composed of four line objects in the shape of a square. You insert the block and then decide it needs to be changed; a small circle must be added in the lower-left corner of the square. If the original BOX block is exploded, all that is left are the four line objects. After drawing the required circle, you can enter the **BLOCK** command and recreate a block named BOX by selecting the four lines and the circle as the component objects. Redefining a block destroys the old definition and creates a new one. Any blocks with the same

Figure 22-17.
A—The correct procedure for redefining a block. B—Redefining a block that has not first been exploded creates an invalid circular reference.

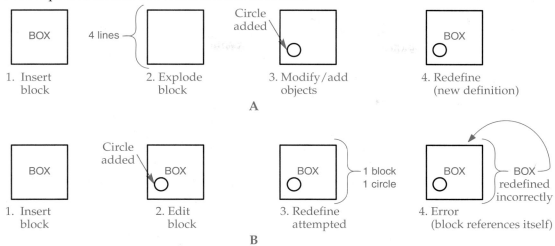

A

B

name are redefined with the updated changes. Make sure you want to redefine the block before agreeing to do so. Otherwise, give the block a new name. The correct way to redefine a block is shown in **Figure 22-17A.**

Alternately, assume you do not explode the block, but still draw the circle and try to redefine the block. By selecting the BOX block *and* the circle, a new block named BOX would now be a block reference of the BOX block with a circle. The old block definition of BOX has not been destroyed, but a new definition has been attempted. Thus, AutoCAD is trying to define a new block named BOX by using an instance of the BOX block. This is referred to as a *circular reference* and is what is meant by a block referencing itself. Refer to **Figure 22-17B.**

Creating a Block from a Drawing File

You can create a block from any existing drawing. This allows you to avoid redrawing the object as a block, thus saving time. Remember, if something has already been drawn, try to use it as a block rather than redrawing it.

To define a block named BOLT from an existing drawing file named fastener.dwg, enter the **INSERT** command and use the **Browse...** button to select the fastener.dwg file. The selected file is then displayed in the **Name:** text box. Use this text box to change the name from fastener to BOLT and pick **OK**. The file can be inserted into the drawing or you can press the [Esc] key to exit the command. A block named BOLT has now been created from the file and can be used as desired.

Exercise
22-7   Complete the Exercise on the Student CD.

Blocks created with the **BLOCK** command are stored in the drawing in which they are made. The **WBLOCK** (write block) command allows you to create a drawing (DWG) file out of a block. You can also use the **WBLOCK** command to create a global block from any object (it does not have to be previously saved as a block). The resulting drawing file can then be inserted as a block into any drawing.

There are several ways to use the **WBLOCK** command. To see how the first method works, open drawing ex22-1. You will convert the CIRCLE block contained within this drawing to a permanent block by making it in a separate drawing file. The first step is to open the **Write Block** dialog box by typing WBLOCK. This dialog box is similar to the **Block Definition** dialog box, **Figure 22-18**.

In the **Source** area, pick the **Block:** radio button and then select the CIRCLE block from the drop-down list. In the **Destination** area, specify the name and location for the wblock in the **File name and path:** text box. By default, the new drawing file has the same name as the block. This is shown with the folder path in the **File name and path:** text box in **Figure 22-18**. Picking the ellipsis (...) button next to the text box displays the **Browse for Drawing File** dialog box. Navigate to the folder where you want to save the file, confirm the name of the file in the **File name:** text box, and then pick the **Save** button. The **Write Block** dialog box is redisplayed with the path and file name shown in the **File name and path:** text box. Next, select the type of units that **DesignCenter** will use to insert the block in the **Insert units:** drop-down list. This is also located in the **Destination** area.

When you are finished, pick **OK**. The block is saved as a wblock in the folder you specified. Now, you can use the **INSERT** command in any drawing to insert the CIRCLE block.

Creating a New Wblock

Suppose you want to create a wblock from a shape you have just drawn, but you have not yet made a block. The following sequence is used to save a selected object as a drawing file. Refer to **Figure 22-19**.

Figure 22-18.
Using the **Write Block** dialog box to create a wblock from an existing block.

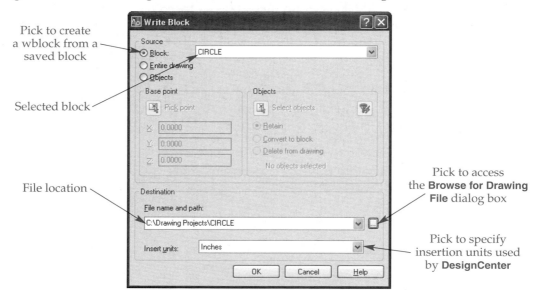

Pick to create a wblock from a saved block

Selected block

File location

Pick to access the **Browse for Drawing File** dialog box

Pick to specify insertion units used by **DesignCenter**

Figure 22-19.
Using the **Write Block** dialog box to create a wblock from selected objects without first defining a block.

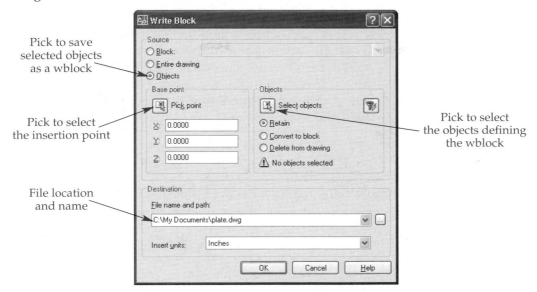

First, enter the **WBLOCK** command and select the **Objects** radio button in the **Write Block** dialog box (it is active by default). Next, pick the **Select objects** button. The dialog box is hidden to allow you to select the objects for the drawing file. Press [Enter] when done selecting objects to redisplay the **Write Block** dialog box.

Next, pick the **Pick point** button to select the insertion point. Again, the dialog box is hidden to allow you to select an insertion point. Once you pick a point, the dialog box is redisplayed. You can also enter coordinates of the insertion point in the **X:**, **Y:**, and **Z:** text boxes instead of picking a point onscreen. Also, specify a path and file name for the block in the **File name and path:** text box.

Finally, select the type of units that **DesignCenter** will use to insert the block in the **Insert units:** drop-down list. Then, pick the **OK** button to create the wblock.

This sequence is the same as that used with the **BLOCK** command. However, the wblock is saved to disk as a drawing file, *not* as a block in the current drawing. Be sure to specify the correct file path in the **File name and path:** text box when using the **Write Block** dialog box. A drawing file named desk that is to be saved in the blocks folder on the c: hard drive, for example, would be saved as c:\blocks\desk.

Storing a Drawing as a Wblock

An entire drawing can also be stored as a wblock. To do this, pick the **Entire drawing** radio button in the **Write Block** dialog box. Specify the name and location to save the wblock using the **File name and path:** text box. Select the type of units **DesignCenter** will use to insert the block in the **Insert units:** drop-down list. Then, pick **OK** when you are through.

In this case, the whole drawing is saved to disk as if you had used the **SAVE** command. However, all unused blocks are deleted from the drawing. If the drawing contains any unused blocks, this method may reduce the size of a drawing considerably.

Using the **Entire drawing** wblock option is a good way to remove unused named objects to reduce the file size. Use this routine when you have completed a drawing and decide the unused blocks, layers, styles, and other unused objects are no longer needed. The **PURGE** command can also be used to remove any unused objects. The process is slower than using the **Entire drawing** wblock option. The **PURGE** command is discussed later in this chapter.

Exercise
22-8   Complete the Exercise on the Student CD.

Revising an Inserted Drawing

You may find that you need to revise a drawing file that has been used in other drawings. If this happens, you can quickly update any drawing in which the revised drawing is used. For example, if a drawing file named pump was modified after being used several times in a drawing, simply enter the **INSERT** command and access the original drawing file with the **Select Drawing File** dialog box. Then, activate the **Specify On-screen** check box in the **Insertion point** area and pick **OK**. When a message from AutoCAD appears and asks if you want to redefine the block, pick **Yes**. All of the pump references are automatically updated. Next, press the [Esc] key. By canceling the command, no new insertions of the pump drawing are made.

If you work on projects in which inserted drawings may be revised, it may be more productive to use reference drawings instead of inserted drawing files. Reference drawings are used with the **XREF** command, which is discussed in Chapter 25. All referenced drawings are automatically updated when a drawing file that contains the externally referenced material is loaded into AutoCAD.

Symbol Libraries

As you become proficient with AutoCAD, you will want to start constructing symbol libraries. A *symbol library* is a collection of related shapes, views, symbols, and other content used repeatedly in drawings. Arranging a storage system for frequently used symbols increases productivity and saves time. First, you need to establish how the symbols are stored (as blocks or drawing files) and then determine where they will be stored for insertion into different drawings.

Blocks versus Separate Drawing Files

As discussed earlier, the **BLOCK** command saves a block with the drawing in which it is created and the **WBLOCK** command saves the block as a separate drawing file. There are two basic options for a symbol library: saving all blocks within a single drawing or saving each block to a separate file (wblock). If you decide to have one drawing that contains all blocks, each person in the office or classroom must have access to that drawing. This is often done by creating the blocks in a template file or a separate drawing file. If individual drawing files (wblocks) are used, each student or employee must have access to the files.

Creating a Symbol Library

Once a set of related block definitions is created, you can arrange the blocks in a symbol library. Each block should be identified with a name and insertion point location. Whether the symbols are being stored in a single drawing file or as individual files, several guidelines can be used to create the symbol library:
- Assign one person to initially create the symbols for each specialty.
- Follow school or company symbol standards.
- When saving multiple blocks in a drawing file, save one group of symbols per drawing file. When using wblocks, name the drawing files accordingly so they can be assigned to separate folders on the hard drive. For example, you may want to create several different symbol libraries based on the following types of symbols: electronic, electrical, piping, mechanical, structural, architectural, landscaping, and mapping.
- Print a hard copy of the symbol library. Include a representation of each symbol, its insertion point, where it is located, and any other necessary information. A sample is shown in **Figure 22-20.** Provide all users of the symbols with a copy of the listing.
- If a network is not in use, place the symbol library file(s) on each workstation in the classroom or office.
- Keep backup copies of all files in a secure place.
- When symbols are revised, update all files containing the edited symbols.
- Inform all users of any changes to saved symbols.

Storing Symbol Drawings

The local or network hard drive is one of the best places to store a symbol library. It is easily accessed, quick, and more convenient to use than portable media. Recordable CDs or other removable media can be used for backup purposes if a network drive with an automatic backup function is not available. In the absence of a network or modem, removable media can also be used to transport files from one workstation to another.

There are several methods of storing symbols on the hard drive. Symbols can be saved as wblocks and organized within folders. It is recommended to store symbols outside of the AutoCAD folder. This will keep the system folder uncluttered and allow you to differentiate which folders and files were originally installed with AutoCAD. A good idea is to create a \Blocks folder for storing your blocks, as shown in **Figure 22-21.**

If multiple symbols are saved within a drawing, they can be inserted using **DesignCenter** or the **Tool Palettes** window. When using this system, several drawing files may be used to group similar symbols. For example, electrical symbols can be saved in an electrical.dwg drawing and piping symbols can be saved in a piping.dwg drawing. Limit the number of symbols within a drawing to a reasonable amount so the symbols can be found relatively easily. If there are too many blocks within a drawing, it may be difficult to locate the desired symbol.

Figure 22-20.
A printed copy of piping flow diagram blocks stored in a symbol library. Each colored dot indicates the insertion point and is not part of the block.

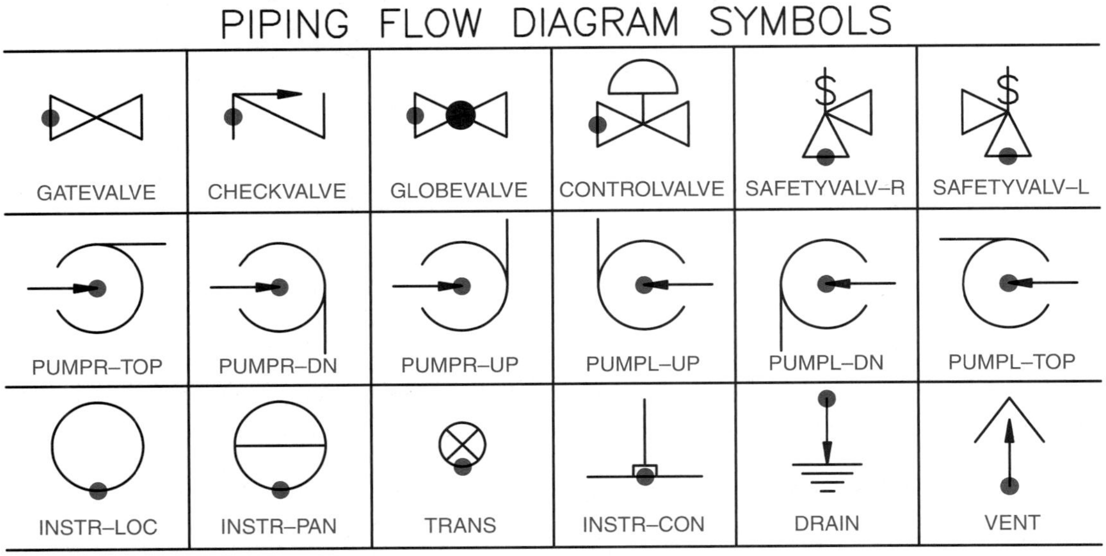

PIPING FLOW DIAGRAM SYMBOLS

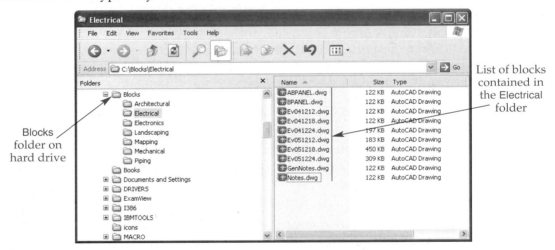

GATEVALVE	CHECKVALVE	GLOBEVALVE	CONTROLVALVE	SAFETYVALV–R	SAFETYVALV–L
PUMPR–TOP	PUMPR–DN	PUMPR–UP	PUMPL–UP	PUMPL–DN	PUMPL–TOP
INSTR–LOC	INSTR–PAN	TRANS	INSTR–CON	DRAIN	VENT

Figure 22-21.
An efficient way to store blocks saved as drawing files is to set up a Blocks folder containing folders for each type of symbol on the hard drive.

Blocks folder on hard drive

List of blocks contained in the Electrical folder

Drawing files saved on the hard drive should be arranged in a logical manner. The following guidelines apply:

- All workstations in the classroom or office should have folders with the same names.
- One person should be assigned to update and copy symbol libraries to all workstations.
- Drawing files should be copied onto each workstation from a master CD or network drive.
- The master and backup versions of the symbol libraries should be kept in separate locations.

Renaming Blocks

RENAME

Type
RENAME
REN

Pull-Down Menu
Format
> Rename...

Blocks can be renamed using the **RENAME** command. Access this command by picking **Format** > **Rename...** in the pull-down menu or typing REN or RENAME. This displays the **Rename** dialog box, Figure 22-22.

To change the name of the CIRCLE block to HOLE, select Blocks from the **Named Objects** list. A list of block names defined in the current drawing then appears in the **Items** list. Highlight CIRCLE in the list. When this name appears in the **Old Name:** text box, type the new block name HOLE in the **Rename To:** text box. Pick the **Rename To:** button and the new block name appears in the **Items** list. Pick **OK** to exit the **Rename** dialog box.

Figure 22-22.
The **Rename** dialog box allows you to change the name of a block and other named objects.

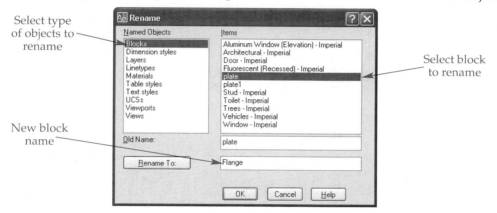

Deleting Named Objects

As discussed earlier, a block is a named object. In many drawing sessions, not all of the named objects defined within a drawing are used. For example, your drawing may contain several layers, text styles, and blocks that are not used. Since these objects increase the drawing file size, it is good practice to delete or *purge* the unused objects from the drawing. The **PURGE** command is used to do this.

PURGE

Type
PURGE
PU

Pull-Down Menu
File
> Drawing Utilities
> Purge...

To access the **PURGE** command, pick **File** > **Drawing Utilities** > **Purge...** from the pull-down menu or type PU or PURGE. The **Purge** dialog box is displayed, Figure 22-23. Select the appropriate radio button at the top of the dialog box to view content that can be purged or to view content that cannot be purged.

Before purging, select the **Confirm each item to be purged** check box to have an opportunity to review each item before it is deleted. If you wish to purge nested items, check the **Purge nested items** check box.

If you want to purge only some items, use the tree view to locate and highlight the items, and then pick the **Purge** button. If you want to purge all unused items, pick the **Purge All** button. Purging may make other named objects unreferenced. Thus, you may need to purge more than once to completely purge the drawing of unused named objects.

Figure 22-23.
The **Purge** dialog box.

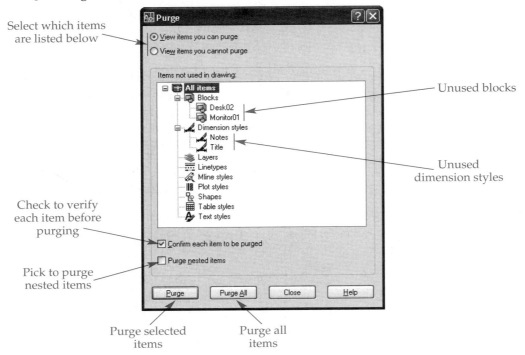

Select which items
are listed below

Unused blocks

Unused
dimension styles

Check to verify
each item before
purging

Pick to purge
nested items

Purge selected
items

Purge all
items

Adding Blocks to Tool Palettes

The **Tool Palettes** window was introduced in Chapter 21. There are four palettes provided in the **Tool Palettes** window that contain block insertion tools—**Architectural**, **Civil/Structural**, **Electrical**, and **Mechanical**. These palettes provide some useful tools for inserting blocks. The blocks can be inserted into a drawing by dragging them from the palette and dropping them into the drawing. However, you can quickly create your own tool palettes and assign block insertion tools to them. Tool palette customization is covered in detail in *AutoCAD and Its Applications—Advanced.*

To create a new, blank tool palette, right-click on the **Tool Palettes** window title bar or in a blank area of a tool palette. Select **New Tool Palette** from the shortcut menu. The new tool palette is added and a text box appears with the default name highlighted. Enter a name for the palette and press [Enter]. Choose a name that identifies the contents of the palette.

One of two methods can be used to add block insertion tools to a new or existing palette. If the blocks are located in a file on the hard drive, you can use **DesignCenter** to locate the file and access the blocks. If the blocks you want to add are displayed in the current drawing, you can drag and drop them into the desired palette.

Using DesignCenter to Create a Palette of Blocks

To create a new palette that contains block insertion tools for all of the blocks within a single drawing file, open **DesignCenter**. Navigate to the drawing and right-click on the drawing file name in the **Folders** tab. Then, select **Create Tool Palette** from the shortcut menu. See **Figure 22-24**. In the example shown, a new palette is created from the Analog Integrated Circuits drawing file. The resulting palette contains block insertion tools for all of the blocks within the file and has the same name as the file. A palette can also be created in this manner by expanding the contents of a drawing file

Figure 22-24.
Right-clicking on a drawing name in **DesignCenter** and selecting **Create Tool Palette** creates a new palette in the **Tool Palettes** window with the name of the drawing file. All of the blocks defined in the drawing become block insertion tools in the palette.

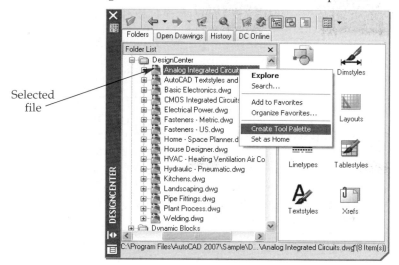

Selected file

in the **Folder List** area and right-clicking on the **Blocks** item in either the **Folder List** area or the content area. When the shortcut menu appears, select **Create Tool Palette**.

Individual block insertion tools can be added to a tool palette from selected blocks in a drawing file by using **DesignCenter**. First, navigate to the drawing file and expand its branch in the **Folder List** of the **Folders** tab. Select the **Blocks** branch so the blocks within the drawing are displayed in the content area. Then, open the **Tool Palettes** window and display the tool palette where you want the block insertion tools. Finally, drag each block from the content area of **DesignCenter** and drop it onto the tool palette. To create a new palette containing a block insertion tool for a single block, right-click on the block in the content area of **DesignCenter** and select **Create Tool Palette** from the shortcut menu. You are then prompted for a new name for the palette.

A block insertion tool of an entire drawing file can be added to a tool palette from **DesignCenter**. First, navigate to the folder that contains the drawing file. Then, select the file in the content area, drag it to the tool palette, and drop it onto the palette. When the new tool is used to insert the drawing file into a drawing, the inserted drawing becomes a block within the current drawing.

A single tool palette can be created that contains block insertion tools for all of the blocks within all of the drawing files in a folder. First, navigate to the folder in the **Folder List** area of **DesignCenter**. Next, right-click on the folder and select **Create Tool Palette of Blocks** from the shortcut menu. A new palette is created in the **Tool Palettes** window with the same name as the folder. This palette contains block insertion tools for all of the blocks contained within all of the drawings in the selected folder.

NOTE

A block that has been added to a tool palette as a block insertion tool is directly linked to the drawing file in which the block resides. If the block has been modified in the source file, inserting it from a tool palette inserts the updated block.

From the Current Drawing

A block in the current drawing can be added to a tool palette as a block insertion tool. Open the **Tool Palettes** window and select the tool palette where the block insertion tool is to be located. Next, pick the block once in the drawing to display grips. The **PICKFIRST** system variable must be set to 1. Then, pick and hold on the block anywhere except on a grip, drag it onto the tool palette, and drop the block. Do not pick the grip of the block for this step. If you pick the block grip, AutoCAD thinks you are trying to move the block in the drawing area.

> **NOTE**
>
> Tool palettes can be used to store many different types of drawing content and tools, such as AutoCAD drawing and editing commands, custom commands, and AutoLISP routines. Examples of command tools are provided in the **Command Tools** tool palette. For a detailed discussion on tool palette customization, refer to *AutoCAD and Its Applications—Advanced.*

Exercise 22-9 Complete the Exercise on the Student CD.

Chapter Test

Answer the following questions. Write your answers on a separate sheet of paper or complete the electronic chapter test on the Student CD.

1. Define *symbol library.*
2. Which color and linetype settings should be used if you want a block to assume the current color and linetype when it is inserted into a drawing?
3. When should a block be drawn to fit inside a one-unit square, and what type of block is this called when it is inserted?
4. A block name cannot exceed _____ characters.
5. What are two ways to access a listing of all blocks in the current drawing?
6. Define the term *nesting* in relation to blocks.
7. How do you preset block insertion variables using the **Insert** dialog box?
8. Describe the effect of entering negative scale factors when inserting a block.
9. What properties do blocks drawn on a layer other than layer 0 assume when inserted?
10. Why would you draw blocks on layer 0?
11. What is a limitation of an array pattern created with the **MINSERT** command?
12. What is the purpose of the **BASE** command?
13. Identify the two methods that allow you to break an inserted block into its individual objects for editing purposes.
14. Suppose you have found that a block was incorrectly drawn. Unfortunately, you have already inserted the block 30 times. How can you edit all of the blocks quickly?
15. What is the primary difference between blocks created with the **BLOCK** and **WBLOCK** commands?

16. Explain two ways to remove all unused blocks from a drawing.
17. What advantage is offered by having a symbol library of blocks in a single drawing, rather than using wblocks?
18. What is the purpose of the **PURGE** command?
19. Identify two ways to add block insertion tools to tool palettes.
20. How can you create a new tool palette that contains block insertion tools for all of the blocks within a drawing file?

Drawing Problems

1. Create a symbol library for one of the drafting disciplines listed below and save it as a template or drawing file. Then, after checking with your instructor, draw a problem using the library. If you save the symbol library as a template, start the problem with the template. If you save it as a drawing file, start a new drawing and insert the symbol library into it. Specialty areas you might create symbols for include:
   • Mechanical (machine features, fasteners, tolerance symbols).
   • Architectural (doors, windows, fixtures).
   • Structural (steel shapes, bolts, standard footings).
   • Industrial piping (fittings, valves).
   • Piping flow diagrams (tanks, valves, pumps).
   • Electrical schematics (resistors, capacitors, switches).
   • Electrical one-line (transformers, switches).
   • Electronics (IC chips, test points, components).
   • Logic diagrams (AND gates, NAND gates, buffers).
   • Mapping, civil (survey markers, piping).
   • Geometric tolerancing (feature control frames).
   Save the drawing as P22-1 or choose an appropriate file name, such as ARCH-PRO or ELEC-PRO.

2. Display the symbol library created in Problem 1 on screen and print a hard copy. Put the printed copy in your notebook as a reference.

3. Open P12-20 from Chapter 12. The sketch for this drawing is shown below. Erase all copies of the symbols that were made, leaving the original objects intact. These include the steel column symbols and the bay and column line tags. Then, do the following:
   A. Make blocks of the steel column symbol and the tag symbols.
   B. Use the **MINSERT** command or the **ARRAY** command to place the symbols in the drawing.
   C. Dimension the drawing as shown in the sketch.
   D. Save the drawing as P22-3.

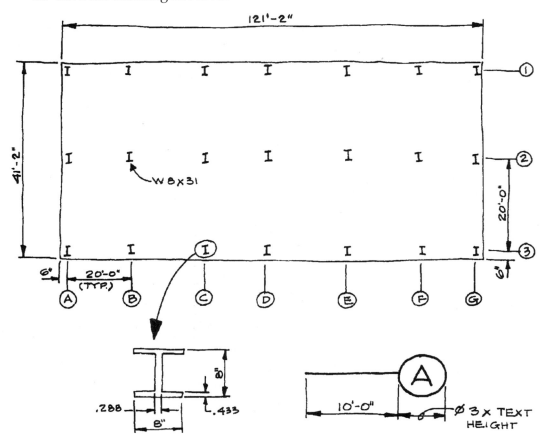

Problems 4–6 represent a variety of diagrams created using symbols as blocks. Create each drawing as shown (the drawings are not drawn to scale). The symbols should first be created as blocks or wblocks and then saved in a symbol library using one of the methods discussed in this chapter. Place a border and title block on each drawing. Save the drawings as P22-4, P22-5, and so on.

4.

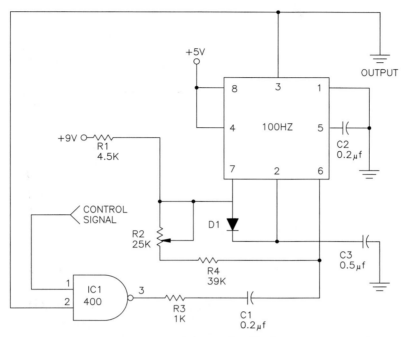

Integrated Circuit for Clock

5.

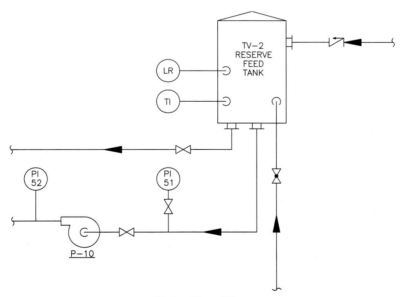

Piping Flow Diagram

6.

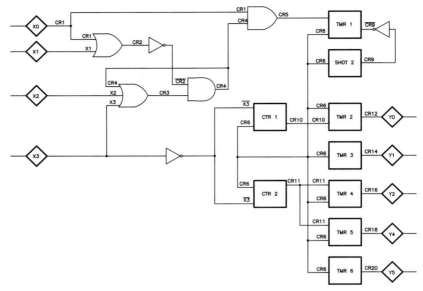

Logic Diagram of Marking System

7. Open P12-21 from Chapter 12. The sketch for this drawing is shown below. Erase all of the desk workstations except one. Then, do the following:
   A. Create a block of the workstation.
   B. Insert the block into the drawing using the **MINSERT** command.
   C. Dimension one of the workstations as shown in the sketch.
   D. Save the drawing as P22-7.

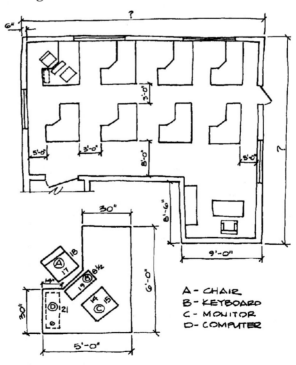

Problems 8–12 are presented as engineering sketches. They are schematic drawings created using symbols and are not drawn to scale. The symbols should first be drawn as blocks and then saved in a symbol library. Place a border and title block on each of the drawings.

8. The drawing shown below is a logic diagram of a portion of a computer's internal components. Create the drawing on a C-size sheet. Save the drawing as P22-8.

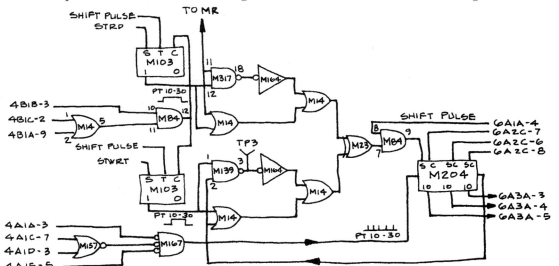

9. The drawing shown below is a piping flow diagram of a cooling water system. Create the drawing on a B-size sheet. Look closely at this drawing. Using blocks and the correct editing commands, it may be easier to complete than you think. Draw the thick flow lines with polylines. Save the drawing as P22-9.

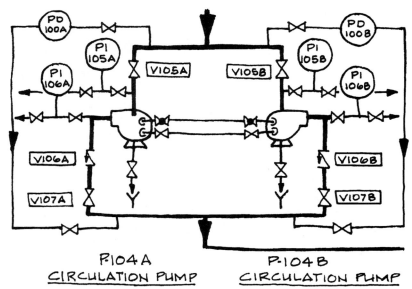

10. The drawing shown below is the general arrangement of a basement floor plan for a new building. The engineer has shown one example of each type of equipment. Use the following instructions to complete the drawing:
   A. Create the drawing on a C-size sheet.
   B. All text should be 1/8″ high, except the text for the bay and column line tags, which should be 3/16″ high. The line balloons for the bay and column lines should be twice the diameter of the text height.
   C. The column and bay line steel symbols represent wide-flange structural shapes, and should be 8″ wide × 12″ high.
   D. The PUMP and CHILLER installations (except PUMP #4 and PUMP #5) should be drawn per the dimensions given for PUMP #1 and CHILLER #1. Use the dimensions shown for the other PUMP units.
   E. TANK #2 and PUMP #5 (P-5) should be drawn per the dimensions given for TANK #1 and PUMP #4.
   F. Tanks T-3, T-4, T-5, and T-6 are all the same size and are aligned 12′ from column line A.
   G. Plan this drawing carefully and create as many blocks as possible to increase your productivity. Dimension the drawing as shown, and provide location dimensions for all equipment not shown in the engineer's sketch.
   H. Save the drawing as P22-10.

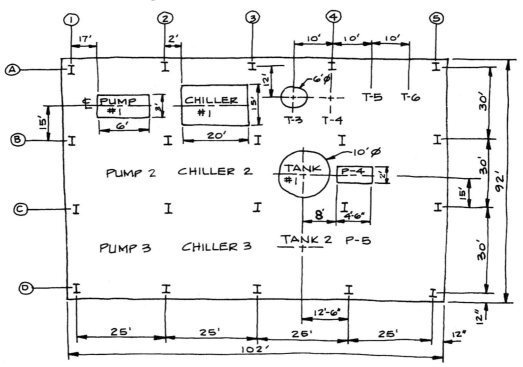

Drawing Problems - Chapter 22

11. The drawing saved as P22-10 must be revised. The engineer has provided you with a sketch of the necessary revisions. It is up to you to alter the drawing as quickly and efficiently as possible. The dimensions shown on the sketch below *do not* need to be added to the drawing; they are provided for construction purposes only. Revise P22-10 so that all chillers and the four tanks reflect the changes. Save the drawing as P22-11.

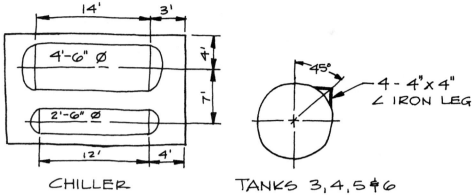

CHILLER   TANKS 3,4,5&6

12. The piping flow diagram shown below is part of an industrial effluent treatment system. Draw it on a C-size sheet. Eliminate as many bends in the flow lines as possible. Place arrowheads at all flow line intersections and bends. The flow lines should not run through any valves or equipment. Use polylines for the thick flow lines. Save the drawing as P22-12.

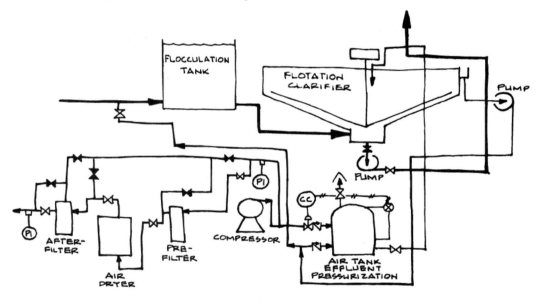

13. Draw the digital logic circuit shown. Create each component in the circuit as a block. Save the drawing as **P22-13**.

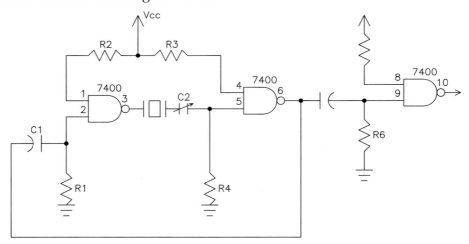

14. Open **P22-13**. Modify the NAND gates to become XNOR gates by modifying the block definition. Save the drawing as **P22-14**.

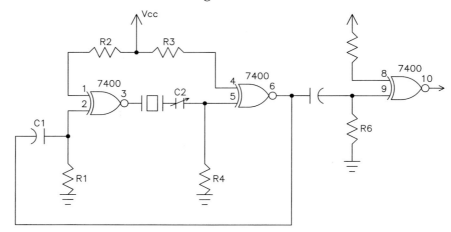

15. Create computer, plotter, and printer/copier blocks and then draw the network diagram. Save the drawing as **P22-15**.

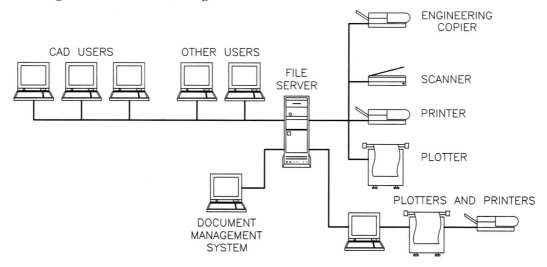

16. Draw the piping diagram shown, creating blocks for each type of fitting. Save the drawing as P22-16.

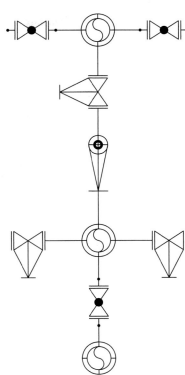

17. Create component blocks based on the dimensions shown. Then, use the blocks to draw the schematic below. Save the drawing as P22-17.

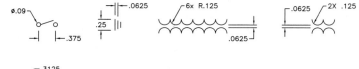

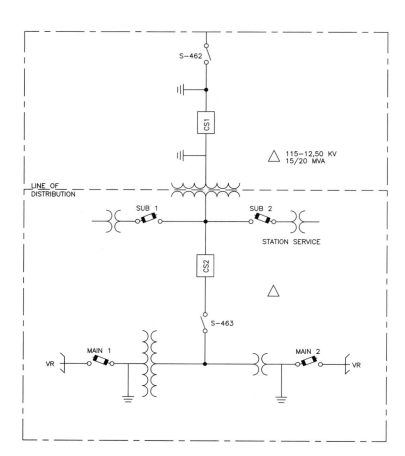

CHAPTER 23

Dynamic Blocks

Learning Objectives

After completing this chapter, you will be able to do the following:

● Use AutoCAD's **Block Editor** to create dynamic blocks.
● Define parameters.
● Define actions.
● List the parameters and actions that can be used to create a dynamic block.
● Insert parameters into blocks.
● Assign actions to parameters.
● Insert and use dynamic blocks.
● Use parameter sets.
● Modify parameters and actions.

Symbol libraries can contain hundreds or even thousands of blocks. The more blocks you have, the more time it takes to manage and work with them. In addition, many blocks may resemble several other blocks with slight variances. For example, you may need to create a block of a bolt that is 1″ long. If the same style of bolt is also available in three other lengths, then three additional blocks need to be created. However, an alternative is to create a single dynamic block.

A *dynamic block* is a normal block that has *parameters* and *actions* assigned to objects within the block. This allows special modifications to be performed on a single block while it is in the drawing without affecting other instances of the same block.

A dynamic block is modified by selecting it in the drawing to display the parameter grip(s). A *parameter grip* can then be selected to modify the block. In **Figure 23-1**, the shaft objects of a bolt block have been assigned a linear parameter with a stretch action. The linear parameter grips are shown in **Figure 23-1A**. To increase the length of the bolt, the right-hand linear parameter grip is selected and dragged to the right. See **Figure 23-1B.** The modification only affects this instance of the bolt block. Other references to the same block in the drawing are *not* updated. In this way, dynamic blocks can be used so only one block is inserted into the drawing, but multiple variations of the symbol can appear in the drawing.

There are various types of parameters and actions that can be used in blocks. This chapter discusses how to create and use dynamic blocks.

Figure 23-1.

A linear parameter and stretch action have been assigned to the shaft objects in this block of a bolt. A—Selecting the block displays the linear grips. B—Selecting a linear grip and dragging it stretches the shaft of the bolt.

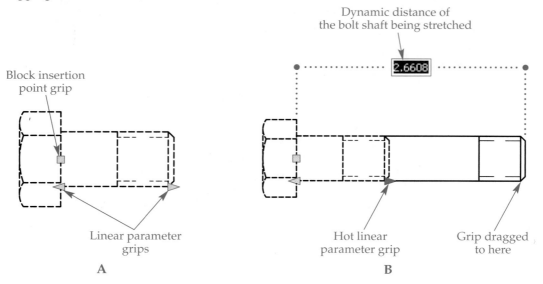

Dynamic distance of the bolt shaft being stretched

2.6608

Block insertion point grip

Linear parameter grips

A

Hot linear parameter grip

Grip dragged to here

B

BEDIT

Type	
BEDIT	
Pull-Down Menu	
Tools > Block Editor	
Toolbar	
Standard	
Block Editor	

Adding Dynamic Properties with Block Editor

Dynamic properties can be assigned to an existing block in the drawing by using the **Block Editor**. To edit a block in the **Block Editor**, pick the **Block Editor** button on the **Standard** toolbar, pick **Tools** > **Block Editor**, type BEDIT, or double-click on a block in the drawing. The **Edit Block Definition** dialog box appears with a list of blocks. See **Figure 23-2**.

Figure 23-2.

The **Edit Block Definition** dialog box.

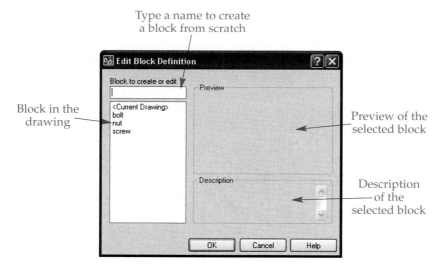

Type a name to create a block from scratch

Block in the drawing

Preview of the selected block

Description of the selected block

Parameters and Actions

To create a dynamic block, a *parameter* is inserted into the block and then an *action* is assigned to the parameter. Each *parameter* contains custom properties for objects within the block that specify the positions, distances, and angles of the block's geometry. An *action* controls how the block's geometry can be modified in the drawing. An action is similar to an editing command. Once a parameter and action have been inserted into a block and the block has been saved, the block is considered a *dynamic block*.

The different types of parameters and actions can be seen in the **Block Authoring Palettes** window by selecting the appropriate tab. The **Parameters** tab and **Actions** tab are shown in Figure 23-3. As mentioned before, only certain actions can be assigned to a given parameter. The following chart lists parameters and the actions that can be assigned to them.

Parameter	Actions that can be associated
Alignment	None
Base Point	None
Flip	Flip
Linear	Move, scale, stretch, and array
Lookup	Lookup
Point	Move and stretch
Polar	Move, scale, stretch, polar stretch, and array
Rotation	Rotate
Visibility	None
XY	Move, scale, stretch, and array

Figure 23-3.
The available parameters and actions can be accessed from the **Block Authoring Palettes** window.

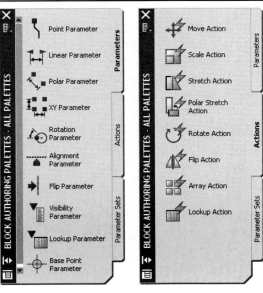

Parameters Tab   Actions Tab

Point Parameter

A *point parameter* defines an XY coordinate location in the drawing and can be used with the move or stretch action. For example, suppose a block of a door includes a door tag as part of the block. A point parameter with a move action can be assigned to the door tag so the tag can be moved independently of the door after the block is inserted into the drawing.

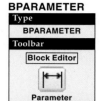

To insert a point parameter, pick the **Parameter** button on the **Block Editor** toolbar or type BPARAMETER. Then, select the **pOint** option. You can also enter this directly by selecting **Point Parameter** from the **Parameters** tab in the **Block Authoring Palettes** window. The following prompt appears on the command line. Refer to **Figure 23-4** while working through the command sequence.

> Specify parameter location or [Name/Label/Chain/Description/Palette]: *(pick the center of the door tag)*
> Specify label location: *(drag the label to the side of the door tag and pick)*
> Command:

The parameter location defines the grip point and the X and Y coordinates. This is the parameter grip that appears when the block is selected in the drawing. Selecting the parameter grip and moving it carries out the action that is assigned to the parameter. In this example it is not important that the center of the door tag be selected as the parameter location, but it makes more sense to put it there. If a point is selected off of the object, it may not be clear what the grip is for when the block is selected. If you want to move the parameter location after it has been inserted, this can be done by selecting the grip in the **Block Editor** and moving it.

The *parameter label* is like a note that indicates the purpose of the parameter. All parameters have a label. It appears only in block editing mode. By default, the label for a point parameter is POSITION. However, this can be changed to a more appropriate label. The parameter label text can be changed when creating the parameter by using the **Label** option before specifying the parameter location. After the parameter is created, the label text can be changed in the **Properties** window. The label can be moved after the parameter has been inserted. This is done by selecting the label text or the label line to highlight the label, selecting the grip next to the label text, and moving the label.

Before specifying the parameter location, the following options are available. All of these options can be modified in the **Properties** window after the label has been inserted.

- **Name.** Allows you to specify a name for the parameter.
- **Label.** Allows you to specify the text for the parameter label. The label is the text that is seen next to the parameter.

Figure 23-4.
A point parameter consists of the grip location and a label.

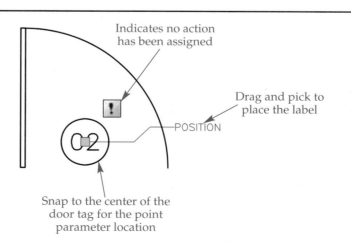

- **Chain.** Determines if the parameter can be affected by a chain action. Chain actions are discussed in more detail later in this chapter.
- **Description.** Allows you to type a description for the parameter. This is longer than the name or label and is used to more fully explain the purpose of the parameter.
- **Palette.** Determines if the label text is displayed in the **Properties** window when the block is selected in the drawing.

Exercise 23-1 Complete the Exercise on the Student CD.

Assigning a Move Action to a Point Parameter

BACTION

Type	
	BACTION
Toolbar	
	Block Editor
	Action

After inserting a point parameter, a move or stretch action needs to be assigned to the parameter to make the block dynamic. The yellow alert icon shown in **Figure 23-4** indicates that no action has been assigned to the parameter. An action can be assigned to a parameter by either picking the **Action** button on the **Block Editor** toolbar, typing BACTION, selecting the action from the **Actions** tab of the **Block Authoring Palette** window, or double-clicking on any part of the parameter.

Depending on the method used, the prompts will be slightly different. When picking the **Action** button from the **Block Editor** toolbar or typing BACTION, the prompts are:

> Select parameter: *(pick the parameter)*
> Enter action type [Move/sTretch]: *(specify the action)*
> Specify selection set for action
> Select objects: *(select the objects to be modified by the action; this prompt differs depending on which type of action is selected)*
> Select objects: ↵
> Specify action location or [Multiplier/Offset]: *(pick a point near the parameter label to place the action icon)*
> Command:

If the action is selected from the **Block Authoring Palette** window, the Enter action type [Move/sTretch]: prompt is not displayed. When double-clicking on the parameter, the Select parameter: prompt is not displayed.

For the door example, select **Move Action** from the **Block Authoring Palette** window to assign a move action to the point parameter. Refer to **Figure 23-5** while following this command sequence:

> Select parameter: *(pick the parameter)*
> Specify selection set for action
> Select objects: *(window around the door tag objects)*
> *n* found
> Select objects: ↵
> Specify action location or [Multiplier/Offset]: *(pick a point near the parameter label to place the action icon)*
> Command:

When prompted to select objects, select all of the objects to be associated with this action. Objects can be picked individually or by using a window/crossing selection. In this example, the objects that make up the door tag need to be selected.

The dynamic block is now ready to be saved and used. To save the block, pick the **Save Block Definition** button on the **Block Editor** toolbar or type BSAVE. An AutoCAD alert appears stating that saving the edits to the block updates any block references in the drawing. Pick the **Yes** button to save the edits. To exit the **Block Editor**, pick the

BSAVE

Type	
	BSAVE
Toolbar	
	Block Editor
	Save Block Definition

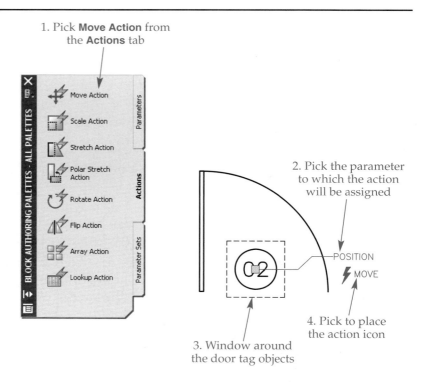

Figure 23-5.
Assigning a move action to a point parameter.

1. Pick **Move Action** from the **Actions** tab

2. Pick the parameter to which the action will be assigned

POSITION

MOVE

4. Pick to place the action icon

3. Window around the door tag objects

Close Block Editor button on the **Block Editor** toolbar or type BCLOSE. Block editing mode is exited and you are returned to the drawing.

PROFESSIONAL TIP

In most cases, when selecting objects to include with an action, also select the parameter with which the action will be associated. If the parameter is not selected, the parameter grip will not be part of the action. Thus, the parameter grip may be left behind when using a move, rotate, or stretch action.

Using the Move Action Dynamically

Once a dynamic block contains the appropriate parameters and actions and it has been saved, the block is ready for use. In **Figure 23-6**, the door block is selected in the drawing. The point parameter grip is displayed as a light blue square and is shown in the center of the door tag. The insertion point that was specified when the block was created is displayed as a darker blue square surrounded by a dark line. It is shown in the lower left corner of the block.

Figure 23-6.
When the block is selected to display grips, the point parameter grip is shown as a light blue square.

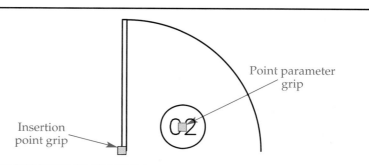

Point parameter grip

Insertion point grip

Figure 23-7.
Dynamically using a move action assigned to a point parameter. A—Select the point parameter grip and move it. B—The door tag is moved to a new location, but is still part of the block.

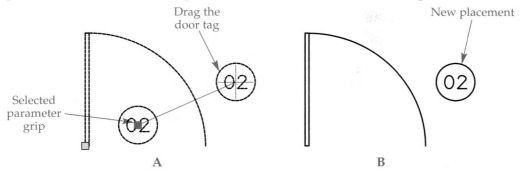

To move the objects composing the door tag within the block, select the block to display grips. Then, select the point parameter grip to make it active. Now, drag the door tag objects to a new location. See **Figure 23-7A.** Pick a point in the drawing area to specify a new location for the door tag. See **Figure 23-7B.**

Being able to move part of a block like this can be very helpful. In the case of the door block, there may be areas in the drawing where other objects pass through the door tag when the tag is in its default location. Being able to quickly move the tag, while maintaining the block definition, results in a drawing that is much cleaner and easier to read. If a normal block is used, the block must be exploded in order for the door tag objects to be moved. Once exploded, the objects are no longer associated with the block definition.

PROFESSIONAL TIP If Dynamic Input is enabled, you can hover the cursor over a parameter grip to display the current value(s) of the parameter.

Exercise 23-2 Complete the Exercise on the Student CD.

Linear Parameter

A *linear parameter* establishes a measurement reference between two points. Inserting a linear parameter into a block is like creating a linear dimension in a drawing. A move, scale, stretch, or array action can be assigned to a linear parameter. The objects that are included in the action selection set can then be modified within the block.

For example, a block of a bolt can have a linear parameter inserted into it. A stretch action can be assigned to the parameter so that the bolt shaft can be lengthened in a drawing. A second linear parameter and stretch action can be assigned to the bolt head so its diameter can be increased.

To insert a linear parameter, pick the **Parameter** button on the **Block Editor** toolbar or type BPARAMETER. Then, use the **Linear** option. You can also enter this directly by selecting **Linear Parameter** from the **Parameters** tab in the **Block Authoring Palettes** window. For the bolt example, use the **Label** option to call the linear parameter SHAFT LENGTH and then assign the parameter to the bolt shaft. Refer to **Figure 23-8**.

Specify start point or [Name/Label/Chain/Description/Base/Palette/Value set]:
    LABEL↵
Enter distance property label: <*current*> **SHAFT LENGTH**↵
Specify start point or [Name/Label/Chain/Description/Base/Palette/Value set]: *(pick the endpoint of the lower edge of the shaft that is connected to the bolt head)*
Specify endpoint: *(using the extension object snap, pick the point where the edge of the shaft would meet the end if extended)*
Specify label location: *(drag the label away from the bolt and pick)*
Command:

Notice that this parameter has many of the same options as the point parameter. There are, however, two different options:
- **Base.** This option allows either the starting point or the midpoint of the linear parameter to be used as the base for the action.
- **Value set.** This option allows specific values to be defined for the action. Both of these options are discussed later in the chapter.

By default a linear parameter has two parameter grips—one at the first pick point and another at the second pick point. These are the grips that are selected in the drawing to carry out the action that is assigned to the parameter.

Assigning a Stretch Action to a Linear Parameter

A stretch action can be assigned to the linear parameter. For the following command sequence, the **Action** button was picked from the **Block Editor** toolbar. Refer to **Figure 23-9**.

Select parameter: *(pick the parameter)*
Enter action type [Array/Move/Scale/sTretch]: **STRETCH**↵
Specify parameter point to associate with action or enter [sTart point/Second point] <*current*>: *(move the cursor close to the parameter point that this action will be associated with; a red snap marker appears at the parameter point; pick to select the point)*
Specify first corner of stretch frame or [CPolygon]: *(pick a point to the upper-right of the end of the bolt shaft; see Figure 23-9A)*
Specify opposite corner: *(pick a point near the lower-middle of the shaft making sure that all the shaft objects are selected; see Figure 23-9A)*

Figure 23-8.
Defining a linear parameter.

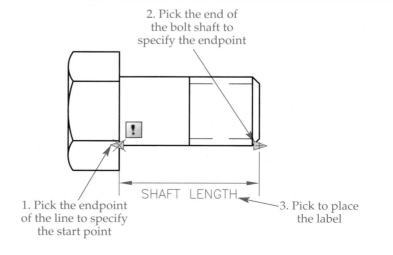

2. Pick the end of the bolt shaft to specify the endpoint

SHAFT LENGTH

1. Pick the endpoint of the line to specify the start point

3. Pick to place the label

Specify objects to stretch
Select objects: *(pick near the first point of the stretch frame; see Figure 23-9B)*
Specify opposite corner: *(pick near the second point of the stretch frame; see Figure 23-9B)*
n found
Select objects: ⏎
Specify action location or [Multiplier/Offset]: *(pick a point near the parameter to place the stretch action icon; see Figure 23-9C)*
Command:

When there is more than one parameter grip, as in the case of the linear parameter, AutoCAD needs to know the grip (parameter point) to which the action is associated. The parameter point can be selected with the cursor. Use the **sTart point** option to select the first point that was picked when creating the linear parameter or use the **Second point** option to select the second point.

To save the changes to the block, pick the **Save Block Definition** button from the **Block Editor** toolbar or type BSAVE. You can now exit block editing mode. The block is ready to be used dynamically.

Using the Stretch Action Dynamically

After inserting the block, select it to display grips. The linear parameter grips are displayed as light blue arrows on screen. In the bolt example shown in **Figure 23-10**, the stretch action is assigned to the grip at the end of the bolt shaft. The block is inserted with its default shaft length. To increase the length, select the parameter grip at the end of the shaft and drag it to the new length. If Dynamic Input is enabled, the distance of the shaft is dynamically updated in the distance field as you stretch the shaft. An

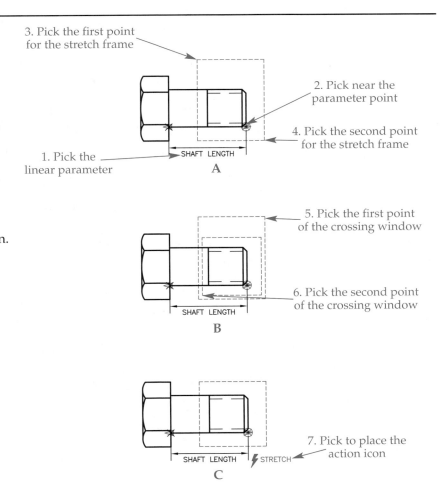

Figure 23-9.
Assigning a stretch action to a linear parameter. A—The parameter, parameter grip, and stretch frame are specified. B—A crossing window is used to specify the objects that will be affected by the stretch action. C—Pick near the parameter point to place the action icon.

3. Pick the first point for the stretch frame

2. Pick near the parameter point

4. Pick the second point for the stretch frame

1. Pick the linear parameter

SHAFT LENGTH

A

5. Pick the first point of the crossing window

6. Pick the second point of the crossing window

SHAFT LENGTH

B

7. Pick to place the action icon

SHAFT LENGTH STRETCH

C

Figure 23-10.
Selecting the block
in the drawing
displays the
parameter grips.

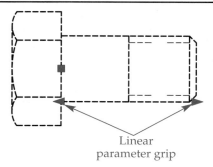

Linear
parameter grip

exact length can be specified by entering a value in the distance field and pressing the
[Enter] key. Relative coordinates can also be specified, which is useful if Dynamic Input
is not enabled.

**PROFESSIONAL
TIP**

The distance field displayed when Dynamic Input is
enabled is a special property of the linear parameter.
This feature allows you to enter an exact distance or
length. Therefore, to get the best results when using the
linear parameter, it is important that the first and second
parameter points are inserted at the correct locations.
Other parameters have similar fields displayed when
Dynamic Input is enabled.

**Exercise
23-3**   Complete the Exercise on the Student CD.

Stretching Objects Symmetrically

For parts of a block that need to stay symmetrical, the **Base** option can be used to
specify a midpoint for the stretch action. This option is used before the first point of
the linear parameter is picked or can be set later in the **Properties** window.

In the following example, a linear parameter with a stretch action is assigned to
the objects composing the bolt head. Refer to **Figure 23-11**. First, open the block in the
Block Editor. Then, pick **Linear Parameter** in the **Parameters** tab of the **Block Authoring
Palette** window. Continue as follows:

Specify start point or [Name/Label/Chain/Description/Base/Palette/Value set]: **BASE**⏎
Enter base location [Startpoint/Midpoint]: <Startpoint>: **MIDPOINT**⏎
Specify start point or [Name/Label/Chain/Description/Base/Palette/Value set]: **LABEL**⏎
Enter distance property label <current>: **HEAD DIAMETER**⏎
Specify start point or [Name/Label/Chain/Description/Base/Palette/Value set]: (pick
    the upper-left corner of the bolt head to specify the start point; the midpoint is auto-
    matically calculated based on the start and endpoints)
Specify endpoint: (pick the lower-left corner of the bolt head to specify the endpoint)
Specify label location: (pick to the left of the bolt to place the label)
Command:

Figure 23-11.
The base point of a linear parameter is displayed as an X. When the **Midpoint** option is used, the base point is in the center between the two parameter grips.

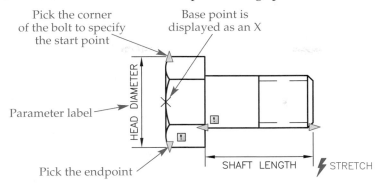

Now, a stretch action must be assigned to the parameter for each side of the bolt head. Refer to **Figure 23-12**. First, pick **Stretch Action** from the **Actions** tab of the **Block Authoring Palette** window. Then, continue as follows:

Select parameter: *(pick the* HEAD DIAMETER *parameter)*
Specify parameter point to associate with action or enter [sTart point/Second point] <Second>: *(pick the upper linear parameter point; see* **Figure 23-12A***)*
Specify first corner of stretch frame or [CPolygon]: *(pick the first corner of the stretch frame above and to the left of the bolt head)*
Specify opposite corner: *(pick just above the midpoint and within the shaft)*
Select objects: *(select the upper objects of the bolt head; see* **Figure 23-12B***)*
Select objects: ↵
Specify action location or [Multiplier/Offset]: *(pick to place the action icon near the parameter point)*
Command:

Repeat this sequence to assign a second stretch action to the parameter. Associate it with the lower parameter point and specify the objects as the lower objects of the bolt head. Then, save the block and exit the **Block Editor**.

Now, dragging one of the parameter grips increases or decreases the opposite side of the bolt head the same length. First, select the block in the drawing area to display grips. Select either of the grips for the HEAD DIAMETER parameter and drag the cursor. Notice how the opposite side of the bolt head is moving the same distance. See **Figure 23-13**. If Dynamic Input is enabled, an exact diameter can be given for the bolt head by typing in a value in the distance field.

Figure 23-12.
Assigning a stretch action to one side of the bolt head. A—Create a stretch frame around the top of the bolt head. B—Use a window to select the objects to be included in the stretch.

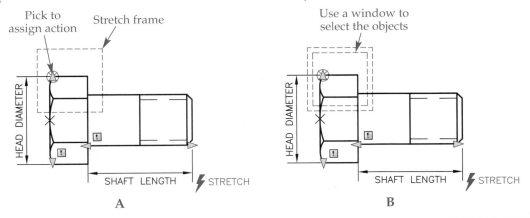

A

B

Figure 23-13.
Dynamically
stretching the
bolt head. Note
that the head is
symmetrically
stretched.

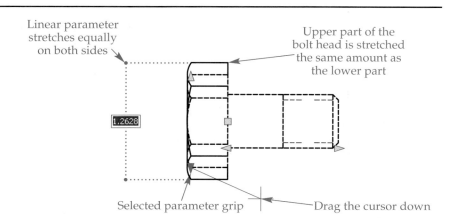

Linear parameter
stretches equally
on both sides

Upper part of the
bolt head is stretched
the same amount as
the lower part

1.2628

Selected parameter grip

Drag the cursor down

Assigning a Scale Action to a Linear Parameter

The scale action allows you to scale some of the objects within a block independently of the other objects. This action is similar to the **SCALE** command, which is discussed in Chapter 12. For example, a block of a countertop consists of the countertop and a sink. The dimensions of the countertop have to remain static, but different size sinks can go in the countertop. Instead of having a different block for each countertop/sink combination, there can be one block that includes both. A linear parameter and scale action can be assigned to the objects that make up the sink. This allows one block to be inserted into the drawing and the sink to be scaled to the correct size as needed.

First, insert a linear parameter along the length of the objects composing the sink. Use the **Base** option to define the midpoint so the sink is scaled symmetrically. Refer to **Figure 23-14.**

Specify start point or [Name/Label/Chain/Description/Base/Palette/Value set]: **BASE**↵
Enter base location [Startpoint/Midpoint] <Startpoint>: **MIDPOINT**↵
Specify start point or [Name/Label/Chain/Description/Base/Palette/Value set]: **LABEL**↵
Enter distance property label <Distance>: **SINK LENGTH**↵
Specify start point or [Name/Label/Chain/Description/Base/Palette/Value set]: *(pick the quadrant on one side of the sink)*
Specify endpoint: *(pick the quadrant on the opposite side of the sink)*
Specify label location: *(pick a location for the label)*
Command:

Now, the scale action needs to be assigned to the parameter. For the following command sequence, pick the **Action** button on the **Block Editor** toolbar. Then, continue:

Select parameter: *(pick the parameter)*
Enter action type [Array/Move/Scale/sTretch]: **SCALE**↵
Specify selection set for action

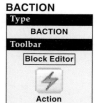

BACTION

Type
BACTION

Toolbar
Block Editor

Action

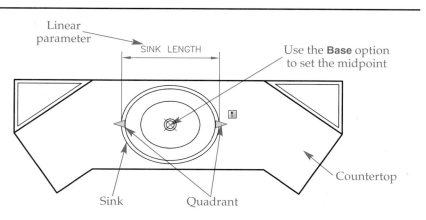

Figure 23-14.
A linear parameter
is inserted into the
block of a sink and
countertop. The base
point is specified as the
center of the sink.

Linear
parameter

SINK LENGTH

Use the **Base** option
to set the midpoint

Countertop

Sink

Quadrant

Select objects: *(select the linear parameter and all of the objects that make up the sink; use a window, crossing, or individual selections)*
n found
Select objects: ↵
Specify action location or [Base type]: **B**↵
Enter base point type [Dependent/Independent] <Dependent>: **I**↵
Specify base point location <current>: *(pick the center of the sink)*
Specify action location or [Base type]: *(pick a point near the parameter to place the scale action icon)*
Command:

When using the scale action, it is critical that the objects are scaled relative to the correct location (base point). If the base point is not in the correct location, undesirable results are produced. For the sink, it is important that the objects are scaled relative to the exact center of the sink. This keeps the sink centered within the countertop.

Notice in the above command sequence that there are two options for the base point of the scale action. The default option is **Dependent**, which results in the objects being scaled relative to the base point of the associated parameter. To specify a different location, use the **Independent** option. You are prompted to specify the base point, which is then used as the base to scale the objects.

The dynamic block is now defined. Save the block and close the **Block Editor**.

PROFESSIONAL TIP

In the above command sequence, the **Independent** option was used to set the center of the sink as the base point for the scale action. This is needed because the base point of the linear parameter is the first pick point, not the midpoint. The midpoint was defined for the parameter so that the parameter (and its grips) are scaled about its midpoint, not its start point. The **Independent** option of the scale action is used to specify the point about which the geometry (not the parameter) is scaled.

Using the Scale Action Dynamically

After inserting the block, select it to display grips. Select either of the linear parameter grips and drag the cursor to dynamically scale the sink objects. Since the center of the sink was selected as the base point, the sink objects are scaled relative to that point. In **Figure 23-15**, the right-hand grip is selected and dragged to the right to increase the size of the sink. Pick a point to resize the sink. If Dynamic Input is enabled, you can also type a value in the distance field.

Figure 23-15.
Dynamically scaling the sink. The scale action is not applied to the countertop.

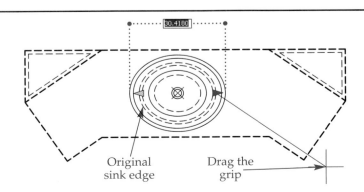

Original sink edge

Drag the grip

Polar Parameter

A *polar parameter* includes two parameter points with a distance property, like a linear property, but also includes an angle property. The action types that can be assigned to a polar parameter are: move, scale, stretch, polar stretch, and array.

For example, a block has been created that consists of a large circle containing a smaller circle. See **Figure 23-16.** A polar parameter can be inserted into the block to specify a distance and angle. Also, a move action can be assigned to the parameter that acts on the smaller circle. Then, the smaller circle can be moved a specified distance and angle without affecting the larger circle.

To insert a polar parameter, pick the **Parameter** button from the **Block Editor** toolbar or type BPARAMETER. Then, select the **Polar** option. You can also enter this directly by selecting **Polar Parameter** from the **Parameters** tab in the **Block Authoring Palettes** window. The following command sequence places a polar parameter in the block shown in **Figure 23-16.**

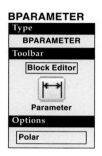

BPARAMETER

Type
BPARAMETER
Toolbar
Block Editor
Parameter
Options
Polar

Enter parameter type
[Alignment/Base/pOint/Linear/Polar/Xy/Rotation/Flip/Visibility/looKup]: **POLAR**↵
Specify base point or [Name/Label/Chain/Description/Palette/Value set]: *(pick the center of the large circle)*
Specify endpoint: *(pick the center of the small circle)*
Specify label location: *(pick a point to place the label)*
Enter number of grips [0/1/2] <2>: ↵
Command:

Notice that you must specify the number of grips. Now that the parameter has been assigned, an action can be associated with it.

Assigning a Move Action to the Polar Parameter

Assigning a move action to a parameter is discussed earlier in this chapter. For this example, the small circle is selected for the move action. In this way, the small circle can be moved independently of the large circle even though they are part of the same block object. Refer to **Figure 23-17** while following these steps:

Figure 23-16.
Inserting a polar
parameter.

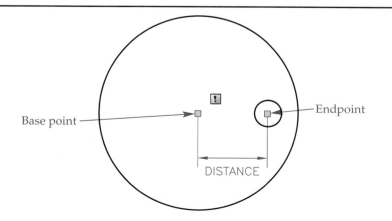

Base point

Endpoint

DISTANCE

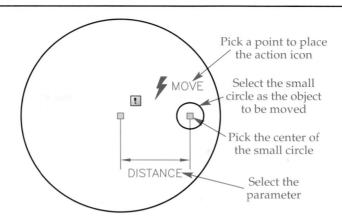

Figure 23-17.
Assigning a move action to a polar parameter.

Pick a point to place the action icon

MOVE

Select the small circle as the object to be moved

Pick the center of the small circle

DISTANCE

Select the parameter

1. Open the block in block editing mode.
2. Pick **Move Action** from the **Actions** tab of the **Block Authoring Palette** window.
3. Select the polar parameter.
4. Select the parameter point in the center of the small circle to associate the move action with this parameter grip.
5. Select the small circle as the object to be included in the move action.
6. Pick a location for the move action icon.
7. Save the block and close the **Block Editor**.

Using the Move Action Dynamically

After the block is inserted, select it to display grips. Select the parameter grip in the center of the small circle and drag it. A point can be picked to place the small circle at a new location, or polar coordinates can be typed to move the circle an exact distance and angle. For example, to move the small circle so it is three inches away from the center of the large circle at 45°, type @3<45 and press [Enter]. Using polar coordinates is covered in Chapter 3. If Dynamic Input is enabled, the distance that the circle is being moved is displayed in the distance field and the angle is displayed next to the distance field. See **Figure 23-18.**

Figure 23-18.
Moving an object with a polar parameter displays the distance and the angle from the base point if Dynamic Input is enabled.

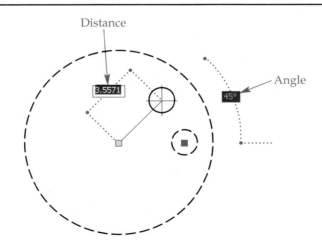

Distance

3.5571

Angle

45°

In this example, the parameter grip for the base point can also be moved by selecting it and dragging. No action or objects are assigned to the base point grip, so only the grip itself is moved. However, this affects the distance and angle to the endpoint.

Exercise 23-5 — Complete the Exercise on the Student CD.

Rotation Parameter

The *rotation parameter* allows objects within a block to be independently rotated. This parameter allows a rotation point and beginning angle to be defined. Only a rotate action can be assigned to a rotation parameter.

For example, look at the speedometer block shown in **Figure 23-19.** The needle pointer should be able to rotate around the circumference of the dial. A rotation parameter with an associated rotation action can be used to allow this.

To insert a rotation parameter, pick the **Parameter** button on the **Block Editor** toolbar or type BPARAMETER. Then, select the **Rotation** option. You can also enter this directly by selecting **Rotation Parameter** from the **Parameters** tab in the **Block Authoring Palettes** window. The following command sequence adds a rotation parameter to the speedometer block:

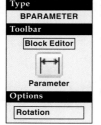

BPARAMETER

Type
BPARAMETER

Toolbar
Block Editor

Options
Rotation

Specify base point or [Name/Label/Chain/Description/Palette/Value set]: *(pick the center of the needle's circular base)*
Specify radius of parameter: *(pick a point to define a circle on which the rotation parameter grip will be placed)*
Specify default rotation angle or [Base angle]: *(pick the tip of the arrow or type 90; the grip will be placed here)*
Specify label location: *(pick a point to place the label)*
Command:

As shown in **Figure 23-20,** an angle of 90° places the parameter grip inline with the arrow. By default, the base angle for a drawing is at 0° to the east. The **Base angle** option allows you to specify a base angle that is different from the current drawing base angle.

Figure 23-19.
By assigning a rotation parameter with a rotate action to the needle, it can be rotated to different points while still remaining part of the speedometer block.

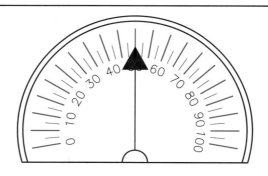

Figure 23-20.
Inserting a rotation parameter into the speedometer block.

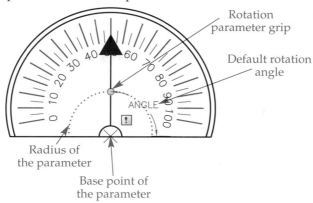

Assigning a Rotate Action to the Rotation Parameter

After a rotation parameter has been inserted, a rotate action can be assigned to the parameter. This action is similar to the **ROTATE** command, which is discussed in detail in Chapter 12. The rotate action allows individual objects within a block to be rotated without affecting the other objects in the block. For the following command sequence, **Rotate Action** was picked from the **Actions** tab of the **Block Authoring Palette** window:

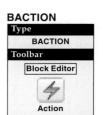

Select parameter: *(pick the rotation parameter)*
Specify selection set for action
Select objects: *(select the rotation parameter and all of the objects that make up the arrow)*
n found
Select objects: ↵
Specify action location or [Base type]: *(pick a point near the parameter to place the rotate action icon)*
Command:

The **Base type** option can be used to define a different rotational base point. By default, the rotation point is the base point of the rotation parameter.

The dynamic block is now defined. Save the block and close the **Block Editor**.

Using the Rotate Action Dynamically

After the block is inserted, select it to display grips. See **Figure 23-21A**. Select the parameter grip and drag. The needle objects are rotated around the base point. Pick to rotate the objects or use relative coordinates. If Dynamic Input is enabled, the angle is displayed dynamically as you drag the grip. In **Figure 23-21B**, the needle is dragged until a value of 45° is displayed.

Figure 23-21.
A—The parameter grip is displayed when the block is selected. B—Dynamically rotating the needle.

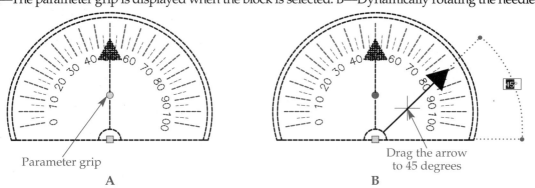

Exercise 23-6 Complete the Exercise on the Student CD.

Alignment Parameter

An *alignment parameter* allows a block to be automatically aligned with another object in the drawing. When the block is moved near another object in the drawing, the block automatically rotates to align with that object based on the angle and alignment line defined within the block. This parameter saves time by not having to determine an angle of rotation and then using the **ROTATE** command on the block. An alignment parameter affects the entire block, not individual components. Therefore, no actions are assigned to the parameter.

Inserting an Alignment Parameter

BPARAMETER

Type
BPARAMETER

Toolbar
Block Editor
⊢═┤
Parameter

Options
Alignment

To insert an alignment parameter, pick the **Parameter** button on the **Block Editor** toolbar or type BPARAMETER. Then, use the **Alignment** option. This can be entered directly by selecting **Alignment Parameter** from the **Parameters** tab in the **Block Authoring Palettes** window. Then, continue as follows. Refer to valve block shown in **Figure 23-22**. By inserting an alignment parameter into the block, the gate valve can be moved near any pipe line and it will automatically rotate to align with the pipe.

Specify base point of alignment or [Name]: *(pick the point in the center of the valve; this is where the parameter grip is located)*
Alignment type = *current*
Specify alignment direction or alignment type [Type] <Type>: **TYPE**↵
Enter alignment type [Perpendicular/Tangent] <*current*>: **TANGENT**↵
Specify alignment direction or alignment type [Type] <Type>: *(pick the endpoint shown in Figure 23-22)*
Command:

The base point is used as the first point in defining the angle of the alignment line. It is also where the alignment parameter grip is located. After specifying the base point, drag the pointer in the direction that is desired for the angle and pick. The angle between the first point and the second point defines the alignment line.

There are two types of alignments—perpendicular and tangent. Use the **Type** option to specify the type of alignment. These options do not affect how the block is aligned; they determine the direction of the alignment grip. When set to perpendicular, the grip is pointing perpendicular to the alignment line and when tangent is used, the grip is pointing tangent to the alignment line.

Figure 23-22.
Inserting an alignment parameter into the gate valve block.

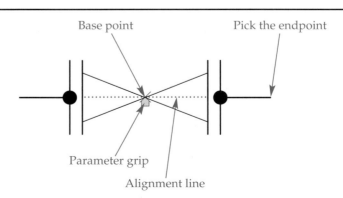

The parameter grip for an alignment parameter looks like a small square with a triangle on one side. See **Figure 23-22**. When the parameter has been assigned to the block, the triangle on the parameter grip points in the direction of alignment. This "arrow" points perpendicular to or tangent to the object in the drawing to which the block is being aligned.

The dynamic block is now defined. Save the block and close the **Block Editor**.

Using the Alignment Parameter Dynamically

Once the block is inserted in the drawing, select it to display grips. Select the parameter grip and drag the block near another object. The block is automatically aligned to the object. The rotation is determined by the alignment path, the type of alignment, and the angle of the other object. In **Figure 23-23**, the gate valve block is dragged near the pipe line.

> **NOTE**
>
> When manipulating a block with an alignment parameter, the **Nearest** object snap is temporarily turned on, if it is not already on.

Exercise 23-7   Complete the Exercise on the Student CD.

Figure 23-23.
When the gate valve block is dragged near the angled line, the block automatically aligns with the line.

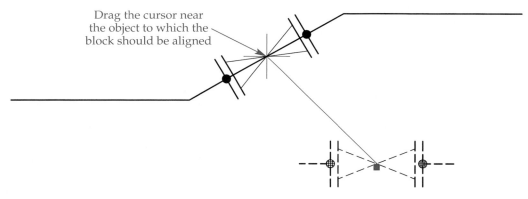

Drag the cursor near the object to which the block should be aligned

Flip Parameter

Using a *flip parameter*, selected objects within a block can be mirrored by simply picking the parameter grip. This is accomplished by inserting a flip parameter, specifying a defining line (mirror line), and assigning a flip action to the parameter, and selecting the objects to be flipped. For example, look at the block of a door shown in **Figure 23-24**. Depending on the side of the swing needed for the door, the block may need to be flipped. By inserting a flip parameter, this can easily be accomplished with a single block.

To insert a flip parameter, pick the **Parameter** button from the **Block Editor** toolbar or type BPARAMETER. Then, use the **Flip** option. You can also enter this directly by selecting **Flip Parameter** from the **Parameters** tab in the **Block Authoring Palettes** window.

Specify base point of reflection line or [Name/Label/Description/Palette]: *(pick the base point shown in Figure 23-24A; the parameter grip is placed here)*
Specify endpoint of reflection line: *(pick the endpoint of the swing arc, as shown in Figure 23-24A)*
Specify label location: *(pick a point to place the label)*
Command:

The block will be mirrored about the reflection line. However, with the line in its current position, an incorrect flip will result. Since a door is placed in a 4″ wall, the reflection line should be 2″ lower than the door. Using the **MOVE** command, select the reflection line and move it 2″ down. The label and parameter grip also move. In addition, you may want to move the parameter grip horizontally to the middle of the door opening. This may help the drafter when the block is inserted into the drawing. The **MOVE** command can be used to move the grip. See **Figure 23-24B.**

Assigning a Flip Action to the Flip Parameter

The objects to which a *flip action* applies are specified when the action is assigned to the flip parameter. The following prompt sequence defines a flip parameter:

Select parameter: *(pick the flip parameter)*
Specify selection set for action
Select objects: *(select all of the objects in the door block)*
n found
Select objects: ↵
Specify action location: *(pick a point near the parameter to place the flip action icon)*
Command:

The dynamic block is now defined. Save the block and close the **Block Editor.**

Using the Flip Action Dynamically

Once the block is inserted, select it to display grips. See **Figure 23-25A.** A pick on the parameter grip flips the objects to the other side of the reflection line, as shown in **Figure 23-25B.** Unlike other parameters and actions discussed to this point, dragging is not required. A single pick initiates the action.

Figure 23-24.
A—Inserting a flip parameter. B—The parameter is moved so the block will correctly flip about the centerline of a wall.

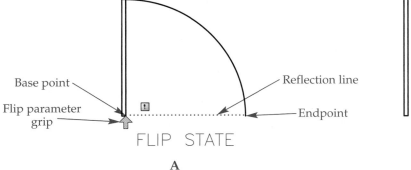
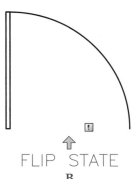

Figure 23-25.
A—The flip parameter grip is displayed when the block is selected. B—Picking the flip parameter grip flips the block about the reflection line. Since all of the objects within the block were selected for the action, the entire block is flipped.

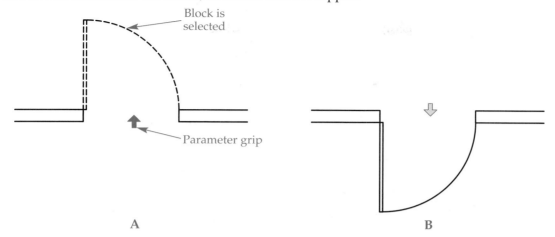

Block is selected

Parameter grip

A

B

PROFESSIONAL TIP

If the door block in **Figure 23-25** has a second flip parameter inserted and action applied, the door can also be flipped from side to side. In this way, one block takes the place of four blocks to accommodate different door positions.

Exercise 23-8   Complete the Exercise on the Student CD.

XY Parameter

The *XY parameter* includes distance properties for both the X and Y directions. With this parameter, four parameter grips are inserted—one at each corner of a 2D box defined by the parameter. A move, scale, stretch, or array action can be assigned to an XY parameter.

To insert an XY parameter, pick the **Parameter** button on the **Block Editor** toolbar or type BPARAMETER. Then, select the **Xy** option. You can also enter this directly by selecting **XY Parameter** from the **Parameters** tab in the **Block Authoring Palettes** window.

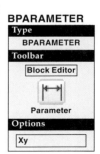

Specify base point or [Name/Label/Chain/Description/Palette/Value set]: *(pick the base point)*
Specify endpoint: *(pick a point to specify the XY grip)*
Command:

The base point is the "origin" for the X and Y distances. The endpoint is where the XY grip is placed. Grips are then automatically created on the X and Y axis aligned with the base point. See **Figure 23-26.**

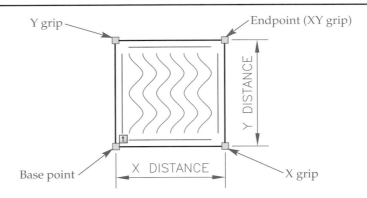

Figure 23-26.
Inserting an XY parameter into a block of architectural glass block. The XY parameter consists of X and Y distance properties and four grips.

Assigning an Array Action to the XY Parameter

An *array action* allows objects within the block to be arrayed based on preset specifications. Objects in the block that do not have the array action assigned are not arrayed. For example, the block of architectural glass block shown in **Figure 23-26** can have an XY parameter and an array action applied to it. Then, by simply manipulating the block dynamically, an architectural feature of glass blocks can be created of any size.

To assign an array action to a parameter, pick the **Action** button from the **Block Editor** toolbar, type BACTION, select **Array Action** from the **Actions** tab of the **Block Authoring Palette** window, or double-click on any part of the parameter.

BACTION
Type
BACTION
Toolbar
Block Editor
Action

    Select parameter: *(pick the parameter)*
    Enter action type [Array/Move/Scale/sTretch]: **ARRAY**⏎
    Specify selection set for action
    Select objects: *(select the objects to be included in the array)*
    n found
    Select objects: ⏎
    Enter the distance between rows or specify unit cell (- - -): *(enter a value for the dis-*
        tance between rows; alternately, pick two points to set the row and column values) ⏎
    Enter the distance between columns (lll): *(type in a value for the distance between*
        columns; this prompt will not appear if you selected two points to define the row
        and column values) ⏎
    Specify action location: *(pick a point near the parameter to place the action icon)*
    Command:

In the example of the glass block, be sure to allow for a grout line when setting the row and column distance. Before assigning the action, you may want to draw a construction point offset from the block by the thickness of the grout line. Then, you can pick two points to define the row and column values. Be sure to erase the construction point before saving the block. Otherwise, the point will be included in the block definition.

The dynamic block is now defined. Save the block and close the **Block Editor**.

Using the Array Action Dynamically

Once the block is inserted, select it to display grips. There are four parameter grips and the block insertion point grip, which may coincide with one of the parameter grips. Selecting any of the parameter grips and dragging them arrays the objects, but the resulting array remains a single block. If Dynamic Input is enabled, the array dimensions are displayed as you drag the grip. In **Figure 23-27**, the block of the architectural glass block is inserted into the drawing. By selecting a parameter grip and dragging, an array is created to fill a space. Notice the grout lines are added because the action was properly defined.

Figure 23-27.
Dynamically creating an array of architectural glass block. The block has an XY parameter and array action. By dragging the XY parameter, a pattern of rows and columns is created. Notice the grout lines between the glass blocks. By properly defining the dynamic block, these lines are automatically added.

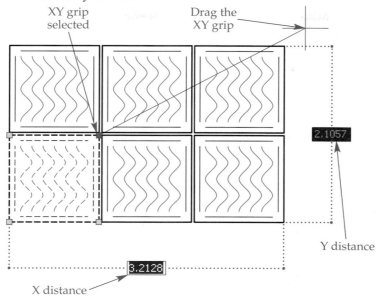

XY grip selected

Drag the XY grip

2.1057

Y distance

3.2128

X distance

Exercise 23-9   Complete the Exercise on the Student CD.

Visibility Parameter

The *visibility parameter* allows different visibility states to be assigned to objects within a block. This allows for multiple views of the same block. Selecting the visibility parameter grip on a block displays a list of the visibility states (views) created for the block. Selecting one of the views changes the block to that view. No action is associated with a visibility parameter.

For example, the four different valves shown in **Figure 23-28A** are created from a single block. When the block is defined, all of the objects representing the different variations need to be drawn. Draw the objects in reference to, or on top of, the other objects within the block. See **Figure 23-28B.** Then, a visibility parameter can be assigned and visibility states defined.

Inserting a Visibility Parameter

BPARAMETER

Type
BPARAMETER

Toolbar
Block Editor

Parameter

Options
Visibility

To insert a visibility parameter pick the **Parameter** button on the **Block Editor** toolbar or type BPARAMETER. Then, use the **Visibility** option. This can also be entered directly by selecting **Visibility Parameter** from the **Parameters** tab in the **Block Authoring Palettes** window.

> Specify parameter location or [Name/Label/Description/Palette]: *(pick a point to place the visibility grip)*
> Enter number of grips [0/1] <1>: ↵
> Command:

Figure 23-28.
A—All four of these different valves can be created from one block by using a visibility parameter. B—All of the objects composing all four valves are drawn together.

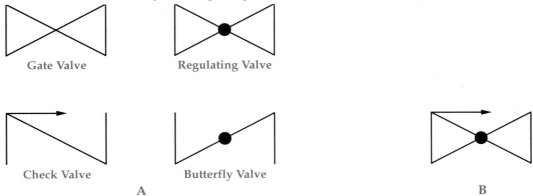

The point picked for the parameter location is where the parameter grip is placed. Picking this grip in the drawing displays the visibility states. A visibility parameter is associated with an entire block, so there is no prompt to select objects.

Creating Visibility States

Once a visibility parameter has been assigned to a block, the visibility tools on the **Block Editor** toolbar are enabled. See **Figure 23-29.** The tools for working with visibility states are located to the far right of the **Block Editor** toolbar. Remember, at lower screen resolutions, these tools may be hidden from view. Either change to a higher screen resolution or use the clean screen option ([Ctrl]+[0]) to allow the tools to be displayed. The tools are:

- **Visibility Mode.** Toggles the visibility mode on and off. When on, the objects that are currently invisible are displayed as semitransparent. When off, only the visible objects are shown. The visibility mode can also be toggled on and off by typing BVMODE.
- **Make Visible.** Prompts you to select objects to be made visible. Invisible objects are temporarily displayed as semitransparent so they can be selected.
- **Make Invisible.** Prompts you to select objects to be made invisible.
- **Manager Visibility States.** Opens the **Visibility States** dialog box. This dialog box can also be opened by typing BVSTATE.
- **Current visibility state.** This drop-down list displays the current visibility state. Picking the button displays all of the visibility states that have been created for the block. Selecting one of the states in the drop-down list makes it current.

To create a visibility state, first open the **Visibility States** dialog box. Then, pick the **New...** button. See **Figure 23-30A.** This opens the **New Visibility State** dialog box, **Figure 23-30B.** In the **Visibility state name:** text box, name the new state visibility state. For the valve

Figure 23-29.
The visibility tools are found on the right-hand end of the **Block Editor** toolbar. You may need to use the "clean screen" option ([Ctrl]+[0]) to allow the tools to be displayed.

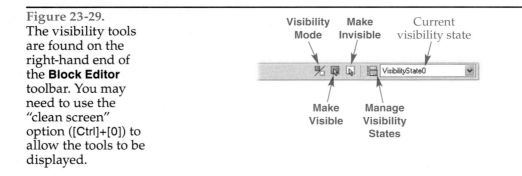

Figure 23-30.
A—The **Visibility States** dialog box is used to manage visibility states. B— The **New Visibility State** dialog box is used to create a new visibility state.

Currently defined visibility states

Pick to create a new visibility state

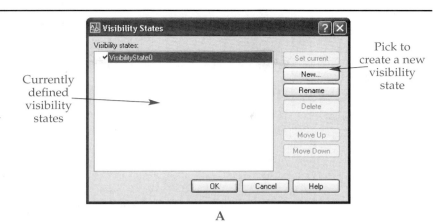

A

Name the new visibility state

Select an option

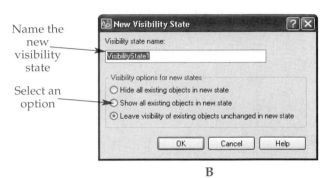

B

block example shown in **Figure 23-28**, this may be GATE VALVE, REGULATING VALVE, CHECK VALVE, or BUTTERFLY VALVE, depending on which valve the visibility state represents. In the **Visibility options for new states** area, select the option that is appropriate for the new state.

- **Hide all existing objects in new state.** When the new visibility state is created, all of the objects in the block are invisible. This allows you to turn on (display) only the objects that you want visible in the visibility state.
- **Show all existing objects in new state.** When the new visibility state is created, all of the objects in the block are visible. This allows you to turn off (hide) any objects that you want invisible for the state.
- **Leave visibility of existing objects unchanged in new state.** When the new visibility state is created, only the currently visible objects are displayed.

When you have entered a name and selected the appropriate option, pick the **OK** button in the **New Visibility State** dialog box to create the new visibility state. The new state is added to the list in the **Visibility States** dialog box and made current, as indicated by the check mark next to the name. Pick the **OK** button in the **Visibility States** dialog box to return to block editing mode.

Now, using the **Make Visible** and **Make Invisible** tools, display only the objects that should be visible in the state. For example, to make a visibility state to depict the gate valve shown in **Figure 23-28A** from the valve block shown in **Figure 23-31A**, use the **Make Invisible** command to turn off the filled circle and the arrow. See **Figure 23-31B**. The changes are automatically saved to the visibility state.

Repeat this process to create additional visibility states for the block. For the valve block, a total of four visibility states are needed. Once all the visibility states have been created, save the block and close the **Block Editor**.

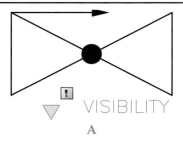
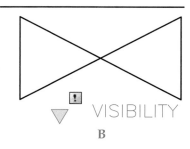

Figure 23-31.
A—The VALVE block with all of the objects visible. B—The VALVE block after the arrow and filled circle are hidden (made invisible) to create the GATE VALVE visibility state.

Using the Visibility Parameter Dynamically

Once the block is inserted, select it to display grips. The visibility grip appears as a horizontal line with a triangle below it. See Figure 23-32A. Selecting the grip displays a shortcut menu that contains the visibility states created for the block. The current visibility state (view) has a check mark next to its name. To switch to a different view of the block, simply select the name of the visibility state in the list. See Figure 23-32B.

Modifying Visibility States

Visibility states can easily be modified in the **Block Editor**. First, set the state to modify current by selecting it in the drop-down list on the **Block Editor** toolbar. Next, use the **Make Visible** and **Make Invisible** tools to change the visibility of objects as needed. New objects can also be drawn in block editing mode using the normal AutoCAD drawing commands. New objects are automatically hidden in all visibility states other than the current state.

The **Visibility States** dialog box can be used to rename, delete, and rearrange the order of the visibility states in the shortcut menu. To change the name of a state, select the state in the list and then pick the **Rename** button. The name is replaced by an edit box. Type the new name and then press the [Enter] key. To permanently remove a state, pick the **Delete** button. The states can be reordered by using the **Move Up** and **Move Down** buttons. The order in which states appear in this dialog box is the same order in which they appear in the shortcut menu displayed when the grip is selected in the drawing. The state at the top of the list is the default view for the block.

Figure 23-32.
A—After selecting the block to display grips, picking the visibility parameter grip displays the available visibility states shortcut menu. The current state is checked. B—Selecting a different visibility state from the shortcut menu changes the block.

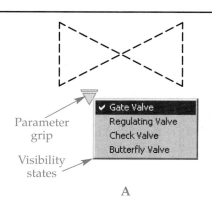
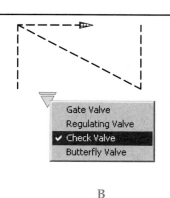

Parameter grip

Visibility states

A   B

Exercise 23-10

Complete the Exercise on the Student CD.

Lookup Parameter

A *lookup parameter* allows custom properties created in a table to be used with existing parameter values. It is used in conjunction with a lookup action. The custom properties can then be displayed in the drawing by selecting the lookup parameter grip. Basically, a lookup action allows you to select a preset group of parameter values to carry out the actions with stored values instead of having to modify the parameter property values one by one.

A lookup parameter is similar to the visibility parameter in that it allows for multiple views of the same block. However, instead of making objects visible and invisible, a lookup parameter actually changes the objects of a block based on assigned parameters and actions.

For example, look at the blocks shown in **Figure 23-33**. These three blocks are created from a single block by adjusting the rotation parameter of the middle line. The different rotation angles are 0, 10, and 20 degrees. The length of the start and end lines automatically adjust to match the rotation of the middle line.

To insert a lookup parameter, pick the **Parameter** button on the **Block Editor** toolbar or type BPARAMETER. Then, use the **looKup** option. This can also be entered directly by selecting **Lookup Parameter** from the **Parameters** tab in the **Block Authoring Palettes** window.

Specify parameter location or [Name/Label/Description/Palette]: *(pick a point to place the parameter)*
Command:

Figure 23-33.
A lookup parameter is used to create these three views of the same block. Notice how the geometry is actually changed.

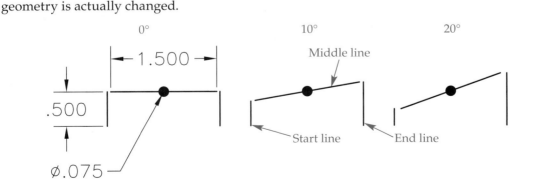

The point picked for the parameter location is where the parameter grip is placed. Picking the grip in the drawing displays a shortcut menu that contains a list of the custom groups. A lookup parameter is associated with the entire block, so no objects are selected.

BACTION

Type
BACTION

Toolbar
Block Editor

⚡

Action

Assigning a Lookup Action to the Lookup Parameter

To assign a lookup action to a lookup parameter, pick the **Action** button from the **Block Editor** toolbar, type BACTION, select **Lookup Action** from the **Actions** tab of the **Block Authoring Palette** window, or double-click on any part of the parameter.

Select parameter: *(pick the lookup parameter)*
Specify action location: *(pick a point near the parameter to place the lookup action icon)*

After specifying the action location, the **Property Lookup Table** dialog box opens. See **Figure 23-34**. This is where the lookup table is created, as described in the next sections.

Example Block

To help explain the lookup parameter and action, create the 0° block shown in **Figure 23-33**. Then, insert parameters and assign actions needed so the 10° and 20° blocks can be created from the same block. Follow these steps:

1. Create the 0° block.
2. Open the block in the **Block Editor**.
3. Insert a linear parameter, label it START LINE, select the start point as bottom of the start line, and select the endpoint as the top of the start line.
4. Assign a stretch action to the START LINE linear parameter. Associate the action with the top parameter grip, create the stretch box around the top of the start line, and select the start line as the object.
5. Insert a linear parameter, label it END LINE, select the start point as the bottom of the end line, and select the endpoint as the top of the end line.
6. Assign a stretch action to the END LINE linear parameter. Associate the action with the top parameter grip, create the stretch box around the top of the line, and select the end line as the object.

Figure 23-34.
The **Property Lookup Table** dialog box.

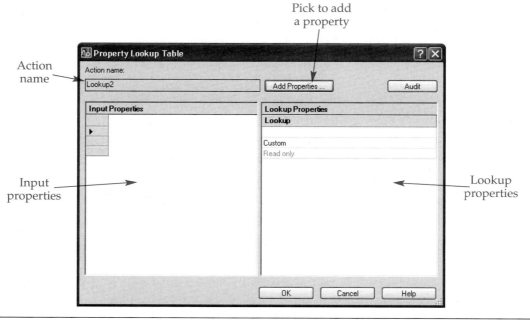

7. Insert a rotation parameter, label it MIDDLE LINE, specify the base point as the center of the circle, select the right-hand endpoint of the middle line to set the radius, and specify the default rotation angle as 0.
8. Assign a rotate action to the MIDDLE LINE rotation parameter. Select the middle line as the object and pick the center of the circle as the rotation base point.
9. Assign a lookup parameter to the block.

The block should look similar to **Figure 23-35** in the **Block Editor**.

Creating a Lookup Table

The first step in creating a lookup table is to assign a lookup action to the lookup parameter. After specifying the action location, the **Property Lookup Table** dialog box is displayed. See **Figure 23-34.**

- **Action name: text field.** Displays the name of the lookup action associated with the table.
- **Add Properties... button.** Opens the **Add Parameter Properties** dialog box, which allows properties to be added to the table.
- **Audit button.** Checks each row (record) in the table to make sure it is unique.
- **Input Properties area.** Once a parameter has been added to the table, it appears in this area and can be given a value.
- **Lookup Properties area.** In this area, the row (record) is named. This name appears in the shortcut menu when the lookup parameter grip is selected in the drawing.

To add a parameter property to the table, pick the **Add Properties...** button to open the **Add Parameter Properties** dialog box, **Figure 23-36.** The parameters that have been assigned to the block appear in the **Parameter properties:** list. Notice that the property name is the parameter label. Only parameters containing property values are displayed in the **Parameter properties:** list. The lookup, alignment, and base point parameters do not contain property values.

The **Property type** area determines which type of property parameters are shown in the list. By default, the **Add input properties** radio button is active, which displays the available input property parameters. To display the available lookup property parameters, select the **Add lookup properties** radio button.

To add a parameter property to the lookup table, select the property in the **Parameter properties:** list and pick the **OK** button. A new column is then added to the **Input Properties** area of the **Property Lookup Table** dialog box. The name of the parameter property is the column header. See **Figure 23-37.** To add values for the parameter, type the value in each cell in the column. A custom name for a row (record) is added on the same row in the **Lookup** column in the **Lookup Properties** area.

Figure 23-35.
The block with linear parameters and stretch actions assigned to the start and end lines and a rotation parameter and rotate action assigned to the middle line.

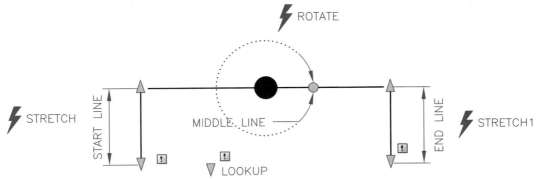

Figure 23-36.
Parameter properties are listed in the **Add Parameter Properties** dialog box.

Select a property to add →

Select the type of property →

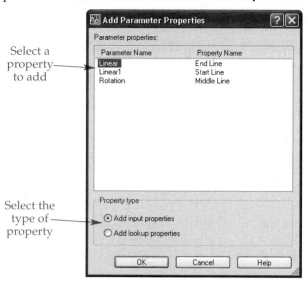

Figure 23-37.
A lookup table with multiple parameters and values added.

Parameter properties

Parameter values for the property →

Custom names for the row (record)

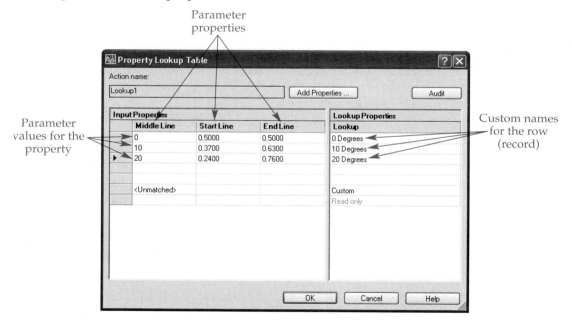

For the example block, add the MIDDLE LINE, START LINE, and END LINE properties to the table. Then, complete the lookup table as shown below. Start with the MIDDLE LINE values. Press [Enter] after typing the value to add a new blank row below it. Then, add the remaining values. Pick in a cell and type the value. Then, press [Enter], pick in a different cell, or use the tab or arrow keys to navigate through the table.

MIDDLE LINE	START LINE	END LINE	Lookup
0	0.5000	0.5000	0°
10	0.3700	0.6300	10°
20	0.2400	0.7600	20°

The row (record) that contains the <Unmatched> value, which is named Custom in the **Lookup** column, is used when the current parameter values of the block do not match any of the records in the table. You cannot add any values to the row, but you can change the name of **Custom**.

Picking in the cell at the bottom of the **Lookup** column, which currently indicates Read only, displays a drop-down list containing two options. The default Read only setting means that the lookup parameter grip is not displayed when the block is selected in the drawing. To have the lookup parameter grip displayed, select Allow reverse lookup from the drop-down list. See Figure 23-38. This can only be selected if all names in the lookup table are unique.

Once all of the properties are added to the table and values assigned to each, pick the **Audit** button in the **Property Lookup Table** dialog box to check the table. Any errors that are found will be reported. If no errors are found, as indicated by a message box, pick the **OK** button to return to the **Block Editor**. Then, save the block and close the **Block Editor**.

Using the Lookup Action Dynamically

Once the block is inserted, select it to display grips. Since Allow reverse lookup was selected in the lookup table, the lookup parameter grip is displayed along with the other parameter grips. Picking the lookup parameter grip displays a shortcut menu that contains a list of the custom named lookup records. See Figure 23-39. The entries in this shortcut menu match the entries in the **Lookup** column of the **Property Lookup Table** dialog box. Picking one of the entries in the shortcut menu changes the geometry in the block based on the parameter values in the lookup table.

Other parameters assigned to the block, linear and rotation in the case of the example block, can still be changed independently. When any of the parameters is changed, the lookup parameter becomes Custom since the current parameter values do not match one of the records in the lookup table.

Modifying a Lookup Table

To modify a lookup table, open the block in the **Block Editor** and double-click on the lookup action icon. The **Property Lookup Table** dialog box is opened. Edits can be made to values and properties in the same way as they were created. Additional

---

Figure 23-38.
The field at the bottom of the **Lookup** column determines if the lookup parameter grip is displayed when the block is selected in the drawing.

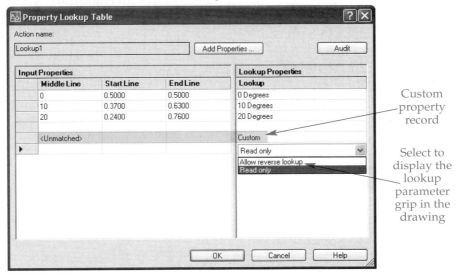

Custom property record

Select to display the lookup parameter grip in the drawing

Figure 23-39.
The lookup parameter grip is displayed when the block is selected. The list of available lookup records is displayed when the lookup parameter grip is selected.

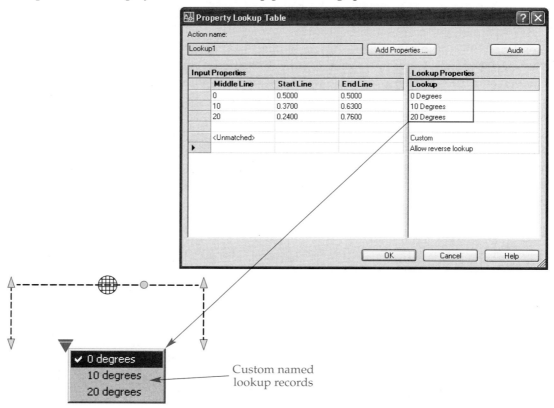

Custom named lookup records

options can be accessed by right-clicking on a column heading or on a row to display a shortcut menu. The column heading shortcut menu is displayed in **Figure 23-40A.** The available options are:

- **Sort.** Sorts the records (rows) by the selected column's values. Picking **Sort** a second time reverses the order of the sort.
- **Maximize all headings.** Adjusts the widths of all columns to the size of the column headings.
- **Maximize all data cells.** Adjusts the widths of all columns to the values in the columns.
- **Size columns equally.** Adjusts the widths of all columns so they are equal.
- **Delete property column.** Deletes the column corresponding to the heading that was right-clicked on.
- **Clear contents.** Deletes all the values entered in the column corresponding to the heading that was right-clicked on.

The row shortcut menu is displayed in **Figure 23-40B.** The available options are:

- **Insert row.** Inserts a new row above the row that was right-clicked on.
- **Delete row.** Deletes the row that was right-clicked on.
- **Clear contents.** Deletes all of the values entered in the row that was right-clicked on.
- **Move up.** Moves the row that was right-clicked up by one row.
- **Move down.** Moves the row that was right-clicked on down by one row.
- **Range syntax examples.** Displays in the online documentation examples of how values can be entered into a lookup table.

Figure 23-40.
A—This shortcut menu is displayed by right-clicking over a column heading. B—This shortcut menu is displayed by right-clicking over a row.

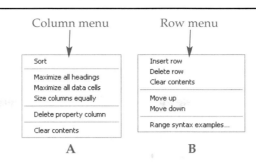

Column menu   Row menu

Sort		Insert row
		Delete row
Maximize all headings		Clear contents
Maximize all data cells		
Size columns equally		Move up
		Move down
Delete property column		
		Range syntax examples...
Clear contents		

A   B

Exercise 23-11

Complete the Exercise on the Student CD.

Base Point Parameter

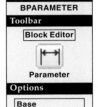

BPARAMETER

| Type |
| BPARAMETER |

Toolbar

Block Editor

Parameter

Options

Base

The *base point parameter* is used to define a base point for the block that is different from the base point that was specified when the block was created. To insert a base point parameter pick the **Parameter** button from the **Block Editor toolbar** or type BPARAMETER. Then, use the **Base** option. This can also be entered directly by selecting **Base Point Parameter** from the **Parameters** tab in the **Block Authoring Palettes** window. The only prompt is:

Specify parameter location:

At this prompt, pick a point to place the base point parameter. The parameter is displayed as a circle with crosshairs. After the block has been saved, the location of the base point parameter becomes the new base point for the block.

No actions can be assigned to a base point parameter. However, the parameter can be included in the selection set for actions.

Parameter Value Sets

A *value set* can be used to limit a parameter to certain values. This ensures that only valid values are used when dynamically modifying the block in a drawing. For example, if a window style is only available in widths of 36″, 42″, 48″, 54″, and 60″, then a value set can be created for a linear parameter with these sizes. Next, a stretch action can be applied to the parameter. Then, when the block is dynamically modified in the drawing, only one of these values can be used for the width. See **Figure 23-41**.

A value set can be used with linear, polar, XY, and rotation parameters. The option to use a value set is available at the first prompt after selecting one of the parameters to insert:

Specify start point or [Name/Label/Chain/Description/Base/Palette/Value set]:
    VALUE↵
Enter distance value set type [None/List/Increment] <None>:

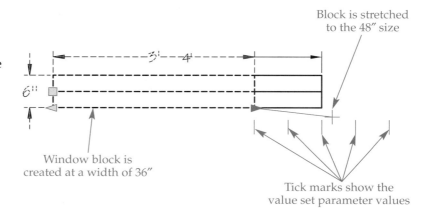

Figure 23-41.
When a value set is used, tick marks appear at locations corresponding to the values in the value set. The block can only be stretched to one of these tick marks.

Block is stretched to the 48″ size

Window block is created at a width of 36″

Tick marks show the value set parameter values

There are two different types of value sets—list and increment. The following command sequence defines a list value set for the available widths for the window example:

Enter distance value set type [None/List/Increment] <None>: **LIST**⏎
Enter list of distance values (separated by commas): **36,42,48,54,60** ⏎ *(type all of the valid values for the parameter separated by commas)*
Specify start point or [Name/Label/Chain/Description/Base/Palette/Value set]:

Next, add the parameter as if a value set is not being used. Once the parameter has been inserted and the value set is specified, the valid values for the parameter appear as tick marks.

The **List** option allows you to create a list of the possible sizes. The **Increment** option allows you to specify an incremental value to be used by the parameter. A minimum and maximum value are also set so there is a limit for the increments. Since the width values for the window are in 6″ increments, the **Increment** option can also be used:

Specify start point or [Name/Label/Chain/Description/Base/Palette/Value set]:
    VALUE⏎
Enter distance value set type [None/List/Increment] <None>: **INCREMENT**⏎
Enter distance increment: **6**⏎
Enter minimum distance: **36**⏎
Enter maximum distance: **60**⏎
Specify start point or [Name/Label/Chain/Description/Base/Palette/Value set]:

The distance increment is the incremental value to be used. The minimum distance is the lowest value that can be used; the maximum distance is the highest value.

Using a Value Set with a Parameter

After the value set and parameter are created, an action needs to be assigned to the parameter. For the window block in Figure 23-41, a stretch action is assigned to the linear parameter. This allows the window to be stretched to the valid widths specified in the value set.

Once the block is inserted, select it to display grips. Then, pick the linear parameter grip (for the window example). Tick marks appear indicating the positions of valid values. As the grip is dragged, the modified block snaps to the nearest tick mark. If Dynamic Input is enabled, a value can also be typed in the input field. If a value is typed that is not in the value set, then the nearest valid value is used.

Modifying a Value Set

To modify a value set, open the block in the **Block Editor**. Then, select the parameter to which the value set is assigned and open the **Properties** window. The value set options are shown in the **Value Set** section. See Figure 23-42. The type of value set can

Figure 23-42.
The value set
options can be
changed by using
the **Properties**
window.

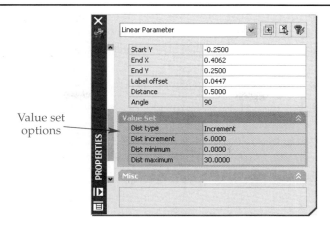

Value set
options

be changed by selecting a different type from the **Dist type** drop-down list. The other options displayed in the **Value Set** section are based on the current type of value set. When done modifying the properties, close the **Properties** window, save the block, and exit the **Block Editor**.

Exercise
23-12   Complete the Exercise on the Student CD.

Parameter Chain Action

A *chain action* can be used to trigger a parameter's action by modifying another parameter. For example, if a table is stretched, the chairs along the table need to be arrayed to match the new table length. See **Figure 23-43**. This can be accomplished in one step by using a chain action. A chain action limits the number of edits that have to be performed by allowing one action to trigger other actions at the same time. Point, linear, polar, XY, and rotation parameters can be part of a chain action.

The option to use a chain action is available at the first prompt after selecting one of the parameters to insert:

> Specify start point or [Name/Label/Chain/Description/Base/Palette/Value set]: **CHAIN**↵
> Evaluate associated actions when parameter is edited by another action? [Yes/No] <No>:

Figure 23-43.
A—A block of
a table with six
chairs. B—Using a
chain action with
a linear parameter,
the table can be
stretched and the
chairs automatically
arrayed.

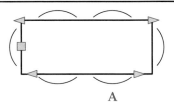

A

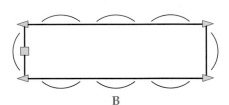

B

The **Chain** option for a parameter is either set to **Yes** or **No**. The default setting is **No**, which means that the action for the parameter cannot be affected by another action. To create a chain action on a parameter, the **Chain** option needs to be set to **Yes**.

Creating and Using a Chain Action

Using the table and chairs example, the following sequence shows how to use a chain action to automatically array the chairs when a table is stretched. First, create a block similar to the block shown in **Figure 23-44**. Then, open the block in the **Block Editor**. Pick **Linear Parameter** from the **Parameters** tab of the **Block Authoring Palette** window and continue as follows.

> Specify start point or [Name/Label/Chain/Description/Base/Palette/Value set]: **CHAIN.↵**
> Evaluate associated actions when parameter is edited by another action? [Yes/No] <No>: **Y.↵**
> Specify start point or [Name/Label/Chain/Description/Base/Palette/Value set]: **LABEL.↵**
> Enter distance property label <Distance>: **CHAIR ARRAY.↵**
> Specify start point or [Name/Label/Chain/Description/Base/Palette/Value set]: *(pick the start point shown in Figure 23-44)*
> Specify endpoint: *(pick the endpoint shown in Figure 23-44)*
> Specify label location: *(pick a location for the parameter label)*

Next, assign an array action to the parameter. Pick **Array Action** from the **Action** tab of the **Block Authoring Palette** window. Then, continue as follows.

> Select parameter: *(pick the linear parameter)*
> Select objects: *(select the chairs on the top and bottom of the table)*
> Select objects: ↵
> Enter the distance between columns (|||): *(use objects snaps to snap to the endpoint of one of the chairs and then snap to the same endpoint on the chair next to it)*
> Specify action location: *(pick a point next to the linear parameter to place the array action icon)*

Now, insert a linear parameter and stretch action for the table. Pick **Linear Parameter** from the **Parameters** tab of the **Block Authoring Palette** window and continue as follows.

> Specify start point or [Name/Label/Chain/Description/Base/Palette/Value set]: **LABEL.↵**
> Enter distance property label <Distance>: **TABLE STRETCH.↵**
> Specify start point or [Name/Label/Chain/Description/Base/Palette/Value set]: *(pick one endpoint of the table, as shown in Figure 23-45A)*
> Specify endpoint: *(pick the opposite endpoint of the table, as shown in Figure 23-45A)*
> Specify label location: *(pick a location for the parameter label)*
> Command: **BACTION.↵**

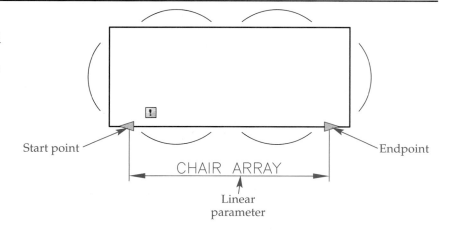

Figure 23-44.
Inserting a linear parameter that will be used with an array action for the chairs.

Start point

Endpoint

CHAIR ARRAY

Linear parameter

Select parameter: *(pick the TABLE STRETCH parameter)*
Enter action type [Array/Move/Scale/sTretch]: **STRETCH.⏎**
Specify parameter point to associate with action or enter [sTart point/Second point]
    <Start>: *(pick the endpoint parameter grip of the TABLE STRETCH parameter)*
Specify first corner of stretch frame or [CPolygon]: *(include the right-hand end of the*
    table and the right-hand parameter grip for the CHAIR ARRAY parameter, as shown
    in Figure 23-45B)
Select objects: *(select the table, the chair at the right-hand end of the table, and the*
    CHAIR ARRAY *parameter)*
Select objects: ⏎
Specify action location or [Multiplier/Offset]: *(pick a location for the action icon)*
Command:

Save the block and exit the **Block Editor**.

Once the block is inserted, select it to display grips. Then, select the right-hand TABLE STRETCH parameter grip. Drag the grip to the right to stretch the table and array the chairs. See **Figure 23-46.** Pick a point to create the new table length with the chairs arrayed automatically.

Figure 23-45.
A—Inserting a linear parameter that will be used to stretch the table. B—Assigning a stretch action to the linear parameter. When specifying the stretch frame, be sure the CHAIR ARRAY parameter grip is within the frame.

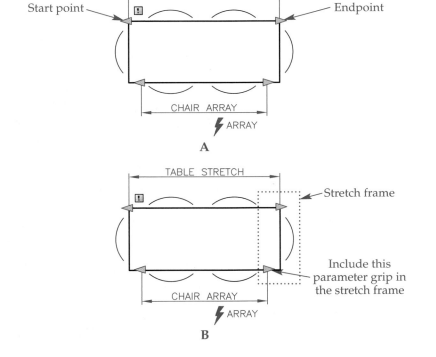

Figure 23-46.
As the parameter grip is dragged, the table is stretched and the chairs are arrayed.

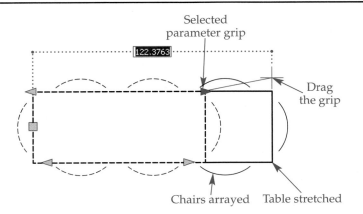

The keys to successfully creating a chain action is to set the **Chain** option to **Yes** for the parameter that is affected automaticall, and to include the parameter in the object selection set when creating the action that will drive chain action.

Multiplier and Offset Options

When inserting a move, stretch, or polar stretch action, the following prompt appears after selecting the objects to which the action applies:

Specify action location or [Multiplier/Offset]:

Entering M for the **Multiplier** option prompts you to enter a distance multiplier. The value entered in the parameter property when the parameter grip is being edited is multiplied by the value entered here. For example, if 2 is entered as the distance multiplier when creating a move action and a value of 4 units is used to move the parameter grip in the drawing, then the object actually moves 8 units.

Entering O for the **Offset** option prompts you to enter an offset angle. This angle is used to increase or decrease the parameter grip angle. For example, if an offset angle value of 45 is specified when a move action is created and a parameter grip is moved at an angle of 10° in the drawing, the object actually moves to an angle of 55°.

Parameter Sets

The **Parameter Sets** tab of the **Block Authoring Palettes** window contains commonly used parameters and actions paired as sets. These are the same parameters and actions that are found in the **Parameters** tab and the **Actions** tab. When one of the sets is used, you are prompted for the normal parameter settings. When the parameter point is specified, the action is automatically associated with the parameter.

The action is created without any objects associated with it, which is indicated by the yellow alert icon. If the parameter set contains an action that needs to have objects associated to it, as most do, double-click anywhere on the action icon. You are then prompted for the missing item(s), such as to select objects. Depending on the type of action, the prompt(s) may differ.

The **BACTIONSET** command can also be used to associate objects to an action. To use this command, type BACTIONSET. You are prompted to select the action and then the objects.

BACTIONSET

Type
BACTIONSET

Modifying Parameters and Actions

After parameters and actions have been created, their location can be edited within the **Block Editor** with grip editing and their settings can be edited using the **Properties** window. To modify the location of a parameter grip, open the block in the **Block Editor** and select the parameter. The parameter grips and the location grip for the parameter label appear. Use normal grip editing procedures to move a grip to a different location.

All of the settings for a parameter or action can be changed in the **Properties** window. In the **Block Editor**, open the **Properties** window and select a parameter or action to modify. Its settings are then displayed in the **Properties** window. The options in the **Properties** window cha ·ge depending on the type of parameter or action that is selected. In **Figure 23-47A** the **Properties** window is shown with a linear parameter selected. For a linear parameter, the main settings are found in the **Property Labels**, **Value Set**, and **Misc** sections. The **Properties** window with a stretch action selected is shown in **Figure 23-47B**.

Any parameter or action can be deleted using the **ERASE** command in the **Block Editor**. Simply select the parameter or action when prompted by the command. A parameter or action can also be deleted by first selecting it and then pressing the [Delete] key.

 **Exercise 23-13** Complete the Exercise on the Student CD.

Complete the Exercise on the Student CD.

Figure 23-47.
A—The **Properties** window with a linear parameter selected in the **Block Editor**. B—The **Properties** window with a stretch action selected in the **Block Editor**.

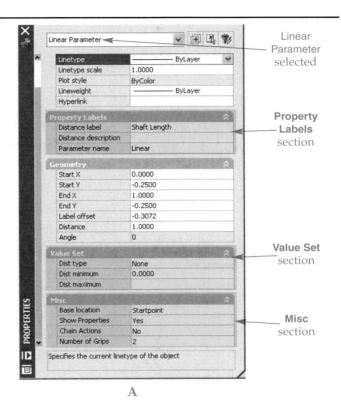

A

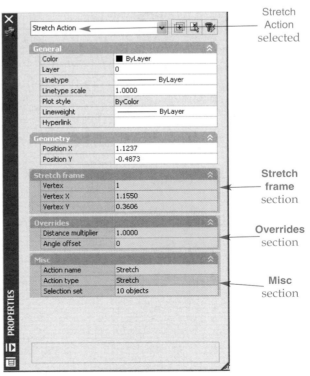

B

Chapter Test

Answer the following questions. Write your answers on a separate sheet of paper or complete the electronic chapter test on the Student CD.

1. Define *dynamic block*.
2. Compare and contrast dynamic blocks and normal blocks.
3. Briefly describe AutoCAD's **Block Editor**.
4. Define *parameter*.
5. List the parameters that can be inserted into a block.
6. Define *action*.
7. What does a point parameter do? Identify the actions that can be assigned to a point parameter.
8. Describe the shape and default color of a point parameter grip.
9. What is the shape and default color of the insertion point specified when a block is created?
10. What does a linear parameter do? Identify the actions that can be assigned to a linear parameter.
11. Describe the shape and default color of a linear parameter grip.
12. What does a stretch action do?
13. Compare and contrast a polar parameter and a linear parameter. Identify the actions that can be assigned to a polar parameter.
14. What does a rotation parameter do? Identify the actions that can be assigned to a rotation parameter.
15. What does an alignment parameter do? Identify the actions that can be assigned to an alignment parameter.
16. Give an example of where an alignment parameter may be used on a block.
17. What is the basic function of the flip parameter?
18. List the function of each grip of an XY parameter. Identify the actions that can be assigned to an XY parameter.
19. How are visibility states defined and used on a dynamic block?
20. What does a base point parameter do?
21. Explain how a lookup parameter differs from a visibility parameter.
22. What is a value set? Give an example of its use.
23. Define *chain action*. Identify the parameters that can be part of a chain action.
24. Explain how the **Multiplier** and **Offset** options can be used.
25. What are parameter sets? Explain how they are used.

Drawing Problems

1. Open P22-3 from Chapter 22. Erase all copies of the steel column symbols except for the one in the lower-left corner. Insert an XY parameter into the steel column block and associate an array action with the parameter. Use the proper values for the array action so the block can be dynamically arrayed to match the drawing. Use the one dynamic block to create the rest of the steel columns in the drawing. Save the drawing as P23-1.

2. Create a block named WIRE ROLL as shown below. Do not include the dimensions. Insert a linear parameter on the entire length of the roll. Use a value set with the following values: 36″, 42″, 48″, and 54″. Assign a stretch action to the parameter and associate the action with either parameter grip. Create a stretch frame that will allow for the length of the role to be stretched. Select all of the objects on one end and the length lines as the objects to be stretched. Insert the WIRE ROLL block four times into a drawing and stretch each block to use a different value set length. Save the drawing as P23-2.

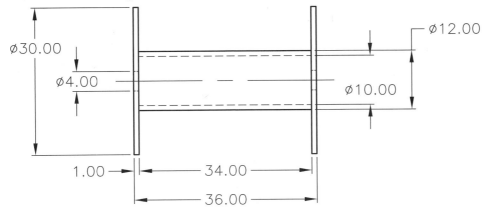

3. Create a single block that can be used to represent each of the three door blocks shown below. Name the block 30 INCH DOOR; do not include labels. Create an appropriately named visibility state for each view: 90 OPEN, 60 OPEN, and 30 OPEN. Insert the 30 INCH DOOR block into the drawing three times. Set each block to a different visibility state. Save the drawing as P23-3.

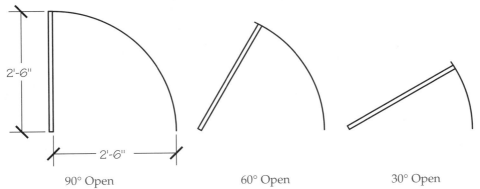

| 90° Open | 60° Open | 30° Open |

Drawing Problems - Chapter 23

4. Create a block named **90D ELBOW** as shown below on the left. Do not include the dimensions. Insert two flip parameters and flip actions. One flip parameter/action combination is for the elbow to flip horizontally. The second flip parameter/action combination is for the elbow to flip vertically. Then, use the dynamic block to create the drawing shown below on the right. Save the drawing as **P23-4**.

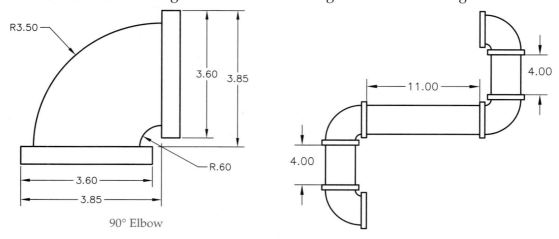

90° Elbow

5. Create a block of the 48″ window shown below on the left. Do not include the dimensions. Insert an alignment parameter so the length of the window can be aligned with a wall. Then, draw the walls shown below on the right. Insert the window block as needed. Use the alignment parameter to align the window to the walls. Windows are centered on wall segments unless dimensioned. Save the drawing as **P23-5**.

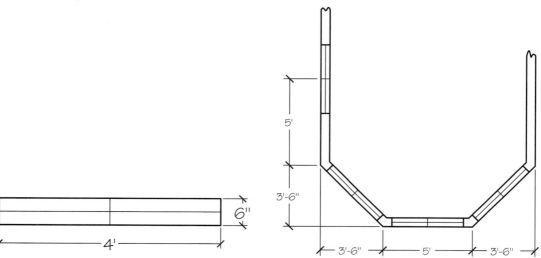

6. Create a block named **FLANGE** as shown below. Do not include dimensions. Insert a rotation parameter specifying the center of the flange as the base point. Assign a rotate action to the parameter selecting the six ⌀0.2 circles as the objects to which the action applies. Insert the **FLANGE** block into the drawing twice. Use the rotation parameter to create the two configurations shown below. Save the drawing as P23-6.

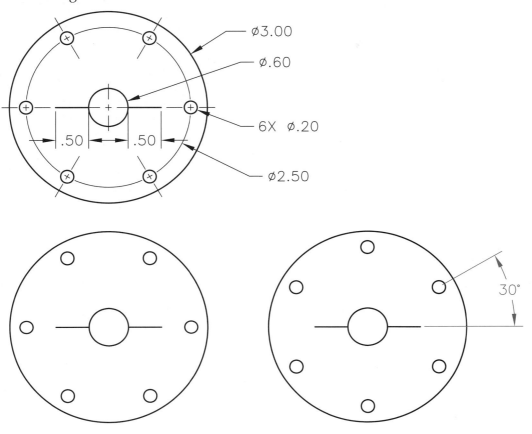

7. Create a block named **CONTROL VALVE** as shown below on the left. Include the label in the block. Insert a point parameter and assign a move action to it. Select the two lines of text as the objects to which the action applies. Then, insert the **CONTROL VALVE** block into the drawing three times. Use the point parameter to move the text to match the three positions shown below. Save the drawing as P23-7.

CONTROL VALVE
PART #336HR

CONTROL VALVE
PART #336HR

CONTROL VALVE
PART #336HR

8. Open P23-6. Save the drawing as P23-8. Open the FLANGE block in the **Block Editor** and use the **Properties** window to give the following settings to the rotation parameter:
   A. **Angle label**—BOLT HOLES
   B. **Angle description**—ROTATION OF BOLT HOLE PATTERN
   C. **Ang type**—INCREMENT
   D. **Ang increment**—30
   E. Save the changes and exit the **Block Editor**. Save the drawing.

9. The drawing below shows a fan with an enlarged view of the motor. There are three different-size motors that go with this fan. Create the fan as a dynamic block.
   A. Draw all the objects. Do not dimension the drawing or draw the enlarged view.
   B. Create a block named FAN consisting of the objects shown in the enlarged view.
   C. Open the block in the **Block Editor** and insert a linear parameter along the top of the motor (the 1.50" dimension). Use a value set with the following values: 1.5, 1.75, and 2.
   D. Assign a scale action to the linear parameter. Select all of the objects that make up the motor as the objects to which the action applies. Use an independent base type and specify the base point as the lower-left corner of the motor (the implied intersection).
   E. Save the block and exit the **Block Editor**.
   F. Insert the block three times into the drawing. Use the linear parameter grip to scale the motor to the three different sizes, as shown below on the right.
   G. Save the drawing as P23-9.

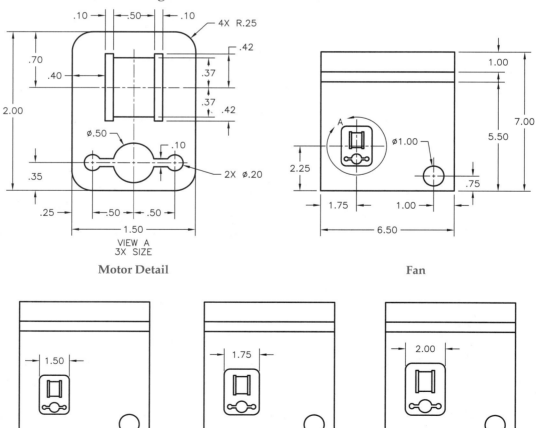

Motor Detail

Fan

AutoCAD and Its Applications—Basics

10. The bolt shown in the drawing below is available in four different lengths. As the length increases, the size of the bolt head increases for added strength. Create a dynamic block that will allow the length of the shaft and the size of the bolt head to be changed in a single operation.
   A. Draw the objects composing the bolt and create a block named BOLT. Do not include dimensions.
   B. Insert a linear parameter along the length of the shaft from the bottom of the bolt head to the end of the shaft. Label it SHAFT LENGTH.
   C. Assign a stretch action to the SHAFT LENGTH parameter. Associate the action with the parameter grip at the end of the shaft. Create a stretch frame around the end of the shaft that includes the threads. Select the end of the shaft, threads, and edges of the shaft.
   D. Insert a linear parameter along the depth of the bolt head (the .3″ dimension). Label it HEAD THICKNESS.
   E. Assign a scale action to the HEAD THICKNESS parameter and select the objects that compose the bolt head. Use an independent base type and specify the midpoint of the vertical line where the shaft meets the bolt head.
   F. Insert a lookup parameter and then assign a lookup action to it.
   G. Add the SHAFT LENGTH and the HEAD THICKNESS parameters to the lookup table. Complete the table with the following properties:

Shaft Length	Head Thickness	Lookup
1	0.3	1″ Length
1.5	0.333	1.5″ Length
2	0.366	2″ Length
2.5	0.4	2.5″ Length

   H. Set the table to allow reverse lookup, save the block, and exit the **Block Editor**.
   I. Insert the block four times into the drawing. Specify a different lookup property for each block.
   J. Save the drawing as P23-10.

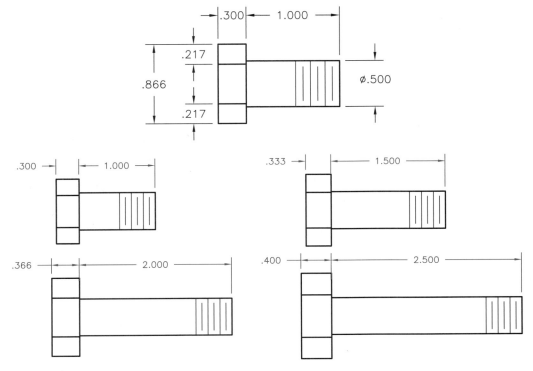

A sample of symbols from eight of the symbol libraries in AutoCAD.

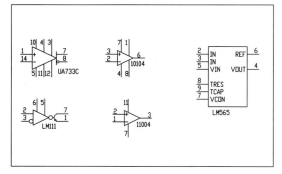

Analog Integrated Circuits

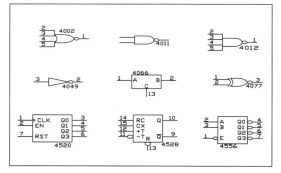

CMOS Integrated Circuits

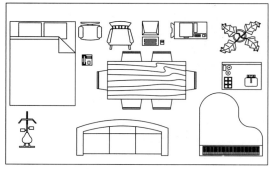

Home-Space Planner

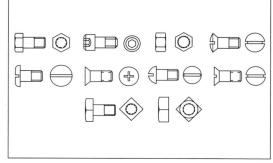

Fasteners-US

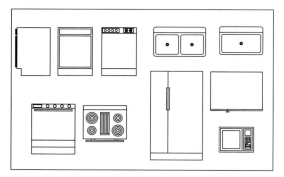

Kitchens

House Designer

Landscaping

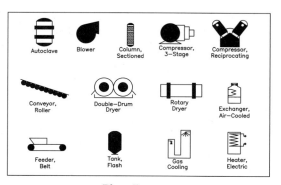

Plant Process

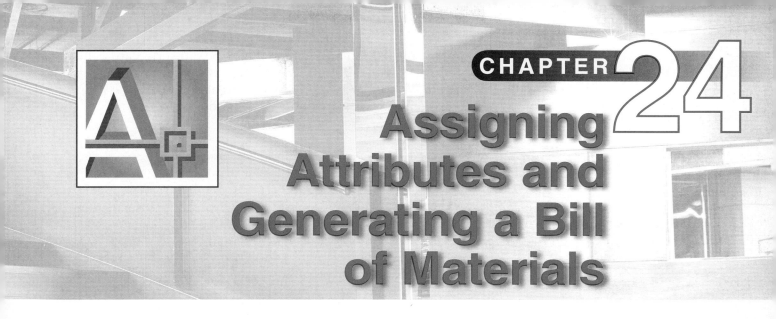

CHAPTER 24

Assigning Attributes and Generating a Bill of Materials

Learning Objectives

After completing this chapter, you will be able to do the following:

- Assign attributes to blocks.
- Edit attributes defined for existing blocks.
- Create a template file for the storage of block attribute data.
- Extract attribute values to create a bill of materials.
- Create a table from attribute information.

Blocks become more useful when written information is provided with them. It is even more helpful to be able to assign information to a block and make it either visible or hidden. From these data, a list very similar to a bill of materials can be requested and printed.

Written or numerical values assigned to blocks are called *attributes*. In addition to being used as text, attribute information can be *extracted* from a drawing. Several blocks with attributes are shown in Figure 24-1.

Figure 24-1.
Examples of blocks with defined attributes.

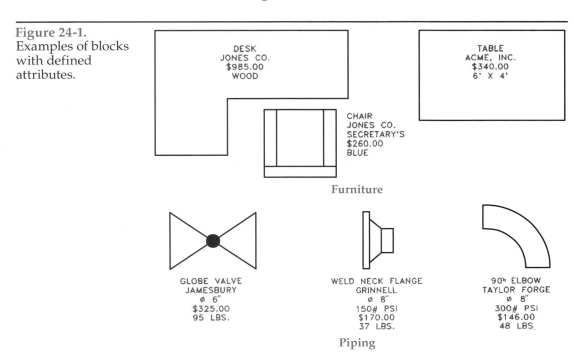

Attributes are created using the **Attribute Definition** dialog box. Inserted attribute values can be modified using the **Enhanced Attribute Editor**. Attribute definitions are modified using the **Block Attribute Manager**. Finally, block and attribute text data can be exported into other applications using the **Attribute Extraction** wizard.

Assigning Attributes to Blocks

The first step in defining attributes for a block is to determine the information needed for the block. In most cases, the name of the object should be the first attribute. This could be followed by other attribute items, such as the manufacturer, type, size, price, and weight. After you determine which attributes to assign, decide how the user should be prompted to enter a value for each attribute. For example, What is the size? might be a typical prompt.

Suppose you are drawing a valve symbol for a piping flow diagram. You might want to list all of the product-related data along with the symbol. The number of attributes needed is limited only by the project requirements.

Once the symbol is drawn, you can use the **ATTDEF** (attribute define) command to assign attributes. To access this command, pick **Draw > Block > Define Attributes...** or type ATT or ATTDEF. This displays the **Attribute Definition** dialog box, **Figure 24-2**.

The **Attribute Definition** dialog box is divided into four areas. Each area allows you to set the specific aspects of an attribute. The four areas, their components, and other features in the **Attribute Definition** dialog box are:

- **Mode area.** Use this area to specify any of the attribute modes you wish to set. If you do not activate any of the attribute modes, the user is prompted to enter values for all attributes and the attributes are visible when the block is inserted.
  - **Invisible.** If this check box is activated, the attribute is not displayed when the block is inserted. Otherwise, the attribute is shown with the inserted block.
  - **Constant.** If the value of the attribute should always be the same, activate the **Constant** check box. All insertions of the block will display the same value for the attribute; the user is not prompted for a new value. Leave this check box inactive to use different attribute values for multiple insertions of the block.

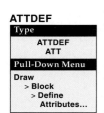

ATTDEF

Type	
ATTDEF	
ATT	

Pull-Down Menu

Draw
  > Block
    > Define
      Attributes...

Figure 24-2.
Attributes can be assigned to blocks using the **Attribute Definition** dialog box.

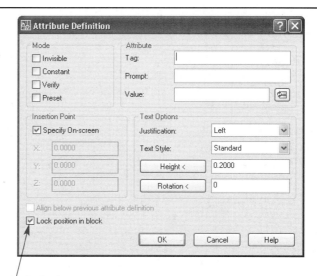

Check to include the attribute in an action set of a dynamic block

- **Verify.** Activate the **Verify** check box if you want a prompt to ask the user whether or not the specified attribute value is correct when the block is inserted.
- **Preset.** Activate the **Preset** check box to have the attribute to assume preset values during block insertion. This option disables the attribute prompt. Leave this check box inactive to display the normal prompt.
- **Attribute area.** This area lets you assign a tag, prompt, and value to the attribute in the corresponding text boxes. The entries in these text boxes can contain up to 256 characters. If the first character in an entry is a space, start the string with a backslash (\). If the first character is a backslash, begin the entry with two backslashes (\\).
  - **Tag: text box.** Use this text box to enter the name, or tag, of the attribute. You must enter a name or number. Any characters can be used except spaces. All text is displayed in uppercase.
  - **Prompt: text box.** Enter a statement in this text box that AutoCAD will use to prompt the user when the block is inserted. For example, if SIZE is specified as the attribute tag, What is the valve size? or Enter valve size: might be entered as the prompt. If the **Constant** attribute mode is inactive, this option is disabled.
  - **Value: text box.** The entry in this text box is used as a *default* attribute value when the block is inserted. You might decide to enter a message regarding the type of information needed, such as 10 SPACES MAX or NUMBERS ONLY. The **Insert field** button can be used to include a field in the default value. The default value is displayed in chevrons (<>) when the user is prompted for the attribute value. The **Value:** text box can be left blank.
- **Text Options area.** This area allows you to specify the justification, style, height, and rotation angle for attribute text.
  - **Justification.** Use this drop-down list to select a justification for the attribute text. The default option is Left.
  - **Text Style.** Use this drop-down list to select a text style defined in the current drawing.
  - **Height.** Specify the height of the attribute text in the text box to the right of the **Height<** button. Alternately, pick the **Height<** button to temporarily return to the drawing area and pick two points to indicate the text height. Once the points are picked, the dialog box returns and the corresponding height is shown in the text box.
  - **Rotation.** To specify a rotation angle for the attribute text, enter an angular value in the text box next to the **Rotation<** button. Alternately, pick the **Rotation<** button and specify a rotation by picking points in the drawing area.
- **Insertion Point area.** This area is used to select the location for the attribute. Coordinates can be entered in the text boxes if the **Specify On-screen** check box is unchecked. If the check box is checked, you must select the attribute location on screen when the **OK** button is picked to close the **Attribute Definition** dialog box.
- **Align below previous attribute definition check box.** If there are no attributes in the drawing, this check box is grayed out. If the drawing contains at least one attribute, this check box is available. Checking it places the attribute that is being created below the most recently created attribute using the justification of that attribute. When this check box is checked, the **Text Options** and **Insertion Point** areas become inactive.
- **Lock position in block check box.** This check box is used for an attribute that will be part of a dynamic block. This check box must be checked for the attribute to be included as part of the action selection set when assigning an action to a dynamic block. If it is unchecked, the attribute is filtered out when the action is assigned to the dynamic block. Dynamic blocks are covered in Chapter 23.

Once all elements of the attribute are defined, pick **OK** to close the **Attribute Definition** dialog box. The attribute tag is then placed on screen if coordinates were specified. Or, you are prompted to select a location if coordinates were not included in the definition. If the attribute mode is set to **Invisible**, do not be dismayed by the fact that the tag is visible; this is the only time the tag appears. When the block is inserted, the user is prompted for information based on the attribute definition.

Using the Properties Window

The **Properties** window provides expanded editing capabilities for attributes. To activate the **Properties** window, pick the **Properties** button on the **Standard** toolbar; pick **Modify** > **Properties** from the pull-down menu; type CH, MO, PROPS, or PROPERTIES; or use the [Ctrl]+[2] key combination. The attribute to be edited can also be selected while no command is active. Then, right-click and select **Properties** from the shortcut menu.

Figure 24-3 shows the **Properties** window with an attribute selected. You can change the color, linetype, or layer of the selected attribute in the **General** section. The attribute tag, prompt, and default value entries are listed in the **Text** section. You can select **Tag**, **Prompt**, or **Value** to change the corresponding values. If the value contains a field, it appears as normal text in the **Properties** window. If you modify the field text, it is automatically converted to text. There are also options to change the text style, justification, height, rotation angle, width factor, and obliquing angle in the **Text** section. You can change the insertion point of the text attribute in the **Geometry** section by using the **Position** options to enter new coordinates. Additional text options are available in the **Misc** section.

PROPERTIES

Type
PROPERTIES
PROPS
CH
MO
[Ctrl]+[2]

Pull-Down Menu
Modify
> Properties

Toolbar
Standard

Properties

Figure 24-3.
The **Properties** window can be used to modify attributes.

Selected object to edit

Pick to change the attribute tag

Pick to change an attribute mode setting

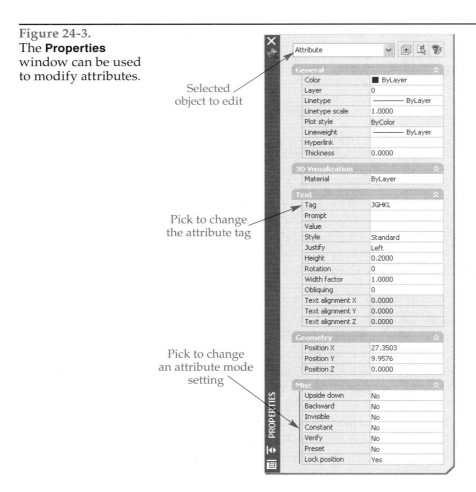

Perhaps the most powerful feature of the **Properties** window for editing attributes is the ability to change the attribute modes that were originally defined. As discussed earlier, an attribute may be defined with the **Invisible, Constant, Verify,** or **Preset** modes active. These settings are located in the **Misc** section of the **Properties** window.

Creating the Block

Once attributes have been created for an object, use the **BLOCK** or **WBLOCK** command to define the block. Blocks are discussed in Chapters 22 and 23. When creating the block, be sure to select all of the objects and attributes that go with the block. The order in which the attribute definitions are selected is the order in which the user is prompted or order in which the attributes appear in the **Enter Attributes** dialog box. If you select the attribute definitions using either the **Window** or **Crossing** selection method, the user will be prompted for the attribute values in the *reverse* order of creation of the attribute definitions.

When creating the block, activate the **Delete** option button in the **Block Definition** dialog box. When the block is created, the selected objects and attributes disappear. If any attributes remain on screen, undo the command and try again, making sure that all of the attributes are selected.

PROFESSIONAL TIP

If you create attributes in the order in which you want to be prompted for their values, and the **Window** or **Crossing** selection method is used to select them for inclusion in the block, the attribute prompting will be in the *reverse* order of the desired prompting. This can be changed by inserting the block, exploding it, and redefining the block. When specifying the new definition, pick the attributes by using the **Window** or **Crossing** selection method. This will reverse the order of the attribute prompting once again, thereby placing the prompts in the initially desired order.

LEGACY NOTE

Attributes can be defined with the **-ATTDEF** by typing -ATT or -ATTDEF. The command sequence then provides all the options found in the **Attribute Definition** dialog box.

Inserting Blocks with Attributes

When the **INSERT** command is used to place a saved block containing attributes into a drawing, the user is prompted for additional information after the block's insertion point, scale factors, and rotation angle are specified. The prompt statement entered with the **ATTDEF** command appears and the default attribute value is shown in brackets. Accept the default by pressing [Enter] or provide a new value and press [Enter]. The attribute is then displayed with the block.

If the attribute value includes a field, the default must be accepted to maintain the field. If the value is changed at the Command: prompt, the field is lost.

Attribute prompts are answered in a dialog box if the **ATTDIA** system variable is set to 1. After issuing the **INSERT** command and entering the insertion point, scale, and rotation angle of a block, the **Enter Attributes** dialog box appears. See **Figure 24-4**. This dialog box can list up to eight attributes. If the block has more than eight attributes, the next page of attributes is displayed by picking the **Next** button at the bottom of the dialog box. When finished entering values for the attributes, pick **OK** to close the dialog box. The inserted block then appears on screen with any visible attributes.

Responding to attribute prompts in a dialog box has distinct advantages over answering prompts on the command line. With the dialog box, you can see at a glance whether all of the attribute values are correct. To change a value, simply move to the incorrect value and enter a new one. If a value includes a field, you can right-click on the field to either edit it or convert it to text. You can quickly move forward through the attributes and buttons in the **Enter Attributes** dialog box by using the [Tab] key. Using the [Shift]+[Tab] key combination cycles through the attributes and buttons in reverse order.

PROFESSIONAL TIP Set the **ATTDIA** system variable to 1 in your template drawings to automatically activate the **Enter Attributes** dialog box whenever a block with attributes is inserted.

Exercise 24-1 Complete the Exercise on the Student CD.

Attribute Prompt Suppression

Some drawings may use blocks with attributes that always retain their default values. In this case, there is no need to be prompted for the attribute values when inserting a block. You can turn off the attribute prompts by setting the **ATTREQ** system variable to 0.

After making this setting, try inserting the VALVE block created in Exercise 24-1. Notice that none of the attribute prompts appear. To display attribute prompts again, change the setting back to 1. The **ATTREQ** system variable setting is saved with the drawing.

Figure 24-4.
The **Enter Attributes** dialog box allows you to enter or change attribute definitions when a block is inserted.

Accept or change the existing attributes

Pick to display the next page of attributes

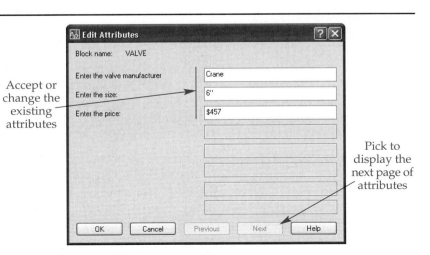

Part of your project and drawing planning should involve the setting of system variables such as **ATTREQ**. Setting **ATTREQ** to 0 before using blocks can save time in the drawing process. Always remember to set **ATTREQ** back to 1 when you want to use the prompts instead of accepting defaults. When anticipated attribute prompts are not issued, you should check the current **ATTREQ** setting and adjust it if necessary.

Controlling the Display of Attributes

Attributes are intended to contain valuable information about the blocks in a drawing. This information is normally not displayed on screen or during plotting. The principal function of attributes is to generate materials lists and to speed accounting. In most cases, you can use the **TEXT** and **MTEXT** commands to create specific labels or other types of text.

To control the display of attributes on screen, use the **ATTDISP** (attribute display) command. This command can be accessed by picking **View > Display > Attribute Display** or by typing ATTDISP. There are three options:

ATTDISP
Type
ATTDISP
Pull-Down Menu
View
> Display
> Attribute
Display

- **Normal.** This option displays attributes exactly as they were created. This is the default setting.
- **ON.** This option displays *all* attributes, including those defined with the **Invisible** mode.
- **OFF.** This option suppresses the display of *all* attributes.

After attributes have been drawn, defined with blocks, and checked for correctness, hide them with the **Off** option of the **ATTDISP** command. If attributes are left on, they clutter the screen and lengthen regeneration time. In a drawing where attributes should be visible but are not, check the current setting of **ATTDISP** and adjust it if necessary.

Changing Attribute Values

As discussed earlier, you can edit attributes before they are included in a block using the **Properties** window. However, once a block with attributes is inserted in a drawing, different commands are used to edit the inserted attributes. Inserted attribute values within a single block can be modified using the **Enhanced Attribute Editor**.

To access the **Enhanced Attribute Editor** dialog box, pick the **Edit Attribute...** button on the **Modify II** toolbar, select **Modify > Object > Attribute > Single...** from the pull-down menu, or type EATTEDIT. You are then prompted to select a block. Pick the block containing the attributes you wish to modify and the **Enhanced Attribute Editor** is displayed. See **Figure 24-5.**

EATTEDIT
Type
EATTEDIT
Pull-Down Menu
Modify
> Object
> Attribute
> Single...
Toolbar
Modify II
Edit Attribute...

Figure 24-5.
Select the attribute to be modified and change its value in the **Attribute** tab of the **Enhanced Attribute Editor**.

Select the attribute to be modified

Value of the selected attribute

Pick to apply changes

Pick to select a different block to be modified

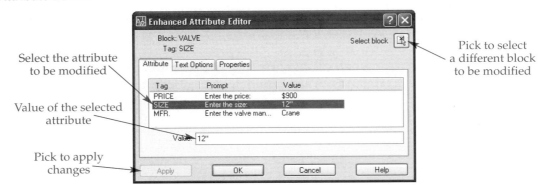

The **Enhanced Attribute Editor** contains three tabs. The **Attribute** tab is displayed when the dialog box is initially accessed with the attributes within the selected block listed in the window. Pick the attribute to be modified. Then, enter a new value for the attribute in the **Value:** text box and pick the **Apply** button.

If you want to select a different block to modify, pick the **Select block** button in the dialog box. The dialog box is temporarily closed. Then, select a different block in the drawing. The dialog box is redisplayed with the attributes for the selected block shown.

Other properties of the selected attribute can be modified using the two other tabs in the **Enhanced Attribute Editor** dialog box. The **Text Options** tab allows you to modify the text properties of the attribute. See **Figure 24-6**. The **Properties** tab contains settings for the object properties of the attribute **Figure 24-7**.

After editing the attribute values and properties, pick the **Apply** button to have the changes reflected on screen. Picking the **OK** button closes the dialog box and applies any changes.

Exercise 24-2   Complete the Exercise on the Student CD.

Figure 24-6.
The **Text Options** tab provides options in addition to those set in the **Attribute Definition** dialog box.

Text modification options

Text options not available in the **Attribute Definition** dialog box

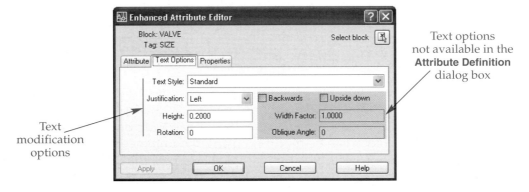

Figure 24-7.
The **Properties** tab can be used to modify an attribute's object properties.

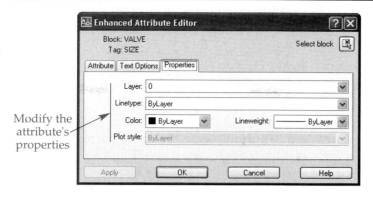

Modify the attribute's properties

Using the Find Command to Edit Attributes

One of the quickest ways to edit attributes is to use the **FIND** command. With no command active, right-click in the drawing area and select **Find...** from the shortcut menu. The **Find and Replace** dialog box is displayed. You can then search the entire drawing or a selected group of objects for an attribute. The **Find and Replace** dialog box is discussed in detail in Chapter 8.

PROFESSIONAL TIP

If you know specific attributes may need to be changed in the future, make a group out of them. Use the **GROUP** command, select all of the attributes, and give the group a name. Then, after picking the **Select objects** button in the **Find and Replace** dialog box, type G and specify the name of the group. All objects in that group are selected.

Editing Attribute Values and Properties Globally

The **Enhanced Attribute Editor** allows you to edit attribute values by selecting blocks one at a time. You can also edit several block attributes at once or edit attributes individually by answering prompts on the command line. This type of attribute editing is done with the **-ATTEDIT** command. To access this command, select **Modify > Object > Attribute > Global** or type **-ATE** or **-ATTEDIT**.

This prompt asks if you want to edit attributes individually. Pressing [Enter] at this prompt to accept the default Yes allows you to select any number of different block attributes for individual editing. AutoCAD lets you edit them all, one at a time, without leaving the command.

It is also possible to change the same attribute on several insertions of the same block. If you enter the **-ATTEDIT** command and respond with No, you can change specific letters, words, and values of a single attribute. This lets you change all other insertions, or instances, of the same block and is known as *global attribute editing*. For example, suppose a block with the attribute RESISTOR was inserted on a drawing in twelve locations. However, you misspelled the attribute as RESISTER. If you enter the **-ATTEDIT** command and specify No when asked whether to edit attributes individually, you can edit the attribute *globally*.

-EATTEDIT

Type
-EATTEDIT
-ATE

Pull-Down Menu

Modify
> Object
> Attribute
> Global

Each **-ATTEDIT** editing technique allows you to determine the exact block and attribute specifications to edit. The following prompts appear after you specify individual or global editing:

    Enter block name specification <*>:
    Enter attribute tag specification <*>:
    Enter attribute value specification <*>:

To selectively edit attribute values, respond to each prompt with the correct name or value. You are then prompted to select one or more attributes. Suppose you receive the following message after entering an attribute value and selecting an attribute:

    0 found

You picked an attribute that was not specified correctly. It is often quicker to press [Enter] at each of the three specification prompts and then *pick* the attribute you need to edit.

In **Figure 24-8A,** the VALVE block from Exercise 24-1 was inserted three times with the manufacturer's name specified as CRANE. Unfortunately, the name was supposed to be POWELL. To change the attribute for each insertion, enter the **-ATTEDIT** command and specify global editing. Then, press [Enter] at each of the three specification prompts and respond to the prompts that follow.

    Command: **-ATE** *or* **-ATTEDIT**⏎
    Edit attributes one at a time? [Yes/No] <Y>: **N**⏎
    Performing global editing of attribute values.
    Edit only attributes visible on screen? [Yes/No] <Y>: ⏎
    Enter block name specification <*>: ⏎
    Enter attribute tag specification <*>: ⏎
    Enter attribute value specification <*>: ⏎
    Select Attributes: *(pick* CRANE *on each of the* VALVE *blocks and press* [Enter] *when completed)*
    3 attributes selected.
    Enter string to change: **CRANE**⏎
    Enter new string: **POWELL**⏎

After pressing [Enter], the CRANE attributes on the selected blocks are changed to the new value POWELL. See **Figure 24-8B.**

Figure 24-8.
Using the global editing technique with the **-ATTEDIT** command allows you to change the same attribute on several block insertions.

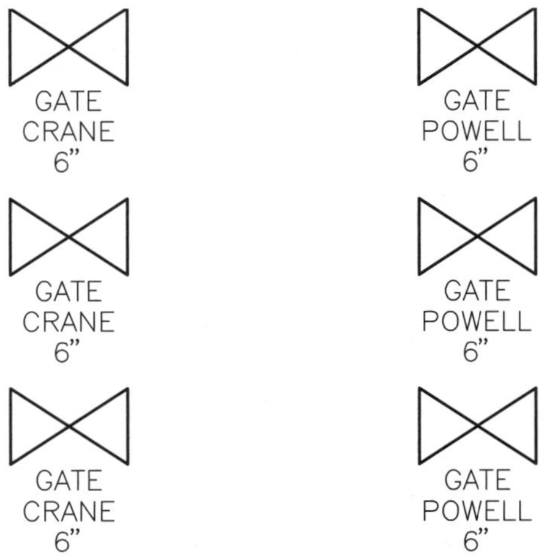

GATE
CRANE
6"

GATE
POWELL
6"

GATE
CRANE
6"

GATE
POWELL
6"

GATE
CRANE
6"

GATE
POWELL
6"

Existing Blocks

After Global Editing

A

B

PROFESSIONAL TIP

Use care when assigning the **Constant** mode to attribute definitions. The **-ATTEDIT** command displays 0 found if you attempt to edit an inserted block attribute with a **Constant** mode setting. The inserted block must then be exploded and redefined. Assign the **Constant** mode only to attributes you know will not change.

NOTE

The **-ATTEDIT** command can also be used to edit individual attribute values and properties. However, it is more efficient to use the **Enhanced Attribute Editor** for changing individual attributes.

Exercise 24-3

Complete the Exercise on the Student CD.

Changing Attribute Definitions

BATTMAN

Before saving an attribute within a block, you can modify the tag, prompt, and default value using the **DDEDIT** command. However, once an attribute is saved in a block definition, you must use the **Block Attribute Manager** to change the attribute definition, as described in this section.

The **Block Attribute Manager** is accessed by picking the **Block Attribute Manager...** button from the **Modify II** toolbar, selecting **Modify** > **Object** > **Attribute** > **Block Attribute Manager...** from the pull-down menu, or typing BATTMAN. The **Block Attribute Manager** is shown in **Figure 24-9**.

The **Block Attribute Manager** lists the attributes for the selected block. To select a block, choose it from the **Block:** drop-down list or pick the **Select block** button to return to the drawing area and pick the block. By default, the tag, prompt, default value, and modes for each attribute are listed.

The attribute list reflects the order in which prompts appear when a block is inserted. To change the order, use the **Move Up** and **Move Down** buttons to change the location of the selected attribute within the list. To delete an attribute, pick the **Remove** button.

You can select the attribute properties to be listed in the **Block Attribute Manager** by picking the **Settings...** button to open the **Settings** dialog box, **Figure 24-10.** Select the properties to list in the **Display in list** area. When the **Emphasize duplicate tags** check box at the bottom of the dialog box is checked, attributes with identical tags are highlighted in red. If you want the changes in the **Block Attribute Manager** applied to existing blocks, check the **Apply changes to existing references** check box. When all settings have been made in the **Settings** dialog box, pick the **OK** button to close it and return to the **Block Attribute Manager**.

To modify an attribute definition, select the attribute in the **Block Attribute Manager** and then pick the **Edit...** button. The **Edit Attribute** dialog box is displayed, **Figure 24-11.** The **Attribute** tab of this dialog box allows you to modify the modes, tag, prompt, and default value. Use the check boxes in the **Mode** area of the tab to select the desired mode(s). Enter new text strings in the **Tag:**, **Prompt:**, and **Default:** text boxes.

Figure 24-9.
Use the **Block Attribute Manager** to change attribute definitions, delete attributes, and change the order of attribute prompts.

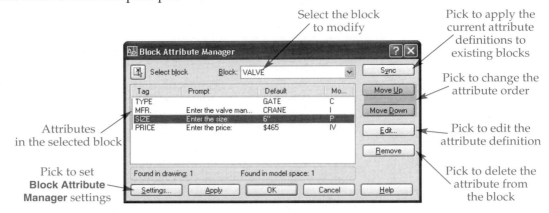

Select the block to modify

Pick to apply the current attribute definitions to existing blocks

Pick to change the attribute order

Attributes in the selected block

Pick to edit the attribute definition

Pick to set **Block Attribute Manager** settings

Pick to delete the attribute from the block

Figure 24-10.
The **Settings** dialog box controls the display of the attribute list in the **Block Attribute Manager**.

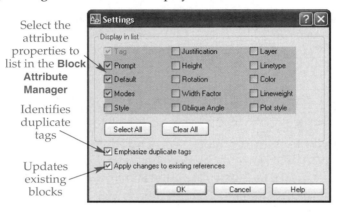

Select the attribute properties to list in the **Block Attribute Manager**

Identifies duplicate tags

Updates existing blocks

Figure 24-11.
Use the **Edit Attribute** dialog box to modify attribute definitions and properties.

Use these tabs to modify attribute properties

Select modes

Modify attribute definition

The **Text Options** and **Properties** tabs of the **Edit Attribute** dialog box are identical to the same tabs found in the **Enhanced Attribute Editor**. These tabs allow you to modify the object properties of the attributes. If the **Auto preview changes** check box at the bottom of the dialog box is checked, changes to attributes are displayed in the drawing area immediately.

After modifying the attribute definition in the **Edit Attribute** dialog box, pick the **OK** button to return to the **Block Attribute Manager**. Then, pick the **OK** button in the **Block Attribute Manager** to return to the drawing. When attributes within a block are modified, all future insertions of the block will reflect the changes. Existing blocks are updated only if the **Apply changes to existing references** check box in the **Settings** dialog box is checked. If this option is not selected, the existing blocks retain the original attribute definitions.

> **NOTE**
> The **Block Attribute Manager** modifies attribute *definitions*, not attribute *values*. Attribute values are modified with the **Enhanced Attribute Editor**.

Redefining a Block and Its Attributes

You may encounter a situation in which an existing block and its associated attributes must be revised. You may need to delete existing attributes, add new attributes, or revise the geometry of the block itself. This could be a time-consuming task, but it is made easy with the **ATTREDEF** command. To access this command, type ATTREDEF. If the command has already been used once in this drawing, you can also type AT. You are then prompted to select the attribute to be redefined.

ATTREDEF
Type
ATTREDEF
AT

When redefining a block and its attributes, a copy of the existing block must be exploded prior to using the **ATTREDEF** command. Otherwise, completely new geometry must be used. If you attempt to select the existing block, this error message is displayed:

New block has no attributes.

Once you explode the existing block (or draw new geometry) and modify the attributes as needed, use the **ATTREDEF** command:

Command: **AT** *or* **ATTREDEF**⏎
Enter name of the block you wish to redefine: *(enter the block name and press* [Enter]*)*
Select objects for new Block…
Select objects: *(select the block geometry and all new and existing attributes; then press* [Enter]*)*
Specify insertion base point of new Block: *(pick the insertion base point)*

After the insertion point is picked, all existing instances of the block and attributes are immediately updated. If any of the attributes were omitted from the redefined block, they are not included in the new version.

Using Attributes to Automate Drafting Documentation

So far you have seen that attributes are extremely powerful tools for assigning textual information to drawing symbols. However, attributes can also be used to automate any detailing or documentation task that requires a great deal of text. Such tasks include the creation of title block information, revision block data, and a parts list or list of materials.

Title Blocks

After a drawing is completely developed and dimensioned, it is then necessary to fill out the information used in the drawing title block. This is usually one of the more time-consuming tasks associated with drafting documentation, and it can be efficiently automated by assigning attributes. The following guidelines are suggested:

- The title block format is first drawn in accordance with industry or company standards. Use the correct layer(s) and be sure to include your company or school logo in the title block. If you work in an industry that produces items for the federal government, also include the applicable Federal Supply Code for Manufacturers (FSCM) in the title block. A typical A-size title block drawn in accordance with the ASME Y14.1 *Decimal Inch Drawing Sheet Size and Format* standard is illustrated in **Figure 24-12**.

NOTE The FSCM is a five-digit numerical code identifier applicable to any organization that produces items used by the federal government. It also applies to government activities that are responsible for the development of certain specifications, drawings, or standards that control the design of items.

- After drawing the title block, create a separate layer for the title block attributes. By placing the attributes on a separate layer, you can easily suppress the title block information by freezing the layer that contains the attributes. This can greatly reduce redraw and regeneration times. Then, when you are ready to plot the finished drawing, simply thaw the frozen layer.

Figure 24-12.
A title block sheet must adhere to applicable standards. This title block is for an A-size sheet and adheres to the ASME Y14.1, *Decimal Inch Drawing Sheet Size and Format* standard.

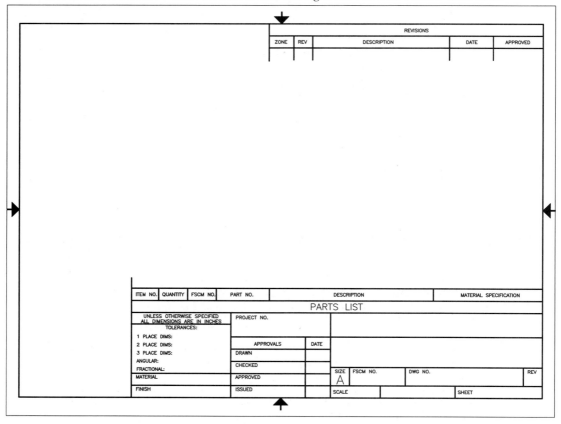

- Define attributes for each area of the title block. As you create the attributes, determine the appropriate text height and justification for each definition. Attributes should be defined for the drawing title, drawing number, drafter, checker, dates, drawing scale, sheet size, material, finish, revision letter, and tolerance information. See **Figure 24-13.** Include any other information that may be specific to your organization or application.
- Assign default values to the attributes wherever possible. For example, if your organization consistently specifies the same overall tolerances on drawing dimensions, the tolerance attributes can be assigned default values.

PROFESSIONAL TIP

The size of each area within the title block limits on the number of characters you can have in a line of text. You can provide a handy cue to yourself by including a reminder in the attribute. When defining an attribute in which you wish to place a reminder, include the information in the attribute prompt. For example, the prompt could read Enter drawing name (15 characters max). Each time a block or drawing containing the attribute is used, the prompt displays the reminder.

Once you have defined each attribute in the title block, the **WBLOCK** command can be used to save the drawing as a file to disk so that it can be inserted into a new drawing. You can also use the **BLOCK** command to create a block of the defined attributes within the current file, which can then be saved as a template or wblock file. Both methods are acceptable and are explained in the next sections.

Regardless of the method used, title block data can be entered quickly and accurately without the use of text commands. **Figure 24-14** shows the completed title block after insertion of the attribute block created in **Figure 24-13.** If the attributes are entered using the **Enter Attributes** dialog box, all the information can be seen at once and mistakes can be corrected quickly. Attributes can be easily edited at a later date if necessary.

Wblock method

The **WBLOCK** command saves a drawing file to disk so that it can be inserted into any drawing that is currently open. Drawings used in this manner should be given descriptive names. An A-size title block, for example, could be named TITLE_A or FORMAT_A. Also, be sure to use 0,0 as the insertion point for the title block.

Figure 24-13.
Attributes should be defined for each area of the title block.

ITEM NO.	QUANTITY	FSCM NO.	PART NO.	DESCRIPTION	MATERIAL SPECIFICATION

PARTS LIST

UNLESS OTHERWISE SPECIFIED ALL DIMENSIONS ARE IN INCHES TOLERANCES:	PROJECT NO. PROJECT		
1 PLACE DIMS: TOL1			
2 PLACE DIMS: TOL2	APPROVALS	DATE	
3 PLACE DIMS: TOL3	DRAWN DRAWN	DATE	TITLE
ANGULAR: ANGL	CHECKED CHECKED	DATE	
FRACTIONAL: FRAC	APPROVED APPROVED	DATE	SIZE A FSCM NO. DWG NO. NUMBER REV REV
MATERIAL MATERIAL			
FINISH FINISH	ISSUED ISSUED	DATE	SCALE SCALE SHEET SHEET

Insertion point

Figure 24-14.
The title block after insertion of the attributes. When the drawing is complete, dates and approvals can be added.

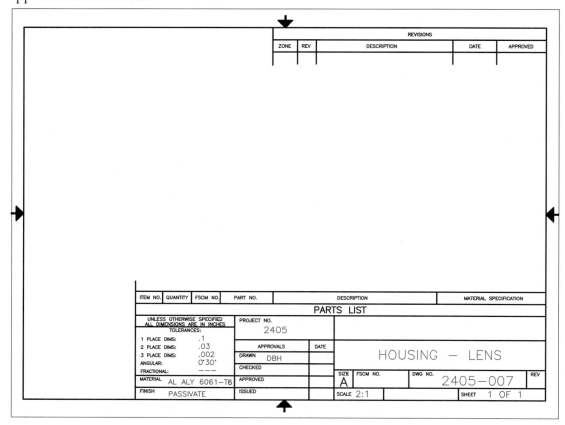

ITEM NO.	QUANTITY	FSCM NO.	PART NO.	DESCRIPTION	MATERIAL SPECIFICATION

PARTS LIST

To use the wblock file, begin a new drawing and insert the template drawing. After locating and scaling the drawing, the attribute prompts are displayed. If the **ATTDIA** system variable is set to 1, all of the attributes can be accepted or edited in the **Enter Attributes** dialog box. When you pick **OK** to close the dialog box, the attributes are placed in the title block. This method requires that you begin with a new drawing and that you know the information requested by the attribute prompts.

Block method

The **BLOCK** command uses the **Block Definition** dialog box to create a block of the defined attributes in the title block. When you select the objects for the block, be sure to select only the *defined attributes*. Do not select the headings of the title block areas or any of the geometry in the title block. When selecting the insertion base point, pick a corner of the title block that will be convenient to use each time the block is inserted into a drawing. The point indicated in **Figure 24-13** shows an appropriate location for the insertion base point.

Finally, activate the **Delete** option button in the **Block Definition** dialog box so the attribute definitions will be removed from the title block. When the block is inserted, the attribute values are inserted where the attribute definitions were located. You can also place the attribute definitions on a separate layer and freeze it so that the original attributes will not be displayed. The current drawing now contains a block of defined attributes for use in the title block.

If you save the drawing as a template file and begin a new drawing using the template, the title block data can be entered at any time during the creation of the new drawing. To do so, issue the **INSERT** command, enter the name of the block in the

Insert dialog box, and pick the proper insertion base point. The attribute prompts are then either displayed on the command line or in a dialog box, depending on the value of the **ATTDIA** system variable.

Revision Blocks

It is almost certain that a detail drawing will require revision at some time. Typical changes that occur include design improvements and the correction of drafting errors. The first time that a drawing is revised, it is usually assigned the revision letter *A*. If necessary, revision letters continue with *B* through *Y*, but the letters *I*, *O*, *Q*, *S*, *X*, and *Z* are not used because they might be confused with numbers.

Title block formats include an area specifically designated to record all drawing changes. This area is normally located at the upper-right of the title block sheet and is commonly called the *revision block*. The revision block provides space for the revision letter, a description of the change, the date, and approvals. These items are entered in columns. A column for the zone is only included if applicable. *Zones* are intended for larger drawings and used to help direct the print reader's attention to the correction location on the drawing. Zones are identified in the margins of a title block sheet by letters and numbers. They are used for reference purposes in the same way reference letters and numbers are used to identify a street or feature on a road map. Although A-size and B-size title blocks may include zones, they are rarely needed.

Block attributes provide a handy means of completing the necessary information in a revision block. Refer to **Figure 24-15** as you follow these steps:

1. Create the drawing geometry for the revision block using the appropriate layer(s).
2. On a separate layer, define attributes that describe the zone (optional), revision letter, description of change, date, and change approval. Use left-justified text for the change description attribute and middle-justified text for the remainder of the attributes.
3. Use the **WBLOCK** command to save the revision block and attributes as a drawing file. Use a descriptive name, such as REVBLK or REV. Keep in mind that each line of the revision block has its own border lines. Therefore, the borders must be saved with the attributes. Use the upper-left endpoint of the revision block as the insertion point.

Now, after a drawing has been revised, simply insert the revision block at the correct location. If the **ATTDIA** system variable is set to 1, the attribute prompts are answered in the **Enter Attributes** dialog box. After providing the change information, pick the **OK** button and the completed revision block is automatically added to the title block sheet. See **Figure 24-16**.

Parts Lists

Assembly drawings require a parts list, or list of materials, that provides information about each component of the assembly or subassembly. This information includes the quantity, FSCM (when necessary), part number, description, and item number for each component. In some organizations, the parts list is generated as a separate document, usually in an 8-1/2″ × 11″ format. In other companies, it is common practice to

Figure 24-15.
The revision block consists of lines and defined attributes. The border lines must be drawn as part of the block, and the upper-left corner is used as the insertion point.

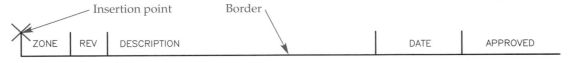

Figure 24-16.
The completed revision block after it is inserted into the drawing.

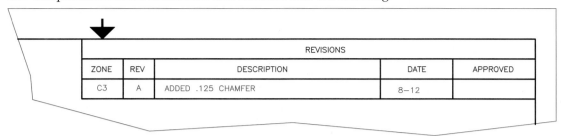

REVISIONS					
ZONE	REV	DESCRIPTION		DATE	APPROVED
C3	A	ADDED .125 CHAMFER		8–12	

include the parts list on the face of the assembly drawing. Whether created as a separate document or as part of the assembly drawing itself, parts lists provide another example of how attributes can be used to automate the documentation process.

Refer to the title block in **Figure 24-12**. Make note of the section located just above the title block area. This area will contain the parts list for this drawing. Now, consider the similar example illustrated in **Figure 24-17** as you follow these steps:

1. Create a parts list block using the appropriate drawing layer(s).
2. On a separate layer, define attributes that describe the quantity, FSCM (when necessary), part number, item description, material specification, and item number for the components of an assembly drawing. Use left-justified text for the item description attribute and middle-justified text for the other attributes.
3. Use the **WBLOCK** command to save the parts list block to disk with a descriptive name, such as PL for parts list or BOM for bill of materials. You can also use the **BLOCK** command to create a block of the parts list in the current drawing. Use the lower-left endpoint of the parts list block as the insertion point, as shown in **Figure 24-17**.

Now, after an assembly drawing has been completed, simply insert the parts list block into the drawing at the correct location. If the **ATTDIA** system variable is set to 1, the attribute prompts are answered in the **Enter Attributes** dialog box. After providing the necessary information, pick the **OK** button and the completed parts list block is automatically added to the title block sheet. See **Figure 24-18**. Repeat the procedure as many times as required until each component of the assembly drawing is included in the parts list.

Fields

You can list attributes in fields. This allows you to display the value of an attribute in a location away from the block.

To display an attribute value in a field, access the **Field** dialog box from within the **MTEXT** or **TEXT** command or by picking **Insert > Field...** from the pull-down menu. In the **Field** dialog box, pick **Objects** from the **Field category:** drop-down list and then pick **Object** in the **Field names:** list box. Next, pick the **Select object** button to return to the drawing window and then select the block containing the attribute.

Figure 24-17.
The parts list block is drawn with defined attributes and the insertion point located at the lower-left endpoint.

	QTY	FSCM	PART_NO.	ITEM_DESC.		MATL_SPEC.	ITEM

Insertion point

Figure 24-18.
The completed parts list block after it is inserted into the drawing.

	1		52451	PLATE, MOUNTING	6061–T6 ALUM	1
	QTY REQ'D	FSCM NO.	PART OR IDENTIFYING NO.	NOMENCLATURE OR DESCRIPTION	MATERIAL SPECIFICATION	ITEM NO.

PARTS LIST

When you select the block, the **Field** dialog box reappears with the available properties listed. Pick the desired attribute tag and the corresponding value is displayed in the **Preview:** box. Select the format and pick **OK** to have the field inserted in the text object.

Collecting Attribute Information

Attribute values and definitions can be extracted from a drawing and organized in a text file. This process, called *attribute extraction*, is useful for creating bills of materials, schedules, and parts lists. AutoCAD creates a text file containing the attribute information in a tabular format. You can select the specific blocks, attributes, and values to be extracted. Block information can also be reinserted into the drawing as a table.

Attributes are extracted using the **Attribute Extraction** wizard. To start this wizard, pick the **Attribute Extraction...** button on the **Modify II** toolbar, pick **Tools** > **Attribute Extraction...** from the pull-down menu, or type EATTEXT. The first step in extracting attributes is to specify whether or not you want to use a previously saved template, or if the extraction options are specified as you go through the **Attribute Extraction** wizard.

EATTEXT
Type: EATTEXT
Pull-Down Menu: Tools > Attribute Extraction...
Toolbar: Modify II — Attribute Extraction...

Begin Page

The **Begin** page of the **Attribute Extraction** wizard is shown in **Figure 24-19**. To create a table or to specify the information to be extracted as you go through the wizard, select **Create table or external file from scratch** and pick the **Next** button. To select a template (BLK), pick the **Use template (schedule, parts list, etc)** radio button, which activates the **Template name:** text box and the ellipsis (...) button to the right of the text box. Pick the ellipsis button to open the **Open Template** dialog box and select the BLK file. Then, pick the **Next>** button to display the next page of the wizard.

Select Drawings Page

In the next page, **Select Drawings,** the objects or drawings from which the information is to be gathered is specified. See **Figure 24-20**. The **Select Drawings** page provides these options:
- **Select objects radio button.** To include only some of the blocks in the current drawing, pick this radio button. The **Select blocks** button is enabled. Pick this button to return to the drawing area and select the blocks to be included. Blocks can only be selected from the current drawing.
- **Current drawing radio button.** Pick this radio button to include all of the blocks in the current drawing.
- **Select drawings/sheet sets radio button.** To gather information from blocks in multiple drawings, pick this radio button. The **Click to browse** button is activated. Pick the button, which opens the **Select Files** dialog box. To select all of the drawings associated with a saved sheet set file, change the **Files of type** option to **.dst**, then navigate to the sheet set file, and select it.

Figure 24-19.
Select a template of preset block and attribute values to be extracted on the **Begin** page.

Pick to create from scratch

Pick to open the **Open Template** dialog box

Enter a template name

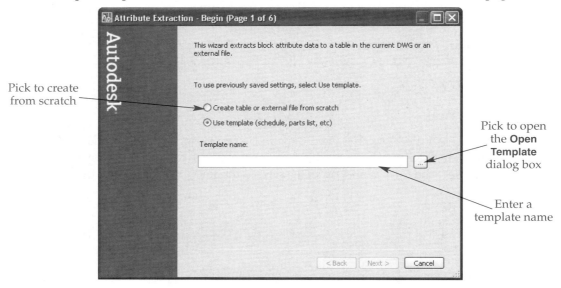

Figure 24-20.
Select the drawings or objects from which to extract information on the **Select Drawings** page.

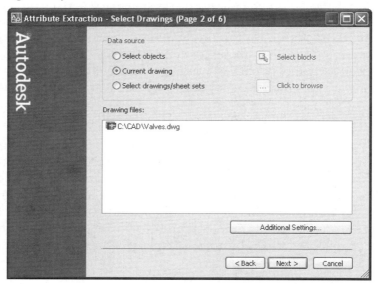

Picking the **Additional Settings...** button on the **Select Drawings** page opens the **Attribute Extraction—Additional Settings** dialog box. The following options are available in this dialog box:

- **Include nested blocks.** If checked, nested block information is included in the extraction.
- **Include blocks in xrefs.** When the drawing contains xrefs, checking this check box includes the blocks within the xrefs. Otherwise, blocks within xrefs are not included.
- **Include xrefs in block count.** Checking this check box causes xrefs to be counted as one of the blocks.
- **Only include blocks in model space.** If checked, only the blocks in model space are extracted. Blocks in paper space are ignored.
- **Include all blocks from entire drawing.** All blocks in the drawing are included in extraction.

Figure 24-21.
Use the **Select Attributes** page to select the items to be extracted.

Check to prevent the display
of general properties

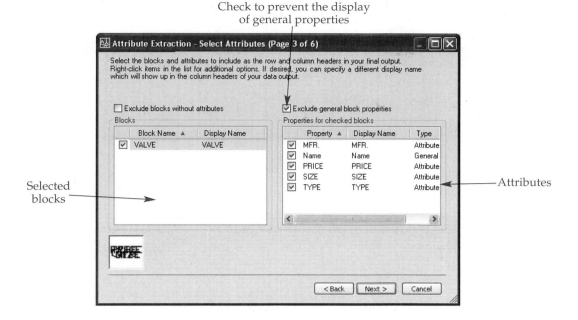

Selected
blocks

Attributes

Select Attributes Page

When settings have been made on the **Select Drawings** page, pick the **Next** button to display the **Select Attributes** page, **Figure 24-21.** This page lists the selected blocks and the attributes contained within those blocks.

You often need to be selective when listing blocks and attributes. In most cases, only certain types of attribute data need to be extracted from a drawing. AutoCAD requires guidelines to use when sorting through a drawing for attribute information. These guidelines are specified on the **Select Attributes** page. This information is then used by AutoCAD to list the attributes when you create an extract file.

On the left of the page is a list of all selected blocks. Check the blocks to be included in the extraction. Blocks without attributes can be filtered out of the list by checking the **Exclude blocks without attributes** check box. The block names appear in the left-hand list with an alias name, or display name, for each block. You can enter or edit an alias by right-clicking in the **Display Name** column for the block and selecting **Edit Display Name** from the shortcut menu.

On the right of the page is a list of the attributes for the blocks in the left-hand list. All of the attributes that were created by using the **ATTDEF** command are listed. Check the attributes to include in the extraction. If a template file was selected on the previous page, the blocks and attributes are automatically selected to match the template.

In addition to extracting attributes, AutoCAD can extract information about certain block characteristics. To display these characteristics in the right-hand list, uncheck the **Exclude general block properties** check box. Block characteristics that can be extracted include X, Y, and Z coordinates of the block insertion point; the name of the layer the block is on and its color, linetype, lineweight, and plot style; the rotation of the block; and the X, Y, and Z insertion scale factors.

> **NOTE**
>
> If an attribute contains a field, the field is automatically converted to text during the extraction process.

Figure 24-22.
The options in the **Finalize Output** page determine how the data are extracted.

Pick a column head
to sort the data

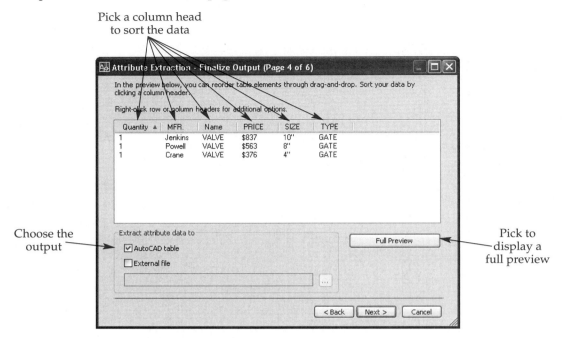

Choose the
output

Pick to
display a
full preview

Finalize Output Page

After selecting the attributes to be extracted, pick the **Next>** button to display the **Finalize Output** page, **Figure 24-22.** The results of the query are shown in table. This page allows you to sort the data by column heading and choose to save the extracted data as an AutoCAD table, external file, or both.

The order of the records (rows) can be changed by picking on the column heading. Picking the heading once sorts the records in ascending order based on that column's information. This is indicated by an up arrow to the right of the column name. Picking the heading twice sorts the records in descending order. Additional options can be accessed by right-clicking on any column heading to display the shortcut menu shown in **Figure 24-23.** The options are:

- **Sort Ascending.** Sorts the records in ascending order based on the information in the column that was right-clicked.
- **Sort Descending.** Sorts the records in descending order based on the information in the column that was right-clicked.
- **Hide Column.** Hides the column that was right-clicked. Hidden columns are not included in the extraction.
- **Show All Columns.** Redisplays any columns that were hidden.
- **Filter Rows.** Opens the **Filter** dialog box. Any rows unchecked in this dialog box are not included in the extraction.
- **Reset Filter.** Resets any filters for the column that was right-clicked.
- **Reset All Filters.** Resets all filters in all columns.
- **Copy to Clipboard.** The information is copied to the Windows Clipboard in the same format as displayed in the table.
- **Rename Column.** The column heading that was right-clicked is replaced with a text box. Type a new name and press [Enter] to rename the column.

To display a preview of the data, pick the **Full Preview** button below the list of data. The window that is opened displays the data as they will appear when extracted. Close the preview window by pressing the [Esc] key or using the Windows control button (X).

Figure 24-23.
Right-clicking on a column in the **Finalize Output** page displays this shortcut menu, which contains options for formatting the data before they are exported.

In the **Extract attribute data to** area at the bottom of the page, pick whether the data are used to create a table within the current drawing, extracted to an external file, or both. To create a table, check the **AutoCAD table** check box. To save the data to an external file, check the **External file** check box. Then, pick the ellipsis (...) button to display the **Save As** dialog box. Specify a file name and folder for the file. The type of file to be saved is selected in the **File of type:** drop-down list. The default file formats are comma separated (CSV) and tab separated (TXT). If Microsoft Excel and Microsoft Access are installed, the XLS and MDB formats are also available. Pick the **Save** button to return to the **Finalize Output** page. The folder location and file name are then displayed in the text box below the **External file** check box.

Pick the **Next>** button to continue with the wizard. If the **AutoCAD table** check box in the **Finalize Output** page is checked, the **Table Style** page is displayed next. If the **AutoCAD table** check box is unchecked, this page is skipped and the wizard continues to the **Finish** page.

Table Style Page

The **Table Style** page is shown in **Figure 24-24.** Tables are discussed in detail in Chapter 9. A title for the table can be entered into the **Enter a title for your table:** text field. A table style can be specified by selecting it from the **Select table style:** drop-down list. The table styles available in the current drawing are listed in the drop-down list. To create a new style or to modify an existing style, pick the ellipsis (...) button to display the **Table Style** dialog box. Then, make the needed changes and pick the **Close** button to return to the **Table Style** page of the wizard.

Figure 24-24.
Select a style for the AutoCAD table on the **Table Style** page.

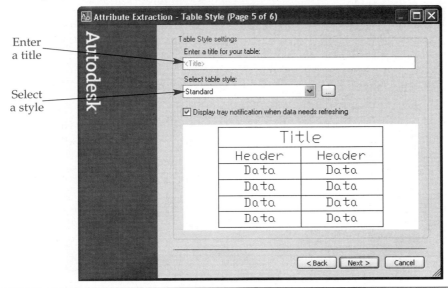

When a table is created from block data, it can be updated when a block is changed in the drawing. For example, if a block is deleted from the drawing, refreshing the table removes the block data from the table. To display a notification when a block is modified, check the **Display tray notification when data needs refreshing** check box. When a block is modified, a notification appears from AutoCAD's system tray area informing you of the change. See **Figure 24-25.** In the notification, pick the **Refresh table data** link to update the table.

Finish Page

The last page of the **Attribute Extraction** wizard is the **Finish** page, shown in **Figure 24-26.** Pick the **Finish** button to finish the attribute extraction. However, this page provides an opportunity to save the settings as a template file (BLK). The template contains the block and attribute selections made in the **Select Attributes** page. It can then be used in the future to automatically make the attribute selection for similar extractions.

To save a template, pick the **Save template...** button to display the **Save As** dialog box. Specify a file name and location for the template. Then, pick the **Save** button.

Output

After the **Finish** button is picked, you are prompted to specify an insertion point for the table if the **AutoCAD table** check box was checked on the **Finalize Output** page. Pick a point or enter coordinates to complete the extraction process.

If an external file was saved, it can be displayed on screen by opening the file in Windows Notepad. Examples of comma- and tab-separated formats are shown in **Figure 24-27.** The file can be printed from the Windows Notepad.

Figure 24-25.
If the **Display tray notification when data needs refreshing** box on the **Table Style** page is checked, this notification appears when block data that are associated with a table are modified.

Pick to update the table

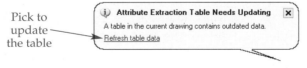

Figure 24-26.
On the **Finish** page of the **Attribute Extraction** wizard, you can save the settings to a template file.

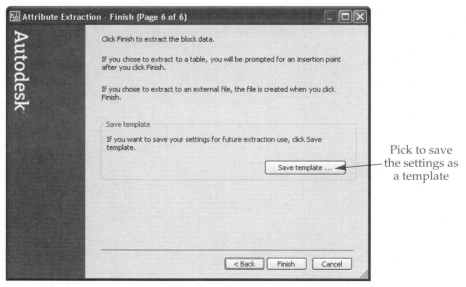

Pick to save the settings as a template

Figure 24-27.
Extracted attribute data that have been saved as files are shown in Windows Notepad.

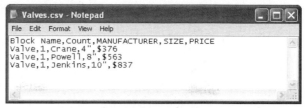

Comma-Separated File (CSV)

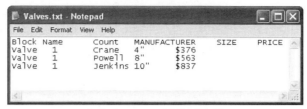

Tab-Separated File (TXT)

PROFESSIONAL TIP

The bill of materials listing discussed in this chapter is a basic list of each block's selected attributes. As you become familiar with AutoCAD, customize it to meet your needs. Study magazines devoted to AutoCAD. You will find numerous software packages that generate specialized bills of material containing information on quantities and totals, rather than just a list of blocks.

Exercise 24-4   Complete the Exercise on the Student CD.

Chapter Test

Answer the following questions. Write your answers on a separate sheet of paper or complete the electronic chapter test on the Student CD.

1. What is an *attribute*?
2. Explain the purpose of the **ATTDEF** command.
3. Define the function of the following attribute modes:
   A. Invisible
   B. Constant
   C. Verify
   D. Preset
4. Which attribute information does the **ATTDEF** command request?
5. Identify two ways to edit attributes before they are included within a block.
6. How can you change an existing attribute from visible to invisible?
7. List the three options for the **ATTDISP** command.
8. What is meant by *global attribute editing*?
9. Explain how to change the value of an inserted attribute.

---

10. How do you modify the prompt statement for an attribute that is saved within a block?
11. After a block with attributes has been saved, what method can you use to change the order of prompts when the block is inserted?
12. How does editing an attribute with **DDEDIT** differ from using the **Properties** window?
13. What purpose does the **ATTREQ** system variable serve?
14. To enter attributes using a dialog box, you must set the **ATTDIA** system variable to _____.
15. List three uses for extracted block and attribute data.
16. What do you have to decide when taking the first step in extracting attributes?
17. Explain the function served by a template file when using the **Attribute Extraction** wizard.
18. Describe the three selection options available in the **Select Drawings** page of the **Attribute Extraction** wizard.
19. In the **Select Attributes** page of the **Attribute Extraction** wizard, how do you filter out blocks without attributes?
20. What are the two general file formats in which extracted attribute data can be saved?

Drawing Problems

1. Start a new drawing. Draw the structural steel wide flange shape shown below using the dimensions given. Do not dimension the drawing. Create attributes for the drawing using the information given. Make a block of the drawing and name it W12 X 40. Insert the block once to test the attributes. Save the drawing as P24-1.

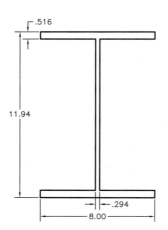

Attributes		
Steel	W12 × 40	Visible
Mfr.	Ryerson	Invisible
Price	$.30/lb	Invisible
Weight	40 lbs/ft	Invisible
Length	10′	Invisible
Code	03116WF	Invisible

2. Open the drawing from Problem 1 (P24-1) and construct the floor plan shown using the dimensions given. Dimension the drawing. Insert the block W12 X 40 six times as shown. Required attribute data are given in the chart below the drawing. Enter the appropriate information for the attributes as you are prompted. Note the steel columns labeled 3 and 6 require slightly different attribute data. You can speed the drawing process by using **ARRAY** or **COPY**. Save the drawing as P24-2.

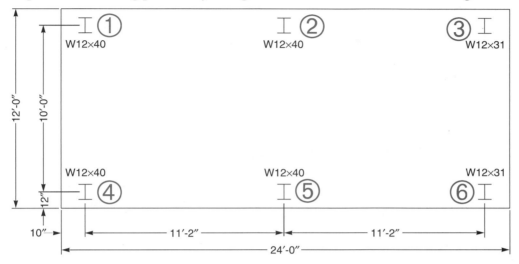

	Steel	Mfr.	Price	Weight	Length	Code
Blocks ①, ②, ④, & ⑤	W12 × 40	Ryerson	$.30/lb	40 lbs/ft	10'	03116WF
Blocks ③ & ⑥	W12 × 31	Ryerson	$.30/lb	31 lbs/ft	8.5'	03125WF

3. Open the drawing from Problem 2 (P24-2). Create a tab-separated extraction file for the blocks in the drawing. Extract the following information for each block:
   - Block name
   - Steel
   - Manufacturer
   - Price
   - Weight
   - Length
   - Code
   Save the file as P24-3.txt.

4. Select a drawing from Chapter 22 and create a bill of materials for it using the **Attribute Extraction** wizard. Use the comma-separated format to display the file. Display the file in Windows Notepad.

Drawing Problems - Chapter 24

5. Create a drawing of the computer workstation layout in the classroom or office in which you are working. Provide attribute definitions for all of the items listed here.
   - Workstation ID number
   - Computer brand name
   - Model number
   - Processor chip
   - Amount of RAM
   - Hard disk capacity
   - Video graphics card brand and model
   - CD-ROM/DVD-ROM speed
   - Date purchased
   - Price
   - Vendor's phone number
   - Other data as you see fit

   Generate an extract file for all of the computers in the drawing.

6. Open one of your template drawings. Define attributes for the title block information, revision block, and parts list, as described in this chapter. Use the **WBLOCK** command to save the entire drawing to disk using 0,0 as the insertion base point. Repeat the procedure for other templates.

7. Open the drawing from Problem 2 (P24-2). Create a table from the block attribute data and insert it into the drawing. Save the drawing as P24-7.

CHAPTER 25
External Reference Drawings

Learning Objectives

After completing this chapter, you will be able to do the following:

- Define the function of external references.
- Reference an existing drawing into the current drawing.
- Use **DesignCenter** and tool palettes to attach external references.
- Bind external references and selected dependent objects to a drawing.
- Edit external references in the current drawing.
- Use external references to create a multiview layout.
- Control the display of layers in viewports using the **Layer Properties Manager** dialog box.

When you create multiple objects in a drawing by copying them, the drawing file grows in size because AutoCAD must maintain a complete description of the geometry of each copied object. On the other hand, when you use a block to represent multiple objects, AutoCAD maintains only one description of the block's geometry. All other instances of the block are recorded as X, Y, and Z coordinates, and AutoCAD refers to the original block definition to obtain the block's data. The size of a drawing is decreased considerably if blocks are used rather than copied objects.

AutoCAD allows you to further control the size of drawing files by using external references. An *external reference (xref)* allows you to incorporate, or reference, existing drawing, design web format, and raster image files into the current drawing without adding new file data. This procedure is excellent for applications in which existing base drawings, complex symbols, images and details are shared by several users, are used often, or can be used to develop new drawings. This chapter describes using external references and introduces the different applications for reference drawings.

Introduction to External References

Any machine or electrical appliance contains a variety of components that are assembled to create the final product. The final product occupies a greater amount of space and weighs more than any of the individual components. In the same way, a drawing composed of a variety of blocks, inserted drawings, and other data such as raster images, is larger than the individual files.

AutoCAD allows you to *reference* existing drawing (DWG), design web format (DWF), and raster image files into the *master drawing* on which you are currently working. When you externally reference a file, the file's geometry is not added to the current drawing, but it is displayed on-screen. This makes for much smaller files. It also allows several people in a class or office to reference the same file, with the assurance that any revisions to the reference file are displayed in any drawing where it is used.

Benefits of External References

In addition to reducing drawing file size, one of the greatest benefits of using xrefs is that whenever the master drawing is opened, the latest versions of the xrefs are displayed. If the original externally referenced files are modified between the time you revise the master drawing and the next time you open and plot the drawing, all revisions are automatically reflected. This is because AutoCAD reloads each xref whenever the master drawing is loaded.

There are other significant advantages to using xrefs. They can be *nested*, and you can use as many xrefs as needed for any drawing. Nesting means a detail referenced to the master drawing can be composed of smaller details that are xrefed. You can also attach other xrefs to the referenced file and have these newly attached xrefs automatically added to the master drawing when it is opened.

Placing External Reference Drawings

Existing drawing (DWG), design web format (DWF), and raster image files can be referenced into the current drawing. DWF files are AutoCAD drawing files or other application files that are compressed for publication and viewing on the Web. A DWF file is usually referenced into a drawing in order to share information from the Web or from an application other than AutoCAD, though the high compression of DWF files may limit their effective use. Raster image files are referenced into a drawing anytime there is a need to add an image to a drawing, such as for a company logo in a title block. Externally referencing an image into a drawing is an excellent tool, especially because the large file size often associated with a raster image is not reproduced in the current drawing. External reference DWF and image files are further described in *AutoCAD and Its Applications—Advanced*.

The primary function of xrefs is to reference another drawing file into the master drawing. External reference drawings can be used to:
- Construct a drawing using predrawn symbols or details, a method similar to the use of blocks.
- Develop a new drawing by using an existing drawing as a pattern or source of needed drawing geometry.
- Layout drawings composed of multiple views or details, using different existing drawings. When working with sheet sets, external references can be used to arrange sheet views in paper space layouts. Sheet sets are described in Chapter 26.

Attaching an Xref Drawing to the Current Drawing

A referenced drawing that is inserted into the current drawing is known as *attached.* To attach an external reference drawing to the current drawing, pick **Insert > DWG Reference...** from the pull-down menu, or pick the **Attach Xref** button from either the **Reference** or **Insert** toolbar. An xref can also be attached using the **External References** palette. To access the **External References** palette, pick **Insert > External References...** from the pull-down menu, pick the **External References** button from the **Reference** toolbar, or type XREF or XR. The **External References** palette, shown

XREF

Type

XREF
XR

Pull-Down Menu

Insert
> DWG
Reference...
Insert
> External
References...

Toolbar

Reference
Insert

Attach Xref

Reference

External References

Figure 25-1.
The **External References** palette provides access to all options for externally referenced files.

Pick to attach an external reference to the current drawing

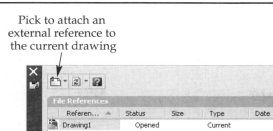

in **Figure 25-1,** is a complete external reference management tool. To attach an xref drawing using the **External References** palette, pick the **Attach DWG** button from the flyout, or right-click on the **File References** pane and select the **Attach DWG...** shortcut menu option. Any of these selection techniques display the **Select Reference File** dialog box. The **Select Reference File** dialog box is a standard file dialog box used to access the drawing file you want to attach. Once you locate and select the drawing file, pick the **Open** button.

Once a file to attach has been specified, the **External Reference** dialog box is displayed, **Figure 25-2.** This dialog box is used to indicate how and where the reference is to be placed in the current drawing. The name and the path of the selected xref are shown in the upper-left corner of the dialog box. To change the drawing to be attached, pick the **Browse...** button and select the new file in the **Select Reference File** dialog box. When attaching an xref, pick the default **Attachment** option in the **Reference Type** area. Working with the **Overlay** option is described later in this chapter.

If there is more than one external reference already in the current drawing, you can attach another copy of an xref by picking the **Name:** drop-down list arrow and choosing the existing drawing file you want to attach again. You can also attach an existing xref by right-clicking on the desired reference name in the **External References** palette and picking the **Attach...** shortcut menu option.

The lower portion of the **External Reference** dialog box contains the options for the xref insertion location, scaling, rotation angle, and block unit settings. The text boxes in the **Insertion point** area allow you to enter 2D or 3D coordinates for insertion of the xref if the **Specify On-screen** check box is inactive. Activate the **Specify On-screen** check box if you want to specify the insertion location on screen. Scale factors for the xref can be set in the **Scale** area. By default, the X, Y, and Z scale factors are set to 1. You can enter new values in the corresponding text boxes, or activate the **Specify On-screen** check box to display scaling prompts on the command line. Checking the **Uniform Scale** check box tells AutoCAD to use the X scale factor for the Y and Z

Figure 25-2.
The **External Reference** dialog box is used to specify how an external reference is placed in the current drawing.

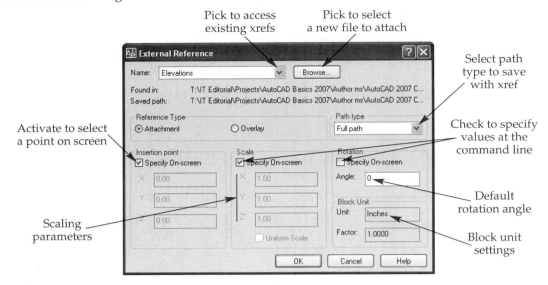

scale factors. The rotation angle for the inserted xref is 0 by default. You can specify a different rotation angle in the **Angle:** text box, or activate the **Specify On-screen** check box to be prompted for the rotation angle at the command line. The **Block Unit** area displays the unit and scale factor stored with the selected drawing file.

The **Path type** drop-down list is used to set how the path to the xref file is stored by AutoCAD. This path is then used to find the xref file when the master file is opened. The resulting path is displayed in the **External References** palette, **Figure 25-3.** It also appears under the xref name in the **Saved path:** listing in the **External Reference** dialog box. The following path options are available:

Figure 25-3.
An xref file attached to the current drawing can be referenced with a full path, a relative path, or no path. The type of path used is displayed in the **Save Path** column in the **External References** palette.

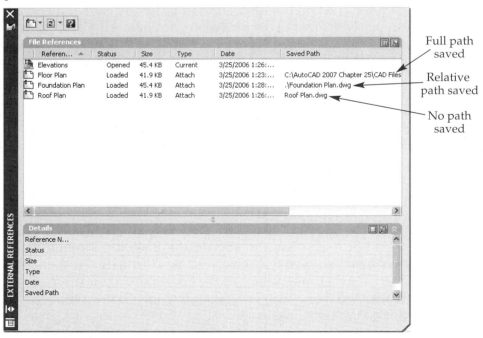

- **Full path.** This option saves the full path to the xref drawing file. The **Full path** option is an *absolute path* and is active by default.
- **Relative path.** This option saves the path relative to the file it is being referenced into (the current file). The **Relative path** option cannot be used if the xref file is on a local or network drive other than the drive that stores the master file.
- **No path.** This option does not save the path to the xref file. When no path is used, the xref file can only be found and loaded if the path to the file is included in one of the Support File Search Path locations or if the xref file is in the same folder as the master file. The Support File Search Path locations are specified in the **Files** tab of the **Options** dialog box.

NOTE

AutoCAD also searches for xref files in all paths of the current project name. These paths are listed under the Project Files Search Path in the **Files** tab of the **Options** dialog box. You can create a new project as follows:

1. Pick Project Files Search Path to highlight it, and then pick the **Add...** button.
2. Enter a project name if desired.
3. Pick the plus sign icon (+), and then pick the word Empty.
4. Pick the **Browse...** button and locate the folder that is to become part of the project search path. Then pick **OK**.

Complete the project search path definition by entering the **PROJECTNAME** system variable and specifying the same name that is used in the **Options** dialog box.

With the **Full path** option, the xref drawing location is defined by its location on the computer system, which means that the xref drawings must be located in the same drive and folder specified in the saved path. The master drawing can be moved to any location, but the xref drawings must remain in the saved path. This option is acceptable if it is unlikely that the master and xref drawings will be copied to another computer or drive or moved to another folder. If you share your drawings with a client or eventually archive the drawings, the **Relative path** option is more appropriate.

The **Relative path** option defines the saved path relative to the location of the master drawing. If the master drawing and xref files are contained within a single folder and subfolders, this folder can be copied to any location without losing the connection between files. For example, the folder can be copied from the C: drive of one computer to the D: drive of another computer, to a folder on a CD, or to an archive server. If these types of transfers are performed with the **Full path** option, you need to open the master drawing after copying, and redefine the saved paths for all xref files.

In the **Saved Path** list in the **External References** palette, AutoCAD uses prefixes to describe the relative paths to xref files. Referring to **Figure 25-3**, the path to the Foundation Plan reference file is preceded by the characters .\. The period (.) represents the folder containing the master drawing. From that folder, AutoCAD "looks in" the House folder, where the Foundation Plan drawing is found. A similar specification is used for the Elevation reference file in **Figure 25-4**. In this instance, the Elevation file is found in the same folder as the master drawing. The specification for the Wall reference file is preceded by the characters ..\. The double period (..) instructs AutoCAD to move up one folder level from the current location. The double period can be repeated to move up multiple folder levels. For example, the Panel reference file in **Figure 25-4** is found by moving up two folder levels from the folder of the master drawing and then opening the Symbols folder.

Figure 25-4.
This figure shows the relationship between symbols in the **Saved Path** list and file locations within the folder structure.

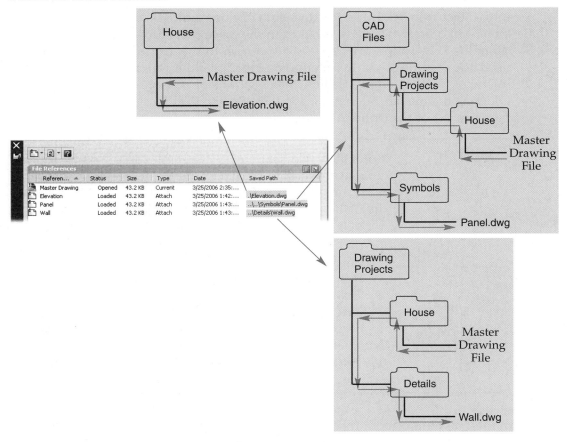

NOTE

The path saved to the xref is one of several locations searched by AutoCAD when a master drawing is opened and an xref must be loaded. When a file containing xrefs is opened, AutoCAD tries several ways to load each xref. The order in which AutoCAD searches path locations for loading xref files is as follows:

1. The path associated with the xref (the full path or a relative path).
2. The current folder of the master drawing.
3. The project paths specified in the Project Files Search Path.
4. The support paths specified in the Support File Search Path.
5. The Start in: folder path specified for the AutoCAD application shortcut, which is accessed with the **Properties** option in the desktop icon right-click menu.

After specifying a reference and path type for an xref in the **External Reference** dialog box, the xref can be inserted into the current drawing. In the example given in **Figure 25-2**, the file C:\Drawing Projects\MKMPlan.dwg is selected for attachment. Because the **Specify On-screen** check box in the **Insertion point** area is activated, the dialog box disappears when you pick **OK**. The xref is attached to your cursor and you are prompted for the insertion point. You can use any valid point specification option, including object snap modes.

The insertion options for attaching an xref are essentially the same as those used when inserting a block. Both commands function in a similar manner, but the internal workings and results are different. Remember that externally referenced files are not added to the current drawing file's database, as are inserted blocks. Therefore, using external references helps keep your drawing file size to a minimum.

PROFESSIONAL TIP

As is the case with inserted blocks, an xref is placed on the current layer when attached to a drawing. When attaching reference files, it is advisable to create an xref layer for each reference that you plan on using. This makes it easier to manage xrefs in your drawing because the individual layers can be frozen or thawed to change the display of different files.

Attaching Xrefs with DesignCenter and Tool Palettes

External references can be quickly attached to the current drawing using **DesignCenter** or the **Tool Palettes** window. Inserting blocks using these features is described in Chapter 22. Similar procedures are used for attaching xrefs. Use the following technique to attach an xref to the current drawing with **DesignCenter**:

1. Find the folder containing the drawing to be attached in the **Tree View** area of **DesignCenter**. Display the drawing files located in the selected folder in the **Content** area.
2. Right-click on the drawing file in the **Content** area and select **Attach as Xref...** from the shortcut menu, or drag and drop the drawing into the current drawing area using the *right mouse button* and select **Attach as Xref...** from the shortcut menu.
3. Enter the appropriate values in **External Reference** dialog box and pick **OK**.

A drawing file can also be attached to the current drawing as an xref from the **Tool Palettes** window. To add an xref to a tool palette, drag an existing xref from the current drawing or an xref from the **Content** area of **DesignCenter** into the **Tool Palettes** window. The xref can then be attached to the current drawing from the palette using drag and drop.

Xref files in tool palettes are identified with an external reference icon. If a drawing file, not an xref, is added to a tool palette from the current drawing or **DesignCenter**, it is designated as a block tool. You can convert the block tool to an xref tool by right-clicking on the image in the **Tool Palettes** window and selecting **Properties...** to display the **Tool Properties** dialog box. Then change the **Insert as** field status from Block to Xref using the drop-down list.

Overlaying the Current Drawing with an Xref

External reference drawings can be used to see what your drawing looks like with another drawing overlaid on top. *Overlaying* the current drawing with an external reference file allows you to temporarily view the xref without attaching it to the current drawing. This is accomplished by picking the **Overlay** radio button in the **Reference Type** area of the **External Reference** dialog box after selecting an xref.

The difference between an overlaid xref and an attached xref is related to the way in which nested xrefs are handled. *Nesting* occurs when an externally referenced file is referenced by an xref file that has been attached to the current drawing. The xref file that is attached is known as the *parent xref*. When an xref is overlaid, any nested xrefs that it contains are displayed as if those xrefs were *attached*, but not if they were *overlaid*. In other words, any nested overlays are not carried into the master drawing with the parent xref.

Managing External References

The **External References** palette is the primary tool used to manage and access current information about external references that have been attached to or overlaid on a drawing. The **External References** palette displays an upper **File References** pane and a lower **Details** pane. See **Figure 25-5**. The **File References** pane can be displayed in either list view or tree view. The list view display mode shown in **Figure 25-5**, is active by default, and can be set by picking the **List View** button, or pressing the [F3] key. The labeled columns displayed in list view are described as follows:

- **Reference Name.** This column displays the current drawing file name followed by the names of all existing external references in alphabetical or chronological order. The current drawing is indicated with the standard AutoCAD drawing file icon, and xrefs appear as a sheet of paper with a paper clip. Pick the **Reference Name** column heading to reverse the xref list order.

Figure 25-5.
The **External References** palette is used to view and manage referenced files. The **File References** pane in **List View** mode and **Details** pane in **Details** mode.

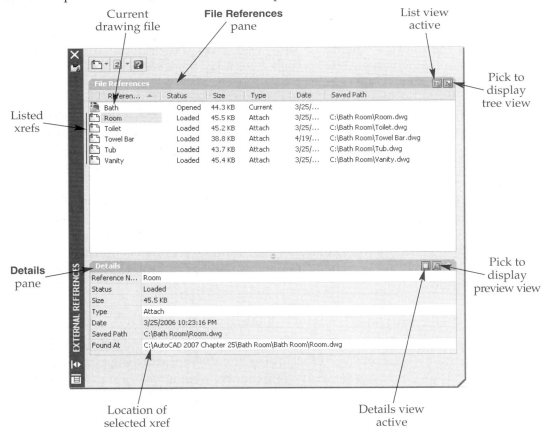

- **Status.** This column describes the current status of each xref. The xref status can be classified as one of the following:
  - **Loaded.** The xref is attached to the drawing.
  - **Unloaded.** The xref is attached but not displayed or regenerated.
  - **Unreferenced.** The xref has nested xrefs that are not found or are unresolved. An unreferenced xref is not displayed.
  - **Not Found.** The xref file is not found in valid search paths.
  - **Unresolved.** The xref file is missing or cannot be found.
  - **Orphaned.** The parent of the nested xref cannot be found.
- **Size.** The file size for each xref is listed in this column.
- **Type.** This column indicates whether the xref was attached or referenced as an overlay.
- **Date.** The last modification date for the file being referenced is indicated in this column.
- **Saved Path.** This column lists the path name saved with the xref. If only a file name appears here, the path has not been saved.

PROFESSIONAL TIP

In the list view display mode, the column widths can be adjusted as necessary to view incomplete information. To adjust the width of a column, move your cursor to the edge of the button at the top of the column until the cursor changes to a horizontal resizing cursor. Press and hold your left mouse button and drag the column to the desired width. The column width adjustments you make are used for subsequent displays of the dialog box. If the columns extend beyond the width of the dialog box window, a horizontal scroll bar appears at the bottom of the list.

To quickly see a listing of externally referenced files in the **File References** pane, and to show nesting levels, pick the **Tree View** button or press the [F4] key. See **Figure 25-6.** Nesting levels are shown in a format that is similar to the arrangement of folders. The xref icon can take on different appearances, depending on the current status of the xref. An xref whose status is unloaded or not found has a grayed-out icon. An upward arrow shown with the icon means the xref has just been reloaded, and a downward arrow means the xref has just been unloaded.

The **Details** pane can be displayed in either details view or preview view. The details view display mode shown in **Figure 25-5,** is active by default, and can be activated by picking the **Details** button. The information listed in the **Details** pane corresponds to the xref selected in the **File References** pane. The rows displayed while in detail view mode are exactly the same as the columns found in the list view mode of the **File References** pane. However, the **Details** pane can be used to modify the reference name by entering a new name in the **Reference Name** text box, and adjust the reference type from an attachment to an overlay or from an overlay to an attachment by picking the appropriate option from the **Type** drop-down list. In addition, the **Details** pane contains a **Found At** row that can be used to update the location of an xref path, as described later in this chapter.

To display an image of the xref selected in the **File References** pane, pick the **Preview** button on the **Details** pane. See **Figure 25-6.**

Figure 25-6.
The **File References** pane in **Tree View** mode shows nested xref levels. The **Details** pane in **Preview** mode provides a display of the selected xref.

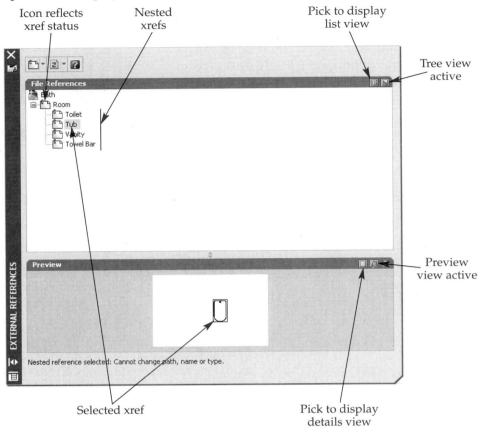

Icon reflects xref status

Nested xrefs

Pick to display list view

Tree view active

Preview view active

Selected xref

Pick to display details view

Nested reference selected: Cannot change path, name or type.

Detaching, Reloading, and Unloading Xrefs

Each time you open a master drawing containing an attached xref, the xref is also loaded and appears on screen. This attachment remains permanent until it is removed, or *detached*. Erasing an xref does not detach it from the master drawing. Detaching an xref is done by right-clicking on the reference name in the **File References** pane of the **External References** palette and picking the **Detach** shortcut menu option. When you detach an externally referenced file, all instances of the xref are erased, and all referenced data is removed from the current drawing. All xrefs nested within the detached file are also removed.

There may be situations where you need to update, or *reload*, an xref file in the master drawing. For example, if an externally referenced file is edited by another user while the master drawing is open, the version on disk may be different from the version currently displayed. To update the xref, right-click on the reference name in the **File References** pane of the **External References** palette and pick the **Reload** shortcut menu option, or pick the **Reload All Reference** button from the flyout to reload all unloaded xrefs. Reloading xrefs forces AutoCAD to read and display the most recently saved version of the drawing.

When you need to temporarily remove an xref without actually detaching it, you can *unload* the xref. To do so, right-click on the reference name in the **File References** pane of the **External References** palette and pick the **Unload** shortcut menu option. When an xref is unloaded, it is not displayed or regenerated, and AutoCAD's performance increases. To display the xref again, right-click on the reference name in the **File References** pane of the **External References** palette and pick the **Reload** shortcut menu option, or pick the **Reload All Reference** button from the flyout to reload all unloaded xrefs.

NOTE You can instruct AutoCAD to create and maintain a *log file* of the attaching, detaching, and reloading functions used in any drawing containing xrefs by setting the **XREFCTL** system variable to 1. At this setting, AutoCAD creates an XLG file having the same name as the current drawing, and the file is saved in the same folder. Each time you load a drawing that contains xrefs, or attach, detach, or reload xrefs, AutoCAD adds information to the log file. A new heading, or title block, is added to the log file each time the related drawing file is opened. The log file provides the following information:

- The drawing name, plus the date, time, and type of each xref operation.
- The nesting level of all xrefs affected by the operation.
- A list of xref-dependent objects affected by the operation, and the names of the objects temporarily added to the drawing.

Updating the Xref Path

A file path saved with an externally referenced file is displayed in the **Saved Path** column of the **File References** pane and **Saved Path** row of the **Details** pane in the **External References** palette. If an xref file is not found in the **Saved Path** location when the master drawing is opened, AutoCAD searches along the *library path*, which includes the current drawing folder and the Support File Search Path locations set in the **Files** tab of the **Options** dialog box. If a file with a matching name is found, it is resolved. In such a case, the **Saved Path** location differs from where the file was actually found. You can check this in the **External References** palette by comparing the path listed in the **Saved Path** column of the **File References** pane and **Saved Path** row of the **Details** pane with the listing in the **Found At** row of the **Details** pane. To update the **Saved Path** location, select the path in the **Found At** edit box and pick the **Browse...** button to the right of the edit box to access the **Select new path** dialog box. Use this dialog box to locate the new folder and select the desired file. Then, press **Open** to update the path.

When a referenced drawing has been moved and the new location is not on the library path, its status is indicated as Not Found. To find the xref file and update the **Saved Path** location, select the path in the **Found At** edit box and pick the **Browse...** button to the right of the edit box to access the **Select new path** dialog box. Use this dialog box to locate the new folder and select the desired file. Then, press **Open** to update the path.

The Manage Xrefs Icon

When changes are made to parent drawings for xrefs used in a master drawing, a notification appears in the AutoCAD status bar tray. This tray is located in the lower-right corner of the drawing window. Changes are indicated by the appearance of the **Manage Xrefs** icon, a balloon message, or both. Notifications in the status bar tray for xref changes and other system updates are controlled by options in the **Tray Settings** dialog box. This dialog box is accessed by selecting **Tray Settings...** from the status bar drop-down menu. If the **Display icons from services** check box is selected in the **Tray Settings** dialog box, the **Manage Xrefs** icon is displayed in the status bar tray next to the **Communication Center** icon when an xref is attached to the current drawing. If an xref in the current file has been modified since the file was opened, the **Manage Xrefs** icon appears with an exclamation sign over it. Picking the **Manage Xrefs** icon, or right-clicking on the **Manage Xrefs** icon and selecting the **External References...** shortcut menu option, opens the **External References** palette so the xref file can be reloaded.

When the **Display notifications from services** check box is selected in the **Tray Settings** dialog box, a balloon message notification appears with the name of the modified xref file. See **Figure 25-7A.** You can then pick on the xref file name in the balloon

---

Figure 25-7.
The **Manage Xrefs** icon in the AutoCAD status bar tray provided a notification when an xref file has been modified and saved. A—A balloon message is displayed with an exclamation point over the icon. B—Reloading the xref file updates the current drawing and changes the appearance of the icon.

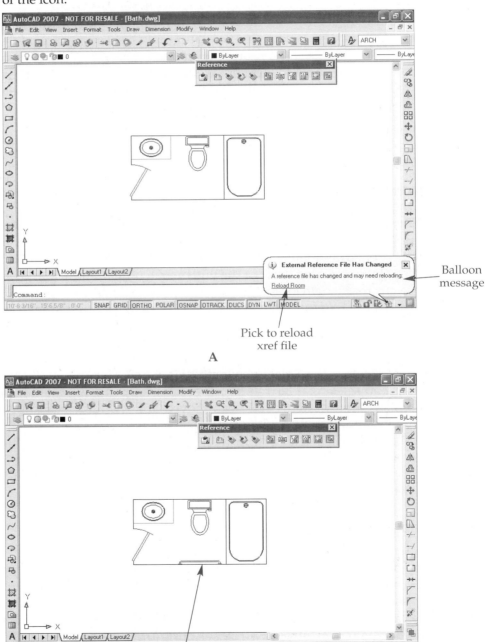

Balloon message

Pick to reload xref file

A

New xref

B

Manage Xrefs icon

AutoCAD and Its Applications—Basics

message to reload the file. In the example shown, a Towel Bar xref has been added to the Room parent xref drawing. The xref is then reloaded in the current drawing named Bath. See **Figure 25-7B.** Xrefs can also be reloaded by right-clicking on the **Manage Xrefs** icon and selecting **Reload DWG Xrefs** from the shortcut menu.

Clipping an Xref

In some cases it may be necessary to display only a specific portion of an external reference drawing. To accommodate this need, AutoCAD allows you to create a boundary that displays a *subregion* of an xref. All geometry occurring outside the border is invisible, while objects that are partially within the subregion appear to be trimmed at the boundary. Although clipped objects appear trimmed, the referenced file is not changed in any way. Clipping is applied to a selected instance of an xref, and not to the actual xref definition.

The **XCLIP** command is used to create and modify clipping boundaries. To access the **XCLIP** command, select an object that is part of the xref file in the drawing area, then right-click and select the **Clip Xref** shortcut menu option, pick the **Clip Xref** button from the **Reference** toolbar, pick **Modify > Clip > Xref**, or type XC or XCLIP. The prompt sequence for creating a rectangular boundary for an xref is as follows:

```
Command: XC or XCLIP↵
Select objects: (select any number of xref objects)
Select objects: ↵
Enter clipping option
[ON/OFF/Clipdepth/Delete/generate Polyline/New boundary] <New>: ↵
```

The Select objects: prompt allows you to select any number of xrefs to be clipped. Then press [Enter] to accept the default **New boundary** option and select the clipping boundary. The other options of the **XCLIP** command include the following:

- **ON** and **OFF.** The clipping feature can be turned on or off as needed by using these options.
- **Clipdepth.** This option allows a front and back clipping plane to be defined. The front and back clipping planes define what portion of a 3D drawing is displayed. Clipping of 3D models is described in *AutoCAD and Its Applications—Advanced.*
- **Delete.** To remove a clipping boundary completely, use this option.
- **generate Polyline.** This option allows you to create a polyline object to represent the clipping border of the selected xref.

After the **New boundary** option is selected, the **XCLIP** command sequence continues as follows:

```
Specify clipping boundary:
[Select polyline/Polygonal/Rectangular] <Rectangular>: (press [Enter] to create a
   rectangular boundary)
Specify first corner: (pick the first corner)
Specify opposite corner: (pick the other corner)
```

An example of using the **XCLIP** command is illustrated in **Figure 25-8.** Note the geometry outside of the clipping boundary is no longer displayed after the command is completed. A clipped xref can be edited just like an unclipped xref. Additionally, the clipping boundary moves with the xref. Note also that nested xrefs are clipped according to the clipping boundary for the parent xref.

If you do not want to create a rectangular clipping boundary after selecting an xref, there are two other options for defining a boundary. These options are described as follows:

- **Select polyline.** This option allows you to select an existing polyline object as a boundary definition. The border can only consist of straight line segments, so any arc segments in the selected polyline are treated as straight line segments. If the polyline is not closed, the start and end points of the boundary are connected.

- **Polygonal.** This option allows an irregular polygon to be drawn as a boundary. This option is similar to the **WPolygon** selection option, and allows a fairly flexible boundary definition.

The clipping boundary, or frame, is invisible by default. The frame can be displayed by setting the **XCLIPFRAME** system variable to 1, by picking the **Xref Frame** button from the **Reference** toolbar, or by picking **Modify** > **Object** > **External Reference** > **Frame**.

Figure 25-8.
A clipping boundary is used to clip selected areas of an xref. A—Using the **Rectangular** boundary selection option. B—The clipped xref.

Rectangular clipping boundary

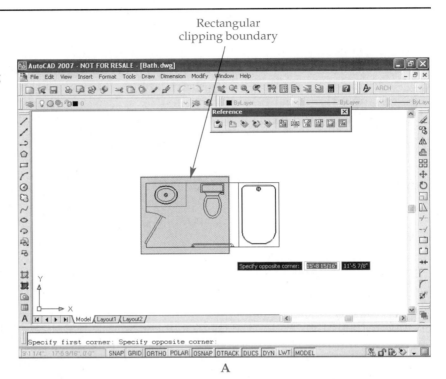

A

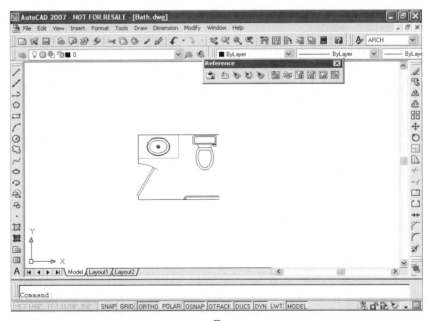

B

If a drawing will be used as an external reference, it is good practice to save the file with spatial and layer indexes. *Spatial indexes* and *layer indexes* are lists that organize objects by their locations in 3D space and their layer names. These lists help improve the performance of AutoCAD when referencing drawings with frozen layers and clipping boundaries. Layers that are frozen are not loaded when demand loading is enabled, and any areas outside clipping boundaries are also not loaded. Demand loading is described in the next section.

You can create spatial and layer indexes using the following procedure:

1. Access the **Save Drawing As** dialog box.
2. Pick **Options...** from the **Tools** flyout button and select the **DWG Options** tab of the **Saveas Options** dialog box.
3. Select the type of index required from the **Index type:** drop-down list.
4. Pick the **OK** button and save the drawing.

Using Demand Loading and Xref Editing Controls

Demand loading controls how much of an external reference file is loaded when it is attached to the master drawing. When demand loading is active, the only portion of the xref file loaded is the part necessary to regenerate the master drawing. This improves performance and saves disk space because the entire xref file is not loaded. For example, any data on frozen layers, as well as any data outside of clipping regions, is not loaded.

Demand loading is enabled by default. To check or change the setting, open the **Open and Save** tab of the **Options** dialog box. The three demand loading options are found in the **Demand load Xrefs:** drop-down list in the **External References (Xrefs)** area. The options are described as follows:

- **Enabled with copy.** When this option is active, demand loading is turned on, and other users can edit the original drawing because AutoCAD uses a copy of the referenced drawing.
- **Enabled.** When this option is active, demand loading is turned on. While the drawing is being referenced, the xref file is kept open and other users cannot edit the file.
- **Disabled.** Enabling this option turns off demand loading.

Two additional settings in the **Open and Save** tab of the **Options** dialog box control the effects of changes made to xref-dependent layers and in-place reference editing. (Reference editing is described later in this chapter.) The settings are controlled by check boxes in the **External References (Xrefs)** area. Each option is explained as follows:

- **Retain changes to Xref layers.** This option allows you to keep all changes made to the properties and states of xref-dependent layers. Any changes to layers take precedence over the layer settings in the xref file. The edited properties are retained even if an xref is reloaded. This option is active by default.
- **Allow other users to Refedit current drawing.** This option controls whether the current drawing can be edited in place by others while it is open and when it is referenced by another file. This option is active by default.

Binding an External Reference

An externally referenced file can be made a permanent part of the master drawing as if it had been inserted with the **INSERT** command. This is called *binding* an xref. Binding is useful when you need to send the full drawing file to another location or user, such as a plotting service or a client.

Before an xref is bound, all dependent objects in the externally referenced file, such as blocks, dimension styles, layers, linetypes, and text styles, are named differently by AutoCAD. When an xref is attached to the master drawing, dependent objects are renamed so the xref name precedes the actual object name. The names are separated by a vertical bar symbol (|). For example, prior to binding, a layer named Notes within an externally referenced drawing file named Title comes into the master drawing as Title|Notes. This is done to distinguish the xref-dependent layer name from the same layer name in the master drawing. When an xref file is bound to the master drawing, the dependent objects are renamed again to reflect that they have become a permanent part of the drawing. There are different renaming methods, depending on the type of binding that is performed.

To bind an xref using the **External References** palette, right-click on the desired reference name and pick the **Bind...** shortcut menu option. This displays the **Bind Xrefs** dialog box, which contains the **Bind** and **Insert** option buttons. See **Figure 25-9**.

The **Insert** option brings the xref into the drawing as if you had used the **INSERT** command to place the file. All instances of the xref are converted to normal block objects. Also, the drawing is entered into the block definition table, and all named objects such as layers, blocks, and styles are incorporated into the master drawing as named in the xref. For example, if an xref named PLATE is bound and it contains a layer named OBJECT, the xref-dependent layer PLATE|OBJECT becomes the locally defined layer OBJECT. All other xref-dependent objects are stripped of the xref name, and they assume the properties of the locally defined objects with the same name. The **Insert** binding option provides the best results for most purposes.

The **Bind** option also brings the xref in as a native part of the master drawing and converts all instances of the xref to blocks. However, the xref name is kept with the names of all dependent objects, and the vertical line in each of the names is replaced with two dollar signs with a number in between. For example, an xref layer named Title|Notes is renamed Title0Notes when the xref is bound using the **Bind** option. The number inside the dollar signs is automatically incremented if a local object definition with the same name exists. For example, if Title0Notes already exists in the drawing, the layer is renamed to Title1Notes. In this manner, unique names are created for all xref-dependent object definitions that are bound. Any of the named objects can be renamed as desired using the **RENAME** command.

In some cases, you may only need to incorporate one or more specific named objects from an xref into the master drawing, rather than the entire xref. If you only need selected items, it can be counterproductive to bind an entire drawing. In this case, you can bind only the named objects you select. This technique is covered later in this chapter.

Figure 25-9.
The **Bind Xrefs** dialog box allows you to specify how the xref is incorporated into the master drawing.

Binding Dependent Objects to a Drawing

Binding an xref allows you to make all dependent objects in an xref file a permanent part of the master drawing. Dependent objects include named items such as blocks, dimension styles, layers, linetypes, and text styles. Before binding, you cannot directly use any dependent objects from a referenced drawing in the master drawing. For example, a layer that exists only in a referenced drawing cannot be made current in the master drawing. The same applies for text styles.

When a drawing is referenced to the master drawing, all dependent named objects are renamed. All xref-dependent layer names are given the name of the referenced drawing, followed by the vertical bar symbol (|), and then the layer name. This naming convention enables you to quickly identify which layers belong to a specific referenced drawing. In **Figure 25-10**, the **Layer Properties Manager** dialog box shows how layer names in the master drawing are distinguished from those belonging to different xref files.

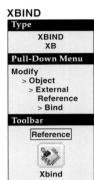

There may be cases where you want to individually bind an xref-dependent named object, such as a layer or block, rather than the entire xref file. This can be done using the **XBIND** command.

To access the **XBIND** command, pick the **Xbind** button from the **Reference** toolbar, pick **Modify > Object > External Reference > Bind...** from the pull-down menu, or type XB or XBIND. This displays the **Xbind** dialog box, **Figure 25-11**. This dialog box allows you to select individual xref-dependent objects for binding.

The xrefs shown are indicated by the AutoCAD drawing file icons. Click the plus sign to expand the listing and display the contents of the xref file.

To select an individually named object from a group, you must first expand the group listing by clicking on the plus sign next to the corresponding icon. To select an object for binding, highlight it and pick the **Add** button. The names of all objects selected and added are displayed in the **Definitions to Bind** list. When all desired objects have been selected, pick the **OK** button. A message displayed on the command line indicates how many objects of each type were bound.

Individual objects that are bound using the **XBIND** command are renamed in the same manner as objects that are bound using the **Bind** option in the **Bind Xrefs** dialog box. In addition to being renamed, a bound layer can also be assigned a linetype that

Figure 25-10.
Xref dependent layer names in the master drawing are preceded by the xref drawing name and the vertical bar symbol (|).

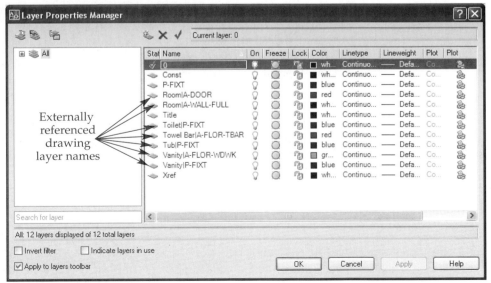

Figure 25-11.
The **Xbind** dialog box is used to individually bind xref-dependent objects to the master drawing.

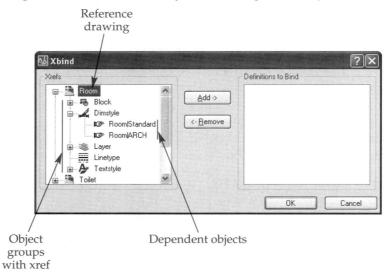

Reference drawing

Object groups with xref

Dependent objects

was not previously defined in the master drawing. An automatic bind is performed so the required linetype definition can be referenced by the new layer. A new linetype name, such as xref1$0$hidden, is created for the linetype. In similar fashion, a previously undefined block may be automatically bound to the master drawing as a result of binding nested blocks.

Bound objects can be renamed using the **RENAME** command.

Editing External Reference Drawings

Reference drawings can be edited *in place*, or within the master drawing. This function, called *reference editing*, allows you to edit reference drawings without opening the original xref file. Any changes can then be saved to the original drawing while remaining inside the master drawing.

> **NOTE**
>
> In-place reference editing is best suited for minor revisions. Larger revisions should be done inside the original drawing. Making major changes with in-place editing can decrease the performance of AutoCAD because additional disk space is used.

REFEDIT

Type
REFEDIT

Pull-Down Menu
Tools
> Xref and Block In-Place Editing
> Edit Reference In-Place

Toolbar
Refedit
Edit Reference In-Place

The **REFEDIT** command is used to edit externally referenced drawings in place. To access the **REFEDIT** command, select an object that is part of the xref file in the drawing area, then right-click and select the **Edit Xref In-place** shortcut menu option, pick the **Edit Reference In-Place** button from the **Refedit** toolbar, pick **Tools > Xref and Block In-Place Editing > Edit Reference In-Place**, or type REFEDIT.

Command: **REFEDIT**↵
Select reference:

This prompt asks you to select a reference to edit; in this case an xref is selected. After you make a selection, the **Reference Edit** dialog box is displayed with the **Identify Reference** tab active, **Figure 25-12.** A preview of the selected xref is shown in the

Figure 25-12.
The **Reference Edit** dialog box lists the name of the selected reference drawing and displays an image preview.

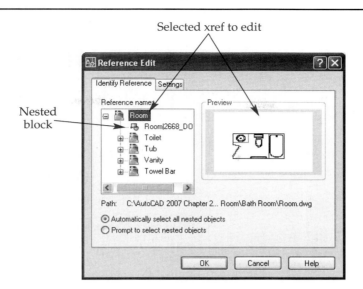

Selected xref to edit

Nested block

Preview panel, and the name of the file is highlighted. In the example shown, the Room reference drawing has been selected. Notice how nested blocks, like the 2668_DOOR block found in the Room reference, are listed under their parent xref.

In the **Path:** area, the radio button labeled **Automatically select all nested objects** is active by default. Using this option makes all the xref objects available for editing. If you want to only edit certain xref objects, then the **Prompt to select nested objects** option can be used. When this option is selected, the Select nested objects: prompt is displayed after picking **OK**. This prompt asks you to pick objects that belong to the previously selected xref. Pick all lines and any other geometry of the object to be edited, and then press [Enter]. The nested objects that you select make up the *working set*. If multiple instances of the same xref are displayed, be sure to pick objects from the one you originally selected.

Additional options for reference editing are available in the **Settings** tab of the **Reference Edit** dialog box. The **Create unique layer, style, and block names** option controls the naming of selected layers and objects that are *extracted*, or temporarily removed from the drawing, for editing purposes. If this check box is selected, layer and object names are given the prefix n, with n representing an incremental number. This is similar to the renaming method used when binding an xref.

The **Display attribute definitions for editing** option is only available if a block object is selected in the **Identify Reference** tab of the **Reference Edit** dialog box. Checking this option allows you to edit any attribute definitions included in the reference. Attributes are covered in detail in Chapter 24.

To prevent accidental changes to objects that do not belong to the working set, you can check the **Lock objects not in working set** option. This makes all objects outside of the working set unavailable for selection when in reference editing mode.

If the selected xref file contains other references, the **Reference name:** area lists all nested xrefs and blocks in tree view. In the example given, Toilet, Tub, Vanity, and Towel Bar are nested xrefs in the Room xref. If you pick the drawing file icon next to Vanity, for example, in the tree view, an image preview is displayed and the selected xref is highlighted in the graphics window. See **Figure 25-13.**

When you are through adjusting settings, pick **OK** to begin editing the xref file and display the **Refedit** toolbar in the drawing area. This toolbar displays the name of the selected reference drawing and is left on screen for the remainder of the reference editing session. See **Figure 25-14.** You can use the toolbar to add objects to the working set, remove objects from the working set, and save or discard changes to the original xref file.

Figure 25-13.
The **Preview** panel displays the Vanity nested xref after it is selected in the tree view.

Selected nested xref

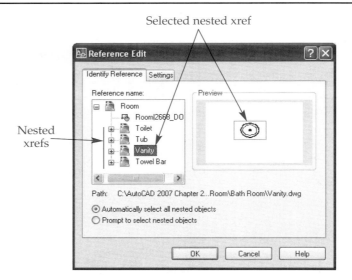

Nested xrefs

Figure 25-14.
The **Refedit** toolbar is used to perform reference editing functions.

Selected xref

Close Reference

Save Reference Edits

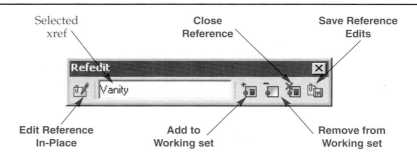

Edit Reference In-Place

Add to Working set

Remove from Working set

Any object that is drawn during the in-place edit is automatically added to the working set. Additional existing objects can also be added to the working set by using the **Add to Working set** button. If an object is added to the working set, it is extracted, or removed, from the host drawing. The **Remove from Working set** button allows you to remove selected objects from the working set. When a previously extracted object is removed, it is added back to the host drawing.

After you define the working set, it appears differently from the rest of the drawing. All nonselected objects are faded, or grayed out, **Figure 25-15A.** The objects in the working set appear in the normal display mode. Once the working set has been defined, you can use any drawing or editing commands to alter the object. In the example given in **Figure 25-15A,** the vanity has been selected from the room so the sink can be redesigned and a faucet added.

Once the necessary changes have been made, pick the **Save Reference Edits** button from the **Refedit** toolbar. If you want to exit the reference editing session without saving changes, pick the **Close Reference** button. If you save changes, pick **OK** when AutoCAD asks if you want to continue with the save and redefine the xref. All instances of the xref are then immediately updated. See **Figure 25-15B.**

CAUTION

All reference edits made in this manner are saved back to the original drawing file, and affect any master drawing that references the file when the master is opened. For this reason, it is critically important that external references be edited only with the permission of your instructor or supervisor.

Figure 25-15.
Figure 25-15.
Reference editing.
A—Objects in the
drawing that are
not a part of the
working set are
grayed out during
the reference editing
session. B—All
instances of the xref
are immediately
updated after
reference editing.

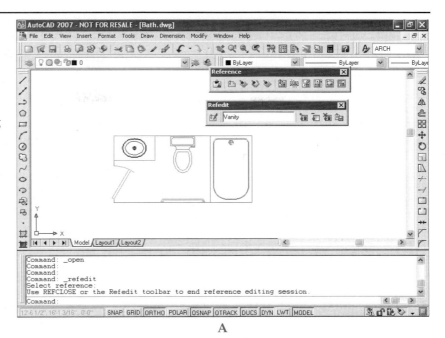

A

B

Opening an Xref File

Using the **REFEDIT** command allows you to edit xref objects within the current drawing. An xref file can also be opened from within its parent drawing into a new AutoCAD drawing window using the **XOPEN** command. This is essentially the same procedure as using the **OPEN** command, but quicker. To use the **XOPEN** command, pick **Tools** > **Xref and Block Editing** > **Open Reference** or type XOPEN.

Command: **XOPEN**↵
Select Xref:

Selecting any object that is a part of an xref opens the xref drawing file into a new AutoCAD drawing window. Picking the **Window** pull-down menu shows all the drawing files that are open in the AutoCAD session.

Once changes are made to the xref file and saved, the xref file needs to be reloaded in the master drawing file. Use the **External References** palette or the **Manage Xrefs** icon to reload the modified xref file. This ensures that the master file you are working in is up-to-date.

Xref files can also be opened by selecting an object that is part of the xref file in the drawing area and followed by right-clicking and selecting the **Open Xref** shortcut menu option. You can also open an xref in the **External References** palette by right-clicking on the xref name and selecting the **Open** shortcut menu option.

Using External References in Multiview Layouts

Mechanical drawings and architectural construction drawings often contain sections and details drawn at different scales. These sections and details can be created as separate drawing files and then attached as xrefs to a master drawing. By controlling the display of layers within multiple viewports, you can create a multiview layout.

The following general procedure is used to create a multiview layout using external references:

1. Create the drawings and details to be displayed in the multiview drawing as separate drawing files.
2. Begin a new master drawing based on a template containing a border and title block.
3. Make a layer for referenced drawings and a layer for viewports.
4. Create viewports in a layout tab.
5. Place external reference drawings in the master drawing.
6. Adjust the drawing display within each viewport according to the required drawing scale and visible layers.

These steps are explained in more detail in the following sections.

Layouts

Creating a multiple viewport layout requires a basic understanding of the two AutoCAD designing environments: model space and paper space. Model space is the environment in which you draw and design. When the **Model** tab is selected, model space is active. Model space is also accessed by double-clicking inside a floating viewport in a layout tab. All drawings and models should be created in model space at full scale.

Paper space is the environment you use when you want to create a layout of the drawing prior to plotting. By default, paper space is active when a layout tab is selected. One powerful aspect of using paper space is that you can create a layout of several different drawings and views, each with different scales. You can even mix 2D and 3D views in the same paper space layout.

Model space and paper space are described in Chapter 10, and a thorough explanation of layouts is provided in Chapter 11.

Viewports

The most important visualization aspect involved in creating a multiview layout is to imagine that the sheet of paper you are creating contains several cutouts, called *viewports*, through which you can see other drawings, which are *models*. See **Figure 25-16**.

Objects and designs should be created at full size in model space. If you are designing a machine part, you are probably using decimal units. For example, a line that is 1″ long should actually be drawn 1″ long in model space. If you are designing a house, you are using architectural units. For example, a line that is 15′ long should actually be drawn 15′ long in model space.

AutoCAD and Its Applications—Basics

Figure 25-16.
Views of other drawings can be seen through viewports cut into paper space.

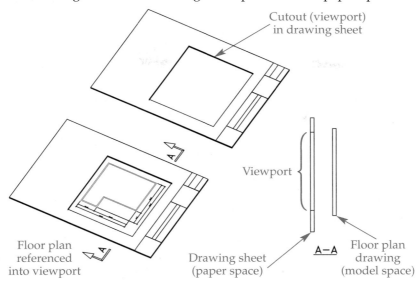

When creating a multiview layout of multiple drawings, double-click inside a viewport to make it active and then *reference* (insert) the drawing to be displayed. This procedure is explained later in this chapter.

Now, imagine a piece of architectural C-size paper (18″ × 24″) is hanging up in front of you, and the first viewport is cut 12″ wide and 12″ high. You want to display the floor plan of a house inside the opening. If you then place the full-size model of the floor plan directly behind the paper, the house will extend many feet beyond the edges of the paper, because a 40′ × 36′ floor plan is much larger than a 18″ × 24″, piece of paper. In order to place the drawing within the viewport the drawing must be scaled. If the floor plan should be displayed inside the viewport at a scale of 1/4″ = 1′-0″, and the scale factor of 1/4″ = 1′-0″ is 48, you need to move the floor plan model away from the paper until it is 1/48 (the reciprocal of 48) the size it is now. When you do that, the entire floor plan fits inside the viewport you cut. This is accomplished with the **XP** (times paper space) option of the **ZOOM** command, which is described later in this chapter. See **Figure 25-17.**

Constructing a Multiview Drawing

Now that you have a good idea of the multiview layout process, the following example leads you through the details of the procedure. This example uses a house floor plan, a stair detail, and a footing detail. This drawing is *not* among the sample drawings furnished with AutoCAD. Instead, the drawing is based on Exercise 25-1. Complete Exercise 25-1 before working through the example.

Exercise 25-1   Complete the Exercise on the Student CD.

Initial Drawing Setup

The first aspect of drawing setup is to place a border and title block in the paper space, or layout, work environment. They should be the proper size for the plot you want to make according to the paper size. This can be accomplished in one of the following ways, depending on the depth of your preparation:

Figure 25-17.
A floor plan placed inside a viewport.

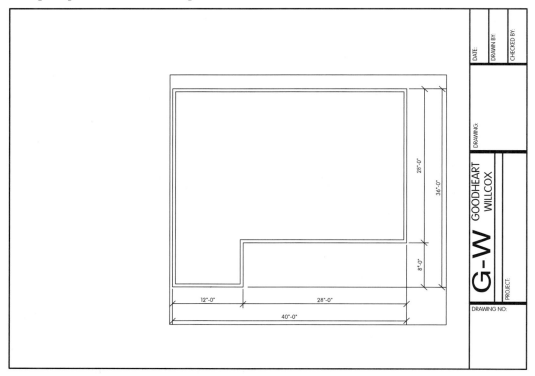

- Draw a border and a title block on separate layers or the same "sheet" layer.
- Draw a border and insert a predrawn title block.
- Insert a predrawn border and title block.
- Open or insert a predrawn standard border and title block template containing all constant text and attributes for variable information. The Architectural, English units template drawing is a D-size sheet, but is appropriate for this example. It contains one viewport, which shows as a thin line just inside the left border line. Erase this viewport before creating a new one.

The method you use is not of primary importance for this example, but it is always best to use existing borders and title blocks, preferably in an existing template, to maximize efficiency and consistency.

PROFESSIONAL TIP

This initial setup phase is unnecessary if your school or company uses preprinted border and title block sheets. You might use a *phantom* border and title block sheet on the screen for layout purposes, and to add additional information to the title block. This phantom information can be frozen before plotting.

When setting up a drawing, first display a paper space layout, then set the units to match the type of drawing you are creating. Be sure the extents of your border and title block match the maximum active plotting area, or *clip limits*, of your plotter. This example uses a standard architectural C-size sheet (18″ × 24″), and assumes that the plotter's active area is .75″ less along the top and bottom and 1.25″ less on the sides, for a total plotting area of 16.5″ × 21.5″.

AutoCAD and Its Applications—Basics

Set the units for the new layout as follows (if you do not use a template):
1. Pick a layout tab.
2. Set the following in the **Drawing Units** dialog box:
   * Architectural units.
   * Units precision = 1/2″.
   * System of angle measure = Decimal degrees.
   * Angle precision = 0.
   * Direction for angle 0 = East.
   * Angles measured counterclockwise.
3. Perform a **Zoom All**.

Creating New Layers

The border and title block should be on a separate layer, so you may want to create a new layer called Border or Title and assign it a separate color. An alternative is to create a Sheet layer on which the border and title block are placed. Be sure to make the new layer current before you draw the border and title block. If you want to use an existing border and title block, insert it now.

One of the principal functions of this example is to use existing drawings in a layout. The house floor plan, stairs, and footing drawings does not become a part of the new drawing, but they are referenced to the current drawing in order to save drawing file space. Therefore, you should also create a new layer for these drawings and name it Xref. Assign the Xref layer the color of 7.

The referenced drawings fit inside viewports that can be any shape. Viewports are added to the layout and can be edited like any other AutoCAD object. Create a layer called Viewports for these objects and assign a color.

The layers of any existing drawings that you reference (xref) into your new drawing remain intact. Therefore, you do not have to create additional layers unless you want to add information to your drawing, such as general notes or other drawing objects.

If you do not have an existing architectural C-size border and title block, you can draw a border at this time. Make the Border layer current and draw a border using the **RECTANG** command at the dimensions of 16.5″ × 21.5″. Draw a title block if you want. Your screen should look similar to **Figure 25-18**.

Creating Viewports

The process of creating viewports is completed in a paper space layout because viewports are cut out of the paper. When creating a drawing in a layout, your screen represents a sheet of paper. Now you create an opening through which you can view a referenced drawing in model space.

Methods of creating viewports are explained in Chapter 10. For this example, you can select the **Single Viewport** button in the **Viewports** toolbar to create each viewport. Be sure to set the Viewports layer current before creating the viewport. This allows the viewports to be turned off for plotting. Select two points to create a 12″ × 12″ viewport positioned as shown in **Figure 25-19**.

Figure 25-18.
The border and title block in paper space.

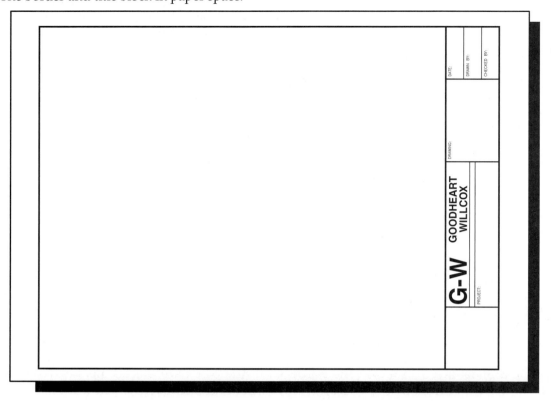

Figure 25-19.
A viewport added to the drawing in paper space.

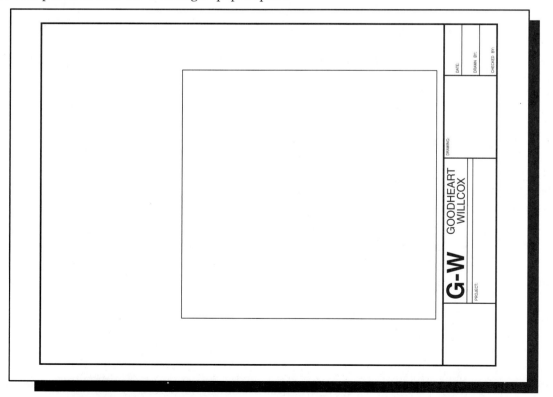

At this point, you can continue creating as many viewports as required. However, this example continues the process and references a drawing into the new viewport.

Placing Views in the Drawing

Use the new viewport to insert the drawing of the floor plan named Floor. Instead of using the **INSERT** command, which combines an existing drawing with the new one, use an external reference (**XREF** command) so that AutoCAD creates a reference to the Floor drawing. This allows the size of the new drawing to remain small because the Floor drawing has not been combined with it.

The following procedure allows you to enter model space, reference an existing drawing to the new one, and zoom the view to see the referenced drawing.

1. If the layout tab is active, double-click inside the viewport to activate model space within the viewport.
2. Set the Xref layer current.
3. Pick **Insert > DWG Reference...** from the pull-down menu. The **Select Reference File** dialog box is displayed. See **Figure 25-20.**
4. Select Floor.dwg in the dialog box, and pick the **OK** button.

The **External Reference** dialog box is displayed. Set the insertion point to 0,0,0, the X, Y, and Z scale to 1.0, and the rotation angle to 0. Pick the **OK** button and perform a **ZOOM Extents**. Your drawing should now resemble the one shown in **Figure 25-21.**

All layers on the referenced drawing are added to the new drawing. These layers can be distinguished from existing layers because the drawing name is automatically placed in front of the layer name and separated by a vertical bar symbol (|). This naming convention is shown in the **Layer Control** drop-down list in the **Object Properties** toolbar and in the **Layer Properties Manager** dialog box.

Scaling a Drawing in a Viewport

When a drawing has been referenced and placed in a viewport, it is ready to be scaled. After using the **Extents** option of the **ZOOM** command, the referenced drawing fills the viewport. However, the drawing is not displayed at the correct scale.

Figure 25-20.
The Floor.dwg drawing is selected in the **Select Reference File** dialog box.

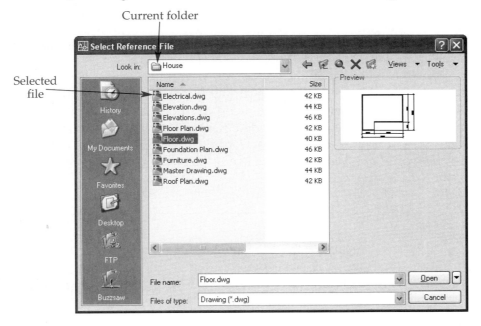

Figure 25-21.
The floor plan is referenced into the first viewport.

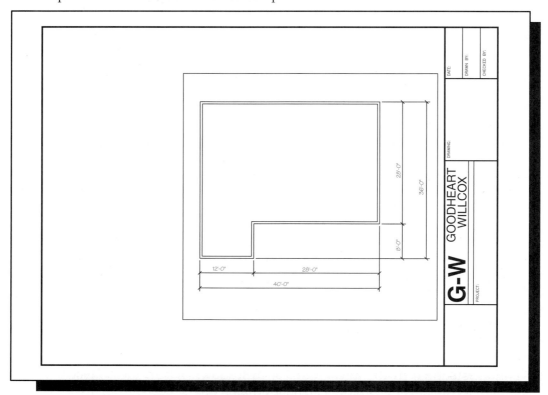

The scale factor of each view of the multiview drawing is important to remember; it is the scale used to size your drawing in the viewport. The scale factor is used in conjunction with the **XP** option of the **ZOOM** command, or it can be selected from the **Viewports** toolbar. Since the intended final scale of the floor plan on the plotted drawing is to be 1/4″ = 1′–0″, the scale factor is 48, or 1/48 of full size. A detailed discussion of determining scale factors is given in Chapter 11.

Be sure you are still in the model space environment within the viewport. Enter the following:

Command: **Z** *or* **ZOOM**↵
Specify corner of window, enter a scale factor (nX or nXP), or [All/Center/Dynamic/Extents/Previous/Scale/Window/Object] <real time>: **1/48XP**↵

The scale can also be set by picking 1/4″ = 1′–0″ from the scale drop-down list in the **Viewports** toolbar. See **Figure 25-22.** The drawing may not change much in size, depending on the size of the viewport. Also, keep in mind the viewport itself is an object that can be moved and stretched if needed. Remember to change to paper space when editing the size of the viewport. If part of your drawing extends beyond the edge of the viewport after applying the scale, use grips or the **STRETCH** command to change the size of the viewport.

PROFESSIONAL TIP

You can use any display command inside a viewport. If a drawing is not centered after scaling, use **PAN** to move it around. If lines of a drawing touch a viewport edge, those lines will not be visible if the viewport layer is frozen or turned off.

Figure 25-22.
The scale can be set
by picking 1/4″ = 1″
from the drop-down
list in the **Viewports**
toolbar.

Pick to display
the scale
drop-down list

Controlling Viewport Layer Visibility

If you create another viewport, the floor plan will immediately fill it. This is because a viewport is just a window through which you can view a drawing or 3D model that has been referenced to the current drawing. One way to control what is visible in addition viewports is to freeze all layers of the Floor drawing in any new viewports that are created. Access the **Layer Properties Manager** dialog box and set all layers from the Floor xref to be frozen in new viewports by picking the icons in the New VP Freeze column. When the snowflake icon appears in this column, the layer is not displayed in any new viewports.

The frozen or thawed status in the current viewport is controlled by the icons in the **Current VP Freeze** column.

PROFESSIONAL TIP

Use the [Shift] and [Ctrl] keys in combination with picking to select multiple layer names. When multiple layers are selected, toggling one setting makes the same new setting apply to all highlighted layer names.

NOTE

The **New VP Freeze** and **Current VP Freeze** settings in the **Layer Properties Manager** dialog box can also be set using the **VPLAYER** command at the Command: prompt.

Creating Additional Viewports

The previous example of creating a viewport and referencing a drawing to it is the same process that is used to create the additional two viewports for the Stair and Footing drawings. In this case, two viewports are created before externally referencing the additional drawing files. If you know the number, size, and location of all viewports needed on a multiview drawing, it may save time to create them all at once.

PROFESSIONAL TIP

Viewports can always be added, deleted, or resized on a drawing. So, if your class or company uses standard sheet layouts containing several views, create and save templates that contain viewports.

Now that the floor plan layers are frozen in new viewports, the other two viewports can be created. Use the following procedure:
1. Double-click outside the viewport to activate paper space.
2. Set the Viewports layer current.

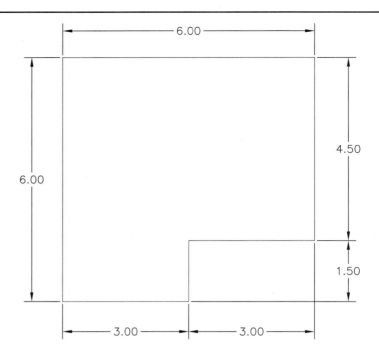

Figure 25-23.
Draw this polygonal
viewport.

3. Draw a viewport to the dimensions shown in **Figure 25-23** using the **Polygonal Viewport** button in the **Viewports** toolbar.

4. Draw a third viewport 6″ wide and 5″ high.

The final arrangement of the three viewports is shown in **Figure 25-24.**

Now that the viewports are complete, you can begin referencing the remaining two drawings. The following procedure uses **DesignCenter** to reference the Stair drawing:

1. Set the current layer to Xref, and double-click in the lower-left viewport to make model space active.

2. Activate **DesignCenter.** Locate the folder that contains the Stair.dwg file and pick it. Files contained in the selected folder are displayed in the **Content** area.

3. Right-click on the Stair.dwg file and select **Attach as Xref...** from the shortcut menu to display the **External Reference** dialog box. Enter 0,0,0 for the insertion point, 1.0 for the scale, and 0 for the rotation angle.

4. Press [Ctrl]+[2] to temporarily dismiss **DesignCenter.**

5. The scale factor for the Stair drawing is 32. Use the **ZOOM** command and enter 1/32XP to scale the drawing correctly.

The drawing now appears as shown in **Figure 25-25.** Notice the Stair drawing is shown in all three viewports. Use the **Layer Properties Manager** dialog box to freeze the stair layers in selected viewports using the following procedure:

1. Pick in the large viewport to make it active.

2. Open the **Layer Properties Manager** dialog box.

3. Select all layers that begin with the name of the referenced drawing you want to freeze in the active viewport. In this case, all layers that begin with Stair are selected.

4. Pick the sun icon in the **Current VP Freeze** column of one of the selected layers. All selected icons change to a snowflake. Pick **OK.** The Stair drawing is now removed from the large viewport.

Repeat this procedure to freeze the stair layers in the upper-left viewport.

Figure 25-24.
Two additional viewports are placed and sized in the drawing.

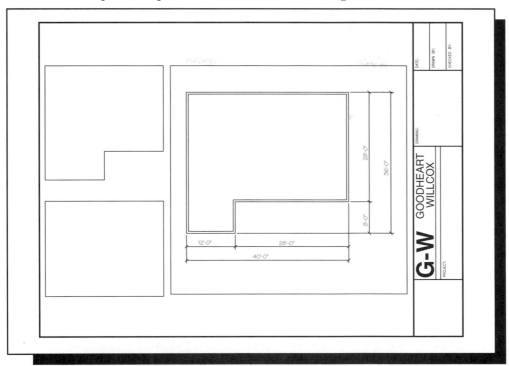

Figure 25-25.
The reference drawing Stair is displayed in all viewports. Use the **Layer Properties Manager** dialog box to restrict its visibility.

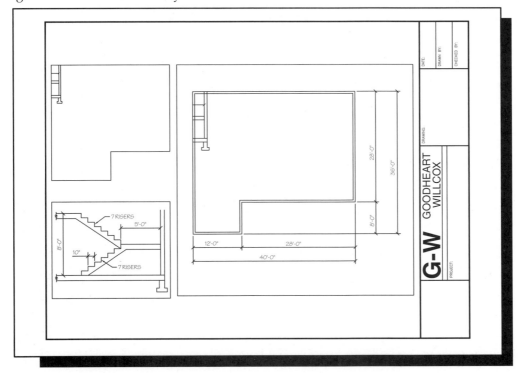

The final drawing can now be inserted into the last viewport. Prepare the third view by following these steps:

1. Double-click in the upper-left viewport.
2. Set the Xref layer current.
3. Attach the Footing drawing as an xref using one of the methods explained earlier in this chapter.
4. Freeze the Footing layers in the other two viewports.
5. Use the **ZOOM** command and enter 1/16XP.

The drawing should now appear as shown in **Figure 25-26**.

NOTE Be sure to set the current layer to Xref when referencing a drawing so the inserted drawing is not placed on another layer, such as Viewports.

Adjusting Viewport Display, Size, and Location

If you need to adjust a drawing within a viewport, first be sure that model space is current. Then, pick the desired viewport to make it active, and use an appropriate display command, such as **ZOOM** or **PAN**.

The entire viewport can be moved to another location, but you must first activate the paper space layout. Pick the viewport border to display its grips. Objects inside the viewport are not selected when picking because they are in model space. After selection, adjust the location of the viewports.

Figure 25-26.
The drawing is completed by referencing the Footing drawing.

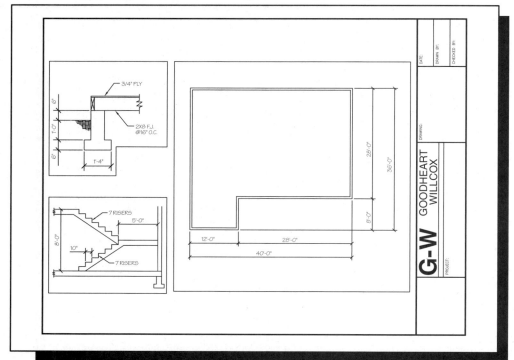

Changing viewport shape and size

Paper space viewport shape and size can be quickly changed using the **VPCLIP** command. To access the **VPCLIP** command, select a viewport in paper space, then right-click and select the **Viewport Clip** shortcut menu option, pick the **Clip Existing Viewport** button from the **Insert** toolbar, pick **Modify > Clip > Viewport**, or type VPCLIP. A viewport can be clipped by either selecting an existing shape that has been drawn or by drawing a new polygon. Use the following procedure to change the shape of a viewport.

1. Activate a paper space layout. Pick the **Clip Existing Viewport** button in the **Viewports** toolbar.
2. Select the outline of the viewport to be resized.
3. Select the new clipping object, such as a circle that has been previously drawn over the current viewport. The old viewport is deleted.

The **Delete** option of the **VPCLIP** command enables you to delete a viewport that was previously clipped. It prompts you to select the clipping object, which is the new shape that was drawn to clip the old viewport. After selecting the viewport and pressing [Enter], the original viewport is redrawn and the clipped version is deleted.

Locking the viewport scale

Once a drawing has been scaled properly inside a viewport, it is important to avoid using a zoom again prior to plotting. AutoCAD provides a viewport locking feature that helps prevent inadvertent zooms. To lock the display in a viewport, access the **Properties** window and then select the viewport from paper space. Change the Display locked property to Yes. Repeat the procedure for all viewports you want to lock.

Adding notes and titles

There are two ways in which titles and notes can be added to a multiview drawing with referenced drawings. The first method is to add the notations to the original drawing. In this manner, all titles and notes are referenced to the new drawing. This is the best system to use if the titles, scale label, and notes will not change.

However, titles may change. You may want to be sure that all titles of views use the same text style, or you might want to add a special symbol. This is easily completed after the drawings are referenced. The most important thing to remember is that the paper space layout must be active to add text. Do not place text in model space. You can use new and existing text styles to add titles and notes to a drawing using the **TEXT** or **MTEXT** command. See **Figure 25-27.**

Removing viewport outlines

Viewport outlines are usually turned off for plotting purposes, as shown in **Figure 25-27.** To turn off viewports before plotting, open the **Layer Properties Manager** dialog box and click on the plot icon for the Viewports layer. A diagonal slash is placed over the symbol, indicating that the layer will not plot.

NOTE If you freeze the Viewports layer and a box surrounds one of the views, you are probably still in model space. Remember that a box outlines the current viewport in model space. Enter PS at the Command: prompt or pick the **Model** button on the status bar to enter paper space and the outline disappears.

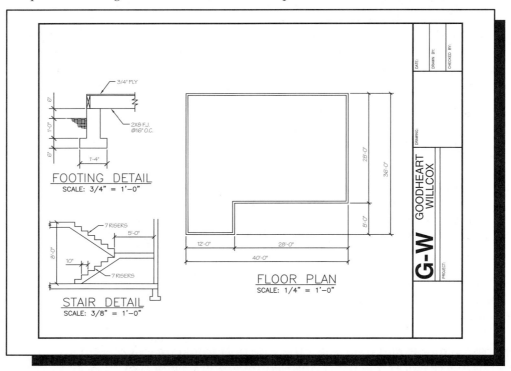

Plotting a Multiview Drawing

You have already taken care of scaling the views because you used the **XP** option of the **ZOOM** command when you referenced them. The drawing that now appears on your screen in paper space must be plotted at full scale, 1 = 1, with the **PLOT** command in order for the correct viewport scales to be plotted.

The process of creating and plotting a properly scaled multiview layout will go smoothly if you planned your drawing at the start of the project. Review the following items, and keep them in mind when starting any drawing or design project—especially one that involves the creation of a multiview paper space layout.

- Determine the size of paper to be used.
- Determine the type of title block, notes, revision blocks, parts lists, etc., that will appear on the drawing.
- Prepare a quick sketch of the view layouts and their plotted scales.
- Determine the scales to be used for each viewport.
- Establish proper text styles and heights based on the drawing scale factors.
- Set the **DIMSCALE** variable using the proper scale factor when creating drawings in model space.

There is no substitute for planning a project before you begin. It may seem like an unnecessary expense of time, but it will save time later in the project, and may help you become more productive in all your work.

You may never have to specify a scale other than full (1 = 1) when plotting. Any object or design, whether 2D or 3D, can be referenced into a border and title block drawing, scaled with **ZOOM XP**, and then plotted. Use the paper space layout procedure for all your drawings, even if they are just a single view. You will find that you need fewer border and title block template drawings, and the process will become much quicker.

**Exercise
25-2**   Complete the Exercise on the Student CD.

Chapter Test

Answer the following questions. Write your answers on a separate sheet of paper or complete the electronic chapter test on the Student CD.

1. When inserting an xref, how does the **Overlay** option differ from the **Attach** option?
2. What effect does the use of referenced drawings have on drawing file size?
3. When are xrefs updated in the master drawing?
4. Why would you want to bind a dependent object to a master drawing?
5. What does the layer name WALL0NOTES mean?
6. What is the purpose of the **Detach** option in the **External References** palette?
7. What are spatial and layer indexes, and what function do they perform?
8. What are the three types of paths that can be used for storing an xref?
9. What command is used to edit external references in place?
10. What command allows you to open a parent xref drawing into a new AutoCAD drawing window by selecting the xref in the master drawing?
11. What is the function of the **VPCLIP** command?
12. What is the purpose of locking a viewport?
13. Indicate the command and value you would use to specify a 1/2″ = 1′-0″ scale inside a viewport.
14. How do you freeze all layers of a referenced drawing inside any new viewports?
15. Do you need to be in paper space or model space in order to resize a viewport?
16. Explain why you should plan your plots.

Drawing Problems

1. Open one of your dimensioned drawings from Chapter 19. Construct a multi-view layout and generate a plot on C-size paper.
   A. Create four viewports of equal size, separated by 1″ of empty space.
   B. Select each viewport and display a different view of the drawing.
   C. Plot the drawing and be sure to use the scale of 1:1.
   D. Save the drawing as P25-1.
2. Open one of your dimensioned drawings from Chapter 19. Construct a multi-view layout and generate a plot on C-size or B-size paper. Plot at the scale of 1:1.
3. Open one of your dimensioned drawings from Chapter 20. Construct a multi-view layout and generate a plot on C-size or B-size paper. Plot at the scale of 1:1.
4. Open one of your dimensioned drawings from Chapter 21. Construct a multi-view layout and generate a plot on C-size or B-size paper. Plot at the scale of 1:1.

CHAPTER 26

Sheet Sets

Learning Objectives

After completing this chapter, you will be able to do the following:

- Identify and describe the functions of the **Sheet Set Manager**.
- Create sheet sets.
- Add sheets and sheet views to a sheet set.
- Plot and publish a set of sheets.
- Insert callout blocks and view labels into sheet views.
- Set up custom properties for a sheet set.
- Create a sheet list table.
- Archive a set of electronic files for a sheet set.

Organizing and distributing drawings during the course of a design project can involve a wide range of tasks. Drawings often need to be shared with clients and other personnel to make sure the design is accurate and any changes are incorporated. As the project is developed, a set of drawings is used to build the design. The design can be relatively simple, such as the views for a mechanical part, or complex, such as the plans for a building or new highway off-ramp. While a simple mechanical part may only call for one drawing sheet for manufacturing, a 10-story office building may require a set of 100 sheets or more. Although design needs vary, the ability to organize drawings for exchange purposes is important because any project typically involves input from a number of sources. This capability becomes critical at the end of the project, when delivery of the drawings must take place in an orderly manner.

AutoCAD provides a tool that helps simplify the management of a project with multiple drawings and views. This tool is the **Sheet Set Manager**. This chapter discusses how to use the **Sheet Set Manager** to structure different drawing layouts into groups of files for reviewing, plotting, and publishing purposes.

Sheet sets combine many AutoCAD features to automate and organize the entire drawing set for a project. To understand and effectively apply sheet sets, you must understand templates (Chapter 2), fields (Chapter 8), views (Chapter 10), layouts (Chapter 11), blocks (Chapter 22), attributes (Chapter 24), and external references (Chapter 25). If you encounter difficulties in understanding an aspect of sheet sets, it may be helpful to review the underlying concept being applied.

Sheet Sets Overview

A *sheet set* is a collection of drawing sheets for a project. The term *sheet* refers to a drawing produced for the project. A sheet is a layout tab in a drawing file and can have additional project-specific properties.

All sheets in a sheet set can use a single template. The template can contain a title block with attributes containing fields. The field values may include items such as project name and sheet number. Thus, if the project name changes during the course of the project, the field can be modified in the template, and the change is automatically applied to all sheets within the set. If a new sheet is inserted into the sheet sets, the sheet numbers and all sheet references update automatically. This automation can save a great deal of time and improve the accuracy of the set of drawings.

Sheets can contain *sheet views*. A sheet view is any referenced portion of a drawing set, such as an elevation, a section, or a detail. Sheet views can be automatically labeled, placed on separate sheets, and referenced to each other through the use of blocks with attributes containing fields. Like the title block fields discussed in the previous paragraphs, these sheet view field values update automatically to reflect changes in sheet numbering.

Once the sheet set is complete, you can easily print, publish, and archive the entire set in a single operation. This is very efficient. For example, it is far easier to plot a sheet set containing twenty sheets than to open and print twenty separate drawings.

Introduction to the Sheet Set Manager

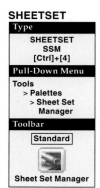

SHEETSET

Type

SHEETSET
SSM
[Ctrl]+[4]

Pull-Down Menu

Tools
> Palettes
> Sheet Set
Manager

Toolbar

Standard

Sheet Set Manager

Sheet sets are created, organized, and accessed using the **Sheet Set Manager**. To open the **Sheet Set Manager**, pick the **Sheet Set Manager** button on the **Standard** toolbar, select **Tools > Palettes > Sheet Set Manager**, type SSM or SHEETSET, or use the [Ctrl]+[4] key combination. See **Figure 26-1A.** The window is divided into three tabs: the **Sheet List** tab, the **Sheet Views** tab, and the **Model Views** tab. The **Sheet Set Control** drop-down list is used to open and create sheet sets. See **Figure 26-1B.** The buttons next to the drop-down list are used to control and manage the items listed in the **Sheet Set Manager** window. These buttons vary depending on the currently selected tab. The area at the bottom of the window (labeled **Details** or **Preview**) is used to show a text description or preview image of a selected sheet or view.

The **Sheet Set Manager** is a modeless dialog box. It can be resized, docked, and set to auto-hide. The **Expand/Collapse** buttons in the upper and lower portions of the **Sheet Set Manager** window can be used to hide or display the information. The **Details** and **Preview** areas can be toggled by picking the appropriate button on the title bar.

Figure 26-1.
The **Sheet Set Manager.** A—The window contains the **Sheet List**, **Sheet Views**, and **Model Views** tabs. B—The **Sheet Set Control** drop-down list contains options for creating and opening a sheet set.

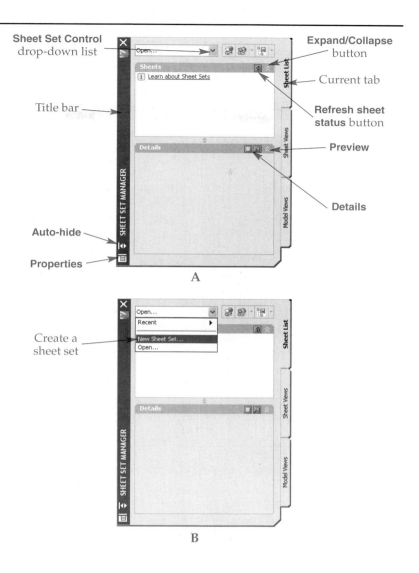

A

B

Creating Sheet Sets

Sheet sets are created with the **Create Sheet Set** wizard. They can be created from an example sheet set or from existing drawing files.

Creating a Sheet Set from an Example Sheet Set

When you create a new sheet using an example sheet set, you select an existing sheet set as a model, and then modify it as needed to fit the needs of the new sheet set. AutoCAD provides several example sheet sets based on different drafting disciplines. You are not limited to the provided examples—you can use any sheet set as the example sheet set.

To create a new sheet set from an example sheet set, open the **Sheet Set Manager** and select **New Sheet Set…** from the **Sheet Set Control** drop-down list. Refer to **Figure 26-1B.** This opens the **Create Sheet Set** wizard. See **Figure 26-2.** This wizard steps you through the process of creating a sheet set.

The **Begin** page of the **Create Sheet Set** wizard provides two options. Pick **An example sheet set** to start your sheet set using an example sheet set. The second option, **Existing drawings**, is discussed in the next section. Pick the **Next** button to display the **Sheet Set Example** page, **Figure 26-3.**

Figure 26-2.
Select **An example sheet set** on the **Begin** page to use an AutoCAD sheet set template.

Pick to use
a template

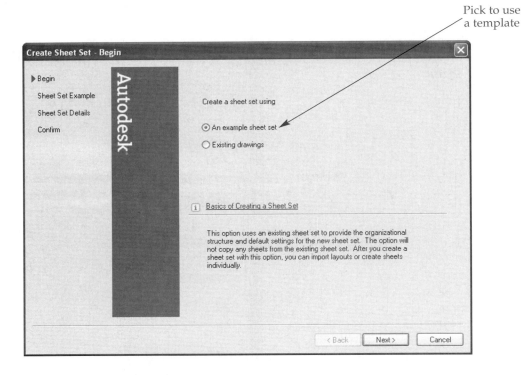

Figure 26-3.
Use the **Sheet Set Example** page to select an example sheet set.

List of sheet sets
in Template folder

Select a template from the
Browse for sheet set dialog box

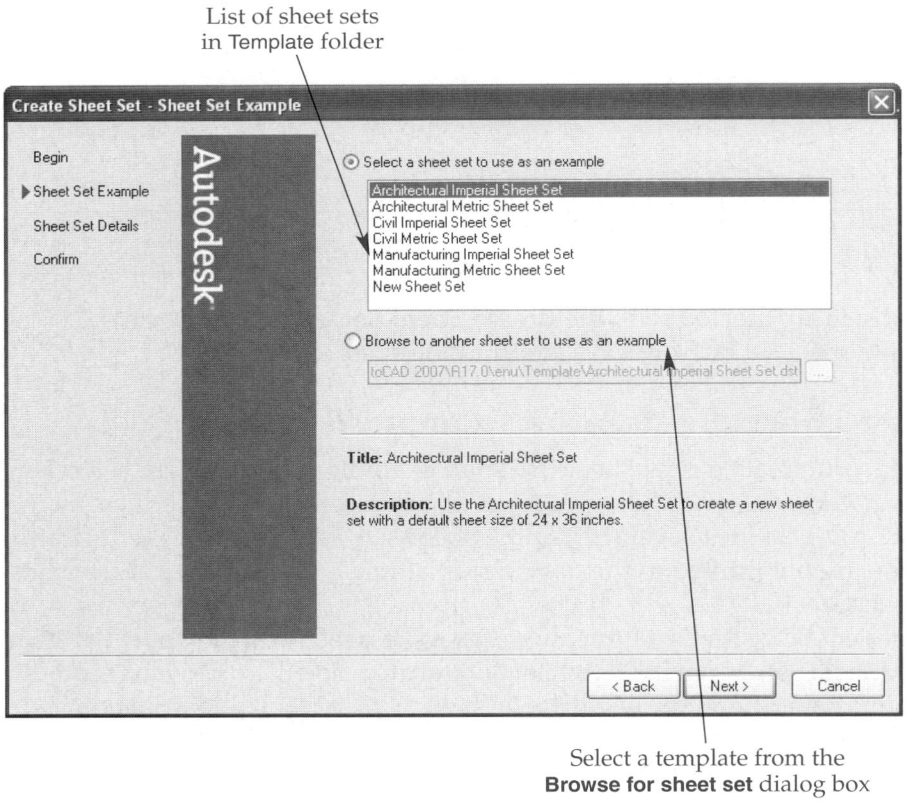

Sheet set information is saved in a DST file (sheet set data file). When creating a sheet set from an example sheet set, you are starting from the existing DST file. The list box on the **Sheet Set Example** page lists all DST files in the default Template folder. You can pick one of these sheet sets, or select the second option and select a DST file from another folder.

After selecting the DST file for the example sheet set, pick the **Next** button to display the **Sheet Set Details** page. See **Figure 26-4.** This page allows you to modify the existing sheet set data and create settings for your new project.

Enter the name of the sheet set in the **Name of new sheet set** text box. This is typically the project number or a short description of the project. A description for the sheet set can be entered in the **Description** area. The **Store sheet set data file (.dst) here** text box determines where the sheet set file is saved on the hard drive. If **Create a folder hierarchy based on subsets** is checked, folders will be created based on subset levels. Picking the **Sheet Set Properties** button opens the **Sheet Set Properties** dialog box. See **Figure 26-5.** The main settings for the sheet set are specified in this dialog box. There are three sections. The properties in the **Sheet Set** section are explained as follows:

- **Name.** This is the title for the sheet set. This can be changed by clicking in the field and modifying the current name.
- **Sheet set data file.** This is the location of the DST file for the sheet set.
- **Description.** This is the description of the sheet set.
- **Model view.** This text box specifies the folder(s) containing drawing files that are used for the sheet set. To modify this setting, pick in the text box, pick the ellipsis (...) button, and select a folder in the dialog box. Objects and views from resource drawings are inserted into sheets as views. This is discussed later in this chapter.
- **Label block for views.** Specifies the block used to label views. This is discussed later in this chapter.

Figure 26-4.
Enter a name, description, and file path location for the new sheet set on the **Sheet Set Details** page.

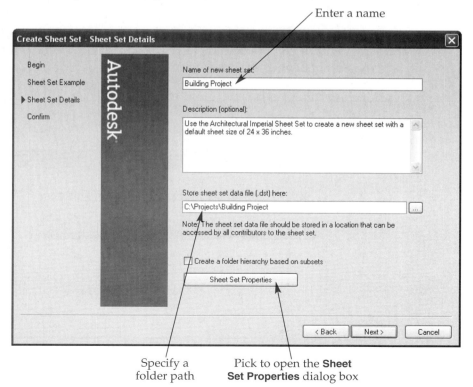

Enter a name

Specify a folder path

Pick to open the **Sheet Set Properties** dialog box

Figure 26-5.
The main properties
of a sheet set are
stored in the **Sheet
Set Properties** dialog
box.

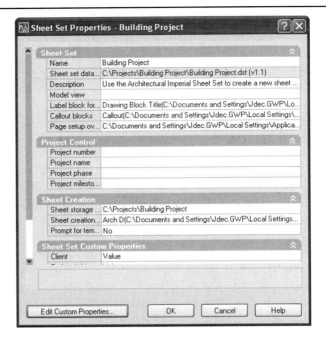

- **Callout blocks.** Specifies blocks available for use as callout blocks. This is discussed later in this chapter.
- **Page setup overrides file.** Specifies the location of an AutoCAD template file (DWT file) containing a page setup to be used to override the existing sheet layout settings.

The properties in the **Project Control** section allow you to store and update information based on the current project. The properties in the **Sheet Creation** section determine the location for the drawing files for new sheets and the template used to create them. When a new sheet is added to a sheet set, AutoCAD creates a new drawing file based on the template and layout specified in the **Sheet creation template** setting. The folder path in the **Sheet storage location** field determines where the new file is saved. It is important to specify the correct location so you know where the files are being saved.

When selecting the **Sheet creation template** value, you must specify both a template file and a layout. To modify this setting, pick in the text box and then pick the ellipsis (...) button. This displays the **Select Layout as Sheet Template** dialog box. See **Figure 26-6.**

Figure 26-6.
An existing layout is
used as a template
for new sheets in a
sheet set.

Pick to select a
different template file

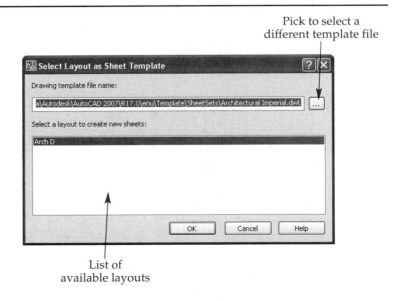

List of
available layouts

All layouts in the selected template are displayed in the list box. Select the layout and then pick **OK**.

If the value in the **Prompt for template** field is set to **No**, the template layout specified in the **Sheet creation template** field is automatically used when a new sheet is created. This is the default setting. If the field value is set to **Yes**, you can select a different layout when creating a new sheet.

Information specific to the project can be set up in the **Sheet Set Custom Properties** section. This topic is discussed later in this chapter.

Once all the values in the **Sheet Set Properties** dialog box are set, pick **OK**. This returns you to the **Sheet Set Details** page. Pick the **Next** button to continue creating the new sheet set. The **Sheet Set Preview** area on the **Confirm** page displays all of the information associated with the sheet set. See **Figure 26-7**. In the example shown, a sheet set named Building Project has been created. This sheet set contains a number of subsets related to the project, such as General and Architectural. After the sheet set is created, sheets can be added to each subset.

After reviewing the information on the **Confirm** page, pick the **Finish** button to create the sheet set. If a setting needs to be changed, use the **Back** button.

PROFESSIONAL TIP
The information in the **Sheet Set Preview** area can be copied to a word processing program to be saved or printed. To do this, highlight all of the text and then use the [Ctrl]+[C] key combination. Open a new document in the word processing program and then use the [Ctrl]+[V] key combination to paste the text into the document.

Figure 26-7.
Use the **Confirm** page to preview settings before creating the sheet set.

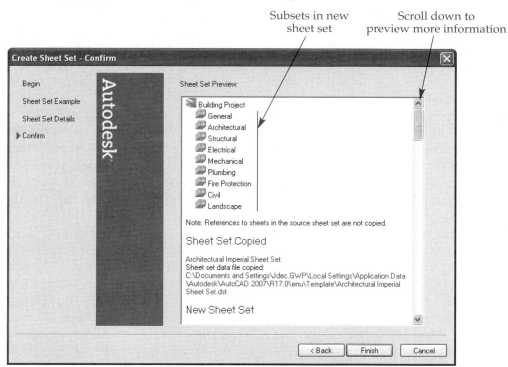

When the **Finish** button is picked, the sheet set data file is saved to the specified location. The sheet set can then be opened in the **Sheet Set Manager**. Since a sheet set is not associated with a particular drawing file, any sheet set can be opened, regardless of the open drawing file.

Exercise 26-1 Complete the Exercise on the Student CD.

Creating a Sheet Set from Existing Drawing Files

You can use existing drawings to create a sheet set. Layouts are imported from the drawing files to create the sheets. Thus, each layout within the drawings becomes a sheet.

When creating a sheet set in this manner, organize all files used in the project in a structured hierarchy of folders. Also, it is recommended to have only one layout in each drawing file so access to different layout tabs is simplified. To ensure all sheets have the same layout settings, a sheet creation template should be created as well. The template is specified in the **Sheet Set Properties** dialog box.

To create a new sheet set from an existing drawing project, open the **Sheet Set Manager**. Then select **New Sheet Set…** from the **Sheet Set Control** drop-down list to open the **Create Sheet Set** wizard. On the **Begin** page, select **Existing drawings** and pick the **Next** button. On the **Sheet Set Details** page, specify a name and description for the sheet set and the location where the data file will be saved. Pick the **Sheet Set Properties** button to specify the sheet set properties.

Picking the **Next** button displays the **Choose Layouts** page. Specify the drawings and layouts to be added to the sheet set. Pick the **Browse…** button to select the folder(s) containing the drawing files with the desired layouts. The selected folder, the drawing files it contains, and all layouts within those drawings are displayed. In **Figure 26-8,** all of the drawing files with layouts in the Commercial folder have been added for selection. Each item has a check box next to it. The layouts that are checked are added to the new sheet set. If a layout should not be part of the new sheet set, uncheck the box next to it. Unchecking a drawing file automatically unchecks all of the layouts within it. If the folder is unchecked, all of the layouts in the drawing files are unchecked. More folders can be added to the **Choose Layouts** page by using the **Browse for Folder** dialog box.

When a sheet set is created using existing layouts, the name for a new sheet can be the same as the layout name, or it can be the drawing file name combined with the layout name. Sheet naming options can be accessed by picking the **Import Options…** button to display the **Import Options** dialog box. See **Figure 26-9.** If the **Prefix sheet titles with file name** check box is checked, the layouts that become sheets are named with the drawing file name and the name of the layout. For example, if a layout named First Floor Electrical is imported from the drawing file Electrical Plan.dwg, the sheet that is created is named Electrical Plan – First Floor Electrical. To have the sheets take on only the layout name, uncheck this check box.

When importing layouts, a sheet set can be organized so that the folders are grouped into subsets of the sheet set. If the **Create subsets based on folder structure** option is checked in the **Import Options** dialog box, all of the folder names added to the sheet set become subsets. The layouts in the folders are added under each subset. The **Ignore top level folder** option determines whether a subset in the sheet set is created for the folder name at the top level. The example in **Figure 26-10A** shows the **Choose Layouts** page with layouts imported from the Residential folder for the Residential Project sheet set. This sheet set has been created with the **Create subsets based on folder structure** and **Ignore top level folder** options checked in the **Import Options** dialog box. The result

Figure 26-8.
Existing layouts can be imported to a new sheet set from the **Choose Layouts** page. Layouts from drawing files in the Commercial folder are imported for addition to the new sheet set. The layouts must have a check next to them to be added to the sheet set.

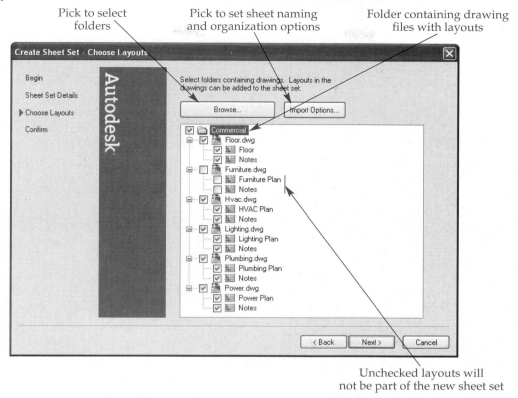

Pick to select folders

Pick to set sheet naming and organization options

Folder containing drawing files with layouts

Unchecked layouts will not be part of the new sheet set

Figure 26-9.
Naming conventions for sheets and folder structuring options are specified in the **Import Options** dialog box.

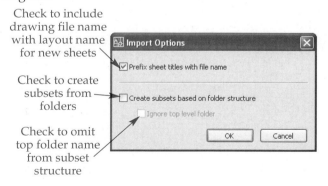

Check to include drawing file name with layout name for new sheets

Check to create subsets from folders

Check to omit top folder name from subset structure

of this configuration is shown in the **Sheet Set Manager** in Figure 26-10B. Creating subsets for sheet sets helps organize the sheets.

Notice how the sheets are named in **Figure 26-10B.** Each sheet has a number preceding its name. By default, a sheet is displayed in the **Sheet Set Manager** with its number, a dash, and then the name of the sheet. In the example shown, the drawing file name is used as a prefix for the sheet name.

When all folders and layouts have been selected for the new sheet set and all settings have been specified, pick the **Next** button on the **Choose Layouts** page. This displays the **Confirm** page. In the **Sheet Set Preview** area, review the sheet set properties. Pick the **Finish** button to create the new sheet set. If a setting needs to be changed, use the **Back** button.

Figure 26-10.
Creating a sheet set named Residential Project with subsets. A—Layouts are imported from the Residential folder. The drawing files are stored in the Architectural and Structural subfolders. The subfolders are designated as subsets for the new sheet set. B—After creating the sheet set and opening it in the **Sheet Set Manager**, the subsets are shown. Notice that the Residential folder is not included as a subset. This was set in the **Import Options** dialog box.

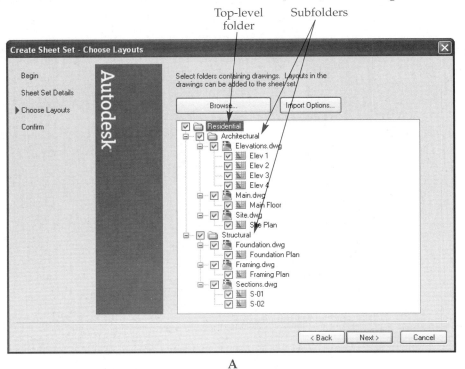

A

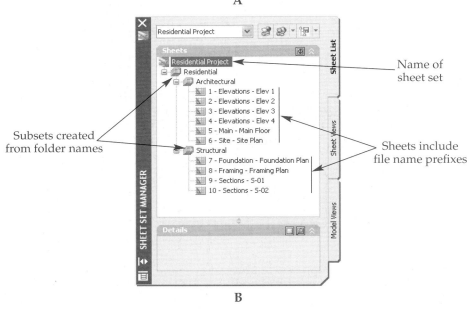

B

Exercise 26-2 Complete the Exercise on the Student CD.

Working with Sheet Sets

Once a sheet set has been created, it can be accessed and edited in the **Sheet Set Manager**. Sheet sets are opened from the **Sheet Set Control** drop-down list. See **Figure 26-11**.

The top area lists the sheet sets that have been opened in the current AutoCAD session. When AutoCAD is closed, this area is cleared. Selecting **Recent** displays a list of the most recently opened sheet sets. Selecting **Open...** displays the **Open Sheet Set** dialog box. You can then navigate to a sheet set data file (DST file) and open it in the **Sheet Set Manager**. A sheet set can also be opened by selecting **File** > **Open Sheet Set...** from the pull-down menu.

Sheets in a sheet set are managed in the **Sheet List** tab of the **Sheet Set Manager**. Sheet views are managed in the **Sheet Views** tab, and drawing files with layouts are managed in the **Model Views** tab. Almost all of the options for working with sheet sets are available from shortcut menus. Right-clicking on a sheet set displays the shortcut menu shown in **Figure 26-12**. The menu options are explained as follows:

- **Close Sheet Set.** Removes the sheet set from the **Sheet Set Manager**.
- **New Sheet.** Creates a new sheet in the sheet set.

Figure 26-11.
The **Sheet Set Control** drop-down list displays recently opened sheet sets. Picking **Open...** allows you to browse for a sheet set that is not in the list.

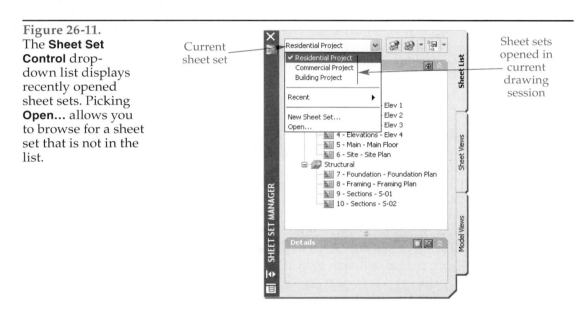

Current sheet set

Sheet sets opened in current drawing session

Figure 26-12.
This shortcut menu is displayed by right-clicking over a sheet set name in the **Sheet List** tab.

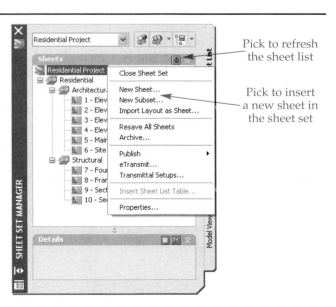

Pick to refresh the sheet list

Pick to insert a new sheet in the sheet set

- **New Subset.** Creates a new subset in the sheet set.
- **Import Layout as Sheet.** Creates a new sheet containing an existing layout.
- **Resave All Sheets.** Updates the drawing files that are part of the current sheet set. All of the drawing files that are part of the sheet set need to be closed first. An open drawing file cannot be updated.
- **Archive.** Saves all drawing files and associated files to one location. Archiving a sheet set is discussed later in this chapter.
- **Publish.** Displays the **Publish** cascading menu. Different options for publishing and plotting a sheet set are available. These options are discussed later in this chapter.
- **eTransmit.** Displays the **Create Transmittal** dialog box for use with the **eTransmit** feature. This option is very similar to the **Archive** option. It is used to package together files and associated files for Internet exchange. The **eTransmit** feature is discussed in Chapter 28.
- **Transmittal Setups.** Displays the **Transmittal Setups** dialog box, which is used to configure **eTransmit** settings.
- **Insert Sheet List Table.** Gathers information about all the sheets in the sheet set and inserts the data into the drawing as a table. This option is only available when a drawing file with a layout in the sheet set is open with the layout tab current. Creating a sheet list table is discussed later in this chapter.
- **Properties.** Opens the **Sheet Set Properties** dialog box.

To manually update changes to the sheet list, pick the **Refresh Sheet Status** button. See Figure 26-12.

Working with Subsets

As previously discussed, *subsets* are subgroups within a sheet set created to help organize the sheets. Creating subsets is similar to creating subfolders under a top-level folder in Windows Explorer. The subsets are created to help manage the contents of the sheet set. For example, if there are ten architectural sheets, ten electrical sheets, and ten plumbing sheets in a sheet set, the three subsets Architectural, Electrical, and Plumbing can be created to store the related sheets.

Creating a New Subset

A new subset can be created by right-clicking over the sheet set name or an existing subset in the **Sheet Set Manager** and selecting **New Subset...** from the shortcut menu. This opens the **Subset Properties** dialog box. See Figure 26-13. The name of the new subset is entered in the **Subset name** text box. If a subset is being created for all of the electrical sheets in a sheet set, for example, then the subset can be named Electrical. When a new sheet is added to the subset using a template, the sheet is saved as a drawing file to the hard drive. A new folder can be created for the subset by checking **Create folders relative to parent subset storage location**. By doing this, the folder structure will mimic the subset structure. The **Store new sheet DWG files in** setting determines the path to which new sheets are saved. The default value is the location specified when the sheet set was initially created.

Each subset can also have its own template and layout for new sheets. This is specified in the **Sheet creation template for subset** setting. For example, if the electrical sheets use their own title block and notes, a template sheet with these settings should be used. Specifying the template and layout for a subset is identical to the procedure used in selecting the sheet set properties.

Figure 26-13.
Settings for a new subset are made in the **Subset Properties** dialog box.

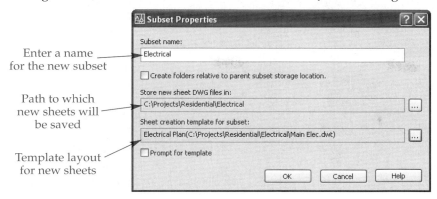

Enter a name for the new subset

Path to which new sheets will be saved

Template layout for new sheets

Modifying a Subset

After a subset has been created, its settings can be modified by right-clicking on the subset and selecting **Properties...** from the shortcut menu. This displays the **Subset Properties** dialog box. The **Rename Subset...** shortcut menu option also opens the **Subset Properties** dialog box.

A subset can be deleted by right-clicking over the subset and selecting **Remove Subset** from the shortcut menu. If the subset contains sheets, this option is grayed out. In this case, the sheets need to be moved to a different subset or deleted before the subset can be removed.

 Exercise 26-3   Complete the Exercise on the Student CD.

Working with Sheets

One of the most useful features of the **Sheet Set Manager** is the ability to open a sheet quickly for reviewing or modifying. A sheet can be opened by double-clicking on the sheet, or by right-clicking over the sheet and selecting **Open** from the shortcut menu. The drawing file that contains the referenced layout tab is then opened in AutoCAD, and the layout is set current.

> **NOTE**
> When files are opened from the **Sheet Set Manager**, they are added to the open files list. If many files are opened, it can affect the performance of AutoCAD. Use the **Window** pull-down menu to view all of the open files. Save and close files that are no longer needed.

Adding a Sheet Using a Template

A new sheet can be added to a sheet set by using the template layout sheet or by importing an existing layout. To add a sheet using the template, right-click on the sheet set name or the subset where the sheet needs to be added, and then select **New Sheet...** from the shortcut menu. This displays the **New Sheet** dialog box. See **Figure 26-14.**

Figure 26-14.
When creating a new sheet from a template, the sheet is defined in the **New Sheet** dialog box.

Enter a
sheet number

Enter a sheet
name (layout name)

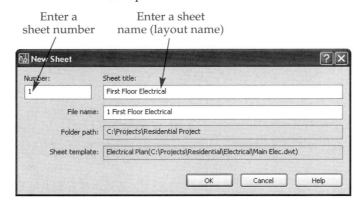

Enter the sheet number in the **Number** text box and the sheet name in the **Sheet title** text box (for example, First Floor Electrical). A new drawing file is created. The sheet title becomes the name of the layout in the drawing file. Enter the name for the file in the **File name** text box. By default, this is the sheet number and title. The **Folder path** field shows where the drawing file will be saved. This path is specified in the **Subset Properties** or **Sheet Set Properties** dialog box.

Adding an Existing Layout as a Sheet

To add an existing layout to a sheet set, right-click on the sheet set name or the subset in which the sheet needs to be added. Then select **Import Layout as Sheet...** from the shortcut menu. This displays the **Import Layouts as Sheets** dialog box. See **Figure 26-15.** Pick the **Browse for Drawings** button to select a drawing file. The layouts from the drawing file are then listed in the list box. The **Status** field indicates whether the layout can be imported into the sheet set. If a layout is already part of a sheet set, it cannot be imported. By default, all of the layouts in the drawing are checked in the list. Uncheck the box to exclude a layout from being imported as a sheet. If the

Figure 26-15.
Existing layouts can be added as sheets to a sheet set from the **Import Layouts as Sheets** dialog box. The layouts from the selected drawing file are listed.

Uncheck to
exclude a layout
from being imported

Pick to select
drawing file

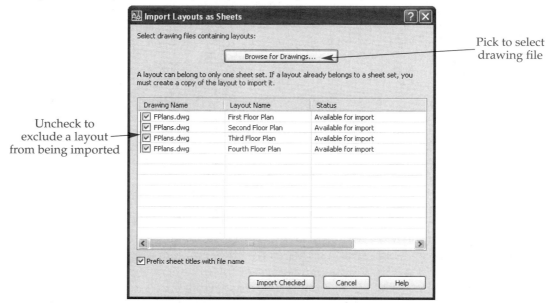

AutoCAD and Its Applications—Basics

Prefix sheet titles with file name check box is checked, the name of the file is included in the sheet title. To import the sheets, pick the **Import Checked** button.

Exercise 26-4   Complete the Exercise on the Student CD.

Modifying Sheet Properties

The properties of a sheet, such as the name, number, and description, can be modified by right-clicking over the sheet name in the **Sheet Set Manager** to display the sheet shortcut menu. The sheet name and number can be changed by selecting **Rename & Renumber...** from this menu. This displays the **Rename & Renumber Sheet** dialog box. This dialog box is similar to the **New Sheet** dialog box. If the sheet is one of several in a subset, picking the **Next** button moves to the next sheet in the subset. If the last sheet in the subset is current, the **Next** button is grayed out.

The **Sheet Properties** dialog box also allows you to change the sheet name and number, along with the description and the publish option. Publishing a sheet set is discussed in the next section. To open the **Sheet Properties** dialog box, right-click on the sheet name and select **Properties...** from the shortcut menu. The **Sheet Properties** dialog box is shown in **Figure 26-16.** A description of the sheet can be entered in the **Description** text box. The **Include for publish** option determines whether the sheet is included when the sheet set is published or plotted. The default value is **Yes.**

The **Expected layout** and **Found layout** text boxes display the file path where the sheet was originally saved and the file path where the sheet was found. If the paths are different, you can update the **Expected layout** field by picking the ellipsis (**...**) button.

If custom property fields have been set up for the sheet, they are displayed. Custom property fields are discussed later in this chapter.

A sheet can be deleted from a sheet set by selecting **Remove Sheet** from the sheet shortcut menu. This does not delete the drawing file from the hard drive; it only removes the sheet from the sheet set.

Figure 26-16.
The properties of a sheet can be modified in the **Sheet Properties** dialog box.

Determines whether the sheet is published or included in plot

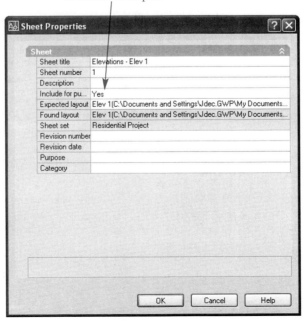

NOTE If the hard drive location of a drawing file is modified, and the drawing file has layouts that are associated with a sheet set, the association is broken. The layouts need to be reimported into the sheet set, or the specified path to the drawing file must be updated in the **Sheet Properties** dialog box.

Publishing a Sheet Set

In AutoCAD, *publishing* refers to the creation of electronic files for distribution purposes or the plotting of hard copy prints. As is the case with other collections of drawing files, sheet sets can be published by creating drawing web format (DWF) files. DWF files are compressed, vector-based files that can be viewed with the Autodesk DWF Viewer, which is installed with AutoCAD. A sheet set can also be published by sending it to a plotter. AutoCAD's plotting and publishing functions were introduced in Chapter 11. For more information about outputting DWF files, refer to *AutoCAD and Its Applications—Advanced*.

An entire sheet set can be published to a DWF file or plotted using the options in the **Publish** shortcut menu in the **Sheet Set Manager**. The **Publish** shortcut menu can be accessed by picking the **Publish** button on the **Sheet Set Manager** toolbar or by selecting **Publish** from the sheet shortcut menu. See **Figure 26-17**.

NOTE A sheet set, a subset, or individual sheets can be selected for publishing at a time. Simply select the appropriate items using the [Shift] and [Ctrl] keys in the **Sheet Set Manager**.

Figure 26-17.
The **Publish** shortcut menu options are used to prepare a sheet set for publishing or plotting.

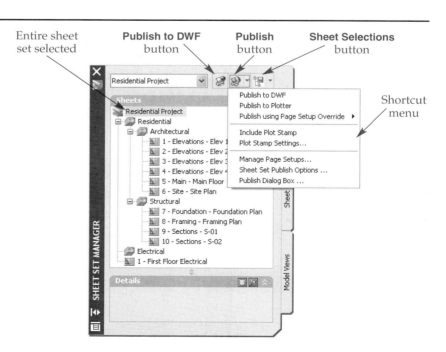

The options in the **Publish** shortcut menu are explained as follows:

- **Publish to DWF.** Creates a DWF file from the sheet set or the selected sheets. In the **Select DWF File** dialog box, specify a name and location for the file. The file is then created with each sheet having its own page in a multisheet file. When the file is completed, a balloon notification is displayed in the AutoCAD status bar tray.
- **Publish to Plotter.** Plots the sheet set or selected sheets to the default plotter or printer. This is done automatically using the plot settings from each layout. When the plot is completed, a balloon notification is displayed in the AutoCAD status bar tray.
- **Publish using Page Setup Override.** Displays the page setups that are available for use as overrides. Selecting a page setup from the list forces the sheet to use the selected page setup settings instead of the plot settings that are saved with the layout. If a page setup override has not been specified for the sheet set or subset, this option is grayed out.
- **Include Plot Stamp.** If checked, places the plot stamp information for the layout on the sheet when it is plotted.
- **Plot Stamp Settings.** Opens the **Plot Stamp** dialog box to specify the plot stamp settings.
- **Manage Page Setups.** Opens the **Page Setup Manager**. A new page setup can be created or an existing one can be modified.
- **Sheet Set Publish Options.** Displays the **Sheet Set Publish Options** dialog box. This displays the available settings for creating a DWF file.
- **Publish Dialog Box.** Opens the **Publish** dialog box. All of the sheets that are in the current sheet set or the sheet selection are listed.

Creating Sheet Selection Sets

During the course of a project, the same set of sheets may need to be published many times. A selection of sheets can be saved so that it can be accessed again quickly for publishing. To save a sheet selection set, select the sheets to be included in the set. Remember, if you want to select all of the sheets in a subset, simply select the subset. Then pick the **Sheet Selections** button on the **Sheet Set Manager** toolbar and select **Create...** from the shortcut menu. In the **New Sheet Selection** dialog box, enter a name for the selection set and pick **OK**. The new selection set is then listed when the **Sheet Selections** button is picked. In **Figure 26-18**, three different sheet selection sets are shown. When a selection set is selected from the shortcut menu, the sheets are automatically highlighted in the **Sheet Set Manager**.

Figure 26-18.
Sheet selection sets can be created from selected sheets or subsets in a sheet set. They are accessed from the **Sheet Selections** shortcut menu.

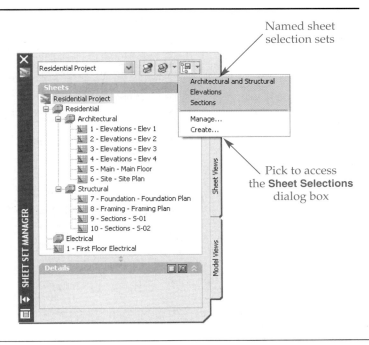

To rename or delete a sheet selection set, pick **Manage...** from the **Sheet Selections** shortcut menu. In the **Sheet Selections** dialog box, select the sheet selection set and then pick the **Rename** or **Delete** button.

Sheet Views

As previously discussed, sheet views are views within sheets that are typically referenced at another location in the sheet set. Sheet views are typically sections, elevations, and details. The **Sheet Views** tab of the **Sheet Set Manager** is used to manage sheet views. Using this tab, views can be grouped by category and opened for viewing and editing.

Special tools in the **Sheet Set Manager** can be used to identify views with numbers, labels, and callout blocks. This section discusses the methods used to create and manage views in the **Sheet Set Manager**.

Adding a View Category

View categories are used to organize views in the **Sheet Views** tab. View categories are similar to subsets created in the **Sheet List** tab. To create a new view category, make the **Sheet Views** tab current. See **Figure 26-19**. Pick the **New View Category** button or right-click on the sheet set name and select **New View Category...** from the shortcut menu. This opens the **View Category** dialog box. See **Figure 26-20**. In the **Category name** text box, enter a name for the category. For example, if there are going to be four elevation views added to the new category, it could be named Elevations.

The **View Category** dialog box lists all of the available callout blocks for the current view category. Check the box next to the callout block to have it available for all of the views that are added to this category. If a block is not in the list, use the **Add Blocks...** button to select it from a drawing file. Once the necessary callout blocks are selected, pick the **OK** button to create the new category. Callout blocks are discussed later in this chapter.

Figure 26-19.
View categories and views are created in the **Sheet Views** tab of the **Sheet Set Manager**.

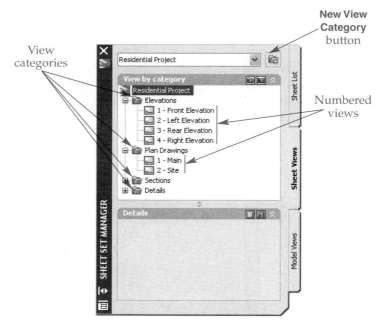

Figure 26-20.
When creating a new view category, the **View Category** dialog box is used to name the category and select callout blocks for use with views.

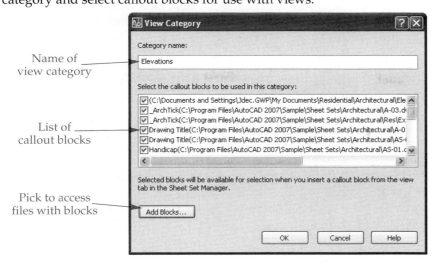

Name of view category

List of callout blocks

Pick to access files with blocks

Modifying a Category

The properties for a category can be modified by right-clicking over the category name in the **Sheet Set Manager** and selecting **Rename...** or **Properties...** from the shortcut menu. Selecting either one of these options opens the **View Category** dialog box. The category name can be changed and different callout blocks can be added to the category.

A category can be deleted by right-clicking over the category name and selecting **Remove Category** from the shortcut menu. If there are views under the category, this option is grayed out. In this case, the views need to be removed before the category can be deleted.

Creating Sheet Views in an Existing Sheet

New views can be added to sheets and organized within sheet sets from the **Sheet Set Manager**. Use the following procedure to add a view to an existing sheet set:

1. Open the desired sheet set and add a category for the view if it is not already created.
2. To add a view to a sheet, the sheet has to be a part of the sheet set. If the sheet has not been added to the sheet set, add it now.
3. Open the drawing file and set the layout tab current where the new view will be created.
4. Use display commands to orient the view as needed and then enter the **VIEW** command.
5. In the **View** dialog box, pick the **New...** button to open the **New View** dialog box.
6. Select the category that you want the view to be a part of from the **View category** drop-down list. See **Figure 26-21.**
7. Specify the rest of the view settings and pick **OK** to save the view.

The newly saved view now appears in the **Sheet Set Manager** under the view category that was selected in the **New View** dialog box.

Once a view has been added to a sheet set, it can be displayed from the **Sheet Set Manager** by double-clicking on the view name or by right-clicking over the name and selecting **Display** from the shortcut menu. If the drawing file is already open, the view is set current. If the file is not open, the drawing file is opened so that the view can be set current.

Figure 26-21.
The **View category** drop-down list displays the available view categories for the view being defined.

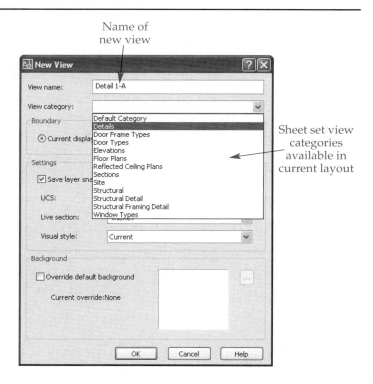

Name of new view

Sheet set view categories available in current layout

The view list can be displayed by category or by sheet. Refer to **Figure 26-19.** The first button, **View by category**, displays all of the categories. The views are accessed by expanding the category and then the sheet. Picking the second button, **View by sheet**, displays the sheet name. Expand the sheet name to display the saved views within the sheet.

Creating Sheet Views from Resource Drawings

Sheet views can be created from drawing files listed in the **Model Views** tab. The sheet view can be the entire model space drawing or a model space view. When a model space view or drawing is inserted into a sheet, the resource drawing becomes an external reference of the sheet drawing.

The **Model Views** tab is shown in **Figure 26-22.** Folders containing reference drawings are listed. To add a new folder, double-click on the Add New Location entry or pick the **Add New Location** button and select a folder. You cannot select specific drawing files—you must select the folder containing the drawing.

Only drawings listed in the **Model Views** tab can be inserted into a sheet to create a new sheet view. If the drawing you wish to use is not listed, you must add the folder containing the drawing to the resource drawing list.

The folder and all of the drawing files that are in it are now listed in the **Locations** list area. The model space views saved in the drawing are listed under the drawing file.

The options available for a drawing file are located in the drawing file shortcut menu. To display the menu, right-click on a drawing file. The options are explained as follows:

- **Open.** Opens the drawing file and sets the model space tab current. Double-clicking on the drawing file also opens the file.
- **Place on Sheet.** Inserts the file into the current sheet as a sheet view. You are prompted to specify an insertion point. When the point is selected, a viewport is automatically created in the sheet.
- **See Model Space Views.** Expands the list of model space views in the drawing. This is the same as picking the + sign next to the drawing file.
- **eTransmit.** Opens the **Create Transmittal** dialog box, so the selected file and its associated files can be packaged together.

Figure 26-22.
Sheet views can be created by inserting model space views and drawings from the **Model Views** tab.

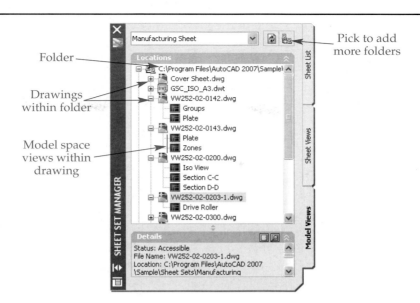

Folder

Drawings within folder

Model space views within drawing

Pick to add more folders

If a model space view has been saved in the drawing, it is listed under the drawing file name. You can insert the model space view as a sheet view in a sheet. To do so, right-click on the model space view name and select the **Place on Sheet** option. Pick an insertion point in the sheet.

When you insert a model space view or drawing into a sheet, AutoCAD creates a viewport and an external reference to the selected drawing. AutoCAD will assign a scale for the viewport, or you can right-click before selecting the insertion point and select the scale for sheet view. The scale for the sheet view is stored as the **ViewportScale** property of the **SheetView** field, and is often displayed in the view label block.

When sheet views are created from resource drawings, an entry is added to the **Sheet Views**. If you insert a model space view, the view name is added to the **Sheet Views** tab. If you insert a drawing, the drawing name is added to the **Sheet Views** tab. You can modify the sheet view name and add a sheet view number in the **Sheet Views** tab. This is discussed in the next section.

To delete a location from a sheet set, right-click on the location and select **Remove Location** from the shortcut menu.

Naming and Numbering Sheet Views

In most projects, you will have several elevations, sections, or details. These items are typically numbered within the drawing set for easier reference. For example, the drawing set may include a foundation plan and a sheet with foundation details. On the foundation detail sheet, each detail is identified by a unique number. The foundation plan includes references to these numbers.

Once a sheet view has been assigned a number, view label blocks and callout blocks can use the number as part of the identification. These blocks are discussed in the next section.

To change the name or number of a sheet view, right-click on the sheet view name in the **Sheet Set Manager** and select **Rename & Renumber...** from the shortcut menu. The **Rename & Renumber View** dialog box is displayed, **Figure 26-23.** Enter a number for the view in the

Figure 26-23.
A view can be numbered in the **Rename & Renumber View** dialog box.

View number

Name of view

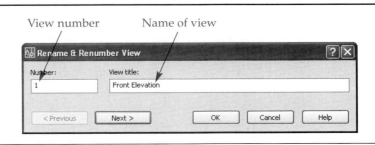

Number text box. The name of the view can be modified in the **View title** text box. Picking the **Next** button moves to the next view in the view category. Pick **OK** when you are done. The view number is displayed in front of the view name in the **Sheet Set Manager**.

Exercise 26-5   Complete the Exercise on the Student CD.

Sheet View Callout and Label Blocks

Sheet views are used for elevations, sections, and details. Often, these drawing components are located on one sheet and referenced on a different sheet. When using sheet views, you can insert blocks to identify the sheet view name, number, and scale on both the sheet with the sheet view and also the sheet that refers to the sheet views.

Typically, two types of blocks are used: callout blocks and view label blocks.

Callout blocks

A callout block is used to refer to the sheet view. For example, when a section line is drawn through a building, a callout block is placed at the end of the section line. The callout block indicates the sheet or location where the section view is found and information about the viewing direction. A callout block would also be used on a foundation plan to identify an area addressed by a detail drawing. The callout block is typically located on a different sheet from the sheet view it references.

AutoCAD provides several styles of callout blocks for use in different types of sheet views. See **Figure 26-24.** The upper value in a callout block is typically the sheet view number, and the lower value is the drawing on which the sheet view appears. For

Figure 26-24.
Callout blocks provide reference information for views and sheets. A—An elevation symbol identifying the viewing direction, view number, and sheet number. B—A sampling of predefined callout blocks available in AutoCAD. Elevation and section blocks are selected based on the type of view and the viewing direction for the reference view.

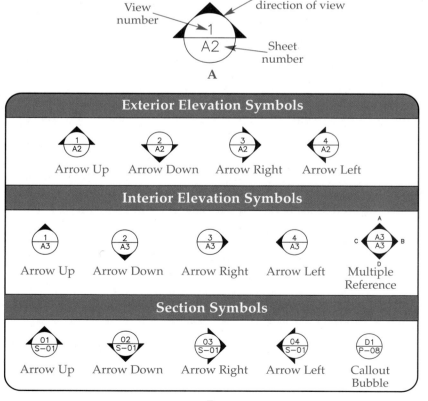

Figure 26-25.
The **ViewNumber** property displays the sheet view number. This field property is used in callout blocks.

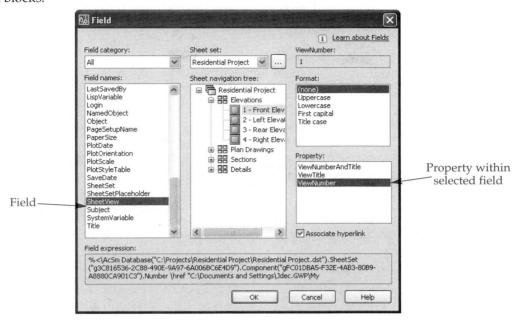

the default callout blocks, the upper value is an attribute containing the **ViewNumber** property of the **SheetView** field. See **Figure 26-25.** This lists the sheet view number specified for the sheet view. The lower value is the **SheetNumber** property of the **SheetSet** value. This lists the sheet number of the sheet containing the sheet view.

By using fields in the sheet view blocks, the values displayed are automatically updated if there are changes in the sheet set. For instance, if a new sheet is added in the middle of a sheet set, all subsequent sheets may need to be renumbered. The sheet view block values update automatically as the sheet numbers change.

View label blocks

View label blocks are placed below the sheet view. The view label typically includes the name and number of the section, elevation, or detail and the scale. See **Figure 26-26.** Like callout blocks, view label blocks include attributes containing fields that automatically update to reflect changes to the sheet set or sheet views. View label blocks typically include three properties of the **SheetView** fields: **ViewNumber**, **ViewTitle**, and **Viewport Scale.**

Figure 26-26.
View labels normally appear below the view on a sheet. They indicate information such as the view name, number, and scale.

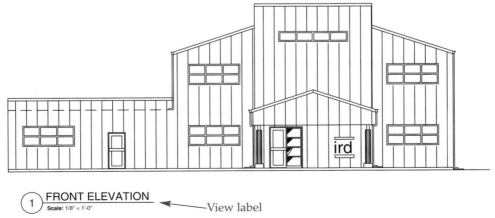

Block hyperlinks

The sample callout and view label blocks provided with AutoCAD also include hyperlink fields. You can pick the hyperlink on a callout block to instantly access the detail, section, or elevation being referenced. This greatly simplifies the process of accessing sheet views.

Associating callout and view label blocks

To insert a callout or view label block from the **Sheet Set Manager**, the block first needs to be available to the sheet set in which the view is defined. These blocks are specified in the **Sheet Set Properties** dialog box. To access this dialog box, right-click on the sheet set name in the **Sheet Set Manager** and select **Properties...** from the shortcut menu. The available blocks are specified in the **Callout blocks** text box and **Label block for views** text box. The name of each block is listed, followed by the path to the drawing file where the block is saved.

PROFESSIONAL TIP A sheet set or view category can have multiple callout blocks available, but only one view label block.

To add a callout block to a sheet set, pick in the **Callout blocks** text box and then pick the ellipsis (...) button. This opens the **List of Blocks** dialog box. See **Figure 26-27**. Pick the **Add...** button to display the **Select Block** dialog box. In this dialog box, pick the ellipsis (...) button to select the drawing file that contains the block. The block can then be selected from the block list area of the **Select Block** dialog box. If the drawing file only consists of the objects that make up the drawing file, use the **Select the drawing file as a block** option.

A block can be deleted from the block list by selecting it in the **List of Blocks** dialog box and picking the **Delete** button.

Specifying a view title block is similar to specifying a callout block. However, there is only one view title block specified for the sheet set, so the **List of Blocks** dialog box is not displayed.

Each view category can have its own callout blocks assigned to it. This way, only the blocks that are needed for the views in a category are available. For example, a category named Section may only need a section callout bubble, while a category named Elevation may need ten different types of elevation symbols. To modify the callout blocks available for a view category, right-click on the category name and select **Properties...** from the shortcut menu. This opens the **View Category** dialog box.

Figure 26-27.
All callout blocks available to a sheet set are listed in the **List of Blocks** dialog box.

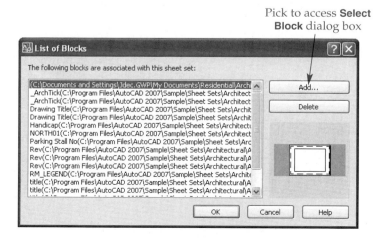

Pick to access **Select Block** dialog box

By default, the callout blocks and view title block assigned to the sheet set are displayed in the block list area. To make a block available to the view category, check the box next to the block. Refer to **Figure 26-20.** This makes the block available to all of the views within the view category.

New blocks can be added to the view category by picking the **Add Blocks...** button and accessing the **Select Block** dialog box.

Inserting callout and view label blocks

To insert a callout block into a drawing, open the sheet where the reference is to be placed. In the **Sheet Views** tab of the **Sheet Set Manager,** right-click on the sheet view name and select the block from the **Place Callout Block** cascading menu. See **Figure 26-28A.** You are then prompted to specify an insertion point for the block. The block can be scaled or rotated by using the options on the command line. When the block is inserted, it is given the same sheet view number and sheet number as the reference view and sheet. See **Figure 26-28B.** If the reference information changes, the block is automatically renumbered by AutoCAD.

Figure 26-28.
Placing callout blocks in a view. A—Right-click on the reference view name and select **Place Callout Block** to display a shortcut menu with all of the callout blocks available. B—Callout blocks are placed in the 1-Main Floor Plan view in the A-01 sheet to reference the section view named 1-Section in the A-05 sheet.

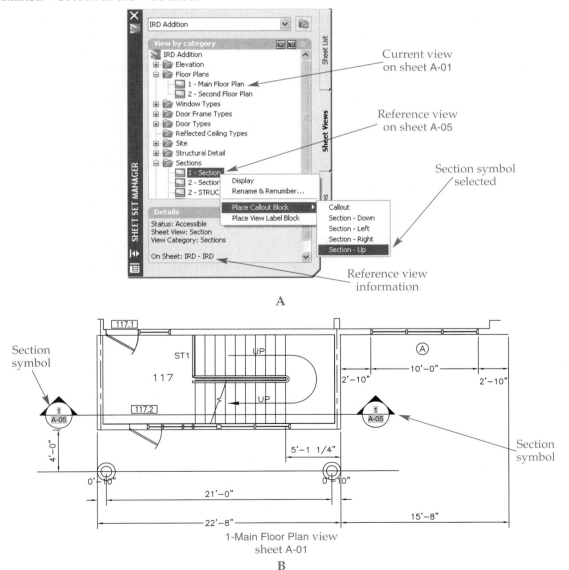

The process of inserting a view label block is similar to that for inserting a callout block. In the **Sheet Set Manager**, right-click on the sheet view name and select **Place View Label Block** from the shortcut menu. You are then prompted to specify an insertion point. The block can be scaled or rotated by using the options on the command line. When the block is inserted, the label appears with the view name and number. If the view name or number is later changed in the sheet set, the information is automatically updated by AutoCAD.

Exercise
26-6   Complete the Exercise on the Student CD.

Sheet Set Fields

Information about a sheet is usually placed in the title block area of the drawing. The information may include items such as the client's name and address, the project number, the person who checked the sheet, and the date the sheet was plotted. You can create fields on sheets to display this information. As previously discussed, fields are special text objects that display updateable values. A field value can change as a result of a change to the value of the field setting. Fields are valuable features for sheet sets, because text items on sheets can be set up to display up-to-date information if changes occur as the project develops.

There are specific field types available in AutoCAD for use with sheet sets. To create a field for a text value on a sheet, select **Insert > Field...** from the pull-down menu. This displays the **Field** dialog box, Figure 26-29. Selecting **SheetSet** from the **Field category:** drop-down list displays a list of predefined field types in the **Field names:** list box. These fields can be inserted to display values that have been defined

Figure 26-29.
Many fields related to sheet sets are available.

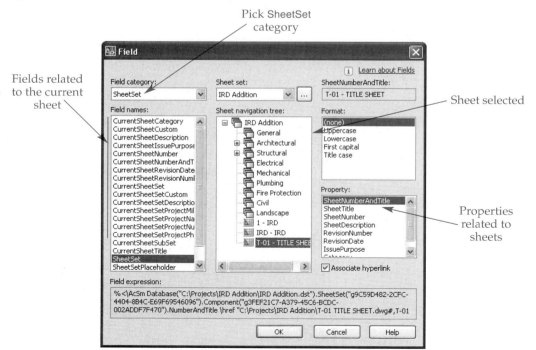

in the sheet, sheet view, or sheet set, such as the sheet title, number, or description. Some of the fields also have several properties. Selecting one of the field types or properties displays the related value in the **Field** dialog box.

For example, selecting the **CurrentSheetNumber** field allows you to insert a field that displays the sheet number of the current sheet. If the sheet is renumbered at a later date, the field changes to display the most current information.

Selecting the **SheetSet** field provides options for inserting many values. When you select the **SheetSet** field, the **Sheet navigation tree** is displayed. If you select the sheet set at the top of the tree, a set of properties related to the entire set is displayed in the **Property** list box. These properties include settings that can be applied to all sheets in the set, such as project information and client information. These settings will not change from sheet to sheet, but will be the same on all sheets. When these field properties are included in the sheet set title block, all sheets display the same values.

If you select a sheet in the **Sheet navigation tree**, properties related to sheets are displayed. These properties include **SheetTitle**, **SheetNumber**, **Drawn By**, and **Checked By** settings. When these field properties are included in the sheet set template title block, each sheet can have a unique value displayed. If a new sheet is added to a sheet set, the fields automatically update.

Selecting the **SheetSetPlaceholder** field allows you to insert a field that acts as a placeholder. A *placeholder* is a temporary value for a field. Selecting a placeholder in the **Placeholder type:** list box assigns a temporary value to the associated field, such as SheetNumber. Placeholders can be used to insert temporary field values in user-defined callout blocks and view labels. When defined with attributes in a callout block, placeholders are updated to display the correct values automatically when the block is inserted onto a sheet from the **Sheet Set Manager**.

Like the **SheetSet** field, the **SheetView** field has many options. When you select the **SheetView** field, the **Sheet navigation tree** displays the view list for the sheet set. If you pick the sheet set name in the **Sheet navigation tree**, the sheet set properties are displayed. These properties are identical to those displayed with the **SheetSet** field. If you pick a sheet view name in the **Sheet navigation tree**, sheet view properties are displayed. These properties are specific to a sheet view, and include **ViewTitle**, **ViewNumber**, and **ViewScale**. As discussed earlier in this chapter, these field properties are used in callout and view label blocks.

Selecting the **CurrentSheetCustom** or **CurrentSheetSetCustom** field allows you to insert a field that is linked to a custom property defined for a sheet or sheet set. Custom property fields for sheet sets are discussed in the next section.

Custom Properties

Information about the sheet set or a specific sheet can be stored electronically with fields and custom properties. This information can then be viewed from the **Sheet Set Manager**. The data can also be inserted into the drawing using the **Field** command, which creates a link between the text data and the custom field data. By doing this, the data can be modified in the **Sheet Set Manager** and the linked data is updated in the drawing files.

Adding a custom property field

Custom properties are managed in the **Sheet Set Properties** dialog box. To add a custom property field to a sheet set, right-click on the sheet set name in the **Sheet Set Manager** and select **Properties...** from the shortcut menu. In the **Sheet Set Properties** dialog box, pick the **Edit Custom Properties...** button to open the **Custom Properties** dialog box. This dialog box is shown in **Figure 26-30**.

Figure 26-30.
Information can be attached to a sheet set in the **Custom Properties** dialog box.

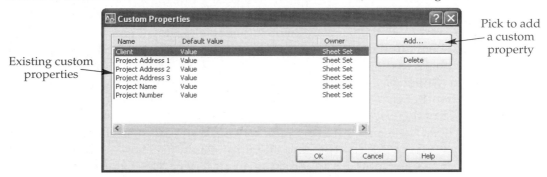

Existing custom properties

Pick to add a custom property

To add a custom property field to the sheet set, pick the **Add...** button. This displays the **Add Custom Property** dialog box. Enter a name for the custom property in the **Name** field. See **Figure 26-31.** Some examples of a custom property may be Job Number, Client Name, Checked By, and Date. If the data for the custom property is usually the same value, this can be entered in the **Default value** field. For example, if the custom property is Checked by, and most of the sheets in this project are checked by ST, then ST could be entered as the default value. The **Owner** area has two options: **Sheet Set** and **Sheet**. If the custom property pertains to the entire project, then **Sheet Set** should be selected. If the custom property pertains to each individual sheet, select **Sheet**. When **Sheet** is selected, the custom property is available in the **Sheet Properties** dialog box. This way, the data is attached to each individual sheet. Pick the **OK** button to add the custom property to the sheet set. The custom property is then listed in the **Sheet Set Properties** dialog box.

Entering custom property data

To modify or enter information into a custom property field for a sheet set, open the **Sheet Set Properties** dialog box. Modify the value.

If custom properties have been added for a sheet, the individual sheets display the custom property fields. To modify or enter information into a sheet custom property field, right-click on the sheet and select **Properties...** from the shortcut menu. The custom properties are listed under the **Sheet Custom Properties** heading of the **Sheet Properties** dialog box. See **Figure 26-32.**

Deleting a custom property

If a custom property field is no longer needed, it can be deleted from the sheet set. To do this, right-click on the sheet set and select **Properties...** to open the **Sheet Set Properties** dialog box. Pick the **Edit Custom Properties...** button. In the **Custom Properties** dialog box, select the custom property and then pick the **Delete** button.

Figure 26-31.
Enter the information for the custom property in the **Add Custom Property** dialog box.

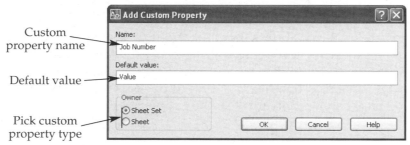

Custom property name

Default value

Pick custom property type

Figure 26-32.
Sheet custom
properties are
available in the
Sheet Properties
dialog box after they
have been added to
the sheet set.

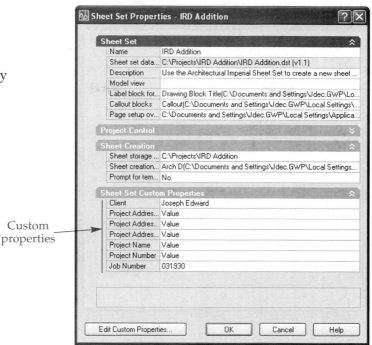

Custom
properties

 NOTE

If a sheet set is created from an example sheet set, any custom properties from the example sheet set are added to the new sheet set.

Exercise 26-7

Complete the Exercise on the Student CD.

Creating a Sheet List Table

One of the first pages of a sheet set typically includes a sheet list. A *sheet list* is like the table of contents for the sheet set. It lists all of the pages in the sheet set and what type of information can be found on the sheet. The **Sheet List Table** command inserts a table object using information from the sheet properties. The information in the table is directly linked to the sheet properties, so if the sheet information is updated in the **Sheet Set Manager**, the sheet list table will also be automatically updated.

Inserting a Sheet List Table

A sheet list table can only be inserted into a drawing from the **Sheet Set Manager**. To insert a sheet list table, open the **Sheet Set Manager** and open the sheet where a table needs to be inserted. Right-click on the sheet set name and select **Insert Sheet List Table...** from the shortcut menu. This opens the **Insert Sheet List Table** dialog box shown in **Figure 26-33**.

Figure 26-33.
Properties for the sheet list table are set up in the **Insert Sheet List Table** dialog box.

Pick to select new table style

Table style to be used

Table title

Preview area

Column headings

Pick to show subheader

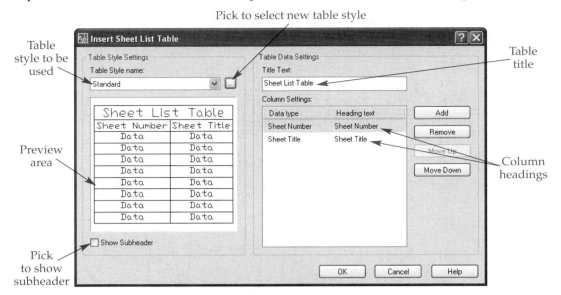

A preset table style for the sheet list can be selected from the **Table Style name** drop-down list. A preview of the table is displayed in the preview area. The **Show Subheader** check box determines if the table will include a subheader row.

The information displayed in the table is set in the **Table Data Settings** area. The title for the sheet list is entered into the **Title Text** text box. The information the table contains is specified in the **Column Settings** area. Pick the **OK** button to insert the table. You are then prompted to specify the insertion point for the table. **Figure 26-34** shows a sheet list table that uses the sheet number and sheet description fields.

> **NOTE**
>
> A sheet list table can only be inserted into a layout tab of a drawing file that is a part of the sheet set. The **Insert Sheet List Table...** options are grayed out if the drawing file is not part of the sheet set or if model space is current.

Figure 26-34.
A sheet list table displays information about each sheet in the sheet set.

SHEET INDEX	
Sheet Number	Sheet Description
T−01	SHEET INDEX, VICINITY MAP, BUILDING CODE ANALYSIS
Architectural	
AS−01	ARCHITECTURAL SITE PLAN, NOTES
A−01	MAIN FLOOR PLAN, SECOND FLOOR PLAN, WALL TYPE NOTES
A−02	EXTERIOR ELEVATIONS
A−03	DOOR & FRAME SCHEDULE, ROOM FINISH SCHEDULE, DOOR, DOOR FRAME & WINDOW TYPES
A−04	MAIN & SECOND FLOOR REFLECTED CEILING PLANS
A−05	STAIR SECTIONS AND DETAILS
Structural	
S−01	FOUNDATION PLAN, PILE SCHEDULE, PILE TYPICAL DETAIL
S−02	STRUCTURAL SECTIONS AND DETAILS
S−03	FLOOR FRAMING PLAN AND SECTIONS
S−04	STRUCTURAL SECTIONS

Modifying the Column Heading Data

A sheet list table can include various types of information from the drawing file and the sheet set. By default, the Sheet Number and Sheet Title fields are included. The sheet list table information is specified in the **Column Settings** area of the **Insert Sheet List Table** dialog box.

A new column can be added to the sheet list by picking the **Add** button. The new column is then placed under the last column in the list. To specify the data type, pick on the name in the **Data type** column to activate the drop-down list. Pick the drop-down list button to display the information that can be used in the sheet list table. Select the type of data you want to include. Then type the heading for the sheet list column in the **Heading text** column. The data types that are available in the drop-down list come from sheet set properties and drawing properties. To have a different data type added to the list, you need to add a custom property to the sheet set.

To delete a data column from the list, select the data column and pick the **Remove** button. To reposition the order of the columns, use the **Move Up** and **Move Down** buttons. The column at the top of the list is inserted as the first column in the sheet list table.

Editing a Sheet List Table

The information in the sheet list table is directly linked to the data source field. For example, if the sheet numbers are modified in the **Sheet Set Manager**, the sheet list table can be updated to reflect those changes. To do this, select the sheet list table in the drawing file, then right-click and select **Update Sheet List Table** from the shortcut menu.

The properties for the table can be modified by selecting the table, right-clicking, and selecting **Edit Sheet List Table Settings...** from the shortcut menu. This opens the **Edit Sheet List Table Settings** dialog box. After making the changes, pick the **OK** button to update the sheet list table.

> **NOTE**
>
>
>
> A sheet list table can be modified the same as any other table. For example, text can be modified, and columns and rows can be added. When the **Update Sheet List Table** command is used on the modified table, a warning dialog box is displayed stating that any manual modifications will be discarded.

Sheet List Table Hyperlinks

If the **Sheet Number** or **Sheet Title** columns are included in the sheet list table, hyperlinks are automatically assigned to the data. *Hyperlinks* are links in a text document connected to related information in other documents or to the Internet. To use a hyperlink, move the crosshairs over a sheet number or sheet title. Hold the pointing device still for a moment and the hyperlink icon and tool tip appear. The tool tip displays the message CTRL + click to follow link. Hold the [Ctrl] key on the keyboard and pick the hyperlink. The selected sheet is opened. This is another way to open a sheet quickly.

Exercise 26-8   Complete the Exercise on the Student CD.

At different periods throughout a project, you may want to gather up all of the electronic drawing files that pertain to a project and store them. This is called *archiving* the drawing set. For example, when a set of drawings in a project is presented to the client for the first time, the client probably wants to make some changes. At this point it may be wise to archive the files for future reference, before the modifications are made.

All files in a sheet set can be archived by using the **ARCHIVE** command. This copies all of the drawing files and their related files to a single location. *Related files* include external references, font files, plot style table files, and template files.

Setting up an Archive

To archive a sheet set, right-click on the sheet set name and select **Archive...** from the shortcut menu, or type ARCHIVE. The **Archive a Sheet Set** dialog box opens. See **Figure 26-35.**

The **Sheets** tab displays all of the subsets and sheets in the sheet set. Check the sheets to be archived. The drawing files and their related files are listed in the **Files Tree** tab. Pick the + sign next to a file to display its related files. A file that is not part of the sheet set can be included in the archive by picking the **Add a File** button. See **Figure 26-36.** This opens the **Add File to Archive** dialog box. Any type of a file can be added to the archive. The archive is not limited to only AutoCAD files. Notes can be included in the archive by typing them in the **Enter notes to include with this archive** text box. The **View Report** button lists all of the files included in the archive. This information can be saved to a text file by picking the **Save As...** button.

The location where the archive is saved, the type of archive that is created, and additional settings are specified in the **Modify Archive Setup** dialog box. See **Figure 26-37.** To open this dialog box, pick the **Modify Archive Setup...** button. The options in the **Archive type and location** area are explained below:

- **Archive package type.** The files can be archived in one of three formats. The options available from the drop-down list are explained as follows:
  - **Folder (set of files).** This option copies all of the archived files into a single folder.

Figure 26-35.
The files to be archived and the archive settings are specified from the **Archive a Sheet Set** dialog box.

File display tabs

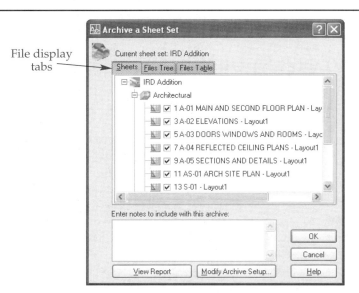

Figure 26-36.
Documents that
relate to a project
can be archived
along with the
AutoCAD files.

List of
files to be
archived

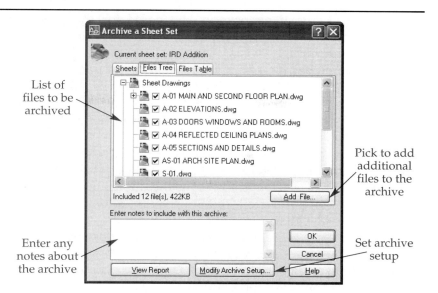

Pick to add
additional
files to the
archive

Enter any
notes about
the archive

Set archive
setup

Figure 26-37.
The archive
file settings are
specified in the
**Modify Archive
Setup** dialog box.

File type

File format

File location

File name

Organization
options

Miscellaneous
options

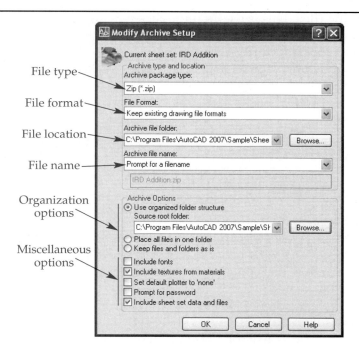

- **Self-extracting executable (*.exe).** This option compresses all of the files
  into a self-extracting zip (EXE) file. The files can be extracted at a later time
  by double-clicking on the file. A *zip file* is a file that has been compressed
  to take up less file space. The utility is used to unzip, or return the file to its
  original size.
- **Zip (*.zip).** With this option, all of the files are compressed into a ZIP file. A
  program that works with ZIP files must be used to extract the files.
- **File Format.** The files can be converted to an earlier version of AutoCAD by
  selecting one of the options from the drop-down list.
- **Archive file folder.** This is the location where the archive is saved. Pick the
  Browse... button to select a different location.
- **Archive file name.** The drop-down list gives the options for how the archive
  package is named. The following options are available:
  - **Prompt for a filename.** The **Specify Zip File** dialog box is displayed, and a
    name for the archive package can be specified.

- **Overwrite if necessary.** The name for the resulting archive file can be entered in the text box below the drop-down list. If a file with the same name already exists, that file is automatically overwritten.
- **Increment file name if necessary.** The name for the resulting archive file can be entered in the text box below the drop-down list. If a file with the same name already exists, a new file is created and an incremental number is added to the file name. With this option, multiple versions of the archive package are saved.

Additional settings for the archive package are specified in the **Archive Options** area. The first option determines how the folder structure is saved. If **Use organized folder structure** is selected, the archive file duplicates the folder structure for the files. When this option is selected, the **Source root folder** setting is used to determine the root folder for files that use relative paths, such as xrefs. To archive all of the files into one single folder, use the **Place all files in one folder** option. The **Keep files and folders as is** option uses the same folder structure for all the files that are in the sheet set.

The other settings in the **Archive Options** area include the following:
- **Include fonts.** All fonts used in the drawings are included in the archive.
- **Set default plotter to 'none'.** This disassociates the plotter name from the drawing files. This is useful if the files will be sent to someone using a different plotter.
- **Prompt for password.** Allows a password to be set for the archive. The password is then needed to open the archive package.
- **Include sheet set data and files.** Selecting this includes the sheet set data file with the archive package.

Chapter Test

Answer the following questions. Write your answers on a separate sheet of paper or complete the electronic chapter test on the Student CD.

1. What is a *sheet set*?
2. What does the term *sheet* refer to in relation to a sheet set and a drawing file?
3. What are *sheet views* and how can they be referenced to each other within a sheet set?
4. What wizard is used to create a sheet set? What two types of ways can a new sheet set be created?
5. What file extension is a sheet set saved with?
6. What are *subsets* in relation to a sheet set?
7. What is the purpose of the **Create subsets based on folder structure** option in the **Import Options** dialog box?
8. Explain how to create a new subset in a sheet set and specify a template file and layout for creating new sheets in the subset.
9. List two ways to open a sheet from the **Sheet Set Manager**.
10. What is the purpose of the **Import Layouts as Sheets** dialog box?
11. How do you modify a sheet name or number?
12. Briefly explain how to publish a sheet set to a DWF file. How are the sheets organized in the resulting file?
13. How do you create a sheet selection set?
14. What tab in the **Sheet Set Manager** is used to manage sheet views?
15. Briefly explain how to create a view category for a sheet set and associate callout blocks to the category.
16. Explain how to add a drawing file to a sheet set so that views in the drawing can be placed on a sheet.
17. Explain why AutoCAD callout blocks and view labels are automatically updated when they appear on sheets and changes are made to the related sheet set.

18. What information is typically provided by the upper and lower values displayed in a callout block?
19. Explain how to insert a callout block into a drawing.
20. Give three examples of fields that can be used in a sheet set.
21. What is the purpose of custom sheet set properties?
22. How do you add a custom property to a sheet set?
23. What is a *sheet list table*?
24. Can column headings be added to a sheet list?
25. How is a table updated to reflect changes that are made in the **Sheet Set Manager**?
26. If a sheet list table is edited manually, will the edits be preserved if the **Update Sheet List Table** command is used? Explain.
27. What is the purpose of archiving a sheet set?
28. List the three packaging types available for archiving a sheet set.
29. What is a *zip file*?
30. How can you password-protect an archive?

Drawing Problems

1. Create a new sheet set using the **Create Sheet Set** wizard and the **Existing drawings** option. Name the new sheet set Schematic Drawings. On the **Choose Layouts** page, pick the **Browse...** button and browse to the folder where the P11-10.dwg file from Chapter 11 is saved. Import all of the layouts from the file into the new sheet set. Continue creating the sheet set as follows:

   A. In the **Sheet Set Properties** dialog box, assign the ISO A2 Title Block layout from the ISO A2-Color Dependent Plot Styles.dwt template file in the AutoCAD 2006 Template folder as the sheet creation template.

   B. Open a new drawing file using the template of your choice and create a block for a view label. Save the drawing file and then assign the block to the sheet set using the **Label block for views** setting in the **Sheet Set Properties** dialog box.

   C. Create a new view category and name it Schematics.

   D. Open the 3 Wire Control layout, create a new view, and add it to the Schematics view category. Double-click on the new view name in the **Sheet Views** tab and then insert the view label block you previously created. Renumber the view and save the drawing.

   E. Add a custom property to the sheet set named Checked by and set the **Owner** type to **Sheet**. Add another custom property named Client and set the **Owner** type to **Sheet Set**.

2. Create a new sheet set using the **Create Sheet Set** wizard and an example sheet set. Use the Architectural Imperial Sheet Set example sheet set. Name the new sheet set Floor Plan Drawings. Finish creating the sheet set. Under the Architectural sub-set, create a new sheet named Floor Plan. Number the sheet A1. In the **Model Views** tab, add a new location by browsing to the folder where the P17-17.dwg file from Chapter 17 is saved. Next, open the P17-17.dwg file and continue as follows:

   A. Create three model space views named Kitchen, Living Room, and Dining Room. Orient each display as needed to describe the area of the floor plan. Save and close the drawing.

   B. Open the A1-Floor Plan sheet. Create a new layer named Viewport and set it current.

   C. In the **Model Views** tab, expand the listing under the P17-17.dwg file. For each view name, right-click on the name and select **Place on Sheet**. Insert each view into the layout. Delete the default view labels inserted with the views. Double-click inside each viewport and set the viewport scale as desired.

   D. In the **Sheet Views** tab, renumber the views. Insert a new view label block under each view and save the drawing.

   E. Close the drawing.

3. Open the Floor Plan Drawings sheet set created in Problem 26-2. Create an archive of the sheet set using the self-extracting zip executable (EXE) file format.

Learning Objectives

After completing this chapter, you will be able to do the following:
● Describe the nature of isometric and oblique views.
● Set up an isometric grid.
● Construct isometric objects.
● Create isometric text styles.
● Demonstrate isometric and oblique dimensioning techniques.

Being able to visualize and draw three-dimensional shapes is a skill that every drafter, designer, and engineer should possess. This is especially important in 3D modeling. However, there is a distinct difference between drawing a view that *looks* three-dimensional and creating a *true* 3D model.

A 3D model can be rotated on the display screen and viewed from any angle. The computer calculates the points, lines, and surfaces of the objects in space. For information on 3D modeling, see *AutoCAD and Its Applications—Advanced*. The focus of this chapter is creating views that *look* three-dimensional using some special AutoCAD functions and two-dimensional coordinates and objects.

Pictorial Drawing Overview

The word *pictorial* means "like a picture." It refers to any realistic form of drawing. Pictorial drawings illustrate height, width, and depth. Several forms of pictorial drawings are used in industry today. The least realistic is oblique. However, this is the simplest type. The most realistic, but also the most complex, is perspective. Isometric drawing falls midway between the two as far as realism and complexity are concerned.

Oblique Drawings

An *oblique drawing* shows objects with one or more parallel faces having true shape and size. A scale is selected for the orthographic, or front faces. Then, an angle for the depth (receding axis) is chosen. The three types of oblique drawings are *cavalier*, *cabinet*, and *general*. See **Figure 27-1**. These vary in the scale of the receding axis. The receding axis is drawn at half scale for a cabinet view and at full scale for a cavalier. The general oblique is normally drawn with a 3/4 scale for the receding axis.

Figure 27-1.
The three types of
oblique drawings
differ in the scale of
the receding axis.

Cavalier   Cabinet   General

Isometric Drawings

Isometric drawings are more realistic than oblique drawings. The entire object appears as if it is tilted toward the viewer. The word *isometric* means "equal measure." This equal measure refers to the angle between the three axes (120°) after the object has been tilted. The tilt angle is 35°16′. This is shown in **Figure 27-2.** The 120° angle corresponds to an angle of 30° from horizontal. When constructing isometric drawings, lines that are parallel in the orthogonal views must be parallel in the isometric view.

The most appealing aspect of isometric drawing is that all three axis lines can be measured using the same scale. This saves time, while still producing a pleasing pictorial of the object. This type of drawing is produced when you use Isometric Snap mode, which is discussed later.

Closely related to isometric drawing are dimetric and trimetric. These forms of pictorial drawing differ from isometric in the scales used to measure the three axes. *Dimetric* drawing uses two different scales and *trimetric* uses three scales. Using different scales is an attempt to create *foreshortening.* This means the lengths of the sides appear to recede. The relationship between isometric, dimetric, and trimetric drawings is illustrated in **Figure 27-3.**

Perspective Drawing

The most realistic form of pictorial drawing is a *perspective drawing.* The eye naturally sees objects in perspective. Look down a long hall and notice that the wall and floor lines seem to converge in the distance at an imaginary point. That point is called the *vanishing point.* The most common types of perspective drawing are

Figure 27-2.
An object is tilted
35°16′ to achieve
an isometric
view having 120°
between the three
axes. Notice the
highlighted face in
each view.

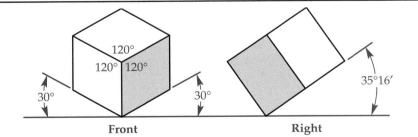

Front   Right

Figure 27-3.
Isometric, dimetric,
and trimetric differ
in the scales used to
draw the three axes.
The isometric shown
here has the scales
represented as one.
You can see how
the dimetric and
trimetric scales vary.

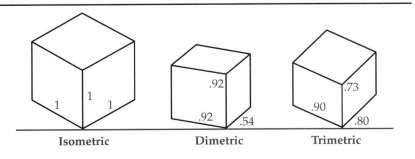

Isometric   Dimetric   Trimetric

Figure 27-4.
An example of one-point perspective and two-point perspective.

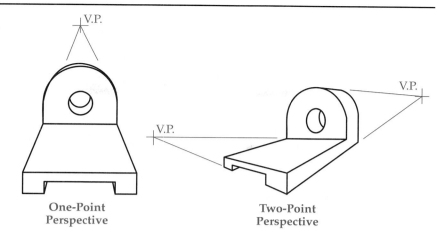

One-Point
Perspective

Two-Point
Perspective

one-point and *two-point*. These forms of pictorial drawing are often used in architecture. They are also used in the automotive and aircraft industries. Examples of one-point and two-point perspectives are shown in **Figure 27-4.** A perspective of a true 3D model can be produced in AutoCAD using the **3DORBIT** command. See *AutoCAD and Its Applications—Advanced* for complete coverage of **3DORBIT.**

Isometric Drawing

The most common method of pictorial drawing used in industry is isometric. These drawings provide a single view showing three sides that can be measured using the same scale. An isometric view has no perspective and may appear somewhat distorted. Two of the isometric axes are drawn at 30° to horizontal; the third at 90°. See **Figure 27-5.**

The three axes shown in **Figure 27-5** represent the width, height, and depth of the object. Lines that appear horizontal in an orthographic view are placed at a 30° angle. Lines that are vertical in an orthographic view are placed vertically. These lines are parallel to the axes. Any line parallel to an axis can be measured and is called an *isometric line.* Lines that are not parallel to the axes are called *nonisometric lines* and cannot be measured. Note the two nonisometric lines in **Figure 27-5.**

Circular features shown on isometric objects must be oriented properly or they appear distorted. The correct orientation of isometric circles on the three principal planes is shown in **Figure 27-6.** Circles appear as ellipses in an isometric drawing. The small diameter (minor axis) of the ellipse must always align on the axis of the circular feature. Notice that the centerline axes of the holes in **Figure 27-6** are parallel to one of the isometric planes.

Figure 27-5.
Layout of the isometric axes. Lines that are not parallel to any of the three axes are called nonisometric lines.

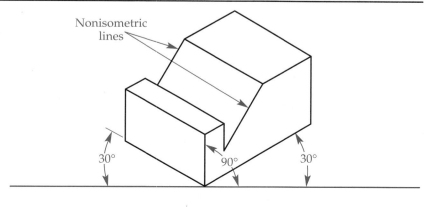

Nonisometric lines

30°   90°   30°

Figure 27-6.
Proper isometric circle (ellipse) orientation on isometric planes. The minor axis always aligns with the axis centerline.

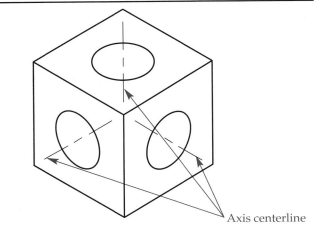

Minor Axis

Major Axis

Axis centerline

A basic rule to remember about isometric drawing is that lines parallel in an orthogonal view must be parallel in the isometric view. AutoCAD's **ISOPLANE** feature makes that task, and the positioning of ellipses, easy.

PROFESSIONAL TIP

If you are ever in doubt about the proper orientation of an ellipse in an isometric drawing, remember that the minor axis of the ellipse must always be aligned on the centerline axis of the circular feature. This is shown clearly in **Figure 27-6.**

Settings for Isometric Drawing

DSETTINGS

Type
DSETTINGS
DS
SE
DDRMODES

Pull-Down Menu
Tools
> Drafting
Settings...

You can quickly set your isometric variables in the **Snap and Grid** tab of the **Drafting Settings** dialog box. See **Figure 27-7.** To access this dialog box, enter DS, SE, DSETTINGS, or DDRMODES, or select **Tools > Drafting Settings...** from the pull-down menu. This dialog box can also be accessed by right-clicking on the **SNAP** or **GRID** status bar button and then selecting **Settings...** from the shortcut menu.

Figure 27-7.
The **Drafting Settings** dialog box allows you to make settings needed for isometric drawing.

Pick to activate isometric snap grid

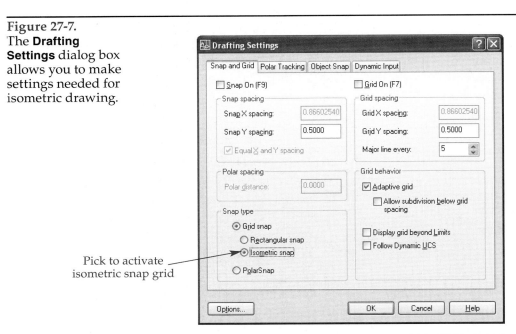

To activate the isometric snap grid, pick the **Isometric snap** radio button in the **Snap type** area. Notice that the **Snap X spacing** and **Grid X spacing** text boxes are now grayed-out. Since X spacing relates to horizontal measurements, it is not used in the isometric mode. You can only set the Y spacing for grid and snap in isometric. Be sure to check the **Snap On (F9)** and **Grid On (F7)** check boxes if you want Snap and Grid modes to be activated. Pick the **OK** button and the grid dots on the screen are displayed in an isometric orientation, as shown in **Figure 27-8.** If the grid dots are not visible, turn the grid on. You may also need to zoom in or out to display the grid.

Notice that the crosshairs appear angled. This aids you in drawing lines at the proper isometric angles. Try drawing a four-sided surface using the **LINE** command. Draw the surface so that it appears to be the left side of a box in an isometric layout. See **Figure 27-9.** To draw nonparallel surfaces, you can change the angle of the crosshairs to make your task easier, as discussed in the next section.

To turn off the Isometric Snap mode, pick the **Rectangular snap** radio button in the **Snap type** area. The Isometric Snap mode is turned off and you are returned to the drawing area when you pick the **OK** button.

>
> **NOTE**
>
> You can also set the Isometric Snap mode by typing SNAP or SN, selecting the **Style** option, and then typing I to select **Isometric**.

Changing the Isometric Crosshairs Orientation

Drawing an isometric shape is possible without ever changing the angle of the crosshairs. However, the drawing process is easier and quicker if the angles of the crosshairs align with the isometric axes.

Whenever the isometric snap style is enabled, simply press the [F5] key or the [Ctrl]+[E] key combination and the crosshairs immediately change to the next isometric plane. AutoCAD refers to the isometric positions or planes as *isoplanes.* As you change between isoplanes, the current isoplane is displayed on the prompt line as a reference. The three crosshairs orientations and their angular values are shown in **Figure 27-10.**

Figure 27-8.
An example of an isometric grid setup in AutoCAD.

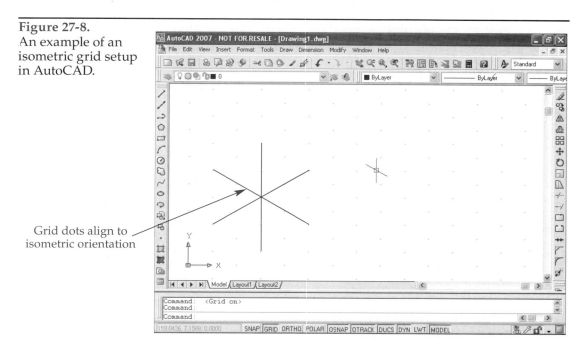

Grid dots align to isometric orientation

Figure 27-9.
A four-sided object drawn with the **LINE** command can be used as the left side of an isometric box.

Draw the left side of an isometric box

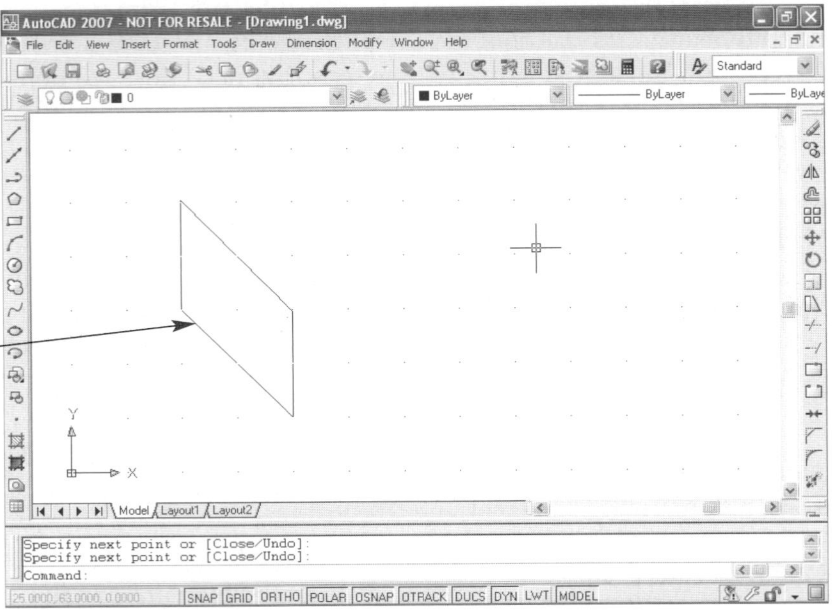

Another method to toggle the crosshairs position is with the **ISOPLANE** command. Enter ISOPLANE as follows.

> Command: **ISOPLANE**↵
> Current isoplane: *current*
> Enter isometric plane setting [Left/Top/Right] <*current*>: ↵

Press [Enter] to toggle the crosshairs to the next position. The command line displays the new isoplane setting. You can toggle immediately to the next position by pressing [Enter] to repeat the **ISOPLANE** command and pressing [Enter] again. To specify the plane of orientation, type the first letter of that position. The **ISOPLANE** command can also be used transparently.

The crosshairs are always in one of the isoplane positions when Isometric Snap mode is in effect. An exception occurs during a display or editing command when a multiple selection set method (such as a window) is used. In these cases, the crosshairs change to the normal vertical and horizontal positions. At the completion of the display or editing command, the crosshairs automatically revert to their former isoplane orientation.

PROFESSIONAL TIP

The quickest way to change the isoplane is to press the [F5] function key or press the [Ctrl]+[E] key combination.

Exercise 27-1

Complete the Exercise on the Student CD.

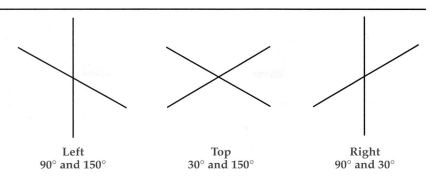

Figure 27-10.
The three isometric crosshairs positions can be changed using the [F5] function key, the [Ctrl]+[E] key combination, or using the **ISOPLANE** command.

| Left 90° and 150° | Top 30° and 150° | Right 90° and 30° |

Isometric Ellipses

Placing an isometric ellipse on an object is easy with AutoCAD because of the **Isocircle** option of the **ELLIPSE** command. An ellipse is positioned automatically on the current isoplane. To use the **ELLIPSE** command, first make sure you are in Isometric Snap mode. Then, pick the **Ellipse** button on the **Draw** toolbar, select **Draw > Ellipse > Axis, End**, or type EL or ELLIPSE. Once the **ELLIPSE** command is initiated, type I for the **Isocircle** option. Once you select the **Isocircle** option, pick the center point and then set the radius or diameter. The **Center** option does not allow you to create isocircles. Also, the **Isocircle** option only appears when you are in Isometric Snap mode.

Always check the isoplane position before placing an ellipse (isocircle) on your drawing. You can dynamically view the three positions that an ellipse can take. Initiate the **ELLIPSE** command, enter the **Isocircle** option, pick a center point, and press [F5] to toggle the crosshairs orientation. See **Figure 27-11**. The ellipse rotates each time you toggle the crosshairs.

The isometric ellipse (isocircle) is a true ellipse. If selected, grips are displayed at the center and four quadrant points. See **Figure 27-12**. However, do not use grips to resize or otherwise adjust an isometric ellipse. As soon as you resize an isometric ellipse in this manner, its angular value is changed and it is no longer isometric. You can use the center grip to move the ellipse. Also, if you rotate an isometric ellipse while Ortho mode is on, it will not appear in a proper isometric plane. You *can* rotate an isometric ellipse from one isometric plane to another, but you must enter a value of 120°.

Figure 27-11.
The orientation of an isometric ellipse is determined by the crosshairs orientation.

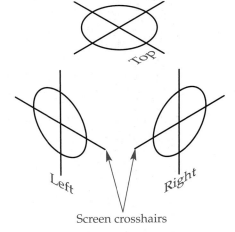

Top

Left

Right

Screen crosshairs

Figure 27-12.
An isometric ellipse
has grips at its four
quadrant points and
center.

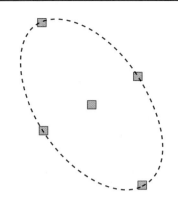

<table>
<tr><td>PROFESSIONAL
TIP</td><td></td><td>Prior to drawing isometric ellipses, it is good practice to first place a marker at the ellipse center point. A good technique is to draw a point at the center using an easily visible point style. This is especially useful if the ellipse does not fall on grid or snap points.</td></tr>
</table>

**Exercise
27-2**   Complete the Exercise on the Student CD.

Constructing Isometric Arcs

ELLIPSE

Type
ELLIPSE
EL

Pull-Down Menu
Draw
> Ellipse
> Arc

Toolbar
Draw
Ellipse Arc

The **ELLIPSE** command can also be used to draw an isometric arc of any included angle. To construct an isometric arc, use the **Arc** option of the **ELLIPSE** command while in **Isometric mode**. To access the **Arc** option, pick the **Ellipse Arc** button on the **Draw** toolbar, type EL or ELLIPSE followed by A for the **Arc** option, or select **Draw** > **Ellipse** > **Arc**. Once the **Arc** option is initiated, the following prompts appear:

Specify axis endpoint of elliptical arc or [Center/Isocircle]: I↵
Specify center of isocircle: *(pick the center of the arc)*
Specify radius of isocircle or [Diameter]: *(pick the radius or type a value and press* [Enter]*)*
Specify start angle or [Parameter]: *(pick a start angle or type a value and press* [Enter]*)*
Specify end angle or [Parameter/Included angle]: *(pick an end angle or type an included angle value and press* [Enter]*)*
Command:

A common application of isometric arcs is drawing fillets and rounds. Once a round is created in isometric, the edge (corner) of the object sits back from its original, unfilleted position. See **Figure 27-13A.** You can draw the complete object first and then trim away the excess after locating the fillets. You can also draw the isometric arcs and then the connecting lines. Either way, the center point of the ellipse is a critical feature, and should be located first. The left-hand arc in **Figure 27-13A** was drawn first and copied to the back position. Use Ortho mode to help quickly draw 90° arcs.

The next step is to move the original edge to its new position, which is tangent to the isometric arcs. You can do this by snapping the endpoint of the line to the quadrant point of the arc. See **Figure 27-13B.** Notice the grips on the line and on the arc. The endpoint of the line is snapped to the quadrant grip on the arc. The final step is to trim away the excess lines and arc segment. The completed feature is shown in **Figure 27-13C.**

                                              AutoCAD and Its Applications—Basics

Figure 27-13.
Fillets and rounds can be drawn with the **Arc** option of the **ELLIPSE** command. A broken line is used to represent an edge that is viewed straight on.

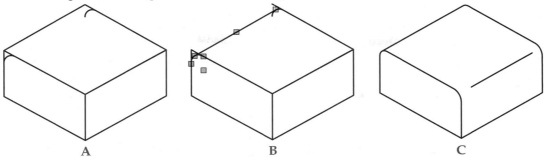

A   B   C

Rounded edges, when viewed straight on, cannot be shown as complete-edge lines that extend to the ends of the object. Instead, a good technique to use is a broken line in the original location of the edge. This is clearly shown on the right-hand edge in **Figure 27-13C.**

Exercise 27-3   Complete the Exercise on the Student CD.

Creating Isometric Text Styles

Text placed in an isometric drawing should appear to be parallel to one of the isometric planes. Text should align with the plane to which it applies. Text may be located on the object or positioned away from it as a note. Drafters and artists occasionally neglect this aspect of pictorial drawing and it shows on the final product.

Properly placing text on an isometric drawing involves creating new text styles. **Figure 27-14** illustrates possible orientations of text on an isometric drawing. These examples were created using only two text styles. The text styles have an obliquing angle of either 30° or –30°. The labels in **Figure 27-14** refer to the chart below. The angle in the figure indicates the rotation angle entered when using one of the text commands. For example, ISO-2 90 means that the ISO-2 style was used and the text was rotated 90°. This technique can be applied to any font.

Figure 27-14.
Isometric text applications. The text shown here indicates which style and angle were used.

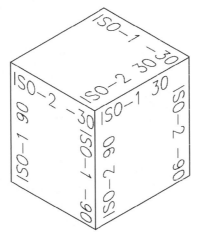

Name	Font	Obliquing Angle
ISO-1	Romans	30°
ISO-2	Romans	−30°

Exercise 27-4 Complete the Exercise on the Student CD.

Isometric Dimensioning

An important aspect of dimensioning in isometric is to place dimension lines, text, and arrowheads on the proper plane. Remember these guidelines:

✓ Extension lines should always extend in the plane being dimensioned.
✓ The heel of the arrowhead should always be parallel to the extension line.
✓ Strokes of the text that would normally be vertical should always be parallel with the extension lines or dimension lines.

These techniques are shown on the dimensioned isometric part in **Figure 27-15**. AutoCAD does not automatically dimension isometric objects. You must first create isometric arrowheads and text styles. Then, manually draw the dimension lines and text as they should appear in each of the three isometric planes. This is time-consuming when compared to dimensioning normal 2D drawings.

You have already learned how to create isometric text styles. These can be set up in an isometric template drawing if you draw isometrics often. Examples of arrows for the three isometric planes are shown in **Figure 27-16**.

Isometric Arrowheads

Arrowheads can be drawn and filled-in with a solid hatch pattern, or you can use the **SOLID** command to create a filled arrowhead. A variable-width polyline cannot be used because the heel of the arrowhead will not be parallel to the extension lines.

Every arrowhead does not need to be drawn individually. First, draw two isometric axes, as shown in **Figure 27-17A**. Then, draw one arrowhead like the one shown in **Figure 27-17B**. Use the **MIRROR** command to create additional arrows. As you create new arrows, move them to their proper plane.

Figure 27-15.
A dimensioned isometric part. Note the text and arrowhead orientation in relation to the extension lines.

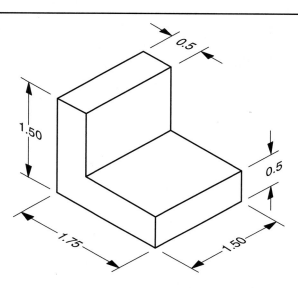

Figure 27-16.
Examples of
arrowheads in
each of the three
isometric planes.

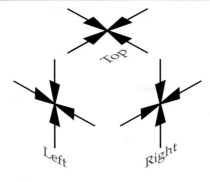

Figure 27-17.
Creating isometric
arrowheads.
A—Draw the two
isometric axes
for arrowhead
placement. B—Draw
the first arrowhead
on one of the axis
lines. Then, mirror
the arrowhead to
create others.

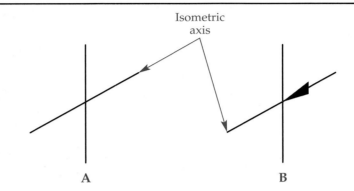

Save each arrowhead as a block in your isometric template or prototype. Use block names that are easy to remember.

Oblique Dimensioning

AutoCAD has a way to semiautomatically dimension isometric and oblique lines. First, the dimensions must be drawn using any of the linear dimensioning commands. **Figure 27-18A** illustrates an object dimensioned using the **DIMALIGNED** and **DIMLINEAR** commands. Then, use the **Oblique** option of the **DIMEDIT** command to rotate the extension lines. See **Figure 27-18B**.

To access the **Oblique** option, type DED or DIMEDIT and then type O for **Oblique**. You can also select **Dimension > Oblique**. When prompted, select the dimension and enter the obliquing angle.

This technique creates suitable dimensions for an isometric drawing and is quicker than the previous method discussed. However, this method does not rotate the arrows so the arrowhead heels are aligned with the extension lines. It also does not draw the dimension text aligned in the plane of the dimension. Therefore, this method does not produce technically correct dimensions.

Figure 27-18.
Using the **Oblique** option of the **DIMEDIT** command, you can create semiautomatic isometric dimensions by editing existing dimensions.

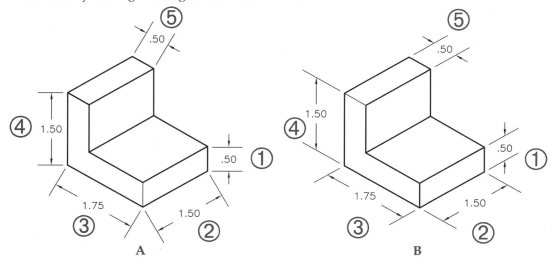

A

B

Dimension	Obliquing Angle
1	30°
2	−30°
3	30°
4	−30°
5	30°

Chapter Test

Answer the following questions. Write your answers on a separate sheet of paper or complete the electronic chapter test on the Student CD.

1. The simplest form of pictorial drawing is _____.
2. How does isometric drawing differ from oblique drawing?
3. How do dimetric and trimetric drawings differ from isometric drawings?
4. The most realistic form of pictorial drawing is _____.
5. What must be set in the **Drafting Settings** dialog box to turn on Isometric Snap mode and set a snap spacing of 0.2?
6. What function does the **ISOPLANE** command perform?
7. Which pull-down menu contains the command to access the **Drafting Settings** dialog box?
8. What factor determines the orientation of an isometric ellipse?
9. Name the command and option used to draw a circle in isometric.
10. Which text style setting allows you to create text that can be used on an isometric drawing?
11. How are isometric arcs drawn?
12. Where are grips located on a circle drawn in isometric?
13. Can grips be used to correctly resize an isometric circle? Explain your answer.
14. What technique does AutoCAD provide for dimensioning isometric objects?

Drawing Problems

Create an isometric template drawing. Items that should be set in the template include grid spacing, snap spacing, ortho setting, and text size. Save the template as **isoproto.dwt.** *Use the template to construct the isometric drawings in Problems 1–10. Save the drawing problems as* **P27-***(problem number).*

1.

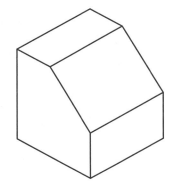

2.

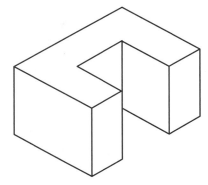

3.

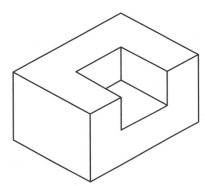

4.

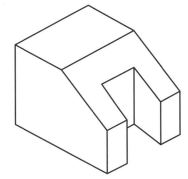

5.

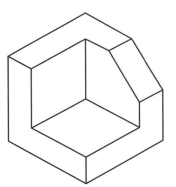

6.

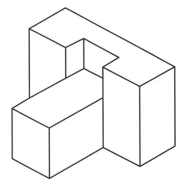

7.

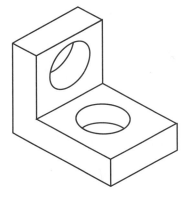

8.

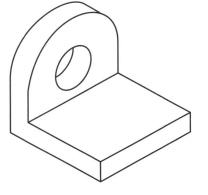

9.

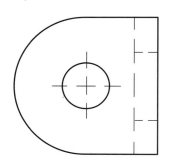

10.

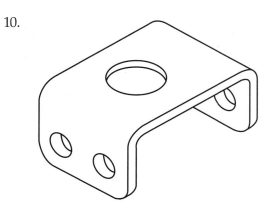

For Problems 11–14, create isometric drawings using the views shown. Measure the drawings to obtain the dimensions.

11.

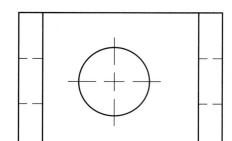

12.

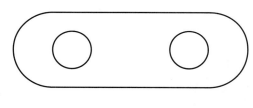

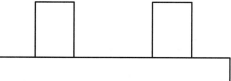

13.

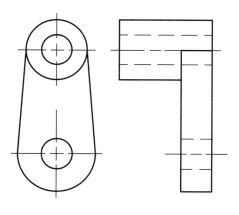

14.

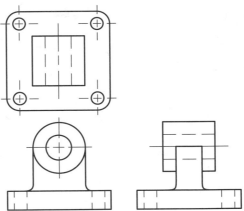

15. Construct a set of isometric arrowheads to use when dimensioning isometric drawings. Load your isometric template drawing. Create arrowheads for each of the three isometric planes. Save each arrowhead as a block. Name them with the first letter indicating the plane: T for top, L for left, and R for right. Also, number them clockwise from the top. See the example below for the right isometric plane. Do not include the labels in the blocks. Save the template again when finished.

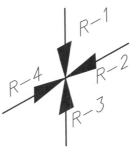

16. Create a set of isometric text styles like those shown in **Figure 27-14.** Load your template drawing and make a complete set in one font. Make additional sets in other fonts if you wish. Enter a text height of 0 so that you can specify the height when placing the text. Save the template when finished.

17. Begin a new drawing using your isometric template. Select one of the following problems from this chapter and dimension it: Problem 5, 7, 8, or 9. When adding dimensions, be sure to use the proper arrowhead and text style for the plane on which you are working. Save the drawing as P27-17.

18. Create an isometric drawing of the switch plate shown below. Select a view that best displays the features of the object. Do not include dimensions. Save the drawing as P27-18.

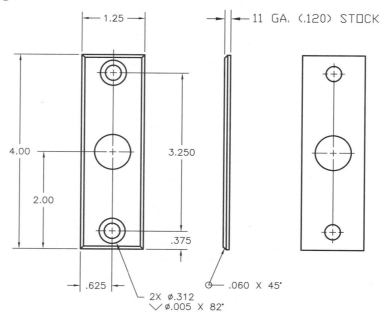

19. Create an isometric drawing of the retainer shown below. Select a view that best displays the features of the object. Do not include dimensions. Save the drawing as P27-19.

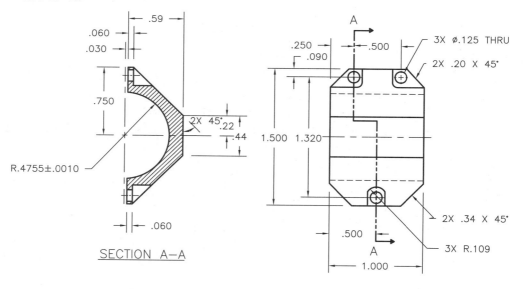

CHAPTER 28

Advanced Topics

Learning Objectives

After completing this chapter, you will be able to do the following:

- Edit the acad.pgp file.
- Use a text editor to create script files.
- Transmit drawing files using e-mail.
- Copy and reference AutoCAD drawing data to other Windows applications using Object Linking and Embedding (OLE).
- Describe the differences between linking and embedding.
- Copy and reference AutoCAD drawing data to other Windows applications using Object Linking and Embedding (OLE).
- Describe the differences between linking and embedding.

The ACAD.PGP File

The acad.pgp (program parameters) file controls such features of AutoCAD as command aliases and external commands. *External commands* carry out functions that are not part of AutoCAD. The acad.pgp file is simply a text file, which can be edited with a word processor text editor. During the AutoCAD installation procedure, this file is placed in the Documents and Settings*User*\\Application Data\\Autodesk\\AutoCAD 2007\\R17.0\\enu\\Support folder. A portion of the acad.pgp file is shown in Windows Notepad in **Figure 28-1**.

Modifying the acad.pgp file can be accomplished through the **Tools** pull-down menu. Select **Tools > Customize > Edit Program Parameters (acad.pgp)**. This procedure opens Notepad (if this is the default editor) and displays the acad.pgp file.

Command Aliases

AutoCAD allows you to abbreviate command names. This feature is called *command aliasing*. A list of predefined aliases furnished with AutoCAD can be displayed by viewing the contents of the acad.pgp file. You can do this by loading the file into Notepad or another text editor. Scroll down past the list of external commands and you will see the list of command aliases. This is an extensive list containing over

Figure 28-1.
The acad.pgp file
opened in Windows
Notepad.

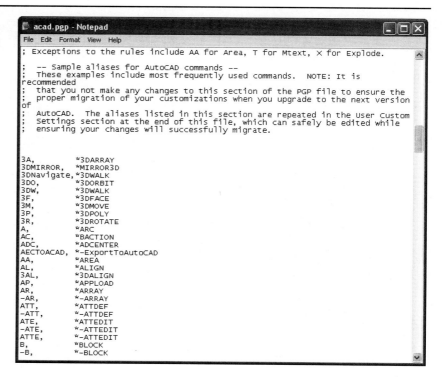

```
acad.pgp - Notepad

File  Edit  Format  View  Help

; Exceptions to the rules include AA for Area, T for Mtext, X for Explode.

;   -- Sample aliases for AutoCAD commands --
;   These examples include most frequently used commands.  NOTE: It is
recommended
;   that you not make any changes to this section of the PGP file to ensure the
;   proper migration of your customizations when you upgrade to the next version
of
;   AutoCAD.  The aliases listed in this section are repeated in the User Custom
;   Settings section at the end of this file, which can safely be edited while
;   ensuring your changes will successfully migrate.


3A,          *3DARRAY
3DMIRROR,    *MIRROR3D
3DNavigate,  *3DWALK
3DO,         *3DORBIT
3DW,         *3DWALK
3F,          *3DFACE
3M,          *3DMOVE
3P,          *3DPOLY
3R,          *3DROTATE
A,           *ARC
AC,          *BACTION
ADC,         *ADCENTER
AECTOACAD,   *-ExportToAutoCAD
AA,          *AREA
AL,          *ALIGN
3AL,         *3DALIGN
AP,          *APPLOAD
AR,          *ARRAY
-AR,         *-ARRAY
ATT,         *ATTDEF
-ATT,        *-ATTDEF
ATE,         *ATTEDIT
-ATE,        *-ATTEDIT
ATTE,        *-ATTEDIT
B,           *BLOCK
-B,          *-BLOCK
```

200 aliases. Some command aliases are provided here. See the *Command Aliases* chart in the *Reference Material* section on the Student CD for the complete listing.

CO,	*COPY
E,	*ERASE
L,	*LINE
P,	*PAN
Z,	*ZOOM

You can easily create your own aliases by editing this file. For example, if you want to add an alias **PP** for the **PLOT** command, enter the following below the **POLYGON** command in the acad.pgp file:

PP,   *PLOT

Be sure to include the asterisk since it indicates to AutoCAD that this is an alias. Then, save the file. The revised acad.pgp file will not work until you restart AutoCAD or reload the acad.pgp file by entering the **REINIT** command. This command displays the **Re-initialization** dialog box shown in **Figure 28-2**. Pick the **PGP File** check box in this dialog box and then pick **OK** to reinitialize the acad.pgp file. After you reinitialize the acad.pgp file, your new command alias will work.

NOTE

The **Re-initialization** dialog box can also be used if you have one of your serial ports, such as COM1, configured for both a plotter and a digitizer. If you change the cable from plotter to digitizer, pick the **Digitizer** check boxes in both areas of the dialog box to reinitiate the digitizer.

Figure 28-2.
The **Re-initialization**
dialog box.

Check to reload
the acad.pgp file

PROFESSIONAL
TIP

In a professional environment, place additions to the acad.pgp file at the end of the file, in the section titled User Defined Command Aliases. By doing so, you can easily find the modifications and migrate the settings when you upgrade to a new version of AutoCAD.

Editing the ACAD.PGP File

There are several tools available to edit the acad.pgp file. Notepad, MS-DOS EDIT, WordPad, or another text editor may be used. The easiest method of editing is to open the file with Notepad by picking **Tools** > **Customize** > **Edit Program Parameters (acad.pgp)** from the pull-down menu.

PROFESSIONAL
TIP

Always make backup copies of AutoCAD files before editing them. If you "corrupt" one of these files through incorrect editing techniques, simply delete that file and restore the original.

The acad.pgp file can be easily altered to specify your personal text editor. For this example, an external command will be set up to access an imaginary editor called TextEditor. If you are currently running AutoCAD, use the method described above to open the acad.pgp file in Notepad.

Once the acad.pgp file is displayed in Notepad, you can move the flashing text cursor around the screen with the left, right, up, and down arrows, as well as the [Home], [Page Up], [Page Down], [Insert], [Delete], and [End] keys. You can also move the text cursor with your pointing device. Use the down arrow key or your pointing device to move the text cursor to the end of the line labeled:

DIR,   DIR,   8,File specification: ,

Hit the [Enter] key to start a new line in the file. Type in the following new line of text:

TE,   START TEXTEDITOR,   9,File to edit: ,

The first word on each line is the text that is entered at the Command: prompt in order to execute the external command. The second word represents the DOS command or program to be executed. Use the space bar to line up the new text with the text on the previous line to make it easier to read. These changes allow you to run TextEditor by entering TE. When you are done, the acad.pgp file should appear as shown in **Figure 28-3**.

Figure 28-3.
TE has been added
as a new command
that will execute
the program named
TextEditor.

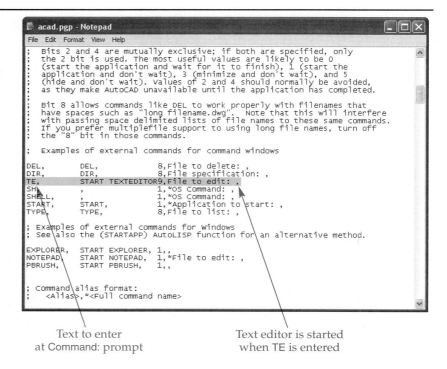

Text to enter
at Command: prompt

Text editor is started
when TE is entered

To save the edited file, select Save from Notepad's File pull-down menu. Use the [Alt]+[Tab] key combination or the Windows task bar to return to AutoCAD.

If you try using the new **TE** command in AutoCAD now, it will not work because AutoCAD is still using the previous version of the acad.pgp file. Before the **TE** command can function, you must reinitialize the acad.pgp file by restarting AutoCAD or executing the **REINIT** command.

> **NOTE**
>
>
> If you add an external command that references a new program, such as the text editor example given here, you must make sure that the path to the program is listed in the **Support File Search Path** area in **Files** tab of **Options** dialog box. If the path to the program is not listed, it must be added before the command will work.

Exercise 28-1 Complete the Exercise on the Student CD.

Creating Script Files to Automate AutoCAD

A *script file* is a list of commands that AutoCAD executes in sequence without input from the user. Scripts enable nonprogrammers to automate AutoCAD functions. Scripts can be used for specific functions, such as plotting a drawing with the correct **PLOT** command values and settings, or creating a slide show. A good working knowledge of AutoCAD commands is needed before you can confidently create a script file.

When writing a script file, use one command or option per line in the text file. This makes the file easier to fix if the script does not work properly. A return is specified by pressing [Enter] after typing a command. If the next option of a command is a default value to be accepted, press [Enter] again. This leaves a blank line in the script file, which represents pressing [Enter].

Creating a Script

The following example shows how a script file can be used to save a drawing in AutoCAD 2000 DWG format. Write the script with Notepad or another text editor. Save the file as convert.scr in the Documents and Settings*User*\Application Data\Autodesk\ AutoCAD 2007\R17.0\enu\Support folder.

CAUTION

A single incorrect entry in a script file can cause it to malfunction. Test the keystrokes at the keyboard as you write the script file and record them for future reference.

Many text editors and word processors save documents with .txt or .doc file extensions by default. Since scripts must end with the .scr file extension, you may have to use the Save As option in the text editor or word processor. Then, select All Files from the Save as type: menu in the Save As dialog box and save the file by including the .scr extension.

A comment can be inserted in a script file to provide information to the reader. Simply place a semicolon as the first character on the line and AutoCAD will not process that line. For example, the first line in the following script is a comment for information only:

> ; Saves the current drawing in AutoCAD 2000 DWG format. *(comment only)*
> FILEDIA   *(sets the system variable that controls file dialog boxes)*
> 0 *(disables file dialog boxes)*
> SAVEAS   *(command that saves the drawing in a format of your choice)*
> 2000   *(specifies the drawing is to be saved in the AutoCAD 2000 DWG format)*
>   *(Enter accepts default file name and location)*
> Y *(replaces the original file with the converted file)*
> FILEDIA   *(sets the system variable that controls file dialog boxes)*
> 1 *(enables file dialog boxes)*
>   *(this line is required to "enter" the previous line)*

Figure 28-4 shows how the script file appears in the Windows Notepad.

PROFESSIONAL TIP

Avoid pressing the space bar at the end of a line in the script file. This adds a space and, since the space bar and the [Enter] key are often equivalent at the Command: prompt, can cause the script to crash. Plus, finding spaces in a script file can be tedious work.

Figure 28-4.
The conversion script file as it appears in Windows Notepad.

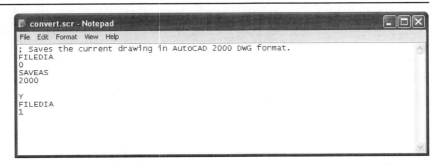

Running a Script

SCRIPT

Type

SCRIPT
SCR

Pull-Down Menu

Tools
> Run Script...

Make sure the drawing has been saved before running the convert.scr script. To run the script, select **Tools** > **Run Script...** from the pull-down menu or enter SCR or SCRIPT. Next, select the file name convert.scr from the **Select Script File** dialog box. See **Figure 28-5**. Then, sit back and watch the script run.

All the commands, options, and text screens associated with the commands in the script are displayed in rapid succession on the screen. If the script stops before completion, a problem has occurred. Flip the screen to the **AutoCAD Text Window** ([F2]) to determine the last command executed. Return to your text editor and correct the problem. Most often, there are too many or too few blank lines, or "enters." Another problem is spaces at the end of a line. If you suspect these errors, retype the line.

Exercise 28-2   Complete the Exercise on the Student CD.

Figure 28-5.
The **Select Script File** dialog box.

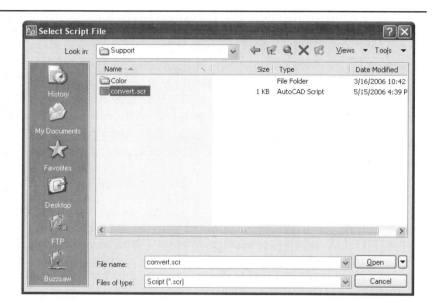

Preparing E-Mail Transmittals

Pull-Down Menu

File
> Send...

There are many instances when drawing files are transmitted using e-mail. To do this, select **File** > **Send...** from the pull-down menu in AutoCAD. This automatically starts your default e-mail service and supplies the current drawing as an attachment file. If e-mail service has not been set up, this option is unavailable.

However, the recipient of your drawing may not have the font files, plot style table files, and xref files associated with the transmitted drawing. When this occurs, at best the drawing features will be displayed differently on the recipient's computer. At worst, critical components can be absent from the drawing.

The **eTransmit** feature of AutoCAD simplifies the process of sending a drawing file by e-mail by creating a transmittal file. The *transmittal file* contains the DWG file and all font files, plot style table files, and xrefs associated with the drawing.

Figure 28-6.
The **Create Transmittal** dialog box.

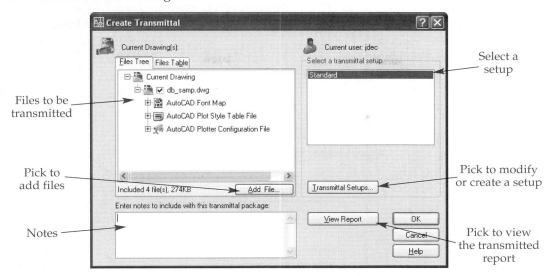

Files to be transmitted

Pick to add files

Notes

Select a setup

Pick to modify or create a setup

Pick to view the transmitted report

eTransmit

To use the **eTransmit** feature, select **File** > **eTransmit...** from the pull-down menu or type ETRANSMIT. This opens the **Create Transmittal** dialog box, **Figure 28-6.**

- **Files Tree tab.** This tab shows the current drawings and associated files to be transmitted. Font maps, shape files, plot style table files, and xrefs can be included in the transmittal. The **Add File...** button opens the standard file selection dialog box. Select any other files to be included in the transmittal. These do not need to be drawing files.
- **Files Table tab.** This tab shows the same files in the **Files Tree** tab, but in a list format.
- **Enter notes to include with this transmittal package.** Text entered in this text box is included in the transmittal report, which is a text file included in the transmittal.
- **Select a transmittal setup.** This box contains a list of available transmittal setups. Highlight the desired setup. A setup is a template used for the transmittal. The **Transmittal Setups...** button is used to create or modify setups, which is discussed in the next section.
- **View Report button.** A transmittal report is included in the transmittal. Picking this button displays the report in a new window, **Figure 28-7.** The report records the time and date when the transmittal is created, lists the files included in the transmittal, and includes some general notes regarding the file types included in the transmittal. You can save the report as a separate text file by picking the **Save As...** button in the **View Transmittal Report** dialog box. A standard "save" dialog box is displayed.

ETRANSMIT

Type
ETRANSMIT
Pull-Down Menu
File
> eTransmit...

Transmittal Setup

A transmittal setup includes various settings related to the creation of a transmittal file. Selecting the **Transmittal Setups...** button opens the **Transmittal Setups** dialog box, **Figure 28-8A.** A list of the available setups appears in the list box on the left. The **Rename** and **Delete** buttons are used to rename or delete the highlighted setup. The **Standard** transmittal setup cannot be renamed or deleted.

Figure 28-7.
The **View Transmittal Report** dialog box. This displays the report that will be included with the transmittal.

Figure 28-8.
A—The **Transmittal Setups** dialog box. To create a new setup, pick the **New...** button. B—Naming a new transmittal setup and selecting the existing setup on which to base the new setup.

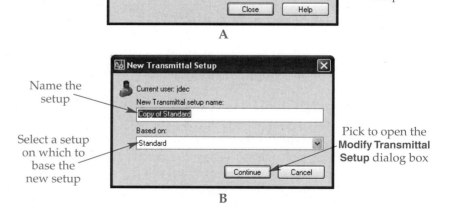

Pick to create a new setup

Pick to modify the highlighted setup

A

Name the setup

Select a setup on which to base the new setup

Pick to open the **Modify Transmittal Setup** dialog box

B

Creating or modifying a transmittal setup

To modify an existing setup, highlight the setup name and pick the **Modify...** dialog box. This opens the **Modify Transmittal Setup** dialog box, which is discussed later.

Picking the **New...** button opens the **New Transmittal Setup** dialog box, **Figure 28-8B**. Enter a name for the setup and select an existing setup on which to base the new setup. Select a setup that most closely resembles the new setup. Then, pick the **Continue** button to open the **Modify Transmittal Setup** dialog box.

Figure 28-9.
The **Modify
Transmittal Setup**
dialog box.

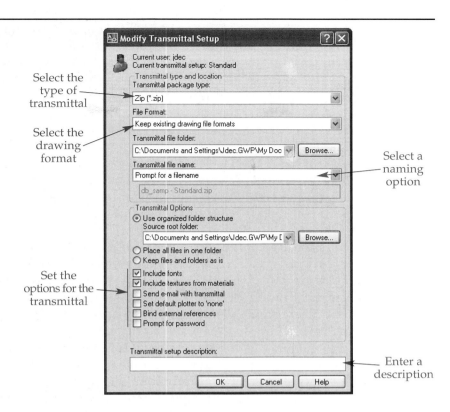

Select the
type of
transmittal

Select the
drawing
format

Select a
naming
option

Set the
options for the
transmittal

Enter a
description

Modify Transmittal Setup dialog box

The **Modify Transmittal Setup** dialog box contains all the options for storing the settings of a transmittal, Figure 28-9. This dialog box is where the transmittal setup is defined.

The transmittal can be created in one of three formats. The files can be compressed into a self-extracting executable (EXE) file. The transmittal recipient can then simply double-click on the file and the individual files are automatically extracted. If the transmittal recipient has unzipping software, you may choose to send the transmittal compressed into a single ZIP file. The third option is to create a folder containing all files to be transmitted. The EXE and ZIP transmittals are smaller in size than the transmittal created with the "folder" option. Select the option you want to use in the **Transmittal package type:** drop-down list.

You also need to select the format for the drawing files. This is done in the **File Format:** drop-down list. You can choose to keep the drawings in their original format, or you can convert to AutoCAD 2007, 2004, or 2000 format. When you choose a conversion option, the files that are transmitted are converted, not your saved files. If you are sending the transmittal to a user who has an older version of AutoCAD, you will need to select the appropriate conversion.

To specify where the transmittal is saved, type the path in the **Transmittal file folder:** text box. This functions as a drop-down list if previous locations have been specified. You can pick the **Browse...** button to locate the folder. Also, select a naming option for the transmittal in the **Transmittal file name:** drop-down list. When the **Prompt for a file name** option is selected, a standard "save" dialog box is displayed when the transmittal file is created. When the **Overwrite if necessary** option is selected, a previously created transmittal file with the same name is overwritten. When the **Increment file name if necessary** option is selected, a space and an incremental number is added to the end of the file name if a transmittal file with the same name already exists. When either of the last two options is selected, the default file name text box below the drop-down list is enabled and the name can be edited.

At the top of the **Transmittal Options** area of the **Modify Transmittal Setup** dialog box are three radio buttons. These three options control the file and folder structure of the files in the transmittal. The **Use organized folder structure** option creates a relative folder structure. The source folder is specified in the **Source root folder:** text box. This source folder becomes the parent folder of all files and folders to be included in the transmittal. The folders of any files that are stored in subfolders of other parent folders or on other drives become subfolders of the source folder. When the **Place all files in one folder** option is selected, all files are stored in a single folder. This option lets the transmittal recipient move the files to different folders. The **Keep files and folders as is** option creates an absolute, or "hard," folder structure that maintains the folder locations of the transmitted files. When the transmittal is extracted, the folder structure from which the transmitted files originated is duplicated on the transmittal recipient's computer.

The bottom of the **Transmittal Options** area of the **Modify Transmittal Setup** dialog box contains five check boxes. When the **Include fonts** check box is checked, font map files and shape files are included in the transmittal. When the **Send e-mail with transmittal** check box is checked, the default e-mail program is automatically started when a transmittal is created. When the **Set default plotter to none** check box is checked, the page setups stored in the drawing files have the plotter set to "none." This may reduce error messages for the recipient. If the **Bind external references** check box is checked, any external reference files are bound to their source drawings. This reduces the need to send the actual external references as individual files, but it does merge all data stored in the external reference files and the source drawings. When the **Prompt for password** check box is checked, you are prompted to create a password when the transmittal is created. The recipient must have the password to unzip the transmittal file.

The setup can have a description that is displayed in the **Transmittal Setups** dialog box and in the **Create Transmittal** dialog box when the transmittal name is highlighted. Enter the description in the **Transmittal setup description:** text box in the **Modify Transmittal Setup** dialog box.

When all settings are made in the **Modify Transmittal Setup** dialog box, pick the **OK** button. The **Transmittal Setups** dialog box is redisplayed. If you created a new setup, the name now appears in the list. Pick the **Close** button to return to the **Create Transmittal** dialog box.

Completing the Transmittal

After the files have been added to the transmittal, a setup has been selected, and any notes entered, you need to complete the transmittal. Pick the **OK** button in the **Create Transmittal** dialog box. Depending on your settings, you may be prompted for a file name and location. Then, the **Transmittal Package Creation is in Progress** dialog box appears indicating the progress, **Figure 28-10.** When the transmittal is created, this dialog box and the **Create Transmittal** dialog box are closed. You can now locate the transmittal and send it to the intended recipient.

Exercise 28-3   Complete the exercise on the Student CD.

Figure 28-10.
Completing the
transmittal.

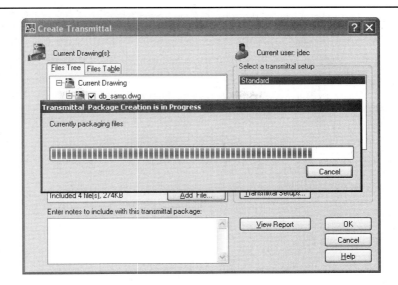

Introduction to Object Linking and Embedding (OLE)

Object linking and embedding (OLE) is a feature of the Windows operating system that allows data from many different source applications to be combined into a single document. A technical document will often present data in several forms to ensure effective communication. For example, the technical documentation for a product might include formatted text from a word processor, technical drawings from AutoCAD, charts and graphs from a spreadsheet program, and even graphic images from a paint program. Understanding the use of OLE will help you to produce high-quality documentation to communicate your ideas effectively.

As implied by the name, there are two distinct aspects to OLE: *linking* and *embedding*. Both linking and embedding allow you to insert data from one application into another, but they differ in the way information is stored. The following terms are important to understand.

- **Object.** A piece of data created by a Windows application that supports OLE server functions. Such data can be text from a word processor, an AutoCAD drawing, or a graphic image.
- **OLE server.** A source application. For example, when using OLE to bring an AutoCAD drawing into your word processor, AutoCAD becomes the OLE server.
- **OLE client.** A destination application. AutoCAD is an OLE client when you use OLE to bring an object into AutoCAD from another application.

Object Embedding

The term *embedding* refers to storing a copy of an OLE object in a client document. Embedding differs from importing because an imported object maintains no association with its source application. An embedded object is edited using the source application, or server. For example, if a Photoshop picture is embedded in an AutoCAD drawing, double-clicking on the picture starts the Photoshop application and loads the selected picture. On the other hand, using the **IMAGE** command to bring an image file into AutoCAD brings in the graphic image, but the image has no association with the original application.

Embedding Objects in AutoCAD

A simple way to embed an OLE object in an AutoCAD drawing is to first copy it to the Clipboard from the source application. Then, return to AutoCAD and paste the Clipboard contents using **PASTECLIP**. When the content of the Clipboard is not AutoCAD data and contains OLE information, it is embedded in the AutoCAD drawing.

One application for using embedded graphics is placing a picture in a title block for a logo design. In **Figure 28-11**, the Paint program has been used to design a logo graphic. Selecting the graphic image and pressing [Ctrl]+[C] copies the selected image to the Clipboard.

Once you have copied the image to the Clipboard, return to AutoCAD. Now press [Ctrl]+[V] to paste the Clipboard contents into the AutoCAD drawing. A rectangle that is the size of the object appears at the cursor and you are prompted:

Specify insertion point:

Specify a point and the OLE object is placed into the drawing. The OLE object can be moved, copied, or rotated just like any other AutoCAD object. **Figure 28-12** shows the image in its final position within the title block.

When the OLE object is selected, grips appear at the corners. You can make the object larger by making a grip hot and moving the cursor. The object remains proportional. However, you can use the **Properties** window to change the height and width of the OLE object, **Figure 28-13.**

By default, the aspect ratio is locked. This means that the object remains proportional. However, you can unlock the aspect ratio in the **Properties** window if you want to change the size of the object disproportionately.

Because the image is embedded, it maintains an association with the original application. You can use the original application whenever you need to edit the image. The application can be initiated by double-clicking on the image. You can also select the object in AutoCAD, right-click to display the shortcut menu, and select **OLE** then **Open**. See **Figure 28-14.** The OLE object is opened in the associated application. In the case of the logo, Windows Paint is opened (unless the default BMP association has been changed).

Figure 28-11.
A graphic image can be designed in Microsoft Paint.

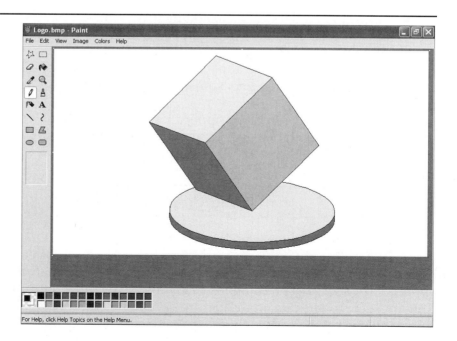

Figure 28-12.
The image is moved to the proper location.

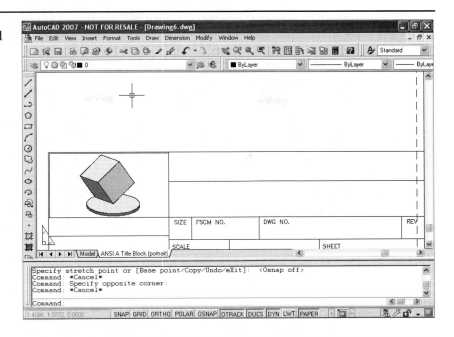

Figure 28-13.
To change the size of an OLE object, use the **Properties** window.

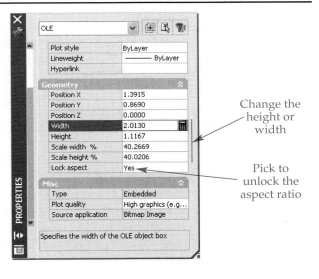

Change the height or width

Pick to unlock the aspect ratio

Figure 28-14.
To open an OLE object in the original application, select the object, right-click, and select **OLE** then **Open** from the shortcut menu.

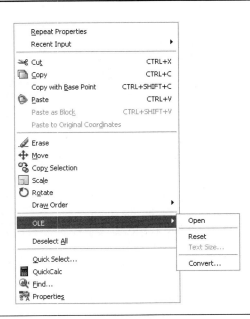

It is possible to embed virtually any OLE object into an AutoCAD drawing. This includes word processing documents, charts, graphs, spreadsheets, audio clips, and video clips. Using these various OLE data types can transform a standard technical drawing into a complete multimedia presentation. As you use these techniques, try to use only objects that have significant communication value, rather than cluttering up a drawing with unnecessary "bells and whistles."

PROFESSIONAL TIP

OLE objects that are linked or embedded in an AutoCAD drawing only print on printers or plotters that use the Windows system printer driver. They will still be displayed on screen, but cannot be printed using non-Windows drivers.

Embedding AutoCAD Drawings in Other Applications

AutoCAD provides both client and server OLE functions. This means that in addition to using embedded OLE objects, AutoCAD can provide objects for other applications. A common use for this feature is to combine technical drawings and illustrations with text in a technical document created with a word processing program.

If you already have a drawing created that you need to embed in another document, first open the drawing in AutoCAD. Press [Ctrl]+[C] or select **Edit** > **Copy** and select the desired objects to place them on the Clipboard. For this example, the entire AutoCAD drawing is copied to the Clipboard.

In this example, the Windows WordPad program is used as the client application. Open the destination document in WordPad, **Figure 28-15A.** Then, select the Edit menu and pick the Paste option to embed the AutoCAD drawing. The embedded drawing is placed at the current cursor location. You are not prompted for a location or a size. If you need to change either the location or the size, you can do so by picking on the drawing or on the grips at the edges or corners and dragging the image. **Figure 28-15B** shows the document with the drawing embedded, resized, and moved to the center of the document.

Embedding an OLE object in an application also modifies the "edit" menu to display new options when the object is highlighted. The Edit pull-down menu in the WordPad program appears as shown in **Figure 28-16** after highlighting the embedded drawing.

Once the drawing is embedded, it loses all connection with the original drawing file. This means that subsequent editing of this drawing will not affect the original source file. In order to edit the embedded drawing, highlight the image in WordPad and select Edit AutoCAD Drawing Object from the Edit pull-down menu or simply double-click on the drawing. When the AutoCAD window opens, examine the title bar and note the specified file name. The title bar shows the drawing name as Drawing in Document. If you access the **SAVEAS** command, the current file name is set to something similar to A$C37DA7DFF.DWG. This is a temporary name assigned to the drawing while it is being edited, and may change from one editing session to another. Also, if you switch back to the client (WordPad) while the drawing is open, the drawing in the client is grayed out or highlighted.

Updating refers to recording your changes to the embedded object within the client document. There are two ways to update the file when you have finished editing it. Picking the **File** pull-down menu in AutoCAD displays a new option, such as **Update WordPad**. Selecting this option replaces the currently embedded drawing with the revised version. You can also simply close the current drawing or exit AutoCAD. If changes have been made, the dialog box shown in **Figure 28-17** is displayed. Selecting the **Yes** button updates the client document.

Figure 28-15.
Inserting an AutoCAD drawing object into a WordPad document. A—The original
document. B—The document after the drawing is embedded.

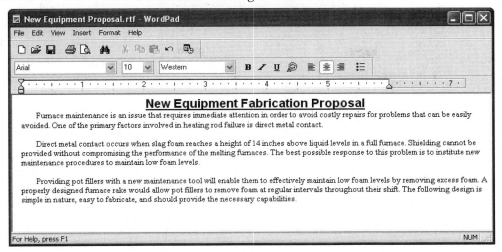

A

B

Figure 28-16.
New options are available in the Windows Notepad Edit pull-down menu when the
embedded drawing is selected.

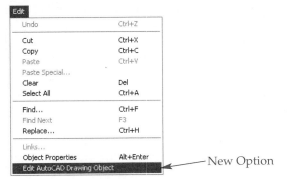

Figure 28-17.
If there are unsaved changes in your drawing, this dialog box is displayed.

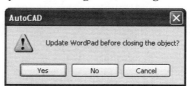

Object Linking

Linking is similar to embedding in that objects from one application are brought into another application. With linking, however, a direct link is maintained between the source data and the OLE object in the client application. Linked objects support *dynamic data exchange (DDE)*. As the source data is modified, the link in the client application is updated.

Linking Objects in AutoCAD

To link an object within AutoCAD, it must first be copied to the Clipboard. When bringing the object into AutoCAD, select **Edit** > **Paste Special...** from the pull-down menu. Using this option activates the **Paste Special** dialog box. See **Figure 28-18**.

The source of the information currently on the Clipboard is displayed in the upper-left area of the dialog box. Two radio buttons allow you to specify whether or not to copy the information as a link. If **Paste** is active, the object will be embedded. If the

Figure 28-18.
The **Paste Special** dialog box. The Clipboard in this example contains text from a Microsoft Word document. A—The **Paste** option embeds the object; several formats are available. B—The **Paste Link** option creates a link to the object; only a single format can be used.

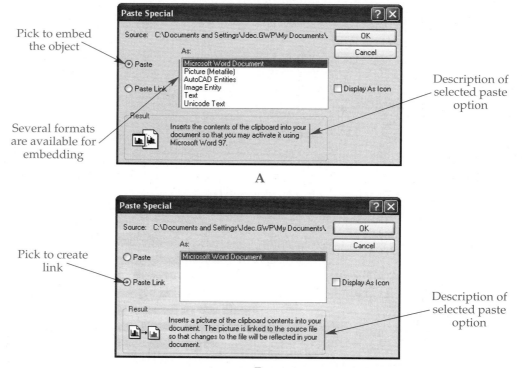

Paste Link option is active, the object will be brought in as a link. If you are embedding the object, you may have several format options, depending on the type of data being pasted. These formats are shown in the **As:** list box. An object that is being linked, on the other hand, is pasted as the file type associated with the server application.

PROFESSIONAL TIP

Objects can only be linked through OLE if they exist as a file on disk. If you copy data from an application without first saving it to disk, the **Paste Link** radio button is disabled (grayed out). In addition, you may not be able to link to files across a network. A link maintains a direct association with the original source file, meaning that editing a linked OLE object changes its source file as well. Pasting an object when the **Paste Link** option is not available creates an embedded OLE object.

Inserting Linked Objects into AutoCAD

A linked object can also be inserted into AutoCAD using the **INSERTOBJ** command. Select this command by picking the **OLE Object...** button on the **Insert** toolbar, selecting **Insert > OLE Object...** from the pull-down menu, or typing IO or INSERTOBJ. The following example shows how to use this command.

First, create a simple image in Windows Paint and save the image as a bitmap (BMP) file. Then, in AutoCAD, initiate the **INSERTOBJ** command. The **Insert Object** dialog box appears, **Figure 28-19A**.

The **Create New** radio button is selected by default. The **Object Type:** list box shows the registered applications that support OLE functions. This list varies based on the software installed on your system. Read each selection carefully, because some programs can produce varied types of data. For example, if you have Microsoft Word installed, you may see options for producing a picture or a document. The option you select affects how the specified program is started, and the data type it will be sending back to AutoCAD.

To create a new object from scratch, highlight the desired program and pick the **OK** button. The appropriate application is opened and you can create the object. When you are finished creating the OLE object, select the Update option from the File menu or just exit the application. If you exit before you save, the application will ask if you want to update the object before you exit.

If the object is already created and saved, as in this example, select the **Create from File** radio button. The dialog box appears as shown in **Figure 28-19B**. Enter the path and file name in the **File:** edit box or pick the **Browse...** button to select the file from a selection dialog box. Activate the **Link** check box to create a link between the object file and the AutoCAD drawing. Then, pick the **OK** button and the object appears in the drawing.

To edit the linked OLE object, select it, right-click to display the shortcut menu, and select **OLE** then **Open**. This opens the server application, which is Paint in this example. Any changes you make to the image are updated in both the OLE object in the drawing and in the source file.

All linked OLE objects behave in much the same manner as the previous example. In certain applications, the updates may be slower, but they are still automatic. To change the way a link is updated or to adjust current links in a drawing, select **Edit > OLE Links...** from the pull-down menu. This opens the **Links** dialog box, as shown in **Figure 28-20**. If no links are present in the current drawing, this item is grayed-out in the pull-down menu.

Figure 28-19.
The **Insert Object** dialog box can be used to link an object to an AutoCAD drawing. A—To create a new object, select the type of object and pick **OK**. B—To create a link to an existing object file, pick the **Create from File** radio button, select the file, and pick the **Link** check box.

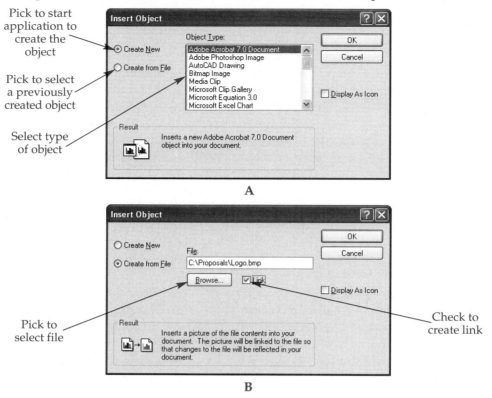

Pick to start application to create the object

Pick to select a previously created object

Select type of object

A

Pick to select file

Check to create link

B

Figure 28-20.
The **Links** dialog box displays all active links.

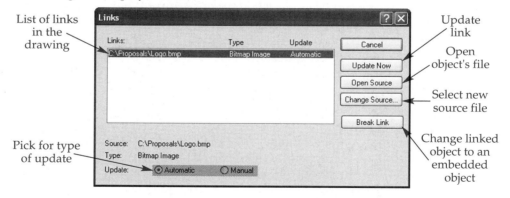

List of links in the drawing

Pick for type of update

Update link

Open object's file

Select new source file

Change linked object to an embedded object

The **Links:** list box in the **Links** dialog box displays all active links in the current drawing. The file name (source) of the highlighted link and the update method are shown at the bottom of the dialog box. By default, a link is automatically updated. If you do not want the updates to be automatic, pick the **Manual** radio button. To force an update, select the **Update Now** button on the right side of the dialog box. The **Break Link** button removes link information from the OLE object, and removes any association with the source file, effectively converting a linked object into an embedded object. Select the **Change Source...** button to change the source file with which the link is associated. Selecting **Open Source** opens the linked file using the originating application.

Some types of files (such as sound files, video clips, and animations) offer additional options within the AutoCAD drawing.

Linking AutoCAD Drawings in Other Applications

To embed an AutoCAD drawing in another application, the AutoCAD object is copied to the Clipboard using the **COPYCLIP** command and then pasted into the other application. However, to insert a linked AutoCAD object into another application, the **COPYLINK** command is used to place the data on the Clipboard.

The **COPYLINK** command is accessed by selecting **Edit > Copy Link** or by typing COPYLINK. Using **COPYLINK** differs from **COPYCLIP** in that there is no selection process. All currently visible objects are automatically selected as they appear on screen. Similar to **COPYCLIP**, the selected objects are displayed in a client application in the view that was active when the copy was made.

The Paste Special... selection found in the Edit pull-down menu of most Windows applications is used to paste a linked OLE object. The Paste Special dialog box displayed by picking this option may vary slightly from one application to the next, but several basic features are standard. See **Figure 28-21.** You can also select Object from the Insert pull-down menu in most applications. This is similar to using the **INSERTOBJ** command in AutoCAD.

Remember that the Paste Link option is only available if the source drawing has been saved to a file. Selecting AutoCAD Drawing Object as the data type maintains the pasted material as AutoCAD drawing data. Selecting Picture brings the information in as a WMF file and Bitmap converts the incoming data to a BMP file. Using bitmaps ensures that what you see on the screen is exactly what will print, but tends to make the client files very large and uses more memory. Your choice for the incoming data type has no effect on the original file, and the link is still maintained if the data type supports linking.

Figure 28-21.
The Paste Special dialog box is similar in most Windows applications. This is the dialog box in Microsoft Word.

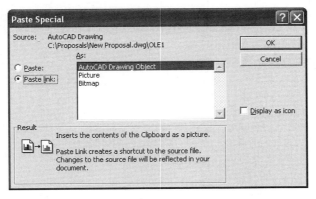

Chapter Test

Answer the following questions. Write your answers on a separate sheet of paper or complete the electronic chapter test on the Student CD.

1. Name the parts of a command listing found in the acad.pgp file.
2. What is a command alias, and how would you write one for the **POLYGON** command?
3. Define *script file.*
4. Why is it a good idea to put one command on each line of a script file?
5. List two common reasons why a script file might not work.
6. Other than simply attaching a drawing to an e-mail message, how can you send drawing data via e-mail?
7. What are some advantages of the method in Question 6?
8. What are the three "package type" options for the method in Question 6?
9. What does *OLE* stand for?
10. Define the following terms.
    A. Object
    B. OLE server
    C. OLE client
11. What does *embedding* mean?
12. How can you edit an object that has been embedded into an application?
13. What does *linking* mean?
14. How do you insert a new OLE object that has not yet been created into an AutoCAD drawing?

Drawing Problems

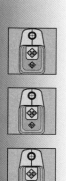

1. If you use a text editor or word processor other than MS-DOS EDIT or Notepad, create a new command in the acad.pgp file that loads the text editor.

2. Create a new command for the acad.pgp file that activates the Windows Calculator.

3. Write a script file called notes.scr that does the following:
    A. Executes the **TEXT** command.
    B. Selects the **Style** option.
    C. Enters a style name.
    D. Selects the last point using the "@" symbol.
    E. Enters a text height of .25.
    F. Enters a rotation angle of 0.
    G. Inserts the text: NOTES:.
    H. Selects the **TEXT** command again.
    I. Enters location coordinates for first note.
    J. Enters a text height of .125.
    K. Enters a rotation angle of 0.
    L. Inserts the text: 1. INTERPRET DIMENSIONS AND TOLERANCES PER ASME Y14.5.
    M. Enters an [Enter] keystroke.
    N. Inserts the text: 2. REMOVE ALL BURRS AND SHARP EDGES.
    O. Enters the [Enter] twice at the Command: prompt to exit the command.

Immediately before this script file is used, select the **ID** command and pick the point where you want the notes to begin. That point will be the "last point" used in the script file for the location of the word NOTES:. The script file, when executed, should draw the following:

NOTES:
1. INTERPRET DIMENSIONS AND TOLERANCES PER ASME Y14.5.
2. REMOVE ALL BURRS AND SHARP EDGES.

4. Open one of your drawings from a previous chapter. Then, do the following.
   A. Copy the object to the Clipboard.
   B. Open a word processing program and paste the Clipboard contents to create an embedded object.
   C. Create a memo to a coworker or instructor in which you describe the process used to create the document.
   D. Save the document as P28-4 but do not close the application. Return to AutoCAD and close the drawing without saving.
   E. Return to the word processor and double-click on the pasted object.
   F. Edit the object in some way and save the drawing.
   G. Return to the document and save it.

5. Open one of your drawings from a previous chapter. Perform the same functions outlined in Problem 4, but this time create a link between the AutoCAD drawing and the word processing document. Edit the drawing in AutoCAD and observe the results in the document file. Save the document as P28-5 and close the word processor.

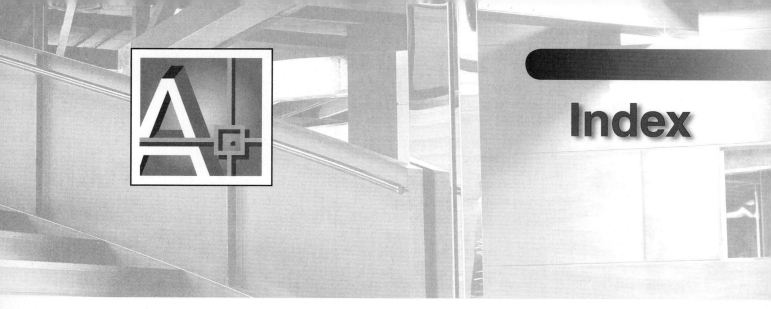

Index

AutoCAD and Its Applications—Basics
